Garage Sale & Flea Market ANNUAL

SIXTH EDITION

CASHING IN ON
TODAY'S LUCRATIVE
COLLECTIBLES MARKET

COLLECTOR BOOKS
A Division of Schroeder Publishing Co., Inc.

The current values in this book should be used only as a guide. They are not intended to set prices, which vary from one section of the country to another. Auction prices as well as dealer prices vary greatly and are affected by condition as well as demand. Neither the Editors nor the Publisher assumes responsibility for any losses that might be incurred as a result of consulting this guide.

Searching For A Publisher?

We are always looking for knowledgeable people considered to be experts within their fields. If you feel that there is a real need for a book on your collectible subject and have a large comprehensive collection, contact Collector Books.

On the Front Cover:

McCoy Jardiniere, $125.00
Coca-Cola VW Van, 1950s, 7½", $350.00
1990 Happy Holidays Barbie Doll, $145.00
Julia Paper Doll, MIB, $50.00
Beatles Disk Go Case, $160.00
Suki Skediddle, $15.00 – 25.00
Royal Copley Bear Planter, $50.00
Lady's Head Vase, $60.00
Welch's Howdy Doody Glass, $15.00 each
Fiesta Fruit Bowls, $22.00 – 28.00

Cover Design by Beth Summers
Book Layout by Karen Smith, Beth Ray, Kent Henry, and Donna Ballard

Additional copies of this book may be ordered from:

Collector Books
P.O. Box 3009
Paducah, Kentucky 42002-3009

@$19.95. Add $2.00 for postage and handling.

Copyright © 1998 by Schroeder Publishing Co.

A Word From the Editor

I may not need the psychiatrist's couch yet, but there are days when I can almost hear it calling my name, and I'll bet there are times you feel the same way. Know what I've found to be one of the best 'stress reducers' around? You guessed it exactly right — garage sales! To me, on a warm summer morning, there's nothing like that adrenalin surge that comes with the sight of a big 'Garage Sale' sign to loosen you up, lay you back, and usher you into a glorious, sunny Saturday after a long, nerve-jangling workweek punctuated here and there with a family crisis or two. If I factor in all the exercise I get, it's not only mentally theraputic but a great way to get in some physical activity as well.

But lest you think that those are the reasons I love garage sales, let me set you straight! I love the hunt. Sure, I love the find even better, but not every sale will hold a particularly delightful surprise. In fact, I'd guess that even on a good day, only one sale in ten will be fruitful, but that's not to say I don't enjoy checking out the other nine. (Here's where you fall back on the sunshine and exercise thing.)

Flea markets are a close second, at least in my book. Not everyone would agree with me, though, preferring a simple stroll through organized rows of dealers' tables to sorting through tons of used clothing, old shoes, chipped dinnerware, and nonfunctioning kitchen appliances at yard sales. But not all the dinnerware will be chipped, you can occasionally find some great vintage clothing, and in case you didn't know it, kitchen appliances from as late as the 1950s and '60s are often very desirable collectibles.

This summer I bought partial sets of Russel Wright and Metlox, some Blue Ridge and Harlequin, a little Fiesta, and several pieces of the brown drip glaze dinnerware lines by McCoy, Hull, and Pfaltzgraff. I also noticed how well Pfaltzgraff's Village pattern went with my almond and forest green kitchen, and over the summer I managed to accumulate a very nice assortment of it which I really enjoy using. It has so many wonderful, varied pieces that are just not available in any of today's modern dinnerware lines. Besides that, it was great fun to find new and 'uncharted' items now and then.

If you're into vintage clothing, you're apt to find anything. I once bought a Harley-Davidson leather jacket (one of the older styles in perfect condition) for $5.00, a beautiful '40s-era peach lace and rayon satin nightie, and a great '50s poodle skirt (thick pink felt with a poodle-cloth dog). I've seen crinolines and nylon gloves from the same era, not to mention the beaded and sequined sweaters and collars or the hand-embroidered aprons like the ones Mom always wore.

So I found it pays to be humble. And considering the recent influx of imposter Roseville pottery, new 'Nippon,' reproduction cast iron, and scores of other fakes that are especially prevelent at most flea markets nowadays, that level of shopping can get to be very frustrating and unproductive. (To their credit, though, there are still some promoters who do their best to keep this sort of garbage out of their show or at least separate from the area allocated to the bonafide collectibles dealers.) I can't discount the good buys we were able to pick up this past season, though. Most came from the larger flea markets, though we did get a pair of Kay Finch squirrels for $4.00 (they book at $175.00 to $200.00) at a small local market last summer. Add to that a $400.00 Cambridge Banjo Lady in green for $90.00, a Homer Laughlin nude vase for $18.00 (she lists for more than $350.00 now), an amber Moon and Star mini lamp for $25.00 (minimum value $100.00), and I can't complain.

But by far, the vast majority of our 'finds' came from garage sales, and they were bought for pennies on the dollar. Some of what we found went into our own collections (which are legion, by the way), but eventually most of these things found their way onto Bob's flea market tables last fall. Like scores of collectors everywhere, we always end up with good saleable items we personally have no use for, so once a year and only once, Bob sets up his tent and becomes a bonafide flea-market dealer. We have only one important festival a year here in west-central Indiana, but it draws tens of thousands of visitors — mostly city folk who find our covered bridges, fall foliage, pumpkins, and corn stalks something special to look at. So for the ten days of the festival, he deals. All those garage-sale goodies are packed on tables in the tent, along the sides of the tent, and he'll even put more tables out in front of the tent. By the middle of the first week, he's beginning to get low on merchandise. By the second weekend, he runs his famous 'half-price' sale; and by the time we tear down and pack up, there's very little to drag back home. As a rule, he will pocket about $2,500.00 of clear profit — the fruits not of our labor but of something we both enjoy very much!

We're certainly not alone in our garage sale/flea market pursuits. Even if you're not 'one of us,' many of your friends probably are. It's been estimated that there are more than 20,000,000 collectors/dealers in this country, turning millions of dollars back into the economy each year. Though some confine their interests to genuine antiques, a very high percentage of that figure prefers collectible items from about World War II on, and that's where the emphasis of our *Garage Sale and Flea Market Annual* lies.

If you're a novice but interested in learning about collectibles, this book is a good place to start. One of our goals is to introduce new collectibles as they begin to catch on, so you'll often find categories in our guide several seasons before they're introduced anywhere else. By tipping you off early, you can get in on the 'ground floor' and snap those bargains up well before prices begin to take off.

Because so many of today's hot collectibles date from the 1950s on, the garage sale/flea market venue is often the perfect place to discover fabulous treasures that can easily go unnoticed unless you're a well-versed shopper. Belive me, it's very satisfying to learn that the Kitchen Prayer Lady egg timer I bought for 25¢ books for a cool $150.00 (actually, I got it *and* the toothpick holder for the quarter), and that the Italian glass clown ashtray that cost me $5.00 is listed at about $100.00. I was also very pleased to find two of my Annalee dolls for $1.00 each (but, of course, I won't sell those), a Ceramic Arts Studio 'Mary' for a quarter (she's about a $25.00 item), a Howard Pierce three-piece quail family for $2.50 (they book for about $60.00), and a McCoy Yosemite Sam cookie jar (the $200.00+ cylinder) for $3.00 — in mint condition. I recently spoke on the phone with a man who told me he'd bought a $1,500.00 Weller Louwelsa lamp base at a garage sale for just $5.00. Unbelievable prices, you say? Of course they are, but finds like these are possible. You can do it too! If you'll take the time to do your homework, your chances at making fantastic buys such as these are as good as mine or anyone else's! Whether you're a natural-born collector or just looking for a second source of income, there's money to be made by the person who is willing to study the collectibles market.

We'll make it easy! In addition to the background narration we've provided at the beginning of each cate-gory, we will reference other sources of helpful information as well. We'll suggest specialized books that are compiled and written by today's leading experts and authorities. (By the way, you'll find your money well spent if you begin immediately to build a substantial library on a broad range of subjects.) We'll also list clubs, newsletters, and tradepapers. There's much to be learned by sharing with other collectors, and newsletters and tradepapers often carry timely, informative articles.

If you yearn to start collecting but find that money is a little tight, we'll suggest ways to help you get the ball rolling. This is one hobby that can literally fund itself! To help you get started, we'll give you suggestions on how to hold a successful garage sale and some basic tips about flea market selling. In the back of the book, you'll even find a listing of potential buyers, sorted for you by alphabetized, topical subjects — and we'll clue you in to what's 'hot' on the market right now. We'll provide you with the information you need to become a wise and confident collector or dealer. Keep in mind that without a doubt there is profit to be gained following the advice we have to offer on the following pages, regardless of whether you're wanting to supplement your income or simply support your 'habit,' as many collectors do. It's a fundamental investment premise: buy low, sell for a profit.

How to Hold Your Own Garage Sale

Just as we promised we would, here are our suggestions for holding your own garage sale. If you're toying with the idea of getting involved in the business of buying and selling antiques and collectibles but find yourself short of any extra cash to back your venture, this is the way we always recommend you get started. Everyone has items they no longer use; get rid of them! Use them to your advantage. Here's how.

Get Organized. Gather up your merchandise. Though there's not a lot of money in selling clothing, this is the perfect time to unload things you're not using. Kids' clothing does best, since it's usually outgrown before it's worn out, and there's lots of budget-minded parents who realize this and think it makes good sense to invest as little as possible in their own children's wardrobes. Everything should of course be clean and rel-atively unwrinkled to sell at all, and try to get the better items on hangers. Leave no stone unturned. Clean out the attic, the basement, the garage — then your parent's attic, basement, and garage. If you're really into it, bake cook-ies, make some crafts. Divide your house plants; pot the starts in attractive little containers — ladies love 'em. Discarded and outgrown toys sell well. Framed prints and silk flower arrangements you no longer use, recipe books and paperbacks, tapes, records, and that kitchen appliance that's more trouble to store than it's worth can be turned into cash to get you off and running!

After you've gathered up your merchandise, you'll need to price it. Realistically, clothing will bring at the most about 15% to 25% of what you had to pay for it, if it's still in excellent, ready-to-wear shape and basically still in style. There's tons of used clothing out there, and no one is going to buy much of anything with buttons miss-ing or otherwise showing signs of wear. If you have good brand-name clothing that has been worn very little, you would probably do better by taking it to a resale or con-signment shop. They normally price things at about one-third of retail, with their cut being 30% of that. Not much difference money-wise, but the garage-sale shopper that passes up that $150.00 suit you're asking $25.00 for will probably give $50.00 for it at the consignment shop, sim-ply because like department stores, many have dressing rooms with mirrors so you can try things on and check them for fit before you buy. Even at $25.00, the suit is no bargain if you can't use it when you get it home.

Remember that garage-sale buyers expect to find low prices. Depending on how long you plan on staying open, you'll have one day, possibly two to move everything. If you start out too high, you'll probably be stuck with a lot of leftover merchandise, most of which you've already decided is worthless to you. The majority of your better buyers will hit early on; make prices attractive to them and you'll do all right. If you come up with some 'low-end' collectibles — fast-food toys, character glasses, played-with action figures, etc. — don't expect to get much out of them at a garage sale. Your competition down the block may underprice you. But if you have a few things you think have good resale potential, offer them at about half of 'book' price. If they don't sell at your garage sale, take them to a flea market or a consignment shop. You'll probably find they sell better on that level, since people expect to find prices higher there than at garage sales.

You can use pressure-sensitive labels or masking tape for price tags on many items. But *please* do not use either of these on things where damage is likely to occur when they are removed. For instance, (as one reader pointed out) on boxes containing toys, board games, puzzles, etc.; on record labels or album covers; or on ceramics or glass with gold trim or unfired, painted decoration. Unless a friend or a neighbor is going in on the sale with you, price tags won't have to be removed; the profit will all be yours. Of course, you'll have to keep tabs if others are involved. You can use a sheet of paper divided into columns, one for each of you, and write the amount of each sale down under the appropriate person's name, or remove the tags and restick them on a piece of poster board, one for each seller. I've even seen people use straight pins to attach small squares of paper which they remove and separate into plastic butter tubs. When several go together to have a sale, the extra help is nice, but don't let things get out of hand. Your sale can get *too* big. Things become too congested, and it's hard to display so much to good advantage.

Advertise. Place your ad in your local paper or on your town's cable TV information channel. It's important to make your ad interesting and upbeat. Though most sales usually start early on Friday or Saturday mornings, some people are now holding their sales in the early evening, and they seem to be having good crowds. This gives people with day jobs an opportunity to attend. You *might* want to hold your sale for two days, but you'll do 90% of your selling during the first two or three hours, and a two-day sale can really drag on. Make signs — smaller ones for street corners near your home to help direct passers-by, and a large one for your yard. You might even want to make another saying 'Clothing ½-Price after 12:00.' (It'll cut way down on leftovers that you'll otherwise have to dispose of yourself.) Be sure that you use a wide-tipped felt marker and print in letters big enough that the signs can be read from the street. Put the smaller signs up a few days in advance unless you're expecting rain. (If you are, you might want to include a rain date in your advertising unless your sale will be held under roof.) Make sure you have lots of boxes and bags, and plenty of change. If you price your items in increments of 25¢, you won't need anything but a few rolls of quarters, maybe ten or fifteen ones, and a few five-dollar bills. Then on the day of the sale, put the large sign up in a prominent place out front with some balloons to attract the crowd. Take a deep breath, brace yourself, and raise the garage door!

What to Do with What's Left. After the sale, pack up any good collectibles that didn't sell. Think about that consignment shop or setting up at a flea market. (We'll talk about that later on.) Sort out the better items of clothing for Goodwill or a similar charity, unless your city has someone who will take your leftovers and sell them on consignment. This is a fairly new concept, but some of the larger cities have such 'bargain centers.'

Learning to Become a Successful Bargain Hunter

Let me assure you, anyone who takes the time to become an informed, experienced bargain hunter will be successful. There is enough good merchandise out there to make it well worthwhile, at all levels. Once you learn what to look for, what has good resale potential, and what price these items will probably bring for you, you'll be equipped and ready for any hunting trip. You'll be the one to find treasures. They are out there!

Garage sales are absolutely wonderful for finding bargains. But you'll have to get up early! Even non-collectors can spot quality merchandise, and at those low, low garage sale prices (unless held by an owner who's done his homework) those items will be the first to move.

In order for you to be a successful garage sale shopper, you have to learn how to get yourself organized. It's important to conserve your time. The sales you hit during the first early-morning hour will prove to be the best nine times out of ten, so you must have a plan before you ever leave home. Plot your course. Your local paper will have a section on garage sale ads, and local cable TV channels may also carry garage sale advertising. Most people hold their sales on the weekend, but some may start earlier in the week, so be sure to turn to the 'Garage Sales' ads daily. Write them down and try to organize them by areas — northwest, northeast, etc. At first, you'll probably need your city map, but you'll be surprised at how quickly the streets will become familiar to you. Upper middle-class neighborhoods generally have the best sales and the best merchandise, so concentrate on those areas. When you've decided where you want to start, go early! If the ad says 8:00, be there at 7:00. This may seem rude and pushy, but if you can bring yourself to do it, it will pay off. And chances are when you get there an hour early, you'll not be their first customer. If they're obviously not ready for business, just politely inquire if you may look. If you're charming and their nerves aren't completely frayed from trying to get things ready, chances are they won't mind.

Competition can be fierce during those important early-morning hours. Learn to scan the tables quickly, then move to the area that looks the most promising. Don't be afraid to ask for a better price if you feel it's too high, but most people have already priced garage sale merchandise so that it will sell. Keep a notebook to jot down items you didn't buy the first time around but think you might be interested in if the price were reduced later on. After going through dozens of sales (I've done as many as thirty or so in one morning), you won't remember where you saw what! Often by noon, at least by mid-afternoon, veteran garage sale buyers are finished with their rounds and attendance becomes very thin. Owners are usually much more receptive to the idea of lowering their prices, so it may pay you to make a second pass. In fact some people find it advantageous to go to the better sales on the last day as well as the first. They'll make an offer for everything that's left, and since most of the time the owner is about ready to *pay* someone to take it at that point, they can usually name their price. Although most of the collectibles will normally be gone at this point, there are nearly always some useable household items and several pieces of good, serviceable clothing left. The household items will sell at flea markets or consignment shops, and if there are worthwhile clothing items, take them to a resale boutique. They'll either charge the 30% commission fee or buy the items outright for about half of the amount they feel they can ask, a new practice some resale shops are beginning to follow. Because they want only clothing that is in style, in season, and like new, their prices may be a little higher than others shops, so half of that asking price is a good deal.

Tag sales are common in the larger cities. They are normally held in lieu of an auction, when estates are being dispersed, or when families are moving. Sometimes only a few buyers are admitted at one time, and as one leaves another is allowed to take his place. So just as is true with garage sales, the early bird gets the goodies. Really serious shoppers begin to arrive as much as an hour or two before the scheduled opening time. I know of one who will spend the night in his van and camp on the 'doorstep' if he thinks the sale is especially promising. And he can tell you fantastic success stories! But since it's customary to have tag sale items appraised before values are set, be prepared to pay higher prices. That's not to say, though, that you won't find bargains here. If you think an item is overpriced, leave a bid. Just don't forget to follow through on it, since if it doesn't sell at their asking price, they may end up holding it for you. It's a good idea to check back on the last day of the sale.

Often the prices on unsold items may have been drastically reduced.

Auctions can go either way. Depending on the crowd and what items are for sale, you can sometimes spend all day and never be able to buy anything anywhere near 'book' price. On the other hand, there are often 'sleepers' that can be bought cheaply enough to resell at a good profit. Toys, dolls, Hummels, Royal Doultons, banks, cut glass, and other 'high-profile' collectibles usually go high, but white ironstone, dinnerware sets from the '20s through the '50s, silverplated hollow ware, books, records, and linens, for instance, often pass relatively unnoticed by the majority of the buyers.

If there is a consignment auction house in your area, check it out. These are usually operated by local auctioneers, and the sales they hold in-house often involve low-income estates. You won't find something every time, so try to investigate the merchandise ahead of schedule to see if it's going to be worth your time to attend. Competition is probably less at one of these than in any of the other types of sales we've mentioned, and wonderful buys have been made from time to time.

Flea markets are often wonderful places to find bargains. I don't like the small ones — not that I don't find anything there, but I've learned to move through them so fast (to beat the crowd), I don't get my 'fix'; I just leave wanting more. If you've never been to a large flea market, you don't know what you're missing. Even if you're not a born-again collector, I guarantee you will love it. And they're excellent places to study the market. You'll be able to see where the buying activity is, you can check and compare prices, talk with dealers and collectors, and do hands-on inspections. I've found that if I first study a particular subject by reading a book or a magazine article, this type of exposure to that collectible really 'locks in' what I have learned.

Because there are many types of flea market dealers, there are plenty of bargains. The casual, once-in-a-while dealer may not always keep up with changing market values. Some of them simply price their items by what they themselves had to pay for it. Just as being early at garage sales is important, here it's a must. If you've ever been in line waiting for a flea market to open, you know that cars are often backed up for several blocks, and people will be standing in line waiting to be admitted hours before the gate opens. Browsers? Window shoppers? Not likely. Competition. So if you're going to have a chance at all, you'd better be in line yourself. Take a partner and split up on the first pass so that you can cover the grounds more quickly. It's a common sight to see the serious buyers conversing with their partners via walkie-talkies, and if you like to discuss possible purchases with each other before you actually buy, this is a good way to do it.

Learn to bargain with dealers. Their prices are usually negotiable, and most will come down by 10% to 20%. Be polite and fair, and you can expect the same treatment in return. Unpriced items are harder to deal for. I have no problem offering to give $8.00 if an item is marked $10.00, but it's difficult for me to have to ask the price and then make a counter offer. So I'll just say 'This isn't marked. Will you take...?' I'm not an aggressive barterer, so this works for me.

There are so many reproductions on the flea market level (and at malls and co-ops), that you need to be suspicious of anything that looks too new! Some fields of collecting have been especially hard hit. Whenever a collectible becomes so much in demand that prices are high, reproductions are bound to make an appearance. For instance, Black Americana, Nippon, Roseville, banks, toys of all types, teddy bears, lamps, glassware, doorstops, cookie jars, prints, advertising items, and many other fields have been especially vulnerable. Learn to check for telltale signs — paint that is too bright, joints that don't fit, variations in sizes or colors, creases in paper that you can see but not feel, and so on. Remember that zip codes have been used only since 1963, and this can sometimes help you date an item in question. Check glassware for areas of wavy irregularities often seen in new glass. A publication we would highly recommend to you is called *Antique and Collector Reproduction News*, a monthly report of fakes, frauds, and facts. To subscribe, call 1-800-227-5531. Rates are very reasonable compared to the money you may save by learning to recognize reproductions.

Antique malls and co-ops should be visited on a regular basis. Many mall dealers restock day after day, and traffic and buying competition is usually fierce. As a rule, you won't often find great bargains here; what you do save on is time. And if time is what you're short of, you'll be able to see a lot of good merchandise under one roof, on display by people who've already done the leg work and invested *their* time, hence the higher prices. But there are always underpriced items as well, and if you've taken the time to do your homework, you'll be able to spot them right away.

Unless the dealer who rents the booth happens to be there, mall and co-op prices are usually firm. But often times they'll run sales — '20% off everything in booth #101.' If you have a dealer's license, and you really should get one, most will give you a courtesy 10% discount on items over $10.00, unless you want to pay with a credit card.

Antique shows are exciting to visit, but obviously if a dealer is paying several hundred dollars to set up for a three-day show, he's going to be asking top price to offset expenses. So even though bargains will be few, the merchandise is usually superior, and you may be able to find that special item you've been looking for.

Mail order buying is not only very easy, but most of the time economical as well. Many people will place an ad in 'For Sale' sections of tradepapers. Some will describe and price their merchandise in their ad, while others offer lists of items they have in exchange for a SASE (stamped, self-addressed envelope). You're out no gas or food expenses, their overhead is minimal so their prices are usually very reasonable, so it works out great for both buyer and seller. I've made lots of good buys this way, and I've always been fairly and honestly dealt with. You may want to send a money order or cashier's check to save time, otherwise (especially on transactions involving larger sums of money) the seller might want to wait until your personal check clears.

Goodwill stores and re-sale shops are usually listed in the telephone book. When you travel, it will pay to check them out. If there's one in your area, visit it often. You never know what may turn up there.

What's Hot on Today's Market

If you haven't already, you're going to find the '90s to be an exciting time to become involved in collecting. Today's collectibles are 'tomorrow's antiques' and values can only go up. But how much more satisfying (and economical) it is to buy at today's prices and be able to sit back and watch your investments appreciate. The trick is to look for trends; and to ferret them out, you'll have to spend some time. Attend shows; observe. For this, specialized shows are best. Go to toys shows — you'll learn which toys are hot and where the main thrust of interest is concentrated. There are advertising shows, pottery shows, glass shows, Art Deco shows, etc. General shows and sales can be a good arena for buying, but when you have many dealers with the same type of merchandise, you can't as easily mistake personal preferences for solid indications of market activity. Read tradepapers and magazines, and check out the 'antiques and collectibles' aisle of your bookstore. Any type of material that publicizes a collectible serves to draw attention to it, and many times that's all it takes to get it off and running. Co-ops are wonderful for 'trend watching.' These dealers generally have high overheads and to stay in the 'black' must stock merchandise that sells. I've become aware of several on-coming collectibles just by noting their first appearance at co-ops — initially only a few pieces; a few months later, a tablefull.

Many of the areas that were 'hot' last year still dominate the scene.

Ceramics imported from Japan. Here's what you need to be watching for:

1) Lefton China — exquisite giftware that has been imported since the 1940s. Workmanship is of the highest quality. Most pieces carry either a fired-on trademark or

a paper label. In particular, these pieces are good — the Christmas line called 'Green Holly'; animals, angels, and figurines; pieces with applied flowers and figures; figural banks; and the kitchenware lines of cookie jars, salt and pepper shakers, teapots, etc., called 'Miss Priss' (the blue kitten), and similar figural designs.

2) Enesco — This is an importer whose goods are really hot! Lots of it is whimsical and funky, and dealers tell us it's the 'off the wall' things that are selling! There are 'Human Beans,' little slug-like bean-people banks, cookie jars, and figurines that sport inscribed messages across their tummies. And they have a license to produce a line of Garfield the Cat items — cookie jars, salt and pepper shakers, bookends, a variety of banks, etc., all of which are bringing very good prices. Their 'Kitchen Prayer Ladies' are still going strong! This line was originally called 'Mother-in-the-Kitchen,' and they're easily identified by the prayer inscribed on their white aprons. They're often wearing a pink dresses, but if you find one in blue, she'll be worth even more. Some pieces are common, but the hard-to-find cookie jars, for instance, are up to $350.00 for the pink one, $495.00 for the blue (a considerable increase over the $250.00 minimum we reported last year). Kitchen Independence with Betsy Ross and George Washington is another of their lines to watch for.

3) Holt Howard — There are several styles of these figural ceramic novelties, and they're just as hot as we told you they were last year! From the late 1950s, collectors search for the Pixie kitchenware items such as cruets, condiments, etc., all with flat, disk-like pixie heads for stoppers. In the sixties, the company designed and distributed a line of roosters — egg cups, napkin holders, salt and pepper shakers, candle holders, plates, and bowls. Items with Christmas themes featuring Santa or angels, for instance, were sold from the fifties through the seventies, and you'll also find a line decorated with comical white cats. There are bobbin' head banks, desk accessories, and cookie jars. Virtually all are marked and most are dated as well. Be wary of unmarked but very similar items. Copy-cat lines abound. Rare items are pricey, especially from their Pixie line. A friend of ours sold his Pixies through an auction on the Internet, and the prices they brought were astonical. Some pieces such as the mayonnaise and the instant coffee jars fetch an easy $250.00, if not more!

4) Kreiss Ceramics — Here's a new one! Remember, you heard it here first! This line is full of some of the strangest ceramic items you'll ever care to see. I like the series with the cute little drunk and his pink elephant friend, but there are other lines that dealers tell us are selling very well for them too, for instance, the beatniks and the Psycho Ceramics. Figural banks are always good, and Kreiss's are certainly no exception. You'll also want to watch for their napkin holder dolls and their salt and pepper shakers.

These are only a few highlights in this wide field. Watch for items marked Vandor and Fitz & Floyd. Both are importers of quality merchandise, much of which is figural, some of it character related. Apart from looking for trademarks of companies such as we mentioned, certain categories of Japanese imports are good as well, for instance, napkin ladies, black cat kitchenware, cookie jars, and salt and pepper shakers. The market is ripe for the pickin' right now, and prices are definitely on their way up!

Advertising. In the advertising field, character collectibles continue to maintain a high profile. Some of the most collectible are Poppin' Fresh, Reddy Killowat, Campbell Kids, Big Boy, Mr. Peanut, and Elsie the Cow. But there are scores of others, old and new, that are well worth your attention as well. Even more recent issues are good: watch for Camel Joe items (now that he's retired, he's even more popular), M&M candy men (especially the 'toppers' from the holiday cylinders), and don't forget the Eveready bunny that keeps on 'going' and 'going' — he already has a lot of fans. Character radios and telephones are good, so are banks and push-button puppets! You'll find that these promotional items appear with suprising frequency at garage sales, even more so at flea markets. They've been distributed in large numbers, since most of them are very inexpensive to produce. Obviously their values hinge on their advertising message rather than their intrinsic worth.

Soda pop memorabilia is coming on strong. Of course, Coca-Cola items are always good, since there are literally tens of thousands of collectors for them and good pieces are easy to find in a price range that suits just about anyone's budget. Pepsi-Cola items are running a close second; and Hires, 7-Up, and Orange Crush are also becoming popular. With so much memorabilia of this type around today, you'll need to do a lot of research. Here's where a good price guide comes in.

Americans like their beer, and breweriana is a hot subdivision of advertising right now. Many collectors like to decorate their rec room with neon signs, clocks, rows of glass mugs, thermometers, signs, statuettes, and trays.

Automobilia collectibles are attracting a following, in fact there are huge cataloged auctions where everything for sale is related in some way to automobilia and gasoline and service station collectibles. The decade of the thirties produced the items that are most in demand today, but things from the fifties and sixties are beginning to accelerate in value as well. Paper ephemera such as brochures and manuals can make an interesting collection in their own right, and they're still not expensive. Motorcycle items have also been in the spotlight this year; we've observed them showing up at shows and auctions all over the country, and there's also been a new book written on the subject. Racing memorabila is another facet of this field where interest seems to be intensifying. This year, we've included information on all of these categories.

Toys. There continues to be a lot of activity in the toy market. Because they're so plentiful at garage sales, here's where you can often find some super deals. They certainly don't have to be old to have value. Some toys are instant collectibles, made by the producer with the collector in mind — for instance, Ertl banks, the new GI Joes, and the Holiday Barbies. Disney movies also generate instant collectibles. *The Rocketeer, Who Framed Roger Rabbit,* and *The Nightmare Before Christmas* casts already have devoted collector followings, and the PVC figures, dolls, watches, etc., representing so many of those characters will turn up every once in awhile on your garage-sale tours. Action figures are hugely popular, and though mint-on-card figures are certainly preferred, some of the loose examples you're more apt to find have considerable worth as well. To find out which are valuable, you'll need to study a book like *Schroeder's Collectible Toys, Antique to Modern,* which contains tons of action figure price listings, as well as thousands more on other types of collectible toys. You'll find it covers every imaginable field in the toy market to some extent, with particularly large, comprehensive sections on currently hot categories such as Model Kits, Japanese Windups and Battery-Ops, Fisher-Price, GI Joe, Star Wars, Celebrity Dolls, Diecast, and Disneyana.

Character collectibles still rule the roost, though, whether in the form of windups and battery-ops whose price tags at toy shows are staggering, or less-expensive, easier to access toys of a more recent vintage such as coloring books, board games, paper dolls, bubble bath containers, and lunch boxes. Besides the staples such as Disney and Western characters, other areas that are hot right now include vintage TV show titles such as *Lost in Space, Flintstones, Laverne and Shirley, Bonanza, Addams Family, Howdy Doody, Man From U.N.C.L.E., Charlie's Angels, CHiPs, Munsters, Batman,* and *I Love Lucy. Star Trek* and *Star Wars* items continue to be in high demand as well. Look for puzzles, playsets, model kits, etc., that were issued with these shows and movies in mind. Board games circa 1960s and '70s routinely go for $25.00 to $50.00, some much higher. And while you might buy a character-related model kit from the same era for under $50.00, on the retail level you can expect to pay $500.00 for a mint-in-the-box Addams Family House #805 by Aurora or their Bride of Frankenstein #482.

The Barbie market continues to be strong, and prices are constantly on the increase. Watch for these dolls on your garage-sale rounds — even nude Barbies of fairly recent manufacture often sell for $8.00 and up, and you may even find a rare vintage doll, it's certainly not out of the realm of possibility. The most sought-after Barbie items are those made before 1970, but Holiday Barbie dolls and of course the Bob Mackie fashion dolls can be very pricey! Remember, though, condition is extremely important in establishing their worth. Because they were mass produced in such huge quantities, only mint-in-box items bring the top prices. Once out of the original pack-

aging, you can immediately deduct about half from the mint-in-box value. Dating your Barbie dolls can be complicated, so you need to study reference books to become knowledgeable. For instance, the date on a doll's back may only indicate a copyright date, not the date of issue.

American-made ceramics. An ever-popular field that shows no evidence of waning interest, art pottery made by companies such as Roseville, Weller, and Rookwood has long been recognized as the cream of the crop, and though you seldom run across it at garage sales, it's certainly in the realm of possibility to pick up a piece now and then. You'll be much more apt to pick up Hall, Hull, McCoy, Pfaltzgraff, Regal, Ceramic Arts Studio, Shawnee, or Royal Haeger, for instance. But if you're buying to resell, you'll find a ready market for the wares of any company that I've mentioned, and similar manufacturers as well. In fact, if you can find a piece of any marked American pottery at garage-sale prices, you can be sure you've found a bargain. (Unmarked items can be good too, but you may have to do your homework to be able to recognize them.) Virtually any pottery you could mention is seeing a steady growth in value. McCoy has been at the top of the heap for the past several years, and we see no signs of it slowing down. From the nondescript flowerpots and Floraline vases to the top-of-the-line cookie jar, if it's marked McCoy, they want it.

Dinnerware is making a comeback, especially anything by Homer Laughlin. Fiesta and the other colored HLC lines have been good for twenty years, but you'll still find a few pieces now and then. The Virginia Rose lines sell well, and patterns from the fifties are becoming popular as well. In Pfaltzgraff, each year we find several good pieces of the brown drip they called 'Gourmet Royal.' Now their Village pattern has been discontinued, and we're finding it easy and lots of fun to reassemble a set of it for ourselves.

You'd have to be from another planet to have missed the furor the California potteries have stirred up! There are many of them, some of them major players, some of them minor. But even the minor companies are attracting more and more of a following. Among the top designer-potters are Kay Finch, Florence, Sascha Brastoff, Marc Bellaire, Cleminson, Howard Pierce, Brayton, and Vernon Kilns. We've dealt with most of these in individual categories, and the others we've touched on in a category called simply California Pottery. You'll do well to become familiar with these companies.

Kitchen Ware. The kitchen has always been at the heart of the home, and many of our favorite childhood memories are of events that happened in the kitchen. After school every afternoon, we'd peel potatoes and prepare food for the evening meal, all the while catching up on events of the day. Back then, families ate together; not only that, they actually talked, right through dessert and until the dishes were washed and the kitchen tidied up.

What was then so mundane is now an ambiance some collectors will go all out at re-creating — the vintage kitchen. You can sometimes still find a fifties breakfast set, the formica-topped, chrome-edged dinette table with its one wide leaf (it was an unheard-of small family that didn't need it all the time) and the six matching chrome-framed chairs with padded backrests and seats. What you do often find are the pottery mixing bowls, flour sifters, egg beaters, rolling pins, reamers, and hundreds of assorted gadgets Mom used to make her life a little easi-er. Clothes sprinkler bottles are priced out of sight at shows, and old appliances are being sought out and restored to look like new. Read through our Kitchen Collectibles category and keep your eyes open. Especially valuable are kitchen glass items in colors like Delphite blue, black, pink, and green. Gene Florence has a wonderful book on the subject titled *Kitchen Glassware of the Depression Years*, a must-have reference if you're drawn to this kind of glassware.

How to Evaluate Your Holdings

When viewed in its entirety, granted, the antiques and collectibles market can be overwhelming. But in each line of glassware, any type of pottery or toys, or any other field I could mention, there are examples that are more desirable than others, and these are the ones you need to be able to recognize. If you're a novice, it will probably be best at first to choose a few areas that you find most interesting and learn just what particular examples or types of items are most in demand within that field. Concentrate on the top 25%. This is where you'll do 75% of your business. Do your home-work. Quality sells. Obviously no one can be an expert in everything, but gradually you can begin to broaden your knowledge. As an added feature of our guide, information on clubs and newsletters, always a wonderful source of up-to-date information on any subject, is contained in each cat-egory when available. (Advisors' names are listed as well. We highly recommend that you exhaust all other resources before you contact them with your inquiries. Their roll is simply to check over our data before we go to press to make sure it is as accurate as we and they can possibly make it for you; they do not agree to answer readers' questions, though some may. If you do write, you must send them an SASE. If you call, please take the time zones into consideration. Some of our advisors are professionals and may charge an appraisal fee, so be sure to ask. Please, do *not* be offended if they do not respond to your contacts, they are under no obligation to do so.)

There are many fields other than those we've already mentioned that are strong and have been for a long time — Depression, Elegant, and carnival glass; photographica; ephemera such as valentines and sheet music; good costume jewelry; Fiesta; dolls; Christmas collectibles; and railroadiana. It's impossible to list them all. But we've left very little out of this book; at least we've tried to represent each category to some extent and where at all possible to refer you to a source of further information. It's up to you to read, observe the market, and become acquainted with it to the point that you feel confident enough to become a part of today's antiques and collectibles industry, if you haven't already. You don't know what you're missing!

The thousands of current values found in this book will increase your awareness of today's wonderful world of buy-ing, selling, and collecting antiques and collectibles. Use it to educate yourself to the point that you'll be the one with the foresight to know what and how to buy as well as where and how to turn those sleepers into cold, hard cash.

In addition to this one, there are several other very fine price guides on the market. One of the best is *Schroeder's Antiques Price Guide*, another is *The Flea Market Trader*. Both are published by Collector Books. *The Antique Trader Antiques and Collectibles Price Guide*, *Warman's Antiques and Their Prices*, and *Kovel's Antiques and Collectibles Price List* are others. You may want to invest in a copy of each. Where you decide to sell will have a direct bearing on how you price your merchandise, and nothing will affect an item's worth more than condition.

If you're not familiar with using a price guide, here's a few tips that may help you. When convenient and reason-able, antiques will be sorted by manufacturer. This is espe-cially true of pottery and most glassware. If you don't find the item you're looking for under manufacturer, look under a broader heading, for instance, cat collectibles, napkin dolls, cookie jars, etc. And don't forget to use the index. Most guides of this type have very comprehensive indexes — a real boon to the novice collector. If you don't find the exact item you're trying to price, look for something similar. For instance, if it's a McCoy rabbit planter you're researching, go through the McCoy section and see what price range other animal planters are in. Or if you have a frame-tray puzzle with Snow White and the Seven Dwarfs, see what other Disney frame-trays are priced at. Just be careful not to com-pare apples to oranges. You can judge the value of a 7" Roseville Magnolia vase that's not listed; just look at the price given for one a little larger or smaller and adjust it up or down. Pricing collectibles is certainly not a science; the bot-tom line is simply where the buyer and the seller finally agree to do business. Circumstances dictate sale price, and we can only make suggestions, which we base on current sales, market observations, and the expert opinions of our advisors.

Once you've found 'book' price, decide how much less you can take for it. 'Book' price represents a high average retail. A collectible will often change hands many times, and obviously it will not always be sold at book price. How quickly do you want to realize a profit? Will you be patient enough to hold out for top dollar, or would you rather price your merchandise lower so it will turn over more quickly? Just as there are both types of dealers, there are two types of collectors. Many are bargain hunters. They shop around — do the legwork themselves. On the other hand, there are those who are willing to pay whatever the asking price is to avoid spending precious time searching out pieces they especially want, but they represent the minority. You'll often see tradepaper ads listing good merchandise (from that top 25% we mentioned before) at prices well above book value. This is a good example of a dealer who knows that his merchandise is good enough to entice the second type of buyer we mentioned and doesn't mind waiting for him (or her) to come along, and that's his prerogative.

Once you have a price range in mind, the next step is to assess condition. Most people, especially inexperienced buyers and sellers, have a tendency to overlook some flaws and to overrate merchandise. Mint condition means that an item is complete and undamaged, in effect, just as it looked the day it was made. Glassware, china, and pottery may often be found in mint condition, though signs of wear will downgrade anything. Unless a toy is still in its original box and has never been played with, you seldom see a toy in mint condition. Paper collectibles are almost never found without deterioration or damage. Most price guides will list values that apply to glass and ceramics that are mint (unless another condition is specifically indicated within some descriptions). Other items are usually evaluated on the assumption that they are in the best as-found condition common to that area of collecting. Grade your merchandise as though you were the buyer, not the seller. You'll be building a reputation that will go a long way toward contributing to your success. If it's glassware or pottery you're assessing, an item in less than excellent condition will be mighty hard to sell at any price. Just as a guideline (a basis to begin your evaluation, though other things will factor in), use a scale of one to five with Good being a one, Excellent being a three, and Mint being a five. As an example, a beer tray worth $250.00 in mint condition would then be worth $150.00 if excellent and $50.00 if only good. Remember, the first rule of buying (for resale or investment) is 'Don't put your money in damaged goods.' And the second rule should be be, 'If you do sell damaged items, indicate 'as is' on the price tag, and don't price the item as though it were mint.' The Golden Rule applies just as well to us as antique dealers as it does in any other phase of interaction. Some shops and co-ops have poor lighting — your honesty will be greatly appreciated. If you include identification on your tags as well, be sure it's accurate. If you're not positive, it's better to let the buyer decide.

Deciding Where to Best Sell Your Merchandise

Personal transactions are just one of many options. Overhead and expenses will vary with each and must be factored into your final pricing. If you have some especially nice items and can contact a collector willing to pay top dollar, that's obviously the best of the lot. Or you may decide to sell to a dealer who may be willing to pay you only half of book. Either way, your expenses won't amount to much more than a little gas or a phone call.

Classified ads are another way to get a good price for your more valuable merchandise without investing much money or time. Place a 'For Sale' ad or run a mail bid in one of the collector magazines or newsletters, several of which are listed in the back of this book. Many people have had excellent results this way. One of the best to reach collectors in general is *The Antique Trader Weekly* (P.O. Box 1050, Dubuque, Iowa 52004). It covers virtually any and all types of antiques and collectibles and has a very large circulation. If you have glassware, china, or pottery from the Depression era, you should have good results through *The Depression Glass Daze* (Box 57, Otisville, Michigan 48463). If you have several items and the cost of listing them all is prohibitive, simply place an ad saying (for instance) 'Several pieces of Royal Copley (or whatever) for sale, send SASE for list. Be sure to give your correct address and phone number.

When you're making out your list or talking with a prospective buyer by phone, try to draw a picture with words. Describe any damage in full; it's much better than having a disgruntled customer to deal with later, and you'll be on your way to establishing yourself as a reputable dealer. Sometimes it's wise to send out photographs. Seeing the item exactly as it is will often help the prospective buyer make up his or her mind. Send a SASE along and ask that your photos be returned to you, so that you can send them out again, if need be. A less expensive alternative is to have your item photocopied. This works great for many smaller items, not just flat shapes but things with some dimension as well. It's wonderful for hard-to-describe dinnerware patterns or for showing their trademarks.

If you've made that 'buy of a lifetime' or an item you've hung onto for a few years has turned out to be a scarce, highly sought collectible, a mail bid is often the best way to get top dollar for your prize. This is how you'll want your ad to read. 'Mail Bid. Popeye cookie jar by American Bisque, slight wear (or 'mint' — briefly indicate condition), closing 6/31/95, right to refuse' (standard self-protection clause meaning you will refuse ridiculously low bids), and give your phone number. Don't commit the sale to any bidder until after the closing date, since some may wait until the last minute to try to place the winning bid.

Be sure to let your buyer know what form of payment you prefer. Some dealers will not ship merchandise until personal checks have cleared. This delay may make the buyer a bit unhappy. So you may want to request a money order or a cashier's check.

Be very careful about how you pack your merchandise for shipment. Breakables need to be well protected. There are several things you can use. Plastic bubble wrap is excellent, or scraps of foam rubber such as carpet padding (check with a carpet-laying service or confiscate some from family and friends who're getting new carpet installed). I've received items wrapped in pieces of egg-crate type mattress pads (watch for these at garage sales!). If there is a computer business near you, check their dumpsters for discarded foam wrapping and other protective packaging. It's best not to let newspaper come in direct contact with your merchandise, since the newsprint may stain certain types of items. After you've wrapped them well, you'll need boxes. Find smaller boxes (one or several, whatever best fits your needs) that you can fit into a larger one with several inches of space between them. First pack your well-wrapped items snugly into the smaller box, using crushed newspaper to keep them from shifting. Place it into the larger box, using more crushed paper underneath and along the sides, so that it will not move during transit. Remember, if it arrives broken, it's still your merchandise, even though you have received payment. You may want to insure the shipment; check with your carrier. Some have automatic insurance up to a specified amount.

After you've mailed it out, it's good to follow it up with a phone call after a few days. Make sure the box arrived in good condition and that your customer is pleased with the merchandise. Most people who sell by mail allow a 10-day return privilege, providing their original price tag is still intact. You can simply initial a gummed label or use one of those pre-printed return address labels that most of us have around the house.

For very large or heavy items such as furniture or slot machines, ask your buyer for his preferred method of shipment. If the distance involved is not too great, he may even want to pick it up himself.

Flea Market Selling can either be a lot of fun, or it can turn out to be one of the worst experiences of your life.

Obviously you will have to deal with whatever weather conditions prevail, so be sure to listen to weather reports so that you can dress accordingly. You'll see some inventive shelters you might want to copy. Even a simple patio umbrella will offer respite from the blazing sun or a sudden downpour. I've recently been seeing stands catering just to the needs of the flea market dealer — how's that for being enterprising! Not only do they carry specific items the dealers might want, but they've even had framework and tarpaulins for shelters they'll erect right on the spot!

Be sure to have plastic table covering in case of rain and some large clips to hold it down if there's much wind. The type of clip you'll need depends on how your table is made, so be sure to try them out before you actually have need for them. Otherwise your career as a flea market dealer may be cut short for lack of merchandise!

Price your things, allowing yourself a little bargaining room. Unless you want to collect tax separately on each sale (for this you'd need a lot of small change), mentally calculate the amount and add this on as well. Sell the item 'tax included.' Everybody does.

Take snacks, drinks, paper bags, plenty of change, and somebody who can relieve you occasionally. Collectors are some of the nicest people around. I guarantee that you'll enjoy this chance to meet and talk to them, and often you can make valuable contacts that may help you locate items you're especially looking for yourself.

Auction Houses are listed in the back of this book. If you have an item you feel might be worth selling at auction, be sure to contact one of them. Many have appraisal services; some are free while others charge a fee, dependent on number of items and time spent. We suggest you first make a telephone inquiry before you send in a formal request.

In Summation

Whatever the reason you've become interested in the antiques and collectibles field, whether to supplement your income part-time, go into it on a full-time basis, or simply because you want to be a wise collector/investor, I'm confident that you will achieve your goals. Aside from monetary gain, it's a wonderful hobby, a real adventure. There's never been a better time to become involved. With study comes knowledge, and knowledge is the key to success. The time you invest in reading, attending shows, talking with experienced collectors, and pursuing understanding of the field in every way you can devise will pay off handsomely as you enjoy the hunt for today's collectibles, tomorrow's antiques.

Abbreviations

dia – diameter	lg – large	MOC – mint on card	qt – quart
ea – each	M – mint condition	NM – near mint	sm – small
EX – excellent	med – medium	oz – ounce	VG – verygood
G – good	MIB – mint in (original) box	pc – piece	w/ – with
gal – gallon		pr – pair	
L – long, length	MIP – mint in package	pt – pint	

Abingdon

You may find smaller pieces of Abingdon around, but it's not common to find many larger items. This company operated in Abingdon, Illinois, from 1934 until 1950, making not only nice vases and figural pieces but some kitchen items as well. Their cookie jars are very well done and popular with collectors. They sometimes used floral decals and gold to decorate their wares, and a highly decorated item is worth a minimum of 25% more than the same shape with no decoration. Some of their glazes also add extra value. If you find a piece in black, bronze, or red, you can add 25% to those as well. Note that if you talk by phone about Abingdon to a collector, be sure to mention the mold number on the base.

See also Cookie Jars.

Advisor: Louise Dumont (See Directory, Abingdon)

Club: Abingdon Pottery Collectors Club
Elaine Westover, Membership and Treasurer
210 Knox Hwy. 5, Abingdon, IL 61410; 309-462-3267

Vase, draped with decals and gold trim, #557, 11", from $65.00 to $75.00.

Ashtray, Trojan, #316, 5x3½", from $50 to **$60.00**
Ashtray, utility, #334, 5½" dia **$15.00**
Bookends, cactus (planter), #374, 6½", pr....................**$75.00**
Bookends, colt, #363, 5¾", pr **$85.00**
Bowl, console; blue, #532, 14½" L..............................**$25.00**
Bowl, hibiscus, #527, 10" dia **$25.00**
Bowl, leaf, beige, #408, 6½" dia...................................**$40.00**
Bowl, morning glory, #393, 7"......................................**$35.00**
Bowl, pineapple, #700D, 14¾" L...................................**$85.00**
Bowl, shell, #506, 6" dia..**$20.00**
Bowl, shell, #610, 9" dia..**$25.00**
Bowl, soup; square, #338, 4¾", w/lid..........................**$40.00**
Box, butterfly, #580, 4¾" **$60.00**
Candle holder, double, Victory Boat, #578.................**$65.00**
Candle holder, single, fern leaf, #434, 5½" L.............**$35.00**
Candle holders, daisy, #384, 4½" dia, pr **$35.00**
Candle holders, star, #714, 4¼", pr.............................**$15.00**
Cornucopia, yellow, #474, 5½".....................................**$18.00**
Dish, square, #337, 5"...**$25.00**
Figurine, goose, #98, 5"...**$25.00**
Figurine, heron, #574, 5¼"..**$30.00**
Figurine, nude, seated, #3903, 7" **$280.00**

Figurine, swan, decorated, #661, 4" **$40.00**
Figurine, swordfish, decorated, #657, 4½"..................**$40.00**
Jug, #201, 1-qt...**$45.00**
Planter, burro, #673, 4½"...**$35.00**
Planter, donkey, #669, 7½" **$25.00**
Planter, fawn, #672, 5"...**$35.00**
Planter, puppy, decorated, #652, 6¾" **$25.00**
Plate, round, #343, 12" dia..**$50.00**
Stringholder, Chinese face, #702D, 5½" **$125.00**
Vase, Arden, #517, 7", from $20 to..............................**$25.00**
Vase, asters, #455, 12"...**$55.00**
Vase, Barre, #522, 9"...**$35.00**
Vase, Blackamoor, #497, 7½"...**$95.00**
Vase, bow knot, blue, #593, 9"......................................**$25.00**
Vase, Classic, #143, 5½" **$20.00**
Vase, Delta, #108, 8"...**$25.00**
Vase, double cornucopia, #581, 8"................................**$30.00**
Vase, Dutch boy, #469, 8"..**$100.00**
Vase, fan form w/ribbon bow, #484, 8½" L...................**$20.00**
Vase, hackney, #659, 8½"..**$30.00**
Vase, Lattice, #458, 5½"..**$30.00**
Vase, Laurel, #600, 12"...**$75.00**
Vase, morning glory, #390, 10" **$40.00**
Vase, poppy, #629, 6½"...**$30.00**

Vase, Laurel, blue, #442, 6", from $35.00 to $40.00.

Vase, swirl, #513, 9", from $15 to.................................**$25.00**
Wall bracket, acanthus, #589, 7"...................................**$50.00**
Wall pocket, cherub bracket, #587, 7½" **$65.00**

Vase, Rope, G4, 14", $175.00.

Wall pocket, Triad, #640, 5½"..**$30.00**
Wall vase, carriage lamp, #711, 10".............................**$45.00**

Advertising Character Collectibles

The advertising field holds a special fascination for many of today's collectors. It's vast and varied, so its appeal is universal; but the characters of the ad world are its stars right now. Nearly every fast-food restaurant and manufacturer of a consumer product has a character logo. Keep your eyes open on your garage sale outings; it's not at all uncommon to find the cloth and plush dolls, plastic banks and mugs, bendies, etc., such as we've listed here. There are several books on the market that are geared specifically toward these types of collectibles. Among them are *Collectible Aunt Jemima* by Jean Williams Turner (Schiffer); *Advertising Character Collectibles* by Warren Dotz and *Zany Characters of the Ad World* by Mary Jane Lamphier (both published by Collector Books); and *Hake's Guide to Advertising Collectibles* by Ted Hake (Wallace-Homestead). *Huxford's Collectible Advertising* offers a more general overview of the market but nevertheless includes many listings and values for character-related items as well. *Schroeder's Collectible Toys, Antique to Modern*, is another source. (The latter two are published by Collector Books.)

See also Breweriana; Bubble Bath Containers; Cereal Boxes and Premiums; Character Clocks and Watches; Character and Promotional Drinking Glasses; Coca-Cola Collectibles; Fast-Food Collectibles; Novelty Radios; Novelty Telephones; Pez Candy Containers; Pin-Back Buttons; Salt and Pepper Shakers; Soda Pop Memorabilia.

Aunt Jemima

One of the most widely recognized ad characters of them all, Aunt Jemima has decorated bags and boxes of pancake flour for more than ninety years. In fact, the original milling company carried her name, but by 1926 it had become part of the Quaker Oats Company. She and Uncle Mose were produced in plastic by the F&F Mold and Die Works in the 1950s, and the salt and pepper shakers, syrup pitchers, cookie jars, etc., they made are perhaps the most sought-after of the hundreds of items available today. (Watch for reproductions.) Age is a big worth-assessing factor for memorabilia such as we've listed below, of course, but so is condition. Watch for very chipped or worn paint on the F&F products, and avoid buying very soiled cloth dolls.

Advisor: Judy Posner (See Directory, Advertising)

Brochure, lists locations of 28 Aunt Jemima's restaurants and planned locations, 1950s, EX **$45.00**
Business card, black graphics on pink ground, Pancakes Made on Famous Automatic Machine..., 4x2¼", EX **$60.00**
Clock, wall; electric **$385.00**
Cookie jar, Aunt Jemima plastic figural, F&F Mold & Die, NM **$400.00**
Cooking set, Junior Chef Pancake Set, w/spatula, griddle, spoon & mix, Argo Industries, ca 1949, 9x10", NMIB **$185.00**

Corn meal sack, multicolor graphics on paper, shows chubby Jemima in full bandana, ca 1950s, 5-lb, unused, M ... **$55.00**
Creamer, Uncle Mose, F&F Mold & Die, EX **$80.00**
Doll, Aunt Jemima Breakfast Bear, blue velour plush, 13", rare, M **$175.00**
Doll, stiched & stuffed oilcloth, premium, ca 1949, 11", EX **$95.00**
Magazine ad, Pancakes in 10 Shakes, features shaker available for 25¢ & box top, 1958, full page, 10½x14", EX ... **$28.00**

Pancake mold, aluminum with center handle, 8½", from $165.00 to $195.00.

Pancake shaker, blue hard plastic, embossed Perfect Pancakes in 10 Shakes, late 1950s, 8½", EX **$85.00**
Poster, Good Old Time Aunt Jemima Buckwheats, Treat the Whole Family, multicolor, for grocery store, 13x20", EX **$165.00**
Poster book, Year Round Parade, ad layouts for store promotions, spiral bound, late 1940s, 17x12¾", rare, EX .. **$550.00**
Recipe booklet, Pancakes Unlimited, multicolor, 1958, 31 pages, 4½x6¼", EX **$75.00**
Recipe box, hard red plastic, shows Aunt Jemima w/red bandana w/red polka dots, EX **$225.00**
Recipe card set, 16 cards + promotional card, ca 1940s, M, from $265 to **$295.00**
Salt & pepper shakers, Aunt Jemima & Uncle Mose, F&F Mold & Die, 3½", pr **$65.00**
Salt & pepper shakers, Aunt Jemima & Uncle Mose, F&F Mold & Die, 5", pr **$75.00**

Salt and pepper shakers, F&F Mold & Die Co., with original flyer, dated 1957, 3½", MIB, from $75.00 to $85.00.

Spatula, hard plastic Bakelite type w/white handle imprinted Hooray! It's Aunt Jemima Day, metal spatula top, 1940s, EX **$125.00**

Spice shaker, plastic figural, F&F Mold & Die, from set of 6, each **$50.00**

Sugar bowl, Aunt Jemima plastic figural, w/lid, premium, F&F Mold & Die, 1950s, EX **$90.00**

Syrup pitcher, Aunt Jemima plastic figural, F&F Mold & Die, 5½" **$70.00**

Big Boy and Friends

Bob's Big Boy, home of the nationally famous Big Boy, the original double-deck hamburger, was founded by Robert C. 'Bob' Wian in Glendale, California, in 1938. He'd just graduated from high school, and he had a dream. With the $300.00 realized from the sale of the car he so treasured, he bought a run-down building and enough basic equipment to open his business. Through much hard work and ingenuity, Bob turned his little restaurant into a multimillion-dollar empire. Not only does he have the double-deck 2-patty burger to his credit, but car hops and drive-in restaurants were his invention as well.

With business beginning to flourish, Bob felt he needed a symbol — something that people would recognize. One day in walked a chubby lad of six, his sagging trousers held up by reluctant suspenders. Bob took one look at him and named him Big Boy, and that was it! It was a natural name for his double-deck hamburger — descriptive, catchy, and easy to remember. An artist worked out the drawings, and Bob's Pantry was renamed Bob's Big Boy.

The enterprise grew fast, and Bob added location after location. In 1969 when he sold out to the Marriott Corporation, he had 185 restaurants in California, with franchises such as Elias' Big Boy, Frisch's Big Boy, and Shoney's Big Boy in other states. The Big Boy burger and logo were recognized by virtually every man, woman, and child in America, and Bob retired knowing he had made a significant contribution to millions of people everywhere.

Since Big Boy has been in business for over sixty years, you'll find many items and numerous variations. Some, such as the large statues, china, and some menus, have been reproduced. If you're in doubt, go to an experienced collector for help. Many items of jewelry, clothing, and kids promotions were put out over the years, too numerous to itemize separately. Values range from $5.00 up to $100.00.

Advisor: Steve Soelberg (See Directory, Advertising)

Dinner plate, 1970s, 8", $100.00. (Photo courtesy Steve Soelberg)

Ashtray, clear w/orange logo, 1969, M **$15.00**
Award, employee, gold 'Oscar' statue........................**$450.00**
Badge, for employee, M..**$10.00**
Cigarette lighter, metal w/embossed image, Zippo, recent, M, from $20 to..**$25.00**
Coffee can, Mocha Boy, running Bob, full................**$100.00**
Comic book, Bob's Big Boy #1, 1940s, M **$250.00**
Comic book, Shoney's Big Boy, NM **$5.00**
Cookie jar, 1950s Big Boy, Wolfe Studio **$600.00**
Counter display, papier-mache, 1960s **$500.00**
Decal, Big Boy for President, M **$5.00**
Doll, Big Boy or Dolly, stuffed cloth, 1978, 14", MIP, each ...**$30.00**
Doll, complete w/hamburger & shoes, Dakin...........**$150.00**
Figure, pewter, good quality, 5" **$50.00**
Figure, PVC, 1994, 3"...**$20.00**
Food bag, Frisch's Big Boy Burger, 1950s, M.............**$15.00**
Food box, cardboard, punch out to assemble vehicle, 1970s, unused, M..**$25.00**
Key chain, flat silver-tone figural, M **$10.00**
Kite, paper w/Big Boy graphics & sticks, 1960s.......**$200.00**
Lunch box, red plastic...**$15.00**
Menu, cardboard w/punch-out puppet, for children, 1970s, M **$45.00**
Night light, Bob's Big Boy, 7", M **$100.00**
Night light, plastic, plug-in-socket type **$20.00**
Pencil, Frisch's Big Boy, M...**$6.00**
Pin-back button, Big Boy for President, M **$7.00**
Pin-back button, National Big Boy Club Member, M..**$20.00**
Pin-back button, Should He Stay or Go?, M...............**$12.00**
Playing cards, from $25 to **$35.00**
Salt & pepper shakers, Big Boy figural, ceramic, 1960s-70s, pr...**$375.00**
Salt & pepper shakers, Big Boy figural, ceramic, 1996, pr...**$10.00**

Salt and pepper shakers, late '50s to early '60s, 4", pr, $350.00. (Photo courtesy Steve Soelberg)

Service pin, man or woman employee, gold-tone, each **$35.00**
Trading cards of famous Americans, set of 30 ....**$40.00**
Transistor radio, Big Boy can, 1960s, M **$300.00**
Watch, Big Boy chasing food on face, 1994, MIP **$25.00**
Watch, Big Boy running, arms as hands, turquoise dots for numbers, 1960s, MIB **$75.00**
Watch, man's, gold quartz, Windert, MIB **$150.00**

Campbell Kids

The introduction of the world's first canned soup was announced in 1897. Later improvements in the manufacturing process created an evolutionary condensed soup. The Campbell's® Soup Company is now the primary beneficiary of this early entrepreneurial achievement. Easily identified by their red and white advertising, the company has been built on a tradition of skillful product marketing through five generations of consumers. Now a household name for all ages, Campbell's Soups have grown to dominate 80% of the canned soup market.

The first Campbell's licensed advertising products were character collectibles offered in 1910 as composition dolls (heads made from a combination of glue and sawdust). The dolls were made by the E.I. Horsman Company and sold for $1.00 each. They were the result of a gifted illustrator, Grace Drayton, who in 1904 gave life to the chubby-faced cherub 'Campbell's Kids.'

In 1994 the Campbell's Soup Kids celebrated their 90th birthday. They have been revised a number of times to maintain a likeness to modern-day children. Over the years hundreds of licensees have been commissioned to produce collectibles and novelty items with the Campbell's logo in a red and white theme.

Licensed advertising reached a peak from 1954 through 1956 with thirty-four licensed manufacturers. Unusual items included baby carriges, toy vacuums, games, and apparel. Many of the more valuable Campbell's advertising collectibles were made during this period. In 1956 a Campbell's Kid doll was produced from latex rubber. Called 'Baby Magic,' it proved to be the most popular mail-in premium ever produced. Campbell's received more than 560,000 requests for this special girl chef doll.

Advisors: David and Micki Young (See Directory, Advertising)

Club: Soup Collector Club
David and Micki Young, Editors and Founders
414 Country Lane Ct.
Wauconda, IL 60084, 847-487-4917; 6 issues per year for $20 donation per address

Calendar, ca 1990, each	**$3.00**
Canister set, ceramic, Westwood, 1991, MIB	**$65.00**
Christmas ornament, Kid atop soup can, plaster, Enesco, 1993, MIB	**$10.00**
Christmas ornament, Kids in bed, 1993	**$5.00**
Clock, tomato soup can face in black frame, 1996, 9¼" dia	**$16.00**
Container, hand lotion, plastic, MIP	**$10.00**
Cookbook, Campbell Soup International, 1980, blue cover	**$9.00**
Cookie jar, ceramic, Westwood, 1991, MIB	**$35.00**
Cup, Bicentennial, 1976	**$7.00**
Cup, Heritage, 1996, set of 4, each	**$12.00**
Cup, microwaveable	**$3.00**
Cup, plastic figural Kid w/yellow hair	**$6.00**
Diecut, baseball player Campbell Kid, cardboard store ad figure, 1980, 18"	**$6.00**

Diecut, Pilgrim Campbell Kids, cardboard store ad figures, 1980, 18"	**$5.00**
Dinnerware, stoneware, plate, bowl, cup & saucer, 1992, 4-pc place setting, child size, MIB	**$9.00**
Dinnerware, tumbler, bowl & spoon, Zak Designs, 1995, M in blister pack	**$19.00**
Doll, Globe, 1988, MIB, each	**$30.00**
Fork & spoon set, Westwood, 1992, MIB	**$8.00**
Hot pad/oven mitt, 1992	**$8.00**

**Jigsaw puzzle, All Aboard, 1986, MIB, $25.00.
(Photo courtesy David and Micki Young)**

Mug, Kid, Westwood, set of 4	**$5.00**
Mug, M'M Good	**$3.00**
Paperweight, etched glass	**$42.50**
Recipe box, 1992	**$6.00**
Salt & pepper shakers, ceramic, Westwood, 1991, pr, MIB	**$9.00**
Salt & pepper shakers, metal, 1996, pr	**$10.00**
Tea set, child's, Chilton, 1993, MIB (Kid graphics)	**$20.00**
Thermometer, Homestyle Soup, tin	**$25.00**
Thimble, Campbell Soup	**$6.00**
Timer, soup can shape, mechanical, 1995, 2x4"	**$4.00**
Tool caddy w/tools, Westwood, 1992	**$5.00**
Towel set, 4-pc	**$13.00**
Train, Campbell's Soup, 1989, MIB	**$150.00**
Tureen, 1½-qt	**$5.00**
Vehicle, semi w/trailer, Campbell's Soup, 1985	**$45.00**
Vehicle, truck in tin can, Ertl, 1996, sm	**$27.00**
Watch, digital w/red face	**$25.00**

Cap'n Crunch

Cap'n Crunch was the creation of Jay Ward, whom you will no doubt remember was also the creator of the Rocky and Bullwinkle show. The Cap'n hails from the sixties and was one of the first heroes of the pre-sweetened cereal crowd. Jean LaFoote was the villian always scheming to steal the Cap'n's cereal.

Advisor: Scott Bruce

Bank, Cap'n Crunch, painted plastic, 1973, VG	**$65.00**
Bank, Treasure Chest, blue plastic, 1984, NM	**$10.00**
Cap'n Crunch Cruiser, plastic, 1987, EX	**$10.00**
Cap'n Rescue Kit, paper, 1986, MIP	**$10.00**

Doll, 1987, Mighty Star Co., 18", NM, $30.00.

Figure, Cap'n Crunch, blue plastic, 1986, 1½", VG.....**$10.00**
Figure, Sog Master, silver plastic robot, 1986, 1½", NM ...**$15.00**
Figure, Soggie, nearly clear plastic, 1986, 1½", EX **$10.00**
Hand puppet, plastic, 1960s, VG..................................**$15.00**
Sea dog spy kit, plastic w/paper instructions, M in original mailer..**$45.00**
Stickers, Chockle, paper, sheet A or B, 1980, M, each ..**$15.00**
Storyscope '72, assembled plastic, w/cut-out story disk, NM **$35.00**

Charlie Tuna

Poor Charlie, never quite good enough for the Star-Kist folks to can, though he yearns for them to catch him; but since the early 1970s he's done a terrific job working for them as the company logo. A dapper blue-fin tuna in sunglasses and a beret, he's appeared in magazines, done TV commercials, modeled for items as diverse as lamps and banks, but still they deny him his dream. 'Sorry, Charlie.'

Alarm clock, blue and white, 1969, 4" diameter, M, $65.00.

Bank, ceramic, 1988, 10", from $50 to.........................**$65.00**
Bathroom scale, painted metal, 1970s, NM, from $65 to ..**$75.00**
Bracelet, embossed raised figure on gold-tone disk, M **$10.00**
Figure, squeeze vinyl, 1974, EX..................................**$40.00**
Key ring, raised design on gold-tone disk, M.............**$10.00**
Lamp, painted plaster figure of Charlie, EX **$75.00**
Pendant, Charlie on anchor, M......................................**$10.00**
Pin, rhinestones, sm...**$10.00**
Wristwatch, stem wind, NM, from $55 to **$75.00**

Colonel Sanders

There's nothing fictional about the Colonel — he was a very real guy, who built an empire on the strength of his fried chicken recipe with 'eleven herbs and spices.' In the 1930s, the Colonel operated a small cafe in Corbin, Kentucky. As the years went by, he developed a chain of restaurants which he sold in the mid-sixties. But even after the sale, the new company continued to use the image of the handsome southern gentlemen as their logo. The Colonel died in 1980.

Bank, plastic figure, no base, white w/black necktie, holding bucket of chicken, 1970s, 8", EX.........................**$40.00**
Bank, plastic figure, 13", NM **$40.00**
Bank, plastic figure w/arm around restaurant building & holding bucket of chicken, white w/red & black trim, 6", EX..**$125.00**
Child's tea set, plastic, 1970s, MIB **$110.00**
Coin, Visit the Colonel at Mardi Gras, M....................**$10.00**
Mask, multicolor plastic, 1960s, M...............................**$38.00**
Name badge, 1960s, M..**$25.00**
Nodder, painted skin tone w/white suit, black trim, cane & glasses, holds bucket of chicken, 1960s, 7", EX...**$85.00**
Playset, Let's Play at Kentucky Fried Chicken, Child Guidance, 1970s, EX (EX box) **$140.00**
Poker chip, plastic w/portrait, 1960s, M **$17.50**
Salt & pepper shakers, plastic figure, pr.....................**$45.00**

Elsie the Cow and Family

She's the most widely recognized cow in the world; everyone knows Elsie, Borden's mascot. Since the mid-1930s, she's been seen on booklets and posters; modeled for mugs, creamers, dolls, etc.; and appeared on TV, in magazines, and at grocery stores to promote their products. Her husband is Elmer (who once sold Elmer's Glue for the same company), and her twins are best known as Beulah and Beauregard, though they've been renamed in recent years (now they're Bea and Beaumister). Elsie was retired in the 1960s, but due to public demand was soon reinstated to her rightful position and continues today to promote the company's dairy products.

Advisor: Lee Garmon (See Directory, Advertising)

Creamer and sugar bowl, molded plastic, marked TBC The Borden Co., Made in USA, 3½", from $45.00 to $55.00. (Photo courtesy Lee Garmon)

Book, Elsie & the Looking Club **$60.00**

Butter mold, Elsie or Beulah, each, M **$28.00**
Charm, Borden's Elsie **$10.00**
Christmas greeting, multicolor litho, intended to be put on milk bottle, old, M **$35.00**
Emery boards, MIP **$15.00**
Game, Elsie the Cow, Junior Edition, complete, EX (EX box)..**$125.00**
Game, Elsie's Ice Cream Cone Pop Game, Wilkening Manufacturing Co, 1958, M (sealed) **$145.00**
Hand puppet, Elsie's baby, vinyl w/cloth body, EX...**$75.00**
Ice cream container, Vanilla & Elsie on blue & white, EX ..**$10.00**
Mug, shows Elsie's face & name, ceramic, 1940s, NM...**$65.00**

**Pin, plastic, 1¾",
M, $75.00.**

Place mat, Elsie w/family, M..**$8.00**
Playing cards, mail-in premium, 1993, MIB (sealed) ..**$22.00**
Postcard, Elsie the Cow & Her Brand New Twins, color, 1957, EX...**$9.00**
Ration book, shows Elsie, given by Borden's Dairy Delivery Co, red, white & blue envelope w/2 ration books & stamps...**$38.00**
Ring, celluloid disc w/raised design, NM **$25.00**
Sign, display; Hey Kids! Free Elsie Ring for Limited Time Only on cardboard, 1950s, NM..............................**$35.00**
Sticker, Elsie in '72, Any Party's Choice, Borden, 1972, MIP **$10.00**
Tie clip, multicolor enameled Elsie in daisy, M **$40.00**
Tin, Borden's Chocolate Flavored Malted Milk, Elsie & ad on front, Elsie's children at back, 1950s, 5¼x3¼" dia, EX...**$40.00**
Toy, Elsie Jumped Over the Moon, wood, NMIB.....**$650.00**
Train, paper, marked Good Food Line, EX (EX envelope)...**$100.00**

Florida Orange Bird

To promote Florida citrus products, the Department of Citrus developed the Orange Bird. An orange was used as an oversized head with leaves for 'hair' and large eyes, and small yellow beak completed this character. Marks may include 'Walt Disney Productions.'

Candle, orange-shaped base, 1980s **$15.00**
Figure, plastic, marked copyright Disney, 2½"............**$14.00**
Figure, rubber, dancing & wearing yellow hat, sm.......**$4.00**
Pin, bird on outline of state **$5.00**

Rain coat, child size, 1980s...**$25.00**
Swim ring, inflatable, 1980s..**$15.00**
Yo-yo, 1980s..**$10.00**

**Bank, plastic,
1980s, 5", M,
from $20.00
to $30.00.**

Funny Face

Pillsbury's answer to Kool-Aid's promotion, the Smiling Pitcher, was the Funny Face series. Each drink flavor was given a name with personality — Jolly Olly Orange, Loud Mouth Punch, Choo-Choo Cherry, Rootin'-Tootin' Raspberry, Goofy Grape, Ruddi Tutti-Frutti, Freckle Face Strawberry, With-It Watermelon, and Lefty Lemonade. Various promotional items have been made since the mid-1960s.

Baseball cap, Rootin' Tootin' Raspberry or Choo-Choo Cherry, 1996, M, each...**$12.00**
Frisbee, Jolly Olly Orange, Goofy Grape, Lefty Lemonade, or Choo-Choo Cherry, white plastic, 1996, M, each, from $7 to..**$10.00**
Kite, features Goofy Grape, 1970s, MIP......................**$45.00**

Mug, Freckle Face Strawberry and Goofy Grape, plastic, marked F&F, EX, each, from $10.00 to $15.00.

Mug, Jolly Olly Orange, Lefty Lemon, Goofy Grape or Loud Mouth Punch, plastic, 1960s, EX, each, from $10 to..**$15.00**
Pitcher, features Goofy Grape, NM **$135.00**
Record, Goofy Grape Sings, 1969, M..........................**$65.00**
T-shirt, Funny Face gang on front, 1996, M **$15.00**

Gerber Baby

Since the late 1920s, the Gerber company has used the smiling face of a baby to promote their line of prepared strained baby food. Several dolls and rubber squeeze toys have been made over the years. Even if you're a novice collector, they'll be easy to spot. Some of the earlier dolls hold a can of product in their hand. Look for the Gerber mark on later dolls. For further information see *A Collector's Guide to the Gerber Baby* by Joan Stryker Grubaugh, Ed.D.

Advisor: Joan Stryker Grubaugh (See Directory, Advertising)

Band-aid dispenser, marked Stamp Out Accidents at Gerber, 1977...**$5.00**
Belt, webbing type, w/Gerber repeated 6 times...........**$7.00**
Booklet, Bringing Up Baby, 1972....................................**$5.00**
Bottle, plastic w/heart design, 1990..............................**$3.00**
Car sun visor, w/Gerber & portrait................................**$15.00**

Cereal bowl and tumbler set, available in pink, yellow, or blue, premium from 1971, 2 pieces, $9.00. (Photo courtesy Joan Stryker Grubaugh)

Doll, Bathtub, foam-filled body, floating eyes, head turns, undressed, premium, 1985, Atlanta Novelty, 12"..**$25.00**

Doll, blue pajamas, with teddy bear and cereal boxes, Mama voice, Atlanta Novelty, 1979–85, 17", MIB, $100.00. (Photo courtesy Joan Stryker Grubaugh)

Doll, Drink & Wet, all vinyl, original outfit w/accessories, Lucky Ltd, 1989, 11"..**$14.00**
Doll, Drink & Wet, vinyl w/cloth & polyester body, floating eyes & molded hair, undressed, retail, 1981, Gerber, 12"...**$35.00**
Doll, Food & Playtime Baby, all original, Toy Biz, 1994, 15"...**$25.00**
Doll, Musical Dreamy Doll, plush body w/vinyl face, sleep eyes, 1984, retail, Atlanta Novelty, 14"..............**$75.00**

Doll, original outfit, premium, Amsco, 1972, 10"........**$50.00**
Doll, original outfit, retail, Sun Rubber, 1955-1958, 12".**$125.00**
Doll, Potty Time Baby, all original, Toy Biz, 1994, 15"....**$25.00**
Jar opener, rubber circle marked Gerber & Safety Pays.....**$2.00**
License plate, metal w/Gerber & portrait, 1981..........**$14.00**
Magnifying glass, marked Medical Marketing Services .**$3.00**
Playing cards, baby's face, double deck, 1990s, MIB ...**$8.00**
Swiss army knife, Gerber screened in silver, 1986......**$18.00**

Green Giant

The Jolly Green Giant has been a well-known ad fixture since the 1950s (some research indicates an earlier date); he was originally devised to represent a strain of European peas much larger than the average-size peas Americans had been accustomed to. At any rate, when Minnesota Valley Canning changed its name to Green Giant, he was their obvious choice. Rather a terse individual himself, by 1974 he was joined by Little Sprout, with the lively white eyes and more talkative personality.

Bank, Little Sprout, composition, plays Valley of the Little Green Giant, 8½"..**$50.00**
Book & tape set, Little Green Sprout's Valley Adventure, M..**$10.00**
Clock, Little Sprout holding round dial in front on round base, w/talking alarm, 10½", EX..........................**$25.00**
Cookware set, Chein, 1960s, metal, complete, MIB..**$175.00**
Dinnerware set, includes: plate, cup, knife & fork, MIB...**$10.00**
Doll, Jolly Green Giant, cloth, 1966, 16", M (original mailer)..**$45.00**
Doll, Little Sprout, plush w/cloth outfit, felt leaf hair, 1970s, 12", NM...**$20.00**
Figure, Little Niblet, 1970s, vinyl, 6½", EX.................**$12.00**
Figure, Little Sprout, vinyl, 6½", from $10 to **$15.00**
Hand puppet, Green Sprout, cloth, NM.......................**$20.00**
Jump rope, Little Green Sprout, MIB...........................**$30.00**
Kite, plastic, mail-in premium, late 1960s, 42x48", M.**$15.00**
Puzzle, jigsaw, 1981, 1,000-pc, M (NM can)...............**$15.00**
Spoon holder, Little Green Sprout, ceramic.................**$20.00**
Squeeze toy, Green Giant, vinyl w/movable upper torso, 1970s, NM+...**$55.00**
Toy, semi & trailer, pressed steel, MIB.........................**$50.00**

Joe Camel

No other characters have been as controversial as Joe Camel and his buddies. Prices are staying stable even though Joe has been banned. Unfortunately, what detractors of Joe have not understood is that Joe is the ultimate Renaissance beast and sex symbol for middle-aged, upper-class women and men — many being nonsmokers. Perhaps, if he were brought back by R.J. Reynolds as a comic-book figure telling people (especially kids) not to smoke, he could have a future. Then collectors wouldn't be feeling so bitter about loosing a role model who had only one flaw.

Advisor: C.J. Russell and Pamela E. Apkarian-Russell (See Directory, Halloween)

Ashtray, camels playing pool, MIB.........................$18.00
Can holder, Camel, face-shaped molded vinyl...........$12.00

Casino tin with chips and playing cards, M, $65.00. (Photo courtesy C.J. Russell and Pamela E. Apkarian-Russell)

License plate, Camel, smooth or suave, each..............$14.00
Mirror, w/Max & Ray, the Wides Guys $55.00
Money clip, brass w/silver finish................................$35.00
Necktie, Joe Camel in green jacket playing saxophone...$25.00
Pool-table light, Camel...$125.00
Salt & pepper shakers, Max & Ray, ceramic, pr..........$45.00
Sign, neon, Joe's face in blue triangle, camel above in yellow $175.00

Stand-up figure, cardboard, Joe Camel 75th Birthday, $150.00. (Photo courtesy C.J. Russell and Pamela E. Apkarian-Russell)

Stein, Joe in alpine outfit playing accordion $125.00
T-shirt, Smooth Character & 75 Years & Still Smoking, 1991 ....$25.00
Translight, Camel, pool-playing Joe w/beautiful gowned woman...$85.00
Tumbler, camels playing pool, plastic.........................$12.00
Windbreaker, Camel Wides, w/box.............................$12.50

Keebler Elf

For more than twenty year, the Keebler Company's choice of spokesman has been Ernie, the Keebler Elf. He's appeared on countless TV commercials and cookie boxes — always dressed in the same red hat, yellow pants and green jacket.

Bank, ceramic, seated, holding barrel, recent, from $15 to..$20.00

Doll, stuffed plush, 1981, 24", VG+.............................$45.00
Figure, vinyl, 1970s, 7", M, from $15 to $20.00
Mug, plastic, Ernie's head, F&F Mold & Die, EX+ $20.00
Wristwatch, battery-op, sweep hand, MIB..................$45.00

M & M Candy Men

Toppers for M&M packaging first appeared about 1988; since then other M&M items have been introduced that portray the clever advertising antics of these colorful characters. Toppers have been issued for seasonal holidays as well as Olympic events.

Advisors: Bill and Pat Poe (See Directory, Fast-Food Collectibles)

Coin holder, set of 6 containers full of mini M&Ms, 1996, per set...$10.00
Cookie cutter, M&M shape, standing w/arms up, red plastic, 3" $4.00
Dispenser, M&M Fun Machine, gumball machine shape, w/candy, 1995, MIB...$20.00
Dispenser, M&M shape, baseball player w/blue cap, glove in left hand & baseball in right, 2nd of series, 1996, lg, MIB.$25.00
Dispenser, peanut or M&M shape, various colors, 1991, sm, each...$5.00
Dispenser, peanut shape w/football & helmet, red nut, 1st in collector series, 1995, lg......................................$18.00
Dispenser, spaceship shape w/letter M, battery-operated, push button to dispense candy, MOC...................$10.00

Dispensers, red plain or yellow peanut shape, 1991, large, each, $15.00. (Photo courtesy Bill and Pat Poe)

Doll, M&M shape, stuffed plush, blue, 4½" $10.00
Doll, M&M shape, stuffed plush, 8" $12.00
Doll, M&M shape w/Santa hat, marked Welcome to the World of M&Ms, 1996, 6", MIP..............................$18.00
Doll, peanut shape, stuffed plush, yellow or green, 14"...$18.00
Light string, M&M Happy Lights, 1996, MIB...............$20.00
Music box, pink Valentine M&M on top, plays Let Me Call You Sweetheart, w/candy, MIP...............................$20.00
Topper, 1988, peanut shape, outstretched hands, red Santa heart, eyebrows on rim of hat, round base $3.50
Topper, 1989, peanut shape, Christmas w/ice skates, red or green nut, round base $3.50
Topper, 1990, M&M shape, Christmas w/snowballs in both hands, pile of snowballs on base, red Santa hat, green candy .$3.50

Topper, 1991, peanut shape on skis w/red Santa hat, round base **$3.50**

Topper, 1992, M&M shape, arrow in left hand w/bow in right hand, arrow-pierced heart on base, red candy **$3.50**

Topper, 1992, M&M shape, Christmas, going down chimney w/toy bag in left hand, green or red candy **$3.50**

Topper, 1992, M&M shape, Christmas w/candy cane, orange or red candy **$3.50**

Topper, 1992, M&M shape, Olympics, red candy w/torch...**$5.00**

Topper, 1992, peanut shape, arrow in left hand & bow in right hand, heart w/arrow on round base **$3.50**

Topper, 1992, peanut shape, Christmas w/candy cane, green nut, round base...**$3.50**

Topper, 1992, peanut shape, Easter egg in left hand, Easter basket on round base **$3.50**

Topper, 1993, peanut shape, sitting on sleigh, round base **$3.50**

Topper, 1994, M&M shape, lavender Easter egg on green base, lime green candy...**$3.50**

Topper, 1994, M&M shape, pink Easter egg on green base, turquoise candy..**$3.50**

Topper, 1995, M&M shape, Christmas w/train at base .**$3.50**

Topper, 1996, M&M shape, postman w/Valentine letter in left hand & red box in right, pink candy **$3.50**

Topper, 1996, peanut shape, Christmas w/snowball in hand, red & white cap, green nut, round base.................**$3.50**

Toppers: Easter, green peanut holding chick and paint brush, 1994; Easter, orange with blue egg and basket on base, 1992; Valentine, red with wings, holding bow and arrow, 1992; each, $3.50. (Photo courtesy Bill and Pat Poe)

Tote bag, M&Ms Plain, brown w/white letters & handles, 1980 ....**$15.00**

Toy, M&M tractor/trailer, Matchbox, 1996, MOC........**$12.00**

Wristwatch, M&M Candies on face, 1993, MIP............**$45.00**

Michelin Man (Bibendum or Mr. Bib)

Perhaps one of the oldest character logos around today, Mr. Bib actually originated in the late 1900s, inspired by a stack of tires that one of the company founders thought suggested the figure of a man. Over the years his image has changed considerably, but the Michelin Tire Man continues today to represent his company in many countries around the world.

Ashtray, molded cream plastic figure sits on black base, ca 1940s, 4¾x6" dia..**$75.00**

Figure, foam-like material, soiled, 3½" **$25.00**

Figure, plastic, 12", NM+...**$100.00**

Flasher squares, M **$5.00**

Nodder, attaches to dashboard, 2 styles, each **$18.00**

Puzzle, Mr Bib on motorcycle, put together to form figure, MIP **$55.00**

Ramp walker, winds up, MIB **$25.00**

Snow dome, Mr Bib in mountains, European issue, MIB ...**$50.00**

Wall clock, white plastic over metal back, yellow letters under white Mr. Bib, 14", EX, $135.00.

Mr. Peanut

The trademark character for the Planters Peanuts Company, Mr. Peanut has been around since 1916. Although his appearance became more stylized in 1961, he is still a common sight on Planters advertising efforts and product containers.

Mr Peanut has been modeled as banks, salt and pepper shakers, whistles, and many other novelty items. His image has decorated T-shirts, beach towels, playing cards, sports equipment, etc.

Today Mr Peanut has his own 'fan club,' the collector's organization for those who especially enjoy the Planters Peanuts area of advertising.

Advisors: Judith and Robert Walthall (See Directory, Advertising)

Club: Peanut Pals
Robert Walthall, President
P.O. Box 4465, Huntsville, AL 35815; 205-881-9198. Dues: $20 per year (+ $3 for each additional member of household.) Annual directory and convention news sent to members. For membership, write to PO Box 652, St Clairsville, OH 43950. Sample newsletter: $2.

Apron, Gold Measure, blue, 1991, M **$6.00**

Ashtray, gold-washed metal w/Mr Peanut at center, marked 1906-56, w/original booklet, MIB......................**$100.00**

Bag, paper, Planter's Roasted Peanuts, 80-oz, unused..**$10.00**

Bank, cast-iron figural, black & tan, fantasy, 1987-90s, 5½" to 11", each, from $6 to **$20.00**

Bank, figural, plastic, Mr Peanut, blue, green, red or tan 1950s-1980, EX, each, from $10 to **$25.00**

Bank, plastic figural, yellow, black & white, 1991, MIB ...**$10.00**

Belt, gold vinyl w/jumbo block design, round metal buckle w/Mr Peanut, late 1960s..................................**$25.00**
Belt buckle, plastic w/2 guns & Mr Peanut, 1950s **$15.00**
Booklet, Mr Peanut's Nutrition, 1970..........................**$5.00**
Case cutter, colored metal w/line drawing, 1963-90, from $5 to...**$10.00**
Charm, plastic figure, 2¼"...**$3.00**
Comic book, The Personal Story of Mr Peanut, 50th anniversary, 16 pages, 7x10", 1956, EX......................**$15.00**
Cuff links, metal, Mr Peanut inside oval, early 1960s.**$75.00**
Doilies, pink or white, plastic, MIP (sealed) **$25.00**
Figure, bendy, 1991, M..**$2.00**
Hand puppet, rubber figural, black & tan, 1950s, EX...**$600.00**
Jar, 8 embossed sides, octagonal lid w/knob, 1924, 12", EX **$250.00**

Jar, glass barrel shape with embossed image and label, peanut finial, 12x9", EX, $250.00.

Key chain, tan Mr Peanut..**$18.00**
Measuring spoon, 4-in-1 style w/figural handle, plastic, 1950s, M..**$6.00**
Night light, plastic, white Mr Peanut figure on aqua base, 1950s, 9½", NM...**$250.00**
Night light, plastic diamond shape w/Mr Peanut face, plug-in type, 1⅞", VG...**$25.00**
Paint palette set, cardboard, 1950s, M **$100.00**
Peanut butter maker, plastic, Emenee, 1967, MIB.......**$65.00**
Pencil, mechanical, black & gold, marked 50th Anniversary, 1956, MIP...**$25.00**
Playing cards, double deck, 1990s, MIB (sealed)........**$10.00**

Salt and pepper shakers, ceramic with rhinestone in monocle, 4½", EX, $100.00 for the pair.

Spoon, nut server, silverplate w/Mr Peanut on handle, 1941-61, 5", MIP..**$15.00**
Stick pin, plastic figural, red, blue, green or tan, 1950s, 1⅛"...**$3.00**
Swizzle stick, green plastic.....................................**$5.00**
Swizzle stick/stirrer, figure w/Everybody Loves a Nut, black & white plastic, 1993..**$10.00**
Toy, Mr Peanut Jet Racer, plastic, 1950s, M (w/mailing bag)...**$350.00**
Whistle, plastic figural, 1950s, 2½"..........................**$4.00**
Whistle, siren, plastic figural, 1950s, 3⅜"...............**$30.00**
Windup, plastic figural, black & tan, 1950s, 8½", EX....**$300.00**

Old Crow

Old Crow collectors have learned to date this character by the cut of his vest and the tilt of his head along with other characteristics of his stance and attire. Advertising Kentucky whiskey, he appears as an elegant gent in his tuxedo and top hat.

Advisor: Geneva Addy (See Directory, Dolls)

Bottle, bright red vest, gold cane, American, 12½" **$65.00**
Bottle, light red vest, yellow cane, Royal Doulton, 12½"..**$100.00**
Bourbon glass **$6.00**
Cocktail glass, Old Crow figural stem, 6", from $15 ...**$20.00**
Doll, stuffed felt w/detailed profile, black only on back, detachable tie, 1970s, 28".......................................**$45.00**
Figure, ceramic, for top of bottle, sm **$35.00**

Figure, composition, 11½", $75.00. (Photo courtesy B.J. Summers)

Figure, Old Crow in birdcage, plastic, 9".....................**$95.00**
Figure, plastic, for top of bottle.................................**$35.00**
Figure, plastic, on white base w/blue letters, 1960s, 5½", from $15 to...**$25.00**
Figure, plastic, round base, 1950s, 10", from $50 to...**$65.00**
Figure, plastic, round base, 1950s, 13½", from $50 to ...**$65.00**
Figure, plastic, square black & white base, 1960s, 10", from $25 to...**$45.00**
Figure, vinyl, 12"...**$45.00**
Key chain **$15.00**
Lamp, red vest w/gold buttons, 14", from $145 to ...**$165.00**
Pitcher, w/logo, 1-pt..**$20.00**
Roly poly, plastic, 9"..**$95.00**
Standee, cardboard, 8"..**$30.00**

Poppin' Fresh (Pillsbury Doughboy) and Family

Who could be more lovable than the chubby blue-eyed Doughboy with the infectious giggle, introduced by the Pillsbury Company in 1965. Wearing nothing but a neck scarf and a chef's hat, he single-handedly promoted the company's famous biscuits in a tube until about 1971. It was then that the company changed his name to 'Poppin' Fresh' and presented him with a sweet-faced, bonnet-attired mate named Poppie. Soon a whole family followed. Many premiums such as dolls, salt and pepper shakers, and cookie jars have been produced over the years, but much of what you see at flea markets today is very recent. Most of the new ceramic items will be marked with a date and sometimes 'Made in Taiwan.'

Club: The Lovin' Connection
Rt. 2, Box 123
Oswego, KS 67356; 316-795-2842

Playhouse, vinyl (example shown lacking top floor), with 4 finger puppets, rare, from $185.00 to (if complete) $225.00. (Photo courtesy Jon Thurmond)

Bank, cardboard biscuit tube w/repeated images of Poppin' Fresh, 1980s, 7", NM..**$15.00**
Bank, Poppin' Fresh, ceramic, 1987, 7½", MIB............**$25.00**
Cookie jar, ceramic, Poppin' Fresh figure, white w/Cookies & blue trim, dated 1973, NM......................................**$50.00**
Cookie jar, glass, Anchor Hocking, 1991.....................**$40.00**
Decal, set of 18, MIP...**$10.00**
Display figure, Poppin' Fresh, styrofoam, 1980s, 2-pc, 50", EX, from $200 to..**$225.00**
Doll, Poppin' Fresh, stuffed cloth, 1970s, 14", VG......**$15.00**
Doll, Poppin' Fresh, stuffed cloth, 1972, 11", EX........**$15.00**
Doll, Poppin' Fresh, stuffed plush, 1982, M................**$50.00**
Figure, Poppin' Fresh, vinyl w/jointed head, 1972, 7", EX+ **$15.00**
Figures, Poppin' & Poppie Fresh, soft vinyl, movable heads, rectangular bases, 1971-72, 7" & 6", NM, pr.........**$35.00**
Finger puppet, Biscuit the Cat, EX.............................**$35.00**
Finger puppet, Flapjack the Dog, EX...........................**$55.00**
Finger puppet, Grandmommer, EX..............................**$50.00**
Finger puppet, Popper, vinyl, 1974, EX......................**$20.00**
Finger puppet, Poppie Fresh, vinyl, 3½", EX...............**$15.00**

Gumball dispenser, plastic Doughboy w/clear body, 25th Anniversary issue, full, unused, M.....................**$400.00**
Hand puppet, Poppin' or Poppie Fresh pop out of refrigerator can, cloth & vinyl, 1974, EX, each..................**$10.00**
Magnet, current, 3", pr..**$6.00**
Mug, ceramic, features Poppin' Fresh, 1979, 5", VG...**$15.00**
Mug, plastic, from $7 to...**$9.00**
Napkin holder, current..**$10.00**
Pencil, blue & white, M...**$20.00**
Radio, Poppin' Fresh, plastic, w/headphones, 1985, 6½", MIB **$125.00**

Salt and pepper shakers, Poppie and Poppin' Fresh, white plastic with blue detail, dated 1974, 3½" and 4", $25.00.

Salt & pepper shakers, Poppin' Fresh, ceramic, 1988, range size, pr, MIB, from $15 to.......................................**$20.00**
Salt & pepper shakers, Poppin' Fresh, white ceramic w/blue details painted over glaze, 1970s, 3½", pr, EX **$22.00**
Soap dispenser, current...**$10.00**
Squeeze toy, Poppin' Fresh, vinyl, 1970s, 6½", VG **$12.00**
Stand-up, Poppin' Fresh, promotional, 1985, from $20 to .**$30.00**
Telephone, Poppin' Fresh, arms extend to hold receiver, 1980s, 14", M..**$90.00**
Timer, digital, 1992, M...**$10.00**
Utensil holder, Poppin' Fresh, ceramic, 1983, 8"........**$18.00**
Wristwatch, gold-tone case, M.....................................**$50.00**

Raid Bug

Rather bizarre and well designed to catch the attention of the consumer, the Raid Bug was created by the S.C. Johnson & Sons Inc. to promote sales for Raid insecticides and repellents.

Banner, Raid Kills Bugs Dead, 48x24", M....................**$28.00**
Beach bag, NM..**$15.00**
Beer stein, shows angry bug, M...................................**$20.00**
Doll, inflatable green vinyl, MIP..................................**$20.00**
Doll, plush, rare, M...**$75.00**
Doll, stuffed cloth, Raid Bug, 1980s, EX, from $15 to....**$20.00**
Memo holder, black plastic w/embossed bug, M **$15.00**
Note pad, Post-It type w/logo, M, from $5 to..............**$8.00**
Playing cards, double deck, MIP (sealed)....................**$10.00**
Puzzle, jigsaw, M (M product-shaped can)..................**$35.00**

Radio, Raid Bug leans against round dial w/both on rectangular digital clock base, ca 1980s, 7", M..............**$225.00**
Robot, Raid Bug, battery-op, 14", w/remote control, EX...**$400.00**
Telephone, standing Raid Bug holds receiver over arm, ca 1980s, 9", EX **$125.00**

Wind-up walker, plastic, 1980s, 4", M, $45.00.

Reddy Kilowatt

Reddy was developed during the late 1920s and became very popular during the fifties. His job was to promote electric power companies all over the United States, which he did with aplomb! Reddy memorabilia is highly collectible today, with the plastic figures sometimes selling for $200.00 or more. Because of high collector demand, new merchandise is flooding the market. Watch for items such as a round mirror, a small hand-held game with movable squares, a ring-toss game, etc., marked 'Made in China.'

Playing cards, double deck, dated 1951, MIB, $45.00.

Ashtray, glass, Reddy's face & K-Listo Kilvatio, round..**$30.00**
Ashtray, glass, square **$10.00**
Bottle capper...**$15.00**
Button cover...**$15.00**
Comic book, Wizard of Light Story of Thomas Edison As Told by Reddy Kilowatt, 1965, NM **$28.00**
Electric bill stub, ca 1950s, each...................................**$5.00**
Figure, plastic Reddy on base, lg head, M, minimum value...**$100.00**
Figure, plastic Reddy on base, sm head, EX.............**$200.00**

Folder, clear plastic w/Reddy in corner, M.................**$20.00**
License plate, Enjoy Electric Living w/Reddy's face, old...**$35.00**
Napkins, 1970, set of 8, MIP.......................................**$32.00**
Pencil holder, gold-tone aluminum, M........................**$42.50**
Postcard, 1¢, Reddy in cowboy hat, M **$8.00**
Poster, Reddy Kilowatt Making Sales Surge, multicolor, 18x10", M...**$25.00**
Pot holder, MIP...**$30.00**
Sales book, Reddy Kilowatt Making Sales Surge, unused..**$40.00**
Sticker, M...**$15.00**

Smokey the Bear

1994 was the 50th anniversary of Smokey the Bear, the spokesbear for the State Foresters, Ad Council, and US Forest Service. After ruling out other mascots (including Bambi), by 1944 it had been decided that a bear was best suited for the job, and Smokey was born. When a little cub was rescued from a fire in a New Mexico national forest in 1950, Smokey's role intensified. Over the years his appearance has evolved from one a little more menacing to the lovable bear we know today.

Salt and pepper shakers (left), unmarked, pr, $70.00; Candy jar (center), Norcrest, minimum value, $350.00; Ashtray (right), Norcrest, MIB, $125.00. (Photo courtesy Judy Posner)

Advisor: Glen Brady (See Directory, Advertising)

Ad, from Pacific Bell Telephone News, July 1964, 4½x6", EX...**$5.00**
Ashtray, metal bucket shape, Smokey Says Use Your Ashtray, for car use, M, from $20 to **$25.00**
Badge, I'm helping Smokey Prevent Forest Fires, tab back, 1950s, NM...**$15.00**
Bell, Prevent Forest Fires on Smokey's sign, ceramic, EX...**$65.00**
Blotter, I Will Be Careful, 1955, 2½x6½", unused, EX..**$8.00**
Blotter, 1960s, unused, M..**$10.00**
Book, Smokey Bear's Camping Book, Golden Book, 45 pages, 10½x12", EX...**$30.00**
Cigarette snuffer, Snuffit, EX......................................**$18.00**
Comic, Smokey March of Comics, Sears, 1970s, M.....**$30.00**
Doll, inflatable vinyl, MIP **$45.00**
Game, Smokey Bear Put Out the Fires Pinball, Gordy, MOC..**$15.00**

Map, California's Golden Chain, the Mother Lode State Highway 49, published by Golden Chain Council, 1949, 22x17", EX **$22.50**

Pamphlet, excerpts from CA laws about fire prevention, Smokey & Woody logos, 1957, 16 pages, 3¾x9", EX **$9.00**

Pathfinder set, complete, Larami, 1978, MIP **$85.00**

Plate, Smokey & friends at center, Melmac, 7", NM....**$25.00**

Playset, Camping the Smokey Bear Way, complete w/figures & papers, Tonka, NMIB **$150.00**

Postcard, Please! Only You Can Prevent Forest Fires, Courtesy National Auto Club of CA, 1965, NM **$11.00**

Poster, 1970s..**$20.00**

Ruler, paper, lettered State of California, shows Smokey & animals praying, 6x2½", EX..**$12.00**

Sign, Flick Your Bick Carefully in My Woods on cardboard, late 1970s, NM...**$25.00**

Song book, Songs From the Ballad of Smokey Bear, 1966, NM..**$25.00**

Spoon, plastic w/figural handle, M **$12.50**

Target set, Smokey Bear Prevents Wildfires, Gordy, MOC **$12.00**

Snap!, Crackle! and Pop!

Rice Krispies, the talking cereal, was first marketed by Kellogg's in 1928. Capitalizing on the sounds the cereal made in milk, the company chose elves named 'Snap,' 'Crackle,' and 'Pop' as their logos a few years later. The first of the Rice Krispie dolls were introduced in 1948. These were 12" tall, printed on fabric for the consumer to sew and stuff. The same dolls in a 16" size were offered in 1954. Premiums and memorabilia of many types followed over the years, all are very collectible.

Binoculars, paper & plastic, 1980s, MIP......................**$15.00**

Canteen, yellow, white & red plastic, 1973, NM.........**$25.00**

Drawing template, yellow plastic, 1970, 3x5", NM **$15.00**

Figures, Crackle!, 1984, 5", MIB, $55.00; Snap! and Pop!, loose, M, $25.00 each. (Photo courtesy June Moon)

Joke machine, 4 in series, 1987, MIP, each...................**$3.00**

Key chain, metal, paper & plastic, 1980s, EX.............**$10.00**

Patch, glow-in-the-dark iron-on cloth, 1974, 2", MIP..**$15.00**

Popper, plastic, 1980s, MIP **$7.00**

Squeeze toy, plastic, 1978, EX....................................**$35.00**

Sticker, Don't Pollute It (air), paper, 1973, NM **$10.00**

Stickers, glow-in-the-dark paper, 1971, M **$10.00**

Trade card, Kellogg's Magic Color Card, 1933, VG+...**$25.00**

Tony the Tiger

Kellogg's introduced Tony the Tiger in 1953, and since then he's appeared on every box of their Frosted Flakes. In his deep, rich voice, he's convinced us all that they are indeed 'Gr-r-r-reat'!

Book, Coloring Fun, w/4 crayons, 1989, MIP **$3.00**

Bowling set, NMIB..**$65.00**

Design maker, Kooky Doodle, 1984, MIP....................**$10.00**

Doll, stuffed cloth, 1973, 14", EX...............................**$40.00**

Doll, stuffed plush, 16", NM **$35.00**

Doll, stuffed plush, 1991, 9", M **$15.00**

Figure, plastic, diving Tony, 1979, MIP........................**$5.00**

Figure, vinyl, arms up, wearing red neckerchief, Kellogg's Frosted Flakes, 1974, 7½", NM **$40.00**

Frisbee, plastic, 1989, MIP...**$2.00**

Hat, plush w/paper tiger face & plush tail, mail-in premium, 1970s, child size, EX...**$28.00**

Hat, white paper w/graphics, given on plant tour in Battlecreek MI, Kellogg's, 1968, M **$25.00**

License plate, orange plastic, for bicycle, 1973, 3x5", EX+ **$12.00**

Padlock, colored plastic, 1987, MIP..............................**$5.00**

Page marker/paper clip, plastic, 1979, NM...................**$3.00**

Patch, glow-in-the-dark cloth, 1965, 4", NM..............**$25.00**

Patch, iron-on, Tony & gang, 1985, 6x8", MIP **$15.00**

Pen, Tony's Secret Message, 1980s, M..........................**$3.00**

Poster, Meet Tony on Tour, paper, 1989, 14x18", NM...**$5.00**

Radio, AM, plastic, battery operated, 1980, 7", MIB, $30.00.

Reflector, Tony's Safe Biking Booster, plastic & paper, 1981, M **$2.00**

Stickers, Tony, Toucan Sam & Cornelius, glow-in-the-dark paper, 1971, M **$10.00**

Tony's Mystery Drawing Disk, paper, 1980, MIP..........**$3.00**

Tony's Safari Cinema, plastic & paper, 1980s, MIP **$5.00**

Tracing template, Tony, Ogg & Toucan Sam, green plastic, 1970, NM **$10.00**

Transfer sheet, Tony, Toucan Sam, Poppy & Dig 'Em, 1980s, MIP...**$10.00**

Valentine cards, set of 30, 1986, MIB.........................**$10.00**

Miscellaneous

Actigall Guy, squeeze toy, gall bladder figure, green vinyl, Summit, 1989, 4", M, $40.00. (Photo courtesy June Moon)

Actigall Guy, memo holder, MIB..................................**$10.00**

Archies, rub-on transfers, paper, Post's, 1970s, MIP ...**$12.00**

Atlas Annie, doll, printed cloth, 1977, 15½", NM........**$10.00**

Baby Ruth, doll, stuffed printed cloth, boy or girl, 1920s, 16", EX...**$20.00**

Baskin Robbins, spoon figure, pink plastic with white hands and feet, embossed 31 logo on body, 4½", M, $5.00.

Blue Bonnet Sue, bank..**$35.00**

Blue Bonnet Sue, booklet, Little Sister Cooks, Blue Bonnet, 1956, 3x6½", NM...**$8.00**

Blue Bonnet Sue, hand puppet, Buttercup the Cow, plush, EX w/original hang tag.................................**$16.00**

Boo Berry, pencil topper, pink rubber, 1973, NM......**$10.00**

Butterfinger Bear, doll, stuffed plush, 1987, 15", M....**$22.50**

Caravelle Man, doll, bendable, 1967, 10", EX..........**$150.00**

Cheesasurus Rex, bank, plastic figure holding treasure chest, M, from $10 to...**$15.00**

Cheesasaurus Rex, camera, Super Sleuth, Kraft mail-in premium, MIB...**$20.00**

Cheesasaurus Rex, figure, NBA or skating outfit, Kraft, M, each, from $6 to...**$8.00**

Chiquita Banana, doll, inflatable, 48".........................**$20.00**

Chiquita Banana, salt & pepper shakers, ceramic, unmarked, 3", pr...**$10.00**

Chiquita Banana, wristwatch, sold at NY Yankee games, MIB...**$15.00**

Chore Boy, figure, vinyl, EX...**$30.00**

Cookie Puss, puppet, plush, marked I'm a CP Celestial Person, made for Caravel, M..............................**$12.00**

Country Yumkin, bolo tie, M..**$15.00**

Country Yumkin, doll, stuffed plush, Del Monte, 1980s, from $10 to...**$12.00**

Crunch Bird, bank, plastic, NM...................................**$50.00**

Dino the Dinosaur, soap, Sinclair Oil, MIB................**$10.00**

Dutch Boy, hand puppet, vinyl & cloth, 1956, 12", NM....**$10.00**

Energizer Bunny, doll, stuffed pink plush, 24", M......**$35.00**

Energizer Bunny, flashlight, squeeze vinyl, 1991, MOC....**$15.00**

Eveready Cat, bank, black plastic, 1981, NM.............**$22.50**

Exxon Tiger, key chain...**$10.00**

Exxon Tiger, puppet, vinyl head, plush body w/felt hands, EX...**$90.00**

Fresh Up Freddie, doll, cloth w/rubber head, 1958, 24", M.**$30.00**

Frito Bandito, eraser, yellow pencil topper, Frito-Lay, 1960s, 1½", M...**$20.00**

Hamm's Bear, figure, porcelain, 1980s, 6", EX...........**$40.00**

Heinz Picnic Ant, figure, bendy type, M.....................**$15.00**

Honey Nut Bee, doll, stuffed plush..............................**$15.00**

Hood Dairyman, doll, squeeze vinyl, 1981, M...........**$65.00**

Jiffaroo Kangaroo, kite, multicolor paper, 1950s, M ...**$35.00**

Jiffaroo Kangaroo, periscope, M..................................**$15.00**

Kaboom Clown, spoon hanger, detailed plastic figural, 1969, 2", M...**$8.00**

Kodak Colorkins, doll, stuffed, ca 1990, 8" to 10", any...**$20.00**

Kraft Cheesasaurus Rex, see Cheesasurus Rex

Lifesaver, figure, bendy type, set of 5, M w/original hang tags...**$15.00**

Little Hans, doll, vinyl w/cloth outfit, 1969, 12½", M.**$40.00**

Little Miss Revlon, doll, vinyl w/outfit, 1950, 10½", M..**$25.00**

Lucky Lymon, doll, talker, battery-op, MIP.................**$25.00**

Lucky Lymon, figure, vinyl, battery-op talker, MIB.....**$25.00**

Meow Mix Cat, figure, vinyl, EX..................................**$35.00**

Miss Curity Nurse, doll, plastic, 24", VG.....................**$85.00**

Miss Sunbeam, store window decal, multicolor, 1960s, 13x10", M...**$20.00**

Mr Buffle, blow bubble maker, w/figural bubble container, 1979, NM...**$65.00**

Mr Wiggle, puppet, hollow red vinyl, General Foods/Jell-O, 1966, w/10x13" newspaper ad for puppet, M....**$179.00**

Naugie, figure, vinyl, M...**$45.00**

Nestle's Quick Bunny, doll, stuffed plush w/Quick necklace, 1985, 16", M...**$20.00**

Nipper, figure, molded plastic, 36", EX.....................**$235.00**

Northern Tissue Girl, doll, M..**$25.00**

Orbie Space Penguin, figure, M...................................**$15.00**

Oreo Cookie Man, figure, bendy type, Dairylea/Oreo, M, from $10 to...**$15.00**

Otto the Orkin, key chain, red plastic, M.....................**$15.00**

Pammy Panda, iron-on sticker, Hallmark, 1981, MIP....**$3.00**

Peerless Amber Beer Elf, salt shaker, celluloid, EX **$50.00**

Pink Panther, 5-in-1 Spy Kit, plastic, 1971, EX...........**$75.00**

Pogo, figure, detailed vinyl w/painted details, posable head & left arm, Proctor & Gamble, 1969, 4", M..........**$12.00**

Sam the Olympic Eagle, playing cards, 1984, MIB (sealed)...**$6.00**

Scrubbin' Bubble, bank, ceramic, M...........................**$20.00**

Scrubbin' Bubble, doll, 1990s, NM $20.00

Shoney's Bear, bank, plastic with red shirt and blue pants, 8", M, $15.00.

Sleepy Bear, doll, stuffed, Travel Lodge, EX $45.00
Sleepy Bear, figure, vinyl, Travel Lodge, EX $65.00
Snorkeldorf, Freakmobile, green plastic, 1974, MIB ...$12.00
Sonny the Cuckoo Bird, bike spinner, brown plastic, 1970s, M on sprue...$45.00
Sonny the Cuckoo Bird, spoon, brown & orange plastic, 1990s, MIP $7.00
Spam Bear, necklace...$10.00
Speedy Alka-Selzer, ornament, clear plastic ball, M......$7.00
Spuds Mackenzie, bank, figure w/bandana & front leg on red heart, unlicensed, sm...$4.00
Spuds Mackenzie, doll, stuffed w/Hawaiian shirt, lg, EX...$50.00
Spuds Mackenzie, key chain, plastic, sm $3.00
Tagamet Stomach, figure, bendy type, EX+.................$15.00
Texaco Cheerleader, doll, 11½", NMIB $65.00
Toys 'R Us, Geoffrey, bank, vinyl, 1980s, NM.............$55.00

Toys 'R Us Geoffrey, music box, NM, $38.00. (Photo courtesy June Moon)

Wally Welch, hand puppet, 9", EX $3.00
Winnie-the-Pooh, Crazy Car, plastic, w/laser cutouts, Great Honey Crunchers, 1973, MIB.................................$40.00
Yogi Bear, lamp shade, yellow plastic head, fits over 40-watt bulb, Arch, 1962, 9", EX+.......................................$48.00
Yogi Bear, spoon, metal, 1961, VG $10.00

Airline Memorabilia

Even before the Wright brothers' historic flight before the turn of the century, people have been fascinated with flying. What better way to enjoy the evolution and history of this amazing transportation industry than to collect its memorabilia. Today, just about any item ever used or made for a commercial (non-military) airline is collectible, especially dishes, glasswares, silver serving pieces and flat-ware, wings and badges worn by the crew, playing cards, and junior wings given to passengers. Advertising items such as timetables and large travel agency plane models are also widely collected. The earlier, the better! Anything pre-war is good; items from before the 1930s are rare and often very valuable.

Advisor: Dick Wallin (See Directory, Aviation)

Baggage sticker, Pan American, blue logo $10.00
Christmas ornament, Capital Airlines Viscount............$35.00
Cup & saucer, British Airways Concorde, blue & yellow design $40.00

Dinnerware, United Airlines, Swirl, by Syracuse China Co: Cup and saucer, $75.00; Plate, sm, $15.00; Bowl, $35.00. (Photo courtesy Dick Wallin)

Flatware set, Eastern Airlines logo on stainless, 3-pc ...$5.00
Flight bag, Mexicana Airlines logo on vinyl $10.00
Glass, cocktail; Piedmont Airlines etched logo..............$8.00
Plate, American Airlines, Collector series, #6 ....$40.00
Plate, American Airlines AirLite, blue eagle & stars, 6"....$200.00
Plate, Pan American, Collector series, #1.....................$80.00
Plate, Pan American, Collector series, #2.....................$50.00
Plate, Pan American, Collector series, #3...................$100.00
Plate, Pan American, Collector series, #4.....................$55.00
Plate, Pan American, Collector series, #5.....................$50.00
Playing cards, Delta oval logo, blue background $75.00
Playing cards, Western Pacific Airline/Thrifty Car Rental....$75.00
Postcard, TWA DC3 in Boulder City Nevada, real photo $85.00
Route map folder, Pan American, winged globe logo, 1950s $10.00
Salt & pepper shakers, Braniff shield logo on silver, heavy, pr...$250.00
Salt & pepper shakers, Singapore Airlines, red & gold on china, pr...$45.00
Timetable, Western Air Express, multicolor, 1929 .....$100.00
Tumbler, Eastern, commerative w/Eddie Rickenbacker name on glass..$20.00
Uniform wings, Capital Airlines, gold color $125.00

Akro Agate

Everybody remembers the 'Aggie' marbles from their childhood; this is the company that made them. They operated in West Virginia from 1914 until 1951, and in addition to their famous marbles they made children's dishes as well as many types of novelties — flowerpots, powder jars with scotty dogs on top, candlesticks, and ashtrays, for instance — in many colors and patterns. Though some of their glassware was made in solid colors, their most popular products were made of the same swirled colors as their marbles. Nearly everything they produced is marked with their logo: a crow flying through the letter 'A' holding an Aggie in its beak and one in each claw. Some children's dishes may be marked 'JP,' and the novelty items may instead carry one of these trademarks: 'JV Co, Inc,' 'Braun & Corwin,' 'NYC Vogue Merc Co USA,' 'Hamilton Match Co,' and 'Mexicali Pickwick Cosmetic Corp.'

In the children's dinnerware listings below, you'll notice that color is an important worth-assessing factor. As a general rule, an item in green or white opaque is worth only about one-third as much when compared to the same item in any other opaque color. Marbleized pieces are about three times higher than solid opaques, and of the marbleized colors, blue is the most valuable. It's followed closely by red, with green about 25% under red. Lemonade and oxblood is a good color combination, and it's generally three times higher item for item than the transparent colors of green or topaz.

For further study we recommend *The Collector's Encyclopedia of Akro Agate Glassware* by Gene Florence and *The Collector's Encyclopedia of Children's Dishes* by Margaret and Kenn Whitmyer.

Club: Akro Agate Collectors Club
Roger Hardy
10 Bailey St., Clarksburg, WV 26301-2524; 304-624-4523

Concentric Ring (Large), 16-pc boxed set, solid opaque colors, MIB, from $160.00 to $185.00.

Chiquita, creamer, baked-on colors, 1½"......................$8.00
Chiquita, creamer, transparent cobalt..........................$16.00
Chiquita, cup, baked-on color, 1½".............................$7.50
Chiquita, cup, transparent cobalt, 1½" $8.00
Chiquita, plate, baked-on colors, 3¾"..........................$3.00
Chiquita, sugar bowl (open), baked-on colors, 1½".....$8.00
Chiquita, sugar bowl (open), opaque green, 1½".........$5.00
Chiquita, teapot, opaque green, 3"..............................$14.00

Concentric Rib, creamer, opaque green or white, sm, 1¼"..$8.00
Concentric Rib, cup, opaque colors other than green or white, sm, 1¼" $8.00
Concentric Rib, plate, opaque colors other than white, sm, 3¼" $7.00
Concentric Rib, sugar bowl (open), opaque colors other than green or white, sm, 1¼"......................................$16.00
Concentric Rib, teapot, opaque colors other than green or white, 3⅜" $18.00
Concentric Rib, teapot, opaque green or white, sm, 3⅜".....$12.00
Concentric Ring, bowl, cereal; transparent cobalt, lg, 3⅜" ...$40.00
Concentric Ring, creamer, opaque colors, lg, 1⅜"......$25.00
Concentric Ring, creamer, opaque colors, sm, 1¼" $20.00
Concentric Ring, cup, yellow, lg, 1⅜".........................$50.00
Concentric Ring, plate, transparent cobalt, sm, 3⅛" ...$15.00
Concentric Ring, sugar bowl (open), any opaque color, sm, 1¼"..$18.00
Concentric Ring, teapot, transparent cobalt, sm, 3⅜".$50.00
Interior Panel, bowl, cereal; azure blue, lg, 3⅜".........$30.00
Interior Panel, creamer, marbleized green & white, lg, 1⅜" $25.00
Interior Panel, creamer, opaque cobalt, white lid, sm, 1¼"..$45.00
Interior Panel, creamer, pink lustre, sm, 1¼" $27.00
Interior Panel, creamer, transparent topaz, lg, 1⅜".....$22.00
Interior Panel, cup, marbleized blue & white, lg, 1⅜"..$25.00
Interior Panel, cup, transparent green or topaz, sm, 1¼"...$10.00

Interior Panel (Large), 21-pc boxed set, blue and white marbleized, MIB, from $600.00 to $700.00.

Interior Panel, plate, lemonade & oxblood, lg, 4¼" ...$14.00
Interior Panel, plate, pink lustre, lg, 4¼" $8.00
Interior Panel, plate, transparent topaz, sm, 3¾".........$4.00
Interior Panel, saucer, lemonade & oxblood, lg, 3⅛".$10.00
Interior Panel, sugar bowl, w/lid, green lustre, lg, 1⅞"..$35.00
Interior Panel, sugar bowl, w/lid, transparent green, lg, 1⅞"..$32.00
Interior Panel, teapot, marbleized green & white, sm, 3⅜"..$35.00
Interior Panel, teapot, w/lid, transparent topaz, sm, 3⅜"..$22.00
Interior Panel, tumbler, green lustre, sm, 2" $9.50
JP, creamer, light blue or crystal, lg, 1½"....................$30.00
JP, plate, transparent green or brown, lg, 4¼" $12.00
JP, sugar bowl, light blue transparent or crystal, lg, 1½"...$32.00
JP, sugar bowl (open), light blue or crystal, lg, 1½"...$30.00
JP, teapot, w/lid, light blue transparent, lg, 2¾" $85.00

Miss America, boxed set, white, 17-pc, MIB **$515.00**
Miss America, creamer, forest green, 1¼"...................**$65.00**
Miss America, creamer, white, 1¼" **$50.00**
Miss America, plate, decal or forest green, 4½".........**$45.00**
Miss America, saucer, white, 3⅝" **$15.00**
Miss America, sugar bowl, w/lid, white, 2" **$65.00**
Miss America, teapot, orange & white, 3¼" **$140.00**
Miss America, white, 1⅝"..**$40.00**
Octagonal, bowl, cereal; green or white, lg, 3⅜" **$10.00**
Octagonal, boxed set, lemonade & oxblood, lg, 17-pc, MIB **$325.00**
Octagonal, creamer, lemonade & oxblood, closed handle, lg, 1¼"...**$30.00**
Octagonal, saucer, dark blue, lg, 4¼" **$4.00**
Octagonal, tumbler, blue or white, sm, 2"..................**$14.00**
Raised Daisy, creamer, yellow, 1¾" **$50.00**
Raised Daisy, cup, blue, 1¾"......................................**$65.00**
Raised Daisy, saucer, beige, 2½" **$9.00**
Raised Daisy, teapot, w/lid, blue, 2⅜".......................**$85.00**
Raised Daisy, tumbler, yellow, sm, 2"........................**$27.00**
Stacked Disc, boxed set, green or white, sm, 21-pc, MIB..**$195.00**
Stacked Disc, creamer, opaque colors other than green or white, sm, 1¼"...**$14.00**
Stacked Disc, cup, opaque green or white, sm, 1¼"....**$6.00**
Stacked Disc, pitcher, opaque colors other than green or white, sm, 2⅞"..**$16.00**
Stacked Disc, plate, opaque green or white, sm, 3¼"..**$3.00**
Stacked Disc, tumbler, opaque colors other than green, 2" **$14.00**
Stacked Disc & Interior Panel, bowl, cereal; transparent green, lg, 3⅜"..**$22.00**
Stacked Disc & Interior Panel, boxed set, any solid color, lg, 21-pc, MIB..**$370.00**
Stacked Disc & Interior Panel, creamer, transparent amber, sm, 1 14"...**$30.00**
Stacked Disc & Interior Panel, cup, marbleized blue, sm, 3¼"..**$35.00**
Stacked Disc & Interior Panel, cup, transparent green, lg, 1⅜"...**$27.50**
Stacked Disc & Interior Panel, cup, transparent green, sm, 1¼"...**$15.00**
Stacked Disc & Interior Panel, pitcher, transparent cobalt, sm, 2⅞"...**$27.00**
Stacked Disc & Interior Panel, plate, marbleized blue, lg, 4¾"..**$35.00**
Stacked Disc & Interior Panel, saucer, opaque colors, lg, 3¼"..**$6.00**
Stacked Disc & Interior Panel, saucer, transparent green, sm, 2¾"...**$8.00**
Stacked Disc & Interior Panel, sugar bowl, w/lid, opaque colors, sm, 1¼" **$18.00**
Stacked Disc & Interior Panel, sugar bowl, w/lid, transparent green, lg, 1⅞"..**$40.00**
Stacked Disc & Interior Panel, teapot, opaque colors, lg, 3¾"..**$45.00**
Stacked Disc & Interior Panel, teapot, opaque colors, lg, 3¾"..**$40.00**
Stacked Disc & Interior Panel, teapot, transparent cobalt, sm, 3⅜"...**$50.00**

Stacked Disc & Interior Panel, transparent green, lg, 4¾"..**$12.00**
Stacked Disc & Interior Panel, tumbler, opaque colors, sm, 2"..**$50.00**
Stippled Band, creamer, transparent amber, lg, 1½"...**$22.00**
Stippled Band, cup, transparent amber, lg, 1½".........**$15.00**
Stippled Band, saucer, sm, transparent amber, sm, 2¼"......**$2.50**
Stippled Band, sugar bowl, w/lid, transparent amber, lg, 1⅞"..**$30.00**

Aluminum

The aluminum items which have become today's collectibles range from early brite-cut giftware and old kitchen wares to furniture and club aluminum cooking pans. But the most collectible, right now, at least, is the giftware of the 1930s through the '50s.

There were probably several hundred makers of aluminum accessories and giftware with each developing their preferred method of manufacturing. Some pieces were cast; other products were hammered with patterns created by either an intaglio method or repousse. Machine embossing was utilized by some makers, many used faux hammering, and lightweight items were often decorated with pressed designs. During one period, spun aluminum and colored aluminum became very popular.

As early as the 1940s, collectors began to seek out aluminum, sometimes to add to the few pieces received as wedding gifts. By the late 1970s and early 1980s, aluminum giftware was found in abundance at almost any flea market, and prices of $1.00 or less were normal. As more shoppers became enthralled with the appearance of this lustrous metal and its patterns, prices began to rise and have not yet peaked for the products of some companies. A few highly prized pieces have brought prices of four or five hundred dollars and occasionally even more.

One of the first to manufacture this type of ware was Wendell August Forge, when during the late 1920s they expanded their line of decorative wrought iron and began to use aluminum, at first making small items as gifts for their customers. Very soon they were involved in a growing industry estimated at one point to be comprised of several hundred companies, among them Arthur Armour, the Continental Silver Company, Everlast, Buenilum, Rodney Kent, and Palmer-Smith. Few of the many original companies survived the WWII scarcity of aluminum.

Prices differ greatly from one region to another, sometimes without regard to quality or condition, so be sure to examine each item carefully before you buy. If you're in doubt as to value, we recommend the newsletter *The Aluminist* published by Dannie Woodard, author of *Hammered Aluminum, Hand Wrought Collectibles*. Another good book on the subject is titled *Collectible Aluminum, An Identification and Value Guide*, by Everett Grist (Collector Books).

Advisor: Dannie Woodard (See Directory, Aluminum)

Newsletter: *The Aluminist*
Dannie Woodard, Publisher
P.O. Box 1346, Weatherford, TX 76086; 817-594-4680

Ashtray, Bruce Fox, square w/horse head, 5½"..........**$38.00**

Basket, Farber & Shlevin, polished w/stamped rose pattern, twisted handle, pottery insert, 7"............................**$18.00**

Bowl, Canterbury, floral bouquet w/carnations & mums....**$20.00**

Bowl, console; Federal Silver, flowers at center, ruffled edge, 12" **$7.00**

Bowl, Everlast, hammered w/fruit pattern, 12½" dia..**$18.00**

Bracelet, unmarked, C-type band w/leaf design.........**$15.00**

Candle holder, Continental #712, leaf handle, 2½".......**$8.00**

Candle holders, Melkraft, flower petal form, pr.......**$10.00**

Candlestick, Everlast, 1 candle, hammered w/scalloped base, 3½"..**$25.00**

Candy dish, Farber & Shlevin #1700 ....**$12.50**

Candy dish, Farber #170, daisies & leaves at center, ruffled edge, 7½" dia...**$12.00**

Candy dish, Farber #1707, handled, w/glass insert, 8" dia **$10.00**

Celery dish, Farberware, raspberries, leaves & flowers at center, 13½x7" **$12.00**

Celery dish, KSC #C334, 13x7"..**$8.00**

Chafing dish, Spain, hammered w/black handle & knob **$12.00**

Coaster, hammered star w/glass insert..........................**$3.50**

Coaster, unmarked, round w/plain rim, embossed goose in flight..**$3.00**

Coaster, unmarked, round w/turned-up plain rim, embossed Scotty dog in center..**$8.00**

Cocktail shaker, Buenilum, double-looped finial, 9½" **$85.00**

Compote, unmarked, deep hammered bowl w/flared rolled rim, low pedestal foot, 5x6" dia **$10.00**

Condiment set, 3 rotating removable baskets, Everlast, 11", $60.00.

Crumber & tray, Everlast, scalloped rims w/leaf design .**$22.00**

Lamp, Wendell August Forge, hammered w/zinnia pattern, silky shade...**$650.00**

Money clip, DeMarsh Forge, embossed lighthouse **$12.00**

Napkin holder, Everlast, hammered trefoil shape w/rose design **$20.00**

Plate, flowers & butterflies at center, fine scalloped edge, 12½" dia **$10.00**

Relish dish, Continental #729, 3-compartment w/chrysanthemums, applied leaf decor **$12.00**

Relish dish, Continental #754, chrysanthemums at center, 9"..**$18.00**

Salad fork & spoon, Wendell August Forge (unmarked), hammered w/twisted handles.......................................**$55.00**

Shot glass set, anodized, 6 assorted colors, palette-form tray, late 1950s to 1960s, $30.00.

Silent butler, Everlast, rose on lid...............................**$36.00**

Silent butler, Rodney Kent, tulips................................**$40.00**

Silent butler, unmarked, hammered w/sunflower on lid, solid hammered handle w/pointed end, 6" dia.............**$20.00**

Toast rack, Wendell August Forge #709, hammered w/wheat pattern..**$75.00**

Tongs, hammered, for ice bucket....................................**$3.50**

Tray, Bread, Everlast, hammered w/anchor design **$18.00**

Tray, Continental #755, mums w/leaves at center, leaf decorated handles, 18¾x12" **$38.00**

Tray, Cromwell, apples, cherries, grapes, other fruits & flowers, fancy lace edge, swirl handles, 21½x12" **$22.50**

Tray, Everlast, roses, 12x12"..**$22.50**

Tray, Farber & Shlevin #1732...**$20.00**

Tray, geese & cattails, 7x4" **$6.50**

Tray, Hand Forged, round w/rod handles wrapped in coiled wire, fruit design, 17" dia......................................**$25.00**

Tray, wild roses, oval w/fluted rim, smooth finish w/stamped design, 12¼"..**$10.00**

American Bisque

This was a West Virginia company that operated there from 1919 until 1982, producing a wide variety of figural planters and banks, cookie jars, kitchenware, and vases. It has a look all its own; most of the decoration was done by the airbrushing method, and some pieces were gold trimmed. Collectors often identify American Bisque items by the 'wedges' or dry-footed cleats on the bottom of the ware. The most valuable pieces are those modeled after copyrighted characters like Popeye and the Flintstones. If you'd like more information, refer to *American Bisque, Collector's Guide With Prices*, by Mary Jane Giacomini.

See also Character Banks; Cookie Jars.

Advisor: Mary Jane Giacomini (See Directory, American Bisque)

Ashtray, Betty Rubble on phone, marked Hanna-Barbera Production, 1961, Arrow Houseware Products, Chicago IL, USA, 8½"..**$110.00**

Ashtray, cream w/gray border, form of Ohio, Made by APCO, flat bottom, 5" across..................................**$20.00**

Bank, Attitude Papa, white w/blue on top, unmarked, 8½"..................................**$75.00**

Bank, Bambi, brown & green, marked Walt Disney Productions, 7½".................................**$65.00**

Bank, Chicken Feed, yellow sack w/black writing, chicken in corner, unmarked, 4½"..............................**$25.00**

Bank, Cinderella, blue over rose dress, holding wand w/yellow star, marked Cinderella USA, Walt Disney 1950, 6½"..................................**$165.00**

Bank, Dumbo, cream w/gold trim, yellow belly, marked Walt Disney, 6¼"..................................**$115.00**

Bank, Figaro, gray, light blue suspenders, unmarked, 6¾"..................................**$75.00**

Bank, Humpty Dumpty, white egg w/yellow bow tie sitting on blue bricks, advertisement pc marked Alice in Philcoland, 6"..................................**$120.00**

Bank, Mr Pig, cream w/green suspenders, Made by APCO, unmarked, 6"..................................**$30.00**

Bank, Roy Rogers & Trigger, rider in rose shirt on brown horse, green base, 7½"..................................**$160.00**

Bank, Sweet Pea, yellow pajamas & blue hat w/black bill, unmarked, 8¼x6½"..................................**$850.00**

Creamer & sugar bowl, Dumbo, white & red w/gold trim, flat bottom, marked Walt Disney, 4" & 4¾".............**$125.00**

Doorstop, English Bobby, white jacket, blue hat & pants, unmarked, original box marked Cardinal, 8¼"..**$200.00**

Figurine, duck, found in different colors, Made by APCO, 1¾"..................................**$3.00**

Gravy boat, 22-24k gold, Genie's lamp style, Produced by APCO, 5"..................................**$60.00**

Grease jar, Churn, brown w/cold-painted flower petals, unmarked, 6½"..................................**$20.00**

Lamp, Baseball Boy, boy on baseball w/bat, unmarked, 7½" (excluding fixture) **$95.00**

Lamp, Davy Crockett hunting bear, original paper shade, unmarked, 7½"..................................**$225.00**

Lamp, nursery; Happy Face Clock, unmarked, 7¼" (excluding fixture)..................................**$55.00**

Lamp, Snow White, green over yellow dress, unmarked, 6½"..................................**$225.00**

Mug, Santa Claus, red & white, unmarked, U-shaped footing, 4"..................................**$25.00**

Night light, Davy Crockett hunting a bear, 4½"..........**$45.00**

Night light, The Shoe, cream w/yellow or blue roof, Made by APCO, unmarked, 6"..................................**$45.00**

Pitcher, cream; white chick w/red bow tie & trim, marked USA, 7¾"..................................**$25.00**

Pitcher, milk; Figaro (on side), greenish brown, tilted style, unmarked, 8¼"..................................**$250.00**

Pitcher, white w/strawberry decoration, cold paint, full circular footing, marked USA, 6¾"..................................**$35.00**

Planter, Donald Duck, blue w/yellow trim, marked Walt Disney Productions, 6½"..................................**$140.00**

Planter, donkey w/cart, multicolored, marked USA, 6"..................................**$12.00**

Planter, Happy Fish, multicolored, unmarked, 4¾"....**$25.00**

Planter, rabbit in log, multicolored, unmarked, 5¾"...**$24.00**

Planter, sailfish, multicolored, unmarked, 8x10½"......**$50.00**

Planter, Thumper, marked Thumper, Walt Disney Production, 6½"..................................**$65.00**

Plate, Christmas tree shape, red cold paint & 22-24k gold, unmarked, 14½"..................................**$75.00**

Refrigerator container, swirl pattern, cream w/floral design, handled, Made by APCO, unmarked, 8¾"..........**$150.00**

Salt & pepper shakers, Donald Duck (standing), cream w/gold trim, U-shape footing, marked Walt Disney, 3¼", pr..................................**$40.00**

Salt & pepper shakers, Mickey/Minnie Mouse, U-shape footing, unmarked, 3½", pr..................................**$40.00**

Salt & pepper shakers, Pluto, cream w/gold trim, U-shape footing, marked Walt Disney, 3¼", pr.................**$125.00**

Sugar bowl, Stanfordware, yellow corn w/green S-shaped leaves, Made by APCO, marked 512 Stanfordware..**$30.00**

Teapot, lattice pattern, wedge-shaped footing, Made by APCO, 7¼"..................................**$30.00**

Vase, thistle motif w/gold trim, 2-handled, Made by APCO, circular footing, 5"..................................**$20.00**

Wall pocket, birdhouse, gold trim, unmarked, 5½", $32.00. (Photo courtesy Mary Jane Giacomini)

Wall pocket, hurricane lamp shape, cream w/light rose top, Made by APCO, marked USA, 6"..................................**$24.00**

Wall pocket, Pluto w/cart, brown w/black trim, marked Pluto, Walt Disney Prod, 6¾"..................................**$120.00**

Angels

Birthday

Not at all hard to find and still reasonably priced, birthday angels are fun to assemble into 12-month sets, and since there are many different series to look for, collecting them can be challenging as well as enjoyable. Generally speaking, angels are priced by the following factors: 1) company — look for Lefton, Napco, Norcrest, and Enesco marks or labels (unmarked or unknown sets are of less value); 2) application of flowers, bows, gold trim, etc. (the more detail, the more valuable); 3) use of rhinestones, which will also increase the price; 4) age; and 5) quality of the workmanship involved, detail, and accuracy of paint.

Advisors: Denise and James Atkinson (See Directory, Angels)

#1194, angel of the month series, white hair, 5", each, from $18 to...**$20.00**

#1294, angel of the month, white hair, 5", each, from $18 to...**$20.00**

#1300, boy angels, wearing suit, white hair, 6", each, from $22 to...**$25.00**

#1600 Pal Angel, month series of both boy & girl, 4", each, from $10 to...**$15.00**

Arnart, Kewpies, in choir robes, w/rhinestones, 4½", each, from $12 to...**$15.00**

Enesco, angels on round base w/flower of the month, gold trim, each, from $15 to........................**$18.00**

High Mountain Quality, colored hair, 7", from $25.00 to $30.00 each. (Photo courtesy Denise and James Atkinson)

Kelvin, C-230, holding flower of the month, 4½", each, from $15 to...**$20.00**

Kelvin, C-250, holding flower of the month, 4½", each, from $15 to...**$20.00**

Lefton, #1323, angel of the month, bisque, each, from $18 to...**$22.00**

Lefton, #2600, birthstone on skirt, 3¼", each, from $25 to..**$30.00**

Lefton, #3332, bisque, w/basket of flowers, 4", each, from $18 to...**$22.00**

Lefton, #489, holding basket of flowers, 4", each, from $25 to...**$30.00**

Lefton, #556, boy w/blue wings, 5", each, from $28 to ...**$32.00**

Lefton, #574, day of the week series (like #8281 but not as ornate), each, from $25 to **$28.00**

Lefton, #6224, applied flower/birthstone on skirt, 4½", each, from $18 to...**$20.00**

Lefton, #627, day of the week series, 3½", each, from $28 to **$32.00**

Lefton, #6883, square frame, day of the week & months, 3¼x4", each, from $20 to.....................................**$25.00**

Lefton, #6949, day of the week series in oval frame, 5", each, from $28 to...**$32.00**

Lefton, #8281, day of the week series, applied roses, each, from $30 to...**$35.00**

Lefton, #985, flower of the month, 5", each, from $25 to ...**$30.00**

Lefton, AR-1987, w/ponytail, 4", each, from $18 to **$22.00**

Lefton, 1987J, w/rhinestones, 4½", each, from $25 to....**$30.00**

Napco, A1360-1372, angel of the month, each, from $20 to **$25.00**

Napco, A1917-1929, boy angel of the month, each, from $20 to **$25.00**

Napco, A4307, angel of the month, sm, each, from $22 to **$25.00**

Napco, C1361-1373, angel of the month, each, from $20 to **$25.00**

Napco, C1921-1933, boy angel of the month, each, from $20 to **$25.00**

Napco, S1291, day of the week 'Belle,' each, from $22 to **$25.00**

Napco, S1307, bell of the month, each, from $22 to..**$25.00**

Napco, S1361-1372, angel of the month, each, from $20 to **$25.00**

Napco, S1392, oval frame angel of the month, each, from $25 to **$30.00**

Napco, S401-413, angel of the month, each, from $20 to.**$25.00**

Napco, S429, day of the week angel (also available as planters), each, from $25 to...............................**$30.00**

Norcrest, F-120, angel of the month, 4½", each, from $18 to **$22.00**

Norcrest, F-15, angel of the month, on round base w/raised pattern on dress, 4", each, from $18 to................**$22.00**

Norcrest, F-167, bell of the month, 2¾", each, from $8 to **$12.00**

Norcrest, F-210, day of the week angel, 4½", each, from $18 to **$22.00**

Norcrest, F-23, day of the week angel, 4½", each, from $18 to **$22.00**

Norcrest, F-340, angel of the month, 5", each, from $20 to **$25.00**

Norcrest, F-535, angel of the month, 4½", each, from $20 to **$25.00**

Relco, 4¼", each, from $15 to **$18.00**

Relco, 6", each, from $18 to..................................**$22.00**

SR, angel of the month, w/birthstone & 'trait' of the month (i.e. April - innocence), each, from $20 to **$25.00**

TMJ, angel of the month, w/flower, each, from $20 to.....**$25.00**

Ucagco, white hair, 5¾", from $12 to **$15.00**

Wales, wearing long white gloves, white hair, Made in Japan, 6⅜", each, from $25 to..**$28.00**

Zodiac

These china figurines were made and imported by the same companies as the birthday angels. Not as many companies made the Zodiac series, though, which makes them harder to find. Because they're older and were apparently never as popular as the month pieces, they were not made or distributed as long as the birthday angels. Examples tend to be more individualized due to each sign having a specific characteristic associated with it.

Advisors: Denise and James Atkinson (See Directory, Angels)

Japan, wearing pastel dress w/applied pink rose on head, standing on cloud base w/stars, 4½", each, from $15 to **$20.00**

Japan, wearing pastel dress w/rhinestones on gold stars, applied pink rose on head, 4", each, from $20 to ..**$25.00**

Josef, holds tablet w/sign written & shown in gold, 1960-62, each, from $30 to.................................**$40.00**

Josef, no wings, sign written in cursive on dress, 4", each, from $30 to.................................**$40.00**

Lefton, K8650, applied flowers & gold stars, 4" when standing (1946-53), each, from $32 to **$38.00**

Semco, gold wings, applied roses & pleated ruffle on front edge of dress, 5", each, from $20 to **$25.00**

Frog, green, Co-op Flint..**$120.00**
Hen, milk glass, Eagle Glass.................................**$90.00**
Hen on woven base, blue, Vallerysthal, 5".........**$85.00**
Hen on woven base, pink, Vallerysthal, 5".........**$155.00**
Horse on split rib base, milk glass, Kemple.............**$200.00**
Lion, creamer, Gillander.......................................**$45.00**
Lion on basketweave base, amber, Kemple, 7½" **$175.00**
Rooster, milk glass, w/paper Kemple label, 5½" **$65.00**
Santa Maria w/dolphins on lid, milk glass, Consolidated...**$135.00**
Seashell w/dolphin final, pink opaque, Vallerysthal.............**$45.00**
Snail on strawberry, milk glass, Vallerysthal.............**$215.00**

Capricorn angels, from left to right: Napco S980, 4", from $23.00 to $28.00; Napco A2646, 5", from $25.00 to $30.00; Napco S1259 planter series, 4", $30.00 to $35.00. (Photo courtesy Denise and James Atkinson)

Duck on wavy base, milk glass, US Glass, 8", $125.00. (Photo courtesy Everett Grist)

Animal Dishes with Covers

Made for nearly two centuries, animal dishes with covers are just about as varied as their manufacturers. Slag, colored, clear, or milk glass types may be found as well as those made of china and pottery. While the hen on the nest (or basketweave base) is the most common theme, birds and animals of nearly every kind have been fashioned into covered dishes. Other figural designs such as ships were produced as well. Note that our listings describe animal dishes made from circa 1930 through 1960. *Covered Animal Dishes* by Everett Grist is an excellent source for more information and covers the products of many manufacturers. Also refer to *Who's Who in the Hen House* by Ruth Grizel, privately published.

See also Degenhart; Duncan and Miller; Fenton; Imperial; Indiana Glass; Kanawha; L.E. Smith; L.G. Wright; St. Clair Glass; Viking Glass; Westmoreland.

Advisor: Everett Grist (See Directory, Animal Dishes)

Acorn w/squirrel finial, milk glass, unmarked, 7".......**$90.00**
Bambi powder jar, crystal, Jeannette...........................**$25.00**
Dominecker Hen, Challinor Taylor **$350.00**
Elephant, green w/flower back, Co-Operative Flint Glass Co.................................**$195.00**
Elephant w/ashtray on back, milk glass, Co-Operative Flint Glass Co **$165.00**
Fox on basketweave base, amber, Kemple, 7½" **$175.00**

Ashtrays

Ashtrays, especially for cigarettes, did not become widely used in the United States much before the turn of the century. The first examples were simply receptacles made to hold ashes for pipes, cigars, and cigarettes. Later, rests were incorporated into the design. Ashtrays were made in a variety of materials. Some were purely functional, while others advertised or entertained, and some were designed to be works of art. They were made to accommodate smokers in homes, businesses, or wherever they might be. Today their prices range from a few dollars to hundreds. Since they are recognized as comparatively new collectibles, prices are still fluctuating. For further information see *Collector's Guide to Ashtrays, Identification and Values,* by Nancy Wanvig.

See also specific glass companies and potteries; Disney; Tire Ashtrays; World's Fairs.

Advisor: Nancy Wanvig (See Directory, Ashtrays)

Advertising, American Express, green & blue stripes & logo at center, 3¾x3¾" **$6.00**
Advertising, Camel, polished gray marble w/name in gold on rise, 3 rests, 6" dia **$25.00**
Advertising, JC Penney Co, black letters on wide yellow rim, white ceramic center, 5¼" dia **$25.00**
Advertising, Liquore Galliano, red letters on white ceramic triangle, Italian, 5½"...................................**$10.00**

Advertising, Masonic, blue & white letters, logo & 1857-1957 on clear glass, 4x4"...**$15.00**

Advertising, Massachusetts Institute of Technology, red & black seal on white ceramic, 7x7".........................**$8.00**

Advertising, Purina Chow, red & white checkerboard center on clear glass octagon, 4½" **$4.00**

Advertising, Schlitz, tan ceramic w/brown logo & picture, 5¼" **$20.00**

Advertising, Sea World, multicolor w/penguin on clear glass, 1985, 4x4" **$9.00**

Advertising, 7-Up, The International Drink, plastic, 5½" square, $10.00. (Photo courtesy Nancy Wanvig)

Advertising, Stork Club, blue letters & stork on beige ceramic, 7¼" dia **$30.00**

Advertising, Whirlpool, gold enamel w/logo at center, 4 rests, 7¾" dia **$30.00**

Advertising, Winston, impressed letters on rectangular aluminum, double rests each side, 8½" L **$9.00**

Cloisonne, bowl form w/brass cells & sm rust flowers, probably China, 3¼" dia **$16.00**

Enamel, free-form w/3 rests, multicolor flowers on bright blue, 5" L **$15.00**

Glass, black amethyst elephant, Greensburg Glass Works, early 1930s, 6" dia....................................**$30.00**

Glass, cobalt cloverleaf, Tiffin, 4¾" L...........................**$28.00**

Glass, crystal horse, Pacemaker, late 1930s, 3x5¼" dia..**$15.00**

Glass, crystal oval w/swirl base, 3 rests each side on spiral rim, Hazel Atlas, 6" L **$9.00**

Glass, crystal shell shape, marked McKee Glass Co Est 1853, Jeannette PA, 5⅝" L **$13.00**

Glass, forest green, hexagonal w/6 rests, Anchor Hocking, 1940s-60s, 5¾"....................................**$8.00**

Glass, forest green, Queen Mary, Hocking, 1950s, 3½" ...**$6.00**

Glass, red, white & blue swirls in round clear base w/2 scallops at top, 3 applied rests, Lenwile Glass/Japan, 4" L **$22.00**

Glass, royal ruby, square w/4 rests, Anchor Hocking, ca 1940-60, 3⅜"...**$5.00**

Glass, 6-point star w/6 rests, star pattern in base, Hazel Atlas, ca 1936-39, 4¾".............................**$15.00**

Horn, bird on oval form, 5⅛" L.........................**$15.00**

Metal, chrome plate w/cut-out pattern & plain handle, cobalt insert, 4¼" dia **$16.00**

Metal, dog on triangle base w/2 rests, 2¾"................**$25.00**

Metal, embossed sterling w/flat rim & 2 rests, enameled shield at center, 3¼" dia.......................................**$18.00**

Metal, hammered copper w/embossed leaves at 1 corner, 5"..**$20.00**

Metal, plain chrome w/2 rests, glass insert, unmarked, 4⅜"..**$10.00**

Metal, plain diamond w/2 rests, American, 3½" **$14.00**

Metal, ship w/mermaid, bronzed pot metal, 4¼" **$23.00**

Novelty, black shoe, metal w/inlaid design, 6" L........**$20.00**

Novelty, ceramic footed tub, Hot Springs Arkansas, 4" L...**$10.00**

Novelty, cowboy hat, metal, souvenir of Las Vegas, 4¼" L...**$10.00**

Novelty, Delft Dutch shoe, Holland, 1 rest, 3" L...........**$8.00**

Novelty, hand w/sm flowers, white porcelain, 5½" L...**$14.00**

Novelty, Indian face, smoke style, smoke comes out nose, Lenwile/Japan, 3"......................................**$45.00**

Novelty, lady on bed, multicolor porcelain, legs nod, 5⅜" **$55.00**

Novelty, Oriental man, sitting on square metal base, head nods, 3¾"...**$60.00**

Novelty, top hat, black glass w/2 rests, 2"...................**$9.00**

Porcelain, classical scene at center, wine border, marked US Zone Germany, 5½" dia...........................**$10.00**

Porcelain, Friar Tuck, Goebel, #ZF 43/II, 1956, 4" ...**$165.00**

Porcelain, green basketweave bowl w/3 rests, Marutomoware-Japan mark, 4½" dia.....................................**$8.00**

Porcelain, Happy Pastimes, Hummel, #62, 3⅜" **$135.00**

Porcelain, Oliver Twist Asks for More, Lancaster & Sandland Ltd, 4x4"...**$17.00**

Porcelain, Quimper, cat as cigarette holder, match holder and ashtray, HB Quimper, 6½" long, old, $140.00. (Photo courtesy Nancy Wanvig)

Porcelain, US Naval Academy, seal at center, 5⅜" dia....**$12.00**

Pottery, leaf shape, cream w/yellow & blue design at center, Winfield, 3¾" L **$5.00**

Pottery, moriage used for gray dragon, unmarked Dragonware, Japan, 3⅝" **$10.00**

Shenango, decorative pattern around rise, match holder at back, 3¾" dia **$25.00**

Soapstone, elephant on back rim, 4¼" L..................**$35.00**

Wedgwood, dark blue & white, laurel leaf border, 4½"..**$30.00**

Autographs

'Philography' is an extremely popular hobby, one that is very diversified. Autographs of sports figures, movie stars, entertainers, and politicians from our lifetime may bring several hundred dollars, depending on rarity and application, while John Adams' simple signature on a document from 1800, for instance, might bring thousands. A signature on a card or photograph is the least valuable type of autograph. A handwritten letter is the most valuable, since in addition to the signature you get the message as well. Depending upon what it reveals about the personality who penned it, content can be very important and can make a major difference in value.

Many times a polite request accompanied by an SASE to a famous person will result in receipt of a signed photo or a short handwritten note that might in several years be worth a tidy sum!

Obviously as new collectors enter the field, the law of supply and demand will drive the prices for autographs upward, especially when the personality is deceased. There are forgeries around, so before you decide to invest in expensive autographs, get to know your dealers.

Over the years many celebrities in all fields have periodically employed secretaries to sign their letters and photos. They have also sent out photos with preprinted or rubber stamped signatures as time doesn't always permit them to personally respond to fan mail. With today's advanced printing, many long-time collectors have even been fooled with a mechanically produced signature.

Advisors: Don and Anne Kier (See Directory, Autographs)

Newspaper: *Autograph Times*
2303 N 44th St., #225, Phoenix, AZ 85008; 602-947-3112 or Fax 602-947-8363

Arnold Schwarzenegger as Commando, signed black and white photo, 10x8", $35.00.

Alexander, Jason; inscribed & signed color bust portrait photo, from Seinfeld, 8x10" $20.00
Allen, Tim; inscribed & signed bust portrait photo, from 'Home Improvement'...$30.00

Ameche, Don; inscribed & signed sepia photo, signed in green ink, 8x10"....................................$55.00
Anderson, Pamela; signed color photo, 8x10".............$80.00
Arnez, Desi; check signed twice, 1954 ....$200.00
Aykroyd, Dan; signed half-length portrait....................$20.00
Bacon, Kevin; inscribed & signed color bust portrait photo $25.00
Bakula, Scott; inscribed & signed half-length color portrait photo $25.00
Baldwin, Alec; inscribed & signed color bust portrait photo..$45.00
Ball, Lucille; & Desi Arnaz, signed contract, 1953 ....$950.00
Ball, Lucille; signed check, 1954 ....$500.00
Bardot, Brigitte; sexy color bust portrait photo...........$45.00
Barrymore, Drew; inscribed & signed color portrait photo, from Bad Girls..$35.00
Basinger, Kim; signed black & white photo, from Batman, 8x10"...$30.00
Bendix, William; inscribed & signed black & white photo, matted, 8x10" $180.00
Berenger, Tom; inscribed & signed half-length color portrait photo $30.00
Bergen, Candice; inscribed & signed color portrait photo, as Murphy Brown...$40.00
Bisset, Jacqueline; full-length color swimsuit pose $10.00
Blaine, Vivian; inscribed & signed black & white photo, matted, 8x10"..$65.00
Bolger, Ray; inscribed & signed sepia photo, 8x10".$110.00
Bolton, Michael; inscribed & signed half-length color portrait photo, in white blazer...$50.00
Brosnan, Pierce; inscribed & signed half-length color portrait photo, in evening clothes $40.00
Cage, Nicholas; inscribed & signed color bust portrait photo..$30.00
Cain, Dean; signed color photo, as Clark Kent, 8x10"...$45.00
Carlin, George; inscribed & signed color bust portrait photo $25.00
Carrey, Jim; inscribed & signed wild color portrait photo, from The Mask...$60.00
Carter, Linda; inscribed & signed color portrait photo, as Wonder Woman $20.00
Close, Glenn; inscribed & signed half-length color portrait photo, from Immediate Family $20.00
Connery, Sean; inscribed & signed color bust portrait photo, as James Bond $115.00
Crawford, Joan; inscribed & signed black & white Laszio Willinger photo, 13x10".......................................$250.00
Crawford, Michael; inscribed & signed color portrait photo, as Phantom of the Opera....................................$30.00
Crystal, Billy; inscribed & signed color bust portrait photo, from City Slickers..$30.00
Delaney, Dana; inscribed & signed color portrait photo, from China Beach $30.00
DeNiro, Robert; inscribed & signed color portrait photo, from Taxi Driver...$75.00
DePardieu, Gerard; inscribed & signed color portrait photo, 8x10"..$40.00
Diamond, Neil; inscribed & signed half-length color portrait photo $75.00

Dillon, Matt; inscribed & signed color portrait photo, from Flamigo Kid, 8x10".....................................**$35.00**

Doherty, Shannen; inscribed & signed color bust portrait photo **$40.00**

Dresher, Fran; inscribed & signed full-length color portrait photo **$45.00**

Eastwood, Clint; inscribed & signed color portrait photo, from Unforgiven.....................................**$60.00**

Elliott, Sam; inscribed & signed rugged Western portrait photo **$35.00**

Englund, Robert; signed color portrait photo, as Freddy Kreuger.....................................**$30.00**

Estevez, Emilio; inscribed & signed color bust portrait photo, holding gun.....................................**$30.00**

Falk, Peter; bust portrait photo, as Columbo **$15.00**

Faye, Alice; inscribed & signed sepia photo, 1942, 8x9" matted to 16x20".....................................**$45.00**

Fonda, Bridget; inscribed & signed color portrait photo, 8x10".....................................**$35.00**

Ford, Harrison; signed color photo, as The Fugitive, matted, 8x10".....................................**$125.00**

Foster, Jodie; inscribed & signed color portrait photo, in backless black gown.....................................**$115.00**

Foster, Jodie; signed color photo, head & shoulders scene, 8x10".....................................**$120.00**

Fox, Michael J; inscribed & signed bust portrait photo, in cowboy duds.....................................**$35.00**

Franz, Dennis; inscribed & signed color portrait photo, from NYPD Blue.....................................**$35.00**

Friends, signed color photo, signed by all 6 cast members, 8x10".....................................**$225.00**

Furlong, Eddie; inscribed & signed color portrait photo, from Terminator 2.....................................**$35.00**

Gibson, Mel; signed color bust portrait photo, from Maverick.....................................**$125.00**

Hanks, Tom; inscribed & signed half-length color portrait photo, as Forrest Gump.....................................**$45.00**

Harrelson, Woody; inscribed & signed color portrait photo, from White Men Can't Jump.....................................**$35.00**

Harris, Neal Patrick; inscribed & signed color portrait photo, as Doogie Howser.....................................**$30.00**

Hatcher, Teri; signed color photo, wearing Superman's cape only, 8x10".....................................**$60.00**

Hayward, Susan; inscribed & signed black & white photo, mid-1940s, 8x10".....................................**$475.00**

Hayworth, Rita; signed black & white photo, from Separate Tables, 8x10".....................................**$475.00**

Holliday, Judy; handwritten note signed, Great Bells Are Ringing content.....................................**$200.00**

Holliday, Judy; signed black & white photo, 2½x4"..**$165.00**

Holyfield, Evander; signed color photo w/champ's belt, 8x10".....................................**$25.00**

Hopper, Dennis; inscribed & signed half-length color portrait photo **$30.00**

Irons, Jeremy; inscribed & signed color portrait photo, as Klaus Von Bulow.....................................**$25.00**

Jackson, Janet; inscribed & signed color performance portrait photo **$75.00**

John, Elton; inscribed & signed color portrait photo..**$75.00**

Jones, Tommy Lee; signed contract.....................................**$50.00**

Judd, Ashley; inscribed & signed half-length color portrait photo **$45.00**

Keaton, Diane; inscribed & signed color portrait photo **$40.00**

Keaton, Michael; signed color portrait photo, as Batman..**$45.00**

Kidman, Nicole; inscribed & signed color bust portrait photo, 8x10".....................................**$50.00**

Knox, Elyse; inscribed & signed black & white photo, signed in 1941, 11x14".....................................**$75.00**

Kristofferson, Kris; inscribed & signed color bust portrait photo **$30.00**

Ladd, Diane; inscribed & signed half-length color portrait photo **$30.00**

Marx, Groucho; signed check.....................................**$210.00**

McNall, Bruce; typed letter signed, to Motown Record's Berry Gordy.....................................**$75.00**

Clayton Moore as the Lone Ranger, signed lobby card, $35.00.

Moore, Demi; signed black & white photo, full-length, sexy, 8x10".....................................**$95.00**

Moranis, Rick; signed contract.....................................**$75.00**

Nagel, Conrad; inscribed & signed sepia photo, George Hurrell photo, 11x14".....................................**$300.00**

Nolin, Gena Lee; signed color photo, in Baywatch swimsuit, 8x10".....................................**$45.00**

Pfeiffer, Michelle; signed color photo, matted, sultry, 8x10".....................................**$100.00**

Powell, Dick; inscribed & signed sepia portrait photo, late '30s, 8x10".....................................**$85.00**

Reeves, Keanu; signed color photo, long hair, 8x10".**$60.00**

Russo, Rene; inscribed & signed half-length color portrait scene.....................................**$35.00**

Ryan, Meg; signed color photo, from The Doors, 8x10"..**$60.00**

Ryder, Winona; inscribed & signed color bust portrait photo **$65.00**

Sarandon, Susan; inscribed & signed color portrait photo, 8x10".....................................**$40.00**

Seagal, Steven; inscribed & signed color portrait photo, w/assault rifle.....................................**$25.00**

Sheedy, Ally; inscribed & signed color portrait photo, in white windbreaker.....................................**$20.00**

Short, Martin; inscribed & signed color portrait scene....**$25.00**

Silverstone, Alicia; signed black & white photo, hard to find, 8x10"..........**$85.00**

Skerritt, Tom; inscribed & signed color bust portrait photo, from Picket Fences **$30.00**

Slater, Christian; inscribed & signed color bust portrait photo **$40.00**

Snipes, Wesley; inscribed & signed half-length color action portrait photo..........**$35.00**

Steenburgen, Mary; signed color portrait, as Miss Firecracker **$25.00**

Stewart, James; signed check..........**$135.00**

Stone, Sharon; inscribed & signed color bust portrait photo..........**$45.00**

Stone, Sharon; signed color photo, sexy, full-length, 8x10"..........**$85.00**

Swayze, Patrick; inscribed & signed half-length color portrait photo **$45.00**

Thurman, Uma; inscribed & signed color portrait photo, from Pulp Fiction, 8x10"..........**$45.00**

Travis, Nancy; inscribed & signed half-length color portrait photo **$20.00**

Van Damme, Jean Claude; inscribed & signed color portrait scene, 8x10" **$35.00**

Van Peebles, Mario; inscribed & signed color bust portrait photo **$35.00**

West, Mae; signed check..........**$100.00**

Williams, Treat; signed half-length color portrait photo **$12.00**

Willis, Bruce; inscribed & signed color portrait scene, from Die Hard, 8x10" **$85.00**

Winger, Debra; inscribed & signed color bust portrait photo..........**$25.00**

Wood, Elijah; inscribed & signed color portrait photo, in Hawaii, 8x10" **$25.00**

Woods, James; inscribed & signed half-length color portrait photo **$25.00**

Wright, Robin; inscribed & signed color portrait photo, from Forrest Gump, 8x10"..........**$45.00**

Young, Paul; inscribed & signed color bust portrait photo.**$30.00**

Automobilia

Automobilia remains a specialized field, attracting antique collectors and old car buffs alike. Automobilia refers to auto-related advertising and accessories like hood ornaments, gear shift and steering wheel knobs, sales brochures, and catalogs. Many figural hood ornaments bring from $75.00 to $200.00 — a Lalique glass radiator attachment recently sold for $55,000.00 at auction. Memorabilia from the high-performance, sporty automobiles of the sixties is very popular with baby boomers at this time. Unusual items have been setting auction records this past year as the market for automobilia heats up.

Note: Badges vary according to gold content — 10k or sterling silver examples are higher than average. Dealership booklets (Ford, Chevy, etc.) generally run about $2.00 per page, and because many reproductions are available, very few owner's manuals sell for more than $10.00.

See also License Plates; Tire Ashtrays.

Advisors: Jim and Nancy Schaut (See Directory, Automobilia)

Badge, chauffeur's; Arizona, copper, 1936, $75.00. (Photo courtesy Jim and Nancy Schaut)

Badge, Studebaker Employee, brass w/celluloid insert, missing pin at back..........**$35.00**

Badge, 1930 Ohio Licensed Chauffeur..........**$35.00**

Badge, 1934 Harrisburg Huckster License #273 ....**$25.00**

Bank, Ford, dog figural, marked Florence Ceramics, 1960s, $35.00. (Photo courtesy Jim and Nancy Schaut)

Blotter, Dodge Brothers Trucks, multicolor, 1929, 4x9", framed, EX..........**$85.00**

Book, automobile payment, 1940, unused **$2.00**

Book, Sign of the 76, Union Oil company history, 1976, hardcover, w/dust jacket..........**$10.00**

Booklet, A Trip Through the Studebaker Factory, Studebaker Corp, ca 1950, 64 pages, VG+ **$10.00**

Booklet, Pontiac, 1978, new product information, NM...**$10.00**

Booklet, Quest: What Does It Take To Make Your Car, black & white photos, late 1960s, 52 pages..........**$5.00**

Bracelet, Goodyear blimp on gold charm w/chain **$10.00**

Brochure, Corvette, for dealer, 1982..........**$5.00**

Change purse, shaped like chauffeur's cap w/embossed mountain scene, driver & passengers, New London NH on side, 2¾"..........**$90.00**

Gear shift knob, orange & white slag glass w/handle..**$20.00**

Key chain, AC-Delco, Space Explorerers in Transportation '70, shows rocket & futuristic car, Apollo 11 on back, MIB .**$35.00**

Key chain, Harsh Hydraulic Hoists, dump truck w/working bed, flasher style, 1950s **$15.00**

Key chain, '66 Olds Super Salesman............................$15.00

Letter opener, Bowser Filtered Gasoline, bronze w/red gas pump at top $50.00

Magazine, Automobile Quarterly, Vol 7 #2, M $15.00

Manual, owner's; Ford, 1960, VG...............................$10.00

Manual, Pinto, Do It Yourself, 1970, EX $7.50

Mug, Chevrolet Truck Sales Award, shows 1947 Stakebed, 1961 ....$15.00

Pencil, mechanical; Kendall Oil can top, NM..............$15.00

Pencil, mechanical; Pontiac, end shaped like shift knob, marked Safety Shift, late 1940s $15.00

Pencil, R&S Oil Co, Crawford NE, phone #9, wood, unused..$5.00

Penholder, Caterpillar, diecast dozer in Lucite w/gravel on top, paper label on base, late 1950s $20.00

Penknife, D-A Lubricant Co, Indianapolis, 1930s........$35.00

Pin, Cadillac Craftsman, gold w/logo, 1947.................$35.00

Pin, Packard, blue & white celluloid over metal, 2¼x1½" ..$75.00

Plate, Ford, 300-500 Club, Wm Rogers silverplate, 6".$10.00

Postcard, 1952 Nash, color, 3x5", unused $4.00

Postcard, 1972 Mustang, black & white real photo, 5x7", unused $2.00

Program, First Century of Studebaker, from company presentation, January 1953, 4 pages, VG.....................$7.50

Tape measure, DeSoto Six, Product of Chrysler, 1½".$50.00

Tie pin, Cadillac crest w/V underneath, sterling........$20.00

Vase, bud; marigold carnival glass, Tree of Life pattern, w/original brackets, 7¼", VG+, pr, from $60 to...$95.00

Watch fob, Good Roads, Road Builders medal $45.00

Watch fob, Link-Belt Speeder Shovel Crane, embossed Allister Equipment, Alsip IL, 1½" square $50.00

Autumn Leaf Dinnerware

A familiar dinnerware pattern to just about all of us, Autumn Leaf was designed by Hall China for the Jewel Tea Company who offered it to their customers as premiums. In fact, some people refer to the pattern as 'Jewel Tea.' First made in 1933, it continued in production until 1978. Pieces with this date in the backstamp are from the overstock that was in the company's warehouse when production was suspended. There are matching pitchers, tumblers, and stemware all made by the Libbey Glass Company, and a set of enameled cookware that came out in 1979. You'll find blankets, tablecloths, metal canisters, clocks, playing cards, and many other items designed around the Autumn Leaf pattern. All are collectible.

Since 1984 Hall Company has been making items for the National Autumn Leaf Collectors Club. These pieces are listed below, designated as such by 'Club' and the date of issue in each of their descriptions.

Limited edition items (by Hall) are being sold by China Specialties, a company in Ohio; but once you become familiar with the old pieces, these are easy to identify, since the molds have been redesigned or were not previously used for Autumn Leaf production. So far, these are the pieces I'm aware of: the Airflow teapot, the Norris refrigerator pitcher, a square-handled beverage mug, a restyled Irish mug, 'teardrop' salt and pepper shakers, a mustard jar, a set of covered onion soup bowls, sherbets, the automobile teapot, a tankard-shaped beer pitcher, fluted salt and pepper shakers, an oval handled relish, a reamer, a round butter dish, a hurricane lamp with a glass shade, a collector's prayer wall plaque, a Hook Cover teapot, a Fort Pitt baker (6" x 4½" x 1¼"), a 7" square wall clock, a small Melody teapot, a 16-oz. chocolate pot, a display shelf sign, 4-oz. footed demitasse cups, a 'Graeter' bud vase, and a 1-handle (2½-pint) bean pot. In glassware they've issued cruets, water and wine goblets, iced tea and juice tumblers, shot glasses, dessert plates, and beer pilsners. These are crystal (not frosted) and are dated at the base of one of the leaves. Their accessory items include playing cards that are dated in the lower right-hand corner.

For further study, we recommend *The Collector's Encyclopedia of Hall China* by Margaret and Kenn Whitmyer. For information on company products see Jewel Tea.

Advisor: Gwynneth M. Harrison (See Directory, Autumn Leaf)

Club: National Autumn Leaf Collectors' Club
Gwynneth Harrison
P.O. Box 1, Mira Loma, CA 91752-0001; 909-685-5434

Newsletter: *Autumn Leaf*
Bill Swanson, Editor
807 Roaring Springs Dr.
Allen, TX 75002-2112; 972-727-5527

Apron, oilcloth, from $600 to $700.00

Baker, cake; Mary Dunbar, Heatflow, 1½-qt, from $40 to...$65.00

Baker, French; 2-pt, from $150 to $175.00

Baker, French; 3-pt, from $18 to $20.00

Baker, pie; from $20 to $35.00

Baker, souffle; 4½", from $40 to.................................$50.00

Bean pot, 2-handled, from $225 to $250.00

Blanket, Vellux, Autumn Leaf, twin-size $175.00

Blanket, Vellux, blue, King-size..................................$250.00

Book, Mary Dunbar Cook Books, from $15 to $20.00

Bottle, Jim Beam..$110.00

Bowl, cream soup; from $25 to....................................$35.00

Bowl, flat soup; 8½", from $16 to $20.00

Bowl, mixing; 3-pc set, from $50 to...........................$65.00

Bowl, refrigerator; 3-pc w/plastic lids, from $200 to ...$275.00

Bowl, Royal Glasbake, milk glass, 4-pc set, from $175 to..$225.00

Bowl, salad; 9", from $15 to $20.00

Bowl, vegetable; Melmac, oval, from $40 to $50.00

Bowl, vegetable; oval, w/lid, from $50 to $75.00

Bowl cover, plastic, 1950-61, 8-pc set, from $75 to..$100.00

Box, oatmeal, from $50 to $100.00

Butter dish, regular, 1-lb, from $350 to.....................$500.00

Butter dish, smooth square top, ¼-lb, from $700 to...$900.00

Cake plate, on metal stand, from $150 to $225.00

Calendar, circa 1920s to 1930s, each, from $40 to......$70.00

Candle holder, Club, Christmas, 1994, each, from $75 to..$100.00

Candle holder, Club, 1989, pr, from $225 to $250.00

Candlestick, metal, 4", pr, from $70 to.....................$100.00

38

Canister, metal, square, 4-pc set, from $250 to **$350.00**

Carrying case, Jewel salesman's, from $150 to..........**$300.00**

Casserole, Mary Dunbar, Heatflow, w/lid, oval, 2-qt, from $85 to...**$125.00**

Casserole, Mary Dunbar, Heatflow, w/lid, round, 1½-qt, from $50 to..**$75.00**

Casserole, round, 2-qt, w/lid, from $30 to...................**$45.00**

Casserole, Royal Glasbake, milk glass, w/lid, round, from $65 to...**$90.00**

Catalog, Jewel, paper cover, from $5 to **$20.00**

Clock, salesman's award, from $300 to......................**$400.00**

Coaster, metal, 3⅛" dia, from $5 to **$8.00**

Coffee dispenser, metal, from $200 to **$400.00**

Coffeepot, Rayed, 9-cup, from $30 to..........................**$45.00**

Cookbook, Club, 1984...**$45.00**

Cookbook, Club, 1988...**$30.00**

Cooker, Mary Dunbar, Waterless, metal, from $50 to .**$75.00**

Cookware, New Metal, 7-pc set, from $400 to..........**$650.00**

Creamer & sugar bowl, Melmac, pr, from $30 to........**$40.00**

Creamer & sugar bowl, Rayed, pr, from $60 to **$80.00**

Creamer & sugar bowl, Ruffled-D, pr, from $25 to.....**$45.00**

Cup, coffee; Jewel's Best..**$25.00**

Cup, custard; Mary Dunbar, Heatflow, from $20 to....**$30.00**

Cup, custard; Radiance, from $6 to **$10.00**

Cup, regular, Ruffled-D, from $4 to...............................**$6.00**

Cup, St Denis, from $25 to **$30.00**

Dripper, metal, for coffeepot, from $20 to **$25.00**

Dutch oven, metal w/porcelain finish, 5-qt, w/lid, from $125 to...**$175.00**

Frying pan, Mary Dunbar, Top Stoveware, from $145 to ..**$175.00**

Goblet, gold & frost on clear, footed, Libbey, 10-oz, from $50 to...**$65.00**

Gravy boat, from $20 to..**$30.00**

Hot pad, metal, oval, 10¾", from $12 to **$15.00**

Hot pad, red or green back, 7¼" dia, from $15 to **$20.00**

Jug, baby ball; Club, 1992, from $60 to **$95.00**

Jug, ball; #3, from $35 to **$40.00**

Jug, batter; Sundial, from $3,000 to **$4,000.00**

Jug, water; Douglas, ice lip, from $450 to.................**$550.00**

Loaf pan, Mary Dunbar, from $40 to...........................**$65.00**

Meat chopper, Griswold, from $250 to **$400.00**

Mug, chocolate; Club, 1992, 4-pc set, from $80 to ...**$100.00**

Mug, Irish coffee; from $90 to.....................................**$150.00**

Mustard condiment, 3-pc set, from $80 to.................**$100.00**

Percolator, Douglas, 1960-62, from $250 to..............**$300.00**

Percolator, electric, from $300 to...............................**$350.00**

Pickle fork, Jewel Tea, from $40 to..............................**$75.00**

Pitcher, syrup; Club, 1995, from $55 to **$95.00**

Plate, bread & butter; 6", from $5 to **$8.00**

Plate, dinner; Melmac, 10", from $15 to......................**$20.00**

Plate, dinner; 10"...**$15.00**

Plate, luncheon; 8"...**$10.00**

Plate, salad; Melmac, 7", from $15 to **$20.00**

Platter, Melmac, oval, 14", from $40 to **$50.00**

Platter, oval, 9", from $20 to **$25.00**

Playing cards, 75th Anniversary, from $25 to.............**$50.00**

Punch bowl, Club, 1993, +12 cups, from $300 to.....**$350.00**

Range set, grease jar w/lid +salt & pepper shakers, 4-pc set, from $50 to..**$60.00**

Salt & pepper shakers, Casper, Ruffled, pr, from $20 to......**$30.00**

Salt & pepper shakers, left or right handled, range-size, pr, from $20 to..**$30.00**

Saucepan, Douglas, 1960-62, w/warmer base, from $300 to...**$500.00**

Saucepan, metal, 2-qt, w/lid, from $70 to **$100.00**

Saucepan, metal w/wood handle, 1½-qt, w/lid, from $100 to...**$150.00**

Saucer, regular, Ruffled-D, from $1 to...........................**$3.00**

Saucer, St Denis, from $6 to..**$8.00**

Shelf liner, plastic, 9-ft, from $125 to **$130.00**

Sherbet, gold & frost on clear, footed, Libbey, 6½-oz, from $50 to...**$65.00**

Shoe polish, white, from $40 to **$55.00**

Silverware, place setting pcs, silverplate, each, from $30 to **$35.00**

Silverware, place setting pcs, stainless steel, each, from $25 to **$30.00**

Silverware, serving pcs, silverplate, each, from $90 to..**$100.00**

Silverware, serving pcs, stainless, each, from $50 to ..**$60.00**

Skillet, metal w/porcelain finish, 9½", from $100 to.....**$125.00**

Stack set, 4-piece, from $100.00 to $125.00. (Photo courtesy Margaret and Ken Whitmyer)

Sugar packet holder, Club, Christmas, 1990, from $75 to **$125.00**

Sweeper, Little Jewel, from $140 to...........................**$175.00**

Tablecloth, muslin, 1930s, 56x81", from $175 to.......**$300.00**

Tablecloth, plastic, 1950-53, 54x54", from $120 to....**$150.00**

Tea for Two set, Club, 1990, from $150 to.................**$175.00**

Tea set, Club, Philadelphia, 1990, from $175 to **$225.00**

Teakettle, metal, w/scale logo, from $100 to **$300.00**

Teakettle, metal w/porcelain finish, from $200 to **$250.00**

Teapot, Aladdin, from $50 to.......................................**$70.00**

Teapot, Club, French, 1992, from $75 to **$95.00**

Teapot, Club, New York, 1984, from $500 to...........**$600.00**

Teapot, Club, Solo, 1991, from $75 to **$100.00**

Teapot, Rayed, long spout, from $50 to **$70.00**

Tin, cocoa, paper label, from $40 to...........................**$70.00**

Tin, fruit cake, tan or white, each, from $7 to...........**$10.00**

Tin, malted milk, paper label, from $50 to.................**$70.00**

Toy, Jewel truck, green, from $175 to **$250.00**

Toy, Jewel truck, orange, from $60 to **$75.00**

Toy, Jewel truck, semi trailer, brown............................**$1,200.00**

Toy, Jewel truck, semi trailer, white, from $275 to...**$375.00**

Tray, metal, oval, from $75 to **$100.00**

Tray, wood & glass, from $125 to............................**$140.00**

Tumbler, Brockway, 13-oz, from $30 to **$45.00**
Tumbler, Brockway, 9-oz, from $30 to **$45.00**
Tumbler, frosted bands, Libbey, 5½", from $25 to......**$40.00**
Vase, bud; Club, 1994.....................................**$40.00**
Vase, bud; sm or regular decal, from $175 to..........**$225.00**
Vase, Club, Edgewater, 1987, from $250 to **$300.00**
Waffle iron, Manning-Bowman, from $75 to **$95.00**
Warmer, round, from $125 to **$160.00**

Teapot, Newport, rectangular lid, 1933, from $175.00 to $200.00.

Avon

You'll find Avon bottles everywhere you go! But it's not just the bottles that are collectible — so are jewelry, awards, magazine ads, catalogs, and product samples. Of course, the better items are the older ones (they've been called Avon since 1939 — California Perfume Company before that), and if you can find them mint in box (MIB), all the better.

For more information we recommend *Hastin's Avon Collector's Price Guide* by Bud Hastin. See also Cape Cod.

Advisor: Tammy Roderick (See Directory, Avon)

Newsletter: *Avon Times*
c/o Dwight or Vera Young
P.O. Box 9868, Dept. P, Kansas City, MO 64134; Inquiries should be accompanied by LSASE

Club: National Association of Avon Collectors
% Connie Clark
6100 Walnut, Dept. P, Kansas City MO 64103; Inquiries should be accompanied by LSASE

Attention Sachet, 57th Ave box, 1943 ....**$10.00**
Avonshire Blue Cologne, blue vase w/white trim, 1971, 6-oz **$7.00**
Baby's 1st Christmas Ornament, 1986 ....**$5.00**
Buttons & Bows Cologne, 2-oz, 1960 ....**$3.00**
Christmas Plate, Country Christmas 1980 ....**$5.00**
Clark Gable as Rhett Butler, porcelain figurine, 1984 ...**$10.00**
Cologne Cruet, clear, 1973, 8-oz..................................**$10.00**
Cotillion Talc Tin, 1956 ....**$2.00**

Dad's Pride & Joy Fostoria Picture Frame, 1982............**$5.00**
Daisies Won't Tell Set, w/case & doll, 1956 ....**$25.00**
Elegante Toilet Water, 1957-59.................................**$35.00**
Endangered Species Stein, 1976 ....**$10.00**

Fair Lady assortment, miniature hatbox with Gardenia, Sweet Pea, Cotillion, and Trailing Arbutus in 4 clear glass minis with label, $60.00. (Photo courtesy Monsen & Baer)

Ferrri 53 Decanter, 1975 ....**$7.00**
Forever Spring Beauty Dust, 1956............................**$5.00**
Fostoria Egg Soap Dish, 1977 ....**$10.00**
Fred Astaire as John Barkley, porcelain figurine, 1984 ....**$7.50**
Gemsio Crystal Set, 1957.......................................**$50.00**
Ginger Rogers as Dinah Barkley, porcelain figurine, 1984 ....**$7.50**
Giving Thanks, porcelain figurine, 1986 ....**$7.50**
Gone Fishing Decanter..**$5.00**
Helping Mom, porcelain figurine, 1986........................**$7.50**
Her Prettiness Pretty Me Doll, 1969...........................**$5.00**
Hummingbird Dinner Bell, lead crystal **$10.00**
Hunters Stein, 1972...**$10.00**
In Style Satin Bag, 1957..**$15.00**
Indian Head Penny Decanter...................................**$5.00**
It's a Blast Decanter, 1970..................................**$7.50**
Jaguar Decanter..**$5.00**
John Wayne as Bob Sexton, porcelain figurine, 1985...**$5.00**
Judy Garland as Dorothy, porcelain figurine, 1985.......**$5.00**
Lavender Toilet Water, 1934-37...............................**$10.00**
Little Folks Perfume Set, 4-pc, boxed, 1911 ....**$500.00**
Mens Travel Kit, 1933-36.....................................**$100.00**
Modern Mood Cosmetic Bag, 1963 ....**$10.00**
Moonlight Glow Bell, 1981 ....**$5.00**
Mount Vernon Sauce Pitcher, 1977..........................**$10.00**
Nail Bleach, 1912...**$100.00**
Nile Blue Bath Urn, 1972 ....**$5.00**
Pepperbox Pistol, 1977..**$10.00**
Perfumed Jewelry a la Glace, 4 styles, 1971, each........**$5.00**
Pretty Peach Cologne, 1964 ....**$5.00**
Pretty Peach Dusting Powder, 1964...........................**$5.00**
Quaintance Rosegay Set, body powder & lotion, 1954....**$5.00**
Rapture Talc Tin, 1965...**$2.00**
Remember When Gas Pump, 1976..............................**$5.00**
Santas Team Set, 1964, set of 2 4-oz bottles...............**$10.00**
Strawberry Bath Foam Pitcher, 1971........................**$5.00**

Sweet Sixteen Face Powder, 1914 ....**$50.00**
Tee Off Decanter, 1973...**$5.00**
Valentine's Day, porcelain figurine, 1986......................**$7.50**
Victorian Washstand, 1973...**$3.00**
Vivian Leigh as Scarlet O'Hara, porcelain figurine, 1984....**$10.00**
Young Hearts Talc, 1952-53 ....**$10.00**

Barbie and Her Friends

Barbie was first introduced in 1959, and soon Mattel found themselves producing not only dolls but tiny garments, fashion accessories, houses, cars, horses, books, and games as well. Today's Barbie collectors want them all. Though the early Barbies are very hard to find, there are many of her successors still around. The trend today is toward Barbie exclusives — Holiday Barbies and Bob Mackies are all very 'hot' items. So are special-event Barbies.

When buying the older dolls, you'll need to do a lot of studying and comparisons to learn to distinguish one Barbie from another, but this is the key to making sound buys and good investments. Remember, though, collectors are sticklers concerning condition; compared to a doll mint in box, they'll often give an additional 20% if that box has never been opened (or as collectors say, 'never removed from box,' indicated in our lines by 'NRFB')! As a general rule, a mint-in-the-box doll is worth twice as much (or there about) as one mint, no box. The same doll, played with and in only good condition, is worth half as much (or even less). If you want a good source for study, refer to one of these fine books: *A Decade of Barbie Dolls and Collectibles, 1981–1991,* by Beth Summers; *The Wonder of Barbie* and *The World of Barbie Dolls* by Paris and Susan Manos; *The Collector's Encyclopedia of Barbie Dolls and Collectibles* by Sibyl DeWein and Joan Ashabraner; *Barbie Doll Fashion*, Vol I and Vol II, by Sarah Sink Eames; *Barbie Exclusives,* Books I and II, by Margo Rana; *The Barbie Doll Boom, 1986–1995,* and *Collector's Encyclopedia of Barbie Doll Exclusives and More* by J. Michael Augustyniak; *The Barbie Years, 1959 to 1995,* by Patrick C. Olds; *The Story of Barbie* by Kitturah Westenhouser; *Barbie, The First 30 Years, 1959 Through 1989,* by Stefanie Deutsch; *Collector's Guide to Barbie Doll Paper Dolls* by Lorraine Mieszala; and *Schroeder's Collectible Toys, Antique to Modern* (Collector Books).

Barbie, 1961, Bubble-Cut, brunette hair, original swimsuit, MIB, $500.00.

Dolls

Allan, 1963, painted red hair, straight legs, NRFB.....**$165.00**
Barbie, #1, 1958-59, blonde hair, MIB **$8,000.00**
Barbie, #2, 1959, brunette hair, MIB **$7,000.00**
Barbie, #3, 1960, blond hair, MIB **$1,350.00**
Barbie, #3, 1960, brunette hair, MIB **$1,550.00**
Barbie, #5, 1961, blond hair, MIB **$550.00**
Barbie, #5, 1961, red hair, MIB...............................**$900.00**
Barbie, Bicyclin', 1993 department store special, NRFB ..**$35.00**
Barbie, Bubble-Cut, 1961, blond hair, MIB...............**$500.00**
Barbie, Bubble-Cut, 1961, red hair, MIB...................**$700.00**
Barbie, California Dream, 1987 department store special, NRFB...**$45.00**
Barbie, Color Magic, 1966, blond hair, NRFB **$1,500.00**
Barbie, Crystal Rhapsody, porcelain, 1992, NRFB.....**$500.00**
Barbie, Cute N' Cool, 1991 department store special, NRFB..**$50.00**
Barbie, Doctor, 1987 department store special, NRFB..**$50.00**
Barbie, Empress Bride, Bob Mackie, 1992, MIB **$800.00**
Barbie, Eskimo, 1981, Dolls of the World series, NRFB..**$75.00**
Barbie, Evening Flame, 1991 department store special, NRFB **$200.00**
Barbie, Gay Parisian, porcelain, 1991, brunette hair, NRFB **$200.00**
Barbie, Gold & Lace, 1989, Target, NRFB...................**$35.00**
Barbie, Hair Happenin's, Sear's Exclusive, 1971, red hair, MIB...**$1,200.00**
Barbie, Hawaiian, 1975, original outfit, rare, VG **$65.00**
Barbie, Holiday, 1989, NRFB......................................**$250.00**
Barbie, Holiday, 1990, NRFB......................................**$200.00**
Barbie, Holiday, 1990, NRFB......................................**$200.00**
Barbie, Holiday, 1990, original dress, VG.....................**$85.00**
Barbie, Holiday, 1992, NRFB......................................**$125.00**
Barbie, Holiday, 1993, Black, MIB **$50.00**
Barbie, Holiday, 1994, NRFB......................................**$175.00**
Barbie, Irish, 1994, Dolls of the World series, NRFB ..**$22.00**
Barbie, Live Action, 1971, NRFB **$200.00**
Barbie, Magic Moves, 1986, original outfit, M.............**$20.00**
Barbie, Malibu, 1971, original blue swimsuit, VG.......**$20.00**
Barbie, Medieval, 1994, Great Eras series, NRFB **$55.00**
Barbie, Neptune Fantasy, Bob Mackie, 1992, NRFB......**$1,000.00**
Barbie, Nigerian, 1989, Dolls of the World series, NRFB.....**$65.00**
Barbie, Oriental, 1980, Dolls of the World series, NRFB..**$150.00**
Barbie, Peaches & Cream, 1984, original outfit, M **$20.00**
Barbie, Pink & Pretty, 1982, originial outfit, M...........**$15.00**
Barbie, Platinum, Bob Mackie, 1991, NRFB **$700.00**
Barbie, Queen of Hearts, Bob Mackie, 1994, NRFB .**$225.00**
Barbie, Royal Splender, porcelain, 1993, MIB **$300.00**
Barbie, Scottish, 1980, Dolls of the World series, NRFB..**$125.00**
Barbie, Snow Princess, 1994 department store special, blond hair, NRFB **$150.00**
Barbie, Sophisticated Lady, porcelain, 1990, NRFB ..**$200.00**
Barbie, Standard, 1970, blond hair, NRFB **$700.00**
Barbie, Standard, 1970, brunette hair, MIB...............**$550.00**
Barbie, Superstar, 1976, original outfit, M...................**$25.00**
Barbie, Superstar, 1993, Walmart, NRFB **$35.00**
Barbie, Sweet 16, blond hair, original pink dress, NM .**$50.00**
Barbie, Swiss, 1983, Dolls of the World series, NRFB.**$85.00**

Barbie, Truly Scrumptious, 1968, original outfit, NM ..**$300.00**

Barbie, Twist N' Turn, 1966, brunette hair, NRFB **$900.00**

Barbie, Twist N' Turn, 1967, blond hair, original pink swim-suit, NM **$225.00**

Barbie, Uptown Chic, 1993, Classique Collections, NRFB .**$65.00**

Barbie, Valentine, 1994 department store special, NRFB...**$50.00**

Barbie, Western, 1980, original outfit, MIB................**$20.00**

Barby, Holiday, 1988, original dress, EX **$325.00**

Cara, Deluxe Quick Curl, 1976, MIB........................**$60.00**

Casey, 1967, blond hair, redressed, VG **$100.00**

Christie, Pink & Pretty, 1982, original outfit, VG.........**$20.00**

Francie, Hair Happenin's 1970, nude, w/3 of 4 hairpieces, NMM **$200.00**

Francie, Twist N' Turn, 1967, brunette hair, nude, NM ...**$275.00**

Ken, as Rhett Butler, Hollywood Legends series, 1994, NRFB **$70.00**

Ken, as Tin Man, Hollywood Legends series, 1995, NRFB...**$65.00**

Ken, Hot Skating, 1994 department store special, NRFB.....**$25.00**

Ken, Malibu, 1971, original swimsuit, VG....................**$20.00**

Ken, Spanish Talking, 1970, MIB **$200.00**

Ken, Western, 1980, original outfit, VG **$20.00**

Ken, 1961, flocked blond or brunette hair, straight legs, NRFB **$350.00**

Ken, 1962, painted brunette hair, straight legs, MIB.**$250.00**

Ken, 1973, Mod Hair, MIB, $60.00.

Midge, 1963, brunette hair, straight legs, original swimsuit, NM **$125.00**

Midge, 30th Anniversary, porcelain, 1992, NRFB......**$300.00**

PJ, Live Action, 1971, nude, EX............................**$75.00**

PJ, Twist N' Turn, 1970, original swimsuit, NM **$150.00**

Ricky, 1965, original outfit, NM **$65.00**

Skipper, Growing Up, 1975, original outfit, VG **$35.00**

Skipper, Super Teen, 1980, MIB **$30.00**

Skipper, 1963, red hair, straight legs, MIB.................**$250.00**

Skooter, blond hair, bendable legs, original outfit, NM **$100.00**

Stacey, Talking, 1968, blond hair, MIB **$385.00**

Steffie, Walk Lively, 1972, brunette hair, bendable legs, redressed, VG...**$85.00**

Teresa, Baywatch, 1994 department store special, NRFB...**$40.00**

Tutti, 1966, blond or brunette hair, MIB....................**$175.00**

Twiggy, 1967, NRFB..**$500.00**

Accessories

Furniture, Barbie Dream Canopy Bed, #5641, 1987, NRFB **$15.00**

Furniture, Barbie Dream Furniture sofa & coffee table, #2475, 1978, M (box worn)..............................**$10.00**

Furniture, Barbie's Room-Fulls Studio Bedroom, #7405, NRFB..**$50.00**

Furniture, Skipper's Jeweled Bed, 1965, MIB...........**$150.00**

Furniture, Skipper's Jeweled Vanity, 1965, NRFB......**$250.00**

Furniture, Suzy Goose Vanity, 1963, G **$25.00**

Outfit, Barbie, Antifreezers, #1464, NRFB................**$125.00**

Outfit, Barbie, Barbie-Q, #962, complete, NM............**$55.00**

Outfit, Barbie, County Fair, Barbie, #1603-1, complete, NM **$45.00**

Outfit, Barbie, Enchanted Evening, #983-4, complete, NM..**$300.00**

Outfit, Barbie, Fab City, #1874-1, shawl only, M **$15.00**

Outfit, Barbie, Fashion Luncheon, #1656, complete, M, $500.00.

Outfit, Barbie, It's Cold Outside, #819, complete, NM **$35.00**

Outfit, Barbie, On the Avenue, #1644, complete, NM..**$300.00**

Outfit, Barbie, Tickled Pink, #1681-1, complete, G ..**$150.00**

Outfit, Francie, #1216, complete, NM **$125.00**

Outfit, Francie, Fresh As a Daisy, #1254, complete, NM ...**$75.00**

Outfit, Francie, Midi Plaid, #3444, NRFB **$50.00**

Outfit, Francie, Quick Shift, #1266, complete, NM ...**$125.00**

Outfit, Francie, Snazz, #1225, complete, EX...............**$65.00**

Outfit, Francie, Wedding Wonder, #1244-1, complete, NM **$125.00**

Outfit, Ken, Campus Hero, #770, NRFB.....................**$95.00**

Outfit, Ken, Casuals, #782-1, complete, NM **$40.00**

Outfit, Ken, College Student, #1416, M....................**$300.00**

Outfit, Ken, Doctor Ken, #793, NRFB **$150.00**

Outfit, Ken, Sailor, #796, NRFB **$125.00**

Outfit, Ken, Shore Lines, #1435, NRFB....................**$50.00**

Outfit, Ken, Ski Champ, #798, NRFB **$125.00**

Outfit, Ken, Special Date, #1401, complete, NM.........**$85.00**

Outfit, Ken, Terry Togs, #784, NRFB.......................**$100.00**

Outfit, Ken, Touchdown, #799, NRFB.......................**$125.00**

Outfit, Ken, Yachtsman, #789, NRFB........................**$100.00**

Outfit, Skipper, Flower Girl, #1904-1, complete, NM..**$50.00**

Outfit, Skipper, Happy Birthday, #1919, dress only, NM..**$25.00**

Outfit, Skipper, Learning To Ride, #1935, NRFB **$250.00**
Outfit, Skipper, Lollapoloozas, #1947, complete, M....**$75.00**
Outfit, Skipper, Posy Party, #1955, complete, NM **$85.00**
Outfit, Skipper, Sledding Fun, #1939, NRFB.............**$300.00**
Outfit, Tutti, Flower Girl, #3615, complete, M **$125.00**
Outfit, Tutti, Pinky PJ's, #3616, M.........................**$75.00**
Outfit, Tutti, Sand Castle, #3603, complete, EX..........**$50.00**
Outfit, Twiggy, Twiggy Gear, #1728, NRFB..............**$325.00**
Vehicle, California Dream Beach Taxi, #4520, 1988, MIB ..**$25.00**
Vehicle, Classy Corvette, 1976, NRFB.........................**$35.00**
Vehicle, Dream Carriage w/Dapple Gray Horses, Europe, 1982, M (seperate boxes)................................**$125.00**
Vehicle, Jaguar XJS, 1994, pink, NRFB.....................**$50.00**
Vehicle, Ken's Hot Rod, Irwin, 1961, NM **$165.00**
Vehicle, Mercedes, 1963, green, NMIB......................**$150.00**
Vehicle, Snowmobile, 1972, Montgomery Ward, MIB.**$50.00**
Vehicle, Sun N' Fun Buggy, 1970, orange, MIB **$75.00**
Vehicle, Ten Speeder, 1973, MIB................................**$15.00**
Vehicle, VW Cabriolet, #3804, 1988, MIB **$35.00**

Gift Sets

Barbie and Ken Campin' Out Set, 1983, MIB, $75.00.

Barbie Denim Fun, #4893, 1989, MIB **$50.00**
Barbie on the Go, 1990, MIB..**$70.00**
Barbie's 35th Anniversary, 1993, blond hair, NRFB ..**$135.00**
Birthday Fun at McDonald's, 1993, NRFB....................**$50.00**
Disney Barbie & Friends, 1991, NRFB **$65.00**
Francie Rise & Shine, 1971, NRFB **$1,000.00**
Jamie Strollin' in Style, 1972, Sears, MIB...................**$425.00**
Ken Red White & Wild, 1970, Sears, MIB.................**$250.00**
Marine Ken & Barbie, 1992, MIB................................**$40.00**
Tennis Star Barbie & Ken, 1988, NRFB.......................**$50.00**
Wedding Party Midge, 1990, NRFB **$150.00**

Miscellaneous

Book, Barbie & Ken, Random House, 1962, EX.........**$25.00**
Booklet, World of Barbie, EX **$30.00**
Box, Ken, 1962, EX..**$50.00**
Box, Miss Barbie, 1964, no liner, VG.......................**$195.00**
Bubbling Bath Milk, 1961, M......................................**$50.00**
Catalog, Timeless Creations, 1990, EX **$10.00**

Embroidery Set, Barbie, Ken & Midge, #7686, 1963, complete, MIB **$225.00**
Francie & Barbie Electric Drawing Set, Lakeside, 1967, NMIB **$50.00**
Magazine, Barbie Bazaar, January/February, 1989, EX .**$75.00**
Magazine, Barbie Bazaar, September, 1988, EX **$125.00**
Ornament, Barbie in Sled, McDonald's, 1995, NRFB ..**$50.00**
Ornament, Holiday Barbie, Hallmark, 1994, 2nd in series, NRFB...**$50.00**
Ornament, Solo in the Spotlight, Hallmark, 1995, 2nd in series, NRFB **$40.00**
Pattern, Barbie, Sightseeing, Sew-Free Fashion Fun, #1713, M..**$30.00**
Photo album, Barbie, 1963, M **$50.00**
Travel case, Barbie, 1979, w/comb & mirror, VG **$15.00**
Wallet, pictures Skipper, 1964, blue, M.....................**$30.00**
Wristwatch, Ponytail Barbie, 1963, blue band, NM...**$150.00**

Barware

Our economy may be 'on the rocks,' but cocktail shakers are becoming the hot new collectible of the nineties. These micro skyscrapers are now being saved for the enjoyment of future generations, much like the 1930s buildings saved from destruction by landmarks preservation committees of today.

Cocktail shakers — the words just conjure up visions of glamour and elegance. Seven hard shakes over your right shoulder and you can travel back in time, back to the glamor of Hollywood movie sets with Fred Astaire and Ginger Rogers and luxurious hotel lounges with gleaming chrome; the world of F. Scott Fitzgerald and *The Great Gatsby*; watch *The Thin Man* movie showing William Powell instruct a bartender on the proper way to shake a martini — the reveries are endless.

An original American art form, cocktail shakers reflect the changing nature of various styles of art, design, and architecture of the era between WWI and WWII. We see the graceful lines of Art Nouveau in the early twenties being replaced by the rage for jagged geometric modern design. The geometric cubism of Picasso that influenced so many designers of the twenties was replaced with the craze for streamline design of thirties. Cocktail shakers of the early thirties were taking the shape of the new deity of American architecture, the skyscraper, thus giving the appearance of movement and speed in a slow economy.

Cocktail shakers served to penetrate the gloom of depression, ready to propel us into the future of prosperity like some Buck Rogers rocket ship — both perfect symbols of generative power, of our perpetration into better times ahead.

Cocktail shakers and architecture took on the aerodynamically sleek industrial design of the automobile and airship. It was as Norman Bel Geddes said: 'a quest for speed.' All sharp edges and corners were rounded off. This trend was the theme of the day, as even the sharp notes of jazz turned into swing.

Cocktail shakers have all the classic qualifications of a premium collectible. They are easily found at auctions, antique and secondhand shops, flea markets, and sales. They can be had in all price ranges. They require little study to identify one manufacturer or period from another, and lastly they are not easily reproduced.

The sleek streamline cocktail shakers of modern design are valued by collectors of today. Those made by Revere, Chase, and Manning Bowman have taken the lead in this race. Also commanding high prices are those shakers of unusual design such as penguins, zeppelins, dumbells, bowling pins, town crier bells, airplanes, even ladies' legs. They're all out there — waiting, waiting to be found, waiting to be recalled to life, to hear the clank of ice cubes, and to again become the symbol of elegance.

For more information we recommend *Vintage Bar Ware, An Identification and Value Guide*, by Stephen Visakay (Collector Books).

Advisor: Steve Visakay (See Directory, Barware)

Book, The Home Bartender's Guide & Song Book, 1930, 94 pages, 8½x11", from $55 to **$85.00**
Book, 900 American Recipes, French, ca 1937, 193 pages..**$35.00**
Bumper sticker, American Beverage Distributors To Elect FDR, Repeal 18th Amendment, cardboard, 4x12", from $25 to...**$35.00**
Canape tray, Five O'Clock No 813, satin chromium over brass, Norman Bel Geddes, ca 1936, 6¾x4⅝", from $7 to...**$10.00**
Cocktail cup, Blue Moon, blue glass on stepped chrome base, 1935-41, 3½x2¼" dia, from $15 to **$20.00**
Cocktail cup, Catalin cup w/chrome stem, stamped Nudawn USA, 6¾", from $8 to **$10.00**
Cocktail cup, head & tail at opposing sides of footed cup, painted details, ca 1930s-40s, 3½x3¼" dia, from $20 to **$25.00**
Cocktail cup, ruby w/applied sterling ring trim, footed, unknown manufacturer, 3⅜", from $7 to..............**$12.00**
Cocktail mixer, clear w/etched vertical lines, glass stirrer w/sterling cap & strainer, Hawks Glass, 18", from $225 to...**$250.00**
Cocktail set, Doric No 90113, white or blue trim, w/shaker, ring tray & 6 cups, 1930s, complete, from $150 to........**$200.00**
Cocktail shaker, chrome-plate pitcher shape w/Catalin handle, Krome Kraft Farber Bros, 1960s, 12¾", from $45 to **$55.00**
Cocktail shaker, chrome-plate skyscraper style w/walnut trim, Steward, part of The Repealer set, ca 1934, from $65 to **$75.00**
Cocktail shaker, clear heavy glass, Caribbean, Duncan Miller, 1936-55, 10½", from $95 to...............................**$100.00**
Cocktail shaker, cobalt dumbell w/wire stand, ca 1937, 13", from $250 to..**$325.00**
Cocktail shaker, cobalt w/applied sterling polo player design, chrome top, ca 1930s, from $125 to **$175.00**
Cocktail shaker, cobalt w/silkscreened dancing sailor, Sportsman Series, Hazel Atlas, from $100 to......**$150.00**
Cocktail shaker, cobalt w/silkscreened recipes, American, 1930s, 10½", from $95 to **$125.00**
Cocktail shaker, cobalt w/silkscreened windmill, Sportsman Series, Hazel Atlas, from $25 to.............................**$35.00**

Cocktail shaker, dumbbell form w/stand, chrome or silver-plate, ca 1935, 40-oz, from $250 to.....................**$350.00**

Cocktail shaker, lady's leg, ruby glass with applied sterling design, chrome top and slipper, West Virginia Specialty Glass Co, ca 1937, from $300.00 to $400.00. (Photo courtesy Steve Visakay)

Cocktail shaker, geometric Art Deco body, Catalin angel handle, stamped recipe base, Forman Bros, '30s, 12", from $65 to..**$95.00**
Cocktail shaker, Manhattan, chrome plate over brass, 1½-qt, 13x3¼" dia, from $300 to....................................**$400.00**
Cocktail shaker, Moonface, chromium on copper w/red or black Bakelite-faced lid, CP Shinn Inc, ca 1936, from $55 to..**$65.00**
Cocktail shaker, pressed glass w/cranberry flashing, silver-plated top, ca 1930s, 11", from $125 to..............**$150.00**
Cocktail shaker, silverplate, marked G Mich Import, 1930s, 9", from $95 to..**$135.00**

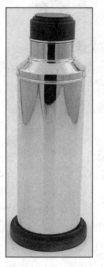

Cocktail shaker, skyscraper-styled chrome with walnut trim, stamped Manning Bowman, ca 1936, from $65.00 to $75.00. (Photo courtesy Steve Visakay)

Cocktail shaker, skyscraper type w/vertical lines, circle lid w/round Catalin knob, unknown maker, 12½", from $150 to..**$175.00**
Cocktail shaker, town crier's bell, chrome w/walnut handle & clapper, ca 1937, 28-oz, 10¼", from $55 to......**$65.00**
Cocktail shaker, 3 stacked chrome balls w/4 attached jingle-bells, wood handle, ca 1935, 14", $175 to.........**$250.00**
Cocktail tumbler, bottoms-up, McKee Glass Co, from $40 to...**$60.00**

Decanter pump, metal top w/O & + for eyes, spigot mouth & top hat, glass cylinder base w/gold trim, 1940s, from $65 to **$75.00**

Decanter set, bowling ball holder opens to reveal decanter & glasses, ca 1940s-50s, from $45 to........................**$65.00**

Highball glass, Artist Model line, decal on clear glass becomes transparent when wet, ca 1941, 4¾", from $10 to **$20.00**

Ice bucket, cobalt w/silkscreened ships, Sportsman Series, Hazel Atlas, 4¼x5½" dia, from $35 to **$45.00**

Ice tongs, nickle plate, ca 1928, 7½", from $35 to......**$45.00**

Sheet music, In Our Cocktail Love, Harry Von Tizer Music Publishing Co, NY, 1936, from $20 to...................**$25.00**

Soda syphon, chrome w/enamel top, stamped Soda King Syphon, Walter Kidder Sales Co, 10", from $125 to **$195.00**

Swizzle stick, bottoms up, plastic, 6", from $8 to **$12.00**

Tin, Huntley & Palmer's Cocktail Snacks w/martini glass, triangle shape w/rounded corners, England, from $8 to.........**$15.00**

Travel bar set, cocktail shaker holds 4 cups & accessories, nickle plate, stamped Germany, ca 1928, 9-pc, from $75 to **$95.00**

Travel bar set, leather case w/8 decanters, 8 cups & other pcs, marked US Zone Germany, ca 1948, from $250 to **$350.00**

Bauer Pottery

Undoubtedly the most easily recognized product of the Bauer Pottery Company who operated from 1909 until 1962 in Los Angeles, California, was their colorful 'Ring' dinnerware (made from 1932 until sometime in the early sixties). You'll recognize it by its bright solid colors: Jade Green, Chinese Yellow, Royal Blue, Light Blue, Orange-Red, Black, and White, and by its pattern of closely aligned ribs. They made other lines of dinnerware as well. They're collectible, too, although by no means as easily found. Bauer also made a line of Gardenware vases and flowerpots for the florist trade.

To further your knowledge of Bauer, we recommend *The Collector's Encyclopedia of California Pottery* and *Collector's Encyclopedia of Bauer Pottery* by Jack Chipman.

Brusche Al Fresco, cereal bowl, speckled greens & gray, 5½"...**$10.00**

Brusche Al Fresco, cookie jar, speckled colors **$50.00**

Brusche Al Fresco, cup & saucer, coffee brown or Dubonnet..**$18.00**

Brusche Contempo, coffee server, any color, 8-cup ...**$25.00**

Brusche Contempo, cup & saucer, any color..............**$10.00**

Brusche Contempo, platter, any color.........................**$15.00**

Contempo, vegetable bowl, any color, 9½" **$18.00**

El Chico, plate, any color, 9" **$35.00**

La Linda, gravy boat, any color **$20.00**

La Linda, mixing bowl, green, yellow or turquoise, #36, 1-pt..**$12.00**

La Linda, salt shaker, any matt color...........................**$6.00**

La Linda, tumbler, burgundy or dark brown, 8-oz......**$20.00**

Monterey, fruit bowl, white, 6"...................................**$22.00**

Monterey, sugar bowl, white, w/lid **$30.00**

Monterey Moderne, butter dish, all colors but black, round **$45.00**

Monterey Moderne, grill plate, any color but black, round .**$20.00**

Ring, ashtray, black, 3" dia..**$75.00**

Ring, batter bowl, black, 1-qt **$175.00**

Ring, butter dish, light blue, round..........................**$225.00**

Ring, coffee server, Delphinium w/copper handle **$95.00**

Ring, pickle dish, all colors but black........................**$45.00**

Ring, souffle dish, jade green or yellow **$200.00**

Ring, tumbler, black, cylinder w/no handle, 6-oz.......**$45.00**

Ring Gardenware, flowerpot, black, rolled rim, 6" **$50.00**

Ring Gardenware, vase, black, ruffled, 7" **$100.00**

Beanie Babies

Who can account for this latest flash in collecting that some liken to the rush for Cabbage Patch dolls we saw many years ago! The appeal of these stuffed creatures is disarming to both children and adults, and excited collectors are eager to scoop up each new-found treasure. There is much to be learned about Beanie Babies. For instance, there are different tag styles and these indicate date of issue:

#1, Swing Tag   #2, Swing Tag

#3, Swing Tag   #4, Swing Tag

#1, Swing tag: single heart-shaped tag.

#2, Swing tag: heart-shaped; folded, with information inside; narrow letters

#3, Swing tag: heart-shaped; folded, with information inside; wider lettering

#4, Swing tag: heart-shaped; folded, with information inside; wider lettering with no gold outline around the 'ty'; yellow star on front; first tag to include a poem and birthdate (Note: for current Beanies with a #2 or #3 tag, add $30.00 to $40.00 to the prices suggested below.)

Unless information is given to the contrary, the following listings are for current issues in mint condition; discontinued (retired) items will be noted.

Advisors: Jerry and Ellen Harnish (See Directory, Beanie Babies)

Ally, alligator, #4032, from $8 to **$10.00**

Baldy, eagle, #4074, from $10 to..........................**$15.00**

Bernie, St Bernard, #4109, from $8 to.........................**$10.00**

Bessie, brown cow, #4009, from $8 to **$10.00**

Blackie, black bear, #4011, from $8 to.........................**$10.00**

Blizzard, snow tiger, #4163, from $10 to **$15.00**

Bones, brown dog, #4001, from $8 to.........................**$10.00**

Bongo, brown monkey w/matching body & tail color, #4067, retired, from $45 to.......................................**$55.00**

Bongo, brown monkey w/matching paws & face, #4067, from $8 to...**$10.00**

Brownie, brown bear, #4010 ....**$250.00**

Bubbles, yellow & black fish, #4078, retired, from $30 to **$40.00**

Bucky Beaver, #4016, from $8 to **$10.00**

Bumble-Bee, #4045, retired, minimum value **$150.00**

Caw, black crow, #4071, retired, minimum value.....**$150.00**

Chilly, white polar bear, #4012, retired, minimum value ..**$750.00**

Chip, calico cat, #4121, from $10 to **$15.00**

Chocolate, moose, #4015, from $8 to **$10.00**

Chops, white lamb w/black face, retired.....................**$75.00**

Claude, tie-dyed crab, #4083, from $10 to..................**$15.00**

Congo, gorilla, #4160, from $8 to **$10.00**

Coral, tie-dyed fish, #4079, retired **$50.00**

Crunch, shark, #4130, from $8 to **$10.00**

Cubbie, brown bear, #4010, from $10 to....................**$15.00**

Curly, brown bear, #4052, from $10 to **$15.00**

Daisy, black & white cow, #4006, from $8 to.............**$10.00**

Derby, brown horse, #4008, 1st issue, fine yarn mane & tail...**$175.00**

Derby, brown horse, #4008, 2nd issue, from $8 to **$10.00**

Digger, orange crab, #4027, retired, minimum value..**$325.00**

Digger, red crab, #4027, retired.................................**$35.00**

Doby, doberman, #4100, from $8 to **$10.00**

Doodles, tie-dyed rooster, #4171 ....**$50.00**

Dotty, dalmatian, #4100, from $8 to.........................**$10.00**

Ears, brown rabbit, #4018, from $8 to **$10.00**

Echo, dolphin, #4180, from $8 to **$10.00**

Flash, dolphin, #4021, retired **$40.00**

Fleece, lamb w/white face, #4125, from $8 to **$10.00**

Flip, white cat, #4012, from $8 to **$10.00**

Floppity, lilac bunny, #4118.......................................**$20.00**

Flutter, tie-dyed butterfly, #4043, retired, minimum value ..**$400.00**

Freckles, leopard, #4066, from $8 to..........................**$10.00**

Goldie, goldfish, #4023, from $10 to.........................**$15.00**

Gracie, swan, #4126, from $8 to................................**$10.00**

Grunt, red razorback pig, #4092, retired....................**$40.00**

Happy, gray hippopotamus, #4061, 1st issue, retired, minimum value **$325.00**

Happy, lavender hippopotamus, #4061, 2nd issue, from $8 to..**$10.00**

Hippity, mint green rabbit, #4119, minimum value **$20.00**

Hoot, owl, #4073, from $8 to **$10.00**

Hoppity, pink rabbit, #4117.......................................**$25.00**

Humphrey, camel, #4060, retired, minimum value...**$650.00**

Inch, multicolor worm, #4044, from $8 to...................**$10.00**

Inch, worm w/magenta tail, #4044, 1st issue............**$100.00**

Inky, gray octopus, #4028, 1st issue, retired **$250.00**

Inky, pink octopus, #4028, 2nd issue, from $8 to **$10.00**

Jolly, walrus, #4082, from $10 to................................**$15.00**

Kiwi, toucan, #4070, retired, minimum value.............**$50.00**

Lefty, donkey w/American flag, #4057, retired, minimum value **$50.00**

Legs, frog, #4020, from $8 to.....................................**$10.00**

Lizzy, lizard, #4033, 1st issue, retired, minimum value....**$375.00**

Lizzy, lizard, #4033, 2nd issue, from $8 to **$10.00**

Lucky, ladybug w/glued-on felt spots, #4040, 1st issue, retired **$100.00**

Lucky, ladybug w/11 spots, #4040, 2nd issue, from $8 to **$10.00**

Lucky, ladybug w/21 spots, #4040, 3rd issue, from $8 to **$10.00**

Magic, winged dragon, #4088, from $10 to **$15.00**

Manny, manatee, #4081, retired................................**$35.00**

Mel, koala bear, #4162, from $10 to..........................**$15.00**

Mystic, unicorn, #4007, 2nd issue, from $8 to............**$10.00**

Mystic, unicorn w/soft fine mane & tail, #4007, 1st issue...**$100.00**

Nanook, husky dog, #4104, from $10 to **$15.00**

Nip, all gold cat, #4003, retired, minimum value......**$600.00**

Nip, all gold cat, #4003, 2nd issue, retired................**$700.00**

Nip, gold cat w/white paws, #4003, 3rd issue, from $8 to....**$10.00**

Nip, gold cat w/white tummy, #4003, 1st issue, retired, minimum value **$250.00**

Nuts, squirrel, #4114, from $8 to **$10.00**

Patti, hot pink & purple platypus, #4025, 2nd issue, from $10 to..**$15.00**

Patti, maroon platypus, #4025, 1st issue, retired....**$1,000.00**

Peanut, light blue elephant, #4062, 2nd issue, from $8 to ..**$10.00**

Peanut, royal blue elephant, #4062, 1st issue, retired, minimum value **$1,500.00**

Peking, panda bear, #4013, retired, minimum value.....**$700.00**

Pinchers, red lobster, #4026, from $8 to **$10.00**

Pinky, pink flamingo, #4072, from $8 to **$10.00**

Pouch, kangaroo, #4161, from $8 to..........................**$10.00**

Pugsly, pug dog, #4105, from $10 to **$15.00**

Quackers, duck w/wings, #4024, 2nd issue, from $8 to..**$10.00**

Quackers, wingless duck, #4024, retired, minimum value..**$1,000.00**

Radar, bat, #4091, minimum value **$70.00**

Righty, gray elephant w/American flag, #4086, retired, minimum value..**$60.00**

Ringo, raccoon, #4014, from $8 to **$10.00**

Roary, lion, #4069, from $10 to **$15.00**

Rover, red dog, #4101, from $8 to **$10.00**

Scoop, pelican, #4107, from $8 to..............................**$10.00**

Scottie, Scottish terrier, #4102, from $8 to **$10.00**

Seamore, white seal, #4029, from $8 to......................**$10.00**

Seaweed, brown otter, #4080, from $8 to....................**$10.00**

Slither, snake, #4031, retired, minimum value...........**$450.00**

Sly, brown fox w/brown belly, #4115, 1st issue.......**$100.00**

Sly, brown fox w/white belly, #4115, 2nd issue, from $8 to **$10.00**

Snip, Siamese cat, #4120, from $8 to **$10.00**

Snort, red bull w/beige feet, #4002, from $8 to..........**$10.00**

Sparky, dalmatian, #4100 ....**$35.00**

Speedy, turtle, #4030, from $8 to **$10.00**

Spike, rhinoceros, #4060, from $8 to **$10.00**

Splash, black & white whale, #4022, retired **$30.00**

Spooky, white ghost, #4090, minimum value.............**$25.00**

Spot, #4000, 1st issue without spot on back..........**$1,000.00**

Spot, #4000, 2nd issue w/black spot on back, from $8 to..**$10.00**

Squealer, pig, #4005, from $8 to...................................**$10.00**

Sting, tie-dyed stingray, #4077, retired, minimum value..**$55.00**

Stinky, skunk, #4017, from $8 to................................**$10.00**

Stripes, tiger, #4065, 1st issue w/darker color & more black stripes **$300.00**

Stripes, tiger, #4065, 2nd issue, from $8 to..................**$10.00**

Tabasco, red bull w/red feet, #4002, minimum value ..**$225.00**

Tank, armadillo, #4031, 1st issue (7 lines) **$100.00**

Tank, armadillo, #4031, 2nd issue (9 lines), minimum value **$150.00**

Tank, armadillo, #4031, 3rd issue, from $8 to............**$10.00**

Teddy, brown bear, #4050, old face, retired **$400.00**

Teddy, cranberry bear, #4052, new face, retired.......**$500.00**

Teddy, cranberry bear, #4052, old face, retired **$450.00**

Teddy, jade bear, #4057, new face, retired...............**$350.00**

Teddy, jade bear, #4057, old face, retired **$300.00**

Teddy, magenta bear, #4056, new face, retired **$600.00**

Teddy, magenta bear, #4056, old face, retired **$400.00**

Teddy, teal bear, #4051, new face, retired.................**$625.00**

Teddy, teal bear, #4051, old face, retired **$425.00**

Teddy, violet bear, #4055, new face, retired **$675.00**

Top: Teddy, violet bear, old face, #4055, retired, $425.00; Libearty, #4057, retired, minimum value, $65.00; Garcia, #3051, retired, from $50.00 to $75.00; Bottom: Peace, #4053, $50.00; Valentino, #4058, $25.00; Teddy, brown bear, new face, #4050, from $8.00 to $10.00; Maple, Canadian exclusive, $75.00. (Photo courtesy Jerry and Ellen Harnish)

Trap, mouse, #4042, retired, minimum value............**$400.00**

Tuffy, terrier, #4108, from $8 to...................................**$10.00**

Tusk, walrus, #4076, retired, minimum value..............**$65.00**

Twigs, giraffe, #4068, from $8 to.................................**$10.00**

Velvet, black panther, #4064, from $8 to **$10.00**

Waddle, penguin, #4075, from $8 to...........................**$10.00**

Waves, whale, #4084, from $10 to...............................**$15.00**

Web, black spider, #4041, retired, minimum value...**$350.00**

Weenie, brown dachshund, #4013, from $8 to...........**$10.00**

Wrinkles, bulldog, #4103, from $8 to.........................**$10.00**

Ziggy, zebra, #4063, from $8 to..................................**$10.00**

Zip, all black cat, #4004, retired, minimum value .**$1,400.00**

Zip, black cat w/white paws, #4004, from $8 to **$10.00**

Zip, black cat w/white tummy, #4004, retired, minimum value **$300.00**

The 3 dinosaurs: Bronty, blue, #4085, retired, $400.00; Steg, #4087, retired, minimum value, $250.00; Rex, #4086, retired, minimum value, $300.00. (Photo courtesy Jerry and Ellen Harnish)

McDonald's® Happy Meal

Chocolate, moose, from $8 to **$10.00**

Chops, lamb, from $8 to **$10.00**

Goldie, goldfish, from $8 to...**$10.00**

Lizz, lizzard, from $8 to..**$10.00**

Patti, platypus, from $8 to..**$10.00**

Pinky, flamingo, from $15 to **$20.00**

Quacks, duck, from $8 to **$10.00**

Seamore, seal, from $8 to **$10.00**

Snort, bull, from $8 to...**$10.00**

Speedy, turtle, from $8 to **$10.00**

Beatles Collectibles

Possibly triggered by John Lennon's death in 1980, Beatles' fans, recognizing that their dreams of the band ever reuniting were gone along with him, began to collect memorabilia of all types. Recently some of the original Beatles material has sold at auction with high-dollar results. Handwritten song lyrics, Lennon's autographed high school textbook, and even the legal agreement that was drafted at the time the group disbanded are among the one-of-a-kind multi-thousand dollar sales recorded.

Unless you plan on attending sales of this caliber, you'll be more apt to find the commercially produced memorabilia that literally flooded the market during the sixties when the Fab Four from Liverpool made their unprecedented impact on the entertainment world. A word about their 45 rpm records: they sold in such mass quantities that unless the record is a 'promotional,' made to send to radio stations or for jukebox distribution, they have very little value. Once a record has lost much of its originial gloss due to wear and handling, becomes scratched, or has writing on the label, its value is minimal. Even in near-mint condition, $4.00 to $6.00 is plenty to pay for a 45 rpm (much less if it's worn), unless the original picture sleeve is present. (An exception is the white-labeled Swan recording of 'She Loves You/I'll Get You'.) A Beatles picture sleeve is usually valued at $30.00 to $40.00, except for the rare 'Can't Buy Me Love,' which is worth ten times that amount. (Beware of reproductions!) Albums of any top recording star or group from the fifties and sixties are becoming very collectible, and the Beatles are among the most popular. Just be very critical of condition! An album must be in at least excellent condition to bring a decent price.

See also Celebrity Dolls; Magazines; Movie Posters; Records; Sheet Music.

Advisor: Bojo/Bob Gottuso (See Directory, Character and Personality Collectibles)

Newsletter: *Beatlefan*
P.O. Box 33515, Decatur, GA 30033; Send SASE for information

Apron, portraits w/instruments, green, black & white, unlicensed, 1964, VG **$180.00**
Beach hat, blue & white, NM **$125.00**

Binder, 3-ring; Yellow Submarine, multicolored paper cover, EX, $330.00. (Photo courtesy Bojo/Bob Gottuso)

Bookmark, multicolor cardboard w/Old Fred or Apple Bonker, from Yellow Submarine, 9" **$10.00**
Booty bag, clear vinyl w/cord handle, yellow paper inserts, blue drawstring, 10x15", NM..............................**$150.00**
Cake decoration, multicolor die-pressed plastic bust portraits w/signatures, 4½" L **$125.00**
Calendar, 12 different glossy black & white photos, Star Pics, UK, 1960s, 2½x5", M **$100.00**
Calendar card, Paladium doorway photo & 1964-65 on sides, 2¼x3½", NM **$20.00**
Candy, record form w/single photo on sleeve, licorice record, 4½", EX..**$50.00**

Candy dish, pottery w/EX George decal, gilt at scalloped edge, Washington Pottery, UK, 4½", EX.............**$160.00**
Charm, metal disk w/portraits & MCMLXIV on sides & top loop hanger, 1¼" dia.................................**$18.00**
Coin holder, black rubber squeeze purse w/white portraits & first names, 2x3", EX................................**$50.00**
Concert booklet, black & white photos w/multicolor photo cover, 1965, 12x12", EX...........................**$30.00**
Cup, ceramic w/blue, gray & black decal, Broadhurst Bros, UK, EX..**$125.00**
Doll, inflatable purple, white & orange vinyl w/instrument, 13", set of 4, M (original brown bag mailer)......**$150.00**
Eyeglasses case, w/John Lennon facsimile signature..**$75.00**
Figurine, hand-painted metal w/instrument, from Sgt Pepper, UK issue, 2½", set of 4+black & white cardboard backdrop **$100.00**
Figurine, hand-painted resin, Ringo, Abbey Road, marked Gardlan USA, 4" **$50.00**
Game, Flip Your Wig, complete, VG+ (VG+ box)....**$200.00**
Headband, I Love the Beatles w/music notes on red cloth, unmarked, 1960s...**$90.00**
Mug, paper portrait insert between clear & white plastic, 4" **$20.00**
Napkin, black & white photo w/blue lettering, Australian, 1963, EX...**$30.00**

Nylons, head portraits and signatures on yellow, blue, and white ground, Ballito, UK, MIP, $130.00. (Photo courtesy Bojo/Bob Guttuso)

Oil paintings, set of 4 9x12" prints, Beatles Fan Club Membership card on header, MIP (sealed)..........**$80.00**
Ornament, Hallmark, set of 5, M (M gift box)..........**$110.00**
Paperweight, Official Beatles Fan logo w/photos & names under thick acrylic, 1970s, 3½x4½"......................**$85.00**
Pen, drum & autographs on barrel, w/metal cluster of 4 heads attached to lapel holder, VG+....................**$80.00**
Pennant, I Love the Beatles w/hearts in white on red felt, 29", VG...**$120.00**
Poster, Dell #2, banner style w/4 lg black & white portraits on red, 19x54", EX...**$32.00**
Press book, Yellow Submarine, w/ad slicks, publicity material & list of merchandisers, United Artists, 13x17½"..........**$85.00**
Promotional display, Baby It's You, for 45 rpm records, unused, M (original shipping box)......................**$45.00**
Ring, brass w/black & white photo, adjustable band, VG+ **$65.00**

Scarf, white w/colorful records, faces & instruments, square, VG **$40.00**

School report cover, green or yellow w/portraits, instruments & border, thin cardboard, EX, each **$100.00**

Stationery, Turtle Turk, from Yellow Submarine, set of 20 sheets w/20 envelopes, MIP (sealed)....................**$45.00**

Switch plate cover, cardboard, Yellow Submarine, group shot, 6x11¾", MIP (sealed) **$75.00**

Tray, multicolor portraits with musical notes and stars at rim, Great Britain, 13x13", VG, $50.00. (Photo courtesy Bojo/Bob Gottuso)

Tumbler, plastic w/multicolor paper insert of group & lips at top under rim, original issue, VG **$70.00**

Wall plaque, white ceramic of Paul, test pressing for Kelsboro, UK, 4", M...**$75.00**

Wallet, beige vinyl, complete w/all but comb, Standard Products, VG+ **$90.00**

Wallpaper, multicolor graphics w/signatures, 1 complete pattern, 21" **$35.00**

Beatnik Collectibles

The 'Beats,' later called 'Beatniks,' consisted of artists, writers, and others disillusioned with Establishment mores and values. The Beatniks were noncomformists, Bohemian free-thinkers who expressed their distain for society from 1950 to 1962. From a collector's point of view, the most highly regarded Beat authors are Allen Ginsberg, Lawrence Ferlinghetti, and Jack Kerouac. Books, records, posters, pamphlets, leaflets, and other items associated with them are very desirable. Although in their day they were characterized by the media as a 'Maynard G. Krebs' (of Dobie Gillis TV fame), today the contributions they made to American literature and the continuation of Bohemianism are recognized for their importance and significance in American culture.

In the listings that follow values are for examples in excellent to near-mint condition.

Advisor: Richard Synchef (See Directory, Beatnik and Hippie Collectibles)

Beatnik kit, w/beret, cigarette holder & beard, 1950s, in 12x11" package **$35.00**

Book, Chicago Trial Testimony, by Allen Ginsberg, San Francisco: City Lights, 1975, 74 pages, scarce **$150.00**

Booklet, Beat Talk, Tulsa OK: Studio Press, 1960, 30 pages, Beatnik glossary.......................................**$35.00**

Cigarette holder, black plastic, 12", mounted on cardboard display card, 1950s **$25.00**

Folder, The Beat Generation, MGM promotional item, 1959, w/Mamie Van Doren, Ray Danton & Steve Cochoran, 4 pages, rare..**$250.00**

Magazine, *City Lights,* #3, Spring 1953, San Francisco: City Lights, very early Ferlinghetti publication, $125.00. (Photo courtesy Richard Synchef)

Magazine, Evergreen Review, #2, The San Francisco Scene, NY: Grove Press, 1959, gave important national exposure..**$90.00**

Magazine, Fruitcup, San Francisco: Beach Books Texts & Documents, 1969, Burroughs, Ginsberg & other writers, only issue **$85.00**

Magazine, Playboy, The Beat Issue, July 1959, Kerouac, Ginsberg, Coroso & other writers.........................**$75.00**

Magazine, Reflections From Chapel Hill, Vol 1 #3, November 1961, Chapel Hill NC, early Ferlinghetti **$100.00**

Magazine, The Second Coming, Vol 1 #2, July 1961, NY, 65 pages, early Ginsberg, scarce **$125.00**

Paperback, Beat Beat Beat, by William Brown, NY: Signet, 1959, cartoons of Beatnik life **$35.00**

Paperback, *Dharma Bums,* by Jack Kerouac, NY: Avon, 1960, 1st printing, $75.00. (Photo courtesy Richard Synchef)

Paperback, Planet News 1961-1967, by Allen Ginsberg, San Francisco: City Lights, 1968, Pocket Poet Series #23 ..**$75.00**

Paperback, Starting From San Francisco, by Lawrence Ferlinghetti, Norfork CT: New Directions, 1961, w/33⅓ rpm record **$100.00**

Paperback, The Beat Generation & The Angry Young Men; by Gene Feldman, NY: Dell, 1959, important early Beat anthology...**$50.00**

Paperback, The Beats, edited by Krim Seymour, Greenwich CT: Dell, 1959, significant Beat anthology............**$50.00**

Paperback, The Subterraneans, by Jack Kerouac, NY: Grove Press, 1958, 1st printing **$85.00**

Poster, The Beard, by Michael McClure, for San Francisco showing of controversial play (later banned), 1965, important **$500.00**

Record, Ginsberg, Allen; Kaddish, NY: Atlantic Verbum Series (4001), 1965, monaural, Ginsberg reading entire poem...**$125.00**

Record, Greenwich Village Cafe Bizarre, NY: Musitron Autiotron Fidelity, no date, Beats reading poetry in coffeehouse **$80.00**

Record, Kerouac, Jack; Blues & Haikus, NY: Hanover 5008, 1959, 33⅓ rpm, w/Zoot Sims, classic.................**$500.00**

Record, San Francisco Poets, NY: Hanover M5001, 1959, monaural, 33⅓ rpm, Rexroth, Whalen, Ginsberg, Ferlinghetti, etc **$150.00**

Record, The Beatniks, ASCAP 19075, 45 rpm, movie tie-in, scarce...**$100.00**

Beatrix Potter

Since 1902 when *The Tale of Peter Rabbit* was published by Fredrick Warne & Company, generations have enjoyed the adventures of Beatrix Potter's characters. Beswick issued ten characters in 1947 that included Peter Rabbit, Benjamin Bunny, Squirrel Nutkin, Jemima Puddleduck, Timmy Tiptoes, Tom Kitten, Mrs Tittlemouse, Mrs. Tiggywinkle, Little Pig Robinson, and Samuel Whiskers. The line grew until it included figures from other stories. Duchess (P1355) was issued in 1955 with two feet that were easly broken. Later issues featured the Duchess on a base and holding a pie. This was the first figure to be discontinued in 1967. Color variations on pieces indicate issue dates as do the different backstamps that were used. Backstamps have changed several times since the first figures were issued. There are three basic styles: Beswick brown, Beswick gold, and Royal Albert — with many variations on each of these. Unless stated otherwise, figures listed here are Beswick brown.

Advisor: Nicki Budin (See Directory, Beatrix Potter)

Amiable Guinea Pig, P2061, 1963-83, brown backstamp, 3½"...**$375.00**

Apply Dapply, P2333, 1980 to present, brown backstamp, 3¼", $75.00.

Aunt Petitoes, P2276, 1969-93, brown backstamp, 3¾".......**$85.00**

Babbitty Bumble, P2971, 1989-93, brown backstamp, 2¾"..**$85.00**

Benjamin Bunny, P1105, 1947-present, brown backstamp, 4"...**$70.00**

Benjamin Bunny & Peter Rabbit, P2509, 1974-95, brown backstamp, 4"...**$250.00**

Benjamin Bunny Sat on a Bank, P2803, 1982-present, head turned, brown backstamp, 3¾" **$125.00**

Cecily Parsley, P1941, 1964-93, brown backstamp, 4"......**$125.00**

Chippy Hackee, P2627, 1978-93, brown back stamp, 3¾"..**$45.00**

Cottontail, P2878, 1985-present, brown backstamp, 3¾".....**$95.00**

Cousin Ribby, P2284, 1969-93, brown backstamp, 3½".......**$60.00**

Diggory Delvet, P2713, 1981-present, brown backstamp, 2¾"...**$65.00**

Duchess Pie, P2601, 1977-82, brown backstamp, 4"..**$350.00**

Fierce Bad Rabbit, P2586, 1977-present, 2nd version, brown backstamp, 4¾"...**$75.00**

Flopsey, Mopsey & Cottontail, P1274, 1952-present, gold backstamp, 2½"...**$275.00**

Foxy Whiskered Gentleman, P1277, 1952-present, brown backstamp, 4¾"...**$75.00**

Gentleman Mouse Made a Bow, P3200, 1990-96, Royal Albert backstamp, 3"...**$75.00**

Ginger, P2559, 1976-82, brown backstamp, 3¾".......**$650.00**

Hunca Munca, P1198, 1950-present, brown backstamp, 2¾"...**$65.00**

Hunca Munca Sweeping, P2584, 1977-present, brown backstamp, 3½"...**$75.00**

Hunca Spills the Beans, P3288, 1992-present, brown backstamp, 3¾"...**$95.00**

Jemima Puddleduck, P1092, 1947-present, brown backstamp, 4¾"...**$85.00**

Jemima Puddleduck, P1092, 1947-present, gold backstamp, 4¾"..**$175.00**

Jemima Puddleduck Made a Feathered Nest, P2823, 1983-97, brown backstamp, 2¼".......................................**$65.00**

Jeremy Fisher, P1157, 1949-present, brown backstamp, 3"..**$70.00**

Jeremy Fisher Digging, P3090, 1988-94, brown backstamp, 3¾"...**$250.00**

Johnny Townmouse, P1276, 1952-93, Beswick & Royal Albert marks, gold backstamp **$175.00**

Lady Mouse, P1183, 1950-present, brown backstamp, 4"..**$75.00**

Little Pig Robinson, P1104, 1947-present, brown backstamp, 3½"...**$45.00**

Miss Dormouse, P3251, 1991-95, brown backstamp, 4" **$95.00**

Miss Tittlemouse, P1103, 1947-93, brown backstamp, 3½".**$65.00**

Mr Drake Puddleduck, P2678, 1978-present, brown backstamp, 4"...**$65.00**

Mr Tod, P3091, 1988-93, brown backstamp, 4¾" **$250.00**

Mrs Tiggy Winkle, P1107, 1947-present, brown backstamp, 3¼"...**$45.00**

Mrs Tiggy Winkle Takes Tea, P2877, 1985-present, brown backstamp, 3¼"...**$110.00**

Peter Rabbit, P1098, 1947-present, brown backstamp, 4½" **$60.00**

Pickles, P2334, 1970-82, brown backstamp, 4½" **$450.00**

Poorly Peter Rabbit, P2560, 1976-present, brown backstamp, 3¾"...**$60.00**

Sally Henny-Penny, P2452, 1973-93, brown backstamp, 4"...**$75.00**

Samuel Whiskers, P1106, 1947-present, brown backstamp, 3¾"..**$45.00**

Squirrel Nutkin, P1102, 1947-present, brown backstamp, 3¾"..**$45.00**

Timmy Tiptoes, P1101, 1947-present, 2nd version, brown backstamp, 3¾"...................................**$95.00**

Tom Kitten, P1100, 1947-present, brown backstamp, 3½"...**$95.00**

Tom Thumb, P2898, 1987-1997, brown backstamp, 3¼"..**$125.00**

Tommy Brock, P1348, 1954-present, brown backstamp, 3½"...**$65.00**

Beer Cans

In the mid-1930s, beer came in flat-top cans that often carried instructions on how to use the triangular punch-type opener. The 'cone-top' can was patented about 1935, and in the 1960s both types were replaced by the aluminum beer can with the pull-tab opener. There are hundreds of brands and variations available to the collector today. Most are worth very little, but we've tried to list a few of the better ones to help you get a feel for the market.

Condition is very, very important! Collectors grade them as follows: 1) rust-free, in 'new' condition; 2) still no rust, but a few scratches or tiny dents are acceptable; 3) a little faded, minor scratching, maybe a little rusting; 4) all of the above only more pronounced. The numbers you'll see at the end of our description lines refer to these grading numbers. The letters 'IRTP' in some lines stand for 'Internal Revenue Tax Paid.'

Advisor: Steve Gordon (See Directory, Beer Cans and Breweriana)

Newsletter: Beer Cans and Brewery Collectibles
Beer Can Collectors of America
747 Merus Ct., Fenton, MO 63026-2092
Phone or Fax 314-343-6486; Subscription: $30 per year for US residents; includes 6 issues and right to attend national CANvention®

Club: National Association Breweriana Advertising
2343 Met-To-Wee Lane, Wauwatosa, WI, 53226
414-257-0158; Membership: $20 (U.S.), $30 (Canada), $40 (Overseas); Publishes The Breweriana Collector and membership directory; Holds annual convention

ABC Dry Beer, Maier Brewing, red, white & blue, flat top, 12-oz, 1...**$40.00**

Acme, Acme Brewing, red & blue letters on white banners across light blue oval, dark blue ground, flat top, 12-oz, 1..**$30.00**

Ambassador Beer, G Kreuger Brewing, flat top, 12-oz, 1..**$30.00**

American Dry Beer, Eastern Brewing, red, white & blue banner on gold, pull tab, 12-oz, 1............................**$8.00**

Atlantic Ale, Altantic Brewing, black lettered band on red circle, red ground w/gold trim, cone top, 12-oz, 1..**$110.00**

Augustiner Beer, Wagner Brewing, red letters w/gold on white, cone top, 12-oz, 1 ....**$70.00**

Barbarossa Beer, Red Top Brewing, red, tan & cream, gold bands at top & bottom, cone top, 12-oz, 1..........**$70.00**

Beer Can Collectors of America, 1973 Commemorative, cone top, 12-oz, 1 ....**$25.00**

Belair Beer, Horlacher Brewing, gold script letters & banner on oval w/logo, gold-striped ground, flat top, 12-oz, 1..**$60.00**

Berghoff 1887 Beer, white script letters on black, gold & yellow shield, band trim, cone top, 12-oz, 1.............**$30.00**

Big Apple Premium Beer, Waukee Brewing, red, white & blue w/silver trim, flat top, 12-oz, 1.....................**$90.00**

Big E Brand Beer, Colonial Brewing, red & white, flat bank top, 12-oz, 1...**$85.00**

Billy Beer, by Cold Spring, Fall City or West End Brewing, pull tab, any, from 50¢ to **$1.00**

Black Label Beer, Carling Brewing, Boston Bruins 1971-72 Champions, bank top, 12-oz, 1............................**$20.00**

Blackhawk Beer, white letters w/Indian's head on black circle, red ground w/top & bottom gold bands, cone top, 12-oz, 1 ....**$38.00**

Blackhawk Premium Beer, letters across silhouetted Indian's head, flat top, 12-oz, 1 ....**$125.00**

Bock Brand Beer, Metropolis Brewery, bold letters & red eagle on black oval, red & gold ground, flat top, 12-oz, 1...**$175.00**

Breidt's Pilsner Beer, white letters on red oval, white lettered band at bottom, cream ground, cone top, 12-oz, 1..**$90.00**

Breverwyck Ale, red, silver & gray, cone top, 12-oz, 1 ...**$75.00**

Brown Derby, Humboldt Malt & Brewing, flat top, IRTP, w/instructions on how to open, 12-oz, 1 ....**$50.00**

Brown Derby Pilsner Beer, Los Angeles Brewing, letters & derby hat in oval on silver, flat top, 12-oz, 1.......**$50.00**

Burger Bohemian Beer, white & gold letters on red oval w/gold trim, cone top, 12-oz, 1............................**$65.00**

Camden Lager Beer, gold-lettered red banner w/circle logo on white, gold & red bands at top & bottom, flat top, 12-oz, 1 ....**$85.00**

Canadian Ace Bock Beer, gold & red on white, flat top, 12-oz, 1 ....**$50.00**

Cardinal Premium Beer, Standard Brewing, red script letters & diagonal gold stripes on cream, cone top, 12-oz, 1 ...**$90.00**

Colonial Premium Beer, lettered white oval w/logo on red, flat bank top, 12-oz, 1 ....**$55.00**

Dart Premium Beer, Eastern Brewing, white & gold letters on red, pull tab, 12-oz, 1......................................**$15.00**

Davidson Premium Beer, Colonial Brewing, red & white, flat top, 12-oz, 1...**$60.00**

Dawson Diamond Ale, lettered oval on silver ground, dated 1956, zip tab, 12-oz, 1 ....**$25.00**

Dis-Go Non Alcholic Beer, Eastern Brewing, guitar player on pink, white letters, pull tab, 12-oz, 1 ....**$10.00**

Dukesa, Eastern Brewing, red, blue & gold letters on cream, pull tab, 12-oz, 1..**$15.00**

Duquesne Can-O Beer, cream script letters on brown w/gold band trim at top & bottom, cone top, 12-oz, 1....**$35.00**

Eastside Beer, red, gold & black logo & letters in oval on blue, cone top, Los Angeles Brewing, 12-oz, 1....**$40.00**

Edelweiss Light Beer, script letters on white rectangle w/logo, white letters on red ground, cone top, 12-oz, 1.......**$30.00**

Ehrets Extra Near Beer, Metropolis Brewery, blue-lettered white banners on red, flat top, 12-oz, 1 ....**$50.00**

El Sol, Colonial Brewing, red, white & yellow, 12-oz, 1 ...**$20.00**

Embassy Club Beer, Metropolis Brewery, white & blue letters on red shield w/logo, white ground, flat top, 12-oz, 1 ....**$20.00**

Erin Brew Standard Beer, white letters on blue-banded red circle, gold & white ground, flat top, 12-oz, 1 .....**$40.00**

Esslinger's Ale, red, orange & blue, cone top, flat bottom, 12-oz, 1 ....**$100.00**

Falstaff Beer, red letters on gold-trimmed white shield, cone top, 12-oz, 1 ....**$25.00**

Feigenspan XXX Amber Ale, red- & black-lettered oval on gold, flat top, IRTP, 12-oz, 1 ....**$70.00**

Fort Pitt Beer, black letters w/logo on white, red letters on gold background, cone top, 12-oz, 1 ....**$45.00**

Fox Deluxe Beer, Peter Fox Brewing, white letters w/fox hunter on gold, flat top, w/instructions, IRTP, 12-oz **$55.00**

Fox Head Bock Beer, Kingsbury Brewing, white letters on brown band, gold fox head on white, flat top, 12-oz, 1 ....**$45.00**

Gambrinus Pale Beer, Wagner Brewing, red, white & gold, cone top, 12-oz, 1 ....**$80.00**

Garden State Beer, red & silver, flat top, 12-oz, 1 .....**$10.00**

Genesee 12 Horse Ale, flat top, IRTP, w/instructions on how to open, 12-oz, 1 ....**$35.00**

Goebel, red & black letters on copper, flat top, IRTP, w/instructions on how to open, 12-oz, 1 ....**$25.00**

Gold Star, Hoff-Brau Brewing, blue letters on silver star in red circle on gold, cone top, 12-oz, 1 ....**$42.00**

Gold Star Beer, Hoff-Brau Brewing, blue letters on silver star in red oval, cone top, 12-oz, 1 ....**$75.00**

Gretz Beer, silver & dark gold letters on gold, man's silhouette at top, cone top, 12-oz, 1 ....**$180.00**

Haffenreffer Lager Beer, white letters on blue circle w/gold band trim, white ground, pull tab, 12-oz, 1 ....**$25.00**

Hamm's, malting scene, flat top, IRTP, w/instructions, 12-oz, 2 ....**$28.00**

Hensler Light Beer, white letters on red oval, white ground w/gold & black letters, gold trim, flat top, 12-oz, 1 ..**$50.00**

Holland Premium Beer, Eastern Brewing, blue & red letters w/logo on white, flat top, 12-oz, 1 ....**$20.00**

Horton Beer, Metropolis Brewery, black, white & silver on red, flat top, 12-oz, 1 ....**$30.00**

Hudepohl Pure Lager Beer, blue and white on red, cone top, 12-oz, Grade 1, from $40.00 to $50.00.

JR Beer, Pearl Brewing Co, pull tab ....**$.50**

Keglet Beer, Esslinger Inc, red letters on gold-trimmed keg, white ground, flat top, 12-oz, 1 ....**$40.00**

Kentucky Malt Liquor, Oertel Brewing, red letters on white, flat top, PA taxed lid, 12-oz, 1 ....**$45.00**

Koehler's Beer, white lettered banner w/eagle on white, cone top, 12-oz, 1 ....**$100.00**

M*A*S*H 4077 Beer, pull tab ....**$.50**

National Bohemian Pale Beer, National Brewing, white lettered banner on black & red, cone top, 12-oz **$30.00**

Old Bohemian Bock Beer, Eastern Brewing, white letters on black banner w/red letters on white band, flat top, 12-oz, 1 ....**$100.00**

Old Crown Ale, Centlivre Brewing, flat top, IRTP, w/instructions on how to open, Ohio tax stamp, 12-oz, 1.**$50.00**

Old Dutch Beer, Aztec Brewing, Dutchman's portrait on gold, white letters on brown, cone top, 12-oz, 1.**$75.00**

Ortliebs Beer, lettered banner on rectangle, gold background, cone top, 12-oz, 1 ....**$40.00**

Ox-Bow Beer, Walter Brewing, white letters w/red & blue logo on gold, pull tab, 12-oz, 1 ....**$22.00**

Peerless Premium Beer, Lacrosse Brewing, red script letters on white shield, red & gold band trim, cone top, 12-oz, 1 ....**$60.00**

Peter Doelger Ale, blue & gold on silver, flat top, w/instructions on how to open, 12-oz, 1 ....**$225.00**

Pilsners Maltcrest Brew, white lettered blue band w/blue & red letters on white ground, flat top, 12-oz, 1 .....**$30.00**

Rex, Fitger Brewing, letters on red insignia w/crown, red letters on cream ground, cone top, 12-oz, 1 ....**$55.00**

Richbrau Beer, Home Brewing, white letters on red horizontal band, cone top, 12-oz, 1 ....**$65.00**

Spearman Ale, red and white on green ground, 12-oz, Grade 1, $25.00.

Stallion XII, Gold Medal Brewing, red letters & horse on white & gold, pull tab, 12-oz, 1 ....**$25.00**

Tamo'Shanter Ale, American Brewing, flat top, open top, IRTP, w/instructions, 12-oz, 1 ....**$95.00**

Trommers, gold letters on red band over logo, gold ground w/red band at bottom, flat top, 12-oz, 1 ....**$25.00**

Tudor Beer, Metropolis Brewery, white letters on blue shield, red ground w/white trim, flat top, 12-oz, 1...........**$9.00**

Tudor Cream Ale, Metropolis Brewery, white & green, flat top, 12-oz, 1 ....**$8.00**

Utica Club Pilsner Beer, West End Brewing, red, gold & blue letters on white, cone top, 12-oz, 1 ....**$35.00**

Wiedemann Beer, red & blue letters on white w/gold band trim, cone top, 12-oz, 1 ....**$40.00**

Wilco Beer, Colonial Brewing, gold & blue letters on golf scene, pull tab, 12-oz, 1 ....$10.00

Wooden Shoe Lager Beer, white letters on blue diagonal banner, red letters on cream, cone top, 12-oz, 1 ....$45.00

Bells

Bell collectors claim that bells rank second only to the wheel as being useful to mankind. Down through the ages bells have awakened people in the morning, called them to meals and prayers, and readied them to retire at night. We have heard them called rising bells, Angelus bells (for deaths), noon bells, Town Crier bells (for important announcements), and curfew bells. Souvenir bells are often the first type collected, with interest spreading to other contemporaries, then on to old, more valuable bells. As far as limited edition bells are concerned, the fewer made per bell, the better. (For example a bell made in an edition of 25,000 will not appreciate as much as one from an edition of 5,000.)

For further information we recommend *World of Bells #5, Bell Tidings, Lure of Bells, Collectible Bells, More Bell Lore, Bells Now and Long Ago*, and *Legendary Bells* by Dorothy Malone Anthony.

Advisor: Dorothy Malone Anthony (See Directory, Bells)

Newsletter: *The Bell Tower*
The American Bell Association
Charles Blake
P.O. Box 172, Shoreham, VT 05770

Benjamin Beal, brass, 3¾" $45.00
Biblical theme, Assyrians slaying Hittites, 3" $24.00
Female Goddess, Lakshmi w/4 arms, not old, 6¼" $18.00
Fenton, milk glass w/holly, 5½"..................................$15.00
Martha Gunn, brass, 2¾"...$37.50
NE Collectors, Donald Duck, silver, 2¾" $10.00
NE Collectors, Lady (dog), silver, 2¾" $10.00
NE Collectors, Mickey Mouse, silver, 2¾".....................$10.00
Pilgrim Glass, hand blown, 7¾" $24.00
Sarna 2nd Christmas, brass, 9"......................................$70.00

**Titanic, brass, replica, 6",
$30.00. (Photo courtesy
Dorothy Malone Anthony)**

Vishnu, Buddhist, not old, 6¼" $18.00
West Virginia centennial, clear glass, 4".......................$38.00
Winnie the Pooh, china...$8.00

Bicycle Collectibles

Over the last ten year, we've seen an explosion of interest in collecting old bicycles. Many are continually being discarded and end up at specialized auctions, swap meets, and vintage cycle collecting clubs where they always attract bicycle enthusiasts.

Historically, the bicycle is directly responsible for many of the innovations in automobiles, airplanes, and motorcycles. To mention a few of these traceable developments, consider the pneumatic tire, the automotive differential, and advanced gearing. The bicycle can even be linked to social changes such as the emancipation of women.

Since many of the collectibles cross over from category to category, items that fall into one field can be even more desirable in another. An example of this is photographic images. These images can be worth much more to the cycling collector who owns the type of bike or bikes depicted in the image than a collector who just collects old photographs.

The hobby itself generally splits into three areas: those collecting pre-1910, those devoted to the development of the classic, and a smaller group who covet lightweight racing machines. Of course, there are always those who collect 'all' and those who are specialists in a particular area.

Nowadays you might see collections of paper ephemera, accessories, watches, photographica, the actual bikes and trikes, rare and unusual parts, cycling radios, prints, and so much more.

Bikes from the 1950s can dramatically exceed the prices of those from the 1880s or 1890s. Much of this has to do with nostalgia, the affluence of the baby boomers, design, and mechanical achievement.

Advisor: Lorne Shields (See Directory, Bicycles and Tricycles)

Bicycles

**Dixie Flyer-Pained, 26" Men's Balloon, complete
with rear carrier, fenders, chain guard, saddle, pedals, and lamp, circa 1939, all original, VG, $2,200.00.
(Photo courtesy Lorne Shields)**

Columbia, Highwheel or Pennyfarthing, Expert, 52" front wheel w/nameplate, brake mechanism missing, 1880s, VG $1,700.00

Columbia, 5 Star, Men's 26" Balloon Tire, w/tank, rear carrier, pedestal mount fender, light & leather saddle, 1953, VG..**$750.00**

Elgin Bluebird, Men's 26" Balloon, original overall w/fender mascot, ca 1936, EX **$4,000.00**

Hawthorne, Men's 26" Balloon Tire, w/tank & rear rack, front fender light & front fork struts, original, 1952, VG .**$250.00**

Huffy, 10 Speed Racer, 27" wheels w/derailleurs, 1970s, rideable, VG..**$20.00**

Raleigh Racer Superbe, 26x1⅜", 3 speed, w/fenders & chainguard, 1960s, VG **$80.00**

Rudge Highwheeler, 52" front wheel, brake mechanism, complete with nameplate, EX, $2,600.00. (Photo courtesy Lorne Shields)

Schwinn Black Phantom, Men's 26" Balloon Tire, w/original rear carrier, tank & front shock fork, 1952, EX ..**$1,700.00**

Schwinn Sting Ray, Boys' 20" rear, 16" front, 5-speed, 1970s, VG...**$450.00**

Westfield, Ladies 26" Balloon, 50th Anniversary model w/stand & headlight, ca 1937, EX **$225.00**

Wolf-American, Men's Safety, regular style, 26" wheels, intact wood rims, original paint, pedals & saddle, 1890s, VG **$325.00**

Tricycles

Converto, Anthony Bros, Inglewood CA, aluminum, 1970s (looks 1950s), EX...**$125.00**

Mercury, 20" front wheel, steel saddle, 1950s, VG......**$45.00**

Montgomery Ward, 12" front wheel, white paint w/red seat, 1970s, VG **$8.00**

Miscellaneous

Bell, American flag, embossed, 1920s, VG **$25.00**

Bell, Mickey Mouse decal, 1970s, EX..........................**$10.00**

Carrier, AMF-Roadmaster, rear, stamped w/rod supports, all chrome, 1963, EX...**$25.00**

Carrier, Hawthorne, rear, stamped & painted, original equipment, 1939, G..**$40.00**

Catalog/flyer, Schwinn, fold-out w/actors & actresses, 1950s, EX...**$50.00**

Cup, cyclist, collapsible, embossed w/couple on tandem, 1897, VG...**$35.00**

Cyclometer, American Waltham Watch, enamel dial, 1920s, 3" dia, MIP **$150.00**

Cyclometer, Lucas, England, 1930s-60s, 26", VG **$10.00**

Grips, Ohio Plastic, Grip-O-Lite, battery-operated, 1950s, 5", MIP...**$50.00**

Grips, w/streamers, pre-1970, MIP **$5.00**

Head badge, Pierce, Angola NY, 1930s, EX................**$25.00**

Head badge, Schwinn, raised enamel, black & white, 1960s, EX...**$8.00**

Headlamp, Delta USA, torpedo style, front fender mount, painted, battery-operated, 1950s, EX....................**$60.00**

Headlamp, jet style, handlebar mount, chrome plated, 1950s, MIP...**$20.00**

Headlamp, Monark, aerodynamic style, pedestal front fender mount, 1950s, VG **$200.00**

Horn, Seiss, handlebar mount w/top plunger, Klaxton type, white paint, 1930s, VG **$50.00**

Horn, Tanita, Japan, electric D cell, w/handlebar mount button, chrome & paint, 1970s, EX....................**$10.00**

Horn, 9" bulb, chrome plated, handlebar mount, 3-trumpet, 1950s, EX...**$12.00**

License plate, Akron Ohio, aluminim, scalloped rounded shape, 1937, VG...**$25.00**

License plate, Buffalo NY, rectangular, 1952, VG........**$12.00**

Light set, Miller, England, Dynamo w/headlight & taillight, chrome plated, 1960s, EX...................................**$25.00**

Lock, Compass, rear frame mount, hoop style, w/combination & 2 reflectors, painted, 1940s, EX.................**$40.00**

Lock, Slaymaker, 9" shackel w/key, 1970s, EX.............**$3.00**

Mirror, 4" round w/rear reflector, chrome plated, 1960s, VG **$3.00**

Mudflaps, Raceway, lg & sm pr, skull & crossbones, MIP **$10.00**

Owner's manual, Huffy, 1950s, MIP..........................**$15.00**

Photo, Bowden Spacelander, 1960, M........................**$20.00**

Photo, family w/boy & his new balloon bike at Christmas, 1950s, EX...**$10.00**

Postcard, comic, multicolor, 1950s, VG......................**$3.00**

Pump, hand operated, telescopic, painted, w/connector, 1950s, VG...**$5.00**

Radio, w/light & horn built into handlebar mount, battery-operated, working, 1960s, VG **$35.00**

Repair kit, Firestone tin w/bicycle graphics, complete, 1940s, EX...**$20.00**

Repair kit, Goodyear, round cardboard w/serrated top, incomplete contents, 1960s, VG **$7.00**

Saddle, Banana, w/standard chromed support bar, glitter & ribbed saddle, 1970s, VG **$30.00**

Saddle, Columbia, pan type, 2 long rear springs at back, circular hairpin spring in front, brown vinyl top, 1952, VG ...**$35.00**

Saddle, Troxel, 2-tone vinyl, adult size, 1960s, EX **$10.00**

Siren, Persons Majestic, chain pull, fork mount, round, internal revolving, chrome, 1950s, EX......................**$60.00**

Speedometer, Stewart Warner, black plastic, mounts to handlebar, 1960s, 26", VG **$15.00**

Tool bag, leather seat mount, plain, w/2 wrenches, tire repair kit & tire levers, 1940s, 5x6", VG+ **$20.00**

Tool bag, vinyl seat mount w/1 reflector, 1970s, 11x8", EX...**$5.00**

Black Americana

There are many avenues one might pursue in the broad field of Black Americana and many reasons that might entice one to become a collector. For the more serious, there are documents such as bills of sale for slaves, broadsides, and other historical artifacts. But by and far, most collectors enjoy attractive advertising pieces, novelties and kitchenware items, toys and dolls, and Black celebrity memorabilia.

It's estimated that there are at least 50,000 collectors around the country today. There are large auctions devoted entirely to the sale of Black Americana. The items they feature may be as common as a homemade pot holder or a magazine or as rare as a Lux Dixie Boy clock or a Mammy cookie jar that might go for several thousand dollars. In fact, many of the cookie jars have become so valuable that they're being reproduced; so are salt and pepper shakers, so beware.

For further study, we recommend *Black Collectibles Sold in America* by P.J. Gibbs, and *Black Dolls, An Identification and Value Guide, 1820–1991,* by Myla Perkins.

See also Advertising, Aunt Jemima; Condiment Sets; Cookie Jars; Postcards; Salt and Pepper Shakers; Sheet Music; String Holders.

Advisor: Judy Posner (See Directory, Black Americana)

Ashtray, Dinah's Pancake & Chicken House, red graphics on clear glass, ca 1940s, 4¼" dia, EX **$70.00**

Ashtray, grotesque native w/white woman in cooking pot, she wears bathing suit & looks happy, 1930s, 4" dia, unused **$50.00**

Ashtray, lg mouth, brown skin tone, exaggerated features, Japan..**$85.00**

Book, color & fun; Sambo's Circus, by Bill Woggon, includes paper dolls, early 1960s, 8½x11", M (uncut)........**$90.00**

Book, Story of Little Black Sambo/Story of Topsy, Reilly & Lee, color, hardcover, 57 pages, 5¼x7", EX **$150.00**

Book, Story of the Mississippi, Harper, 1941, multicolor, hardcover, 40 pages, 10x11", EX....................................**$75.00**

Bottle, Del-Tox cleaning product, amber, colored label & lid, trademark of Mammy w/clothes basket, ca 1920s, 9½", EX **$135.00**

Candy box, Amos N' Andy, black & white w/orange on cardboard, 1930, 8¼x11¾", VG...................................**$350.00**

Card, get well, girl w/lg ribbon proclaims Some Things Look Darkest Jes' Befo' de Dawn, 1934, EX...................**$25.00**

Creamer, toby style, Mammy in white dress w/blue & green details, orange & yellow apron, rare & old, EX ...**$75.00**

Dart board, multicolor Sambo litho on tin, Wyandotte, ca 1940s, 14x23", EX **$145.00**

Doll, Betty Boop type, celluloid, brown skin tone, side glance googly eyes, feather outfit, ca 1930s, 6¾", EX........**$65.00**

Doll, pecan nut head, Folk Art, handmade, simulated straw crocheted hat, applied gray hair, colorful, 1930s, 6", EX..**$60.00**

Figure, cast iron, barefoot man on fence eating watermelon slice, exaggerated features, Manoil, 3", EX.........**$150.00**

Figure, cast metal, brown skin barefoot boy, red shorts, has roped angry bull, detailed, 1930s, 3x1½", EX **$165.00**

Figure, cast metal, gray outfit, red cap, gold buttons & badges, w/satchel, suitcases & golf clubs, 1930s, 3", M **$42.00**

Figure, cast metal, porter w/whisk broom, blue outfit w/gold buttons, embossed Made in USA, EX details, 1930s, 3", M..**$45.00**

Figure, diecut cardboard Mammy, detailed litho face, red & yellow bandana, draped crepe apron, 6¼", EX ...**$65.00**

Figures, chalkware, Amos N' Andy, multicolor, ca 1930s, EX, pr **$275.00**

Handkerchief, embroidered w/Sambo, multicolor, 1930s, set of 3, MIB (circus box)...**$135.00**

Handkerchief, Golliwogg, cotton, tan & brown on white background, Made in Ireland label, 1940s............**$95.00**

Lawn ornament, diecut wood Sambo hose caddy, 33", EX **$275.00**

Matchsafe/striker, metal, Coon Chicken logo, matches in hat, striker on back, ethnic caricature, ca 1930s, 3¼x3", EX...**$245.00**

Menu, souvenir; Club Plantation, w/naughty exaggerated ethnic female w/chain & lock on panties, ca 1940s, 5x6½"...**$70.00**

Menu, souvenir; Sambo's Resturants, glossy full color, 1967, 4x6¾" folded or 15x6¾" w/all 4 panels open, EX..**$85.00**

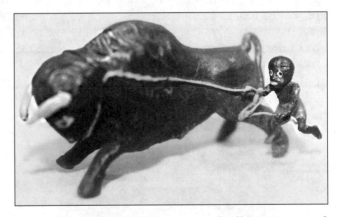

Miniature, boy roping angry bull, cast metal, detailed, ca 1930s, 1½x3", $165.00. (Photo courtesy Judy Posner)

Miniature, 2 boys climbing lamppost, cast metal, hand-painted details, 1930s, 5", $150.00. (Photo courtesy Judy Posner.)

Mug, Golliwogg's Joy Ride, minor gold wear around rim, no mark, 1930s, EX $125.00

Mug, 40th-anniversary commemorative for Uncle Ben's Rice, 1943-83, colorful logo on front, M $65.00

Nodder, colorful dressed minstrel, side-glancing, ca 1930s, 6¼", EX...$185.00

Noisemaker, tin litho, brown skin banjo player & fat sax player, red wooden handle, Made in Germany, 1930s, 3½x6½"...$95.00

Notepad holder, Mammy w/hard plastic torso, skirt forms pad, 1940s, 8½", EX...$95.00

Paper hat, Sambo's Restaurant, colorful logo, Cellucap PA, 1960s, 11¼x5½" $85.00

Photo folder, Memories of Club Plantation, shows cotton bale & banjo player on cover, souvenir, ca 1940s, EX..$40.00

Pin, bellhop, Bakelite, Art Deco style w/1 lg googly eye & red cap tilted over other eye, ca 1930s, 5", M ...$155.00

Pin, costume jewelry, gold-tone regal male profile, detailed headgear & shoulder wear, 1930s, 2", EX.............$70.00

Plate, cake; Coon Chicken Inn logo, blue & red on beige, Inca Ware, Shenango China, New Castle PA USA, 5½", EX..$195.00

Plate, dinner; Sambo's Resturant, aqua graphics on white ground, Jackson China, 10", EX.............................$85.00

Plate, Famous & Dandy, Amos N' Andy knock-offs, multicolor, 1930s, EX $95.00

Plate, Golliwogg's Joy Ride, Shenango China (heavy), full color, 1930s, 5½" dia, EX $135.00

Pot holder caddy, chalkware, hangs on wall w/1 hook for pot holders, boy chef w/red lips, white outfit, 6¼", MIB...$50.00

Pot holders with caddy, embroidered folk art, $75.00 for set. (Photo courtesy Judy Posner)

Puzzle, Sambo, wooden diecut pcs, Judy's Toys, 1930s, 11¾x8¾"..$125.00

Sack, Fisher's Cake Flour, cloth w/chef, blue, brown & red logo, 1930s, 2-lb size, 5½x10", EX $90.00

Sheet music, Blue Boogie, black & blue graphics, 1944, 12x9", EX $32.00

String holder, handmade stitched felt Mammy w/applied features, hole in mouth for string, 1930s, 8¼", M.....$75.00

Teapot, figural Mammy w/brown curly hair, googly eyes, & white chef hat, pink spout, ca 1930s, Japan, 4¼", EX $195.00

Toothpick holder, fellow in diaper eating watermelon, black pot holder, ceramic on wood base, 1930s, 8x3¾", EX $95.00

Tumbler, Black men shooting craps, red devil looking on, frosted w/red & black fired-on decor, 7", M $25.00

Wall plaque, chalkware, woman w/fruit basket, 1940-50s, 7", EX..$95.00

Whisk broom, figural Mammy, hand-painted wood handle torso, red bristles form skirt, 1930s, 4½", EX $75.00

Record album, Delta Rhythm Boys, Dry Bones, 4 record set with album cover, 78 rpm, EX, $65.00. (Photo courtesy Judy Posner)

Black Cats

Kitchenware, bookends, vases, and many other items designed as black cats were made in Japan during the 1950s and exported to the United States where they were sold by various distributors who often specified certain characteristics they wanted in their own line of cats. Common to all these lines were the red clay used in their production and the medium used in their decoration — their features were applied over the glaze with 'cold (unfired) paint.' The most collectible is a line marked (or labeled) Shafford. Shafford cats are plump and pleasant looking. They have green eyes with black pupils; white eyeliner, eyelashes, and whiskers; and red bow ties. The same design with yellow eyes was marketed by Royal, and another fairly easy-to-find 'breed' is a line by Wales with yellow eyes and gold whiskers. You'll find various other labels as well. Some collectors buy only Shafford, while others like them all.

When you evaluate your black cats, be critical of their paint. Even though no chips or cracks are present, if half of the paint is missing, you have a half-price item. Remember this when using the following values which are given for cats with near-mint to mint paint.

Ashtray, flat face, Shafford, hard to find size, 3¾"......$30.00

Ashtray, flat face, Shafford, 4¾" $18.00

Ashtray, head shape, not Shafford, several variations, each, from $12 to..$15.00

Ashtray, head shape w/open mouth, Shafford, 3" $18.00

Bank, seated cat w/coin slot in top of head, Shafford .$125.00

Bank, upright cat, Shafford-like features, marked Tommy, 2-part, from $150 to...$175.00

Cigarette lighter, Shafford, 5½", from $150 to **$175.00**

Cigarette lighter, sm cat stands on book by table lamp..**$65.00**

Condiment set, upright cats, yellow eyes, 2 bottles & pr of matching shakers in wireware stand, row arrangement **$85.00**

Condiment set, 2 joined heads, J & M bows w/spoons (intact), Shafford, 4"..**$75.00**

Condiment set, 2 joined heads yellow eyes (not Shafford)..**$65.00**

Cookie jar, cat's head, fierce expression, yellow eyes, brown-black glaze, heavy red clay, lg, rare **$250.00**

Cookie jar, lg head cat, Shafford **$85.00**

Creamer & sugar bowl, cat-head lids are salt & pepper shakers, yellow-eyed variation, 5⅜" **$50.00**

Creamer & sugar bowl, Shafford **$45.00**

Cruet, slender form, gold collar & tie, tail handle **$12.00**

Cruet, upright cat w/yellow eyes, open mouth, paw spout..**$30.00**

Cruets, oil & vinegar; cojoined cats, Royal Sealy, 1-pc (or similar examples w/heavier yellow-eyed cats), 7¼"..**$40.00**

Cruets, upright cats, she w/V eyes for vinegar, he w/O eyes for oil, Shafford, pr, from $50 to **$60.00**

Decanter, long cat w/red fish in his mouth as stopper .**$50.00**

Decanter, upright cats holds bottle w/cork stopper, Shafford, from $40 to..**$50.00**

Decanter set, upright cat, yellow eyes, +6 plain wines ..**$35.00**

Decanter set, upright cat, yellow eyes, +6 wines w/cat faces **$45.00**

Demitasse pot, tail handle, bow finial, Shafford, 7½"...**$95.00**

Desk caddy, pen forms tail, spring body holds letters, 6½" .**$8.00**

Egg cup, cat face on bowl, pedestal foot, Shafford....**$30.00**

Grease jar, sm cat head, Shafford, scarce, from $65 to...**$75.00**

Ice bucket, cylindrical w/embossed yellow-eyed cat face, 2 sizes, each **$75.00**

Measuring cups, 4 sizes on wooden wall-mount rack w/painted cat face, Shafford, rare **$300.00**

Mug, Shafford, scarce, 4"...**$65.00**

Mug, Shafford, 3½"...**$50.00**

Paperweight, cat's head on stepped chrome base, open mouth, yellow eyes, rare......................................**$75.00**

Pincushion, cushion on cat's back, tongue measure ..**$25.00**

Pitcher, milk; seated upright cat, ear forms spout, tail handle, Shafford, 6", or 6½", each, from $85 to **$100.00**

Planter, cat sits on knitted boot w/gold drawstring, Shafford-like paint, Elvin, 4¼x4½" **$30.00**

Planter, upright cat, Shafford-like paint, Napco label, 6"...**$20.00**

Pot holder caddy, 'teapot' cat, 3 hooks, Shafford.....**$125.00**

Salad set, spoon & fork, funnel, 1-pc oil & vinegar cruet & salt & pepper shakers on wooden wall-mount rack, Royal Sealy...**$200.00**

Salt & pepper shakers, long crouching cat, shaker in each end, Shafford, 10", from $75 to **$85.00**

Salt & pepper shakers, range size; upright cats, Shafford, scarce, 5", from $40 to...**$50.00**

Salt & pepper shakers, round-bodied 'teapot' cat, Shafford, pr, from $40 to...**$50.00**

Salt & pepper shakers, seated, blue eyes, Enesco label, 5¾", pr...**$15.00**

Salt & pepper shakers, upright cats, Shafford, 3¾" (watch for slightly smaller set as well), pr **$25.00**

Spice set, triangle, 3 rounded tiers of shakers, 8 in all, in wooden wall-mount triangular rack, very rare...**$350.00**

Spice set, 4 upright cat shakers hook onto bottom of wireware cat-face rack, Shafford, rare........................**$350.00**

Spice set, 6 square shakers in wooden frame, Shafford...**$145.00**

Spice set, 6 square shakers in wooden frame, yellow eyes..**$125.00**

Stacking tea set, mamma pot w/kitty creamer & sugar bowl, yellow eyes..**$65.00**

Stacking tea set, 3 cats w/red collar, w/gold ball, yellow eyes, 3-pc **$65.00**

Sugar bowl/planter, sitting cat, red bow w/gold bell, Shafford-like paint, Elvin, 4" **$25.00**

Teapot, bulbous body, head lid, green eyes, Shafford, med size, from $40 to..**$45.00**

Teapot, bulbous body, head lid, green eyes, Shafford, 4-4½"..**$30.00**

Teapot, bulbous body, head lid, green eyes, Shafford, 7" .**$75.00**

Teapot, cat face w/double spout, Shafford, scarce, 5" **$125.00**

Teapot, cat's face, yellow hat, blue & white eyes, pink ears, lg, from $40 to **$50.00**

Teapot, crouching cat, paw up to right ear is spout, inset green jewel eyes, 8½" L **$60.00**

Teapot, panther-like appearance, gold eyes, sm........**$20.00**

Pitcher, squatting cat, pour through mouth, Shafford, 3 sizes: 5½", 17" circumference, very rare, $200.00; 5", 14½" circumference, rare, $75.00; 4½", 13" circumference, scarce, $65.00.

Planter, cat & kitten in a hat, Shafford-like paint........**$30.00**

Teapot, upright cat with paw spout, yellow eyes and red bow, Wales, 8¼", $65.00.

Teapot, upright, slender cat (not ball-shaped), lift-off head, Shafford, rare, 8"..**$175.00**

Teapot, yellow-eyed cat face embossed on front of standard bulbous teapot shape, wire bale, from $50 to **$60.00**

Teapot, yellow eyes, 1-cup **$30.00**

Thermometer, cat w/yellow eyes stands w/paw on round thermometer face **$30.00**
Toothpick holder, cat on vase atop book, Occupied Japan ..**$12.00**
Tray, flat face, wicker handle, Shafford, lg **$125.00**
Utensil (fork, spoon or strainer), wood handle, Shafford, rare, each..**$90.00**
Utensil rack, flat-backed cat w/3 slots for utensils, cat only **$90.00**
Wall pocket, flat-backed 'teapot' cat, Shafford **$95.00**
Wine, embossed cat's face, green eyes, Shafford, sm.**$20.00**

Blair Dinnerware

American dinnerware has been a popular type of collectible for several years, and the uniquely styled lines of Blair Ceramics, who operated in Ozark, Missouri, for a few years from the mid-forties until the early fifties are especially appealing, though not often seen except in the Midwest. Gay Plaid, recognized by its squared-off shapes and brush-stroke design (in lime, brown, and dark green on white), is the one you'll find most often. Several other lines were made as well. You'll be able to recognize them easily enough, since most pieces (except for the smaller items) are marked.

Bowl, fruit/cereal; Gay Plaid, square, from $8 to **$10.00**
Bowl, onion soup; Bamboo, rope handle, w/lid **$22.00**
Bowl, sauce; Gay Plaid, double spout, handled **$16.00**
Bowl, serving; Autumn Leaf..**$12.50**
Bowl, vegetable; Bird, divided, rectangular w/tab handles **$32.50**
Celery dish, Bird, from $20 to **$25.00**
Coffee server, Bamboo, rope handle, from $40 to......**$50.00**
Cruet, Bird, cone form w/ring handle **$27.50**
Cup & saucer, Autumn Leaf...**$12.00**
Cup & saucer, Bamboo, rope handle...........................**$12.00**
Mug, Gay Plaid **$18.00**
Pitcher, utility; Gay Plaid, bulbous body, smooth curved handle, sm...**$15.00**
Pitcher, water; Gay Plaid, rope handle, ice lip............**$45.00**

Plate, dinner; Bamboo, $12.50.

Plate, dinner; Bird, square **$17.50**
Platter, Yellow Plaid, 3-compartment **$27.50**
Salt & pepper shakers, Bird, pr.....................................**$16.00**
Sugar bowl, Gay Plaid, rope handle, w/lid **$17.50**

Blue Ridge Dinnerware

Blue Ridge has long been popular with collectors, and prices are already well established, but that's not to say there aren't a few good buys left around. There are! It was made by a company called Southern Potteries, who operated in Erwin, Tennessee, from sometime in the latter thirties until the mid-fifties. They made literally hundreds of patterns, all hand decorated. Some collectors prefer to match up patterns, while others like to mix them together for a more eclectic table setting.

One of the patterns most popular with collectors (and one of the most costly) is called French Peasant. It's very much like Quimper with simple depictions of a little peasant fellow with his staff. But they also made many lovely floral patterns, and it's around these where most of the buying and selling activity is centered. You'll find roosters, plaids, and simple textured designs, and in addition to the dinnerware, some vases and novelty items as well.

Nearly every piece is marked 'Blue Ridge,' though occasionally you'll find one that isn't. Watch for a similar type of ware often confused with Blue Ridge that is sometimes (though not always) marked Italy.

The values suggested below are for the better patterns. To evaluate the French Peasant line, double these figures; for the simple plaids and textures, deduct 25% to 50%, depending on their appeal.

If you'd like to learn more, we recommend *The Collector's Encyclopedia of Blue Ridge Dinnerware, Identification and Values*, by Betty and Bill Newbound.

Advisors: Bill and Betty Newbound (See Directory, Dinnerware)

Newsletter: *National Blue Ridge Newsletter*
Norma Lilly
144 Highland Dr., Blountsville, TN 37617

Ashtray, individual **$14.00**
Ashtray, w/rest **$18.00**
Baking dish, oven proof, Japan, 2½x5" **$35.00**
Bowl, cereal/soup; 6" **$10.00**
Bowl, flat soup; 8" **$15.00**
Bowl, fruit; 5¼" **$5.00**
Bowl, mixing; 8½" **$35.00**
Bowl, salad; Square Dancers, 11½"...............................**$90.00**
Bowl, salad; 10½" **$50.00**
Bowl, vegetable; divided, oval, 9"................................**$25.00**
Bowl, vegetable; 8" dia **$17.00**
Box, cigarette **$75.00**
Butter dish **$45.00**
Butter pat/coaster **$30.00**
Cake lifter **$25.00**
Carafe, w/lid **$60.00**
Casserole, w/lid **$45.00**
Celery, Skyline **$30.00**
Coffeepot...**$150.00**
Creamer, demitasse **$35.00**
Creamer, regular..**$8.00**
Cup, dessert; glass **$12.00**

Cup & saucer, demitasse......................................$25.00
Cup & saucer, jumbo..$40.00
Cup & sugar, regular $12.00
Custard...$15.00
Dish, baking; 8x13"...$25.00
Egg cup, double...$30.00
Gravy boat...$28.00
Gravy boat underplate.......................................$25.00
Jug, batter; w/lid...$75.00
Jug, syrup; w/lid...$90.00
Lazy susan, 6-pc w/tray $650.00
Pitcher, Betsy...$90.00
Pitcher, Spiral $70.00
Plate, aluminum edge, 12" $25.00
Plate, cake; 10½"...$30.00
Plate, Christmas or Turkey................................$75.00

Plate, dinner; Floral Spray or Apple Tart pattern, $20.00. (Photo courtesy Betty and Bill Newbound)

Plate, Language of Flowers.............................$75.00
Plate, party; w/cup well & cup $30.00
Plate, pie; 7"...$10.00
Plate, snack; 3-compartment.........................$20.00
Plate, square, novelty pattern, 6"..................$50.00
Plate, wallpaper advertising.........................$325.00
Plate, 6"...$5.00
Plate, 8"...$10.00
Platter, artist signed $900.00
Platter, 11" $18.00
Platter, 12½" $22.00
Platter, 15" $28.00
Ramekin, w/lid, 5" $30.00
Ramekin, w/lid, 7½"...$35.00
Salad fork $45.00
Salad spoon..$40.00
Salt & pepper shakers, Blossom Top, pr...................$35.00
Salt & pepper shakers, Chickens, pr......................$95.00
Salt & pepper shakers, Mallards, pr.....................$155.00
Salt & pepper shakers, regular, short, pr...................$18.00
Sconce $65.00
Server, center handle.......................................$30.00
Sherbet...$22.00
Sugar bowl, regular, w/lid................................$15.00
Sugar bowl, wide, open....................................$20.00
Tea tile, round or square, 3"...........................$25.00
Tea tile, round or square, 6"...........................$35.00

Teapot, Ball shape...$50.00
Teapot, Charm House $150.00
Teapot, Colonial shape......................................$95.00
Teapot, demitasse; earthenware $90.00
Teapot, Piecrust...$95.00
Teapot, Square Round......................................$75.00
Teapot, Woodcrest...$125.00
Tidbit tray, 2-tier...$30.00
Tidbit tray, 3-tier...$40.00
Toast, covered...$100.00

Tray, cake; Verna, Maple Leaf shape, from $50.00 to $60.00.

Tray, waffle set...$55.00
Tumbler, glass $14.00
Vase, Boot, 8"..$85.00
Vase, bud..$90.00

Blue Willow Dinnerware

Blue Willow dinnerware has been made since the 1700s, first by English potters, then Japanese, and finally American companies as well. Tinware, glassware, even paper 'go-withs' have been produced over the years — some fairly recently, due to on-going demand. It was originally copied from the early blue and white wares made in Nanking and Canton in China. Once in awhile you'll see some pieces in black, pink, red, or even multicolor.

Obviously the most expensive will be the early English wares, easily identified by their backstamps. You'll be most likely to find pieces made by Royal or Homer Laughlin, and even though comparatively recent, they're still collectible, and their prices are very affordable.

For further study we recommend *Blue Willow Identification and Value Guide* by Mary Frank Gaston.

See also Homer Laughlin; Royal China.

Advisor: Mary Frank Gaston (See Directory, Dinnerware)

Newsletter: *American Willow Report*
Lisa Kay Henze, Editor
P.O. Box 900, Oakridge, OR 97463. Bimonthly newsletter, subscription: $15 per year, out of country add $5 per year

Newsletter: *The Willow Word*
Mary Berndt, Publisher
P.O. Box 13382, Arlington, TX 76094; Send SASE for information about subscriptions and the International Willow Collector's Convention

Bisquit jar, silverplated lid and bail handle, English, unmarked, 7", $225.00 to $250.00. (Photo courtesy Mary Frank Gaston)

Biscuit jar, w/lid & cane handle, Moriyama mark.....**$175.00**
Bone dish, crescent shape, Wood & Sons, 7½x4½" ...**$55.00**
Bowl, salad; unmarked Japan, 3½x10", w/matching fork & spoon (wooden handles)......................................**$140.00**
Bowl, soup/cereal; scalloped rim, Doulton mark, 7½" ..**$120.00**
Bowl, soup/cereal; Shenango China **$20.00**
Bowl, vegetable; Shenango China, 8" **$30.00**
Bowl, vegetable; w/lid, unmarked, 10½x6" **$150.00**
Butter dish, rectangular, holds ¼-lb, Japan **$75.00**
Butter warmer, sm handled pot on 3-legged metal frame w/ceramic candle holder in center, unmarked Japan..**$100.00**
Canister set, graduated set of 4 barrels w/identified contents, Japan...**$500.00**
Carafe & warmer, w/stopper, Japan, 10" overall.......**$275.00**
Compote, footed, Shenango China, 3x6" **$60.00**
Creamer, hotel ware, Shenango China, 2½" **$35.00**
Creamer & sugar bowl, gold trim, w/lid, unmarked Japan, 3½"..**$60.00**
Cup, chile; unmarked Japan, 4x4½"..........................**$55.00**
Cup, lg (referred to as Texas Cup), Japan, 5½x8½" ...**$90.00**
Egg cup, double; Allerton's Made in England, 4½" **$32.50**
Egg cup, double; unmarked Japan, 3¾".......................**$20.00**
Egg cup, single, gold trim, unmarked Japan...............**$35.00**
Flatware, 4-pc place setting, stainless w/patterned plastic handles, Japan..**$55.00**
Horseradish dish, marked Doulton, 5½"......................**$65.00**
Lamp, electric, resembles oil lamp, Made in Japan, 7¼" .**$55.00**
Mug, heavy, Japan, 4"..**$40.00**
Pie plate, unglazed base for baking, Moriyama Made in Japan mark, 10" **$75.00**
Pie server, Moriyama Made in Japan mark, 10" **$40.00**
Plate, cake; Mandarin pattern w/Dagger border, Shore & Coggins mark, 9½x9½" **$70.00**
Plate, grill; Booth's center pattern w/Bow Knot border, marked Booth's, 10¾" **$30.00**
Plate, grill; Turner pattern w/Scroll & Flower border, marked Shenango China, 10"..................................**$25.00**
Plate, Traditional w/gold trim, marked HM Williamson & Sons, 6½" square **$25.00**

Plate, Two Temples II, Butterfly border, gold trim, GL Ashworth mark, 8½"..**$65.00**
Plate, Variant center pattern w/Pictorial border, unmarked, 6"...**$12.00**
Platter, Traditional, marked Made in Occupied Japan, 12¾x9½"...**$55.00**
Relish, rectangular w/scalloped edge, marked John Maddock, 11" **$65.00**

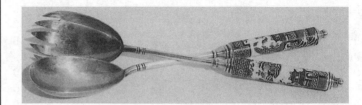

Salad fork and spoon, ceramic and silverplate, unmarked, 11½", from $200.00 to $225.00 for the set. (Photo courtesy Mary Frank Gaston)

Salt box, wooden lid, unmarked Japan, 5x5"............**$135.00**
Spoon rest, double style, unmarked Japan, 9" L.........**$50.00**
Sugar bowl, w/lid, marked Japan, 3½" **$35.00**
Tea strainer, unmarked, 4" dia...................................**$200.00**
Teapot, marked North Staffordshire Pottery Co Ltd, 1940s, 4-cup..**$75.00**
Teapot, musical type, unmarked Japan **$140.00**
Toothbrush holder, marked Doulton Made in England, 5" **$175.00**
Vase, cylindrical w/handles, marked Doulton Made in England, 5¼"..**$150.00**
Wall pocket, teapot form w/Traditional pattern & floral border, Japan, 6"..**$50.00**

Bookends

You'll find bookends in various types of material and designs. The more inventive their modeling, the higher the price. Also consider the material. Cast-iron examples, especially if in original polychrome paint, are bringing very high prices right now. Brass and copper are good as well, though elements of design may override the factor of materials altogether. If they are signed by the designer or marked by the manufacturer, you can about triple the price. Those with a decidedly Art Deco appearance are often good sellers. See *Collector's Guide to Bookends* by Louis Kuritzky for more information.

Antique cars, redware, Japan, 1960s, pr **$18.00**
Asters, cast iron w/worn original paint, pr................**$155.00**
Aviators, cast iron w/bronze finish, pr.......................**$50.00**
Bulldogs' heads, cast bronze, EX details, 4⅝", pr.......**$85.00**
Cathedrals, cast iron w/multicolor paint, 5⅜", EX, pr...**$85.00**
Cowboys on broncos, cast iron w/old gold paint, marked CFW, 5½", pr...**$50.00**
Elephants, cast iron w/multicolor trim, #112, 4", pr ...**$80.00**
Flamenco dancers, Deco style, signed Herzel, pr.....**$185.00**
Floral reliefs on crescents, cast iron, #54 C Albany Fdy Co, pr...**$60.00**

Galleon ships, lead, pr **$45.00**
Indian chiefs, cast iron w/red & gold paint, 4¾", pr..**$50.00**
John F Kennedy, pewter look, marked FMC, 6" pr ...**$30.00**
Lindbergh, cast iron w/bronze finish, 5⅝", pr.............**$40.00**
Lovebirds, cast iron w/multicolor paint, Acorn #600, pr...**$125.00**
Nudes in shells, painted chalkware, EX, pr.................**$45.00**
Parrots on rings, cast iron w/multicolor paint, NM, pr....**$185.00**
Pirates, bronze, EX, pr..**$45.00**
Shakespeare, cast iron w/bronze finish, 1920s, pr......**$50.00**
Spirit of Freedom, painted cast iron, pr.....................**$200.00**
Terriers, cast iron w/brass finish, Copr 1930, 5¾", pr...**$25.00**
Thinker, painted metal, NM, pr **$35.00**
Wolfhounds, cast iron, white & gold paint, 2⅝", pr ...**$45.00**

Ancestral Home of George Washington, brass, 4", $45.00.

Books

Books have always fueled our imaginations. Before television lured us out of the library into the TV room, everyone enjoyed reading the latest novels. Western, horror, and science fiction themes are still popular to this day — especially those by such authors as Louis L'Amour, Steven King, and Ray Bradbury, to name but a few. Edgar Rice Burrough's Tarzan series and Frank L. Baum's Wizard of Oz books are regarded as classics among today's collectors. A first edition of a popular author's first book (especially if it's signed) is especially sought after, so is a book that 'ties in' with a movie or television program.

Dick and Jane readers are fast becoming collectible. If you went to first grade sometime during the 1930s until the mid-1970s, you probably read about their adventures. These books were used all over the United States and in military base schools over the entire world. These books were published here as well as in Canada, the Philippine Islands, Australia, and New Zealand; there were special editions for the Roman Catholic parochial schools and the Seventh Day Adventists', and even today they're in use in some Mennonite and Amish schools.

On the whole, ex-library copies and book club issues (unless they are limited editions) have very low resale values.

For further information we recommend *Huxford's Old Book Value Guide* by Sharon and Bob Huxford. This book is designed to help the owners of old books evaluate their holdings. It also lists the names of prospective buyers.

Magazine: *AB Bookman's Weekly*
P.O. Box AB, Clifton, NJ 07015; 201-772-0020 or FAX 201-772-9281. Sample copies: $10

Big Little Books

The Whitman Publishing Company started it all in 1933 when they published a book whose format was entirely different than any other's. It was very small, easily held in a child's hand, but over an inch in thickness. There was a cartoon-like drawing on the right-hand page, and the text was printed on the left. The idea was so well accepted that very soon other publishers — Saalfield, Van Wiseman, Lynn, World Syndicate, and Goldsmith — cashed in on the idea as well. The first Big Little Book hero was Dick Tracy, but soon every radio cowboy, cartoon character, lawman, and space explorer was immortalized in his own adventure series.

When it became apparent that the pre-teen of the fifties preferred the comic-book format, Big Little Books were finally phased out; but many were saved in boxes and stored in attics, so there's still a wonderful supply of them around. You need to watch condition carefully when you're buying or selling. For further information we recommend *Big Little Books, A Collector's Reference and Value Guide*, by Larry Jacobs.

Newsletter: *Big Little Times*
Big Little Book Collectors Club of America
Larry Lowery
P.O. Box 1242, Danville, CA 94526; 415-837-2086

Ace Drummond, #1177, 1935, EX.................................**$40.00**
Blondie & Baby Dumpling, #1415, EX+ **$38.00**
Buck Jones & the Rock Creek Cattle War, 1938, VG+ ..**$25.00**
Buck Rogers on the Moons of Saturn, 1934, EX.........**$60.00**
Captain Easy Behind Enemy Lines, Whitman #1474, 1943, NM **$60.00**
Chester Gump, Silver Creek Ranch, #734, 1933, EX...**$30.00**
Dan Dunn & the Crime Master, #1171, 1937, EX........**$35.00**
Dick Tracy & Yogee Yamma, 1946, EX........................**$40.00**
Don Winslow, USN; #1107, 1935, EX...........................**$30.00**

Flash Gordon and the Water World of Mongo, 1930, EX+, $50.00; Jungle Jim and the Vampire Woman, EX, $35.00; Zane Grey's King of the Royal Mounted Gets His Man, #1452, 1938, EX, $20.00.

Flash Gordon on the Planet Mongo, Whitman #1469, 1943, NM **$95.00**
G-Man Breaking the Gambling Ring, #1493, 1938, EX .**$30.00**

Little Orphan Annie & the Junior Commandos, Whitman #1457, 1943, EX..............................**$45.00**

Lost Patrol, Whitman, 1934, EX **$40.00**

Mandrake the Magician, Whitman #1167, 1935, EX+..**$35.00**

Popeye Sees the Sea, Whitman #1163, 1936, EX **$45.00**

Skeezix at the Military Academy, #1408, 1938, EX......**$30.00**

Tiny Tim in the Big Big World, Whitman, 1945, EX...**$30.00**

Zip Saunders King of the Speedway, 1939, VG+........**$18.00**

Children's Miscellaneous Books

America's Abraham Lincoln, May McNeer, Houghton Mifflin, 1957, 1st edition, Lynd Ward illustrator, w/dust jacket, NM **$40.00**

Animal ABC by Sally Lee Woodall, US Camera, 1946, photos, VG+..**$20.00**

Anno's Counting Book, Anno Mitsumasa, Crowell, 1977, 1st American edition, w/dust jacket, VG+ **$30.00**

Anno's Counting House, Mitsumasa Anno, Philomel, 2nd printing, 1983, color pictorial boards, NM **$20.00**

At the Back of the North Wind, George MacDonald, Macmillan, 1924, 1st edition thus, 13 full-page illustrations, VG ..**$55.00**

Bedtime Stories, Thornton Burgess, Grosset Dunlap, 1959, Carl & Mary Haige illustrators, 105 pages, NM.....**$40.00**

Birds Christmas Carol, Kate Douglas Wiggins, Houghton Mifflin, 1929, Helen Mason Grose illustrator, w/dust jacket, VG+ **$30.00**

Blue Ridge Billy, Lois Lenski, Lippincott, 1946, 1st edition, 203 pages, w/dust jacket, VG **$60.00**

Borrowers Afloat, Mary Norton, Harcourt Brace, 1959, 191 pages, w/dust jacket, VG+ **$35.00**

Bouncing Betsy, Dorothy Lathrop, Macmillan, 1946, 1st edition, unpaged, w/dust jacket, VG........................**$50.00**

Boy's King Arthur, Scribner Classic, 1947, NC Wyeth illustrator, color plate on black cloth, VG......................**$30.00**

Busy ABC, Eloise Wilkin, Whitman, 1950, color pictorial boards, VG **$30.00**

Celery Stalks at Midnight, James Jowe, Atheneum, 1983, 1st edition, 111 pages, cloth, w/dust jacket, NM **$30.00**

Children's Corner, Marie Penny, Greenberg, 1933, 1st edition, Mary Sarg illustrator, calico cover, w/dust jacket, NM...**$35.00**

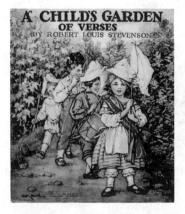

A Child's Garden of Verses, Saalfield, 1929, 12 color illustrations by Clara M. Burd, VG+, $35.00. (Photo courtesy Marvelous Books)

Cucumber, the Story of a Siamese Cat, Enid Colfer, Thomas Nelson, 1961, 1st edition, 98 pages, w/dust jacket, VG **$20.00**

Favorite Uncle Remus, Joel Chandler Harris, Houghton Mifflin, 1948, 11th printing, w/dust jacket, NM....**$30.00**

Frisky, Try Again...An Easy To Read Photo Story Book for Children, Charles Fox, Reilly & Lee, 1959, w/dust jacket, EX+...**$20.00**

Good Master, Kate Seredy, Viking, 1935, 1st edition, w/dust jacket, VG...**$55.00**

Hansel & Gretel, Fern Bisel Peat, Harper, 1932, 8 color plates, VG..**$60.00**

Honey the City Bear, Madalena Paltenghi, Grosset Dunlap, CW Anderson illustrator, 1937, VG........................**$40.00**

How the Moon Began, James Reeves, Abelard-Schuman, 1971, 1st American edition, Ardizzone illustrator, w/dust jacket, NM...**$30.00**

Jane Withers, Her Life Story, Twentieth-Century Fox/Whitman, #976, 1936, VG, $15.00.

Just a Dream, Chris Van Allsburg, Houghton Mifflin, 1990, 1st edition, w/dust jacket, NM.....................................**$45.00**

Little Brown Koko Has Fun, Blance Seale Hunt, American Colortype, 1945, Dorothy Wagstaff illustrator, VG..**$55.00**

Little Princess, Frances Hodgson Burnett, Lippincott, 1963, 1st edition, Tasha Tudor illustrator, w/dust jacket, VG+.......**$325.00**

Look at a Gull, Dare Wright, Random House, 1967, unpaged, pictorial boards, VG...**$22.00**

Lost Teddy Bear & Other Stories, Edith Mason Armstrong, Rand McNally, possible 2nd printing, 1943, pictorial boards, VG **$25.00**

Mary Poppins in the Park, PL Travers, Harcourt Brace, 1952, 1st edition, Mary Shepard illustrator, w/dust jacket, VG+ **$75.00**

Molly Cottontail, Erskine Caldwell, Little Brown, 1958, 1st edition thus, William Sharp illustrator, VG............**$65.00**

More Once Upon a Time Stories, Rose Dobbs, Random House, 1961, 1st edition, Flavia Gag illustrator, w/dust jacket, VG+ **$30.00**

Mother Goose, Gabriel, 1924, various illustrators, 12 linen pages, VG **$25.00**

Mrs Mallard's Ducklings, Clelia Delafield, Lothrop Lee & Shepard, 1946, 1st edition, unpaged, w/dust jacket, VG...**$25.00**

Norman Rockwell's Americana ABC by George Mendoza, Abrams, 1971, color illustrations, w/dust jacket, NM ..**$40.00**

Nursery Rhymes for Children, Muriel Dawson, Samuel Lowe, 1940, 20 pages, NM **$60.00**

Nursery Tales Children Love, Watty Piper, Platt & Munk, 1933, color plate on blue boards, VG+.................**$55.00**

Penny Fiddle, Poems for Children, Robert Graves, Doubleday, 1960, 1st edition, Ardizzone illustrator, w/dust jacket, VG **$20.00**

Pied Piper of Hamelin, Jack Perkins, McLoughlin, 1931, color pictorial boards, NM **$15.00**

Pig-Tale, Lewis Carroll, Little Brown, 1975, 1st edition thus, Leonard Lubin illustrator, 30 pages, w/dust jacket, VG+ **$25.00**

Pinocchio, the Tale of a Puppet, Carlo Collodi, Dent & Dutton, 1919, 2nd edition, 12 color plates, stamped cloth, VG...**$110.00**

Restless Robin, Marjorie Flack, Houghton Mifflin, 1937, unpaged, w/dust jacket, VG **$25.00**

Soon We'll Be Three Years Old (Dionne Quintuplets), Whitman, 1936, unpaged, VG................................**$30.00**

Tale of Peter Rabbit, Beatrix Potter, Fideler, 1946, color pictorial boards, w/dust jacket, VG......................**$85.00**

Tasha Tudor's Favorite Christmas Carols, McKay, 1978, 1st edition, 52 pages, w/dust jacket, VG+ **$75.00**

Teddy Bear Tales, Joan Walsh Anglund, Random House, 1st edition, 1985, NM...**$18.00**

Three Bears, Frances Brundage, Saalfield, 1928, VG ..**$95.00**

Three Christmas Trees, Juliana Horatia Ewing, Macmillan, 1930, Pamela Bianco illustrator, VG **$25.00**

Topsy Turvy & the Tin Clown, Bernice Anderson, Rand McNally, not 1st edition, 1934, pictorial boards, VG **$48.00**

Travels of Babar, Jean DeBrunhoff, Random House, 1934, w/dust jacket, VG **$65.00**

Turkey for Christmas, Marguerite deAngeli, Westminster, 1949, 1st edition, unpaged, w/dust jacket, VG+ ..**$50.00**

We Live by the River, Lois Lenski, Lippincott, 1956, 1st edition, Roundabout America series, VG+ **$35.00**

What Color Is Love?, Joan Walsh Anglund, Harcourt, 1st edition, 1966, w/dust jacket, NM..............................**$25.00**

Witch on the Corner, Felice Holman, WW Norton, 1966, 1st edition, Arnold Lobel illustrator, w/dust jacket, VG+ **$22.00**

Yogi Bear Makes a Wish, Modern Promotions, 1974, 4 multi-dimensional pop-ups, VG **$25.00**

Juvenile Series Books

Air Combat: Yankee Flier in the RAF, Al Avery, Grosset Dunlap, 1941, 214 pages, w/dust jacket, VG **$25.00**

Air Combat: Yankee Flier Over Berlin, Al Avery, Grosset Dunlap, 1944, 212 pages, w/dust jacket, VG+ **$27.00**

Barbara Ann & the Mystery at Mountain View, Ruth Grosby, Grosset Dunlap, 1940, 243 pages, w/dust jacket, VG ..**$22.00**

Belgian Twins, Lucy Fitch Perkins, Houghton Mifflin, 1917, NM **$35.00**

Beverly Gray's Problem, Clair Blank, Grosset Dunlap, 1943, 1st edition, 214 pages, w/dust jacket, VG+ **$37.00**

Black Stallion Revolts, Walter Farley, Random House, 1953, 1st edition, w/dust jacket, VG **$30.00**

Blue Grass Seminary Girls on the Water, Carolyn Judson Burnett, AL Burt, 1916, 244 pages, w/dust jacket, VG.............**$22.00**

Bomba the Jungle Boy & the Perilous Kingdom, Roy Rookwood, Cupples Leon, 1937, 208 pages, w/dust jacket, VG...**$22.00**

Bronc Burnett & Grand-Slam Homer, Wilfred McCormick, Putnam, 1951, 1st edition, 183 pages, w/dust jacket, VG..........**$42.00**

Cherry Ames, Cruise Nurse, #9, Grosset Dunlap, 1948, pictorial hardcover, EX, from $5.00 to $7.00.

Dana Girls & the Riddle of the Frozen Fountain, Carolyn Keene, Grosset Dunlap, 1964, 173 pages, w/dust jacket, VG+ **$22.00**

Dave Fearless After a Sunken Treasure, Roy Rookwood, Sully, 1918, 252 pages, VG.....................................**$27.00**

Dick & Jane, Fun With Dick & Jane, hardcover, 1946, NM, from $325 to..**$350.00**

Dick & Jane, Fun With Dick & Jane, hardcover, 1946, VG **$125.00**

Dick & Jane, Happy Days With Our Friends, Scott Foresman, 1954, VG..**$60.00**

Dick & Jane, More Dick & Jane Stories, Elson-Gray, 1934, EX+, from $250 to **$275.00**

Dick and Jane, The New We Look and See, Scott Foresman, 1956, soft cover, NM, from $60.00 to $75.00.

Dick & Jane, Our Big Book, teacher's edition, easel size, M, from $250 to..**$275.00**

Dick & Jane, Our New Friends, Scott Foresman, 1946, 191 pages, cloth, VG+ **$60.00**

Dick & Jane, The New We Work & Play, Scott Foresman, 1956, soft cover, VG **$65.00**

Dick & Jane, We Read Pictures, Scott Foresman, 1951, 48 pages, soft cover, VG **$50.00**

Don Sturdy in the Land of Volcanoes, Victor Appleton, Grosset Dunlap, 1925, w/dust jacket, VG............**$27.00**

Don Sturdy in the Tombs of Gold, Victor Appleton, Grosset Dunlap, 1925, 214 pages, w/dust jacket, VG **$32.00**

Grace Harlowe's Overland Riders in the Great North Woods, Jessie G Flower, Altemus, 1921, 255 pages, w/dust jacket, VG...**$17.00**

Hal Keen & the Copperhead Trail Mystery, Lloyd Hugh, Grosset Dunlap, 1931, 218 pages, w/dust jacket, VG **$82.00**

Hardy Boys & a Figure in Hiding, Franklin W Dixon, Grosset Dunlap, 1937, 212 pages, w/dust jacket, VG **$67.00**

Hardy Boys & the Mystery of the Flying Express, Franklin W Dixon, Grosset Dunlap, 1941, 1st edition, w/dust jacket, VG **$52.00**

Jerry Todd & the Flying Flapdoodle, Leo Edwards, Grosset Dunlap, 1934, 244 pages, w/dust jacket, VG **$42.00**

Judy Bolton & the Forbidden Chest, Margaret Sutton, Grosset Dunlap, 1953, 210 pages, w/dust jacket, VG **$42.00**

Judy Bolton & the Phantom Friend, Margaret Sutton, Grosset Dunlap, 1959, 1st edition, 174 pages, w/dust jacket, VG+ **$100.00**

Lone Ranger & the Gold Robbery, Fran Striker, Grosset Dunlap, 1939, 185 pages, w/dust jacket, VG **$37.00**

Lone Ranger & the Outlaw Stronghold, Fran Striker, Grosset Dunlap, 1939, 214 pages, w/dust jacket, VG+ **$42.00**

Motor Boys Over the Ocean, Clarence Young, Cupples Leon, 1911, 241 pages, w/dust jacket, VG **$50.00**

Nancy Drew & the Sign of the Twisted Candles, Carolyn Keene, Grosset Dunlap, 1935B edition, w/dust jacket, VG...**$125.00**

Outdoor Girls Along the Coast, Laura Lee Hope, Grosset Dunlap, 1926, 210 pages, w/dust jacket, VG+ **$37.00**

Radio Boys With the Iceberg Patrol, Allen Chapman, Grosset Dunlap, 1922, 218 pages, w/dust jacket, VG **$47.00**

Red Randall on Active Duty, R Sidney Bowen, Grosset Dunlap, 1944, 211 pages, w/dust jacket, VG **$17.00**

Ted Scott in Over the Rockies With the Air Mail, Franklin W Dixon, Grosset Dunlap, 1927, 214 pages, w/dust jacket, VG...**$32.00**

Tom Swift & His Airline Express, Victor Appleton, Grosset Dunlap, 1926, 1st edition, 218 pages, w/dust jacket, VG **$48.00**

Tom Swift in the Land of Wonders, Victor Appleton, Grosset Dunlap, 1917, 1st edition, 218 pages, w/dust jacket, VG **$67.00**

Trixie Belden & the Gatehouse Mystery, Julie Campbell, Whitman, 1951, 250 pages, w/dust jacket, VG.....**$12.00**

Little Golden Books

Everyone has had a few of these books in their lifetime; some we've read to our own children so many times that we still know them word for word, and today they're appearing in antique malls and shops everywhere. The first were printed in 1942. These are recognizable by their blue paper spines (later ones had gold foil). Until the early 1970s, they were numbered consecutively; after that they were unnumbered.

First editions of the titles having a 25¢ or 29¢ cover price can be identified by either a notation on the first or second pages, or a letter on the bottom right corner of the last page (A for 1, B for 2, etc.). If these are absent, you probably have a first edition.

Condition is extremely important. To qualify as mint, these books must look just as good as they looked the day they were purchased. Naturally, having been used by chil-

dren, many show signs of wear. If your book is only lightly soiled, the cover has no tears or scrapes, the inside pages have only small creases or folded corners, and the spine is still strong (though its cover may be missing), it will be worth about half as much as one in mint condition. Additional damage would of course lessen the value even more.

A series number containing an 'A' refers to an activity book, while a 'D' number identifies a Disney story. Our values are for examples in excellent condition.

For more information, we recommend *Collecting Little Golden Books* by Steve Santi (who provided us with our narrative material).

Advisor: Ilene Kayne (See Directory, Books)

Newsletter: *The Pokey Gazette*
Steve Santi
19626 Ricardo Ave., Hayward, CA 94541; 501-481-2586; a *Little Golden Book* collector newsletter

Animal Orchestra, #334, 3rd edition, VG **$5.00**
Animal's Merry Christmas #329, A edition, VG/EX **$4.00**
Baby Looks, #404, 3rd edition, VG/EX **$17.00**
Bambi, #106-9, F edition, VG/EX **$2.00**
Bednobs & Broomsticks, #D93, 1st edition, EX **$8.00**
Ben & Me, #D37, A edition, VG/EX.............................**$22.00**
Big Brown Bear, #335, 6th edition, blue cover, VG/EX..**$6.00**
Bobby the Dog, #440, A edition, VG/EX......................**$28.00**
Bozo the Clown, #446, C edition, VG/EX.....................**$8.00**
Buffalo Bill Jr, #254, A edition, VG/EX **$14.00**
Bugs Bunny Pioneer, #111-66, A edition, VG/EX..........**$6.00**
But You're a Duck, #206-64, 1992, VG/EX **$2.00**
Captain Kangaroo & the Beaver, #427, A edition, EX...**$12.00**
Christmas ABC, #478, A edition, VG/EX......................**$14.00**

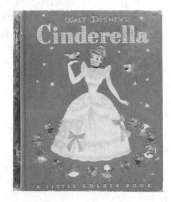

Cinderella, #13, 1950, NM, $12.00.

Color Kittens, #496, 5th edition, VG/EX **$22.00**
Corky, #486, A edition, VG/EX....................................**$14.00**
Country Mouse & City Mouse, #426, D edition, VG/EX.**$3.00**
Dale Evans & the Coyote, #253, A edition, VG/EX **$12.00**
Day at the Zoo, #324, 9th edition, VG/EX....................**$8.00**
Donald Duck & Santa Claus, #D27, C edition, VG/EX.**$18.00**
Donald Duck Christmas Tree, #460-13, 1993, VG/EX...**$3.00**
Donald Duck Toy Sailboat, #D40, 17th edition, VG/EX.**$4.00**
Emerald City of Oz, #151, A edition, VG....................**$13.00**
Farmyard Friends, #429, B edition, VG/EX...................**$9.00**

First Bible Stories, #198, A edition, VG/EX.................$22.00
Floating Bananas, #208-65, 1993, VG/EX......................$4.00
Four Little Kittens, #322, 6th edition, VG/EX...............$3.00
Gingerbread Man, #165, A edition, VG/EX..................$22.00
Golden Goose, #200, A edition, VG/EX.....................$14.00
Goodbye Tonsils, #327, 4th edition, VG/EX.................$3.00
Hansel & Gretel, #217, A edition, VG/EX..................$10.00
Hopalong Cassidy, #147, A edition, VG/EX................$15.00
Hymns, #34, C edition, VG/EX............................$12.00
I Have a Secret, #494, A edition, VG/EX..................$14.00
Jetsons, #500, B edition, VG.............................$15.00
Lady Lovely Locks, #107-57, A edition, VG/EX.............$8.00
Little Book, #583, 3rd edition, VG/EX.....................$5.00
Little Fat Policeman, #91, A edition, VG/EX..............$14.00
Little Red Riding Hood, #309-31, 14th edition, Les Grey illus-
    trations, VG/EX....................................$2.00
Love Bug, #D130, 4th edition, VG/EX......................$8.00
Magilla Gorilla, #547, A edition, VG/EX..................$12.00
Mary Poppins, #D113, B edition, VG/EX..................$10.00

**Mickey Mouse's Picnic,
#15, 1949, EX, $15.00.**

Mickey's Christmas Carol, #459-09, H edition, VG/EX..$2.00
Mister Ed, #483, A edition, VG/EX.......................$17.00
Mother Goose, #D36, B edition, VG......................$14.00
My Christmas Treasury, #144, 1st edition, VG/EX.........$6.00
Naughty Bunny, #377, A edition, VG/EX.................$26.00
New Baby, #41, D edition, VG/EX........................$30.00
Noah's Ark, A edition, 1952, VG.........................$6.00
Nursery Tales, #14, 3rd edition, blue spine, EX.........$18.00
Our Flag, #388, A edition, VG/EX........................$8.00
Pantaloon, #114, A edition, VG/EX......................$15.00
Pebbles Flintstone, #531, A edition, VG/EX..............$24.00
Peter Pan, #104-68, 1989, VG/EX.........................$4.00
Peter Rabbit, #505, 9th edition, VG/EX..................$7.00
Pinocchio, #D8, D edition, VG/EX.......................$18.00
Poky Little Puppy, #506, 41st edition, VG/EX.............$2.00
Prayers for Children, #301-9, X edition, red cover, VG/EX...$5.00
Rabbit & His Friends, #169, 4th edition, VG/EX...........$2.00
Raggedy Ann & the Cookie Snatcher, #107-3, 8th edition,
    VG/EX...$2.00
Rocky & His Friends, #408, 2nd edition, VG/EX.........$10.00
Rootie Kazootie Detective, #150, A edition, VG/EX...$22.00
Ruff & Reddy, #477, C edition, VG/EX..................$10.00
Seven Sneezes, #51, B edition, VG......................$12.00
Shy Little Kitten, #23, blue spine, VG/EX...............$18.00
Smokey Bear & the Campers, #423, 2nd edition, VG/EX...$10.00

So Big, #574, 5th edition, VG/EX........................$12.00
Tawny Scrawny Lion, #138, 11th edition, VG/EX.........$4.00
Three Bears, #47, 38th edition, VG/EX...................$8.00
Three Little Pigs, #D120, K edition, VG/EX.............$10.00
Tom & Jerry, #561, E edition, VG/EX.....................$6.00
Tom & Jerry Meet Little Quack, #181, 2nd edition, VG/EX.$5.00
Tweety, #141, 2nd edition, VG/EX........................$5.00
Uncle Mistletoe, #175, A edition, VG/EX................$15.00
Uncle Wiggily, #148, A edition, VG/EX..................$14.00
Velveteen Rabbit, #307-68, 1993, VG/EX..................$3.00
We Help Daddy, #305-57, A edition, VG/EX...............$8.00
Wheels, #141, A edition, VG/EX.........................$10.00
Whispering Rabbit, #312-03, A (50th Anniversary) edition,
    VG/EX...$7.00
Wild Kingdom, #151, 1st edition, VG/EX..................$8.00
Winnie the Pooh, #101-24, 2nd edition, VG/EX...........$3.00
Wonders of Nature, #293, B edition, VG/EX.............$12.00
Woody Woodpecker, #330, E edition, VG..................$5.00
Yogi Bear, #395, G edition, VG/EX.......................$7.00
Zorro, #D68, B edition, VG/EX..........................$13.00

Movie and TV Tie-Ins

Academy Award Winners, Ronald Bergan, Crescent, 1986, 1st
    edition, 312 pages, hardcover, w/dust jacket, M....$9.00
All-Time Movie Favorites, Joel W Finler, Norwalk, 1975, 1st
    American edition, 250+ photos, 189 pages, w/dust jack-
    et, NM...$12.00
Anastasia, Marcelle Maurette, Signet #S1356, 1956, VG.....$3.00
April Fools, William Johnston, Popular Library #60-8086,
    1969, VG...$1.50
Bachelor Party, Paddy Chayefsky, Signet #S1385, 1957,
    VG...$3.25
Basil Rathbone: His Life & Films, Michael Druxman, Barnes, 1975,
    1st edition, 359 pages, hardcover, w/dust jacket, VG..$50.00
Battle of the Bulge, Michael Tabor, Popular Library #PC1062,
    1965, VG+..$2.25

**Beverly Hillbillies,
Saga of Wildcat Creek,
Whitman, 1963, hard-
cover, EX, $10.00.**

Bonanza: Treachery Trail, Leonard Wibberley, Whitman,
    1968, hardcover, VG...............................$20.00
Boots & Saddles, Edgar Jean Bracco, Berkley #G-180, 1958,
    VG+..$4.00
Charles Chaplin: My Autobiography, Simon & Schuster,
    1964, 1st edition, 512 pages, hardcover, w/dust jacket,
    VG...$7.00

Complete Night of the Living Dead File, John Russo, Harmony Books trade paperback, 1985, EX.........**$15.00**

Count Dracula, Gerald Savory, Corgi #20135, 1982, 3rd printing, VG.................**$8.00**

DeMille: The Man & His Pictures, Gabe Essoe, Castle, 1970, 319 pages, hardcover, w/dust jacket, NM...............**$8.00**

Divine Garbo, Frederick Sands, Grosset Dunlap, 1979, 1st edition, 243 pages, hardcover, w/dust jacket, NM **$15.00**

Doctors, Michael Avallone, Popular Library #08115, 1970, VG.................**$2.00**

Don't Go Near the Water, William Brinkley, Signet #D1458, 1957, VG.................**$3.00**

Everybody Does It, James M Cain, Signet #759, 1949, G+..**$3.50**

Films of Bing Crosby, Robert Bookbinder, Citadel, 1977, 256 pages, hardcover, w/dust jacket, NM.................**$9.00**

Films of Laurel & Hardy, William K Everson, Citadel, 1972, 4th printing, 223 pages, NM.................**$7.50**

Films of Mae West, Jon Tuska, Citadel, 1973, 1st edition, w/dust jacket, VG.................**$20.00**

Films of Marilyn Monroe, Michael Conway, Citadel, 1964, 1st edition, 160 pages, hardcover, w/dust jacket, VG..**$20.00**

Fondas: A Hollywood Dynasty, Peter Collier, Putnam, 1991, 1st edition, 336 pages, hardcover, w/dust jacket, VG...**$10.00**

Frank Sinatra: My Father, Nancy Sinatra, Doubleday, 1985, 1st edition, 340 pages, hardcover, w/dust jacket, EX ..**$20.00**

Ghost & Mrs Muir, Alice Denham, Popular Library 60-2348, 1968, VG+.................**$1.75**

Grace of Monaco: An Interpretive Biography, Steve Englund, Doubleday, 1984, 392 pages, hardcover, w/dust jacket, NM **$10.00**

Harold Lloyd's World of Comedy, William Cahn, Duell Sloan, 1964, 1st edition, hardcover, w/dust jacket, NM ..**$25.00**

Hatful of Rain, Michael Vincente Gazzo, Signet #S1412, 1957, VG.................**$3.50**

High Wind in Jamaica, Richard Hughes, Signet #P2648, 1965, VG+.................**$3.50**

I'm All Right Jack, Alan Hackney, Signet #D1876, 1960, VG **$3.25**

Indiana Jones & the Temple of Doom, Les Martin, Random House #87040, 1984, EX.................**$3.00**

It Takes a Thief, Gil Brewer, Ace #37598, 1969, 1st edition, NM **$10.00**

James Dean, William Bast, Ballantine #180, 1956, 1st printing, VG **$12.50**

John Wayne & the Movies, Allen Eyles, Grosset Dunlap, 1978, 320 pages, hardcover, w/dust jacket, NM...**$15.00**

Judgment at Nuremberg, Aby Mann, #D2025, 1961, VG+ **$5.00**

Last Tango in Paris, Robert Alley, Dell #4653, 1973, VG **$4.00**

League of Gentlemen, John Boland, Beacon-Envoy #103, G+ **$3.00**

Letters to Star Trek, Susan Sackett, Ballantine #25522, 1977, NM **$10.00**

Man Who Shot Liberty Valance, JW Bellah, Perma #M4238, NM.................**$12.00**

Many-Splendored Thing, Han Suyin, Signet #D1183, 1955, 2nd printing, VG+.................**$3.00**

Markham, Lawrence Block, Belmont #236, 1st edition, NM.................**$20.00**

Marlene: The Life of Marlene Dietrich, Charles Higham, Norton, 1977, 1st edition, photos, hardcover, w/dust jacket, EX.................**$8.00**

Meet Me in St Louis, Sally Benson, Bantam #15, 1945, EX **$9.00**

My Fair Lady, Alan Jay Lerner, Signet #S1551, 1958, VG+.................**$4.00**

Natalie: A Memoir by Her Sister, Lana Wood, Putnam's, 1984, 1st edition, 240 pages, hardcover, w/dust jacket, NM.......**$8.00**

Night Gallery, Rod Serling, Bantam #S7160, 1971, VG .**$8.00**

Night of the Iguana, Tennessee Williams, Signet #D2481, 1964, VG.................**$2.00**

Not With My Wife You Don't, Evan Lee Heyman, Popular Library #60-2143, 1966, VG+.................**$2.00**

Picture of Dorian Gray, Oscar Wilde, Tower, 1945, 4th printing, w/dust jacket, VG.................**$20.00**

Return of Tarzan, Edgar Rice Burroughs, Ballantine #U-2002, 1967, 3rd printing, VG.................**$6.00**

Russians Are Coming, the Russians Are Coming, Peter Benchley, Popular Library #60-8020, VG+ **$2.25**

Sierra Baron, TW Blackburn, Bantam #1798, VG.........**$4.50**

Some Came Running, James Jones, Signet #T1637, 1958, VG+ **$5.00**

Some Like It Hot, Wilder & Diamond, Signet #S1656, 1959, Marilyn Monroe, VG.................**$10.00**

Spock Must Die, James Blish, Bantam #08075, 1972, 11th printing, VG+.................**$5.00**

Star Trek #5, James Blish, Bantam #S7300, 1972, 1st edition, NM.................**$10.00**

Star Trek II: The Wrath of Khan, Richard Anobile, Pocket #45912, 1982, 1st printing, VG.................**$5.00**

Strange Report, John Burke, Lancer #73219, 1970, VG.**$7.50**

Streetcar Named Desire, Tennessee Williams, Signet #917, 1953, 6th printing, VG.................**$1.50**

Sweet Bird of Youth, Tennessee Williams, Signet #D2121, 1962, VG.................**$3.00**

Tammy Tell Me True, Cid Ricketts Sumner, Popular Library #50-439, VG+.................**$1.75**

Tarzan & the Leopard Men, Edgar Rice Burroughs, New English Library #1132, 1967, 3rd printing, VG........**$6.00**

Tea & Sympathy, Robert Anderson, Signet #1343, 1956, 3rd printing, VG+.................**$2.00**

Teahouse of the August Moon, Vern Sneider, Signet #S1348, VG.................**$2.75**

Thinking Machine Affair, Joel Bernard, Ace #51704, VG ..**$9.00**

Twilight Zone the Movie, Robert Bloch, Warner #30840, 1st edition, VG.................**$2.00**

Ugliest Girl in Town, Burt Hirschfeld, Popular Library #60-2340, 1968, VG.................**$2.00**

Vintage Science Fiction Films 1896-1949, Michael Benson, McFarland, 1985, 1st edition, 219 pages, hardcover, NM.................**$15.00**

We Were Strangers, Robert Sylvester, Signet #716, 1949, VG+.................**$7.50**

What's New Pussycat?, Marvin H Albert, Dell #9461, VG .**$5.00**

Why Me? The Sammy Davis Jr Story, Sammy Davis, 1989, 1st edition, 374 pages, hardcover, w/dust jacket, EX ..**$10.00**

Wicked Dreams of Paula Schultz, Alton Harsh, Popular Library #60-8057, 1968, VG+.................**$3.00**

Will Rogers in Hollywood, Bryan Sterling, Crown, 1984, 1st edition, 182 pages, hardcover, w/dust jacket, EX ..**$12.00**

Tell-A-Tale Books

Bambi, Whitman #2541, 1972, VG/EX............................**$4.00**
Bible Stories, Whitman #828, 1947, Story Hour series, VG/EX...**$7.00**
Cinderella, Whitman #22, 1972, VG/EX **$3.00**
Clip Clop, Whitman #2569, 1958, VG/EX **$4.00**
Daffy Duck, Whitman #2453-36, 1977, VG/EX..............**$5.00**
Ernie the Cave King, Whitman #2604, 1975, VG/EX.....**$5.00**
I Like To See, Whitman #2422, 1973, VG/EX **$3.00**
Johnny Appleseed, Whitman #2544, VG/EX.................**$5.00**
Lady, Whitman #2552, 1954, VG/EX **$7.00**
Little Red Hen, Whitman #2651, VG/EX **$5.00**
Magic Zoo, Whitman #2474-32, 1972, VG/EX **$4.00**
Mother Goose, Whitman #2638, 1958, VG/EX **$6.00**
Mr Jolly, Whitman #868, 1948, VG **$4.00**
Pete's Dragon, Whitman #2428-3, 1977, VG/EX...........**$3.00**
Polka Dots Tots, Whitman #864, 1946, VG/EX **$10.00**
Sleepy Puppy, Whitman #2400, 1961, VG/EX **$4.00**
Three Bears, #2551, 1955, VG/EX **$10.00**
Tweety & Sylvester at the Farm, Whitman #2642, 1978, VG/EX..**$3.00**

Bottle Openers

A figural bottle opener is one where the cap lifter is an actual feature of the subject being portrayed — for instance, the bill of a pelican or the mouth of a four-eyed man. Most are made of painted cast iron or aluminum; others were chrome or brass plated. Some of the major bottle-opener producers were Wilton, John Wright, L&L, and Gadzik. They have been reproduced, so beware of any examples with 'new' paint. Condition of the paint is an important consideration when it comes to evaluating an opener.

For more information, read *Figural Bottle Openers, Identification Guide*, by the Figural Bottle Opener Collectors. Number codes in our descriptions correlate with their book.

Advisor: Charlie Reynolds (See Directory, Bottle Openers)

Club: Figural Bottle Opener Collectors
Linda Fitzsimmons
9697 Gwynn Park Dr., Ellicott City, MD 21043; 301-465-9296

Newsletter: *Just for Openers*
John Stanley
3712 Sunningdale Way, Durham, NC 27707-5684; 919-419-1546. Quarterly newsletter covers all types of bottle openers and corkscrews

Alligator, F-136, cast iron, multicolor paint, EX...........**$85.00**
Alligator, F-137, pot metal, worn gold paint................**$15.00**
Auto Jack, F-211, chrome, NM, from $35 to **$45.00**
Bear, F-426, cast iron, repainted, EX.........................**$150.00**
Beer Drinker, F-406, CI, NM original paint, wall mount ..**$600.00**

Caddy, F-44, painted cast iron, $430.00; brass, $300.00. (Photo courtesy Charlie Reynolds)

Canada goose, F-105, cast iron, multicolor paint, EX, from $65 to...**$75.00**
Clown, F-417, brass, EX **$55.00**
Cowboy & Signpost, F-14, cast iron, multicolor paint, EX.**$130.00**
Cowboy w/Guitar, G-27, cast iron, EX original paint **$110.00**
Donkey, F-60, cast iron, EX original paint....................**$32.00**
Elephant, F-49, cast iron, pink paint, EX **$45.00**
False teeth, F-420, cast iron, EX original paint............**$80.00**
Fish, F-154, aluminum, EX.......................................**$25.00**
Fish, F-164, abalone shell, EX...................................**$50.00**
Fisherman, F-30, brass...**$45.00**
Hanging Drunk, F-415, cast iron, EX original paint....**$80.00**
Lamppost Drunk, F-1, leg up, cast iron, muticolor paint, EX...**$20.00**
Lamppost Drunk, F-2A, bronze, NM **$25.00**
Leg, F-206, brass **$38.00**
Lobster, F-168, brass **$22.00**
Lobster, F-169, white metal, EX.................................**$45.00**
Lock, F-214, brass **$48.00**
Monkey, F-89A, brass, 2½" **$42.00**
Nude, F-171, brass, Russwood, 1946..........................**$55.00**
Nude, F-172, standing w/wreath over head, brass, EX details...**$45.00**
Palm Tree Drunk, F-19, brimmed hat, cast iron, multicolor paint, EX...**$60.00**
Pelican, F-129, cast iron, bright multicolor paint **$65.00**
Pheasant, F-104, aluminum **$20.00**
Pheasant, F-104, CI, EX original paint **$225.00**
Pretzel, F-230, aluminum, EX paint **$42.50**
Sea Gull, F-123, cast iron, bright 3-color paint............**$60.00**
Shoe, F-209, aluminum, no paint, 3¾" **$100.00**
Signpost Drunk, F-11, cast iron, multicolor paint, EX....**$25.00**
Skunk, F-92, cast iron, EX original paint **$165.00**
Streetwalker, F-5, aluminum, NM original paint, 4½" ...**$160.00**
Trout, F-159, cast iron, multicolor paint, EX **$120.00**
4-Eyed Man, F-413, cast iron, EX original paint, from $60 to **$70.00**
4-Eyed Man, F-414, cast iron, wall mount, EX **$50.00**

Boyd Crystal Art Glass

After the Degenhart glass studio closed (see the Degenhart section for information), it was bought out by the Boyd family, who added many of their own designs to the molds they acquired from the Degenharts and other defunct glasshouses. They are located in Cambridge, Ohio, and the glass they've been pressing in the more than 225 colors they've developed since they opened in 1978 is marked with their 'B in diamond' logo. Since 1988, a line has been added under the diamond. All the work is done by hand, and each piece is made in a selected color in limited amounts — a production run lasts only about six weeks or less. Items in satin glass or an exceptional slag are expecially collectible, so are those with hand-painted details.

Note: An 'R' in the following lines indicates a color or item that has been retired.

Advisor: Joyce Pringle (See Directory, Boyd)

Club: Boyd's Art Glass Collectors Guild
P.O. Box 52, Hatboro, PA 19040-0052

Airplane, Cobalt	$23.00
Airplane, Mirage	$17.50
Angel, Capri Blue	$18.00
Angel, Vaseline (R)	$27.50
Bear, Chocolate	$8.00
Bear, Yellow	$10.00
Bingo (deer), Caramel	$8.00
Bird Shaker, Forest Green	$7.00
Bird Shaker, Tomato Creme Slag	$7.00
Bow Slipper, Caramel	$6.00
Brian Bunny, Kumquat (R)	$9.00
Candy Mini Carousel Horse, Maverick Blue	$9.00
Chick Salt, Bermuda	$28.50
Chick Salt, Crystal Carnival	$8.50
Chick Salt, Spinnaker Blue Carnival	$10.50
Chick Salt, Sunkist Carnival	$9.00
Chicken Dish, Ruby Mist, 2½"	$30.00
Colonial Doll, Candyland (R)	$20.00
Colonial Doll, Caramel	$12.00
Colonial Doll, Milk White	$12.00
Duckling, Kumquat	$5.00
Elephant Head Toothpick, Capri Blue	$8.00
Elephant Head Toothpick, Green Whisper	$12.00
Elephant Head Toothpick, Willow Blue	$14.00
Gypsy Pot, Classic Black	$7.00
Hand Dish, Chocolate Carnival	$6.50
Hand Dish, Pippin Green	$9.50
Hen on Nest, Mint Julep, 5"	$16.00
JB Scotty, Confetti (R)	$38.50
JB Scotty, Cornsilk (R)	$9.00
JB Scotty, Green Bouquet, special club piece (R)	$25.00
JB Scotty, Sunburst	$17.50
Jennifer Doll, Purple Frost Carnival	$9.25
Jeremy Frog, Green Bouquet	$8.50
Joey the Horse, Cobalt Carnival	$40.00
Lamb Dish, Ruby Mist, 2½"	$30.00
Louise Doll, Crystal (R)	$20.00
Louise Doll, Ice Blue	$36.50
Louise Doll, Olde Ivory (R)	$12.50
Louise Doll, Purple Slag	$12.00
Louise Doll Bell, Jadite, 1989	$16.00

Marguerite Doll, Teal (R)	$16.00
Nancy Doll, Cobalt	$12.50
Nancy Doll, Spring Sunrise	$8.50
Parlour Pup, Mulberry Mist	$10.00
Pooch, Buttercup Slag	$24.00
Rex Dinosaur, Aqua Diamond	$11.00
Robin, Golden Delight, 5"	$15.00
Swan, Amberina, Cambridge mold, 4"	$35.00
Swan, Blue Slag, Cambridge mold, 5"	$45.00
Swan, Green Slag, Cambridge mold, 5"	$55.00
Swan, Vaseline, open back, 4"	$15.00
Taffy Carousel Horse, Spring Surprise	$16.50
Tractor, Heather Gray (R)	$11.00
Train set, hand painted, Classic Black Satin, Christmas limited edition	$125.00
Train set, Plum Carnival, 6-pc	$65.00
Woodchuck, Bermuda Slag	$15.00
Zak the Elephant, Crown Tuscan	$15.00
Zak the Elephant, Flame	$35.00
Zak the Elephant, Lilac	$10.00

Zak the Elephant, Pippin Green (R), $12.50.

Boyd's Bears and Friends

In 1992 Gary Lowenthal began designing cold-cast sculptural interpretations of his now-famous bears, tabbies, moose, etc. These sculptures are extraordinary in detail and highly sought after by collectors. For more information, color photos, and an extensive listing of current values, we recommend *Rosie's Secondary Market Price Guide to Boyd's Bears and Friends* by Rosie Wells.

Values are given for examples in mint condition and retaining their original boxes.

Advisor: Rosie Wells (See Directory Boyd's Bears)

Bearstone, 1993, Victoria, 1E/2004	$225.00
Bearstone, 1994, Bailey, 2E/2020-09	$70.00
Bearstone, 1994, Charlotte & Bebe, 1E/229	$110.00
Bearstone, 1994, Elgin, 2E/2236	$50.00
Bearstone, 1994, Grenville & Beatrice, 2E/2016	$65.00
Bearstone, 1994, Justin & M Harrison, 1E/2015	$95.00
Dollstones, 1996, Ashley w/Christie, 2E/3506	$30.00
Dollstones, 1996, Betsy w/Edmund, 1E/3503	$60.00

Dollstones, 1996, Courtney w/Phoebe, 1E/3512 ....**$65.00**
Dollstones, 1996, Jennifer w/Priscilla, Prem Ed/3500 ...**$140.00**
Folkstones, 1994, Nicholai, 1E/2800 ....**$75.00**
Folkstones, 1994, Slik Nick, 1E/2803 ....**$55.00**
Folkstones, 1996, Angel of Love, 3E/2821 ....**$55.00**
Folkstones, 1996, Egon, 2E/2837 ....**$25.00**
Folkstones, 1996, St Nick, 1E/2808 ....**$40.00**

Brastoff, Sascha

When Sascha Brastoff died on February 4, 1993, the world lost a Renaissance man. His talent spanned the globe, and his life touched people of all walks of life. In 1953 Sascha's friend, Nelson Rockefeller, built Sascha a pottery complex on Olympic Boulevard in Los Angeles, California. Sascha's talents were so diversified that he could work in almost any medium, whether resins, textiles, paintings, or enamels. He designed and made dinnerware as well as art-ware and jewelry.

In the beginning (1947–1952), he marked his wares simply 'Sascha B.' or 'Sascha Brastoff,' with his full signature. Today it matters little what item you're evaluating; if it has a full signature, it's worth much more than one without. After 1952 and before 1962, employees marked pieces 'Sascha B.' (on the top side), and these items almost always carried a Chanticleer backstamp in gold. This Chanticleer mark is confusing to collectors today, since it incorporates the full signature below the rooster. Sellers often make the mistake of pricing Chanticleer-marked items as though they were a full-signature Brastoff. The Chanticleer is not on the pieces with Sascha's full signature. The 'Sascha B.' mark with the 'R' in a circle was used on later pieces made after 1962.

During his career, Sascha created hand-painted china with names such as La Jolla, Allegro, Night Song, and Roman Coin. A pottery dinnerware line called Surf Ballet was made in pink, blue, and yellow (there were also others), dipped in real gold or platinum to produce a marbelized swirl effect. Pink or blue with platinum are the most common glazes seen in Surf Ballet; any of the other combinations are more difficult to find. Artwork bore different patterns such as Star Steed, a leaping fantasy horse, and Rooftops, a series of houses where the roofs were predominant. In just the last year, the Merbaby (a child-like mermaid) pattern has become increasingly popular, even though it is hard to find. However, at this point, rarity has not yet pushed values as high as they will probably go in the near future.

Enamel and resin pieces are important to the Brastoff history; both are evident to the diverse talent of the man. Textiles were another facet of Sascha's abilities. One could never say of him that he merely 'dabbled' in any medium. Whatever interest he chose, he would be literally consumed whenever an idea would strike him, even in his later years when he worked with holograms.

For more information we recommend *The Collector's Encyclopedia of California Pottery* by Jack Chipman and *The Collector's Encyclopedia of Sascha Brastoff* by Steve Conti, A. DeWayne Bethany, and Bill Seay both published by Collector Books.

Advisor: Susan Cox (See Directory, California Pottery)

Ashtray, Alaska, hooded, #H1.............................**$55.00**
Ashtray, Aztec or Mayan design, #H8 ....**$85.00**
Ashtray, Chi Chi Birds, #07, 10".........................**$80.00**
Ashtray, grapes, enamel **$45.00**
Ashtray, Jewel Bird design, #F6, personalized to RM Francis, commercial signature, 12" **$100.00**
Ashtray, Poodle, #H1, 5" **$75.00**
Bowl, enamel green w/white flowers, metal pedestal...**$55.00**
Bowl, Minos, 9x6"..**$125.00**
Bowl, salad; Surf Ballet, blue & platinum, +6 sm bowls, 7-pc...**$175.00**
Bowl, white shell, Aztec or Mayan........................**$95.00**
Box, free-form, Jewel Bird, w/lid, 7" **$60.00**
Cache pot, Early Fish, scalloped rim, 4" **$75.00**
Candle holders, blue-green diamond resin, 6", pr **$55.00**
Candy dish, Rooftops, 5½x5½" **$40.00**
Dish, Aztec or Mayan, #C2, 7"............................**$45.00**
Dish, free-form, Mosaic, fish pattern, 12" **$125.00**
Dish, sgraffito Mayan design on matt white, unsigned, 7x7" **$500.00**
Figurine, rooster, matt white pebble finish, 17" **$290.00**
Mug, Alaska, igloo, #077, marked Sascha B **$35.00**
Obelisk w/lid, blue & yellow stripes, full signature, 20".**$800.00**
Plate, abstract rooster w/gold, full signature, dated 1952, 10" **$750.00**
Plate, African dancer, full signature, 11" **$450.00**
Plate, free-form w/court jester, full signature, 10".....**$900.00**
Plate, Merbaby, 9"..**$65.00**
Platter, sgraffito fish, 12x19"...........................**$400.00**
Platter, Surf Ballet, 3-compartment, pink & gold, 21".**$80.00**
Switch plate, lion's head, dull brass finish, marked Sascha in mold, 9½"..**$115.00**
Tankard, Alaska, totem, early, signed Sascha B..........**$65.00**
Tile, Rooftops, created as fabric design, unsigned, 6x6", set of 3 ....**$150.00**
Tray, Chi Chi Birds, #052, 15"...........................**$100.00**
Tray, fish design & shape, 6½" dia **$85.00**

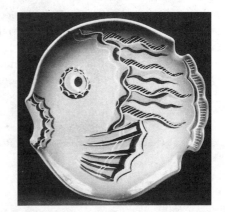

Tray, pink and blue fish form with brown and white details, 8", $95.00. (Photo courtesy Susan Cox)

Vase, Provincial Rooster, #F20, faux raku background, 5"...**$350.00**
Vase, Star Steed design, #F21, 7" **$95.00**

Brayton Laguna

Durlin E. Brayton, a graduate of the Chicago Art Institute, was at first inclined toward architecture and design. But in 1927, he installed a kiln in his Laguna, California, home and turned to pottery. He wheel turned plates, dinnerware, vases, and so on, then created his own glazes, giving them appetizing names such as purple eggplant and lettuce green. Other glazes he used were gold, turquoise, burnt orange, burgundy, and a combination of white and silky black.

When he married Ellen (Webb) Webster Grieve a short time later, it soon became obvious that in every sense of the word, they were meant for each other. Webb was a talented woman with a propensity for color combinations and decorating by hand. The couple hired many top artists to create or expand various lines for their business. Andy Anderson created comical figures such as the hillbilly shotgun wedding group; jockey on horseback; and the purple cow, bull, and calf family. Though these items are plentiful in some color combinations, they were also made in harder-to-find colors, providing a challenge for today's collectors.

Peter Ganine created the giant chessmen; the Blackamoors and fighting cocks were the inspiration of Ruth Peabody; Lietta Helen Dodd was responsible for many of the children figurines which are so popular today. It seems that Durlin and Webb had a talent for choosing the right artists for the products that ultimately made Brayton Pottery successful.

Walt Disney Studios arranged for Brayton to make a line of figurines that would portray the entire array of Disney characters including Donald Duck, Pluto, Mickey and Minnie Mouse, Bambi, Figaro, and all the others.

Their Webton Ware is just now beginning to draw the interest of many collectors. (The name was erroneously reported in an early publication as Welton Ware, probably because the mark was sometimes obscure.) Backgrounds are white with blue, maroon, and yellow decorations in the forms of leaves, flowers, or as is sometimes the case, people engaged in various activities such as planting seeds, hoeing, shoveling, etc.

Webb Brayton died in 1948 and Durlin died just three years later. Brayton employees attempted to keep the business operating, but when the market became flooded with foreign imports, it soon became evident that it was doomed. The plant closed in 1968, and by 1970 the property had been sold.

For further study, read *The Collector's Encyclopedia of California Pottery* by Jack Chipman (Collector Books).

Advisor: Susan Cox (See Directory, California Pottery)

Ashtray, plain w/indented center, 1 rest, 4¼" dia.......**$20.00**
Bookends, clown, Circus series, 6x4¾" L, pr...........**$250.00**
Bowl, burgundy, wavy lip, sm.....................................**$55.00**
Bowl, fern green glaze, Calasia pattern, #A15, oval, 2¼x14x11½"...**$60.00**
Candle holder, Blackamoor, seated, multicolor w/gold trim, 5"...**$85.00**
Candle holder, round, plain woodtone glaze, Model No D-8, 3½x4½" dia **$18.00**

Figurine, African-American babies, 4¼", pr..............**$155.00**

Figurine, Ann, Childhood series, 4", $135.00. (Photo courtesy Susan Cox)

Figurine, Butch, boy standing w/present under each arm, short pants w/suspenders, 7½"..............................**$85.00**
Figurine, cat, lying down, head up, yellow body w/brown trim, green eyes, stamped Copyright 1941, 4¼x6½".........**$55.00**
Figurine, circus ringmaster w/4 horses, 5-pc.............**$230.00**
Figurine, Dorothy, girl w/hands at sides, pigtails w/tied ribbons, Childhood series, 4" **$105.00**
Figurine, duck, textured bisque body, glossy green face, marked Model No 4138, 5x5½" **$65.00**
Figurine, Dweedle Dee, non-Disney, 3" **$28.00**
Figurine, elephant, standing, upturned trunk, Circus series, 7", from $110 to **$135.00**
Figurine, Ellen, standing, pigtails & hat, arms bent & palms forward, Childhood series, 7¼" **$90.00**

Figurine, Gay '90s Honeymoon, 9", from $100.00 to $125.00.

Figurine, Gay Nineties, lady holding up dress w/1 hand & umbrella in other, ruffled skirt, ca 1930, 9½".....**$115.00**
Figurine, man standing & woman sitting w/baby, Wedding series, 1-pc **$150.00**
Figurine, Millie, bent over w/legs apart & head between legs, Childhood series, 3¾" **$155.00**
Figurine, monkey, male & female, woodtone w/crackle face, 12", pr...**$325.00**
Figurine, Oriental girl w/baby on back **$90.00**
Figurine, owl, woodtone w/white crackle face, 6" **$45.00**
Figurine, Pat, standing, freckled face w/hat, short dress, holds doll in back between legs, Childhood series, 7"....**$85.00**
Figurine, peacock, #41-47, matt black w/red crest & wings, 17"...**$125.00**

Figurine, peacock, white body w/blue & white feathers, green base, 5x5".....................................**$60.00**

Figurine, Petunia, African-American girl w/basket of flowers, Childhood series, 6¼" **$155.00**

Figurine, piano player, piano & singer, 3-pc.............**$750.00**

Figurine, Pluto, howling, Walt Disney, 6", from $175 to ..**$200.00**

Figurine, rooster, teal & gold, 14½" **$90.00**

Figurine, Sambo, standing w/chicken under arm, Childhood series, 7½" **$155.00**

Figurine, toucan, polychrome high glaze, in-mold marks, 1950s-60s, 9" **$125.00**

Figurine, Weezy, from $100 to....................................**$125.00**

Figurine, 3 Blackamoors, standing w/bowl, polychrome, 1-pc, 8" **$140.00**

Figurines, Bride & Groom, woman standing, man seated, 8" largest, pr..**$100.00**

Figurines, cow, calf, bull, purple, 3-pc family, from $350 to..**$450.00**

Figurines, dice players, African-American boys on hands & knees, 4¾" tallest, set of 3 ....**$225.00**

Planter, Blackamoor, w/holder, pr...............................**$75.00**

Planter, Dutch girl pushing cart, 8x8" **$25.00**

Planter, peasant woman figural, 8".................................**$65.00**

Planter, woman w/baskets...**$100.00**

Plate, eggplant glaze, early, 9" dia **$40.00**

Salt & pepper shakers, clown & dog, Circus series, pr, from $225 to..**$250.00**

Salt & pepper shakers, clowns, white body, black shoes, blue ruffles at ankles, wrist & collar, 6½", pr **$100.00**

Salt & pepper shakers, Gingham Dog & Calico Cat, pr...**$75.00**

Salt & pepper shakers, Mammy & chef, green, pr....**$150.00**

Salt & pepper shakers, Swedish children, pr **$125.00**

Sugar bowl & creamer, wheelbarrow & watering can shape, 3¼", pr...**$37.00**

Vase, slightly bulbous body w/feather design, round foot w/raised circle design, Calasia pattern, 7" **$75.00**

Wall plaque, woman w/arms above head, Webton Ware mark, 13½"...**$175.00**

Breweriana

'Breweriana' is simply a term used by collectors to refer to items (usually freebies) given away by breweries to advertise their products. Some people prefer pre-prohibition era bottles, pocket mirrors, foam scrapers, etched and enameled glasses, mugs, steins, playing cards, postcards, pin-back buttons, and the like; but many collectors like the more available items from the past few decades as well. Some specialize either in breweries from a particular state, specific items such as foam scrapers (used to clean the foam off the top of glasses or pitchers of beer), or they might limit their buying to just one brewery.

The books we recommend for this area of collecting are *Back Bar Breweriana* by George J. Baley and *Huxford's Collectible Advertising* (Collector Books).

See also Beer Cans.

Club: National Association of Breweriana Advertising
Robert E. Jaeger, Executive Secretary

2343 Met-To-We Ln., Wauwatosa, WI 53226, 414-257-0158; Annual dues: $20 US, $30 Canada, $40 overseas; with paid membership receive Membership Directory and certificate as well as two recent issues of *Breweriana Collector*

Ashtray, Cambden Beer, red painted logo on clear glass....**$8.00**

Bottle opener, Barbarossa Beer, wooden bottle shape w/foil label, 1950s, 4½x1"..**$20.00**

Calendar, Black Label Beer, 1969, complete, 12x5½", NM, $60.00.

Clock, Busch, plastic, lights up, working, dated Jan 3, 1992, 4x13x19" **$16.00**

Clock, Duboise Budweiser, reverse-painted face, working, 1950s, 4x19" **$125.00**

Clock, Gibbons, Is Good Anytime, plastic, working, 1950s, 3x14", EX...**$45.00**

Coaster, Burgh Brau, black & gold logo, pressed paper, 4" dia, NM **$17.50**

Coaster, Busch, red & green logo, pressed paper, 3x3½", NM **$10.00**

Coaster, Elk Head, 3-color logo, pressed paper, 4" dia, EX **$7.00**

Display, Blatz Beer, man with bottle torso carries pitcher on tray, round base, plastic, 1960, 12", M, $40.00.

Display, Goldcrest 51 Beer, cardboard bottle topper, late 1950s, 10x7"...**$5.00**

Door push, Pabst Blue Ribbon Beer, painted metal, 4x9", VG **$55.00**

Foam scraper, Ballantine Ale-Beer, clear blue, 1-sided, light wear **$10.00**

Foam scraper, Hampden Mild Ale, plastic, light wear ..**$25.00**

Foam scraper, Hull's Ale-Beer, yellow marbled, beveled edges, EX..**$25.00**

Foam scraper, Pickwick Ale, clear plastic, 2-sided......**$35.00**

Foam scraper holder, Crown Premium Lager Beer, plastic, 1950s..**$25.00**

Foam scraper holder, Krueger Beer, plastic, 6", EX **$50.00**

Glass, Falstaff, red & white painted label on clear glass, 3½"..**$15.00**

Glass, Freestate Beer, blue & red painted label on clear glass, 5½"..**$16.00**

Glass, Gennessee Beer & Ale, etched logo 1 side on clear glass, 4½" **$29.00**

Glass, Gold Coast Pale Beer, blue & red painted label on clear glass, 4¾" **$17.00**

Glass, Golden Glow XXX Beer, red painted label on clear glass, 4½", NM **$15.00**

Glass, Gunther's Beer, red painted label (scuffed) on clear glass, 5½"..**$8.00**

Glass, Hensler Beer, red painted label on milk glass, 4¼", NM **$12.00**

Glass, Huber Premium Beer, red painted label on clear glass, 5½" **$10.00**

Glass, National Premium Beer, blue painted label on clear glass, 5½" **$10.00**

Glass, pilsner; Atlantic Premium Beer, painted label on clear glass, 5½" **$12.00**

Glass, pilsner; Hanley Pilsner, 4-color painted label on clear glass, 6½" **$12.00**

Glass, pilsner; Matt's Premium Beer, red painted label on clear glass, 8½" **$15.00**

Globe, Schlitz Beer, plastic, revolves, wall mounted, lights up, 1960s, 16" dia, EX **$15.00**

Jug, Gunther Premium Beer, 3-color painted label on clear glass, 8½" **$25.00**

Letterhead, Anheuser-Busch, To Shareholders, 1966, 8½x11" **$10.00**

Letterhead, Leisey Brewing Co, factory scene, 1949, 8½x11" **$20.00**

Lighter, O'Keefe-Ale, Brynnite, 2-sided, 2x2", EX........**$20.00**

Measuring stick/ruler, Eilert's Supreme Lager, 6x1"....**$18.00**

Menu cover, Hull's Beer & Ale, w/insert, 1950s, 8½x11", unused **$3.00**

Mirror, Wiedemann Fien Beer, reverse-painted glass, 1981, 14x20" **$5.00**

Mug, Iroquois Beer & Ale, 3-color painted label on glass, 6"..**$10.00**

Mug, Lowenbrau, lion logo, ceramic, Coors USA on bottom, 4½"..**$7.00**

Mug, Meister Brau Lite, blue & gold painted label on glass, 5"..**$12.00**

Mug, Schlitz Brewing, 125th Anniversary, ceramic, Ceramarte, 1974, 7½"..**$70.00**

Necktie, Schlitz Beer, 1950s, NM **$20.00**

Pitcher, Blackberry Julep, clear glass, 5x5" **$5.00**

Playing cards, Ballantine Beer, 3-ring red & yellow design on backs, 1960s, complete, MIB **$22.50**

Poster, Acme Beer, colorful western scene, 1950s, 19x25", EX **$50.00**

Poster w/calendar, Horlacher Brewing Co, paper w/poor wooden frame, complete, 20x38", VG **$30.00**

Print, Reingold Beer, Miss Reingold, oil on canvas, brass plaque on wooden frame, 1958, 20x16" **$35.00**

Sign, Ambassador Beer, plastic stein w/tin plate for hanging on back, 1960s, 15x8", EX................................**$20.00**

Sign, Ballantine Draught Beer, pressed wood, 1951, 14x10", G **$25.00**

Sign, Budweiser, red neon, 11x18", w/plastic base **$55.00**

Sign, Budweiser King of Beer, lighted wall plaque, early 1960s, 19x14", EX..**$55.00**

Sign, Budweiser King of Beers, lights up, wall mounted, 1970s, 14x14x14", EX..**$50.00**

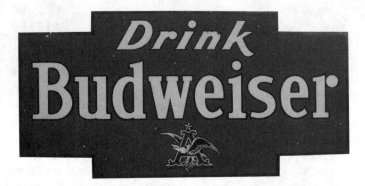

Sign, Budweiser, porcelain, double-sided, white on red, 36x72", EX, $110.00.

Sign, Old Milwaukee Beer, Tastes Like Draught Beer, reverse-painted glass, 1940s, replaced frame, 12x15"..........**$50.00**

Sign, Old Shay Ale, It's Like Champagne, cardboard, 1950s, 6x11", EX **$20.00**

Sign, Pabst Blue Ribbon Beer, reverse-painted glass w/cardboard, stands up, 1950s, 12x9", VG **$25.00**

Sign, Schaefer Beer, plastic w/heavy metal back, lights up, 1950s, 16" dia, EX **$70.00**

Sign, Schlitz, Take Home...Half Quarts, shows 16-oz cans, tin on cardboard, self standing, 1956, 13x16", EX **$25.00**

Sign, Schmidt's, plastic, lights up, 1980, 13x20", NM **$5.00**

Sign, Schmidt's of Philadelphia, wildlife scene, cardboard, 1970s, 20x14"..**$25.00**

Sign, Stroh's Beer, plastic, lights up, 1980s, 10x23x5", EX...**$15.00**

Sign, Stroh's Fire-Brewed Beer, plastic, lights up, 1970s, 19x11", EX **$12.00**

Sign/clock, Falstaff Beer, composite back-bar display, lights up, working, 1980s, 11x7x3"................................**$10.00**

Stein, Budweiser, sports scenes, ceramic, Ceramarte, 1980, 7½", MIB..**$10.00**

Tap handle, Walter's Premium Draft Beer, 1960s, EX.**$32.00**

Tap knob, Cooper's Old Bohemian, plastic w/metal insert, EX..**$32.00**

Tap knob, Duquesne, plastic, EX................................**$20.00**

Tip tray, Hamm's Beer, cartoon bear, 1981, NM **$10.00**

Tip tray, Lone Star Beer, Our Saloon Serves, dated 1981, 3½", NM..**$5.00**

Tip tray, Simon Pure Beer, center logo, early 1980s, NM ..**$5.00**

Token, Falstaff Beer, Golden Anniversary, 1903-53, M in 3x2½" plastic case..**$4.00**

Tray, Cambden Beer, It's Cambden Beer song, 1953, 12" dia, EX..**$16.00**

Tray, Falls City Lager Beer, 70th Anniversary, 1975, 12" dia, EX..**$10.00**

Tray, Gettelman Milwaukee Beer, logo on white, 1940s, 12" dia, NM......................................**$70.00**

Tray, Narragansett Lager & Ale, Dr Suess art, 1960, NM ...**$125.00**

Tray, Trenton Old Stock Beer, 12" dia, EX **$50.00**

Breyer Horses

Breyer horses have been popular children's playthings since they were introduced in 1952, and you'll see several at any large flea market. Garage sales are good sources as well. The earlier horses had a glossy finish, but after 1968 a matt finish came into use. You'll find smaller domestic animals too. They are evaluated by condition, rarity, and desirability; some of the better examples may be worth a minimum of $150.00.

For more information and listings, see *Schroeder's Collectible Toys, Antique to Modern* (Collector Books) and *Breyer Animal Collector's Guide* by Felicia Browell. Our advisor is the author of a continually updated value guide as well as several articles for *The Model Horse Gazette* on model collecting, values, and care.

Advisor: Carol Karbowiak Gilbert (See Directory, Breyer Horses)

Action Stock Horse Foal, bay pinto, 1984-86, Traditional scale...**$20.00**

American Saddlebred, red chestnut, 1985-88, Classic scale...**$15.00**

Andalusian Mare, dapple gray, 1979-93, Classic scale ..**$15.00**

Appaloosa Gelding, #97, Traditional scale, 1971–80, $35.00. (Photo courtesy Carol Karbowiak Gilbert)

Appaloosa Performance Horse, 1974-80, Traditional scale...**$40.00**

Arabian Foal (Proud), glossy alabaster, 1956-60, Traditional scale...**$40.00**

Arabian Mare, red bay, 1992-94, Classic scale............**$15.00**

Arabian Stallion, alabaster, 1975-81, Stablemates Saddle Club scale...**$13.00**

Arabian Stallion, alabaster, 1989-94, Little Bit scale **$10.00**

Arabian Stallion (Proud), dapple rose gray, 1991-94, Traditional scale...**$40.00**

Belgian, woodgrain, 1964-65, Traditional scale......**$1,000.00**

Bucking Bronco, bay, 1967-70, Classic scale............**$100.00**

Buckshot, Cody, 1995, Traditional scale **$25.00**

Clydesdale Foal, light bay, 1990-91, Traditional scale...**$25.00**

Donkey, w/red baskets, 1958-60, Traditional scale.....**$75.00**

Draft Horse, sorrel, 1976-81, Stablemates Saddle Club scale...**$10.00**

Family Arabian Mare, glossy charcoal, 1961-67, Traditional scale...**$35.00**

Fighting Stallion, bay, Toys 'R Us, 1993, Traditional scale..**$30.00**

Foundation Stallion, American Indian Pony, 1988-91, Traditional scale...**$35.00**

Ginger, alabaster, 1990-91, Classic scale **$15.00**

Grazing Mare, Buttons, black, 1964-70, Traditional scale ...**$100.00**

Haflinger, sorrel, 1979-84, Traditional scale.................**$40.00**

Hanoverian, bay, 1980-84, Traditional scale **$55.00**

Indian Pony, brown pinto, 1970-76, Traditional scale....**$75.00**

Johar, alabaster, 1980-93, Classic scale........................**$15.00**

Jumping Horse, Stonewall, 1965-88, Traditional scale ..**$60.00**

Justin Morgan, dark bay, 1990-92, Traditional scale....**$35.00**

Kelso, dark bay, 1975-90, Classic scale.......................**$20.00**

Legionario, Spanish Pride bay, 1991-92, Traditional scale..**$35.00**

Lipizzan Stallion, Pegasus, wings attached, 1984-87, Classic scale...**$60.00**

Lying Foal, chestnut, 1975-76, Stablemates Saddle Club scale...**$15.00**

Merrylegs, alabaster, 1990-91, Classic scale **$15.00**

Midnight Sun, Tennessee Walking Horse, red bay, 1988-89, Traditional scale...**$40.00**

Morgan (stretched), Show Stance Morgan, red chestnut, 1990-91, Traditional scale...**$40.00**

Morgan Mare, red chestnut, 1995, Stablemates Saddle Club scale...**$10.00**

Morgan Stallion, black, 1976-88, Stablemates Saddle Club scale...**$10.00**

Morgan Stallion, sorrel, 1989-94, Little Bit scale..........**$10.00**

Mustang Foal, roan, 1994-96, Classic scale **$15.00**

Old Timer, alabaster, 1966-76, Traditional scale..........**$50.00**

Quarter Horse Foal, red bay, 1975-82, Classic scale ...**$20.00**

Quarter Horse Mare, chestnut, 1976, Stablemates Saddle Club scale...**$40.00**

Quarter Horse Stallion, bay pinto, 1985-88, Little Bit scale...**$15.00**

Quarter Horse Yearling, Thunder Bay, bay, 1995-96, Traditional scale...**$20.00**

Rearing Stallion, bay, 1965-80, Classic scale **$30.00**

Ruffian, Lula palomino, 1991-92, Classic scale **$25.00**

Running Foal, alabaster, 1963-71, Traditional scale.....**$45.00**

San Domingo, Camanche Pony, 1990-92, Traditional scale **$35.00**

Shetland Pony, bay pinto, 1989-91, Traditional scale .**$20.00**

Silky Sullivan, T-bone flea-bit gray, 1991-92, Classic scale.**$20.00**

Stock Horse Mare, black blanket appaloosa, 1983-88, Traditional scale...**$35.00**

Stock Horse Stallion, Quarter Horse, bay, 1981-88, Traditional scale...**$40.00**

Terrang, buckskin, 1995, Classic scale **$15.00**

Thoroughbred Stallion, red bay, 1984-88, Little Bit scale ..**$15.00**

Unicorn, alabaster, 1984-94, Little Bit scale **$10.00**

Welsh Pony (cantering), bay w/yellow ribbons, 1971-73, Traditional scale...**$100.00**

Western Horse, glossy palomino, 1950-70, Traditional scale **$40.00**

Western Prancer, buckskin, 1961-73, Traditional scale..**$60.00**

British Royal Commemoratives

While seasoned collectors may prefer the older pieces using 1840 (Queen Victoria's reign) as their starting point, even present-day souvenirs make a good inexpensive beginning collection. Ceramic items, glassware, metalware, and paper goods have been issued on the occasion of weddings, royal tours, birthdays, christenings, and many other celebrations. Food tins are fairly easy to find, and range in price from about $30.00 to around $75.00 for those made since the 1950s.

We've all seen that items related to Princess Diana have appreciated rapidly since her untimely and tragic demise, and in fact collections are being built exclusively from memorabilia marketed both before and after her death. For more information, we recommend *British Royal Commemoratives* by Audrey Zeder.

Advisor: Audrey Zeder (See Directory, British Royalty Commemoratives)

Bank, Elizabeth II coronation, crown shape, red & gold-tone iron..**$50.00**

Bell, Queen Elizabeth II Silver Jubilee, ceramic with wooden handle, $35.00.

Book, Victoria, text, 28 full-page etchings, hardback, 1897, pr **$125.00**

Booklet, Vol 1 Golden Cord Souvenirs Royalty, Pitkins, 1950..**$20.00**

Bowl, Edward VII coronation, multicolored portrait, yellow lustre, shell form, 7" **$175.00**

Bowl, George V coronation, 2 joined bowls w/multicolor portrait, 9½" **$105.00**

Bowl, Victoria 1897, sepia portrait, young/old queen, 5½" **$225.00**

Bust, George V 1935 jubilee, hand painted w/black pedestal, 7½" **$125.00**

Calendar, Edward VIII 1937, booklet w/months & portrait, 2x3" **$25.00**

Compact, Elizabeth II coronation, multicolor portrait, gold tone, 3½" dia...**$50.00**

Cup & saucer, Elizabeth II 1959 Canada visit, portrait & leaves **$35.00**

Cup & saucer, Princesses Elizabeth & Margaret, from 1937 toy set **$50.00**

Ephemera, Elizabeth II coronation, coloring book, partly colored..**$25.00**

Ephemera, Elizabeth II New Zealand visit, ice-cream box..**$15.00**

First Day Cover, George VI 1939 Canada visit **$15.00**

Framed picture, George VI portrait painted on butterfly wings, 3½"...**$75.00**

Jewelry, George V coronation brooch, brass frame w/king & queen photos **$50.00**

Magazine, Edward VII coronation, ILN Record Number...**$75.00**

Matchbook, Elizabeth II jubilee, black w/silver portrait, Britannia **$15.00**

Medal, Edward VII coronation, embossed portrait, brass, w/case, 2¼"..**$135.00**

Miniature, Edward VII coronation, ceramic plaque, green glaze, 3" **$75.00**

Mug, Victory 1897 jubilee, blue & gray overall transfer, JC&N **$195.00**

Novelty, Elizabeth II coronation, Viewmaster, w/3 coronation reels **$50.00**

Photograph, Victoria & family 1861 cabinet photo.....**$60.00**

Pin-back button, Princesses Elizabeth & Margaret 1937, black & white, 1¼"..**$45.00**

Pitcher, Victoria 1897 jubilee, black w/gold portrait & enamel, 6"..**$225.00**

Plate, Edward VIII coronation, embossed portrait on brown glaze, 10" **$50.00**

Plate, Edward 1911 Prince of Wales investiture, multicolor portrait, 8" **$125.00**

Plate, George V coronation, multicolor king or queen, Royal Doulton, 7", pr **$295.00**

Plate, King George and Queen Elizabeth's 1939 Canada visit, Royal Winton, 10½", $55.00.

Plate, Victoria 1847, black transfer w/multicolor, hexagon, 7½"...**$695.00**

Plate, Victoria 1897 jubilee, sepia portrit w/multicolor, Allerton, 7½" **$150.00**

Pocketknife, George V/Prince of Wales, multicolor portrait, 2-blade, 3" **$60.00**

Postcard, George V WWI w/European generals **$20.00**

Postcard, George V 1911 w/24 European royals.........**$25.00**

Postcard, Prince of Wales 1911 investiture, black & white, unused **$15.00**

Postcard, Queen Victoria memorial, multicolor portrait & decor, Tuck.................................**$25.00**

Puzzle, Princess Elizabeth 1947, multicolor portrait, Grafton **$50.00**

Spoon, Victoria 1897, crown top, embossed portrait bowl, silverplate, 6".................................**$100.00**

Tea set, Princesses Elizabeth & Margaret, 1927, child size, 15-pc.................................**$350.00**

Textile, Edward VIII, multicolor portrait & flag (vibrant), 10x10".................................**$45.00**

Textile, Elizabeth II coronation handkerchief, multicolor crown, crepe.................................**$20.00**

Tin, Edward VII coronation, green portrait, domed lid, Rowntree, sm.................................**$50.00**

Tin, Prince Charles 1969 investiture, multicolor, 5x3x4".**$55.00**

Tray, Elizabeth II jubilee, multicolor portrait, 10x15".**$30.00**

Bubble Bath Containers

By now, you're probably past the state of being incredulous at the sight of these plastic figurals on flea market tables with price tags twenty time higher than they carried when new and full. (There's no hotter area of collecting today than items from the fifties through the seventies that are reminiscent of early kids' TV shows and hit movies.) Most of these were made in the 1960s. The Colgate-Palmolive Company produced the majority of them — they're the ones marked 'Soaky' — and these seem to be the most collectible. Each character's name is right on the bottle. Other companies followed suit; Purex also made a line, so did Avon. Be sure to check for paint loss, and look carefully for cracks in the brittle plastic heads of the Soakies. For more information, we recommend *Schroeder's Collectible Toys, Antique to Modern* (Collector Books).

Advisors: Matt and Lisa Adams (See Directory, Bubble Bath Containers)

Dick Tracy, Soaky, 1965, 10", NM, 45.00.

Alvin (Chipmunks), Colgate-Palmolive, 1960s, white w/red cap head, NM.................................**$25.00**

Baba Louie, Soaky, w/original tag, M.................................**$20.00**

Bamm-Bamm, Purex, 1960s, black & white, NM.......**$30.00**

Barney Rubble, Soaky, MIB.................................**$20.00**

Batman, Soaky, VG.................................**$50.00**

Beatles, Ringo Starr, blue, EX, from $100 to.............**$125.00**

Broom Hilda, Landers, 1977, EX.................................**$25.00**

Casper the Friendly Ghost, EX.................................**$30.00**

Cecil the Serpent, Purex, 1960s, green, NMIB (w/1 of 9 disguises).................................**$75.00**

Cinderella, Colgate-Palmolive, 1960s, movable arms, NM.................................**$35.00**

Deputy Dawg, Colgate-Palmolive, 1960s, brown & yellow outfit, lg, NM.................................**$30.00**

Donald Duck, Colgate-Palmolive, 1960s, white, blue & yellow w/cap head, NM.................................**$25.00**

Dopey, Colgate-Palmolive, 1960s, bank, purple & yellow, NM.................................**$30.00**

El Cabong, Knickerbocker, 1960s, black, yellow & white, rare, VG.................................**$75.00**

Elmer Fudd, Soaky, in hunting outfit, NM.................**$30.00**

Felix the Cat, Soaky, red body, EX+.................................**$35.00**

Frankenstein, Soaky, 1960s, 10", EX.................................**$90.00**

Fred Flintstone, Purex, 1960s, black & red, NM..........**$30.00**

Huckleberry Hound, Knickerbocker, 1960s, powder/bank, red & black, 15", NM.................................**$50.00**

Jiminy Cricket, Colgate-Palmolive, 1960s, green, black & red, NM.................................**$30.00**

Mickey Mouse, band leader, Soaky, 1960s, red, NM..**$30.00**

Mighty Mouse, Soaky, NM.................................**$25.00**

Mr Jinx w/Pixie & Dixie, Colgate-Palmolive, EX, from $30 to.................................**$35.00**

Muskie, Soaky, 1960s, NM, from $25 to.................**$35.00**

Peter Potamus, Soaky, w/original tag, M.................**$25.00**

Pluto, Colgate-Palmolive, 1960s, orange w/cap head, NM.................................**$25.00**

Popeye, Soaky, white suit w/blue accents, 1960s, MIB.......**$55.00**

Punkin' Puss, Purex, NM, $40.00.

Quick Draw McGraw, Purex, 1960s, orange & blue or orange only, NM, each.................................**$40.00**

Ricochet Rabbit, Purex, 1960s, movable or non-movable arm, NM.................................**$50.00**

Sailor, Avon, VG.................................**$10.00**

Secret Squirrel, Purex, 1960s, yellow & purple, NM...**$60.00**

Snoopy, Avon, retains original label, 5½", EX.............**$15.00**

Speedy Gonzales, Colgate-Palmolive, 1960s, blue & red, NM.................................**$30.00**

Superman, Avon, 1978, 8", NM, minimum value.......**$35.00**

Thumper (Bambi), Colgate-Palmolive, 1960s, light blue & white, NM.................................**$30.00**

Top Cat, Soaky, NM.................................**$35.00**

Tweety Bird, Colgate-Palmolive, 1960s, slipover only, NM **$25.00**

Winsome Witch, Purex, 1960s, blue & black, NM **$30.00**

Woody Woodpecker, Colgate-Palmolive, 1960s, blue, yellow & white, w/red flume cap, NM.............................**$25.00**

Yogi Bear, Knickerbockers (Purex), 1960s, powder/bank, brown, w/tag & card, VG+ **$30.00**

Calculators

It is difficult to picture the days when a basic four-function calculator cost hundreds of dollars, especially when today you get one free by simply filling out a credit application. Yet when they initially arrived on the market in 1971, the first of these electronic marvels cost from $300.00 to $400.00. All this for a calculator that could do no more than add, subtract, multiply, and divide.

Even at that price there was an uproar by consumers as calculating finally became convenient. No longer did you need to use a large mechanical monster adding machine or a slide rule with all of its complexity. You could even put away your pencil and paper for those tough numbers you couldn't 'do' in your head.

With prices initially so high and the profit potential so promising, several hundred companies jumped onto the calculator bandwagon. Some made their own; many purchased them from other (often overseas) manufacturers, just adding their own nameplate. Since the product was so new to the world, most of the calculators had some very different and interesting body styles.

Due to the competitive nature of all those new entries to the market, prices dropped quickly. A year and a half later, prices started to fall below $100.00 — a magic number that caused a boom in consumer demand. As even more calculators became available and electronics improved, prices continued to drop, eventually forcing many high-cost makers (who could not compete) out of business. By 1978 the number of major calculator companies could be counted on both hands. Fortunately calculators are still available at almost every garage sale or flea market for a mere pittance — usually 25¢ to $3.00.

For more information refer to *A Guide to HP Handheld Calculators and Computers* by Wlodek Mier-Jedrzejowicz and *Collector's Guide to Pocket Calculators* by Guy Ball and Bruce Flamm (both published by Wilson/Barnette), and *Personal Computers and Pocket Calculators* by Dr. Thomas Haddock.

Note: Due to limited line length, we have used these abbreviations: flr — flourescent; fct — function.

Advisor: Guy D. Ball (See Directory, Calculators)

Club: International Association of Calculator Collectors
P.O. Box 345, Tustin, CA 92781-0345

Adler, #82M, 4-fct, metric conversions, green flr, 4-AAA batteries, ca 1974, Japan, 3x4¾", from $45 to **$50.00**

American, L180, 4-fct, red LED, 9V battery, black case, USA, 2½x4½", from $40 to.................................**$50.00**

Berkey, #100, 4-fct, %, flr, 4 AA batteries, USA, 3¼x5¼", from $45 to **$55.00**

Brother, #408AX, 4-fct, green flr, 5 AA batteries, ca 1972, Japan, 3¾x6", from $45 to **$55.00**

Calstar, #DT-10, 4-fct, %, memory, 10 digit flr, 2-D batteries, Tiawan, 6½x7", from $25 to.........................**$35.00**

Candle, #800N, 4-fct, %, square root, sign change, green flr, 2-AA batteries, Korea, 3x5½", from $45 to **$55.00**

Canon Pocketronic, $80.00; Busicom Handy-LE 120A, $150.00; Texas Instruments (TI-2500), $20.00. (Photo courtesy Guy Ball)

Casio, #AL-8S, 4-fct, memory, date fct, flr, 2 AA batteries, 1977, Japan, 3¼x5½", from $25 to **$45.00**

Cybernet, #6PD, 4-fct, memory, %, green flr, paper printer, sealed battery, Japan, 3¼x6¾", from $35 to.........**$45.00**

Litronix, #2140, 4-fct, memory, red LED, 3 AA batteries, ca 1974, Malaysia, 3x6½", from $50 to **$60.00**

Melcor, #390, 4-fct, memory, %, red LED, 9V battery, 2 keypad variations, ca 1973, USA, 3¼x6", from $45 to..........**$55.00**

Monroe-Litton, #30, 4-fct, %, red LED, sealed battery, ca 1973, USA, 3½x6", from $40 to..**$50.00**

National Semiconductor, Mathematician, science fct, memory, exponent, red LED, 9V battery, 3x6", from $25 to.**$35.00**

Olympia, CD-45, 4-fct, %, square root, green flr, 2 AA batteries, Japan, 2¾x4¾", from $35 to **$45.00**

Panasonic, JE-8220U, 4-fct, memory, %, square root, sign change, flr, 2 AA batteries, Japan, 2¾x7", from $25 to.............**$35.00**

Radio Shack, EC-225, 4-fct, red LED, 4 AA batteries, Canada, 3x6½", from $40 to...**$50.00**

Rapid Data, #804, 4-fct, red LED, 9V battery, Canada, 3½x5¾", from $30 to...**$40.00**

Rockwell, #31R, 4-fct, memory, %, square fct, sign change, red LED, sealed battery, Mexico, 3x6", from $15 to **$25.00**

Sanyo, CZ-8101, science fct, flr, sealed battery, ca 1974, from $45 to..**$55.00**

Sharp, EL-8008, 4-fct, %, sign change, COS-LCD, 1 AA battery, ca 1975, Japan, 3¼x5", from $40 to.............**$50.00**

Sinclair, Oxford #300, science fct, purple LED, 9v battery, black case, ca 1975-76, England, 3x6¼", from $70 to..........**$80.00**

Soundsign, #8280, 4-fct, flr, 4-C batteries, Japan, 4½x5¾", from $35 to..**$45.00**

Teal, #110PD, 4-fct, printer, flr, sealed battery, 3½x8¾", from $20 to $25.00

Texas Instruments, Spelling B, game calculator, flr, 9v battery, USA, 3½x6¼", from $15 to $25.00

Texas Instruments, TI-1025, 4-fct, memory, %, sign change, blue flr, 9v battery, 1978, USA, 3x5¾", from $15 to............$20.00

Texas Instruments, TI-2500-II, 4-fct, %, red LED, 2 AA batteries, USA, 3x5½", from $35 to................................$45.00

Toko, Mini 8, 4-fct, flr, 4 AA batteries, Japan, 3½x6", from $25 to $30.00

Toshiba, BC-815, 4-fct, memory, %, square root, blue flr, 4 AA batteries, Japan, 3¼x7", from $25 to $35.00

Triumph, #80C, 4-fct, %, green flr, 4 AAA batteries, 3x4¾", from $40 to $50.00

Unisonic, #1299R-A, science fct, green flr, 4 AA batteries, Japan, 3½x6", from $10 to $20.00

Unisonic, #739SQ, 4-fct, %, square fct, reciprical, green flr, 4 AA batteries, Japan, 3½x6", from $10 to.............$20.00

Unitrex, #800D, 4-fct, %, 4 AA batteries, horizontal, Japan, 6½x6", from $20 to $30.00

California Potteries

This is a sampling of the work of several potteries and artists who operated in California from the 1940s to the 1960s. Today good examples are among the most highly collectible pottery items on the market. As you begin to observe their products, you will see a certain style emerge. Figural pieces account for a large percentage of their work, and very often their glazes tended toward beautiful pastels, more vivid than the norm and often used in striking combinations. Some of the more renowned companies are listed elsewhere in this book.

For more information we recommend *The Collector's Encyclopedia of California Pottery* by Jack Chipman.

See also Sascha Brastoff; Brayton Laguna; Cleminson Pottery; Kay Finch; Brad Keeler; Howard Pierce; Hedi Schoop; Twin Winton; Weilware.

Advisors: Pat and Kris Secor (See Directory, California Pottery)

Bellaire, Marc; ashtray, multicolored clown on cream, 7", $45.00. (Photo courtesy Marty Webster)

Adams, Matthew; bowl, vegetable; hand-painted, old mark..$65.00

Adams, Matthew; bowl, walrus, #190A $50.00

Adams, Matthew; candle holder, polar bear design....$35.00

Adams, Matthew; tile, baby seal, knotty pine frame, 10x8"..**$135.00**

Adams, Matthew; tile, Eskimo child, 5" dia **$35.00**

Avia of Hollywood, figurine, crawling baby, 4" **$10.00**

Ball Art, figurines, pheasants, #285 & #286, pr **$115.00**

Bellaire, Marc; ashtray, Island Native, boomerang form, 14x7"..**$110.00**

Bellaire, Marc; console bowl, bird (swan?) modeling, black w/pink & blue (Mardi Gras colors)......................**$425.00**

Bellaire, Marc; plaque, man stacking coconuts, palm tree at back, 12" dia...**$150.00**

Block, figurine, Heidi **$30.00**

Brock of California, butter dish, w/lid...................**$15.00**

Brock of California, cup & saucer, Country Meadow ...**$2.50**

Brock of California, cup & saucer, Forever Yours........**$2.50**

Brock of California, lamp, rooster figural, pr **$70.00**

Brock of California, plate, Rooster, 10" **$5.00**

Brock of California, tea & toast set **$25.00**

Cochran, Anne; ashtray, 13", w/matching kidney-shaped cigarette box, winged ballerinas, gold, black & white on green..**$95.00**

Decora, wall plaque, engagement, wedding & baby, 3-pc...**$45.00**

DeForest of California, condiment jar, BBQ sauce **$50.00**

DeForest of California, condiment jar, Onions or Mustard..**$50.00**

DeForest of California, jam jar, boy's head figural, w/spoon..**$50.00**

DeForest of California, relish jar, hamburger figural, w/spoon..**$50.00**

DeForest of California, tureen, Chicken Soup, w/ladle..**$250.00**

DeForest of California, wall plaque, poodle w/rhinestones, pr..**$65.00**

DeForest of California, wall pocket, rolling pin w/face..**$45.00**

Dorothy Kindell, ashtray, nude................................**$75.00**

Dorothy Kindell, mug, nude handle, from $28 to.......**$35.00**

Flintwood, hors d'oeuvres, horse form **$55.00**

Freeman-McFarlan, ashtray, turquoise.........................**$15.00**

Freeman-McFarlan, figurine, bald eagle, 13" **$185.00**

Freeman-McFarlan, figurine, Mickey, pomeranian dog..**$70.00**

Freeman-McFarlan, figurine, snow owl, 5" **$45.00**

Johann Brahms of California, Easter egg, purple, 2-pc..**$35.00**

Johann Brahms of California, wall pocket, w/fancy applied flower..**$60.00**

Kaye of Hollywood, figurine, blond lady in strapless dress, vase beside, #311, 12", $85.00. (Photo courtesy Pat and Kris Secor)

Kaye of Hollywood, planter, boy w/bow tie...............**$25.00**

Kaye of Hollywood, wall pocket, lady w/full skirt, 9" **$45.00**
KTK of California, dish, leaf form, chartreuse mottle, 6" ..**$35.00**
KTK of California, flower bowl, mauve mottle, 12½"...**$45.00**
Lerner, Claire; figurine, heron, green **$30.00**

Madeline Originals, figurine, peacock, shades of blues and greens, 12x12", from $125.00 to $165.00.

Madeline Originals, vase, blue stripes, 3" **$20.00**
McCarty Bros, figurine, boy making pottery................**$30.00**
McCarty Bros, figurine, girl w/apples..........................**$30.00**
McCulloch, figurine, deer, sitting.................................**$25.00**
McCulloch, figurine, heron, pink, 12", pr **$45.00**
Modglins Originals, figurine, tiger..............................**$40.00**
Modglins Originals, lamp, lady w/muff **$60.00**
Pacific, bowl, mixing; black, orange & yellow, 8"....**$125.00**
Pacific, casserole, Hostessware, Apache red, w/trivet...**$175.00**
Pacific, figurine, rooster, yellow, 17"..........................**$300.00**
Pacific, planter, white shell form................................**$15.00**
Pacific, planter, white swan, lg...................................**$80.00**
Pacific, plate, chop; Hostessware, red, 15" **$55.00**
Pacific, platter, embossed fish, turquoise, Hostessware, oval, 15¾"..**$245.00**
Robert Simmons, figurine, Nutsy or Frisky squirrel, each ..**$12.00**
Robert Simmons, figurine, Pals, spotted dog, w/original silver label, 4¾", pr...**$30.00**
Robert Simmons, figurine, Skidoo, giraffe, #2021, 7"..**$25.00**
Santa Anita Ware, bowl, cereal; Trellis, lg.....................**$9.00**
Sara Hume of California, bank, owl figural, multicolor glaze, 3½"..**$35.00**
Stewart of California, planter, Chinaman, pr **$25.00**

West Coast Pottery, figurine, Hawaiian lady, topless, pink floral skirt, applied flowers in hair, 17¼", $275.00. (Photo courtesy Pat and Kris Secor)

West Coast Pottery, vase, leaf form, aqua & rose, #117..**$15.00**
West Coast Pottery, vase, shell form, aqua **$12.50**
West Coast Pottery, vase, white, #209.......................**$14.00**
Will-George, figurine, cardinal on branch, 10"..........**$65.00**
Will-George, figurine, flamingo, head up, 12"..........**$135.00**
Will-George, pitcher, chicken figural, multicolor, 7"..**$125.00**
Will-George, wine, chicken figural, multicolor, 5" **$55.00**
Winfield, bowl, Bird of Paradise, 4x9" dia.................**$50.00**
Winfield, bowl, Garden City, ruffled rim, 8"..............**$45.00**
Winfield, plate, Bird of Paradise, 10" **$20.00**
Winfield, plate, Dragon Flower, 8" **$10.00**
Yona, figurine, mother & daughter, 9½" & 7½", pr..**$175.00**
Yona, planter, embossed man & woman, 2 handles, footed, 6x8" **$35.00**
Yona, sugar bowl, clown **$20.00**
Yona, wall pocket, clown & pig, tub forms pocket, dated 1957, 7" **$55.00**

California Raisins

Since they starred in their first TV commercial in 1986, the California Raisins have attained stardom through movies, tapes, videos, and magazine ads. Today we see them everywhere on the secondary market — PVC figures, radios, banks, posters — and they're very collectible. The PVC figures were introduced in 1987. Originally there were four, all issued for retail sales — a singer, two conga dancers, and a saxaphone player. Before the year was out, Hardee's, the fast-food chain, came out with the same characters, though on a slightly smaller scale. A fifth character, Blue Surfboard (horizontal), was created, and three 5½" Bendees with flat pancake-style bodies appeared.

In 1988 the ranks had grown to twenty-one: Blue Surfboard (vertical), Red Guitar, Lady Dancer, Blue/Green Sunglasses, Guy Winking, Candy Cane, Santa Raisin, Bass Player, Drummer, Tamourine Lady (there were two styles), Lady Valentine, Boy Singer, Girl Singer, Hip Guitar Player, Sax Player with Beret, and four Graduates (styled like the original four, but on yellow pedestals and wearing graduation caps). And Hardee's issued an additional six: Blue Guitar, Trumpet Player, Roller Skater, Skateboard, Boom Box, and Yellow Surfboard.

Eight more characters came out in 1989: Male in Beach Chair, Green Trunks with Surfboard, Hula Skirt, Girl Sitting on Sand, Piano Player, AC, Mom, and Michael Raisin. They made two movies and thereafter were joined by their fruit and vegetable friends, Rudy Bagaman, Lick Broccoli, Banana White, Leonard Limabean, and Cecil Thyme. Hardee's added four more characters in 1991: Anita Break, Alotta Stile, Buster, and Benny.

All Raisins are dated with these exceptions: those issued in 1989 (only the Beach Scene characters are dated, and they're actually dated 1988), and those issued by Hardee's in 1991.

For more information we recommend *Schroeder's Collectible Toys, Antique to Modern* (Collector Books).

Applause, Captain Toonz, w/blue boom box, yellow glasses & sneakers, Hardee's Second Promotion, 1988, sm, M....**$3.00**

Applause, FF String, w/blue guitar & orange sneakers, Hardee's Second Promotion, 1988, sm, M **$3.00**

Applause, Michael Raisin (Jackson), w/silver microphone & studded belt, Special Edition, 1989, M **$15.00**

Applause, Rollin' Rollo, w/roller skates, yellow sneakers & hat marked H, Hardee's Second Promotion, 1988, sm, M **$3.00**

Applause, SB Stuntz, w/yellow skateboard & blue sneakers, Hardee's Second Promotion, 1988, sm, M **$3.00**

Applause, Trumpy Trunote, w/trumpet & blue sneakers, Hardee's Second Promotion, 1988, sm, M **$3.00**

Applause, Waves Weaver I, w/yellow surfboard connected to foot, Hardee's Second Promotion, 1988, sm, M **$4.00**

Applause, Waves Weaver II, w/yellow surfboard not connected to foot, Hardee's Second Promotion, 1988, sm, M.....**$6.00**

Applause-Claymation, Banana White, yellow dress, Meet the Raisins First Edition, 1989, M **$15.00**

Applause-Claymation, Lick Broccoli, green & black w/red & orange guitar, Meet the Raisins First Edition, 1989, M..**$15.00**

Applause-Claymation, Rudy Bagaman, purple shirt and flipflops, Meet the Raisins 1st Edition, 1989, M, $15.00. (Photo courtesy Larry DeAngelo)

CALRAB, Blue Surfboard, board connected to foot, Unknown Production, 1988, M..**$35.00**

CALRAB, Blue Surfboard, board in right hand, not connected to foot, Unknown Production, 1987, M **$50.00**

CALRAB, Guitar, red guitar, First Commercial Issue, 1988, M **$8.00**

CALRAB, Hands, left hand points up, right hand points down, Post Raisin Bran Issue, 1987, M.............................**$4.00**

CALRAB, Hands, pointing up w/thumbs on head, First Key Chains, 1987, M...**$5.00**

CALRAB, Hands, pointing up w/thumbs on head, Hardee's First Promotion, 1987, sm, M **$3.00**

CALRAB, Microphone, right hand in fist w/microphone in left, Post Raisin Brand Issue, 1987, M **$6.00**

CALRAB, Microphone, right hand points up w/microphone in left, Hardee's First Promotion, 1987, sm, M............**$3.00**

CALRAB, Microphone, right hand points up w/microphone in left, First Key Chains, 1987, M **$7.00**

CALRAB, Santa, red cap & green sneakers, Christmas Issue, 1988, M **$9.00**

CALRAB, Saxophone, gold sax, no hat, First Key Chains, 1987, M **$5.00**

CALRAB, Saxophone, gold sax, no hat, Hardee's First Promotion, 1987, sm, M **$3.00**

CALRAB, Saxophone, inside of sax painted red, Post Raisin Bran Issue, 1987, M **$4.00**

CALRAB, Singer, microphone in left hand not connected to face, First Commercial Issue, 1988, M **$6.00**

CALRAB, Sunglasses, holding candy cane, green glasses, red sneakers, Christmas Issue, 1988, M **$9.00**

CALRAB, Sunglasses, index finger touching face, First Key Chains, 1987, M..**$5.00**

CALRAB, Sunglasses, index finger touching face, orange glasses, Hardee's First Promotion, 1987, M......................**$3.00**

CALRAB, Sunglasses, right hand points up, left hand points down, orange glasses, Post Raisin Bran Issue, 1987, M...**$4.00**

CALRAB, Sunglasses II, eyes not visible, aqua glasses & sneakers, First Commercial Issue, 1988, M **$6.00**

CALRAB, Sunglasses II, eyes visible, aqua glasses & sneakers, First Commercial Issue, 1988, M **$16.00**

CALRAB, Winky, in hitchhiking pose & winking, First Commercial Issue, 1988, M **$6.00**

CALRAB-Applause, AC, 'Gimme 5' pose, tall pompadour & red sneakers, Meet the Raisins Second Edition, 1989, M..**$150.00**

CALRAB-Applause, Alotta Stile, w/purple boom box, pink boots, Hardee's Fourth Promotion, 1991, sm, MIP..**$12.00**

CALRAB-Applause, Anita Break, shopping w/Hardee's bag, Hardee's Fourth Promotion, 1991, sm, M **$12.00**

CALRAB-Applause, Bass Player, w/gray slippers, Second Commercial Issue, 1988, M **$8.00**

CALRAB-Applause, Benny, w/bowling ball, orange sunglasses, Hardee's Fourth Promotion, 1991, sm, MIP **$20.00**

CALRAB-Applause, Boy in Beach Chair, orange glasses, brown base, Beach Theme Edition, 1988, M........**$10.00**

Calrab-Applause, Boy w/Surfboard, purple board, brown base, Beach Theme Edition, 1988, M....................**$10.00**

CALRAB-Applause, Cecil Tyme (Carrot), Meet the Raisins Second Promotion, 1989, M................................**$175.00**

CALRAB-Applause, Drummer, black hat with yellow feather, 2nd Commercial Issue, 1988, M, $8.00.

CALRAB-Applause, Girl w/boom box, purple glasses, green shoes, brown base, Beach Theme Edition, 1988, M **$10.00**

CALRAB-Applause, Girl w/Tambourine, green shoes & bracelet, Raisin Club Issue, 1988, M......................**$12.00**

CALRAB-Applause, Girl w/Tambourine (Ms Delicious), yellow shoes, Second Commercial Issue, 1988, M....**$12.00**

CALRAB-Applause, Hands, Graduate w/both hands pointing up & thumbs on head, Graduate Key Chains, 1988, M...**$85.00**

CALRAB-Applause, Hip Band Guitarist (Hendrix), w/headband & yellow guitar, Third Commercial Issue, 1988, M.........**$22.00**

CALRAB-Applause, Hip Band Guitarist (Hendrix), w/headband & yellow guitar, Second Key Chains, 1988, sm, M.........**$65.00**

CALRAB-Applause, Hula Girl, yellow shoes & bracelet, green skirt, Beach Theme Edition, 1988, M **$10.00**

CALRAB-Applause, Lenny Lima Beans, purple suit, Meet the Raisins Second Promotion, 1989, M **$125.00**

CALRAB-Applause, Microphone (female), yellow shoes & bracelet, Third Commercial Edition, 1988, M..........**$9.00**

CALRAB-Applause, Microphone (female), yellow shoes & bracelet, Second Key Chains, 1988, sm, M...........**$45.00**

CALRAB-Applause, Microphone (male), left hand extended w/open palm, Third Commercial Issue, 1988, M ...**$9.00**

CALRAB-Applause, Microphone (male), left hand extended w/open palm, Second Key Chains, 1988, sm, M..**$45.00**

CALRAB-Applause, Mom, yellow hair, pink apron, Meet the Raisins Second Promotion, 1989, M **$125.00**

CALRAB-Applause, Piano, blue piano, red hair, green sneakers, Meet the Raisins First Edition, 1989, M **$25.00**

CALRAB-Applause, Saxophone, black beret, blue eyelids, Third Commercial Issue, 1988, M **$15.00**

CALRAB-Applause, Saxophone, Graduate w/gold sax, no hat, Graduate Key Chain, 1988, M **$85.00**

CALRAB-Applause, Singer (female), reddish purple shoes & bracelet, Second Commercial Issue, 1988, M........**$12.00**

CALRAB-Applause, Sunglasses, Graduate w/index finger touching face, orange glasses, Graduate Key Chains, 1988, M **$85.00**

CALRAB-Applause, Valentine, Be Mine, girl holding heart, Special Lover's Issue, 1988, M.....................................**$8.00**

CALRAB-Applause, Valentine, I'm Yours, boy holding heart, Special Lover's Issue, 1988, M.....................................**$8.00**

CALRAB-Claymation, Sunglasses/Singer/Hands/Saxophone or Graduate on yellow base, Post Raisin Bran, 1988, each, from $45 to...**$65.00**

Miscellaneous

Balloon, Congo line, 1987, M **$12.00**
Belt, lead singer w/mike on buckle, 1987, EX...........**$15.00**
Book, Birthday Boo Boo, 1988, EX..............................**$10.00**
Bubble bath, Rockin' Raisin, 24-oz, M **$4.00**
Cap, 1988, EX...**$5.00**
Coloring book, Sports Crazy, 1988, EX **$5.00**
Costume, Collegeville, 1988, MIB...............................**$10.00**
Game, California Raisin board game, MIB...................**$25.00**
Mugs, Christmas Issue, 1988, set of 4, MIB **$60.00**
Party invitations, M **$15.00**
Postcard, Claymation/Will Vinton, 1988, M...................**$5.00**
Poster, California Raisin Band, 22x28", M **$8.00**
Sticker album, Diamond Publishing, 1988, M..............**$15.00**
Sunshield, Congo Line, 1988, EX................................**$10.00**
Video, Hip To Be Fit, M **$18.00**
Wallet, yellow plastic, 1988, EX.................................**$20.00**
Wind-up toy, figure w/right hand up & orange glasses, 1987, MIB..**$8.00**
Wind-up toy, w/left hand up & right hand down, plastic, 1987, MIB..**$8.00**

Wristwatch, Official Fan Club, w/3 different bands, Nelsonic, 1987, MIB **$50.00**

Camark Pottery

Camark Pottery was manufactured in CAMden, ARKansas, from 1927 to the early 1960s. The pottery was founded by Samuel J. 'Jack' Carnes, a native of east central Ohio familiar with Ohio's fame for pottery production. Camark's first wares were made from Arkansas clays shipped by Carnes to John B. Lessell in Ohio in early to mid-1926. Lessell was one of the associates responsible for early art pottery-making. These wares consisted of Lessell's lustre and iridescent finishes based on similar ideas he pioneered earlier at Weller and other potteries. The variations made for Camark included versions of Weller's Marengo, LaSa, and Lamar. These 1926 pieces were signed only with the 'Lessell' signature. When Camark began operations in the spring of 1927, the company had many talented, experienced workers including Lessell's wife and stepdaughter (Lessell himself died unexpectedly in December 1926), the Sebaugh family, Frank Long, Alfred Tetzschner, and Boris Trifonoff. This group produced a wide range of art pottery finished in glazes of many types including lustre and iridescent (signed LeCamark), Modernistic/Futuristic, crackles, and combination glaze effects such as drips. Art pottery manufacture continued until the early 1930s when emphasis changed to industrial castware (molded wares) with single-color, primarily matt glazes.

In the 1940s Camark introduced its Hand-Painted line by Ernst Lechner. This line included the popular Iris, Rose, and Tulip patterns. Concurrent with the Hand-Painted Series (which was made until the early 1950s), Camark continued mass production of industrial castware — simple, sometimes nondescript pottery and novelty items with primarily glossy pastel glazes — until the early 1960s.

Some of Camark's designs and glazes are easily confused with those wares of other companies. For instance, Lessell decorated and signed a line in his lustre and iridescent finishes using porcelain (not pottery) blanks purchased from the Fraunfelter China Company. Camark produced a variety of combination glazes including the popular drip glazes (green over pink and green over mustard/brown) closely resembling Muncie's — but Muncie's clay is generally white while Camark used a cream-colored clay for its drip-glaze pieces. Muncie's are marked with a letter/number combination, and the bottoms are usually smeared with the base color. Camark's bottoms have a more uniform color application.

For more information, we recommend the *Collector's Guide to Camark Pottery* by David Edwin Gifford, Arkansas pottery historian and author of *Collector's Encyclopedia of Niloak Pottery*. (Both books are published by Collector Books.)

Advisor: David Edwin Gifford (See Directory, Camark)

Art Ware

Jug, orange & green, ball form, clay stopper, 6½" ...**$100.00**
Tray, blue & white matt, ruffled rim, sm die stamp, 13½" ..**$75.00**

TV lamp, polar bear balancing fishbowl, maroon glaze, $125.00.

Vase, Aztec red mottled design, brown Arkansas sticker, 6", from $180 to...**$200.00**
Vase, coralene on brick red, signed JL, 6", from $400 to ..**$500.00**
Vase, crackle finish, white, gold mark, 8"..................**$275.00**
Vase, fish form, orange & brown mottle, 8"..............**$150.00**
Vase, green over pink, horizontally ribbed & fluted, 6¼" ..**$45.00**

Vase, LeCamark Jonquil, glossy black with gold and red lustre, gold Arkansas ink stamp, 8", $600.00. (Photo courtesy David Gifford)

Vase, Lessell, lustre palm trees & pyramids on gold lustre, LeCamark, 8¾", from $700 to **$900.00**
Vase, lustre tree on gold lustre ground, signed Lessell, concave neck, shouldered, 10", from $600 to **$800.00**
Vase, Old English, plum & cream, signed LeCamark, 8½" ..**$500.00**
Vase, orange crackle design, handled, gold Arkansas ink stamp, Arkansas die stamp, 5¼x7¾", from $350 to.............**$400.00**
Vase, Sandpaper, matt red with coralene, molded-in ring handles, bulbous, 4½", from $180 to **$200.00**
Vase, Tiger Lady, brown Arkansas sticker, 13¼", from $900 to **$1,100.00**

Hand-Painted Ware

Bowl, orchid flower, #624.......................................**$38.00**
Pitcher, cat figural, detailed features, tail forms handle, #145, 8"...**$75.00**
Pitcher, embossed iris, scalloped lip **$125.00**
Vase, embossed cornflowers, handled, #563, 7½" **$50.00**
Vase, embossed iris each side, basket handle **$60.00**

Industrial Castware

Ashtray, flower form, blue, 8".......................................**$18.00**

Ashtray, leaf form, #88, 10"..**$25.00**
Bottle, water; #365, 7½x8x2" **$95.00**
Cup & saucer, flower form, Arkansas sticker **$15.00**
Figurine, cat, beside fishbowl, white, 8"....................**$50.00**
Figurine, cat, climbing, black gloss, 12".....................**$75.00**
Jug, mini whiskey; golden brown gloss, Pure Corn, 5" ..**$60.00**
Novelty, cotton dispenser, rabbit, orange, 3".............**$20.00**
Pitcher, parrot handle, blue gloss, 6½" **$90.00**
Pitcher, pelican spout, ball shape, green, 5¾" **$20.00**
Planter, swans, black, double neck, 8" **$15.00**
Planter, turkey figural, #381, 8x8½" **$50.00**
Planter/bowl, melon ribs, #620, 3x6" **$50.00**
Salt & pepper shakers, S & P shapes, pr **$15.00**
Sign, Arkansas state shape, paper label.....................**$60.00**
Wall pocket, flour scoop, pink, 8".............................**$12.00**

Cambridge Glassware

If you're looking for a 'safe' place to put your investment dollars, Cambridge glass is one of your better options. But as with any commodity, in order to make a good investment, knowledge of the product and its market is required. There are two books we would recommend for your study, *Colors in Cambridge Glass,* put out by the National Cambridge Collectors Club, and *The Collector's Encyclopedia of Elegant Glass* by Gene Florence.

The Cambridge Glass Company (located in Cambridge, Ohio) made fine quality glassware from just after the turn of the century until 1958. They made thousands of different items in hundreds of various patterns and colors. Values hinge on rarity of shape and color. Of the various marks they used, the 'C in triangle' is the most common. In addition to their tableware, they also produced flower frogs representing ladies and children and models of animals and birds that are very valuable today. To learn more about them, you'll want to read *Glass Animals of the Depression Era* by Lee Garmon and Dick Spencer.

Advisor: Debbie Maggard (See Directory, Elegant Glassware)

Newsletter: *The Cambridge Crystal Ball*
National Cambridge Collectors, Inc.
P.O. Box 416, Cambridge, OH 43725-0416. Dues: $15 for individual member and $3 for associate member of same household

Apple Blossom, bowl, crystal, oval, 4-footed, 12" **$40.00**
Apple Blossom, crystal, bowl, baker; 10" **$50.00**
Apple Blossom, crystal, bowl, cream soup; w/liner plate..**$40.00**
Apple Blossom, crystal, candlestick, keyhole; 1-light .**$17.50**
Apple Blossom, crystal, tumbler, footed, #3130, 8-oz.**$15.00**
Apple Blossom, crystal, vase, 2 styles, 8" **$40.00**
Apple Blossom, pink or green, ashtray, heavy, 6"......**$40.00**
Apple Blossom, pink or green, plate, sandwich; 2-handled, 12½"...**$37.50**
Apple Blossom, pink or green, tumbler, footed, #3400 12-oz **$37.50**
Apple Blossom, yellow or amber, bowl, bonbon; 2-handled, 5½"...**$25.00**

Apple Blossom, yellow or amber, creamer, tall, footed ..**$20.00**

Apple Blossom, yellow or amber, plate, salad; square ...**$12.00**

Apple Blossom, yellow or amber, plate, square, 2-handled, 6" **$9.00**

Apple Blossom, yellow or amber, tumbler, footed, #3135, 10-oz **$25.00**

Candlelight, crystal, bowl, footed, 2-handled, #3900/130, 7" **$30.00**

Candlelight, crystal, candle, #3900/67, 5" **$37.50**

Candlelight, crystal, creamer, individual; #3900/40 .....**$20.00**

Candlelight, crystal, icer, cocktail; #968, 2-pc.............**$65.00**

Candlelight, crystal, plate, torte; 4-toed, #3900/33, 13" ..**$55.00**

Candlelight, crystal, salt & pepper shakers, #3900/1177, pr...**$45.00**

Candlelight, crystal, stem, oyster cocktail; #3111, 4½-oz...**$27.50**

Candlelight, crystal, stem, sherbet; low, #3776, 7-oz ..**$16.50**

Candlelight, crystal, sugar bowl, #3900/41 ....**$17.50**

Candlelight, crystal, tumbler, iced tea; footed, #3111, 12-oz ..**$25.00**

Candlelight, crystal, vase, keyhole; footed, #1237, 9"..**$55.00**

Candlestick, milk glass, swan, 4½" **$175.00**

Caprice, blue or pink, bowl, salad; 4-footed, #57, 10"..**$125.00**

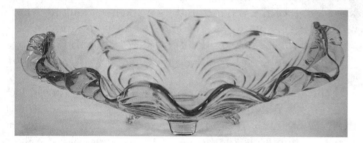

Caprice, blue or pink, bowl, #66, 4-footed, 13", $135.00.

Caprice, blue or pink, candlestick, keyhole; #646, 5", each **$55.00**

Caprice, blue or pink, cigarette box, w/lid, #208, 4½x3½"..**$75.00**

Caprice, blue or pink, ice bucket, #201.....................**$165.00**

Caprice, blue or pink, plate, bread & butter; #20, 5½"...**$25.00**

Caprice, blue or pink, plate, 4-footed, 15" **$110.00**

Caprice, blue or pink, stem, wine; blown, #300, 2½-oz ..**$62.50**

Caprice, blue or pink, sugar bowl, #38, med.............**$20.00**

Caprice, blue or pink, vase, crimped top, #345, 5½"..**$200.00**

Caprice, crystal, bowl, crimped, 4-footed, #66, 13" ...**$40.00**

Caprice, crystal, bowl, square, footed, #50, 8" **$40.00**

Caprice, crystal, candlestick, keyhole; 2-light, #647, 5"...**$16.00**

Caprice, crystal, candy jar, w/lid, footed, #165, 6"......**$42.50**

Caprice, crystal, creamer, #41, lg...............................**$13.00**

Caprice, crystal, oil cruet, w/stopper, #100, 5-oz **$70.00**

Caprice, crystal, plate, cabaret; 4-footed, #32, 11" **$30.00**

Caprice, crystal, salt & pepper shakers, individual; ball shape, #90, pr..**$45.00**

Caprice, crystal, stem, sherbet; blown, #301, 6-oz **$13.00**

Caprice, crystal, vase, ball shape, #239, 8½" **$50.00**

Chantilly, crystal, bowl, relish/pickle; 7".....................**$30.00**

Chantilly, crystal, bowl, 4-footed, flared, 12"...............**$40.00**

Chantilly, crystal, candlestick, 3-light, 6"...................**$37.50**

Chantilly, crystal, cup **$20.00**

Chantilly, crystal, marmalade, w/lid............................**$55.00**

Chantilly, crystal, plate, cake; tab handled, 13½" **$40.00**

Chantilly, crystal, plate, salad; crescent shape............**$80.00**

Chantilly, crystal, stem, cordial; #3775, 1-oz.............**$50.00**

Chantilly, crystal, stem, sherbet; tall, #3775, 6-oz.......**$17.50**

Chantilly, crystal, stem, water; #3600, 10-oz **$20.00**

Chantilly, crystal, tumbler, juice; footed, #3775, 5-oz .**$14.00**

Chantilly, crystal, vase, flower; footed, 11".................**$45.00**

Cleo, blue, bowl, cranberry; 6½".................................**$40.00**

Cleo, blue, bowl, finger; w/liner, #3077 ....**$50.00**

Cleo, blue, mayonnaise jar, footed.............................**$55.00**

Cleo, blue, stem, cocktail; #3077, 2½-oz **$45.00**

Cleo, blue, sugar bowl, Decagon style **$25.00**

Cleo, blue, tumbler, footed, #3077, 10-oz...................**$55.00**

Cleo, pink, green, yellow, or amber, bowl, pickle; Decagon style, 9"..**$30.00**

Cleo, pink, green, yellow or amber, bowl, relish; 2-part...**$22.00**

Cleo, pink, green, yellow or amber, comport, tall, #3115, 7" **$40.00**

Cleo, pink, green, yellow or amber, ice tub.................**$50.00**

Cleo, pink, green, yellow or amber, plate, dinner; Decagon style, 9½" **$65.00**

Cleo, pink, green, yellow or amber, stem, sherbet; low, #3115, 6-oz **$15.00**

Cleo, pink, green, yellow or amber, vase, 11" **$130.00**

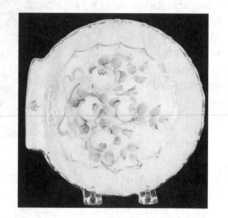

Crown Tuscan, tray, shell form, hand-painted roses, gold trim, 7¼", $45.00.

Decagon, pastel colors, bowl, bonbon; 2-handled, 6¼" ..**$10.00**

Decagon, pastel colors, French dressing bottle, Oil/Vinegar...**$65.00**

Decagon, pastel colors, plate, 2-handled, 7" **$9.00**

Decagon, pastel colors, salt dip, footed, 1½".............**$15.00**

Decagon, pastel colors, tumbler, footed, 5-oz.............**$10.00**

Decagon, red or blue, bowl, fruit; flat rim, 5¾" **$11.00**

Decagon, red or blue, bowl, vegetable; oval, 10½" ...**$30.00**

Decagon, red or blue, comport, 5¾" **$20.00**

Decagon, red or blue, creamer, lightning bolt handles ..**$20.00**

Decagon, red or blue, mayonnaise, 2-handled, w/2-handled liner & ladle **$40.00**

Decagon, red or blue, plate, bread & butter; 6¼" **$6.00**

Decagon, red or blue, plate, service; 10"....................**$30.00**

Decagon, red or blue, tray, service; 2-handled, 13"....**$30.00**

Decagon, red or blue, tumbler, footed, 10-oz.............**$25.00**

Diane, crystal, bowl, bonbon; 2-handled, 5¼".............**$18.00**

Diane, crystal, bowl, celery/relish; 3-part, 9"..............**$30.00**

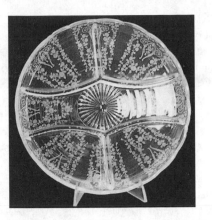

Diane, crystal, plate, relish; 5-part, 10½" dia, $75.00.

Diane, crystal, plate, torte; 4-footed, 13".................**$35.00**
Diane, crystal, plate, 2-handled, 6"...........................**$10.00**
Diane, crystal, tumbler, juice; footed, 5-oz..............**$27.00**
Diane, crystal, tumbler, water; footed, #3106, 12-oz...**$29.00**
Diane, crystal, vase, bud; 10".....................................**$45.00**
Elaine, crystal, basket, 2-handled, upturned sides, 6".**$15.00**
Elaine, crystal, bowl, celery/relish; 3-part, 9" **$25.00**
Elaine, crystal, bowl, 4-footed, oval, ear handles, 12"...**$40.00**

Elaine, crystal, bowl, open handles, gold encrusted, 15", $135.00.

Elaine, crystal, ice bucket, w/chrome handle.............**$60.00**
Elaine, crystal, plate, service; 4-footed, 12" **$25.00**
Elaine, crystal, stem, claret; #1402, 5-oz **$27.50**
Elaine, crystal, stem, cocktail; #3121, 3-oz.................**$22.00**
Elaine, crystal, stem, water; #3500, 10-oz **$22.00**
Elaine, crystal, stem, wine; #3500, 2½-oz **$30.00**
Elaine, crystal, tumbler, water; footed, #3121, 10-oz ..**$25.00**
Elaine, crystal, vase, footed, 6" **$35.00**
Figurine, Bashful Charlotte, green, flower frog, 11½"..**$375.00**
Figurine, Bashful Charlotte, Moonlight Blue, flower frog, 11½"'...**$525.00**
Figurine, bird, crystal satin, 2¾" L............................**$30.00**
Figurine, blue jay, flower holder...............................**$125.00**
Figurine, Buddha, amber, 5½".....................................**$225.00**
Figurine, Draped Lady, green frost, flower frog, 8½".**$150.00**
Figurine, Draped Lady, light pink, flower frog, 8½".**$125.00**
Figurine, Draped Lady, pink frost, flower frog, 8½".**$150.00**
Figurine, eagle, cobalt, bookend, Cambridge Club, 1986, each **$100.00**
Figurine, frog, crystal satin..**$25.00**
Figurine, heron, sm, 9"...**$75.00**
Figurine, Mandolin Lady, green, flower frog.............**$400.00**
Figurine, Pencil Pup, emerald or amber, w/sticker, each.**$50.00**

Figurine, Pouter pigeon, crystal.................................**$75.00**
Figurine, Rose Lady, green, flower frog, 8½"............**$200.00**
Figurine, Scottie, crystal, bookend, w/label, each.......**$80.00**
Figurine, sea gull, flower block....................................**$60.00**
Figurine, swan, ebony, 12½" **$300.00**
Figurine, swan, ebony, 3" **$65.00**
Figurine, swan, ebony, 8½" **$165.00**
Figurine, swan, emerald, 8½" **$125.00**
Figurine, swan, milk glass, 6½" **$550.00**
Figurine, turkey, blue, w/lid.......................................**$550.00**
Figurine, Two Kids, flower frog, 9½" **$200.00**
Gloria, crystal, bowl, cranberry; 4-footed, 3½" **$25.00**
Gloria, crystal, bowl, salad; tab handled, 9" **$20.00**
Gloria, crystal, comport, fruit cocktail; 4" **$10.00**
GLoria, crystal, comport, low, 7"..................................**$30.00**
Gloria, crystal, cup, square, 4-footed **$25.00**
Gloria, crystal, plate, bread & butter; 6" **$6.00**
Gloria, crystal, stem, sherbet; tall, #3035, 6-oz............**$12.50**
Gloria, crystal, tray, relish; 2-part, center handled......**$25.00**
Gloria, crystal, tumbler, footed, used w/cocktail shaker, #3120, 2½-oz..**$22.00**
Gloria, green, pink or yellow, bowl, footed, flared rim, 12" **$55.00**
Gloria, green, pink or yellow, icer, w/insert **$85.00**
Gloria, green, pink or yellow, plate, salad; square.....**$12.00**
Gloria, green, pink or yellow, saucer, round **$5.00**
Gloria, green, pink or yellow, stem, water; #3120, 9-oz..**$25.00**
Gloria, green, pink or yellow, tumbler, tea; #3135, 12-oz.**$30.00**
Imperial Hunt Scene, colors, creamer, footed **$30.00**
Imperial Hunt Scene, colors, ice bucket.....................**$75.00**
Imperial Hunt Scene, colors, plate, 8".........................**$22.00**
Imperial Hunt Scene, colors, sugar bowl, footed........**$30.00**
Imperial Hunt Scene, colors, tumbler, footed, #3085, 10-oz **$30.00**
Imperial Hunt Scene, crystal, bowl, 8".......................**$35.00**
Imperial Hunt Scene, crystal, stem, #1402, 18-oz........**$60.00**
Imperial Hunt Scene, crystal, tumbler, flat, tall, #1402, 10-oz **$25.00**
Mt Vernon, amber or crystal, ashtray, #63, 3½"............**$8.00**
Mt Vernon, amber or crystal, bowl, bell shape, #128, 11½" **$30.00**
Mt Vernon, amber or crystal, bowl, finger; #23...........**$10.00**
Mt Vernon, amber or crystal, bowl, flanged, rolled edge, #45, 12½" **$35.00**
Mt Vernon, amber or crystal, box, w/lid, footed, round, #15, 4½" **$37.50**
Mt Vernon, amber or crystal, candlestick, 2-light, #110, 5"..**$20.00**
Mt Vernon, amber or crystal, coaster, ribbed, #70, 3" ...**$5.00**
Mt Vernon, amber or crystal, comport, #81, 8" **$25.00**
Mt Vernon, amber or crystal, lamp, hurricane; #1607, 9"..**$70.00**
Mt Vernon, amber or crystal, pitcher, ball shape, #95, 80-oz **$95.00**
Mt Vernon, amber or crystal, plate, handled, #37, 11½"..**$20.00**
Mt Vernon, amber or crystal, salt & pepper shakers, short, #88, pr...**$20.00**
Mt Vernon, amber or crystal, stem, cocktail; #26, 3½-oz.......**$9.00**
Mt Vernon, amber or crystal, sugar bowl, individual; #4.....**$12.00**
Mt Vernon, amber or crystal, tumbler, barrel shape, 14-oz.**$20.00**
Mt Vernon, amber or crystal, tumbler, footed, #21, 5-oz.....**$12.00**

Mt Vernon, amber or crystal, vase, squat, #107, 6½" ..**$27.50**

Portia, crystal, bowl, bonbon; 2-handled, 5¼" **$15.00**

Portia, crystal, bowl, flared, 4-footed, 12"...................**$45.00**

Portia, crystal, celery/relish; tab handled, 3-part, 9" ...**$30.00**

Portia, crystal, cigarette holder, urn shape..................**$65.00**

Portia, crystal, comport, blown, 5⅜"...........................**$35.00**

Portia, crystal, mayonnaise set, divided bowl, w/liner & 2 ladles..**$50.00**

Portia, crystal, plate, bonbon; tab handled, footed, 8"....**$20.00**

Portia, crystal, stem, cordial; #3121, 1-oz...................**$60.00**

Portia, crystal, stem, goblet; #3126, 9-oz.....................**$22.50**

Portia, crystal, stem, sherbet; tall, #3124, 7-oz.............**$15.00**

Portia, crystal, stem, tea; #3130, 12-oz.......................**$25.00**

Portia, crystal, tumbler, bar; #3121, 2½-oz..................**$30.00**

Portia, crystal, tumbler, water; #3124, 10-oz...............**$22.50**

Portia, crystal, vase, flower; 11"................................**$55.00**

Primrose, yellow opaque, candy box, #96-½, w/lid...**$50.00**

Rosalie, amber, bowl, 2-handled, 10".........................**$27.00**

Rosalie, amber, comport, 5¾".....................................**$15.00**

Rosalie, amber, plate, salad; 7½"..................................**$6.00**

Rosalie, amber, stem, sherbet; high, #3077, 6-oz **$14.00**

Rosalie, amber, vase, 6"..**$40.00**

Rosalie, blue, pink or green, bowl, bonbon; 2-handled, 5½"...**$20.00**

Rosalie, blue, pink or green, bowl, oval, 15½"...........**$95.00**

Rosalie, blue, pink or green, ice tub..........................**$70.00**

Rosalie, blue, pink or green, salt dip, footed, 1½" **$50.00**

Rosalie, blue, pink or green, tumbler, footed, #3077, 5-oz .**$25.00**

Rose Point, crystal, ashtray, #3500/125, 3½" **$35.00**

Rose Point, crystal, ashtray, oval, #3500/131, 4½" **$65.00**

Rose Point, crystal, basket, footed, 2-handled, square, #3500/55, 6"...**$37.50**

Rose Point, crystal, bowl, bonbon; deep cupped, #3400/204, 3½"...**$80.00**

Rose Point, crystal, bowl, finger; w/liner, #3121.........**$85.00**

Rose Point, crystal, bowl, flared, #3400/168, 10½" **$65.00**

Rose Point, crystal, bowl, tab handled, #3900/34, 11" ..**$67.50**

Rose Point, crystal, bowl, 3-part, #221, 8½".............**$150.00**

Rose Point, crystal, candelabrum, 3-light w/#19 bobeche & #1 prisms, #1545, 5½" **$125.00**

Rose Point, crystal, candlestick, #3500/108, 2½".........**$30.00**

Rose Point, crystal, candy box, w/lid, blown, #3500/103, 5⅜"...**$155.00**

Rose Point, crystal, celery tray, 5-part, #3400/67, 12" .**$75.00**

Rose Point, crystal, cocktail shaker, w/glass stopper, #101, 32-oz..**$175.00**

Rose Point, crystal, comport, scalloped edge, #3900/136, 5½"...**$55.00**

Rose Point, crystal, creamer, footed, #3900/41...........**$20.00**

Rose Point, crystal, icer, cocktail; #968 or #18 ....**$72.50**

Rose Point, crystal, plate, rolled edge, footed, #3900/33, 13"...**$70.00**

Rose Point, crystal, relish tray, 2-part, #3500/68, 5½".**$25.00**

Rose Point, crystal, relish tray, 2-part, #3900/124, 7"..**$37.50**

Rose Point, crystal, stem, cocktail; #3500, 3-oz...........**$35.00**

Rose Point, crystal, stem, sherbet; low, #3106, 7-oz ...**$25.00**

Rose Point, crystal, stem, sherry; #3106, 2-oz..............**$45.00**

Rose Point, crystal, sugar bowl, flat, #137................**$110.00**

Rose Point, crystal, vase, globe shape, #3400/102, 5"....**$85.00**

Rose Point, crystal, vase, keyhole; footed, #1233, 9½"..**$75.00**

Rose Point, crystal, vase, slender, #274, 10" **$55.00**

Valencia, crystal, ashtray, round, #3500/126, 4" **$14.00**

Valencia, crystal, bowl, footed, 2-handled, #3500/115, 9½" .**$35.00**

Valencia, crystal, comport, #3500/36, 6"......................**$27.50**

Valencia, crystal, mayonnaise set, #3500/59, 3-pc.......**$40.00**

Valencia, crystal, relish tray, 3-compartment, #3500/69, 6½"...**$20.00**

Valencia, crystal, relish tray, 4-compartment, #3500/65, 10"...**$30.00**

Valencia, crystal, stem, cocktail; #1402......................**$20.00**

Valencia, crystal, stem, goblet; #1402........................**$20.00**

Valencia, crystal, stem, sherbet; tall, #3500, 7-oz **$15.00**

Valencia, crystal, tumbler, #3400/92, 2½-oz...............**$17.50**

Valencia, crystal, tumbler, footed, #3500, 13-oz **$22.50**

Wildflower, crystal, bowl, bonbon; 2-handled, #3400/1180, 5¼"...**$18.00**

Wildflower, crystal, bowl, celery/relish; 5-part, 12" ..**$35.00**

Wildflower, crystal, bowl, mayonnaise; w/underplate, #3400/11...**$55.00**

Wildflower, crystal, bowl, relish; 2-part, #3900/124, 7"..**$22.00**

Wildflower, crystal, bowl, w/tab handle, footed, #3900/28, 11½"...**$45.00**

Wildflower, crystal, candlestick, #3400/646, 5"...........**$35.00**

Wildflower, crystal, ice bucket, w/chrome handle, #3900/671...**$75.00**

Wildflower, crystal, plate, #3400/176, 7½" **$9.00**

Wildflower, crystal, plate, service; 4-footed, #3900/26, 12"..**$35.00**

Wildflower, crystal, stem, claret; #3121, 4½-oz **$65.00**

Wildflower, crystal, sugar bowl, #3900/41...................**$12.50**

Wildflower, crystal, tumbler, tea; #3121, 12-oz............**$25.00**

Rose Point, crystal, pitcher, #3900/15, 76-oz, $200.00.

Cameras

Camera collecting as an investment or hobby has boomed, as evidenced by price increases and by the interest shown in current publications and at numerous camera shows that emphasize both user and classic collectible types.

Buying at garage sales, flea markets, auctions, or estate sales are ways to add to collections, although it is rare to find an expensive classic camera offered through these outlets. But buying at such sales to resell to dealers or collectors can be profitable, if one is careful to buy quality items and not common worn, cheap cameras. A very old camera is not necessarily valuable, as value depends on availability and the number orginally made. Knowing how to check out a camera or to judge quality will pay off when building a collection.

There are many distinct types of cameras to consider: large format (such as Graflex and large view cameras), medium format, early folding and box styles, 33mm single-lens-reflex (SLR), 35mm range finders, twin-lens-reflex (TLR), miniature or sub-miniture, novelty, and other types — including the more recent 'point-and-shoot' styles, Polaroid types, and movie cameras. Although no sizeable market has developed for Polaroids or movie cameras, interest is beginning to mount for certain types. Yet caution is advised on buying these types for resale, as there is very little market at this time. Most pre-1900 cameras will be found in large-format view camera or studio camera types. In the 1920s to the 1930s, folding-and box-type cameras were produced, which today make good collector items. Most have fairly low values because of their vast numbers. Many of the more expensive classics were manufactured in the 1930 through 1955 period and primarily include the range-finder type of camera and those with the first built-in meters. The most prized of these are of German or Japanese manufacture, valued because of their innovative designs and great optics. The key to collecting these types of cameras is to find a mint-condition item or one still in the original box. In camera collecting, quality is the most important aspect.

This listing includes only a few of the various categories and models of cameras from the many thousands available and gives current average retail prices for working models with average wear. A (+) at the end of the line indicates cameras that are generally considered as the most popular user-type cameras with standard 50mm lenses and does not include the later model Auto-Focus or 'point-and-shoot' cameras. Note that cameras in mint condition or mint with their original boxes may be valued much higher, while very worn examples with defects (scratches, dents, torn covers, poor optics, nonworking meters or range finders) would be valued far less. If buying for resale, remember that a dealer will pay considerably less than these values considering his expenses for refurbishing, cleaning, etc. Again, remember that quality is the key to value, and prices on some cameras vary widely according to condition. Typical collector favorites are old Contax, Nikon, Canon, or Leica rangefinders, Rolleiflex TLR's, some Zeiss-Ikon models, Exakta, and certain Voigtlander models. For information about these makes as well as models by Alpa and Conley (early view cameras) please consult the advisor.

Advisor: Gene's Cameras (See Directory, Cameras)

Agfa, Billy, early 1930s	$25.00
Agfa, Isolette	$30.00
Agfa, Karat 3.5, 1940	$35.00
Aires, 35III, 1958	$40.00
Ansco, Memar, 1956-59	$25.00
Ansco, Speedex, Standard, 1950	$15.00
Ansco, Super Speedex, 75/3.5 lens, 1953-58	$175.00
Argoflex Seventy-five, TLR, 1949-58	$7.00
Argus A2F, 1939-41	$20.00

Argus C3, black brick type, 1940-50	$15.00
Argus C4, 50/2.8 lens w/flash	$30.00
Asahi Pentax, original, 1957	$200.00
Asahiflex I, 1st Japanese SLR	$400.00
Baldi, by Balda-Werk, Germany, 1930s	$35.00
Bolsey, B2	$30.00
Braun Paxette I, 1952	$40.00
Canon A-1 (+)	$200.00
Canon AE-1 (+)	$110.00
Canon AE-1P (+)	$140.00
Canon F-1 (+)	$250.00
Canon IIB, 1949-52	$275.00
Canon III, 1951-53	$225.00
Canon J, Seiki Kogaku, 1939-40	$7,000.00
Canon S-II, Seiki Kogaku, 1946-47	$800.00
Canon 7, 1961-64	$300.00
Ciroflex, TLR, 1940s	$40.00
Compass Camera, 1938	$1,300.00
Contax II or III, 1936-42, from $300 to	$400.00
Contessa 35, 1950-55	$150.00

Detrola Model D, Detroit Corp., 1938 – 40, $30.00. (Photo courtesy Gene's Cameras)

Eastman Folding Brownie Six-20	$15.00
Eastman Premo, many models available, any	$35.00
Edinex, by Wirgin	$50.00
Exakta II, 1949-50	$150.00
Exakta VX, 1951	$80.00
Fujica AX-3 (+)	$110.00
Fujica AX-5 (+)	$145.00
Fujica ST-701 (+)	$80.00
Graflex Pacemaker Crown Graphic, various sizes	$175.00
Graflex Speed Graphic, various sizes	$150.00
Hasselbland 1000F, 1952-57	$700.00
Hit Camera, sm novelty, Japan, various names, any	$20.00
Kodak Baby Brownie, Bakelite	$12.00
Kodak Bantam, Art Deco design, 1935-38	$35.00
Kodak Box Brownie 2A	$7.00
Kodak Box Hawkeye No 2A	$8.00
Kodak Hawkeye, plastic	$10.00
Kodak Medalist, 1941-48	$150.00
Kodak No 1 Folding Pocket	$30.00
Kodak No 3A Folding Pocket	$50.00
Kodak Retina I	$50.00
Kodak Retina II	$70.00

Kodak Retina IIa $90.00
Kodak Retina IIIC $500.00

Kodak Retina Model IIIc, 35mm, Germany, 1954 – 57, $150.00. (Photo courtesy Gene's Cameras)

Kodak Retinette, various models, from $30 to $45.00
Kodak Signet 35 ....$30.00
Kodak Vest Pocket Folding, various models, from $25 to...$35.00
Kodak View, early 1900s, from $150 to $175.00
Kodak 35, w/rangefinder, 1940-51 ....$30.00
Konica Autoreflex TC, various models, from $60 to...$90.00
Konica Autoreflex T4 ....$135.00
Konica FS-1 (+) $100.00
Konica III, 1956-59 ....$80.00
Leica IIc, 1940-46 ....$200.00
Leica IID, 1932-38 ....$270.00
Leica IIIa, 1935-50 ....$250.00
Leica IIIf, 1950-56 ....$350.00
Leica M3, 1954-66 ....$600.00
Mamiya-Sekor 500TL, 1966 ....$35.00
Mamiyaflex 1, TLR, 1951 ....$140.00
Mercury, Model II, CX, 1945 ....$40.00
Minolta Autocord, TLR $100.00
Minolta HiMatic Series, various models $20.00
Minolta SR-7 ....$50.00
Minolta SRT 101 (+) $75.00
Minolta SRT 202 (+) $90.00
Minolta XD-11, 1977 ....$175.00
Minolta XE-5 (+) $180.00
Minolta XG-1 (+) $60.00
Minolta X700 (+) $145.00
Minolta 35, early models, 1947-50, from $300 to......$500.00
Minolta-16, miniature, various models $25.00
Minox B (Spy Camera) $125.00
Miranda Automex II, 1963 ....$85.00
Nikkormat FTN (+) $130.00
Nikon EM (+) $75.00
Nikon F, various finders & meters $175.00
Nikon FA (+) $280.00
Nikon FG (+) $135.00
Nikon FM (+) $195.00
Nikon S, 1951-54 ....$425.00
Nikon S2, 1954-58 ....$400.00
Nikon S3, 1958-60 ....$800.00
Olympus OM-1 (+) $120.00

Olympus OM-10 (+) $80.00
Olympus OM-2 (+) $150.00
Olympus Pen EE, compact half frame $35.00
Olympus Pen F, compact half frame SLR $150.00
Olympus 35 IV, 1949-53 ....$50.00
Pax-M3, 1957 ....$50.00
Pentax K-1000 (+) $110.00
Pentax ME (+) $100.00
Pentax Spotmatic (+) $80.00
Pentax Super Program (+) $160.00
Petri FT, FT1000 or FT-EE, each $70.00
Petri 7, 1961 ....$20.00
Plaubel-Makina II, 1933-39 ....$200.00
Polaroid, most models, from $5 to $10.00
Polaroid, SX-70 ....$35.00
Polaroid, 110, 110A or 110B Pathfinder, each $40.00
Polaroid, 180, 185, 190 or 195 Professional, each, from $150 to. $300.00
Praktica FX, 1952-57 ....$50.00
Praktica Super TL, 1968-74 ....$60.00
Realist Stereo, 3.5 lens $120.00
Regula, King, various models, fixed lens $40.00
Regula, King, w/interchangeable lenses $90.00

Ricoh Diacord L, TLR, built-in meter, 1958, $80.00. (Photo courtesy Gene's Cameras)

Ricoh KR-30 (+) $115.00
Rolleicord II, 1936-50 ....$90.00
Rolleiflex Automat, 1937 ....$125.00
Rolleiflex 3.5E, 1956-59 ....$300.00
Rolleiflex 3.5F, 1960-81 ....$600.00
Samoca 35, 1950s $35.00
Seroco 4x5, Folding Plate, Sears, 1901 ....$125.00
Supersport Dolly, w/rangefinder, 1936 ....$130.00
Tessina, miniature, chrome $500.00
Tessina, miniature, colors $700.00
Topcon Super D, 1963-74 ....$135.00
Topcon Uni $50.00
Tower 45 (Sears), w/Nikkor lens $200.00
Tower 50 (Sears), w/Cassar lens $18.00
Univex, Universal Camera Co, 1935-39 ....$25.00
Voigtlander Bessa, various folding models, 1931-49 ...$40.00

Voigtlander Bessa, w/rangefinder, 1936....................**$140.00**
Voigtlander Vitessa L, 1954 ....**$175.00**
Voigtlander Vito II, 1950.............................**$50.00**
Yashica A, TLR.......................................**$45.00**
Yashica Electro 35, 1966.............................**$30.00**
Yashica FX-1, 1975...................................**$50.00**
Yashica FX-70 (+)....................................**$85.00**
Yashicamat 124G, TLR.................................**$190.00**

Zeiss Baldur Box Tengor, Frontar lens, ca 1935, from $35.00 to $50.00. (Photo courtesy Gene's Cameras)

Zeiss-Ikon Box Tengor 43/2, 1934-38 ....**$40.00**
Zeiss-Ikon Juwell (275/11), 1927-39.........................**$500.00**
Zeiss-Ikon Nettar, folding roll film, various sizes........**$35.00**
Zeiss-Ikon Super Ikonta B (532/16), 1937-56...........**$160.00**
Zenit E, Russian **$35.00**
Zorki 4, Russian **$70.00**

Candlewick Glassware

This is a beautifully simple, very diverse line of glassware made by the Imperial Glass Company of Bellaire, Ohio, from 1936 to 1982. (The factory closed in 1984.) From all explored written material found so far, it is known that Mr. Earl W. Newton brought back a piece of the French Cannonball pattern upon returning from a trip. The first Candlewick mold was derived using that piece of glass as a reference. As for the name Candlewick, it was first introduced at a Wheeling, West Virginia, centennial celebration in August of 1936, appearing on a brochure promoting the craft of 'Candlewick Quilts.'

Imperial did cuttings on Candewick; several major patterns are Floral, Valley Lily, Starlight, Princess, DuBarry, and Dots. So remember, these are *cuts* and should not be confused with etchings. (Cuts that were left unpolished were called Gray Cut — an example of this is seen with the Dot cut.) The most popular Candlewick etch was Rose of Sharon (Wild Rose). All cutting was done on a wheel, while etching utilized etching paper and acid. Many collectors confuse these two processes. Imperial also used gold, silver, platinum, and hand painting to decorate Candlewick, and they made several items in colors.

With over 740 pieces in all, Imperial's Candlewick line was one of the leading tableware patterns in the country. Due to its popularity with collectors today, it is still number one and has the distinction of being the only single line of glassware to ever have two books written about it, a national newsletter, and over 15 collector clubs across the USA devoted to it exclusively.

There are reproductions on the market today — some are coming in from foreign countries. Look-alikes are often mistakenly labeled Candlewick, so if you're going to collect this pattern, you need to be well informed. Most collectors use the company mold numbers to help identify all the variations and sizes. The *Imperial Glass Encyclopedia, Vol. 1,* has a very good chapter on Candlewick. Also reference *Candlewick, The Jewel of Imperial,* by Mary Wetzel-Tomalka. The National Imperial Glass Collectors' Society newsletter, *Glasszette,* October 1993 issue has an excellent history of Candlewick by Willard Knob, glass historian.

Advisor: Joan Cimini (See Directory, Imperial Glass)

Newsletter: *The Candlewick Collector*
Virginia R. Scott
275 Milledge Terrace, Athens, GA 30306; 404-548-5966

Creamer and sugar bowl on tray, #400/2930, $30.00.

Ashtray, heart, #400/173, 5½"......................................**$12.00**
Ashtray/jelly, round, #400/33, 4" **$12.00**
Basket, beaded handle, #400/273, 5" **$225.00**
Basket, handled, #400/73/0, 11"..................................**$210.00**
Bowl, #400/7F, 8"...**$37.50**
Bowl, baked apple; rolled edge, #400/53X, 6½" **$27.50**
Bowl, belled (punch base), #400/128B, 10" **$85.00**
Bowl, belled rim, #400/63B, 10½".............................**$48.00**
Bowl, cottage cheese; #400/85, 6"...........................**$30.00**
Bowl, float; cupped edge, #400/75F, 10" **$40.00**
Bowl, lily; 4-toed, #400/74J, 7".................................**$215.00**
Bowl, mayonnaise; 2 sections, #400/84, 6½" **$30.00**
Bowl, nappy, 3-toed, #400/206, 4½"..........................**$60.00**
Bowl, square, #400/232, 6" **$115.00**
Bowl, 2 handles, #400/52B, 6½".................................**$18.00**
Bowl, 3-toed, #400/182, 8½".......................................**$110.00**
Butter dish, #400/144, 5½" dia **$32.50**
Calendar, desk; 1947 ....**$200.00**
Candle holder, flower, crimped, #400/40C, 5"............**$35.00**
Candle holder, flower, 2-bead stem, #400/66F, 4".......**$70.00**

Candle holder, heart shape, #400/40HC, 5" **$75.00**
Candle holder, mushroom, flat edge, #400/86 ....**$35.00**
Candle holder, rolled edge, #400/79R, 3½" **$14.00**
Candle holder, 3-toed, #400/207, 4½" **$65.00**
Candy box, 3-compartment, #400/158, 7" dia **$190.00**
Celery boat, oval, #400/46, 11" **$70.00**
Clock, 4" dia **$300.00**
Coaster, w/spoon rest, #400/226 ....**$16.00**
Compote, beaded stem, #400/48F, 8" **$85.00**
Compote, crimped rim, footed, #400/67C, 9" **$120.00**
Compote, plain stem, #400/63B, 4½" **$45.00**
Creamer, domed foot, #400/18 ....**$115.00**
Creamer, flat, beaded handle, #400/126....................**$35.00**
Cruet, handled, bulbous bottom, #400/279, 6-oz.......**$65.00**
Cup, coffee; #400/37...**$7.50**
Dish, 3-part, oblong, w/lid, #400/216, 10"................**$335.00**

Dresser set: Cologne bottles, each, $85.00; Powder box with star cutting, $120.00.

Hurricane lamp, 2-pc candle base, #400/79 ....**$110.00**
Ice tub, 2 handles, #400/168, 7" **$195.00**
Jar tower, 3-compartment, #400/655 ....**$325.00**
Ladle, mayonnaise; 2-bead handle, #400/135, 6¼" **$12.00**
Mustard jar, w/lid & spoon, #400/156.......................**$40.00**
Pitcher, Manhattan, #400/18, 40-oz **$235.00**
Pitcher, short, round, no beads, #400/330, 14-oz......**$170.00**
Plate, #400/34, 4½" **$8.00**
Plate, crescent salad; #400/120, 8½" **$50.00**
Plate, dinner; #400/10D, 10½" **$40.00**
Plate, oval, #400/124, 12½" **$75.00**
Plate, oval w/indent, #400/98, 9" **$16.00**
Plate, salad; #400/3D, 7"..**$8.00**
Plate, torte; #400/17D, 14" **$42.50**
Plate, torte; 2 handles, #400/113D, 14" **$45.00**
Plate, 2 handles, #400/62D, 8½"................................**$12.00**
Platter, oval, #400/131D, 16"....................................**$200.00**
Relish bowl, oblong, 4-compartment, #400/215, 12" ..**$70.00**
Salt & pepper shakers, #400/109, individual, pr **$16.00**
Salt & pepper shakers, bulbous w/1-bead stems, plastic lids,
    #400/116, pr **$115.00**
Sauce boat, w/8" oval underplate, #400/169.............**$150.00**
Saucer, tea or coffee; #400/35 or #400/37 ....**$2.50**

Stem, brandy, 2-bead stem, #3800............................**$32.00**
Stem, claret, #3400, 5-oz **$50.00**
Stem, cocktail, #400/190, 4-oz **$20.00**
Stem, dinner wine, #400/190, 5-oz **$26.00**
Stem, goblet, #400/190, 10-oz **$20.00**
Stem, goblet, 2-bead stem, #3800, 10-oz **$30.00**
Stem, sherbet, low, 1-bead stem, #3800....................**$25.00**
Sugar bowl, flat, bead handle, #400/126 ....**$35.00**
Sugar bowl, plain foot, #400/31 ....**$10.00**
Teacup, #400/35..**$8.00**
Tray, fruit; center handle, #400/68F, 10½"................**$115.00**
Tray, relish; 5-compartment, #400/102, 13" **$75.00**

Tray, relish; 5-part, #400/56, 10½", $55.00.

Tray, upturned handles, #400/42E, 5½" **$16.00**
Tumbler, cocktail; footed, #400/19, 3-oz....................**$18.00**
Tumbler, juice; #400/19, 5-oz **$15.00**
Tumbler, juice; 1-bead stem, #3800, 5-oz **$30.00**
Tumbler, sherbet; #400/18, 6-oz **$40.00**
Tumbler, tea; #400/19, 14-oz **$22.00**
Tumbler, water; #400/18, 9-oz **$40.00**
Tumbler, 1-bead stem, #3800, 12-oz **$30.00**
Vase, #400/198, 6" dia **$260.00**
Vase, beaded foot, inward rim, #400/27, 8½" **$215.00**
Vase, bud; footed, #400/187, 7" **$200.00**
Vase, fan; open beaded handles, #400/87F, 8" **$35.00**
Vase, footed, #400/193, 10".....................................**$170.00**
Vase, mini bud; beaded foot, #400/107, 5¾"...............**$70.00**

Candy Containers

Most of us can recall buying these glass toys as a child, since they were made well into the 1960s. We were fascinated by the variety of their shapes then, just as collectors are today. Looking back, it couldn't have been we were buying them for the candy, though perhaps as a child those tiny sugary balls flavored more with the coloring agent than anything else were enough to satisfy our 'sweet tooth.'

Glass candy containers have been around since our country's centennial celebration in 1876 when the first two, the Liberty Bell and the Independence Hall, were introduced. Since then they have been made in hundreds of styles, and some of them have become very expensive. The leading manufacturers were in the East — Westmoreland, Victory

Glass, J.H. Millstein, Crosetti, L.E. Smith, Jack Stough, T.H. Stough, and West Bros. made perhaps 90% of them — and collectors report finding many in the Pennsylvania area. Most are clear, but you'll find them in various other colors as well.

If you're going to deal in candy containers, you need a book that will show you all the variations available. *The Compleat American Glass Candy Containers Handbook* by Eikelberner and Agadjaninian (recently revised by Adele Bowden) uses a numbering system that has become universal among collectors. Numbers in our listings refer to this book, except for the few 'L' numbers which correspond with Jenny Long's *Album of Candy Containers, Vol. 1 and Vol. 2,* published in 1978 – 83.

Because of their popularity and considerable worth, many of the original containers have been reproduced. Beware of any questionable glassware that has a slick or oily touch. Among those that have been produced are Amber Pistol (#283), Auto (#48 and #33), Carpet Sweeper (#132 and #133), Chicken on Nest (#149), Display Case (#177), Dog (#179), Drum Mug (#543), Fire Engine (#213), Independence Hall (#342), Jackie Coogan (#345), Kewpie (#539), Mail Box (#521), Mantel Clock (#164), Mule and Waterwagon (#539), Peter Rabbit (#618), Piano (#577), Rabbit Pushing Wheelbarrow (#601), Rocking Horse (#651), Safe (#661), Santa (#674), Santa's Boot (#111), Station Wagon (#567), Uncle Sam's Hat (#303). Others are possible.

Our values are given for candy containers that are undamaged, in good original paint, and complete (with all original parts and closure). Repaired or repainted containers are worth much less. A very comprehensive new book, *Collector's Guide to Candy Containers,* by Douglas M. Dezso, J. Leon Poirier, and Rose D. Poirier, was released early in 1998. D&P numbers in our listings refer to that book. Published by Collector Books, it is a must for beginners as well as seasoned collectors.

See also Christmas; Easter; Halloween.

Advisor: Doug Dezso (See Directory, Candy Containers)

Club/Newsletter: *The Candy Gram*
Candy Container Collectors of America
Joyce L. Doyle
P.O. Box 426
North Reading, MA 01864-0426

Airplane, US Army B-51, w/wings, L #591	**$120.00**
Amos 'N Candy Fresh Air Taxi, clear glass w/painted figures & wheels, EX	**$450.00**
Basket, clear glass w/grape design, L #223 (E&A #81)	**$45.00**
Bear on Circus Tub, original blades, L #1 (E&A #81)	**$45.00**
Bureau, L #125 (E&A #112)	**$200.00**
Camel, D&P #4, 6"L, from $75 to	**$100.00**
Candlestick, L #201	**$300.00**
Car, Long Hood Coupe #3, L #359 (E&A #51)	**$110.00**
Chick Baby, standing, D&P #7, yellow w/black beak & legs, from $100 to	**$125.00**
Coal Car, w/tender, L #402 (E&A #170)	**$350.00**
Decorettes, L #655	**$200.00**
Dog, Puppy; D&P #33, from $25 to	**$40.00**

Felix by Barrel, L #85 (E&A #211)	**$625.00**
Fire Engine, Victory Glass, L #386	**$35.00**

Flossie Fisher's Bed, L #127 (E&A #234), EX, $2,000.00. (Photo courtesy Doug Dezso)

Horn, Millstein's, L #282 (E&A #311)	**$25.00**
Jack-O-Lantern, black cat, L #158 (E&A #349-1)	**$450.00**
Locomotive 888, no wheels, L #395 (E&A #485)	**$50.00**
Poodle Dog, glass head, L #471, from $20 to	**$30.00**
Rabbit Crouching, L #41 (E&A #615), EX paint	**$105.00**
Rabbit Nibbling Carrot, L #53 (E&A #609), w/original candy	**$60.00**
Rabbit on Dome, gold paint, L #46 (E&A #607)	**$450.00**
Rabbit on Eggshell, gold-painted top, L #48, 5½"	**$75.00**
Racer #12 (E&A #151)	**$275.00**

Skookum by Stump, L#106 (E&A #681), $250.00.

Taxi, L #366, 4¼" L	**$100.00**
Telephone, Victory Glass (E&A #397), 5"	**$50.00**
Trunk, L #218 (E&A #789)	**$125.00**
Wagon or Stagecoach, L #441	**$125.00**
Will's Jeep Scout Car, L #391 (E&A #350)	**$30.00**
Windmill, shaker top, original blades, L #445 (E&A #842)	**$200.00**

Cape Cod by Avon

You can't walk through any flea market or mall now without seeing volumes of this ruby red glassware. It was made by Wheaton Glass Co. and sold by Avon since the seventies. The small cruet and tall candlesticks, for instance, were filled originally with one or the other of their fragrances, the wine and water goblets were filled with scented candlewax, and the dessert bowl with guest soap. Many 'campaigns' have featured accessory tableware items such as plates, cake stands, and a water pitcher. Obviously the line was very good seller for them, judging from the sheer volume of it around. Until very recently it was still featured in their catalogs, but it has now been discontinued, and you can look for interest in it to increase.

Some nice pieces can be found at garage sales, the glassware is of good quality, there's a nice assortment of items in the line, and it's readily available. Even at mall prices, it's not expensive. That's about all it takes to make a collectible.

Advisor: Debbie Coe (See Directory, Cape Cod)

Bell, hostess; marked 1979, 6½"....................................$22.50
Bell, hostess; unmarked, 1979-1980, 6½".......................$17.50
Bowl, dessert; 1978-1990, 5" $14.50
Bowl, rimmed soup; 1991, 7½" $18.00
Bowl, vegetable; to commemorate Avon's 100th anniversary of business, marked Centennial Edition 1886-1986, 8¾" $34.50
Bowl, vegetable; unmarked, 1986-1990, 8¾" $24.50
Box, heart form, w/lid, 1989-1990, 4" wide................$18.00
Butter dish, w/lid, 1983-84, ¼-lb, 7" L........................$22.50
Cake knife, plastic handle, Regent Sheffield, 1981-84 ..$9.50

Candle holder, hurricane type with clear chimney, 1985, 13", $35.00.

Candlestick, 1975-1980, 8¾", each $12.50
Candlestick, 1983-1984, 2½", each................................$9.75
Candy dish, 1987-1990, 3½x6" dia $19.50
Christmas ornament, 6-sided, marked Christmas 1990, 3¼"..$10.00
Creamer, footed, 1981-84, 4".......................................$12.50
Cruet, oil; w/stopper, 1975-1980, 5-oz $12.50
Cup & saucer, commemorates 15th anniversary, marked 1975-1990 on cup, 7-oz...$24.50
Cup & saucer, 1990-1993, 7-oz $19.50
Decanter, w/stopper, 1977-80, 16-oz...........................$20.00
Goblet, champagne; footed, 1991, 8-oz, 5¼" $9.50
Goblet, claret; footed, 1992, 5-oz, 5¼"..........................$8.50
Goblet, water; footed, 1976-1990, 9-oz $9.50
Goblet, wine; footed, 1977-1980, 3-oz $5.00
Gravy boat w/attached liner, 1988 only......................$28.50

Mug, pedestal foot, 1982-1984, 6-oz, 5"......................$12.50
Napkin ring, 1989-1990, 1¾" dia $9.50
Pie plate, server, 1992-93, 10¾" dia $19.50
Pitcher, water; footed, 1984-1985, 60-oz $50.00
Plate, bread & butter; 1992-1993, 5½"...........................$7.50
Plate, cake; pedestal foot, 1991, 3¼x10¾" dia...........$50.00
Plate, dessert; 1980-1990, 7½".....................................$9.50
Plate, dinner; 1982-1990, 11"......................................$19.50
Platter, oval, 1986, 13" $35.00
Relish, 2-part, 1985-86, 9½" $19.50

Salt and pepper shakers, marked May 1978 on bottom, pair, MIB, from $18.00 to $22.00.

Salt & pepper shakers, marked 1978, each....................$8.50
Salt & pepper shakers, unmarked, 1978-1980, each $5.00
Sugar bowl, footed, 1980-83, 3½" $12.50
Tidbit tray, 2-tiers (7" & 10" dia), 1987, 9¾" $49.50
Tumbler, straight sided, footed, 1988, 8-oz, 3¾"...........$8.50
Tumbler, straight sided, 1990, 12-oz, 5½"......................$9.50
Vase, footed, 1985, 8" $20.00

Cardinal China Company

This was the name of a distributing company who had their merchandise made to order and sold it through a chain of showrooms and outlet stores in several states from the late 1940s through the 1950s. (Although they made some of their own pottery early on, we have yet to find out just what they themselves produced.) They used their company name to mark cookie jars (some of which were made by the American Bisque Company), novelty wares, and kitchen items, many of which you'll see as you make your flea market rounds. *The Collector's Encyclopedia of Cookie Jars* by Joyce and Fred Roerig (Collector Books) shows a page of their jars, and more can be seen in *American Bisque* by Mary Jane Giacomini (Shiffer).

See also Cookie Jars.

Condiment jar, Onion lettered on hat of sad clown head, unmarked, 5¼"..$65.00
Dresser dish, Doxie-dog..$18.00
Flower holder, doughnut shape, turquoise on white, 7" .$8.00
Measuring spoon holder, flowerpot shape w/basketweave base, w/spoons $15.00
Measuring spoon holder, windowsill planter shape ...$15.00

Salt & pepper shakers, Chinese man & lady, green & yellow, pr $22.00
Scissors holder, nest w/chicken figural $25.00
Shrimp boat set, 4 colors, EX $75.00
Spoon rest, yellow flower shape $6.00
String holder, nest w/chicken figural $25.00
Tray, dresser; dachshund $16.00

Measuring spoon holder, flowerpot shape with plain base, with spoons, $12.00; Sprinkler bottle, Chinaman Sprinkle Plenty, from $20.00 to $30.00.

Carnival Chalkware

From about 1910 until the 1950s, winners of carnival games everywhere in the United States were awarded chalkware figures of Kewpie dolls, the Lone Ranger, Hula girls, comic characters, etc. The assortment was vast and varied. The earliest were made of plaster with a pink cast. They ranged in size from about 5" up to 16".

They were easily chipped, so when it came time for the carnival to pick up and move on, they had to be carefully wrapped and packed away, a time consuming, tedious chore. When stuffed animals became available, concessionists found that they could simply throw them into a box without fear of damage, and so ended an era.

Today the most valuable of these statues are those modeled after Disney characters, movie stars, and comic book heroes.

Chalkware figures are featured in *The Carnival Chalk Prize, Vols I and II,* written by Thomas G. Morris, who has also included a fascinating history of carnival life in America.

See also Cat Collectibles.

Advisor: Tom Morris (See Directory, Carnival Chalkware)

Bathing Beauty, hand painted, oversized bonnet, 1920s, 12" $95.00
Bell Hop, tipping hat, copyrighted June Yates Jenkins, November 21, 1946, 13", from $45 to $55.00
Betty Boop, several variations made, ca 1930-40, 14½", each, from $265 to $285.00
Black Boy, eating watermelon, marked By Buelah, ca 1930-40, 7½" $80.00
Cave Girl, pink chalk, hand painted, holds club, marked 1929 Harvey Lee, 11½" $90.00

Child, yawning, sitting w/legs tucked under, ca 1920-30, unmarked, 6" $35.00
Clown, full-figure bank, colorful paint, ca 1940-50, 12", from $45 to $50.00
Cowboy, 10-gallon hat, illegible mark, ca 1940s, 12", from $35 to $45.00
Disney's Donald Duck, head bank, ca 1940-50, 10½" ..$80.00
El Matador, stern face, signed Riverview Park, Chicago, dated 1939, 14" $95.00
Girl & Goat, ca 1930, 9½" $45.00
Girl in Horseshoe, marked Baby Luck, signed, Riverview Park, Chicago, July 1947, 10½" $75.00
Hula Hula Girl, marked Oakland Statuary Co, 1947, 10", from $45 to $55.00
I Love Me Girl, pink chalk, hand-painted features, 1915-30, 11½", from $45 to $55.00
Indian Chief, full figure, unmarked, ca 1930-45, 19" ..$50.00
Indian on Horse (rearing), ca 1930-50, 11" $50.00
Lady w/Horse, leads horse w/dog at side, marked Friends, 1930-40, 9¾x8½" $70.00
Little Red Riding Hood, marked Connie Mamat, ca 1930-40, 14" $45.00

Mae West, many variations, unmarked, 1934 – 45, 13" to 14½", from $95.00 to $120.00. (Photo courtesy Tom Morris)

Mexican Girl, hand painted, white chalk, Jenkins, July 27, 1925, 14½" $135.00
Miss America, blond in swimsuit, unmarked, ca 1940-50, 15¾", from $55 to $65.00
Papa, marked Call Me Papa, ca 1935-45, 14" $40.00
Piano Baby, ca 1910-25, 9½x10½" $120.00
Pinocchio, unmarked, ca 1940, 10", from $35 to $40.00
Popeye, left arm across chest, 1929-50, 13½" or 15½", each, from $95 to $120.00
Sailor, arms folded, legs wide, ca 1935-45, 13", from $55 to $65.00
Sailor, saluting, flat-back figure, ca 1930, 13½", from $30 to $35.00
Sailor Boy, partially hand painted, Jenkins, 1934, 9" ..$35.00
Sea Hag, multicolor paint, ca 1930-40, 8" $90.00
Shirley Temple, dressed as Little Colonel, unmarked, ca 1935-45, 14½" $190.00
Shriner, Kewpie type, marked Portland 1920 on front base, 10½" $110.00

Sitting Girl, pink chalk, hand painted, 1920s, 12½"....**$85.00**
Snow White, no marks, ca 1939-50, 14" or 15", each.**$85.00**
Superman, unmarked, ca 1940-50, 15", from $185 to..**$225.00**
US Sailor, Navy picture frame, 1940s, 7¼x5½" **$45.00**
Wimpy, holds mug of beer, Jenkins, ca 1940s, 9½", from $55
 to...**$60.00**

Pirate girl, by William Rainwater, 1936, 10¾", $65.00; same, 14¼", $95.00. (Photo courtesy Tom Morris)

Cat Collectibles

Cat collectibles continue to grow in popularity as cats continue to dominate the world of household pets. Cat memorabilia can be found in almost all categories, and this allows for collections to grow rapidly! Most cat lovers/collectors are attracted to all items and to all breeds, though some do specialize. Popular categories include Siamese, black cats, Kitty Cucumber, Kliban, cookie jars, teapots, books, plates, postcards, and Louis Wain.

Because cats are found throughout the field of collectibles and antiques, there is some 'crossover' competition among collectors. For example: Chessie, the C&O Railroad cat, is collected by railroad and advertising buffs; Felix the Cat, board games, puppets, and Steiff cats are sought by toy collectors. A Weller cat complements a Weller pottery collection just as a Royal Doulton Flambe cat fits into a Flambe porcelain collection.

Since about 1970 the array and quality of cat items have made the hobby explode. And, looking back, the first half of the twentieth century offered a somewhat limited selection of cats — there were those from the later Victorian era, Louis Wain cats, Felix the Cat, those on postcards, and the kitchen-item black cats of the 1950s. But prior to 1890, cats were few and far between, so a true antique cat (100-years old or more) is scarce, much sought after, and when found in mint condition, pricey. Examples of such early items would be original fine art, porcelains, and bronzes.

There are several 'cat' books available on today's market; if you want to see great photos representing various aspects of 'cat' collecting, you'll enjoy *Cat Collectibles* by Pauline Flick, *Antique Cats for Collectors* by Katharine Morrison McClinton, *American Cat-alogue* by Bruce Johnson, and *The Cat Made Me Buy It* and *The Black Cat Made Me Buy It* by Muncaster and Yanow.

See also Black Cats; Character Collectibles; Cookie Jars; Lefton.

Advisor: Marilyn Dipboye (See Directory, Cat Collectibles)

Club: Cat Collectors
Newsletter: *Cat Talk*
Marilyn Dipboye, President
33161 Wendy Dr., Sterling Hts., MI 48130; 810-264-0285.
Subscription $20 per year US or $27 Canada.

Ashtray, lustreware, black & white kitten on dish, 6 rests,
 Made in Japan, 3¼x3¾" **$25.00**
Bell, Christmas Eve at the Farmhouse, porcelain, Bing &
 Grondahl, 1985...**$42.00**
Bookends, cat w/yarn ball, antique white composition,
 marked Universal Statuary c31366, 6¼", pr..........**$50.00**
Box, cat figural, Oriental blue design w/pink flowers, ceramic, marked Made in China, 7½" L........................**$65.00**
Cat in the Hat, alarm clock....................................**$175.00**
Cat in the Hat, book bag, cloth, 1970s, 9x12", NM.....**$15.00**
Cat in the Hat, bookstand, red plastic **$15.00**
Cat in the Hat, doll, talker (non-working), rag & plush,
 Mattel, G..**$100.00**
Cat in the Hat, infant's rocking chair, EX....................**$50.00**
Cat in the Hat, jack-in-the-box, Mattel, 1970............**$150.00**
Cat in the Hat, stuffed cat, Coleco, 1983, in box, from $25
 to..**$50.00**
Cat in the Hat, thermos..**$75.00**
Chessie, playing cards, double deck, MIB..................**$30.00**
Chessie, scarf, silk, sleeping Chessie pattern, 1949-50..**$50.00**
Chessie, set of 3 prints from original work by Guido
 Gruenewald, 11½x10", 1970s, in original envelope.**$65.00**
Coin, Isle of Man, Manx cat, 1 crown, proof silver, 1975, in
 presentation box **$30.00**
Coin, Isle of Man, Manx cat, 1 crown, 1970, uncirculated...**$15.00**
Coin, Singapore Mint, tiger, 999 silver proof, 1986.....**$25.00**

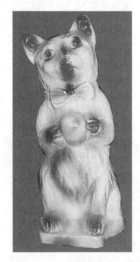

Figurine, carnival chalkware, 7¼", $25.00. (Photo courtesy Marilyn Dipboye)

Figurine, cat, brass, Made in Korea paper label, 4¾", pr..**$12.00**
Figurine, cat playing fiddle, pewter, 1½"....................**$25.00**
Figurine, cat's head, pottery, tan w/mosaic design in gold,
 aqua & white, signed Sascha B, 7½" **$300.00**

Figurine, Catnapping Too?, black & white cat on chair, Lowell Davis, 1984, 4¼" **$98.00**

Figurine, ceramic, mother cat disciplines baby, tabby cats, on base, And Don't Do It Again, Japan hallmark, 6¾x2½" **$68.00**

Figurine, Egyptian cat, bronze-like composition on wood base, marked Austin Prod 1965, 12" **$95.00**

Figurine, kitten, ceramic, covered w/fuzzy material, Josef Originals, 2½"..**$6.00**

Figurine, kitten atop green basket, porcelain covered w/fuzzy material, Josef Originals, 2½".................................**$8.00**

Figurine, kitten playing tennis, Viennese bronze, 2½"...**$195.00**

Figurine, Persian listens to old-fashioned radio, cold-cast porcelain, Border Fine Arts, 1987, 4¼" **$65.00**

Figurine, porcelain, white & brown, various poses by Karner, Rosenthal Hallmark, from $295 to.......................**$325.00**

Figurine, pottery, curled up & sleeping, Chester Nicodemus, #640, 7½" L **$200.00**

Figurine, Siamese, Beswick #1559B-1A, M **$55.00**

Figurine, tabby in pink dress w/umbrella, bisque, marked Hallmark Cards 1987, 4"................................**$9.50**

Food bowl, cat figural w/open back, white w/blue details, Lillian Vernon Corp, Taiwan, 5½" dia **$8.50**

Food dispenser, cat figural, orange & beige tabby w/blue bib, 12x5½" wide **$68.00**

Garfield, bank, bowling **$65.00**

Garfield, bank, in blue & red cap holding bat, ceramic....**$35.00**

Garfield, bank, in chair, ceramic, Enesco, from $110 to .**$125.00**

Garfield, bank, on skis, ceramic, Enesco.....................**$70.00**

Garfield, bank, the graduate, Enesco, 1978, 5½" **$55.00**

Garfield, bank, vinyl, San Diego Chargers, MIB..........**$16.00**

Garfield, bib, image of Garfield riding in sleigh, MOC...**$2.00**

Garfield, book, Scary Tales, Grosset Dunlap................**$4.00**

Garfield, bookends, w/Odie, ceramic, Enesco, pr, from $100 to...**$125.00**

Garfield, cookie jar, Enesco, dated 1978 & 1981, M.**$125.00**

Garfield, cookie tin, Garfield tangled in lights **$6.00**

Garfield, creamer, I love moo juice, stamped on bottom, Enesco, early 1980s.....................................**$30.00**

Garfield, Dakin figure, stuffed Garfield, Spaghetti Attack...**$15.00**

Garfield, doll, dressed as Santa Claus, plush, original tag, M **$16.00**

Garfield, figurine, Class of '84, from $10 to.................**$15.00**

Garfield, figurine, on roller skates, ceramic, 2", EX....**$10.00**

Garfield, growth chart, 3 sheets, MIB **$16.00**

Garfield, lamp, ceramic, party shade, Prestigeline, MIB .**$40.00**

Garfield, mug, Ho Ho Ho, Garfield as Santa, standing beside toy sack..**$5.00**

Garfield, music box, Baby's First Christmas, train circles Garfield & plays 'Toyland,' M **$20.00**

Garfield, night light, Off the Wall, Prestigeline PT-5658 ..**$15.00**

Garfield, ornament, on a star, Hallmark, 1991, MIB ...**$20.00**

Garfield, pin, cloisonne, Garfield sitting **$2.00**

Garfield, PVC figure, in duck innertube **$3.50**

Garfield, salt & pepper shakers, Garfield Santa heads, Enesco, 1993, pr...**$15.00**

Garfield, slide-tile puzzle, MIP....................................**$4.00**

Garfield, soap, Twincraft/Canada, MIB **$4.00**

Garfield, switch plate, Garfield in a tree throwing apples to Odie, Prestigeline, PT 5658..................................**$15.00**

Garfield, trinket box, Be My Valentine, ceramic, Enesco..**$30.00**

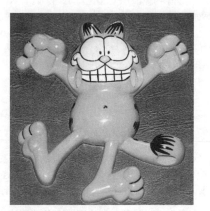

Garfield, wall-mount toothbrush holder, United Features, copyright 1978, from $10.00 to $15.00.

Kitty Cucumber, figurine, Kitty & JP on tricycle, Away We Go, 1988-90, 4"..**$16.00**

Kitty Cucumber, figurine, Kitty bride & Albert groom in hot air balloon, Up, Up & Away, 6½" **$15.00**

Kitty Cucumber, figurine, Kitty graduate in blue gown ..**$8.00**

Kitty Cucumber, music box, cat w/hearts & flowers, plays Love Me Tender, porcelain, 1987-88, 5¼"............**$38.00**

Kitty Cucumber, ornament, Kitty & JP on tricycle, #333264...**$12.00**

Kliban, bank, wearing red sneakers, Sigma, 1979, 6½", $50.00.

Kliban, cookie jar, cat in long pants, Sigma, from $165 to ..**$180.00**

Kliban, cookie jar, cat playing guitar, Sigma, from $165 to..**$180.00**

Kliban, cookie jar, cat sitting upright w/kitten, marked Taste Setter Sigma..**$485.00**

Kliban, cookie jar, Mom cat, Sigma, from $335 to....**$360.00**

Kliban, mug, England...**$30.00**

Kliban, mug, I Love LA, MIB **$8.00**

Kliban, mug, picture of cat playing guitar, from $15 to..**$18.00**

Kliban, pillow, stuffed figural, 22".............................**$22.00**

Kliban, plate, 1995...**$35.00**

Kliban, salt & pepper shakers, cat w/red shoes, composition, pr **$130.00**

Kliban, teapot, cat in blue airplane, from $225 to....**$250.00**

Kliban, teapot, cat in tuxedo, from $175 to **$200.00**

Match holder, bisque, white w/black mother cat & white kitten, dotted bows, Don't Scratch Me..., Germany, 1925, 3½x4"..**$185.00**

Match striker/ashtray, porcelain, black cat & white cat on green, Germany, ca 1925, 3½x5".....................**$145.00**

Match striker/ashtray, pottery, red tabby cat w/blue collar, holds basket on oval base, # incised, Germany, 1880, 5"..**$175.00**

Music box, brown kitten in basket, Sisters Are Forever & I'm So Glad You're Mine, ceramic, 4½"..................**$17.00**

Night light, cat looking down into mirror & flowers on base, white bisque, Neiman Marcus, 5¾".................**$28.00**

Paperweight, 2 curled-together cats, aluminum, Arthur Court Design, 1992, 2¾"..**$35.00**

Perfume container, yellow cat under plastic dome holds 1-oz bottle marked Golden Woods Sophisti-Cat, Max Factor, M..**$25.00**

Planter, Beckoning Cat (Good Luck Cat), marked Elvin Hand Painted Japan on paper label, 4¼", $30.00. (Photo courtesy Marilyn Dipboye)

Plate, Mothers Make the World a Happier Place, white cat w/kitten on red & blue, American Greetings, 6"....**$8.50**

Plate, 3 Kittens, gold trim, from $35.00 to $40.00. (Photo courtesy Marbena Fyke)

Plate, Three Kittens, milk glass, no gold **$25.00**

Playing cards, canasta; white angora cat on blue background, 1950s, double deck, NM..............................**$12.50**

Ring holder, stylized cat, brass, 6" tail..................**$5.00**

Sugar bowl & creamer, yellow tabby cats, Norcrest, late 1980s, 4½", pr **$12.00**

Teapot, brown cat curled next to blue desk phone w/receiver off hook, Coppercraft, Made in England, 1992, 10" L...**$50.00**

Teapot, Siamese w/paw spout & tail handle, Norcrest, late 1980s, 7" L...**$25.00**

Thermometer, hammered aluminum, white metal cat on base, 5¼"...**$40.00**

Toy, lion, fuzzy tan color, Line MAR Toys Japan, wind-up, head nods & tail wags, 6", working condition, VG.........**$160.00**

Tray, metal cat's face shape, The Cat's Meow, A Everette & Son Pattern Letters Auburn NY, ca 1915...............**$85.00**

Tray, sleeping cat figural, blue & cream pottery, marked Sautler 76, 9½"...**$22.00**

Cat-Tail Dinnerware

Cat-tail was a dinnerware pattern popular during the late twenties until sometime in the forties. So popular, in fact, that ovenware, glassware, tinware, even a kitchen table was made to coordinate with it. The dinnerware was made primarily by Universal Potteries of Cambridge, Ohio, though a catalog from Hall China circa 1927 shows a three-piece coffee service, and others may have produced it as well. It was sold for years by Sears Roebuck and Company, and some items bear a mark that includes their name.

The pattern is unmistakable: a cluster of red cattails (usually six, sometimes one or two) with black stems on creamy white. Shapes certainly vary; Universal used at least three of their standard mold designs, Camwood, Old Holland, Laurella, and possibly others. Some Cat-tail pieces are marked Wheelock on the bottom. (Wheelock was a department store in Peoria, Illinois.)

If you're trying to decorate a forties vintage kitchen, no other design could afford you more to work with. To see many of the pieces that are available and to learn more about the line, read *The Collector's Encyclopedia of American Dinnerware* by Jo Cunningham.

Advisors: Barbara and Ken Brooks (See Directory, Dinnerware).

Gravy boat with liner, $35.00. (Photo courtesy Barbara and Ken Brooks)

Batter jug, metal top..**$80.00**

Bowl, Old Holland shape, marked Wheelock, 6".........**$6.00**

Butter dish, w/lid, 1-lb.................................**$45.00**
Cake cover & tray, tinware **$30.00**
Canister set, tinware, 4-pc..........................**$45.00**
Casserole, w/lid **$30.00**
Coffeepot, 3-pc **$65.00**
Cookie jar..**$85.00**
Cracker jar, barrel shape **$75.00**
Creamer, Laurella shape **$16.00**
Custard cup **$7.00**
Gravy boat, w/liner **$35.00**
Jug, refrigerator; w/handle..........................**$30.00**
Jug, side handle, cork stopper.....................**$32.00**
Kitchen scales, tinware................................**$37.00**
Match holder, tinware..................................**$35.00**
Pie plate..**$25.00**
Pie server, hole in handle for hanging, marked Universal
    Potteries **$25.00**
Pitcher, ice lip; glass.................................**$100.00**
Pitcher, utility or milk................................**$25.00**
Plate, dinner; Laurella shape, from $12 to...**$15.00**
Plate, dinner; 3-compartment.......................**$25.00**
Plate, salad or dessert; round........................**$5.00**
Plate, serving; early, marked Universal Potteries-Oven Proof,
    Cambridge Ohio, from $30 to...............**$35.00**
Platter, oval..**$25.00**
Salad set (fork, spoon & bowl) **$50.00**

Salt and pepper shakers, different styles, each pair, $15.00. (Photo courtesy Barbara and Ken Brooks)

Saucer, Old Holland shape, marked Wheelock.............**$6.00**
Shaker set (salt, pepper, flour & sugar shakers), glass, on red
    metal tray..**$40.00**
Stack set, 3-pc w/lids..................................**$40.00**
Sugar bowl, 2-handled, w/lid **$16.00**
Tablecloth..**$85.00**
Teapot, w/lid, from $30 to...........................**$35.00**
Tumbler, iced tea; glass...............................**$35.00**
Tumbler, marked Universal Potteries, scarce..............**$65.00**
Tumbler, water; glass...................................**$30.00**
Waste can, step-on, tinware **$30.00**

Catalin Napkin Rings

Plastic (Catalin) napkin rings topped with heads of cartoon characters, animals, and birds are very collectible, especially examples in red and orange; blue is also good, and other colors can be found as well.

Band, lathe turned, amber, red or green, 1¾" **$10.00**
Band, plain, amber, red, or green, 2", each.............**$8.00**

Band, plain, colors, 2", set of 6, MIB **$40.00**
Camel, inlaid eye rod **$72.00**
Chicken, no inlaid eyes................................**$30.00**
Donald Duck, w/decal, from $65 to **$80.00**
Duck, no inlaid eyes **$30.00**
Elephant, ball on head **$35.00**
Elephant, no ball on head **$30.00**
Fish, no inlaid eyes......................................**$30.00**
Mickey Mouse, w/decal, from $70 to............**$85.00**

Rabbit, inlaid eye rod, $40.00; Elephant, inlaid eye rod, $40.00.

Rabbit, no inlaid eyes..................................**$30.00**
Rocking horse, inlaid eye rod.......................**$72.00**
Schnauzer dog, no inlaid eyes......................**$30.00**
Scotty dog, inlaid eye rod **$40.00**

Catalogs

Right now, some of the most collectible catalogs are those from the the fifties, sixties, and seventies, especially those Christmas 'wish books.' They're full of the toys that are so sought after by today's collectors — battery-ops, Tonkas, and of course, GI Joes and Barbies. No matter what year the catalog was printed, its value will hinge on several factors: subject, illustrations and the amount of color used, collector demand, size, rarity, and condition (grade them carefully and be sure to adjust their values accordingly). Generally, manufacturer's catalogs are more valuable than those put out by a jobber.

Adrian Baby Shoppe, ca early 1930s, 32 pages, VG...**$42.00**
Aldens, 1976, NM.......................................**$22.00**
American Mask Mfg Co, 1948, 23 pages, VG **$28.00**
American Wholesale Corp, Div of Butler Bros, 1931, household items, shoes, hardware & general line, 338 pages,
    EX...**$70.00**
B Altman & Co, 1927, Fall/Winter, clothing & accessories,
    G+ **$25.00**
Ball Company, 1931, jewelry & fine gift items, 664 pages,
    hardcover, 9x12", EX **$140.00**
Banta Refrigerator Co, 1932, counter displays for stores, 23
    pages, 9x11", EX **$55.00**
Beardslee Chandelier Mfg Co, 1921, lighting fixtures, 32
    pages, EX **$35.00**

Bennett Bros, 1963, general merchandise, 786 pages, 8½x11", EX..**$35.00**

Big Smith, 1958, clothing, 32 pages, VG.....................**$20.00**

Bill Bartlett Food Merchant Extraordinary, 1936, specialty foods, 182 pages, 5½x8", VG................................**$36.00**

Brown Fence & Wire Co, 1931, farm building materials, 162 pages, EX...**$45.00**

Butler Bros, 1926, Spring **$65.00**

Butler Furniture Specialties, 1941, 32 pages, VG **$12.00**

CE Ward Co, 1927, furniture for fraternal lodges, 12 pages, VG..**$58.00**

Chicago Millwork Supply, 1929, 96 pages, VG **$28.00**

Craftsman Wood Service Co, 1935, 92 pages, VG.......**$18.00**

Dennison Mfg Co, 1928, party supplies, 20 pages, G+..**$20.00**

Electric Storage Battery, 1936, 14 pages, VG...............**$40.00**

Enterprise Mfg Co, 1941, fishing tackle, 116 pages, NM......**$85.00**

Eugene Dietzgen Co, 1931, drafting tools, 520 pages, VG..**$36.00**

FM Thorpe Mfg Co, 1933, grocery & general merchandise display items, 8 pages, VG......................................**$42.00**

Ford Motor Co, model information, 1928, 20 pages, G .**$50.00**

Fordson Tractor Parts, 1931, NM **$20.00**

Franklin Owner's Instruction Manual & Parts Price List, Franklin Automobile Service Co, ca 1930s, 16 pages, VG+....**$22.50**

Fulton Metal Bed Mfg Co, 1927, 36 pages, VG **$32.00**

Harry & David of Bear Creek Orchards, 1960, fruit baskets and nature's gifts, 24 pages, EX.............................**$35.00**

Horder's Stationery Stores, 1922, office supplies & furniture, 224 pages, 8½x11", VG **$87.00**

House of Gurney Inc, 1940, seed supply, 84 pages, VG ..**$10.00**

Imperial Wallpapers, 1940, Book 2 ....**$45.00**

International Harvester Co of America, dairy farm supplies, 1934, 112 pages, VG...**$22.50**

Janesville Machine Co, farming repair parts, ca 1930, 218 pages, VG **$30.00**

JC Penney, 1969, Fall-Winter, 1,082 pages, 8x11", EX...**$70.00**

JC Penney, 1974, Christmas, EX..................................**$30.00**

JC Penney, 1976, 1,154 pages, VG **$55.00**

JC Penney, 1983, 1,332 pages, EX..............................**$45.00**

JC Penney, 1985, Christmas **$20.00**

Jim Brown's Catalog of Home & Farm Equipment, 1946, Fall & Winter, 170 pages, VG....................................**$8.00**

Johnson Smith & Co, 1920s, adolescent goods & ventriloquism, 64 pages, 5x7½", EX **$42.00**

JW Miller Co, 1920s, poultry supplies, 20 pages, VG .**$20.00**

Larkin Co, 1933, 222 pages, G+..................................**$30.00**

Lilley Co, 1927, fraternal items, 16 pages, VG............**$32.00**

Lionel Corp, 1956, toy trains & accessories, 22 pages, 11x8", EX...**$62.00**

LL Bean, 1943, Fall, hunting & fishing, 68 pages, EX.**$27.50**

Lufkin Precision Tools No 7, 1930s, EX.....................**$15.00**

Manhattan Gun & Repair, 1935, 16 pages, VG.............**$7.00**

Montgomery Ward, 1941, Spring & Summer, 607 pages, EX.**$40.00**

Montgomery Ward, 1951, Christmas, 272 pages, VG ..**$40.00**

Montgomery Ward, 1953, Christmas............................**$50.00**

Montgomery Ward, 1953-1954, Winter, 1,072 pages, 9x13½", EX...**$65.00**

Montgomery Ward, 1981 ....**$20.00**

Norm Thompson's Anglers Guide, 1962, fishing equipment, 64 pages, VG+...**$10.00**

Old Fisherman's Bait Co, 1950, 4th Annual edition, 30 pages, VG..**$32.00**

Oshkosh B'Gosh, Inc, 1968, 14 pages, VG..................**$20.00**

Parke, Davis & Co, 1930, medical supplies, VG **$40.00**

Pathe, Ince, NYC, 1926, cameras, projectors & accessories, 16 pages, EX...**$42.00**

Pittsburgh Plate Glass Co, 1930s, 80 pages, VG.........**$20.00**

Prentiss Vice Co, 1926, tools, 8 pages, EX..................**$45.00**

RC Nichols, 1949, hunting & fishing, 40 pages, NM...**$22.00**

Reading Wallpaper Co, 1928, 12 pages, VG **$16.00**

SC Toof & Co, 1928, stationery & office supplies, 16 pages, 8x11", EX...**$25.00**

Scars Paint, 1916, 40 pages w/4 paint chip pages, EX .**$60.00**

Sears, 1919, sporting goods, 96 pages, VG **$225.00**

Sears, 1931, 980 pages, VG...**$85.00**

Sears, 1960, Christmas **$55.00**

Sears, 1967, Christmas **$60.00**

Sears, 1976, Christmas **$25.00**

Sears, 1983, Christmas Wish Book, 610 pages, 8x11", NM..**$35.00**

Shoe & Leather Lexicon, 1952, leather & shoe repair, 114 pages, EX...**$32.00**

Snap-On-Tools, 1982, NM..**$10.00**

Spiegel, 1938, Fall & Winter..**$45.00**

Spiegel, 1978, Christmas..**$25.00**

Structo Manufacturing Co., No. 1, Bobby's Adventures in Structoland, toys, 1956, EX, $25.00.

The Movies, 1930s, current movie releases for theaters, 20 pages, NM...**$28.00**

Thompson's Pure Food Journal, 1928, published by & for restaurant chain, 24 pages, EX................................**$28.00**

Western Auto, 1975, Christmas, VG.............................**$15.00**

Westinghouse Electric & Supply, 1928, VG **$40.00**

Winchester Sporting Goods & Ammo, 1970, EX **$7.00**

Wm Henry Maule Seed Book, 1937, 82 pages, 8x10", EX.....**$32.00**

World's Greatest Artists Are on Victor Records, 1940-41, M ..**$25.00**

WW Grainger Motor Book, 1957, electric motors, fans & sm appliances, 136 pages, VG....................................**$10.00**

Ceramic Arts Studio

American-made figurines are very popular now, and these are certainly among the best. They have a distinctive look you'll soon learn to identify with confidence, even if you happen to pick up an unmarked piece. They were first designed in the forties and sold well until the company closed in 1955. (After that, the new owner took the molds to Japan and produced them over there for a short time.) The company's principal designer was Betty Harrington, who modeled the figures and knicknacks that so many have grown to love. In addition to the company's marks (there were at least seven, possibly more), some of the character pieces she designed also carry their assigned names on the bottom.

The company also produced a line of metal items to accessorize the figurines; these were designed by Liberace's stepmother, Zona.

Though prices continue to climb, once in awhile there's an unmarked bargain to be found, but first you must familiarize yourself with your subject!

CAS collectors will be sad to learn that Betty Harrington passed away on Good Friday, 1997.

Advisor: BA Wellman (See Directory, Ceramic Arts Studio)

Catalog Reprints: BA Wellman
P.O. Box 673, Westminster, MA 01473-1435

Newsletter/Club: CAS Collectors Association
CAS Collector bimonthly newsletter
P.O. Box 46
Madison, WI 53701; 608-241-9138
Newsletter $15; Annual membership, $15; Inventory record and price guide listing 800+ works, $12 postage paid

Bank, Paisley pig, 3"	$125.00
Bank, Tony, razor disposal, 4¾"	$70.00
Bell, Lillibelle, 6½"	$85.00
Bell, Summer Bell, 5¼"	$80.00
Bell, Winter Bell, 5¼"	$80.00
Bowl, scalloped, rectangular, 2"	$35.00
Candle holder, Triad girl, left or right, 7"	$90.00
Canoe, for Indian set, 8"	$125.00
Figurine, Al, hunter, 6¼"	$85.00
Figurine, Alice & white rabbit, 4½", 6", pr	$300.00

Figurine, Archibald the Dragon, 8", minimum value, $200.00

Figurine, Bali-Loa, 8½"	$125.00
Figurine, bass viol boy, 4¾"	$70.00

Figurine, Bedtime boy, 4¾"	$75.00
Figurine, Bird of Paradise male & female, pr	$200.00
Figurine, bride & groom, 4¾", 5", pr	$165.00
Figurine, Bright Eyes cat, 3"	$38.00
Figurine, bunny mother & baby, snuggle type, pr	$75.00
Figurine, Calico Cat, 3"	$35.00
Figurine, camel, standing, 5½"	$125.00
Figurine, child w/towel, 5"	$95.00
Figurine, Chinese boy & girl, 4¼", 4", pr	$35.00
Figurine, Cinderella & Prince Charming, 6½", pr	$145.00
Figurine, Comedy & Tragedy, 10", pr	$180.00
Figurine, Daisy ballerina, standing, 5¼", from $85 to	$110.00
Figurine, Dinky girl skunk	$25.00
Figurine, Elsie elephant, 5"	$75.00
Figurine, fawn, 4¼"	$50.00
Figurine, fish up on tail, 4"	$25.00
Figurine, flute lady, standing, 8½"	$265.00
Figurine, Frisky lamb, w/garland, 3"	$28.00
Figurine, guitar boy, 5"	$70.00
Figurine, Hands & Katrinka, chubby, 6½", 6¼", pr	$110.00
Figurine, harem girl, kneeling, 4½", from $60 to	$70.00
Figurine, Harry & Lillibeth, 6½", pr	$100.00
Figurine, Jim & June, 4¾", 4", pr, from $70 to	$80.00
Figurine, Little Bo Peep, 5½"	$28.00
Figurine, Little Boy Blue	$28.00
Figurine, Little Jack Horner, 4"	$75.00
Figurine, Madonna w/Bible, 9½", from $125 to	$140.00
Figurine, mermaid baby, sitting, 2½"	$85.00
Figurine, Mexican girl, 6½"	$75.00
Figurine, mouse & cheese, snuggle type, pr	$25.00
Figurine, Mr Monk, 4"	$45.00
Figurine, Mr Skunk, 3" L	$50.00
Figurine, palomino colt, 5¾"	$125.00
Figurine, Pansy ballerina, standing, 5¾"	$95.00
Figurine, Peek & Boo Siamese cats, snuggle type, 3x3", pr	$125.00
Figurine, Peter Pan & Wendy, 5¼", pr	$165.00
Figurine, Petrov & Petruskha (Russians), 5", pr	$75.00
Figurine, Pioneer Sam & Suzie, 5", 5½", pr	$95.00
Figurine, Pixie, sitting, 2½"	$22.00
Figurine, Poncho & Pepita, 4½", pr	$95.00
Figurine, skunk baby, 2"	$24.00
Figurine, Spanish rhumba couple, 7", 7½", pr	$135.00
Figurine, Square Dance boy & girl, pr, from $125	$135.00
Figurine, St George on charger, 8½"	$185.00
Figurine, Summer Sally, 3½", from $65 to	$75.00
Figurine, Tembino elephant baby, 2½"	$125.00
Figurine, toadstool, 3"	$20.00
Figurine, tortoise w/cane, 3¼", from $65 to	$70.00
Figurine, Wee Dutch boy & girl, 3", pr	$32.00
Figurine, Wee Eskimo boy & girl, 3¼", 3", pr	$60.00
Figurine, Wee French boy & girl, 3", pr	$55.00
Figurine, Wee Indian boy & girl, 3", 3¼", pr	$55.00
Figurine, Winter Willy, 4", from $60 to	$70.00
Figurine, zebra, 5"	$150.00
Head vase, African man, 8"	$160.00
Head vase, Becky, 5¼", from $110 to	$125.00
Head vase, Bonnie, 7"	$200.00
Pitcher, Adam & Eve, 3"	$60.00
Pitcher, Diana the Huntress, 3½", from $42 to	$58.00

Planter, flowerpot, round, 1".................................$20.00
Planter, Lorelei on seashell, 6"........................$185.00
Plaque, Attitude & Arabesque, 9½", pr.....................$110.00
Plaque, Comedy, 5"..$75.00
Plaque, Harlequin & Columbine, 8", pr..................$160.00
Plaque, Neptune, 6".....................................$165.00
Plaque, Shadow Dancers, 7", pr.........................$120.00
Salt & pepper shakers, bear & cub, snuggle type, black, 4¼" overall, pr, from $245 to $260.00
Salt & pepper shakers, bear & cub, snuggle type, brown, pr $65.00
Salt & pepper shakers, boy in chair, snuggle type, 2¼", pr ..$75.00
Salt & pepper shakers, Butch & Billy pup, pr...........$125.00
Salt & pepper shakers, cat, stylized, 4¼", 2⅝", pr....$200.00
Salt & pepper shakers, Chihuahua & doghouse, snuggle type, 1¾" overall, pr $75.00
Salt & pepper shakers, Chirp & Chip, 4", pr $95.00
Salt & pepper shakers, doe & fawn, stylized, snuggle type, 3¾", 2", pr $150.00
Salt & pepper shakers, fox & goose, 3¼", 2¼", pr...$150.00
Salt & pepper shakers, frog & toadstool, 2", 3", pr, from $55 to $65.00
Salt & pepper shakers, giraffe mother & baby, pr....$235.00
Salt & pepper shakers, leopards fighting, 3½", 6¼", pr ..$225.00
Salt & pepper shakers, mouse in cheese, snuggle type, 2½", pr...$38.00
Salt & pepper shakers, Mr & Mrs Penguin, 3¾", pr...$80.00
Salt & pepper shakers, native boy on alligator, pr ...$250.00
Salt & pepper shakers, Oakie on spring leaf, snuggle type, 3" overall, pr...$180.00
Salt & pepper shakers, pixie boy & toadstool, 2½", 3", pr..$65.00
Salt & pepper shakers, Santa & evergreen, 2¼", 2½", pr $275.00
Salt & pepper shakers, spaniel mom & pup, 2¼", 1¾", pr, from $70 to..$80.00
Salt & pepper shakers, Spanish rhumba couple, 7", 7½", pr $300.00
Salt & pepper shakers, Wee Indian boy & girl, 3", pr.....$60.00
Shelf sitter, Bali boy & girl, 5½", pr...................$125.00
Shelf sitter, Billy, w/ball down, black, 4½"............$135.00
Shelf sitter, boy w/dog, 4¼" $65.00
Shelf sitter, Budgie & Pudgie parakeets, 5", pr $150.00
Shelf sitter, Collie mother, 5", from $55 to.............$60.00
Shelf sitter, En Pos, ballerina, 4½".....................$70.00
Shelf sitter, farm girl, 4¾"..............................$50.00
Shelf sitter, Fluffy & Tuffy cats, 7", pr................$175.00
Shelf sitter, Greg & Grace, 6", pr......................$125.00
Shelf sitter, harmonica boy, 4"..........................$70.00
Shelf sitter, Jack & Jill, 4¾", 5", pr.....................$80.00
Shelf sitter, Maurice, 7"..................................$75.00
Shelf sitter, Pierrot & Pierette, green, 6½", pr..........$185.00
Shelf sitter, setter dog, prone, paws hang over, 5" L .$125.00
Shelf sitter, Sun-Li & Lun-Lin, chubby, 5½", pr, from $65 to..$70.00
Teapot, swan, Wedgwood, 3".............................$75.00
Vase, bird motif, round, 2"...............................$50.00
Vase, Lu Tang on bamboo bud, 7"........................$45.00
Vase, modern, square, 2".................................$22.00
Vase, rose motif, round, 2¼" $30.00

Cereal Boxes and Premiums

Yes, cereal boxes — your eyes aren't deceiving you. But think about it. Cereal boxes from even the sixties have to be extremely scarce. The ones that are bringing the big bucks today are those with a well-known character emblazoned across the front. Am I starting to make more sense to you? Good. Now, say the experts, is the time to look ahead into the future of your cereal box collection. They recommend going to your neighborhood supermarket to inspect the shelves in the cereal aisle today! Choose the ones with Batman, Quisp, Ninja Turtles, or some other nineties' phenomenon. Take them home and (unless you have mice) display them unopened, or empty them out and fold them up along the seam lines. If you want only the old boxes, you'll probably have to find an old long-abandoned grocery store or pay prices somewhere around those in our listings when one comes up for sale.

Store displays and advertising posters, in-box prizes or 'send-a-ways,' coupons with pictures of boxes, and shelf signs and cards are also part of this field of interest.

Our values are based on recent selling prices. If you want to learn more about this field of collecting, we recommend *Toys of the Sixties* by Bill Bruegman and *Cereal Box Bonanza, The 1950s, ID and Values*, by Scott Bruce.

Advisor: Scott Bruce (See Directory, Cereal Boxes and Premiums)

Newsletter: *FLAKE, The Breakfast Nostalgia Magazine*
P.O. Box 481
Cambridge, MA 02140; 617-492-5004

Alpha Bits, Mighty Mouse merry-pack, overwrap, 1958, NM+ $75.00
Alpha Bits, Roll-a-Word game (big mouth), 1960, VG ..$20.00
Big G's & Raisin-Flavor Flakes, empty, 1964, EX..........$5.00
C-3POs, Storm Trooper mask, flat, 1984, M $50.00
Cabbage Patch Kids Cereal, stickers, kids pouring, flat, 1985, EX...$30.00
Cheerios, Eddie Cantor Famous Comedian Hall of Fun cutout, 1949, NM...$70.00
Cheerios, tricky tracer toy, flat, 1977, NM $15.00
Choco Krispis (Mexico), fencing cutout, flat, 1966, EX...$35.00
Cocoa Pebbles, bird kite, 1972, no flaps otherwise EX ..$50.00
Cocoa Pebbles, metallic dinosaur coins, flat, 1979, EX...$35.00
Corn Chex box, Chex brittle recipe, 1960s, EX+.........$12.00
Corn Flakes, Jimmy Jet (toy cockpit) & Suzy Smart (doll), 1962, VG+...$50.00
Corn Flakes, Magic Mary (magnetic) doll, 1963, VG+ ..$50.00
Corn Flakes, Vanessa Williams Miss America, flat, 1984, NM+ $65.00
Corny Snaps, Fun & Games book, turtle wears hat, flat, 1977, EX $125.00
Country Corn Flakes, American Gothic couple picture, 1965, EX $9.00
Crisp, Mighty Mouse TV game, 1958, EX $95.00
Crispy Critters, 8 delicious shapes, single-serving overwrap, 1963, M $25.00
Freakies, Freakmobile, 1975, no flaps otherwise EX ..$150.00

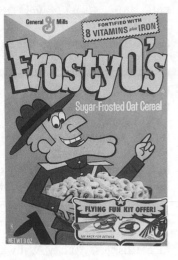

Dudley Do-Right Frosty O's, 1970, $600.00. (Photo courtesy Scott Bruce)

Frosted Flakes, Hokus-Pokus Fun #1, Tony's mug, bowl & spoon on side, flat, 1966, M $75.00

Frosted Flakes, Tony the Tiger's HO train set, flat, 1979, M $45.00

Frosted Flakes (Canadian), Tony Tiger & Swimming Tiger shark, flat, 1966, M $85.00

Frosted Rice, Tony Jr mask, flat, 1981, M $15.00

Frosty O's, Million-Dollar offer, pitcher, 1961, EX.......$20.00

Fruity Pebbles, Flintmobile, overwrap, 1972, NM $95.00

Grape Nuts, football cards (Grier, McDonald, Morral), overwrap, 1962, EX $85.00

Honeycombs, Honeycomb Kid & Flood picture puzzle #6, overwrap, 1966, EX $75.00

Honeycombs, miniature license plates, overwrap, 1968, NM..$75.00

Kellogg's Corn Flakes, Mattel's Toc'l Toys, flat, 1971, M ...$25.00

Kellogg's Corn Flakes, Pick-Presidents game (12 pictures including Lincoln), flat, 1968, M $50.00

Kellogg's Corn Flakes (Australia), Cutty Sark (clipper ship) picture, flat, 1967, M.......................................$15.00

Kellogg's Corn Flakes (Canadian), totem mask cutout, flat, 1956, M $45.00

Kellogg's Cracklin Bran, flat, 1978, M $10.00

Kellogg's Frosties (British), Spitfire & ME 109 models, 1967, M $85.00

Kellogg's Raisin Bran, Win a GE Portable TV, flat, 1967, M $25.00

Kellogg's Shredded Wheat, Mariner IV space picture, flat, 1965, M $40.00

Kix, Treasure Island tell-a-vision cutouts, flat, 1949, EX $25.00

Krinkles, Mighty Mouse blow pipe (clown), overwrap, 1954, NM $75.00

Oks, Yogi Bear & Gemini capsule picture, flat, 1966, M $350.00

Pink Panther Flakes, 5-in-1 spy kit, 1971, no flaps otherwise EX $275.00

Post Toasties, Billy Bird, You Can Draw Me (back), flat, 1966, M $55.00

Post Toasties, Indian escape trick, wax overwrap, 1952, VG $9.00

Post's Corn Flakes & (freeze-dried) Strawberries, flat, 1966, M $20.00

Post's 40% Bran Flakes, couple dancing, wax overwrap, 1954, NM+ $10.00

Post's 40% Bran Flakes, Li'l Abner's Name Honest Abe's Sweetheart contest, flat, 1958, EX.........................$85.00

Post's 40% Bran Flakes, single-serving overwrap, 1961, NM $2.00

Raisin Bran, Barnum & Bailey Circus toy, wax overwrap, 1956, NM $65.00

Rice Honeys, Rinty Barrels-of-Fun, 1958, VG+ $65.00

Rice Krinkles, ballpoint pen, Pushme-Pullyu Critters on side, flat, 1968, M..$25.00

Rice Krispies, Dennis the Menace treasure hunt, laser top flaps, 1960, VG...$20.00

Rice Krispies, Win Jeep or Aruba vacation contest, 1960, EX $15.00

Rice Krispies, Woody Woodpecker swimmer toy, flat, 1967, 6-oz size, M $135.00

Rice Krispies (Canadian), Ball 'n Jack (Snap head), 1959, M...$50.00

Rice Krispies (Canadian), Tony Tiger dangle-dandy, flat, 1954, M $50.00

Shredded Wheat, Niagara Falls on front, ballpoint pens, flat, 1950s, NM $12.00

Shredded Wheat, Rin Tin Tin televiewer, flat, 1953, EX....$125.00

So-Hi Krinkles, football player (kicker inpacts), overwrap, 1963, EX...$125.00

So-Hi Krinkles, single-serving wax overwrap, 1966, NM ..$50.00

So-Hi Krinkles, 1960 Plymouth Fury, overwrap, 1960, EX+ $95.00

Sugar Crisp, Bear bowl & mug sets, full box, 1960, NM...$75.00

Sugar Crisp, inflatable Sugar Bear, overwrap, 1964, EX..$135.00

Sugar Crisp, Mammy's Power Punch cutouts, flat, 1958, uncut, NM $40.00

Sugar Crisp, Sugar Bear & giraffe, magic riddle rub picture, flat, 1966, M $95.00

Sugar Pops, Stretch Pete, back only, 1972, EX............$12.00

Sugar Pops, Sugar Pops Pete & magic aquarium, flat, 1963, M $125.00

Sugar Pops, Sugar Pops Pete cutout, 1959, EX $80.00

Sugar Smacks, Admiral TV coloring contest, flat, 1957, M...$135.00

Sugar Smacks, magic flute, 1974, NM $75.00

Sugar Sparkled Flakes, crossword & Rory Raccoon plugging ears, flat, 1966, M $145.00

Super Sugar Crisp, NBA Oscar Robertson's ball offer, overwrap, 1970, NM...$70.00

Wheat Honeys, Buffalo Bee connect-the-dots picture, 1954, VG $40.00

Wheat Honeys, Rinty & Indian war medals, full box, 1960, NM $75.00

Wheaties, Chief Big Eagle fun mask, flat, 1940s, EX ..$25.00

Wheaties, Larry Byrd, full box, 1995, M $15.00

Wheaties, Minnesota Twins, full box, 1987, NM+ $9.00

Wheaties, Paul Bunyan fun mask, flat, 1940s, EX+.....$25.00

Premiums

Alpha Bits, Big Smile Trophy, plastic, 1970s, MIP $15.00

Alpha Bits, bike streamers, plastic, 1970s, MIP $7.00

Alpha Bits, Mercury Cougar, plastic, F&F, 1967, NM ..$10.00

Alpha Bits, Pocket Printer, plastic, 1970s, MIP **$10.00**
Alpha Bits, Rear-View Mirror Glasses, plastic, 1970s, MIP...**$12.00**
Alpha Bits, Silly Sign, paper, 1970s, MIP.......................**$7.00**
Amazin' Raisin Bran, Crispy's Pals Jig Saw Story Book, 1988,
    MIP...**$10.00**
Bill & Ted's Excellent Cereal, phone booth (on back), plastic
    w/sticker, 1991, NM...**$7.00**
C-3POs, Rebel Rockets (popper), white plastic w/stickers,
    1984, MIP...**$15.00**
C-3POs, trading card, Han Solo, cardboard, 1984, MIP .**$10.00**
Cheerios, Magic Hats Trick, plastic, 1973, MIP............**$12.00**
Cherrios, Polaris Snowmobile, red plastic, 1972, MIP.**$10.00**
Cookie Crisp, Balloon Launcher, plastic w/balloon, 1977,
    MIP...**$10.00**
Corn Flakes, baseball card, Blyleven, 1974, MIP........**$10.00**
Corny Snaps, Fun & Games Booklet #2, paper, 1978, M in
    paper envelope..**$25.00**
Frosted Mini-Wheats, Kellogg's NFL Touchdown Game Piece,
    1990s, MIP...**$3.00**
Frosty O's, Fun Ruler, plastic, 1973, NM.......................**$3.00**
Honeycomb, Around-the-Corner-Viewer, plastic, 1970s,
    MIP...**$10.00**
Honeycomb, Dot-'n-Dash Flasher, plastic w/foil mirror,
    1970s, MIP...**$10.00**
Honeycomb, Glow-in-the-Dark Yo-Yo, plastic w/string,
    1970s, MIP...**$10.00**
Honeycomb, license plate, metal w/Arkansas, 1970, MIP..**$5.00**
Honeycomb, Mini-Phoney Baloney Puzzle, brown plastic
    w/rubber band, 1970s, MIP...................................**$10.00**
Honeycomb, Monster Mitt, red plastic w/eyeball, 1974,
    M **$20.00**
Honeycomb, Pocket Calculator, plastic, 1970s, MIP ...**$10.00**
Kix, Whirly Pop (propeller toy), plastic, 1973, M on sprue..**$15.00**
Krinkles, Mustang, plastic, F&F, 1965, set of 3: fastback, con-
    vertible & hardtop, EX..**$20.00**
Lucky Charms, EZ Haul, gyro truck, green plastic & paper,
    1973, MIP...**$15.00**
Maltex, All Year Round Food Ruler Card, multicolor paper,
    1930s, EX..**$2.00**
Pebbles, Crazy Hi-Bounce Rock Ball, green rubber, 1971,
    MIB **$10.00**

Puffa Puffa Rice, Power Drill Toolie Bird, purple plastic,
    1971, MIP...**$35.00**
Raisin Bran, Hasbro's Dial Art (template) Set, plastic w/pen,
    1974, 7x8", MIP **$15.00**
Raisin Bran, Punch-Out Chess, 1973, MIP **$5.00**
Raisin Bran, Zany Raisin Stickers, 1988, MIP...............**$3.00**
Rice & Wheat Honeys, Jolly Clown Glass Hanger, plastic,
    1961, M...**$12.00**
Rice & Wheat Honeys, Octopus (sea creature series), blue
    plastic, 1969, M **$12.00**
Rice Krispies, Talking Skull, white plastic, 1988, MIP...**$5.00**
Rice Krispies, Trumpet, colored plastic & paper, 1980s,
    MIP...**$5.00**
Rice Krispies, Volcano (add baking powder & vinegar), green
    plastic, 1989, MIP **$5.00**
Rice Krispies, Wacky Wallwalker, soft sticky rubber, 1980s,
    MIP...**$9.00**
Sugar Smacks, Police Officer Daffy Dawg, green plastic,
    1970, MIP...**$15.00**
Sugar Smacks, Snozzing Funny Fringe, pink plastic, 1970s,
    MIP...**$35.00**
Super Sugar Crisp, Dynamite Mag's Book of Yuks, paper,
    1979, M...**$8.00**
Super Sugar Crisp, Glow Ballpoint Pen, plastic, 1970s,
    MIP...**$10.00**
Super Sugar Crisp, Mini Terrarium & Seeds, plastic w/sponge,
    1970s, MIP..**$10.00**
Toasties, Zingone-the-Magician Card Trick 78-rpm Record,
    1940, VG...**$10.00**
Wheaties, card, Skippy at the Gym, paper, 1932, any of 12,
    VG...**$3.00**

Character and Promotional Drinking Glasses

In any household, especially those with children, I would venture to say, you should find a few of these glasses. Put out by fast-food restaurant chains or by a company promoting a product, they have for years been commonplace. But now, instead of glass, the giveaways are nearly always plastic. If a glass is offered at all, you'll usually have to pay 99¢ for it.

You can find glasses like these for small change at garage sales, and at those prices, pick up any that are still bright and unfaded. They will move well on your flea market table. Some are worth more than others. Among the common ones are Camp Snoopy, B.C. Ice Age, Garfield, McDonald's, Smurfs, and Coca-Cola. The better glasses are those with super heroes, characters from Star Trek and thirties movies such as Wizard of Oz, sports personalities, and cartoon characters by Walter Lantz and Walt Disney. Some of these carry a copyright date, and that's all it is. It's not the date of manufacture.

Many collectors are having a good time looking for these glasses. If you want to learn more about them, we recommend *Tomart's Price Guide to Character and Promotional Drinking Glasses* by Carol Markowski, and *Collectible Drinking Glasses, Identification and Values*, by Mark Chase and Michael Kelly (Collector Books).

Post Grape-Nuts Flakes, Ford scale model cars, F&F mold, five different ones, from $10.00 to $40.00 each. (Photo courtesy Scott Bruce)

There are some terms used in the descriptions that may be confusing. 'Brockway' style refers to a thick, heavy glass that tapers in from top to bottom. 'Federal' style, on the other hand, is thinner, and the top and bottom diameters are the same.

Advisors: Mark Chase and Michael Kelly (See Directory, Character and Promotional Drinking Glasses)

Newsletter: *Collector Glass News*
P.O. Box 308
Slippery Rock, PA 16057; 412-946-2838; e-mail: cgn@glass-news.com

Amazing Spider-Man, Super Heroes, Marvel/7-Eleven, 1978 ....**$30.00**

Apollo 11, 12, 13, or 14, Apollo Series, Marathon Oil, from $3 to **$5.00**

Aquaman, Wonder Woman, Superman, Supergirl or Flash, Super Heros (Moon) Series, Pepsi/DC Comics or NPP, 1976, each **$15.00**

Arby's, Bicentennial Cartoon Character Series, 1976, 10 different, 6", each, from $15 to **$18.00**

Arby's, Currier & Ives, 1978, 4 different, numbered, each, from $3 to **$5.00**

Arby's Actor Series, smoke-colored glass w/black & white images, silver trim, numbered, each, from $5 to....**$7.00**

Archies, Welch's, 1971, 6 different w/many variations, each, from $3 to **$5.00**

Atlanta Falcons, McDonald's/Dr Pepper, 1980-81, 4 different, each, from $4 to **$6.00**

Avon, Christmas Issues, 1969-72, 4 different, each, from $2 to **$5.00**

Bagheera or Shere Kahn, Jungle Book, Disney/Pepsi, unmarked, 1970s, each, from $60 ....**$90.00**

Battlestar Galactica, Universal Studios, 1979, 4 different, each, from $7 to **$10.00**

Beatles, group photo & signatures in white starburst, Dairy Queen, Canadian, gold trim, from $100 to.........**$150.00**

Beatles, John Lennon or Paul McCartney, United Kingdom, full-color decal, gold trim, 4", each, from $140 to.......**$170.00**

Boris Badenov, Natasha, and Rocky, P.A.T. Ward/Holly Farms, each, from $45.00 to to $65.00. (Photo courtesy Collector Glass News)

Broom Hilda, Sunday Funnies, 1976, from $100 to ..**$150.00**

Bugs, Daffy, Porky, Road Runner, Sylvester or Tweety, Looney Tunes/Warner Bros/Pepsi, 1973, 16-oz, each, from $5 to..**$10.00**

Bugs, Daffy, Porky, Sylvester, Tweety or Road Runner, Warner Bros, Collector Series/Pepsi, 1979, round bottom, each, $7 to..**$10.00**

Bugs, Daffy, Porky, Sylvester or Tweety, Warner Bros, Arby's, 1988, each, from $15 to................................**$20.00**

Burger Chef, Presidents & Patriots, 1975, 6 different, each, from $3 to..**$5.00**

Burger Chef & Jeff, Burger Chef, Now We're Glassified!, from $15 to..**$25.00**

Burger King, Dallas Cowboys, Dr Pepper, 2 sets each w/6 different, each, from $7 to................................**$10.00**

Burger King, Disney Collector's Series, 1994, multicolored images on clear plastic, 8 different, MIB, each **$3.00**

Buzz Buzzard/Space Mouse, Walter Lantz, Pepsi, 1970s-80s, 2-sided, from $25 to **$35.00**

Captain America, Fantastic Four, Howard the Duck or Thor, Super Heros, Marvel/7-Eleven, 1977, each **$20.00**

Casper, Baby Huey, Wendy or Hot Stuff, action poses, Harvey Cartoons, 1970s, 5", each, from $8 to **$12.00**

Casper, Baby Huey, Wendy or Hot Stuff, static poses, Harvey Cartoons/Pepsi, 1970s, from $12 to......................**$15.00**

Caterpillar D-10 Tractor, Pepsi, 5⅛", NM **$10.00**

Chilly Willy or Wally Walrus, Walter Lantz, Pepsi, 1970s, each, from $35 to..**$55.00**

Coca-Cola, Christmas, McCrory's, 1982-89, 8 different, various styles, each, from $2 to **$4.00**

Coca-Cola, Heritage Collector Series, 1976, 4 different, tall pedestal bottom, each, from $3 to........................**$6.00**

Coca-Cola, Wild West Series, Buffalo Bill, Annie Oakley or Calamity Jane, each, from $12 to......................**$15.00**

Cuddles, Walter Lantz, Pepsi, 1970s, from $60 to **$90.00**

Dick Tracy, 1940s, frosted, 8 different, 3" or 5", each, from $50 to..**$75.00**

Disney's All-Star Parade, 1939, 10 different, each, from $25 to..**$60.00**

Elsie the Cow, yellow daisy image, Borden, 1960s, from $10 to..**$12.00**

Elsie the Cow & Family, Borden, Elsie in 1976 Bicentennial parade, red, white & blue graphics, from $5 to **$7.00**

ET, Pepsi/MCA Home Video, 1988, 6 different, each, from $15 to..**$25.00**

Flintstone Kids, Freddy, Wilma, Barney or Betty, each, from $2 to..**$4.00**

Fonz, Happy Days/Dr Pepper/Pizza Hut, 1977, from $10 to..**$15.00**

Ghostbusters II, Sunoco/Canada, 1989, 6 different, each, from $5 to..**$7.00**

Giant Panda, Burger Chef, Endangered Species Collector's Series, 1979, from $7 to................................**$9.00**

Glinda, Wizard of Oz, Swift's, 1950-60s, fluted bottom, from $15 to..**$25.00**

Great Muppet Caper, McDonald's, 1981, 4 different, 6", each..**$2.00**

Green Arrow, Super Heroes (Moon) Series, Pepsi/DC Comics, 1976, from $20 to **$30.00**

Hopalong Cassidy's Western Series, 4½", each, from $35 to..**$50.00**

Horace & Clarabelle, Happy Birthday, Pepsi, 1978, from $15 to **$20.00**

Howdy Doody, Welch's/Kagran, early 1950s, 6 different w/many color variations & bottom embossings, each, from $25 to...................**$35.00**

Indiana Jones; The Last Crusade, white plastic w/4 different images, each, from $2 to.....................**$4.00**

Joe Btsptflk, Al Capp, 1975, flat bottom, 16-oz, from $40 to...................**$60.00**

Joe Btsptflk, Al Capp, 1975, footed, 16-oz, from $40 to....**$60.00**

Jungle Book, Disney/Canada, 1966, 6 different, numbered, 4⅞", each, from $40 to......................**$60.00**

Jungle Book, Disney/Canadian, 6 different in set, numbered, 6½", each, from $30.00 to $50.00. (Photo courtesy Collector Glass News)

Keebler, 135th Birthday, 1988..........................**$3.00**

Lucy or Snoopy, Peanuts, Camp Snoopy, McDonald's, 1983, white plastic, each, from $5 to **$8.00**

Masters of the Universe, Mattel, plastic, 4 different, each..**$3.00**

McVote, McDonald's, 1986, 3 different, 5⅞", each......**$10.00**

Mickey, Minnie, Donald, Goofy, Pluto or Uncle Scrooge, Happy Birthday, Pepsi, 1978, each, from $6 to......**$8.00**

Mickey Mouse, Mickey's Christmas Carol, Coca-Cola, 1982, 3 different, each **$10.00**

Mickey Mouse, Through the Years, 1928, 1938, 1940, 1955, 1983 or 1988, Sunoco/Canada, each, from $6 to ...**$8.00**

Mister Magoo, Polamar Jelly, many different variations & styles, each, from $25 to **$35.00**

Mowgli, Jungle Book, Disney/Pepsi, 1970s, unmarked, each, from $40 to....................**$50.00**

NFL, Mobil Oil, 1988, single band, tall, footed, each, from $4 to....................**$5.00**

Night Before Christmas, Pepsi, 1982-83, 4 different, each, from $4 to....................**$6.00**

Norman Rockwell, Country Time Lemonade, Saturday Evening Post Series, 4 different, w/authorized logo, each, from $7 to.....................**$10.00**

Norman Rockwell, Summer Scenes, Arby's, 1987, 4 different, tall, each, from $3 to **$5.00**

Orko, He-Man, Skeletor/Panthor or Man-at-Arms, Masters of the Universe, Mattel, 1986, each, from $3 to..........**$5.00**

Pinocchio, Dairy Promo/Libbey, 1938-40, 12 different, 4¾", each **$20.00**

Popeye, King Sealy Features, Kollect-A-Set, Coca-Cola, 1975....................**$7.00**

Popeye, 10th Anniversary Series, Popeye's Famous Fried Chicken/Pepsi, 1982, 4 different, each, from $10 to ..**$15.00**

Porky, Bugs, Taz or Sylvester, Warner Bros, Marriott's Great America, 1989, 4 different, each, from $5 to........**$10.00**

Ralph, Joanie or Potsie, Happy Days/Dr Pepper, 1977, each, from $6 to.....................**$8.00**

Return of the Jedi, Burger King/Coca-Cola, 1983, each, from $4.00 to $6.00. (Photo courtesy Collector Glass News)

Richie or Fonz on his motorcycle, Happy Days/Dr Pepper, 1977, each, from $8 to..........................**$12.00**

Riddler, Green Lantern, Joker or Penguin, Super Heroes (Moon) Series, Pepsi/NPP, 1976, each, from $20 to.............**$40.00**

Ringling Bros Circus Clown Series, Pepsi/Federal, 1976, 8 different, each, from $15 to......................**$20.00**

Sad Sack, static poses, Harvey Cartoon/Pepsi, 1970s, scarce, 6", from $25 to **$30.00**

Sleeping Beauty, American, late 1950s, 6 different, each..**$15.00**

Smurf's, Hardee's, 1982, 8 different, from $1 to............**$3.00**

Snoopy in pool, Lucy on swing, Snoopy on surfboard or Charlie Brown flying a kite, Peanuts, Kraft, 1988, each....................**$2.00**

Snoopy sitting on lemon or Snoopy sitting by lg red apple, Peanuts, pedestal bottom, each, from $2 to **$3.00**

Snow White, Pinocchio, Alice, Lady & the Tramp, Bambi or 101 Dalmatians, Wonderful World of Disney, Pepsi, 1980s, each....................**$25.00**

Snow White & the 7 Dwarfs, Bosco, 1938, 3", from $25 to..**$45.00**

Star Trek, Dr Pepper, 1976, 4 different, each, from $15 to **$20.00**

Star Trek III: The Search for Spock, Taco Bell, 1984, 4 different, each, from $3 to **$5.00**

Star Wars Trilogy: Star Wars; Burger King/Coca-Cola, 1977, 4 different, each, from $12 to **$15.00**

Star Wars Trilogy: The Return of the Jedi; Burger King/Coca-Cola, 1983, 4 different, each, from $4 to **$6.00**

Superman the Movie, Pepsi, 1978, 6 different, each, from $7 to **$10.00**

Tom & Jerry, Tom chasing Jerry or Jerry trapping Tom's tail, MGM Collector Series, Pepsi, 1975, 5", each, from $6 to....................**$10.00**

Underdog, Leonardo TTV Collector Series, Pepsi, blue lettering, w/ or w/out logo, 6", from $20 to.................**$25.00**

Underdog, Sweet Polly or Simon Bar Sinister, Leonardo TTV Collector Series, Pepsi, each, from $8 to **$12.00**

Welches, Dinosaur Series, 1989, 4 different, each..........**$2.00**

Wendy's, New York Times, 1981, 4 different, each, from $3 to...**$5.00**

Wicked Witch of the West, Wizard of Oz, Swift's, 1950-60s, fluted bottom, from $35 to....................................**$50.00**

Winnie the Pooh, Sears/WDP, 1970, 4 different, each, from $7 to...**$10.00**

Wizard of Oz, 50th Anniversary Series, Coca-Cola/Krystal, 1989, 6 different, each, from $8 to........................**$10.00**

Woody Woodpecker, Walter Lantz, Pepsi, 1970s, from $10 to..**$15.00**

Yogi/Huck, Josie/Pussycats, Mumbly, Scooby, Flintstones or Dynomutt, Hanna-Barbera, 1977, each, from $25 to..**$35.00**

Ziggy, 7-Up Collector's Series, 4 different, each, from $4 to...**$7.00**

Plastic Mugs

For over forty years, children's plastic cups have been a favorite of advertisers as well as children at the breakfast table. In the 1950s the Wander Company, makers of Ovaltine, offered Beetleware plastic cups depicting comic characters such as Howdy Doody, Little Orphan Annie, and Captain Midnight. They were very popular and sold in large quantities, and good examples can still be found today.

In the 1960s other companies such as Walt Disney Studios, Kellogg's, Pillsbury, and Planters, to name only a few, found this a successful form of advertising for their products, and many thousands of cups found their way into homes through special offers on cereal boxes and through other promotions. The cups were designed after the likenesses of favorite cartoon or advertising characters. Few children would eat breakfast without first having their cup at the table by them.

Look at the bottoms of these cups and you will see the imprints of manufacturers such as F&F Mold and Die Works Company of Dayton, Ohio; Deka of Elizabeth, New Jersey; Beacon Plastics; and others. Some have dates; others don't.

Advisors: Lee and Cheryl Brown (See Directory, Character and Personality Collectibles)

Club/Newsletter: Children's Cups America
Cheryl and Lee Brown
7377 Badger Ct.
Indianapolis, IN 46260

Flintstones (Hanna-Barbera), Pebbles or Bamm-Bamm, F&F, 1972, $18.00 each; Dino or Fred, F&F, 1968, $24.00. (Photo courtesy Lee and Cheryl Brown)

Bugs Bunny, F&F, Warner Bros, VG **$18.00**

Cowboy Boot, E-Z Por Corp, M **$12.00**

Cowboy Pistol, E-Z Por Corp, M **$18.00**

Dennis the Menace, F&F, Hall Syn, VG **$35.00**

Dukes of Hazzard, Deka, Warner Bros, 1981, EX.......**$11.00**

Flintstones, all, Deka, Hanna-Barbera, 1978, EX.........**$12.00**

Frosty the Snowman, F&F, G **$15.00**

Incredible Hulk, Deka, Marvel Comics, 1977, G.........**$15.00**

Indianapolis 500, Whirley IN, G **$9.00**

Jiminy Cricket, Walt Disney Productions, flickering eyes, M **$38.00**

Keebler Elf, F&F, Keebler Co, 1972, M **$26.00**

Kool Aid, F&F, clear, General Foods, M **$28.00**

Kool Aid, F&F, frosted, General Foods, M...................**$35.00**

Kool Aid, unmarked, red, M **$7.00**

Masters of the Universe, Deka, Mattel Inc, 1983, G....**$18.00**

Mickey Mouse, Walt Disney Productions, flickering eyes, rare, EX **$55.00**

Mickey Mouse Club, Deka, Walt Disney Productions, EX...**$14.00**

Nestles Quik Bunny, Nestles Co, VG **$12.00**

Pilgrim, F&F, Quaker Oats, G **$35.00**

Popeye, Deka, King Features Syn, 1971, G **$11.00**

Porky Pig, Eagle, blue, M..**$35.00**

Quaker Oats Man, F&F, M **$18.00**

Roy Rogers 'King of the Cowboys,' F&F, EX...............**$60.00**

Smurfs, Deka, SEPP, 1980, EX......................................**$10.00**

Snoopy, Knickerbocker, United Features, 1958, G......**$50.00**

Star Trek, The Motion Picture, Deka, Paramount Pictures Corp, 1979, VG **$24.00**

Star Wars, Deka, 20th Century Fox, 1977, G **$22.00**

Strawberry Shortcake, Deka, American Greetings, 1980, EX...**$7.00**

Tony the Tiger, F&F, Kellogg's, 1964, EX....................**$37.00**

Woody Woodpecker, F&F, WLP, 1965, G **$18.00**

Yogi Bear, F&F, Hanna-Barbera, 1961, VG **$28.00**

Character Banks

Since the invention of money there have been banks, and saving it has always been considered a virtue. What better way to entice children to save than to give them a bank styled after the likeness of one of their favorite characters! Always a popular collectible, banks have been made of nearly any conceiveable material, mechanical or still. Cast-iron and tin banks are often worth thousands of dollars. The ones listed here are from the past fifty years or so, when ceramics and plastics have been the materials of choice. Still, some of the higher-end character-related examples can be quite pricey!

See also Advertising Character Collectibles; Cowboy Collectibles; MAD Collectibles; Star Trek; Star Wars.

Addams Family, Thing, Pointer Products, 1964, hand pops out to grab coin, battery-operated, EX (EX box) .**$45.00**

Batman, Penguin bust, Mego, w/original sticker, NM.**$60.00**

Beatnik, Put Your Money Where Your Mouth Is, fur hair, coin slot forms mouth, 6" **$35.00**

Benji, vinyl, 1970s, NM..**$25.00**

Big Bird, in fire truck, Enesco, MIB $22.00
Big Bird, w/toy chest, painted ceramic, Applause, MIB....$35.00

Bozo the Clown, composition, 1960s, 19", VG, $85.00.

Bozo the Clown, vinyl, 1972, EX.................................$25.00
Brother Juniper, ceramic, marked Help the Cause, 1995,
    NM...$95.00
Bugs Bunny, vinyl figural in bushel of carrots, 1972, 13",
    EX+..$35.00
Bugs Bunny & Elmer Fudd, talking, Janex, 1978, M ..$60.00

Casper the Ghost, marked USA, American Bisque, 8½", minimum value, $475.00. (Photo courtesy Mary Jane Giacomini)

Davy Crockett, bust, holding his rifle, copper-like metal,
    1950s, EX...$150.00
Dr Dolittle, hard pink plastic w/blue & black details, ChiChi
    the Chimp & Jip the Dog at either side, AJ Renzi, 1976,
    NM $50.00
Dr Dolittle, Sea Snail, AJ Reniz Plastic Corporation, 1971,
    pink, NM..$40.00
Dressed-Up Piggy, 1950s, 4½" $25.00
Felix the Cat, Applause, 1989, 6¾" $50.00
Flintstones, Barney w/bowling ball, Homecraft, 1973, NM ..$30.00
Flintstones, Fred, Homecraft, 1973, NM $35.00
Flintstones, Pebbles, vinyl, sleeping, EX+.................$25.00
Flintstones, Pebbles on Dino, vinyl, NM.....................$45.00
Galen (Planet of the Apes), vinyl, NM.........................$50.00
Herbert the Lion, Lefton, 7½" $35.00

Howdy Doody, atop pig, ceramic, Bob Smith USA, 1950s, no
    closure otherwise NM...$235.00
Howdy Doody, sitting on barrel, hand painted, Lefton, 1950s,
    6", NM...$335.00
Huckleberry Hound & Yogi Bear, Help Us Help the Children,
    Royal Russell School, England, 1960s, 9", EX.....$490.00
Humpty Dumpty, Clay Art, M.....................................$35.00
Incredible Hulk, hollow green plastic bust w/painted details,
    Renzi, 1979, 15"...$12.00
King Kong, atop Empire State Bldg, train in 1 hand, house in
    other, Ricogen Inc, 1977, 13", EX $40.00
King Kong, plastic, 20", EX+....................................$45.00
Kirby Kangaroo, vinyl, 1984, EX $35.00
Laurel & Hardy, Hardy figural, Play Pal, 1974, 7", VG..$22.00
Little Orphan Annie & Sandy, Applause, 1982............$45.00
Lord of the Rings, Samwise or Frodo, MIB, each $35.00
Magic Chef, vinyl, EX...$15.00
Mammy & Pappy Yokum, multicolored composition figures,
    Capp Enterprises Inc Dogpatch USA, 1975, 7¼", M..$95.00
Mary Poppins, round w/graphics, 1964, M.................$32.00
Mickey Mouse, in armored car, painted ceramic, Enesco,
    MIB $20.00
Mr Magoo, pink plastic w/painted details, Renzi, 1960, 16",
    EX+..$65.00
Nodder Pig w/Flasher Eyes, porcelain, vintage import,
    4½x8½"...$95.00
Oscar the Grouch, ceramic, Gorham, MIB $35.00
Oscar the Grouch, in trash can, vinyl, M.....................$15.00
Paddington Bear, ceramic, Gorham, 1978, 5½", EX....$45.00
Paddington Bear, Eden, NM.......................................$75.00
Peanuts, Snoopy, as engineer in locomotive, Willets, 1980s,
    MIB $35.00
Peanuts, Snoopy, as Uncle Sam, Willets, 11"............$150.00
Peanuts, Snoopy figure, silverplate, Leonard #9669, MIB ..$30.00
Peanuts, Snoopy's doghouse, papier-mache, slot on side,
    Korea, 6", EX..$10.00
Peanuts, Snoppy, ceramic, marked Italy.....................$95.00
Peanuts, Woodstock figure, signed Schultz, dated 1972,
    6"...$55.00

Pink Panther Bubble Gum Bank, deposit coin for gum reward, Tarco, 1970s, M (EX box), $40.00. (Photo courtesy John Thurmond)

Planet of the Apes, plastic, M......................................$45.00
Popeye, dime register, litho tin, King Features, 1929, 2½"
    square, VG..$55.00
Porky Pig, metal, 1940s, light paint chips, VG.........$150.00
Porky Pig, That's All Folks, ceramic, Warner Bros/Applause ..$195.00

Raggedy Ann, musical, no mark, vintage import, 6½"..**$40.00**
Rainbow Brite, vinyl, M...**$15.00**
Rocky Squirrel, ceramic, 1961, NM **$325.00**
Scooby Doo, vinyl figure w/felt vest, NM **$25.00**
Shirt Tails, Hallmark **$50.00**
Shmoo, plastic, 1948, MIP...**$85.00**
Simpsons, Bart standing plastic figure, Street Kids, MIB ...**$12.00**
Snuffy Skunk, ceramic, Walter Lantz, 1950s, NM **$70.00**
Space: 1999, Commander Koenig/Martin Landau, vinyl figure
 w/slot at back, 1975, 11", EX+.............................**$30.00**
Spider-Man, molded plastic figure climbing web w/Amazing
 Spider-Man on base, painted details, Renzi, 1979, 12",
 NM **$40.00**
Spider-Man, red plastic bust w/painted details, Renzi, 1979,
 15", VG+ **$10.00**
Stan Laurel, plastic figural sitting on treasure chest, 1970s,
 NM **$60.00**
Star Wars, Yoda, Sigma, 7½".....................................**$95.00**
Superman, plastic, Mego, 1974, EX **$30.00**
Sylvester & Tweety Bird w/jukebox, Warner Brothers, 1994,
 M **$45.00**
Tasmanian Devil, Applause, Warner Bros, 1988, 6"....**$50.00**
Topo Gigio, ceramic figure sitting between pineapples,
 MIB..**$80.00**
Topo Gigio, ceramic w/painted overalls & stripped shirt,
 furry felt-covered head, nodder, ca 1962, 6", VG.**$32.00**
Underdog, Imco, 1977, MIP **$100.00**
Underdog, vinyl, Playpal, 8", NM **$55.00**
Wizard of Oz, Dorothy figure, hand painted, Arnat Imports,
 1960s, 7", NMIB **$825.00**
Woody Woodpecker, Walter Lantz/Applause, MIB, from $25
 to **$30.00**
Yogi Bear, plastic, 14", EX..**$35.00**
Yosemite Sam, Applause, 1988....................................**$125.00**
Ziggy on safe, 1981, M..**$45.00**

Character Clocks and Watches

There is growing interest in the comic character clocks and watches produced from about 1930 into the 1950s and beyond. They're in rather short supply simply because they were made for children to wear (and play with). They were cheaply made with pin-lever movements, not worth an expensive repair job, so many were simply thrown away. The original packaging that today may be worth more than the watch itself was usually ripped apart by an excited child and promptly relegated to the wastebasket.

Condition is very important in assessing value. Unless a watch is in like-new condition, it is not mint. Rust, fading, scratching, or wear of any kind will sharply lessen its value, and the same is true of the box itself. Good, excellent, and mint watches can be evaluated on a scale of one to five, with excellent being a three, good a one, and mint a five. In other words, a watch worth $25.00 in good condition would be worth five times that amount if it were mint ($125.00). Beware of dealers who substitute a generic watch box for the original. Remember that these too were designed to appeal to children and (99% of the time) were printed with colorful graphics.

Some of these watches have been reproduced, so be on guard. For more information, we recommend *Comic Character Clocks and Watches* by Howard S. Brenner, and *Schroeder's Collectible Toys, Antique to Modern* (Collector Books).

Advisor: Howard Brenner (See Directory, Character Clocks and Watches)

Batman, lg image of Batman in center, other characters at 12, 3, 6 & 9, plastic, Electro-Optix, 1989, 9", NM.......**$40.00**
Big Bird Alarm Clock, Bradley, 1970s, VG **$35.00**

Bugs Bunny Talking Alarm Clock, Janex, MIB, $75.00.

Chipmunks, w/wind-up alarm, 1990, EX....................**$40.00**
Doc (Snow White & The 7 Dwarfs), plastic figure w/dial in
 stomach, wind-up pendulum, 1970s, 7", unused .**$50.00**
Flintstones Alarm Clock, ceramic standing figure of Fred
 w/dial in middle, Sheffield, 1960s, 8½", VG+ **$185.00**
Kermit the Frog, w/alarm, Casio, 1988, NM **$15.00**
Lady & the Tramp, plastic figure of Lady w/dial under chin,
 wind-up pendulum, 1970s, 7", unused, NM **$50.00**
Little Sprout Talking Alarm Clock, Little Sprout holds round
 dial in front on round base, 10½", EX..................**$25.00**

Mickey Mouse travel alarm, Walt Disney Productions/Bradley (Japan), EX, $75.00.

Peanuts Alarm Clock, round dial next to Charlie Brown & Snoopy sleeping, Janex, EX..................................**$25.00**
Pluto Alarm Clock, image of Pluto in front of doghouse on round dial, Bayard/France, 1978, 5", MIB..........**$265.00**

Sesame Street Talking Alarm Clock, round dial in building w/Big Bird reading to Ernie & Oscar the Grouch, 11", EX...**$25.00**

Sleepy (Snow White & the 7 Dwarfs), plastic figure w/dial in middle, eyes move, Miken, 1950s (?), 8½", VG..**$100.00**

Snow White Alarm Clock, Snow White w/bird in center, dwarfs, etc next to numbers, 4½", MIB..............**$350.00**

Star Wars Talking Alarm Clock, round dial on base next to figures of R2-D2 & C-3PO, 8½x6½", EX+ (EX+ box)...........**$175.00**

Thundercats Talking Alarm Clock, molded characters on base w/round dial, 7", EX................................**$25.00**

Woody Woodpecker, animated, w/alarm, EX............**$225.00**

Pocket Watches

Betty Boop, Ingraham, 1934, very rare, VG...........**$1,250.00**

Bozo, plastic, tin & paper, toy only, Larry Harman/Japan, 1960s, MIP **$6.00**

Buck Rogers and Wilma, Ingraham, 1935, M, $500.00. (Photo courtesy Dunbar Gallery)

Dan Dare, double animation, 1953, EX...................**$275.00**

Dizzy Dean, New Haven, 1935, EX **$900.00**

Donald Duck, Ingersoll, 1939, EX...........................**$950.00**

GI Joe Combat Watch, w/compass & sighting lenses, Gilbert, EXIB..**$250.00**

Marilyn Monroe, portrait on black, 2" dia, M............**$60.00**

Mickey Mouse, image w/lg arms (as watch hands), round chrome case, MIB...**$75.00**

Popeye, shows arms as hands, second hand is Wimpy, King Features Syndicate/New Haven, 1935, EX, minimum value $400.00.

Mickey Mouse, lapel style, 1938, M.....................**$1,500.00**

Mickey Mouse, 1976 Bicentennial, MIB.................**$250.00**

Mighty Mouse, flexing muscles, nickel-plated case, 1⅞" dia, EX+ **$100.00**

Roy Rogers, embossed portrait fob, Bradley, 1959, M..**$150.00**

Superman, Bradley, 1959, EX **$395.00**

Three Stooges, Moe pulling Curley's tooth out w/pliers, nickle-plated case, marked FTCC, 2" dia, EX **$75.00**

Wristwatches

Alien, figural w/wraparound tail wristband, MIP........**$15.00**

Alvin & Chipmunks, digital, MIP **$15.00**

Amazing Spider-Man, digital, MOC **$20.00**

Archie, Betty & Veronica orbit Archie, plastic case & band, Cheval/Archie Comic Pub/Hong Kong, 1989, MIB..**$30.00**

Archie, his face spins around on clear plastic disk, red band, Rowan, 1970s, MIB (w/Archie & Jughead insert).**$75.00**

Bart Simpson, multicolored plastic, 5-funtion, Nelsonics, LCD, MOC **$12.00**

Big Jim, figure in red shorts w/arms as hands, Big Jim in blue & red lettering, black vinyl band, Bradley, 1973, NM..**$150.00**

Bozo, Bozo's arm stretched across yellow dial, gives illusion of Bozo juggling, replaced red band, 1960s, NM.**$80.00**

Bugs Bunny, image w/lg carrots for hands, chrome case, red leather strap, Timex/Warner Bros, EX................**$100.00**

Captain America, digital, MIP **$15.00**

Captain Marvel, w/original tags, unused, MIB **$475.00**

Captain Planet, digital, MIP...**$15.00**

Casper the Friendly Ghost, Casper flies over mountains on blue dial, white vinyl band, Bradley, 1960s, NM .**$150.00**

Chucky (Child's Play), MIP **$35.00**

Cinderella, on plastic figure, US Time, 1951, EX **$115.00**

Cinderella, US Time, 1951, pink band, complete with Cinderella figure, MIB, from $300.00 to 400.00. (Photo courtesy Dunbar Gallery)

Cool Cat, replaced red band, Sheffield/Warner Bros, 1960s, NM **$80.00**

Dan Quayle, his tie as hands that runs backwards, M (original 'Quayle' egg-carton box) **$150.00**

Daniel Boone, cream w/black image of powder horn below name, replaced band, 1960s, EX **$50.00**

Dennis the Menace, image of Dennis & Ruff w/name in red, replaced band, 1960s, EX......................**$75.00**

Donald Duck, image w/lg dial arms, round chrome case, red leather strap, Topolino/Swiss/WDP, EXIB.............**$30.00**

Donald Duck, 50th Birthday commemorative, registered edition, Bradley, original papers, MIB.....................**$150.00**

Dukes of Hazzard, stainless steel band, LCD Quartz, Unisonic, 1981, NRFB..**$40.00**

Elmer Fudd, waving hand & holding shotgun, Sheffield, 1960s, MIB..**$150.00**

Gene Autry Six Shooter, New Haven, NM (NM box), $450.00.

George of the Jungle, Jay Ward, NMIB......................**$495.00**

Hopalong Cassidy, bust image, round chrome case, black leather western strap, US Time, 1950s, EX.........**$150.00**

Jetson's Movie, Elroy & Astro in saucer on face, digital, MIP...**$15.00**

Jughead, plastic case & band, burger & soda orbit Jughead, Cheval/Archie Comic Pub/Hong Kong, 1989, MIB..**$30.00**

Lamb Chop, MOC..**$12.00**

Lassie, image of Lassie sitting, white w/name in blue, 1960s, EX...**$60.00**

Little Orphan Annie & Sandy, comic strip illustrated on dial, gold-tone band, 1970s, M......................................**$28.00**

Lone Ranger, Hi-Yo Silver, image of Lone Ranger on Silver, rectangular chrome case, tan leather strap, VG .**$125.00**

Madonna, recalled, MOC..**$35.00**

Man From UNCLE, blue w/black & white line drawing of Napolean using communicator, UNCLE Secret Agent in white, 1966, EX...**$100.00**

Mary Marvel, VG...**$175.00**

Mickey Mouse, Mickey on face, red band, Ingersoll, 1950s, NM (NM box w/5" plastic Mickey figure)...........**$225.00**

Mickey Mouse, moving head, Bradley, 1982, MIB....**$350.00**

Mighty Mouse, digital, MOC **$15.00**

Mighty Mouse, Fossil, MIB..**$30.00**

Minnie Mouse, moving head, Bradley, 1982, MIB....**$450.00**

Nascar's Richard Petty, digital, MIP **$12.00**

New Kids on the Block, metal w/leather band, working, EX..**$12.00**

Pluto, moving head, Bradley, 1982, very rare, MIB..**$750.00**

Popeye, opening can of spinach w/name in red, replaced band, 1960s, EX **$60.00**

Raggedy Ann, image w/arms as watch hands, replaced band, Bobbs-Merrill, 1971, EX...................................**$50.00**

Real Ghostbusters, digital, flicker dial w/Egan's face, MIP ..**$15.00**

Real Ghostbusters, flasher style, M...........................**$10.00**

Robin Hood, Sheffield, EX+.......................................**$325.00**

Robocop, 2-dimensional, digital, MIP **$15.00**

Rocketeer, Disney Channel promotion, MIP...............**$30.00**

Rudolph the Red Nosed Reindeer, rectangular chrome case, red vinyl strap, USA, EX...................................**$75.00**

Snoopy, playing tennis, tennis ball as second hand, Timex #86211, M..**$100.00**

Tweety Bird, image w/lg arms as watch hands, round chrome case, red leather strap, Topolino/Swiss, EXIB......**$50.00**

Underdog, hands point out time, blue vinyl band, Lafayette, 1973, MIB (w/Underdog insert).........................**$250.00**

Voltron Timekeeper Robot, MIP **$15.00**

X-Men, Wolverine, digital, MIP **$20.00**

Yogi Bear, image w/arms as watch hands, chrome case, blue leather strap, Swiss/Hanna-Barbera, EXIB **$50.00**

Character Collectibles

Any popular personality, whether factual or fictional, has been promoted through the retail market to some degree. Depending on the extent of their success, we may be deluged with this merchandise for weeks, months, even years. It's no wonder, then, that the secondary market abounds with these items or that there is such wide-spread collector demand for them today. There are rarities in any field, but for the beginning collector, many nice items are readily available at prices most can afford. Disney characters, Western heroes, TV and movie personalities, super heroes, comic book characters, and sports greats are the most sought after.

For more information, we recommend *Character Toys and Collectibles* by David Longest; *Toys of the Sixties* and *Superhero Collectibles: A Pictorial Price Guide,* both by Bill Bruegman; *Collector's Guide to TV Memorabilia, 1960s and 1970s,* by Greg Davis and Bill Morgan; and *Howdy Doody* by Jack Koch. *Schroeder's Collectible Toys, Antique to Modern,* published by Collector Books contains extensive listings of character collectibles with current market values.

See also Advertising Characters; Beatles Collectibles; Bubble Bath Containers; California Raisins; Character and Promotional Drinking Glasses; Character Watches; Coloring Books; Cookie Jars; Cowboy Character Collectibles; Disney Collectibles; Dolls, Celebrity; Elvis Presley Memorabilia; Movie Posters; Paper Dolls; Pez Candy Containers; Pin-Back Buttons; Premiums; Puzzles; Rock 'n Roll Memorabilia; Shirley Temple; Star Trek Memorabilia; Star Wars; Toys; Vandor.

Note: Our listings are often organized by the leading character with which they're associated (for example, Pokey is in the listings that begin Gumby) or the title of the production in which they appear. (Mr. T is with A-Team listings.)

Club: Smurf Collectors
24ACH, Cabot Rd. W, Massapequa, NY 11758
Membership includes newsletter; LSASE required for information

A-Team, air freshener, Mr T, 1983, MIP.........................**$8.00**

A-Team, party hat, set of 4 assorted, EX......................**$8.00**

A-Team, vehicle, diecast, 1983, 1/64 scale, M (NM card) **$5.00**

Addams Family, key chain, Thing, EX **$5.00**

Alf, lap tray, Let's Do Lunch!, How About Yours?, 1987, EX **$15.00**

Alf, memo board, w/pen, MIP **$8.00**

Alf, sleeping bag, MIP **$15.00**

Alf, tablet, M **$8.00**

Alice in Wonderland, record player, Bakelite, VG **$175.00**

Alvin & the Chipmunks, Curtain Call Theatre, Ideal, 1983, MIB **$25.00**

Alvin & the Chipmunks, On Tour Van, Ideal, 1983, MIB..**$28.00**

Alvin & the Chipmunks, soap dispenser, Alvin figure, Helm Products, 1984, MIB................................**$10.00**

Andy Griffith Show, nodder, Andy or Barney, ceramic w/name on base, 1992, 7", each **$65.00**

Andy Panda, doll, stuffed cloth w/vinyl hands, 18", early, VG **$90.00**

Annie, doll, w/party dress & shoes, Knickerbocker, 1982, MIB, from $25 to..**$35.00**

Annie, napkins, Happy Birthday, 1980s, MIP **$6.00**

Annie's Sandy, stuffed plush, Knicker-bocker, 1982, 10", MIB, $45.00.

Annie, tray, lithographed metal, 1982, 17x12", EX......**$15.00**

Arachnophobia, figure, Big Bob Spider, Remco, 1990, MOC **$8.00**

Archies, activity set, Archies Gang at Pops, Whitman, 1970, MIB **$30.00**

Archies, carrying case, Marx, EX, from $30 to **$35.00**

Archies, tattoo, gum pack w/tattoo sheet & gum, Topps, 1969, 2x4", unused, M..**$20.00**

Aristocats, Colorforms, 1960s, NM (EX box) **$38.00**

Aristocats, doll case, vinyl, for Barbie-type dolls, 1970, 12x9", EX..**$30.00**

Astro Boy, squirt gun, plastic, VG **$12.00**

Atom Ant, trickey trapeze, push-button action, M......**$45.00**

Avengers, folder, comic book page reproduced on back, Meade, 1975, 9½x12½", NM **$15.00**

Babar the Elephant, soap, England, 1970s, MIB **$20.00**

Banana Splits, bowl, red plastic w/graphics on sides, 1969, 5½" dia, EX **$38.00**

Banana Splits, doll, Fleegle, stuffed pillow type, 1970s, 10", EX..**$35.00**

Banana Splits, flute set, plastic, Larami, 1973, MOC...**$42.00**

Banana Splits, Kut-Up Kit, Larami 1973, MIP (sealed)..**$8.00**

Banana Splits, sign, Tattoo Bubble Gum, multicolor, for gum machine, 1970s, M..**$42.00**

Batgirl, slipper socks, knit w/red soles, 1979, unused, M..**$35.00**

Batman, Bat Chute, metallic blue figure & working parachute, CDC, 1966, NMOC.......................................**$55.00**

Batman, Batcuffs, Ideal, 1966, NM **$100.00**

Batman, Batmobile, Ertl, 1989, 1/64 scale, MOC...........**$8.00**

Batman, Batmobile w/figures, black plastic w/blue Batman & yellow Robin, Duncan, 1970s, 8", EX...................**$35.00**

Batman, bicycle ornament, 1966, 10", EX...................**$45.00**

Batman, charm bracelet, 5 multicolor charms on gold-tone chain, DC Comics, 1966, EX **$50.00**

Batman, Colorforms Cartoon Kit, 1966, MIB, $35.00.

Batman, figure, Batman Bend-N-Flex, molded rubber, Mego, 1970s, 5", NMOC...**$50.00**

Batman, figure, vinyl w/cloth cape, all-black version, China, in original bag, 12", M..**$25.00**

Batman, gloves, imitation leather, Wells Lamont, 1966, MIP **$85.00**

Batman, jackknife, yellow plastic w/Batman logo, 1972, 3½", NM **$90.00**

Batman, lamp, multicolor figure w/cloth cape, 1966, 11", NM **$125.00**

Batman, license plate, diecut metal w/Gotham City skyline background, Groff Signs, 1966, 12x16", NM.........**$30.00**

Batman, magazine, Look, 1966, EX+...........................**$45.00**

Batman, magic slate, diecut top w/Batman logo & images of Batman & Robin, Watkins/Strathmore, 1966, VG .**$35.00**

Batman, marionette, jointed plastic w/strings, cloth & felt costume, Hazelle, 1966, 15", EX+......................**$400.00**

Batman, paddle ball, white plastic paddle w/Batman & Joker, 1966, 10x4", EX **$20.00**

Batman, party hat, stiff cardboard, shows heroes running, Gotham City background, Amscan/Canada, 1972, 7", unused, M..**$10.00**

Batman, pencil case, pink vinyl w/colorful image of Batman & Robin in Batmobile, 1977, 5x8", NM **$30.00**

Batman, pillow, white felt w/plain back, shows Batman, marked With Robin the Boy Wonder, 1966, 11x12", NM **$65.00**

Batman, placemat, textured vinyl w/foam backing, shows Robin, 1966, 13x18", NM...............................**$79.00**

Batman, roller skates, 1966, EX **$15.00**

Batman, slippers, boot-style blue leatherette, Batman graphics, blue fabric lining w/cushioned heel, unused, M, pr..**$129.00**

Batman, slot car, black hard plastic Batmobile w/red & silver details, BZ, 1966, 8", EX+.....................................**$220.00**

Batman, snow-cone cup, cardboard, 1960s, 5½", M.....**$4.00**

Batman, stamper kit, set of 6 w/stamping pad in hard black plastic case, mail-in premium, Kellogg's, 1966, VG+ **$30.00**

Batman, String Art Kit, Smith, 1976, MIB.....................**$35.00**

Batman, sunglasses, licensed in 1966, w/paper label, scarce, M **$90.00**

Batman, toy, Junior Speed Boat, AHI, 1979, MOC......**$30.00**

Batman & Robin, society member button, Charter Member, Button World, 1966, 3" dia, EX................................**$12.00**

Batman Returns, Colorforms, Sparkle Art, MIB...........**$10.00**

Batman Returns, pencil topper, Penguin, MOC.............**$6.00**

Battlestar Galactica, Poster Art Set, Craft Master, 1978, MIP **$30.00**

Battlestar Galactica, wallet, w/Cylon Raider, EX **$10.00**

Beany & Cecil, Disguise Kit, w/18" doll, Mattel, 1962, NMIB **$80.00**

Beany & Cecil, jack-in-the-box, lithographed tin, Mattel, 1961, EX...**$85.00**

Beany & Cecil, music box, Mattel, M.........................**$150.00**

Beany & Cecil, music box, not working, otherwise EX..**$40.00**

Ben Casey, charm bracelet, steel w/plastic pearls, Sears, 1962, NMOC...**$25.00**

Ben Casey, doctor kit, w/8 accessories, Transogram, 1960s, EX...**$30.00**

Betty Boop, doll, bisque, movable head, jointed arms & legs, Vandor, 1981, 10", NM..**$250.00**

Betty Boop, figure, bendable, 1989, MOC...................**$10.00**

Betty Boop, greeting card, Betty as cowgirl, Sands, 1989, M **$4.00**

Beverly Hillbillies, Colorforms, 1963, complete, EX ...**$40.00**

Billy Baloney, puppet, MIB...**$65.00**

Bionic Woman, Paint-By-Number Set, MIB.................**$45.00**

Bionic Woman, slide-tile puzzle, American Publishing, 1977, MOC..**$30.00**

Bionic Woman, Tattoos & Stickers, Kenner, 1976, MOC.**$8.00**

Blondie & Dagwood, sandwich bag, shows Dagwood w/armfuls of sandwiches, 1952, 7x5", unused, M **$25.00**

Blue Knight, toy watch, 1976, MOC............................**$12.00**

Bozo, puppet, talker, Mattel, 1963, EX.......................**$30.00**

Bozo the Clown, doll, bendable, Knickerbocker, 1960, MIP..**$45.00**

Bozo the Clown, doll, Mattel, talker (non-working), G..**$10.00**

Brady Bunch, Fishing Fun Set, 1973, MOC **$40.00**

Brother Juniper, planter, figure riding donkey pulling cart, w/embossed comic scenes, 1958, M **$95.00**

Buck Rogers, Colorforms Adventure Set, 1979, MIB...**$27.00**

Buck Rogers, Super Sonic Glasses, 1950s, NMIB......**$125.00**

Bugs Bunny, birthday napkins, Reed, 1980s, MIP........**$5.00**

Bugs Bunny, candle holder, ceramic, NMIB...............**$25.00**

Bugs Bunny, Cartoon Pals Paint-By-Number, Craft, 1979, MIB **$22.00**

Bugs Bunny, Cartoon-O-Graph Sketch Board, 1950s, NMIB..**$50.00**

Bugs Bunny, cup dispenser, 1989, MIP........................**$8.00**

Bugs Bunny, doll, rubber head w/stuffed body, talker (not working), 1964, EX...**$35.00**

Bugs Bunny, pull-string talker, Mattel/Hong Kong, 1976, 7½", from $15.00 to $18.00.

Bugs Bunny, jack-in-the-box, Mattel, 1970s, VG.........**$15.00**

Bugs Bunny, slippers, EX, pr..**$10.00**

Bugs Bunny, tattoos, unopened gum wrapper w/sheet & gum, Topps, 1971, 2x4", unused, M.....................**$24.00**

Captain America, figure, rubber bendy w/painted features & removable red plastic shield, Lakeside, 1966, unused, M...**$40.00**

Captain America, kite, red & blue graphics, Pressman, 1966, original package, EX..**$35.00**

Captain America, sweatshirt, white w/multicolor graphics, Marvel Comics, 1960s, child size, unused, NM.....**$60.00**

Captain Kangaroo, activity set, Lowe, 1977, EX..........**$15.00**

Captain Kangaroo, doll, pull-string talker (non-working), 1967, EX...**$55.00**

Captain Kangaroo, Fundamental Activity Set, Lowe, 1977, MIB **$20.00**

Captain Kangaroo, TV Eras-O-Board Set, Hasbro, 1956, complete, MIB..**$35.00**

Captain Marvel, greeting card, illustration from comic book, blank inside, Third Eye, 1971, 6x9", w/envelope, M .**$8.00**

Captain Marvel, music box, ceramic figure on round base lettered Shazam!, DC Comics, 1978, 8", MIB.........**$125.00**

Captain Marvel, pencil bag, vinyl, EX+.......................**$25.00**

Casper the Friendly Ghost, candy bucket, plastic, EX+ ..**$30.00**

Casper the Friendly Ghost, doll, stuffed plush w/Casper sweater, 1960s, VG...**$20.00**

Casper the Friendly Ghost, figure, inflatable vinyl, 1981, 12", MIP...**$12.00**

Casper the Friendly Ghost, kite, folder w/punch-out pieces to make kite, Saalfield, 1960, M **$18.00**

Casper the Friendly Ghost, lamp shade, ca 1950s, M, from $75.00 to $100.00.

Charlie Chaplin, musical statue, pays The Entertainer, Hamilton, 1992, MIB **$20.00**

Charlie McCarthy, soap, figural, NM (NM box) **$65.00**

Charlie McCarthy, spoon, silverplate, figural handle ..**$12.00**

Charlie's Angels, carrying cases, cream vinyl w/show's & girl's names in repeated brown designs, 1970s, 3-pc set, EX **$50.00**

Charlie's Angels, Colorforms, 1978, NM (EX box) **$28.00**

Charlie's Angels, cosmetic kit, w/mirror & bag, 1970s, MIB **$65.00**

Charlie's Angels, purse, vinyl box style, black names on beige, 8" L, NM **$20.00**

Child's Play, doll, Chucky, stuffed cloth w/suction cups on hands & feet, real hair, 1992, 12", EX **$30.00**

Child's Play, doll, Chucky, 1991, 18", M **$25.00**

CHiPs, Emergency Medical Kit, complete w/multicolor photo case, 1980, MIB **$36.00**

CHiPs, motorcycle, riding toy w/pedals, Empire Toys, 1977, NMIB **$165.00**

Curious George, magic slate, Fairchild, 1968, 9x12", M ..**$10.00**

Daffy Duck, placemat, Warner Bros/Pepsi, EX **$7.00**

Daredevil, pennant, The man Without Fear, cardboard in plastic sleeve, Marvel Comics, 1966, 3x7", M **$40.00**

Dennis the Menace, bookends, pr **$165.00**

Dennis the Menace, doll, 14", EX **$100.00**

Dennis the Menace, hand puppet, red cotton body w/plastic head, 1950s, NM **$32.00**

Dennis the Menace, napkin box, yellow & red w/graphics, Monogram, 1954, 5x5x1", EX **$25.00**

Dennis the Menace, xylophone, battery-op, plays London Bridge, Universal Toy/Sears, ca 1960, MIB **$345.00**

Dennis the Menace & Ruff, composition, Determined, 1974, EX, pr **$65.00**

Deputy Dawg, pencil case, red cardboard w/decal, inside sectioned tray w/5 pencils & tools, Hasbro, 1961, 8x4", EX+ **$24.00**

Dick Tracy, bookmark, diecut, 1950s, EX **$45.00**

Dick Tracy, calendar, Copy Express of Woodstock, black & white cover, 1988, NM **$25.00**

Dick Tracy, camera, Seymour Sales, 1950s, NMIB **$75.00**

Dick Tracy, charms, Sam Catchem, Gravel Gertie or Sparkle Plenty, from gumball machine, each.....................**$20.00**

Dick Tracy, Colorforms Adventure Kit, 1962, NMIB ...**$65.00**

Dick Tracy, Dick Tracy Special Agent Set, w/badge & handcuffs, Larami, 1972, NMOC **$35.00**

Dick Tracy, figure, Jr, Rubb'r Niks, poseable w/magnetic space car, 1968, 6", NMOC.................................**$35.00**

Dick Tracy, flashlight, blue w/red top, image of Tracy on side, 1950s, EXIB **$50.00**

Dick Tracy, gun, Rattattat Machine Pistol, blue & gray plastic, Larami, 1973, 8", MIB **$55.00**

Dick Tracy, holster, rubber, Mattel, 1961, NM **$20.00**

Dick Tracy, magazine, NEMO, Chester Gould & Dick Tracy Special Issue, February 1986, NM **$15.00**

Dick Tracy, magnifying glass, Larami, 1979, MOC **$22.00**

Dick Tracy, pocketknife, Dick Tracy Detective, single blade, white case w/Tracy holding gun, 1950s, 2¾", EX ..**$75.00**

Dick Tracy, postcard, Ruben Award Winner Series, Tracy in lab w/Measles, Sleet & Larceny Lou, 1987, NM ...**$20.00**

Dick Tracy, Secret Service Patrol Promotion Certificate, 1938, EX **$38.00**

Dick Tracy, 2-way wrist radios, Remco, plastic, battery powered, 1960s, complete, MIB, $95.00.

Dick Tracy, wallet, black vinyl w/Tracy profile, 1973, 3½x2½", w/6 Crimp Stopper Textbook cards, NM **$20.00**

Dick Tracy, yo-yo, MOC..**$8.00**

Ding Dong School, Mr Bumps figure set, Barry Products, 1955, MIB **$60.00**

Ding Dong School, scrapbook, Whitman, 1953, unused, EX+ **$20.00**

Ding Dong School, Shopping Chime Cart, 1954, M (VG box) **$100.00**

Dr Dolittle, bath toy, sponge type, Amsco #1591, M..**$30.00**

Dr Dolittle, Cartoon Kit, Colorforms #456, NMIB **$40.00**

Dr Dolittle, lawn shower spray, pink sea snail, AJ Renzi, 1975, NM **$50.00**

Dr Dolittle, magic set, Mystery Chamber, Remco, 1939, MIB **$30.00**

Dr Dolittle, music box, Ge-Tar, Mattel #4716, M.........**$50.00**

Dr Dolittle, music box, jack-in-the-box style, Giraffe, Mattel #4747, NMIB **$50.00**

Dr Dolittle, numbered pencil & paint set, Hasbro #3673, MIB **$25.00**

Dr Dolittle, party cup, plastic, Hallmark, NM.............**$10.00**

Dr Dolittle, periscope, Bar-Zim #609, NMIP...............**$30.00**

Dr Dolittle, playhouse, vinyl w/characters pictured, Mattel #5125, NM **$60.00**

Dr Dolittle, postcard, black & white, Personality Posters Manufacturing Co, 25 per set, each, from $5 to...**$10.00**

Dr Dolittle, riding stick, Pushmi-Pullyu Lama, AJ Renzi Plastic Corp, 1972, M...**$40.00**

Dr Dolittle, stamp & paint set, School House #D-100, MIB .**$25.00**

Dr Dolittle, wrist flashlight, Bantamlite #DW-30, NM .**$30.00**

Dr Kildare, magic slate, w/lift-up erasable film sheet, Lowe, 1962, unused, NM **$50.00**

Dr Seuss, jewelry set, The 5,000 Fingers of Dr T, Cullen, MOC..**$98.00**

Dracula, doll, vinyl w/cloth cape, Hamilton Presents, 1992, 14", EX **$30.00**

Dukes of Hazzard, tray, litho metal, 1981, 17x12", EX ..**$20.00**

Dukes of Hazzard, Wrist Racer, Police Cruiser, Knickerbocker, 1980, MOC **$10.00**

Elvira, belt, 1986, MIP...**$18.00**

Elvira, make-up kit w/earrings, MOC...........................$10.00

ET, Colorforms, 1982, MIB $20.00

ET, ring, 1982, EX $5.00

ET, tray, litho metal, 1982, 17x12", EX.....................$15.00

Evel Knievel, Sky Cycle, diecast metal & plastic, Ideal, 1976, MIB...$60.00

Fall Guy, truck, motorized take-apart model, Fleetwood, 1981, NMOC...$8.00

Fantastic Four, notebook, 1975, EX...........................$20.00

Fat Albert, figure, PVC, 1980s, NM $8.00

Felix the Cat, bop bag, inflatable vinyl w/image of Felix, Dartmore Corp, 1950s, 11", EX $25.00

Felix the Cat, figure, cardboard, holding fish, diecut, 1950s, 10", EX $20.00

Felix the Cat, Magna-Slide Cartoon Drawing Set, Multiple Toys, 1960s, EX...$70.00

Flash Gordon, beanie w/fins & goggles, 1950s, NM...$400.00

Flash Gordon, Colorforms, 1980, MIB $30.00

Flash Gordon, postcard, 1967, M................................$15.00

Flash Gordon, Strato-Kite Kit, MIP $85.00

Flash Gordon, tray, litho metal, Flash battling lizard creatures, 1979, 17½x13", EX $8.00

Flintstones, barometer, Bamm-Bamm, stone-like figure in tube changes color w/weather change, Schall, 1966, 4", NMIB $75.00

Flintstones, bubble pipe, Bamm-Bamm, Transogram, 1960s, EX...$25.00

Flintstones, clothes hanger, Bamm-Bamm, 1975, EX ..$20.00

Flintstones, doll, Barney, cloth, Knickerbocker, 7", MIB .$20.00

Flintstones, doll, Pebbles, stuffed, Knickerbocker, 6", NMIB..$30.00

Flintstones, doll, Pebbles, vinyl head, arms & legs, stuffed cloth body, Mighty Star Ltd, 1982, 12", MIB $55.00

Flintstones, earring tree, Fred, EX+ $35.00

Flintstones, figure, Barney, w/lawn mower, Mattel, 1993, MOC...$5.00

Flintstones, figures, all characters, bendable, Just Toys, MOC, each $10.00

Flintstones, night light, Barney, Electricord, 1979, MOC..$6.00

Flintstones, ornament, Fred & Barney in car, Hallmark, MIB $30.00

Flintstones, Pebbles & Bamm-Bamm in cradle, plastic, Ideal, 14½" L, EX...$125.00

Flintstones, pencil holder, Fred, plastic, comes in various colors, 1974, M...$5.00

Flintstones, Rotodraw, plastic discs, felt tip pens & drawing paper, England, 1969, NMIB.............................$45.00

Flintstones, squeeze toy, Barney, Lanco, 1950s, 6", NMIP..$135.00

Flintstones, Super Putty, 1980, MOC $15.00

Flintstones, tablecloth, 52x96", MIP...........................$12.00

Flintstones, wastebasket, lithographed tin, EX $60.00

Flipper, magic slate, w/lift-up erasable film sheet, Lowe, 1963, 12x8", unused, M $45.00

Flying Nun, Oil Painting by Numbers, Hasbro, 1967, MIB..$140.00

Friday the 13th, spitball, Jason, 1989, MOC................$10.00

Froggy the Gremlin, figure, Rempel, 1950s, 9", VG..$150.00

Full House, doll, Michelle, talker, Meritus, 1991, MIB...$40.00

Ghostbusters, figure, Green Hornet, charm bracelet, w/5 charms, NMOC...$90.00

Goofy, Tricky Trapeze, 1977, EX+.............................$35.00

Green Hornet, charm bracelet, w/5 charms, 1966, MOC..$90.00

Green Hornet, poster, Black Beauty from Aurora model kit box, heavy stock, glossy paper, limited edition, 1990, 14x22" $15.00

Green Hornet, spoon, 1966, NM $25.00

Green Hornet, wallet, vinyl, Mattel, M.......................$95.00

Gremlins, doll, Gizmo, Spain, plush, 8", MIB $100.00

Gremlins, figure, hard rubber, 1984, 4", EX................$7.00

Gumby, Colorforms, 1988, MIB $10.00

Gumby, doll, stuffed cloth, w/guitar & headband, Applause, 1989, 6", M $10.00

Gumby, figure, Pokey, bendable, 3", EX $4.00

Gumby, pencil topper, Pokey's head, marked Copyright LIL, 1967, 1½", M $15.00

Gumby and Pokey, figures, Perma Toy Co., 1984, 12" and 9", from $10.00 to $12.00 each. (Photo courtesy Lee Garmon)

Harry & the Hendersons, doll, talker, Galoob, 1990, 24", MIB $50.00

Heathcliff, doll, stuffed, Knickerbocker, 1981, VG $8.00

Hector Heathcote, magic slate, Lowe, 1964, 12x8", EX..$60.00

Hong Kong Phooey, candle, 1976, MIP......................$25.00

Hong Kong Phooey, tablecloth, 1975, MIP..................$15.00

Howdy Doody, bubble pipe, Clarabell, plastic, 5", NM..$35.00

Howdy Doody, dexterity puzzle, Howdy holds marionettes of Mr Bluster & Dilly, Japan, 1950s, 3" dia, EX $150.00

Howdy Doody, doll, molded plastic w/movable head & arms, black cloth jacket & pants, Ideal, 1965, 9", NM......$60.00

Howdy Doody, doll, stuffed body w/hard plastic head & vinyl hands, 12", EX $45.00

Howdy Doody, doll, talker, stuffed cloth w/plastic head, movable eyes & jaw, 1950s, EX................................$325.00

Howdy Doody, football, white w/black line drawing of Howdy, 1950s, 7", EX $85.00

Howdy Doody, key chain puzzle, M $40.00

Howdy Doody, Oil Painting Set for Beginners, Simple as ABC, Kagran, 1950, unused, MIB $120.00

Howdy Doody, pen, posable plastic w/pen in foot, NBC-KFS/Leadworks, 1988, 6" $5.00

Howdy Doody, pencil holder, ceramic Howdy in cowboy hat, Leadworks/NBC/KFS, 1988, 6", MIB.............$45.00

Howdy Doody, Sand Forms, plastic heads of Howdy, Clarabell, Flub-a-Dub & Mr Bluster, w/hand shovel, Kagran, 1952, NMOC $130.00

Howdy Doody, stationery, individual characters on each sheet, w/envelopes, Graphic Products, 1971, MIB.............$25.00

Howdy Doody, swim ring, vinyl, VG.........................$20.00

Howdy Doody, toy watch set, contains wristwatch & pocket watch, Ja-Ru, 1980s, MOC....................................$15.00

Huckleberry Hound, riding toy, VG...........................$85.00

Huckleberry Hound, bowling pin, hollow plastic figure, 7", VG...$2.00

Huckleberry Hound, doll, Boo Boo, vinyl head w/plush body, Knickerbocker, 1960s, 10", EX...................$30.00

Huckleberry Hound, flashlight, MIP..........................$20.00

Huckleberry Hound, napkins, 1959, MIP....................$15.00

Huckleberry Hound, pencil box, cardboard, Hanna-Barbera, 1960s, VG+...$45.00

Huckleberry Hound, push puppet, EX $25.00

Huckleberry Hound, tablecloth, multicolor paper, 1960s, MIP (sealed), from $25 to $35.00

Huckleberry Hound, TV tray, lithographed metal w/legs, 17x13", EX..$55.00

Huckleberry Hound, wastebasket, lithographed tin, EX ..$60.00

Huckleberry Hound & Yogi Bear, glasses case, 5", EX.$8.00

Hunter, Police Accessory Set, handcuffs, walkie-talkie, pistol, Police badge & ID card, Largo, 1984, MOC..........$27.00

Inch High Private Eye, mini gun set, 1973, MOC $12.00

Incredible Hulk, figure, orange plastic, Marx, NM......$20.00

Incredible Hulk, figure, rubber, 1979, 5", EX.............$8.00

Incredible Hulk, Halloween bucket, green plastic w/painted details, Renzi, 1979, 10", EX..............................$12.00

Incredible Hulk, roller skates, green, Larami, 1970s, MIB $25.00

Incredible Hulk, Rub 'n Play Set, Colorforms, 1979, MIB ..$27.00

Incredible Hulk, showerhead & shampoo set, 1990, MIB..$35.00

Incredible Hulk, switchplate, glow-in-the-dark plastic w/hand-painted details, 1976, MIP (sealed) $22.50

Indiana Jones, playset, Streets of Cairo, Kenner, 1983, MIB...$78.00

Indiana Jones & the Temple of Doom, sticker sheet, Topps uncut...$15.00

James Bond, action toy, Largo's boat & dragon, Gilbert, 1965, EX+ $30.00

James Bond, Electric Drawing Set, Lakeside, 1966, complete, EX (EX box) $50.00

James Bond, hair dressing, Colgate-Polmolive, 1965, M.$50.00

James Bond, ID tags, Imperial, 1980s, MOC $22.00

James Bond, talcum powder, 1960s, NM.....................$35.00

Jetsons, doll, Elroy, plush w/plastic hat, original tag, 1985, 14", NM $15.00

Jetsons, Slate & Chalk Set, 1960s, MIB........................$95.00

Jetsons, socks, Elroy, 1980, EX, pr $10.00

Knight Rider, Colorforms Rub 'N' Play Set, 1982, MIB (sealed)...$35.00

Knight Rider, diecast car, Ertl, 1/25 scale, 1982, MIB .$20.00

Knight Rider, KITT Dashboard, battery-operated, Illco, NMIB...$65.00

Knight Rider, sun visor hat w/sunglasses, Larami, 1982, MOC...$18.00

Land of the Giants, Movie Viewer, Kenner, 1969, MOC .$360.00

Laurel & Hardy, figure, Stan, plastic, 1972, 14", NM...$28.00

Li'l Abner, tray, Dogpatch USA, 1968, EX..................$45.00

Li'l Abner Venda-Bar, vending machine, coin-operated, 26x12x11", NM, $1,300.00. (Photo courtesy Dunbar Gallery)

Little Audrey, tote bag, vinyl w/Little Audrey & countries, 1960, 8x6x5", EX+..$60.00

Little House on the Prairie, Paint-By-Number Set, 1979, MIB..$45.00

Little Lulu, jewelry box, Larami, 1973, NMIP..............$12.00

Little Orphan Annie & Sandy, figure, plaster, copyright 1973, M...$350.00

Looney Tunes, Cartoon-O-Graph Sketch Board, Metal Moss Man Co, 1950s, unused, MIB.................................$70.00

Lost in Space, postcard, Official Fan Club, 1965, unused, M...$45.00

Love Boat, doctor's set, Fleetwood, 1979, MOC $30.00

Lucille Ball, ashtray, Desilu Sales Inc, 1950s $150.00

Lucille Ball, board game, Body Language, Milton Bradley, 1975 ....$20.00

Lucille Ball, book, Lucy & the Madcap Mystery, Whitman, 1963 ....$20.00

Lucille Ball, magazine, Life, April 6, 1953, Lucy & Desi on cover...$25.00

Lucille Ball, magazine, Quick, October 13, 1952, Lucy & Desi on cover $25.00

Lucille Ball, magazine ad, Philip Morris cigarettes, 1950s...$10.00

Lucille Ball, poster, Forever Darling, Lucy-Desi Films, 1956, 1-sheet...$75.00

Lucille Ball, sheet music, There's a Brand New Baby, 1953...$45.00

M*A*S*H, air freshener, Gibbs Manufacturing, MOC...$10.00

M*A*S*H, dog tags, NMOC......................................$20.00

M*A*S*H, sunglasses, plastic, MOC..........................$10.00

Magnum PI, tray, litho metal, 1982, 17x12", EX..........$15.00

Man From UNCLE, flasher ring, silver-colored base w/black & white flasher, Vari-Vue, 1965, NM $30.00

Man From UNCLE, Secret Cap Shooting Lighter, EX...$45.00

Masters of the Universe, Paint & Play Set, diecast figures w/paints, MIB...$15.00

Masters of the Universe, toothpaste topper, MOC $15.00

Max Headroom, puppet, Fingertronic, Bendy Toys, MIB ..$20.00

Mighty Mouse, Launcher Gun, Ja-Ru, 1981, MOC.......$15.00

Mighty Mouse, magic slate, w/erasable lift-up film sheet, Lowe, 1950s, 11x8", NM $30.00

Mork & Mindy, doll, Mork, rag-type talker (non-working), EX...$12.00

Mork & Mindy, sleeping bag, 1979, EX+ $18.00

Mr Magoo, doll, cloth & vinyl, Ideal, 1961, 16", NM ..$68.00

Mr Magoo, doll, plush & vinyl w/cloth clothes, Ideal, 1962, 14", EX...$50.00

Mr Magoo, magic slate, Rand McNally, 1975, EX........**$18.00**

Mr Magoo & Waldo, ring, comes w/2 interchangeable heads, Macman Ent, 1956, MIP...**$32.00**

Mummy, figure, Playco, 1991, 10", MIB...................**$12.00**

Munsters, baby figure, Ideal, Lily or Eddie, nude, 1964, EX each **$25.00**

Munsters, figures, Lily and Herman, Remco, 1964, $225.00 each. (Photo courtesy June Moon)

Munsters, hand puppet, vinyl head w/painted details on cloth body, Kayro, 1964, EX+ **$90.00**

Muppets, oven mitt, Miss Piggy, 1981, EX.....................**$8.00**

Nancy & Sluggo, music box, Sluggo figural, Schmid, 1970s, EX **$125.00**

Nightmare on Elm Street, figure, Stick-Up, 4", MOC.....**$6.00**

Olive Oyl, push puppet, Kohner No 3991, NM **$43.00**

Partridge Family, shopping bag, 1972, M **$12.00**

Peanuts, banner, Snoopy, America You're Beautiful on white, 13x28", M...**$20.00**

Peanuts, beach bag, Beagle Beach, Colgate premium, white w/zipper, 9x8", M **$20.00**

Peanuts, bell, Snoopy atop doghouse, Schmid, Christmas 1973, EX...**$6.00**

Peanuts, bookends, Snoopy, red plastic hearts, Hong Kong, EX, pr..**$18.00**

Peanuts, charm bracelet, gold-tone metal w/5 cloisonne charms, Applause, M **$20.00**

Peanuts, Colorforms, How's the Weather Lucy, EXIB.**$20.00**

Peanuts, comb & brush set, silverplate, Godinger, 1980s, MIB **$18.00**

Peanuts, cymbals, silver w/red wood knob, Chein, 4½" dia, EX, pr...**$45.00**

Peanuts, doll, Charlie Brown, red shirt, black pants, Hungerford, 10", EX...**$55.00**

Peanuts, doll, Linus, w/hand out, red shirt, Hungerford, 8½", EX...**$60.00**

Peanuts, doll, Peppermint Patty, rag type, Determined Toys, 1970s, 14", MIB **$20.00**

Peanuts, doll, Peppermint Patty, 1982, 15", NM..........**$15.00**

Peanuts, doll, Snoopy, black & white plush w/red necktie, Determined, 1969, 10", MIP **$40.00**

Peanuts, doll, Snoopy, cloth w/cloth clothes, United Features, 1968, 7", EX...**$14.00**

Peanuts, doll, Snoopy, inflatable, 1969, 18", VG **$8.00**

Peanuts, doll, Snoopy, movable head, Hasbro, 12", EX...**$12.00**

Peanuts, earring tree, Snoopy, enameled metal doghouse, 1979, 5", MIB...**$10.00**

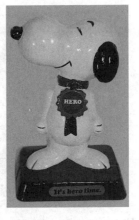

Peanuts, figure, Snoopy, It's Hero Time, composition, 1960s, 5", M, $25.00. (Photo courtesy June Moon)

Peanuts, fishing rod, Snoopy, Zebco, VG...................**$10.00**

Peanuts, jack-in-the-box, Snoopy, NMIB **$75.00**

Peanuts, kitchen set, w/3 metal plates & 3 pots & pans featuring Charlie Brown & Snoopy, Ohio Art, VG....**$65.00**

Peanuts, music box, Snoopy, plays Home Sweet Home, Schmid, 1985, 5", M...**$50.00**

Peanuts, paint set, 8 pictures w/paints, 1966, MIB (sealed) **$30.00**

Peanuts, pin, Lucy, gold-tone, Knott's Camp Snoopy, 1992, 2¾", M..**$30.00**

Peanuts, pitcher, Linus on chair, ceramic, Willets, 1966, M....**$40.00**

Peanuts, scissors, battery-op, blades in mouth, Snoopy Snippers, Mattel #7410, VG **$20.00**

Peanuts, Snoopy's Scooter Shooter, Child Guidance #51720, MIB **$40.00**

Peanuts, soap dish, Snoopy, rubber, w/soap, Avon, 7½", MIB **$15.00**

Peanuts, toothbrush, battery-op, Kenner, 1972, MIB ..**$35.00**

Peanuts, toothbrush holder, Willets, 1980s, MIB.........**$25.00**

Peanuts, waste can, Charlie Brown & Snoopy, tin, 1969, EX **$14.00**

Pee Wee Herman, puppet, pull-string type, 24", NM..**$65.00**

Phantom, iron-on transfer, thin paper for use on T-shirt, ca 1965, unused, NM..**$15.00**

Pink Panther, candle climber, ceramic, w/original hang tag, M **$60.00**

Pink Panther, jewelry set, 1989, MOC........................**$12.00**

Planet of the Apes, Colorforms Adventure Set, 1967, original box, EX...**$25.00**

Planet of the Apes, kite, Hi-Flier, MIP.........................**$75.00**

Popeye, bowl, cereal; plastic, 1979, EX **$8.00**

Popeye, bubble pipe, plastic, Hong Kong, 1960s, 6", EX ..**$15.00**

Popeye, can, Popeye Spinach label on tin can, 1965, unused, EX...**$18.00**

Popeye, figure, painted & jointed wooden body w/composition head, black shirt & blue pants, Jaymar, 8", VG **$65.00**

Popeye, figure, Wimpy, ceramic, 1980s, M.................**$45.00**

Popeye, flashlight, pocket size, Larami, 1983, MOC...**$16.00**

Popeye, kaleidoscope, w/4 changeable lenses, 1978, MOC..**$15.00**

Popeye, knapsack, multicolor canvas w/tags, 1979, M...**$12.00**

Popeye, magic slate, Lowe, 1957, 12x8", unused, NM..**$30.00**

Popeye, party cup, waxy paper, shows Popeye riding whale & other characters w/Happy Birthday, 1950s, 3", M **$8.00**

Popeye, pencil box, King Features Syndicate, 1934, EX, $55.00. (Photo courtesy Dunbar Gallery)

Popeye, Power Strength Toy, 1950s, MIP **$60.00**
Popeye, record player, Dynamite Music Machine, EX ..**$25.00**
Popeye, wallet, vinyl w/flasher square, NM **$55.00**

Popeye, Wimpy chalkware figure, copyright KFS, 13½", EX, from $300.00 to $450.00. (Photo courtesy Dunbar Gallery)

Porky Pig, cookie mold, 1978, EX **$5.00**
Prince Valiant, charm, plastic w/top loop, ½", EX **$5.00**
Punky Brewster, doll, Galoob, 1984, 18", MIB **$40.00**
Quick Draw McGraw, doll, plush w/felt hat, scarf & gun belt, Nanco, 1989, 12", NM **$12.00**
Quick Draw McGraw, wastebasket, lithographed tin, EX..**$60.00**
Raggedy Andy, doll, Playschool, 1987, 12", MIB.........**$12.00**
Raggedy Ann, bulletin board, 1970s, 23", VG **$15.00**
Raggedy Ann, Colorforms, 1967, MIB **$25.00**
Raggedy Ann, doll, Hasbro, 1983, 17", MIB **$25.00**
Raggedy Ann, doll, Knickerbocker, 1970s, 14", NM....**$30.00**
Raggedy Ann, figure, bisque, 1988, 4", M...................**$15.00**
Raggedy Ann, quilt, baby's, NM **$15.00**
Rat Finks, decal, 1990, M **$7.00**
Rat Finks, ring, sm, M..**$8.00**
Rat Patrol, hat, red w/logo, 1966, EX..........................**$85.00**
Ricochet Rabbit, change purse, pink vinyl, early 1960s, NMOC **$50.00**
Ricochet Rabbit, doll, stuffed plush w/vinyl face, felt hat & vest, Ideal, 1960s, 16", EX **$85.00**
Road Runner, placemat, Pepsi/Warner Brothers, 10x17", M **$22.00**

Rocky & Bullwinkle, Dudley Do-Right, figure, Fun-E-Flex, 1972, 5", MOC...**$25.00**
Rocky & Bullwinkle, figure, Rocky, Wham-O, MOC ..**$25.00**
Rocky & Bullwinkle, marbles, 1988, M **$3.00**
Rocky & Bullwinkle, plate, Melmac, 1960s, 8", EX **$16.00**

Rocky & Bullwinkle, Snidely Whiplash bendy, Wham-O, 4½", M, $25.00.

Rocky & Bullwinkle, Spelling & Counting Board, Larami, 1969, M (EX card)...**$28.00**
Rocky & His Friends, Colorforms, 1961, NMIB **$90.00**
Rodan, figure, Toho Co, 1979, lg, EX/NM **$85.00**
Rudolph the Red-Nosed Reindeer, magic slate, Lowe, 1964, 8x12", M..**$32.00**
Saturday Night Live, doll, Conehead, Broadway Video, 1991, w/tag & stand, 10", EX..**$12.00**
Scooby Doo, doll, stuffed cloth, paper label w/Scooby image, 1970, 11", EX..**$22.00**
Secret Agent 002, grab bag & candy, bag w/3 plastic toys & candy, Best, 1966, unused, M **$8.00**
Secret Sam, shooting cane, plastic w/sculpted lion's head top, Topper, 1965, 32", NM **$89.00**
Sesame Street, doll, Big Bird, pull-string talker, Playskool, 1970s, 22", VG...**$25.00**
Sesame Street, figures, PVC, Applause, set of 8 ....**$20.00**
Sesame Street, tray, lithographed metal, 1971, 17x12", EX **$12.00**
Simpsons, bulletin board, cork, Roseart, 1990, 16x20"..**$15.00**
Simpsons, doll, Bart, stuffed body w/vinyl head, arms & legs, Dandee, 16", MIB...**$15.00**
Simpsons, doll, Bubble Blowin' Lisa, blows bubbles w/saxaphone, Mattel, 18", MIB......................................**$35.00**
Simpsons, figure, bendable, Jesco, 5 different, MOC, each..**$5.00**
Simpsons, frisbee, white w/image of Bart's head, Betras Plastics **$5.00**
Simpsons, magnet, Marge dancing w/jello salad, ceramic, Presents, 2¾x1¾"...**$4.00**
Simpsons, paper plates, Chesapeake, 8 per package, 9", MIP **$4.50**
Simpsons, pogs, complete set of 50, EX.....................**$15.00**
Simpsons, yo-yo, white w/image of Bart on skateboard Spectra Star, MOC **$8.00**
Sinbad Jr, belt, red plastic w/blue & white hard plastic diamond buckle, battery-op light w/code book, Voplex, 1965, MIB **$160.00**

Six Million Dollar Man, Give-A-Show Projector, 1977, MIB $25.00

Smokey & the Bandit, diecast figure, Bandit, Ertl, 1982, M (EX+ card) $12.00

Smothers Brothers, yo-yo, wood, Kodak, M..................$7.00

Smurfs, banner, Happy Smurfday, MIP $20.00

Smurfs, Colorforms, EXIB $35.00

Smurfs, doll, Smurf boy, stuffed, 1981, 12", VG $8.00

Smurfs, doll, Smurfette, stuffed, 1981, 8", EX $10.00

Smurfs, figures, PVC, several different, NM, each, from $2 to..$4.00

Smurfs, Paint-By-Number #263, complete, EXIB.........$30.00

Smurfs, record player, 1982, EX...................................$20.00

Smurfs, serving tray, VG...$15.00

Smurfs, sewing cards, MIB $25.00

Smurfs, Shrinky Dinks, MIB $20.00

Smurfs, Travel Twin Mirror & Comb Set, 1980s, NMIB...$15.00

Smurfs, Wrap-an-Egg set, MIB $10.00

Sonic the Hedgehog, bubble pipe, plastic, Sega, 1990, M ..$12.00

Space: 1999, Sonic Powered megaphone, battery-op, Vanity Fair, 1970s, original box, VG $25.00

Speedy Gonzales, doll, cloth, Mighty Star/Looney Tunes, 1971, EX+ $15.00

Spider-Man, Colorforms Adventure Set, 1974, M (VG+ box) $15.00

Spider-Man, comb & brush set, 1970s, MIB $45.00

Spider-Man, doll, stuffed cloth w/Velcro hands & feet, Knickerbocker, 1978, 20", NM $27.00

Spider-Man, Fly 'Em High Parachutist & Launcher, 6" figure w/parachute & sling-shot launcher, AHI, 1979, MOC.$27.00

Spider-Man, Halloween bucket, red hard plastic head, Renzi, 1979, 10", VG $15.00

Spider-Man, Mix 'N Mold Set, 1970s, MIB $45.00

Spider-Man, pencil sharpener, Nasta, 1970, 4", MOC....$5.00

Spider-Man, scissors, figural handle w/metal blades, Nasta, 1980, 3½", MOC $4.00

Spider-Man, vehicle set, Buddy L, 1984, MIB $35.00

Spider-Woman, Under-oos, 2-pc polyester underwear costume, Union Underwear, 1979, 11x11" package, M...........$20.00

Steve Canyon, membership card, w/place for a photo, 1959, 3½x2¼", M $10.00

Steve Canyon, T-shirt, Shir Tees, ca 1959, MIP (sealed) .$98.00

Steve Uerkel, doll, 18", EX $10.00

Super Heroes, beach tote bag, 1978, EX $15.00

Super Heroes, postcard book, perforated, shows miscellaneous characters, DC Comics, 1978, EX+ $10.00

Superman, belt buckle, heavy bronze metal, 1970s, 4", M..$7.50

Superman, belt buckle, multicolor, 1970s, NM.............$25.00

Superman, Cartoonist Stamp Set, complete, 1966, M (EX+ card)..$35.00

Superman, container, Sunnyland California Raisins, multicolor, Sunnyland, 1982, 1½x2", EX+ $15.00

Superman, hairbrush, Avon, MIB $10.00

Superman, horseshoe set, Super Slim Inc, 1954, EX (VG box)..$40.00

Superman, ornament, Hallmark, MIB..........................$35.00

Superman, pencils, National Periodical, 1966, set of 12", EX (VG package) $30.00

Superman, planter, ceramic, Superman flying & word balloon w/Super Plants, 1976, 3", NM $15.00

Superman, tattoos, Topps, 1962, 1½x3½" wrapper, NM ..$30.00

Superman, Thingmaker Accessory Kit, w/mold, Plastigoop, paint, brush & pins, Mattel, 1960s, MOC $85.00

Superman, token, Happy Birthday 50 Years, blue, flasher type, 1982, 1¾", M..$10.00

Superman, tote bag, 1982, EX $12.00

Superman, wallet, brown leather, 1976, M $10.00

SWAT, bullhorn, 1975, EX $12.00

Sylvester, blow-up figure, 1970, 8", EX $8.00

Tarzan, magic slate, 1968, EX.....................................$20.00

Tasmanian Devil, doll, stuffed, 1980, 13", EX.............$12.00

Teddy Ruxpin, doll, complete w/cassette, 1989, 14", M .$50.00

Teenage Mutant Ninja Turtles, key chain, Hope Industries, 1989, MOC..$8.00

Thor, folder, allover comic illustrations, Meade, 1975, 9½x12½", NM...$15.00

Thor, patch, cloth w/embroidered portrait & yellow stitched border, EX detail, ca 1970s, 3" dia, NM..................$6.00

Three Stooges, doll set, stuffed cloth, Collins, 1982, on separate cards, M, 3 for $200.00

Three Stooges, folder, Bright-Ideas, 1984, 9½x12", NM..$12.00

Three Stooges, photos, set of 4, 1977, 11x14", NM $48.00

Three Stooges, puffy stickers, 1984, MIP $8.00

Tom & Jerry, ring, cloisonne, 1970s, M.......................$12.00

Top Cat, doll, stuffed cloth body, soft vinyl head w/tongue sticking out, Ideal, 1960s, 6", MIB......................$150.00

Topo Gigio, eraser, rubber figure, hands behind his head, looking up, 1960s, 2", VG.....................................$20.00

Tweety Bird, doll, Mighty Star, stuffed, 1971, EX........$15.00

Underdog, harmonica, embossed Simon Bar Sinister or Underdog at each end, 1975, 8", NM....................$15.00

Welcome Back Kotter, calculating wheel, 1976 MOC .$12.50

Welcome Back Kotter, Colorforms, 1976, NMIB..........$22.00

Welcome Back Kotter, greeting card, set of 6, MIB $25.00

Winky Dink, Super Magic TV Kit, Winky Dink & You!, Standard Toycraft, 1968, NMIB $125.00

Wizard of Oz, Cowardly Lion push-button jigger, plastic, Mattel, 15", $50.00.

Wizard of Oz, doll, Dorothy, Presents, 14", MIB $35.00

Wizard of Oz, doll, Glenda, Presents, 15", MIB $45.00

Wizard of Oz, doll, Lowes Inc, 1988, 6 different, MIB, each, from $20 to..$30.00

Wizard of Oz, doll, Scarecrow, MC toilet tissue premium, 1960s, 16", NM $25.00

Wizard of Oz, night light, Scarecrow, 1989, MIB........**$25.00**

Wizard of Oz, wastebasket, characters & Oz map graphics, Cheinco, 1975, 10x13", G......................**$265.00**

Wolfman, doll, vinyl w/cloth outfit, Hamilton Presents, 1992, 14", EX......................**$30.00**

Wolfman, eraser top, rubber, 1960s, 1", NM................**$12.00**

Wolfman, figure, Playco Products, 1991, 10", MIB......**$12.00**

Wolfman, pencil sharpener, 3" tall bust of Wolfman sets on pencil sharpener base, green plastic, UP Co, 1960s, M..**$24.00**

Wolfman, statue lamp, plaster, Universal Studios, 1973, 19", EX **$200.00**

Wonder Woman, paint set, complete w/picture, brushes, paint & instructions, Craft Master, 1984, MIB **$20.00**

Wonder Woman, sunglasses, Nasta, MOC....................**$20.00**

Woody Woodpecker, flannel board set, VG **$45.00**

Woody Woodpecker, purse, vinyl w/image of Woody as Uncle Sam, 1970s, NM....................**$18.00**

Woody Woodpecker, sheet music, As Recorded by Kay Kyser, 1974, EX+ **$12.00**

Yogi Bear, camera, 1976, MOC....................**$20.00**

Yogi Bear, doll, pillow type w/bells inside, 1977, 15", EX ..**$20.00**

Yogi Bear, flashlight, MIP....................**$20.00**

Yogi Bear, Lovable Smoking Traveler's Pet, plastic, MOC..**$18.00**

Yogi Bear & Boo Boo, curtains, brown chenille w/fuzzy red letters, 1967, 67x38", EX, pr....................**$15.00**

Ziggy, mirror, 1970s, MIP....................**$10.00**

Spike Jones, drum, 19", $85.00.

Christmas Collectibles

Christmas is nearly everybody's favorite holiday, and it's a season when we all seem to want to get back to time-honored traditions. The stuffing and fruit cakes are made like Grandma always made them, we go caroling and sing the old songs that were written a hundred years ago, and the same Santa that brought gifts to the children in a time long forgotten still comes to our house and yours every Christmas Eve.

So for reasons of nostalgia, there are thousands of collectors interested in Christmas memorabilia. Some early Santa figures are rare and may be very expensive, especially when dressed in a color other than red. Blown glass ornaments and Christmas tree bulbs were made in shapes of fruits and vegetables, houses, Disney characters, animals, and birds. There are

Dresden ornaments and candy containers from Germany, some of which were made prior to the 1870s, that have been lovingly preserved and handed down to our generation. They were made of cardboard that sparkled with gold and silver trim.

Artificial trees made of feathers were produced as early as 1850 and as late as 1950. Some were white, others blue, though most were green, and some had red berries or clips to hold candles. There were little bottle-brush trees, trees with cellophane needles, and trees from the sixties made of aluminum.

Collectible Christmas items are not necessarily old, expensive, or hard to find. Things produced in your lifetime have value as well. To learn more about this field, we recommend *Christmas Collectibles* by Margaret and Kenn Whitmyer, and *Christmas Ornaments, Lights and Decorations* Volumes I through III by George Johnson.

Assorted electric lights, 1950s, $90.00 – 100.00.

Bubble light, Noma Biscuit (also known as Glo-Lite, Yule Glo, Amoco), most common form, ca 1946-60, from $3 to..**$5.00**

Bubble light, Noma snowman, 1985, from $8 to **$9.00**

Bubble light, Noma Tulip, ca 1948-60, from $5 to........**$7.00**

Bubble light, Renown (also known as Gem, Everlite, & Santa), 3-color, ca 1957, from $8 to **$12.00**

Bubble light, snowman, made in Taiwan/marketed by Noma, 1980s, 4½", boxed set, from $15 to......................**$20.00**

Candle, painted milk glass, electric, Japan, 2½", from $10 to **$15.00**

Candy cane holder, molded cardboard, American, 1940s – 50s, 10", from $50.00 to $60.00. (Photo courtesy Margaret and Kenn Whitmyer)

Candy container, bell, foil over pressed paper, Japan, 1920s-50s, 3", from $25 to **$35.00**

Candy container, feather tree w/decorations, base opens, 6¾", from $100 to................**$125.00**

Candy container, globe, paper map over cardboard ball, opens at equator, 1½" dia, from $95 to..............**$115.00**

Candy container, National League baseball, printed paper over cardboard, 1" dia, from $90 to...................**$100.00**

Candy container, printed paper over cardboard, Germany, 1950-60, 3", from $10 to **$15.00**

Candy container, Santa, chenille strips form suit, crepe-paper bag over shoulder, Germany, 1935, 9", from $60 to **$75.00**

Candy container, Santa on skis, hard plastic, American, ca 1955, 3½", from $12 to **$15.00**

Candy container, snowman, plastic, Rosbro Plastics, 1955, 5", from $12 to **$15.00**

Candy container, suitcase, paper w/applied leather straps & metal latch, 4", from $50 to **$60.00**

Candy container, top hat, fabric over paper, candy bag inside, 2", from $175 to **$200.00**

Candy container, white net stocking w/clay Santa face, Japan, 5½", from $50 to **$60.00**

Chain of beads, glass berries, Blumchen & Co, ca 1990-94, 108", from $22 to **$30.00**

Chain of beads, plastic, round or oval, Japan or China, 1960s-70s, up to 108" L, from $3 to **$4.00**

Chain of beads, round, glass, common Japanese type, from ¼" to ½", price per foot: $1 to **$1.25**

Chain of beads, Santa heads, glass, price per foot: from $50 to **$60.00**

Game, Rudolph the Red-Nosed Reindeer, Parker Brothers, copyright, 1948, MIB, from $70 to **$80.00**

Light, candle w/embossed flame, painted clear glass, standard base, Austria, 4½", from $15 to **$20.00**

Light, cross w/exhaust tip, painted clear glass, standard unmarked base, 5½x3½", from $90 to **$100.00**

Light bulb, bell, Christmas Greetings, painted milk glass, Japan, ca 1950, 1¼", from $10 to **$15.00**

Light bulb, bell, flattened form w/5-pointed star embossed in center, electric, base marked Mazda, 1¾", from $20 to ...**$25.00**

Light bulb, Betty Boop in strapless gown, painted milk glass, Japan, 2¼", from $30 to **$35.00**

Light bulb, bird in a birdcage, painted milk glass, Japan, 1935-55, 2", from $10 to **$15.00**

Light bulb, cats (2) in basket, painted milk glass, Japan, 2¼", from $55 to.......................................**$65.00**

Light bulb, cow jumping over moon, painted milk glass, Japan, ca 1955, 2¼", from $35 to **$40.00**

Light bulb, cross, painted clear glass tubular arms, Japan, 2¾", from $10 to.......................................**$15.00**

Light bulb, dragon on a lantern, painted milk glass, Japan, 2¼", from $10 to.......................................**$15.00**

Light bulb, Fiddler pig (of 3 pigs), painted milk glass, DiaBrite, Japan, ca 1970, 2¾", from $14 to **$18.00**

Light bulb, Humpty Dumpty, painted milk glass, Paramount, 2½", from $15 to **$25.00**

Light bulb, Kewpie w/wavy hair, painted milk glass, Japan, 3", from $50 to **$60.00**

Light bulb, monkey head, double-faced, painted clear glass, Japan, 1½", from $20 to.......................................**$30.00**

Light bulb, morning glory, muted colors, marked Mazda on base, ca 1940, 2½", from $60 to **$75.00**

Light bulb, parrot, celluloid, 3¾", from $40 to...........**$50.00**

Light bulb, pine cone, lacquered clear glass w/crushed glass trim, Czechoslovakia, recent, 2¼", from $5 to......**$10.00**

Light bulb, pouter pigeon, painted clear glass, base in tail, Japan, 2½", from $8 to **$10.00**

Light bulb, rabbit in a suit, painted clear glass, ears up, Japan, 1¾", from $30 to **$35.00**

Light bulb, rooster in a tub, painted milk glass, Japan, 2¼", from $40 to.......................................**$50.00**

Light bulb, Santa standing w/bag over left shoulder, painted milk glass, Japan, 3¾", from $10 to **$15.00**

Light bulb, Scottie sitting, painted milk glass, angular face & head, Japan, 2½", from $35 to.............................**$45.00**

Light bulb, snow-covered cottage, painted milk glass, Japan, 2" to 2¾", from $8 to.......................................**$12.00**

Light bulb, square w/Santa & sleigh embossed on sides, painted milk glass, Japan, ca 1950, 2", from $25 to **$35.00**

Light bulbs, Walt Disney characters, unauthorized issue, $30.00 each. (Photo courtesy Margaret and Kenn Whitmyer)

Light cover, Santa figural, hard plastic, rabbit fur trim, ca 1950, 4¾", from $15 to.......................................**$18.00**

Light reflector, cardboard & foil, Tinselite, 3½" dia, boxed set, from $4 to.......................................**$5.00**

Light reflector, snowflake, hard plastic, 2-sided, metal clip to hold light, late 1940s, 5", from $7 to.....................**$8.00**

Light shade, Noma bells w/Christmas scenes, boxed set w/light string, from $55 to **$65.00**

Light-up figure, Santa, plastic, General Porducts, ca 1950, 8¼", from $30 to.......................................**$40.00**

Light-up figure, Santa on reindeer, plastic, unmarked, ca 1955, 11", from $25 to **$30.00**

Light-up figure, Santa w/outstretched arms holding wreath, opening for light in back, ca 1955, 10¼", from $45 to........**$55.00**

Ornament, angel standing, hard plastic, lg wings, American, late 1940s-50s, 3¼", from $10 to **$12.00**

Ornament, angel w/harp, reproduction scrap, ca 1989, 12", from $25 to.......................................**$35.00**

Ornament, ball, hard plastic w/snowflakes filigree, Made in USA, ca 1955, 2½", from $3 to.................................**$4.00**

Ornament, basket, wooden w/glass fruit, 3", from $40 to **$50.00**

Ornament, bell, paper honeycomb, red or green, American made, 1920s-60s, 3" to 4", from $2 to **$3.00**

Ornament, bird, cardboard, flat, sm, from $20 to.......**$35.00**

Ornament, butterfly, filigree wings, flat or double, Dresden, 1980s-90s, 4½", from $5 to.................................**$10.00**

Ornament, butterfly on a leaf, mold blown, Radko, 1994, from $20 to.......................................**$30.00**

Ornament, cockateel, mold blown w/spun glass wings, 3¼x5" wingspan, from $75 to..............................**$90.00**

Ornament, cow mooing, silver, Dresden, 3x5¼", from $95 to...**$115.00**

Ornament, cross, cardboard, flat, from $20 to **$35.00**

Ornament, deer w/raised leg, celluloid, Japan, ca 1950, 4½", from $4 to...**$5.00**

Ornament, dog w/basket (begging), mold blown, multicolor paint, ca 1970s, 5", from $20 to..........................**$25.00**

Ornament, dove w/olive branch, scrap, 6½x7", from $30 to...**$35.00**

Ornament, heart on a quilted heart, pink paint on milk glass, 2", from $10 to...**$18.00**

Ornament, horse, tin lead, recast by Wm J Rigby Co from original mold, 2½", from $12 to....................**$25.00**

Ornament, house, cardboard, Czechoslovakia, 1¾" to 2¼", from $10 to...**$12.00**

Ornament, house, painted cardboard, Japan, sm, from $5 to **$6.00**

Ornament, icicle, flanged, glow-in-the-dark type, w/loop, American, late 1950s-50s, 5½", from $1.50 to.........**$2.00**

Ornament, lady bug, gold & silver or natural, flat or double, Dresden, recently made, 2½", from $3 to..............**$5.00**

Ornament, lion walking, gold or silver, flat or double, Dresden, 1980s-90s, 2½x3½", from $3 to **$5.00**

Ornament, manger, cut metal w/wax figure of Jesus, 2¾", from $100 to...**$125.00**

Ornament, moose head, silver, flat, Dresden, ca 1988, 3¾", from $3 to...**$4.00**

Ornament, nativity scene, scrap type w/tinsel, generic type w/figures of 1½" to 3", from $8 to........................**$18.00**

Ornament, oyster shell w/pearl, silver paint on clear, Italy, 1950s, 2½", from $75 to..**$90.00**

Ornament, peasant girl wearing apron & scarf, multicolor on clear, 3¼", from $50 to.......................................**$60.00**

Ornament, pine cone, foil over paper, resembles 3-dimensional Dresden ornament, Wilmsen of Philadelphia, ca 1935, 2"...**$15.00**

Ornament, pineapple slice, gold paint on clear glass, mold blown, 4½", from $8 to...**$12.00**

Ornament, Red Star, Russian Dresden, ca 1960, 1½", from $30 to...**$40.00**

Ornament, Russian Santa, mold blown w/fur trim, Radko, 7", from $25 to...**$35.00**

Ornament, Santa, vinyl w/flocking, Japan, ca 1970s-80s, 4½", from $3 to...**$4.00**

Ornament, Santa going down the chimney, mold blown, red, white & silver, Radko, 1993, 4", from $20 to........**$30.00**

Ornament, Santa w/boughs, spun cotton w/porcelain face, D Blumchen & Co, 1989, 5", from $40 to.................**$50.00**

Ornament, Santa w/Christmas tree (standard form), mold blown, red coat, 4½", from $40 to.......................**$50.00**

Ornament, Santa w/hand behind his back, celluloid, Japan, 7", from $75 to...**$100.00**

Ornament, Santa w/tree, girl & lamb, scrap w/tinsel trim, 6", from $20 to...**$25.00**

Ornament, slipper, gold, flat w/tinsel & lithographs, toe contains net candy container, Dresden, 1980s, from $10 to...**$15.00**

Ornament, snowflake, paper honeycomb w/beads, red, pink or white, ca 1925, 6½", from $25 to.....................**$30.00**

Ornament, songbird, painted spun cotton w/painted paper wings, 2½", from $55 to..**$85.00**

Ornament, spun glass rosette w/scrap angel (walking) on 1 side, 7½", from $55 to...**$65.00**

Ornament, spun glass rosette w/scrap Santa each side, 4¾" dia, from $40 to...**$50.00**

Ornament, star, cardboard w/applied Santa head, 3¾", from $20 to...**$25.00**

Ornament, star, gold or silver, flat or double, tinsel tail, Dresden, 1980s-90s, 2" to 3¼", from $1 to.............**$2.00**

Ornament, star w/a face, double, painted milk glass, 2¼", from $30 to...**$35.00**

Ornament, star w/hammer & sickle embossed in center, Dresden, ca 1935, 3½", from $70 to.....................**$80.00**

Ornament, teapot, silvered plastic, embossed details, ca 1960, 3", from $8 to...**$9.00**

Ornament/reflector, tin lead, round, 2½", from $25 to ...**$35.00**

Ornaments, nativity scene, scrap fold-out type, Germany, approximately 4½x7", from $10 to.......................**$15.00**

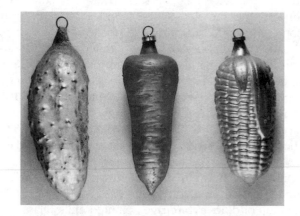

Ornaments, pickle, carrot, or ear of corn, silvered, 1920s – 30s, 3½" to 4", from $35.00 to $60.00 each. (Photo courtesy Margaret and Ken Whitmyer)

Rope, red & silver foil, DoubleGlo, 1950s, 120", from $3 to..**$4.00**

Tree stand, cast iron w/Merry Christmas cast into 1 side, thumb screws, 12" dia, from $20 to **$25.00**

Tree stand, common 3- or 4-legged, round pan w/ring & thumb screws, 1950s-60s, 18" to 32" leg spread, from $1 to ...**$6.00**

Tree stand, metal, 4-legged, Harras, marked Germany, 11¾", from $35 to...**$45.00**

Tree stand, metal cone shape w/Christmas scenes, red string of lights around base, Noma, 13", from $175 to ..**$200.00**

Tree stand, musical & electrical, Cameo, ca 1960, 13" dia, from $20 to...**$25.00**

Tree stand, 8-Light Automatic by Noma, ca 1948, 19" dia, from $20 to...**$25.00**

Tree top, angel in cloud wreath, plastic & silver foil, Majestic, ca 1958, 8", from $5 to.......................................**$6.00**

Tree top, Carillon Spire, plastic, electrified, Bradford Plastics on base, ca 1960, from $5 to.............................**$7.00**

Tree top, Paramount Star, metal w/plastic tips, 3¼", MIB, from $10 to...**$15.00**

Tree top, Santa w/tree, molded & free-blown glass, Inge Glass, late 1980s, 11", from $20 to **$25.00**

Tree top, star, foil, 5-pointed, National Tinsel, 9", MIB, from $6 to...**$8.00**

Cigarette Lighters

Collectors of tobacciana tell us that cigarette lighters are definitely hot! Look for novel designs (figurals, Deco styling, and so forth), unusual mechanisms (flint and fuel, flint and gas, battery, etc.), those made by companies now defunct, those with advertising, and quality lighters made by Ronson, Dunhill, Evans, Colibri, and Zippo. For more information we recommend *Collector's Guide to Cigarette Lighters, Books I and II,* by James Flanagan.

Newsletter: *On the Lighter Side*
Judith Sanders
Route 3, 136 Circle Dr.
Quitman, TX 75783; 903-763-2795; SASE for information

Advertising, Camel Cigarettes, enamel work cigarette pack on chromium, Japan, early 1960s, 2¼", from $10 to.......**$15.00**

Advertising, General Electric, black letters w/red logo on chromium, Zippo, ca 1963, 2¼", from $10 to **$15.00**

Advertising, It's a Great Gang That Sells the Maytag, musical, MIB, $75.00. (Photo courtesy Nate Stroller)

Advertising, Jim Beam Bourbon Whiskey bottle, plastic, butane, Korea, 1980s, 3", from $5 to.....................**$10.00**

Advertising, Playboy, white bunny logo & black enamel on brass, Korea, ca mid-1960s, 2½x¾", from $10 to.**$20.00**

Advertising, Raritan Oil Co, silver metal w/red letters, 3½x2x1½"..**$45.00**

Advertising, Switch to Dodge Trucks & Save...Up to $95 a Year on Gas Alone, barrel shaped tin, 3x1¾" dia..**$40.00**

Advertising, table-top, Coors Beer can, holds disposable butane lighter, ca 1970s, 3½x1¾" dia, from $10 to...............**$20.00**

Advertising, table-top, Winston, red & white painted metal w/gold trim & crown logo, Gillette, 1980s, 4¼", from $5 to..**$10.00**

Advertising, VW Volkswagen, MW Motors, Etna PA in blue & white on silver, Made in Japan, MIB.....................**$12.50**

ATC, Super de Lux, brushed satin chromium, ca mid-1950s, 2¼", MIB, from $10 to...**$20.00**

Beetland/Toho (Japan), Godzilla Lite, painted die-cast metal figural, Special 30th Birthday Edition, 3", MIB **$50.00**

Berkley, Director, chromium w/vertical stripe design, ca late 1940s, 1¾", from $25 to **$40.00**

Colibri, brushed chromium, lift-arm replica, ca 1986, 2⅝", MIB, from $40 to..**$60.00**

Colibri, enameled bird & black on gold plate, hinged top, ca mid-1970s, 2½x¾", from $30 to............................**$50.00**

Crown, musical, engraved gold plate, plays Home on the Range, late 1940s, 2⅝", from $45 to.....................**$60.00**

Crown, musical, plays On the Atchison, Topeka & Santa Fe, black letters w/Santa Fe in circle on brass, late '40s, 2⅝" ...**$60.00**

Dunhill, gold plated, lift-arm style, marked Made in Switzerland, mid-1950s, 2½x⅞", from $225 to ...**$300.00**

Dunhill, Turn-O-Top Lighter-Dispenser, turn top & cigarette pops up, round leather body, 1940s, 3¾x4" **$75.00**

Elgin, American Beauty, gold plate w/fine vertical lines, ca mid-1950s, 1¼x2⅛", w/display stand, from $40 to.........**$60.00**

Elgin, American Lite-O-Matic, M...................................**$20.00**

Evans, Lucite cube shows building & antenna, RCA Tubes on roof, EX **$45.00**

Evans, Spitfire, US army insignia on black enamel, ca 1940s **$30.00**

Evans, table-top, footed marble base w/brass top, ca late 1930s, 3¾", from $25 to **$30.00**

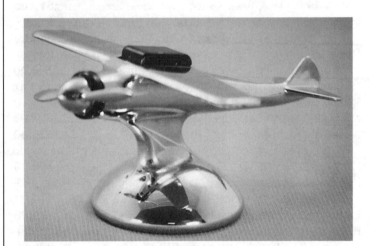

Figural, airplane, table model, chromium, made by Negbaur in Germany, 6½" long, from $60.00 to $80.00.

Figural, bellows, brass & leather, squeeze handles to light, mid-1960s, 2x7¼", from $20 to..............................**$30.00**

Figural, book, flip-out style chromium, ca late 1950s, 1½", from $5 to...**$15.00**

Figural, Book of Smoking, Corona...............................**$20.00**

Figural, bulldog, metal w/detachable head to reveal lighter, marked Austria, April 1912, 2¼x2¾", from $75 to ...**$100.00**

Figural, canteen, plastic w/metal chain on cap, remove cap to reveal lighter, Germany, 2¼", from $15 to.......**$25.00**

Figural, cowboy boot w/spur, Evans **$15.00**

Figural, donkey, brass, Japan, mid-1950s, 2x2½", from $15 to..**$20.00**

Figural, gas pump, painted metal w/round globe top, push pump handle down & top pops up w/light, 3½x2¼" dia **$35.00**

Figural, golf ball, Bogey, Ronson, 1930s......................**$25.00**

Figural, gun, automatic machine type on tripod, chromium & metal, butane, ca 1985, 5½x11⅞" L, from $35 to.**$50.00**

Figural, gun, Henry 42 caliber derringer, Swank.........**$20.00**

Figural, kangaroo w/lighter pouch, metal, Japan, late 1960s, 3¾x3½", from $15 to......................................**$20.00**

Figural, outboard motor, black, red & white enamel on chrome, Swank, early 1960s, 5", from $50 to.......**$90.00**

Figural, spark plug, plastic w/key chain, marked PLA, early 1990s, 3", from $5 to **$10.00**

Figural, table-top, bomb, brass, ca early 1930s, 4x1¼" dia, from $40 to..**$60.00**

Figural, table-top, cowboy w/chaps, silverplated w/hinged head, Occupied Japan, ca 1948, 4", from $75 to....**$100.00**

Figural, table-top, elephant, painted ceramic w/chromium howdah, Occupied Japan, ca 1948, 3½x4" L, from $60 to..**$90.00**

Gibson, Windproof, ostrich leather w/engravable shield, 1950s..**$10.00**

Golden Wheel, Spin-Type, watch in side, engine-turned & hand engraved, 24-hour movement, 1930s...........**$50.00**

Hyalyn, ceramic w/brown & orange on cream, table size.**$15.00**

Marvel Pocket Lighter, metal, w/Ray-O-Lite Fluid, MIB ..**$35.00**

Miniature, chromium w/mesh band & chain, Occupied Japan, ca 1949, 1½", from $25 to **$40.00**

Miniature, engraved vertical striped brass w/chain, Pereline, ca 1955, 1¼", from $5 to......................................**$10.00**

Miniature, leather band w/chromium top, lift-arm, Occupied Japan, ca 1948, 1", from $30 to **$45.00**

Miniature, mother-of-pearl card suit design w/chromium top, lift-arm, Occupied Japan, ca 1948, 1¼", from $25 to.......**$40.00**

Miniature, pinup portrait on plastic band w/chromium top, lift arm, Japan, ca 1955, ⅞", from $20 to..............**$35.00**

Nimrod, Sportsman Pipeliter, chromium, ca early 1970s, w/instruction booklet, MIB, from $10 to **$25.00**

PAC, gold plate w/mother-of-pearl inserts, musical, key-wind back, early 1950s, 2⅝", from $65 to.......................**$90.00**

Parker, Flaminaire, plain polished chromium, ca 1951, 2¾", MIB, from $25 to..**$40.00**

Partlow Kase Liter, polished chrome, MIB..................**$20.00**

Penguin, chromium w/engraved checkerboard design, lift-arm, late 1970s, 2⅝", from $10 to **$20.00**

Ronson, Adonis, black enamel w/engravable shield on chromium, ca 1947, 1⅞", from $15 to...................**$25.00**

Ronson, Banker, 14k gold, engine-tuned, 1950s.......**$150.00**

Ronson, Capri, ivory cherubs on blue enamel, ca 1954, 2⅛", MIB, from $15 to..**$25.00**

Ronson, Essex, leather w/metal shield for engraving on chromium, ca 1954, 2⅛", from $10 to...................**$20.00**

Ronson, Mini Cadet, chromium w/embossed leaf design, ca 1959, 1⅜", from $10 to...**$20.00**

Ronson, Princess, black w/multicolor jewel effects, ca 1930s..**$50.00**

Ronson, Princess, enameled florals on black, 1950s...**$45.00**

Ronson, Princess, leather band on chromium, 1950s, 1⅞x1½", from $25 to..**$40.00**

Ronson, table-top, Spartan, black & white enamel stripes on chromium, ca 1950, 2⅜x3", from $10 to..............**$20.00**

Ronson, table-top, Varaflame Optic, cut grooved aluminum band & black satin finish, late 1960s **$25.00**

Ronson, Typhoon, brushed chromium w/polished top, ca 1960, 2¼", from $15 to....................................**$25.00**

Ronson, Varaflame, chromium w/fine engraved stripes, ca 1960s, 2¾x1", MIB, from $20 to **$30.00**

Ronson, Whirlwind, chromium w/engraved vertical stripes & shield for engraving, ca 1941, 2⅛", from $25 to ..**$40.00**

Royale, 2500 Automatic Fuel Finder, embossed chromium, w/instructions, late 1950s, 1⅛x2⅝", MIB, from $20 to ..**$30.00**

Spesco, C-Thru, clear base w/floating fishing lure, chrome top...**$15.00**

Supreme, pinup on plastic band w/chromium top, ca 1950s, 2", from $15 to...**$30.00**

Vulcan, military emblem & Every Man a Tiger on chromium, ca 1956, 2¼", from $15 to....................................**$20.00**

Weston, Ball of Flint, pen form w/ball top, M...........**$40.00**

Weston, Mighty Midgett, 3" **$35.00**

Wisner, Trickette, allover prong-set rhinestones on brass, early 1950s, 1½", from $25 to **$40.00**

Zippo, Civil War, Cherokee rifleman, 1991.................**$25.00**

Zippo, Golden Elegance, polished finish w/engraved traditional designs, 1976, from $25 to **$30.00**

Zippo, Golden Tortoise, w/shield for engraving, 1977, from $25 to..**$30.00**

Zippo, Landing on the Moon, 1969, from $25 to........**$30.00**

Zippo, Pittsburgh Steelers, 1974-1975 World Champions, vinyl applique on polished metal, from $25 to....**$30.00**

Zippo, Presidential, Dwight D Eisenhower, 1990, from $25 to..**$30.00**

Zippo, Scrimshaw, whaling scene w/masted ship, 1980s, from $25 to..**$30.00**

Zippo, Town & Country, enameled pheasant on polished chrome, late 1940s, from $25 to **$30.00**

Zippo, 50th Anniversary, official Zippo seal & diagonal lines at corners on brass, 1982, from $25 to **$30.00**

Cleminson Pottery

One of the several small potteries that operated in California during the middle of the century, Cleminson was a family-operated enterprise that made kitchenware, decorative items, and novelties that are beginning to attract a considerable amount of interest. At the height of their productivity, they employed 150 workers, so as you make your rounds, you'll be very likely to see a piece or two offered for sale just about anywhere you go. Prices are not high; this may be a 'sleeper.'

They marked their ware fairly consistently with a circular ink stamp that contains the name 'Cleminson.' But even if you find an unmarked piece, with just a little experience you'll easily be able to recognize their very distinctive glaze colors. They're all strong, yet grayed-down, dusty tones. They made a line of bird-shaped tableware items that they marketed as 'Distlefink' and several plaques and wall pockets that are decorated with mottoes and Pennsylvania Dutch-type hearts and flowers.

In Jack Chipman's *The Collector's Encyclopedia of California Pottery*, you'll find a chapter devoted to Cleminson Pottery. Roerig's *The Collector's Encyclopedia of*

Cookie Jars has some more information.

See also Clothes Sprinkler Bottles.

Advisor: Robin Stine (See Directory, California Pottery)

Ashtray, fish, 2 rests at bottom edge, 2¾x7½" dia......**$28.00**
Blade bank, man shaving framed w/4-leaf clovers, from $25 to...**$30.00**
Bobbie Guard, figure of a man, hat lifts off, to hold bobbie pins, 4"...**$50.00**

Butter dish, lady figure, 2-piece, $65.00.

Dinner bell, Fancy Pants maid, light blue dress, fancy leggings, clapper, w/original tag **$85.00**
Match holder, Cherries, wall-hanging style..................**$25.00**

Marmalade, green-dotted flowerpot with strawberry finial, $28.00.

Mug, Morning After, w/ice-bag lid **$35.00**
Mug, soup; Indian boy w/dog, 4" dia.........................**$40.00**
Oyster dish, The World Is Our Oyster on easel shape, 6½" dia **$25.00**
Plaque, girl w/floral bouquet & butterflies, 4¾x3½" dia ..**$15.00**
Plaque, heart form w/girl's face, Stay As Sweet As You Are **$16.00**
Plaque, Rhett & Scarlett, pr...**$35.00**
Plaque, 2 flowers w/buds & leaves, square w/flanged sides, 6½" **$20.00**
Plate, molded scalloped rim, painted florals, 7" dia, from $20 to...**$25.00**
Plate, silhouetted woman at spinning wheel or churning butter, 6½", from $18 to **$22.00**
Recipe holder, hearts & flowers on footed rectangular base, scalloped sides & rim, 4" L **$28.00**

Salt & pepper shakers, Distlefink, lg, pr, from $20 to...**$25.00**
Salt & pepper shakers, Gala Gray, figural, pr **$55.00**
Salt & pepper shakers, kangaroos, w/original label, pr **$50.00**
String holder, Friends From Afar..., house shape, 6½"...**$65.00**
Tea bag holder, Let Me Hold the Bag, 4" **$10.00**
Wall pocket, barrel form **$25.00**
Wall pocket, frying pan..**$30.00**
Wall pocket, Kitchen Bright & Singing Kettle Make Home the Place You Want To Settle, teapot shape, 6x9", from $30 to...**$35.00**
Wall pocket, scoop w/painted flowers, 9" L..............**$35.00**
Wall pocket, The Kitchen Is the Heart of the Home, footed kettle w/bail handle, 4" **$28.00**

Plaque, kitchen; 7¼x8½", $20.00.

Clothes Sprinkler Bottles

With the invention of the iron, clothes were sprinkled with water, rolled up to distribute the dampness, and pressed. This created steam when ironing, which helped to remove wrinkles. The earliest bottles were made of hand-blown clear glass. Ceramic figurals were introduced in the 1920s; these had a metal sprinkler cap with a rubber cork. Later versions had a true cork with an aluminum cap. More recent examples contain a plastic cap. A 'wetter-downer' bottle had no cap, but contained a hole in the top to distribute water to larger items such as sheets and tablecloths. Water was filled through a large opening in the bottom and plugged with a cork. Some 'wetter-downers' are mistaken for shakers and vice versa. In the end, with the invention of more sophisticated irons that produced their own steam (and later their own sprayers), the sprinkler bottle was relegated to the attic or, worse yet, the trash can.

The variety of subjects depicted by figural sprinkler bottles runs from cute animals to laundry helpers and people who did the ironing. Because of their whimsical nature, their scarcity and desirability as collectibles, we have seen a rapid rise in the cost of these bottles over the last couple of years.

See also Kitchen Prayer Ladies.

Advisor: Ellen Bercovici (See Directory, Clothes Sprinkler Bottles)

Cat, marble eyes, ceramic, American Bisque, from $150 to **$195.00**

Cat, Siamese, tan, ceramic, from $100 to...................**$125.00**

Cat, variety of designs & colors, homemade ceramic, from $50 to..**$60.00**

Chinese man, holding iron, from $125 to.................**$150.00**

Chinese man, Sprinkle Plenty, white, green & brown, holding iron, ceramic, from $125 to...........................**$145.00**

Chinese Man, Sprinkle Plenty, yellow & green, ceramic, Cardinal China Co, from $20 to............................**$30.00**

Chinese man, towel over arm, from $125 to............**$150.00**

Chinese man, variety of designs & colors, handmade ceramic, from $30 to..**$60.00**

Chinese man, white & aqua, ceramic, Cleminson, from $30 to..**$40.00**

Chinese man, white & aqua w/paper shirt tag, ceramic, Cleminson's, from $65 to **$75.00**

Clothespin, aqua, yellow & pink w/smiling face, ceramic, from $100 to...**$125.00**

Clothespin, hand decorated, ceramic, from $50 to.....**$60.00**

Clothespin, red, yellow & green plastic, from $15 to.**$25.00**

Dearie Is Weary, ceramic, Enesco, minimum value..**$200.00**

Dutch boy, green & white ceramic, from $125 to **$145.00**

Dutch girl, white w/green & pink trim, wetter-downer, ceramic, from $125 to **$145.00**

Elephant, pink & gray, ceramic, from $45 to **$55.00**

Elephant, trunk forms handle, ceramic, American Bisque, from $225 to..**$250.00**

Elephant, white & pink w/shamrock on tummy, ceramic, from $65 to...**$75.00**

Emperor, variety of designs & colors, handmade ceramic, from $50 to..**$100.00**

Iron, blue flowers, ceramic, from $50 to **$60.00**

Iron, green ivy, ceramic, from $30 to **$40.00**

Iron, green plastic, from $15 to...................................**$25.00**

Iron, lady ironing, ceramic, from $60 to......................**$70.00**

Iron, man & woman farmer, ceramic, from $100 to .**$125.00**

Iron, souvenir of Aquarena Springs, San Marcos TX, ceramic, from $100 to..**$125.00**

Iron, souvenir of Florida, pink flamingo, ceramic, from $85 to **$95.00**

Iron, souvenir of Wonder Cave, ceramic, from $85 to...**$95.00**

Mammy, ceramic, possibly Pfaltzgraff, from $225 to ...**$250.00**

Mary Maid, all colors, plastic, Reliance, from $15 to ..**$35.00**

Mary Poppins, ceramic, Cleminson, from $150.00 to $175.00. (Photo courtesy Ellen Bercovici)

Myrtle, ceramic, Pfaltzgraff, from $195.00 to $225.00. (Photo courtesy Ellen Bercovici)

Peasant woman, w/laundry poem on label..............**$150.00**

Poodle, gray & pink or white, ceramic, from $125 to ..**$150.00**

Queen or King, ceramic, Tilso, Japan, from $100 to ..**$125.00**

Rooster, red or green, ceramic, from $100 to...........**$125.00**

Clothing and Accessories

Watch a 'Golden Oldie' movie, and you can't help admiring the clothes — what style, what glamour, what fun! Due in part to the popularity of classic movies and the retro spectaculars like 'Evita!,' there's a growing fascination with the fabulous styes of the past — and there's no better way to step into the romance and glamour of those eras than with an exciting vintage piece!

Clothes of the 1940s through the 1970s are not as delicate as their Victorian and Edwardian counterparts; they're easier to find and much more affordable! Remember, the more indicative of its period, the more desirable the item. Look for pieces with glitz and glamour — also for young, trendy pieces that were expensive to begin with. Look for designer pieces and designer look-alikes. Noted fifties designers include Dior, Balenciaga, Balmain, Chanel, Norell, Clare McCardell, Heim, Adele Simpson, Eisenberg, and Ann Fogarty. In the sixties, Mary Quant, Betsey Johnson, Pucci, Givenchy, Yves St. Laurent, Pierre Cardin, Rudi Gernreich, Paco Rabanne, Courreges, Geoffrey Beene, and Gunne Sax were some of the names that made fashion headlines.

Levi jeans and jackets made circa 1971 and before have a cult following, especially in Japan. Among the most sought-after denim Levi items are jeans with a capitol 'E' on a *red* tab or back pocket. The small 'e' jeans are collectible as well; these were made during the late 1960s and until 1970 (with two rows of single stitching inside the back pocket) and in the 'red line' style of the eighties (these have double-stitched back pockets). Other characteristics to look for in vintage Levis are visible rivets inside the jeans and single pockets and silver-colored buttons on jackets with vertical pleats. From the same era, Lee, Wrangler, Bluebell, J.C. Penney, Oxhide, Big Yanks, James Dean, Doublewear, and Big Smith denims are collectible as well.

Running and basketball shoes from the 1970s and 1980s such as Nike 'Air Jordans' and 'Terminators' are also becoming popular. Look for an orange logo on the tongue, 'NIKE' in block letters on the heel, or a date inside the shoe.

While some collectors buy with the intent of preserving their clothing and simply enjoy having it, many buy it to wear. If you do wear it, be very careful how you clean it. Fabrics may become fragile with age.

For more information, refer to *Vintage Hats and Bonnets, 1770 – 1970, Identifications and Values,* by Sue Langley; *Clothing and Accessories from the '40s, '50s and '60s,* by Jan Lindenberger; *Vintage Denim* by David Little; *Shoes* by Linda O'Keefe; *Plastic Handbags* by Kate E. Dooner; *Fit To Be Tied, Vintage Ties of the '40s and Early '50s,* by Rod Dyer and Ron Spark; and *The Hawaiian Shirt* by H. Thomas Steele.

Advisors: Sue Langley and Pat Compensa (See Directory, Clothing and Accessories)

Newsletter: *Costume Society of America*
55 Edgewater Dr., P.O. Box 75
Earleville, MD 21919
Phone 301-275-2329 or Fax 301-275-8936

1940s Women's Day Wear

Dress, 'snails' rayon print	**$65.00**
Dress, multicolor rayon 'hands' print	**$135.00**
Halter top, green checked cotton print	**$20.00**
Housedress, cotton print w/rickrack trim	**$24.00**
Playsuit, printed cotton, 1-pc short style	**$25.00**
Suit, burgundy wool	**$145.00**
Suit, Lilli Ann, navy, eyelet-trimmed jacket	**$250.00**
Suit, New Look, black wool, late 1940s	**$110.00**
Suit, pink wool gabardine	**$115.00**
Suit blouse, white rayon	**$15.00**
Tennis shorts, pleated wide leg, cotton twill	**$32.00**

1940s Women's Coats and Jackets

Coat, Pauline Trigere, wool tweed, fitted waist	**$300.00**
Coat, red wool, fitted	**$65.00**
Coat, swing style, beige wool	**$115.00**
Dress, 'Broadway' motif print	**$145.00**
Jacket, black wool, braid trim	**$75.00**
Jacket, tan wool, plain, excellent tailoring	**$35.00**
Suit blouse, purple rayon, open-work neckline	**$55.00**

1940s Women's Evening Wear

Cocktail dress, sequins, peplum, knee length	**$75.00**
Dinner dress, cotton floral w/bustle back, long	**$165.00**
Dinner gown, purple rayon crepe, beaded neckline	**$200.00**
Evening coat, black rayon velvet w/hood, long	**$125.00**
Gown, black rayon crepe, sequin trim, long	**$145.00**

1940s Women's Intimate Apparel/Lounge Wear

Bra, peach rayon satin	**$6.00**
Corset, 'Waspy' New Look	**$25.00**
Corset, long, back-laced, peach color	**$12.00**

Dinner gown, purple rayon crepe, beaded neckline	**$200.00**
Dress & jacket, Hawaiian print, Made in Hawaii	**$125.00**
Lounging pajamas, wide leg, rayon, Hawaiian print	**$95.00**
Nightie, satin (rayon) floral print	**$45.00**
Nightie, sheer black silk, strategic decorations	**$75.00**
Panties, satin 'See No Evil'	**$55.00**
Panties, wide leg 'step-in' style, peach rayon	**$10.00**
Robe, cotton seersucker butterfly print, long	**$55.00**
Slip, peach rayon satin	**$8.00**

1940s Women's Accessories

Hat, yellow 'Casablanca' fedora, $85.00. (Collection of Sue Langley/copyright John Dowling 1997)

Gloves, black velvet evening mitts, jewelled, long	**$125.00**
Gloves, gauntlet, brown cotton	**$15.00**
Hat, black straw 'topper,' lg red 'wing' & back-tied veil	**$55.00**
Hat, green felt petals, 'doll' style	**$60.00**
Hat, red felt w/wide brim	**$115.00**
Hat, sm, each, from $20 to	**$95.00**
Hat, sm straw 'toy' style, flowers & veil	**$35.00**
Hat, wide brim, each, from $55 to	**$150.00**
Hat w/wimple (scarf across chin)	**$115.00**
Purse, alligator bag, Cuba	**$75.00**
Purse, clutch, red plastic squares	**$30.00**
Purse, pearl evening clutch	**$30.00**
Purse, rayon ribbed cord, plastic zipper ornament	**$35.00**
Purse, silver clutch, Whiting & Davis, rhinestone clasp	**$50.00**
Scarf, silk, 'hats' print	**$15.00**
Shoes, alligator slingbacks, 'Minnie ear' clips, pr	**$75.00**
Shoes, gold satin evening slippers, pr	**$35.00**
Shoes, pr, from $30 to	**$110.00**

1950s Women's Day Wear

Bathing suit, cotton plaid	**$25.00**
Blouse, cotton, sleeveless	**$10.00**
Coat, Lilli Ann, pink wool, full-skirted style	**$275.00**
Dress, lounging style, scenic 'Paris' cotton print	**$35.00**
Dress, shirtwaist style, pink cotton gingham	**$45.00**
Skirt, circle style, 'masques' print	**$35.00**
Skirt, circle style, flocked floral trim, sequins	**$45.00**
Skirt, tight sheath, pink wool flannel	**$25.00**
Sweater, beaded cardigan, from $35 to	**$85.00**

Sweater, beige cashmere, fur collar.............................$85.00
Sweater shell & cardigan set, purple orlon $35.00

Bathing suit, gold lame, $55.00. (Collection of Sue Langley/copyright John Dowling 1997)

1950s Women's Evening Wear

Ballgown, strapless, velvet & net w/sequin trim, long...$300.00
Coat, swing style, navy silk faille, mid-calf length......$55.00
Dress, 'Suzy Wong' Chinese style, short, tight, from $45 to $95.00
Dress, cocktail style, bateau neck, red velvet, full skirt...$125.00
Dress, cocktail; black lace, strapless, full skirt $45.00
Dress, pink silk halter style, circle skirt $65.00
Dress, short white chiffon, hand-painted orchids $55.00

Dress, velvet top with rhinestones and pearls, taffeta circle skirt, $75.00. (Collection of Sue Langley/copyright John Dowling 1997/model: Marcia Cohen)

Gown, chartreuse chiffon w/spaghetti straps, long ..$150.00

1950s Women's Intimate Apparel/Lounge Wear

Bra, Locket, strapless & boned, pointed 'Wonder Woman' look...$15.00
Net crinoline, Florele label..$20.00
Pajamas, 'Baby Doll' style, pink cotton print.................$8.00

1950s Women's Accessories

Collar, detachable, gold/jeweled, from India..............$15.00
Collar, detachable, white cotton pique $6.00
Gloves, short white cotton, from $5 to.......................$10.00
Hat, black felt, red poinsettia trim, sm......................$32.00
Hat, fine straw, wide brim..$110.00
Hat, jewels, pearls & rhinestones, sm $75.00
Hat, mink, sm...$22.00
Hat, profile style, red plaid cellophane straw $28.00
Hat, straw, cherry trim, sm..$45.00
Hat, velvet, pink w/ostrich feather trim, sm................$55.00
Hat, velvet wide brim, edged w/maribou $125.00
Necklace, plastic pop-it beads $5.00
Purse, gray marbleized hard plastic $85.00
Purse, hard plastic or Lucite, from $25 to $125.00
Purse, velvet bag, jewels & sequin poodle..................$85.00
Purse, velvet evening clutch, gold 'India' embroidery ...$35.00
Purse, whimsical w/poodles, etc, from $45 to $85.00
Purse, wooden box style w/decoupage design, from $35 to...$55.00
Scarf/kerchief, silk, Moulin Rouge scene.....................$75.00
Shoes, 'flats' ballet style, black suede $22.00
Shoes, Lucite 'Cinderella' heels, from $25 to...............$55.00
Shoes, saddle style...$20.00
Shoes, stiletto heels $25.00

1960s – 70s Women's Day Wear

Coat, acid green polka-dot polyester, 1960s...............$35.00
Coat dress, Adele Simpson, faux leopard..................$125.00
Coat dress, Galanos Couture, black wool knit..........$325.00
Coat dress, Twiggy label, yellow polka-dot $55.00
Dress, Gunne Sax (Jessica McClintock) calico print, 1970s ..$45.00
Dress, halter style, paisley tricot print, 1970s, long.....$25.00

Mini dress, metallic blue quilted paper, $45.00. (Collection of Sue Langley/copyright John Dowling 1997/model: Dana Kleiber)

Dress, Oleg Cassini, orange polyester mini................$75.00

1960s – 70s Women's Evening Wear

Coat, black sequin, long $150.00
Cocktail ensemble, short dress & coat, beaded $125.00

Dress, Ann Fogarty, brown velvet, long **$85.00**
Dress, white cocktail mini, allover beadwork **$55.00**
Dress, white crepe mini, rhinestone zippers on neck & sleeves **$65.00**
Dress, white polyester wide-leg culotte style, long **$65.00**
Dress & coat, white poppies brocade, long **$150.00**
Gown, red satin sheath style, plain, good tailoring, long **$45.00**
Pantsuit, 'Disco' satin bell-bottom style, 1970s **$45.00**
Top, sequined & beaded knit, sleeveless **$45.00**

1960s – 70s Women's Accessories

Hat, feathered bubble toque, Jack McConnell **$125.00**
Hat, net 'whimsey,' Sally Victor, w/Sally Victor hatbox ..**$24.00**
Hat, pink metallic brocade toque **$12.00**
Hat, red velvet pillbox, gold 'India' embroidery **$45.00**
Purse, 'magazine' style **$45.00**
Purse, clear plastic over embroidered & jeweled print...**$22.00**
Purse, lg 'silver' faux leather bag, plastic handles.......**$12.00**
Shoes, 'Disco' platforms, gunmetal multicolor, 1970s .**$65.00**
Shoes, snakeskin go-go boots, late 1960s.....................**$85.00**
Shoes, square-toed silk evening style, gold & beaded lion heads..**$55.00**

1940s – 70s Men's Wear

Blue jean jacket, Lee Riders 101J................................**$90.00**
Blue jeans, Levi Big E...**$80.00**
Blue jeans, Levi Big E, S-type, dark **$100.00**
Blue jeans, Levi 501...**$22.00**
Blue jeans, Wrangler Bluebell, dark **$175.00**
Hawaiian shirt, rayon or cotton print, ca 1940s-50s, from $55 to...**$150.00**
Hawaiian shirt, red print, 100% cotton, Made in Hawaii...**$150.00**

Hawaiian shirt, silk, 'Hookano' label, print by Frank MacIntosh, $600.00 – 800.00. (Collection of John Dowling/copyright John Dowling 1997/model: John Dowling)

Jacket, gabardine, zip front, 1950s, from $45 to **$400.00**
Jacket, souvenir, reversible **$500.00**
Jacket, souvenir, 1940s-60s, from $75 to....................**$500.00**
Leisure suit, polyester, bell-bottoms, 1960s **$55.00**
Shirt, 'Disco' style, photo scenes, prints, 1970s, from $20 to...**$55.00**
Shirt, bowling; from $25 to **$95.00**

Shoes, platform style, 1970s, from $35 to....................**$75.00**
Ties, from $6 to **$75.00**

Coca-Cola Collectibles

Coca-Cola was introduced to the public in 1886. Immediately an advertising campaign began that over the years and to the present day has literally saturated our lives with a never-ending variety of items. Some of the earlier calendars and trays have been known to bring prices well into the four figures. Because of these heady prices and the extremely wide-spread collector demand for good Coke items, reproductions are everywhere, so beware! Some of the items that have been reproduced are pocket mirrors (from 1905, 1906, 1908 – 11, 1916, and 1920), trays (from 1899, 1910, 1913 – 14, 1917, 1920, 1923, 1926, 1934, and 1937), tip trays (from 1907, 1909, 1910, 1913 – 14, 1917, and 1920), knives, cartons, bottles, clocks, and trade cards. Currently being produced and marketed are an 8" brass 'button,' a 27" brass bottle-shaped thermometer, cast-iron toys and bottle-shaped door pulls, Yes Girl posters, a 12" 'button' sign (with one round hole), a rectangular paperweight, a 1949-style cooler radio, and there are others. Look for a date line.

In addition to reproductions, 'fantasy' items have also been made, the difference being that a 'fantasy' never existed as an original. Don't be deceived. Belt buckles are fantasies. So are glass doorknobs with an etched trademark, bottle-shaped knives, pocketknives (supposedly from the 1933 World's Fair), a metal letter opener stamped 'Coca-Cola 5¢,' a cardboard sign with the 1911 lady with fur (9" x 11"), and celluloid vanity pieces (a mirror, brush, etc.).

When the company celebrated its 100th anniversary in 1986, many 'centennial' items were issued. They all carry the '100th Anniversary' logo. Many of them are collectible in their own right, and some are already high priced.

If you'd really like to study this subject, we recommend these books: *Goldstein's Coca-Cola Collectibles* by Sheldon Goldstein; *B.J. Summers' Guide to Coca-Cola* by B.J. Summers; *Huxford's Collectible Advertising* by Sharon and Bob Huxford; *Collector's Guide to Coca-Cola Items, Vols I and II*, by Al Wilson; *Collectible Coca-Cola Toy Trucks* by Gael and Lara de Courtivron; and *Petretti's Coca-Cola Collectibles Price Guide* by Allan Petretti.

Advisor: Craig and Donna Stifter (See Directory, Soda Pop Collectibles)

Club: Coca-Cola Collectors Club International
P.O. Box 49166
Atlanta, GA 30359. Annual dues: $25

Information Hotline: 941-355-COLA or 941-359-COLA

Book, 100 Best Posters, hardcover, 1941, EX+...........**$40.00**
Bookmark, celluloid owl figural, 1906, EX...............**$675.00**
Bottle carrier, aluminum, lift handle, holds 12 bottles, 1950s, NM **$110.00**
Bottle case, yellow & red painted wood, holds 24 bottles, 1930s, EX...**$45.00**

Bottle opener, metal, Shirts for the Coke Set on solid handle, EX+ **$25.00**

Bottle topper, We Let You See the Bottle, plastic, 1950s, EX **$375.00**

Bowl, green pottery, 1930s, EX **$500.00**

Bowl, pretzel; aluminum, 3 bottles as legs, 1936, EX ..**$250.00**

Buckle, chrome plate w/applied gold truck, Year 5 Record No Accident **$130.00**

Calendar, 1919, complete, EX **$2,000.00**

Calendar, 1924, complete, EX **$1,000.00**

Calendar, 1925, complete, NM, from $750 to **$1,000.00**

Calendar, 1933, complete, EX **$625.00**

Calendar, 1936, complete, EX **$700.00**

Calendar holder, Coke Refreshes You Best, embossed fishtail logo, tin, 1960s, EX **$250.00**

Carrier, aluminum w/red side panels, for 12 pack, 1950s **$85.00**

Carrier, cardboard w/metal handle, +6 bottles, 1950s, miniature, EX **$65.00**

Cigarette lighter, musical, 1950s, MIB **$150.00**

Clock, plastic & metal, Things Go Better, disk logo, 16" square, VG **$75.00**

Clock, wood & metal, 15" dia center w/wood side panels, 1948, 36", NM, from $250 to **$400.00**

Cooler, picnic, red vinyl box type, fishtail logo, NM ..**$40.00**

Cooler, red metal picnic box, metal handle and hardware, 1950s, 6-pack size, with original box, $325.00. (Photo courtesy Craig and Donna Stifter)

Decal, Things Go Better... (receding words), 1960s, NM ..**$25.00**

Display, bottle w/cap, glass, dated December 25, 1923, EX **$275.00**

Display, window; soda fountain scene w/soda jerk, 1950s, 24x36", EX **$400.00**

Festoon, bathing beauties theme, 3-D, cardboard, 1946, 5-pc, NM (NM envelope) **$1,700.00**

Festoon, birthday theme, 3-D cardboard, 5-pc w/plastic jewels, 1960s **$475.00**

Festoon, sports car theme, cardboard, 1950s, 5-pc ...**$900.00**

Festoon, state trees theme, cardboard, 1950s, 5-pc, NM (NM envelope) **$425.00**

Fountain dispenser, outboard boat engine form, 1940s, EX **$375.00**

Game, Bingo, Milton Bradley, 1940s, EX **$65.00**

Game, Shanghai, MIB **$20.00**

Game set, includes Checkers, Acey-Ducey & Backgammon, Milton Bradley, 1940s, EX **$125.00**

Ice pick, Coca-Cola in Bottles Delicious & Refreshing, 1930s, NM, from $10 to **$20.00**

Ice pick/bottle opener, metal w/wood handle, Compliments..., 1940s-50s **$40.00**

Menu board, To-Day w/diamond-shaped logo, tin, 1930s ..**$275.00**

Music box, plastic, 1940s, 2¾x2⅝x2¼", $275.00. (Photo courtesy Phil Helley)

Paper cup, Things Go Better... in red on white square, 1960s, 3½" **$3.00**

Picnic cooler, Acton, 1950s, 6-pack size, MIB **$325.00**

Pin, 10 Year Service, 1950s, EX **$65.00**

Pin, 20 Year Service, 1950s, EX **$100.00**

Plate, Knowles, Taylor, Knowles China Company, 1931, 7¼", NM, $375.00. (Photo courtesy Gary Metz)

Playing cards, Gibson girls, 52 cards w/jokers, 1909, MIB **$2,500.00**

Playing cards, girl drinking from straw in bottle, 52 cards w/jokers, 1928, EX (EX box) **$475.00**

Playing cards, girl in pink w/parasol, 52 cards w/jokers, 1950, NMIB, from $750 to **$1,250.00**

Playing cards, girl lacing ice skates, 52 cards w/jokers, 1956, EX (EX box) **$85.00**

Playing cards, It's the Real Thing, party scene, 1972, NMIB ..**$25.00**

Postcard, bottling plant photo, black & white, NM **$30.00**

Sewing kit, girl w/fox stole on cardboard, complete w/contents, 1925, EX **$75.00**

Sign, Accepted Home Refreshment, cardboard, 1942, 29x56", EX **$375.00**

Sign, cardboard, bathing beauty sitting on beach, 1940, 29x50", EX **$675.00**

Sign, cardboard, Best of Taste, girl w/umbrella, 1956, 30x52", EX **$400.00**

Sign, cardboard, diving board girl, 1939, 29x50", EX....**$575.00**

Sign, cardboard, girl w/Scottie dog, Sundblom artwork, 1938, 30x52", EX...**$900.00**

Sign, cardboard, Play Refreshed, tennis girl at cooler, 1949, 16x27", EX **$375.00**

Sign, cardboard, Santa diecut, Good Taste for All, leaning on grandfather clock, 19", EX **$225.00**

Sign, cardboard, Santa diecut, Greetings, reading from list, 1945, 14", EX...**$200.00**

Sign, cardboard, Santa diecut, paint brush behind ear & holding toy rabbit, 1947, 48", EX..**$275.00**

Sign, cardboard, Santa diecut, Sign of Good Taste, 60", EX..**$250.00**

Sign, cardboard, Things Go Better With Coke, girl w/skates, 1964, 16x27", EX..**$85.00**

Sign, cardboard, You Taste Its..., lady w/bottle, 1942, 20x36", EX **$485.00**

Sign, cardboard diecut, hand-held bottle, 1950s, 9", M...**$85.00**

Sign/clock, 'Lunch With Us,' counter-top, glass and metal, lights up, 1950s, $475.00. (Photo courtesy Craig and Donna Stifter)

Sign, girl running w/bottles in hands, cardboard, 1937, 14x30", EX **$425.00**

Sign, lantern shape w/4 plastic panels showing logos, lights up, 1960s, EX **$150.00**

Sign, paper, Plastic Cooker for Picnics..., 1950s, 27x16", NM...**$40.00**

Sign, porcelain, Drink Coca-Cola, 1950s, 36", EX **$350.00**

Sign, porcelain, fountain service, green & red, 1950s, 10x28", EX **$250.00**

Sign, porcelain, shows fountain dispenser, 1950s, 28x28", EX **$675.00**

Sign, porcelain w/bottle, 1950s, 24", EX....................**$375.00**

Sign, tin, Coca-Cola Sign of Good Taste, shows fishtail & bottle, 1960s, 11x28", EX **$150.00**

Sign, tin, diecut bottle, 1933, 36", EX.......................**$675.00**

Sign, tin, flange, Sign of Good Taste, image of fishtail, 1960s, EX..**$225.00**

Sign, tin, Take Home a Carton, shows 6-pack, 1930s, 19x54", EX **$425.00**

Sign, tin, Things Go Better With Coke, shows button & bottle, 1960s, 18x54", EX **$225.00**

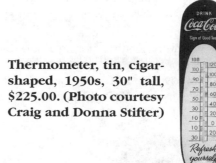

Thermometer, tin, cigar-shaped, 1950s, 30" tall, $225.00. (Photo courtesy Craig and Donna Stifter)

Thermometer, tin, shows 2 bottles, 1941, EX...........**$325.00**

Toy delivery truck, yellow with red lettering, Marx, 1950s, 12½" long, NM, $325.00. (Photo courtesy Dunbar Gallery)

Tray, girl w/bottle, screened background, 1950, 13x10½", NM **$125.00**

Tray, serving; tin, 1926, EX.......................................**$500.00**

Tray, serving; tin, 1931, EX.......................................**$700.00**

Tray, serving; tin, 1936, EX.......................................**$350.00**

Tray, serving; tin, 1938, EX.......................................**$200.00**

Tray, serving; tin, 1940, EX.......................................**$250.00**

Tray, serving; tin, 1961, EX...**$35.00**

Vendor's stadium carrier, curved to fit waist, w/leather strap, 1930s, EX..**$350.00**

Watch fob, Gibson girl on celluloid, 1909, EX.........**$850.00**

Coloring and Activity Books

Coloring and activity books representing familiar movie and TV stars of the 1950s and 1960s are fun to collect, though naturally unused examples are hard to find. Condition is very important, of course, so learn to judge their values accordingly. Unused books are worth as much as 50% to 75% more than one only partially colored.

Adventures of Electro-Man Coloring Book, Lowe, 1967, 48 pages, 8x11", EX+ **$10.00**

Adventures of Rin Tin Tin Coloring Book, Whitman, 1955, EX, from $10 to..**$15.00**

Agent Zero M Coloring Book, Whitman, #1155, unused, M.**$40.00**

Aladdin & His Magic Lamp Coloring Book, Saalfield, 1970, unused, EX **$20.00**

Alley Oop Coloring Book, Treasure, 1962, unused, NM...**$30.00**

Animal Stamps Book, Golden, #6102, 1980, unused, EX..**$18.00**

Army Coloring Book, Lowe, 1965, 20 pages, 8x11", unused, NM..**$12.00**

Barney Google & Snuffy Smith Coloring Book, Lowe, 1963, 80 pages, 8x11", EX.....................................**$20.00**

Batman & Robin Dot-To-Dot & Color Book, Bertdan International Publishing, 1967, 17 pages, 8x10½", unused, NM..**$20.00**

Batman Coloring Book, Whitman, 1967, NM, $30.00.

Batman, Meets Blockbuster Coloring Book, Whitman, 1966, 8x11", EX..**$12.00**

Batman, Robin & Penguin Giant Comics To Color, Whitman, 1976, unused, NM..**$10.00**

Beetle Bailey Coloring Book, Lowe, 1961, 100+ pages, 11x8", EX+ **$24.00**

Ben Hur Coloring Book, Lowe, 1959, 8x11", few pages colored, EX..**$15.00**

Ben-Hur Punch-Out Book, Golden, 1959, unused, NM.**$45.00**

Billy the Kid & Oscar Funny Animal Paint Book, Fawcett, 1940s, 7x11", unused, EX, from $10 to **$15.00**

Bob Hope Coloring Book, Saalfield, 1954, unused, NM ...**$55.00**

Bobby Benson's B-Bar-Riders Coloring Book, Whitman, 1950, unused, EX...**$15.00**

Boots & Saddles TV Show Coloring Book, 1958, M, from $35 to **$45.00**

Brady Bunch Coloring Book, Whitman, 1973, few pages colored, EX...**$50.00**

Bronco Coloring Book, Saalfield, 1961, EX **$25.00**

Buckaneer Coloring Book, Saalfield, 1959, 8x11", few pages colored, EX...**$15.00**

Buffalo Bill Jr & Calamity Jane Coloring Book, Whitman, 1957, VG **$18.00**

Bugs Bunny Private Eye Coloring Book, Whitman, 1957, 8x11", unused, NM..**$15.00**

Bullwinkle Coloring Book, 1969, M **$25.00**

Bullwinkle's How To Have Fun Outdoors Without Getting Clobbered Coloring Book, General Mills, 1963, unused, EX...**$50.00**

Candid Camera Coloring Book, Lowe, 1963, unused, NM..**$25.00**

Captain America Coloring Book, Whitman, 1966, 8x11", EX **$25.00**

Captain Kangaroo Fun-Damental Activity Set, Lowe, 1977, 11x8", set of 3, M (sealed) **$18.00**

Centurions Giant Coloring Book, 1985, NM **$10.00**

Chitty-Chitty Bang-Bang Coloring Book, Watkins-Strathmore, EX...**$12.00**

Christmas Coloring Book, Lowe, 1959, 20 pages, 8x11", unused, M...**$15.00**

Circus Boy Coloring Book, Whitman, 1957, few pages colored, VG..**$45.00**

Cisco Kid Coloring Book, Saalfield, 1954, few pages colored, VG...**$25.00**

Elsworth Elephant Coloring Book, Saalfield, 1962, 8x11", mostly colored, VG..**$12.00**

Family Affair Coloring Book, Whitman, 1968, unused, NM..**$52.00**

Fat Albert Coloring Book, 1978, EX **$25.00**

Felix Sticker Book, 1957, M.......................................**$58.00**

Flash Gordon Coloring Book, Saalfield, 1958, M **$55.00**

Flash Gordon & His Adventures in Space, #9545, M, $45.00.

Flintstones Great Big Punchout Book, Whitman, 1961, unused, NM...**$35.00**

Flipper Coloring Book, Whitman, 1965, few pages colored, EX...**$20.00**

Funday School Coloring Book, Lowe, 1950s, 8x11", unused, M **$8.00**

Fuzzy Bear Funny Animal Paint Book, Fawcett, 1940s, 16 pages, 7x11", unused, EX......................................**$10.00**

Get Smart Coloring Book, Saalfield, 1965, unused, M ...**$40.00**

Gumby & Pokey Coloring Book, Western Publishing, 1966, 8½x11", unused, NM...**$30.00**

Heroes of the West Coloring Book, Lowe, 1959, unused, NM..**$8.00**

Hokey Wolf & Ding-A-Ling Coloring Book, Golden, 1961, few pages colored, EX **$40.00**

Hopalong Cassidy Coloring Book, Whitman, 1951, few pages colored, from $55.00 to $75.00.

Humpty Dumpty Coloring Book, Lowe, 1950s, 10x11", unused, NM **$10.00**

I Love Lucy Coloring Book, Whitman, 1954, unused, EX..**$150.00**

Jungle Boy Coloring Book, Artcraft, 1967, unused, EX+.......**$12.00**

Lassie Magic Paint Book, Whitman, 1957, 60+ pages, 8x11",
EX **$25.00**

Laugh-In Coloring Book, Artcraft, 1968, few pages colored,
NM **$25.00**

Laugh-In Punch-Out & Paste Book, 1968, M...............**$30.00**

Magic Land of Alla-Kazam With Mark Wilson Coloring Book,
Whitman, 1962, EX **$12.00**

Make Way for Bullwinkle Coloring Book, Whitman, 1972, lg
diecut, unused, EX.....................................**$15.00**

Man From UNCLE Coloring Book, Watkins-Strathmore, 1965,
M, from $30 to **$40.00**

Masters of the Universe Coloring Book, 1985, NM.....**$10.00**

Mighty Mouse Activity Book, cardboard cover, stickers & activity
pages, Lowe, 1954, 10x12", unused, NM, from $60 to..**$70.00**

Monroes Coloring Book, shows story by brief captions,
Saalfield, 1966, 8x11", unused, NM **$30.00**

My Paint Book, Saalfield, 1950s, 16 pages, 14x11", unused,
M **$12.00**

Nanny & the Professor Coloring Book, Artcraft, 1971, several
pages colored, EX+....................................**$25.00**

Oliver Punch-Out & Paste Book, 1968, M **$18.00**

Ozzie & Harriet, David & Ricky Coloring Book, Saalfield,
1954, M...**$45.00**

Partridge Family Color & Activity Book, Artcraft, 1973, NM,
from $25 to...**$35.00**

Pebbles Flintstone Coloring Book, Whitman, 1963, 8x11",
unused, VG **$25.00**

Pip the Piper Coloring Book, Whitman, 1962, few pages colored, EX..**$12.00**

Play Safe Coloring Book, Lowe, 1968-72, 20 pages, 8x11",
unused, M..**$6.00**

**Popeye Color and Read,
Whitman, 1972, 16x7½",
unused, $10.00.**

Popeye Coloring & Paint Book, Whitman, 1961, 48 pages,
8x11", EX **$50.00**

Popeye Great Big Paint & Crayon Book, McLoughlin Bros,
early 1930s, 200 pages, 9½x12", EX....................**$40.00**

Porky Pig Coloring Book, Saalfield, 1938, 11x15", EX+ ..**$70.00**

Quiet, Artist at Work!, Lowe, 1950s, 11x12", unused, M .**$8.00**

Racing Cars Coloring Book, cutout of model racer on back,
Lowe, 8x11", unused, NM **$10.00**

Ramar of the Jungle Coloring Book, Saalfield, 1955, few
pages colored, EX.....................................**$20.00**

Robin Hood Coloring Book, Saalfield, early 1950s, 16 pages,
11x14", unused, EX+..................................**$12.00**

Rudolph the Red-Nosed Reindeer Coloring Book, Lowe,
1963, 120+ pages, 11x8", unused, EX **$15.00**

Sabrina Coloring Book, Whitman, 1971, 8½x11", EX .**$20.00**

School Days Coloring Book, Lowe, 1965, 8x11", unused, M.**$10.00**

Simpsons Rainy Day Fun Book, unused, NM.............**$15.00**

Six Million-Dollar Man Activity Book, Rand McNally, 1976,
unused, M...**$25.00**

Sky Rocket Coloring Book, Lowe, 1959, 50+ pages, 8x11",
unused, NM **$15.00**

Spin & Marty Coloring, Book, Whitman, 1956, several pages
colored, EX+...**$30.00**

Steve Canyon Coloring Book, Saalfield, 1952, 11x15", EX+,
from $30 to...**$40.00**

Sugarfoot Coloring Book, Saalfield, 1959, few pages colored,
G **$15.00**

**Super Friends Coloring
Book, Nat'l Periodicals
Publications, Whitman,
1975, NM, $12.00.**

Tales of the Vikings Coloring Book, Saalfield, 1960, unused,
EX...**$22.00**

Tarzan Punch-Out Book, 1967, M **$35.00**

Tennesse Tuxedo Coloring Book, 1975, M.................**$20.00**

Tommy Tortoise & Moe Hare Coloring Book, Saalfield, 1966,
8x11", EX **$12.00**

Tonto Coloring Book, Whitman, 1957, few pages colored,
VG+...**$12.00**

Top Cat Coloring Book, 1971, M...............................**$20.00**

Treasure Island Adventure Coloring Book, Lowe, 1950s,
11x8", unused, M **$8.00**

Tweety Coloring Book, Whitman, 1955, 30+ pages, 6x7",
EX...**$20.00**

Underdog Coloring Book, 1972, M, from $20 to........**$25.00**

Wagon Train Coloring Book, Whitman, 1959, few pages colored, EX..**$20.00**

101 Dalmatians Coloring Book, Whitman, 1960, few pages
colored, EX...**$15.00**

Comic Books

Though just about everyone can remember having stacks
and stacks of comic books as a child, few of us ever saved
them for more than a few months. At 10¢ a copy, new ones

quickly replaced the old, well-read ones. We'd trade them with our friends, but very soon, out they went. If we didn't throw them away, Mother did. So even though they were printed in huge amounts, few survive, and today they're very desirable collectibles.

Factors that make a comic book valuable are condition (as with all paper collectibles, extremely important), content, and rarity, but not necessarily age. In fact, comics printed between 1950 and the late 1970s are most in demand by collectors who prefer those they had as children to the earlier comics. They look for issues where the hero is first introduced, and they insist on quality. Condition is first and foremost when it comes to assessing worth. Compared to a book in excellent condition, a mint issue might be worth six to eight times as much, while one in only good condition should be priced at less than half the price of the excellent example. We've listed some of the more collectible (and expensive) comics, but many are worth very little. You'll really need to check your bookstore for a good reference book before you actively get involved in the comic book market.

Advisor: Larry Curcio, Avalon Comics (See Directory, Comic Books)

Abbott & Costello, #15, EX+	**$9.00**
Adventures in Paradise, Dell Four-Color #1301, 1962, EX	**$15.00**
Adventures of Rex the Wonder Dog, #11, VG	**$30.00**
Adventures of the Jaguar, #1, VG	**$35.00**
Adventures of the Jaguar, #7, 1962, NM	**$30.00**
Alley Oop, #12, 1948, EX	**$34.00**
Alley Oop, 1948, #12, VG+	**$28.00**
Amazing Spider-Man, Marvel Comics #1, 1963, EX	**$5,400.00**
Andy Panda, #280, Dell Four-color, EX+	**$20.00**
Annie Oakley & Tagg, #575, EX	**$25.00**
Aquaman, #26, VG+	**$8.00**
Archie, #82, VG	**$5.00**
Archie's Mad House, Comic Book Annual #9, VG	**$10.00**
Aristokittens, #2, EX+	**$5.00**
Avengers, Gold Key #1, 1968, EX	**$45.00**
Banana Splits, Gold Key, April 1971, G	**$12.00**
Banana Splits #8, 1971, NM	**$25.00**
Bat Masterson, #2, VG+	**$15.00**
Batman, #115, 1958, 10¢ cover price, G	**$35.00**
Battle of the Planets, #2, EX	**$2.00**
Ben Bowie & Mountain Men, #11, VG	**$6.00**
Ben Casey, #9, EX+	**$12.00**
Beneath the Planet of the Apes, Gold Key Movie Comics, 1962, NM	**$28.00**
Bobby Sherman, #5, 1972, NM	**$15.00**
Bonanza, Dell #1221, NM+	**$60.00**
Bonanza, Gold Key #10, 1964, EX	**$12.00**
Bonanza, Gold Key #27, G	**$5.00**
Bugs Bunny, #200, 1948, EX+	**$45.00**
Bugs Bunny Halloween Parade, Dell Giant #1, 1953, EX+	**$115.00**
Bullwinkle, Gold Key #1, 1962, EX	**$35.00**
Captain Johner & the Aliens, #1, NM	**$15.00**
Captain Marvel Adventures, Fawcett #24, EX+	**$160.00**
Captain Midnight, Fawcett #37, NM	**$150.00**
Captain Venture, Gold Key #1, 1968, EX	**$15.00**

Casper the Friendly Ghost, #18, VG	**$18.00**
Casper the Friendly Ghost, #23, 1960, EX	**$10.00**
Charlie Chan, Dell #1, 1965, EX+	**$24.00**
Cheyenne, Dell #6, EX+	**$30.00**
Christmas w/Mother Goose, Dell #201, EX	**$35.00**
Cisco Kid, #21, 1954, 10¢ cover price, VG	**$10.00**
Cisco Kid, #23, NM	**$15.00**
Colt .45, Dell #5, 1960, EX+	**$20.00**
Courtship of Eddie's Father, #2, NM	**$18.00**
Daisy Duck's Diary, #659, EX+	**$15.00**
Dark Shadows, Gold Key #1, 1961, 1st issue, no poster otherwise EX	**$30.00**
Dark Shadows, Gold Key #15, 1972, EX	**$10.00**
David Cassidy, Charlton #1, 1972, photo cover, NM	**$18.00**
Death Valley, #7, 1955, 10¢ cover price, EX	**$15.00**
Dick Tracy, Dell Monthly #5, EX+	**$80.00**
Dick Tracy, Harvey Monthly #111, NM	**$40.00**
Dick Tracy, Little Orphan Annie & Other Super Comics, #87, 1945, NM	**$45.00**
Doc Savage, #12, 1943, EX+	**$92.00**
Don Winslow, #61, 1948, EX	**$25.00**
Donald Duck Beach Party, Dell Giant #1, EX	**$30.00**
Dr Who & the Daleks, Dell #1, 1966, photo cover, VG	**$15.00**
Dracula, #2, EX	**$12.00**
Drag n' Wheels, #58, 1978, NM	**$10.00**
F-Troop, #7, 1967, EX	**$20.00**
Felix the Cat, Dell #6, 1964, EX	**$20.00**

Flash, DC Comics #17, September 1967, EX, from $12.00 to $15.00.

Flintstones, #10, 1963	**$20.00**
Flintstones, Gold Key #33, 1966, VG+	**$8.00**
Flintstones, March of Comics #243, 1963, NM	**$50.00**
Flying Nun, #3, VG+	**$8.00**
Funky Phantom, #3, NM	**$4.00**
Gang Busters, DC Comics #58, VG	**$14.00**
Gene Autry, Dell #24 through #44, EX+, each, from $30 to	**$35.00**
Gene Autry, Dell #59 through #74, EX+, each, from $18 to	**$22.00**
Gentle Ben, Dell #1, 1968, VG	**$10.00**
Gentle Ben, Dell #4, 1968, photo cover, EX	**$5.00**
George of the Jungle, Dell #2, 1969, EX+	**$30.00**
Get Smart, Dell #1, 1965, EX+	**$10.00**
Gomer Pyle, #3, 1967, VG+	**$7.00**
Governor & JJ, #1, EX	**$20.00**
Great Grape Ape, #2, 1976, NM	**$5.00**
Great Locomotive Chase, Dell Four-Color #712, Fess Parker photo cover, EX	**$20.00**

Gunsmoke, Dell Four-Color #679, NM **$110.00**
Gunsmoke, Dell Four-Color #720, EX...........................**$27.00**
Hardy Boys, Gold Key #2, 1970, photo cover, NM.......**$8.00**
Harlem Globetrotters, #3, 1972, EX.............................**$3.00**
Hennessey, Dell Four-Color #1200, 1961, VG+...........**$10.00**
Henry, #27, VG+..**$6.00**
Hopalong Cassidy, Fawcett #54, 1951, VG **$8.00**
House of Secrets, Dell #50, EX...................................**$38.00**
HR Pufnstuf, Gold Key #1, 1970, VG+.......................**$20.00**
HR Pufnstuf, Gold Key #2, NM...................................**$25.00**
Huckleberry Hound, Dell #3, EX+ **$15.00**
I Dream of Jeannie, Dell #1, photo cover, EX+ **$60.00**
I Love Lucy, #23, VG...**$22.00**
I Spy, Gold Key #1, 1966, photo cover, VG **$15.00**
I Spy, Gold Key #3, 1967, NM+..................................**$30.00**
I Spy, Gold Key #5, EX **$25.00**
Incredible Hulk, #2, 1976, NM.....................................**$5.00**

Invisible Man, Superior Stories #1, 1955, NM, $65.00.

It's About Time, Gold Key #1, EX...............................**$12.00**
Jerry Lewis, DC Comics #108, 1968, EX......................**$5.00**
Jesse James, #25, 1956, 10¢ cover price, EX..............**$20.00**
Jetsons, #14, VG+...**$18.00**
Jiggs & Maggie, Standard #12, 1949, EX **$15.00**
Jiminy Cricket, #701, 1956, 10¢ cover price, VG.........**$10.00**
Journey Into Mystery, Marvel #116, VG+....................**$12.00**
Kid Colt, Marvel #5, G...**$18.00**
King of Kings, Dell Four-Color #1236, 1961, EX.........**$30.00**
Krofft Supershow, #1, 1978, EX..................................**$12.00**
Lancer, Gold Key #1, 1968, EX+ **$10.00**
Larami, Dell Four-Color #1223, EX+............................**$32.00**
Lassie, Dell #11, VG+..**$8.00**
Linus the Lionhearted, Gold Key #1, 1965, EX............**$25.00**
Little Lulu Christmas Diary, Gold Key #166, 1963, EX...**$40.00**
Little Monsters, Gold Key #13, 1964, EX......................**$3.00**
Lone Ranger, #61 through #74, EX+, each...................**$30.00**
Lone Ranger, #70, 1954, EX+ **$22.00**
Lost in Space, #35, 1969, VG **$2.00**
Lost in Space, #41, 1974, VG+......................................**$2.00**
Man From UNCLE, Gold Key #10, 1966, VG+...............**$5.00**
Man From UNCLE, Gold Key #13, 1966, EX.................**$8.00**
Margie, Dell #2, 1962, VG...**$4.00**
Maverick, Dell #16, 1960, VG+....................................**$16.00**
Maverick, Dell Four-Color #930, VG+ **$25.00**
McHale's Navy, #3, VG+ **$15.00**
Mighty Mouse, Pines, May 1957, EX+ **$20.00**

Mission Impossible, Dell #3, 1967, photo cover, NM .**$25.00**
Mr Ed, Gold Key #2, 1963, G..**$5.00**
Mr Ed, Gold Key #3, 1963, EX......................................**$25.00**
Munsters, #3, 1965, EX+...**$30.00**
My Favorite Martian, Gold Key #4, EX+ **$35.00**
My Favorite Martian, Gold Key #5, EX **$22.00**
My Favorite Martian, Gold Key #8, EX **$18.00**
Old Ironsides With Johnny Tremain, Dell #874, 1957, VG...**$8.00**
Our Gang, Dell #20, G...**$15.00**
Patridge Family, #10, EX+..**$12.00**
Peter Potamus, Gold Key #1, 1964, G **$15.00**
Playful Little Audrey, Harvey #1, EX+...........................**$75.00**
Playful Little Audrey, Dell #1, 1957, EX+ **$6.00**
Pogo Possum, Dell #8, NM..**$75.00**
Range Rider, Dell #13, 1955, VG.....................................**$8.00**
Rawhide Kid, Dell #34, VG..**$12.00**
Red Ryder, Dell #69, 1949, EX......................................**$25.00**
Restless Gun, Dell Four-Color #1089, VG.....................**$12.00**
Rex Allen, Dell #13, EX+...**$28.00**
Rifleman, #20, 1949, EX **$20.00**
Rifleman, #20, 1949, G..**$12.00**
Rin-Tin-Tin & Rusty, Dell #18, April 1957, EX+ **$15.00**
Road Runner, #25, VG+..**$2.00**
Roy Rogers, Dell #1239, 1950s, NM.............................**$35.00**
Roy Rogers, Dell #27, VG+ **$25.00**
Run Buddy Run!, Gold Key #1, 1967, photo cover, G..**$3.00**
Secret Agent, Gold Key #1, 1966, NM **$100.00**
Secret Agent, Gold Key #1, 1966, VG **$25.00**
Shotgun Slade, #111, G...**$12.00**
Sir Walter Raleigh, Dell #644, 1955, G+ **$10.00**
Smokey Bear, #9, EX...**$3.00**
Sports Thrills, Accepted #12, 1951, G **$8.00**
Star Trek, Gold Key #13, 1972, VG **$20.00**
Star Trek, Gold Key #19, 1969, EX...............................**$35.00**
Star Wars, #1, 1978, NM **$15.00**
Sugar Cops, Red Circle #1, July 1974, NM....................**$3.50**
Super Mouse, Dell #36, EX..**$12.00**
Superman, #114, 1957, 10¢ cover price, VG.................**$35.00**
Superman's Pal Jimmy Olsen, Dell #32, EX..................**$30.00**
Tales From the Crypt, #26, EX+ **$145.00**
Tales of Wells Fargo, Dell Four-Color #876, 1st issue, photo cover, EX **$45.00**
Tarzan, Dell #10, 1949, VG...**$40.00**

Tarzan, Dell #112, 1959, EX, $25.00.

Tarzan, Dell #116, 1960, EX..**$10.00**

Tarzan, Dell #28, 1952, photo cover, EX $45.00
Tarzan, Dell #38, VG $22.00
Tarzan, Dell #60, EX+...$20.00
Tarzan's Jungle Annual, Dell #7, 1958, VG+...............$10.00
Tex Ritter Western, Fawcett/Charlton #33, EX............$28.00
Texas Rangers in Action, #8, VG+ $12.00
That Darn Cat, Movie Comics, NM..................................$45.00
Thief of Baghdad, #1229, VG $28.00
Three Stooges, Dell #1170, 1961, VG..........................$20.00

Three Stooges, Dell, 1962, EX, $30.00.

Three Stooges, Dell Comic Album #4, 1958, VG+ $15.00
Tom & Jerry Funhouse, Gold Key #213, 1962, 1st Funhouse
    issue, EX..$15.00
Tom Mix, Fawcett #10, 1948, VG $35.00
Top Cat, #24, EX..$10.00
Underdog, #1, 1974, VG+ $20.00
Untouchables, Dell #207, 1962, EX $25.00
Untouchables, Dell #876-210, 1962, VG.......................$20.00
Wagon Train, Dell Four-Color #1019, 1959, 3rd issue, VG+ ..$10.00

Walt Disney's Old Yeller, Dell #869, 1957, EX, $25.00.

Walt Disney's Treasure Island, Dell #624, 1955, EX....$22.00
Warlock, Marvel Premiere #1, 1972, NM.....................$12.00
Western Marshall, #613, G+ $12.00
Western Roundup, #1, VG+ $55.00
Western Roundup, Dell Giant #14, 1956, VG+ $15.00
Woody Woodpecker, Dell Four-Color #288, 1950, EX ...$20.00
World of Wheels, #23, 1978, NM...................................$10.00
X-Men, Marvel #60, 1969, EX...$15.00
Zorro, Dell #11, 1960, EX..$20.00
Zorro, Dell Four-Color #617, 1955, G+ $15.00
Zorro, Gold Key #1, 1957, EX $14.00

Compacts and Purse Accessories

Very new to the collectibles scene, compacts are already making an impact. When 'liberated' women entered the workforce after WWI, cosmetics, previously frowned upon, became more acceptable, and as a result the market was engulfed with compacts of all types and designs. Some went so far as to incorporate timepieces, cigarette compartments, coin holders, and money clips. All types of materials were used, mother-of-pearl, petit-point, cloisonne, celluloid, and leather among them. There were figural compacts, those with wonderful Art Deco designs, souvenir compacts, and some with advertising messages.

Carryalls were popular from the 1930s to the 1950s. They were made by compact manufacturers and were usually carried with evening wear. They contained compartments for powder, rouge, and lipstick, often held a comb and mirror, and some were designed with a space for cigarettes and a lighter. Other features might have included a timepiece, a tissue holder, a place for coins or stamps, and some even had music boxes. Solid perfumes and lipsticks are becoming increasingly popular as well.

For further study, we recommend *Vintage Ladies' Compacts, Vintage Vanity Bags and Purses*, and *Vintage and Contemporary Purse Accessories* by Roselyn Gerson; and *Collector's Encyclopedia of Compacts, Carryalls, and Face Powder Boxes Vols. I* and *II* by Laura Mueller.

Advisor: Roselyn Gerson (See Directory, Compacts)

Newsletter The Compacts Collector Chronicle
Powder Puff
P.O. Box 40
Lynbrook, NY 11563. Subscription: $25 (4 issues, USA or Canada) per year

Carryalls

DF Briggs Co, engine-turned silvered metal w/lady in oval
    disk in center, compartments, carrying chain, from $150
    to..$200.00
Evans, metal w/pink, yellow & white basketweave, 1940s-
    50s, from $125 to...$150.00
Volupte, mother-of-pearl Swinglok, ca 1940-50s, from $150
    to $200.00
Volupte, Oval Sophisticase, silver-embossed gilt lid, black
    faille carrying case, 1950s, from $125 to.............$150.00

Compacts

Columbia Fifth Avenue, mesh vanity pouch w/orange & blue
    1939 NY World's Fair on lid, from $80 to...........$125.00
Compact, gift package form, gold-tone w/raised card & bow
    on lid, 3" square, from $50 to..............................$75.00
Coro, gold-tone half-moon w/enameled Persian design on
    lid, from $40 to $60.00
Coty, gold-tone vanity, wishbone & star w/rhinestones
    embossed on lid, compartments, 3¾x2¼", from $80
    to $100.00

Elgin American, gold-tone with harlequin masks on lid, 2¾x2¾", from $40.00 to $60.00. (Photo courtesy Roselyn Gerson)

Elgin, brushed gold-tone, thermometer centered on lid, incised ladies playing sports, 2¾" square, from $120 to.......**$150.00**

Elgin, gold-tone w/multicolor enameled Eastern Star emblem, 3" dia, from $40 to...**$60.00**

Elgin, heart shape, brushed gold-tone w/engraved Cupid, hearts & I Love You in different languages, 3¼", from $60 to..**$100.00**

Elgin, mother-of-pearl vanity, rouge compartment w/mother-of-pearl centered on lid, 2¾" square, from $60 to.......**$100.00**

Elgin, petit-point city scene on lid, floral petit-point border, gold-tone trim, 3½x3", from $80 to.....................**$120.00**

Evans, gilt mesh, white enamel vanity bag w/metal mirror, compartments, 1940s-50s, from $150 to.............**$225.00**

Evans, gilt-mesh white cloisonne vanity pouch, 1930s, miniature, from $75 to..**$95.00**

Evans, gold-tone compact/watch combination w/engraved design on lid, ca 1930s-40s, from $150 to **$225.00**

Evans, gold-tone tap-sift model, 2" dia, w/matching lighter, M in tan suede fitted 5x3" box, from $60 to...........**$100.00**

Evans, petit-point gold-tone mesh vanity bag w/metal mirror, compartments, 1940-50s, from $150 to **$225.00**

Evans, pink & yellow gold-tone basketweave, ca 1946, from $150 to..**$225.00**

Figu, flying saucer form, blue celestial scene each side, from $350 to...**$400.00**

France, black silk w/beaded pink fan, from $60 to....**$80.00**

Great Britain, gold-tone, plastic textured dog w/movable head applied to pearlized plastic lid, 3" dia, from $80 to..**$150.00**

Gwenda, gold-tone & enameled painted foil, round, from $80 to..**$100.00**

Hudnut, gilt w/embossed tulip design, lipstick encased in lid cover, from $40 to **$60.00**

Hudnut, gold-tone vanity/cigarette case combination, white enamel w/purple orchids, compartments, 3x4½", from $150 to..**$175.00**

Italy, brown gold-tooled leather, square, from $150 to..**$200.00**

Italy, owl face figural, textured gold-tone w/faux emerald eyes, w/mirror, 2¾x2", from $250 to **$350.00**

K&K, brass-colored basket form, engine tooled, swing handle, metal interior, 2⅛" dia, from $80 to.............**$120.00**

K&K, brushed gold-tone case, attached lipstick, red & turquoise stones form band, beveled mirror, 2¼x3", from $100 to...**$150.00**

Kigu, gold-tone & blue enamel with heart-shaped flower on lid, ca 1940-50s, from $50 to................................**$75.00**

Lesco Bond Street, green alligator, square, sm, from $70 to **$90.00**

Marathon, gold-tone w/heart on lid, locket inside, opens from plastic side panels, from $60 to...................**$80.00**

Mary Dunhill, satin gold-tone w/rhinestones & green stones, from $60 to..**$80.00**

Maxley, mother-of-pearl w/inlaid black diagonal stripes & mother-of-pearl cameo, 1930s, from $175 to......**$200.00**

Melba, gold-tone vanity w/blue enameled flower on lid, compartments, carrying chain, from $80 to........**$125.00**

Paloma Piccaso, silver and gold-tone case, domed lid w/red stone & signature, mirror, 2½x¾", from $125 to...**$175.00**

Rex, brushed silver w/polished gold-tone flowers, lipstick attached by chain, 3½" dia, from $175 to...........**$200.00**

Rex, gilt mesh vanity pouch w/white plastic mini beads, ca 1930s, from $40 to...**$60.00**

Rex Fifth Avenue, multicolor-striped taffeta vanity pocket w/mirror on outside base, 1940s, from $75 to...**$100.00**

Rex Fifth Avenue, red enamel oval w/mother-of-pearl Army hat on lid, inscribed, 1940s, from $80 to............**$100.00**

Schiaparelli, gold-tone triangle w/figure on dark pink enamel, w/mirror, puff & rouge compartment, 2", from $60 to...**$100.00**

Stratton, gold-tone w/scenic transfer on lid, 1950s, from $40 to..**$60.00**

Tangee, dresser/vanity, white enameled lid w/stylized red lips, compartments, 5x5", from $75 to **$125.00**

Unmarked, alligator covered w/gold-tone lipstick tube attached to side, square, from $80 to **$100.00**

Unmarked, Army officer's cap form, khaki-colored plastic, 1940s, from $50 to...**$80.00**

Unmarked, Bakelite, yellow w/pink flowers, mirror & well, 1½" Bakelite tube in tassel, 1¾" dia, from $150 to........**$190.00**

Unmarked, beaded vanity pouch w/silvered lid, 1930s, from $50 to...**$60.00**

Unmarked, black & white mother-of pearl vanity w/attached lipstick, 1930s, from $50 to **$75.00**

Unmarked, book form w/mother-of-pearl checkerboard lid, from $50 to...**$75.00**

Unmarked, brown fur vanity pouch w/collapsible bottom, from $50 to...**$75.00**

Unmarked, cigarette/compact combination, plastic w/metal cut-out Scottie on lid, 1940s, from $80 to...........**$100.00**

Unmarked, fan form, gold-tone w/multicolor flowers, pearl twist lock, w/mirror & well, 2½x1½", from $40 to ..**$60.00**

Unmarked, gilt-mesh vanity pouch w/butterfly on lid, 1930s, from $60 to...**$80.00**

Unmarked, gold-tone mother-of-pearl vanity, resembles book, lipstick tube in spine, compartments, 2x2½", from $60 to...**$100.00**

Unmarked, gold-tone triangle w/embossed elephants, from $40 to...**$60.00**

Unmarked, gold-tone w/micro-mosaic flowers on lid & 4 stones set around base, from $60 to.....................**$80.00**

Unmarked, green lizard w/lipstick hinged on top of lid, round, from $150 to **$200.00**

Unmarked, hat box form, red faux leather cover, snaps open, mirror & puff, w/carrying handle, 3x2¾", from $75 to...**$125.00**

Unmarked, heart shape, gold-tone w/brocade lid, 1930s, from $40 to..**$60.00**

Unmarked, heart shape resembling lock, gold-tone w/enameling, from $120 to...**$150.00**

Unmarked, horseshoe form, blue leather, 2-pc, from $40 to...**$60.00**

Unmarked, silver-tone & maroon w/Buick Eight logo applied to lid, 3" dia from $70 to..................................**$85.00**

Unmarked, suitcase form, blue enameled w/gold-tone snap opening, 3x2¼x¾", from $80 to.........................**$100.00**

Unmarked, white enamel w/mesh bottom, black poodle on lid, 2½" dia, from $60 to.....................................**$80.00**

USA, suitcase form, brushed gold-tone w/blue and red straps & corners, 3x2¼", from $150 to.........................**$175.00**

Volupte, brushed gold-tone, red/white/blue enamel stripes & stones, 3" square, from $60 to...........................**$80.00**

Volupte, brushed silver-tone 'Lucky Purse,' polished flap, w/mirror, 3½x2¾", from $80 to...........................**$100.00**

Volupte, hand shape, gold-tone, 1940s, from $150 to .**$175.00**

Volupte, mink covered, 3x3" square, from $75 to **$100.00**

Volupte, white enamel with red anchor & blue rope, 2½" dia, from $50 to..**$70.00**

Wadsworth, envelope shape, cobra skin covering, from $120 to...**$150.00**

Wadsworth, fan form, gold-tone w/hand-painted flowers on yellow enamel, 1940s, from $80 to....................**$100.00**

Zell, hat box form, maroon w/gold-tone hardware, anchor & USN emblem on lid, 3" dia, from $150 to.........**$175.00**

Zell Fifth Avenue, black suede vanity clutch w/compact, 2 lipstick tubes & comb, snap closure, 1940s, from $60 to..**$80.00**

Zell Fifth Avenue, gold-tone w/picture locket in lid, from $40 to..**$60.00**

Lipsticks

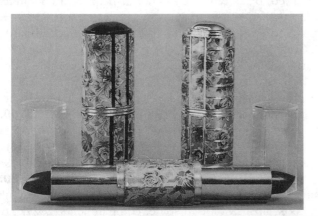

Lipsticks, Tri-Delta, gold-tone with painted flowers, 3", from $5.00 to $25.00; Tri-Delta, dual tube, 4½", from $25.00 to $35.00. (Photo courtesy Roselyn Gerson)

Charles of the Ritz, petit-point pink & yellow roses on black fabric, 2¼", from $15 to **$25.00**

Charles of the Ritz, white enamel & rose on gold-tone, 2¼", from $30 to..**$45.00**

Florenza, brushed gold-tone w/green cabachon stones, 2", from $35 to...**$50.00**

Halston, gold-tone heart-shaped tube, 2¾", from $35 to ..**$50.00**

Hampden, applied filigree w/red, blue & green stones on gold-tone, 2", from $35 to.....................................**$50.00**

Hudnut, Du Barry, gold-tone w/square Lucite base & top, faceted square rhinestone, 2½", from $25 to........**$35.00**

Lillie Dache, brushed gold-tone w/applied plastic couple in swing, 2½", from $45 to.......................................**$55.00**

Lucien Lelong, rabbit fur cover, 2¼", from $45 to......**$65.00**

Prince Matchabelli, gold-tone w/crown top, 2½", from $35 to..**$50.00**

Tangee, gold-tone case w/Lucite base, 2", from $15 to ..**$25.00**

Mirrors

Celluloid, lady holding out full skirt w/beveled mirror, floral trim, 3½x2¼", from $50 to....................................**$75.00**

France, gold-tone filigree w/rhinestones & cabachon turquoise stones, silk tassle at center, beveled mirror, 3" dia.....**$60.00**

Limoges, cobalt blue enamel w/courting scene, gold-tone wire retainer & handle, 4¾x2¼", from $35 to......**$45.00**

Mattel, Barbie, glitter, red rose & cabachon stones on gold-tone, 2¼x2¼"..**$40.00**

Petit-point, gold-tone wire retainer, florals on handle, 3¾x1¼", from $20 to..**$30.00**

Stratton, gold-tone, black & multicolor florals, handle folds up against mirror, 2½" dia, from $20 to...............**$30.00**

West Germany, red & white enamel, regular & magnifying mirrors, metal swing hinge, 2⅜" dia, from $15 to.......**$20.00**

Solid Perfumes

Solid perfume, Sarah Coventry, gold-tone turtle with faceted amethyst stone, 1¾x1½", from $30.00 to $40.00. (Photo courtesy Roselyn Gerson)

Avon, cameo & gold-tone ring, from $15 to **$25.00**

Avon, polished gold-tone book shape w/engraved design, 1⅜x1¼", from $25 to...**$35.00**

Carolee, antique gold-tone walnut pendant, 1½", from $40 to..**$50.00**

Coty, jeweled gold-tone flower w/blue cabachon stone, Imprevu fragrance, 1½" dia, w/fitted presentation box............**$35.00**

Estee Lauder, gold-tone w/raised florals, pink stones & cameo at center, 1¼" dia, from $25 to.................**$35.00**

Guy Laroche, gold-tone shell figural, Fidji fragrance, 2½x2½", from $30 to..**$40.00**

Helena Rubinstein, oval gold-tone w/faceted green stone, 1x1½", from $15 to..**$20.00**

Matchabelli, antique gold-tone pendant, strapwork design, Aviance fragrance, 1½x1½" square, from $30 to..**$40.00**

Max Factor, textured antique gold-tone teddy bear figural, rhinestone bow tie, yellow stone eyes, 1½x1", from $45 to..**$55.00**

Revlon, filigree gold-tone octagon w/portrait, Ciara fragrance, 1¾", from $30 to..............................**$40.00**

Revlon, striated gold-tone hippopotamus figural, Charlie scent, 1⅞" L, from $45 to........................**$55.00**

Vanda, antique gold-tone owl figural pin, green stone eyes, 1¾", from $40 to..............................**$50.00**

Condiment Sets

Whimsical styling make these sets lots of fun to collect. Any species of animal, plant, bird, or mammal that ever existed and many that never did or ever will are represented, so an extensive collection is possible, and prices are still reasonable. These sets are usually comprised of a pair of salt and pepper shakers and a small mustard pot on a tray, though some sets never had a tray, and others were figurals that were made in three parts. For more information, we recommend *Collector's Guide to Made in Japan Ceramics, Books I and II*, by Carole Bess White; *Salt and Pepper Shakers, Vols I through IV*, by Helene Guarnaccia; and *Collector's Encyclopedia of Salt and Pepper Shakers, Figural and Novelty*, by Melva Davern.

See also Black Americana.

Art Deco, angular black & white block design, sugar shaker, pitcher, salt & pepper shakers, lustre, largest: 6½" ..**$40.00**

Art Deco, angular form w/rickrack & dot design, cruets, shakers & mustard sit in wells on tray, multicolor lustre **$100.00**

Art Deco castle mustard w/black cat finial, shakers as part of building, multicolor matt finish, rare, from $90 to ..**$125.00**

Art Deco form w/built-in mustard pot & salt dip, triangular pepper shaker sits in 4" L tray, blue lustre, from $28 to ..**$42.00**

Art Deco shakers w/ovoid body & round foot, mustard w/round finial, +9" L gondola tray, blue & black glossy finish **$45.00**

Bear mustard, baby bear shakers & round rimmed tray, blue & multicolor lustre, Noritake, largest: 3", from $90 to...**$125.00**

Beer barrel shakers & mustard on tray w/standing bartender figure, multicolor glossy finish, 5¾", from $18 to ..**$25.00**

Bird mustard w/pr baby bird shakers, on narrow 7¼" tray, from $32 to..**$42.00**

Bird nodder salt & pepper shakers w/mustard pot & spoon sit in log base, from $45 to..............................**$55.00**

Boat tray w/bluebird & flower on side, shakers & mustard sit on top, blue & multicolor lustre, 6½", from $25 to.......**$35.00**

British telephone booth & mailboxes on tray, Japan, 1950, from $60 to..**$80.00**

Cats on tray, arched backs, tan & multicolor lustre, black tail is mustard spoon, Japan, 6-pc, from $65 to.........**$85.00**

Chicken nodder shakers w/baby chick as mustard lid, from $45 to..**$55.00**

Desert scene w/camel & pyramid beyond, cruets, shakers & mustard, +9" oval tray, multicolor glossy finish, from $60 to..**$100.00**

Dog figural mustard w/ladle tongue, sm dog shakers, on narrow handled tray, tan & blue lustre, from $35 to ..**$50.00**

Dogs on tray, mustard spoon as tail, lustre w/red & black trim, from $65 to..**$75.00**

Dogs on tray after cat atop lg oval mustard, multicolor lustre, from $75 to..**$90.00**

Donkey nodder shakers in condiment base w/inset mustard pot at center, from $45 to............................**$55.00**

Dutch boy & girl shakers w/ball form mustard on tray, multicolor & cream matt finish, Noritake, from $90 to..**$125.00**

Elephant figural w/upturned trunk, shaker basket each side, round finial lid, tan & multicolor lustre, 4", from $20 to..**$35.00**

Elephants w/trunks pointed down on tray, lustre, German, 1930s, from $80 to..**$120.00**

Fish, top quarter of head & tip of tail are shakers, lg fin is mustard lid, silver lustre, from $95 to.................**$120.00**

Fish w/shakers & mustard pot sitting in back, lustre w/Havana capitol scene on side, German, from $65 to..............**$85.00**

Floral-painted oil & vinegar cruets, mustard, salt & pepper shakers, +9" tray w/handles & gold trim, from $60 to **$100.00**

Flower basket form tray, pr oval shakers & floral mustard w/bee finial sit on top, teal & multicolor lustre, 4"..............**$38.00**

Fort & 2 cannons sit on moat base, multicolor, Japan, 1950, from $80 to..**$100.00**

Galleon, 3 sails as shakers & mustard, blue & tan lustre, marked souvenir of Albany NY, Japan, from $35 to................**$55.00**

Horse shakers pulling carriage mustard on realistic tray base, Japan, 1950s, from $80 to..............................**$100.00**

Houses on tray, ½-timbered style w/brown gabled roofs, green tray, from $45 to..............................**$65.00**

Indian chief w/headdress, seated w/2 children as shakers, multicolor matt finish, from $35 to........................**$50.00**

Kangaroo family, tall vinegar & oil, sm mustard, salt & pepper shakers, on 7" dia tray, tan & blue lustre finish.......**$95.00**

Loch-Ness monster, black, English, 1970, 4-pc, from $40 to..**$50.00**

Lotus blossom shakers, mustard w/frog finial, +5½" cupped base, cream & tan lustre finish, from $25 to............................**$45.00**

Monks on tray, Carlton Ware, English, 1950s, from $80 to..**$100.00**

Monks on tray, comic expressions, Japan, 1960s, from $40 to..**$50.00**

Ocean liner, 3 smokestacks on mustard lid, pink lustre w/souvenir scene in oval on side, from $55 to....**$85.00**

Rabbit figural, salt cellars as ears, tan & blue lustre, 4½", from $25 to..**$45.00**

Rabbit figural mustard, figural salt & pepper shakers at sides, on tray, marked Germany, largest: 3¾", from $35 to.......**$50.00**

Salt dip, bird on perch finial on center handle, double flower wells, 3¼", from $25 to..............................**$40.00**

Tomatoes on leaf form tray, marked #4040 Germany, 6-pc, from $40 to..**$50.00**

Train engine & 2 cars on track base, multicolor glossy finish, Japan, 1950s, from $60 to..............................**$80.00**

3 Wise Monkeys, figural mustard, salt & pepper shakers, on 5½" L tray w/leaf handle, tan & blue lustre, from $50 to..**$75.00**

3 Wise Monkeys, realistic figural mustard & shakers, blue, tan & cream lustre, on narrow ring-handled tray, from $35 to $50.00

Cookbooks and Recipe Leaflets

If you've ever read a nineteenth-century cookbook, no doubt you've been amused by the quaint way the measurements were given. Butter the size of an egg, a handfull of flour, a pinch of this or that — sounds like a much more time-efficient method, doesn't it? They'd sometimes give household tips or some folk remedies, and it's these antiquated methods and ideas that endear those old cookbooks to collectors, although examples from this era are not easily found.

Cookbooks from the early twentieth century are scarce too, but even those that were printed thirty and forty years ago are well worth collecting. Food and appliance companies often published their own, and these appeal to advertising buffs and cookbook collectors alike, especially if they illustrate kitchen appliances pre-1970. Some were diecut to represent the product, perhaps a pickle or a slice of bread. Cookbooks that focus on unusual topics and those that have ethnic or regional recipes are appealing, too. The leaflets we list were nearly all advertising giveaways and premiums. Condition is important in any area of paper collectibles, so judge yours accordingly.

Perhaps no single event in the 1950s attracted more favorable attention for the Pillsbury Flour Company than the one first staged in 1949. Early in the year, company officials took the question to its advertising agency. Together they came up with a plan that would become an American institution — the Pillsbury Bake-Off Contest. On December 12, 1949, in the grand ballroom of the Waldorf Astoria Hotel in New York City, ninety-seven women and three men were standing nervously over one hundred ranges ready to compete for $100,00 in cash prizes. Philip Pillsbury, Eleanor Roosevelt, and Art Linkletter presented the awards to the winners. The Duke and Duchess of Windsor were in attendance as guests. The bake-offs have been held each year since that time.

Betty Crocker, the ultimate, eternal, and supreme housewife was fabricated by the Washburn Crosby Company, who in 1928 became part of the merger that was General Mills, Inc. She was introduced to the public in 1917 via the *Gold Medal Flour Cook Book*, an 8½"x11" softcover book that was published twice in 1917. Betty appeared in the second printing. She soon became a most believable entity complete with radio voice, signature, and a black and white composite drawing for advertising purposes. Hundreds of Betty Crocker/General Mills cookbooks and advertising booklets have been printed over the years, many displaying Betty's portrait, which has been modified from time to time to keep her hairstyle and clothing attune with current fashions. Today there are many collectors who vie for not only the cookbooks but package inserts, magazine ads, and any other material where Betty's likeness appears.

For further study, we recommend *A Guide to Collecting Cookbooks* by Colonel Bob Allen and *Price Guide to Cookbooks and Recipe Leaflets* by Linda Dickinson. Our values are based on cookbooks in excellent condition.

Advisor: Bob Allen (See Directory, Cookbooks)

Club/Newsletter: *Cookbook Gossip*
Cookbook Collectors Club of America, Inc.
Bob and Jo Ellen Allen
P.O. Box 85
St. James, MO 65559

Newsletter: *The Cookbook Collector's Exchange*
Sue Erwin
P.O. Box 32369
San Jose, CA 95152-2369

American Home All Purpose Cookbook, 1966, hardcover, 563 pages, EX..$15.00
American Indian Cooking & Herb Lore, 1973, 32 pages, EX..$10.00
Amy Vanderbilt's Complete Cookbook With Illustrations by Andy Warhol, 1961, hardcover, 811 pages, EX.....$20.00
Around the World Cookery With Electric Housewares, 1962, leaflet, 48 pages $4.00
Aunt Sammy's Radio Recipes, 1976, 24 pages, EX........$7.00
Bakers Chocolate & Coconut Favorites, 1962, paperback, 64 pages, VG $7.50
Better Homes & Gardens, Bread Cookbook, 1967, hardcover, 160 pages, VG.......................................$7.50
Better Homes & Gardens, Hot & Spicy Cooking, 1984, hardcover, 96 pages, VG..................................$7.00
Betty Crocker, Baking to Your Heart's Content, 1988, 10 pages, EX..$1.00
Betty Crocker, Cake Decorating, 1984, hardcover, 1960 pages, EX..$10.00
Betty Crocker, Cakes Kids Love, 1969, 24 pages, EX....$2.00
Betty Crocker, Dinner in a Dish Cookbook, 1st edition, 1965, hardcover w/spiral back, 152 pages, EX...............$10.00
Betty Crocker, Fifteen Ways to a Man's Heart, General Mills Inc, 1932, stiff covers, 24 pages, 3½x5", EX.........$25.00
Betty Crocker, How To 'Simplify' Your Baking, ca 1929, soft cover, EX $20.00
Betty Crocker, New Boys' & Girls' Cookbook, 1971, 156 pages, EX..$10.00
Betty Crocker, 42 Hot Potato Ideas, 1967, leaflet, VG ..$4.00
Betty Crocker, Picture Cookbook, 1st state ca 1950, 1st ed, yellow end papers, blue cloth binding/sleeve, limited to 400..$400.00
Betty Crocker, Picture Cookbook, 2nd state c 1950, 1st edition, yellow end papers, blue cloth bound, limited to 2,500..$75.00
Betty Crocker, Picture Cookbook, 3rd state c 1950, 1st edition, brown end papers, red cloth bound, dust jacket, 449 pages..$35.00
Betty Crocker, Picture Cookbook, 4th state ca 1950, 1st edition, red with cloth covers, hardcover 5-ring binder, 449 pages..$25.00
Betty Crocker, 12 Famous Stars of Cookery, 'All Star' recipes, package insert, 1932, EX.....................$10.00
Betty Crocker, $25,000 Recipe Set, recipes from world famous chefs, spiral bound, aluminum-clad covers, 60 pages, EX..$45.00

Betty Crocker, Vitality Demands Energy, 109 Smart New Ways To Serve Bread…, 1934, softcover, 54 pages +2, EX.......**$15.00**

Betty Crocker, Vitality Demands Energy, 109 Smart New Ways To Serve Bread…, 1934, hardbound, 54 pages +2, EX **$35.00**

Betty Crocker's Cake Mix Magic, 1951, leaflet, 27 pages, G **$5.00**

Betty Crocker's 101 Delicious Bisquick Creations Made… by Well-Known Gracious Hostesses…, 1933, softcover, 32 pages...**$15.00**

Betty Crocker's Party Book, 1960, 1st edition, spiral binding, 176 pages, NM **$10.00**

Big Baking News From Swans Down & Calumet, 1944, 19 pages, EX...**$6.00**

Big Green Salad Book, 1977, paperback, 125 pages, EX..**$5.00**

Boston Cooking School Cookbook, Fannie Farmer, 1944, 824 pages, EX...**$20.00**

Brer Rabbit, Modern Recipes for the Modern Hostess, 1930s, 48 pages **$10.00**

California Dairy Products, New Idea Cookbook, 18 pages, EX...**$3.00**

California Fresh Mushrooms Cookbook, 1963, 28 pages, EX **$4.00**

Calumet, Kate Smith's Favorite Recipes, 1939, 47 pages, EX **$10.00**

Campbell's, Easy Ways to Delicious Meals, 1970, spiral binding, 204 pages, NM...**$6.00**

Campbell's, Wonderful Ways With Soup, 1948, paperback, 64 pages, VG **$4.50**

Campfire Marshmallow Cookery, 1934, 19 pages, EX ...**$10.00**

Carnation, Cooking for the Crowd, 1963, 23 pages, EX ..**$6.00**

Carnation, Fun To Cook Book, 1925, 32 pages, VG...**$12.00**

Certo/Sure Jell, What Makes Jelly Jell?, 1945, 23 pages, EX..**$6.00**

Cheese Book, Viviene Marquie & Patricia Haskell, 1964, hardcover, 314 pages, EX **$10.00**

Chiquita Banana Recipe Book, 1950, 24 pages, EX......**$6.00**

Chocolate Cookbook, JE Hamelecourt, 1985, hardcover, 214 pages, EX...**$12.00**

Clabber Girl Baking Book, 1934, 18 pages, EX...........**$12.50**

Complete Encyclopedia of Chinese Cooking, 1979, hardcover, 224 pages, EX **$15.00**

Complete International Jewish Cookbook, Evelyn Rose, 1977, paperback, 320 pages, EX...**$12.00**

Confident Cook, 1975, hardcover, 240 pages, VG.........**$5.00**

Cookies & Cakes, Jane Solmson, 1980, hardcover, 64 pages, EX...**$8.00**

Cooking Across the South, 1980, hardcover, 272 pages, EX...**$15.00**

Cooking With Kenny Rogers, 1987, paperback, 96 pages, EX...**$8.00**

Cooking With the Pennsylvania Dutch, 1961, leaflet, 64 pages **$4.00**

Corning Glass Works, Getting the Most Out of Foods, 1920s, leaflet, 32 pages, EX...**$10.00**

Creative Breads the Easy Oster Way, 48 pages, NM **$1.50**

Crisco, A Few Cooking Suggestions, 1928, 15 pages..**$10.00**

Diamond Walnut Recipe Gems, 1960s, 88 pages, VG...**$3.00**

Diamond Walnuts, Menu Magic in a Nutshell, 1938, 32 pages, VG+...**$5.00**

Durkee Coconut Cookbook, 1971, 31 pages, EX..........**$5.00**

Eating in Bed Cookbook, Barbara Ninde Byfield, 1962, hardcover, 103 pages, EX **$10.00**

Excellent Recipes for Baking With Fleischman's Yeast, 1910, 52 pages, EX...**$10.00**

Farm Journal's Complete Pie Cookbook, 1965, hardcover, 308 pages, EX...**$10.00**

Farm Journal's Country Cookbook, 1959, hardcover, 420 pages, VG...**$8.00**

Farm Journal's Friendly Food Gifts From Your Kitchen, 1978, hardcover, 255 pages, EX...**$10.00**

Farm Journal's Homemade Candy, 1970, hardcover, 224 pages, VG+...**$9.00**

Farmer's Almanac Cookbook, 1964, hardcover, 390 pages, EX...**$12.00**

Feast Without Fuss, 1977, hardcover, 399 pages, EX+ **$10.00**

Fifty Ways To Cook Most Everything, Andrew Schloss, 1992, hardcover, 477 pages, EX...**$20.00**

Fish & Game Cooking, Joan Cone, 1980s, paperback, 382 pages, EX...**$10.00**

Food Processor Cookbook, 1977, paperback, 183 pages, EX...**$5.00**

Galloping Gourmet Cookbook, Graham Kerr, 1969, hardcover, 284 pages, EX **$6.00**

General Foods Kitchens, All About Home Baking, 1963, leaflet, 36 pages, G...**$3.00**

Gold Medal Flour Cookbook, 1917, Betty Crocker introduced on page 73, softcover, EX **$30.00**

Gold Medal Flour Cookbook, 1917, softcover, EX......**$20.00**

Gold Medal Foods Recipe Book, ca 1923, softcover, 24 pages, EX...**$20.00**

Good Things To Eat, 1934, 64 pages, EX **$8.00**

Guide to Better Canning, 1951, 30 pages, EX **$8.00**

Heinz Book of Salads, 1925, 90 pages, EX.................**$15.00**

Hershey's Bitter-Sweet Chocolate Recipes, 1940, leaflet, 14 pages, EX...**$8.00**

Hershey's 1934 Cookbook, 1971, spiral binding, 96 pages, EX...**$4.00**

House & Garden's New Cookbook, 1967, hardcover, 404 pages, EX...**$10.00**

How To Be Easy on Your Ration Book, 1943, 24 pages, EX...**$5.00**

Hungarian Cooking, 1979, hardcover, 64 pages, EX.....**$4.00**

I Hate To Cook Book, Peg Bracken, 1960, hardcover, 176 pages, EX...**$10.00**

Jack Bailey's What's Cookin', 1949, hardcover, 187 pages, EX...**$15.00**

Japanese American Cookbook, 1972, hardcover, 222 pages, EX...**$10.00**

Jello, Dessert Magic, 1944, 26 pages, EX **$8.00**

Jello, Make Ice Cream in a Jiffy!, 1932, 8 pages, EX.....**$5.00**

Joy of Cooking, Irma Rombauer, 1976, hardcover, 915 pages, EX...**$25.00**

Joy of Cooking, 1943, hardover, 884 pages, EX..........**$17.50**

Kellogg's, A New Way of Living, 1932, leaflet, 32 pages, G...**$6.00**

Kelvinator Book of Recipes, 1928, 32 pages, VG+ **$15.00**

Kerr Presents Let's Eat!, 1940, 22 pages, EX...............**$10.00**

Kraft, Cheese the Ideal Food, 1930s, 32 pages, VG+....**$8.00**

Kraft, Wonderful Ways To Serve Kraft Cottage Cheese, 1940s, leaflet, EX $2.00

Lipton, Souped Up Recipes From Lipton, 1978, spiral binding, 128 pages, EX $5.00

Lipton, The Secret's in the Soup, 1983, paperback, 128 pages, VG $5.50

Lobel Brothers Meat Cookbook, 1980, paperback, 254 pages, EX...$5.00

Lover's Dining, 1970, 47 pages, EX $3.00

Magic of Wheat Cookery, 1977, spiral binding, 146 pages, EX...$6.00

Mazola, Recipes for Your Good Health, leaflet, 6 pages ..$2.00

McCormick, How To Use Spices, 1958, 48 pages, EX ..$6.00

Minute Tapioca, Adding Variety to the Menu, 1925, leaflet, 16 pages, EX..$16.00

More Mom's Cookin', Les Blair, 1986, leaflet, 64 pages, VG $3.50

Mrs Knox Sugarless Desserts & Salads, leaflet, VG $1.50

Mrs Knox's Top 20 Delicious Salads & Desserts, 1942, 14 pages, EX..$10.00

Nancy Drew Cookbook, 1976, hardcover, 159 pages, EX...$25.00

Natural Cooking, 1971, leaflet, 47 pages, EX $20.00

New Casserole Cookery, Marian Tracey, 1967, hardcover, 229 pages, EX..$6.00

New Party Cakes for All Occasions, message from Betty Crocker inside front cover, ca 1934, 24 pages, EX $15.00

North American Hunting Club Wild Game Cookbook, 1991, paperback, 219 pages...$10.00

Northern Exposure Cookbook, 1993, paperback, 176 pages, EX...$15.00

Nut Cookbook, William Kaufman, 1964, hardcover, 194 pages, EX...$10.00

Ocean Spray Cranberry Juice Cocktail, 1950s, leaflet, VG...$3.00

Old Favorite Honey Recipes, 1945, 42 pages, VG $7.50

Pace Picante 40th Anniversary Recipe Collection, 1987, spiral binding, 158 pages, VG $6.50

Parkay Margarine, Flavor Touches, 1940s, leaflet, EX...$2.00

Parkay Margarine, New Recipes for Cookies, Cakes, 'n Muffins, 1950s, 15 pages, EX $3.00

Peanut Cookbook, Dorothy C Frank, 1976, hardcover, 110 pages, EX...$8.00

Pennsylvania Dutch Cooking, 1960, leaflet, 48 pages, EX ..$6.00

Pillsbury's, Ann Pillsbury's Baking Book, Includes the Winning Recipes, 1st Grand National, hardcover, 1950 ....$50.00

Pillsbury's, 1950 Grand National Recipe & Baking Contest, 100 Prize Winning Recipes...................................$65.00

Pillsbury's, 1950s Grand National Recipe & Baking Contest, Nos 3 through 10, each...$10.00

Pillsbury's, 1960s Grand National Recipe & Baking Contest, Nos 11 through 20, each $8.00

Pillsbury's, 1970s Grand National Recipe & Baking Contest, Nos 21 through 30, each $5.00

Pillsbury's Butter Cookie Booklet, 1961, leaflet, 22 pages, EX...$4.00

Pillsbury's Let's Have a Barbecue, paperback, 9x6", VG ..$3.50

Pillsbury's Recipes You'll Use Over & Over Again, leaflet ..$10.00

Pillsbury's 100 New Bundt Ideas, 1977, softcover, 90 pages, EX...$4.00

Pillsbury's 100 Prize-Winning Recipes, 2nd Grand National, 1951, from $15.00 to $20.00. (Photo courtesy Bob Allen)

President's Own White House Cookbook, 1973, hardcover, 110 pages, EX...$10.00

Queen of Hearts Cookbook, Peter Pauper Press, 1955, hardcover, 64 pages, EX $10.00

Recipes for Country Cookin' by Methodist Churches of Idaho, 1989, spiral binding, 72 pages, EX $6.00

Richard Nelson's American Cooking, 1983, hardcover, 445 pages, EX..$12.00

Robert L Green's Live With Style, 1978, hardcover, 282 pages, EX...$10.00

Roquefort Chefmanship Recipes, 1970, 39 pages, EX...$3.00

Royal Cookbook, 1939, 65 pages, EX $12.00

Saturday Evening Post's Time To Entertain Cookbook, 1978, hardcover, 306 pages, EX.......................................$8.00

Sealtest Food Advisor, 1942, leaflet, 11 pages, EX $3.00

Someone's in the Kitchen With Dinah, Dinah Shore, 1972, hardcover, 179 pages, EX.......................................$15.00

Spry, Aunty Jenny's 12 Pies Husbands Like Best, 1952, 20 pages, EX..$5.00

Star-Kist Tuna, Food and Fun, endorsed by Arthur Godfrey, 1953, $45.00. (Photo courtesy Bob Allen)

Star Kist Tuna, 22 pages, VG+ $2.50

Sun Maid, Downright Delicious Sun Maid Raisin Recipes, 1949, 32 pages, EX $10.00

Sunset Menu Cookbook, 1969, hardcover, 208 pages, EX..$5.00

Take a Can of Salmon, leaflet, 17 pages, VG+ $1.00

Twelve Days of Christmas Cookbook, Suzanne Huntley, 1965, hardcover, 143 pages, EX...........................$10.00

Utitarian Universalist Cookbook of Desserts, Montgomery AL, spiral binding, 382 pages, EX $8.00

Velvetta, Fresh Ideas, 1986, 29 pages, EX....................$2.00

Waring Cookbook for 8 Push Button Blender, 1967, 128 pages, EX...$6.00

Wesson Oil, Quicker Ways to Better Eating, 1955, 100 pages,
EX..**$5.00**

What Cooks at Stillmeadow, Gladys Taber, 1958, hardcover,
250 pages, EX...**$30.00**

What's for Dinner, 1975, paperback, 104 pages, EX.....**$4.00**

Williamsburg Art of Cookery, 1938, hardcover, 276 pages,
EX..**$20.00**

Working Couple's Cookbook, 1971, paperback, 175 pages,
EX..**$5.00**

World Book of Meat Dishes, 1965, hardcover, 127 pages,
EX..**$5.00**

World of Baking, Dolores Casella, 1968, hardcover, 371
pages, EX..**$10.00**

Wright's Mayonnaise, Recipes for Salads & Sandwiches,
1920s, leaflet, EX......................................**$4.00**

Young Children's Mix & Fix Cookbook, 1975, hardcover, 125
pages, EX...**$8.00**

Your Community Cookbook, 1949, hardcover, 395 pages,
EX..**$20.00**

Cookie Cutters

Cookie cutters have come into their own in recent years as worthy kitchen collectibles. Prices on many have risen astronomically, but a practiced eye can still sort out a good bargain. Advertising cutters and product premiums, especially in plastic, can still be found without too much effort. Aluminum cutters with painted wood handles are usually worth several dollars each, if in good condition. Red and green are the usual handle colors, but other colors are more highly prized by many. Hallmark plastic cookie cutters, especially those with painted backs, are always worth considering, if in good condition.

Be wary of modern tin cutters being sold for antique. Many present-day tinsmiths chemically antique their cutters, especially if done in a primitive style. These are often sold by others as 'very old.' Look closely because most tinsmiths today sign and date these cutters.

Molds, instead of cutting the cookie out, impressed a design into the dough. To learn more about both types (and many other old kitchenware gadgets as well), we recommend *300 Years of Kitchen Collectibles* by Linda Campbell Franklin and *Kitchen Antiques, 1790 to 1940*, by Kathryn McNerney. Also read *The Cookie Shaper's Bible* by Phyllis Wetherill and our advisor, Rosemary Henry.

Advisor: Rosemary Henry (See Directory, Cookie Cutters)

Newsletter: *Cookies*
Rosemary Henry
9610 Greenview Ln.
Manassas, VA 20109-3320; Subscription: $12.00 per year for 6 issues

Newsletter: *Cookie Crumbs*
Cookie Cutter Collectors Club
Ruth Capper
1167 Teal Rd. SW
Dellroy, OH 44620; 216-735-2839 or 202-966-0869

Animal Snacks, yellow soft plastic lion, elephant, hippo, and zebra, impression lines, Hallmark, 1978, MIP, $15.00. (Photo courtesy Rosemary Henry)

Chicken, aluminum, strap handle, 3½".........................**$5.00**
Christmas Tree, aluminum, strap handle, 4".................**$5.00**
Circus Animals, Hultzer, 1960s, MIP............................**$5.00**
Easter Duck w/Daisy, Hallmark, 1979, MIP..................**$5.00**
Easter Egg, Hallmark, 1981..**$5.00**
Easter Flower, Hallmark, 1980.......................................**$5.00**

Formay rabbit, machine-formed metal with self handle, ca 1930, 6", G, $10.00. (Photo courtesy Rosemary Henry)

Gingerbread Boy, blue or red, Betty Crocker Gingerbread
Mix **$3.50**
Halloween Cat, dark orange hard plastic w/eyelet, 1976 ..**$5.00**
Heart, tin, strap handle, marked Kreamer, 3¼".............**$7.50**
Heart, tin, strap handle, 2¼"..**$6.00**
Heart, tin, 2"..**$4.00**
KO Biscuit & Cookie, spring-action handle, VG...........**$8.00**
Lamb, aluminum, 4"...**$5.00**
Lion, anodized aluminum, strap handle, 4"..................**$3.00**
Lucy & Gift, blue hard plastic, Hallmark......................**$9.00**
Mr Peanut, blue, Planters Peanuts, set of 2.................**$40.00**
Mr Peanut, red, Planters Peanuts, set of 2...................**$25.00**
NFL Football Shaper, Hallmark, 1995, set of 10.........**$25.00**
Owl, gold soft plastic w/eyelet, Hallmark, 1980...........**$2.00**
Precious Moments, Christmas, pink plastic, Enesco, 1991, set
of 6, MIP..**$18.00**
Rabbit, aluminum, strap handle, 4" **$5.00**
Raggedy Ann & Andy, marked Bobbs-Merrill, Hallmark, 5",
set of 2...**$10.00**
Raggedy Ann & Andy, marked Bobbs-Merrill, Hallmark, 8",
set of 2...**$25.00**
Robin Hood Flour, various colors, marked, set of 7...**$35.00**
Santa, Hallmark, 1982, MIP..**$5.00**
Santa in Sleigh, Hallmark, 1979, MIP **$7.00**

Snoopy in Space Helmet, red hard plastic, Hallmark, 1971...**$25.00**
Snoopy w/Ball Ornament, green hard plastic, Hallmark ..**$9.00**
St Patrick's Day Hat w/Shamrocks, Hallmark, 1981, MIP..**$4.00**
Star, aluminum, 2¾"...**$2.50**
Sun Giant, graduated sun faces, Hallmark, 1981, set of 3..**$15.00**
Tom & Jerry, Lowe's, 1956, set of 6............................**$24.00**
Valentine Dove, Hallmark, 1979 ....**$8.00**
Valentine w/Love, Hallmark, 1981, MIP.....................**$8.00**

Cookie Jars

This is an area that for years saw an explosion of interest that resulted in some very high prices. Rare cookie jars sell for literally thousands of dollars. Even a common jar from a good manufacturer will fall into the $40.00 to $100.00 price range. At the top of the list are the Black-theme jars, then come the cartoon characters such as Popeye, Howdy Doody, or the Flintstones — in fact, any kind of a figural jar from an American pottery is collectible right now.

The American Bisque company was one of the largest producers of these jars from 1930 until the 1970s. Many of their jars have no marks at all; those that do are simply marked 'USA,' sometimes with a mold number. But their airbrushed colors are easy to spot, and collectors look for the molded-in wedge-shaped pads on their bases — these say 'American Bisque' to cookie jar buffs about as clearly as if they were marked.

The Brush Pottery (Ohio, 1946 – 71) made cookie jars that were decorated with the airbrush in many of the same colors used by American Bisque. These jars are strongly holding their values, and the rare ones continue to climb in price. McCoy was probably the leader in cookie-jar production. Even some of their very late jars bring high prices. Abingdon, Shawnee, and Red Wing all manufactured cookie jars, and there are lots of wonderful jars by many other companies. Joyce and Fred Roerig's books *The Collector's Encyclopedia of Cookie Jars, Books I, II, and III*, cover them all beautifully, and you won't want to miss Ermagene Westfall's *An Illustrated Value Guide to Cookie Jars II*. All are published by Collector Books.

Warning! The market place abounds with reproductions these days. Roger Jensen of Rockwood, Tennessee, is making a line of cookie jars as well as planters, salt and pepper shakers, and many other items which he marks McCoy. Because the 'real' McCoys never registered their trademark, he was able to receive federal approval to begin using this mark in 1992. Though he added '#93' to some of his pieces, the majority of his wares are undated. He is using old molds, and novice collectors are being fooled into buying the new for 'old' prices. Here are some of his reproductions that you should be aware of: McCoy Mammy, Mammy with Cauliflower, Clown Bust, Dalmatians, Indian Head, Touring Car, and Rocking Horse; Hull Little Red Riding Hood; Pearl China Mammy; and the Mosaic Tile Mammy. Recently he has been known to use the marks 'Brush-McCoy' (though this mark was never used on an authentic cookie jar) and 'B.J. Hull.' Several Brush jars have been reproduced — see *Schroeder's Antiques Price Guide* for information — and there are others.

Cookie jars from California are getting their fair share of attention right now, and then some! We've included several from companies such as Brayton Laguna, Treasure Craft, Vallona Starr, and Twin Winton. Roerig's books have information on all of these. Advisor Mike Ellis is the author of *Collector's Guide to Don Winton Designs* (Collector Books), and advisor Bernice Stamper has written *Vallona Starr Ceramics*, which we're sure you will also enjoy.

Advisors: Phil and Nyla Thurston, Fitz & Floyd (See Directory, Figural Ceramics); Pat and Ann Duncan, Holt Howard (See Directory, Holt Howard); Mike Ellis, Twin Winton (See Directory, California Pottery); Bernice Stamper, Vallona Starr (See Directory, California Pottery); Lois Wildman, Vandor (See Directory, Vandor).

Newsletter: *The Cookie Jar Express Newsline*
Paradise Publications
P.O. Box 221, Mayview, MO 64071-0221

Newsletter: *Cookie Jarrin' With Joyce*
R.R. 2, Box 504
Walterboro, SC 29488

A Company of Two, Higby Butler, from $85 to........**$125.00**
A Company of Two, Sister Chubby Cheeks, from $135 to..**$170.00**
A Little Company, Fats, from $200 to **$250.00**
A Little Company, Santa Fe Station, from $125 to **$150.00**
Abindon, Windmill, #678 ....**$185.00**
Abingdon, Baby, Black, decorated, #561...................**$300.00**
Abingdon, Bo Peep, #694 ....**$240.00**
Abingdon, Choo Choo (locomotive), #651................**$150.00**
Abingdon, Clock, #653, from $85 to **$100.00**
Abingdon, Daisy, #677, 1949 ....**$45.00**
Abingdon, Hippo, decorated, #549, 1942 ....**$225.00**
Abingdon, Hobby Horse, #602, from $185 to **$225.00**
Abingdon, Humpty Dumpty, decorated, #663..........**$250.00**
Abingdon, Jack-in-Box, #611 ....**$275.00**
Abingdon, Little Girl, #693, from $60 to **$80.00**
Abingdon, Miss Muffet, #622 ....**$250.00**
Abingdon, Money Bag, #588, 1947.............................**$70.00**
Abingdon, Mother Goose, #695...................................**$295.00**
Abingdon, Old Lady, green, #471, rare.....................**$195.00**
Abingdon, Old Lady, plain or decorated, #471, 1942.**$210.00**

Abingdon, Pineapple, #664, from $75.00 to $95.00.

Abingdon, Pumpkin, #674, 1949 ....**$310.00**

Abingdon, Three Bears, #696 ....$120.00
Abingdon, Witch, #692, minimum value $350.00
Advertising, Avon House w/lady at door, from $175 to.......$225.00
Advertising, Avon Panda Bear, upside down, from $65 to $100.00
Advertising, Benjamin & Medwin, Blue Bonnet Sue, from $45 to $70.00
Advertising, Benjamin & Medwin, Little Green Sprout .$90.00
Advertising, Benjamin & Medwin, Mr Peanut, from $65 to.$90.00
Advertising, Benjamin & Medwin, Pillsbury Doughboy Funfetti, from $50 to................................$65.00
Advertising, Coca-Cola Polar Bear, no sweater, from $30 to $45.00
Advertising, Disneyland Cinderella Castle, from $65 to ..$95.00
Advertising, F&F, Ernie head, plastic, from $95 to....$125.00
Advertising, Famous Amos Bag of Cookies, from $55 to.$80.00
Advertising, Heritage Mint, Mushroom House, recent grocery store premium $30.00
Advertising, Holiday Designs, Almost Home House, from $70 to..$110.00
Advertising, Little Debbie, glass cylinder, from $25 to..$35.00
Advertising, Mrs Fields Cookie Sack, from $35 to.......$50.00
Advertising, Nabisco Milk Bone, figural bone, from $30 to..$60.00
Advertising, Nabisco Oreo Cookie Stack, from $30 to..$60.00
Advertising, Nestles', Disneyland's 40th Anniversary Sleeping Beauty Castle..............................$75.00
Advertising, Pillsbury Doughboy, Benjamin & Medwin, 1988, from $35 to..$50.00
Advertising, Proctor & Gamble USA Soccer Ball, from $40 to..$55.00
Advertising, Wade China, Tetley Tea, cylinder w/head...$180.00
Aladdin, Paddy Pig, from $25 to $40.00
Alfano Art Pottery, King Arthur, from $250 to..........$275.00
American Bisque, Beehive, plain................................$50.00

American Bisque, Blackboard Saddle, marked USA, from $275.00 to $300.00.

American Bisque, Butter Churn, w/flowering vine $30.00
American Bisque, Castle, marked Cardinal 310 USA ..$175.00
American Bisque, Cat, w/tail finial, (Ungemach) marked USA $145.00
American Bisque, Collegiate Owl, marked Cookies, gold trim..$150.00
American Bisque, Cookieville Bus Co $350.00
American Bisque, Cow & Moon (flasher).................$995.00
American Bisque, Cow/Lamb Turnabout..................$195.00

American Bisque, Crowing Rooster, spaced tail..........$85.00
American Bisque, Dancing Pig, multicolor dotted dress ..$195.00
American Bisque, Farmer Pig $145.00
American Bisque, French Chef.................................$125.00
American Bisque, Gift Box.......................................$150.00
American Bisque, Jack-In-The-Box $150.00
American Bisque, Kitten on Quilt Base, marked Cookies..$175.00
American Bisque, Moon Rocket, marked Cookies Out of This World $275.00
American Bisque, Oaken Bucket, spoon finial, bail handle $195.00
American Bisque, Pennsylvania Dutch Boy, in straw hat.$425.00
American Bisque, Sad Clown, I Want Some Cookies, marked Cardinal USA..$125.00
American Bisque, Seal on Igloo $350.00
American Bisque, Sentry, in striped guard house.....$135.00
American Bisque, Stern Wheeler, tugboat $250.00
American Bisque, Sweethearts, 2 children under umbrella ..$350.00
American Bisque, Yarn Doll, gold trim.....................$250.00
American Greetings, Strawberry Shortcake, from $700 to..$750.00
American Pottery/Celadon, Owl, from $20 to $30.00
Applause, '57 Chevy, from $80 to.............................$100.00
Applause, Sylvester Head w/Tweety, from $75 to......$90.00
Applause, Tasmanian Devil, from $65 to....................$80.00
Benjamin & Medwin, Snoopy on Doghouse, from $45 to....$60.00
Brayton Laguna, Calico Dog.....................................$595.00
Brayton Laguna, Christina (Swedish Maiden)............$425.00
Brayton Laguna, Gingerbread House..........................$250.00
Brayton Laguna, Mammy, burgundy base, turquoise bandana, not reproduction................................$1,300.00
Brayton Laguna, Matilda, blue & green skirt.............$475.00
Brayton Laguna, Provincial Lady...............................$295.00
Brayton Laguna, Wedding Ring Granny (Grandma), not reproduction..$500.00
Brechner, Donald Duck head, from $400 to $500.00
Brush, Boy w/Balloons, minimum value...................$850.00
Brush, Chick in Nest...$400.00
Brush, Cinderella Pumpkin, #W32 ....$250.00
Brush, Circus Horse, green.......................................$950.00
Brush, Clown Bust, #W49, minimum value...............$325.00
Brush, Cookie House, #W31......................................$125.00
Brush, Covered Wagon, dog finial, #W30, minimum value..$550.00
Brush, Cow w/Cat on Back, purple, minimum value..$1,000.00
Brush, Davy Crockett, gold trim, minimum value $800.00
Brush, Davy Crockett, no gold, marked USA...........$300.00
Brush, Dog & Basket..$300.00
Brush, Donkey w/Cart, ears down, gray, #W33 ....$400.00
Brush, Donkey w/Cart, ears up, #W33, minimum value ..$800.00
Brush, Elephant w/Baby Bonnet & Ice Cream Cone, white $500.00
Brush, Fish, #W52...$500.00
Brush, Formal Pig, green hat & coat..........................$300.00
Brush, Gas Lamp, #K1..$75.00
Brush, Granny, pink apron, blue dots on skirt.........$325.00
Brush, Granny, plain skirt, minimum value $400.00
Brush, Happy Bunny, white, #W25............................$225.00
Brush, Hen on Basket $125.00
Brush, Hillbilly Frog, minimum value, not reproduction $4,500.00

Brush, Little Angel $800.00
Brush, Little Boy Blue, gold trim, #K25, sm..............$700.00
Brush, Little Girl, #017..$800.00
Brush, Little Red Riding Hood, gold trim, marked, lg, minimum value $850.00
Brush, Little Red Riding Hood, no gold, #K24 USA, sm..$550.00
Brush, Old Clock, #W10 ....$165.00
Brush, Peter Pan, gold trim, lg $800.00
Brush, Sitting Pig $400.00

Brush, Squirrel on Log, marked USA, from $90.00 to $100.00. (Photo courtesy Ermagene Westfall)

Brush, Stylized Siamese, #W41 ....$400.00
Brush, Treasure Chest, #W28......................................$150.00
California Originals, Bear, #2648 ....$75.00
California Originals, Bulldog, from $35 to..................$50.00
California Originals, Monkey w/Bananas $160.00
California Originals, Sheriff w/hole in hat, from $40 to...$60.00
California Originals, Strawberry Jar $25.00

California Originals, Superman, marked Cal. Original USA 876 D.C. Comics, Inc., 1978, from $425.00 to $475.00. (Photo courtesy Ermagene Westfall)

California Originals, Taxi Cab, from $85 to $125.00
Cardinal, Sack 'O Cookies, from $45 to......................$60.00
Certified International, Barney Rubble.........................$45.00
Certified International, Daffy Duck, from $40 to $50.00
Certified International, Neiman-Marcus '93 Panda Bear Cowboy $125.00
Certified International, Wyle E Coyote, from $40 to...$50.00
Clay Art, Chicken Racer, from $50 to...........................$65.00

Clay Art, Humpty Dumpty, from $100 to $135.00
Clay Art, Wizard of Oz, from $75 to $110.00
Cleminson, Carrot Head...$165.00
Cleminson, Christmas House $150.00
Cleminson, Gingerbread House..................................$200.00
Cleminson, The Way to a Man's Heart, heart shape.$175.00
Coco Dowley, Polar Bear, from $40 to $45.00
Cooks Bazare, Cat, from $35 to..................................$45.00
Cumberland Ware, WC Fields, from $600 to.............$750.00
Dayton Hudson, Christmas Snowman, from $60 to....$75.00
Dayton Hudson, Pinocchio..$60.00
DeForest, Buddha, from $100 to $145.00
DeForest, Clown, wood grain......................................$90.00
Delft, Dutch Girl, from $45 to $55.00
Demand Marketing, Cookie Monster, from $50 to......$60.00
Department 56, Fishing Creel Basket, from $45 to.....$65.00
Doranne of California, Basset Hound, marked J1 USA...$50.00
Doranne of California, Dinosaur, from $200 to.........$250.00

Doranne of California, Fancy Cat, from $35.00 to $45.00.

Doranne of California, Ketchup Bottle, from $55 to...$70.00
Doranne of California, School Bus.............................$200.00
Doranne of California, Strawberry Pie, from $45 to ...$50.00

Enesco, Betsy Ross, $225.00. (Photo courtesy Pat Duncan)

Enesco, Century Brothers Circus Wagon, from $100 to ..$150.00
Enesco, Coca-Cola Vending Machine, from $50 to $60.00
Enesco, Gingerbread House, from $30 to....................$40.00
Enesco, Here Comes Trouble, from $175 to $200.00
Enesco, Human Bean, from $140 to $150.00
Enesco, Jack & the Bean Stalk, from $40 to...............$50.00
Enesco, Mother in Kitchen (Kitchen Prayer Lady), blue & white $495.00

Enesco, Precious Moments Rose Basket, from $60 to ..**$75.00**

Enesco, Precious Moments Sugar Town Tea Time, from $50 to..**$65.00**

Enesco, Woodland Commune, from $125 to............**$145.00**

Expressive Designs, Mustang Car, from $85 to **$115.00**

Fitz & Floyd, Ballooning Bunnies................................**$85.00**

Fitz & Floyd, Berry Patch Lamb, from $50 to............**$65.00**

Fitz & Floyd, Black Boy in Turban **$600.00**

Fitz & Floyd, Bunny Bloomers, from $150 to **$175.00**

Fitz & Floyd, Bunny Bonnet.......................................**$110.00**

Fitz & Floyd, Bunny Hop Pink Cadillac...................**$295.00**

Fitz & Floyd, Busy Bunnies, from $100 to................**$125.00**

Fitz & Floyd, Car w/Flat Tire.....................................**$275.00**

Fitz & Floyd, Cat Holding Fish **$65.00**

Fitz & Floyd, Caterine the Great, Reigning Cats & Dogs Series, 1990 ....**$125.00**

Fitz & Floyd, Cinderella Fairy Godmother................**$100.00**

Fitz & Floyd, Cookie Factory **$85.00**

Fitz & Floyd, Cotton Tailor's Hatbox, from $65 to......**$90.00**

Fitz & Floyd, Dot Kangaroo.......................................**$175.00**

Fitz & Floyd, English Garden Wheelbarrow, from $100 to...**$125.00**

Fitz & Floyd, Famous Amos, signed **$150.00**

Fitz & Floyd, Halloween Hoedown Witch, w/cauldron, cat & lizard, from $100 to **$140.00**

Fitz & Floyd, Halloween Witch, black robe, basket on arm, from $100 to **$130.00**

Fitz & Floyd, Hampshire Hog......................................**$175.00**

Fitz & Floyd, Harvest Farm Piggly Pig.......................**$135.00**

Fitz & Floyd, Hat Box Bunnies....................................**$160.00**

Fitz & Floyd, Hat Party Bear......................................**$175.00**

Fitz and Floyd, Haunted House, $150.00. (Photo courtesy Pat Duncan)

Fitz & Floyd, Hippo Limpix, from $60 to **$85.00**

Fitz & Floyd, Holiday Leaves Deer, from $160 to.....**$195.00**

Fitz & Floyd, Hydrangea Bear **$150.00**

Fitz & Floyd, Jungle Elephant....................................**$250.00**

Fitz & Floyd, Kittens of Knightsbridge......................**$100.00**

Fitz & Floyd, Man Playing Bass Viol (older jar)........**$195.00**

Fitz & Floyd, Mayfair Bunny, from $80 to..................**$95.00**

Fitz & Floyd, Old McDonald's Cow, from $75 to **$100.00**

Fitz & Floyd, Old Woman in Shoe, from $85 to **$110.00**

Fitz & Floyd, Paint Party Hedda Gobbler Turkey **$80.00**

Fitz & Floyd, Panda w/plaid scarf & holly-decorated red hat..**$150.00**

Fitz & Floyd, Parrots...**$15.00**

Fitz & Floyd, Petting Zoo Hippo...............................**$150.00**

Fitz & Floyd, Pink Dinosaur, from $120 to...............**$140.00**

Fitz & Floyd, Plaid Teddy (figural bear)...................**$175.00**

Fitz & Floyd, Polka-Dot Witch, from $250 to...........**$325.00**

Fitz & Floyd, Prunella Pig..**$125.00**

Fitz & Floyd, Queen of Hearts **$175.00**

Fitz & Floyd, Rolls Royce, Christmas, Signature collection, 1986 ....**$895.00**

Fitz & Floyd, Santa & Reindeer in Rolls Royce, lg....**$875.00**

Fitz & Floyd, Santa in Airplane, lg, from $1,800 to..**$2,000.00**

Fitz & Floyd, Santa in Chair......................................**$125.00**

Fitz & Floyd, Santa in Sleigh, from $150 to...............**$175.00**

Fitz & Floyd, Santa on Motorcycle, from $500 to **$600.00**

Fitz & Floyd, Scarlet O'Hare, from $100 to **$125.00**

Fitz & Floyd, Sheepdog..**$125.00**

Fitz & Floyd, Sheriff, black & white full figure, minimum value **$450.00**

Fitz & Floyd, Sock Hoppers, from $275 to................**$300.00**

Fitz & Floyd, Southwest Santa, from $500 to **$575.00**

Fitz & Floyd, The Runaway (older jar) **$475.00**

Fitz & Floyd, Three Little Kittens...............................**$175.00**

Fitz & Floyd, Wanda the Witch...................................**$190.00**

Fitz & Floyd, Woodland Santa Centerpiece, from $475 to...**$500.00**

Fredericksburg Art Pottery (FAPCO), Bartender, from $250 to...**$300.00**

Fredericksburg Art Pottery (FAPCO), Hen w/Chick, from $45 to..**$55.00**

Ganz Co, Little Cheezer, from $100 to......................**$125.00**

Gilner, Mother Goose, from $250 to **$275.00**

Gilner, Rooster, from $60 to..**$70.00**

Gorham, Tom & Jerry, from $275 to **$325.00**

Grant Howard, School Bus, from $50 to **$75.00**

Great American Housewares, Transformer, from $160 to .**$190.00**

Gustin, Wedding Pineapple, from $25 to....................**$45.00**

Hallmark, Christmas Bear, from $60 to **$75.00**

Hallmark, Maxine...**$125.00**

Hallmark, Shirt Tales Ricky Raccoon Bandit, from $250 to ....:...**$300.00**

Happy Memories, James Dean **$300.00**

Happy Memories, Marilyn Monroe.............................**$300.00**

Hearth & Home, Carousel Horse, from $50 to............**$70.00**

Hearth & Home, Stagecoach, from $60 to...................**$75.00**

Hearth & Home, Wild 'Bull' Hickok, from $45 to.......**$60.00**

Hirsch, Covered Wagon, from $65 to..........................**$85.00**

Holiday Designs, Snoopy, from $60 to **$75.00**

Home Collection, Goldilocks & Three Bears, from $40 to..**$55.00**

Home Collection, Old World Santa, from $50 to **$65.00**

House of Lloyd, Christmas Sleigh, from $30 to...........**$45.00**

House of Webster, Coffee Grinder, from $30 to..........**$35.00**

Hull, Daisy, cylinder, from $35 to **$45.00**

Inarco, Raggedy Andy, from $60 to **$70.00**

International Silver, Norfin Troll, from $75 to **$100.00**

Japan, Raggedy Andy Bust..**$450.00**

JC Miller, Grandfather Washington, from $100 to .**$135.00**

JC Miller, Sister Ruth, from $115 to **$140.00**

Judy of California, Sweet Shop, from $35 to..............**$50.00**

Lane, Cowboy, from $450 to **$550.00**

Lane, Sheriff, from $650 to **$700.00**

Larry Zimpleman, Mary & Her Lamb, from $350 to .**$360.00**

Lefton, Santa in Rocking Chair, from $75 to..............**$95.00**
Lillian Vernon, School Bus...**$35.00**
Lotus, Witch **$50.00**
Lotus International, Cowboy Santa, from $55 to.........**$60.00**
Lotus International, Train Santa..................................**$60.00**
Louisville Stoneware, Belle of Louisville Paddle Boat, from
    $185 to..**$200.00**
Macy's Dept Store, Covered Wagon, from $45 to.......**$60.00**
Maddux of California, Bear, #2101 ....**$75.00**
Maddux of California, Beatrix Potter Rabbit.............**$100.00**
Maddux of California, Calory Hippy **$300.00**
Maddux of California, Humpty Dumpty, #2113 ....**$300.00**
Maddux of California, Koala **$75.00**
Maddux of California, Raggedy Andy, #2108 ....**$300.00**
Maddux of California, Scottie.....................................**$75.00**
Maddux of California, Snowman **$75.00**
Maddux of California, Strawberry...............................**$35.00**
Maddux of California, Walrus **$65.00**
Market Square, Hound Dog, from $25 to **$30.00**
Marshall Field, Frango Mint Chip Cookies, from $100 to..**$125.00**
Maurice of California, Koala Bear, from $75 to...........**$95.00**
Maurice of California, Train, from $60 to **$65.00**
McCoy, Animal Crackers, from $100 to **$120.00**
McCoy, Apollo Age, minimum value......................**$1,400.00**
McCoy, Apple, 1950-64, from $50 to..........................**$65.00**
McCoy, Apple on Basketweave....................................**$70.00**
McCoy, Asparagus..**$50.00**
McCoy, Astronauts..**$650.00**
McCoy, Bananas, from $100 to....................................**$125.00**
McCoy, Barnum's Animals **$400.00**

McCoy, Baseball Boy, $225.00. (Photo courtesy Judy Posner)

McCoy, Basket of Eggs..**$60.00**
McCoy, Basket of Potatoes, from $30 to.....................**$50.00**
McCoy, Bear, cookie in vest, no 'Cookies' **$95.00**
McCoy, Bicentennial Milk Can, silver or brown, each..**$30.00**
McCoy, Black Kettle, w/immovable bail, hand-painted flow-
    ers **$40.00**
McCoy, Blue Willow Pitcher.......................................**$50.00**
McCoy, Bobby Baker, from $80 to..............................**$100.00**
McCoy, Bugs Bunny, cylinder **$225.00**
McCoy, Burlap Sack, from $25 to................................**$35.00**
McCoy, Caboose..**$165.00**
McCoy, Cat on Coal Scuttle **$200.00**
McCoy, Chairman of the Board, minimum value......**$400.00**

McCoy, Chef..**$140.00**
McCoy, Chilly Willy **$85.00**
McCoy, Chinese Lantern...**$75.00**
McCoy, Chipmunk..**$150.00**
McCoy, Clown (Little), from $80 to...........................**$100.00**
McCoy, Clown Bust **$85.00**
McCoy, Clyde Dog..**$200.00**
McCoy, Coca-Cola Can, from $75 to **$100.00**
McCoy, Coca-Cola Jug, from $60 to **$85.00**
McCoy, Coffee Grinder..**$45.00**
McCoy, Coffee Mug...**$40.00**
McCoy, Colonial Fireplace **$95.00**
McCoy, Cookie Barrel..**$40.00**
McCoy, Cookie Boy..**$225.00**
McCoy, Cookie Cabin, from $100 to............................**$125.00**
McCoy, Cookie Jug, double loop.................................**$30.00**
McCoy, Cookie Jug, single loop, 2-tone green rope...**$25.00**
McCoy, Cookie Log **$75.00**
McCoy, Cookie Safe...**$65.00**
McCoy, Cookstove, black, from $25 to **$50.00**
McCoy, Corn **$200.00**
McCoy, Covered Wagon..**$150.00**
McCoy, Cylinder, w/red flowers **$45.00**
McCoy, Dalmatians in Rocking Chair..........................**$450.00**
McCoy, Drum...**$100.00**
McCoy, Duck on Basketweave, from $75 to.............**$100.00**
McCoy, Dutch Boy...**$55.00**
McCoy, Dutch Boy & Girl, image on each side, rare ..**$125.00**
McCoy, Dutch Treat Barn...**$75.00**
McCoy, Eagle on Basket..**$35.00**
McCoy, Elephant..**$200.00**
McCoy, Elephant w/Split Trunk, rare, minimum value...**$450.00**
McCoy, Engine, black...**$175.00**
McCoy, Fireplace (Colonial)..**$95.00**
McCoy, Flowerpot, plastic flower on top **$500.00**
McCoy, Football Boy..**$225.00**
McCoy, Forbidden Fruit..**$75.00**
McCoy, Friendship...**$250.00**
McCoy, Frog on Stump **$45.00**
McCoy, Frontier Family **$60.00**
McCoy, Fruit in Bushel Basket.....................................**$80.00**
McCoy, Gingerbread Boy, cylindrical.........................**$75.00**
McCoy, Globe **$325.00**
McCoy, Grandfather Clock **$80.00**
McCoy, Granny **$85.00**
McCoy, Green Pepper, from $35 to..............................**$45.00**
McCoy, Happy Face **$75.00**
McCoy, Honey Bear **$120.00**
McCoy, Humpty Dumpty, decal..................................**$100.00**
McCoy, Indian..**$400.00**
McCoy, Kangaroo, blue..**$300.00**
McCoy, Keebler Tree House, from $75 to **$95.00**
McCoy, Kissing Penguins...**$110.00**
McCoy, Kittens (2) on Low Basket, minimum value ..**$800.00**
McCoy, Kookie Kettle, black **$45.00**
McCoy, Lemon...**$50.00**
McCoy, Liberty Bell...**$100.00**
McCoy, Mac Dog..**$95.00**
McCoy, Mammy, 'Cookies' on base **$300.00**

McCoy, Monk $75.00
McCoy, Mr & Mrs Owl $110.00
McCoy, Mushrooms on Stump, from $25 to $40.00
McCoy, Oaken Bucket $35.00
McCoy, Pears on Basketweave $70.00
McCoy, Picnic Basket, from $75 to $85.00
McCoy, Pineapple $100.00
McCoy, Pirate's Chest $110.00
McCoy, Popeye, cylinder $225.00
McCoy, Potbellied Stove, black, from $25 to $50.00
McCoy, Rabbit on Stump $45.00
McCoy, Red Bird on Burlap Sack $40.00
McCoy, Rooster, white, 1970-74 ....$75.00
McCoy, Snoopy on Doghouse $295.00
McCoy, Snow Bear $100.00
McCoy, Spaniel in Doghouse, pup finial $295.00
McCoy, Squirrel on Stump $40.00
McCoy, Stagecoach, minimum value $1,000.00
McCoy, Strawberry, 1955-57 ....$55.00
McCoy, Strawberry, 1971-75 ....$60.00
McCoy, Tepee, straight top $350.00
McCoy, Timmy the Tortoise $40.00
McCoy, Tomato $55.00
McCoy, Touring Car $130.00
McCoy, Traffic Light $65.00
McCoy, Tulip on Flowerpot $225.00
McCoy, Upside Down Bear, panda $75.00
McCoy, Wedding Jar $125.00
McCoy, Woodsy Owl $300.00
McCoy, Wren House $175.00
McMe, Cathy $150.00
McMe, Roy Rogers or Dale Evans, each $200.00
Metlox, Bluebird on Stump, glaze decoration, from $150
  to $175.00
Metlox, Calico Cat, green w/pink ribbon, from $300 to .$325.00
Metlox, Chef Pierre Mouse, from $100 to $125.00
Metlox, Cook Mammy, yellow, from $450 to $500.00
Metlox, Cookie Boy, from $325 to $350.00
Metlox, Cow, purple w/pink flowers & butterfly, yellow bell,
  from $600 to $700.00
Metlox, Dina-Stegasaurus, any color except lavender, from
  $150 to $175.00
Metlox, Dottie Hippo, white w/yellow dots, minimum
  value $500.00
Metlox, Dutch Boy, from $300 to $325.00
Metlox, Golden Delicious Apple, from $125 to $150.00
Metlox, Grapefruit, from $175 to $200.00
Metlox, Happy the Clown, minimum value $350.00
Metlox, Kangaroo, minimum value $1,000.00
Metlox, Lamb, white, from $275 to $300.00
Metlox, Little Piggy, bisque, from $150 to $175.00
Metlox, Loveland, from $65 to $75.00
Metlox, Merry Go Round, blue, white & green, from $200
  to $225.00
Metlox, Mouse Mobile, color glazed, from $175 to ..$200.00
Metlox, Noah's Ark, bisque, from $125 to $150.00
Metlox, Pear, yellow, from $150 to $175.00
Metlox, Pumpkin, boy on lid, minimum value $500.00
Metlox, Rag Doll, boy, from $200 to $225.00

Metlox, Rex-Tyrannosaurus Rex, rose, from $150 to ..$175.00
Metlox, Scottie Dog, white, from $175 to $200.00

Metlox, Slenderella Pig, $150.00. (Photo courtesy Carl Gibbs)

Metlox, Space Rocket, minimum value $1,000.00
Metlox, Teddy Bear, brown, from $45 to $50.00
Metlox, Topsy, red polka dots, minimum value $800.00
Metlox, Tulip, minimum value $500.00
Metlox, Woodpecker on Acorn, from $375 to $400.00
Monmouth, Cookie Jug, from $15 to $25.00
Montgomery Ward, Lady Chef Hippo $30.00
NAPCO, Little Bo Peep, from $225 to $250.00
NAPCO, Miss Cutie Pie, from $225 to $275.00
Neiman Marcus, King Bear, from $85 to $100.00
Newcor, Cookie Monster $45.00
Newcor, Ernie, from $55 to $70.00
Newcor, Ernie, w/black or blond hair $75.00
Nintendo, Princess, from $35 to $45.00
Norcrest, Chipmunk $65.00
North American Ceramics, Andretti Race Car, from $300
  to $350.00
North American Ceramics, Porsche Convertible, from $100
  to $125.00
NS Gustin, Snowman, gold trim $45.00
Omnibus, Cabbage Patch Rabbit, from $25 to $35.00
Omnibus, European Santa $50.00
Omnibus, Halloween Pumpkin, from $45 to $50.00
Omnibus, Pirate, from $50 to $75.00
Omnibus, Russian Santa, from $60 to $80.00
Omnibus, Studebaker, from $80 to $110.00
Otagiri, Cook w/Spoon, from $20 to $25.00
Otagiri, Penguin, from $150 to $175.00
Otagiri, Santa's Cookie House, from $40 to $55.00
Pacific Stoneware, Dog, from $45 to $55.00
Pamona, Alien Pig, from $35 to $50.00
Pan American Art, Bartender, from $250 to $300.00
Pantry Pride, Tomato, from $50 to $65.00
Papal, Cathy, from $75 to $100.00
People Lovers, Rooster, from $45 to $50.00
Pfaltzgraff, Chef, from $425 to $475.00
Pfaltzgraff, Derby Dan, from $225 to $275.00
Pottery Guild, Dutch Girl, from $65 to $85.00
Pottery Guild, Girl Holding Chest, from $125 to $145.00
Purinton, Apple, from $75 to $100.00

Red Wing, Chef (Pierre), brown..................$195.00
Red Wing, Chef (Pierre), pink, marked $450.00
Red Wing, Crock, white $60.00
Red Wing, Friar Tuck, green, marked..................$295.00
Red Wing, Grapes, cobalt or dark purple $450.00
Red Wing, Jack Frost..................$750.00
Red Wing, King of Tarts, pink w/blue & black trim,
  marked $950.00
Red Wing, Pineapple, yellow $200.00
Red Wing, Queen of Tarts, marked $550.00
Regal China, Cat..................$425.00
Regal China, Clown, green collar..................$675.00
Regal China, Churn Boy..................$275.00

Regal China, Davy Crockett, $550.00.

Regal China, Dutch Girl, peach trim..................$800.00
Regal China, Fifi Poodle..................$650.00
Regal China, French Chef..................$375.00
Regal China, Hubert Lion..................$775.00
Regal China, Little Miss Muffett..................$385.00
Regal China, Old McDonald's Barn..................$275.00
Regal China, Oriental Lady w/Baskets..................$600.00
Regal China, Toby Cookies..................$750.00
Regal China, Uncle Mistletoe..................$850.00
Rick Wisecarver, Christmas Day, from $200 to..........$225.00
Rick Wisecarver, Cookstove Mammy, from $150 to..$200.00
Rick Wisecarver, Geronimo, from $175 to..................$200.00
Rick Wisecarver, Hill Folk, from $200 to..................$225.00
Rick Wisecarver, Snow White, from $200 to............$250.00
Robinson Ransbottom, Cow Jumped Over Moon.....$275.00
Robinson Ransbottom, Sheriff Pig, w/gold trim, from $150
  to..................$175.00
Robinson Ransbottom, Wise Owl (Hootie), gold trim, from
  $150 to..................$175.00
Roman Ceramics, C-3PO..................$450.00
Roman Ceramics, R2-D2, from $175 to..................$200.00
Rose Collection, Cotton Ginny, from $140 to............$150.00
Rose Collection, Watermelon Girl, from $150 to.......$175.00
Schmid, Gingerbread House Bakery, from $55 to $65.00
Schmid, Pumbaa, musical..................$150.00
Schmid, 101 Dalmatians, from $100 to..................$135.00
Sears, Mickey Mouse Driving Car, from $300 to.......$350.00
Share the Joy, Santa Claus, from $55 to..................$60.00
Shawnee, Cottage, marked USA 6, minimum value...$650.00
Shawnee, Dutch Boy, white w/blue pants & trim, marked
  USA, minimum value..................$80.00

Shawnee, Dutch Girl, green, marked Great Northern 1026,
  minimum value..................$250.00
Shawnee, Dutch Girl, plain white head & bodice, marked
  USA, minimum value..................$50.00
Shawnee, Jug, Pennsylvania Dutch design, marked USA,
  minimum value..................$150.00
Shawnee, Muggsy, decals & gold trim, marked Pat Muggsy
  USA, minimum value..................$550.00
Shawnee, Puss 'N Boots, cold-painted trim, minimum
  value $150.00

Shawnee, Puss 'n Boots, gold trim, minimum value, $375.00. (Photo courtesy Marilyn Dipboye)

Shawnee, Sailor Boy, decals & gold trim, marked USA, min-
  imum value $550.00
Shawnee, Smiley the Pig, blue bib, marked USA, minimum
  value $150.00
Shawnee, Smiley the Pig, mums, gold trim, marked USA,
  minimum value..................$325.00
Shawnee, Snowflake, bean pot, yellow, marked USA, mini-
  mum value..................$50.00
Shawnee, Winnie the Pig, peach collar, minimum value..$225.00
Shawnee, Winnie the Pig, red collar & gold trim, marked
  USA, minimum value..................$350.00
Sierra Vista, Circus Wagon, w/head..................$200.00
Sierra Vista, Clown Bust, from $55..................$75.00
Sierra Vista, Elephant, from $95 to..................$110.00

Sierra Vista, Tugboat, from $150.00 to $165.00.

Sierra Vista, Train, from $100 to..................$125.00
Sigma, Beaver Fireman, from $250 to..................$300.00
Sigma, Cat Playing Guitar, from $165 to..................$180.00
Sigma, Cat Sitting Upright w/Kitten..................$485.00
Sigma, Christmas Tree, from $150 to..................$175.00

Sigma, Kabuki Dancer, from $200 to **$225.00**

Sigma, Kliban Cat in Long Pants, from $165 to **$180.00**

Sigma, Miss Piggy on Couch.................................**$85.00**

Sigma, Mom Cat, from $335 to.............................**$360.00**

Sigma, Panda Chef, from $100 to..........................**$135.00**

Sigma, Santa w/Toy Sack, from $60 to **$75.00**

Sigma, Wind in the Willows, from $125 to...............**$150.00**

Star Jars, Tin Man, from $175 to...........................**$200.00**

Starnes, Gangster Car, from $150 to.......................**$175.00**

Starnes, Noah's Ark, from $195 to.........................**$235.00**

Storyteller Art, Cowboy Boot, from $60 to **$80.00**

Taiwan, Hippo, from $40 to **$50.00**

Takahashi, Granny, from $45 to **$60.00**

Terrace Ceramics, Fluffy Cat **$25.00**

Terrace Ceramics, Muggsy Dog, from $95 to **$120.00**

Terrace Ceramics, Smiley Pig, from $100 to..............**$110.00**

Treasure Craft, Aladdin Genie Bust, from $70 to **$90.00**

Treasure Craft, Big Al, Disney, from $125 to............**$165.00**

Treasure Craft, Birdhouse.....................................**$45.00**

Treasure Craft, Bulldog Cafe, Disney, from $150 to .**$165.00**

Treasure Craft, Cactus, from $35 to **$50.00**

Treasure Craft, Cruisin' Dog, discontinued **$95.00**

Treasure Craft, Dopey, from $40 to........................**$55.00**

Treasure Craft, Fozzie Bear **$45.00**

Treasure Craft, Gardener Bunny.............................**$55.00**

Treasure Craft, Ice-Cream Cone, from $45 to **$65.00**

Treasure Craft, Jackpot Slot Machine, from $50 to......**$75.00**

Treasure Craft, Katrina, from $450 to **$475.00**

Treasure Craft, Kermit the Frog, playing banjo, from $55 to....**$70.00**

Treasure Craft, Mrs Owl, from $40 to **$50.00**

Treasure Craft, Nick at Nite/Nickelodeon, from $400 to ..**$475.00**

Treasure Craft, Noah's Ark, from $50 to **$75.00**

Treasure Craft, Pink Panther, w/certificate of authenticity......**$250.00**

Treasure Craft, Pluto in Doghouse, Disney, limited edition...**$250.00**

Treasure Craft, Storyteller Bear, from $50 to **$75.00**

Treasure Craft, Sweetheart Cat, from $50 to...............**$75.00**

Treasure Craft, Tugboat, from $50 to **$75.00**

Treasure Craft, Tulip Time, from $45 to **$60.00**

Twin Winton, Apple w/Worm, wood stain w/painted detail **$120.00**

Twin Winton, Bambi w/Squirrel Finial, wood stain w/painted detail..................................**$175.00**

Twin Winton, Barrel of Cookies (no mouse), wood stain w/painted detail **$75.00**

Twin Winton, Barrel of Cookies w/Mouse Finial, wood stain w/painted detail **$75.00**

Twin Winton, Butler, wood stain w/painted detail, minimum value **$375.00**

Twin Winton, Cookie Barn, Collector Series, fully painted...**$175.00**

Twin Winton, Cookie Barn, wood stain w/painted detail or gray, each **$80.00**

Twin Winton, Cookie Catcher, wood stain w/painted detail or gray, each **$100.00**

Twin Winton, Cookie Elf, Collector Series, fully painted..**$250.00**

Twin Winton, Cookie Elf (on Stump), wood stain w/painted detail, avocado green, pineapple yellow or orange, each................................**$65.00**

Twin Winton, Cookie House, wood stain w/painted detail **$175.00**

Twin Winton, Cop, wood stain w/painted detail or gray, each **$100.00**

Twin Winton, Cop (Policeman), Collector Series, fully painted...**$250.00**

Twin Winton, Dinosaur, wood stain w/painted detail, minimum value **$400.00**

Twin Winton, Dog w/Lg Bow, wood stain w/painted detail or gray, each **$125.00**

Twin Winton, Donkey w/Cart, wood stain w/painted detail, avocado green, pineapple yellow or orange, each..**$90.00**

Twin Winton, Donkey w/Straw Hat, Collector Series, fully painted..**$175.00**

Twin Winton, Dutch Girl, Collector Series, fully painted ..**$250.00**

Twin Winton, Dutch Girl, wood stain w/painted detail....**$100.00**

Twin Winton, Elf Bakery, wood stain w/painted detail **$90.00**

Twin Winton, Fire Truck, wood stain w/painted detail.......**$85.00**

Twin Winton, Foo Dog, wood stain w/painted detail, avocado green, pineapple yellow, orange or red, each **$350.00**

Twin Winton, Gorilla, wood stain w/painted detail, minimum value **$350.00**

Twin Winton, Grandma w/Bowl of Cookies (Lg), wood stain w/painted detail....................................**$110.00**

Twin Winton, Grandma w/Bowl of Cookies (Sm), wood stain w/painted detail......................................**$80.00**

Twin Winton, Gunfighter Rabbit, Collector Series, fully painted...**$200.00**

Twin Winton, Hen on Basket, wood stain w/painted detail **$125.00**

Twin Winton, Hobby Horse, Collector Series, fully painted...**$250.00**

Twin Winton, Jack-in-the-Box, wood stain w/painted detail, minimum value **$350.00**

Twin Winton, Lamb, Collector Series, fully painted .**$175.00**

Twin Winton, Lighthouse, wood stain w/painted detail ..**$250.00**

Twin Winton, Mother Goose, Collector Series, fully painted...**$275.00**

Twin Winton, Ole King Cole, wood stain w/painted detail, minimum value **$450.00**

Twin Winton, Owl, Collector Series, fully painted ...**$100.00**

Twin Winton, Peanut Man, wood stain w/painted detail...**$1,000.00**

Twin Winton, Pear w/Worm, wood stain w/painted detail, avocado green, pineapple yellow, orange or red, each...**$120.00**

Twin Winton, Persian Cat, wood stain w/painted detail...**$140.00**

Twin Winton, Pirate Fox, Collector Series, fully painted...**$250.00**

Twin Winton, Pirate Fox, wood stain w/painted detail.......**$85.00**

Twin Winton, Pot O' Cookies, wood stain w/painted detail, avocado green, pineapple yellow or orange, each........**$40.00**

Twin Winton, Potbellied Stove, earlier version, marked Twin Winton Designs..................................**$150.00**

Twin Winton, Potbellied Stove, wood stain w/painted detail, avocado green, pineapple yellow, orange or red, San Juan Capistrano, each **$85.00**

Twin Winton, Raggedy Andy (Flopsy), Collector Series, fully painted...**$250.00**

Twin Winton, Raggedy Ann (Mopsy), Collector Series, fully painted...**$250.00**

Twin Winton, Ranger Bear, Collector Series, fully painted..**$100.00**

Twin Winton, Rooster, Collector Series, fully painted **$100.00**

Twin Winton, Sailor Elephant, Collector Series, fully painted..**$175.00**

Twin Winton, Sailor Mouse, Collector Series, fully painted..**$250.00**

Twin Winton, Sheriff Bear, Collector Series, fully painted.....**$200.00**

Twin Winton, Sheriff Bear, wood stain w/painted detail **$75.00**

Twin Winton, Snail w/Elf Finial, wood stain w/painted detail..**$250.00**

Twin Winton, Squirrel w/Acorns, wood stain w/painted detail or gray, each..**$75.00**

Twin Winton, Teddy Bear, wood stain w/painted detail .**$85.00**

Twin Winton, Tug Boat, wood stain w/painted detail ..**$250.00**

Twin Winton, Ye Olde Cookie Bucket, wood stain w/painted detail **$60.00**

United Silver, Nerd, w/reindeer antlers, from $75 to ..**$85.00**

United Silver, Nose Marie Pound Puppy, from $75 to .**$100.00**

Vallona Starr, Peter, Peter Pumpkin Eater, orange w/hand-painted details, minimum value **$375.00**

Vallona Starr, Peter Pumpkin Eater, Design Pat copyright 49 Ct 49 California **$425.00**

Vallona Starr, Squirrel on Stump, #86..............................**$75.00**

Vallona Starr, Winkie, original pink & yellow w/blush (mold was sold, beware of other colors), from $600 to...**$900.00**

Vandor, Baseball **$48.00**

Vandor, Betty Boop, as cook **$75.00**

Vandor, Betty Boop, standing, minimum value.........**$600.00**

Vandor, Betty Boop Head, marked Copyright 1983 KFS, w/paper label, from $75 to **$100.00**

Vandor, Betty Boop Holiday 1994.............................**$125.00**

Vandor, Betty Boop Holiday 1995.............................**$50.00**

Vandor, Betty Boop Kitchen **$40.00**

Vandor, Betty Boop w/Top Hat.................................**$150.00**

Vandor, Cow Beach Woody.......................................**$475.00**

Vandor, Cowboy, from $60 to...................................**$80.00**

Vandor, Cowmen Mooranda **$850.00**

Vandor, Fred Flintstone, standing.............................**$125.00**

Vandor, Happy Trails...**$70.00**

Vandor, Howdy Doody Bumper Car, 1988, minimum value...**$325.00**

Vandor, Howdy Doody Bust, winks eye, w/paper label, minimum value **$375.00**

Vandor, I Love Lucy, 1996..**$135.00**

Vandor, Jukebox, booth style **$150.00**

Vandor, Jukebox, 1985 ....**$125.00**

Vandor, Mona Lisa **$65.00**

Vandor, Popeye Head, w/winking eye, marked 1980 King Features Syndicate, from $400 to **$450.00**

Vandor, Radio, from $80 to **$95.00**

Vandor, Socks, from $50 to **$65.00**

Vandor, Tasmanian Devil **$325.00**

Warner Brothers, Daffy Duck Head **$85.00**

Warner Brothers, Marc Anthony in Doghouse, from $60 to **$80.00**

Warner Brothers, Michael Jordan/Bugs Bunny, Space Jam...**$150.00**

Warner Brothers, Olympic Torch..............................**$135.00**

Warner Brothers, Sylvester, w/trash can, from $70 to.**$80.00**

Warner Brothers, Tasmanian Devil as Santa, from $60 to .**$90.00**

Watt Pottery, Tulip, from $350 to **$400.00**

Weiss, Bear, many variations, from $30 to..................**$60.00**

Weiss, Mother Goose, from $150 to **$175.00**

Wolfe Studio, Purdue Pete **$150.00**

Wolfe Studio, Rainbow Troup, from $65 to **$70.00**

Yona, Clown, from $135 to **$165.00**

Zimpleman, Little Red Riding Hood, limited edition, 1994..**$350.00**

Zimpleman, Mary & Her Lamb, limited edition, 1994..........**$350.00**

Coors Rosebud Dinnerware

Golden, Colorado, was the site for both the Coors Brewing Company and the Coors Porcelain Company, each founded by the same man, Adolph Coors. The pottery's beginning was in 1910, and in the early years they manufactured various ceramic products such as industrial needs, dinnerware, vases, and figurines, but their most famous line and the one we want to tell you about was 'Rosebud.'

The Rosebud 'Cook 'n Serve' line was introduced in 1934. It's very easy to spot, and after you've once seen a piece, you'll be able to recognize it instantly. It was made in solid colors — rose, blue, green, yellow, ivory, and orange. The rose bud and leaves are embossed and hand painted in contrasting colors. There are nearly fifty different pieces to collect, and bargains can still be found, but prices are accelerating, due to increased collector interest. For more information we recommend *Coors Rosebud Pottery* by Robert Schneider and *Collector's Encyclopedia of Colorado Pottery, Identification and Values,* written by Carol and Jim Carlton.

Note: To evaluate pieces in blue and ivory, add 10% to the prices below.

Advisor: Rick Spencer (See Directory, Regal China)

Newsletter: *Coors Pottery Newsletter*
Robert Schneider
3808 Carr Pl. N
Seattle, WA 98103-8126

Bean pot, lg..**$60.00**

Bowl, batter; handled, no lid, 3½-pt...............................**$65.00**

Bowl, batter; 7-pt...**$80.00**

Bowl, cream soup; 4"...**$30.00**

Bowl, mixing; 6"..**$28.00**

Bowl, mixing; 9"..**$48.00**

Bowl, pudding; tab handles, 5" **$35.00**

Casserole, French; 7½", w/lid...**$80.00**

Casserole, straight-sided, 8", w/lid **$65.00**

Casserole, triple service; w/lid, 2-pt...............................**$54.00**

Creamer **$35.00**

Cup & saucer...**$35.00**

Custard...**$18.00**

Egg cup..**$44.00**

Honey pot, no spoon, w/lid, from $150 to **$170.00**

Jar, utility; rope handle, w/lid, 2½-pt.............................**$45.00**

Loaf pan, from $40 to...**$55.00**

Pie plate, from $35 to...**$45.00**

Pitcher, w/lid, lg...**$150.00**

Plate, 10"...**$30.00**

Plate, 9¼" $24.00
Platter, 9x12" $40.00
Ramekin, 4¼" $32.00
Salt & pepper shakers, straight, range size, pr............$45.00
Salt & pepper shakers, tapered, range size, pr, from $35
  to $40.00
Shirred egg dish, 6½" $35.00
Sugar shaker..$65.00
Teapot, sm...$125.00
Teapot, 6-cup...$145.00
Tumbler, footed or handled, from $100 to...............$125.00

Casserole, Triple Service; with undertray and lid, 3½-pint, $75.00.

Cottage Ware

Made by several companies, cottage ware is a line of ceramic table and kitchen accessories, each piece styled as a cozy cottage with a thatched roof. At least four English potteries made the ware, and you'll find pieces marked 'Japan' as well as 'Occupied Japan.' From Japan you'll also find pieces styled as windmills and water wheels, though the quality is inferior. The better pieces are marked 'Price Brothers' and 'Occupied Japan.' They're compatible in coloring as well as in styling, and values run about the same. Items marked simply 'Japan' are worth considerably less.

Bowl, salad; English $65.00
Butter dish, English..$45.00
Butter pat, embossed cottage, rectangular, Occupied Japan....$17.50
Chocolate pot, English $135.00
Condiment set, 2 shakers & mustard on tray, Occupied
  Japan $45.00
Cookie jar, pink, brown & green, square, Japan,
  8½x5½" $65.00
Cookie jar/canister, cylindrical, English $85.00
Creamer, windmill, Occupied Japan, 2⅝".................$15.00
Creamer & sugar bowl, English, 2½x4½" $45.00
Creamer & sugar bowl, w/lid, on tray, Occupied Japan..$65.00
Cup & saucer, English, 2½", 4½".............................$45.00
Demitasse pot, English $100.00
Dish w/cover, Occupied Japan, sm...........................$35.00
Grease jar, Occupied Japan.....................................$35.00
Marmalade, English...$40.00

Mug, Price Bros..$50.00
Pin tray, English, 4" dia $20.00

Pitcher, tankard style, rare, English, $135.00.

Pitcher, water; English...$150.00
Salt & pepper shakers, windmill, Occupied Japan, pr...$20.00
Sugar bowl, windmill, w/lid, Occupied Japan, 3⅞"....$25.00
Sugar box, for cubes, English, 5¾" L $45.00
Tea set, child's, Japan, serves 4................................$150.00
Teapot, English or Occupied Japan, 5" $45.00
Teapot, English or Occupied Japan, 6½"......................$50.00

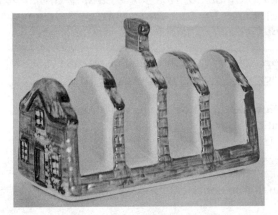

Toast rack, 4-slot, English, 5½" long, from $65.00 to $75.00.

Tumbler, Occupied Japan, 3½"...................................$25.00

Cowboy Character Collectibles

When we come across what are now called cowboy character toys and memorabilia, it rekindles warm memories of childhood days for those of us who once 'rode the range' (often our backyards) with these gallant heroes. Today we can really appreciate them for the positive role models they were. They sat tall in the saddle, reminded us never to tell an un-truth, to respect 'women-folk' as well as our elders, animal life, our flag, our country, and our teachers; to eat all the cereal placed before us in order to build strong bodies; to worship God, and have (above all else) a strong value system that couldn't be compromised. They were Gene, Roy, and Tex, along with a couple dozen other names, who rode beautiful steeds such as Champion, Trigger, and White Flash.

They rode into a final sunset on the silver screen only to return and ride into our homes via television in the 1950s. The next decade found us caught up in more western adventures such as Bonanza, Wagon Train, The Rifleman, and many others. These set the stage for a second wave of toys, games, and western outfits.

Annie Oakley was one of only a couple of cowgirls in the corral; Wild Bill Elliott used to drawl, 'I'm a peaceable man'; Ben Cartwright, Adam, Hoss, and Little Joe provided us with thrills and laughter. Some of the earliest collectibles are represented by Roy's and Gene's 1920s predecessors — Buck Jones, Hoot Gibson, Tom Mix, and Ken Maynard. There were so many others, all of whom were very real to us in the 1930s – 60s, just as their memories and values remain very real to us today.

Remember that few items of cowboy memorabilia have survived to the present in mint condition. When found, mint or near-mint items bring hefty prices, and they continue to escalate every year. Unless otherwise noted, our values are for examples in good to very good condition.

For more information we recommend these books: *Roy Rogers*, *Singing Cowboy Stars*, *Silver Screen Cowboys*, *Hollywood Cowboy Heroes*, and *Western Comics: A Comprehensive Reference*, all by Robert W. Phillips; the *Collector's Guide to Hopalong Cassidy Memorabilia* by Joseph J. Caro; *The Lone Ranger* by Lee Felbinger; and *W.F. Cody Buffalo Bill* by James W. Wojtowicz.

Advisor: Robert W. Phillips, Phillips Archives (See Directory, Character and Personality Collectibles)

Club/Newsletter: Roy Rogers – Dale Evans Collectors Association
Nancy Horsley
P.O. Box 1166, Portsmouth, OH 45662-1116
Annual membership: $15 per year, includes free admission to annual convention

Club/Newsletter: Cowboy Collector
Joseph J. Caro, Publisher
P.O. Box 7486
Long Beach, CA 90807

Club/Newsletter: Hopalong Cassidy Fan Club International and *Hopalong Cassidy Newsletter*
Laura Bates, Editor
6310 Friendship Dr.
New Concord, OH 4362-9708; 614-826-4850
Subscription: $15 US, $20 Canadian; includes quarterly newsletter and information about annual festival

Newsletter: *Gene Autry Star Telegram*
Gene Autry Development Association
Chamber of Commerce
P.O. Box 158, Gene Autry, OK 73436

Newsletter: *The Lone Ranger Silver Bullet*
P.O. Box 553, Forks, WA 98331; 206-327-3726
Subscription: $12 per year

Buffalo Bill, perforated roll caps, NMIB $10.00
Dale Evans, album, My Personal Picture Album, 1971, EX..$10.00
Dale Evans, Colorforms, NMIB....................................$85.00

Davy Crockett, bank, bronze-color metal, 1950s bank giveaway, EX $25.00. (Photo courtesy June Moon)

Davy Crockett, card, Happy Birthday Grandson, 1950s, EX...$10.00
Davy Crockett, display card, Frontier Badge, cardboard w/6 (of 9) badges, 1950s, 11x16", NM......................$90.00
Davy Crockett, flannel material, 1 yard, NM $22.00
Davy Crockett, hat, coonskin......................................$10.00
Davy Crockett, lariat tie, NMOC $45.00
Davy Crockett, moccasin kit, marked Old Town Crafts Corp Kittery for Gabriel, MIB...$75.00
Davy Crockett, neckerchief, dark blue.......................$25.00

Davy Crockett, toy watch, hands move as stem winds, marked Made in USA on card, M, from $35.00 to $45.00.

Davy Crockett, T-shirt transfer, NM $15.00
Davy Crockett, wallet, 1950s, EX................................$100.00
Gabby Hayes, sheriff's set, 1950s, NMOC....................$80.00
Gene Autry, frame-tray puzzle, Whitman No 2610-29, 1957, NM $47.00
Gene Autry, postcard, black & white photo, advertising Gene Autry shirts, M...$16.00
Gene Autry, shoe box, Cowboy Footwear, unknown maker, 1950s, NM..$85.00
Gene Autry, song book, color covers, black & white photos, Western Music Publishing, 1942, M.....................$42.00
Hopalong Cassidy, ad photo, for Mary Jane Bread, 8x10", M $20.00
Hopalong Cassidy, badge, w/pinback clasp, original, EX..$50.00
Hopalong Cassidy, bicycle horn w/handlebar clamp, NM $150.00

Hopalong Cassidy, display, Langendorf Bread loaf, 1951, 5x5x12", EX $25.00

Hopalong Cassidy, film, Danger Trail, 16mm, Castle Films, 1950s, 7" reel, M $30.00

Hopalong Cassidy, greeting card, w/lead boot attached to front, M $65.00

Hopalong Cassidy, knife, 1950s, EX $125.00

Hopalong Cassidy, magazine, International Photographer, 1937, Hoppy & Topper on cover, EX $165.00

Hopalong Cassidy, magazine, Memories, 1989, M $20.00

Hopalong Cassidy, magazine ad, Arvin TV, ½-page, NM .$15.00

Hopalong Cassidy, magazine ad, Grape Nuts Cereal, color, full page, EX $35.00

Hopalong Cassidy, magazine ad, ½-page, from $10 to ..$15.00

Hopalong Cassidy, money clip, silver w/photo insert ..$50.00

Hopalong Cassidy, outfit, black skirt w/Hoppy on front pockets, blouse w/horse head & piping, 2-pc set, EX ..$125.00

Hopalong Cassidy, pencil box, NM $195.00

Hopalong Cassidy, penny arcade card, closeup photo, 1950s, 3½x5", NM $18.00

Hopalong Cassidy, photo album, black & white, NM ..$275.00

Hopalong Cassidy, photo frame, diecut cardboard, w/black & white photo, EX $120.00

Hopalong Cassidy, postcard, Happy Birday, Hopalong Cassidy Savings Club, 1950 ....$3.00

Hopalong Cassidy, record album, Singing Bandit, 78 rpm, set of 2 in original sleeve, NM $145.00

Hopalong Cassidy, roller skates, EX+ $325.00

Hopalong Cassidy, sheet music, Wide Open Spaces, w/photo of Hoppy & Topper, VG $45.00

Hopalong Cassidy, sunglasses, girl's, white, VG $185.00

Hopalong Cassidy, sweater, Hoppy on front w/mountain range scene on sleeves, Topper on back, ca 1951-52, child size, M $250.00

Hopalong Cassidy, tie and scarf set, printed silk, MIB, $350.00. (Photo courtesy Phil Helley)

Hopalong Cassidy, tie tack, NM+ $225.00

Hopalong Cassidy, wood-burning set, complete w/instructions & unused paints, NMIB $275.00

John Wayne, photo, Rooster Cogburn press release, black & white glossy w/Katherine Hepburn, 1975, 8x10", M ..$16.00

Lone Ranger, Action Arcade, Durham, 1974, EX $60.00

Lone Ranger, holster, leather, EX $80.00

Lone Ranger, matchbook, advertising Lone Ranger Ice Cream, 1938, EX $30.00

Lone Ranger, neckerchief w/mask, EX $115.00

Lone Ranger, scrap book, VG+ $40.00

Lone Ranger, tattoos, wrapper w/Lone Ranger fighting Indian, Philadelphia Gum Corp, 1966, 1½x3½", EX+ $32.00

Pecos Bill, figure, metal, 6", NM $35.00

Pecos Bill, statue, metal, EX detail, 6", NM $35.00

Red Ranger, holster, 1930s $20.00

Reno Browne, photo, color w/German Shepherd, signed, 5x7", EX $15.00

Rex Allen, commemorative coin, copper, Rex Allen Days, 1971, Wilcox AZ $10.00

Rex Allen, mat, shows movie ads, 1954, 12½x9½", EX ...$10.00

Rin-Tin-Tin, dexterity puzzle, Sgt Biff O'Hara, Nabisco Shredded Wheat premium $25.00

Rin-Tin-Tin, erasable picture set, Trans-O-Graph, 1956, unused, NMIB $45.00

Roy Rogers, ad sheet, Dream of Santa, shows toys, 1950s, 4 pages, EX $35.00

Roy Rogers, binoculars, MIB, $295.00.

Roy Rogers, contest sheet, Post Toasties Name the Pony, 1955, 11x14", EX $10.00

Roy Rogers, lariat, MIP $325.00

Roy Rogers, lucky horseshoe, black rubber, NM $22.50

Roy Rogers, modeling clay set, Toycraft, 1950s, NMIB ..$50.00

Roy Rogers, mutoscope card, ca 1940, VG $12.00

Roy Rogers, salt & pepper shakers, boot shape, EX, pr $95.00

Roy Rogers, scarf, silk w/facsimile signature, 1950s, EX ...$40.00

Roy Rogers, song book, Roy Rogers' Own Songs, Roy on cover, full-page Roy & Trigger, 1942, 30 pages, VG $25.00

Roy Rogers, tablet, EX $30.00

Roy Rogers, window card, Man From Oklahoma, w/Gabby Hayes, Dale Evans, Sons of the Pioneers & Trigger, 14x22", EX $175.00

Roy Rogers & Dale Evans, Paint-By-Number set, ca 1950, 8x10", EX $125.00

Roy Rogers & Dale Evans, postcard, King & Queen of the Rodeo, 1960s, NM $7.50

Straight Arrow, manuscript, The Stage Rider, for Nabisco Puppet Theater, 1952, EX $5.00

Straight Arrow, punch-out puppets, color, ca 1950s, 7½" square, unused, M $20.00

Tex Ritter, photo, black & white w/guitar, printed signature, EX...**$15.00**

Texas Pete, soap-on-a-rope, cowboy shape, unused, NM...**$35.00**

Will James, book, Lone Cowboy, Scribner's, 1st edition, EX...**$25.00**

Wyatt Earp, guitar, 24", EX...**$120.00**

Cracker Jack Toys

In 1869 Frederick Rueckheim left Hamburg, Germany, bound for Chicago, where he planned to work on a farm for his uncle. But farm life did not appeal to Mr. Rueckheim, and after the Chicago fire, he moved there and helped clear the debris. With another man whose popcorn and confectionary business had been destroyed in the fire, Mr. Rueckheim started a business with one molasses kettle and one hand popper. That following year, Mr. Rueckheim bought out his original partner and sent for his brother, Louis. The two brothers formed Rueckheim & Bro. and quickly prospered as they continued expanding their confectionary line to include new products. It was not until 1896 that the first lot of Cracker Jack was produced — and then only as an adjunct to their growing line. Cracker Jack was sold in bulk form until 1899 when H.G. Eckstein, an old friend, invented the wax-sealed package, which allowed them to ship it further and thus sell it more easily. Demand for Cracker Jack soared, and it quickly became the main product of the factory. Today millions of boxes are produced — with a prize in every box.

The idea of prizes came along during the time of bulk packaging; it was devised as a method to stimulate sales. Later, as the wax-sealed package was introduced, a prize was given (more or less) with each package. Next, the prize was added into the package, but still, not every package received a prize. It was not until the 1920s that 'a prize in every package' became a reality. Initially the prizes were put in with the confection, but the company feared this might pose a problem, should it inadvertently be mistaken for the popcorn. To avoid this, the prize was put in a separate compartment and finally into its own protective wrapper. Hundreds of prizes have been used over the years, and it is still true today that there is 'a prize in every package.' Prizes have ranged from the practical girl's bracelet and pencils to tricks, games, disguises, and stick-anywhere patches. To learn more about the subject, you'll want to read *Cracker Jack Toys, The Complete Unofficial Guide for Collectors*, written by our advisor, Larry White.

Advisor: Larry White (See Directory, Cracker Jack)

Newsletter: *The Prize Insider*
Larry White
108 Central St.
Rowley, MA 01969
508-948-8187

Cloth, iron-on patch (Beware, Shucks, No Riders, etc), 1970, each..**$7.00**

First row: NIT, plastic, $20.00; Sundial, metal, $27.00; Cracker Jack Nursery Rhymes booklet, paper, $95.00; Second row: Game, Smallest Ring Toss, $65.00; Snap-together railroad, plastic, $12.00; Top, metal, $8.00; Third row: Cracker Jack 512 locomotive, metal, $175.00; Game, Big League Baseball at Home, paper with metal spinner, $90.00. (Photo courtesy Larry White)

Foil on paper, Fun Shiny Sticker, 1980, 15 in set, each..**$2.00**

Metal, presidential coin, 1930, 31 in set, each.............**$10.00**

Metal, thimble, For a Good Girl, japanned, 1930..........**$6.00**

Metal, top, Keep 'Em Flying, Let's Do It, black planes, 1940 ....**$45.00**

Metal, whistle, cat shape & picture, multicolor, 1930.**$19.00**

Metal & plastic, ring, split back w/faux colored jewel, 1950 ....**$4.00**

Paper, Action Acrobats cards, multicolor, 1980, 10 in set, each...**$3.00**

Paper, Bess & Bill of Cracker Jack Hill series, multicolor, 1930, each **$90.00**

Paper, book, Cracker Jack Wise Cracks, 1960, 18 in set, each...**$9.00**

Paper, card game, Cracker Jack, 1960, each.................**$8.00**

Paper, Cracker Jack Painting Book, 1920....................**$80.00**

Paper, Cracker Jack Picture Dominoes, yellow & black, 1970, each **$10.00**

Paper, Cracker Jack Trick Mustache, red or black, 1940, each **$20.00**

Paper, Cracker Jack/Donruss Series 1 baseball cards, common, 1990, each...**$2.00**

Paper, Cracker Jack/Nickelodeon, Ren & Stimpy, 1990, 8 in set, each...**$1.00**

Paper, Cracker Jack/Sega, tattoos, pencil toppers or stickers, 1990, each...**$1.00**

Paper, Cracker Jack/Topps Series 1 baseball cards, common, 1990, each...**$2.50**

Paper, Cracker Jack/Topps Series 2 baseball cards, common, 1990, each...**$2.00**

Paper, hat, Me for Cracker Jack, 1920......................**$125.00**

Paper, Monkey Ring Toss Game, red & green, 1940..**$30.00**

Paper, Mysticolor Paint Set, 1970, 24 in set, each.........**$8.00**

Paper, Strange Facts Card, red or green border, 1950, 30 in set, each..**$6.00**

Paper, Tiny Tattoos, 1970, 6 in set, each **$5.00**

Plastic, charm (swan, donkey, water can, etc) on silk cord, 1940, each..**$2.00**

Plastic, comic badge (BO Plenty, Dick Tracy, Smitty, etc), 1930, each...**$18.00**

Plastic, cylinder whistle, figure (cow, bird, squirrel, etc) on top, 1950, each.......................................**$8.00**

Plastic, magnifier, clear w/various designs, 1950, each...**$1.00**

Plastic, Pocket Clips (monkey, Indian, astronaut, etc), 1970, each..**$6.00**

Plastic, put-together buildings, cars or badges, 1960, each, from $6 to..**$10.00**

Plastic, Squeeze Sides figures (boxers, monkey, clown, etc), 1960, each.......................................**$8.00**

Plastic & paper, alphabet tilt card, 1980, 26 in set, each ..**$6.00**

Plastic & paper, Fun Mirror, reflective surface w/funny face, 1980, each.......................................**$5.00**

Plastic & paper, maze puzzles, 1980, 20 in set, each....**$8.00**

Plastic & paper, tilt card (magician, elephant, pirate, etc), 1950, each...**$7.00**

Pot metal, battleship, 1¼" L.......................................**$15.00**

Sheet metal, Baggage & Smoker pullman car, multicolor, 1930...**$95.00**

Crackle Glass

At the height of productivity from the 1930s through the 1970s, nearly five hundred companies created crackle glass. As pieces stayed in production for several years, dating items may be difficult. Some colors such as ruby red, amberina, cobalt, and cranberry were more expensive to produce. Smoke gray was made for a short time, and because quantities are scarce, prices on these pieces tend to be higher than on some of the other colors, amethyst, green, and amber included. Crackle glass is still in production today by the Blenko Glass Company, and it is being imported from Taiwan and China as well. For further information on other glass companies and values we recommend *Crackle Glass, Identification and Value Guide, Book I and Book II*, by Stan and Arlene Weitman (Collector Books).

See also Kanawha.

Advisors: Stan and Arlene Weitman (See Directory, Crackle Glass)

Candy dish, tangerine, wide ruffled rim, footed, Pilgrim, 1949-69, 5½", from $105 to...............................**$130.00**

Creamer & sugar bowl, blue, matching drop-over handle, Pilgrim, 1949-69, 3½", from $55 to.................**$80.00**

Cruet, amberina, yellow pulled-back handle, 2-ball yellow stopper, Rainbow, late 1940s-60s, 7", from $50 to .**$80.00**

Cruet, sea green, matching ball stopper, Pilgrim, 1949-69, 6", from $45 to...**$75.00**

Cup, light sea green, clear drop-over ring handle, unknown company & date, 2½", from $30 to....................**$35.00**

Decanter, light amethyst (lilac), teardrop form, clear teardrop stopper, Pilgrim, 1949-69, 12", from $80 to..........**$90.00**

Decanter, topaz, bulbous, matching ball stopper, Blenko, 1963, 8¾", from $65 to.......................................**$80.00**

Decanter, topaz, stick neck, matching lg-ball stopper, Rainbow, late 1940s-60s, 8½", from $80 to........**$105.00**

Decanter, topaz, waisted form w/yellow ball stopper, Rainbow, late 1940s-60s, 14", from $80 to.........**$105.00**

Hat, blue, Pilgrim, 1949-69, 5", from $40.00 to $45.00. (Photo courtesy Stan and Arlene Weitman)

Jug, blue, clear drop-over handle, Pilgrim, 1949-69, 4", from $35 to...**$40.00**

Jug, topaz, crystal drop-over handle, Pilgrim, 1949-69, 4", from $30 to...**$35.00**

Novelty, apple, cobalt, Blenko, 1950s-60s, 4½", from $60 to...**$85.00**

Novelty, fish bottle (wine), topaz, applied green eyes, unknown company & date, 15", from $80 to.....**$105.00**

Novelty, fish vase, topaz, Hamon, 1940s-70s, 9", from $80 to...**$90.00**

Novelty, pear, light sea green, Blenko, 1950s-60s, 5", from $55 to...**$80.00**

Perfume bottle, light blue teardrop shape w/matching flower-shaped stopper, unknown company & date, 4½", from $50 to...**$65.00**

Pitcher, amberina, clear drop-over handle, Pilgrim, 1949-69, 3½", from $35 to.......................................**$40.00**

Pitcher, blue flared cylinder w/square mouth, clear drop-over handle, unknown company & date, 4", from $45 to...**$50.00**

Pitcher, emerald green, clear drop-over handle, Pilgrim, 4", from $30 to...**$35.00**

Pitcher, golden amber, matching drop-over handle, Rainbow, late 1940s-50s, 3½", from $30 to.........**$35.00**

Pitcher, light amethyst (lilac), matching pulled-back handle, pear shape, Pilgrim, 1949-69, 4½", from $45 to...**$50.00**

Pitcher, ruby, amber drop-over handle, Pilgrim, 1949-69, 3½", from $35 to.......................................**$40.00**

Pitcher, tangerine, amber pulled-back handle, Pilgrim, 1949-69, 4", from $35 to.......................................**$40.00**

Pitcher, tangerine, clear drop-over handle, bulbous, 3¾", Pilgrim, 1949-69, from $35 to.............................**$40.00**

Pitcher, topaz, matching drop-over handle, flared rim, unknown company & date, 3¾", from $30 to......**$35.00**

Salt & pepper shakers, amethyst, original metal lids, unknown company & date, 3¼", pr, from $55 to...................**$80.00**

Salt & pepper shakers, crystal, original metal lids, unknown company & date, 4", pr, from $35 to **$55.00**

Tumbler, topaz, unknown company & date, 6¾", from $40 to.. **$55.00**

Vase, amberina w/yellow top, appled red decor at neck, unknown company & date, 5¼", from $80 to...... **$90.00**

Vase, amethyst, pinched rim forms double neck, Blenko, late 1940s-50s, 4", from $55 to **$70.00**

Vase, black amethyst, unknown maker, 1940s, 8¼", from $130.00 to $155.00. (Photo courtesy Stan and Arlene Weitman)

Vase, blue, flared cylinder w/crimped rim, Bischoff, 1940-63, 10½", from $105 to **$130.00**

Vase, blue, inverted cylinder w/applied decor at waist, scalloped rim, Pilgrim, 1949-69, 3½", from $40 to **$50.00**

Vase, bud; crystal, unknown maker & date, 8", from $40 to... **$45.00**

Vase, crystal w/applied blue rosettes, flared cylinder, Blenko, 1940s-50s, 7", from $80 to.................................. **$105.00**

Vase, Jonquil (yellow), crimped top, footed, Blenko, 1950s, 7¼", from $105 to **$130.00**

Vase, lemon-lime, bulbous form w/pinched sides, Pilgrim, 1949-69, 5", from $40 to **$45.00**

Vase, sea green, bulbous w/pinched rim, Blenko, late 1940s-50s, 3¾", from $55 to **$80.00**

Vase, sea green, clear drop-over angle handles, Blenko, 1940s-50s, 7½", from $80 to................................. **$90.00**

Vase, tangerine, stick neck, applied decor, ruffled rim, Pilgrim, 1949-69, 4½", from $55 to........................ **$80.00**

Cuff Links

Many people regard cuff links as the ideal collectible. Cuff links are very available; they can be found at almost every garage sale, flea market, thrift store, and antique shop. Cuff links can also be very affordable. Collectors take pride in showing off great looking pairs which they bought for only a dollar or two. Some of these cuff links turn out to be worth a lot more! The possibility of such 'finds' is one of the many joys of cuff link collecting. Cuff link collecting is also educational. In use for centuries as cuff fasteners and an item of fashion, cuff links have always mimicked the art of their period.

It is easy to display a cuff link collection. Their small size is convenient for curio cabinets, shadow boxes, wall framing, and shelf arrangements. Storing a cuff link collection is also simple. Entire collections can often be stored on a closet shelf or a dresser drawer. Cuff link collecting is a fun hobby which the whole family can enjoy. Some cuff-linking families devote weekend days to garage sales and flea markets. Often individual family members have their own areas of cuff link specialization. These include antique, modern, large, small, fraternal, advertising themes, metal, wood, glass, etc. Some collectors even specialize in cuff link 'singles' — they enjoy the art form and the search for the mate. It's no wonder that cuff links are one of the fastest-growing collectibles in the world.

Advisor: Gene Klompus (See Directory, Cuff Links)

Club: The National Cuff Link Society

Newsletter: *The Link*
Gene Klompus, President
P.O. Box 346
Prospect Hts., IL 60070-0346
Phone or Fax: 847-816-0035

Acme, silver-colored plating, w/3 matching studs, 1965, 4-pc set, G **$75.00**

Anson, Masonic emblem, gold filled, 1970, G............. **$45.00**

Anson, Scorpio motif, sterling, 1965, 1x1", original box, G **$100.00**

Confucius, metal and wood, ca 1950, from $45.00 to $75.00. (Photo courtesy Gene Klompus)

Dante, oval, jade stone, silver rim, swivel closure, 1970, original box... **$45.00**

Fenwick & Sailors, sterling microphones, 1960.......... **$85.00**

HICKOK, gold colored, fluer-de-lis motif, square, 1955, w/magazine ad, G **$25.00**

Kum-A-Part, separable (Snappers), round w/multicolor enamel dome, sterling, 1925, M........................... **$55.00**

Squirt beverage, toggle closure, matching tie bar, 1970, w/original box (torn bottom), G **$65.00**

SWANK, Buddha design, Arts of the World series, 1972, original box... **$80.00**

SWANK, initial L, 1955, w/tie bar, original box, EX....**$25.00**

SWANK, wrap-around style, round w/rose-colored stone, removable wrap, 1972, M..**$35.00**

Thermometer, w/matching tie bar, 1950, original box, EX..**$105.00**

Other Accessories

Collar button container, celluloid, 1920, from $145.00 to $175.00. (Photo courtesy Gene Klompus)

Collar pins, 1" to 2" lengths, 1950, box of 8, EX.........**$20.00**

Cuff links, tie bar & matching ballpoint pen set w/ink refill, 1950, original faux pigskin box............................**$100.00**

Cuff links & matching bow tie set, Blue Bell brand, 1955, original box (poor condition), M..............................**$90.00**

Shirt studs, Krementz, gold colored w/brushed finish, 1950, set of 4...**$50.00**

Shirt studs, unbranded, old Dutch Boy paint advertising logo, enameled, 1940, M, set of 4....................................**$90.00**

SWANK coach, multicolor ceramic, w/cuff link & coin reservoir, 1950, 8", M...**$125.00**

Tie bar, marcasite, initial F, 1950, original box, M....**$100.00**

Tie tack, gold colored, square, 1970, M......................**$20.00**

Czechoslovakian Glass and Ceramics

Established as a country in 1918, Czechoslovakia is rich in the natural resources needed for production of glassware as well as pottery. Over the years it has produced vast amounts of both. Anywhere you go, from flea markets to fine antique shops, you'll find several examples of their lovely pressed and cut glass scent bottles, Deco vases, lamps, kitchenware, tableware, and figurines.

More than thirty-five marks have been recorded; some are ink stamped, some etched, and some molded in. Paper labels have also been used. *Czechoslovakian Glass and Collectibles* by Diane and Dale Barta and Helen Rose and *Made in Czechoslovakia* by Ruth Forsythe are two books we highly recommend for further study.

Club: Czechoslovakian Collectors Guild International
P.O. Box 901395
Kansas City, MO 64190

Ceramics

Creamer, chicken (dressed hen) figural, multicolor details, 4"..**$40.00**

Creamer, cow (recumbent) figural, white w/orange tail handle, 3"..**$48.00**

Creamer, cow figural, yellow & white, tail handle, mouth spout, 6¼"...**$85.00**

Creamer, moose figural, brown & beige w/black trim, full antlers, open mouth, 4"....................................**$50.00**

Cup & saucer, demitasse; white w/yellow, blue or green trim, 2¾", each...**$7.50**

Cup & saucer, floral band on white, 2¼"..................**$15.00**

Dish, gold overlay w/embossed flower basket design, 2 handles, 7" L...**$50.00**

Figurine, Art Deco lady, white, 9¾".........................**$250.00**

Figurine, cat, white w/pink details, 5", from $40 to ...**$45.00**

Figurine, hound dog, brown & white, 5"....................**$35.00**

Flower holder, rust, yellow and blue bird on double branch yellow base, 2 holes, 5½", from $45.00 to $50.00. (Photo courtesy Dale and Diane Barta and Helen M Rose)

Napkin ring, girl figural, yellow bonnet, black shoes, 4"..**$25.00**

Nut bowl, flower shape, blue, white & orange, 5½", from $15 to..**$20.00**

Nut bowl, tulip shape, 5-color, glossy, 6½", from $15 to..**$20.00**

Pitcher, burgundy w/black and white mottling, black handle & rim, tricorner spout, 5¼", from $45 to..............**$50.00**

Pitcher, chicken figural, white w/red & black details, 7½", from $50 to...**$55.00**

Pitcher, embossed wide leaves, rust, blue & yellow, 4", from $25 to..**$30.00**

Pitcher, milk; blue rim shaded to yellow at base, multicolor flowers in center, blue stripe at rim & handle, 6" ...**$75.00**

Pitcher, multicolor feather-like geometric design on dark teal, bulbous, 6¼"...**$50.00**

Pitcher, yellow w/blue rim and handle, trumpet form, 7½", from $40 to...**$50.00**

Planter, bird perched beside open stump, 3½"...........**$40.00**

Planter/bowl, white pearlescent w/bluebird on each side, 2 applied birds on rim, 6½" dia...............................**$55.00**

Plate, chicks, yellow on white, 6½".............................**$30.00**

Plate, lady's portrait on brown w/gold trim, 11".........**$65.00**

Sprinkling can, white w/painted floral decor, 4½".....**$35.00**

Sugar bowl, pink lustre, w/lid, 4".............................**$20.00**

Sugar bowl, swans back to back form body of bowl, necks form handles, white w/multicolor details, w/lid, 2½".........**$55.00**

Toby mug, woman, multicolor w/black details, 1¾", from $40 to...**$45.00**

Vase, pearlized pale blue mottle, 8", from $45 to **$50.00**

Vase, swirled multicolor on white, fan form, 7½", from $65 to......**$75.00**

Vase, yellow lustre w/flared black rim, handles, 10", from $45 to......**$40.00**

Wall pocket, bird perched beside birdhouse, 5½"......**$45.00**

Wall pocket, woodpecker perched at side of tree trunk, 7¾"......**$65.00**

Glassware

Bowl, satin, mottled colors, cased in amber, 3-footed, 4⅛"......**$145.00**

Candlestick, red flared rim over black base, 3"......**$60.00**

Candy basket, light green varicolored, green handle, 8" .**$190.00**

Candy basket, yellow w/black rim, plain crystal handle, 6½"......**$200.00**

Candy jar, green w/blue foot & applied blue serpentine ornamentation, green lid w/clear finial, 6"......**$325.00**

Cologne bottle, cranberry opalescent hobnail, w/white stopper, 5½"......**$85.00**

Perfume bottle, blue, simple base w/matching fan-form stopper, 4¾"......**$145.00**

Perfume bottle, clear w/blue foot, pale blue frosted flower stopper, 5¾"......**$300.00**

Perfume bottle, crystal stepped base w/frosted lovebird stopper, 4⅜"......**$165.00**

Perfume bottle, simple amethyst base w/frosted nude stopper, 6⅝"......**$800.00**

Pitcher, exotic bird painted on orange, black handle, 11½"......**$285.00**

Puff box, blue satin w/molded floral decor, 3¼"......**$35.00**

Puff box, green w/red finial, 7⅛"......**$40.00**

Puff box, red w/black linear decor & finial, 3¾"......**$110.00**

Vase, blue w/applied red decor forming handles & spiral up neck, 8½"......**$175.00**

Vase, bud; red w/silver & black decor, 11¼"......**$110.00**

Vase, cane decoration on black, red interior, classic form, 5½"......**$150.00**

Vase, green cased w/applied apple green ornaments on trumpet form, 5½"......**$85.00**

Vase, green, yellow & blue mottle, stick form, 8½" ...**$55.00**

Vase, orange w/silver painted bird scene, classic form, 7¾"......**$95.00**

Vase, painted desert scene on yellow, slim form, sm foot, 8½"......**$125.00**

Vase, red, bulbous w/can neck, 3 applied cobalt handles, cobalt at rim, 5½"......**$450.00**

Vase, red varicolored, crystal twisted thorn handle, 5½"...**$250.00**

Vase, red w/applied black serpentine decor, slim cylinder, 6½"......**$100.00**

Vase, varicolored, double cased, bulbous, 5½"......**$120.00**

Vase, white classic form, applied light amber handles, 5"......**$65.00**

Vase, white opaque w/red opaque overlay, bulbous w/short neck, 5½"......**$110.00**

Vase, yellow w/black trim along ruffled rim, slim form, 8½"......**$75.00**

Vase, yellow w/multicolor mottle at base, 8"......**$85.00**

Wine, red w/black stem & foot, silver trim along rim, 7½"......**$55.00**

Dairy Bottles

Between the turn of the century and the 1950s, milk was bought and sold in glass bottles. Until the twenties, the name and location of the dairy was embossed in the glass. After that, it became commonplace to pyro-glaze (paint and fire) the lettering onto the surface. Farmers sometimes added a cow or some other graphic that represented the product or related to the name of the dairy.

Because so many of these glass bottles were destroyed when paper and plastic cartons became popular, they've become a scarce commodity, and today's collectors have begun to take notice of them. It's fun to see just how many you can find from your home state — or try getting one from every state in the union!

What makes for a good milk bottle? Collectors normally find the pyro-glaze decorations more desirable, since they're more visual. Bottles from dairies in their home state hold more interest for them, so naturally New Jersey bottles sell better there than they would in California, for instance. Green glass examples are unusual and often go for a premium; so do those with the embossed baby faces. (Watch for reproductions here!) Those with a 'Buy War Bonds' slogan or a patriotic message are always popular, and cream-tops are good as well.

Some collectors enjoy adding 'go-alongs' to enhance their collections, so the paper pull tops, advertising items that feature dairy bottles, and those old cream-top spoons will also interest them. The spoons usually sell for about $6.00 to $10.00 each.

For more information, we recommend *Udderly Delightful* by John Tutton, whose address may be found in the Directory under Bottles.

Newsletter: *The Milk Route*
National Association of Milk Bottle Collectors, Inc.
Thomas Gallagher
4 Ox Bow Rd., Westport, CT 06880-2602; 203-277-5244

Newsletter: *Creamers*
Lloyd Bindscheattle
P.O. Box 11, Lake Villa, IL 60046-0011; Subscription: $5 for 4 issues

Burroughs Brothers, red pyro, cream top, from $35.00 to $45.00; Stueber's, orange pyro, cream top, from $28.00 to $35.00

Anderson Bros, Drink Milk For Health, Worchester, blue pyro, round, qt...**$8.00**
Angola Dairy, red letters, qt...**$7.50**
Arden Certified Milk, Los Angeles CA, embossed, round, qt...**$15.00**
Beltz Dairy, Palmerton PA, farm scene, red pyro, round, qt...**$14.00**
Borden's, square Elsie logo on front & back, lg seat, red pyro, ½-pt...**$6.00**
Brunskill Dairy, Cedar Falls IA, banner across world, red pyro, round, qt...................................**$50.00**
Carrigan's Niagara Dairy, Niagara Falls NY, embossed, round, qt...**$14.00**
City Dairy Ltd, Canadian Imperial, embossed, round, ¼-pt...**$20.00**
Cloverdale Farms, Milk Is Your Best Food Buy, cream top, pyro, square, qt...........................**$14.00**
DeCracker's Dairy Products, Lyons NY, red pyro, round, qt...**$45.00**
Ellerman Dairy, Athens WI, red pyro, round, qt.........**$14.00**
Farm Fresh Maine Milk, cow in oval frame on front, blue pyro, square, pt.............................**$7.00**
Fostoria Dairy, Buy at Home Help Fostoria, red pyro, qt..**$35.00**
Gates Homestead Farms 1798, amber, ½-gal.................**$8.50**
Good-Rich Dairy, baby top, embossed, round, ½-pt, minimum value...**$25.00**
Haleake Dairy, Makawao, Alameda CA, embossed, round, ¼-pt...**$25.00**
Hammes Dairy, LaCrosse WI, cows in pasture w/barn & sunrise in background, red & black pyro, round, qt............**$50.00**
Haskel's, Augusta GA, Back Their Attack Buy More War Bonds, soldiers firing guns, pyro, round, qt.........**$50.00**
Hazel Return My Bottle or I'll Bust, cow w/dripping udder, red pyro, round, qt...**$20.00**
Heiss & Sons Dairy, Rochelle Park NJ, orange pyro, tall neck, round, qt...**$12.00**
Hickory Grove Dairy Milk, From Mineral Fed Cows, Mt Ulla NC, blue pyro, round, qt.................................**$35.00**
Highland Dairy, Rochester NY, cream top, pyro, round, qt, minimum value...**$50.00**
Hollandia Dairy, Escondido CA, windmill, red pyro, round, qt...**$45.00**
Imperial Dairy Co, crown, embossed, round, ½-pt......**$9.00**
It's Pure We're Sure, seated baby w/bottle, brown pyro, round, qt...**$25.00**
Mapleleaf Dairy, Cleveland OH, maple leaf, embossed, round, ½-pt...**$10.00**
Marshall Dairy, Ithaca NY, sundae, red pyro, round, qt..**$14.00**
Mirror Lake Farm, CL Purdy & Son, Herkimer NY, baby top, embossed, round, qt, minimum value.................**$50.00**
Oddo's, Rochester NY, orange letters, qt.......................**$8.00**
Orchard Farms Dairy, Dalles PA, cream top, embossed, round, qt, minimum value.....................................**$25.00**
Radel Dairy, Rochester NY, red letters, qt.....................**$7.50**
Reiss' Dairy Milk, Little Jack Horner..., pyro, round, qt, minimum value...**$20.00**
Riverside Dairy, Milldale CT, on shield, pyro, round, qt...**$35.00**
Ross Jersey Dairy, North Vernon OH, soda fountain scene w/customer, pyro, round, qt.................................**$20.00**

Senica Dairy, Buffalo NY, Indian chief, embossed, round, qt...**$12.00**
St Mary's Dairy, St Mary's PA, barn scene, brown pyro, round, qt...**$14.00**
Sunrise Dairy, Joe Gourde, Jackman ME, red pyro, qt..**$14.00**
Try Our Old Fashioned Buttermilk, Dutch girl, round, qt.**$25.00**
Vermont Country Egg Nog, cow's head, holly on shoulder & back, maroon pyro, square, qt.................................**$9.00**
Wash & Return to Mrs B Mansfield, embossed, round, ½-pt...**$10.00**
Webster Schutts Dairy, Webster NY, red letters, qt........**$7.50**
Whiting Milk Co, Boston MA, embossed, round, ½-pt..**$6.00**
Yes Sir It's Good for Grown-Ups Too, girl w/parents drinking milk, red & black pyro, round, qt.......................**$20.00**

Dakin

Dakin has been in the toy-making business since the 1950s and has made several lines of stuffed and vinyl dolls and animals, but the Dakins that collectors are most interested in today are the licensed characters and advertising figures made from 1968 through the 1970s. Originally there were seven Warner Brothers characters, each with a hard plastic body and a soft vinyl head, all under 10" tall. The line was very successful and eventually expanded to include more than fifty cartoon characters and several more that were advertising related. In addition to the figures, there are banks that were made in two sizes. Some Dakins are quite scarce and may sell for over $100.00 (a few even higher), though most will be in the $30.00 to $60.00 range.

Condition is very important, and if you find one still in the original box, add about 50% to its value. Figures in the colorful 'Cartoon Theatre' boxes command higher prices than those that came in a clear plastic bag or package (MIP). More Dakins are listed in *Schroeder's Collectible Toys, Antique to Modern*, published by Collector Books.

Advisor: Jim Rash (See Directory, Dakins)

Baby Puss, Hanna-Barbera, 1971, EX+ **$100.00**
Bamm-Bamm, Hanna-Barbera, w/club, 1970, EX **$35.00**

Banana Splits, Fleegle, 1970, 7", NM, $75.00.

Bay View, bank, 1976, EX+ **$30.00**
Benji, cloth, 1978, 10", VG **$30.00**
Bob's Big Boy, missing hamburger o/w VG **$80.00**

Bozo the Clown, Larry Harmon, 1974, EX..................$35.00

Bugs Bunny, Warner Bros, 1976, MIB (TV Cartoon Theater box) $40.00

Bugs Bunny, Warner Bros, 1978, MIP (Fun Farm bag)..$20.00

Bull Dog, Dream Pets, EX....................................$15.00

Christian Bros Brandy, St Bernard, 1982, VG $30.00

Cool Cat, Warner Bros, w/beret, 1970, EX+ $40.00

Daffy Duck, Warner Bros, 1976, MIB (TV Cartoon Theater box) $40.00

Deputy Dawg, Terrytoons, 1977, EX..........................$40.00

Dewey Duck, Disney, straight or bent legs, EX..........$40.00

Donald Duck, Disney, 1960s, straight or bent legs, EX ..$20.00

Dumbo, Disney, 1960s, cloth collar, MIB $25.00

Elmer Fudd, Warner Bros, 1968, tuxedo, EX..............$30.00

Foghorn Leghorn, Warner Bros, 1970, EX+ $75.00

Freddy Fast, 1976, M $100.00

Goofy, Disney, 1960s, EX..$20.00

Goofy Gram, Dog, You're Top Dog, EX......................$20.00

Goofy Gram, Kangaroo, World's Greatest Mom!, EX..$20.00

Hokey Wolf, Hanna-Barbera, 1971, EX+...................$250.00

Huckleberry Hound, Hanna-Barbera, 1970, EX+ $75.00

Jack-in-the-Box, bank, 1971, EX..............................$25.00

Kangaroo, Dream Pets, EX......................................$15.00

Kernal Renk, American Seeds, 1970, rare, EX+.........$350.00

Louie Duck, Disney, straight or bent legs, EX $30.00

Merlin the Magic Mouse, Warner Bros, 1970, EX+.....$25.00

Mickey Mouse, Disney, 1960s, cloth clothes, EX $20.00

Midnight Mouse, Dream Pets, w/original tag, EX.......$15.00

Mighty Mouse, Terrytoons, 1978, EX $100.00

Minnie Mouse, Disney, 1960s, cloth clothes, EX........$20.00

Miss Liberty Belle, 1975, MIP..................................$75.00

Monkey on a Barrel, bank, 1971, EX $25.00

Olive Oyl, King Features, 1976, MIB (TV Cartoon Theater box) $40.00

Opus, 1982, cloth, w/tag, 12", EX $15.00

Pepe Le Peu, Warner Bros, 1971, EX $55.00

Pink Panther, Mirisch-Frelong, 1976, MIB (TV Cartoon Theater box)..$50.00

Popeye, King Features, 1974, cloth clothes, MIP $50.00

Porky Pig, Warner Bros, 1968, EX+...........................$30.00

Quasar Robot, bank, 1975, NM $150.00

Road Runner, Warner Bros, 1968, EX+ $30.00

Rocky Squirrel, Jay Ward, 1976, MIB (TV Cartoon Theater box) $60.00

Sambo's Boy, 1974, EX+ $75.00

Sambo's Tiger, 1974, EX+...$125.00

Scooby Doo, Hanna-Barbera, 1980, EX $75.00

Seal on a Box, bank, 1971, EX..................................$25.00

Second Banana, Warner Bros, 1970, EX $35.00

Smokey Bear, 1974, MIP $20.00

Smokey Bear, 1976, MIB (TV Cartoon Theater box) ..$30.00

Snagglepuss, Hanna-Barbera, 1971, EX $100.00

Speedy Gonzales, Warner Bros, MIB (TV Cartoon Theater box) $50.00

Stan Laurel, Larry Harmon, 1974, EX+ $30.00

Swee' Pea, beanbag doll, King Features, 1974, VG $20.00

Sylvester, Warner Bros, 1968, EX+..............................$20.00

Sylvester, Warner Bros, 1978, MIP (Fun Farm bag) $20.00

Tiger in a Cage, bank, 1971, EX................................$25.00

Top Banana, NM...$25.00

Tweety Bird, Warner Bros, 1966, EX+.........................$20.00

Tweety Bird, Warner Bros, 1976, MIB (TV Cartoon Theater box) $40.00

Wile E Coyote, bank, 1971, EX $230.00

Wile E Coyote, Warner Bros, 1968, MIB $30.00

Woodsey Owl, 1974, MIP $60.00

Yosemite Sam, Warner Bros, 1968, MIB.....................$40.00

Sylvester, Warner Bros, 1976, MIB, $40.00.

Decanters

The first company to make figural ceramic decanters was the James Beam Distilling Company. Until mid-1992 they produced hundreds of varieties in their own US-based china factory. They first issued their bottles in the mid-fifties, and over the course of the next twenty-five years, more than twenty other companies followed their example. Among the more prominent of these were Brooks, Hoffman, Lionstone, McCormick, Old Commonwealth, Ski Country, and Wild Turkey. In 1975, Beam introduced the 'Wheel Series,' cars, trains, and fire engines with wheels that actually revolved. The popularity of this series resulted in a heightened interest in decanter collecting.

There are various sizes. The smallest (called miniatures) hold two ounces, and there are some that hold a gallon! A full decanter is worth no more than an empty one, and the absence of the tax stamp doesn't lower its value either. Just be sure that all the labels are intact and that there are no cracks or chips. You might want to empty your decanters as a safety precaution (many collectors do) rather than risk the possibility of the inner glaze breaking down and allowing the contents to leak into the porous ceramic body.

All of the decanters we've listed are fifths unless we've specified 'miniature' within the description.

See also Elvis Presley Collectibles.

Advisor: Art and Judy Turner, Homestead Collectibles (See Directory, Decanters)

Newsletter: *Beam Around the World*
International Association of Jim Beam Bottle and Specialties Club
Shirley Sumbles, Secretary
2015 Burlington Ave., Kewanee, IL 61443; 309-853-3370

Newsletter: *The Ski Country Collector*
1224 Washington Ave., Golden, CO 80401

Aesthetic Specialist (ASI), 1909 Stanley Steamer, green ..**$40.00**

Aesthetic Specialist (ASI), 1910 Oldsmobile, black **$70.00**

Aesthetic Specialist (ASI), 1910 Oldsmobile, gold.....**$125.00**

Beam, Casino Series, Circus Circus Clown **$50.00**

Beam, Casino Series, Golden Gate, 1970....................**$10.00**

Beam, Casino Series, Harrah, gray **$500.00**

Beam, Casino Series, Harrah, silver..........................**$700.00**

Beam, Casino Series, HC Man in Barrel #2 ....**$150.00**

Beam, Casino Series, HC Slot, gray............................**$10.00**

Beam, Casino Series, HC VIP, 1974 ....**$15.00**

Beam, Casino Series, Reno, Prima Donna **$10.00**

Beam, Centennial Series, Cheyenne............................**$10.00**

Beam, Centennial Series, Colorado Centennial **$10.00**

Beam, Centennial Series, Hawaii 200th.......................**$15.00**

Beam, Centennial Series, Laramie...............................**$10.00**

Beam, Centennial Series, New Mexico Bicentennial...**$10.00**

Beam, Centennial Series, St Louis Arch, 1967 ....**$15.00**

Beam, Centennial Series, Washington Bicentennial **$17.00**

Beam, Centennial Series, Yellowstone Park................**$10.00**

Beam, Club Series, Akron Club **$20.00**

Beam, Club Series, Beaver Valley................................**$10.00**

Beam, Club Series, Chicago Loving Cup.....................**$10.00**

Beam, Club Series, Fox, Uncle Sam **$15.00**

Beam, Club Series, Gem City.......................................**$25.00**

Beam, Club Series, Pennsylvania Dutch **$10.00**

Beam, Club Series, Rocky Mountain **$10.00**

Beam, Club Series, Tiffany Poodle..............................**$20.00**

Beam, Club Series, Twin Bridges **$25.00**

Beam, Convention Series, #1 Denver, 1971.................**$10.00**

Beam, Convention Series, #2 Anaheim, 1972.............**$25.00**

Beam, Convention Series, #3 Detroit, 1973 ....**$10.00**

Beam, Convention Series, #4 Lancaster, 1974.............**$25.00**

Beam, Convention Series, #5 Sacramento, 1975..........**$10.00**

Beam, Convention Series, #6 Hartford, 1976...............**$10.00**

Beam, Convention Series, #7 Louisville, 1977 ....**$10.00**

Beam, Convention Series, #8 Chicago, 1978 ....**$10.00**

Beam, Convention Series, #9 Houston, 1979...............**$25.00**

Beam, Convention Series, #10 Norfolk, USS Beam.....**$20.00**

Beam, Convention Series, #11 Showgirl, blond or brunette, each **$40.00**

Beam, Convention Series, #12 Buccaneer, gold **$40.00**

Beam, Convention Series, #13 Gibson Girl, blue or yellow, each **$50.00**

Beam, Convention Series, #14 Mermaid, blond or burnette, each **$40.00**

Beam, Convention Series, #15 Las Vegas....................**$45.00**

Beam, Convention Series, #16 Minuteman **$50.00**

Beam, Convention Series, #17 Kentucky Colonel, blue or gray, each **$65.00**

Beam, Convention Series, #18 Portland Rose, red or yellow, each **$25.00**

Beam, Convention Series, #19 Kansas City.................**$45.00**

Beam, Convention Series, #20 Florida **$45.00**

Beam, Customer Series, Armanette First Award **$10.00**

Beam, Customer Series, Broadmoor Hotel **$10.00**

Beam, Wustomer Series, Foremost, black.................**$200.00**

Beam, Customer Series, Harley-Davidson Eagle **$300.00**

Beam, Customer Series, Harry Hoffman **$10.00**

Beam, Customer Series, Hyatt House, New Orleans...**$10.00**

Beam, Customer Series, Jewel T Man 50th Anniversary....**$75.00**

Beam, Customer Series, Oregon Liquor Commission .**$30.00**

Beam, Customer Series, Ponderosa Ranch..................**$15.00**

Beam, Customer Series, Poulan Chainsaw...................**$25.00**

Beam, Customer Series, Sheraton Inn **$10.00**

Beam, Customer Series, Zimmerman Oatmeal Jug **$45.00**

Beam, Customer Series, Zimmerman 50th Anniversary ..**$25.00**

Beam, Executive Series, Carolier Bell, 1984 ....**$20.00**

Beam, Executive Series, Cherub, gray, 1958 ....**$150.00**

Beam, Executive Series, Fantasia, 1971.......................**$15.00**

Beam, Executive Series, Golden Chalice, 1961 ....**$30.00**

Beam, Executive Series, Golden Jubilee, 1977 ....**$15.00**

Beam, Executive Series, Italian Marble Urn.................**$15.00**

Beam, Executive Series, Presidential, 1968 ....**$15.00**

Beam, Executive Series, Prestige, 1967 ....**$15.00**

Beam, Executive Series, Sovereign, 1969....................**$15.00**

Beam, Executive Series, Tavern Scene, 1959...............**$35.00**

Beam, Executive Series, Titian, 1980............................**$15.00**

Beam, Executive Series, Twin Cherubs, 1974..............**$15.00**

Beam, Foreign Series, Australia, Galah Bird **$25.00**

Beam, Foreign Series, Australia, Koala........................**$15.00**

Beam, Foreign Series, Australia, Sydney Opera **$25.00**

Beam, Foreign Series, Australia, Tiger **$15.00**

Beam, Foreign Series, Boystown **$10.00**

Beam, Foreign Series, Fiji Islands................................**$10.00**

Beam, Foreign Series, Germany, Hansel & Gretel **$10.00**

Beam, Foreign Series, Germany, Wiesbaden...............**$10.00**

Beam, Foreign Series, Kiwi Bird...................................**$8.00**

Beam, Foreign Series, New Zealand, Kiwi....................**$5.00**

Beam, Foreign Series, Queensland...............................**$22.00**

Beam, Foreign Series, Richard Hadlee **$95.00**

Beam, Foreign Series, Samoa.......................................**$10.00**

Beam, Opera Series, Boris Godinov, w/base & paperweight..**$195.00**

Beam, Opera Series, Don Giovanni, w/base & paperweight..**$125.00**

Beam, Opera Series, Falstaff, w/base.........................**$125.00**

Beam, Opera Series, Figaro, w/base & paperweight ..**$125.00**

Beam, Opera Series, Nutcracker, w/paperweight **$95.00**

Beam, Organization Series, Blue Goose Order **$10.00**

Beam, Organization Series, BPO Does **$10.00**

Beam, Organization Series, Devil Dog.........................**$35.00**

Beam, Organization Series, Ducks Unlimited #1, Mallard, 1974 ....**$50.00**

Beam, Organization Series, Ducks Unlimited #11, Pintail Pr, 1985 ....**$65.00**

Beam, Organization Series, Ducks Unlimited #14, Gadwalls, 1988 ....**$50.00**

Beam, Organization Series, Ducks Unlimited #17, Tundra Swan, 1991 ....**$40.00**

Beam, Organization Series, Ducks Unlimited #2, Wood Duck, 1975 ....**$45.00**

Beam, Organization Series, Ducks Unlimited #6, Teal, 1980..**$50.00**

Beam, Organization Series, Legion Music....................**$10.00**

Beam, Organization Series, Pearl Harbor, 1976..........**$10.00**

Beam, Organization Series, Phi Sigma Kappa $15.00
Beam, Organization Series, Telephone #1, Wall, 1907..$20.00
Beam, Organization Series, Telephone #3, Cradle, 1928...$25.00
Beam, Organization Series, Telephone #7, Digital Dial.....$40.00
Beam, Organization Series, Trout Unlimited...............$15.00
Beam, Organization Series, Yuma Rifle Club..............$20.00
Beam, People Series, Captain & Mate.........................$10.00
Beam, People Series, Emmet Kelley, Native Son $55.00
Beam, People Series, General Stark $15.00
Beam, People Series, Hannah Dustin..........................$30.00
Beam, People Series, Hone Heke $150.00
Beam, People Series, John Henry...............................$18.00
Beam, People Series, King Kamehameha $15.00
Beam, People Series, Leprechaun $15.00
Beam, People Series, Petroleum Man $15.00
Beam, People Series, Rocky Marciano $40.00
Beam, People Series, Santa Claus, w/paperweight ...$150.00
Beam, Political Series, Campaigner Donkey, 1960......$20.00
Beam, Political Series, Election Demecrat, 1988..........$30.00
Beam, Political Series, Election Republican, 1988.......$35.00
Beam, Political Series, New York Donkey, 1976........$20.00
Beam, Political Series, San Diego Elephant, 1972 ......$25.00
Beam, Regal China Series, AC Sparkplug $40.00
Beam, Regal China Series, Antique Clock...................$30.00
Beam, Regal China Series, Big Apple..........................$20.00
Beam, Regal China Series, Christmas Tree, w/paperweight .$175.00
Beam, Regal China Series, Expo 1974........................$10.00
Beam, Regal China Series, Franklin Mint $10.00
Beam, Regal China Series, Hawaii Aloha....................$10.00
Beam, Regal China Series, Jukebox............................$60.00
Beam, Regal China Series, Musicians on Cask $10.00
Beam, Regal China Series, Permian Oil Show............$10.00
Beam, Regal China Series, Seattle World's Fair $10.00
Beam, Regal China Series, Stone Mountain $20.00
Beam, Regal China Series, Tombstone.......................$10.00
Beam, Regal China Series, Vendome Wagon..............$50.00
Beam, Sports Series, AT&T Pebble Beach, 1991 ....$250.00

Beam, Sports Series, Bing Crosby National Pro-Am, 29th, $10.00.

Beam, Sports Series, Bing Crosby 29th, 1970 ....$10.00
Beam, Sports Series, Bing Crosby 37th, 1978 ....$35.00
Beam, Sports Series, Bing Crosy 32nd, 1973 ....$35.00
Beam, Sports Series, Bob Hope 14th, 1973 ....$15.00
Beam, Sports Series, Bowling Pin.............................$10.00
Beam, Sports Series, Clint Eastwood $25.00
Beam, Sports Series, Fiesta Bowl...............................$10.00

Beam, Sports Series, Hula Bowl $15.00
Beam, Sports Series, Kentucky Derby 95th, pink or red roses,
    each $20.00
Beam, Sports Series, Louisiana Superdome $15.00
Beam, Sports Series, Mint 400, metal stopper, 1970 ...$10.00
Beam, Sports Series, PGA $15.00
Beam, Sports Series, Ruidoso Downs..........................$15.00
Beam, Sports Series, Seattle Seafair $15.00
Beam, Sports Series, WGA Western Open..................$15.00
Beam, State Series, Alaska...$40.00
Beam, State Series, Delaware....................................$10.00

Beam, States Series, Arizona, 12½", $10.00.

Beam, State Series, Florida.......................................$10.00
Beam, State Series, Hawaii, 1959...............................$32.00
Beam, State Series, Maine $10.00
Beam, State Series, Nevada $40.00
Beam, State Series, North Dakota.............................$45.00
Beam, State Series, Ohio $10.00
Beam, State Series, Pennsylvania...............................$15.00
Beam, State Series, Washington $15.00
Beam, State Series, West Virginia $125.00
Beam, Trophy Series, Armadillo $15.00
Beam, Trophy Series, Bird, Blue Goose $10.00
Beam, Trophy Series, Bird, Cardinal Female $15.00
Beam, Trophy Series, Bird, Robin $10.00
Beam, Trophy Series, Bird, Snow Goose....................$15.00
Beam, Trophy Series, Bird, Woodpecker...................$10.00
Beam, Trophy Series, Cat, Burmese $10.00
Beam, Trophy Series, Doe $15.00
Beam, Trophy Series, Dog, Poodle, gray or white, each ..$10.00
Beam, Trophy Series, Dog, St Bernard $30.00
Beam, Trophy Series, Fish, Bluegill............................$20.00
Beam, Trophy Series, Fish, Muskie $15.00
Beam, Trophy Series, Fish, Northern Pike...................$15.00
Beam, Trophy Series, Harp Seal $20.00
Beam, Trophy Series, Horse, mare & foal $45.00
Beam, Trophy Series, Horse, white, 1967...................$15.00
Beam, Trophy Series, Jaguar.....................................$20.00
Beam, Wheel Series, Duesenberg Convertible, dark blue ..$125.00
Beam, Wheel Series, Dump Truck $40.00
Beam, Wheel Series, Tractor Trailer, orange or yellow,
    each...$65.00
Beam, Wheel Series, Train (Casey Jones), Tank Car...$30.00
Beam, Wheel Series, Train (General), Caboose, gray ..$65.00
Beam, Wheel Series, Train (General), Locomotive ...$110.00

Beam, Wheel Series, Train (Grant), Caboose, red.......**$65.00**
Beam, Wheel Series, Train (Turner), Caboose, yellow .**$85.00**
Beam, Wheel Series, Train (Turner), Locomotive **$125.00**
Beam, Wheel Series, Volkswagen, blue or red, each..**$75.00**
Beam, Wheel Series, 1930 Ford Paddy Wagon **$150.00**
Beam, Wheel Series, 1935 Ford Fire Pumper Truck ...**$90.00**
Beam, Wheel Series, 1953 Chevy Corvette, white **$175.00**
Beam, Wheel Series, 1956 Ford T-Bird, green or yellow, each **$110.00**
Beam, Wheel Series, 1957, Chevy Corvette, red.......**$195.00**
Beam, Wheel Series, 1957 Chevy, turquoise **$70.00**
Beam, Wheel Series, 1957 Chevy Convertible, black..**$70.00**
Beam, Wheel Series, 1959 Cadillac, blue...................**$150.00**
Beam, Wheel Series, 1969 Chevy Camaro, green **$175.00**
Beam, Wheel Series, 1969 Chevy Camaro, silver......**$125.00**
Beam, Wheel Series, 1986 Chevy Corvette, bronze **$90.00**
Brooks, Automobiles & Transportation Series, Indy Racer Penske #3 ....**$75.00**
Brooks, Automobiles & Transportation Series, Ontario Racer #10 ....**$25.00**
Brooks, Automobiles & Transportation Series, 1957 Corvette, blue................**$125.00**

Brooks, Quail, 1970, $12.00.

Budweiser, Grant's Farm C515, short.......................**$325.00**
Budweiser, Jim Beam 83 Convention, brown **$125.00**
Budweiser, Jim Beam 92 Convention, celadon **$45.00**
Budweiser, Panda GM6...**$130.00**
Budweiser, Sea World, Dolphin CS187 ....**$25.00**
Davis Country, Automobiles & Transportation Series, Jeep CJ-7, red................**$45.00**
Davis County, Automobiles & Transportation Series, IML Tractor Trailer................**$50.00**
Famous First, Automobiles & Transportation Series, Duesenberg **$95.00**
Famous First, Automobiles & Transportation Series, Duesenberg, red, rare................**$245.00**
Famous First, Automobiles & Transportation Series, Renault Racer #3................**$50.00**
Famous First, Automobiles & Transportation Series, 1953 Corvette **$95.00**
Hoffman, Lucky Lindy................**$95.00**
Lionstone, Automobiles & Transportation Series, Corvette (1.75L), white **$95.00**
Lionstone, Barber................**$25.00**
Lionstone, Buffalo Hunter................**$20.00**
Lionstone, Calamity Jane................**$15.00**

Lionstone, Chinese Laundryman................**$20.00**
Lionstone, Circut Judge **$12.00**
Lionstone, Dancehall Girl................**$25.00**
Lionstone, Firefighter w/Child #2................**$50.00**
Lionstone, Jesse James................**$15.00**
Lionstone, Molly Brown **$15.00**
Lionstone, Saturday Nite Bath................**$45.00**
Lionstone, Sodbuster **$10.00**
Lionstone, Tribal Chief **$20.00**
Lionstone, Wells Fargo Man **$15.00**
McCormick, Elvis, See Elvis Presley category
McCormick, Jimmy Durante................**$55.00**
Mike Wayne, Christmas Tree, white **$75.00**

Mike Wayne, John Wayne Bust, $65.00.

Mike Wayne, John Wayne Statue, bronze................**$125.00**
Pacesetter, Ahrens Fox, red & white................**$125.00**
Pacesetter, American La France **$65.00**
Pacesetter, Mack, white & red **$150.00**
Wade, District Teapot, blue or cream, each **$45.00**
Wade, Fire Station Teapot................**$40.00**
Wade, German Beamers Club, 1995................**$40.00**
Wade, Jim Beam Convention Moneybox, blue or cream, each................**$65.00**
Wade, Lipton Tea Cookie Jar................**$45.00**
Wade, Westie Dog................**$30.00**
Wade, 200th Anniversary Barrel, blue................**$45.00**
Wild Turkey, #1, in flight................**$40.00**
Wild Turkey, #1, in flight, mini **$40.00**
Wild Turkey, #5, w/Raccoon, mini................**$30.00**
Wild Turkey, #10, w/Coyote................**$40.00**
Wild Turkey, #10, w/Coyote, mini **$40.00**
Wild Turkey, Turkey on Log, 1972, mini................**$15.00**
Wild Turkey, Turkey Taking Off, 1977 ....**$15.00**

Degenhart

John and Elizabeth Degenhart owned and operated the Crystal Art Glass Factory in Cambridge, Ohio. From 1947 until John died in 1964 they produced some fine glassware; John was well known for his superior paperweights. But the glassware that collectors love today was made after '64, when Elizabeth restructured the company, creating many lovely moulds and scores of colors. She hired Zack Boyd, who had previously worked for Cambridge Glass, and between the two of them, they developed almost 150 unique and original color formulas.

Complying with provisions she had made before her death, close personal friends at Island Mould and Machine Company in Wheeling, West Virginia, took Elizabeth's moulds and removed the familiar 'D in heart' trademark from them. She had requested that ten of her moulds be donated to the Degenhart Museum, where they remain today. Zack Boyd eventually bought the Degenhart factory and acquired the remaining moulds. He has added his own logo to them and is continuing to press glass very similar to Mrs. Degenhart's.

For more information, we recommend *Degenhart Glass and Paperweights* by Gene Florence, published by the Degenhart Paperweight and Glass Museum, Inc., Cambridge, Ohio.

Advisor: Linda K. Marsh (See Directory, Degenhart)

Club: Friends of Degenhart
Degenhart Paperweight and Glass Museum
P.O. Box 186, Cambridge, OH 43725; Individual membership: $5 per year; membership includes newsletter, *Heartbeat*, a quarterly publication, and free admission to the museum

Baby (Hobo) Shoe, Milk Blue	$15.00
Baby (Hobo) Shoe, Toffee Slag	$20.00
Baby (Hobo) Shoe Toothpick, Cobalt	$15.00
Baby (Hobo) Shoe Toothpick, Taffeta	$15.00
Basket Toothpick, Sparrow Slag	$22.50
Beaded Oval Toothpick, Bittersweet Slag, 1976	$45.00
Beaded Oval Toothpick, Fawn	$20.00
Beaded Oval Toothpick, Ivory	$20.00
Beaded Oval Toothpick, Lemon Custard	$45.00
Beaded Oval Toothpick, Vaseline	$15.00
Bicentennial Bell, Canary	$12.00
Bicentennial Bell, Crown Tuscan	$16.00
Bicentennial Bell, Crystal	$8.00
Bicentennial Bell, Custard	$25.00
Bicentennial Bell, Elizabeth's Lime Ice	$15.00
Bicentennial Bell, Rose Marie Pink	$12.00
Bird Salt & Pepper, Gun Metal	$40.00
Bird Salt & Pepper, Nile Green	$35.00
Bird Salt & Pepper, Ruby	$50.00
Bird Salt w/Cherry, Autumn	$22.00
Bird Salt w/Cherry, Bernard Boyd's Ebony	$30.00
Bird Salt w/Cherry, Brown	$15.00
Bird Salt w/Cherry, Forest Green	$16.00
Bird Toothpick, Red	$45.00
Bow Slipper, Champagne	$15.00
Bow Slipper, Opal	$16.00
Bow Slipper, Rose Marie	$17.50
Buzz Saw Wine, Amberina	$35.00
Buzz Saw Wine, Cobalt	$38.00
Buzz Saw Wine, Willow Blue	$30.00
Chick Covered Dish, Lemon Custard, 2"	$60.00
Chick Covered Dish, Light Powder Blue, 2"	$27.00
Chick Covered Dish, White, 2"	$20.00
Child's Mug, Amberina	$22.50
Child's Mug, Apple Green	$23.00
Child's Mug, Blue Green	$25.00

Child's Mug, Opal	$20.00
Coaster, Amber	$6.00
Colonial Drape Toothpick, Amberina	$20.00
Colonial Drape Toothpick, Cobalt	$22.00
Daisy & Button Creamer & Sugar, Cobalt	$90.00
Daisy & Button Hat, Frosty Jade	$15.00
Daisy & Button Salt, Custard, unmarked	$13.50
Daisy & Button Salt, Gold	$13.50
Daisy & Button Salt, Vaseline	$12.00
Daisy & Button Toothpick, Baby Blue Slag	$25.00
Daisy & Button Toothpick, Cobalt Carnival, hand stamped	$30.00
Daisy & Button Toothpick, Light Amberina	$22.00
Daisy & Button Toothpick, Pink	$16.00
Daisy & Button Toothpick, Vaseline	$17.50
Elephant Head Toothpick, Blue Green	$30.00
Forget-Me-Not Toothpick, Bloody Mary (#1 or #2)	$45.00
Forget-Me-Not Toothpick, Bluebell	$20.00
Forget-Me-Not Toothpick, Caramel	$32.50
Forget-Me-Not Toothpick, Dark Chocolate Creme	$25.00
Forget-Me-Not Toothpick, Dogwood	$40.00
Forget-me-Not Toothpick, Fog	$18.00
Forget-Me-Not Toothpick, Lavender Blue	$25.00
Forget-Me-Not Toothpick, Milk Blue	$15.00
Forget-Me-Not Toothpick, Misty Green	$20.00
Forget-Me-Not Toothpick, Peach-Opaque	$22.00
Forget-Me-Not Toothpick, Toffee	$25.00
Forget-Me-Not Toothpick, Twilight Blue	$20.00

Gypsy pot, Bittersweet, 2¼", $35.00.

Gypsy Pot Toothpick, Bloody Mary	$50.00
Gypsy Pot Toothpick, Cobalt, hand stamped	$25.00
Gypsy Pot Toothpick, Tomato	$40.00
Hand, April Green	$12.00
Hand, Bernard's Boyd Ebony	$22.50
Hand, Ivorene	$15.00
Hand, Persimmon	$8.00
Hand, Sapphire	$6.00
Heart & Lyre Cup Plate, Amethyst, unmarked	$6.00
Heart & Lyre Cup Plate, Blue Green	$10.00
Heart & Lyre Cup Plate, Emerald Green, unmarked	$6.00
Heart & Lyre Cup Plate, Mulberry	$20.00
Heart Jewel Box, Baby Pink	$26.00
Heart Jewel Box, Chocolate Creme	$32.00
Heart Jewel Box, Elizabeth Blue	$44.00
Heart Jewel Box, Royal Violet	$25.00
Heart Toothpick, Amethyst	$15.00
Heart Toothpick, Buttercup Slag	$35.00

Heart Toothpick, Dark Blue Jay Slag $35.00
Heart Toothpick, Gray Tomato....................................$25.00
Heart Toothpick, Seafoam Green $25.00
Hen Covered Dish, Amberina, unmarked, 3" $30.00
Hen Covered Dish, Caramel Custard Slag, 3" $50.00
Hen Covered Dish, Crystal, 5" $25.00
Hen Covered Dish, Pigeon Blood, 3".........................$50.00
Hen Covered Dish, Sparrow Slag, 3" $25.00
High Boot, Ruby $40.00
Kat Slipper, Jabe's Amber...$25.00
Lamb Covered Dish, Canary $35.00
Lamb Covered Dish, Sapphire $30.00
Mini Pitcher, Opal Milk Blue......................................$20.00
Mini Slipper w/Sole, Champagne $30.00
Owl, Apple Green, old..$50.00
Owl, Bluebell $35.00
Owl, Bluebird #2 ....$50.00
Owl, Chad's Blue...$50.00
Owl, Custard Opal $45.00
Owl, Fog Opaque $55.00
Owl, Frosted Shamrock $35.00
Owl, Heliotrope $100.00
Owl, Ivorene $50.00
Owl, Lemon Chiffon..$40.00
Owl, Limeade $75.00
Owl, Mauve $38.00
Owl, Pearl Gray $35.00
Owl, Pigeon Blood $45.00
Owl, Teal...$22.00
Pooch, April Day $20.00
Pooch, Bittersweet $30.00
Pooch, Buttercup Slag $35.00
Pooch, Charcoal $22.00
Pooch, Fantastic $45.00
Pooch, Gray Tomato...$32.00
Pooch, Green Caramel Slag $45.00
Pooch, Gun Metal $22.00
Pooch, Milk Blue $16.00
Pooch, Milk White $13.50
Pooch, Old Lavender $20.00
Pooch, Red $30.00
Pooch, Snow White $13.50
Pottie Salt, Amethyst...$6.00
Pottie Salt, Vaseline $12.00
Priscilla Doll, Blue & White $125.00
Priscilla Doll, Daffodil $100.00
Priscilla Doll, Jade $125.00
Priscilla Doll, Smoky Blue $88.00
Robin, Crown Tuscan, unmarked, 5" $70.00
Roller Skate (Skate Shoe), Ice Blue Carnival $40.00
Seal of Ohio Cup Plate, Elizabeth's Blue.....................$25.00
Star & Dew Drop Salt, Crystal $10.00
Star & Dew Drop Salt, Custard, unmarked...................$17.50
Star & Dew Drop Salt, Heatherbloom..........................$30.00
Texas Boot, Sapphire $12.00
Texas Creamer & Sugar, Milk White.............................$50.00
Turkey Covered Dish, Amberina $70.00
Turkey Covered Dish, Amethyst....................................$40.00
Turkey Covered Dish, Bittersweet.................................$75.00

Turkey Covered Dish, Crown Tuscan $80.00
Turkey Covered Dish, Gray Slag, unmarked...............$85.00
Wildflower Candle Holder, Crown Tuscan $30.00
Wildflower Candy Dish, Amethyst, unmarked $25.00
Wildflower Candy Dish, Crown Tuscan, unmarked....$30.00
Wildflower Candy Dish, Crystal, unmarked................$18.50
Wildflower Candy Dish, Twilight Blue $25.00

deLee Art Pottery

Jimmie Lee Adair Kohl founded her company in 1937, and it continued to operate until 1958. She was the inspiration, artist, and owner of the company for the 21 years it was in business. The name deLee means 'of or by Lee' and is taken from the French language. She trained as an artist at the San Diego Art Institute and UCLA where she also earned an art education degree. She taught art and ceramics at Belmont High School in Los Angeles while getting her ceramic business started. In 1997 she turned 91 years old and is still a working artist, doing commissioned pieces and other creations for fun.

The deLee line included children, adults, animals, birds, and specialty items such as cookie jars, banks, wall pockets, and several licensed Walter Lantz characters. Skunks were a favorite subject, and more of her pieces were modeled as skunks than any other single animal. Her figurines are distinctive for their design, charm, and excellent hand painting; when carefully studied, they can be easily recognized. Jimmie Lee modeled almost all the pieces — more than 350 in all.

The beautiful deLee colors were mixed by her and remained essentially the same for 20 years. The same figurine may be found painted in different colors and patterns. Figurines were sold wholesale only. Buyers could select from a catalog or visit the deLee booth in New York and Los Angeles Gift Marts. All figurines left the factory with name and logo stickers. The round Art Deco logo sticker is silver with the words 'deLee Art, California, Hand Decorated.' Many of the figures are incised 'deLee Art' on the bottom.

The factory was located in Los Angeles during its 21 years of production and in Cuernavaca, Mexico, for four years during WWII. Production continued until 1958, when Japanese copies of her figures caused sales to decline. For further study we recommend *deLee Art* by Joanne and Ralph Schaefer and John Humphries.

Advisors: Joanne and Ralph Schaefer (See Directory, deLee)

Bank, Henny Penny...$85.00
Bank, Money Bunny, rabbit w/purse, pink clay, from $90
    to..$125.00
Candle holder, Twinkle or Star, each, from $25 to.....$35.00
Figurine, adult Cuban couple, Panchita dancing & Pedro
    playing bongos, 13", pr, from $225 to $300.00
Figurine, Annabelle, holds out skirt/planter at side & hat
    w/other hand, 8", from $35 to............................$45.00
Figurine, Babe, deer, from $30 to................................$45.00
Figurine, Danny, boy in top hat & wearing vest, matches
    Hattie, 9", from $35 to...$50.00

Figurine, girl doing somersault, on head, 5" **$50.00**
Figurine, girl doing somersault, 5" **$60.00**
Figurine, girl on her head, 5" **$60.00**
Figurine, Hans & Katrina, Dutch boy & girl, pink clay, 7", pr, from $70 to..**$90.00**
Figurine, Hattie, girl in long skirt w/fan & planter, 7½", from $30 to...**$45.00**
Figurine, Katrina, planter, 6½" **$35.00**
Figurine, Kitty, sitting w/painted closed eyes, floral decor, 4", from $35 to...**$45.00**
Figurine, Kitty (girl w/kitten) & Kenny (boy w/dog), 7", pr, from $70 to...**$85.00**
Figurine, Lizzie, lady w/lg hat & full skirt, planter, 9", from $35 to...**$50.00**
Figurine, Mr & Mrs Skunk, w/hats, planter, original label, pr, from $70 to...**$85.00**
Figurine, Mr Chips, squirrel, 4½", from $25 to............**$35.00**
Figurine, Oswalt the Rabbit, w/tag, from $80 to.......**$100.00**
Figurine, Pat, blond girl holds skirt/planter at front, head turned to right, 7", from $25 to **$40.00**
Figurine, poodle, applied spaghetti, from $70 to........**$90.00**
Figurine, Sandy, Airedale, 3¾", pr, from $75 to........**$100.00**
Figurine, Siamese cat, 12" **$60.00**
Figurine, Zombie, zebra, from $60 to **$75.00**

Figurines, Cuban couple, Panchita and Pedro, 7½" and 8½", from $50.00 to $75.00 for the pair. (Photo courtesy Joanne and Ralph Schaefer)

Flower frog, girl atop rounded base, 5" **$60.00**
Match holder, DeStinker, skunk figural, wall mount...**$35.00**

Depression Glass

Since the early sixties, this has been a very active area of collecting. Interest is still very strong, and although values have long been established, except for some of the rarer items, Depression Glass is still relatively inexpensive. Some of the patterns and colors that were entirely avoided by the early wave of collectors are now becoming popular, and it's very easy to reassemble a nice table setting of one of these lines today.

Most of this glass was produced during the Depression years. It was inexpensive, mass produced, and was available in a wide assortment of colors. The same type of glassware was still being made to some extent during the fifties and sixties, and today the term 'Depression glass' has been expanded to include the later patterns as well.

Some things have been reproduced, and the slight variation in patterns and colors can be very difficult to detect. For instance, the Sharon butter dish has been reissued in original colors of pink and green (as well as others that were not original); and several pieces of Cherry Blossom, Madrid, Avocado, Mayfair, and Miss America have also been reproduced. Some pieces you'll see in antique malls and flea markets today have been recently made in dark uncharacteristic carnival colors, which, of course, are easy to spot.

For further study, Gene Florence has written several informative books on the subject, and we recommend them all: *The Pocket Guide to Depression Glass, The Collector's Encyclopedia of Depression Glass,* and *Very Rare Glassware of the Depression Years.*

Publication: *Depression Glass Daze*
Teri Steel, Editor/Publisher
Box 57, Otisville, MI 48463; 810-631-4593. The nation's market place for glass, china, and pottery

Adam, ashtray, green, 4½" **$25.00**
Adam, bowl, cereal; pink or green, 5¾"......................**$42.00**
Adam, bowl, green, oval, 10" **$32.00**
Adam, bowl, pink, w/lid, 9" **$65.00**
Adam, butter dish, pink, w/lid **$80.00**
Adam, candy jar, green, w/lid, 2½" **$100.00**
Adam, lamp, pink..**$275.00**
Adam, plate, cake; pink, footed, 10".............................**$25.00**
Adam, plate, dinner; pink, square, 9" **$33.00**
Adam, plate, grill; green, 9"...**$22.00**
Adam, plate, sherbet; green, 6" **$10.00**
Adam, relish dish, pink, divided, 8".............................**$20.00**
Adam, saucer, pink or green, square, 6".......................**$6.00**
Adam, sugar bowl, pink, w/lid....................................**$42.50**
Adam, tumbler, green, 4½" **$28.00**
Adam, tumbler, iced tea; pink, 5½"............................**$60.00**

Adam, water pitcher, pink, $40.00.

American Pioneer, bowl, crystal, pink or green, handled, 5" **$20.00**
American Pioneer, bowl, crystal or pink, w/lid, 9¼"..**$95.00**
American Pioneer, bowl, green, handled, 9" **$27.50**
American Pioneer, candlestick, green, 6½", pr...........**$90.00**

American Pioneer, candy jar, crystal or pink, w/lid, 1-lb ..**$85.00**

American Pioneer, cheese & cracker set (indented platter & comport), green **$65.00**

American Pioneer, creamer, crystal or pink, 2¾" **$25.00**

American Pioneer, cup, green...........................**$12.00**

American Pioneer, goblet, cocktail; amber, 3-oz, 3¾"...**$40.00**

American Pioneer, goblet, water; crystal or pink, 8-oz, 6"..**$45.00**

American Pioneer, goblet, wine; green, 3-oz, 4".........**$50.00**

American Pioneer, lamp, crystal or pink, tall, 8½" ...**$100.00**

American Pioneer, mayonaise, green, 4¼" **$90.00**

American Pioneer, pilsner, crystal, pink or green, 11-oz, 5¾" **$125.00**

American Pioneer, pitcher, green, covered urn style, 5" ..**$210.00**

American Pioneer, plate, crystal or pink, 6" **$12.50**

American Pioneer, plate, green, 8"......................**$12.00**

American Pioneer, saucer, green.........................**$5.00**

American Pioneer, sugar bowl, crystal or pink, 2¾"...**$20.00**

American Pioneer, tumbler, crystal or pink, 8-oz, 4" ..**$30.00**

American Sweetheart, bowl, cereal; cremax, 6" **$10.00**

American Sweetheart, bowl, soup; monax, flat, 9½" ..**$80.00**

American Sweetheart, bowl, soup; smoke & other trims, 9½" **$125.00**

American Sweetheart, cup, blue...........................**$125.00**

American Sweetheart, cup, pink..........................**$18.00**

American Sweetheart, lamp shade, cremax...............**$450.00**

American Sweetheart, pitcher, pink, 80-oz, 8"..........**$695.00**

American Sweetheart, plate, luncheon; monax, 9"......**$12.00**

American Sweetheart, plate, salad; red, 8"...................**$85.00**

American Sweetheart, plate, salver; blue, 12" **$210.00**

American Sweetheart, plate, server; red, 15½"..........**$300.00**

American Sweetheart, salt & pepper shakers, monax, footed, pr **$400.00**

American Sweetheart, sugar bowl, smoke & other trims, footed **$95.00**

American Sweetheart, tumbler, pink, 5-oz, 3½" **$95.00**

American Sweetheart, tumbler, pink, 9-oz, 4¼" **$80.00**

Aunt Polly, bowl, berry; green or iridescent, 4¾".........**$8.00**

Aunt Polly, bowl, green or iridescent, oval, 8⅜" **$45.00**

Aunt Polly, bowl, pickle; blue, handled, oval, 7¼" **$40.00**

Aunt Polly, butter dish, blue, w/lid......................**$210.00**

Aunt Polly, candy dish, blue, footed, 2-handled........**$45.00**

Aunt Polly, candy dish, green or iridescent, w/lid, 2-handled..**$75.00**

Aunt Polly, creamer, blue..................................**$50.00**

Aunt Polly, plate, sherbet; blue, 6".......................**$14.00**

Aunt Polly, sherbet, green or iridescent...................**$10.00**

Aunt Polly, sugar bowl, blue, w/lid.......................**$190.00**

Aunt Polly, tumbler, blue, 8-oz, 3⅝".....................**$30.00**

Aunt Polly, vase, green or iridescent, footed, 6½"......**$30.00**

Aurora, bowl, cobalt or pink, 4½" deep...................**$55.00**

Aurora, cup, green...**$7.50**

Aurora, saucer, green.......................................**$2.50**

Aurora, tumbler, cobalt or pink, 10-oz, 4¾"..............**$25.00**

Avocado, bowl, crystal, 2-handled, 5½".................**$10.00**

Avocado, bowl, green, 2-handled, oval, 8"..............**$27.50**

Avocado, bowl, preserve; pink, handled, 7".............**$20.00**

Avocado, creamer, pink, footed.............................**$30.00**

Avocado, pitcher, pink, 64-oz.............................**$800.00**

Avocado, plate, luncheon; crystal, 8¼" **$7.00**

Avocado, saucer, pink, 6⅜" **$22.00**

Avocado, sugar bowl, green, footed **$35.00**

Beaded Block, bowl, amber, flared, round, 7¼"........**$14.00**

Beaded Block, bowl, canary yellow, plain edge, round, 7½" **$30.00**

Beaded Block, bowl, green, round, 6" deep..............**$15.00**

Beaded Block, bowl, jelly; pink, 2-handled, 4⅞-5" **$10.00**

Beaded Block, bowl, opalescent, square, 5½" **$24.00**

Beaded Block, bowl, red, round, 6½" **$28.00**

Beaded Block, creamer, pink.................................**$18.00**

Beaded Block, plate, green, round, 8¾"...................**$22.00**

Beaded Block, sugar bowl, red............................**$30.00**

Beaded Block, vase, bouquet; amber, 6" **$14.00**

Block Optic, bowl, berry; pink, lg, 8½"...................**$35.00**

Block Optic, bowl, green, 1½x4½"........................**$27.50**

Block Optic, butter dish, blue, w/lid, 3x5".............**$495.00**

Block Optic, candy jar, pink, w/lid, 6¼".................**$135.00**

Block Optic, cup, yellow, 4 styles...........................**$8.00**

Block Optic, goblet, wine; green or pink, 4½" **$37.00**

Block Optic, goblet, yellow, thin, 9-oz, 7¼" **$38.00**

Block Optic, mug, green....................................**$33.00**

Block Optic, pitcher, green or pink, 80-oz, 8" **$90.00**

Block Optic, plate, green or yellow, 12¾" **$30.00**

Block Optic, sherbet, yellow, 5½-oz, 3¼" **$10.00**

Block Optic, tumbler, green, flat, 10- or 11-oz, 5".....**$22.00**

Block Optic, tumbler, green or pink, flat, 12-oz, 4⅞"..**$25.00**

Block Optic, tumbler, pink, flat, 5-oz, 3½"..............**$25.00**

Block Optic, tumbler, pink, footed, 10-oz, 6".............**$32.00**

Block Optic, tumbler, yellow, footed, 9-oz...............**$22.00**

Block Optic, whiskey, green or pink, 2-oz, 2¼".........**$30.00**

Bowknot, bowl, berry; green, 4½"..........................**$16.00**

Bowknot, cup, green...**$8.00**

Bowknot, plate, salad; green, 7"...........................**$12.00**

Bowknot, sherbet, green, low footed **$17.50**

Bowknot, tumbler, footed, 10-oz, 5".......................**$22.50**

Cameo, bowl, berry; green, lg, 8¼".......................**$37.50**

Cameo, bowl, cream soup; green, 4¾"....................**$130.00**

Cameo, bowl, sauce; crystal, 4¼".............................**$6.00**

Cameo, bowl, soup; pink, rimmed, 9"....................**$135.00**

Cameo, bowl, vegetable; yellow, oval, 10"................**$42.00**

Cameo, butter dish, yellow, w/lid......................**$1,500.00**

Cameo, cookie jar, green, w/lid **$52.00**

Cameo, creamer, yellow, 3¼" **$20.00**

Cameo, cup, green, 2 styles.................................**$14.00**

Cameo, decanter, crystal, w/stopper, 10"..................**$225.00**

Cameo, goblet, water; pink, 6"............................**$175.00**

Cameo, goblet, wine; green, 4" **$75.00**

Cameo, pitcher, juice; green, 36-oz, 6" **$60.00**

Cameo, plate, cake; green, flat, 10½" **$100.00**

Cameo, plate, dinner; pink, 9½"..........................**$85.00**

Cameo, plate, green, square, 8½".........................**$42.00**

Cameo, plate, salad; crystal, 7" **$3.50**

Cameo, plate, sandwich; green, 10" **$13.00**

Cameo, plate, sherbet; green, 6".............................**$4.00**

Cameo, salt & pepper shakers, green, footed, pr **$70.00**

Cameo, sherbet, pink, blown, 3⅛"..........................**$75.00**

Cameo, sugar bowl, green, 4¼"............................**$27.50**

Cameo, sugar bowl, yellow, 3¼"...........................**$18.00**

Cameo, tumbler, water; crystal, 9-oz, 4".....................**$9.00**

Cameo, tumbler, yellow, footed, 9-oz, 5" **$16.00**

Cherry Blossom, bowl, berry; delphite, round, 8½" ..**$50.00**

Cherry Blossom, bowl, berry; pink, 4¾" **$16.00**

Cherry Blossom, bowl, soup; green, flat, 7¾" **$80.00**

Cherry Blossom, butter dish, pink, w/lid..............**$75.00**

Cherry Blossom, coaster, green **$13.00**

Cherry Blossom, cup, delphite **$18.00**

Cherry Blossom, mug, green, 7-oz............**$195.00**

Cherry Blossom, plate, grill; green, 10" **$95.00**

Cherry Blossom, plate, salad; pink, 7" **$20.00**

Cherry Blossom, platter, pink, oval, 11"............**$40.00**

Cherry Blossom, platter, pink, oval, 9"............**$850.00**

Cherry Blossom, saucer, pink, green or delphite **$5.00**

Cherry Blossom, sugar bowl, pink, w/lid............**$33.00**

Cherry Blossom, tray, sandwich; pink or green, 10½"..**$30.00**

Cherry Blossom, tumbler, green, pattern at the top, flat, 12-oz, 5"............**$75.00**

Cherryberry, bowl, berry; crystal, 4"............**$6.50**

Cherryberry, bowl, berry; pink or green, 7½"............**$25.00**

Cherryberry, butter dish, pink or green, w/lid..........**$175.00**

Cherryberry, comport, pink or green, 5¾" **$25.00**

Cherryberry, creamer, crystal, lg, 4⅝" **$15.00**

Cherryberry, pickle dish, pink or green, oval, 8¼".....**$18.00**

Cherryberry, plate, sherbet; crystal, 6" **$6.00**

Cherryberry, sherbet, pink or green............**$10.00**

Cherryberry, sugar bowl, crystal, lg............**$15.00**

Cherryberry, tumbler, pink or green, 9-oz, 3⅝" **$35.00**

Chinex Classic, bowl, castle decal, 11" **$45.00**

Chinex Classic, bowl, cereal; brownstone or plain ivory, 5¾"............**$5.50**

Chinex Classic, bowl, soup; decal decorated, 7¾" **$22.00**

Chinex Classic, butter dish, decal decorated............**$75.00**

Chinex Classic, creamer, brownstone or plain ivory.....**$5.50**

Chinex Classic, cup, decal decorated............**$6.50**

Chinex Classic, plate, dinner; castle decal, 9¾" **$20.00**

Chinex Classic, plate, sandwich/cake; decal decorated, 11½"............**$13.50**

Chinex Classic, saucer, brownstone or plain ivory **$2.00**

Chinex Classic, sherbet, decal decorated, low footed...**$11.00**

Circle, bowl, green or pink, 4½"............**$8.00**

Circle, bowl, green or pink, 8"............**$18.00**

Circle, cup, green or pink, 2 styles **$5.00**

Circle, goblet, water; green or pink, 8-oz............**$11.00**

Circle, plate, luncheon; green or pink, 8¼"............**$4.00**

Circle, sherbet, green or pink, 3⅛"............**$4.00**

Circle, tumbler, iced tea; green or pink, 10-oz, 5" **$16.00**

Cloverleaf, ashtray, black, match holder in center, 4"...**$65.00**

Cloverleaf, ashtray, black, match holder in center, 5¾"...**$85.00**

Cloverleaf, bowl, cereal; yellow, 5"............**$35.00**

Cloverleaf, bowl, green, 8"............**$60.00**

Cloverleaf, bowl, salad; green, 7" deep **$45.00**

Cloverleaf, creamer, yellow, footed, 3⅝"............**$18.00**

Cloverleaf, cup, pink **$7.00**

Cloverleaf, plate, luncheon; yellow, 8" **$14.00**

Cloverleaf, plate, sherbet; green, 6"............**$5.00**

Cloverleaf, salt & pepper shakers, black, pr............**$95.00**

Cloverleaf, saucer, pink or green............**$3.00**

Cloverleaf, sugar bowl, yellow, footed, 3⅝" **$18.00**

Cloverleaf, tumbler, green, flat, flared, 10-oz, 3¾".....**$40.00**

Cloverleaf, tumbler, yellow, footed, 10-oz, 5¾".........**$35.00**

Colonial, bowl, berry; pink, 4½"............**$16.00**

Colonial, bowl, soup; pink or green, low, 7"............**$65.00**

Colonial, bowl, vegetable; crystal, oval, 10"............**$22.00**

Colonial, butter dish, pink, w/lid............**$650.00**

Colonial, celery/spoon holder, pink, 5½"............**$130.00**

Colonial, cheese dish, green............**$225.00**

Colonial, cup, white............**$7.00**

Colonial, pitcher, pink, w/ or w/out ice lip, 54-oz, 7"..**$50.00**

Colonial, plate, grill; crystal, 10"............**$15.00**

Colonial, plate, sherbet; green, 6"............**$8.00**

Colonial, salt & pepper shakers, crystal, pr............**$60.00**

Colonial, saucer/plate, sherbet; green............**$8.00**

Colonial, stem, wine; crystal, 2½-oz, 4½"............**$16.00**

Colonial, tumbler, juice; pink, 5-oz, 3"............**$20.00**

Colonial, tumbler, lemonade; pink, 15-oz............**$65.00**

Colonial, tumbler, pink or green, footed, 10-oz, 5¼"..**$47.00**

Colonial, tumbler, water; pink or green, 9-oz, 4"............**$20.00**

Colonial, whiskey, crystal, 1½-oz, 2½"............**$11.00**

Colonial Block, bowl, pink or green, 4"............**$6.50**

Colonial Block, butter dish, pink or green, w/lid.......**$45.00**

Colonial Block, candy jar, pink or green, w/lid..........**$40.00**

Colonial Block, creamer, white............**$7.00**

Colonial Block, goblet, pink or green............**$12.50**

Colonial Block, sugar bowl, white, w/lid............**$10.00**

Colonial Fluted, bowl, berry; green, lg, 7½"............**$20.00**

Colonial Fluted, bowl, cereal; green, 6"............**$10.00**

Colonial Fluted, creamer, green............**$6.50**

Colonial Fluted, plate, luncheon; green, 8" **$5.00**

Colonial Fluted, sugar bowl, green, w/lid............**$21.00**

Columbia, bowl, cereal; crystal, 5"............**$18.00**

Columbia, bowl, crystal, ruffled edge, 10½"............**$20.00**

Columbia, butter dish, ruby flashed, w/lid............**$22.00**

Columbia, cup, pink............**$25.00**

Columbia, plate, bread & butter; pink, 6"............**$15.00**

Columbia, plate, chop; crystal, 11"............**$12.00**

Columbia, saucer, pink............**$10.00**

Columbia, tumbler, juice; crystal, 4-oz, 2⅞"............**$25.00**

Coronation, bowl, berry; pink, handled, 4¼"............**$4.50**

Coronation, bowl, nappy; Royal Ruby, handled, 6½"...**$12.00**

Coronation, pitcher, pink, 68-oz, 7¾"............**$550.00**

Coronation, plate, luncheon; green, 8½"............**$45.00**

Coronation, saucer, pink **$2.00**

Coronation, tumbler, green, footed, 10-oz, 5"............**$175.00**

Cremax, bowl, cereal; ivory, 5¾"............**$3.50**

Cremax, bowl, vegetable; blue or ivory w/decal, 9" ..**$15.00**

Cremax, cup, demitasse; blue or ivory w/decal..........**$25.00**

Cremax, cup, ivory **$4.00**

Cremax, plate, dinner; ivory, 9¾"............**$4.50**

Cremax, plate, sandwich; blue or ivory w/decal, 11½"..**$12.00**

Cremax, saucer, ivory............**$2.00**

Cremax, sugar bowl, blue or ivory w/decal............**$8.00**

Cube, bowl, dessert; green, 4½"............**$7.00**

Cube, bowl, pink, 4½" deep............**$8.00**

Cube, bowl, salad; ultramarine, 6½"............**$70.00**

Cube, butter dish, pink or green, w/lid............**$65.00**

Cube, candy jar, green, w/lid, 6½"............**$33.00**

Cube, creamer, pink, 2⅝"............**$2.00**

Cube, cup, green............**$9.00**

Cube, plate, luncheon; pink, 8".................................$6.50
Cube, salt & pepper shakers, pink or green, pr $35.00
Cube, sherbet, pink, footed $7.00
Cube, sugar bowl, green, 3"......................................$8.00
Cube, tumbler, pink, 9-oz, 4"..................................$67.50
Diamond Quilted, bowl, blue or black, crimped edge, 7"..$18.00
Diamond Quilted, bowl, cereal; pink or green, 5"........$7.50
Diamond Quilted, bowl, cream soup; blue or black, 4¾" ..$20.00
Diamond Quilted, cake salver, pink or green, tall, 10" dia ..$60.00
Diamond Quilted, candlestick, blue or black, 2 styles, pr...$50.00
Diamond Quilted, compote, pink or green, 6x7¼" $45.00
Diamond Quilted, creamer, blue or black $17.50
Diamond Quilted, cup, pink or green $9.50
Diamond Quilted, goblet, cordial; pink or green, 1-oz..$12.00
Diamond Quilted, goblet, pink or green, 3-oz...........$12.00
Diamond Quilted, ice bucket, pink or green $55.00
Diamond Quilted, pitcher, pink or green, 64-oz.........$50.00
Diamond Quilted, plate, luncheon; blue or black, 8"..$12.00
Diamond Quilted, plate, salad; blue or black, 7"..........$9.00
Diamond Quilted, plate, sandwich; pink or green, 14"..$15.00
Diamond Quilted, plate, sherbet; blue or black, 6" $5.00
Diamond Quilted, saucer, blue or black $5.00
Diamond Quilted, sherbet, pink or green.....................$5.00
Diamond Quilted, sugar bowl, blue or black.............$17.50
Diamond Quilted, tumbler, pink or green, footed, 12-oz ..$15.00
Diamond Quilted, tumbler, water; pink or green, 9-oz ..$9.00
Diamond Quilted, whiskey, pink or green, 1½-oz $8.00
Diana, ashtray, crystal, 3½"......................................$2.50
Diana, bowl, amber, scalloped edge, 12" $20.00
Diana, bowl, cereal; pink, 5" $10.00
Diana, bowl, console fruit; pink, 11" $40.00
Diana, bowl, cream soup; amber, 5½".......................$17.50
Diana, bowl, salad; crystal, 9"..................................$10.00
Diana, candy jar, crystal, w/lid, round......................$16.00
Diana, coaster, pink, 3½" $7.00
Diana, cup, amber $7.00
Diana, plate, pink, 9½" $16.00
Diana, platter, crystal, oval, 12" $9.00
Diana, saucer, pink $5.00
Diana, sugar bowl, crystal, oval.................................$5.00
Diana, tumbler, pink, 9-oz, 4⅛" $45.00
Dogwood, bowl, berry; green, 8½" $120.00
Dogwood, bowl, cereal; pink, 5½" $32.00
Dogwood, bowl, fruit; monax or cremax, 10¼" $110.00
Dogwood, creamer, green, flat, thin, 2½"..................$47.50
Dogwood, cup, pink, thick.......................................$18.00
Dogwood, plate, bread & butter; pink, 6" $8.00
Dogwood, plate, salver; monax or cremax, 12".........$15.00
Dogwood, saucer, monax or cremax $20.00
Dogwood, sugar bowl, green, flat, thin, 2½" $45.00
Dogwood, tumbler, green, decorated, 12-oz, 5" $115.00
Dogwood, tumbler, pink, decorated, 10-oz, 4" $40.00
Doric, bowl, berry; delphite, lg, 8¼" $125.00
Doric, bowl, berry; pink, 4½" $9.00
Doric, bowl, cereal; green, 5½" $75.00
Doric, bowl, green, 2-handled, 9" $20.00
Doric, butter dish, pink, w/lid..................................$70.00
Doric, candy dish, pink, w/lid, 8" $37.50
Doric, cup, pink..$9.00

Doric, pitcher, green, flat, 32-oz, 5½"......................$42.50
Doric, plate, sherbet; green, 6".................................$5.00
Doric, salt & pepper shakers, green, pr.....................$37.50
Doric, sherbet, delphite, footed................................$7.00
Doric, sugar bowl, pink $12.00
Doric, tray, green, handled, 10".................................$18.00
Doric, tray, serving; pink, 8x8".................................$22.00
Doric, tumbler, green, footed, 10-oz, 4".....................$90.00
Doric & Pansy, bowl, berry; green or teal, lg, 8"........$80.00
Doric & Pansy, bowl, pink or crystal, handled, 9"......$17.50
Doric & Pansy, cup, pink or crystal...........................$10.00
Doric & Pansy, plate, dinner; green or teal, 9" $35.00
Doric & Pansy, sugar bowl, green or teal $110.00
English Hobanil, candy dish, pink or green, 3-footed ..$55.00
English Hobnail, ashtray, turquoise or ice blue, 4½" .$22.50
English Hobnail, bowl, cranberry; pink or green, 3"..$17.00
English Hobnail, bowl, finger; turquoise or ice blue, footed,
    square, 4½"..$35.00
English Hobnail, bowl, grapefruit; pink or green, 6½"..$22.00
English Hobnail, bowl, pink or green, crimped, 6"....$18.00
English Hobnail, bowl, pink or green, rolled edge, 11"..$45.00
English Hobnail, bowl, turquoise or ice blue, 2-handled,
    hexagonal foot, 8" $110.00
English Hobnail, cigarette jar, turquoise or ice blue, w/lid,
    round $60.00
English Hobnail, creamer, pink or green, square foot.......$42.50
English Hobnail, ice tub, turquoise or ice blue, 4"....$80.00
English Hobnail, marmalade, pink or green, w/lid.....$40.00
English Hobnail, plate, pink or green, round, 5½".......$9.50
English Hobnail, saucer, pink or green, round $4.00
English Hobnail, stem, cocktail; pink or green, round foot, 3-
    oz..$20.00
English Hobnail, sugar bowl, turquoise or ice blue, hexago-
    nal foot $45.00
English Hobnail, tumbler, water; pink or green, 8-oz...$22.00
Floragold, bowl, iridescent, square, 4½"....................$5.50
Floragold, butter dish, iridescent, w/lid, round..........$42.50
Floragold, creamer, iridescent $9.00

**Floragold, plate,
13½", $20.00.**

Floragold, tumbler, iridescent, footed, 15-oz.............$100.00
Floral, bowl, berry; pink, 4"......................................$20.00
Floral, bowl, vegetable; green, w/lid, 8".....................$50.00
Floral, butter dish, pink, w/lid...................................$85.00
Floral, canister set: coffee, tea, cereal & sugar; jadite, 5¼",
    each $55.00
Floral, comport, pink, 9"...$800.00

Floral, creamer, green, flat **$15.00**
Floral, lamp, green **$275.00**
Floral, plate, dinner; green, 9" **$18.00**
Floral, plate, sherbet; pink, 6" **$6.00**
Floral, platter, delphite, oval, 10¾" **$150.00**
Floral, refrigerator dish, jadite, w/lid, 5" square..........**$22.00**
Floral, salt & pepper shakers, pink, footed, 4", pr......**$45.00**
Floral, sherbet, green......................................**$20.00**
Floral, tumbler, green, footed, 3-oz, 3½"...............**$175.00**
Floral, tumbler, water; footed, 7-oz, 4¾" **$18.00**
Floral, vase, green, 8-sided, 6⅞"......................**$435.00**
Floral, vase, rose bowl; green, 3-legged...................**$525.00**
Floral & Diamond Band, bowl, berry; pink, 4½" **$8.00**
Floral & Diamond Band, bowl, berry; pink or green, lg, 8" ...**$15.00**
Floral & Diamond Band, butter dish, pink, w/lid.....**$140.00**
Floral & Diamond Band, compote, green, 5½"...........**$18.00**
Floral & Diamond Band, creamer, pink, 4¾" **$17.50**
Floral & Diamond Band, pitcher, green, 42-oz, 8"....**$100.00**
Floral & Diamond Band, sherbet, pink **$7.00**
Floral & Diamond Band, sugar bowl, green, sm.........**$11.00**
Floral & Diamond Band, sugar bowl, pink or green, 5¼" ..**$15.00**
Floral & Diamond Band, tumbler, iced tea; green, 5".**$45.00**
Floral & Diamond Band, tumbler, water; pink, 4" **$20.00**
Florentine No 1, ashtray, crystal or green, 5½"...........**$22.00**
Florentine No 1, bowl, berry; yellow or pink, 5"........**$15.00**
Florentine No 1, bowl, cream soup; pink, 5" **$18.00**
Florentine No 1, bowl, vegetable; yellow or pink, w/lid, oval, 9½"..**$65.00**

Florentine #1, butter dish, green, $120.00.

Florentine No 1, coaster/ashtray, crystal or green.............**$18.00**
Florentine No 1, creamer, pink, ruffled **$37.50**
Florentine No 1, plate, dinner; yellow or pink, 10"..**$25.00**
Florentine No 1, plate, salad; crystal or green, 8½"......**$7.50**
Florentine No 1, platter, yellow or pink, oval, 11½" ..**$25.00**
Florentine No 1, saucer, cobalt blue **$17.00**
Florentine No 1, sugar bowl, yellow or pink **$12.00**
Florentine No 1, tumbler, iced tea; yellow or pink, footed, 12-oz, 5¼"...**$30.00**
Florentine No 1, tumbler, juice; crystal or green, footed, 5-oz, 3¾"...**$16.00**
Florentine No 1, tumbler, water; yellow or pink, footed, 10-oz, 4¾"...**$24.00**
Florentine No 2, bowl, berry; crystal or green, lg, 8".**$25.00**
Florentine No 2, bowl, berry; crystal or green, 4½" ...**$12.00**

Florentine No 2, bowl, cereal; yellow, 6" **$40.00**
Florentine No 2, bowl, cream soup; pink, 4¾"..........**$16.00**
Florentine No 2, bowl, vegetable; yellow, w/lid, oval, 9".**$75.00**
Florentine No 2, butter dish, crystal or green, w/lid ..**$100.00**
Florentine No 2, candlesticks, yellow, 2¾", pr..........**$67.50**
Florentine No 2, coaster, pink, 3¼".......................**$16.00**
Florentine No 2, coaster/ashtray, crystal or green, 5½" ..**$17.50**
Florentine No 2, custard cup, yellow........................**$85.00**
Florentine No 2, pitcher, pink, 48-oz, 7½" **$135.00**
Florentine No 2, plate, grill; crystal or green, 10¼"....**$12.00**
Florentine No 2, plate, salad; pink, 8½" **$8.50**
Florentine No 2, plate, sherbet; yellow, 6" **$6.00**
Florentine No 2, platter, crystal or green, oval, 11" **$16.00**
Florentine No 2, platter (for gravy boat), yellow, 11½"..**$45.00**
Florentine No 2, salt & pepper shakers, yellow, pr....**$50.00**
Florentine No 2, sugar bowl, crystal or green, w/lid..**$25.00**
Florentine No 2, tumbler, juice; 5-oz, 3⅜"...............**$21.00**
Florentine No 2, tumbler, pink, footed, 5-oz, 3¼"......**$17.50**
Florentine No 2, tumbler, water; cobalt blue, 9-oz, 4"..**$70.00**
Florentine No 2, vase/parfait, yellow, 6" **$62.50**
Flower Garden w/Butterflies, bowl, black, flying saucer shape, w/lid, 7¼" **$375.00**
Flower Garden w/Butterflies, bowl, console; black, rolled edge, w/base, 12" **$200.00**
Flower Garden w/Butterflies, candlesticks, amber or crystal, 8", pr **$77.50**
Flower Garden w/Butterflies, candy dish, blue or canary yellow, heart-shaped, w/lid.....................**$1,300.00**
Flower Garden w/Butterflies, cigarette box, black, w/lid, 4⅜" **$150.00**
Flower Garden w/Butterflies, comport, amber or crystal, fits 10" plate, 3" **$20.00**
Flower Garden w/Butterflies, comport, blue or canary yellow, 5⅞x11" **$95.00**
Flower Garden w/Butterflies, cup, pink, green or blue-green **$65.00**
Flower Garden w/Butterflies, plate, amber or crystal, 7" ..**$16.00**
Flower Garden w/Butterflies, plate, pink, green or blue-green, 10" **$42.50**
Flower Garden w/Butterflies, powder jar, pink, green or blue-green, flat, 3½" **$80.00**
Flower Garden w/Butterflies, saucer, pink, green or blue-green **$27.50**
Flower Garden w/Butterflies, vase, black, Dahlia, cupped, 8" **$200.00**
Flower Garden w/Butterflies, vase, blue, canary yellow, 10½" **$225.00**
Fortune, bowl, dessert; pink or crystal, 4½".................**$9.00**
Fortune, bowl, pink or crystal, handled, 4½"..............**$9.00**
Fortune, bowl, salad or lg berry; pink or crystal, 7¾"..**$18.00**
Fortune, plate, luncheon; pink or crystal, 8" **$22.00**
Fortune, plate, sherbet; pink or crystal, 6" **$3.00**
Fortune, tumbler, juice; pink or crystal, 5-oz, 3½"........**$9.00**
Fruits, bowl, berry; green, 8" **$75.00**
Fruits, bowl, berry; pink, 5" **$22.00**
Fruits, cup, pink...**$7.00**
Fruits, plate, luncheon; green or pink, 8" **$6.50**
Fruits, saucer, pink.......................................**$4.00**
Fruits, sherbet, green.....................................**$9.00**

Fruits, tumbler, green, 1 fruit decoration, 4".................$17.50

Fruits, tumbler, juice; pink, 3½" $40.00

Fruits, tumbler, pink, 12-oz, 5" $95.00

Georgian, bowl, berry; green, 4½"..................................$8.50

Georgian, bowl, green, 6½"...$65.00

Georgian, bowl, vegetable; green, oval, 9"................$60.00

Georgian, creamer, green, footed, 3".............................$12.00

Georgian, hot plate, green, center design, 5".............$47.50

Georgian, plate, green, center design only, 9¼".........$22.00

Georgian, plate, luncheon; green, 8"...............................$9.00

Georgian, sherbet, green...$12.00

Georgian, sugar bowl, green, w/lid, 3".........................$50.00

Georgian, tumbler, green, flat, 12-oz, 5¼"................$115.00

Hex Optic, bowl, berry; pink or green, ruffled, 4¼"....$5.50

Hex Optic, bowl, mixing; pink or green, 8¼" $17.50

Hex Optic, bucket reamer, pink or green $55.00

Hex Optic, cup, pink or green, 2 styles of handles......$4.50

Hex Optic, pitcher, pink or green, flat, 70-oz, 8" $225.00

Hex Optic, plate, luncheon; pink or green, 8".............$5.50

Hex Optic, refrigerator dish, pink or green, 4x4" $10.00

Hex Optic, saucer, pink or green.....................................$2.50

Hex Optic, sherbet, pink or green, footed, 5-oz...........$4.50

Hex Optic, tumbler, pink or green, footed, 5¾".........$10.00

Hobnail, cup, pink or crystal $4.50

Hobnail, decanter, crystal, w/stopper, 32-oz $27.50

Hobnail, pitcher, crystal, 67-oz $25.00

Hobnail, plate, luncheon; pink or crystal, 8½".............$3.50

Hobnail, plate, sherbet; pink, 6"......................................$2.00

Hobnail, sugar bowl, crystal w/red trim, footed $5.00

Hobnail, tumbler, iced tea; crystal, 15-oz.....................$7.00

Hobnail, whiskey, crystal, 1½-oz....................................$6.00

Holiday, creamer, pink, footed $8.00

Holiday, pitcher, pink, 6¾", $35.00.

Holiday, plate, chop; pink, 13¾".................................$95.00

Holiday, saucer, pink, 2 styles $4.50

Homespun, bowl, pink or crystal, closed handles, 4½"...$11.00

Homespun, butter dish, pink or crystal, w/lid $60.00

Homespun, cup, pink or crystal.....................................$10.00

Homespun, platter, pink or crystal, closed handles, 13"..$15.00

Homespun, tumbler, iced tea; pink or crystal, 12½-oz, 5⅜" $30.00

Homespun, tumbler, pink or crystal, footed, 15-oz, 6¼"....$27.50

Homespun, tumbler, pink or crystal, straight edge, 7-oz, 3⅞" $20.00

Indiana Custard, bowl, cereal; ivory, 6½"...................$24.00

Indiana Custard, butter dish, ivory, w/lid...................$60.00

Indiana Custard, plate, luncheon; ivory, 8⅞" $18.00

Indiana Custard, sugar bowl, ivory, w/lid $35.00

Iris, bowl, fruit; iridescent, ruffled, 11½"...................$14.00

Iris, bowl, salad; green or pink, ruffled, 9½" $125.00

Iris, bowl, sauce; crystal, ruffled, 5" $9.00

Iris, bowl, soup; iridescent, 7½"...................................$60.00

Iris, butter dish, crystal, w/lid......................................$47.50

Iris, candy jar, crystal, w/lid..$155.00

Iris, creamer, green or pink, footed $110.00

Iris, fruit or nut set, crystal..$75.00

Iris, goblet, crystal, 4-oz, 5½" $27.50

Iris, pitcher, iridescent, footed, 9½"...........................$40.00

Iris, saucer, crystal..$12.00

Iris, tumbler, iridescent, footed, 6" $16.00

Iris, vase, green or pink, 9" $150.00

Jubilee, bowl, fruit; yellow, handled, 9" $125.00

Jubilee, candlestick, pink or yellow, pr...................$185.00

Jubilee, creamer, yellow..$17.50

Jubilee, plate, luncheon; pink, 8¾"...........................$27.50

Jubilee, vase, pink or yellow, 12" $350.00

Lace Edge, bowl, cereal; pink, 6⅜"............................$24.00

Lace Edge, bowl, pink, plain, 9½"...............................$26.00

Lace Edge, butter dish or bonbon, pink, w/lid, each..$67.50

Lace Edge, comport, pink, 7"..$25.00

Lace Edge, cup, pink $25.00

Lace Edge, plate, luncheon; pink, 8¼".......................$23.00

Lace Edge, plate, relish; pink, 3-part, 10½"...............$25.00

Lace Edge, plate, salad; pink, 7¼"...............................$25.00

Lace Edge, saucer, pink..$11.00

Lace Edge, tumbler, pink, flat, 9-oz, 4½"....................$20.00

Laced Edge, bowl, fruit; opalescent, 4⅜-4¾" $30.00

Laced Edge, bowl, soup; opalescent, 5⅞" $80.00

Laced Edge, candlestick, double; opalescent, pr........$35.00

Laced Edge, cup, opalescent $35.00

Laced Edge, plate, bread & butter; opalescent, 6½"...$18.00

Laced Edge, saucer, opalescent $15.00

Laced Edge, tumbler, opalescent, 9-oz.........................$55.00

Lake Como, bowl, cereal; white, 6" $25.00

Lake Como, plate, salad; white, 7¼".............................$18.00

Lake Como, platter, white, 11".......................................$70.00

Lake Como, saucer, white, St Denis $12.00

Laurel, bowl, berry; blue, lg, 9"...................................$45.00

Laurel, bowl, berry; white opalescent or jade green, 4¾" $6.50

Laurel, bowl, ivory, 11"..$38.00

Laurel, bowl, ivory, 3-leg, 6"...$15.00

Laurel, bowl, vegetable; white opalescent, jade green or ivory, oval, 9¾"..$25.00

Laurel, creamer, blue, tall..$35.00

Laurel, plate, dinner; white opalescent, 9⅛" $15.00

Laurel, saucer, blue..$7.50

Laurel, sugar bowl, ivory, short $9.00

Laurel, tumbler, white opalescent or jade green, flat, 9-oz, 4½"..$45.00

Lincoln Inn, ashtray, blue or red..................................$17.50

Lincoln Inn, bonbon, blue or red, oval, handled........$16.00

Lincoln Inn, bowl, blue or red, footed, 9¼"...............$65.00

Lincoln Inn, bowl, colors other than blue or red, crimped, 6" **$8.50**
Lincoln Inn, comport, blue or red **$30.00**
Lincoln Inn, goblet, water; colors other than blue or red ..**$15.50**
Lincoln Inn, nut dish, blue or red, footed **$20.00**
Lincoln Inn, plate, blue or red, 6" **$7.50**
Lincoln Inn, sandwich server, colors other than blue or red, center handle **$90.00**
Lincoln Inn, sherbet, blue or red, 4¾" **$19.00**
Lincoln Inn, tumbler, blue or red, footed, 12-oz **$45.00**
Lincoln Inn, tumbler, blue or red, footed, 9-oz **$30.00**
Lincoln Inn, tumbler, juice; blue or red, flat, 4-oz **$30.00**
Lorain, bowl, cereal; crystal or green, 6" **$45.00**
Lorain, bowl, cereal; green, 6" **$40.00**
Lorain, creamer, crystal or green, footed **$16.00**
Lorain, cup, yellow **$15.00**
Lorain, plate, luncheon; crystal or green, 8⅜" **$17.50**
Lorain, plate, sherbet; yellow, 5½" **$11.00**
Lorain, platter, green, 11½" **$25.00**
Lorain, platter, yellow, 11½" **$45.00**
Lorain, saucer, crystal or green **$4.50**

Lorain, sugar bowl and creamer, yellow, $45.00 for the pair.

Lorain, tumbler, yellow, footed, 9-oz, 4¾" **$33.00**
Madrid, bowl, cream soup; amber, 4¾" **$16.00**
Madrid, bowl, salad; green, 8" **$17.50**
Madrid, bowl, sauce; amber or pink, 5" **$6.50**
Madrid, bowl, vegetable; blue, oval, 10" **$40.00**
Madrid, creamer, blue, footed **$20.00**
Madrid, cup, amber **$6.50**
Madrid, hot dish coaster, amber or green **$40.00**
Madrid, pitcher, pink, 60-oz, square, 8" **$35.00**
Madrid, plate, luncheon; amber, 8⅞" **$8.00**
Madrid, plate, relish; green, 10¼" **$16.00**
Madrid, plate, sherbet; amber or green, 6" **$4.00**
Madrid, saucer, blue **$10.00**
Madrid, sherbet, amber, 2 styles **$7.50**
Madrid, tumbler, amber, 5-oz, 3⅞" **$14.00**
Madrid, tumbler, green, 9-oz, 4¼" **$20.00**
Manhattan, ashtray, crystal, round, 4" **$11.00**
Manhattan, bowl, berry; crystal, lg, 7½" **$15.00**
Manhattan, bowl, sauce; crystal, handles, 4½" **$9.00**
Manhattan, candlesticks, crystal, square, 4½", pr **$15.00**
Manhattan, candy dish, pink, 3-leg **$12.00**
Manhattan, creamer, pink, oval **$11.00**

Manhattan, relish tray insert, crystal **$5.50**
Manhattan, saucer, crystal, 6" **$7.00**
Manhattan, sugar bowl, pink, oval **$11.00**
Manhattan, wine, crystal, 3½" **$5.50**
Mayfair (Open Rose), bowl, cereal; green or yellow, 5½" ..**$85.00**
Mayfair (Open Rose), bowl, vegetable; pink, 10" **$28.00**
Mayfair (Open Rose), cake plate, pink, footed, 10" **$32.50**
Mayfair (Open Rose), cake plate, pink, handles, 12" ..**$50.00**
Mayfair (Open Rose), celery dish, green or yellow, 10" ..**$125.00**
Mayfair (Open Rose), cookie jar, yellow, w/lid **$895.00**
Mayfair (Open Rose), cup, blue **$55.00**
Mayfair (Open Rose), goblet, blue, thin, 9-oz, 7¼" ..**$195.00**
Mayfair (Open Rose), goblet, cocktail; pink, 3-oz, 4" ..**$85.00**
Mayfair (Open Rose), goblet, wine; green, 3-oz, 4½" ..**$450.00**
Mayfair (Open Rose), pitcher, pink, 80-oz, 8½" **$100.00**
Mayfair (Open Rose), pitcher, yellow, 80-oz, 8½" **$750.00**

Mayfair (Open Rose), pitchers, blue, 8½", $200.00; 8", $170.00.

Mayfair (Open Rose), plate, grill; green or yellow, 9½" ..**$85.00**
Mayfair (Open Rose), plate, luncheon; blue, 8½" **$55.00**
Mayfair (Open Rose), plate, sherbet; pink, round, 6½" ..**$12.50**
Mayfair (Open Rose), relish, blue, 4-part, 8⅜" **$65.00**
Mayfair (Open Rose), sandwich server, green, center handle **$40.00**
Mayfair (Open Rose), sherbet, green or yellow, footed, 4¾" **$165.00**
Mayfair (Open Rose), tumbler, iced tea; blue, 13½-oz, 5¼" **$240.00**
Mayfair (Open Rose), tumbler, water; pink, 9-oz, 4¼" ..**$30.00**
Mayfair (Open Rose), tumbler, yellow, footed, 10-oz, 5¼" ..**$180.00**
Mayfair Federal, bowl, cereal; crystal, 6" **$9.50**
Mayfair Federal, bowl, sauce; amber, 5" **$9.00**
Mayfair Federal, cup, green **$9.00**
Mayfair Federal, plate, dinner; crystal, 9½" **$10.00**
Mayfair Federal, plate, salad; crystal, 6¾" **$4.50**
Mayfair Federal, saucer, amber **$4.00**
Mayfair Federal, sugar bowl, crystal, footed **$11.00**
Miss America, bowl, berry; green, 4½" **$12.00**
Miss America, bowl, cereal; crystal, 6¼" **$10.00**
Miss America, bowl, Royal Ruby, shallow, 11" **$800.00**
Miss America, butter dish, pink, w/lid **$595.00**
Miss America, coaster, crystal, 5¾" **$15.00**
Miss America, creamer, pink, footed **$19.00**
Miss America, cup, green **$12.00**

Miss America, goblet, juice; Royal Ruby, 5-oz, 4¾"..**$255.00**

Miss America, goblet, wine; pink, 3-oz, 3¾" **$85.00**

Miss America, pitcher, crystal, 65-oz, 8" **$46.00**

Miss America, plate, salad; Royal Ruby, 8½"............**$150.00**

Miss America, plate, sherbet; pink, 5¾" **$10.50**

Miss America, platter, crystal, oval, 12¼"...................**$14.00**

Miss America, relish, pink, 4-part, 8¾" **$25.00**

Miss America, salt & pepper shakers, pink, pr............**$60.00**

Miss America, saucer, crystal..**$4.00**

Miss America, sugar bowl, pink **$17.50**

Miss America, tumbler, iced tea; pink, 14-oz, 5¾"......**$85.00**

Miss America, tumbler, water; crystal, 10-oz, 4½".......**$15.00**

Moderntone, bowl, berry; cobalt, lg, 8¾"...................**$50.00**

Moderntone, bowl, cream soup; amethyst, ruffled, 5"..**$33.00**

Moderntone, bowl, cream soup; cobalt, 4¾" **$22.50**

Moderntone, creamer, amethyst...............................**$10.00**

Moderntone, cup/custard, cobalt, handleless **$20.00**

Moderntone, plate, luncheon; cobalt, 7¾"..................**$12.50**

Moderntone, plate, salad; amethyst, 6¾" **$10.00**

Moderntone, plate, sandwich; amethyst, 10½"............**$40.00**

Moderntone, platter, cobalt, oval, 12" **$77.50**

Moderntone, saucer, amethyst **$4.00**

Moderntone, tumbler, amethyst, 5-oz.........................**$32.00**

Moderntone, whiskey, cobalt, 1½-oz **$42.50**

Moondrops, ashtray, blue or red...................................**$32.00**

Moondrops, bowl, berry; colors other than red or blue, 5¼" **$10.00**

Moondrops, bowl, console; colors other than red or blue, w/wings, 13" **$42.00**

Moondrops, bowl, pickle; red or blue, 7½" **$22.00**

Moondrops, bowl, red or blue, handled, oval, 9¾"....**$52.50**

Moondrops, bowl, relish; colors other than red or blue, 3-footed, divided, 8½" **$18.00**

Moondrops, candle holders, red or blue, ruffled, 2", pr....**$40.00**

Moondrops, candlesticks, colors other than red or blue, wings, 5", pr **$50.00**

Moondrops, comport, blue or red, 4" **$27.50**

Moondrops, creamer, colors other than red or blue, miniature, 2¾" **$11.00**

Moondrops, decanter, red or blue, med, 8½" **$70.00**

Moondrops, goblet, wine; red or blue, metal stem, 4-oz, 5½" **$20.00**

Moondrops, mug, colors other than red or blue, 12-oz, 5⅛" **$23.00**

Moondrops, plate, red or blue, 5⅞"............................**$11.00**

Moondrops, plate, sandwich; red or blue, round, 14" ..**$18.00**

Moondrops, saucer, red or blue **$6.00**

Moondrops, sugar bowl, red or blue, 3½" **$16.00**

Moondrops, tumbler, red or blue, 7-oz, 4⅜" **$16.00**

Moondrops, vase, red or blue, rocket style, 9¼" **$250.00**

Mt Pleasant, bonbon, amethyst, rolled-up, handled, 7" ..**$23.00**

Mt Pleasant, bowl, black, 2-handled, square, 8" **$35.00**

Mt Pleasant, bowl, fruit; cobalt, scalloped, 10" **$42.00**

Mt Pleasant, bowl, pink or green, rolled-out edge, 3-footed, 7" **$16.00**

Mt Pleasant, bowl, rose; pink or green, 4" opening ...**$18.00**

Mt Pleasant, candlesticks, single; pink, or green, pr...**$20.00**

Mt Pleasant, mint dish, pink or green, center handle, 6" ..**$16.00**

Mt Pleasant, plate, amethyst, scalloped or square, 8"..**$15.00**

Mt Pleasant, plate, black, 2-handled, 12" **$33.00**

Mt Pleasant, plate, pink or green, 2-handled, 8"........**$11.00**

Mt Pleasant, saucer, pink or green **$2.50**

Mt Pleasant, sherbet, cobalt, 2 styles.........................**$17.50**

Mt Pleasant, vase, amethyst, 7¼".................................**$32.00**

New Century, ashtray/coaster, green or crystal, 5⅜" ..**$28.00**

New Century, bowl, berry; green or crystal, lg, 8" **$22.00**

New Century, creamer, green or crystal.........................**$8.50**

New Century, pitcher, all colors, w/ or w/out ice lip, 60-oz, 7¾" **$35.00**

New Century, plate, salad; green or crystal, 8½"........**$10.00**

New Century, plate, sherbet; green or crystal, 6".........**$3.50**

New Century, sherbet, green or crystal, 3" **$9.00**

New Century, tumbler, green or crystal, 9-oz, 4¼".....**$15.00**

New Century, tumbler, pink, cobalt or amethyst, 10-oz, 5"...**$20.00**

New Century, tumbler, pink, cobalt or amethyst, 5-oz, 3½" **$15.00**

New Century, whiskey, green or crystal, 1½-oz, 2½"...**$20.00**

Newport, all in amethyst: Plate, sherbet, $6.00; Plate, luncheon, 8½", $12.00; Tumbler, 4½", 9-oz., $32.00; Sherbet, $13.00; Bowl, cereal, 5¼", $30.00. (Photo courtesy Gene Florence)

Newport, bowl, berry; cobalt, 4¾".............................**$20.00**

Newport, bowl, cream soup; amethyst, 4¾" **$18.00**

Newport, cup, amethyst **$10.00**

Newport, plate, dinner; cobalt or amethyst, 8¾" **$30.00**

Newport, plate, sherbet; cobalt, 5⅞"............................**$7.00**

Newport, salt & pepper shakers, cobalt, pr................**$47.50**

Newport, saucer, cobalt & amethyst............................**$5.00**

Newport, sugar bowl, amethyst...................................**$14.00**

No 610 Pyramid, bowl, berry; crystal, 4¾" **$11.00**

No 610 Pyramid, bowl, pickle; pink, 9½"....................**$35.00**

No 610 Pyramid, ice tub, green................................**$100.00**

No 610 Pyramid, relish tray, yellow, 4-part, handled .**$65.00**

No 610 Pyramid, sugar bowl, pink or green **$30.00**

No 610 Pyramid, tray, pink or green, for creamer & sugar bowl...**$30.00**

No 612 Horseshoe, bowl, berry; green, 4½" **$28.00**

No 612 Horseshoe, bowl, vegetable; green or yellow, 8½" **$35.00**

No 612 Horseshoe, creamer, yellow, footed...............**$18.00**

No 612 Horseshoe, cup, green.....................................**$12.00**

No 612 Horseshoe, plate, luncheon; yellow, 9⅜"........**$15.00**

No 612 Horseshoe, plate, sherbet; green, 6" $8.00

No 612 Horseshoe, saucer, green or yellow.................$5.00

No 612 Horseshoe, sugar bowl, green.......................$16.00

No 612 Horseshoe, tumbler, green or yellow, footed, 9-oz...$25.00

No 616 Vernon, cup, green or yellow.........................$17.50

No 616 Vernon, plate, luncheon; crystal, 8" $6.00

No 616 Vernon, saucer, green or yellow.....................$4.00

No 616 Vernon, tumbler, crystal, footed, 5"..............$15.00

No 618 Pineapple & Floral, ashtray, crystal, 4½".........$17.50

No 618 Pineapple & Floral, bowl, salad; red, 7".........$10.00

No 618 Pineapple & Floral, creamer, crystal, diamond shaped $7.50

No 618 Pineapple & Floral, plate, sandwich; crystal, 11½" $17.50

No 618 Pineapple & Floral, plate, sherbet; amber or red, 6"...$6.00

No 618 Pineapple & Floral, saucer, crystal, amber or red $4.00

No 618 Pineapple & Floral, tumbler, amber or red, 8-oz, 4¼"...$25.00

Normandie, bowl, berry; amber, 5" $6.50

Normandie, creamer, pink, footed $12.00

Normandie, cup, iridescent $6.00

Normandie, plate, grill; iridescent, 11".........................$9.00

Normandie, plate, luncheon; pink, 9¼".......................$14.00

Normandie, plate, sherbert; amber, 6".........................$4.50

Normandie, saucer, amber or pink...............................$4.00

Normandie, sugar bowl, pink $9.00

Normandie, tumbler, water; amber, 9-oz, 4¼" $20.00

Old Cafe, bowl, berry; crystal or pink, 3¾"..................$5.00

Old Cafe, bowl, cereal; Royal Ruby, 5½" $13.00

Old Cafe, bowl, crystal or pink, closed handles, 9"....$12.00

Old Cafe, cup, crystal or pink $7.00

Old Cafe, pitcher, crystal or pink, 36-oz, 6" $80.00

Old Cafe, plate, sherbet; crystal or pink, 6"..................$2.50

Old Cafe, sherbet, crystal, pink, low foot, ¾" $12.00

Old Cafe, vase, Royal Ruby, 7¼"...............................$25.00

Old English, bowl, pink, green or amber, flat, 4".......$17.50

Old English, candlesticks, pink, green or amber, 4", pr...$32.50

Old English, compote, pink, green or amber, 3½x7" .$22.00

Old English, egg cup, crystal $8.00

Old English, pitcher, pink, green or amber, w/lid....$125.00

Old English, tumbler, pink, green or amber, footed, 4½" ...$25.00

Old English, vase, pink, green or amber, footed, 8¼x4¼"..$45.00

Ovide, bowl, cereal; decorated white, 5½" $13.00

Ovide, cup, green $3.50

Ovide, fruit cocktail, black, footed..............................$5.00

Ovide, plate, luncheon; green, 8".................................$3.00

Ovide, saucer, black $3.50

Ovide, sugar bowl, Art Deco......................................$85.00

Oyster & Pearl, bowl, fruit; crystal or pink, 10½" deep..$25.00

Oyster & Pearl, bowl, Royal Ruby, handled, 5½" $15.00

Oyster & Pearl, bowl, Royal Ruby, heart-shaped, handled, 5¼"...$17.00

Oyster & Pearl, candle holder, crystal or pink, 3½", pr.$25.00

Oyster & Pearl, plate, sandwich; crystal or pink, 13½"...$20.00

Parrot, bowl, berry; amber, 5".....................................$18.00

Parrot, butter dish, green, w/lid $365.00

Parrot, cup, amber or green.......................................$40.00

Parrot, plate, dinner; amber, 9"..................................$40.00

Parrot, plate, grill; green, round, 10½".......................$32.00

Parrot, plate, sherbet; amber, 5¾".............................$23.00

Parrot, platter, amber, oblong, 11¼"..........................$75.00

Parrot, saucer, amber or green $15.00

Parrot, tumbler, amber, heavy, footed, 5¾".............$110.00

Parrot, tumbler, green, 10-oz, 4¼".............................$135.00

Patrician, bowl, berry; amber or crystal, 5" $12.50

Patrician, bowl, berry; pink, lg, 8½"..........................$25.00

Patrician, butter dish, green, w/lid............................$110.00

Patrician, creamer, pink or green, footed $12.00

Patrician, jam dish, green...$40.00

Patrician, plate, grill; pink or green, 10½".................$15.00

Patrician, plate, luncheon; pink, 9" $10.00

Patrician, plate, sherbet; amber or crystal, 6" $10.00

Patrician, saucer, amber, crystal, pink or green...........$9.50

Patrician, sherbet, pink or green $14.00

Patrician, tumbler, green, 9-oz, 4¼"..........................$25.00

Patrick, bowl, fruit; pink, handled, 9"........................$175.00

Patrick, candlesticks, pink or yellow, pr...................$150.00

Patrick, cheese & cracker set, pink...........................$150.00

Patrick, cup, yellow $35.00

Patrick, goblet, juice; pink, 6-oz, 4¾".........................$80.00

Patrick, mayonnaise, pink, 3-pc $195.00

Patrick, plate, salad; yellow, 7½"...............................$20.00

Patrick, saucer, pink $20.00

Patrick, tray, yellow, 2-handled, 11"..........................$60.00

Petalware, bowl, cereal; pink, 5¾".............................$11.00

Petalware, bowl, cream soup; crystal, 4½"..................$4.50

Petalware, cup, pink..$7.00

Petalware, plate, dinner; pink, 9".................................$14.00

Petalware, plate, salad; red trim floral, 8".................$25.00

Petalware, plate, salver; monax florette, 11"..............$18.00

Petalware, plate, sherbet; cremax, 6" $6.00

Petalware, saucer, pink or monax plain......................$2.00

Petalware, sugar bowl, crystal, footed.........................$3.00

Petalware, tumbler, red trim floral, 6-oz, 3⅝" $35.00

Primo, bowl, yellow or green, 4½" $18.00

Primo, coaster/ashtray, yellow or green $8.00

Primo, creamer, yellow or green $12.00

Primo, plate, yellow or green, 6¼"..............................$10.00

Primo, plate, yellow or green, 7½"..............................$10.00

Primo, saucer, yellow or green $3.00

Primo, sugar bowl, yellow or green...........................$12.00

Princess, bowl, berry; green or pink, 4½"..................$25.00

Princess, bowl, vegetable; pink, oval, 10" $28.00

Princess, coaster, topaz or apricot............................$100.00

Princess, cup, blue $125.00

Princess, cup, green or pink.......................................$12.00

Princess, pitcher, green or pink, 60-oz, 8"..................$55.00

Princess, plate, dinner; topaz or apricot, 9½" $15.00

Princess, plate, grill; green or pink, 9½".....................$15.00

Princess, plate, sherbet; green or pink, 5½"...............$10.00

Princess, platter, green or pink, closed handles, 12" ..$25.00

Princess, relish, topaz or apricot, plain, 7½"............$250.00

Princess, sherbet, green or pink, footed....................$24.00

Princess, spice shakers, green, 5½", pr......................$40.00

Princess, tumbler, green, footed, 10-oz, 5¼".............$30.00

Princess, tumbler, water; pink, topaz or apricot, 9-oz, 4"....**$25.00**
Queen Mary, ashtray, crystal, round, 3½".....................**$3.00**
Queen Mary, bowl, berry; pink, 4½" **$6.00**
Queen Mary, bowl, crystal, sm, 7" **$7.00**
Queen Mary, butter dish, pink, w/lid......................**$135.00**
Queen Mary, candlesticks, double branch; crystal, 4", pr..**$15.00**
Queen Mary, coaster, pink, 3½".....................................**$4.00**
Queen Mary, comport, crystal, 5¾".................................**$8.00**
Queen Mary, creamer, pink, oval....................................**$7.50**
Queen Mary, cup, crystal, sm..**$8.00**
Queen Mary, plate, sandwich; crystal, 12"....................**$9.00**
Queen Mary, relish tray, pink, 3-part, 12" **$18.00**
Queen Mary, saucer, crystal..**$2.50**
Queen Mary, sugar bowl, pink, oval..............................**$7.50**
Queen Mary, tumbler, water; crystal, 9-oz, 4" **$6.00**
Raindrops, bowl, fruit; green, 4½" **$6.00**
Raindrops, cup, green..**$5.50**
Raindrops, plate, luncheon; green, 8".............................**$5.50**
Raindrops, saucer, green..**$2.00**
Raindrops, tumbler, green, 4-oz, 3" **$5.00**
Raindrops, tumbler, green, 9½-oz, 4⅛"..........................**$9.00**
Raindrops, whiskey, green, 1-oz, 1⅞" **$7.00**
Ribbon, bowl, berry; black, lg, 8" **$35.00**
Ribbon, bowl, berry; green, 4" **$25.00**
Ribbon, plate, sherbet; green, 6¼".................................**$2.50**
Ribbon, saucer, green...**$2.50**
Ribbon, tumbler, green, 10-oz, 6"................................**$30.00**
Ring, bowl, berry; crystal, 5"...**$3.50**
Ring, bowl, berry; green or crystal w/decoration, lg, 8" ..**$12.00**
Ring, cup, crystal...**$4.50**
Ring, goblet, green or crystal w/decoration, 9-oz, 7¼"...**$15.00**
Ring, ice bucket, crystal **$20.00**
Ring, plate, sandwich; crystal, 11¼" **$7.00**
Ring, plate, sherbet; green or crystal w/decoration, 6¼" ..**$2.50**
Ring, saucer, green or crystal w/decoration **$2.00**
Ring, sugar bowl, crystal, footed **$4.50**
Ring, tumbler, green or crystal w/decoration, 5-oz, 3½" .**$6.50**
Ring, tumbler, water; crystal, footed, 5½"......................**$6.00**
Rock Crystal, bowl, celery; red, oblong, 12" **$85.00**
Rock Crystal, bowl, crystal, scalloped edge, 4½".........**$14.00**
Rock Crystal, candlesticks, blue, yellow or black, low, 5½", pr..**$65.00**
Rock Crystal, creamer, crystal, flat, scalloped edge **$37.50**
Rock Crystal, parfait, blue, yellow or black, low footed, 3½-oz **$37.50**
Rock Crystal, plate, blue, yellow or black, scalloped edge, 11½"...**$25.00**
Rock Crystal, plate, red, plain or scalloped edge, 7½" ..**$21.00**
Rock Crystal, salt dip, crystal......................................**$40.00**
Rock Crystal, saucer, crystal...**$7.50**
Rock Crystal, stemware, cocktail, red, footed, 3½-oz **$40.00**
Rock Crystal, stemware, cordial, blue, yellow or black, footed, 1-oz...**$45.00**
Rock Crystal, stemware, goblet, blue, yellow or black, lg foot, 8-oz **$26.00**
Rock Crystal, syrup, crystal, w/lid..............................**$150.00**
Rock Crystal, vase, crystal, footed, 11".......................**$60.00**
Rose Cameo, bowl, berry; green, 4½"...........................**$10.00**
Rose Cameo, bowl, green, straight sides, 6".................**$22.00**

Rose Cameo, sherbet, green **$12.00**
Rosemary, bowl, berry; amber, 5" **$6.00**
Rosemary, bowl, cereal; green, 6".................................**$30.00**
Rosemary, creamer, pink, footed..................................**$18.00**
Rosemary, cup, amber...**$5.50**
Rosemary, plate, dinner; green.....................................**$14.00**
Rosemary, plate, grill; pink..**$22.00**
Rosemary, platter, amber, oval, 12"..............................**$17.00**
Rosemary, saucer, green...**$5.00**
Roulette, bowl, fruit; crystal, 9"....................................**$9.50**
Roulette, plate, sherbet; pink or green..........................**$4.50**
Roulette, saucer, crystal...**$1.50**
Roulette, tumbler, juice; crystal, 5-oz, 3¼".....................**$7.00**
Roulette, tumbler, water; pink or green, 9-oz, 4⅛".....**$30.00**
Roulette, whiskey, pink or green, 1½-oz, 2½" **$17.00**
Round Robin, bowl, berry; green or iridescent, 4" **$5.00**
Round Robin, creamer, green, footed **$7.50**
Round Robin, plate, sherbet; green or iridescent, 6" **$2.50**
Round Robin, sugar bowl, iridescent **$6.00**
Roxana, bowl, cereal; yellow, 6"..................................**$17.50**
Roxana, bowl, white, 4½x2⅜".......................................**$15.00**
Roxana, plate, yellow, 5½"...**$8.50**
Roxana, tumbler, yellow, 9-oz, 4¼".............................**$12.00**
Royal Lace, bowl, berry; crystal, 5" **$15.00**
Royal Lace, bowl, vegetable; green, oval, 11"............**$40.00**

Royal Lace, butter dish, crystal, $75.00.

Royal Lace, creamer, blue, footed **$55.00**
Royal Lace, cup, pink..**$15.00**
Royal Lace, plate, luncheon; green, 8½" **$16.00**
Royal Lace, platter, blue, oval, 13" **$55.00**
Royal Lace, tumbler, pink, 9-oz, 4⅛"...........................**$20.00**
Royal Ruby, bonbon, 6½" **$8.50**
Royal Ruby, bowl, cereal; 5½"......................................**$13.00**
Royal Ruby, bowl, handled, 8".....................................**$15.00**
Royal Ruby, marmalade, crystal w/ruby lid, 5⅛" **$7.50**
Royal Ruby, mint dish, low, 8".....................................**$16.00**
Royal Ruby, vase, 2 styles, 9" **$16.00**
S Pattern, bowl, cereal; crystal, 5½" **$5.00**
S Pattern, plate, luncheon; crystal, 8¼"........................**$4.50**
S Pattern, saucer, crystal..**$2.00**
S Pattern, tumbler, crystal, 10-oz, 4¾"..........................**$7.00**
Sandwich, bowl, console; pink or green, 9"................**$40.00**
Sandwich, creamer, amber or crystal............................**$9.00**
Sandwich, cup, red..**$27.50**

Sandwich, plate, dinner; pink or green, 10½".............$20.00
Sandwich, plate, sherbet; amber or crystal, 6" $3.00
Sandwich, saucer, teal blue.................................$4.50
Sandwich, wine, red, 4-oz, 3"..............................$12.50
Sharon, bowl, berry; amber, 5"..............................$8.50
Sharon, bowl, cereal; pink or green, 6"....................$27.50
Sharon, bowl, vegetable; green, oval, 9½"..................$35.00
Sharon, butter dish, amber, w/lid..........................$47.50
Sharon, creamer, pink, footed $18.00
Sharon, plate, bread & butter; amber, 6" $5.00
Sharon, saucer, green......................................$12.00
Sharon, tumbler, green, thin, 9-oz, 4⅛"....................$75.00
Sierra, bowl, cereal; pink, 5½" $15.00
Sierra, creamer, pink......................................$20.00
Sierra, plate, dinner; pink, 9"............................$22.00
Sierra, salt & pepper shakers, pink or green, pr.........$40.00
Sierra, sugar bowl, pink, w/lid............................$36.00
Spiral, bowl, berry; green, 4¾".............................$5.00
Spiral, plate, sherbet; green, 6"...........................$2.00
Spiral, sherbet, green......................................$4.00
Spiral, tumbler, water; green, 9-oz, 5".....................$7.50
Starlight, bowl, cereal; pink, closed handles, 5½" $12.00
Starlight, cup, crystal or white $4.00
Starlight, plate, luncheon; crystal or white, 8½"...........$5.00
Starlight, plate, sandwich; crystal or white, 13"..........$15.00
Starlight, sugar bowl, crystal or white, oval..............$5.00
Strawberry, bowl, berry; crystal, 4".......................$6.50
Strawberry, bowl, berry; pink or green, 7½"...............$30.00
Strawberry, comport, crystal, 5¾"..........................$14.00
Strawberry, pitcher, pink or green, 7¾"..................$165.00
Strawberry, tumbler, pink or green, 8-oz, 3⅝"............$35.00
Sunburst, bowl, berry; crystal, 4¾".........................$8.00
Sunburst, cup, crystal......................................$6.00
Sunburst, relish, crystal, 2-part..........................$12.00
Sunflower, ashtray, pink, center design only, 5"...........$9.00
Sunflower, cup, opaque $75.00
Sunflower, plate, dinner; pink, 9".........................$17.00
Sunflower, tumbler, green, footed, 8-oz, 4¾"..............$32.00
Swirl, bowl, salad; pink, 9"...............................$20.00
Swirl, candy dish, ultramarine, open, 3-legged...........$20.00
Swirl, cup, delphite or pink $10.00
Swirl, plate, salad; ultramarine, 8" $15.00
Swirl, saucer, pink...$3.50
Swirl, sugar bowl, delphite, footed $12.00
Swirl, tumbler, pink, footed, 9-oz.........................$22.00
Tea Room, bowl, finger; green..............................$55.00
Tea Room, bowl, vegetable; pink, oval, 9½"................$60.00
Tea Room, goblet, green, 9-oz $75.00
Tea Room, parfait, pink....................................$70.00
Tea Room, relish, green, divided...........................$25.00
Tea Room, sherbet, green, low foot.........................$25.00
Tea Room, sundae, pink, ruffled top, footed $70.00
Tea Room, tumbler, green or pink, footed, 6-oz........$35.00
Tea Room, tumbler, pink, footed, 11-oz.....................$45.00
Tea Room, vase, green, straight sides, 9½" $75.00
Thistle, bowl, fruit; pink, lg, 10¼" $325.00
Thistle, plate, cake; pink, heavy, 13" $135.00
Thistle, plate, grill; pink, 10¼".........................$20.00
Tulip, bowl, amethyst, 6" $20.00

Tulip, candy jar, amber, crystal or green, footed, w/lid..$50.00
Tulip, decanter, amethyst or blue, w/stopper $95.00
Tulip, plate, amethyst, 7¼" $14.00
Tulip, tumbler, juice; amber, crystal or green.............$20.00
Twisted Optic, bowl, console; pink, green or amber, 10½"..$20.00
Twisted Optic, bowl, cream soup; blue or yellow, 4¾" ..$16.00
Twisted Optic, candlesticks, blue or yellow, 8", pr $60.00
Twisted Optic, mayonnaise, pink, green or amber.....$20.00
Twisted Optic, plate, sherbet; blue or yellow, 6"..........$4.00
Twisted Optic, powder jar, blue or yellow, w/lid.......$65.00
Twisted Optic, tumbler, pink, green or amber, 9-oz, 4½"...$6.00
US Swirl, bowl, green, handled, 5½" $9.50
US Swirl, butter dish, green or pink, w/lid $110.00
US Swirl, comport, green...................................$20.00
US Swirl, creamer, pink....................................$16.00
US Swirl, salt & pepper shakers, green or pink, pr....$50.00
US Swirl, tumbler, green or pink, 8-oz, 3⅝"..............$10.00
Victory, bonbon, amber, pink or green, 7".................$11.00
Victory, bowl, amber, pink or green, flat edge, 12½"...$30.00
Victory, bowl, soup; black or blue, flat, 8½".............$50.00
Victory, bowl, vegetable; amber, pink or green, oval, 9"..$32.00
Victory, creamer, black or blue $50.00
Victory, plate, bread & butter; amber, pink or green, 6"....$6.00
Victory, platter, black or blue, 12".......................$75.00
Vitrock, bowl, cereal; white, 7½"...........................$6.00
Vitrock, bowl, cream soup; white, 5½"......................$15.00
Vitrock, bowl, vegetable; white, 9½".......................$15.00
Vitrock, plate, soup; white, 9"............................$30.00
Vitrock, sugar bowl, white..................................$5.00
Waterford, ashtray, crystal, 4".............................$7.50
Waterford, butter dish, pink, w/lid.......................$220.00
Waterford, creamer, crystal, oval...........................$5.00
Waterford, cup, pink, Miss America style $45.00
Waterford, plate, dinner; 9⅝".............................$11.00
Waterford, saucer, crystal..................................$3.00
Waterford, tumbler, crystal, footed, 10-oz, 4⅞"..........$12.00
Windsor, ashtray, crystal, 5¾"............................$13.50
Windsor, bowl, cream soup; pink, 5"........................$22.00
Windsor, bowl, green, 2-handled, 8"........................$25.00
Windsor, coaster, pink, 3¼"................................$15.00
Windsor, plate, dinner; crystal, 9".........................$6.00
Windsor, sherbet, green, footed $15.00
Windsor, tumbler, crystal, footed, 7¼"....................$18.00
Windsor, tumbler, pink, 5-oz, 3¼"..........................$25.00

Disney

The largest and most popular area in character collectibles is without doubt Disneyana. There are clubs, newsletters, and special shows that are centered around this hobby. Every aspect of the retail market has been thoroughly saturated with Disney-related merchandise over the years, and today collectors are able to find many good examples at garage sales and flea markets.

Disney memorabilia from the late twenties and thirties was marked either 'Walt E. Disney' or 'Walt Disney Enterprises.' After about 1940 the name was changed to 'Walt Disney Productions.' This mark was in use until 1984 when the 'Walt Disney Company' mark was introduced, and this last mark has remained in use up to the present time. Some of the earlier items have become very expensive, though many are still within the reach of the average collector.

During the thirties, Mickey Mouse, Donald Duck, Snow White and the Seven Dwarfs, and the Three Little Pigs (along with all their friends and cohorts) dominated the Disney scene. The last of the thirties' characters was Pinocchio, and some 'purists' prefer to stop their collections with him.

The forties and fifties brought many new characters with them — Alice in Wonderland, Bambi, Dumbo, Lady and the Tramp, and Peter Pan were some of the major personalities featured in Disney's films of this era.

Even today, thanks to the re-release of many of the old movies and the popularity of Disney's vacation 'kingdoms,' toy stores and department stores alike are full of quality items with the potential of soon becoming collectibles.

If you'd like to learn more about this fascinating field, we recommend *Stern's Guide to Disney Collectibles, First, Second,* and *Third Series,* by Michael Stern; *The Collector's Encyclopedia of Disneyana* by Michael Stern and David Longest; *Character Toys and Collectibles* and *Toys, Antique and Collectible*, both by David Longest; and *Schroeder's Collectible Toys, Antique to Modern*. All are published by Collector Books.

Advisor: Judy Posner (See Directory, Character and Personality Collectibles)

Alice in Wonderland, figurine, ceramic, Shaw, EX....**$395.00**
Alice in Wonderland, figurine, United China & Glass, Walt Disney Productions, 1970s, 5½" **$35.00**
Alice in Wonderland, note paper, full color folder w/16 sheets & 11 envelopes, Whitman, 1951, 8x9¼", EX **$95.00**
Alice in Wonderland, punch-out book, Whitman, Walt Disney Productions, 1951, EX **$175.00**
Alice in Wonderland, tea set, china, Walt Disney Productions, 1960s, MIB...**$150.00**
Alice in Wonderland, 3-D plastic cutouts, Aldon Industries, 1950s, MIP **$150.00**
Aristocats, figurine, Berlioz (kitten), painted bisque, Enesco..**$25.00**
Aristocats, hooked rug, dates from original release of film, 46x60", EX...**$375.00**
Bambi, bank, ceramic, airbrushed colors, Keystone Dairy advertising on bottom, Leeds, 1940s, 7"................**$95.00**
Bambi, bicycle ornament, thin celluloid figure, 1940s, M...**$125.00**
Bambi, figure, velvet plush, Character Novelty Co Licensee, Walt Disney Productions on label, 1940s, 12½", EX **$85.00**
Bambi, mirror, molded plastic frame w/Bambi & related characters, 1960s, 20x24".......................................**$175.00**
Bambi & Flower, figurine, hand decorated, Walt Disney Productions, Goebel, W Germany, #17214-72, 5¼" ..**$125.00**
Big Bad Wolf, figurine, painted bisque, 1930s, 3½", EX.....**$85.00**
Blue Fairy, mechanical valentine, 1939, EX.................**$40.00**
Bongo & Lulubelle, figurine, in typical clothing, Japan, 1940s, 4x4½"...**$95.00**
Captain Hook, costume jewelry pin, full color, 1950s, EX ..**$35.00**

Cinderella, bedspread, chenille, pastels on white, 1950s, twin size, EX...**$155.00**
Cinderella, sheet music, A Dream Is a Wish Your Heart Makes, 1949, EX...**$35.00**
Cinderella's castle, night light, figural pottery, Sears, 1988, 11x9¼", MIB...**$95.00**
Disney Studio, Christmas card, 1978, unused, M **$75.00**
Disneyland, bracelet, Little Miss Disneyland, character charms, souvenir, 1950s, MIB **$35.00**
Disneyland, pennant, red w/white & blue trim, 1950s ...**$40.00**
Disneyland, tray, multicolor litho map of early Disneyland on tin, EX...**$150.00**
Disnleyland, publication, Vacationland Magazine, Frontierland Mine Train on cover, 20-page, 1958-59, 8½x10¾", EX..**$85.00**

Donald Duck, bank, composition, tent scene with skunk, mushrooms, and flowers, 1960s, Japan, M, $55.00. (Photo courtesy June Moon)

Donald Duck, bicycle ornament, thin celluloid jointed figure, 1940s, M **$125.00**
Donald Duck, costume jewelry charm, long bill, enameled metal, 1930s...**$65.00**
Donald Duck, figural perfume bottle, med bill, minor paint wear, 1940s, 4", EX..**$60.00**
Donald Duck, figurine, marked Dan Brechner, Walt Disney Productions WD 26, 1961, 5½", from $45 to........**$85.00**
Donald Duck, planter, airbrushed pastels, Leeds, 1940s, 7"..**$75.00**
Donald Duck, planter, dressed as Santa, sack forms planter, airbrushed colors, Leeds, 1940s, EX....................**$125.00**
Donald Duck, postcard, Hearty Birthday Greetings, holds heart w/verse, Valentine & Sons, 1930s, EX.........**$40.00**
Donald Duck, toy, Donald the Bubble Duck, as 1950s soda jerk, Walt Disney, 1950s, MIB............................**$85.00**
Donald Duck & Nephews, hooked rug, w/instruments, bright colors, 1950s, 43x60", EX **$150.00**
Donald's Nephew, figurine, as baseball catcher, Shaw, 2⅞", EX...**$95.00**
Dumbo, figurine, w/clown hat, china w/gold trim & floral decals, 1940s, 2¾"..**$45.00**
Dumbo, wall pocket/planter, Dumbo in tree, hangs or sits on shelf, 1940s, 4¼", EX..**$40.00**
Dutch boy, figurine, on tulip, It's a Small World, 5¾", MIB **$70.00**
Figaro, figurine, ceramic, standing, Brayton, 1940s, 3" ..**$95.00**
Figaro, figurine, porcelain, pale blue tones, National, 1940, 2½"..**$39.00**

Goofy, birthday card, Hallmark, 1943, M w/unused envelope **$40.00**

Goofy, figurine, frosted glass, Cristallerie Antonia Imperatore, Italy, 1960s, 7", MIB **$55.00**

Goofy, model sheet, dated 1937, EX **$175.00**

Jiminy Cricket, tin clicker, green graphics on yellow, You Help More the United Way, 1940s, M **$45.00**

Kaa, cloth figure, 1967, M **$39.00**

Lady & the Tramp, tankard, restaurant advertising, Buffalo China **$75.00**

Mad Hatter, figurine, Evan K Shaw, 1950s, 4", EX **$395.00**

Mary Poppins, dinner plate, plastic, Sun Valley Melmac, 9½" **$29.00**

Mary Poppins, spoon, silverplate, figural handle, 1964, EX **$32.00**

Mary Poppins, tea set, plastic, 1964, MIB **$95.00**

Mickey Mouse, baby spoon, embossed Mickey on handle, Branford Silverplate, WD mark, 1930s, 4¼" **$60.00**

Mickey Mouse, bookends/banks, painted cast iron, Walt Disney Productions, 1960s, 5x4", pr....................**$275.00**

Mickey Mouse, ceiling light shade, painted figures on glass, 1950s, 14" dia, M..**$79.00**

Mickey Mouse, Christmas ornament, blown glass figural, silver glitter & hand-painted details, late 1940s, 6"..**$95.00**

Mickey Mouse, Colorforms Sew-Ons, Lace & Dress Mickey...Swell New Clothes, 1960s, MIB **$45.00**

Mickey Mouse, costume jewelry pin, celluloid, full color, early **$75.00**

Mickey Mouse, Donald & Pluto, switch plate, multicolor hard plastic, 1950s, MIP **$32.00**

Mickey Mouse, figurine, as vegetable gardener, marked Goebel W Germany, Walt Disney Productions, 1970s, 4" **$75.00**

Mickey Mouse, figurine, bisque, green shorts, brown shoes, pie eyes, Japan, 1930s, 11¾", EX **$75.00**

Mickey Mouse, Goofy & Pluto, figurine set, Dan Brechner Imports, 3 figures attached by gold-tone chain, 1961, M **$175.00**

Mickey Mouse, lantern, Official Walt Disney's..., battery operated, 1977, 7", MIB **$90.00**

Mickey Mouse, magic slate/blackboard, multicolor graphics on cardboard, Strathmore Co, ca 1943, 12½x18½", MIB **$95.00**

Mickey Mouse, marionette, composition, plastic, wood & cloth, Pelham Puppets, 11", EX **$150.00**

Mickey Mouse, marionette, hard plastic, Walt Disney Productions, 4½" figure, 7" overall, M **$40.00**

Mickey Mouse, Mickey's Roadster, cloth doll & plastic car, Mickey Mouse Club/Walt Disney Productions, Knickerbocker, MIB **$85.00**

Mickey Mouse, Minnie & Pluto, tea set, litho tin, Chein, 1940s, 12-pc, serves 4, EX....................................**$195.00**

Mickey Mouse, music box, as cowboy, Schmid, M **$75.00**

Mickey Mouse, music box, as magician, 50th birthday, plays It's a Small World, M **$75.00**

Mickey Mouse, music box, Bicentennial, plays Yankee Doodle Dandy, Schmid, EX **$75.00**

Mickey Mouse, music box, 60th birthday, limited edition, plays club song, M...**$75.00**

Mickey Mouse, pendulum clock, diecut wood, marked W Germany, Walt Disney Productions, 1960s, 11½", MIB **$175.00**

Mickey Mouse, plaque, as band leader, Cermica De Cuernavaca, 1970s Disneyland souvenir..............**$95.00**

Mickey Mouse, plate, Bicentennial, Schmid, MIB **$55.00**

Mickey Mouse, recipe bread card, full color, Now I Lay Me Down, Bell Bread, 1934, 3½x5", M **$38.00**

Mickey Mouse, tea set, lustreware w/rare divided grille plates, 1930s, 17-pc, M..**$595.00**

Mickey Mouse, toothbrush holder, plastic, red & black figural, stands, ca 1949, EX...**$125.00**

Mickey Mouse & characters, luncheon set, Dan Brechner Exclusive foil label, Walt Disney Productions, 1961, MIB **$275.00**

Mickey Mouse & Minnie, bookends, heavy composition figurals, multicolor, Determined Productions, ca 1970, 6½", pr...**$95.00**

Mickey Mouse & Minnie, hairbrush, wooden handle, Hughes/Walt Disney, 1930s, EX...........................**$50.00**

Mickey Mouse & Minnie, music box, Love Makes the World Go Round, 1970s, M..**$75.00**

Mickey Mouse & Minnie, snow dome, Wonderful World of Disney, in front of castle, 1960s, M......................**$89.00**

Mickey Mouse & the Beanstalk, napkin holder, pottery, Royal Orleans, Walt Disney Productions, 1970s, 4½x5¾", MIB...**$75.00**

Mickey Mouse Club, Dance-a-Tune toy, battery operated, Jamar, No 800 Walt Disney Productions Patent Pending, MIB **$85.00**

Mickey Mouse Club, night light, multicolor plastic TV shape, 1950s **$90.00**

Mickey Mouse w/Donald & Goofy, child's feeding set, Come & Get It, chuck wagon scene, 1970s, MIB **$95.00**

Mickey Mouse/Disneyland, Happy Birthday Carousel, tin litho cake decoration, 9", 1940s, EX (EX original box) **$150.00**

Minnie Mouse, baby fork, embossed handle, Winthrop Silverplate, 1930s, 4¼", EX..................................**$60.00**

Minnie Mouse, pillow case, stitched, Vogue, 23x20", framed, M, from $100.00 to $150.00.

Mouseketeer, doll, blond girl, vinyl, all original, Horsman, M **$55.00**

Pegasus (baby), figurine, marked Copyright Disney, Japan, 4" **$40.00**

Peter Pan, costume jewelry pin, multicolor, 1950s, EX..**$35.00**

Peter Pan, figurine, painted bisque, Magic Memories, limited edition...**$125.00**

Peter Pan, towel set, Styled by Gildex, 1950s, MIP (sealed) **$65.00**

Pinocchio, figurine, Evan K Shaw, 1940s, EX **$295.00**

Pinocchio, jointed wood doll, Ideal, 1939, 11", $350.00. (Photo courtesy Dunbar Gallery)

Pinocchio, lunch pail, tin litho, multicolor graphics on red, cylindrical, 1939, 6½x4¾", EX **$235.00**

Pluto, costume jewelry pin, silver-tone, Alpha-Craft, A Walt Disney Character Pin, 1940, 2x1½", MIB **$60.00**

Shaggy Dog, figurine, WDE 192, Enesco paper label, 1960s, 5" **$89.00**

Sleeping Beauty, figurine, Flora (fairy), Hagen-Renaker, 1959 ....**$250.00**

Sleeping Beauty, sheet music, I Wonder, 1954, EX.....**$45.00**

Snow White, milk pitcher, heavy pottery, Treasure Craft, 1970s, 6¼"..**$225.00**

Snow White, night light, multicolor figural plastic, 1950s, EX, from $75 to...**$125.00**

Snow White, sheet music, Whistle While You Work, 1938, EX **$35.00**

Snow White & Doc, costume jewelry pin, enamel on gold-tone, WD, 1938..**$150.00**

Snow White & Dopey, glow-in-the-dark print, 1940s, M in original frame...**$48.00**

Snow White & the Seven Dwarfs, birthday/record card, 33 ⅓-rpm, Walt Disney Productions, 1960s, M in envelope **$50.00**

Snow White & the Seven Dwarfs, booklet, Dairy Recipes, American Dairy Association, Walt Disney Productions, 1955, EX...**$60.00**

Snow White & the Seven Dwarfs, child's purse, red silk w/printed characters, metal frame, 1930s, EX....**$135.00**

Snow White & the Seven Dwarfs, child's purse, silky cloth w/cloth handle, Bakelite frame, 1930s, EX...........**$95.00**

Snow White & the Seven Dwarfs, fan card, multicolor theater promotional item, ca 1938, EX **$95.00**

Three Little Pigs, ashtray, lustreware, 1930s, M...........**$90.00**

Three Little Pigs, switch plate, hard plastic, 1950s, M in cellophane package..**$32.00**

Thumper, cotton ball dispenser, original cold paint, Leeds, 5", EX...**$49.00**

Tinkerbell, bell, gold-tone metal, souvenir, 1950s, 3⅛", EX...**$59.00**

Tinkerbell, change purse, Disneyland souvenir, w/original price tag, 1960s, M..**$29.00**

Tinkerbell, figurine, Goebel stylized bee mark, 5½"...**$395.00**

Tinkerbell, figurine, Walt Disney Productions, Enesco paper label, 1970s, 4¼"...**$65.00**

Tramp, figurine, ceramic, tan tones, no mark, 1950s, 4½"..**$49.00**

Tramp, plush figure, w/hang tag, 1950s, 12", EX........**$30.00**

Tweedle Dum, figurine, ceramic, Shaw, w/paper label, EX...**$295.00**

Vulture (Jungle Book), cloth figure, 1967, M **$39.00**

Winnie the Pooh, figurine, Beswick, EX.....................**$95.00**

Winnie the Pooh, figurine, Eeyore, painted ceramic, 1960s, EX..**$55.00**

Winnie the Pooh, figurine, Kanga, Beswick...............**$95.00**

Winnie the Pooh, figurine, Owl, redware, marked Canada/Walt Disney Productions on foil label, 1960s, 5½"...**$225.00**

Winnie the Pooh, figurine, Piglet, Beswick **$95.00**

Winnie the Pooh, figurine, Tigger, Beswick **$95.00**

Winnie the Pooh, lamp, figural, original shade, Dolly Toy Co, 1960s, 17½", EX **$75.00**

Winnie the Pooh, Old Maid card game, Jaymar, 1965, MIB **$50.00**

Winnie the Pooh, top, tin litho w/wooden handle, Ohio Art, 1960s, EX...**$75.00**

101 Dalmatians, figurine, Penny, Enesco, 1960s, 4¾"...**$125.00**

101 Dalmatians, figurine, puppy, paper label w/double-D mark, Walt Disney Productions, 1½x3"................**$39.00**

Dog Collectibles

Dog lovers appreciate the many items, old and new, that are modeled after or decorated with their favorite breeds. They pursue, some avidly, all with dedication, specific items for a particular accumulation or a range of objects, from matchbook covers to bronzes.

Perhaps the Scottish Terrier is one of the most highly sought-out breeds of dogs among collectors; at any rate, Scottie devotees are more organized than most. Both the Aberdeen and West Highland Terriers were used commercially; often the two are found together in things such as magnets, Black & White Scotch Whiskey advertisements, jewelry, and playing cards, for instance. They became a favorite of the advertising world in the 1930s and 1940s, partly as a result of the public popularity of President Roosevelt's dog, Fala.

Poodles were the breed of the 1950s, and today items from those years are cherished collectibles. Trendsetter teeny-boppers wore poodle skirts, and the 5-&-10¢ stores were full of pink poodle figurines with 'coleslaw' fur. For a look back at these years, we recommend *Poodle Collectibles of the '50s and '60s* by Elaine Butler (L-W Books).

Many of the earlier collectibles are especially prized, making them expensive and difficult to find. Prices listed here may vary as they are dependent on supply and demand, location, and dealer assessment.

Advisor: Elaine Butler, Poodles (See Directory, Poodle Collectibles)

Advisor: Donna Palmer, Scotties (See Directory, Scottie Dog Collectibles)

Newsletter: *Canine Collectibles Quarterly*
Patty Shedlow, Editor
736 N Western Ave., Ste. 314
Lake Forest, IL 60045; Subscription: $28 per year

Newsletter: *Colliectively Speaking!*
Joan L. Neidhardt, Editor
428 Philadelphia Rd.
Joppa, MD 21085; 410-679-7224; Specializing in 'old, new, Lassie too' — anything collies; Subscription $20 per year

Newsletter: *Scottie Sampler*
David Bohnlein
P.O. Box 2597, Winchester, VA 22604-2597

Magazine: *Great Scots Magazine*
Tartan Scottie
1028 Girard NE
Albuquerque, NM 87106

Basset Hound, Beswick, #2045, glossy, M...................**$60.00**
Poodle, apron, linen w/nylon ruffled trim, shows poodle w/baby carriage on pocket......................**$20.00**
Poodle, book, The Different Dog, Scholarship Books, 1960, softcover.................**$6.00**
Poodle, bookends, begging w/paws on book & pen holder, black glossy finish on red clay, gold trim, 6", pr, from $12 to.................**$20.00**
Poodle, clothes hamper, poodle beneath the Eiffel tower ..**$75.00**
Poodle, curtains, lacy vinyl w/poodles admiring themselves in mirror, pr.........................**$20.00**
Poodle, dish towel, heavy cotton, It's a Dog's Life, w/scenes of clothed lady poodle doing household chores .**$10.00**
Poodle, dress, rayon, sleeveless shift type, applique of lg black & white gingham poodle w/terry cloth trim..........**$40.00**
Poodle, drink mixer, poodle & other party animals drinking champagne, lg.................**$8.00**
Poodle, figurine, Indian chief, ceramic w/spaghetti, Japan **$48.00**

Poodle, figurine, as Indian chief, Japan, $48.00. (Photo courtesy Elaine Butler)

Poodle, figurine, reclining in chaise lounge, wearing sash & tiara, ceramic w/spaghetti, Japan.........................**$55.00**
Poodle, figurine, standing, ceramic w/coleslaw, paper label marked Hardie Arnita of California, 10" **$250.00**
Poodle, hankerchief, poodle strolling w/closed parasol ..**$10.00**
Poodle, luggage, Miss Traveler w/poodle on vinyl, child size, 3-pc.................**$100.00**
Poodle, puzzle, frame-tray; girl in convertible w/teddy bear & poodle, Whitman **$10.00**
Poodle, salt & pepper shakers, kissing, seated on wooden bench, 3-pc.................**$20.00**
Poodle, scarf, silk w/multicolor stylized poodles, lg ..**$12.00**
Poodle, skirt, quilted satin w/poodle smoking in chaise lounge.................**$125.00**
Poodle, squeeze toy, Sun Rubber.................**$15.00**
Poodle, tray, metal w/Parisian scenes, set of 4...........**$40.00**
Pug, bookends, Van Briggle, pr.................**$150.00**
Pug, night light, ceramic, light shines through eyes, heat vents at top & sides, marked Germany, 6¼", VG+.........**$30.00**
Schnauser, china, standing, marked The Kennel Club of Shafford, 11x12".................**$85.00**
Scottie, bookends, brass, sitting figural, 5½x3", EX, pr..**$80.00**
Scottie, bookends, caramel slag glass, Imperial, 6x5x3", EX, pr **$195.00**
Scottie, bookends, white Scottie w/black points & red bow tie, multicolor lustre finish, Japan, 6½", pr...........**$35.00**
Scottie, box, black lacquered wood w/silver Scotties on lid, red & silver decor at corners, Japan, 10½x3½", VG **$42.00**
Scottie, cigarette case, green w/black enamel & marcasite Scottie, 1920-30s, 3x4", EX.................**$80.00**
Scottie, coaster, white paper w/black Scottie & red polka-dots, 3½", EX, set of 6.........................**$25.00**
Scottie, condiment set, mustard & shaker figurals on tray, orange matt finish, largest: 4", from $35 to...........**$50.00**
Scottie, cuff links, Scotties behind convex glass, pr, VG..**$40.00**
Scottie, decanter, glass w/reverse-painted Scotties at center of inverted dome, signed Czechoslovakia, 10", NM .**$290.00**

Scottie, figurines, orange with black collar, Goldscheider, 6", pr, $50.00.

Scottie, lamp, square milk glass base, stenciled Scottie on square shade, 9½", EX **$175.00**
Scottie, napkin holder, carved wood, 5½x4", VG **$25.00**
Scottie, pen holder, brass Scottie on marble base, 3½x2½", EX.................**$95.00**

Scottie, pincushion, recumbent Scottie on satin cushion, 4x5", EX...**$55.00**

Scottie, purse, vinyl triangular form w/brass Scottie on front, leather handle, 3½x6", VG........................**$45.00**

Scottie, salt & pepper shakers, black, Japan, M (EX box), pr...**$25.00**

Scottie, thermometer, carved wood figural, marked Taft Calif, 4x6", EX...**$30.00**

Scottie, tumbler, juice; black Scottie border at base, red decor at top, 1930s, 3", EX.............................**$7.50**

Dollhouse Furniture

Some of the mass-produced dollhouse furniture you're apt to see on the market today was made by Renwal and Acme during the 1940s and Ideal in the 1960s. All three of these companies used hard plastic for their furniture lines and imprinted most pieces with their names. Strombecker furniture was made of wood, and although it was not marked, it has a certain recognizable style to it. Remember that if you're lucky enough to find it complete in the original box, you'll want to preserve the carton as well.

Acme/Thomas, seesaw, red w/white horse head or blue w/yellow horse head................................**$8.00**

Acme/Thomas, wagon, blue w/red handle & wheels ..**$25.00**

Allied, stove, white..**$4.00**

Allied, vanity, red...**$3.00**

Blue Box, chair, caramel w/red back & seat...............**$3.00**

Blue Box, vanity, w/heart-shaped mirror, tan..............**$3.00**

Ideal, chair, kitchen; ivory w/red or blue seats...........**$5.00**

Ideal, mangle, white or black..................................**$15.00**

Ideal, night stand, light blue..................................**$10.00**

Ideal, sewing machine, dark marbleized maroon.......**$20.00**

Ideal, tub, corner; blue w/yellow faucets..................**$15.00**

Ideal Petite Princess, boudoir chaise lounge, blue, #4408-1, MIB..**$21.00**

Ideal Petite Princess, chair, dining; host, #4413-1.........**$8.00**

Ideal Petite Princess, chair, dressing table; blue, w/accessories...**$25.00**

Ideal Petite Princess, grandfather clock, #4423-0........**$18.00**

Ideal Petite Princess, hamper.................................**$20.00**

Ideal Petite Princess, pedestal table set, #4427, MIB ..**$20.00**

Ideal Petite Princess, Royal buffet, #4419-8, MIB........**$25.00**

Ideal Petite Princess, Royal candelabra, #4439-6, MIB..**$18.00**

Ideal Petite Princess, Salon coffee table, #4433-9..........**$5.00**

Ideal Petite Princess, table, occasional; #4437-0............**$5.00**

Ideal Young Decorator, sofa section, middle, rose.....**$10.00**

Imagination, dresser, green, long.............................**$2.00**

Imagination, TV, green...**$2.00**

Jaydon, buffet, reddish brown.................................**$4.00**

Jaydon, piano, reddish brown swirl, w/bench...........**$12.00**

Marklin, bed, blue tin, scrolled headboard, footboard & side rails, gold trim, springs & canvas mattress, 8", EX..**$250.00**

Marklin, toilet, porcelain w/wood-look tank & lid, mounted on tin floor, 5", NM....................................**$600.00**

Marx, accessory, double boiler, metallic gold..............**$4.00**

Marx, accessory, pitcher, metallic tan.......................**$4.00**

Marx, bed, bright yellow, hard plastic, ¾" scale..........**$5.00**

Marx, buffet, dark maroon swirl, hard plastic, ¾" scale.**$5.00**

Marx, chair, bedroom; soft yellow, soft plastic, ¾" scale...**$3.00**

Marx, chair, dining; maroon, hard plastic, ½" scale.....**$2.00**

Marx, chair, tufted back, bright yellow, hard plastic, ¾" scale...**$5.00**

Marx, crib, light blue, soft plastic, ½" scale................**$3.00**

Marx, dining room set, soft brown, soft plastic, table/buffet/hutch/4 chairs (2 w/arms), ¾" scale, 6-pc......**$18.00**

Marx, doll, baby w/rattle, flesh, soft plastic................**$3.00**

Marx, garbage can, light yellow, soft plastic, ½" scale.**$2.00**

Marx, hassock, soft yellow, soft plastic, ¾" scale..........**$3.00**

Marx, hobby horse, light blue, soft plastic, ½" scale....**$3.00**

Marx, kitchen set, dark ivory, hard plastic, sink/stove/refrigerator/sm counter/4 charis, ¾" scale, 8-pc..........**$32.00**

Marx, night stand, ivory or yellow, hard plastic, ¾" scale.**$5.00**

Marx, playground pail, bright yellow, hard plastic, ¾" scale...**$6.00**

Marx, potty chair, pink, hard plastic, ½" scale............**$4.00**

Marx, refrigerator, white, hard plastic, ½" scale...........**$2.00**

Marx, sink, ivory, hard plastic, ½" scale....................**$2.00**

Marx, sofa, blue, curved, for game room, soft plastic, ½" scale...**$5.00**

Marx, sofa, light blue, soft plastic, 3-pc, ½" scale.........**$5.00**

Marx, stove, light ivory, soft plastic, ¾" scale.............**$3.00**

Marx, table, coffee; curved, red, soft plastic, ¾" scale.**$5.00**

Marx, table, kitchen; white, hard plastic, ½" scale........**$2.00**

Marx, toilet, ivory, hard plastic, ½" scale..................**$3.00**

Marx, tub, corner; ivory, hard plastic, ½" scale............**$3.00**

Marx, TV/phonograph, bright yellow, blue or light blue, hard plastic, ¾" scale...**$5.00**

Marx, umbrella table, yellow hard plastic, no umbrella, ½" scale...**$3.00**

Marx, vanity, yellow or blue, hard plastic, ½" scale.....**$2.00**

Mattel Littles, armoire..**$8.00**

Mattel Littles, sofa...**$8.00**

Plasco, bathroom set, tub/toilet/sink/vanity/bench/hamper, w/paper floor plan, MIB...............................**$65.00**

Plasco, birdbath/fountain, ivory.............................**$12.00**

Plasco, chair, living room; light green w/brown base..**$6.00**

Plasco, grandfather clock, brown, cardboard face........**$8.00**

Plasco, kitchen counter, white, blue base, rectangular.**$5.00**

Plasco, refrigerator, white, blue base.......................**$5.00**

Plasco, sofa, light blue, brown base.........................**$8.00**

Plasco, table, coffee; brown marbleized...................**$3.00**

Plasco, tub, various colors.....................................**$4.00**

Plasco, vanity, pink, no-mirror style, w/bench...........**$8.00**

Renwal, baby bath, blue w/bear decal, #122.............**$15.00**

Renwal, buffet, brown, #D55..................................**$6.00**

Renwal, chair, barrel; turquoise or blue w/brown base, stenciled, #77...**$10.00**

Renwal, chair, rocking; red or yellow, #65................**$8.00**

Renwal, china closet, brown, stenciled, #K52............**$15.00**

Renwal, doll, brother, tan, metal rivets, #42..............**$25.00**

Renwal, doll, mother, all pink, plastic rivets, #43.......**$25.00**

Renwal, doll, sister, ivory, plastic rivets, #41.............**$25.00**

Renwal, garbage can, red w/yellow lid, no decal, #64...**$8.00**

Renwal, highboy, pink, #35....................................**$15.00**

Renwal, ironing board, blue or pink, w/iron, #32.......**$22.00**

Renwal, Jolly Twins Kitchen Set, MIB, $100.00 to $125.00. (Photo courtesy Judith Mosholder)

Renwal, lamp, table; brown or reddish brown, stenciled, #73 ....$10.00
Renwal, piano, brown marbleized, #74 ....$30.00
Renwal, radio, floor; brown, #79............................$20.00
Renwal, refrigerator, ivory w/black, nonopening door, #66...$10.00
Renwal, sink, bathroom; pink w/blue, stenciled, #T96...$8.00
Renwal, sink, ivory w/blue, opening door, 368..........$10.00
Renwal, smoking stand, red w/ivory or ivory w/red, #13 .$12.00
Renwal, stool, red w/ivory seat or ivory w/red seat, #12 ..$10.00
Renwal, stroller, pink w/blue wheels, #87...................$35.00
Renwal, table, cocktail; reddish brown, #72 ....$8.00
Renwal, toilet, various colors, #T97.............................$9.00
Renwal, vacuum cleaner, red or yellow, w/decal, #37 ..$25.00
Renwal, washing machine, blue or pink w/decal, #31 ..$30.00
Strombecker, chair, kitchen; aqua, ¾" scale $8.00
Strombecker, grandfather clock, walnut w/gold trim, ¾" scale $15.00
Strombecker, piano bench, walnut, ¾" scale $30.00
Strombecker, table, coffee; wood, for 8" dolls, 1950s, MIB $45.00
Strombecker, table, kitchen; aqua, ¾" scale $10.00
Superior, chair, kitchen; yellow or pink, soft plastic.....$1.00
Superior, hutch, pink or red, ¾" scale $5.00
Superior, refrigerator, white, soft plastic $1.00
Superior, table, ivory, soft plastic $1.00
Thomas, doll, baby w/diaper, 1¼" $3.00
Thomas, doll, baby w/diaper, 3" $4.00
Tomy Smaller Homes, accessory, hamper, white $6.00
Tomy Smaller Homes, bar..$6.00
Tomy Smaller Homes, crib..$15.00
Tomy Smaller Homes, refrigerator, 2 drawers $10.00
Tootsietoy, bench, vanity, pink w/pink-flocked seat..$10.00
Tootsietoy, cupboard, ivory $20.00

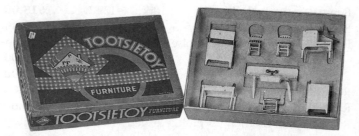

Tootsietoy, kitchen set, complete, MIB, $325.00.

Tootsietoy, medicine cabinet, lavender, no mirror......$15.00

Tootsietoy, table, living room; long w/bottom strut, green w/ivory crackle $25.00
Wolverine, crib $8.00
Wolverine, playpen...$8.00

Dolls

Doll collecting is one of the most popular hobbies in the United States. Since many of the antique dolls are so expensive, modern dolls have come into their own and can be had at prices within the range of most budgets. Today's thrift-shop owners know the extent of 'doll mania,' though, so you'll seldom find a bargain there. But if you're willing to spend the time, garage sales can be a good source for your doll buying. Granted most will be in a 'well loved' condition, but as long as they're priced right, many can be re-dressed, rewigged, and cleaned up. Swap meets and flea markets may sometimes yield a good example or two, often at lower-than-book prices.

Modern dolls, those made from 1935 to the present, are made of rubber, composition, magic skin, synthetic rubber, and many types of plastic. Most of these materials do not stand up well to age, so be objective when you buy, especially if you're buying with an eye to the future. Doll repair is an art best left to professionals, but if yours is only dirty, you can probably do it yourself. If you need to clean a composition doll, do it very carefully. Use only baby oil and follow up with a soft dry cloth to remove any residue. Most types of wigs can be shampooed with wig shampoo and lukewarm water. Be careful not to matt the hair as you shampoo, and follow up with hair conditioner or fabric softener. Comb gently and set while wet, using small soft rubber or metal curlers. Never use a curling iron or heated rollers.

In our listings, unless a condition is noted in the descriptions, values are for dolls in excellent condition.

For further study, we recommend these books by Patricia Smith: *Patricia Smith's Doll Values, Antique to Modern; Modern Collector's Dolls* (eight in the series); *Vogue Ginny Dolls, Through the Years With Ginny;* and *Madame Alexander Collector's Dolls*. Patsy Moyer's books, *Modern Collectible Dolls, Volume 1 and 2,* and *Doll Values, Volume II,* are also highly recommended. Patikii Gibbs has written the book *Horsman Dolls, 1950 – 1970;* and Estelle Patino is the author of *American Rag Dolls, Straight From the Heart;* both contain a wealth of information on those particular subjects. Myla Perkins has written *Black Dolls: 1820 – 1991* and *Black Dolls, Book II; Chatty Cathy Dolls* is by Kathy and Don Lewis; and Judith Izen is the author of *Collector's Guide to Ideal Dolls*. Cindy Sabulis and Susan Weglewski have written the *Collector's Guide to Tammy* and Paris Langford's book, *Liddle Kiddles, An Identification Guide,* includes other doll lines as well. The *Collector's Guide to Vogue Dolls* by Judith Izen and Carol J. Stover includes information on those dolls from the earliest times to the present. All these references are published by Collector Books.

See also Barbie and Friends; Shirley Temple; Toys (Action Figures and GI Joe); Trolls.

Magazine: *Doll Castle News*
37 Belvidere Ave., P.O. Box 247
Washington, NJ 07882
908-689-7042 or Fax 908-689-6320; Subscription $16.95 per
year

Newsletter: Doll Collectors of America
14 Chestnut Rd., Westford, MA 01886; 617-692-8392

Newsletter: *Doll Investment Newsletter*
P.O. Box 1982, Centerville, MA 02632

Newsletter: *Doll News*
United Federation of Doll Clubs
P.O. Box 14146, Parkville, MO 64152

Newsletter: *Modern Doll Club Journal*
Jeanne Niswonger
305 W Beacon Rd., Lakeland, FL 33803

Annalee

Barbara 'Annalee' Davis' was born in Concord, New Hampshire, on February, 11, 1915. She started dabbling at dollmaking at an early age, often giving her creations to friends. She married Charles 'Chip' Thorndike in 1941 and moved to Meredith, New Hampshire, where they started a chicken farm and sold used auto parts. By the early 1950s, with the chicken farm failing, Annalee started crafting her dolls on the kitchen table to help make ends meet. She designed her dolls by looking into the mirror, drawing faces as she saw them, and making the clothes from scraps of material.

The dolls she developed are made of wool felt with hand-painted features and flexible wire frameworks. The earlier dolls from the 1950s had a long white red-embroidered tag with no date. From 1959 to 1964, the tags stayed the same, except there was a date in the upper right-hand corner. From 1965 to 1970, this same tag was folded in half and sewn into the seam of the doll. In 1970 a transition period began. The company changed to a white satiny tag with a date preceded by a copyright symbol in the upper right-hand corner. In 1975 they made another change to a long white cotton strip with a copyright date. In 1982 the white tag was folded over, making it shorter. Many people mistake the copyright date as the date the doll was made — not so! It wasn't until 1986 that they finally began to date the tags with the year of manufacture, making it much easier for collectors to identify their dolls. Besides the red-lettered white Annalee tags, numerous others were used in the 1990s, but all reflect the year the doll was actually made.

The company has held an annual auction on the premises in June since 1983. Recently they have added a second fall auction, which they hold in selected areas around the East Coast. Annalee's signature on a doll increases its value by as much as $300.00, sometimes more. The dolls that are signed on the body can only be purchased at their June auction.

Remember, these dolls are made of wool felt. To protect them, store them with moth balls, and avoid exposing them to too much sunlight, since they will fade. Our advisor has been a collector for fifteen years and a secondary market dealer since 1988. Most of these dolls have been in her collection at one time or another. She recommends 'If you like it, buy it, love it, treat it with care, and you'll have it to enjoy for many years to come.'

Our values are suggested for dolls in very good to excellent condition, not personally autographed by Annalee herself.

Advisor: Jane Holt (See Directory, Dolls)

Newsletter: *The Collector*
Annalee Doll Society
P.O. Box 1137, 50 Reservoir Rd., Meredith, NH 03253-1137
1-800-433-6557

1957, square dancers, came w/assorted clothes, hand-painted faces, 10", pr, minimum value.........................**$950.00**
1958, red elf w/tinsel trim holding instrument, 10" ..**$225.00**
1963, bellhop, assorted colors, 24"...........................**$750.00**
1963, bellhop, red only, 32" **$1,200.00**
1966, monk in green robe carries sm tree in burlap bag, 10" **$250.00**

1966, Yum Yum bunny, 12", $550.00; 7", $300.00. (Photo courtesy Jane Holt)

1967, Fancy Nancy Cat, came in yellow or white & hot pink **$450.00**
1968, painter mouse (flat face) holds paint can & brush, 7"..**$250.00**
1970, elf w/black hair & red outfit, 10" **$75.00**
1970, mailman mouse (flat face), by US mail box, 7"..**$250.00**
1970, monkey (came in chartreuse, blue & hot pink), 10"..**$325.00**
1971, yellow boy bunny w/butterfly on nose, 18" ...**$350.00**
1971, yellow girl bunny in turquoise bandana w/lg white polka dots, missing straw basket........................**$350.00**
1972, donkey head pin **$100.00**
1973, mouse head pin...**$50.00**
1974, Willie Wog Frog, going fishing (missing pole), 42" .**$900.00**
1976, Colonial girl's head pick **$100.00**
1976, gnome, 12"..**$225.00**
1976, Yankee Doodle on horse, 18"..........................**$550.00**
1977, Jack Frost, white outfit, 22"............................**$90.00**
1978, pilgrim couple, 10" **$160.00**
1979, frog boy or girl, 18", each...............................**$125.00**
1979-80, gnome, 18"...**$160.00**
1980, mouse pilot, 7"..**$110.00**
1980, Santa frog, red-striped bag, 18".......................**$150.00**

1980, Valentine mouse, 7" **$40.00**
1981, frog bride & groom, 10", pr **$250.00**
1981, Jack Frost w/5" snowflake, 10" **$110.00**
1981, monkey boy or girl, 12", each **$200.00**
1981, Santa card holder (only year w/suspenders), 29" ..**$150.00**
1982, bunny boy or girl head pick or pin, each **$45.00**
1982, I'm a Ten, 10" **$95.00**
1983, pj baby, 3" **$150.00**
1984, Bob Cratchet & Mrs Cratchet, 18", pr **$300.00**
1984, monk w/jug, 16" **$150.00**
1984, skier, 10" **$95.00**
1985, clown head ornament **$50.00**
1986, angel head ornament......................................**$35.00**
1986, elf skier, green outfit w/red skis, 10" **$75.00**
1986, skier ornament, 3" **$35.00**
1987, baby witch kid, 3" **$100.00**
1987, balloon mobile w/3" Cupid **$135.00**
1987, barbeque mouse, 7"..**$40.00**
1987, clown, pink or blue, 10", each **$50.00**
1987, fall elf, orange, brown or moss green outfit, 10",
   each..**$35.00**
1987, Indian boy & girl, 7", pr..................................**$60.00**
1987, mouse w/watering can, 7" **$40.00**
1987, Santa frog, 10" **$55.00**
1987, stick horse ornament, 5" **$40.00**
1988, Americana couple, 18", pr **$250.00**
1988, artist bunny, 10" **$50.00**
1988, artist bunny w/egg, 18" **$85.00**
1988, country boy & girl rabbits, 10", pr **$85.00**
1988, Huck Finn, Folk Hero Series, 10" **$225.00**
1988, Mom bunny w/baby, 18" **$100.00**
1988, Mr or Mrs Claus in rocking chair, 18", each **$100.00**
1988, skeleton kid, 7" **$50.00**
1988, toy soldier, 10" **$50.00**
1988, toy soldier, 18" **$85.00**
1989, caroller mouse, 12" **$50.00**
1989, duck in pink or teal egg, 5", each....................**$40.00**
1989, Eskimo bear, 10" **$65.00**
1989, kitten on sled, 10"..**$65.00**
1989, Santa pig, 10" **$50.00**
1989, Workshop Santa, animated, 30" **$350.00**
1990, angel, 30" **$145.00**
1990, pj kid, 12" **$45.00**
1990, pj kid, 18", in 24" stocking...............................**$90.00**
1990, strawberry bunny, 18" **$95.00**
1990, Valentine dragon, 5" **$55.00**
1991, Desert Storm head pin **$25.00**
1991, gingerbread boy, 10" **$35.00**
1991, huskies in toboggan, 10"...................................**$75.00**
1991, Thorney the Ghost, 18" **$100.00**
1991, turkey, sm...**$55.00**
1992, Halloween pumpkin kid, 7" **$50.00**
1992, pink flower pick **$10.00**
1992, skater rabbit in pink, 10"..................................**$60.00**
1993, baby Jesus in crib, 5".......................................**$35.00**
1993, Christmas owl, 5" **$45.00**
1993, Halloween kid butterfly, black & orange, 7".....**$50.00**
1993, Jesus in manger ornament, 3"..........................**$25.00**
1994, champagne mouse in glass, 7" **$40.00**

1994, fishing Santa ornament.....................................**$35.00**
1994, Hershey witch pin **$150.00**
1994, marble kid, 7"...**$50.00**
1994, Victorian Santa ornament, 5" **$30.00**
1995, Christmas Morn' Itsie Vignette (only purchased at 1995
   Annalee events), 3"...**$175.00**
1995, fishing boy, 7" **$50.00**
1996, bride & groom mice, 7", pr...............................**$50.00**
1996, butterfly pick **$30.00**

Aurora Dolls by Tonka

The advertising theme of Aurora's #6700 line of Aurora dolls was 'the future looks beautiful.' Their bodies were made of colored, shiny metallic material, and their faces are flesh-colored with colored rhinestone eyes. Hair colors are blond, pink, purple, or blue. There appear to be four dolls in this series; all are made to stand alone, and they each came with a styling brush. Dolls are marked 'Creata-1984.' Boxes are marked with the Tonka logo and are dated 1987. Note that Mattel made similar dolls in 1986 — but they had no rhinestone eyes and tinsel was sprinkled through their hair. Loose dolls in excellent condition are worth only $8.00 to $10.00 each.

Aurora, amber rhinestone eyes, blond hair, gold body, MIB, $25.00. (Photo courtesy Lee Garmon)

Aurora, flesh-colored face w/amber rhinestone eyes, gold body, long blond hair, MIB...................................**$25.00**
Crysta, flesh-colored face w/pink rhinestone eyes, silver body, pink hair, MIB **$25.00**
Lustra, flesh-colored face w/purple rhinestone eyes, silver body, purple hair, MIB..**$25.00**
Mirra, flesh-colored face w/blue rhinestone eyes, silver body, long blue hair, MIB...**$25.00**

Betsy McCall

The tiny 8" Betsy McCall doll was manufactured by the American Character Doll Company from 1957 through 1963. She was made from high-quality hard plastic with a bisque-like finish and hand-painted features. Betsy came in four hair colors — tosca, red, blond, and brunette. She had blue sleep eyes, molded lashes, a winsome smile, and a fully jointed body with bendable knees. On her back there is an identification circle which reads McCall Corp. The basic doll wore a sheer chemise, white taffeta panties, nylon socks, and Maryjane-style shoes and could be purchased for $2.25.

There were two different materials used for tiny Betsy's hair. The first was a soft mohair sewn into fine mesh. Later the rubber scullcap was rooted with saran which was more suitable for washing and combing.

Betsy McCall had an extensive wardrobe with nearly one hundred outfits, each of which could be purchased separately. They were made from wonderful fabrics such as velvet, taffeta, felt, and even real mink. Each ensemble came with the appropriate footwear and was priced under $3.00. Since none of Betsy's clothing was tagged, it is often difficult to indentify other than by its square snap closures (although these were used by other companies as well).

Betsy McCall is a highly collectible doll today but is still fairly easy to find at doll shows. The prices remain reasonable for this beautiful clothes horse and her many accessories.

Advisor: Marci Van Ausdall (See Directory, Dolls)

Newsletter: *Betsy's Fan Club*
Marci Van Ausdall
P.O. Box 946, Quincy, CA 95971; e-mail: dreams707@aol.com; Subscription $12.50 per year or send $4 for sample copy

American Character, extra joints at ankles, knees, waist & wrists, marked McCall 1961, all original, 29", minimum value **$400.00**
American Character, hard plastic, jointed knees, original ballgown, 1958, 8", M, minimum value **$200.00**
American Character, hard plastic, jointed knees, original bathing suit or romper, 1958, 8", M **$100.00**
American Character, hard plastic, jointed knees, original street dress, 1958, 8", M **$165.00**
American Character, hard plastic, jointed knees, riding habit, 1958, 8", M **$200.00**
American Character, vinyl, rooted hair, all original, 36", M, minimum value **$550.00**
American Character, vinyl, rooted hair, med high heels, sleep eyes, marked McCall 1958 (made in '61), 14", M, minimum value **$265.00**
American Character, vinyl, rooted hair, slim limbs, 20" (allow higher value for flirty eyes), M **$300.00**
American Character, vinyl, rooted hair, 29" to 30", M...**$400.00**
American Character (unmarked), extra joints at waist, ankles, wrists & knees, all original, 22", M.....................**$250.00**
Horsman, marked BMC Horsman 1971, all original, 29", M **$175.00**
Horsman Dolls, Inc 1967 on head, 13", M..................**$65.00**
Ideal, marked McCall 1959, all original, 36", minimum value **$550.00**
Ideal, Sandy McCall, marked McCall 1959, all original, 39", M, minimum value **$650.00**
Ideal, vinyl & hard plastic, rooted hair, marked P-90 on body, all original, 14", minimum value..........................**$250.00**
Ideal, vinyl & plastic, extra joints, 22", M, minimum value **$275.00**
Uneeda (unmarked), vinyl & plastic, brown sleep eyes, reddish rooted hair, all original, 11½", M..................**$95.00**

Betsy McCall, outfit #8204 Birthday Party, MOC, $95.00 (also shown, 8" doll). (Photo courtesy Marci Van Ausdall)

Celebrity Dolls

Celebrity and character dolls have been widely collected for many years, but they've lately shown a significant increase in demand. Except for rarer examples, most of these dolls are still fairly easy to find at doll shows, toy auctions, and flea markets, and the majority are priced under $100.00. These are the dolls that bring back memories of childhood TV shows, popular songs, favorite movies, and familiar characters. Mego, Mattel, Remco, and Hasbro are among the largest manufacturers.

Condition is a very important worth-assessing factor, and if the doll is still in the original box, so much the better! Should the box be unopened (NRFB), the value is further enhanced. Using mint as a standard, add 50% for the same doll mint in the box and 75% if it has never been taken out. On the other hand, dolls in only good or poorer condition drop at a rapid pace.

See also Elvis Presley Memorabilia.

Advisor: Henri Yunes (See Directory, Dolls)

Angie Dickinson, Police Woman, Horsman, 1976, 9", M (VG box), $45.00. (Photo courtesy June Moon)

Beatles, hard body w/instrument, Remco, set of 4, EX...**$400.00**
Beatles, Raggedy Ann style w/multicolor Sgt Pepper uniform, w/hang tags, metal stands & promo display, 22", set of 4, M..**$420.00**
Boy George, LJN, 1984, 11½", MIB..........................**$125.00**
Brooke Shields, 2nd Issue, suntan & swimsuit, LJN, 1983, 11½", MIB (sealed) **$95.00**

Carol Channing (as Hello Dolly), vinyl, Nasco Dolls, 1962, 11½", MIB $300.00

Charlie Chaplin, 100th Anniversary, World Doll, 1989, 11½", MIB (sealed)..............................$45.00

Cher, 2nd issue, Growing Hair, Mego, 1977, 12¼", MIB (sealed) $80.00

Dolly Parton, red gown, World Doll, 1987, 18", MIB (sealed) $90.00

Dolly Parton, 2nd issue, cowgirl outfit, Eegee, 1987, 11½", MIB (sealed)..............................$50.00

Dorothy Hamill, red Olympic outfit w/medal, 1977, 11½", MIB (sealed) $75.00

Elizabeth Taylor, The Bluebird, w/3 outfits, Horsman, 1976, 12", MIB (sealed) $150.00

Farrah Fawcett (as Jill from Charlie's Angels), jumpsuit w/scarf, Hasbro, 1977, 8½", MOC $40.00

Flip Wilson/Geraldine, talker, Shindana, 1976, 16", MIB...$65.00

Fred Gwynne (as Herman Munster), Remco, #1820, 1964, MIB $150.00

James Dean, Rebel Rouser or City Streets outfit, DSI, 1994, 12", MIB (sealed), each $75.00

John Wayne, Great Legends Series, Guardian of the West cavalry outfit, Effanbee, 1982, 18", MIB $120.00

Macaully Caulkin (as Home Alone's Kevin), vinyl, screams, MIB $20.00

Marie Osmond, Mattel, 1976, 11", MIB $50.00

Marilyn Monroe, issued in 6 different outfits, DSI, 1993, 11½", MIB (sealed), each $60.00

Marilyn Monroe, issued in 8 different outfits, Tri-Star, 1982, 11½", MIB (sealed), each..................................$100.00

Mr. T, first issue, Galoob, 1983, 12", MIB, $50.00. (Photo courtesy June Moon)

New Kids on the Block, 1st issue, Hangin' Loose, vinyl, 5 different dolls, 12", MIB, each....................................$35.00

Parker Stevenson (as Frank Hardy), Kenner, 1978, 12", MIB (sealed) $50.00

Princess Diana, wedding gown, Goldberger, 1982, 11½", MIB (sealed)..$125.00

Rex Harrison (as Dr Dolittle), vinyl & cloth, talker, Mattel, 24", MIB...$130.00

Rex Harrison (as Dr Dolittle), w/Polynesia parrot, Mattel, 1967, 6", MIB (sealed) $65.00

Roger Moore (as James Bond from Moonraker movie), Mego, 1979, 12", MIB..$100.00

Suzanne Sommers (from Three's Company), Mego, 1975, 12½" MIB...$65.00

Twiggy, Mattel, 1967, 11½", MIB..............................$350.00

Vanna White in wedding dress, Totsy Toys, 1990, rare, MIB, $100.00. (Photo courtesy Henry Yunes)

Vince Edwards (as Ben Casey), vinyl, Bing Crosby Productions, 1962, 12", MIB, rare $400.00

Vivian Leigh (as Scarlett O'Hara), 1st issue, World Dolls, 1980, 12", MIB (sealed) $65.00

Chatty Cathy and Other Mattel Talkers

One of the largest manufacturers of modern dolls is the Mattel company, the famous maker of the Barbie doll. But besides Barbie, there are many other types of Mattel dolls that have their own devotees, and we've tried to list a sampling of several of their more collectible lines.

Next to Barbie, the all-time favorite doll was Mattel's Chatty Cathy. She was first made in the 1960s, in blond and brunette variations, and much of her success can be attributed to that fact that she could talk! By pulling the string on her back, she could respond with eleven different phrases. The line was expanded and soon included Chatty Baby, Tiny Chatty Baby and Tiny Chatty Brother (the twins), Charmin' Chatty, and finally Singin' Chatty. They all sold successfully for five years, and although Mattel reintroduced the line in 1969 (smaller and with a restyled face), it was not well received. For more information we recommend *Chatty Cathy Dolls, An Identification & Value Guide,* by our advisors, Kathy and Don Lewis.

In 1960 Mattel introduced their first line of talking dolls. They decided to take the talking doll's success even further by introducing a new line — cartoon characters that the young TV viewers were already familiar with.

Below you will find a list of the more popular dolls and animals available. Most MIB (mint-in-box) toys found today are mute, but this should not detract from the listed price. If the doll still talks, you may consider adding a few more dollars to the price.

Advisors: Kathy and Don Lewis (See Directory, Dolls)

Animal Yacker, Bernie Bernard, MIB $250.00

Animal Yacker, Bernie Bernard, played with, nontalking ...$25.00

Animal Yacker, Chester O'Chimp, MIB $375.00

Animal Yacker, Chester O'Chimp, played with, nontalking $35.00

Animal Yacker, Crackers the Talking Plush Parrot, MIB..$450.00

Animal Yacker, Crackers the Talking Plush Parrot, played with, nontalking..................**$100.00**

Animal Yacker, Larry the Talking Plush Lion, MIB ...**$325.00**

Animal Yacker, Larry the Talking Plush Lion, played with, nontalking.......................**$20.00**

Storybook Small-Talk, Cinderella, MIB **$250.00**

Storybook Small-Talk, Cinderella, played with, nontalking..**$10.00**

Storybook Small-Talk, Goldilocks, MIB **$250.00**

Storybook Small-Talk, Goldilocks, played with, nontalking.**$10.00**

Storybook Small-Talk, Little Bo Peep, MIB...............**$250.00**

Storybook Small-Talk, Little Bo Peep, played with, nontalking.......................**$10.00**

Storybook Small-Talk, Snow White, MIB.................**$250.00**

Storybook Small-Talk, Snow White, played with, nontalking..**$10.00**

Talk Up, Casper, MIB **$75.00**

Talk Up, Casper, played with, nontalking **$15.00**

Talk Up, Funny Talk, MIB......................**$75.00**

Talk Up, Funny Talk, played with, nontalking............**$10.00**

Talk Up, Mickey Mouse, MIB **$125.00**

Talk Up, Mickey Mouse, played with, nontalking **$10.00**

Talk Up, Silly Talk, MIB **$75.00**

Talk Up, Silly Talk, played with, nontalking **$5.00**

Talk Up, Tweety Bird, MIB **$75.00**

Talk Up, Tweety Bird, played with, nontalking **$5.00**

Talker, Baby First Step, MIB **$225.00**

Talker, Baby First Step, played with, nontalking.........**$25.00**

Talker, Baby Say 'n See, MIB......................**$200.00**

Talker, Baby Say 'n See, played with, nontalking.......**$30.00**

Talker, Baby Secret, MIB......................**$175.00**

Talker, Baby Secret, played with, nontalking..............**$20.00**

Talker, Baby Small Talk, MIB **$125.00**

Talker, Baby Small Talk, played with, nontalking......**$10.00**

Talker, Black Chatty Baby, M......................**$650.00**

Talker, Black Chatty Cathy, pageboy-style hair, M...**$1,000.00**

Talker, Black Chatty Cathy, w/pigtails, M...............**$2,000.00**

Talker, Black Drowsy, MIB **$200.00**

Talker, Black Drowsy, played with, nontalking **$10.00**

Talker, Black Tiny Chatty Baby, M......................**$650.00**

Talker, Bozo the Clown, MIB **$300.00**

Talker, Bozo the Clown, played with, nontalking.......**$10.00**

Talker, Bozo the Clown hand puppet, MIB **$300.00**

Talker, Bozo the Clown hand puppet, played with, nontalking......................**$10.00**

Talker, Buffy & Mrs Beasley, MIB **$250.00**

Talker, Buffy & Mrs Beasley, played with, nontalking..**$50.00**

Talker, Bugs Bunny, MIB **$300.00**

Talker, Bugs Bunny, played with, nontalking **$10.00**

Talker, Bugs Bunny hand puppet, MIB **$275.00**

Talker, Bugs Bunny hand puppet, played with, nontalking......................**$10.00**

Talker, Casper the Friendly Ghost, MIB....................**$450.00**

Talker, Casper the Friendly Ghost, played with, nontalking......................**$25.00**

Talker, Cat in the Hat, rag & plush, MIB..................**$375.00**

Talker, Cat in the Hat, rag & plush, played with, nontalking......................**$100.00**

Talker, Cecil the Seasick Serpent, MIB.................**$325.00**

Talker, Cecil the Seasick Serpent, played with, nontalking......................**$45.00**

Talker, Charmin' Chatty, auburn or blond hair, blue eyes, 1 record, M......................**$250.00**

Talker, Chatty Baby, brunette, red pinafore over white romper, MIB......................**$250.00**

Talker, Chatty Baby, early, blond hair, blue eyes, ring around speaker, M......................**$250.00**

Talker, Chatty Baby, early, brunette hair, blue eyes, M.....**$300.00**

Talker, Chatty Baby, early, brunette hair, brown eyes, M.**$350.00**

Talker, Chatty Baby, open speaker, blond hair, blue eyes, M......................**$250.00**

Talker, Chatty Baby, open speaker, brunette hair, blue eyes, M......................**$250.00**

Talker, Chatty Baby, open speaker, brunette hair, brown eyes, M......................**$250.00**

Talker, Chatty Cathy, brunette hair, brown eyes, M, $800.00. (Photo courtesy Kathy and Don Lewis)

Talker, Chatty Cathy, later issue, open speaker grille, blond hair, blue eyes, M......................**$750.00**

Talker, Chatty Cathy, later issue, open speaker grille, brunette hair, blue eyes, M......................**$750.00**

Talker, Chatty Cathy, later issue, open speaker grille, brunette hair, brown eyes, M......................**$800.00**

Talker, Chatty Cathy, mid-year or transitional, brunette hair, blue eyes, M......................**$600.00**

Talker, Chatty Cathy, mid-year or transitional, brunette hair, brown eyes, M......................**$650.00**

Talker, Chatty Cathy, mid-year or transitional, open speaker, blond hair, blue eyes, M......................**$600.00**

Talker, Chatty Cathy, Patent Pending, brunette hair, blue eyes, M......................**$850.00**

Talker, Chatty Cathy, Patent Pending, cloth over speaker or ring around speaker, blond hair, blue eyes, M..**$850.00**

Talker, Chatty Cathy, porcelain, 1980, MIB **$700.00**

Talker, Doctor Dolittle, MIB......................**$250.00**

Talker, Doctor Dolittle, played with, nontalking.........**$10.00**

Talker, Doctor Dolittle hand puppet, MIB................**$200.00**

Talker, Doctor Dolittle hand puppet, played with, nontalking......................**$25.00**

Talker, Herman Munster hand puppet, MIB.............**$300.00**

Talker, Herman Munster hand puppet, played with, nontalking......................**$50.00**

Talker, King Kong & Bobby Bond, rag & plush, MIB.....**$350.00**

Talker, King Kong & Bobby Bond, rag & push, played with, nontalking......................**$50.00**

Talker, King Kong & Bobby Bond hand puppet, MIB ..**$350.00**

Talker, King Kong & Bobby Bond hand puppet, played with, nontalking...**$25.00**

Talker, Larry Lion hand puppet, MIB..........................**$225.00**

Talker, Larry Lion hand puppet, played with, nontalking..**$10.00**

Talker, Linus the Lionhearted, MIB **$200.00**

Talker, Linus the Lionhearted, played with, nontalking..**$10.00**

Talker, Maurice Monkey, MIB...................................**$250.00**

Talker, Monkees finger puppet, MIB **$300.00**

Talker, Monkees finger puppet, played with, nontalking..**$75.00**

Talker, Mother Goose, rag & plush, MIB...................**$150.00**

Talker, Mother Goose, rag & plush, played with, nontalking..**$5.00**

Talker, Mrs Beasley, rag & plush, MIB **$250.00**

Talker, Mrs Beasley, rag & plush, played with, nontalking.**$5.00**

Talker, Off To See the Wizard finger puppet, MIB...**$350.00**

Talker, Off To See the Wizard finger puppet, played with, nontalking..**$50.00**

Talker, Patootie, rag & plush, MIB **$325.00**

Talker, Patootie, rag & plush, played with, nontalking, MIB **$10.00**

Talker, Porky Pig, MIB **$225.00**

Talker, Scooba-Doo, MIB **$150.00**

Talker, Scooba-Doo, played with, nontalking **$35.00**

Talker, Shrinkin' Violette, MIB **$350.00**

Talker, Shrinkin' Violette, played with, nontalking **$40.00**

Talker, Singin' Chatty, blond hair, M........................**$250.00**

Talker, Singin' Chatty, brunette hair, M....................**$250.00**

Talker, Sister Belle the Talking Doll, MIB.................**$375.00**

Talker, Sister Belle the Talking Doll, played with, nontalking..**$25.00**

Talker, Tatters, MIB **$150.00**

Talker, Tatters, played with, nontalking.....................**$10.00**

Talker, Timey Tell, MIB...**$125.00**

Talker, Timey Tell, played with, nontalking **$5.00**

Talker, Tiny Chatty Baby, blond hair, blue eyes, M..**$250.00**

Talker, Tiny Chatty Baby, brunette hair, blue eyes, M......**$350.00**

Talker, Tiny Chatty Baby, brunette hair, brown eyes, M..**$375.00**

Talker, Tom & Jerry, rag & plush, MIB.....................**$275.00**

Talker, Tom & Jerry, rag & plush, played with, nontalking..**$25.00**

Dawn Dolls by Topper

Made by Deluxe Topper in the 1970s, this 6" fashion doll was part of a series sold as the Dawn Model Agency. They're becoming highly collectible, especially when mint in the box. They were issued already dressed in clothes of the highest style, or you could buy additional outfits, many complete with matching shoes and accessories.

Advisor: Dawn Parrish (See Directory, Dolls)

Case, Dawn, pink w/stars & clouds, NM....................**$10.00**

Colorforms, Dawn & Angie dolls, MIB **$50.00**

Doll, Dawn, #0500, MIB (sealed) **$35.00**

Doll, Dawn Majorette, MIB (sealed)..........................**$75.00**

Instructions, #PG0966 or #PG1004, How To Make Your Doll Walk, original, each **$5.00**

Outfit, Black Tie 'n Tux, #8393, MIB (sealed)............**$65.00**

Outfit, Bluebell, #0722, dress & shawl, M **$10.00**

Outfit, Fuchsia Flash, #0612, MIB (sealed) **$35.00**

Outfit, Glimmering Stardust Coat, M (sealed half-box w/modeling agency purse) **$50.00**

Outfit, Gold Glow Swirl, #0721, dress & shawl, M.....**$10.00**

Outfit, Long 'n Leather, #8125, white version, MIB (sealed) **$40.00**

Outfit, Skinny Mini, #0611, MIB (sealed)....................**$30.00**

Dolly Darlings

Hasbro created the short-lived Dolly Darlings in 1965 when they brought out the first series of six dolls that were known as the Hat Box series because of the shape of their cases. Dolly Darlings are approximately 4" and were made in four different series until they were discontinued in 1967. For more information see *Liddle Kiddles, An Identification and Value Guide* by Paris Langford.

Advisor: Paris Langford (See Directory, Dolls)

Beth at the Supermarket, orange hair, vest & gingham slacks, w/accessories, Hat Box Series, 1965, MIB, from $25 to **$35.00**

Boy Trap, #8523, blond bobbed hair, pink dress w/lace inset, Blue Box Series, 1967, MIB, from $12 to.............**$15.00**

Boy Trap, #8545, orange hair, white shirt, long green vest & white painted legs, Playtime Series, 1967, MOC, from $12 to..**$15.00**

Casual, #8513, dark brown hair w/orange elastic headband, gingham outfit, Dark Pink Box Series, 1967, MIB, from $12 to..**$15.00**

Cathy Goes to a Party, orange hair w/red bow, w/birthday cake & accessories, Hat Box Series, 1965, from $25 to **$35.00**

Dolly Darlings, Hipster, Sugar 'n Spice, and Casual, MIB and MOC, from $12.00 to $15.00 each. (Photo courtesy Paris Langford)

Dreamy, #8535, blond hair w/pink ribbon, pink, purple & white dress, Partytime Series, 1968, MOC, from $12 to........**$15.00**

Fancy Pants, #8543, blond hair w/side ponytail & blue bow, blue & white outfit, Playtime Series, 1967, MOC, from $12 to **$15.00**

First Aid, #8515, brown ponytail, blue & white gingham dress w/white apron, Dark Pink Box Series, 1967, MIB, from $12 to **$15.00**

Flying Nun, dark brown hair, long white robe, belt & plastic flying hat, MIB (sealed pink or blue box)............**$25.00**

Go-Team-Go, #8511, blond hair, cheerleader outfit, w/one yarn pom-pon, Blue Box Series, 1967, MIB, from $12 to....................**$15.00**

Go-Team-Go, #8511, blond hair, cheerleader outfit w/1 yarn pom-pon, Dark Pink Series, 1967, MIB, from $12 to....................**$15.00**

Hipster, #8520, brown hair w/braid to side, green & purple outfit w/beret, Blue Box Series, 1967, MIB, from $12 to....................**$15.00**

Honey, #8533, blond hair w/yellow flower on headband, white dress, Partytime Series, 1968, MOC, from $12 to....................**$15.00**

John & His Pets, brown hair, checked jacket & blue shorts, 5 pets & accessories, Hat Box Series, 1965, MIB, from $25 to....................**$35.00**

Karen Has a Slumber Party, brown hair, 2-pc pjs, w/accessories, Hat Box Series, 1965, MIB, from $25 to....**$35.00**

Lemon Drop, #8544, short brown hair, yellow shirt & overalls, Playtime Series, 1967, MOC, from $12 to......**$15.00**

Powder Puff, #8532, brown hair w/lilac ribbon, lilac dress w/fur trim, Partytime Series, 1968, MOC, from $12 to........**$15.00**

School Days, #8514, blond hair, green vest, blue shirt & plaid skirt, Dark Pink Box Series, 1967, MIB, from $12 to..**$15.00**

Shary Takes a Vacation, blond hair w/orange bow, pink & white outfit, w/accessories, Hat Box Series, 1965, from $25 to....................**$35.00**

Slick Set, #8521, orange pigtails, yellow, orange & purple rain outfit, Blue Box Series, 1967, MIB, from $12 to...**$15.00**

Slick Set, #8541, orange pigtails, yellow, orange & purple rain outfit w/hat, Playtime Series, 1967, MOC, from $12 to....................**$15.00**

Slumber Party, #8512, auburn hair, 2-pc pjs, Blue Box Series, 1967, MIB, from $12 to....................**$15.00**

Sugar 'n Spice, #8534, blond hair w/3 ponytail curls, green & white dress, Partytime Series, 1968, MOC, from $12 to....................**$15.00**

Sunny Day, #8542, blond hair, white dress w/flower applique, Playtime Series, 1967, MOC, from $12 to................**$15.00**

Susie Goes to School, brown hair w/red headband, plaid school uniform, w/accessories, Hat Box Series, 1965, from $25 to....................**$35.00**

Sweetheart, #8531, white hair w/pink hearts, pink & white dress w/heart trim, Partytime Series, 1968, MOC, from $12 to....................**$15.00**

Tea Time, #8510, blond hair, black & white party dress, Blue Box Series, 1967, MIB, from $12 to....................**$15.00**

Tea Time, #8510, blond hair w/red headband, black & white party dress, Dark Pink Box Series, 1967, MIB, from $12 to **$15.00**

Tea Time, #8530, blond hair, black & white party dress, Partytime Series, 1968, MOC, from $12 to **$15.00**

Technicolor, #8524, blond hair, purple, yellow & orange dress w/hair ribbon, Blue Box Series, 1967, MIB, from $12 to....................**$15.00**

Teeny Bikini, #8522, blond braided ponytail, pink & green floral outfit w/hat, Blue Box Series, 1967, MIB, from $12 to....................**$15.00**

Teeny Bikini, #8540, blond braided ponytail, green & pink floral dress, Partytime Series, 1967, MOC, from $12 to........**$15.00**

Holly Hobbie

In the late 1960s a young homemaker and mother, Holly Hobbie, approached the American Greeting Company with some charming country-styled drawings of children as proposed designs for greeting cards. Her concepts were well received by the company, and since that time thousands of Holly Holly items have been produced. Nearly all are marked HH, H. Hobbie, or Holly Hobbie.

Advisor: Donna Stultz (See Directory, Dolls)

Newsletter: *Holly Hobbie Collectors Gazette*
c/o Donna Stultz
1455 Otterdale Mill Rd.
Taneytown, MD 21787-3032; 410-775-2570
Subscription: $25 per year for 6 issues; includes free 50-word ad per issue

Bank, Holly Hobbie holding cat, 1980, from $25 to...**$35.00**

Bank, letters spell Baby as base, Holly at top w/Robby standing to side, 1983, from $25 to................**$35.00**

Bank, Robbie Hobbie holding dog, 1980, from $25 to...**$35.00**

Cake pans, aluminum, made by Wilton: Holly, 1976, 14½", from $20.00 to $30.00; Robbie, 1976, 14½", from $25.00 to $35.00; Holly, 1975, 17", from $10.00 to $15.00; Far right: from child's baking set, circa unknown, 9¾", from $15.00 to $20.00. (Photo courtesy Donna Stultz)

Cookie cutter set, 7 plastic shapes w/mixing bowl, spoon, rolling pin & booklet, Pillsbury, 1976, complete, from $75 to....................**$100.00**

Cookie jar, lithographed tin w/Love Is a Good Cook's Secret Ingredient & Robby, w/plastic lid, Cheinco, from $20 to....................**$30.00**

Cookie jar, white glass w/Holly carring tray & It's Cookie Time, w/blue lid, 1980, from $65 to....................**$75.00**

Doll, Grandma Holly, cloth, Knickerbocker, 14", MIB..**$25.00**

Doll, Holiday Holly Hobbie, berry scented, w/clear ornament at neck, 1988, 18", MIB (sealed)....................**$35.00**

Doll, Holly Hobbie, Heather, Amy or Carrie, cloth, Knickerbocker, 16", MIB, each **$20.00**

Doll, Holly Hobbie, Heather, Amy or Carrie, cloth, Knickerbocker, 27", MIB, each..............................**$30.00**

Doll, Holly Hobbie, Heather, Amy or Carrie, cloth, Knickerbocker, 33", MIB, each..............................**$40.00**

Doll, Holly Hobbie, Heather, Amy or Carrie, Knickerbocker, cloth, 6", MIB, each **$6.00**

Doll, Holly Hobbie, Heather, Amy or Carrie, Knickerbocker, 9", MIB, each...**$10.00**

Doll, Holly Hobbie Talker, cloth, 4 sayings, Knickerbocker, 16", MIB, from $25 to **$35.00**

Doll, Robby, cloth, Knickerbocker, 9", MIB................**$15.00**

Doll, Robby, cloth, Knickerbocker, 16", MIB..............**$25.00**

Knife & fork set, stainless w/figural handle, Oneida, 2-pc, junior size, MIB, from $25 to **$35.00**

Lamp, blue girl w/cat, painted ceramic, unauthorized issue, 23", from $75 to **$100.00**

Plate, Love Is a Precious Thing w/Holly & cat in relief, sterling, Franklin Mint, 1973, 9", MIB, from $350 to..**$500.00**

Server, stainless w/Holly cutout, Oneida, from $25 to..**$35.00**

Spoon, feeding; stainless w/figural handle, Oneida, from $25 to **$35.00**

Teddy bear, pastel patchwork material, ribbon at neck marked Holly Hobbie, Knickerbocker, 1981, 14", from $35 to...**$45.00**

Jem

The glamorous life of Jem mesmerized little girls who watched her Saturday morning cartoons, and she was a natural as a fashion doll. Hasbro saw the potential in 1985 when they introduced the Jem line of 12" dolls representing her, the rock stars from Jem's musical group, the Holograms, and other members of the cast, including the only boy, Rio, Jem's road manager and Jerrica's boyfriend. Each doll was poseable, jointed at the waist, head, and wrists, so that they could be positioned at will with their musical instruments and other accessory items. Their clothing, their makeup, and their hairdos were wonderfully exotic, and their faces were beautifully modeled. The Jem line was discontinued in 1987 after being on the market for only two years.

Aja, blue hair, complete w/accessories, MIB...............**$40.00**

Ashley, curly blond hair, w/stand, 11", MIB................**$25.00**

Banee, straight black waist-length hair, w/stand, 11", MIB .**$25.00**

Clash, straight purple hair, complete, MIB **$40.00**

Danse, pink & blond hair, invents dance routines, MIB..**$40.00**

Jem, Roll 'N Curl, 12", MIB (sealed)............................**$25.00**

Jem/Jerrica, Glitter & Gold, w/accessories, MIB **$50.00**

Jetta, black hair w/silver streaks, complete, MIB........**$40.00**

Kimber, red hair, w/stand, cassette, instrument & poster, 12½", MIB...**$40.00**

Krissie, dark skin w/dark brown curly hair, w/stand, 11", MIB **$25.00**

Pizzaz from Misfits, chartreuse hair, complete, MIB ...**$40.00**

Raya, pink hair, complete, MIB **$40.00**

Rio, Glitter & Gold, complete, 12½", MIB **$50.00**

Roxy, blond hair, complete, MIB..................................**$40.00**

Shana, of Holograms Band, purple hair, complete, EX, from $30 to...**$40.00**

Stormer, curly blue hair, complete, MIB **$40.00**

Liddle Kiddles

These tiny little dolls ranging from ¾" to 4" tall were made by Mattel from 1966 until 1979. They all had poseable bodies and rooted hair that could be restyled, and they came with accessories of many types. Some represented storybook characters, some were flowers in perfume bottles, some were made to be worn as jewelry, and there were even spacemen 'Kiddles.'

Our prices range from excellent and complete to mint with no packaging. A doll whose accessories are missing is worth from 65% to 70% less. Serious collectors prefer examples that are still in their original packaging and will often pay a minimum of 30% (to as much as 100%) over the price of a doll in excellent condition with all her original accessories.

For more information, we recommend *Liddle Kiddles, An Identification and Value Guide* by Paris Langford and *Schroeder's Collectible Toys, Antique to Modern* (both published by Collector Books).

Advisor: Dawn Parrish (See Directory, Dolls)

Club: Liddle Kiddle Klub
Laura Miller
3639 Fourth Ave., La Crescenta, CA 91214

Bunson Bernie, #3501, red hair, yellow vinyl slicker w/Fire Chief hat, truck & accessories, 1966-67, 3", from $60 to...**$70.00**

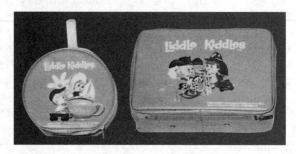

Cases, from $30.00 to $35.00 each. (Photo courtesy Dawn Parrish)

Cherry Blossom Skeddiddle, #3790, black hair w/orange headband, green parasol, tunic dress, 1969-70, 4", from $60 to..**$75.00**

Freezy Sliddle, #3516, auburn hair, blue jacket w/hot pink fur trim, pink stretch tights, 1967, 3½", from $50 to..**$60.00**

Funny Bunny Kiddle, #3532, pink, yellow or blue bunny suit w/ribbon trim, 1968-69, from $15 to....................**$20.00**

Gretta Griddle, #3508, doll, only, blond ponytail, bangs & side curls, 1966, 3½", from $15 to........................**$20.00**

Heather Hiddlehorse, #3673, auburn hair w/ponytail & sideburns, 1969-70, 4", from $65 to **$75.00**

Howard Biff Boodle, #3502, blond hair, T-shirt, jeans & red baseball cap, 1966, 3½", from $60 to....................**$70.00**

Lenore Limousine, #3643, doll only, blond hair w/curly up-do, 1969-70, from $20 to......................................**$25.00**

Lickety Spliddle & Her Traveliddles, #3771, doll only, blond hair & blue eyes, 1968-69, 4", from $15 to..........**$20.00**

Liddle Diddle, complete, from $50.00 to $60.00. (Photo courtesy Cindy Sabulis)

Liddle Middle Muffet, #3545, doll only, auburn hair, 1967-68, 3½", from $75 to.....................................**$85.00**

Lola Liddle, #3504, long blond hair, sailor outfit w/sailboat, 1966-67, 3½", from $60 to......................................**$70.00**

Loretta Locket, #3722, doll only, dark brown hair, 1968, from $5 to...**$10.00**

Lorna Locket, #3535, blond hair w/side braid, red satin jumper, red jewel locket, 1967, from $15 to........**$25.00**

Robin Hood & Maid Marian, #3785, dolls only, marked Mattel Inc Hong Kong or Taiwan, 1969-70, 2", pr, from $65 to..**$75.00**

Rosebud Kologne, #3702, dolls only, red hair, 1968-69, from $15 to..**$25.00**

Santa Kiddle, Christmas ornament, MIB, $65.00. (Photo courtesy Dawn Parrish)

Shelia Skediddle, #3765, long hair w/yellow ribbon, yellow dress w/white lace trim, 1968-70, 4", from $15 to .**$25.00**

Shirley Strawberry Kola Kiddle, #3727, doll only, red hair to ankles, 1968-69, from $15 to...................................**$20.00**

Sleeping Biddle, #3527, doll only, blond hair, closed eyes w/rooted lashes, 1968, 3½", from $35 to..............**$50.00**

Telly Viddle, #3751, doll only, long brown hair, octagon shaped eyes, 3½", from $25 to **$35.00**

Tiny Tiger Animiddle, #3636, 2-pc brushed nylon tiger suit w/yarn bangs & tail, 1969-70, from $30 to..........**$40.00**

Yellow Fello Kozmic Kiddle, #3650, yellow glow-in-the-dark body w/painted features, w/spaceship, 1969-70, from $135 to...**$150.00**

Littlechaps

In 1964 Remco Industries created a family of four fashion dolls that represented an upper-middle class American family. The Littlechaps family consisted of the father, Dr. John Littlechap, his wife, Lisa, and their two children, teenage daughter Judy and pre-teen Libby. Interest in these dolls is on the rise as more and more collectors discover the exceptional quality of these fashion dolls and their clothing.

Advisor: Cindy Sabulis (See Directory, Dolls)

Accessories, Family Room, Bedroom or Dr John's Office, complete, EX, each..**$125.00**
Carrying case..**$25.00**
Doctor John, MIB (sealed)..**$60.00**
Dr John, outfits, MIB (sealed), from $30 to.................**$50.00**
Judy, MIB (sealed)..**$65.00**
Libby, MIB (sealed)...**$45.00**
Lisa, MIB (sealed)...**$60.00**
Outfit, Dr John, MIB (sealed), from $30 to..................**$50.00**
Outfit, Judy, MIB (sealed), from $35 to **$75.00**
Outfit, Libby, MIB (sealed), from $35 to......................**$50.00**
Outfit, Lisa, MIB (sealed), from $35 to.........................**$75.00**

Remco's Littlechap Family: Libby (front), Judy (left), John (back), and Lisa (right), EX, from $15.00 to $20.00 each. (Photo courtesy Cindy Sabulis)

Petal People

Uneeda Petal People are approximately 3" tall, Kiddle-like vinyl dolls with rooted hair and fabric clothing. Each doll has plastic shoes and comes inside a 12" flower attached to a flowerpot base. There are six different flowers and dolls — each a different color flower with a molded seat inside the petals. Each pot has a color-coordinated sticker with the accompanying doll's name, stock number, and a short poem. For further information we recommend *Liddle Kiddles, An Identification and Value Guide,* by Paris Langford.

Advisor: Paris Langford (See Directory, Dolls)

Petal People, any, from $15.00 to $20.00. (Photo courtesy Paris Langford)

Carrying case, Flower Shoppe, vinyl, holds 3 dolls, M w/original hang tag **$25.00**
Doll, Daffi Dill, #30130, brown hair, yellow & black short suit, white pearlized shoes, w/green daffodill, from $15 to...**$20.00**
Doll, Dizzy Daisy, #30131, blond hair, yellow outfit, pink pearlized shoes, w/white daisy, from $15 to........**$20.00**
Doll, Polly Poppy, #30128, brown hair, black & orange outfit, white pearlized shoes, w/orange poppy, from $15 to...**$20.00**
Doll, Rosy Rose, #30127, blond hair w/orange headband, red & black outfit, red shoes, w/red rose, from $15 to......**$20.00**
Doll, Sunny Flower, #30129, brown hair w/yellow bow, yellow outfit & shoes, w/yellow sunflower, from $15 to....**$20.00**
Doll, Tiny Tulip, #30126, blond hair w/black bow, pink & black outfit, pink pearlized shoes, w/pink tulip, from $15 to...**$20.00**
Paper dolls, uncut, original folder, M...........................**$15.00**

Strawberry Shortcake and Friends

Strawberry Shortcake came on the market with a bang around 1980. The line included everything to attract small girls — swimsuits, bed linens, blankets, anklets, underclothing, coats, shoes, sleeping bags, dolls and accessories, games, and many other delightful items. Strawberry Shortcake and her friends were short lived, lasting only until the mid-1980s.

Advisor: Geneva Addy (See Directory, Dolls)

Newsletter: *Berry-Bits*
Strawberry Shortcake Collector's Club
Peggy Jimenez
1409 72nd St., N Bergen, NJ 07047

Doll, Almond Tea, 5½", MIB...................................**$25.00**
Doll, Angel Cake, 5½", MIB....................................**$25.00**
Doll, Berry Baby Lemon Meringue, 5½", MIB.............**$25.00**
Doll, Blueberry Muffin, 5½", MIB.............................**$25.00**
Doll, Butter Cookie, 5½", MIB.................................**$25.00**
Doll, Cherry Cuddler, 5½", MIB...............................**$25.00**

Doll, Lemon Meringue, 5½", MIB...............................**$25.00**
Doll, Lime Chiffon, 5½", MIB **$25.00**
Doll, Orange Blossom Party Pleaser, 6", MIB.............**$55.00**
Doll, Raspberry Tart, 5½", MIB.................................**$25.00**
Doll, stuffed pillow type, NM **$8.00**
Game, Strawberry Shortcake Housewarming, cards, MIB...**$6.00**
Gift ribbon, Christmas, 1982, MIP, from $2.50 to **$4.00**

Huckleberry Pie and Pup-Cake, $65.00. (Photo courtesy June Moon)

School desk, w/attached seat **$65.00**
Sheet set, twin size, MIP **$15.00**
Slacks, printed graphics, girl's size, EX **$7.00**
Store display, molded plastic, 2-sided, Kenner, 1981, NM...**$25.00**

Wonderful World cabinet with 17 scented figures, $100.00. (Photo courtesy June Moon)

Tammy and Friends

In 1962 the Ideal Novelty and Toy Company introduced their teenage Tammy doll. Slightly pudgy and not quite as sophisticated-looking as some of the teen fashion dolls on the market at the time, Tammy's innocent charm captivated consumers. Her extensive wardrobe and numerous accessories added to her popularity with children. Tammy had a car, a house, and her own catamaran. In addition, a large number of companies obtained licenses to issue products using the 'Tammy' name. Everything from paper dolls to nurses' kits were made with Tammy's image on them. Her success was not confined to the United States; she was also successful in Canada and several other European countries. See *Collector's Guide to Tammy, the Ideal Teen* (Collector Books), by Cindy Sabulis and Susan Weglewski for more information.

Advisor: Cindy Sabulis (See Directory, Dolls)

Black Tammy, MIB **$400.00**
Dodi, suntan version, 1977, 9", MIB........................**$40.00**
Grown-Up Tammy, MIB...**$75.00**
Patty, Montgomery Ward's Exclusive, MIB **$200.00**
Pepper, slim body, 1965, MIB...................................**$50.00**
Pepper, 1963, 9", MIB..**$45.00**
Pos'n Pepper, original clothes, 1964, 9", VG **$20.00**
Pos'n Pete, MIB..**$125.00**
Pos'n Salty, MIB...**$100.00**
Pos'n Tammy & Her Phone Booth, MIB, from $75 to ..**$95.00**

Tammy, doll, rare 'carrot top,' MIB, $75.00. (Photo courtesy Cindy Sabulis)

Tammy, MIB, from $45 to...**$65.00**
Tammy's Dad, MIB **$65.00**
Tammy's Mom, MIB...**$65.00**
Ted, re-dressed, 12½", VG **$25.00**
Ted, 1964, 12½", MIB...**$65.00**

Tiny Teens

Uneeda Tiny Teens are approximately 7" tall with rooted hair and eyelashes. Each doll came packaged in an oval-shaped card with a gold scalloped bubble that resembled a locket frame. These dolls were very well dressed and came with one or more accessories, a posing stand, and removable shoes. The dolls were marked UD, CO 1967 on the back of the shoulders. There are twelve dolls in the series.

Advisor: Paris Langford (See Directory, Dolls)

Beau Time, blond hair w/headband, blue & white dress, purse & blue shoes, 1967, 7", MOC, from $10 to **$15.00**
Bride Time, blond hair, white lace dress & shoes w/bouquet, 1967, 7", MOC, from $10 to **$15.00**
Date Time, auburn hair, green & white evening gown w/glitter trim & silver bag, white shoes, 1967, 7", MOC, from $10 to..**$15.00**
Fun Time, brown hair, gingham-trimmed dress, w/hat, purse & shoes, 1967, 7", MOC, from $10 to....................**$15.00**
Mini Time, brown hair, navy jumpsuit w/striped overdress, blue shoes & TV, 1967, 7", MOC, from $10 to **$15.00**
Party Time, auburn hair w/pink ribbon, sheer pink & white dress, Paris-type hat & pink shoes, 1967, 7", MOC, from $10 to...**$15.00**

Prom Time, brown hair w/silver crown, blue velvet gown w/glitter trim & Tiny Teen banner, 1967, 7", MOC, from $10 to..**$15.00**
Shower Time, blond hair, black rain outfit w/hat, boots & umbrella, 1967, 7", MOC, from $10 to **$15.00**
Sport Time, blond hair, brown & gold outfit w/hat, brown ice skates & shoes, 1967, 7", MOC, from $10 to........**$15.00**
Tea Time, blond hair, blue gingham dress w/hat, white shoes & telephone, 1967, 7", MOC, from $10 to **$15.00**
Vacation Time, black hair w/yellow headband, coat & hat w/blue trim, 1967, 7", MOC, from $10 to **$15.00**
Winter Time, blond hair, green jacket w/blue collar & hat, black shoes & dog, 1967, 7", MOC, from $10 to..**$15.00**

Tressy

Tressy was American Character's answer to Barbie. This 11½" fashion doll was made from 1963 to 1967. Tressy had a unique feature — her hair 'grew' by pushing a button on her stomach. She and her little sister, Cricket, had numerous fashions and accessories. Note that never-removed-from-box Tressy and Cricket items are rare, so unless indicated, values listed are for loose, mint items.

Advisor: Cindy Sabulis (See Directory, Dolls)

Apartment, M **$150.00**
Beauty Salon, M...**$125.00**
Case, features Cricket, M..**$35.00**
Case, features Tressy, M...**$30.00**
Doll, Cricket, M...**$30.00**
Doll, Pre-Teen Tressy, M..**$75.00**
Doll, Tressy, M..**$25.00**
Doll, Tressy w/Magic Makeup Face, M.......................**$20.00**
Doll Clothes Pattern, M **$10.00**
Gift Paks w/Doll & Clothing, MIB (sealed), each, minimum value **$100.00**
Hair Accessory Paks, MIB (sealed), each.....................**$20.00**
Hair Dryer, M..**$45.00**
Hair or Cosmetic Accessory Kits, M, each, minimum value ..**$50.00**
Millinery, M **$150.00**
Outfits, MIB (sealed), each, minimum value **$40.00**
Outfits, MOC, each **$25.00**

Tressy, doll, original dress, M, $25.00; Mary Makeup, doll, re-dressed, G, $15.00. (Photo courtesy Cindy Sabulis)

Vogue Dolls, Inc.

Vogue Dolls Incorporated is one of America's most popular manufacturer of dolls. In the early 1920s through the mid-1940s, Vogue imported lovely dolls of bisque and composition, dressing them in the fashionable designs hand sewn by Vogue's founder, Jennie Graves. In the late forties through the early fifties they became famous for their wonderful hard plastic dolls, most notably the 8" Ginny doll. This adorable toddler doll skyrocketed into nationwide attention in the early fifties as lines of fans stretched around the block during store promotions, and Ginny dolls sold out regularly. A Far-Away-Lands Ginny was added in the late fifties, sold well through the seventies, and is still popular with collectors today. In fact, a modern-day version of Ginny is currently being sold by Vogue.

Many wonderful dolls followed through the years, including unique hard-plastic, vinyl, and soft-body dolls. These dolls include teenage dolls Jill, Jan, and Jeff, Ginnette the 8" baby doll, Miss Ginny, and the famous vinyl, and soft-bodied dolls by noted artist and designer, E. Wilkin. It is not uncommon for these highly collectible dolls to turn up at garage sales and flea markets.

Over the years, Vogue developed the well-deserved reputation as 'The Fashion Leaders in Doll Society' based on their fine quality sewing and on the wide variety of outfits designed for their dolls to wear. These outfits included frilly dress-up doll clothes as well as action-oriented sports outfits. The company was among the first in the doll industry to develop the concept of marketing and selling separate outfits for their dolls, many of which were 'matching' for their special doll lines. The very early Vogue outfits are most sought after, and later outfits are highly collectible as well. It is wise for collectors to become aware of Vogue's unique styles, designs, and construction methods in order to 'spot' these authentic Vogue 'prizes' on collecting outings.

Values here are for these lines in complete, mint condition and are only a general guide. For further information we recommend *Collector's Guide to Vogue Dolls* by Judith Izen and Carol J. Stover (Collector Books).

Advisors: Judith Izen and Carol J. Stover (See Directory, Dolls)

Baby Dear, 12", EX	**$95.00**
Baby Dear, 12", MIB	**$145.00**
Baby Dear, 12", Musical, M	**$200.00**
Baby Dear, 17", EX	**$180.00**
Baby Dear, 17", MIB	**$225.00**
Baby Dear, 17", Musical, M	**$250.00**
Ginnette, Cries Real Tears, MIB	**$125.00**
Ginnette, Meritus, MIB, minimum value	**$40.00**
Ginnette, outfits, early (1955-59), MIB, from $25 to	**$75.00**
Ginnette, outfits, later (1960s), MIB, from $35 to	**$100.00**
Ginnette, painted eyes, EX	**$75.00**
Ginnette, painted eyes, MIB, from $100 to	**$150.00**
Ginnette, porcelain, MIB, minimum value	**$60.00**
Ginnette, sleep eyes, EX	**$60.00**
Ginnette, sleep eyes, MIB, from $75 to	**$150.00**
Jan, outfits for Lovable or Sweetheart Jan, MIB, from $50 to	**$60.00**
Jan, 1959-60, M	**$75.00**
Jan, 1959-60, MIB	**$120.00**
Jan, 1963, Lovable Jan, MIB	**$150.00**
Jan, 1963-64, M	**$95.00**
Jan, 1964, Sweetheart Jan, MIB	**$150.00**
Jeff, M	**$75.00**
Jeff, MIB	**$150.00**
Jeff, outfits, MIB, from $25 to	**$40.00**
Jill, accessories, from $10 to	**$50.00**
Jill, furniture, from $45 to	**$75.00**
Jill, MIB, minimum value	**$225.00**
Jill, outfit, MIB, from $45 to	**$65.00**
Jill, 1957-1959 head locket w/chain, rhodium plated	**$300.00**
Jill, 1957-58, basic dress, M, from $125 to	**$160.00**
Jill, 1959-60, basic outfit, M, from $150 to	**$175.00**
Jill, 1959-60, hard-to-find outfits including rodeo or cookout, M, from $195 to	**$200.00**
Littlest Angel, 1961-63, hard plastic body, M	**$65.00**
Littlest Angel, 1961-63, hard plastic body, MIB	**$100.00**
Littlest Angel, 1969-80, 11", all vinyl, M	**$25.00**
Littlest Angel, 1969-80, 11", all vinyl, MIB	**$45.00**
Littlest Angel, 1969-80, 15", all vinyl, M	**$30.00**
Littlest Angel, 1969-80, 15", all vinyl, MIB	**$55.00**
Miss Ginny, 1962-64, hard plastic, 15", from $35 to	**$65.00**
Miss Ginny, 1965-75, vinyl, Far-Away Lands, 12", from $20 to	**$40.00**
Miss Ginny, 1965-75, vinyl, 15", from $25 to	**$55.00**
Miss Ginny, 1975, vinyl, contemporary, 15", from $25 to	**$45.00**
Miss Ginny, 1976-80, vinyl, 15", from $25 to	**$45.00**
8" Dolls, 1948-50, hard plastic, painted eyes, minimum value	**$300.00**
8" dolls, 1950-53, Ginny, sleep eyes, minimum value, from $325 to	**$375.00**
8" Dolls, 1954, Ginny, sleep eyes, straight leg walker, painted lashes, from $260 to	**$350.00**
8" Dolls, 1955-1956, Ginny, sleep eyes, straight leg walker, molded lashes, from $225 to	**$350.00**
8" Dolls, 1957-62, Ginny, sleep eyes, bent-knee walker, molded lashes, from $150 to	**$225.00**
8" Dolls, 1963-65, Ginny, sleep eyes, bent knee, vinyl head, minimum value	**$150.00**
8" Dolls, 1965-72, Ginny, sleep eyes, all vinyl (last USA doll), minimum value	**$100.00**

Door Knockers

Though many of the door knockers you'll see on the market today are of the painted cast-iron variety (similar in design to doorstop figures), they're also found in brass and other metals. Most are modeled as people, animals and birds, and baskets of flowers are common. All items listed are cast iron unless noted otherwise. Prices shown are suggested for examples without damage and in excellent original paint.

Advisor: Craig Dinner (See Directory, Doorstops)

Buster Brown & Tige, creme shirt & pants, creme dog w/black spots, #200, 4¾x2"	**$600.00**

Butterfly, black, green, yellow & blue butterfly under pink rose, creme & purple backplate, 3½x2½" **$125.00**

Cardinal, red feathers w/black highlights on light brown branch, black & yellow berries, creme & green backplate, 5x3" **$285.00**

Cardinal, yellow & brown bird (female) on light brown branch, black & yellow berries, creme & green backplate, 5x3" **$285.00**

Castle, creme w/3 flags, blue sky, green trees, gold band, white oval backplate, 4x3" **$250.00**

Cottage, white w/peak & 2 chimneys, red roof, dark green trees behind cottage, creme oval backplate, 3½x2½".....**$385.00**

Dancing Cupid, brown hair, white wings, 3 red roses, purple scarf on blue, creme oval backplate, Hubley #618, 3x4¼" **$425.00**

Flower basket, deep basket w/blue bow, yellow & blue flowers w/2 pink roses, creme oval backplate, 4x3" ..**$65.00**

Flower basket, yellow ribbon on white basket, pink & blue flowers, green leaves, yellow & white backplate, 4x2½" **$95.00**

Flowers in a basket, yellow, pink & blue flowers white backplate, 4x2" **$85.00**

Ivy basket, light & dark green ivy in yellow basket, white backplate, 4¼x2½" **$135.00**

Laundry mammy, red & white bandana, red & yellow blouse, brown basket on head, knocking causes breasts to move, 7x4⅜" **$1,750.00**

Morning Glory, purple-blue single flower w/1 bud, green leaves as backplate, 3x3" **$300.00**

Owl, yellow, light & dark brown & white feathers, black eyes & highlights on face, creme & green backplate, 4¾x3" **$265.00**

Parrot, faces right, on brown branch, creme/pink/blue/yellow feathers, green leaves, creme & green backplate, 4¾x2¾" **$100.00**

Peacock, blue, green, yellow & black feathers outstretched, black bird, white backplate, 3x3" **$625.00**

Rooster, holding branch, red comb & waddle, red, yellow & brown feathers, creme & green oval backplate, 4½x3" **$235.00**

Roses, pink & creme flowers, green leaves, brown stems, creme oval backplate, signed Hubley #626, 3x4" .**$325.00**

Ship, gold waves & ship w/highlights, oval backplate w/blue waves, 4x2¾" **$275.00**

Snow owl, mostly white feathers, black eyes & highlights on face, creme & green backplate, 4¾x3" **$285.00**

Spider on web, gray web background w/black strings, orange, black, yellow spider, yellow, black & brown fly, 3½x1⅞" **$775.00**

Woodpecker, red head w/black & white feathers, backplate is tree, brown & green leaves w/pink flowers, 3¾x2½" **$135.00**

Doorstops

There are three important factors to consider when buying doorstops — rarity, desirability, and condition. Desirability is often a more important issue than rarity, especially if the doorstop is well designed and detailed. Subject matter often overlaps into other areas, and if they appeal to collectors of Black Americana and advertising, for instance, this tends to drive prices upward. Most doorstops are made of painted cast iron, and value is directly related to the condition of the paint. If there is little paint left or if the figure has been repainted or is rusty, unless the price has been significantly reduced, pass it by.

Be aware that Hubley, one of the largest doorstop manufacturers, sold many of their molds to the John Wright Company who makes them today. Watch for seams that do not fit properly, grainy texture, and too bright paint; all are indicative of recent manufacture.

The doorstops we've listed here are all of the painted cast-iron variety unless another type of material is mentioned in the description. Values are suggested for examples in near-mint condition and paint and should be sharply reduced if heavy wear is apparent. For further information, we recommend *Doorstops, Identification and Values*, by Jeanne Bertoia.

Club: Doorstop Collectors of America
Jeanie Bertoia
2413 Madison Ave.
Vineland, NJ 08630; 609-692-4092; Membership $20.00 per year, includes 2 *Doorstoppers* newsletters and convention. Send 2-stamp SASE for sample

Amish Man, full-figured, solid, 8½x3¾", from $225 to....**$250.00**

Basket of Kittens, 10x7", NM, from $350.00 to $425.00. (This pristine example realized $575.00 at auction.) Basket of Puppies, 7x7¼", pristine, at auction: $425.00.

Boston Bulldog, sitting pose, glass eyes, Greenblatt Studios, 13x5½", from $200 to **$250.00**

Boston Terrier w/Paw Up, full-figured, 9½x7", from $275 to **$350.00**

Camel, full-figured, 7x9", from $250 to **$325.00**

Carian Terrier, Bradley & Hubbard, 9x6", from $200 to..**$275.00**

Cat, rubber, unmarked, 8¾x4⅜", from $125 to.........**$150.00**

Cat, standing w/back arched high, tail straight up, marked Sculptured Metal Studios 1928, 13x9", from $225 to **$300.00**

Cinderella Carriage, 9¾x19", from $150 to **$225.00**

Conestoga Wagon, marked #100, 8x11", from $100 to ...**$175.00**

Cow, standing, marked New Holland Machine Co, Compliments of AM Zimmerman, 12½x8½", from $325 to **$375.00**

Crocodile, stylized w/open mouth & curved tail, wedge, 5¾x11½", from $75 to **$125.00**

Deco Girl, wearing strapless gown, butterfly pose, semicircle stepped base, cJo mark & #1251, 9x7½", from $300 to...**$375.00**

Doll on Base, wearing bonnet & dress w/ruffled tiers, full-figured, solid, 5½x4⅞", from $75 to........................**$125.00**

Dolly Dimple, full-figured, Hubley, 7¾x3¾", from $275 to...**$325.00**

Donald Duck, standing w/stop sign, marked Walt Disney Productions 1971, 8¼x5¼", from $200 to...........**$250.00**

Duck by Bush, stepped base, 7½x10½", from $325 to ...**$375.00**

Elephant, trunk on base, Bradley & Hubbard, 10x11¾", from $200 to...**$250.00**

Elephant, trunk on head, Hubley, 8¼x12", from $100 to...**$150.00**

Fantail Fish, Hubley, 9¾x5⅞", from $150 to.............**$175.00**

Fawn, stylized, standing pose, marked No 6 Copyright 1930, Taylor Cook, 10x6", from $175 to **$250.00**

Fisherman in Boat, 6¾x4", from $175 to...................**$225.00**

Flower Basket, basketweave pot, round pedestal base, marked Hubley, National or Albany Foundries, 5⅞", from $50 to...**$125.00**

Fox Terrier, rectangular base, 10⅜x10½", from $225 to..**$275.00**

Frog on Mushroom, full-figured, solid, 4½x3⅝", from $175 to...**$200.00**

Fruit Basket, w/pomegranetes, pineapple & grapes, 11⅝x11⅜", from $275 to......................................**$350.00**

Geisha, seated on pillow w/instrument, Hubley, 7x6", from $200 to...**$275.00**

Giraffe, full-figured, Hubley, 12½x9", minimum value ..**$750.00**

Grandpa Rabbit, dressed in tux jacket & bow tie, 8⅝x4⅞", minimum value **$750.00**

Horse Jumping Fence, marked Eastern Specialty Co #79, 7⅞x11¾", from $325 to......................................**$400.00**

Lighthouse, full-figured, 13½x8", from $150 to.........**$175.00**

Lilies of the Valley, marked Hubley #189, 10½x7½", from $150 to...**$200.00**

Lion, full-figured, 7x8", from $100 to........................**$175.00**

Maid of Honor, wearing lg hat, holds flowers & skirt hem w/hands, lg footed base, Hubley, 8½x5" dia, from $275 to...**$350.00**

Mayflower, marked Eastern Specialty, 8x9", from $100 to...**$175.00**

Owl on Books, Eastern Specialty Mfg Co, 9x6½", from $475 to...**$550.00**

Pinocchio, solid lead, full-figured, 9½x2¾", from $600 to **$700.00**

Poinsettia, single bloom in pot, square base, marked cJo #1232, 10x5", from $200 to **$275.00**

Poppies & Cornflowers, marked Hubley #265, 7¼x6½", from $100 to...**$150.00**

Primrose, marked Hubley #488, 7⅜x6¼", from $100 to...**$175.00**

Rabbit Garden Ornament, full-figured, Hubley, 11⅝x10", from $250 to...**$300.00**

Rebecca at the Well, English, 10x14¼", from $250 to..**$275.00**

Reclining Kitten, w/bow at neck, full-figured, National Foundry, 8x4", from $200 to...............................**$250.00**

Roses, marked Hubley #445, 8¾x7⅞", from $125 to..**$200.00**

Scottie, sitting pose, full-figured, Hubley, 12x16", from $300 to...**$350.00**

Soldier, Revolutionary War dress, standing w/trees at back, Albany Foundry, 9½x5", from $175 to...............**$250.00**

Southern Belle, holds bonnet w/flowers in left hand, National Foundry, 11¼x6", from $150 to............**$175.00**

Stork, Hubley, 12¼x7", from $325 to........................**$400.00**

Swallows, on semicircle base of berries & leaves, marked Hubley #480, from $300 to **$375.00**

Terrier, rubber, Holest Rubber Products label, 12¾x11", from $150 to...**$225.00**

Tulip Vase, marked Hubley #443, 10x8", from $125 to...**$175.00**

Turtle, 2x7½", up to **$85.00**

Vase of Flowers, rubber knobs, Bradley & Hubbard, 11¾x6", from $175 to...**$250.00**

Violet Bowl, marked Hubley #9, 6¼x4¼", from $100 to...**$150.00**

Wirehaired Fox Terrier, marked Hubley #467, 10½x12¾", from $450 to...**$525.00**

Duncan and Miller Glassware

Although the roots of the company can be traced back as far as 1865 when George Duncan went into business in Pittsburgh, Pennsylvania, the majority of the glassware that collectors are interested in was produced during the twentieth century. The firm became known as Duncan and Miller in 1900. They were bought out by the United States Glass Company, who continued to produce many of the same designs through a separate operation which they called the Duncan and Miller Division.

In addition to crystal, they made some of their wares in a wide assortment of colors including ruby, milk glass, some opalescent glass, and a black opaque glass they called Ebony. Some of their pieces were decorated by cutting or etching. They also made a line of animals and bird figures. For information on these, see *Glass Animals of the Depression Era* by Lee Garmon and Dick Spencer, as well as specific glass manufacturers in this book such as Fenton, Fostoria, Heisey, etc.

Advisor: Roselle Schleifman (See Directory, Elegant Glass)

Caribbean, water pitcher, ice lip, crystal, $200.00.

Canterbury, ashtray, crystal, 5" **$12.00**

Canterbury, bowl, gardenia; crystal, 12x2¾" **$30.00**

Canterbury, bowl, nappy; crystal, 5" **$8.00**

Canterbury, candle, crystal, low, 3".............................**$12.50**

Canterbury, cigarette jar, crystal, w/lid, 4"..................**$20.00**

Canterbury, pitcher, martini; crystal, 32-oz, 9¼" **$45.00**

Canterbury, plate, cake; crystal, 14" **$25.00**

Canterbury, salt & pepper shakers, crystal, pr **$22.50**
Canterbury, saucer, crystal...**$3.00**
Canterbury, stem, cocktail; crystal, 3½-oz, 4¼"......**$10.00**
Canterbury, urn, crystal, 4½x4½".............................**$15.00**
Canterbury, vase, crystal, crimped, 4"......................**$17.50**
Canterbury, vase, crystal, flared, 12"........................**$65.00**
Caribbean, bowl, salad; blue, 9"................................**$75.00**
Caribbean, candelabrum, crystal, 2-light, 4¾"..........**$40.00**
Caribbean, cocktail shaker, crystal, 33-oz, 9".............**$85.00**
Caribbean, cruet, crystal..**$37.50**
Caribbean, ladle, punch; blue **$165.00**
Caribbean, mustard, crystal, w/lid & underplate.........**$57.50**
Caribbean, plate, egg; #30, 12"................................**$120.00**
Caribbean, plate, luncheon; blue, 8½".......................**$35.00**
Caribbean, plate, torte; crystal, 16"...........................**$45.00**
Caribbean, salt dip, crystal, 2½"................................**$10.00**
Caribbean, syrup, crystal, metal cut-off top.................**$80.00**
Caribbean, tray, blue, round, 12¾".............................**$50.00**
Caribbean, tumbler, shot glass; blue, 2-oz, 2¼".........**$55.00**
Caribbean, vase, blue, footed, 10"............................**$135.00**
Cigarette box, duck, red, 6"......................................**$150.00**
Figurine, Bird of Paradise **$700.00**
Figurine, dove, head down, 11½" L...........................**$175.00**
Figurine, duck, ashtray, crystal, 4"............................**$22.00**
Figurine, Fat Goose, blue, 6x6"................................**$325.00**
Figurine, Fat Goose, crystal, 6x6"............................**$295.00**
Figurine, heron, crystal satin, 7"..............................**$120.00**
Figurine, ruffled grouse, crystal, very rare **$2,000.00**
Figurine, swan, blue opalescent, W&F, spread wings,
  10x12½"..**$245.00**
Figurine, swan, crystal, 3" **$30.00**
Figurine, swan, crystal, 5" **$40.00**
Figurine, swan, open, 7"..**$45.00**
Figurine, swan, solid, 5"...**$30.00**
Figurine, swordfish...**$300.00**
Figurine, Sylvan swan, blue or pink, 6½" **$125.00**
Figurine, Sylvan swan, yellow opalescent, 7½" **$100.00**
Figurine, Tropical Fish, ashtray, blue, 3½" **$40.00**
First Love, bowl, finger; crystal, #30, 4x1½".............**$32.00**
First Love, candle holder, cornucopia; crystal, #117, 4" ..**$25.00**
First Love, cheese stand, crystal, #115, 5¾x3½" **$27.00**
First Love, decanter, crystal, w/stopper, #5200, 16-oz ..**$145.00**
First Love, ice bucket, crystal, #30, 6".......................**$90.00**
First Love, plate, crystal, square, #111, 6".................**$14.00**
First Love, salt & pepper shakers, crystal, #30, pr **$40.00**
First Love, tray, celery; crystal, #91, 11"...................**$40.00**
First Love, vase, crystal, crimped, #115, 5x5".............**$35.00**
Sandwich, ashtray, crystal, square, 2½"......................**$8.00**
Sandwich, bowl, console; crystal, oblong, 12"...........**$40.00**
Sandwich, bowl, fruit salad; crystal, 6" **$12.00**
Sandwich, bowl, nut; crystal, 3½"...............................**$10.00**
Sandwich, butter dish, crystal, w/lid, ¼-lb.................**$40.00**
Sandwich, candlestick, crystal, 3-light, 5" **$50.00**
Sandwich, comport, crystal, low footed, 5" **$20.00**
Sandwich, oil bottle, crystal, 5¾".............................**$37.00**
Sandwich, plate, cracker; crystal, w/ring, 13"...........**$40.00**
Sandwich, saucer, crystal, w/ring, 6"..........................**$5.00**
Sandwich, stem, goblet; 9-oz, 6" **$16.00**
Sandwich, urn, crystal, w/lid, footed, 12".................**$135.00**

Sandwich, vase, crystal, footed, 10" **$65.00**
Spiral Flutes, bowl, bouillon; amber, 3¾"...................**$15.00**
Spiral Flutes, bowl, grapefruit; green, footed **$20.00**
Spiral Flutes, bowl, lily pond; pink, 10½" **$40.00**
Spiral Flutes, cigarette holder, amber, 4"...................**$32.00**
Spiral Flutes, mug, pink, handled, 9-oz, 6½" **$30.00**
Spiral Flutes, platter, amber, 13"...............................**$40.00**
Spiral Flutes, sweetmeat, green, w/lid, 7½" **$110.00**
Spiral Flutes, tumbler, soda; pink, flat, 5½-oz, 4¾" **$35.00**
Spiral Flutes, vase, amber, 10½"................................**$25.00**
Tear Drop, bowl, dessert; crystal, 6" **$6.00**
Tear Drop, bowl, salad; crystal, 12" **$40.00**
Tear Drop, candy basket, crystal, 2-handled, oval, 5½x7½" ..**$75.00**
Tear Drop, creamer, crystal, 3-oz.................................**$5.00**
Tear Drop, marmalade, crystal, w/lid, 4" **$35.00**
Tear Drop, nut dish, crystal, 2-part, 6".......................**$10.00**
Tear Drop, plate, canape; crystal, 6" **$10.00**
Tear Drop, plate, lazy susan; crystal, 18"...................**$75.00**

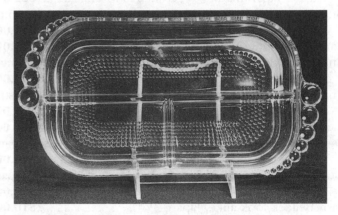

Tear Drop, relish, crystal, 3-part, 12" long, from $24.00 to $28.00.

Tear Drop, saucer, demitasse; crystal, 4½" **$3.00**
Tear Drop, stem, sherry; crystal, 1¾-oz, 4½" **$30.00**
Tear Drop, tumbler, party; crystal, footed, 8-oz, 5".......**$9.00**
Tear Drop, tumbler, whiskey; crystal, flat, 2-oz, 2¼"..**$17.00**
Tear Drop, vase, crystal, fan shape, footed, 9"...........**$25.00**
Terrace, bowl, amber, footed, 9x4½".........................**$42.00**
Terrace, candy urn, red, w/lid..................................**$350.00**
Terrace, nappy, cobalt, handled, 6x1¾" **$35.00**
Terrace, plate, cake; amber, footed, 13" **$75.00**
Terrace, plate, red, 8½"...**$30.00**
Terrace, relish, red, handled, 2-part, 6x1¾"................**$40.00**
Terrace, stem, ice cream; amber, #5111½, 5-oz, 4".....**$14.00**
Terrace, sugar bowl lid only, crystal **$12.50**

Egg Cups

Egg cups were once commonplace kitchen articles that were often put to daily use. Recent trends include changes in dietary patterns that have caused egg cups to follow butter pats and salt dishes into relative obscurity. These small egg holders were commonly made in a variety of shapes from many metals, wood, plastic, and ceramics. They were used as early as ancient Rome and were very common on Victorian tables. Many were styled like whimsical animals or made in other shapes that would specifically appeal to children. Some were commemorative or sold as souvenirs. Still others were part of extensive china or silver services.

They're easy to find today, and though most are inexpensive, some are very pricey! Single egg cups with pedestal bases are the most common, but shapes vary and include doubles, egg hoops, buckets, and sets of many types. Pocillivists, as egg cup collectors are known, are increasing in numbers every day. For more extensive listings we recommend *Schroeder's Antiques Price Guide* (Collector Books).

Newsletter: *Egg Cup Collector's Corner*
Dr. Joan George, Editor
67 Stevens Ave., Old Bridge, NJ 08857; Subscription $18 per year for 4 issues; sample copies available at $5 each

Bunny standing to side of house-form cup, multicolor & tan lustre, Japan mark, 3¼", from $16 to $22.00
Bunny supports cup on back, tan lustre w/multicolor trim, glossy, 2", from $12 to..$18.00
Carlton, Walking Ware..$15.00
Chicken pecking, cup on back, tan & yellow lustre w/orange & black trim, Japan mark, 2½", from $16 to........$23.00
Chickens (2) stand at sides of basket cup, multicolor lustre matt, 2½", from $20 to $25.00
Clown face w/attached saucer base, pepper shaker hat..$20.00
Duck beside lg egg, white w/multicolor trim, glossy, Japan, 2", from $8 to...$15.00
Duck figural w/cup at top, multicolor glossy finish, Japan mark, 3", from $18 to $26.00
Irish Belleek look-alike, Japan, 3¼".............................$10.00
Ironstone, hand-painted boy & girl, red & yellow flower..$7.00
Ironstone, raised grape pattern....................................$18.00
Lady, earthenware, w/salt shaker, red Japan mark, 3¾" ...$45.00
Lady, light crazing, earthwenware, black mark numbers underside of shaker, no mark on egg cup portion, 5" $35.00

Man with blue hat as lid, $15.00; Lady, missing pink lid, $8.00; Salt and pepper shaker, from $8.00 to $12.00 for the pair.

Milk glass, flared base, marked Hazel Atlas $10.00
Phoenix Bird, white interior $20.00
Porcelain, child's, colorful fired decal of girl & puppy w/flower cart, gold trim, no mark, 2¼" $22.00

Porcelain, child's, hand-painted image of little doll boy, gold trim, Made in Japan blue ink stamp, 2½"............$18.00
Porcelain, hand-painted image of little chicks, Japan blue ink stamp, gold trim, 2½"...$18.00
Porcelain, heavy enameled blue flowers w/light blue leaves, some gold trim, 2⅜"..$20.00
Porcelain, marked November & Hutschenreuther $18.00
Rabbit, pink ceramic, marked English Royal Art........$18.00
Restaurant ware, white w/blue & gold Greek Key band..$8.00
Roosters w/orange waddles stand at sides of basketweave cup, multicolor & matt finish, Japan, 2½", from $16 to.....$26.00
Roosterware, hand-painted image, earthenware, no mark, 3¾"...$19.00
Scenic, mountain range on ovoid form w/conical foot, tan lustre & multicolor glossy finish, Noritake, 3", from $12 to...$18.00
Stainless steel, from $5 to...$6.00

Swan, Japanese lustreware, $14.00.

Wood, green trim, marked Made in France.................$5.00

Egg Timers

Egg timers are comprised of a little glass tube, pinched in the center and filled with sand, attached to a figural base, usually between 3" and 5" in height. They're all the rage today among collectors. Most figural egg timers reached their heyday in the 1940s. However, Germany produced many beautiful and detailed timers much earlier. Japan followed suit by copying many German designs. Today, one may find timers from the United Kingdom as well as many foreign ports. The variety of subjects represented by these timers is endless. Included are scores of objects, animals, characters from fiction, and people in occupational or recreational activities. Timers have been made in many materials including bisque, china, ceramic, chalkware, cast iron, tin, brass, wood, and plastic.

Although they were originated to time a 3-minute egg, some were also used to limit the duration spent on telephone calls as a cost-saving measure. Frequently a timer is designed to look like a telephone or a phone is depicted on it.

Since the glass tubes were made of thin, fine glass, they were easily broken. You may recognize a timer masquerading as a figurine by the empty hole that once held the tube. Do not pass up a good timer just because the glass is missing. These can be easily replaced by purchasing a cheap egg timer with a glass tube at your local grocery store.

Listings are for timers in excellent to mint condition with their glass tubes attached.

Advisor: Ellen Bercovici (See Directory, Egg Timers)

Bear dressed as chef w/towel over arm, ceramic, Japan, 4" **$65.00**

Bellhop, green, ceramic, Japan, 4½" **$60.00**

Bellhop on phone, ceramic, Japan, 3" **$40.00**

Black chef sitting w/raised right hand holding timer, ceramic, many sizes & shadings, German, from $95 to......**$120.00**

Black chef standing w/fry pan in right hand, chalkware, Japan, 5½" **$125.00**

Black chef standing w/lg fish, timer in fish's mouth, ceramic, Japan, 4¾" **$125.00**

Boy, Mexican playing guitar, ceramic, German, 3½" ..**$45.00**

Boy skiing, ceramic, German, 3" **$65.00**

Boy stands on head (plastic) which fills w/sand, ceramic, Cooley Lilley sticker, 3¾" **$35.00**

Boy w/black cap stands & holds black bird, ceramic, unmarked, 3½" **$50.00**

Boy w/black cloak & cane, ceramic, German, 3¾" **$65.00**

Boy w/red cap stands & holds different glass tubes in both hands, wooden, unmarked, 4½" **$20.00**

Cat, standing by base of grandfather clock, ceramic, German, 4¾" **$65.00**

Cat w/ribbon at neck, ceramic, marked Germany......**$85.00**

Chef, standing in blue w/white apron, towel over right arm, timer in jug under left, ceramic, Japan, 4½" **$35.00**

Chef holding plate w/hole to hold timer which removes to change, ceramic, Japan, 3¾" **$35.00**

Chef in white on blue base holding spoon, ceramic, German, 4" **$60.00**

Chef in yellow pants, white jacket, blue trim, holds platter of food, ceramic, Japan, 3½" **$35.00**

Chef winking, white clothes, timer in back, turn upside-down to tip sand, ceramic, 4"......................................**$35.00**

Chicken, wings hold tube, ceramic, German, 2¾"......**$50.00**

Chicken on nest, green plastic, England, 2½"............**$15.00**

Chimney sweep carrying ladder, ceramic, German, 3¼" ..**$65.00**

Clown on phone, standing, yellow suit, ceramic, Japan, 3¾" **$50.00**

Clown sitting w/legs to side, timer in right hand, ceramic, German, 3¼" **$65.00**

Colonial lady w/bonnet, variety of dresses & colors, ceramic, German, 3¾" **$65.00**

Colonial man in knickers, ruffled shirt, waistcoat hides hat, ceramic, Japan, 4¾" **$65.00**

Dutch boy kneeling, ceramic, Japan, 2½" **$40.00**

Dutch boy standing, ceramic, German, 3½".............**$65.00**

Dutch girl on phone, standing, blue & white, ceramic, Japan, 3¾"..**$50.00**

Dutch girl w/flowers, walking, chalkware, unmarked, 4½" **$45.00**

Geisha, ceramic, German, 4½" **$65.00**

Goebel, double, chefs, man & woman, ceramic, German, 4" **$100.00**

Goebel, double, Mr Pickwick, green, ceramic, German, 4" **$150.00**

Goebel, double, rabbits, various color combinations, ceramic, German, 4½"..**$100.00**

Goebel, double, roosters, various color combinations, ceramic, German, 4" **$100.00**

Goebel, single chimney sweep, ceramic, German, 4¼"..**$70.00**

Goebel, single Friar Tuck, ceramic, German, 4" **$70.00**

Golliwog, bisque, English, 4½", $150.00. (Photo courtesy Ellen Bercovici)

Housemaid w/towel, standing, earthenware, Japan, 4" ..**$69.00**

Humpty Dumpty, sits on brick wall, vintage hard plastic, M (unsold store stock)..**$65.00**

Isle of Mann, vintage hard plastic, M (unsold store stock) .**$32.00**

Kitten w/ball of yarn, chalkware................................**$50.00**

Leprechaun, shamrock on base, brass, Ireland, 3¼" ..**$30.00**

Lighthouse, blue, cream & orange lustre, ceramic, German, 4½"..**$65.00**

Mammy, tin, lithographed picture of her cooking, pot holder hooks, unmarked, 7¾" **$95.00**

Mouse, yellow & green, chalkware, Josef Originals, Japan, 1970s, 3¼" **$35.00**

Newspaper boy, ceramic, Japan, 3¾" **$50.00**

Parlor maid w/cat, ceramic, Japan, 4".........................**$50.00**

Penguin, chalkware, England, 3¾"...............................**$50.00**

Pixie, ceramic, Enesco, Japan, 5½" **$40.00**

Sailor, blue, ceramic, German, 4" **$65.00**

Sailor w/sailboat, ceramic, German, 4" **$65.00**

Santa Claus and present, ceramic, Sonsco, Japan, 5½", $75.00. (Photo courtesy Ellen Bercovici)

Scotsman w/bagpipes, plastic, England, 4½" **$50.00**

Sultan, Japan, 3½"..**$75.00**

Telephone, black glaze on clay, Japan, 2"..................**$20.00**

Telephone, candlestick type on base w/cup for timer, wooden, Cornwall Wood Prod, So Paris ME.................**$25.00**

Veggie man or woman, bisque, Japan, 4½" **$60.00**

Welsh woman, ceramic, German, 4½" **$65.00**
Windmill, yellow w/bird on top, ceramic, unmarked, 4"..**$60.00**
Windmill w/dog on base, ceramic, Japan, 3¾" **$60.00**

Elvis Presley Memorabilia

Since he burst upon the fifties scene wailing 'Heartbreak Hotel,' Elvis has been the undisputed 'King of Rock 'n Roll.' The fans that stood outside his dressing room for hours on end, screamed themselves hoarse as he sang, or simply danced till they dropped to his music are grown-up collectors today. Many of their children remember his comeback performances, and I'd venture to say that even their grandchildren know Elvis on a first-name basis.

There has never been a promotion in the realm of entertainment to equal the manufacture and sale of Elvis merchandise. By the latter part of 1956, there were already hundreds of items that appeared in every department store, drugstore, specialty shop, and music store in the country. There were bubble gum cards, pin-back buttons, handker-chiefs, dolls, guitars, billfolds, photograph albums, and hundreds of other items. You could even buy sideburns from a coin-operated machine. Look for the mark 'Elvis Presley Enterprises' (along with a 1956 or 1957 copyright date); you'll know you've found a gold mine. Items that carry the 'Boxcar' mark are from 1974 to 1977, when Elvis's legendary manager, Colonel Tom Parker, promoted another line of merchandise to augment their incomes during the declining years. Upon his death in 1977 and until 1981, the trademark became 'Boxcar Enterprises, Inc., Lic. by Factors ETC. Bear, DE.' The 'Elvis Presley Enterprises, Inc.' trade-mark reverted back to Graceland in 1982, which re-opened to the public in 1983.

Due to the very nature of his career, paper items are usually a large part of any Elvis collection. He appeared on the cover of countless magazines. These along with ticket stubs, movie posters, lobby cards, and photographs of all types are sought after today, especially those from before the mid-sixties.

Though you sometime see Elvis 45s with $10.00 to $15.00 price tags, unless the record is in near mint to mint condition, this is just not realistic, since they sold in such volume. In fact, the picture sleeve itself (if it's in good condition) will be worth more than the record. The exceptions are, of course, the early Sun label records (he cut five in all) that collectors often pay in excess of $500.00 for. In fact, at an auction held last year, a near-mint copy of 'That's All Right' (his very first Sun recording) realized $2,800.00! And some of the colored vinyls, promotional records, and EPs and LPs with covers and jackets in excellent condition are certainly worth researching further. For instance, though his *Moody Blue* album with the blue vinyl record can often be had for under $25.00 (depending on condition), if you find one of the rare ones with the black record you can figure on about ten times that amount! For a thorough listing of his records as well as the sleeves, refer to *Official Price Guide to Elvis Presley Records and Memorabilia* by Jerry Osborne.

For more general information and an emphasis on the early items, refer to *Elvis Collectibles* and *Best of Elvis Collectibles* by Rosalind Cranor, P.O. Box 859, Blacksburg, VA 24063 ($19.95+$1.75 postage each volume).

Special thanks to Art and Judy Turner, Homestead Collectibles (see Directory, Decanters) for providing information on decanters.

See also Magazines; Movie Posters; Pin-back Buttons; Records.

Advisor: Lee Garmon (See Directory, Elvis Presley)

Beach hat, w/original photo hang tag, 1956 ....**$125.00**
Board game, Elvis, metal playing pieces, guitar-shaped board, record game cards, 1987, complete, EX (EX box) **$75.00**
Book, If I Can Dream, by Larry Geller, hardcover, M...**$20.00**
Book, Solid Gold Memories, The Elvis Presley Scrapbook, by James Robert Paris, Ballantine, 1975, soft cover, M ..**$20.00**
Book, souvenir 2nd tour, 1956, w/photos, NM.........**$350.00**
Booklet, from A Legendary Performer Volume 2, M ..**$10.00**
Bracelet, Elvis Presley Enterprises, 1977, M.................**$15.00**
Charm, RCA record, 1956, miniature, M **$28.00**
Charm bracelet, Loving You, on 1956 card, but 1977 issue...**$50.00**
Christmas ornament, Hallmark, 1992, MIB **$20.00**
Concert pennant, red felt w/yellow stripe, blue & white King of Rock 'n Roll w/photo, 31", VG **$130.00**
Concert ticket, Savannah GA, September 28, 1977, unused, M...**$35.00**
Concert ticket, Terre Haute IN, September 26, 1977, unused, complete, M...**$35.00**
Decanter, McCormick, 1978, Elvis '77, Plays Love Me Tender...**$125.00**
Decanter, McCormick, 1978, Elvis Bust, no music box, 750 ml...**$75.00**
Decanter, McCormick, 1979, Elvis '55, plays Loving You, 750 ml...**$125.00**
Decanter, McCormick, 1979, Elvis '77 Mini, plays Love Me Tender, 50 ml **$55.00**
Decanter, McCormick, 1979, Elvis Gold, plays My Way, 750 ml..**$175.00**
Decanter, McCormick, 1980, Elvis '55 Mini, plays Loving You, 50 ml **$65.00**
Decanter, McCormick, 1980, Elvis '68, plays Can't Help Falling in Love, 750 ml...................................**$125.00**
Decanter, McCormick, 1980, Elvis Silver, plays How Great Thou Art, 750 ml **$175.00**
Decanter, McCormick, 1981, Aloha Elvis, plays Blue Hawaii, 750 ml..**$150.00**
Decanter, McCormick, 1981, Elvis '68 Mini, plays Can't Help Falling in Love, 50 ml **$55.00**
Decanter, McCormick, 1981, Elvis Designer I White (Joy), plays Are You Lonesome Tonight, 750 ml..........**$150.00**
Decanter, McCormick, 1982, Aloha Elvis Mini, plays Blue Hawaii, 50 ml **$175.00**
Decanter, McCormick, 1982, Elvis Designer II White (Love), plays It's Now or Never, 750 ml.........................**$125.00**
Decanter, McCormick, 1982, Elvis Karate, plays Don't Be Cruel, 750 ml...**$350.00**
Decanter, McCormick, 1983, Elvis Designer III White (Reverence), plays Crying in the Chapel, 750 ml..**$250.00**

Decanter, McCormick, 1983, Elvis Gold Mini, plays My Way, 50 ml..$125.00

Decanter, McCormick, 1983, Elvis Silver Mini, plays How Great Thou Art, 50 ml $95.00

Decanter, McCormick, 1983, Sgt Elvis, plays GI Blues, 750 ml..$295.00

Decanter, McCormick, 1984, Elvis & Rising Sun, plays Green, Green Grass of Home, 750 ml............................$495.00

Decanter, McCormick, 1984, Elvis Designer I Gold, plays Are You Lonesome Tonight, 750 ml.....................$175.00

Decanter, McCormick, 1984, Elvis Designer II Gold, plays It's Now or Never, 750 ml.....................................$195.00

Decanter, McCormick, 1984, Elvis Karate Mini, plays Don't Be Cruel, 50 ml...$125.00

Decanter, McCormick, 1984, Elvis on Stage, plays Can't Help Falling in Love, 50 ml (decanter only)...............$195.00

Decanter, McCormick, 1984, Elvis w/Stage, 50 ml (complete w/separate stage designed to hold decanter).....$450.00

Decanter, McCormick, 1984, Elvis 50th Anniversary, plays I Want You, I Need You, I Love You, 750 ml.......$495.00

Decanter, McCormick, 1984, Sgt Elvis Mini, plays GI Blues, 50 ml..$95.00

Decanter, McCormick, 1985, Elvis Designer I White Mini, plays Are You Lonesome Tonight, 50 ml............$125.00

Decanter, McCormick, 1985, Elvis Designer III Gold, plays Crying in the Chapel, 750 ml......................$250.00

Decanter, McCormick, 1985, Elvis' Teddy Bear, plays Let me Be Your Teddy Bear, 750 ml...............$695.00

Decanter, McCormick, 1986, Elvis & Gates of Graceland, plays Welcome to My World, 750 ml.................$150.00

Decanter, McCormick, 1986, Elvis & Rising Sun Mini, plays Green, Green Grass of Home, 50 ml...................$250.00

Decanter, McCormick, 1986, Elvis Designer I Gold Mini, plays Are You Lonesome Tonight, 50 ml.............$150.00

Decanter, McCormick, 1986, Elvis Designer I Silver Mini, plays Are You Lonesome Tonight, 50 ml............$135.00

Decanter, McCormick, 1986, Elvis Hound Dog, plays Hound Dog, 750 ml $695.00

Decanter, McCormick, 1986, Elvis Season's Greetings, plays White Christmas, 375 ml......................................$195.00

Decanter, McCormick, 1986, Elvis Teddy Bear Mini, plays Let Me Be Your Teddy Bear, 50 ml...................$295.00

Decanter, McCormick, 1986, Elvis 50th Anniversary Mini, plays, I Want You, I Need You, I Love You, 50 ml.........$250.00

Decanter, McCormick, 1987, Elvis Memories, cassette player base, lighted top, extremely scarce, 750 ml, from $1,000 to..$1,200.00

Doll, Eugene, 1984, issued in 6 different outfits, 12", MIB, each, from $60 to......................................$65.00

Doll, Hasbro, Teen Idol, Jail House Rock or '68 Special, 12", MIB, each $40.00

Doll, World Doll, 1984, Burning Love, vinyl, 21", EX-..$110.00

Doll, World Doll, 1984, Joyce Christofer designer, rooted hair, 21", M, from $400 to................................$500.00

Drinking cup, plastic, 1979 ....$7.50

Frisbee, yellow & blue, M...................................$20.00

Guitar, plastic, Lapin Productions, M (EX card), lg.....$65.00

Guitar, plastic, Lapin Productions, 1984, M (EX card), sm ..$45.00

Guitar, toy, Selcol, 1959, rare, EX..............................$700.00

Gum cards, Holland, set of 5 w/gum, MIP (sealed).....$2.50

Gum cards, 1978, complete set of 66, M.................$65.00

Key chain, Elvis Presley Boulevard, 1980s..................$4.50

Locket, gold plated, Elvis picture on front.................$15.00

Magazine, Silver Screen, April 1960, EX/NM, from $15.00 to $18.00.

Menu, Las Vegas International Hotel, black & white photo, 1970, 8x11", M...$95.00

Necklace, dog tag w/blue letters on silver, M.............$45.00

Newspaper, National Enquirer, Exclusive Edition, September 6, 1977, shows coffin on cover, +6-page feature story, EX $18.00

Overnight case, brown, '56 on outside, interior mirror, VG $400.00

Paper dolls, 1982, uncut, M $15.00

Pen, from 1956 Tickle Me promotion w/feathers at top..$18.00

Pencil, Sincerely Yours Elvis Presley '56 on side, unused, M $18.00

Pennant, Elvis & Roger Moore on sides, marked Printed in Spain, EX-, 12" L $70.00

Pennant, The King of Rock 'n Roll in blue & white on red felt w/yellow stripe, 1960s, 31" L, VG $130.00

Photo, 1970s tour, color photo in caped jumpsuit, 11x14", VG+...$12.00

Photo tray, early photo, part of eulogy on back, 1977 ....$20.00

Pin-back button, Elvis Presley Fan Club, black & white..$15.00

Pin-back button, Love Me Tender, black & white flasher, 3"..$20.00

Plate, Elvis Goes Country, by Susie Morton, RJ Ernst Enterprises, 8½", M..$50.00

Plate, Jailhouse Rock, by Bruce Emmett, #2 in series, 1989, 8½", MIB $110.00

Pocket calendar, Strictly Elvis Generation, 1977, M $15.00

Poster, color, toy bears on back, 1970s, 7x12", M.......$15.00

Poster, Easy Come, Easy Go, 1-sheet, EX $90.00

Promo kit, Tickle Me, w/feather.............................$65.00

Ring, flasher type w/Elvis & Doris Day, 1950s, M....$200.00

Scarf, blue or purple w/silkscreen signature, M..........$15.00

Sheet music, Hurt/For the Heart, NM $18.00

Sheet music, King Creole/Lover Doll, 1958, M...........$25.00

Song book, Love Me Tender, marked Copyright 1956, M..$65.00

Standee, Elvis, for video promotions, EX $95.00

Standee, Elvis Lives!, MIB (sealed) $60.00

Stein, 1968 Comeback Special, M.............................$18.00

Stick pin, Elvis, gold or silver $7.50

Sticker, sideburns, Elvis Sideburns Are Here, 1950s, from vending machine, M $45.00

Ticket, Elvis in Concert, Memphis, August 28, 1977, complete, M..$75.00

Pitcher and four mugs, multicolored decals of Elvis, from $100.00 to $125.00.

Enesco

Enesco is an importing company based in Elk Grove, Illinois. They're distributors of ceramic novelties made for them in Japan.

One of their most collectible lines, Mother-in-the-Kitchen, or as collectors refer to it, Kitchen Prayer Ladies, has become so popular that it's been given its own category later on in this guide, but several other groupings are starting to catch on, and we'll list them here. One is Kitchen Independence which features George Washington with the Declaration of Independence scroll held at his side and Betsy Ross wearing a blue dress and holding a large flag. Another line is called Snappy the Snail, then there's the winking-eye cat, the Dutch boy and girl, and several others. You'll find them turning up as kitchen wares such as teapots, salt and pepper shakers, cookie jars, and spoon rests, as well as banks and other novelties.

See also Cookie Jars; Kitchen Prayer Ladies; Salt and Pepper Shakers.

Advisor: April Tvorak (See Directory, Figural Ceramics)

Bank, Human Bean series, w/golf club $40.00

Bank, Human Beans series, This Is a Retired Human Being, 1981, from $15 to...$20.00

Bank, Miss Piggy baby $65.00

Console set, swans, turquoise-tipped black wings, 5⅜x7" center swan + pr candlesticks, 3-pc......................$25.00

Cookie jar, Kitchen Independence, Betsy Ross, sm, from $200 to..$250.00

Creamer & sugar bowl, Snappy the Snail, wearing bow tie...$35.00

Cup & saucer, Dutch boy & girl...................................$45.00

Egg timer, Kitchen Independence, George Washington...$50.00

Figurine, cat or dog w/sad eyes, 6", each, from $6 to..$8.00

Figurine, Moon Girl, dyed rabbit fur hair w/black antennas, matching outfit, various poses, each, from $8 to .$12.00

Music box, Mary Poppins, blue dress, white apron, plays 'A Spoonful of Sugar,' minimum value....................$150.00

Napkin holder, Kitchen Independence, George Washington, from $18 to...$22.00

Plaque, Paddington Bear, 1990, MIB..........................$20.00

Salt & pepper shakers, Dutch shoes, boy on 1, girl on other, kissing, E-5816, sm, pr $25.00

Salt and pepper shakers, Kitchen Independence, Betsy Ross and George Washington, 4¼", $20.00 for the pair.

Salt & pepper shakers, Mickey Mouse w/pot of gold, Irish costume, pr, MIB..$22.00

Salt & pepper shakers, rocket to Mars & passenger, Going Up & to Mars, multicolor ceramic, 1950s, pr, NM $89.00

Salt & pepper shakers, Snappy the Snail, wearing bow tie, pr...$22.00

Snowdome, Paddington Bear, Christmas, 1992, MIB ..$15.00

Spoon holder, Betsy Ross, marked Spoon Storage on skirt, 5¾", from $22 to...$28.00

Spoon rest, Granny, blue dress, white gloves, blue hat with flowers, glasses sliding off nose, 6¾" $28.00

Spoon rest, Snappy the Snail $12.00

Tea bag holder, Snappy the Snail................................$6.00

Tea set, Snappy the Snail, w/creamer & sugar bowl...$125.00

Toothpick holder, Dutch boy & girl, E-6803 ....$30.00

Toothpick holder, George Washington (drummer), scarce .$35.00

Eye Winker

Designed along the lines of an early pressed glass pattern by Dalzell, Gilmore and Leighton, Eye Winker was one of several attractive glassware assortments featured in the catalogs of L. G. Wright during the sixties and seventies. The line was extensive and made in several colors: amber, blue, green, crystal, and red. It was probably pressed by Fostoria, Fenton, and Westmoreland, since we know these are the companies who made Moon and Star for Wright, who was not a glass manufacturer but simply a distributing company. Red and green are the most desirable colors and are priced higher than the others we mentioned. The values given here are for red and green, deduct about 20% for examples in clear, amber, or light blue.

Advisor: Sophia Talbert (See Directory, Eye Winker)

Ashtray, allover pattern, 4½" dia $15.00

Bowl, 4 toes, 2½x5" **$20.00**
Butter dish, allover pattern, 4½" dia lid, 6" base **$40.00**
Candy dish, allover pattern, disk foot, w/lid, 5¼x5½"....**$28.00**
Candy dish, oval, 4-toed, 5x3½"................................**$21.00**
Celery or relish, ruffled rim, oblong, 9½x5", from $25 to ..**$30.00**
Compote, allover pattern except for plain flared rim, pat-
    terned lid, 10½x6"+finial **$55.00**
Compote, allover pattern except for plain flared rim & foot,
    patterned lid, 7x5", w/lid **$40.00**
Compote, allover pattern except for plain flared rim & foot,
    7x7" **$30.00**
Compote, ruffled rim, plain foot, 4-sided, 7x6"..........**$32.00**
Compote, ruffled rim, 4-sided, 6x10" **$45.00**
Fairy lamp, allover pattern, disk foot, 2-pc **$45.00**
Goblet, plain rim & foot, 6¼" **$22.00**
Jelly dish, patterned lid, plain foot & rim, 6¼x3½"....**$36.00**
Marmalade, w/lid, 5¼x4" **$36.00**
Pickle tray, scalloped edge, 9½"................................**$35.00**
Pitcher, ruffled rim, plain foot, 1-qt, from $50 to........**$60.00**
Salt & pepper shakers, allover pattern w/metal lids, 3¾", pr,
    from $22 to...**$25.00**
Salt cellar, allover pattern, ruffled rim, 1¾" **$12.00**
Sherbet, plain rim & foot, 4½"..................................**$16.00**
Tumbler, 8-oz...**$18.00**
Vase, ruffled rim, 3-sided, 3-toed, 7¾".......................**$40.00**
Vase, 3-footed, scalloped, 6" **$35.00**

Toothpick holder, allover pattern, ruffled rim, 2¼", $12.00; Creamer and sugar bowl, allover pattern, disk foot, small, 3¼", from $35.00 to $45.00. (From the collection of Sophia Talbert)

Fast-Food Collectibles

Since the late 1970s, fast-food chains have been catering to their very young customers through their kiddie meals. The toys tucked in each box or bag have made a much longer-lasting impression on the kids than any meal could. Today it's not just kids but adults (sometimes entire families) who're clammoring for them. They're after not only the kiddie meal toys but also boxes, promotional signs used by the restaurant, the promotional items themselves (such as Christmas ornaments you can buy for 99¢, collector plates, glass tumblers, or stuffed animals), or the 'under 3' (safe for children under 3) toys their toddler customers are given on request.

There have been three kinds of promotions: 1) national — every restaurant in the country offering the same item, 2) regional, and 3) test market. While, for instance, a test market box might be worth $20.00, a regional box might be $10.00, and a national, $1.00. Supply dictates price.

To be most valuable, a toy must be in the original package, just as it was issued by the restaurant. Beware of dealers trying to 'repackage' toys in plain plastic bags. Most original bags were printed or contained an insert card. Vacuform containers were quickly discarded, dictating a premium price of $10.00 minimum. Toys without the original packaging are worth only about one-half to two-thirds as much as those mint in package.

Toys representing popular Disney characters draw cross-collectors, so do Star Trek, My Little Pony, and Barbie toys. It's not always the early items that are the most collectible, because some of them may have been issued in such vast amounts that there is an oversupply of them today. At the same time, a toy only a year or so old that might have been quickly withdrawn due to a problem with its design will already be one the collector will pay a good price to get.

As I'm sure you've noticed, many flea market dealers are setting out huge plastic bins of these toys, and no one can deny they draw a crowd. It's going to be interesting to see what develops here! If you'd like to learn more about fast-food collectibles, we recommend *Tomart's Price Guide to Kid's Meal Collectibles* by Ken Clee; *The Illustrated Collector's Guide to McDonald's® Happy Meal® Boxes, Premiums and Promotions©, McDonald's® Happy Meal Toys in the USA, McDonald's® Happy Meal Toys Around the World*, and *Illustrated Collector's Guide to McDonald's® McCAPS*, all by Joyce and Terry Losonsky; *Schroeder's Collectible Toys, Antique to Modern;* and *McDonald's® Collectibles* by Gary Henriques and Audre Duvall (Collector Books).

See also California Raisins.

Note: Unless noted MIP, values are given for M, no-package items.

Club: McDonald's® Collector Club
c/o Joyce and Terry Losonsky
7506 Summer Leave Ln., Columbia, MD 21046-2455; 301-381-3358

Club: McDonald's® Collector's Club, SUNSHINE Chapter
c/o Bill and Pat Poe
220 Domica Cir. E, Niceville, FL 32578-4068; 904-987-4163 or FAX 904-897-2606. Annual membership is $10 per individual or $15 per family (includes 6 newsletters and 2 McDonald's only shows)

Newsletter: *Collecting Tips*
Meredith Williams
Box 633, Joplin, MO 64802. Send SASE for information

Newsletter: *McDonald's® Collector Club*
c/o Tenna Greenberg
5400 Waterbury Rd., Des Moines, IA 50312; 515-279-0741

Arby's, Babar's World Tour, finger puppets, 1990, M each .**$2.00**
Arby's, Looney Tunes Car Tunes, 1989, each................**$3.00**
Arby's, Snowdomes, 1995, MIP, each **$5.00**
Burger King, Beetle Juice, 1990, each..........................**$2.00**

Burger King, box, Fairy Tales Cassettes, 1989, each.....**$6.00**
Burger King, Cool Stuff, 1995, MIP, each, from $2 to...**$3.00**
Burger King, Gargoyles (1st set), 1995, MIP, each, from $2 to **$3.00**
Burger King, Good Gobblin', 1989, 3 different, each ...**$3.00**
Burger King, Hunchback of Notre Dame, 1995, hand puppets, 4 different, MIP, each **$10.00**
Burger King, Lion King, 1994, 7 different, MIP, each....**$3.00**
Burger King, Nerfuls, 1989, 3 different, each **$4.00**
Burger King, Pumbaa & Timon, 1996, set of 4, MIP ..**$20.00**
Burger King, Silverhawks, 1987, pencil topper **$5.00**

Burger King, Simpsons, Lisa plays saxaphone with rabbit in it; Maggie on turtle, 1990, 3", M, $2.00 each.

Burger King, Super Powers, 1987, door shield..............**$8.00**
Burger King, Toy Story, 1995, Woody, MIP **$8.00**
Denny's, Flintstones, vehicles, 3 different......................**$4.00**
Denny's, Flintstones Dino-Racers, 3 different, MIP, each ..**$4.00**
Dominoes, Donnie Domino, figure, 4", M.....................**$6.00**
Hardee's, box, Eureka's, Castle, 1994, each...................**$1.00**
Hardee's, box, Micro Soakers, 1994, each **$1.00**
Hardee's, Dinosaur in My Pocket, 4 different, MIP, each..**$3.00**
Hardee's, Homeward Bound II, 1996, 5 different, MIP, each..**$3.00**
Hardee's, Pound Puppies, 1986, plush, 4 different, each...**$5.00**
Hardee's, Pound Puppies & Pur-R-Ries, 1987, plush, 5 different, each **$5.00**
Hardee's, Tattoads, 1995, 4 different, MIP, each............**$3.00**
Hardee's, X-Men, 1995, 6 different, MIP, each..............**$3.00**
Long John Silver's, Sea Watchers, 1991, mini kaleidoscope, 3 different, MIP, each...**$5.00**
Long John Silver's, Water Blasters, 1990, 4 different, each..**$4.00**
McDonald's, Animaniacs, 1995, any except under age 3, MIP, each..**$3.00**
McDonald's, Barbie/Hot Wheels, 1993, Barbie, any except under age 3, MIP, each...**$3.00**
McDonald's, Barbie/Hot Wheels, 1994, any including under age 3, MIP, each..**$4.00**
McDonald's, Barbie/Hot Wheels, 1995, under age 3, Key Force truck, MIP...**$4.00**
McDonald's, Barbie/Hot Wheels, 1996, under age 3, mini steering wheel, MIP **$4.00**
McDonald's, Barbie/Mini Streex, 1992, Barbie, under age 3, Sparkle Eyes, MIP, each.......................................**$4.00**

McDonald's, Batman (Animated), 1993, under age 3, Batman, MIP **$4.00**
McDonald's, Bedtime, 1989, wash mitt, blue foam, MIP.....**$5.00**
McDonald's, box, Batman, 1992, each **$1.00**
McDonald's, box, Beach Toy, 1990, each......................**$3.00**
McDonald's, box, Carnival, 1990, rides.......................**$2.00**
McDonald's, box, Dink the Dinosaur, 1990, each.......**$10.00**
McDonald's, box, Fraggle Rock, 1988, each **$3.00**
McDonald's, box, Gravedale High, 1991, each.............**$3.00**
McDonald's, box, Hook, 1991, each.............................**$3.00**
McDonald's, box, Littlest Pet Shop Transformers, 1996, 4 different, M, each **$1.00**
McDonald's, box, Marvel, 1996, each...........................**$1.00**
McDonald's, box, Mickey's Birthdayland, 1989, each...**$4.00**
McDonald's, box, Oliver & Co, 1988, each...................**$5.00**
McDonald's, box, Real Ghostbusters, 1987, each..........**$5.00**
McDonald's, box, Space Rescue, 1995, each **$1.00**
McDonald's, box, Tiny Toon Adventures, 1992, each...**$1.00**
McDonald's, box, Valentine From the Heart, 1990, Play Matchmaker **$3.00**
McDonald's, Cabbage Patch Kids/Tonka Trucks, under age 3, Tonka Trucks, dump truck, MIP, each **$4.00**
McDonald's, Crayola Stencils, 1987, any except under age 3, each...**$2.00**
McDonald's, Ghostbusters, 1987, pencil case, Containment Chamber **$5.00**
McDonald's, Halloween McNuggets, 1993, under age 3, McBoo McNugget, MIP, each **$4.00**
McDonald's, Jungle Book, 1989, Baloo, King Louie, Kaa & Shere Khan windups, set of 4, NMIP.................**$15.00**
McDonald's, Lego Motion, 1989, under age 3, Giddy Gator or Tuttle Turtle, MIP..**$6.00**
McDonald's, Mac Tonight, 1988, under age 3, skateboard, MIP...**$8.00**
McDonald's, McDonaldland Dough, 1990, M, each **$5.00**
McDonald's, Mickey's Birthdayland, 1988, under age 3, MIP...**$6.00**
McDonald's, Muppet Workshop, 1995, MIP, each.........**$2.00**
McDonald's, New Archies, 1988, 6 different characters ..**$8.00**
McDonald's, Peanuts, 1990, any except under age 3, MIP, each..**$3.00**
McDonald's, Power Rangers, 1995, under age 3, MIP ..**$4.00**
McDonald's, Safari Adventure, 1980, sponge, Ronald sitting cross-legged..**$5.00**
McDonald's, School Days, 1984, pencil sharpener, Grimace or Ronald, each...**$8.00**
McDonald's, Space Rescue, 1995, under age 3, Astro Viewer, MIP...**$4.00**
McDonald's, Stomper Mini 4x4, 1986, 15 different, each..**$8.00**
McDonald's, Super Mario Brothers, 1990, under age 3, Super Mario standing, MIP..**$4.00**
McDonald's, Totally Toy Holiday, 1995, MIP, each, from $3 to **$4.00**
McDonald's, Totally Toys, 1993, under age 3, Key Force car, MIP...**$3.00**
McDonald's, VR Troopers, 1996, any except under age 3, MIP, each...**$3.00**
McDonald's, Winter Worlds, 1983, ornaments, Birdie or Mayor McCheese, each **$8.00**

McDonald's, Zoo Face, 1988, 4 different, MIP..............**$4.00**
Pizza Hut, Eureeka's Castle, 1990, hand puppets, Batley, Eureeka or Magellan, rubber, each.........................**$5.00**
Sonic, Animal Straws, 1995, 4 different, MIP, each **$3.00**
Sonic, Creepy Strawlers, 1995, 4 different, MIP, each ...**$5.00**
Sonic, Monster Peepers, 1994, 4 different, MIP, each ...**$3.00**
Sonic, Wacky Sackers, 1994, green or yellow sets of 6, MIP, each set..**$20.00**
Subway, Tale Tale, 1995, any except under age 3, MIP, each...**$4.00**
Taco Bell, The Tick, 1995, finger puppet, Arthur Wall Climber or Trakkorzog Squirter, MIP, each **$4.00**
Wendy's, All Dogs Go to Heaven, 1989, 6 different, each......**$2.00**
Wendy's, box, Carmen Sandiego Code Cracker, 1994, each ..**$2.00**
Wendy's, box, Rhyme Time, 1991, each **$2.00**
Wendy's, box, Wendy & the Good Stuff Gang, 1989, each..**$3.00**
Wendy's, Definitely Dinosaurs, 1988, 4 different, each.**$4.00**
Wendy's, Fast-Food Racers, 1990, 6 different, each **$3.00**
Wendy's, Gear Up, 1992, handlebar streamers of Back-Off license plate, each...**$2.00**

**Wendy's, George Jetson in Spaceship,
1st series, 1989, M, $3.50.**

Wendy's, Good Stuff Gang, 1985, each.........................**$3.00**
Wendy's, Kids 4 Parks, compass, magnifying glass or belt pouch, each..**$2.00**
Wendy's, Rocket Writers, 1992, 4 different, each...........**$2.00**
Wendy's, Speed Writers, 1991, under age 3, paint w/water book...**$4.00**
Wendy's, Wacky Windups, 1991, under age 3, Wacky Roller **$3.00**
Wendy's, Write & Sniff, 1994, any except under age 3, each **$2.00**
White Castle, Castle Dude Squirters, 1994, 3 different, MIP, each..**$3.00**
White Castle, Holiday Huggables, 1990, 3 different, MIP, each..**$6.00**

Fenton Glass

Located in Williamstown, West Virginia, the Fenton company is still producing glassware just as they have since the early part of the century. Nearly all fine department stores and gift shops carry an extensive line of their beautiful products, many of which rival examples of finest antique glassware. The fact that even some of their fairly recent glassware has collectible value attests to its fine quality.

Over the years they have made many lovely colors in scores of lines, several of which are very extensive. Paper labels were used exclusively until 1970. Since then some pieces have been made with a stamped-in logo.

Numbers in the descriptions correspond with catalog numbers used by the company. Collectors use them as a means of identification as to shape and size. If you'd like to learn more about the subject, we recommend *Fenton Glass, The Second Twenty-Five Years,* and *Fenton Glass, The Third Twenty-Five Years,* by William Heacock; *Fenton Glass, The 1980s,* by James Measell; and *Fenton Art Glass, 1907 to 1939,* by Margaret and Kenn Whitmyer. For an inclusive listing and suggested values of Fenton animals made from 1967 until 1993, refer to *A Digest of Fenton Glass Animals,* by Ruth Grizel, privately published. (Mrs. Grizel's address is in the Directory under Westmoreland.)

Advisor: Ferill J. Rice (See Directory, Fenton Glass)

Club: Fenton Art Glass Collectors of America, Inc.
P.O. Box 384
Williamstown, WV 26187

Club: Pacific Northwest Fenton Association
8225 Kilchis River Rd.
Tillamook, OR 97141

Baskets

Antique Rose, #7630AF...**$38.00**
Cactus, Sunset Red (red carnival), #3431RN.................**$60.00**
Cherry Chain, plum opalescent, lg...............................**$60.00**

Cranberry opalescent swirl, 12", $125.00.

Custard w/hand-painted daisies, #7437 ....**$65.00**
Daisy & Button, amethyst, #QVC16916.........................**$45.00**
Dianthus Paneled, #9035DN, 7½".................................**$47.00**
Hobnail, carnival topaz opalescent, 8½" **$50.00**
Kristen's Floral, #2788YB..**$48.00**
Lily of the Valley, plum opalescent, #8437PO **$75.00**
Mary Gregory, red, #8637RG **$55.00**
Milk glass w/hand-painted pink roses, roses on handle..**$70.00**
Poppy, Lime Sherbet, deep, #9138, 7" **$75.00**
Rose Garden, #2737EG...**$32.00**

Roses, red carnival, crimped edges, round..................$30.00
Vase Murrhina, green & blue, 4"................................$45.00

Bells

Aurora, Steigel Green stretch, #9667SS...............$20.00
Beauty, Blue Royale, #9665KK..............................$15.00
Beauty, Dusty Rose, #9665DK................................$15.00
Bicentennial, Patriot Red, #8467............................$25.00
Butterflies Are Free, #8267....................................$35.00
Christopher Columbus, ruby carnival, #6576RN..........$25.00
Custard w/hand-painted coral daisies, #7564..............$15.00
Daisy & Button, blue satin......................................$23.00
Dusty Rose w/hand-painted tulips, #767H6................$20.00
Elizabeth, #9266ES, miniature................................$25.00
Faberge, Crystal Velvet, #8466VE..........................$15.00
Hearts & Flowers, #7662, 4½"................................$15.00
Hobnail, purple slag, #3667....................................$25.00
Hobnail, ruby, #3667RU..$20.00
Holiday Green w/hand-painted poinsettia, #8761GP .$20.00
July, Petite, w/flowers..$8.00
Juniper Train, #7564TP..$75.00
Kristen's Floral, #6761YB......................................$28.00
Light House, #7667..$85.00
Mary Gregory, Petite, blue w/hand-painted white trim ..$15.00
Milk glass w/hand-painted rose & Love, #7362LW $25.00
Mother's Day, New Born, 1980................................$25.00
Peking Blue, #7564PK, 1980 only............................$18.00
Roses, ruby carnival, #9262RN................................$25.00
Sable Arches, light amethyst carnival, #9065DT..........$25.00
Silver Crest, Spanish Lace, #3567MI........................$20.00
Syndenham, cobalt carnival, #9063NK......................$20.00
Syndenham, green w/cobalt crest, #9063GK...............$25.00
Whitton, blue opalescent, #9064BO..........................$25.00

Carnival Glass

Note: Carnival glass items listed here were made after 1970.

Bowl, basketweave w/open lattice top, amethyst, #8222CN..$45.00
Box, Twilight Blue, heart form w/lid, #8200...............$65.00
Comport, Open Heart, red, #9780............................$35.00
Nappy, Heavy Grape, purple....................................$48.00
Pitcher, red..$100.00
Planter, Hexagon, amethyst, #8226CN $65.00
Tobacco jar, amethyst, #3700CN, w/lid....................$175.00
Vase, Atlantis, topaz opalescent, #5150....................$65.00
Vase, Peacock, Champagne Pink Satin, 8".................$40.00

Crests

Emerald, comport, #7228EC....................................$25.00
Emerald, comport, flared rim, footed, 3⅛x6" dia........$37.50
Gold, bowl, double-crimped, 14"..............................$40.00
Gold, bowl, 7½" square..$38.00
Peach, pitcher, Beaded Melon, handled, #7166PC......$85.00
Peach, vase, #7156PC..$70.00
Peach, vase, cornucopia, #7274SC...........................$75.00
Peach, vase, Tulip, #7250PC...................................$65.00

Rose, jug, #192, 5"..$20.00
Rose, vase, double-crimped, 5½"..............................$50.00
Silver, bonbon, 5½"..$12.00
Silver, bowl, high foot, 12¼"..................................$68.00
Silver, cake plate, #7213..$25.00
Silver, candlesticks, 6", pr......................................$70.00
Silver, candy dish, #7274, w/lid..............................$58.00
Silver, cup, punch; #7306......................................$8.50
Silver, cup & saucer, #7209....................................$30.00
Silver, mayonnaise set w/spoon, #7203....................$25.00
Silver, plate, #7217, 8½"..$25.00
Silver, plate, bread & butter; #7219........................$15.00
Silver, punch bowl set w/glass ladle, #7306..............$500.00
Silver, relish, divided, #7234..................................$40.00
Silver, tray, tid-bit; 2-tier, #7296............................$32.00
Silver, vase, cornucopia, #7274SC...........................$60.00
Silver, vase, fan form, #7262, 12"............................$58.00

Figurines and Novelties

Alley cat, teal marigold, #5177 0I, 11"......................$85.00
Bear, teal marigold carnival, sitting, #5151 0I.............$20.00
Bird, lavender satin, #5163LN, short tail....................$45.00
Bunny, white carnival, #5162..................................$20.00
Cardinal head, ruby, 6½"..$95.00
Donkey, custard w/hand-painted daisies, 4½"............$45.00
Duck, milk glass w/hand-painted berries & flowers, swimming..$35.00
Egg, custard w/hand-painted orange roses, #5145RC.$40.00
Fawn, milk glass w/hand-painted poinsettias, #5160..$22.50
Fawn, white satin w/hand-painted berries & flowers.$50.00
Fish, paperweight, red carnival, limited edition..........$65.00
Fish, vase, milk glass w/black tail & eyes, 7"..........$425.00
Frog, custard w/hand-painted orange roses, #1191RC..$37.00
Girl, Burmese, #5141BG, 8"....................................$75.00
Hat, Violets in Snow, #7293DV, 4"..........................$110.00
Hen on nest, blue, #5186KL, 5"..............................$25.00
Hen on nest, Champagne, #5186PQ, 5"......................$25.00
Lion, ruby carnival, #5141RN..................................$50.00
Lion, Shell Pink iridescent......................................$40.00
Mallard duck, iridized mother-of-pearl, #5147PT........$15.00
Owl ring tree, Crystal Velvet, #9299VE....................$25.00
Owl ring tree, custard, #9299CU..............................$15.00
Praying boy & girl, Frosted Asters, #5100FA..............$70.00
Praying boy & girl, Old White Satin, #5100WS..........$27.00
Rooster, Special Milk Glass w/hand-painted decor, #468NJ, 8½"..$95.00
Scottie, milk glass w/hand-painted gray details..........$35.00
Snail, teal, #5134OC..$70.00
Snow Bird, crystal, #5163CY..................................$22.50
Swan, Bairly Blue Satin, #5161BA...........................$40.00

Hobnail

Banana basket, plum opalescent..............................$450.00
Basket, blue opalescent, 3½" dia.............................$42.00
Bonbon, French opalescent, crimped........................$15.00
Bowl, cranberry opalescent, crimped, 7"...................$49.00
Bowl, milk glass, crimped, 8"..................................$20.00

Candle bowl, milk glass, crimped, ftd $25.00
Candle epergne, milk glass, #3746, 2-pc....................$65.00
Candle holder, milk glass, #3745, 7" $30.00
Candle holder, milk glass, 2-light, #3672 ....$28.00

Comport, Blue Marble, #3731MB, made in 1970 only, 6½", from $35.00 to $45.00.

Creamer & sugar bowl, blue opalescent, footed.........$35.00
Creamer & sugar bowl, French opalescent, individual, 3½" $22.00
Cruet, blue opalescent, w/stopper $48.00
Cruet, French opalescent, w/stopper $35.00
Cup, punch; milk glass, #3847....................................$15.00
Epergne, blue opalescent, apartment size $90.00
Ginger jar (salt jar), French opalescent......................$45.00
Hat, milk glass, #3991...$7.00
Jam set, milk glass, 3-pc..$30.00
Lamp, courting; milk glass, #3793 ....$128.00
Lamp, student; milk glass...$200.00
Lamp shade, cranberry opalescent..............................$40.00
Pitcher, juice; blue opalescent, squat, +6 juice tumblers..$105.00
Planter, milk glass, #3697, 8½" $10.00
Relish dish, milk glass, divided, #3740, 12" $32.00
Relish dish, milk glass, heart form, handled, #3722....$25.00
Salt & pepper shakers, French opalescent, #3806, pr.$20.00
Sugar & creamer, milk glass, lg spout, #3906, pr........$12.50
Toothpick holder, Colonial Blue, 3-footed $10.00
Tray, clear, fan shape $29.00
Tumbler, juice; blue opalescent..................................$15.00
Tumbler, water; milk glass, footed, lg.........................$12.50
Vase, blue opalescent, double-crimped, 5"..................$55.00
Vase, bud; plum opalescent, 8" $45.00
Vase, cranberry opalescent, crimped, mini $30.00
Vase, green opalescent, smooth rim, mini...................$30.00
Vase, Honey Amber, #3752HA, 11" $85.00
Vase, milk glass, flat base, #3759, tall $22.00
Vase, milk glass, footed, #3753, med $12.00
Vase, milk glass, pitcher form, #3760.........................$27.50
Vase, milk glass, ruffled edge, #3852, 4" $8.00
Vase, plum opalescent, #3756, 8" $32.50
Vase, Powder Blue, #3856BV, 6" $48.00

Lamps

Fairy, blue, owl, #5108, satin.....................................$22.00

Fairy, blue Burmese, FAGCA souvenir, 1-pc $125.00
Fairy, Clydesdale, Cameo, satin.................................$55.00
Fairy, custard, owl, #5108 ....$24.00
Fairy, custard w/hand-painted pink flowers, #7300PY ..$35.00
Fairy, Heart, Rosalene, #8406RE $75.00
Fairy, Heart Optic, cranberry opalescent, #2903CR, 1996 Valentine Collection, 3-pc $135.00
Fairy, Lime Sherbet, owl, #5108.................................$22.00
Fairy, Rosalene, owl, #5180 ....$55.00
Gone With the Wind, Spanish Lace Optic, cranberry, #9219CC, 23" $265.00
Hurricane, cranberry, #2830CC, 10" $50.00
Hurricane, Dusty Rose overlay, #2830OD, 10"...........$90.00
Hurricane, Spanish Lace Optic, cranberry, #2830CC, 10" ..$110.00
Student, Burmese, Hammered Colonial base, hand-painted roses, 20" $285.00
Student, custard, Hammered Colonial base, hand-painted roses, 20" $250.00
Table, reverse-painted poppies, #6805EA, limited edition (1 of 400), 33x17" W...$750.00
Table, Springwoods, reverse painted, #2780CX, 1993, limited edition (1 of 500)..$550.00

Louise Piper Decorated Pieces

Basket, amethyst carnival w/hand-painted flowers ..$150.00
Basket, strawberry, ruby w/white birds & flowers, #9537...$50.00
Bowl, milk glass w/hand-painted yellow roses..........$40.00
Candy box, pink daffodils on custard, L Piper, March 1975, #7380 ....$160.00

Plates

Anniversary, white satin...$15.00
Christmas 1970, blue satin $20.00
Christmas 1974, white satin..$20.00
Country Cottage, #7418..$55.00
Juniper Train, #7418TP...$100.00
Light House, #7418...$125.00
Mother's Day 1972, blue satin $12.00
Mother's Day 1990, hand-painted swan......................$75.00
Nativity, Blue Florentine, #9412................................$75.00
Smoke & Cinders, #7618TL......................................$200.00
Statue of Liberty, #7618LO.......................................$110.00

Miscellaneous

Bowl, Basketweave, lavender satin, open lattice edge, #8222LN...$45.00
Bowl, Grape & Cable, aqua opalescent, crimped edge, made from base of tobacco jar, ca 1989 ....$65.00
Cake salver, Violets in the Snow, 13".........................$70.00
Candlesticks, Diamond Optic, green, low, pr $35.00
Candy box, Heritage Green, w/butterfly lid, #9280....$20.00
Comport, custard w/hand-painted orange roses, #7429RC ..$38.00
Comport, Peking Blue, #7528PK $23.00
Cornucopia candlesticks, Ming Pink, #950, pr $70.00
Creamer & sugar bowl, Daisy & Button, amber, w/lid, #1900 ....$42.50

Cruet, Dot Optic, topaz opalescent, w/stopper, 6½" ..**$85.00**
Epergne, #389MI, 1950-1977, miniature, 4-pc..............**$35.00**
Goblet, Plymouth, red, 5¾" **$32.00**
Ivy ball, purple w/milk glass foot, #1021 ....**$60.00**
Marmalade, Lamb's Tongue, green pastel....................**$37.50**
Mug, black, FAGCA souvenir......................................**$20.00**
Nut dish, custard w/hand-painted daisies, #7229........**$18.00**
Pitcher, Daisy & Fern, yellow opalescent, water size ..**$170.00**
Pitcher, Lattice, Burmese, #2729BR, 10" **$95.00**
Plate, Diamond Optic, amber, #1502, 4" dia................**$8.00**
Rose bowl, Beaded Melon, green opalescent, 3½"....**$35.00**
Stein, Bicentennial, Patriotic Red................................**$45.00**
Tobacco jar, Sea Mist slag, w/lid, #3007 ....**$140.00**
Top hat, Daisy & Button, blue, 2½".............................**$40.00**
Tumbler, iced tea; Plymouth, red, 6"...........................**$32.00**
Tumbler, Roses, Colonial Blue **$8.00**
Vanity set, Burmese, #2905BG....................................**$225.00**
Vase, Atlantis, Sea Mist slag, #5150 ....**$80.00**
Vase, Beaded Melon, Gold Overlay, #711, 3½"...........**$20.00**
Vase, bud; Florentine, green stretch, #251, 12" **$40.00**
Vase, jack-in-the-pulpit; Beaded Melon, light green, 9" ..**$42.00**
Vase, Mandarin Red, fan form, 7½x11".........................**$65.00**
Vase, Melon Rib, custard w/daisies, #7451 ....**$24.00**
Vase, Melon Rib, lavender satin, #7451LN, 6"..............**$32.00**
Vase, Old Mosaic, cobalt handles, 8" **$800.00**
Vase, Pinch Bubble Optic, Honey Amber, #1356HA, 8" .**$85.00**
Vase, Roses, Burmese, #7252RB, 7".............................**$90.00**
Vase, Thumbprint, ebony, #4454BK, 8" **$37.00**
Vase, Wheat, Apple Green, #5858AG, 8"......................**$40.00**
Vase, Wheat, Honey Amber, #5858HA, 8" **$30.00**
Vase, Wild Rose & Bow Knot, coral, #2855CL, 5".......**$45.00**
Vase, Wild Rose & Bow Knot, Powder Blue, #2855BV, 5" **$40.00**

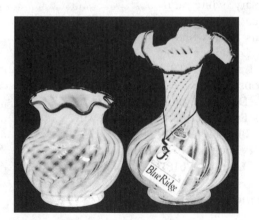

Vases, Blue Ridge, 1930s, 5½", from $65.00 to $75.00; 1985 reissue, 8", $50.00.

Wine, Plymouth, red..**$32.00**

Fiesta

You still can find Fiesta, but it's hard to get a bargain. Since it was discontinued in 1973, it has literally exploded onto the collectibles scene, and even at today's prices, new collectors continue to join the ranks of the veterans.

Fiesta is a line of solid-color dinnerware made by the Homer Laughlin China Company of Newell, West Virginia. It was introduced in 1936 and was immediately accepted by the American public. The line was varied. There were more than fifty items offered, and the color assortment included red (orange-red), cobalt, light green, and yellow. Within a short time, ivory and turquoise were added. (All these are referred to as 'original colors.')

As tastes changed during the production years, old colors were retired and new ones added. The colors collectors refer to as 'fifties' colors are dark green, rose, chartreuse, and gray, and today these are very desirable. Medium green was introduced in 1959 at a time when some of the old standard shapes were being discontinued. Today, medium green pieces are the most expensive. Most pieces are marked. Plates were ink stamped, and molded pieces usually had an indented mark.

In 1986 Homer Laughlin reintroduced Fiesta, but in colors different than the old line: white, black, cobalt, rose (bright pink), and apricot. Many of the pieces had been restyled, and the only problem collectors have had with the new colors is with the cobalt. But if you'll compare it with the old, you'll see that it is darker. Turquoise, periwinkle blue, yellow, and seamist green were added next, and though the turquoise is close, it is a little greener than the original. Lilac and persimmon were later made for sale exclusively through Bloomingdale's department stores. Production was limited on lilac (not every item was made in it), and now that it's been discontinued, collectors are already clammoring for it, often paying several times the original price. The newest color is sapphire blue. It's also a Bloomingdale's exclusive and the selection will be limited. Probably another 'instant collectible' in the making!

Items that have not been restyled are being made from the original molds. This means that you may find pieces with the old mark in the new colors (since the mark is an integral part of the mold). When an item has been restyled, new molds had to be created, and these will have the new mark. So will any piece marked with the ink stamp. The new ink mark is a script 'FIESTA' (all letters upper case), while the old is 'Fiesta.' Compare a few, the difference is obvious. Just don't be fooled into thinking you've found a rare cobalt juice pitcher or individual sugar and creamer set, they just weren't made in the old line.

For further information, we recommend *The Collector's Encyclopedia of Fiesta, Eighth Edition,* by Sharon and Bob Huxford.

Note: The term 'original colors' in the following listings refers to light green, yellow, and turquoise; use values for all but the items followed by the asterisk. Those items in turquoise are valued in the range of red, cobalt, and ivory. (Red, cobalt, and ivory are also 'original' colors, but because of high collector demand have been elevated to the next price point.)

Newsletter: *Fiesta Club of America*
P.O. Box 15383, Loves Park, IL 61132-5383

Newsletter: *Fiesta Collector's Quarterly*
China Specialties, Inc.
Box 471, Valley City, OH 44280. $12 (4 issues) per year

Creamer and sugar, individual; on figure-8 tray, see listings for values.

Ashtray, '50s colors $88.00
Ashtray, original colors $47.00
Ashtray, red, cobalt or ivory $60.00
Bowl, covered onion soup; cobalt or ivory $675.00
Bowl, covered onion soup; red $700.00
Bowl, covered onion soup; turquoise, minimum value ..$3,000.00
Bowl, covered onion soup; yellow or light green $575.00
Bowl, cream soup; '50s colors $72.00
Bowl, cream soup; med green, minimum value $4,000.00
Bowl, cream soup; original colors $42.00
Bowl, cream soup; red, cobalt or ivory $60.00
Bowl, dessert; '50s colors, 6" $52.00
Bowl, dessert; med green, 6" $475.00
Bowl, dessert; original colors, 6" $38.00
Bowl, dessert; red, cobalt or ivory, 6" $52.00
Bowl, footed salad; original colors * $270.00
Bowl, footed salad; red, cobalt or ivory $330.00
Bowl, fruit; '50s colors, 4¾" $35.00
Bowl, fruit; '50s colors, 5½" $36.00
Bowl, fruit; med green, 4¾" $450.00
Bowl, fruit; med green, 5½" $68.00
Bowl, fruit; original colors, 11¾" $250.00
Bowl, fruit; original colors, 4¾" $25.00
Bowl, fruit; original colors, 5½" $25.00
Bowl, fruit; red, cobalt or ivory, 11¾" $285.00
Bowl, fruit; red, cobalt or ivory, 4¾" $32.00
Bowl, fruit; red, cobalt or ivory, 5½" $32.00
Bowl, individual salad; med green, 7½" $105.00
Bowl, individual salad; red, turquoise or yellow, 7½" ..$85.00
Bowl, nappy; '50s colors, 8½" $62.00
Bowl, nappy; med green, 8½" $140.00
Bowl, nappy; original colors, 8½" * $40.00
Bowl, nappy; original colors, 9½" * $52.00
Bowl, nappy; red, cobalt or ivory, 8½" $52.00
Bowl, nappy; red, cobalt or ivory, 9½" $65.00
Bowl, Tom & Jerry; ivory w/gold letters $260.00
Bowl, unlisted salad; red, cobalt or ivory $500.00
Bowl, unlisted salad; yellow $105.00
Candle holders, bulb; original colors, pr * $95.00
Candle holders, bulb; red, cobalt or ivory, pr $130.00
Candle holders, tripod; original colors, pr * $465.00
Candle holders, tripod; red, cobalt or ivory, pr $585.00
Carafe, original colors * $220.00

Carafe, red, cobalt or ivory $280.00
Casserole, '50s colors $300.00
Casserole, French; standard colors other than yellow ..$650.00
Casserole, French; yellow $275.00
Casserole, med green $725.00
Casserole, original colors $140.00
Casserole, red, cobalt or ivory $195.00
Coffeepot, '50s colors $350.00
Coffeepot, demitasse; original colors * $340.00
Coffeepot, demitasse; red, cobalt or ivory $435.00
Coffeepot, original colors $195.00
Coffeepot, red, cobalt or ivory $245.00
Compote, original colors, 12" * $148.00
Compote, red, cobalt or ivory, 12" $185.00
Compote, sweets; original colors * $75.00
Creamer, individual; red $240.00
Creamer, individual; turquoise or cobalt $345.00
Creamer, individual; yellow $70.00
Creamer, regular; '50s colors $40.00
Creamer, regular; med green $80.00
Creamer, regular; original colors $22.00
Creamer, regular; red, cobalt or ivory $35.00
Creamer, stick handled, original colors * $45.00
Creamer, stick handled, red, cobalt or ivory $62.00
Cup, demitasse; '50s colors $350.00
Cup, demitasse; original colors $60.00
Cup, demitasse; red, cobalt or ivory $75.00
Cup, see teacup
Egg cup, '50s colors $160.00
Egg cup, original colors $58.00
Egg cup, red, cobalt or ivory $70.00
Lid, for mixing bowl #1-#3, any color, minimum value ..$785.00
Lid, for mixing bowl #4, any color, minimum value $1,000.00
Marmalade, original colors * $230.00
Marmalade, red, cobalt or ivory $285.00
Mixing bowl #1, original colors * $170.00
Mixing bowl #1, red, cobalt or ivory $225.00
Mixing bowl #2, original colors * $110.00
Mixing bowl #2, red, cobalt or ivory $125.00
Mixing bowl #3, original colors * $120.00
Mixing bowl #3, red, cobalt or ivory $130.00
Mixing bowl #4, original colors * $130.00
Mixing bowl #4, red, cobalt or ivory $155.00
Mixing bowl #5, original colors * $155.00
Mixing bowl #5, red, cobalt or ivory $185.00
Mixing bowl #6, original colors * $200.00
Mixing bowl #6, red, cobalt or ivory $265.00
Mixing bowl #7, original colors * $280.00
Mixing bowl #7, red, cobalt or ivory $350.00
Mug, Tom & Jerry; '50s colors $90.00
Mug, Tom & Jerry; ivory w/gold letters $65.00
Mug, Tom & Jerry; original colors $58.00
Mug, Tom & Jerry; red, cobalt or ivory $78.00
Mustard, original colors * $95.00
Mustard, red, cobalt or ivory $250.00
Pitcher, disk juice; gray, minimum value $2,500.00
Pitcher, disk juice; Harlequin yellow $62.00
Pitcher, disk juice; red $450.00
Pitcher, disk juice; yellow $45.00

Pitcher, disk water; '50s colors	$275.00
Pitcher, disk water; med green, minimum value	$1,150.00
Pitcher, disk water; original colors	$115.00
Pitcher, disk water; red, cobalt or ivory	$165.00
Pitcher, ice; original colors *	$125.00
Pitcher, ice; red, cobalt or ivory	$150.00
Pitcher, jug, 2-pt; '50s colors	$145.00
Pitcher, jug, 2-pt; original colors	$80.00
Pitcher, jug, 2-pt; red, cobalt or ivory	$115.00
Plate, '50s colors, 10"	$52.00
Plate, '50s colors, 6"	$9.00
Plate, '50s colors, 7"	$13.00
Plate, '50s colors, 9"	$22.00
Plate, cake; original colors *	$755.00
Plate, cake; red, cobalt or ivory *	$885.00
Plate, calendar; 1954 or 1955, 10"	$45.00
Plate, calendar; 1955, 9"	$50.00
Plate, chop; '50s colors, 13"	$90.00
Plate, chop; '50s colors, 15"	$115.00
Plate, chop; med green, 13"	$275.00
Plate, chop; original colors, 13"	$35.00
Plate, chop; original colors, 15"	$48.00
Plate, chop; red, cobalt or ivory, 13"	$50.00
Plate, chop; red, cobalt or ivory, 15"	$70.00
Plate, compartment; '50s colors, 10½"	$75.00
Plate, compartment; yellow, 12"	$50.00
Plate, compartment; original colors, 10½"	$40.00
Plate, compartment; red, cobalt or ivory, 10½"	$40.00
Plate, compartment; red, cobalt or ivory, 12"	$60.00
Plate, deep; '50s colors	$55.00
Plate, deep; med green	$120.00
Plate, deep; original colors	$40.00
Plate, deep; red, cobalt or ivory	$52.00
Plate, med green, 10"	$110.00
Plate, med green, 6"	$20.00
Plate, med green, 7"	$32.00
Plate, med green, 9"	$45.00
Plate, original colors, 10"	$32.00
Plate, original colors, 6"	$5.00
Plate, original colors, 7"	$9.00
Plate, original colors, 9"	$12.00
Plate, red, cobalt or ivory, 10"	$40.00
Plate, red, cobalt or ivory, 6"	$7.00
Plate, red, cobalt or ivory, 7"	$10.00
Plate, red, cobalt or ivory, 9"	$18.00
Platter, '50s colors	$58.00
Platter, med green	$140.00
Platter, original colors	$35.00
Platter, red, cobalt or ivory	$45.00
Relish tray, gold decor, complete, minimum value	$250.00
Relish tray base, original colors *	$65.00
Relish tray base, red, cobalt or ivory	$85.00
Relish tray center insert, original colors *	$42.00
Relish tray center insert, red, cobalt or ivory	$55.00
Relish tray side insert, original colors *	$40.00
Relish tray side insert, red, cobalt or ivory	$48.00
Salt & pepper shakers, '50s colors, pr.	$45.00
Salt & pepper shakers, med green, pr.	$140.00
Salt & pepper shakers, original colors, pr	$22.00

Salt & pepper shakers, red, cobalt or ivory, pr.	$30.00
Sauce boat, '50s colors	$78.00
Sauce boat, med green	$155.00
Sauce boat, original colors	$45.00
Sauce boat, red, cobalt or ivory	$68.00
Saucer, '50s colors	$6.00
Saucer, demitasse; '50s colors	$95.00
Saucer, demitasse; original colors	$18.00
Saucer, demitasse; red, cobalt or ivory	$22.00
Saucer, med green	$12.00
Saucer, original colors	$4.00
Saucer, red, cobalt or ivory	$5.00
Sugar bowl, individual; turquoise	$350.00
Sugar bowl, individual; yellow	$120.00
Sugar bowl, w/lid, '50s colors, 3¼x3½"	$72.00
Sugar bowl, w/lid, med green, 3¼x3½"	$160.00
Sugar bowl, w/lid, original colors, 3¼x3½"	$45.00
Sugar bowl, w/lid, red, cobalt or ivory, 3¼x3½"	$55.00
Syrup, original colors *	$320.00
Syrup, red, cobalt or ivory	$385.00
Teacup, '50s colors	$38.00
Teacup, med green	$58.00
Teacup, original colors	$25.00
Teacup, red, cobalt or ivory	$35.00
Teapot, lg; original colors *	$180.00
Teapot, lg; red, cobalt or ivory	$220.00
Teapot, med; '50s colors	$310.00
Teapot, med; med green, minimum value	$1,000.00
Teapot, med; original colors	$155.00
Teapot, med; red, cobalt or ivory	$195.00
Tray, figure-8; cobalt	$82.00
Tray, figure-8; turquoise or yellow	$275.00
Tray, utility; original colors *	$38.00
Tray, utility; red, cobalt or ivory	$42.00
Tumbler, juice; chartreuse, Harlequin yellow or dark green	$460.00
Tumbler, juice; original colors	$40.00
Tumbler, juice; red, cobalt or ivory	$45.00
Tumbler, juice; rose	$65.00
Tumbler, water; original colors *	$60.00
Tumbler, water; red, cobalt or ivory	$75.00
Vase, bud; original colors *	$80.00
Vase, bud; red, cobalt or ivory	$100.00
Vase, original colors, 10" *	$720.00
Vase, original colors, 12" *	$950.00
Vase, original colors, 8" *	$560.00
Vase, red, cobalt or ivory, 10"	$800.00
Vase, red, cobalt or ivory, 12", minimum value	$1,100.00
Vase, red, cobalt or ivory, 8"	$640.00

Kitchen Kraft

Bowl, mixing; light green or yellow, 10"	$100.00
Bowl, mixing; light green or yellow, 6"	$65.00
Bowl, mixing; light green or yellow, 8"	$82.00
Bowl, mixing; red or cobalt, 10"	$120.00
Bowl, mixing; red or cobalt, 6"	$75.00
Bowl, mixing; red or cobalt, 8"	$92.00
Cake plate, light green or yellow	$55.00

Cake plate, red or cobalt	**$65.00**
Cake server, light green or yellow	**$130.00**
Cake server, red or cobalt	**$140.00**
Casserole, individual; light green or yellow	**$140.00**
Casserole, individual; red or cobalt	**$155.00**
Casserole, light green or yellow, 7½"	**$85.00**
Casserole, light green or yellow, 8½"	**$100.00**
Casserole, red or cobalt, 7½"	**$90.00**
Casserole, red or cobalt, 8½"	**$110.00**
Covered jar, lg; light green or yellow	**$300.00**
Covered jar, lg; red or cobalt	**$320.00**
Covered jar, med; light green or yellow	**$260.00**
Covered jar, med; red or cobalt	**$280.00**
Covered jar, sm; light green or yellow	**$270.00**
Covered jar, sm; red or cobalt	**$290.00**
Covered jug, light green or yellow	**$250.00**
Covered jug, red or cobalt	**$275.00**
Fork, light green or yellow	**$100.00**
Fork, red or cobalt	**$125.00**
Metal frame for platter	**$26.00**
Pie plate, light green or yellow, 10"	**$40.00**
Pie plate, light green or yellow, 9"	**$40.00**
Pie plate, red or cobalt, 10"	**$45.00**
Pie plate, red or cobalt, 9"	**$45.00**
Pie plate, Spruce Green	**$290.00**
Platter, light green or yellow	**$68.00**
Platter, red or cobalt	**$78.00**
Platter, Spruce Green	**$350.00**
Salt & pepper shakers, light green or yellow, pr	**$95.00**
Salt & pepper shakers, red or cobalt, pr	**$105.00**
Spoon, light green or yellow	**$100.00**
Spoon, red or cobalt	**$125.00**
Stacking refrigerator lid, ivory	**$205.00**
Stacking refrigerator lid, light green or yellow	**$70.00**
Stacking refrigerator lid, red or cobalt	**$80.00**
Stacking refrigerator unit, ivory	**$195.00**
Stacking refrigerator unit, light green or yellow	**$45.00**
Stacking refrigerator unit, red or cobalt	**$55.00**

Finch, Kay

Wonderful ceramic figurines signed by artist-decorator Kay Finch are among the many that were produced in California during the middle of the century. She modeled her line of animals and birds with much expression and favored soft color combinations often with vibrant pastel accents. Some of her models were quite large, but generally they range in size from 12" down to a tiny 2". She made several animal 'family groups' and some human subjects as well. After her death a few years ago, prices for her work began to climb.

She used a variety of marks and labels, and though most pieces are marked, some of the smaller animals are not; but you should be able to recognize her work with ease, once you've seen a few marked pieces.

For more information, we recommend *Collectible Kay Finch* by Richard Martinez, Devin Frick, and Jean Frick; *The Collector's Encyclopedia of California Pottery* by Jack Chipman (both by Collector Books); and *Kay Finch Ceramics, Her Enchanted World,* by Mike Nickel and Cindy Horvath (Schiffer).

Figurines, Owls, all pastel colors: Toot, #188, 5¾", from $100.00 to $125.00; Tootsie, #189, 3¾", from $50.00 to $65.00; Hoot, #187, 8¾", $200.00.

Asthray, dog's head form, green, #4773, from $100 to	**$150.00**
Box, heart shape w/red heart in center, bird perched on heart lid, #5051, from $50 to	**$75.00**
Cigarette jar, attached Yorky, #4766, from $200 to	**$250.00**
Figurine, angel, #114a, #114b, or #114c, 4", each, from $75 to	**$100.00**
Figurine, angel band member, #5151, #5152, #5153, or #5154, each, from $100 to	**$110.00**
Figurine, bride & groom, #201 & #204, 6½", pr, from $400 to	**$500.00**
Figurine, camel, #464, hard to find, 5", minimum value	**$450.00**
Figurine, cat, Jezebel, slip colors, #5302, from $250 to	**$300.00**
Figurine, Chinese court lady, deep turquoise, #402, 10½", from $150 to	**$175.00**
Figurine, choir boy, #210, 7"	**$125.00**
Figurine, cocker spaniel, brown or brown & white, #5201, 8", from $300 to	**$350.00**
Figurine, colt, #4806, 11", from $250 to	**$350.00**
Figurine, dog, Peke, #156, 2½", from $100 to	**$125.00**
Figurine, dog, Pekingese, pink, #154, 14" long, from $450 to	**$550.00**
Figurine, donkey, detailed mane w/decor, #135, from $100 to	**$150.00**
Figurine, elephant, circus; #5364, 3½"	**$200.00**
Figurine, elephant, Peanuts, trunk up, #191, 8½", from $275 to	**$325.00**
Figurine, girl, PJ, w/pigtails, #5002, 5", from $150 to	**$200.00**
Figurine, monkey, Socko (circus), #4841, 4½", from $150 to	**$200.00**
Figurine, peasant boy or girl, #113 through #117, 6", each, from $50 to	**$70.00**
Figurine, pig, Bitsy, #130, from $75 to	**$125.00**
Figurine, pig, Sassy, #166, 3½", from $100 to	**$125.00**
Figurine, rabbit, Cottontail Baby, #152, 2½", from $85 to	**$110.00**
Figurine, rabbit, Cuddles, #4623, 11"	**$450.00**
Figurine, rabbit, pink jacket & flower hat, #5005b, from $150 to	**$200.00**
Figurine, skunks, #4774 & #4775, pr, from $450 to	**$550.00**

Figurine, squirrel, #108a or 108b, 3" to 4", each, from $75 to **$100.00**

Figurine, St Francis, green, #5457, 13", from $200 to..**$250.00**

Figurine, western burro, w/ or w/out baskets on back, #4768 or #4769, each, from $100 to.............................**$150.00**

Figurine, Yorky pups, #170 & #171, pr.....................**$550.00**

Mug, Santa figural, cap forms lid, #4950, 5", from $150 to **$200.00**

Planter, baby & block, Baby's First from California Line, 6½", from $100 to..**$150.00**

Planter, swan figural, pink pearl, #4956, from $75 to.**$125.00**

Planter, Teddy bear w/block **$110.00**

Plaque, sea horse, white w/gold, #5788, 16", from $100 to...**$150.00**

Salt & pepper shakers, Tootsie, owl, #189, 3", pr, from $100 to **$150.00**

Wall plaque, eagle, white, #5904, 16", from $100 to...**$150.00**

Fire-King

This is an area of collecting interest that you can enjoy without having to mortgage the home place. In fact, you'll be able to pick it up for a song, if you keep your eyes peeled at garage sales and swap meets.

Fire-King was a tradename of the Anchor Hocking Glass Company, located in Lancaster, Ohio. As its name indicates, this type of glassware is strong enough to stand up to high oven temperatures without breakage. From the early forties until the mid-seventies, they produced kitchenware, dinnerware, and restaurant ware in a variety of colors. (We'll deal with Jade-ite, the most popular of these colors later on in the book.) Blues are always popular with collectors, and Anchor Hocking made two, Turquoise Blue and Azur-ite (light sky blue). They also made pink, Forest Green, Ruby Red (popular in the Bubble pattern), gold-trimmed lines, and some with fired-on colors. During the late sixties they made Soreno in avocado green to tie in with home-decorating trends.

Bubble (made from the thirties through the sixties) was produced in just about every color Anchor Hocking ever made. You may also hear this pattern refered to as Provincial or Bullseye.

Alice was a mid-forties to fifties line. It was made in Jade-ite and a white that was sometimes trimmed with blue or red. Cups and saucers were given away in boxes of Mother's Oats, but plates had to be purchased (so they're scarce today).

In the early fifties, they produced a 'laurel leaf' design in peach and 'Gray Laurel' lustres (the gray is scarce), followed later in the decade and into the sixties with several lines of white glass decorated with decals — Honeysuckle, Fleurette, Primrose, and Game Bird, to name only a few. (In the listing that follows, look for lines beginning 'Decal Dinnerware' to evaluate any of these patterns.)

Anchor Hocking made ovenware in many the same colors and designs as their dinnerware. Their most extensive line (and one that is very popular today) was made in Sapphire Blue, clear glass with a blue tint, in a pattern called Philbe. Most pieces are still very reasonable, but some are already worth in excess of $50.00, so now is the time to start your collection. These are the antiques of the future! If you'd like to study more about Anchor Hocking and Fire-King, we recommend *Anchor Hocking's Fire King & More* and *Collectible Glassware of the 40s, 50s, and 60s*, both by Gene Florence (Collector Books, and *Fire-King Fever '97* by April Tvorak.

See also Jade-ite; Kitchen Collectibles.

Advisor: April Tvorak (See Directory, Fire-King)

Newsletter: *The '50s Flea!!!*
April and Larry Tvorak
P.O. Box 126
Canon City, CO 81215-0126; 719-269-7230; Subscription: $5 per year for 1 yearly postwar glass newsletter; includes free 30-word classified ad

Alice, cup & saucer, white w/blue trim **$12.00**

Alice, plate, dinner; white w/red trim, 9½" **$24.00**

American Artware, leaf & blossom dessert set, fired-on color **$9.00**

Apple Blossom, bowl, cereal; 5" **$6.00**

Apple Blossom, custard cup **$4.00**

Apple Blossom, mug **$7.00**

Apple Blossom, plate, dinner; from $7 to **$10.00**

Blue Mosaic, bowl, dessert; 4⅝" **$3.50**

Blue Mosaic, cup & saucer...**$6.00**

Blue Mosaic, plate, dinner; 10" **$5.00**

Bubble, bowl, cereal; Forest Green or Ruby Red, 5¼"..**$10.00**

Bubble, bowl, vegetable; crystal or white **$10.00**

Bubble, plate, dinner; crystal or white........................**$6.00**

Bubble, plate, dinner; Forest Green or Ruby Red.......**$20.00**

Bubble, platter, oval, Forest Green or Ruby Red........**$18.00**

Charm/Square, bowl, dessert; Azur-ite or Forest Green, 4¾" **$7.00**

Charm/Square, bowl, soup; Azur-ite or Forest Green, 6"..**$12.50**

Charm/Square, creamer & sugar bowl, Azur-ite or Forest Green, set **$14.00**

Charm/Square, plate, dinner; Azur-ite or Forest Green, 9¼" **$16.00**

Charm/Square, plate, luncheon; Azur-ite or Forest Green, 8½" **$7.00**

Charm/Square, plate, salad; Azur-ite or Forest Green, 6⅝".**$5.00**

Charm/Square, platter, rectangular, Azur-ite or Forest Green, 11x8" **$20.00**

Decal Dinnerware, bowl, cereal; 5"..............................**$6.00**

Decal Dinnerware, creamer & sugar bowl, w/lid **$14.00**

Decal Dinnerware, cup & saucer...................................**$5.00**

Decal Dinnerware, plate, dinner; 9" **$5.00**

Decal Dinnerware, snack set (cup & tray)....................**$6.00**

Fishscale, bowl, deep cereal; ivory or ivory w/trim, 5½"...**$9.00**

Fishscale, bowl, soup; ivory or ivory w/trim, 7½" **$15.00**

Fishscale, plate, dinner; ivory or ivory w/trim, 9¼"......**$9.00**

Fleurette, plate, dinner; white w/decal, 9"...................**$3.50**

Fleurette, platter, white w/decal, 9x12".......................**$12.00**

Fluerette, bowl, dessert; 4⅝"..**$2.00**

Game Bird, ashtray, white w/decal, 5¼" **$7.50**

Game Bird, creamer & sugar w/lid, white w/decal, from $8 to **$10.00**

Game Bird, mug, white w/decal, 8-oz, from $6 to **$8.00**

Game Bird, plate, dinner; white w/decal, 9" **$7.00**

Honeysuckle, creamer & sugar bowl, white w/decal ...**$6.00**

Honeysuckle, cup & saucer, white w/decal $2.50
Jane Ray, bowl, dessert; white or ivory, 4⅞" $4.00
Jane Ray, bowl, soup; white or ivory, 7⅝"..................$10.00
Jane Ray, bowl, vegetable; white or ivory, 8¼".........$12.00
Jane Ray, creamer & sugar w/lid, white or ivory, from $12
  to $15.00
Jane Ray, cup & saucer, white or ivory, from $6 to......$8.00
Jane Ray, plate, dinner; white or ivory, 9"...................$9.00
Laurel, bowl, cereal; ivory......................................$12.00
Laurel, bowl, serving; oval, ivory $22.00
Laurel, bowl, soup; ivory $16.00
Laurel, bowl, vegetable; gray, 8", from $8 to $10.00
Laurel, cup & saucer, gray, from $6 to..........................$8.00
Laurel, cup & saucer, ivory $8.00
Laurel, plate, dinner; ivory, 9" $8.00
Laurel, plate, grill; ivory, 3-compartment....................$12.00
Laurel, platter, ivory, oval, minimum value $25.00
Laurel, salt & pepper shakers, ivory, footed, scarce, pr, mini-
  mum value..$45.00
Laurel, sherbet, ivory $8.00
Peach Lustre, bowl, fruit; 4⅞".....................................$5.00
Peach Lustre, bowl, soup $9.00
Peach Lustre, creamer & sugar bowl, from $6 to..........$8.00

Peach Lustre, cup and saucer, $4.00; Plate, 9", $6.00.

Peach Lustre, mug, household....................................$3.00
Peach Lustre, plate, dinner; 9" $6.00
Peach Lustre, plate, salad; 7⅜", from $3 to $4.00
Peach Lustre, plate, serving, 11" dia............................$12.00
Primrose, bowl, dessert; white w/decal, 4⅝" $2.50
Primrose, bowl, vegetable; white w/decal, 8" $7.50
Primrose, plate, dinner; white w/decal, 9"....................$5.00
Primrose, sugar bowl w/lid, white w/decal....................$5.00
Sheaf of Wheat, cup & saucer, crystal..........................$8.00
Sheaf of Wheat, plate, dinner; crystal $10.00
Swirl/Flat, bowl, cereal; Sunrise (ivory w/red-orange trim)...$9.00
Swirl/Flat, bowl, dessert; Anniversary (white w/gold trim),
  4⅞"...$4.00
Swirl/Flat, bowl, sauce; ivory..$5.00
Swirl/Flat, bowl, soup; Anniversary (white w/gold trim), 7⅝",
  from $3 to $5.00
Swirl/Flat, bowl, vegetable; Azur-ite, 8".......................$12.00
Swirl/Flat, bowl, vegetable; pink, 8", from $10 to $15.00
Swirl/Flat, creamer & sugar bowl, Anniversary (white w/gold
  trim), from $5 to $7.50

Swirl/Flat, creamer & sugar bowl, Sunrise (ivory w/red-
  orange trim)...$9.00
Swirl/Flat, creamer & sugar bowl w/lid, ivory $12.00
Swirl/Flat, cup & saucer, Azur-ite, from $8 to $10.00
Swirl/Flat, cup & saucer, ivory.....................................$8.00
Swirl/Flat, plate, dinner; Anniversary (white w/gold trim), 9",
  from $5 to...$7.00
Swirl/Flat, plate, dinner; pink, 9", from $8 to..............$12.00
Swirl/Flat, platter, Anniversary (white w/gold trim), oval,
  12" $7.00
Turquoise Blue, ashtray, 3½"..$6.50
Turquoise Blue, bowl, cereal; 5" $9.00
Turquoise Blue, bowl, vegetable....................................$12.00
Turquoise Blue, creamer & sugar bowl, from $8 to ...$12.00
Turquoise Blue, cup & saucer $6.00
Turquoise Blue, egg plate, gold trim $12.00
Turquoise Blue, mug, 8-oz...$8.00
Turquoise Blue, plate, bread & butter; 6"....................$10.00
Turquoise Blue, plate, dinner; 9"...................................$8.00
Turquoise Blue, plate, salad; 7" $8.00

Turquoise Blue, relish dish, 3-part, gold trim, $8.00.

Wheat, bowl, vegetable; white w/decal, 8", from $8 to........$10.00
Wheat, creamer & sugar bowl, white w/decal, from $8 to ..$10.00
Wheat, custard cup, white w/decal, 6-oz, from $2 to...$3.00
Wheat, plate, dinner; white w/decal, 10", from $6 to...$8.00
Wheat, plate, salad; white w/decal, from $5 to............$7.00
Wheat, platter, white w/decal, 9x12" $12.00

Fishbowl Ornaments

Prior to World War II, every dime store had its bowl of small goldfish. Nearby were stacks of goldfish bowls — small, medium, and large. Accompanying them were displays of ceramic ornaments for these bowls, many in the shape of Oriental pagodas or European-style castles. The fish died, the owners lost interest, and the glass containers along with their charming ornaments were either thrown out or relegated to the attic. In addition to pagodas and castles, other ornaments included bridges, lighthouses, colonnades, mermaids, and fish. Note that figurals such as mermaids are difficult to find.

Many fishbowl ornaments were produced in Japan between 1921 and 1941, and again after 1947. The older Japanese items often show clean, crisp mold designs with visible detail of the item's features. Others were made in Germany and also by potteries in the United States. Aquarium pieces made in America are not common. Those produced in recent years are usually of Chinese origin and are more crude, less colorful, and less detailed in appearance. In general, the more detail and color, the older the piece. A few more examples are shown in *Collector's Guide to Made in Japan Ceramics* by Carole Bess White (Collector Books).

Advisor: Sara Gifford (See Directory, Fishbowl Ornaments)

Arches, green & red matt, Germany, 4¼x4½" **$24.00**
Castle & tower, details blurred, green, beige, pink, yellow & cobalt, Japan, 4½x4½" **$22.00**
Castle & tower, sharp details, green, beige, pink, yellow & cobalt, Japan, 3½x3¼" **$22.00**

Castles, 2½", $10.00 to $15.00; 3½", from $18.00 to $22.00. (Photo courtesy Carole Bess White)

Colonnade w/palm tree, green, blue & white, 3¾x4" ..**$20.00**
Coral reef, curved, yellow & green, 8x2" **$20.00**
Fish (2), riding waves, white fish, cobalt waves, 3½x3" .**$22.00**
Houses w/water wheel & bridge, yellow, pink, green & brown, 4½x4½" **$26.00**
Lighthouse, detailed, orange, yellow & brown, Japan, 2x2½" ...**$16.00**
Lighthouse, detailed, tan, black, brown & green, 6½x4" **$26.00**
Medieval gate, detailed, ivory, red, lustre, Japan, 3½x 3¾" ..**$26.00**
Pagoda, triple roof, blue, green & maroon, 5½x3¼" ..**$20.00**
Pagodas, joined by bridge, beige, blue & green, 6½x2½" .**$24.00**
Pagodas, joined by bridge, pink, blue, brown & green, Japan (wreath mark), 3¼x3¼" **$22.50**
Sign, No Fishing, on tree trunk, brown, black & white, 2½x4" **$12.00**
Torii, double roof, blue, beige & lavender, Japan, 2¼x3¾" **$20.00**
Torii, triple roof, blue, yellow & peach, lustre, 4½x3½" **$22.00**

Fisher-Price

Probably no other toy manufacturer is as well known among kids of today than Fisher-Price. Since the 1930s they've produced wonderful toys made of wood covered with vividly lithographed paper. Plastic parts weren't used until 1949, and this can sometimes help you date your finds. These toys were made for play, so very few older examples have survived in condition good enough to attract collectors. Watch for missing parts and avoid those that are dirty. Edge wear and some paint dulling is normal and to be expected. Our values are for toys with minimum signs of such wear.

For more information we recommend *Modern Toys, American Toys, 1930 – 1980,* by Linda Baker; *Fisher-Price, A Historical, Rarity Value Guide,* by John J. Murray and Bruce R. Fox (Books Americana); and *Schroeder's Collectible Toys, Antique to Modern,* published by Collector Books.

Advisor: Brad Cassity (See Directory, Toys)

Club: Fisher-Price Collector's Club
Jeanne Kennedy
1442 N Ogden, Mesa, AZ 85205; Monthly newsletter with information and ads; send SASE for more information

Museum: Toy Town Museum
636 Girard Ave., PO Box 238, East Aurora, NY 14052; Monday through Saturday, 10-4.

Adventure People Construction Workers, #0352, 1976-79, complete **$15.00**
Adventure People Cycle Racing Team, #0356, 1977-81, complete **$10.00**
Adventure People Daredevil Sports Van, #0318, 1978-82, complete **$25.00**
Adventure People Turbo Hawk, #0367, 1982-83, complete **$15.00**
Animal Cutouts, duck, elephant, pony or Scotty dog, #0020, 1942, each **$50.00**
Audrey Doll, vinyl face & hands w/cloth body, removable jeans, #0203, 1974-78..**$25.00**
Bossy Bell, w/bonnet, #0656, 1960 ....**$60.00**
Bouncing Buggy, 6 wheels, #0122, 1974-79................**$10.00**
Bunny Racer, #0474, 1942...**$225.00**
Butch the Pup, #0333, 1951 ....**$75.00**
Chick Basket Cart, #0302, 1947 ....**$40.00**
Cry Baby Bear, #0711, 1967-69.....................................**$40.00**
Cuddly Cub, head turns & chimes when rocked, #0719, 1973-77..**$15.00**
Dapper Donald Duck, #0460, 1936.............................**$600.00**
Dinky Engine, black litho, #0642, 1959 ....**$75.00**
Dizzie Donkey, Pop-Up Kritter, #0433, 1939............**$125.00**
Dollhouse, 3-story w/5 rooms, spiral staircase, 2 figures, wallpaper & instructions, #0250, 1978-79 ....**$40.00**
Double-Screen TV Music Box, plays Hey Diddle Diddle, wood & plastic, #0196, 1964-69............................**$30.00**
Ferry Boat, 3 figures, 2 cars & 2 life preservers, #0932, 1979-80 ....**$25.00**
Frisky Frog, squeeze plastic bulb & frog jumps, #0154, 1971-83 ....**$20.00**
Golden Gulch Express, #0191, 1961 ....**$100.00**
Grandfather Clock & Rocker, #0262, 1980, each...........**$2.00**
Honey Doll, yellow & white print, #0208, 1978..........**$20.00**
Humpty Dumpty, plastic, #0736, 1972-79 ....**$8.00**

Jiffy Dump Truck, squeeze bulb & dump moves, #0156, 1971-73 ....$30.00
Jolly Jalopy, circus clown's roadster, #0724, 1965-78..$15.00
Leo the Drummer, #0480, 1952 ....$225.00
Little People Pool, w/2 figures & accessories, #2526, 1986-88 ....$15.00
Lofty Lizzy, Giraffe Pop-Up Kritter, #0405, 1931 ....$225.00
Looky Fire Truck, #0007, 1950 ....$100.00
McDonald's Restaurant, 2nd version, same pcs as 1st version but lg-size figures, #2552, 1991-92 ....$50.00
Milk Wagon, truck w/bottle carrier, #0131, 1964.........$55.00
Mini Copter, blue litho, #0448, 1971-83 ....$25.00
Mini Snowmobile, w/sled, 2 figures & dog, #0705, 1971-73 ....$50.00
Mother Goose, #0164, 1964-66 ....$40.00
Music Box, play's Teddy Bear's Picnic, plastic, #0792, 1980-81 ....$15.00
Music Box Movie Camera, plays This Old Man, w/5 picture disks, #0919, 1968-70..............................$40.00
Musical Sweeper, plays Whistle While You Work, #0100, 1950 ....$250.00
Oscar the Grouch, #0177, 1977-84 ....$30.00

Peter Bunny Engine, #0715, 1941, $225.00. (Photo courtesy Brad Cassity)

Pick-Up & Peek Puzzles, #0500, 1972-86.....................$10.00
Picnic Basket, plastic w/accessories & cotton tablecloth, #0677, 1975-79 ....$30.00
Pinky Pig, litho eyes, #0695, 1958..............................$100.00
Play Family Camper, w/4 figures & accessories, #0994, 1973-76 ....$75.00
Play Family House Decorator Set, w/4 figures & accessories, #0728, 1970..$20.00
Play Family Houseboat, w/2 deck lounges, figures & accessories, #0985, 1972-76..............................$40.00
Play Family Merry-Go-Round, play's Skater's Waltz, w/4 figures, #0111, 1972-76 ....$40.00
Pocket Radio, plays Frere Jacques, wood & plastic, #0778, 1967-68 ....$20.00
Pocket Radio, plays Raindrops, wood & plastic, #0762, 1972-77 ....$15.00
Pocket Radio, plays 12 Days of Christmas, wood & plastic, #0756, 1973..$25.00
Pony Chime, pink plastic wheels, #0137, 1962 ....$40.00
Poodle Zilo, #0739, 1962...$75.00

Pop'n Ring, #0808, 1956..............................$85.00
Prancing Pony, #0617, 1965-70...............................$40.00
Roly Raccoon, waddles side to side, tail bobs & weaves, #0172, 1980-82 ....$15.00
Running Bunny Cart, #0304, 1957......................$75.00
Sesame Street Characters, #0940, 1977.........................$3.00
Snoopy Sniffer, Fisher-Price Commemorative limited edition (3,500), Ponderosa pine, #6588, 1990 ....$150.00
Squeaky the Clown, ToyFest limited edition (5,000), #6593, 1995 ....$150.00
Super Jet, #0415, 1952..$225.00
Three Men in a Tub, w/bell atop spring mast, #0142, 1970-73 ....$20.00

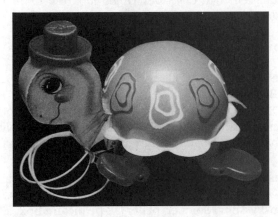

Tip-Toe Turtle, #0773, 1962, $20.00. (Photo courtesy Brad Cassity)

Tip-Toe Turtle, #0773, 1962 ....$20.00
Tote-A-Tune Radio, Toyland, #0795, 1984-91 ....$10.00
Winky Blinky Fire Truck, #0200, 1954......................$100.00
Woodsey Major Goodgrub Mole, w/32-page book, #0605, 1981 ....$20.00
Woodsey's Airport, airplane, hanger, 1 figure & 32-page book, #0962, 1980................................$40.00

Ziggy Zilo, #737, 1958, $75.00. (Photo courtesy Continental Hobby House)

Fishing Lures

There have been literally thousands of lures made since the turn of the century. Some have bordered on the ridiculous, and some have turned out to be just as good as the manufacturers claimed. In lieu of buying outright from a dealer, try some of the older stores in your area — you just might turn up a good old lure. Go through any old tackle boxes that might be around, and when the water level is low, check out the river banks.

If you have to limit your collection, you might want to concentrate just on wooden lures, or you might decide to try to locate one of every lure made by a particular company. Whatever you decide, try to find examples with good original paint and hardware. Though many lures are still very reasonable, we have included some of the more expensive examples as well to give you an indication of the type you'll want to fully research if you think you've found a similar model. For such information, we recommend *Fishing Lure Collectibles* by Dudley Murphy and Rick Edmisten and *Collector's Guide to Creek Chub Lures & Collectibles* by Harold Smith (Collector Books).

Advisor: Dave Hoover (See Directory, Fishing Lures)

Club: NFLCC Tackle Collectors
HC 3, Box 4012
Reeds Spring, MO 65737; Send SASE for more information about membership and their publications: *The National Fishing Lure Collector's Club Magazine* and *The NFLCC Gazette*

Arbogast, Jitterbug, green scale w/black plastic lip, wire hook holder, EX+..**$35.00**
Biff, Musky Spiral Spinner, papers, 2-pc picture box, sm wear on 1 corner, MIB **$225.00**
Brown, Fisheretto, leader & spinner, washer eyes, white body, orange head, red neck, EX..........................**$40.00**
Bud Stewart, Crab, tack eyes, brown scale, blended red spot on belly & red trim, side & nose hook & spinner, EX **$85.00**
Clark, Water Scout, tack eyes, black w/white ribs, EX+......**$30.00**

Crazy Legs, green with yellow eyes, two treble hooks, 3¼", $18.00.

Creek Chub, Baby #1601, glass eyes, perch, MIB................**$45.00**
Creek Chub, Baby Pikie #900, glass eyes, silver flash, NM.**$25.00**
Creek Chub, Baby Pikie #901, glass eyes, perch, MIB **$45.00**
Creek Chub, Baby Pikie #918, glass eyes, silver flash, MIB...**$45.00**
Creek Chub, Beetle, black head w/red wings, EX+ **$250.00**
Creek Chub, Castrolla, glass eyes, golden shriner, minor varnish scratches, light rust on hooks, EXIB **$185.00**
Creek Chub, Crawdad #400, crab, legs intact, EX................**$65.00**
Creek Chub, Crawdad #416, bead eyes, natural crab, legs intact, EX+...**$70.00**

Creek Chub, Darter #2019, plastic eyes, frog spot, NMIB...**$35.00**
Creek Chub, Ding Bat, glass eyes, frog, black tails, EX+..**$75.00**
Creek Chub, Giant Straight Pikie #6034, tack eyes, blue flash, MIB (plastic box) **$75.00**
Creek Chub, Husky Jointed Pikie #3001, tack eyes, perch, MIB **$20.00**
Creek Chub, Injured Minnow #1519, glass eyes, frog, MIB.**$45.00**
Creek Chub, Jointed Snook Pikie #5501, glass eyes, perch, pocket catalog, MIB..**$55.00**
Creek Chub, Jointed Striper Pikie #6808, glass eyes, rainbow, pocket catalog, MIB..**$225.00**
Creek Chub, Pikie #700, glass eyes, silver flash, EX+.**$25.00**
Creek Chub, Pikie #718, glass eyes, silver flash, black lettering on back, EX (rough box)................................**$30.00**
Creek Chub, Pikie Jointed #2600, glass eyes, silver flash, EX+...**$25.00**
Creek Chub, Pikie Midget #2200, glass eyes, no papers, MIB **$35.00**
Creek Chub, Plunker #3200, pikie, glass eyes, MIB....**$35.00**
Creek Chub, Surface Ding Bat, glass eyes, golden shriner, MIB **$185.00**
Creek Chub, Surfster #7400, glass eyes, blue flash, MIB (marked #7402) **$145.00**
Creek Chub, Wigglefish, glass eyes, perch, 1 ding on head, EX- **$65.00**
Creek Chub, Wiggler #100, glass eyes, double line tie, handpainted fins, EX..**$60.00**
Fishcake, Baby #7, frog, MIB **$15.00**
Fly Rod, Shur-Luk Froggie, frog colors, EX+ **$35.00**
Heddon, #150, plastic eyes, VG+ **$45.00**
Heddon, Chugger Spook Jr, plastic eyes, S, yellow shore, EX **$15.00**
Heddon, Crackleback, plastic, brown, EX+ **$20.00**
Heddon, Flap-Tail Jr, glass eyes, 2-pc, green perch scale, EX+...**$55.00**
Heddon, Fly Rod Punkie Spook, carpie, single hook, EX+...**$55.00**
Heddon, Gamefisher, pike scale, sm hook scratch on tail, EX **$65.00**
Heddon, Giant Jointed Vamp #7350, plastic eyes, white w/red head & tail, MIB **$95.00**
Heddon, Meadow Mouse #9800, black, MIB (marked #9800 GM) **$20.00**
Heddon, Pumpkinseed Spook #730, crappie, line tie in mouth, 2-pc, EX+..**$150.00**
Heddon, Pumpkinseed Spook #9630, bluegill, EX+ ...**$50.00**
Heddon, River Runt Spook #9110-M Standard, S, perch, papers, MIB **$20.00**
Heddon, Stingaree, black shore, tiny, EX....................**$25.00**
Heddon, Tadpolly Spook #9000XBW, black shore, papers, MIB **$20.00**
Heddon, Timber Rattler, wooden, glass eyes, perch, MOC...**$15.00**
Heddon, Vamp, salt flash & white w/blended red head, 2-pc, EX+...**$75.00**
Keeling, Baby Tom #201, aluminum & red head, paper & color chart, M (NM box) **$225.00**
Kurz Buckskin Bait, Buckskin Minnow #40, 2-pc, rare pocket catalog, MIB (odd box)................................**$95.00**

Lanes, Wag-Tail, hand painted green & silver w/side lines, EX- **$385.00**

Miller Manufacturing Company, Min-Nix Spoon, silver finish, very old, MOC...**$25.00**

Milsite, Rattle Bug, frog spot, oldest version, EX........**$20.00**

Fitz & Floyd

If you've ever visited a Fitz & Floyd outlet store, you know why collectors find this company's products so exciting. Steven Speilberg has nothing on their designers when it comes to imagination. Much of their production is related to special holidays, and they've especially outdone themselves with their Christmas lines. But there are wonderful themes taken from nature featuring foxes, deer, birds, or rabbits, and others that are outrageously and deliberately humorous. Not only is the concept outstanding, so is quality.

Prices for Fitz & Floyd are on the rise due to the uncertainty of the company's future.

See also Cookie Jars.

Advisors: Phil and Nyla Thurston (See Directory, Figural Ceramics)

Bank, Aviator Airplane **$145.00**
Bank, Cheshire Cat **$55.00**
Bank, Platypus Duck **$45.00**
Candle holder, Kitchen Witch, each.............................**$25.00**
Candy jar, Butler Cat..**$35.00**
Candy jar, Frog w/Crown...**$35.00**
Candy jar, Santa & Reindeer in Rolls Royce **$125.00**
Centerpiece, Sugar Plum Vase **$275.00**
Cookie jar, Runaway...**$375.00**
Lamp, Berenstain Bear **$30.00**
Match holder, little boy w/cannon, for fireplace........**$25.00**
Mug, Polka Dot Witch **$55.00**

Mug, pumpkin face with figural vulture handle, from $50.00 to $75.00. (Photo courtesy Pamela Apkarian Russel)

Planter, Santa figural..**$30.00**
Salt & pepper shakers, Halloween Hoedown Witch, 1992, pr..**$25.00**
Salt & pepper shakers, mice, pr **$20.00**
Salt & pepper shakers, parrots, pr...............................**$75.00**
Salt & pepper shakers, plaid teddy, pr **$25.00**

Salt & pepper shakers, snuggle cats, pr......................**$32.00**
Teapot, Aviator...**$145.00**
Teapot, Bremen Town Musicians, #LE5000, 1993, 9½"...**$75.00**
Teapot, Mad Hatter **$90.00**
Teapot, plaid teddy...**$35.00**
Teapot, Polka Dot Witch...**$175.00**
Trinket box, Catnap...**$45.00**

Florence Ceramics

During the forties, Florence Ward began modeling tiny ceramic children as a hobby at her home in Pasadena, California. She was so happy with the results that she expanded, hired decorators, and moved into a larger building where for two decades she produced the lovely line of figurines, wall plaques, busts, etc., that have become so popular today. The 'Florence Collection' featured authentically detailed models of such couples as Louis XV and Madame Pompadour, Pinkie and Blue Boy, and Rhett and Scarlett. Nearly all of the Florence figures have names which are written on their bases.

Many figures are decorated with 22k gold and lace. Real lace was cut to fit, dipped in a liquid material called slip, and fired. During the firing it burned away, leaving only hardened ceramic lace trim. The amount of lacework that was used is one of the factors that needs to be considered when evaluating a 'Florence.' Size is another. Though most of the figures you'll find today are singles, a few were made as groups, and once in awhile you'll find a lady seated on a divan. The more complex, the more expensive.

There are Florence figurines that are very rare and unusual, i.e., Mark Anthony, Cleopatra, Story Hour, Grandmother and I, Carmen, Dear Ruth, Spring and Fall Reverie, Clocks, and many others. These may be found with a high price; however, there are bargains still to be had.

If you'd like to learn more about the subject, we recommend *The Collector's Encyclopedia of California Pottery* by Jack Chipman; and *The Florence Collectibles, An Era of Elegance,* by Doug Foland.

Advisor: Doug Foland (See Directory, Florence Ceramics)

Dot and Bud, each, $250.00. (Photo courtesy Doug Foland)

Adeline, green or pink, 8¼", from $145 to **$160.00**
Ann, any color other than yellow, 6", from $55 to.....**$90.00**
Artware, Camille lamp, from $300 to **$450.00**
Artware, cardinal, red, from $250 to **$300.00**

Artware, cockatoo, white satin, from $300 to **$350.00**
Artware, Floraline candy dish, from $125 to **$150.00**
Belle, flower holder, green, 8", from $70 to **$75.00**
Charles, white w/gold, 8¾", from $200 to.................**$250.00**
Claudia, pink, 8¼", from $125 to **$200.00**
Darleen, rose, 8¼", from $250 to **$275.00**
Diana, pink, blue or green, 6¼", from $175 to........**$200.00**
Douglas, green or aqua, 8¼", from $175 to **$200.00**
Ellen, violet, 7", from $150 to **$175.00**
Ethel, aqua, 7¼", from $100 to **$150.00**
Gary, rose, royal red, teal, or moss green, 8½", from $175
    to..**$200.00**
Grace, rose or teal, 7¾", from $150 to **$200.00**
Her Majesty, violet, 7", from $175 to **$200.00**
Joy, child, aqua or butterscotch, 6", from $125 to **$150.00**
Joyce, rose or violet, 9", from $200 to **$225.00**
Kay, flower holder, ivory w/blue & white trim, 7", from $50
    to..**$75.00**
Lantern Boy, flower holder, green, 8¼", from $100 to....**$175.00**
Lisa, ballerina, pink, 9¾", from $300 to....................**$400.00**
Louis XV, velvet green, 12½", rare, from $300 to **$325.00**
Lyn, flower holder, green or beige, 6", from $50 to ...**$75.00**
Madeline, violet or moss green, 9", from $200 to.....**$250.00**
Marianne, rose or peacock, 8¾", from $275 to.........**$300.00**
Marilyn, rose, violet or moss green, 8¼", from $275 to..**$300.00**
Martin, moss green, teal or royal red, 10½", from $175
    to **$250.00**
May, white w/blue trim, 6½", from $50 to **$75.00**
Mikado, royal red or white, 14", from $175 to..........**$225.00**
Molly, flower holder, ivory w/peach or ivory w/blue, 6½",
    from $50 to..**$75.00**
Our Lady of Grace, white, blue & green, 9¾", from $175
    to...**$200.00**
Patrice, rose, violet or white w/gold, 7¼", from $150 to..**$250.00**
Peg, flower holder, green or beige, 7", from $50 to ...**$75.00**
Polly, flower holder, ivory w/blue & white or ivory w/pink
    & white, 6", from $50 to......................................**$75.00**
Priscilla, green, 7¼", from $150 to **$175.00**
Rebecca, green w/violet trim or aqua w/violet trim, 7", from
    $175 to..**$200.00**
Sally, flower holder, rose or white w/gold trim, 6¾", from
    $35 to..**$40.00**
Sarah, green w/violet trim, or blue w/white & gold trim, 7½",
    from $100 to...**$150.00**
Sherri, rose, violet or aqua, 8", from $175 to **$250.00**
Sue Ellen, yellow, 8¼", from $200 to.......................**$250.00**
Susanna, white w/gold trim, 8¾", from $250 to **$300.00**
Tess (teenager), pink, blue or green, 7¼", from $150 to.**$200.00**
Victor, royal red, teal, or white w/gold, 9¼", from $200
    to **$225.00**
Vivian, moss green, teal, or coral, 10", from $200 to....**$250.00**
Wood Nymph, pink or aqua, from $175 to **$200.00**
Yvonne, green, 8¾"...**$300.00**

Flower Frogs

Nearly every pottery company and glasshouse in America produced their share of figural flower 'frogs,' and many were

imported from Japan as well. They were probably most popular from about 1910 through the 1940s, coinciding not only with the heyday of American glass and ceramics, but with the gracious, much less hectic style of living the times allowed. Way before a silk flower or styrofoam block was ever dreamed of, there were fresh cut flowers on many a dining room sideboard or table, arranged in shallow console bowls with matching frogs such as we've described in the following lines. See also specific pottery and glass companies.

Advisor: Nada Sue Knauss (See Directory, Flower Frogs)

Bird, black w/white face & breast, orange beak, on forked
    tan stump, lustre finish, Japan, 4½" **$28.00**
Bird, blue lustre songbird w/pale yellow breast, dark red
    beak, orange lustre stump, irregular base, 3".......**$12.00**
Bird, blue w/lilac breast, yellow beak, sitting on branch w/yel-
    low & red flower, Made in Japan on oval base, 3"....**$15.00**
Bird, green, brown & black on brown rocky base, incised
    Made in Japan on bottom, 6x3" dia **$15.00**
Bird, orange lustre on blue lustre base, 2½x1¾" dia....**$8.00**
Bird, pelican-like, yellow w/burgundy beak & legs, orange &
    black wings, turquoise crest & log base, Japan ...**$15.00**
Bird, pelican-like w/yellow lustre body, black beak,
    orange wings & crest, blue lustre stump base, Japan,
    3x2½"..**$12.00**
Bird, red w/black mask & beak, white under tail, blue stump,
    lustre & glossy finish, Japan, 5¼".........................**$28.00**
Bird, red w/yellow breast & orange beak, irregular 2½" dia
    base, Made in Japan, 3¼" **$12.00**
Bird, wings outstretched, aqua semi-matt, 4x3¼", 8x10" leaf-
    design bowl marked Camark...............................**$38.50**
Bird, yellow lustre, orange beak, blue lustre stump, Japan, 2½",
    +4" yellow bowl w/blue lustre interior, from $15 to..**$20.00**
Bird, yellow lustre w/orange beak, blue lustre stump, Made
    in Japan, oval base, 2½"..**$8.00**
Bird, yellow w/turquoise wings, pink breast, brown head, irreg-
    ular blue stump base, marked made in Japan, 4" **$15.00**

Birds, multicolor glossy glazes, marked Made in Japan, 6" tallest, each, $15.00. (Photo courtesy Nada Sue Knauss)

Birds, orange crests w/lavender breasts, orange lustre
    stump, marked Niagara Falls Canada/Japan on irreg-
    ular base, 6"..**$15.00**

Birds, row of 3, blue lustre, yellow breasts, orange & white faces, blue lustre branch, Japan, 4x3¾x2", from $20 to..**$25.00**

Birds, 1 blue & white, 1 white, both w/orange beaks, on tan stump w/ivy & berries, lustre finish, Japan, 5¾"........**$28.00**

Blue jay, blue lustre w/outstretched wings, yellow breast, orange beak & face, orange lustre logs, Japan, 3¾"................**$20.00**

Blue jay, blue lustre w/yellow breast, on orange lustre log, +7½" bowl w/floral & bird decor, Hand-Painted Japan.......**$45.00**

Crane pr on perch, + lotus bowl, white semi-matt, Camark, 11"..**$50.00**

Dancing lady, 6½", attached scalloped 5" dia bowl, white w/hint of yellow on sides, from $15 to................**$25.00**

Duck pr, white w/orange bills on tan stump, lustre finish, Japan, 5"..**$28.00**

Flower bud, yellow w/blue center w/2 green leaves on blue base, lustre & glossy finish, Japan, 2½"................**$22.00**

Frog, blue lustre w/yellow belly, front legs on pink flower, orange lustre base, Hand-Painted Japan, 3", from $15 to..**$20.00**

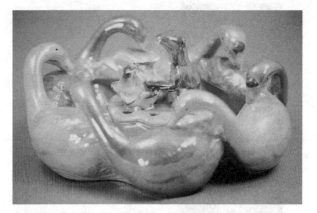

Geese surrounding bird and frog, lustre finish, 7" diameter, from $35.00 to $40.00.

Lotus bud, cupped in 2 rings of green petals, glossy finish, Japan, 4½"..**$18.00**

Oriental lady, 13", lime green, on 3½" dia base, ca 1940s..**$15.00**

Pelican, yellow lustre body, orange glossy wings & crest, blue lustre stump, Made in Japan, 3x2½", from $10 to......**$12.00**

Pelican, yellow w/orange & black wings, turquoise crest, on log pylon, glossy finish, Made in Japan, 4"..........**$12.00**

Penguin pr, blue lustre, pale yellow breasts, on pearl lustre ice & snow base, marked Hand Painted, Made in Japan, 4¾"..**$25.00**

Rosebud, pink w/yellow edges, blue leaf & stem, +3-lobed yellow & blue lustre bowl w/candle holders, Japan, 6", from $35..**$45.00**

Rosebud, pink w/yellow edges, blue leaf & stem, tan base, lustre finish, Japan, 2½"..**$22.00**

Scarf dancer, Deco, lime green, 9", on 4¾x3½" base, from $15 to..**$25.00**

Scarf dancer, nude, white semi-matt, 6½", on 2½x3½" oval base, from $15 to..**$25.00**

Scarf dancer, teal, 7½", w/attached 6x4½" scalloped bowl, Yankoware, ca 1920s..**$20.00**

Scarf dancer, white semi-matt, 6¼x4¾", from $15 to .**$25.00**

Turtle on rock, glossy terra-cotta red finish, Rushmore Pottery, 3½"..**$35.00**

Water lily, orange & yellow, green & yellow center, green leaves at side, irregular square base, 2½x3¼x2¼"..............**$15.00**

Water lily leaf, dark green, old, 1½x4x4"...................**$22.50**

Fostoria

This was one of the major glassware producers of the twentieth century. They were located first in Fostoria, Ohio, but by the 1890s had moved to Moundsville, West Virginia. By the late thirties, they were recognized as the largest producers of handmade glass in the world. Their glassware is plentiful today and, considering its quality, not terribly expensive.

Though the company went out of business in the mid-eighties, the Lancaster Colony Company continues to use some of the old molds — herein is the problem. The ever-popular American and Coin Glass patterns are currently in production, and even experts have trouble distinguishing the old from the new. Before you invest in either line, talk to dealers. Ask them to show you some of their old pieces. Most will be happy to help out a novice collector. Read *Elegant Glassware of the Depression Era* by Gene Florence; *Fostoria, An Identification and Value Guide* Vol I and II, by Ann Kerr; and *Fostoria Stemware, The Crystal for America*, by Milbra Long and Emily Seate. If there is a Fostoria outlet within driving distance, it will be worth your time just to see what is being offered there.

You'll be seeing lots of inferior 'American' at flea markets and (sadly) antique malls. It's often priced as though it is American, but in fact it is not. It's been produced since the 1950s by Indiana Glass who calls it 'Whitehall.' Watch for pitchers with only two mold lines, they're everywhere. (Fostoria's had three.) Remember that Fostoria was hand-made, so their pieces were fire polished. This means that if the piece you're examining has sharp, noticeable mold lines, be leery. There are other differences to watch for as well. Fostoria's footed pieces were designed with a 'toe,' while Whitehall feet have a squared peg-like appearance. The rays are sharper and narrower on the genuine Fostoria pieces, and the glass itself has more sparkle and life. And if it weren't complicated enough, the Home Interior Company sells 'American'-like vases, covered bowls, and a footed candy dish that were produced in a foreign country, but at least they've marked theirs.

Coin Glass was originally produced in crystal, red, blue, emerald green, olive green, and amber. It's being reproduced today in crystal, green (darker than the original), blue (a lighter hue), and red. Though the green and blue are 'off' enough to be pretty obvious, the red is close. Beware. Here are some (probably not all) of the items currently in production: bowl, 8" diameter; bowl, 9" oval; candlesticks, 4½"; candy jar with lid, 6¼"; creamer and sugar bowl; footed comport; wedding bowl, 8¼". Know your dealer!

Numbers included in our descriptions were company-assigned stock numbers that collectors use as a means to distinguish variations in stems and shapes.

Advisor: Debbie Maggard (See Directory, Elegant Glassware)

Newsletter/Club: *Facets of Fostoria*
Fostoria Glass Society of America
P.O. Box 826, Moundsville, WV 26041; Membership: $12.50 per year

American, crystal, ashtray, oval, 5½" $18.00
American, crystal, ashtray, 2⅞" square $10.00
American, crystal, bowl, bonbon, 3-footed, 6" $15.00
American, crystal, bowl, fruit; shallow, 13" $65.00
American, crystal, butter dish, w/lid, ¼-lb $35.00
American, crystal, coaster, 3¾" $10.00
American, crystal, creamer & sugar bowl, tea; pr $23.00
American, crystal, cup, flat $7.50
American, crystal, ice tub, w/liner, 6½" $90.00
American, crystal, picture frame $22.00
American, crystal, platter, oval, 12" $55.00
American, crystal, salt cellar, individual; 1" $9.00
American, crystal, tray, ice cream; oval, 13½" $160.00
American, crystal, tray, mint; 3" $12.00
American, crystal, vase, flared, 7" $75.00
American, crystal, whiskey, 2-oz, 2½" $15.00
Baroque, blue, bowl, rolled edge, 11" $50.00
Baroque, crystal, tray, oval, 11" $15.00
Baroque, yellow, sherbet, 5-oz, 3¾" $17.50
Buttercup, crystal, candlestick, #2594, 5½" $25.00
Buttercup, crystal, syrup, #2586, sani-cut $225.00
Century, crystal, bowl, bonbon; 3-footed, 7¼" $20.00
Century, crystal, bowl, cereal; 6" $25.00
Century, crystal, creamer, individual $9.00
Century, crystal, plate, torte; 14" $30.00
Century, crystal, tumbler, tea; footed, 12-oz, 5⅞" $27.50
Chintz, crystal, candlestick, #2496, 5½" $55.00
Chintz, crystal, platter, #2496, 12" $75.00
Coin, amber, ashtray, #1372/123, 5" $17.50
Coin, amber, decanter, w/stopper, #1372/400, pt, 10¼" ..$120.00
Coin, amber, lamp, courting; w/chimney, oil, handled, #1372/31 ....$110.00
Coin, amber, lamp, patio; electric, #1372/466, 16⅝" ...$160.00
Coin, amber, salver, footed, #1372/630, 6½" $110.00
Coin, amber, urn, w/lid, footed, #1372/829, 12¾" $80.00
Coin, amber or olive, cruet, #531, w/stopper, 7-oz $47.50
Coin, blue, ashtray, oblong, #1372/115 ....$20.00
Coin, blue, creamer, #1372/680 ....$16.00
Coin, blue, lamp, coach or patio; chimney, #1372/461 .....$60.00
Coin, blue, lamp, coach; electric, #1372/321, 13½" ..$195.00
Coin, blue, lamp, patio; oil, #1372/459, 16⅝" $275.00
Coin, blue, salt & pepper shakers, w/chrome lid, #1372/652, 3¼", pr $45.00
Coin, blue, vase, bud; #1372/799, 8" $45.00
Coin, crystal, bowl, round, #1372/179, 8" $25.00
Coin, crystal, condiment tray, #1372/738, 9⅝" $40.00
Coin, crystal, nappy, #1372/495, 4½" $22.00
Coin, crystal, stem, wine; #1372/26, 5-oz, 4" $35.00
Coin, crystal, tumbler, water/scotch & soda; #1372/73, 9-oz, 4¼" $30.00
Coin, crystal, vase, footed, #1372/818, 10" $45.00

Coin, green, bowl, oval, #1372/189, 9" $70.00
Coin, green, cigarette holder, w/ashtray lid, #1372/372 ....$90.00
Coin, green, pitcher, #1372/453, 32-oz, 6¼" $165.00
Coin, green, sugar bowl, w/lid, #1372/673 ....$65.00
Coin, olive, candle holder, #1372/316, 4½", pr $30.00
Coin, olive, candy jar, w/lid, #1372/347, 6¼" $25.00
Coin, olive, plate, #1372/550, 8" $20.00
Coin, olive, stem, sherbet; #1372/7, 9-oz, 5¼" $45.00
Coin, olive, tumbler, iced tea; #1372/58, 14-oz, 5¼" ..$45.00
Coin, ruby, candy box, w/lid, #1372/354, 4⅛" $60.00
Coin, ruby, nappy, w/handle, #1372/499, 5⅜" $30.00
Colony, crystal, plate, dinner; 9" $25.00
Colony, crystal, plate, torte; 18" $15.00
Colony, crystal, stem, goblet; 9-oz, 5¼" $13.00
Fairfax, amber, bouillon, footed $7.00
Fairfax, green or yellow, bowl, cereal; 6", each $12.00
Fairfax, green or yellow, salt & pepper shakers, footed, individual, each pr $25.00
Fairfax, rose, blue or orchid, bowl, 12", each $25.00
Fairfax, rose, blue or orchid, platter, oval, 15", each ..$65.00

Fern, crystal, stem, water; $25.00. (From the collection of John and Peggy Scott)

Heather, crystal, plate, cake; handled, 10" $25.00
Heather, crystal, stem, oyster cocktail; #6037, 4½-oz, 4" ...$19.00
Heather, crystal, vase, flip; #2660, 8" $85.00
Heritage, blue or wisteria, pitcher, #2449, 1-pt, each .$85.00
Hermitage, crystal, tumbler, old fashion; #2449½, 3¼" $6.00
June, crystal, comport, #2400, 5" $20.00
June, crystal, plate, salad; 7½" $6.00
June, pink or blue, parfait, 5¼", each $100.00
June, yellow, bowl, centerpiece; 11" $40.00
June, yellow, candlestick, 5" $30.00
June, yellow, sherbet, low, 6-oz, 4¼" $20.00
Kashmir, blue, candlestick, 5" $27.50
Kashmir, blue, saucer, round $10.00
Kashmir, blue, sugar bowl, footed $20.00
Kashmir, yellow or green, candlestick, 2", each $15.00
Kashmir, yellow or green, plate, salad; 8", each $8.00
Kashmir, yellow or green, stem, oyster cocktail; 4½-oz, each $16.00
Navarre, crystal, ice bucket, #2375, 6" $145.00
Navarre, crystal, plate, luncheon; #2440, 8½" $20.00
Navarre, crystal, stem, cordial; #6106, 1-oz, 3⅞" $55.00
Navarre, crystal, vase, #4108, 5" $85.00

Rogene, crystal: Pitcher, $360.00; Champagne, $20.00; Wine, $25.00; Water glass, footed, $28.00. (From the collection of John and Peggy Scott)

Romance, crystal, cigarette holder, #2364, blown, 2"..**$35.00**
Romance, crystal, stem, goblet; #6017, 9-oz, 7⅜" **$25.00**
Romance, crystal, tumbler, oyster cocktail; #6017, footed, 4-oz, 3⅝" **$17.50**
Royal, amber or green, bowl, #2324, footed, 13", each **$45.00**
Royal, amber or green, comport, jelly; #1861½, 6", each ..**$25.00**
Royal, amber or green, plate, luncheon; #2350, 8½", each..**$8.00**
Royal, amber or green, tumbler, #859, flat, 9-oz, each **$25.00**
Seville, amber, candlestick, #2324, 4" **$12.50**
Seville, amber, plate, luncheon; #2350, 8½" **$6.00**
Seville, green, bowl, cream soup; #2350½, footed **$17.00**
Seville, green, stem, cocktail; #870..............................**$16.00**
Trojan, pink, bowl, mint; #2394, 3-footed, 4½"...........**$25.00**
Trojan, pink or yellow, mayonnaise ladle, each **$30.00**
Trojan, yellow, ice bucket, #2375.................................**$65.00**
Trojan, yellow, whipped cream pail, #2378 ....**$125.00**
Versailles, blue, tumbler, #5098 or #5099, footed, 9-oz, 5¼" **$35.00**
Versailles, pink or green, platter, #2375, 15", each **$95.00**
Versailles, yellow, stem, oyster cocktail; #5098 or #5099, each **$25.00**
Vesper, amber, plate, canape; #2321, 8¾" **$45.00**
Vesper, amber, tumbler, #5100, footed, 2-oz **$40.00**
Vesper, blue, stem, oyster cocktail; #5100 ....**$35.00**
Vesper, green, bowl, grapefruit; #5082½, blown.........**$45.00**
Vesper, green, stem, sherbet; #5093, high **$16.00**

Figurines and Novelties

Cardinal head, Silver Mist, 6½".................................**$125.00**
Chanticleer, black, 10¾"..**$600.00**
Colt, standing, Sea Mist **$45.00**
Colt, standing, Silver Mist..**$45.00**
Deer, reclining, Sea Mist..**$40.00**
Deer, sitting or standing, milk glass **$55.00**
Deer, standing, Sea Mist, set of 7 w/6" sleigh...........**$300.00**
Dolphin, blue, 4¾"..**$25.00**
Duck w/3 ducklings, amber, set......................................**$50.00**
Duckling, head down, crystal, original issue...............**$20.00**
Eagle, bookend, Silver Mist, NM **$150.00**
Elephant, bookend, ebony, 6½", each.........................**$125.00**
Goldfish, crystal, vertical **$95.00**

Madonna, Silver Mist, 10", original issue **$50.00**
Mermaid, crystal, 11½"...**$125.00**
Pelican, amber, 1991, commemorative.........................**$55.00**
Pelican, crystal **$50.00**
Penguin, clear frosted, square base, 4½"....................**$85.00**
Penguin, Sea Mist..**$65.00**
Polar bear, topaz, 4⅝"...**$125.00**
Sea horse, bookend, crystal, 8", each **$115.00**
Sea horse, Sea Mist, pr..**$250.00**
Seal, crystal, w/label..**$65.00**
Sleigh, milk glass, w/old label, 3" **$30.00**
Squirrel, amber, running..**$37.50**
St Francis, Silver Mist, 3½", original issue.................**$350.00**

Franciscan Dinnerware

Franciscan is a tradename of Gladding McBean, used on their dinnerware lines from the mid-thirties until it closed its Los Angeles-based plant in 1984. They were the first to market 'starter sets' (four-place settings), a practice that today is commonplace.

Two of their earliest lines were El Patio (simply styled, made in bright solid colors) and Coronado (with swirled borders and pastel glazes). In the late thirties, they made the first of many hand-painted dinnerware lines. Some of the best known are Apple, Desert Rose, and Ivy. From 1941 to 1977, 'Masterpiece' (true porcelain) china was produced in more than 170 patterns.

Many marks were used, most included the Franciscan name. An 'F' in a square with 'Made in U.S.A.' below it dates from 1938, and a double-line script F was used in more recent years.

For further information, we recommend *The Collector's Encyclopedia of California Pottery* by Jack Chipman.

Note: To evaluate maroon items in El Patio and Coronado, add 10% to 20% to suggested prices.

Advisors: Mick and Lorna Chase, Fiesta Plus (See Directory, Dinnerware)

Apple, ashtray, oval...**$137.50**
Apple, bowl, cereal; 6" **$18.00**
Apple, bowl, fruit...**$14.00**
Apple, bowl, mixing; med **$190.00**
Apple, bowl, rimmed soup **$32.00**
Apple, bowl, salad; 10" **$125.00**
Apple, bowl, straight sides, lg **$55.00**
Apple, bowl, vegetable; divided...................................**$50.00**
Apple, bowl, vegetable; 9"..**$45.00**
Apple, box, cigarette **$137.50**
Apple, box, heart shape or round, each....................**$180.00**
Apple, candle holders, pr..**$82.00**
Apple, casserole, 1½-qt **$95.00**
Apple, coffeepot **$105.00**
Apple, compote, lg **$82.50**
Apple, creamer, individual **$45.00**
Apple, cup & saucer, demitasse **$60.00**
Apple, cup & saucer, tall..**$50.00**
Apple, egg cup **$38.00**

Apple, goblet, footed	$180.00
Apple, gravy boat	$35.00

Apple, individual casserole, $65.00.

Apple, mug, 7-oz	$27.50
Apple, piggy bank	$275.00
Apple, pitcher, milk	$105.00
Apple, pitcher, water; 2½-qt	$137.50
Apple, plate, 9½"	$20.00
Apple, platter, 14"	$72.50
Apple, teapot	$95.00
Apple, tumbler, 10-oz	$35.00
Apple, vase, bud	$75.00
Coronado, bowl, cereal	$12.00
Coronado, bowl, vegetable; serving, round	$15.00
Coronado, candlesticks, pr	$28.00
Coronado, cup & saucer	$12.00
Coronado, gravy boat, w/attached plate	$28.00
Coronado, nut cup, footed	$16.00
Coronado, plate, 6½"	$8.00
Coronado, plate, 8½"	$12.00
Coronado, platter, 11½"	$25.00

Coronado, teapot, $65.00.

Desert Rose, ashtray, oval	$125.00
Desert Rose, bell, Danbury Mint	$125.00
Desert Rose, bowl, bouillon; w/lid	$325.00
Desert Rose, bowl, cereal; 6"	$15.00
Desert Rose, bowl, fruit	$12.00
Desert Rose, bowl, soup; footed	$32.00
Desert Rose, bowl, vegetable; 9"	$40.00

Desert Rose, box, egg	$195.00
Desert Rose, butter dish	$45.00
Desert Rose, candle holders, pr	$75.00
Desert Rose, casserole, 2½-qt	$195.00
Desert Rose, coffeepot	$95.00
Desert Rose, cookie jar	$295.00
Desert Rose, cup & saucer, demitasse	$55.00
Desert Rose, gravy boat	$32.00
Desert Rose, napkin ring	$35.00
Desert Rose, pitcher, syrup	$75.00
Desert Rose, plate, chop; 12"	$75.00
Desert Rose, plate, 10½"	$25.00
Desert Rose, plate, 6½"	$6.00
Desert Rose, platter, 14"	$65.00
Desert Rose, salt shaker & pepper mill, pr	$295.00
Desert Rose, sugar bowl, individual	$125.00
Desert Rose, tea canister	$225.00
Desert Rose, teapot	$85.00
Desert Rose, tile, square	$65.00
Desert Rose, tumbler, juice; 6-oz	$35.00
El Patio, bowl, cereal	$12.00
El Patio, bowl, salad; 3-qt	$25.00
El Patio, bowl, vegetable; oval	$30.00
El Patio, cup	$10.00
El Patio, cup & saucer, demitasse	$45.00
El Patio, plate, 10½"	$15.00
El Patio, relish, handled	$35.00
El Patio, sugar bowl, w/lid	$18.00
Forget-Me-Not, ashtray, individual	$18.00
Forget-Me-Not, bowl, fruit	$10.00
Forget-Me-Not, bowl, soup; footed	$28.00
Forget-Me-Not, bowl, vegetable; 9"	$36.00
Forget-Me-Not, candle holders, pr	$67.50
Forget-Me-Not, plate, 8½"	$16.00
Forget-Me-Not, platter, 14"	$58.00
Forget-Me-Not, tumbler, juice; 6-oz	$32.00
Forget-Me-Not, vase, bud	$67.50
Ivy, candle holders, pr	$97.50
Ivy, coffeepot	$125.00
Ivy, creamer, individual	$52.00
Ivy, egg cup	$42.00
Ivy, mug, 7-oz	$32.50
Ivy, pitcher, milk	$125.00
Ivy, plate, 10½"	$32.50
Ivy, plate, 8½"	$25.00
Ivy, sherbet	$32.50
Ivy, teapot	$110.00
Ivy, tumbler, 10-oz	$42.00
Meadow Rose, bowl, rimmed soup	$25.00
Meadow Rose, bowl, vegetable; 8"	$28.00
Meadow Rose, butter dish	$65.00
Meadow Rose, plate, chop; 12"	$67.50
Meadow Rose, plate, 9½"	$16.00
Meadow Rose, sherbet	$25.00
Meadow Rose, teapot	$195.00
Meadow Rose, tumbler, 10-oz	$28.00
Poppy, bowl, fruit	$40.00
Poppy, butter dish	$165.00
Poppy, cup & saucer	$30.00

Poppy, plate, 10½" **$45.00**
Poppy, salt & pepper shakers, pr..............................**$125.00**
Starburst, bowl, cereal **$8.00**
Starburst, bowl, salad; individual.............................**$25.00**
Starburst, bowl, soup..**$15.00**
Starburst, candlesticks, pr, from $175 to **$200.00**
Starburst, creamer, from $10 to.................................**$15.00**

Starburst, fruit bowl, 5", $7.00; Cup and saucer, $9.00; Bowl, 7¼", from $18.00 to $22.00.

Starburst, ladle, from $25 to..............................**$35.00**
Starburst, pepper grinder, from $150 to....................**$175.00**
Starburst, plate, chop; from $55 to **$65.00**
Starburst, plate, 6½", from $5 to **$6.00**
Starburst, relish, 3-part..**$35.00**
Starburst, sugar bowl, w/lid....................................**$20.00**
Starburst, TV tray, from $60 to **$75.00**

Frankoma

In 1933 John Frank opened a studio pottery in Norman, Oklahoma. Today, even though it is an elusive mark, collectors can find pieces stamped 'Frank Potteries' or 'Frank Pottery, Norman, Oklahoma.' Not only is the mark hard to find, but the items that bear it are expensive. This could be because so few were made before Mr. Frank moved to Sapulpa, Oklahoma, in mid-1938. Still harder to find is the mark 'First Kiln Sapulpa 6-7-38,' which was used only on items fired on that day. It has been estimated that less than one hundred pieces were completed.

Mr. Frank interpreted clay as not many artists have been able to do. He created artware but was also capable of knowing what the public was buying for everyday use. His catalogs are filled with limited editions, advertising, miniatures, sculptures, jewelry, and dinnerware. In 1965 Frankoma became the first American company to produce collector plates. John Frank was always experimenting with glazes and created some unusual color combinations that have never been duplicated. Discontinued glazes are avidly searched out by collectors, with glazes such as the early Ivory, Rosetone, and Rose Bud being at the top of their lists.

Limited edition series such as the Christmas plates, bottle vases, Teenagers of the Bible plates, political mugs, and the bicentennial plates are desired by collectors. However, the political mugs are not as much in demand as the other limited editions. Miniatures and Christmas cards are the most sought-out groups ever produced by Frankoma. Their prices reflect their scarcity and desirability.

The pot and leopard mark was used from 1935 until November 11, 1938, when a fire destroyed the entire Frankoma operation. In 1983, after John Frank's death in 1973, Frankoma was once again destroyed by fire. Joniece Frank, a ceramic designer and daughter of Grace Lee and John Frank, became president of Frankoma when Mr. Frank died. It was under her supervision that an office, showroom, and plant were rebuilt on the same property. In 1991 Richard Bernstein bought the pottery, and the name was changed to Frankoma Industries.

If you'd like to learn more, we recommend *Frankoma Pottery, Value Guide and More*, by Susan Cox; and *Frankoma and Other Oklahoma Potteries* by Phyllis and Tom Bess.

Advisor: Susan Cox (See Directory, Frankoma)

Club/Newsletter: Frankoma Family Collectors Association
c/o Nancy Littrell
P.O. Box 32571, Oklahoma City, OK 73123-0771
Membership dues: $25; includes newsletter and annual convention

Figurine, seated Indian bowl maker, Desert Gold or Prairie Green, Ada clay, $90.00.

Ashtray, Aztec, Woodland Moss, #471, 9"....................**$13.00**
Ashtray, Dutch shoe, Peach Glow, #466, 6"................**$25.00**
Ashtray, individual; Jade Green, #459, 2x3" **$10.00**
Bank, dog, Sapulpa clay, #385, 7½", scarce **$70.00**
Bank, mallard, Sapulpa clay, #382, 4¾"......................**$12.00**
Bookends, bucking bronco, stepped base, Ada clay, #423, each **$150.00**
Bookends, Irish setter, Prairie Green, #430, 6½", each ...**$135.00**
Bowl, dessert; Wagon Wheel, Prairie Green, #94xs, 10-oz .**$7.00**
Bowl, free-form, Woodland Moss, #231a, 11"..............**$18.00**
Bowl, individual vegetable; Sapulpa clay, #244 ....**$3.00**
Bowl, Turquoise, #224, 8" dia....................................**$14.00**
Candle holder, Oral Roberts Easter, 1971, each **$11.00**
Child's set, plate sectioned as elephant's head w/cup, Sapulpa clay, #257, 2-pc.......................................**$28.00**
Christmas card, 1950 – 1960, from $70 to **$85.00**
Christmas card, 1961 – 1970, from $40 to **$60.00**
Christmas card, 1971 – 1975, from $30 to **$40.00**

Christmas card, 1976 – 1977 ....$85.00
Christmas card, 1980 – 1982 ....$25.00
Cornucopia, Ada clay, #215, 15½" $33.00
Creamer & sugar bowl, w/lid, Lazybones, Peach Glow, #4a & #4b, pr $20.00
Creamer & sugar bowl, w/lid, Mayan Aztec, Woodland Moss, #7a & #7b, pr $29.00
Cup, demitasse; Red Bud, #5dc $5.75
Dealer sign, pacing leopard, #1....................$425.00
Decanter, w/lid, Woodland Moss, #330, 24-oz $34.00
Dish, shell, Jade Green, #214, 6" $15.00
Earrings, screw or clip type, pr $25.00
Egg plate, Sapulpa clay, #819, 12"................$27.50
Figurine, bucking bronco, Ivory, #121 ....$200.00
Figurine, deer group of 3, Prairie Green, 1-pc..........$900.00
Figurine, donkey, Ada clay, #164, 3" $90.00
Figurine, English setter, Rosetone or Ivory, #41, lg, 5¼" ..$250.00
Figurine, Farmer boy, blue belted pants..................$95.00
Figurine, Gardener girl, yellow dress................$90.00
Figurine, horse, Sapulpa clay, #162, 3" $45.00
Figurine, pekingese, Ada clay, #112, 7¾".........$325.00
Figurine, puma, Rose Bud, #165, 3"...............$45.00
Flower arranger, wedding ring, Sapulpa clay, #746....$17.00
Flower frog, Red Bud, #804, 6½", scarce.................$30.00
Inkwell, We the People around base, w/quill feather writing pen & litho printing, Bicentennials, #IW $35.00
Jardiniere, Ada clay, #A8, 8½" $12.00
Jug, Uncle Slug, Ada clay, #10, 2¼"................$25.00
Mug, Donkey, Carter-Mondale, Rosetone, 1977 ....$48.00
Mug, Elephant, Bush-Quayle, Peach, 1989 ....$20.00
Mug, Elephant, Reagan-Bush, Celery Green, 1981......$38.00
Napkin ring, butterfly, Sapulpa clay, #263.....................$3.00
Pitcher, eagle, Cherokee Red, #555, 3" $28.00
Pitcher, eagle, Desert Gold, #555, 3"............$16.00
Pitcher, Mayan Aztec, Desert Gold, #7d, 2-qt.............$20.00
Pitcher, water; w/bird & advertising, Club Trade Winds, Woodland Moss, #T12, 2-qt.................$95.00
Planter, Alamo, Desert Gold, 6½", scarce $28.00
Planter, elephant, Sapulpa clay, #390, 6" $8.00
Planter, kettle, Sapulpa clay, #256, 6" $12.00
Planter, mallard, Woodland Moss, #208A, 9½" $18.00
Plate, Bobwhite Quail, Wildlife series, 1972FE, Prairie Green.............................$145.00
Plate, Mary the Mother, Teenagers of the Bible, 1982, Desert Gold, 7" $20.00
Plate, The Guiding Light, Christmas 1988, White Sand, 8½" $30.00
Plate, Victories for Independence, Bicentennials, 1975, White Sand, 8½" $55.00
Plate, Wagon Wheel, Onyx Black, #94fl, 10"..............$18.00
Plate, We the People, Bicentennials, #BC87 ....$22.00
Platter, Lazybones, Sunflower Yellow, #4p, 13"...$13.50
Salt & pepper shakers, bull, Ivory, #166H, 2", pr $75.00
Salt & pepper shakers, elephant, Ada clay, #160H, 3", pr...$70.00
Salt & pepper shakers, Plainsman, Woodland Moss, #5h, pr $14.00
Server, 3 bowls sit in holder w/metal handle at center, Sapulpa clay, #282 ....$19.50
Toby, Uncle Sam, dated 1976, #600 ....$16.00

Toothbrush holder, owl, Sapulpa clay, #404................$9.00
Trivet, American Eagle, dated 1776-1976, blue, #AETR, 6" dia $24.00

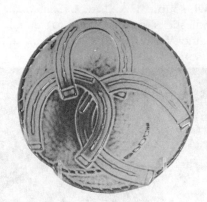

Trivet, Horseshoes, green, #94TRH, 6", $12.00.

Trivet, White Buffalo, Symbol of Indian Survival, Sapulpa clay, #WBTR $7.50
Tumbler, Bamboo, Club Trade Winds, Woodland Moss, #T2, 14-oz, 6½" $12.00
Tureen, Westwind, Country Blue, #6vt, 2½-qt $26.50
Vase, bottle; V-1, 1969, 15" $105.00
Vase, bottle, V-2 through V-15, from $65 to $85.00
Vase, free-form, Sapulpa clay, #21, 8".........................$12.00

Furniture

A piece of furniture can often be difficult to date, since many seventeenth- and eighteenth-century styles have been reproduced. Even a piece made early in the twentieth century now has enough age on it that it may be impossible for a novice to distinguish it from the antique. Sometimes cabinetmakers may have trouble identifying specific types of wood, since so much variation can occur within the same species; so although it is usually helpful to try to determine what kind of wood a piece has been made of, results are sometimes inconclusive. Construction methods are usually the best clues. Watch for evidence of twentieth-century tools — automatic routers, lathes, carvers, and spray guns.

For further information we recommend *Collector's Guide to Oak Furniture* by Jennifer George; *Heywood-Wakefield Modern Furniture* by Steven Rouland and Roger Rouland; *Collector's Encyclopedia of American Furniture, Vol I and II,* and *Furniture of the Depression Era,* both by Robert and Harriett Swedberg; and *American Oak Furniture* by Kathryn McNerney. All are published by Collector Books.

Armchair, Heywood-Wakefield, solid back & seat, late 1950s, 32x18x16", EX+ $65.00
Armchair rocker, oak, straight crest over spindle back, curved arms & legs $265.00
Bench, church; oak, carved flower each end, 1930s, 41x45x19" $350.00

Bookcase, quarter-sawn golden oak, glass door, adjustable shelves, 55x25"..**$300.00**

Cabinet, china; oak w/convex glass panels, claw feet, 1900s, 63x45"...**$1,100.00**

Cabinet, Hoosier; oak, 3 sm doors over 2 doors over counter over lg door & 4 drawers, restored, 69x40x27"....**$700.00**

Chair, desk; Limbert #84, tapered back w/1 wide slat, brand, refinished, 41"..**$425.00**

Chair, office; Eames of Herman Miller, cast aluminum frame w/leather upholstery **$440.00**

Chair, rocker/arm; 3-slat ladder-back, cane seat, restored, 38"..**$120.00**

Chairs, side; Hepplewhite style w/shield back, 20th century, 38½", 6 for...**$465.00**

Chairs, side; oak, triple pressed backs, cane seats, turned legs, 39", 4 for.....................................**$1,500.00**

Chest, cherry, Country, 6 dovetail drawers, turned foot, paneled ends, replacements, 51x42" **$500.00**

Chest, oak, 3-drawer, incised lines, straight apron, 1930s, 32x40x28" **$250.00**

Cupboard, Country, Hoosier type w/dark finish, 2-drawer, bins, breadboard top, 64x42"..............................**$125.00**

Cupboard, oak, 2 glass doors over 3 drawers over 2 panel doors, 2-pc step-back, 83x41"......................**$800.00**

Desk, cherry & maple, S-roll top, 5 dovetail drawers, repairs/refinished, 50x54".............................**$990.00**

Desk, mahogany, Chippendale style, slant front, N Western Cabinet Co, 40x31" **$275.00**

Desk, oak, S-roll top, fitted interior, 4 drawers each pedestal, 60"...**$1,200.00**

Desk, quarter-sawn oak, Mission, dovetail drawer, King Furniture...OH, 45"..................................**$220.00**

Desk, roll-top; Heywood-Wakefield, maple, streamline form on squared legs, top opens to reveal six compartments, rare, 33x32x24", $1,200.00.

Desk, walnut, Chippendale-inspired, slant front, 20th century, 43x31x17"...**$385.00**

Secretary, oak w/bookcase, flat glass door, refinished, 68x38x13" **$340.00**

Sofa, mahogany, Duncan Phyfe style, carved & reeded frame w/striped upholstery, 72" **$440.00**

Stand, magazine; Arts & Crafts, 4-shelf, arched aprons, 38x22"..**$350.00**

Stand, oak w/raised base shelf, 4 turned splay legs, round top..**$250.00**

Table, drop leaf; Heywood-Wakefield, 42" dia, w/leaves down, 42x19½", EX+...**$125.00**

Table, library; quarter-sawed golden oak, 2-drawer, 28x48x30" **$900.00**

Table, tea; mahogany, Duncan Phyfe style, demilune, swivel top opens, 32" L **$330.00**

Vanity, Victory, Heywood-Wakefield, champagne finish, 28x34" mirror, 2 drawers each side 24½x18x44" base, 1943-44, EX+ **$200.00**

Washstand, oak, sm mirror in lyre frame w/simple press carving, drawer over 2 doors, sm **$365.00**

Games

Games from the 1870s to the 1970s and beyond are fun to collect. Many of the earlier games are beautifully lithographed. Some of their boxes were designed by well-known artists and illustrators, and many times these old games are appreciated more for their artwork than for their entertainment value. Some represent a historical event or a specific era in the social development of our country. Characters from the early days of radio, television, and movies have been featured in hundreds of games designed for children and adults alike.

If you're going to collect games, be sure that they're reasonably clean, free of water damage, and complete. Most have playing instructions printed inside the lid or on a separate piece of paper that include an inventory list. Check the contents, and remember that the condition of the box is very important too.

If you'd like to learn more about games, we recommend *Toys, Antique and Collectible*, by David Longest; *Toys of the Sixties* by Bill Bruegman; *Board Games of the '50s, '60s & '70s* by Stephanie Lane; *Baby Boomer Games* by Rick Polizzi; and *Schroeder's Collectible Toys, Antique to Modern*.

Club: American Game Collectors Association
49 Brooks Ave., Lewiston, ME 04240

Newsletter: *Game Times*
Joe Angiolillo
4628 Barlow Dr., Bartlesville, OK 74006

Bionic Woman, Parker Brothers, 1976, MIB, $30.00. (Photo courtesy June Moon)

Across the Continent, Parker Bros, 1952, EX (EX box) .**$50.00**

Air Raid Defense Target, Wyandotte, 1940, NM (VG box) ..**$175.00**

Annie, Parker Bros, 1981, VG (VG box)......................**$22.00**

Auto Drome, skill game, Transogram, 1967, NMIB.....**$45.00**

Baretta, Milton Bradley, 1976, VG (VG box)..............**$20.00**

Baseball, Parker Bros, 1950, VG (VG box)..................**$35.00**

Batman, card game, Whitman, 1966, EX (clear plastic box)..**$55.00**

Battle of the Planets, Milton Bradley, 1979, VG (VG box)..**$35.00**

Billionaire, Parker Bros, 1973, VG (VG box)..............**$25.00**

Blondie, card game, Whitman, 1941, NM (EX box)....**$50.00**

Brownie Horseshoe Game, MH Miller, G.................**$150.00**

Buying & Selling, Milton Bradley, EXIB **$250.00**

Calvin & the Colonel High Spirits, Milton Bradley, 1962, EX..**$30.00**

Candid Camera, Lowell, 1963, NM (EX box)..............**$70.00**

Careers, Parker Bros, 1957, VG (VG box) **$30.00**

Charlie's Angels, Milton Bradley, 1978, NM (EX box) .**$35.00**

Chester Gump Game, Milton Bradley, 1938, NM (EX+ box)...**$145.00**

Chuggedy Chug, Milton Bradley, 1955, VG (VG box)..**$75.00**

Chutes & Ladders, Parker Bros, 1977, VG (VG box) ..**$20.00**

Close Encounters of the Third Kind, Parker Brothers, 1978, EX..**$12.00**

Comical Conversation Cards, Parker Bros, 1890s, EXIB..**$45.00**

Crazy Clock, Ideal, 1964, NM (EX box)......................**$80.00**

Crow Hunt, Parker Bros, 1930, EX (G box) **$75.00**

Deck Derby, Wolverine, 1937, litho tin, rare, NM (VG box)..**$95.00**

Dice Ball, Milton Bradley, 1934, VG (VG box) **$70.00**

Dick Tracy Sunday Funnies, Ideal, 1972, MIB.............**$50.00**

District Messenger Boy, McLoughlin Bros, 1886, VG+ (VG box)...**$250.00**

Dondi Potato Race, Hassenfeld Bros, 1950s, G (G box)..**$28.00**

Dondi Potato Race, Hasbro, 1960, NMIB....................**$50.00**

Dondi Prairie Race, Hasbro, 1960, NMIB....................**$72.00**

Dr Dolittle, card game, Whitman #4851, NMIB...........**$25.00**

Drew Pearson's Predict-A-Word, Dee-Jay, 1949, VG (VG box)..**$25.00**

Electric Bunny Run, Prentice, 1951, NM (EX box)......**$50.00**

Elliot Ness & the Untouchables, Transogram, 1961, NMIB..**$100.00**

ET, the Extra-Terriestrial, Parker Brothers, 1982, unused, M...**$8.00**

F-Troop, Ideal, 1965, NMIB **$165.00**

FBI Game, Transogram, MIB (sealed)........................**$150.00**

Fish Pond, McLoughlin Bros, 1890, VG (2 fish on VG box)..**$150.00**

Flintstone's Big Game Hunt, Whitman, 1962, NMIB.**$100.00**

Frank Buck's Wild Cargo, 1934, EX+ **$145.00**

Frosty the Snowman, Parker Bros, 1979, VG (VG box)..**$25.00**

Game of Politics, Parker Bros, 1952, VG (VG box)....**$45.00**

Game of the States, Milton Bradley, 1940, 2nd edition, VG (VG box) **$35.00**

Games You Like To Play, Parker Bros, 1920s, VG (VG box)..**$30.00**

Godfather, Family Games, 1971, VG (VG box)...........**$30.00**

Godzilla, Mattel, 1978, VG (VG box).........................**$120.00**

Green Ghost, Transogram, 1965, NMIB **$85.00**

Hardy Boys Treasure Game, Parker Bros, 1957, NMIB .**$75.00**

Hector Heathcote, Transogram, 1963, NM (EX box)...**$60.00**

Hopalong Cassidy, Milton Bradley, 1950, MIB..........**$150.00**

Hopalong Cassidy Lasso Game, Transogram, 1950, NM (EX box)..**$230.00**

Howdy Doody Card Game, Russell, 1950s, NM (EX box)..**$25.00**

Huck Hound Western Game, Milton Bradley, 1958, VG **$20.00**

I Spy, card game, Ideal, 1965, NM (EX box)..............**$60.00**

Inspector Gadget, Milton Bradley, 1983, VG (VG box) ..**$20.00**

James Bond 007 Tarot, US Games System, 1973, VG .**$45.00**

Jarts Missile Game, lawn game, Jarts, 1960s, NMIB **$30.00**

John Drake Secret Agent, Milton Bradley, 1966, NM (EX box)..**$40.00**

Ker Plunk, Ideal, 1967, NMIB....................................**$30.00**

Laurel & Hardy, card game, Ed-U,1972, NMIB...........**$20.00**

Leave It to Beaver, Money Maker Game, Hasbro, complete (VG box), $40.00. (Photo courtesy Paul Fink)

Li'l Abner, Parker Bros, 1969, NMIB............................**$50.00**

Little House on the Prairie, Parker Bros, 1978, VG (VG box)..**$20.00**

Little Orphan Annie Board Game, Milton Bradley, 1972, NMIB...**$260.00**

Lone Ranger (The New), Parker Bros, 1956, EXIB **$40.00**

Lost in Space, Milton Bradley, 1965, EXIB **$135.00**

M*A*S*H Trivia, 1984, EXIB.......................................**$25.00**

Mad Magazine Game, Parker Bros, 1979, MIB.............**$20.00**

Make-A-Million, card game, Parker Bros, 1945, VG (VG box)..**$32.00**

Mandrake the Magician, Transogram, 1966, NM (NM box)..**$50.00**

Margie, Milton Bradley, 1961, VG (VG box) **$28.00**

Miami Vice, Pepper Lane, 1984, EXIB........................**$20.00**

Mickey Mouse Canasta Game, 1950s, EXIB................**$60.00**

Mickey Mouse Slugaroo, WDP, 1950s, MIB **$35.00**

Milton the Monster, Milton Bradley, 1966, NM (EX box) ..**$35.00**

Mostly Ghostly, Cadaco, 1975, EX (VG+ box) **$20.00**

Mouse Trap, Ideal, 1963, NM (EX box) **$80.00**

Mr Doodles Dog, Selchow & Righter, 1940, Jr edition, VG (VG box) **$28.00**

Munsters, card game, Milton Bradley, 1964, VG (VG box)..**$20.00**

New Adventures of Gilligan, Milton Bradley, 1974, NM (NM box)..**$55.00**

Northwest Passage, Impact, 1969, G **$20.00**

Off to See the Wizard, Milton Bradley, 1968, EXIB **$50.00**

Old Witch, card game, Whitman/WDP, 1970s, Features Mickey Mouse, MIB (sealed)................................**$15.00**

Park & Shop, Milton Bradley, 1960s, EXIB $50.00

**Patty Duke, Milton Bradley, 1962, NMIB, $45.00.
(Photo courtesy June Moon)**

Patty Duke, Milton Bradley, 1963, EXIB $35.00

Pinocchio, card game, Ed-U, 1960s, MIB (sealed) $18.00

Planet of the Apes, Milton Bradley, 1974, VG (VG box) ..$20.00

Prince Valiant Game of Valor, Transogram, 1957, NM (EX box) $55.00

Quick Draw McGraw, card game, 1961, NMIB $25.00

Radar Search Game, 1969, EXIB...............................$25.00

Rex Morgan MD, Ideal, 1972, NM (EX box)...............$45.00

Rich Uncle, Parker Bros, 1955, VG (VG box) $60.00

Road Runner, Milton Bradley, 1968, VG (VG box).....$35.00

Road Runner & Wile E Coyote, Whitman, 1969, NMIB ..$25.00

Robin Hood, Parker Bros, 1973, VG (VG box) $35.00

Ruf & Reddy Spills & Thrills Circus Game, Transogram, 1962, NM $60.00

Sandlot Slugger, Milton Bradley, 1968, EXIB.............$45.00

Say When!, Parker Bros, 1961, NM (EX box) $30.00

Skipper, Mattel, 1964, NM (NM box)..........................$70.00

Smurf Game, Milton Bradley, 1981, VG (VG box)......$30.00

Snoopy, Selchow & Righter, 1960, EX (EX box) $60.00

Solarquest, Western Publishing, 1986, EXIB $30.00

Space Shuttle 101, Media, 1978, VG (VG box)............$20.00

Steve Canyon, Lowell, 1959, VG (VG box) $70.00

Stock Market, Whitman, 1968, NMIB $40.00

Superman, Hasbro, 1965, EXIB $110.00

Swayze, Milton Bradley, 1955, VG (G box)................$35.00

Three Chipmunks Big Record, Hasbro, 1960, NMIB...$40.00

Thunderbirds, Parker Bros, 1967, NMIB $125.00

Tin Can Alley Electronic Rifle & Target, Ideal, 1976, MIB..$45.00

Tom & Jerry, Milton Bradley, 1977, VG (VG box)......$20.00

Travel With Woody Woodpecker, Cadaco, 1956, VG..$70.00

TV Guide TV Game, Trivia Inc, 1984, VG+ (original box)..$20.00

Uncle Wiggily, Parker Bros, 1967, NMIB $15.00

Wacky Races, Milton Bradley, 1968, NM (EX box) $45.00

Waltons, Milton Bradley, 1974, VG (VG box) $20.00

What's My Line?, Lowell, 1955, NM (EX box) $40.00

Wildlife, ES Lowe, 1971, VG (VG box) $45.00

Wizard of Oz, Cadaco, 1974, VG (VG box) $30.00

Woody Woodpecker Up a Tree Game, Whitman, 1969, EX $32.00

Yogi Bear, Milton Bradley, 1971, VG (VG box) $30.00

Yogi Bear Go Fly a Kite, Transogram, 1961, EX-........$50.00

Zoo Game, Milton Bradley, 1920s, VG (original box)..$55.00

Zorro, Whitman/WD, 1965, EXIB.............................$30.00

Gas Station Collectibles

Items used and/or sold by gas stations are included in this very specialized area of advertising memorabilia. Collectors tend to specialize in memorabilia from a specific gas station like Texaco or Signal. This is a very regional market, with items from small gas companies that are no longer in business bringing the best prices. Memorabilia decorated with Gulf's distinctive 'orange ball' logo may sell more readily in Pittsburgh than in Los Angeles. Gas station 'giveaways' like plastic gas pump salt and pepper sets and license plate attachments are gaining in popularity with collectors. If you're interested in learning more about these types of collectibles, we recommend *Huxford's Collectible Advertising* by Sharon and Bob Huxford and *Gas Station Memorabilia* by B.J. Summers and Wayne Priddy, both published by Collector Books.

See also Ashtrays; Automobilia.

Advisor: Jim and Nancy Shaut (See Directory, Automobilia)

Newsletter: *Petroleum Collectors Monthly*
Scott Benjamin and Wayne Henderson, Publishers
411 Forest St., LaGrange, OH 44050; 216-355-6608.
Subscription: $29.95 per year (Samples: $5).

Antifreeze tester, plastic, metal & rubber, blue, orange & black, minor paint chips, 20", VG $30.00

Bank, Atlantic Premium, pump shape, blue, red & white, tin, 5", NM..$45.00

Bank, Atlas Batteries, metal, red & black, 3", EX........$30.00

Bank, DX-Diamond 760 Motor Oil, can form, cream, red & black, VG..$35.00

Banner, Kendall Oil, red silk w/gold fringe $35.00

Book, Kendall Oil, oil change tags, 1950s, unused $15.00

Booklet, Automobile Lubrication; Standard Oil of Indiana, Chicago IL, cooling, lubrication & troubleshooting, VG $25.00

Bottle, window spray, Mobil, Socony-Vacuum Oil Co, glass, paper label, VG, from $25 to..................................$50.00

Calender, Texaco, 1936, The Texas Co, Port Arthur TX, spiral bound, different art each month, complete, EX+.....$125.00

Can, Thermo Anti-Freeze, red, white & blue, full, ca 1945, 5½x4", VG $55.00

Clock, Firestone, tractor tire shape, working...............$75.00

Clock, Quaker State, green & black on white, battery operated, 1970s-90s, working, 16x16", VG.....................$35.00

Clock, Studebaker Batteries, logo top center, square metal frame, glass front, 1930s-50s, 15¼", EX.............$250.00

Container, Empire Motor Oil, Wolf's Head Oil Refining Co Inc, yellow over red w/black letters, 5-gal, 16" tall, EX $35.00

Container, Magic Rubber Mend, Eastern Rubber Co, red & yellow, dented, 4½x2¼", VG................................$15.00

Container, Standard Electric Motor Oil, plastic spout, ½-pt..$18.00

Display, counter; Hastings Oil Filters, shows Hastings Man, 16", EX..$55.00

Display rack, Micro-Lube, wire, metal sign at top, 20x34", EX $75.00

Display rack, Mohawk Tires, painted tin, arrowhead logo, 13x9", EX..$60.00

Dust cloth, Lastik, lg, M (M tin container) **$10.00**

Gas mileage finder, Bud Husing Texaco, Rockport MO, VG+ **$20.00**

Globe, Aetna Oil Co, red & white lens, all glass, 3-pc, 13½" **$450.00**

Globe, Malco Refining Co, plastic band w/glass lens globe, ca 1950s, 3-pc, 13½", NM **$265.00**

Guide, Mobiloil Lubrication Recommendations, Socony Vacuum Oil Co & Affiliates, paper, ca 1950, 16x28", EX...**$25.00**

Hat, attendant's, Ethyl, cloth, ca 1930s, red w/white letters, EX **$125.00**

Hat, attendant's, Standard Oil, summer-style mesh w/embroidered emblem, 1960s, EX **$175.00**

Hat (toy), Texaco Fire Chief, red plastic w/logo & letters on white shield, 8", EX **$60.00**

License plate reflector, D-X, Dura-Products Mfg Co, Canton OH, 5½x4", EX..**$40.00**

Map holder, Texaco Touring Service, painted metal, red shield, w/maps, EX...**$80.00**

Measuring stick, Gulf Refining Co Inc, used to check gas levels before gauges, EX...............................**$15.00**

Oil can, Around...Motor Oil, Atlas Oil Co, tin, earth encircled by cars, screw lid, 1925-45, 2-gal, 12x9", EX.................**$100.00**

Paperweight mirror, Phillips 66 Silver Anniversary, black & white, ca 1955, 3½" dia, NM..................**$120.00**

Pump glass insert, D-X, painted glass, 13x15⅜", EX ..**$45.00**

Pump nozzle, no company name, brass, #U17, NM...**$55.00**

Pump sign, Atlantic Kerosene, porcelain, EX **$70.00**

Salt & pepper shakers, Conoco Super, decals on plastic pump form, pr **$40.00**

Salt and pepper shakers, Esso, plastic gas pumps, blue, red, and white, 2¼", from $35.00 to $45.00 for the pair.

Service information guide, Texaco, spiral bound, 1995, VG.**$15.00**

Shirt pocket window spritzer, chrome-look metal, unmarked, EX...**$25.00**

Sign, AC Oil Filters, artwork of oil filter in center, yellow, black & white painted tin, 1941, 18x8¾", EX.......**$65.00**

Sign, American Amoco Gas, porcelain, double-sided, Courteous Cards Honored Here, 1940s, 15x24", EX.................**$110.00**

Sign, Danger: No Smoking, Matches or Open Lights, unmarked, 14½x10½", EX...**$20.00**

Sign, Jenny Aero, red, white & blue porcelain, 12x9", NM...**$160.00**

Sign, Pennzoil, painted metal, yellow, red & black, raised frame, 11¾x60", minor scratches........................**$110.00**

Sign, pole; Purolator, red & white porcelain, 7x30", EX ..**$95.00**

Sign, Tenneco, blue, white & red porcelain, 14¾x9½", EX.**$15.00**

Sign, Texaco Sky Chief, red, green, black & white porcelain, marked Made in USA 3-10-47, 18x12", EX.........**$150.00**

Sign, US Tire Co, blue, yellow & white frosted glass, 14¾x11¾", EX...**$35.00**

Sign, Weed Chains Life Savers for Safe-Sure-Traction, chromolithograph standee, 27¼x20½" **$75.00**

Tanker ship (toy), w/display box, Texaco, motorized, plastic, logo on smokestacks, dealer offer, 26½x5" **$180.00**

Thermometer, Pennzoil, Liberty Bell in center, white, red & black, EX+ **$125.00**

Thermometer, Prestone Anti-Freeze, porcelain, ca 1940s, 8¾x36", EX...**$100.00**

Thermometer, Standard Oil, Joe Darnall/Agent, LA 7-4391, Benton KY, metal, 3¼x11½", VG **$45.00**

Thermometer, Valentine & Co, Valentines Varnishes, celluloid, black w/red & white lettering, 20x5½", EX **$110.00**

Tin, American Motors Coolant, 1-qt, unused, M **$25.00**

Tin, Atlantic #1 Lubricant A, red, white & blue lithographed tin, VG **$20.00**

Tin, Champlin S-3, dark blue w/silver logo, 1-qt, unused, NM **$20.00**

Tin, Macmillan Grease, M & Ring Free, red & white, 1-lb.**$15.00**

Toy gas pump, Marx, tin w/milk glass globes, battery-operated, early style, 9½x6", EX **$275.00**

Gaudy Italian

I'm sure you've seen these ceramic items around, marked on the bottom with only 'Italy,' usually handwritten in ink. The ware (circa mid-fifties through the seventies) is handmade and may be decorated with applied flowers and leaves that have been formed a section at a time by the decorator, whose palm prints are sometimes visible. It's hand painted as well, and some of the floral designs remind you of Blue Ridge. Fruit and animal designs were evidently also popular. Just recently collectors have started to show some interest in this type of pottery, which they have christened 'Gaudy Italian' (and most of it is!). Though many items can still be found for $5.00 and under, we've listed values for some of the more interesting pieces below.

Advisor: April Tvorak (See Directory, Fire-King)

Vase, unusual volcanic glaze, geometrics, 7½", $8.00.

Basket, lg, 10" to 8", from $20 to **$22.00**
Basket, med, 6" to 8", from $10 to **$15.00**
Basket, sm, 4", from $6 to...**$8.00**
Bowl, vegetable; w/lid **$15.00**
Bowl, vegetable; 9" **$10.00**
Bowl, 10½" dia **$15.00**
Box, ring; sm...**$5.00**
Cigarette box, square...**$15.00**
Lamp, bedroom; sm, from $20 to.............................**$35.00**
Lamp, living room; lg, minimum value.....................**$45.00**
Plate, dinner **$8.00**

Gay Fad Glassware

What started out as a home-based 'one-woman' operation in the late 1930s within only a few years had grown into a substantial company requiring much larger facilities and a staff of decorators. The company, dubbed Gay Fad by her husband, was founded by Fran Taylor. Originally they decorated kitchenware items but later found instant success with the glassware they created, most of which utilized frosted backgrounds and multicolored designs such as tulips, state themes, Christmas motifs, etc. Some pieces were decorated with 22-karat gold and sterling silver. In addition to the frosted glass which collectors quickly learn to associate with this company, they also became famous for their 'bentware' — quirky cocktail glasses whose stems were actually bent.

Some of their more collectible lines are 'Beau Brummel' — martini glasses with straight or bent stems featuring a funny-faced drinker wearing a plaid bow tie; 'Gay Nineties' — various designs such as can-can girls and singing bartenders; '48 States' — maps with highlighted places of interest; 'Rich Man, Poor Man' (or beggar man, thief, etc.); 'Bartender' (self-explanatory); 'Currier & Ives' — made to coordinate with the line by Royal China; 'Zombies' — extra tall and slim with various designs including roses, giraffes, and flamingos; and the sterling silver- and 22-karat gold-trimmed glassware.

Until you learn to spot it a mile away (which you soon will), look for an interlocking 'G' and 'F' or 'Gay Fad,' the latter mark indicating pieces from the late 1950s to the early 1960s. The glassware itself has the feel of satin and is of very good quality. It can be distinguished from other manufacturers' wares simply by checking the bottom — Gay Fad's are frosted; generally other manufacturers' are not. Hand-painted details are another good clue. (You may find similar glassware signed 'Briard'; this is not Gay Fad.)

This Ohio-based company was sold in 1963 and closed altogether in 1965. Be careful of condition. If the frosting has darkened or the paint is worn or faded, it's best to wait for a better example.

Advisor: Donna S. McGrady (See the Directory, Gay Fad)

Bent tray, Phoenix Bird, clear, signed Gay Fad, 13¾" dia...**$15.00**
Bent trays, classic design, paper label, 2 square trays in metal frame..**$22.00**
Beverage set, magnolia, clear, 86-oz pitcher & 6 13-oz tumblers **$45.00**

Chip n' Dip, Horace the Horse w/cart, knife tail, 3 bowls, double old-fashion glass as head, signed Gay Fad...**$60.00**
Cocktail shaker, ballerina, frosted, 28-oz **$35.00**
Decanter set, Gay '90s, Scotch, Rye, Gin & Bourbon, frosted or white inside **$80.00**
Luncheon set, Fantasia Hawaiian Flower, 1 place setting (square plate, cup & saucer)................................**$15.00**
Mug, Notre Dame, frosted, 16-oz.................................**$15.00**
Pitcher, Currier & Ives, blue & white, frosted, 86-oz..**$50.00**
Pitcher, martini; cardinal & pine sprig, frosted, w/glass stirrer, 42-oz **$35.00**
Pitcher, tulips (rosemaling), white inside, 32-oz **$28.00**
Punch set, turquoise veiling, bowl & 8 cups in metal frame...**$65.00**
Salad set, fruits, frosted, lg bowl, 2 cruets, salt & pepper shakers **$50.00**
Stem, bent cocktail, Beau Brummel, clear, signed Gay Fad, 3½-oz **$12.00**
Stem, bent cocktail, Souvenir of My Bender, frosted, 3-oz.**$11.00**
Tom & Jerry set, Christmas bells, milk white, marked GF, bowl & 6 cups...**$70.00**
Tumbler, Christmas Greetings From Gay Fad, frosted, 4-oz **$12.00**
Tumbler, Derby Winner Citation, frosted, 1948, 14-oz..**$50.00**
Tumbler, grouse, brown, aqua & gold on clear, signed Gay Fad, 10-oz..**$8.00**
Tumbler, Kentucky state map (1 of 48), pink, yellow or lime, frosted, marked GF, 10-oz.......................................**$5.00**
Tumbler, Pegasus, gold & pink on black, 12-oz **$8.00**
Tumbler, Say When, frosted, 4-oz **$5.00**
Tumbler, Zombie, flamingo, frosted, marked GF, 14-oz.**$15.00**

Tumbler, highly stylized cats design, from $4.00 to $6.00. (Photo courtesy Donna McGrady)

Tumblers, Dickens Christmas Carol characters, frosted, 12-oz, set of 8...**$65.00**
Tumblers, French Poodle, clear, 17-oz, set of 8 in original box **$96.00**
Tumblers, Ohio Presidents, frosted, 12-oz, set of 8....**$60.00**
Tumblers, Rich Man, Poor Man (nursery rhyme), frosted, marked GF, 16-oz, set of 8.....................................**$95.00**
Vanity set, butterflies in meadow, pink inside, 5-pc...**$60.00**
Waffle set, Little Black Sambo, frosted, 48-oz waffle batter jug, 11½-oz syrup jug...**$200.00**

Waffle set, red poppy, frosted, 48-oz waffle batter jug, 11½-oz syrup jug **$24.00**

Geisha Girl China

The late nineteenth century saw a rise in the popularity of Oriental wares in the US and Europe. Japan rose to meet the demands of this flourishing ceramics market place by a flurry of growth in potteries and decorating centers. These created items for export which would appeal to Western tastes and integrate into Western dining and decorating cultures, which were distinct from those of Japan. One example of the wares introduced into this market place was Geisha Girl porcelian.

Hundreds of different patterns and manufacturers' marks have been uncovered on Geisha Girl porcelain tea, dinner, dresser, decorative items, etc., which were produced well into the twentieth century. They all share in common colorful decorations featuring kimono-clad ladies and children involved in everyday activities. These scenes are set against a backdrop of lush flora, distinctive Japanese architecture, and majestic landscapes. Most Geisha Girl porcelain designs were laid on by means of a stencil, generally red or black. This appears as an outline on the ceramic body. Details are then completed by hand-painted washes in a myriad of colors. A minority of the wares were wholly hand painted.

Most Geisha Girl porcelain has a colorful border or edging with handles, finials, spouts, and feet similarly adorned. The most common border color is a red which can range from orange to red-orange to a deep brick red. Among the earliest used border colors were red, maroon, cobalt blue, light (apple) green, and Nile green. Pine green, blue-green, and turquoise made their appearance circa 1917, and a light cobalt or Delft blue appeared around 1920. Other colors (e.g. tan, yellow, brown, and gold) can also be found. Borders were often enhanced with guilded lace or floral decoration. The use of gold for this purpose diminished somewhat around 1910 to 1915 when some decorators used economic initiative (fewer firings required) to move the gold to just inside the border or replace the gold with white or yellow enamels. Wares with both border styles continued to be produced into the twentieth century. Exquisite examples with multicolor borders as well as ornate rims decorated with floras and geometrics can also be found.

Due to the number of different producers, the quality of Geisha ware ranges from crude to finely detailed. Geisha Girl porcelain was sold in sets and open stock in outlets ranging from the five-and-ten to fancy department stores. It was creatively used for store premiums, containers for store products, fair souvenirs, and resort memorabilia. The fineness of detailing, amount of gold highlights, border color, scarcity of form and, of course, condition all play a role in establishing the market value of a given item. Some patterns are scarcer than others, but most Geisha collectors seem not to focus on particular patterns.

The heyday of Geisha Girl porcelain was from the 1910s through the 1930s. Production continued until the World War II era. During the 'Occupied' period, a small amount of wholly hand-painted examples were made, often with a black and gold border. The Oriental import stores and catalogs from the 1960s and 1970s featured some examples of Geisha Girl porcelain, many of which were produced in Hong Kong. These are recognized by the very white porcelain, sparse detail coloring, and lack of gold decoration. The 1990s has seen a resurgence of reproductions with a faux Nippon mark. These items are supposed to represent high quality Geisha ware, but in reality they are a blur of Geisha and Satsuma-style characteristics. They are too busy in design, too heavily enameled, and bear poor resemblance to items that rightfully carry Noritake's Green M-in-Wreath Nippon mark. Once you've been introduced to a few of these reproductions, you'll be easily able to recognize them.

Note: Colors mentioned in the following listings refer to borders.

Advisor: Elyce Litts (See Directory, Geisha Girl China)

Berry set, Dragonboat, couple w/boy & girl in sampan, dragon head at bow, cobalt & gold, master+5 individual, 6-pc..**$125.00**

Bisquit jar, Basket of Mums B, lady & child w/mums, 2 ladies on balcony, 3-footed, melon ribbed, red w/gold.**$58.00**

Bonbon, Garden Bench B, 2 ladies on either side of bench, others stroll garden, hand-fluted edge, footed, green & gold..**$42.00**

Bowl, Boy's Processional, ladies w/sm boys walk into distance from iris garden, red-orange w/yellow, 9½"...........**$50.00**

Bowl, Chinese Coin, Battledore, Washday & Flower Gathering scenic reserves, maple leaves & stylized wind, 7½"..**$75.00**

Bowl, dessert; Fan A, 2 to 5 ladies w/fans cross bridge, cobalt w/backdrop of dots, phoenix & mums, 4-lobed..**$14.00**

Bowl, Ikebana in Rickshaw, flower arranger in floral headdress, 3-footed, 6-lobed, scalloped edge, cobalt & gold **$40.00**

Bowl, nut (master); Bamboo Trellis, 3 ladies by water's edge, peony-covered trellis beyond, 9-lobed, 3 feet, dark green **$38.00**

Butter pat, Geisha Face, head or bust of lady, red line as interior frame, geisha in cherry blossom-shape reserve....**$12.00**

Cake platter, International Day, lady w/hand puppet & boy in sailor suit in garden, pierced lobes, cobalt & gold border..**$70.00**

Cocoa pot, Basket A, 4 ladies gathering cockle shells, mums & reeds on bank, conical w/melon ribs, green w/gold, 8"..**$75.00**

Cocoa pot, Battledore, ladies & children playing game, butterflies, cranes & mums, ewer shape, yellow-green, 9"..**$95.00**

Cocoa pot, Courtesan Processional, ladies & manservant w/umbrella cross bridge, lg maple leaves, cobalt & gold border **$90.00**

Cocoa pot, Gardening, 3 ladies tend mum garden, ladies on porch in background, fluted, red-orange w/yellow.**$45.00**

Creamer, Carp C, 2 ladies & girl hold string of rice cakes, mother & infant on opposing bank, ribbed hourglass shape **$25.00**

Creamer, Chinese Coin, Battledore & scenic reserves...**$28.00**

Cup & saucer, bouillon; Garden Bench O, lady on bench w/lady standing by her side, fluted, red w/gold buds **$40.00**

Cup & saucer, cocoa; Fan D, ladies w/round fans in garden, fluted, flower shape, scalloped gold border over cobalt.................**$35.00**

Cup & saucer, demitasse; Chrysanthemum Garden, ladies stroll garden, gold-laced interior, flower shape, red w/yellow.................**$25.00**

Cup & saucer, demitasse; Flower Gathering D, w/2 other patterns, cobalt w/gold slashes & buds, red handle, reserves.................**$25.00**

Cup & saucer, demitasse; Geisha in Cards, sm figure in spade or diamond shapes, bamboo leaf backdrop, wavy red w/gold **$20.00**

Cup & saucer, tea; Bamboo Tree, Processional-type pattern w/green bamboo trees, green band at rim...........**$25.00**

Cup & saucer, tea; Bamboo Trellis, 3 ladies at water's edge, peony-covered trellis beyond, red w/gold & florals inside.................**$15.00**

Cup & saucer, tea; Bamboo Trellis, 3 ladies at water's edge, peony-covered trellis beyond, dark green, #20....**$20.00**

Cup & saucer, tea; Battledore, ladies & children playing game, cranes in cherry blossoms, cherry blossom interior ...**$25.00**

Cup & saucer, tea; Blue Hoo, cobalt hoo perched in tree w/strolling ladies below, diapered diamond border..**$20.00**

Cup & saucer, tea; Boy With Sythe, boy cuts path for 2 ladies, cobalt w/gold **$20.00**

Cup & saucer, tea; Child Reaching for Butterfly, 2 ladies in garden, red-orange band.................**$10.00**

Cup & saucer, tea; Inside the Teahouse, interior view of house w/lady holding bamboo dipper, red-orange w/gold buds **$24.00**

Dresser box, Boat Festival, dragon & rooster-decorated boats, red-orange, #19, gold lacing on interior, 6" dia........**$38.00**

Egg cup, Cherry Blossom Ikebana, artisan arranging blossoms in pot, tradesman approaching, red **$15.00**

Ewer, Garden Bench H, lady w/round fan sitting on bench, lanterns & textile screens at back, gold leaves, red-orange, 5" **$38.00**

Hair receiver, Carp A, school of carp w/lady & child watching from bank, ladies on balcony, scalloped cobalt w/gold.......**$40.00**

Jug, Battledore, ladies & children playing game, butterflies & mums w/cranes in cherry blossoms, ribbed body, 5".............**$45.00**

Marmalade jar, Cloud A, stylized clouds as backdrop for ladies & children w/many accessories, melon ribbed, red-orange **$55.00**

Miniature lamp, painted entirely by hand, Parasol pattern variant with red and gold neck, handles and feet, scarce, $50.00.

Mug, lemonade; Geisha in Sampan B, ladies in sampan poled by manservant, cobalt blue w/gold.................**$15.00**

Mustard jar, Child Reaching for Butterfly, 2 ladies in garden, red.................**$20.00**

Napkin ring, Flower Gathering C, lady w/mums & child in garden, semicircular, red **$25.00**

Nappy, Garden Bench F, 2 ladies leaving bench, boy playing near water, 4-lobed, S-shaped handle, red & gold .**$35.00**

Pitcher, Garden Bench C, seated lady w/open fan near water's edge, child points to water, cobalt & gold border, 4"..**$28.00**

Plate, Duck Watching B, lady & child to left w/lady on bench to right of stream watching ducks, blue-green & white, 7".................**$15.00**

Salt & pepper shakers, Blind Man's Bluff, blindfolded lady in mum garden, swirl-fluted body, light apple green, pr **$20.00**

Salt & pepper shakers, Cloud B, stylized cloud backdrop for ladies w/instruments, green decals, blossoms at top, pr **$20.00**

Sauce dish, Bamboo Trellis, 3 ladies at water's edge, peony-covered trellis beyond, 8-lobed, red w/gold **$15.00**

Toothpick holder, Court Lady, lady w/floral headdress & kimono kneeling on tatami mat, 5-sided, footed, coralene & gold.................**$42.00**

GI Joe

The first GI Joe was introduced by Hasbro in 1964. He was 12" tall, and you could buy him with blond, auburn, black, or brown hair in four basic variations: Action Sailor, Action Marine, Action Soldier, and Action Pilot. There was also a Black doll as well as representatives of many other nations. By 1967, GI Joe could talk, all the better to converse with the female nurse who was first issued that year. The Adventure Team series (1970 – 1976) included Black Adventurer, Talking Astronaut, Sea Adventurer, Talking Team Commander, Land Adventurer, and several variations. At this point, their hands were made of rubber, making it easier for them to hold onto the many guns, tools, and other accessories that Hasbro had devised. Playsets, vehicles and articles of clothing completed the package, and there were kid-size items designed specifically for the kids themselves. The 12" dolls were discontinued by 1976.

Brought out by popular demand, Hasbro's 3¾" GI Joes hit the market in 1982. Needless to say, they were very well accepted. In fact, these smaller GI Joes are thought to be the most successful line of action figures ever made. Loose (removed from the original packaging) figures are very common, and even if you can locate the accessories that they came out with, most are worth only about $3.00 to $10.00. It's the mint-in-package items that most interest collectors, and they pay a huge premium for the package. There's an extensive line of accessories that go along with the smaller line as well. Many more are listed in *Schroeder's Collectible Toys, Antique to Modern,* and *Collector's Guide to Dolls in Uniform* by Joseph Bourgeois, both published by Collector Books.

12" Figures and Accessories

Action Pilot Coveralls, G **$4.00**
Adventure Team Poncho, camouflage, EX.................**$6.00**

Air Cadet Hat, EX..$25.00
Airborne Military Police Pants, tan, EX...................$25.00
Annapolis Cadet Belt, EX......................................$40.00
Annapolis Cadet Jacket, G....................................$25.00
Astro Locker, EX..$190.00
Australian Hat, EX..$25.00
Bivouac Machine Gun Set, #7514, MOC...................$60.00
British Pants, EX...$32.00
Combat Camouflage Netting Set, #7511, MOC...........$25.00
Command Post Poncho, green, #7519, MOC..............$55.00
Crash Crew Jacket & Pants, EX..............................$30.00
Crash Crew Set, #7820, M (VG box)......................$260.00
Deep Sea Diver Sledge Hammer, EX........................$12.00
Demolition Set, complete, M (EX box).....................$85.00
Dog Tag, VG...$20.00
Field Phone, brown vinyl, VG...................................$5.00

Figure, Action Marine, EX, $150.00.

Figure, Action Pilot, 30th Anniversary, 1994, MIB (sealed)..$140.00
Figure, Action Soldier, 30th Anniversary, 1994, MIB (sealed)..$100.00
Figure, Adventure Team Intruder Soldier, original outfit, VG..$30.00
Figure, Astronaut, complete w/accessories, EX.........$185.00
Figure, Deep Sea Diver, complete w/accessories, VG..$160.00
Figure, Fighter Pilot, complete w/accessories, EX....$365.00
Figure, French Resistance Fighter, complete w/accessories, NM...$275.00
Figure, Japanese Imperial Soldier, complete w/accessories, M..$625.00
Figure, Marine Demolition, complete w/accessories, EX..$150.00
Figure, Navy Attack, complete w/accessories, EX....$225.00
Figure, Sabotage Set w/Action Marine, complete w/accessories, EX...$250.00
Figure, Shore Patrol, complete w/accessories, VG...$265.00
Figure, Ski Patrol, complete w/accessories, VG........$175.00
Figure, West Point Cadet, complete w/accessories, EX...$185.00
Fire Fighter Accessories, Action Man, complete, M (VG card)..$18.00
French Greatcoat, French Foreign Legion, Action Man, MOC..$30.00
French 7.65 Light Machine Gun, Action Man, MIP.....$15.00
German Beret Bazooka, w/2 shells, EX....................$32.00
German Field Pack, EX..$25.00

German Lugar Pistol, EX.......................................$20.00
Green Beret French Radio, EX...............................$14.00
Green Beret Pants, VG...$20.00
Highway Hazard Accessories, Action Man, M (VG card)..$20.00
Indian Brave, Action Man, complete, M (EX box)......$60.00
Japanese Jacket, EX...$10.00
Life Ring, MOC...$45.00
Medic Arm Band, EX..$15.00
Mess Kit, EX..$10.00
Military Police Trousers, brown, MOC.....................$70.00

Paths of Danger, 1977, MIP, from $55.00 to $60.00.

Pistol, .45 caliber, revolver-type, black, EX...............$6.00
Russian Grenade, EX..$10.00
Russian Soldier Equipment, #8302B, MIP...............$250.00
Scuba Tank, orange, EX..$8.00
Shore Patrol Sea Bag, #7615, MOC........................$40.00
Space Coveralls, white, EX....................................$30.00
Stethoscope, EX...$8.00
Vehicle, Action Pack Turbo Copter, MIB (sealed).......$50.00
Vehicle, Adventure Team Skyhawk, 1975, MIB (sealed)..$110.00
Vehicle, Big Trapper, VG.......................................$75.00
Vehicle, British Armored Car, Irwin, EX..................$275.00
Vehicle, Iron Knight Tank, Action Man, M (NM box)..$175.00
Vehicle, Survival Raft, Action Man, complete w/accessories, MIB..$45.00

Volcano Jumper, MIP, from $50.00 to $55.00.

White Tiger Set, complete, EX................................$50.00
Wrist Camera, EX...$10.00

3¾" Figures and Accessories

Armadillo Mini Tank, 1984, EX................................$8.00

Battle Gear Accessory Pack #1, 1983, MIP $16.00
Cobra Ferret, 1984, EX $12.00
Cobra Pom Pom Gun, 1983, EX $12.00
Cobra Wolf w/Ice Viper, 1985, EX $18.00
Dictator, 1989, w/instructions, EX $10.00
Figure, Ace, complete w/accessories, 1983, MIP $25.00
Figure, Alpine, complete w/accessories, 1986, MIP $30.00
Figure, Astro Viper, complete w/accessories, MIP $12.00
Figure, Big Boa, complete w/accessories, 1987, MIP .$25.00
Figure, Captain Grid Iron, complete w/accessories, 1990, MIP...$11.00
Figure, Cobra Soldier, complete w/accessories, 1983, MIP .$62.00

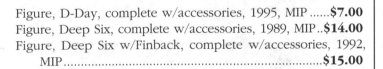

Figure, Crystal Ball, 1986, MIP, $15.00.

Figure, D-Day, complete w/accessories, 1995, MIP $7.00
Figure, Deep Six, complete w/accessories, 1989, MIP..$14.00
Figure, Deep Six w/Finback, complete w/accessories, 1992, MIP $15.00

Figure, Dial Tone, 1985, MIP, $32.00.

Figure, Duck, complete w/accessories, 1984, MIP....$105.00
Figure, Flint, complete w/accessories, 1985, MIP $55.00
Figure, Heavy Duty, complete w/accessories, 1991, MIP ..$8.00
Figure, Iceberg, complete w/accessories, 1986, MIP ..$32.00
Figure, Leatherneck, complete w/accessories, 1983-85, MIP $25.00
Figure, Mainframe, complete w/accessories, 1986, MIP..$32.00
Figure, Raptor, complete w/accessories, 1987, MIP $20.00
Figure, Shockwave, complete w/accessories, 1988, MIP..$22.00
Figure, Snake Eyes, complete w/accessories, 1989, MIP..$30.00
Figure, Sub-Zero, complete w/accessories, 1990, MIP..$10.00
Figure, Tele-Viper, complete w/accessories, 1985, MIP..$42.00
Figure, Zandar, complete w/accessories, 1983-85, MIP...$18.00

Flame Thrower, 1983, EX..$5.00
Locust, complete w/instructions, 1989, EX.................$10.00
Missile Defense Unit, 1984, MIP $20.00
Mountain Howitzer, complete w/accessories, 1984, EX..$8.00
Pogo, complete w/instructions, 1987, EX $8.00
Q Force Battle Gear, Action Force, MIP........................$4.00
Sky Patrol Drop Zone, brown, w/parachute pack, 1990, MIP $18.00
Swamp Skier w/Zartan, complete w/ID card, 1983, EX ..$45.00
Tiger Fish, 1988, w/instructions, EX............................$10.00
Weapons Transport, 1984, EX......................................$12.00

Glass Knives

Popular during the Depression years, glass knives were made in many of the same colors as the glass dinnerware of the era — pink, green, light blue, crystal, and once in awhile even amber, forest green, or white (originally called opal). Some were decorated by hand with flowers or fruit. Collectors will accept reground, resharpened blades as long as the original shape has been maintained. By their very nature, they were naturally prone to chipping, and mint condition examples are uncommon.

Glass knives are often found in original boxes which sometimes included original inserts extolling their virtues — purity of materials for their production and lack of metallic tastes when used in food preparation.

Advisor: Adrienne Escoe (See Directory, Glass Knives)

Club: *Glass Knife Collectors' Club*
Adrienne Escoe
4448 Ironwood Ave.
Seal Beach, CA 90740
562-430-6479 Send SASE for information.

Aer-Flo (Grid), forest green, 7½" $250.00
Aer-Flo (Grid), pink, 7½" $75.00
Block, green...$30.00
Block, pink, Atlantic City engraving, 8¼"....................$30.00
Block, vaseline, rare color $70.00
Butter, green or crystal, 6¼" $25.00

Candlewick, crystal, Imperial, 8½", $350.00. (Photo courtesy Adrienne Escoe)

Dur-X (3-Leaf), crystal, 8½" $12.00
Dur-X (5-Leaf), blue, 9¼"..$20.00
Dur-X (5-Leaf), crystal, 8½" $12.00
Plain handle, light pink, 9" $35.00
Stonex, amber, 8¼" $135.00
Vitex (3-Star), blue, 9¼", MIB......................................$28.00

Vitex (3-Star), crystal, 8½"...............$10.00
Vitex (3-Star), pink, 9¼"..................$28.00

Golden Foliage

In 1935 Libbey Glass was purchased by Owens-Illinois, but continued to operate under the Libbey Glass name. After World War II, the company turned to making tableware and still does today. Golden Foliage is just one of the many patterns made during the 1950s. It is a line of crystal glassware with a satin band that features a golden maple leaf as well as others. The satin band is trimmed in gold, above and below.

Advisor: Debbie Coe (See Directory, Cape Cod)

Drink set, includes 6 jiggers & brass-finished caddy ..**$35.00**
Drink set, includes 8 tumblers (9-oz), ice tub & brass finished
    caddy **$50.00**
Drink set, includes 8 tumblers (9-oz) & brass finished
    caddy **$36.00**
Goblet, cocktail; 4-oz......................**$5.00**
Goblet, cordial; 1-oz.......................**$8.50**
Goblet, pilsner; 11-oz......................**$8.50**
Goblet, sherbet; 6½-oz......................**$3.50**

Goblet, water; 9-oz, $6.50. Tumbler, water; 10-oz, $6.50.

Ice tub **$14.50**
Pitcher, 5¼", w/metal frame **$12.50**
Salad dressing set, includes 3 bowls (4") & brass finished
    caddy..................................**$14.75**
Tumbler, beverage; 12½-oz...................**$8.50**
Tumbler, cooler; 14-oz......................**$9.50**
Tumbler, jigger; 2-oz.......................**$7.00**
Tumbler, juice; 6-oz........................**$5.00**
Tumbler, old fashioned; 9-oz................**$4.50**

Griswold Cast-Iron Cooking Ware

Late in the 1800s, the Griswold company introduced a line of cast-iron cooking ware that was eventually distributed on a large scale nationwide. They also made a line of aluminum. Today's collectors appreciate the variety of skillets, cornstick pans, Dutch ovens, and griddles available to them, and many still enjoy using them to cook with.

Several marks have been used, most contain the Griswold name, though some were marked simply 'Erie.'

If you intend to use your cast iron, you can clean it safely by using any commercial oven cleaner. (Be sure to re-season it before you cook in it.) A badly pitted, rusty piece may leave you with no other recourse than to remove what rust you can with a wire brush, paint the surface black, and find an alternate use for it around the house. For instance, you might use a kettle to hold a large floor plant or some magazines. A small griddle or skillet would be attractive as part of a wall display in a country kitchen.

Advisors: Grant Windsor (See Directory, Griswold)

Aebleskiver pan, marked Griswold, #32 & Erie PA.....**$35.00**
Ashtray, #570A **$30.00**
Brownie cake pan, #9, full writing............**$150.00**
Cake mold, lamb, #866 ....**$125.00**
Cornstick pan, #273...........................**$25.00**
Dutch oven, #8 Tite Top, w/lid................**$50.00**
Dutch oven, #9 Tite-Top, w/trivet & lid **$100.00**
Golfball pan, #9, marked w/pattern #947 only **$100.00**
Grease pot, from $100 to......................**$150.00**

Griddle No. 8, marked Heat Slowly, $125.00.

Griddle, #10, slant logo+EPU..................**$50.00**
Kettle, Erie #812, from $75 to................**$100.00**
Long pan or iron heater, #9...................**$150.00**
Muffin pan, #17, w/narrow center band, from $175 to...**$225.00**
Patty bowl, #871, from $100 to **$125.00**
Platter, oval, tree type, from $100 to........**$125.00**
Plett pan, #34, block logo, from $75 to **$125.00**
Popover pan, #18..............................**$85.00**
Saucepan, aluminum, block logo, 2-qt **$45.00**
Scotch bowl, #3, Erie...USA...................**$50.00**
Skillet, #3, square...........................**$200.00**
Skillet, #6, slant logo+EPU **$40.00**
Skillet, #8, chicken fryer, smooth bottom, w/lid, from $100
    to.....................................**$125.00**
Skillet, #9, Victor...........................**$45.00**
Skillet, #14, bail handle, from $1,200 to.....**$1,400.00**
Skillet, egg; #53, square, from $35 to........**$40.00**

Skillet lid, #8, high-dome, top writing $50.00
Vienna roll pan, #6...$200.00
Waffle iron, #7, May 21, 1901, from $100 to $125.00
Waffle iron, #8, Pat 1901 ....$45.00
Waffle iron, #11, square, high base...........................$150.00
Waffle iron, #11, square, low base............................$200.00

Griddle, cast aluminum, 7½x16½", $45.00.

Hall China Company

Hall China is still in production in East Liverpool, Ohio, where they have been located since around the turn of the century. They have produced literally hundreds of lines of kitchen and dinnerware items for both home and commercial use. Several of these in particular have become very collectible.

They're especially famous for their teapots, some of which were shaped like automobiles, basketballs, donuts, and footballs. Each teapot was made in an assortment of colors, often trimmed in gold. Many were decaled to match their dinnerware lines. Some are quite rare, and collecting them all would be a real challenge.

During the 1950s, Eva Zeisel designed dinnerware shapes with a streamlined, ultra-modern look. Her lines, Classic and Century, were used with various decals as the basis for several of Hall's dinnerware patterns. She also designed kitchenware lines with the same modern styling. They were called Casual Living and Tri-Tone. All her designs are popular with today's collectors.

Although some of the old kitchenware shapes and teapots are being produced today, you'll be able to tell them from the old pieces by the backstamp. To identify these new issues, Hall marks them with the shaped rectangular 'Hall' trademark they've used since the early 1970s.

For more information, we recommend *The Collector's Encyclopedia of Hall China* by Margaret and Kenn Whitmyer.

Newsletter: *Hall China Collector's Club Newsletter*
P.O. Box 360488, Cleveland, OH 44136

Acacia, casserole, Medallion $35.00
Acacia, salt & pepper shakers, handles, pr..................$32.00
Arizona, bowl, coupe soup; Tomorrow's Classic, 9".....$9.00
Arizona, candlestick, Tomorrow's Classic $30.00
Arizona, onion soup, Tomorrow's Classic, w/lid $27.00
Arizona, platter, Tomorrow's Classic, 15"....................$22.00
Beauty, bowl, Radiance, 9"...$27.00
Beauty, bowl, salad; 9½"..$27.00

Beauty, casserole, Thick Rim......................................$37.00
Blue Blossom, casserole, Five Band...........................$60.00
Blue Blossom, casserole, Thick Rim...........................$60.00
Blue Blossom, cookie jar, Five Band $195.00
Blue Blossom, salt & pepper shakers, Five Band, pr .$50.00
Blue Bouquet, bean pot, New England, #4.............$150.00
Blue Bouquet, bowl, Radiance, 6"............................$14.00
Blue Bouquet, cake plate...$30.00
Blue Bouquet, salt & pepper shakers, teardrop shape, pr..$34.00
Blue Bouquet, spoon $125.00
Blue Bouquet, tray, metal, rectangular.......................$30.00
Blue Crocus, salt & pepper shakers, handled, pr $60.00
Blue Floral, bowl, 6¼" $12.00
Blue Floral, bowl, 9"..$18.00
Blue Floral, casserole...$30.00
Blue Garden, casserole, Sundial, #4...........................$25.00
Blue Garden, custard, Thick Rim $15.00
Blue Garden, leftover, loop handle.............................$95.00
Blue Garden, teapot, Sundial...................................$200.00
Blue Willow, teapot, Boston, 2-cup.........................$250.00
Bouquet, casserole, Tomorrow's Classic, 2-qt $42.00
Bouquet, celery dish, oval, Tomorrow's Classic..........$19.00
Bouquet, egg cup, Tomorrow's Classic.......................$30.00
Bouquet, plate, Tomorrow's Classic, 8".......................$7.50
Bouquet, salt & pepper shakers, Tomorrow's Classic, pr..$22.00
Bouquet, teapot, Tomorrow's Classic, 6-cup $95.00
Buckingham, bowl, salad; Tomorrow's Classic, 14½".$32.00
Buckingham, casserole, Tomorrow's Classic, 2-qt.......$37.00
Buckingham, cup & saucer, Tomorrow's Classic..........$8.50
Cactus, bowl, Radiance, 9"..$32.00
Cactus, coffeepot, Viking Drip-o-lator........................$35.00
Cactus, salt & pepper shakers, Five Band, pr $44.00
Cameo Rose, butter dish, E-style, ¼-lb $50.00
Cameo Rose, cup & saucer, E-style $10.50
Cameo Rose, gravy boat w/underplate, E-style...........$32.00
Cameo Rose, plate, E-style, 10" $11.00
Cameo Rose, salt & pepper shakers, E-style, pr..........$25.00
Cameo Rose, teapot, E-style, 8-cup $60.00
Caprice, casserole, Tomorrow's Classic, 2-qt $27.00
Caprice, cup, AD; Tomorrow's Classic.........................$7.50
Caprice, sugar bowl, Tomorrow's Classic, w/lid $16.00
Carrot/Golden Carrot, bowl, Five Band, 6" $18.00
Carrot/Golden Carrot, bowl, Thick Rim, 8½" $27.00
Carrot/Golden Carrot, casserole, oval, 11½" $75.00
Christmas Tree & Holly, bowl, oval, E-style $30.00
Christmas Tree & Holly, bowl, plum pudding; E-style, 4½" ..$14.00
Christmas Tree & Holly, cup & saucer, E-style............$22.00
Christmas Tree & Holly, mug, Irish coffee; E-style, 3-oz .$22.00
Christmas Tree & Holly, tidbit, 2-tier, E-style...............$55.00
Clover (Pink), baker, round, #503, 6"..........................$22.00
Clover (Pink), canister, Radiance...............................$150.00
Clover/Golden Clover, ball jug, #3............................$120.00
Clover/Golden Clover, bowl, Radiance, 10" $37.00
Clover/Golden Clover, casserole, Radiance $42.00
Clover/Golden Clover, stack set $125.00
Crocus, bowl, flat soup; D-style, 8½".........................$22.00
Crocus, cake plate $30.00
Crocus, cake safe, metal..$35.00
Crocus, coffeepot, Meltdown, from $90 to.................$110.00

Crocus, mug, tankard style $45.00
Crocus, pie baker..$38.00
Crocus, plate, D-style, 7¼" $7.00
Crocus, soap dispenser, metal $35.00
Crocus, teapot, Boston, from $150 to $175.00
Eggshell, baker, fish shape, Dot, 13½" $45.00
Eggshell, bowl, Ribbed, Plaid or Swag, 7¼"...............$20.00
Eggshell, bowl, Thin Rim, Dot, 6" $13.00
Eggshell, casserole, Plaid or Swag, 8½" or 9¼" $55.00
Eggshell, mustard, Dot $35.00
Eggshell, salt & pepper shakers, Plaid or Swag, handled,
   pr $44.00

Fantasy, batter bowl, 5½x10½", $275.00.

Fantasy, creamer, morning set $32.00
Fantasy, egg cup, Tomorrow's Classic $25.00
Fantasy, jug, Donut $195.00
Fantasy, marmite, Tomorrow's Classic, w/lid $27.00
Fern, bowl, divided vegetable; Century.................$20.00
Fern, cup & saucer, Century $6.50
Fern, salt & pepper shakers, Century, pr...............$18.00
Five Band, bowl, batter; colors other than red or cobalt ..$30.00
Five Band, carafe, colors other than red or cobalt $90.00
Five Band, carafe, red or cobalt, 8⅞" $25.00
Five Band, jug, red or cobalt, 6¼" $25.00
Five Band, salt & pepper shakers, colors other than red or
   cobalt, pr $22.00
Flamingo, creamer, Viking $28.00
Flamingo, syrup, Five Band $125.00
Flareware, casserole, Gold Lace, 2-qt....................$25.00
Flareware, casserole, Radial, 3-pt $8.00
Floral Lattice, ball jug, #3.......................................$125.00
Floral Lattice, canister, Radiance...........................$125.00
Floral Lattice, onion soup, individual....................$35.00
Floral Lattice, salt & pepper shakers, handled, pr $36.00
French Flower, coffeepot, Washington...................$65.00
French Flower, teapot, French $45.00
Frost Flowers, bowl, open vegetable; square, Tomorrow's
   Classic, 8⅞" $18.00
Frost Flowers, candlestick, Tomorrow's Classic, 8" $35.00
Frost Flowers, cup & saucer, Tomorrow's Classic $9.50
Frost Flowers, plate, Tomorrow's Classic, 8" $6.50
Game Bird, bowl, Thick Rim, 7½" $16.00
Game Bird, casserole..$30.00
Game Bird, creamer, E-style $15.00

Game Bird, mug, coffee..$12.00
Game Bird, platter, E-style $25.00
Game Bird, sugar bowl, E-style, w/lid....................$25.00
Game Bird, teapot, New York $125.00
Gold Label, bowl, Thick Rim, 9" $16.00
Golden Glo, bean pot, New England, #4 ....$50.00
Golden Glo, creamer, Boston $12.00
Golden Glo, mug, Irish coffee..................................$20.00
Harlequin, ashtray, Tomorrow's Classic $7.00
Harlequin, casserole, Tomorrow's Classic, 8" $30.00
Harlequin, gravy boat, Tomorrow's Classic $25.00
Harlequin, plate, Tomorrow's Classic, 11" $12.00
Heather Rose, bowl, cereal; E-style, 6¼" $6.00
Heather Rose, coffeepot, Terrace $40.00
Heather Rose, gravy boat & underplate, E-style $20.00
Heather Rose, plate, E-style, 10".............................$8.50
Heather Rose, platter, oval, E-style, 15½" $20.00
Holiday, bowl, open vegetable; square, Tomorrow's Classic,
   8⅞"..$18.00
Holiday, butter dish, Tomorrow's Classic $85.00
Holiday, creamer, Tomorrow's Classic $9.00
Holiday, plate, Tomorrow's Classic, 8"...................$5.00
Holiday, vase, Tomorrow's Classic $27.00
Homewood, bowl, Radiance, 7½" $15.00
Homewood, coffeepot, Terrace $55.00
Homewood, cup & saucer, D-style...........................$8.50
Homewood, salt & pepper shakers, handles, pr.........$36.00
Lyric, bowl, fruit; Tomorrow's Classic, 5⅞" $5.00
Lyric, coffeepot, Tomorrow's Classic, 6-cup $80.00
Lyric, egg cup, Tomorrow's Classic $25.00
Lyric, plate, Tomorrow's Classic, 8".......................$4.50
Lyric, platter, Tomorrow's Classic, 15"...................$25.00
Meadow Flower, casserole, Sundial, #4..................$55.00
Meadow Flower, custard, Thick Rim........................$16.00
Meadow Flower, salt & pepper shakers, handled, pr .$44.00
Medallion, bowl, Chinese Red, #6, 10" $30.00
Medallion, bowl, ivory, #3, 6"..................................$3.50
Medallion, creamer, ivory...$4.00
Medallion, custard, Chinese Red.............................$9.00
Medallion, drip jar, Lettuce $14.00
Medallion, jug, Chinese Red, 7"..............................$28.00
Medallion, reamer, ivory $250.00
Medallion, stack set, Lettuce $55.00
Morning Glory, bowl, straight-sided, 4⅜"...............$16.00
Morning Glory, casserole, Thick Rim......................$32.00
Morning Glory, teapot, Aladdin...............................$125.00
Mulberry, bowl, cereal; Tomorrow's Classic, 6"............$7.00
Mulberry, cup & saucer, Tomorrow's Classic...............$8.50
Mulberry, plate, Tomorrow's Classic, 11"....................$10.00
Mulberry, teapot, Tomorrow's Classic, 6-cup $85.00
Mums, bowl, D-style, oval, 10¼"..............................$27.00
Mums, bowl, Radiance, 9"...$22.00
Mums, casserole, Medallion $40.00
Mums, coffeepot, Terrace $70.00
Mums, creamer, New York or Medallion, each $16.00
Mums, custard, Medallion $16.00
Mums, plate, D-style, 8¼"...$6.50
Mums, platter, D-style, oval, 13¼"............................$25.00
No 488, ball jug, red & yellow flower decals, #3 .....$125.00

No 488, bowl, flat soup; red & yellow flower decals, D-style, 8½"......**$25.00**

No 488, cup, red & yellow flower decals, D-style......**$14.00**

No 488, left-over, red & yellow flower decals, square..**$75.00**

No 488, platter, red & yellow flower decals, oval, D-style, 13¼"......**$30.00**

No 488, shirred egg dish, red & yellow flower decals..**$35.00**

No 488, sugar bowl, red & yellow flower decals, Art Deco, w/lid......**$32.00**

No 488, teapot, red & yellow flower decals, Radiance..**$225.00**

Orange Poppy, bean pot, New England, #4......**$95.00**

Orange Poppy, bowl, Radiance, 9"......**$22.00**

Orange Poppy, bowl, round vegetable; C-style, 9¼"..**$35.00**

Orange Poppy, bread box, metal......**$50.00**

Orange Poppy, cake safe, metal......**$20.00**

Orange Poppy, coffeepot, Great American......**$55.00**

Orange Poppy, cup & saucer, C-style......**$19.00**

Orange Poppy, custard......**$7.00**

Orange Poppy, mustard, w/liner......**$57.00**

Orange Poppy, plate, C-style, 7¼"......**$8.00**

Orange Poppy, platter, C-style, oval, 11¼"......**$22.00**

Orange Poppy, salt & pepper shakers, handled, pr..**$32.00**

Orange Poppy, salt & pepper shakers, teardrop, pr...**$50.00**

Orange Poppy, teapot, Boston......**$180.00**

Orange Poppy, wastebasket, metal......**$50.00**

Pastel Morning Glory, ball jug, #3......**$110.00**

Pastel Morning Glory, bowl, D-style, oval......**$25.00**

Pastel Morning Glory, bowl, Radiance, 9"......**$22.00**

Pastel Morning Glory, cake plate......**$22.00**

Pastel Morning Glory, coffeepot, Terrace......**$70.00**

Pastel Morning Glory, gravy boat, D-style......**$27.00**

Pastel Morning Glory, leftover, rectangular......**$60.00**

Pastel Morning Glory, platter, D-style, 13¼"......**$25.00**

Pastel Morning Glory, salt & pepper shakers, handled, pr....**$32.00**

Peach Blossom, bowl, coupe soup; Tomorrow's Classic, 9"..**$11.00**

Peach Blossom, bowl, footed fruit; Tomorrow's Classic, lg...**$32.00**

Peach Blossom, creamer, AD; Tomorrow's Classic......**$12.00**

Peach Blossom, ladle, Tomorrow's Classic......**$20.00**

Peach Blossom, salt & pepper shakers, Tomorrow's Classic, pr......**$22.00**

Pert, bean pot, Chinese Red, tab handles......**$60.00**

Pert, bowl, Cadet, straight-sided, 5¼"......**$8.00**

Pert, custard, Cadet, straight-sided......**$5.00**

Pert, salt & pepper shakers, Chinese Red, pr......**$22.00**

Pert, sugar bowl, Cadet......**$7.00**

Pert, teapot, Cadet, 3-cup......**$16.00**

Pinecone, casserole, Tomorrow's Classic, 1¼-qt......**$25.00**

Pinecone, gravy boat, Tomorrow's Classic......**$25.00**

Pinecone, mug, Tomorrow's Classic......**$25.00**

Pinecone, tidbit, 3-tier, E-style......**$45.00**

Primrose, ashtray, E-style......**$10.00**

Primrose, bowl, flat soup; E-style, 8"......**$10.00**

Primrose, creamer, E-style......**$8.00**

Primrose, plate, E-style, 9¼"......**$6.50**

Primrose, sugar bowl, E-style, w/lid......**$14.00**

Radiance, bowl, colors other than red, cobalt or ivory, #6, 10"......**$25.00**

Radiance, bowl, ivory, #3, 6"......**$3.50**

Radiance, bowl, red or cobalt, #1, 3½"......**$10.00**

Radiance, casserole, red or cobalt......**$35.00**

Radiance, drip coffeepot, ivory......**$30.00**

Radiance, salt & pepper shakers, color other than red, cobalt or ivory, canister style, pr......**$45.00**

Radiance, teapot, red or cobalt, 6-cup......**$225.00**

Red Poppy, baker, French; fluted......**$16.00**

Red Poppy, bowl, flat soup; 8½"......**$16.00**

Red Poppy, bowl, round, D-style, 9¼"......**$30.00**

Red Poppy, cake plate......**$25.00**

Red Poppy, cake safe, metal......**$35.00**

Red Poppy, canister, pattern painted on glass, 1-gal..**$30.00**

Red Poppy, coffee dispenser, metal......**$30.00**

Red Poppy, creamer, Daniel......**$15.00**

Red Poppy, cup & saucer, D-style......**$16.00**

Red Poppy, drip jar, Radiance, $22.00; Salt and pepper shakers, Teardrop shape, $36.00 for the pair.

Red Poppy, dust pan, metal......**$40.00**

Red Poppy, gravy boat, D-style......**$30.00**

Red Poppy, pie baker......**$35.00**

Red Poppy, plate, D-style, 10"......**$45.00**

Red Poppy, platter, D-style, 11¼"......**$22.00**

Red Poppy, sugar bowl, Daniel, w/lid......**$25.00**

Red Poppy, teapot, Aladdin......**$125.00**

Red Poppy, tray, metal, round......**$27.00**

Red Poppy, tumbler, pattern painted on clear glass...**$30.00**

Ribbed, baker, color other than russet or red, vertical ribs, 3-qt......**$11.00**

Ribbed, baker, diagonal ribs, russet or red, 8- to 12-oz, each, from $4 to......**$6.00**

Ribbed, baker, russet or red, vertical ribs, 2- or 3-qt, each......**$16.00**

Ribbed, bowl, color other than russet or red, 9½"......**$10.00**

Ribbed, custard, color other than russet or red, 7-oz...**$5.00**

Ribbed, onion soup, color other than russet or red, w/lid......**$14.00**

Ribbed, ramekin, russet or red, 4½-oz......**$7.00**

Ribbed, teapot, russet or red, Globe......**$225.00**

Rose Parade, baker, French; fluted......**$32.00**

Rose Parade, casserole, tab handles......**$35.00**

Rose Parade, jug, Pert, 5"......**$25.00**

Rose White, bowl, Medallion, 7¼"......**$18.00**

Rose White, bowl, salad; 9"......**$25.00**

Rose White, custard, straight-sided......**$15.00**

Rose White, salt & pepper shakers, Pert, pr......**$28.00**

Royal Rose, ball jug, #3..................................$70.00
Royal Rose, bowl, straight-sided, 9" $22.00
Rx, butter dish, ¼-lb....................................$55.00
Rx, cup & saucer $11.00
Sears' Arlington, bowl, covered vegetable; E-style.....$28.00
Sears' Arlington, gravy boat & underplate, E-style......$16.00
Sears' Arlington, platter, oval, E-style, 15½" $20.00
Sears' Arlington, platter, oval, 13¼"..............$15.00
Sears' Fairfax, bowl, flat soup; 8" $8.00
Sears' Fairfax, plate, 10" $7.00
Sears' Monticello, bowl, cereal; 6¼"...............$7.00
Sears' Monticello, platter, oval, 13¼"...........$16.00
Sears' Mount Vernon, bowl, fruit; E-style, 5¼" $6.00
Sears' Mount Vernon, casserole, E-style, w/lid.........$32.00
Sears' Mount Vernon, gravy boat, w/underplate, E-style .$20.00
Sears' Richmond/Brown-Eyed Susan, baker, French; fluted,
    1960s only $15.00
Sears' Richmond/Brown-Eyed Susan, bowl, oval, 9¼" .$15.00
Sears' Richmond/Brown-Eyed Susan, pickle dish, 9"....$5.00
Sears' Richmond/Brown-Eyed Susan, plate, 7¼"..........$5.00
Sears' Richmond/Brown-Eyed Susan, platter, oval, 13¼"..$16.00
Sears' Richmond/Brown-Eyed Susan, sugar bowl, w/lid ..$14.00
Serenade, bowl, cereal; D-style, 6"................$8.50
Serenade, bowl, round, D-style, 9¼" $22.00
Serenade, bowl, salad; 9" $16.00
Serenade, creamer, Art Deco $18.00
Serenade, drip jar, Radiance, w/lid $22.00
Serenade, pie baker $27.00
Serenade, plate, D-style, 9" $8.00
Serenade, sugar bowl, Modern, w/lid..............$15.00
Serenade, teapot, New York $125.00
Shaggy Tulip, custard, Radiance....................$13.00
Shaggy Tulip, drip jar, Radiance, w/lid...........$25.00
Shaggy Tulip, shirred egg dish, 5¼"...............$27.00
Silhouette, bean pot, New England, #4 ....$150.00
Silhouette, bowl, fruit; D-style, 5½"...............$8.00
Silhouette, bowl, Medallion, 7½"..................$18.00

Silhouette, bowl, mixing; Medallion shape, 8½", $24.00; 7½", $18.00.

Silhouette, bowl, oval, D-style..................$32.00
Silhouette, bread box $75.00
Silhouette, coffeepot, Five Band...................$50.00
Silhouette, creamer, Medallion....................$15.00
Silhouette, cup & saucer, D-style..................$16.50
Silhouette, cup & saucer, St Denis................$45.00
Silhouette, gravy boat, D-style.....................$30.00

Silhouette, match safe....................................$40.00
Silhouette, mirror $75.00
Silhouette, mug, beverage..............................$45.00
Silhouette, pitcher, crystal, Federal..................$120.00
Silhouette, plate, D-style, 9".............................$18.00
Silhouette, pretzel jar....................................$125.00
Silhouette, tumbler, painted pattern on clear glass, 10-
    oz $30.00
Spring, bowl, salad; Tomorrow's Classic, 14½"..........$20.00
Spring, candlestick, Tomorrow's Classic, 4½".............$20.00
Spring, coffeepot, Tomorrow's Classic, 6-cup $75.00
Spring, egg cup, Tomorrow's Classic $25.00
Spring, sugar bowl, Tomorrow's Classic, w/lid..........$16.00
Springtime, bowl, flat soup; D-style, 8½"..........$13.00
Springtime, bowl, fruit; D-style, 5½".................$5.50
Springtime, cake plate, D-style......................$16.00
Springtime, creamer, Modern...........................$11.00
Springtime, custard $8.00
Springtime, pie baker $20.00
Springtime, plate, D-style, 6"...........................$4.00
Stonewall, custard, Radiance...........................$14.00
Stonewall, salt & pepper shakers, Novelty Radiance, pr...$75.00
Sundial, batter jug, red or cobalt.....................$125.00
Sundial, casserole, color other than red or cobalt, #3,
    6½"...$20.00
Sundial, syrup, color other than red or cobalt $80.00
Sunglow, bowl, soup; Century, 8".....................$9.00
Sunglow, creamer, Century $8.00
Sunglow, plate, Century, 8".............................$4.50
Sunglow, sugar bowl, Century, w/lid.................$14.00
Teapot, Automobile, red $700.00
Teapot, McCormick, maroon, w/infuser, 6-cup..........$35.00
Teapot, Parade, emerald green w/gold trim, 6-cup $75.00
Teapot, Twinspout, maroon, 6-cup $65.00
Tulip, bowl, flat soup; D-style, 8½"..................$18.00
Tulip, bowl, Thick Rim, 6"..............................$12.00
Tulip, bowl, Thick Rim, 8½".............................$30.00
Tulip, coffeepot, Perk....................................$60.00
Tulip, gravy boat, D-style................................$27.00
Tulip, plate, D-style.......................................$11.00
Tulip, platter, oval, D-style, 11¼"......................$18.00
Tulip, tidbit, 3-tier, D-style.............................$55.00
Wild Poppy, bowl, Radiance, 10".......................$40.00
Wild Poppy, creamer, New York........................$30.00
Wild Poppy, leftover, square............................$85.00
Wild Poppy, sugar bowl, New York, w/lid $50.00
Wildfire, bowl, oval, D-style............................$22.00
Wildfire, bowl, Thick Rim, 8½"..........................$25.00
Wildfire, coffeepot, S-lid................................$55.00
Wildfire, jug, Radiance, #5 ....$37.00
Wildfire, platter, oval, D-style, 13¼"..................$25.00
Wildfire, teapot, Streamline.............................$150.00
Yellow Rose, custard $11.00
Yellow Rose, bowl, Radiance, 9".........................$18.00
Yellow Rose, bowl, salad; 9".............................$16.00
Yellow Rose, plate, D-style, 9"..........................$9.00
Yellow Rose, platter, oval, D-style, 13¼" $22.00
Yellow Rose, platter, oval, 13¼".........................$22.00
Yellow Rose, teapot, New York...........................$85.00

Hallmark

Since the early 1970s when Hallmark first introduced their glass ball and yarn doll ornaments, many lines and themes have been developed to the delight of collectors. Many early ornaments are now valued at several times their original price. This is especially true of the first one issued in a particular series. For instance, Betsy Clark's first edition issued in 1973 has a value today of $125.00 (MIB).

If you'd like to learn more about them, we recommend *The Secondary Price Guide to Hallmark Ornaments* by Rosie Wells.

Our values are for ornaments that are mint and in their original boxes.

Advisor: The Baggage Car (See Directory, Hallmark)

Newsletter: The Baggage Car
3100 Justin Dr., Ste. B
Des Moines, IA 50322; 515-270-9080 or Fax 515-223-1398
Includes show and company information along with current listing

Angel Messenger, QX408-7, brass, handcrafted, dated 1983.**$95.00**
Baby's 1st Xmas Photo Holder, QX461-9, dated 1987 ..**$30.00**
Bearly Reaching, QXL7151, lighted, 1988 ....**$40.00**
Bellringers, 2nd Edition, QX157-4, porcelain, dated 1980..**$85.00**
Betsy Clark, 3rd Edition, QX133-1, glass ball, dated 1975..**$75.00**
Bicentennial '76 Commemorative, QX203-1, satin ball, dated
    1976 ....**$60.00**
Cinnamon Bear, 2nd Edition, QX454-1, porcelain, 1984..**$50.00**
Claus Construction, Keepsake, QX4885, 1989 ....**$40.00**
Colors of Christmas, Santa's Flight, QX308-6, acrylic, dated
    1982 ....**$50.00**
Come All Ye Faithful (church opens), Keepsake, QX6244,
    dated 1996..**$30.00**
Dickens, Tiny Tim, Keepsake, QX5037, porcelain, 1991 ..**$40.00**
Dr Seuss: The Grinch's Xmas, QX287-3, glass ball, 1987 ..**$95.00**
First Christmas Together, QX505-5, acrylic, dated 1981.....**$25.00**
Fraggle Rock, QX265-5, glass ball, dated 1985 ....**$30.00**
Friendship Line, Keepsake, QX503-4, handcrafted, 1992..**$30.00**
Gift Bringers, 4th Edition, Keepsake, QX212-4, glass ball,
    dated 1992..**$22.50**
Godchild, QX242-1, glass ball, dated 1984 ....**$20.00**
Grandson, QX210-7, satin ball, Peanuts design, dated 1979 .**$35.00**
Heart of Christmas, 4th Edition, Keepsake, QX448-2, hand-
    crafted, dated 1993 ....**$32.50**

Holiday Barbie, 1st in series, 1993, MIB, $125.00.

Holiday Horn, QX5146, porcelain, 1986......................**$32.50**
Holiday Wildlife #7 Purple Finch, QX3711, 1988........**$27.50**
Kitty's Best Pal, QX4716, 1990...................................**$25.00**
Lion King, Simba & Nala, Keepsake, QX1303, handcrafted,
    1994, set of 2..**$26.00**
Locomotive, 2nd Edition, QX404-9, pressed tin, dated
    1983 ....**$295.00**
Refreshing Gift (Coca-Cola Santa), Keepsake, QX4067, dated
    1995 ....**$30.00**
Sailing Santa, QX439-5, handcrafted, dated 1981........**$30.00**
Santa & Sparky, 2nd Edition, QX701-9, dated 1987....**$75.00**
Sharing a Ride, Miniature, QXM5765, 1989 ....**$17.00**
Star Trek, Captain James T Kirk, Keepsake, QX15539, dated
    1995 ....**$22.50**
Thimble, 7th Edition, QX430-4, handcrafted, 1984 .....**$60.00**
Twirl-About, Weather House, QX191-5, handcrafted, dated
    1977 ....**$95.00**
Woodland Babies, 1st Edition, Miniature, QXM5667, 1991 .**$25.00**
10 Years Together Bell, QX4013, dated 1986 ....**$25.00**
25th Christmas Together, QX269-6, glass ball, dated 1978 ..**$35.00**

Halloween

Halloween collectors are very inclusive. Anything that lends itself at all to the spirit of the holiday is generally acceptable to them. It's not just monsters or ghosts and haunted houses that holds a fascination for them. Items representing Nightmare Before Christmas, The Addams Family, or the Munsters are popular, so is anything relating to Salem witches, fortune telling, spiritualism, and the occult. Whether modern or vintage, they're incorporating it into their collections. Halloween is a special mix of fun and fright that has left many children with wonderful memories, so it's not surprising that there are so many collectors today. There are two levels of pricing: auction prices and show prices. Show prices are decidedly lower than specialty Halloween auctions, and vintage items — especially in the month of October — are available in most areas. Most dealers are still reasonable, but you'd do well to shop around. Modern items of good quality have become very popular as well. For further information we recommend *Collecting Halloween* and *Salem, Witchcraft, and Souvenirs*, by Pamela E. Apkarian-Russell.

Advisors: Pamela E. Apkarian-Russell (See Directory, Halloween)

Newsletter: *Trick or Treat Trader*
P.O. Box 499, Winchester, NH 03470; 603-239-8875; Subscription: $15 per year for 4 quarterly issues

Advertising piece, Nightmare Before Christmas, house for
    A&W, lg **$600.00**
Apron, crepe paper, Dennison **$20.00**
Bag, mylar, MaGruff Crime Dog **$4.00**
Banner, Elvira for Coors Beer, lg................................**$95.00**
Book, Bogie, Dennison, 1924 ....**$95.00**
Book, Peanuts Book of Pumpkin Carols **$4.00**
Bottle, perfume; blown glass w/devil inside **$35.00**
Box, cardboard, elongated witch, 1950s.....................**$15.00**

Boxer shorts, Nightmare Before Christmas.................**$15.00**

Bucket, Casper the Ghost..**$20.00**

Candy container, cat in pink w/chenille tail, Western Germany..**$65.00**

Candy container, glass, jack-o'-lantern.......................**$85.00**

Candy container, glass, jack-o'-lantern face on bell shape...**$450.00**

Candy container, glass, jack-o'-lantern face on policeman..**$750.00**

Candy container, witch, Germany, 1930s.................**$400.00**

Candy holder, cardboard, cat pulling pumpkin house coach, double-sided..**$45.00**

Candy pail, Casper the Friendly Ghost.......................**$20.00**

Chocolate mold, 3 pumpkin men..............................**$125.00**

Cookie cutters, tin, Trick or Treat, MIB....................**$45.00**

Costume, Alf, Collegeville, MIB.................................**$20.00**

Costume, Barbie, Ben Cooper, MIB............................**$45.00**

Costume, Big Bird, Ben Cooper, in box.....................**$20.00**

Costume, Glow Worm, Ben Cooper, 1984..................**$20.00**

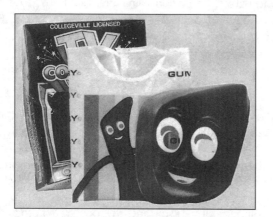

Costume, Gumby, Collegeville, EX (G box), $35.00.

Costume, Little Mermaid, in original bag...................**$15.00**

Costume, Oscar the Grouch, Ben Cooper, in box......**$20.00**

Cup & saucer, cocoa; devil..**$45.00**

Diecut, devil's head, Germany....................................**$85.00**

Diecut, owl in tree branch, Germany, 12x12"..........**$125.00**

Diecut, witch walking, Germany.................................**$110.00**

Earrings, Trick or Troll, pr, MOC................................**$4.00**

Figurine, celluloid, scarecrow, orange & black...........**$95.00**

Figurine, celluloid, witch pulling cart w/ghost in it..**$250.00**

Figurine, composition, witch that wiggles on base, West Germany...**$100.00**

Figurine, hard plastic, donkey w/jack-o'-lantern in his mouth, orange & black...**$95.00**

Figurine, hard plastic, witch on rocket ship.............**$100.00**

Figurine, pulp, witch w/lg hat, 1950s.......................**$140.00**

Figurine, Santa, Nightmare Before Christmas, MIB.....**$85.00**

Fingernails, Elvira, MIP..**$5.00**

Game, Romany, fortune telling, Parker Bros, 1899...**$175.00**

Horn, cardboard, 1921..**$20.00**

Horn, tin, cats & witches, short...................................**$15.00**

Horn, tin w/plastic mouthpiece, cat on house, skeleton, depending on size, from $12 to...............................**$25.00**

Jack-o'-lantern, tin w/plastic horn nose.....................**$50.00**

Lantern, cardboard, cat's face, double-sided..............**$95.00**

Lantern, cardboard, skeleton, double-sided..............**$125.00**

Light, outdoor; Casper the Ghost & friend.................**$25.00**

Light bulb, skull & crossbones, milk glass.................**$35.00**

Mask, multicolored gauze, w/hair & mustache............**$5.00**

Mask, painted & molded paper, fat-faced white baby..**$75.00**

Milk carton, Unicef, from the 1960s...........................**$25.00**

Money collector, Unicef trick or treat........................**$25.00**

Noisemaker, tin, black cat face, $15.00; Sexy Art Deco witch and skyline, $20.00. (Photo courtesy Pamela E. Apkarian-Russell)

Noisemaker, tin, frying pan shape w/cat face, sm......**$14.00**

Noisemaker, tin, ratchet type w/witch, jack-o'-lantern, owl on moon..**$12.50**

Organ pipes, Nightmare Before Christmas scenes, John Moreno, lg set...**$1,400.00**

Plate, collector's; Wicked Witch of Oz.....................**$150.00**

Point of sale, McDonald's Happy Meals, w/plastic buckets...**$45.00**

Popcorn bucket, Nightmare Before Christmas..........**$200.00**

Postcard, beautiful woman w/masks, Winch...............**$75.00**

Postcard, mechanical, Black boy in white sheet, jack-o'-lantern in hand, Clappsaddle...............................**$175.00**

Postcard, Whitney, green-haired pumpkin child.........**$15.00**

Postcards, Gottschaulk series #2279, heavily embossed, set of 6, each..**$25.00**

Poster, Unicef, little boy in black outfit.....................**$95.00**

Posters, Kewpies around jack-o'-lantern, Hallmark Cards..**$285.00**

Puzzle, black cat in orange costume, 1920s...............**$25.00**

PVC, Skull rock bank from Hook.................................**$12.00**

PVC ornament, Wicked Witch of Oz............................**$5.00**

Rattle, tin, 2 cats on fence..**$12.00**

Standup, Elvira, Coors Beer, lg....................................**$95.00**

Talcum powder can, White Witch.................................**$45.00**

Tambourine, tin, jack-o'-lantern w/dancing trick or treaters..**$50.00**

Tambourine, tin, laughing devil face...........................**$95.00**

Tambourine, tin, lg scared black cat face...................**$85.00**

Tambourine, tin, 2 black cats & jack-o'-lantern..........**$95.00**

Tie, bolo; Nightmare Before Christmas, Jack in coffin..**$50.00**

Toy, celluloid, pumpkin man, balancing type...........**$200.00**

Toy, wooden, witch, balancing type.............................**$25.00**

Translight, McDonald's, w/plastic buckets.................**$30.00**

Tumbler, Hot Stuff, glass...**$20.00**

Watch, Timex, Nightmare Before Christmas, Jack's face, digital, MIP...**$45.00**

Harker Pottery

Harker was one of the oldest potteries in the country. Their history can be traced back to the 1840s. In the thirties, a new plant was built in Chester, West Virginia, and the company began manufacturing kitchen items and dinnerware lines, eventually employing as many as three hundred workers.

Several of these lines are popular with collectors today. One of the most easily recognized is Cameoware. It is usually found in pink or blue decorated with white silhouettes of flowers, though other designs were made as well. Colonial Lady, Red Apple, Amy, Mallow, and Pansy are some of their better-known lines that are fairly easy to find and reassemble into sets.

If you'd like to learn more about Harker, we recommend *The Collector's Encyclopedia of American Dinnerware* by Jo Cunningham and *The Collector's Guide to Harker Pottery* by Neva Colbert, both published by Collector Books.

Amy, creamer	**$8.00**
Amy, server	**$22.00**
Amy, teapot, w/lid	**$37.00**
Basket, creamer	**$8.00**
Bird & Flowers, pitcher, Regal, tall, 8"	**$35.00**
Blue Blossoms, pitcher, Regal	**$22.00**
Cactus, cake plate	**$24.00**
Calico Tulip, baking dish, individual	**$8.00**
Calico Tulip, creamer	**$10.00**
Calico Tulip, sugar bowl, w/lid	**$10.00**

Cameo Rose, plate, 9½", from $12.00 to $15.00.

Cameo Rose, meat platter	**$20.00**
Cameo Rose, rolling pin, white handles	**$130.00**
Cameo Rose, salad set, spoon & fork	**$60.00**
Cameo Rose, salt & pepper shakers, pr	**$10.00**
Cameo Shellware, cup & saucer	**$12.00**
Carnival, cake plate	**$20.00**
Cherry Blossom, meat platter	**$10.00**
Chesterton, creamer, blue w/white scalloped rim	**$8.00**
Chesterton, gravy boat, yellow w/floral design	**$15.00**
Colonial Lady, casserole, w/lid	**$30.00**
Colonial Lady, cookie jar, w/lid	**$40.00**
Colonial Lady, rolling pin	**$130.00**
Cottage, casserole, w/lid	**$15.00**
Cottage, fork	**$25.00**
Cottage, plate, 8¼"	**$8.00**
Countryside, rolling pin	**$130.00**
Countryside, server	**$22.00**
Countryside, shaker	**$18.00**

Deco Dahlia, jug, utility; 6"	**$20.00**

Deco Dahlia, platter, 9½", $18.00.

Deco Dahlia, plate, utility; 12"	**$22.00**
Duchess, creamer	**$8.00**
Fruits, pitcher, Regal, 7"	**$40.00**
Godey Print, plate, 10"	**$8.00**
Godey Print, platter, 11⅞"	**$15.00**
Ivy Vine, plate, 8"	**$6.00**
Ivy Vine, platter	**$20.00**
Mallow, bake set in wire frame	**$42.00**
Mallow, lard jug, w/lid	**$22.00**
Mallow, plate, 8"	**$14.00**
Mallow, serving spoon	**$27.00**
Modern Tulip, lifter	**$24.00**
Modern Tulip, syrup	**$24.00**
Pansy, bowl, 6"	**$8.00**
Pastel Tulip, cake plate, 11"	**$25.00**
Pastel Tulip, pie baker, 10"	**$22.00**
Pastel Tulip, plate, Gadroon, 9"	**$8.00**
Petit Point II, pie plate	**$28.00**
Red Apple I, server	**$22.00**
Red Apple I, serving plate, utility, 12"	**$25.00**
Red Apple I, teapot, w/lid	**$27.00**
Red Apple II, bowl, swirl design w/red trim, 9"	**$32.00**
Red Apple II, casserole, individual	**$8.00**
Red Border, bowl, oval, gold trim, 9"	**$12.00**
Red Border, plate, 6"	**$4.00**
Rooster, plate, beige	**$5.00**
Rose I, cake server	**$22.00**
Rose I, plate, 6"	**$4.00**
Rose II, cake server	**$22.00**
Rose II, casserole, w/lid, 8"	**$30.00**
Rose II, individual custard	**$6.00**
Rose II, utility bowl, 6x11½"	**$32.00**
Rose Spray, creamer	**$14.00**
Rose Spray, cup & saucer	**$12.00**
Rose Spray, plate, dinner; 10"	**$12.00**
Royal Rose, cake set: cake plate, server, saucer	**$43.00**
Ruffled Tulip, pitcher, Arches, w/lid	**$35.00**
Shellridge, creamer	**$8.00**
Shellware, plate, 9"	**$12.00**
Slender Leaf, plate, 8"	**$6.00**
Slender Leaf, serving plate	**$15.00**
Springtime, plate, 10"	**$6.00**

Springtime, saucer...$3.00
Vine, plate, tan..$8.00
White Rose, drippings jar, w/white lid.........................$20.00
White Rose, teapot, w/lid $30.00

Hartland Plastics, Inc.

The Hartland company was located in Hartland, Wisconsin, where during the fifties and sixties they made several lines of plastic figures: Western and Historic Horsemen, Miniature Western Series, and the Hartland Sport Series of Famous Baseball Stars. Football and bowling figures and religious statues were made as well. The plastic, virgin acetate, was very durable and the figures were hand painted with careful attention to detail. They're often marked.

Hartland prices have decreased some this past year, although the rare figures and horses are still in high demand. Dealers using this guide should take these factors into consideration when pricing their items: values listed here are for the figure, horse (unless noted gunfighter), hat, guns, and all other accessories for that particular figure in near-mint condition with no rubs and all original parts. All parts were made exclusively for a special figure, so a hat is not just a hat — each one belongs to a specific character! Many people do not realize this, but it is important for the collector to be knowledgable. An excellent source of information is *Hartland Horses and Riders* by Gail Fitch. In our listings, for sports figures, mint to near-mint condition values are for figures that are white or near-white in color; excellent values are for those that are off-white or cream-colored.

For more information see *Schroeder's Collectible Toys, Antique to Modern* (Collector Books).

Advisor: James Watson, Sports Figures (See Directory, Hartland)

Advisors: Judy and Kerry Irvin, Western Figures (See Directory, Hartland)

Sports Figures

Babe Ruth, NM/M, from $200 to $250.00
Dick Groat, EX, from $800 to..................................$1,000.00
Dick Groat, NM/M, from $1200 to $1,500.00
Don Drysdale, EX, from $275 to $300.00
Don Drysdale, NM/M, from $325 to $400.00
Duke Snider, EX, from $300 to.................................$325.00
Duke Snider, M, from $500 to $600.00
Eddie Mathews, NM/M, from $125 to $150.00
Ernie Banks, EX, from $200 to $225.00
Ernie Banks, NM/M, from $250 to $350.00
Harmon Killebrew, NM/M, from $400 to..................$550.00
Henry Aaron, EX, from $150 to................................$175.00
Henry Aaron, NM/M, from $200 to $250.00
Little Leaguer, 6", EX, from $100 to.........................$125.00
Little Leaguer, 6", NM/M, from $200 to....................$250.00
Louie Aparacio, EX, from $200 to $225.00
Louie Aparacio, NM/M, from $250 to $350.00
Mickey Mantle, NM/M, from $250 to $350.00

Minor Leaguer, 4", EX, from $50 to............................$75.00
Minor Leaguer, 4", NM/M, from $100 to...................$125.00
Nellie Fox, NM/M, from $200 to $250.00
Rocky Colavito, NM/M, from $600 to $800.00
Roger Maris, EX, from $300 to $350.00
Roger Maris, NM/M, from $350 to............................$450.00
Stan Musial, EX, from $150 to $175.00
Stan Musial, NM/M, from $200 to............................$250.00

Ted Williams, NM/M, $225.00 to $300.00; Yogi Berra, without mask, NM/M, from $150.00 to $175.00.

Warren Spahn, NM/M, from $150 to $175.00
Willie Mays, EX, from $150 to $200.00
Willie Mays, NM/M, from $225 to $300.00
Yogi Berra, w/mask, EX, from $150 to $175.00
Yogi Berra, w/mask, NM/M, from $175 to $250.00

Horsemen and Gunfighters

Alkine Ike, NM..$150.00
Bill Longley, NM..$600.00
Brave Eagle, NMIB $300.00
Bret Maverick, gunfighter, NMIB...........................$175.00
Bret Maverick, w/gray horse, rare, NM....................$500.00
Cheyenne, miniature series, NM..............................$75.00
Chief Thunderbird, rare shield, NM $150.00

Chris Colt, Gunfighter series, NM, $150.00. (Photo courtesy of Ellen and Jerry Harnish.)

Dale Evans, blue version, rare, NM.........................$400.00
Dale Evans, purple, NM..$250.00

General Custer, NMIB..$200.00
General Custer, reproduction flag, NM.....................$150.00
General George Washington, NMIB.........................$150.00
General Robert E Lee, NMIB $175.00
Jim Bowie, w/tag, NM..$250.00
Lone Ranger, rearing, NMIB....................................$300.00
Matt Dillon, w/tag, NMIB.......................................$275.00
Rebel, miniature series, reproduction hat, NM..........$100.00
Rifleman, NMIB...$350.00

Ronald MacKenzie, NM, $1,200.00. (Photo courtesy of Kerry and Judy's Toys)

Roy Rogers, semi-rearing, rare, NMIB.......................$500.00
Roy Rogers, walking, NMIB.....................................$250.00
Seth Adams, NM $175.00
Sgt Lance O'Rourke, NMIB $250.00
Sgt Preston, reproduction flag, NM $750.00
Tonto, miniature series, NM.....................................$75.00
Warpaint Thunderbird, w/shield, NMIB.....................$350.00

Head Vases

These are fun to collect, and prices are still reasonable. You've seen them at flea markets — heads of ladies, children, clowns, even some men, and a religious figure now and then. A few look very much like famous people — there's a Jackie Onassis vase by Inarco that leaves no doubt as to who it's supposed to represent!

They were mainly imported from Japan, although a few were made by American companies and sold to florist shops to be filled with flower arrangements. So if there's an old flower shop in your neighborhood, you might start your search with their storerooms.

If you'd like to learn more about them, we recommend *Head Vases, Identification and Values*, by Kathleen Cole.

Newsletter: *Head Hunters Newsletter*
Maddy Gordon
P.O. Box 83H, Scarsdale, NY 10583, 914-472-0200;
Subscription: $20 per year for 4 issues

Baby, Relpo, #6744, blond boy in blue cap & top w/white
collar, dark eyes, 5½"..$55.00
Baby, unmarked, #TP-2113, blond w/pink bows in hair, pink
bodice w/white collar, 6"..$60.00

Bonnie, Ceramic Arts Studios, from $150.00 to $175.00.

Girl, Enesco (paper label), brunette w/yellow bow in flip
hairdo, flower on blue bodice, 4½".....................$32.00
Girl, Nancy Pew (paper label), blond w/red telephone in left
hand, purple bodice w/white ruffle, 6"................$45.00
Girl, Napco, #C4072G, blond graduate, dressed in white w/gold
trim, brown eyes, holds diploma, 1959, 6".............$55.00
Girl, no mark, #4138, blond w/sm yellow flowers in hair, 1
pearl earring, green bodice, lg dark eyes, 6½"....$60.00
Girl, no mark, blond w/ponytail, brown bodice & derby-style
hat, hand to face, thick black lashes, 6½"............$48.00
Girl, Relpo, #K1613, blond frosted hair, white-rimmed hat
w/black trim, matching bodice, pearl earrings, 5½".$45.00
Girl, Relpo, #K1836, blond in hat w/upturned brim & bow at
side, black V-neck bodice, 1 pearl earring, 7"......$80.00
Girl, Relpo, #1695, blond w/curls high on head, long curved
bangs, black sleeveless bodice, brown eyes, 7"...$60.00
Girl, Relpo, #2207, blond ponytails w/blue bows, white hat
w/pink flower, pearl earrings, black bodice w/bow,
5½"..$45.00
Girl, Rubens (paper label), #4137, blond w/long ponytails,
pearl earrings, black bodice w/white ruffle & gold bow,
7"..$80.00
Lady, Atlas (paper label), white hair w/gold, bow at front of
bonnet, pearl necklace & earrings, ruffled pink bodice,
6" $55.00
Lady, Glamour Girl, white w/gold painted details, simply
styled, 6½"...$28.00
Lady, Inarco, #E-191/M/c, blond in pink & white, feather in
hat, pearl necklace & earrings, thick lashes, 5½".$40.00
Lady, Inarco, #E193/S, blond w/pink rose in hair, pearl necklace, pink bodice, hand to face, 4½"....................$45.00
Lady, Inarco, #E402, blond in flat-rimmed hat, pearl necklace
& earrings, hand to face, thick lashes, 5½".........$48.00
Lady, Japan, blond in pink bonnet w/bow tied at neck, plain
pink bodice, 3"..$25.00
Lady, Japan, white hair on long curls, white ruffled bodice,
thick lashes, hand to face, 5½"............................$55.00
Lady, Japan (paper label), white hair w/gold details, flat
hat & green bodice, pearl necklace & earrings, hand
up, 6" $35.00
Lady, Napco, #C3815, blond in green flat wide-rimmed hat,
pearl earrings, green & white bodice w/high collar,
5½"..$55.00
Lady, Napco, #C5046, light brown hair, flat hat, pearl necklace
& earrings, gloved hands crossed at chin, 4½"......$48.00

Lady, Napcoware, #C6431, blond w/hair curled under at chin, black bodice w/3 flowers, thick lashes, 6"..**$55.00**

Lady, no mark, #S353A, blond in black hat & bodice, black-gloved hand to face, 4¼" **$48.00**

Lady, no mark, blond in flat-rimmed white hat w/bow, pearl necklace & earrings, pin on bodice, gloved hand up, 5" **$40.00**

Lady, no mark, blond w/flat white hat w/gold decor, black bodice, hand to face, thick gold lashes, 4"..........**$40.00**

Lady, no mark, white hair in ornate style, pearl earrings, white bodice w/bow at neck, blue-gloved hand to face, 6"..**$55.00**

Lady, Relpo, #D936B, short brown hair w/flower at left temple, white bodice w/red painted flowers, pearl earrings, 6" **$60.00**

Lady, Relpo, #K1335, white hair in long curls, low ruffled bodice w/bow in center, brown eyes, 8" **$160.00**

Lady, Rubens, #497/M, white dress w/gold leaves, flower in blond hair, pearl necklace & earrings, 6½" **$60.00**

Heisey Glass

From just before the turn of the century until 1957, the Heisey Glass Company of Newark, Ohio, was one of the largest, most successful manufacturers of quality tableware in the world. Though the market is well established, many pieces are still reasonably priced; and if you're drawn to the lovely patterns and colors that Heisey made, you're investment should be sound.

After 1901, much of their glassware was marked with their familiar trademark, the 'Diamond H' (an H in a diamond), or a paper label. Blown pieces are often marked on the stem instead of the bowl or foot.

Numbers in the listings are catalog reference numbers assigned by the company to indicate variations in shape or stem style. Collectors use them, especially when they buy and sell by mail, for the same purpose. Many catalog pages (showing these numbers) are contained in *The Collector's Encyclopedia of Heisey Glass* by Neila Bredehoft. This book and *Elegant Glassware of the Depression Era* by Gene Florence are both excellent references for further study. If you're especially interested in the many varities of glass animals Heisey produced, you'll want to get *Glass Animals of the Depression Era* by Lee Garmon and Dick Spencer. All of these books are published by Collector Books.

Advisor: Debbie Maggard (See Directory, Elegant Glassware)

Newsletter: *The Heisey News*
Heisey Collectors of America
169 W Church St., Newark, OH 43055; 612-345-2932

Banded Flute, crystal, stem, cocktail; 3-oz.................**$17.00**
Banded Flute, crystal, tray, 12½" **$42.00**
Cabochon, crystal, plate, 8"...**$6.00**
Charter Oak, crystal, compote, #3362, low foot, 6".....**$45.00**
Charter Oak, green, finger bowl, #3362......................**$20.00**
Charter Oak, pink, tumbler, #3362, flat, 12-oz **$17.50**

Chintz, crystal, bowl, jelly; footed, 2-handled, 6"........**$25.00**
Chintz, yellow, bowl, Nasturtium, 7½" **$35.00**
Cleopatra, crystal, plate, 6"...**$5.00**
Colonial, crystal, compote, shallow, footed, #300, 8⅞x8½" dia **$85.00**
Colonial, crystal, nappy, shallow, #341, 4⅞" **$8.50**
Colonial, crystal, plate, #1150, 9"..............................**$15.00**
Colonial, crystal, plate, #341, 6"...................................**$7.50**
Colonial, crystal, sherbet, high foot, ruffled, #300, 6-oz **$9.00**
Colonial, crystal, stem, cordial; #300, 1-oz **$15.00**
Colonial, crystal, syrup, spring-hinged lid, #353, 7-oz ..**$75.00**
Columbia, crystal, bowl, fruit; 12"............................**$110.00**
Crystolite, crystal, ashtray, w/book match holder, 5"..**$25.00**
Crystolite, crystal, cheese dish, footed, 5½" **$22.00**
Crystolite, crystal, coaster, 4".......................................**$6.00**
Crystolite, crystal, jar, cherry, w/lid..........................**$90.00**
Crystolite, crystal, nut dish, individual; handled, #52-1503..**$12.00**
Empress, alexandrite, ashtray **$200.00**
Empress, green, plate, square, 6" **$15.00**

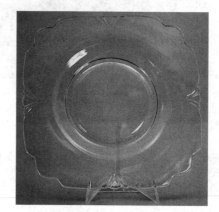

Empress, plate, yellow, 10", $150.00.

Empress, yellow, plate, 8"..**$17.00**
Empress, yellow, platter, 14".......................................**$50.00**
Empress, yellow, stem, oyster cocktail; 2½-oz............**$25.00**
Flat Panel, crystal, almond dish, individual; #353 ....**$10.00**
Flat Panel, crystal, horseradish w/stopper, #352, 5½" ...**$45.00**
Flat Panel, crystal, soap dish w/lid, #353...................**$35.00**
Greek Key, crystal, candy dish, w/lid, 1-lb **$150.00**
Greek Key, crystal, sherbet, low footed, 6-oz **$15.00**
Ipswich, crystal, tumbler, straight rim, flat bottom, 10-oz..**$40.00**
Lariat, crystal, basket, 10"..**$150.00**
Lariat, crystal, bowl, nougat; flat, 8".........................**$15.00**
Lariat, crystal, bowl, relish; 3-part, handled, 11" **$28.00**
Lariat, crystal, coaster, 4" **$7.00**
Lariat, crystal, plate, 8" **$12.00**
Lariat, crystal, plate, cookie; 11"...............................**$25.00**
Lariat, crystal, sugar bowl **$17.00**
Lodestar, Dawn, candy jar, w/lid, 5" **$135.00**
Mercury, crystal, candlesticks, #112, 3½", pr..............**$22.50**
Minuet, crystal, comport, #5010, 5½"..........................**$35.00**
Minuet, crystal, stem, cocktail; #5010, 3½-oz **$28.00**
Minuet, crystal, stem, saucer champagne; #5010, 6-oz.**$18.00**
Minuet, crystal, stem, water; #5010, 8", 9-oz **$30.00**
Minuet, crystal, tumbler, iced tea; footed, #5010, 12-oz.**$40.00**
Narrow Flute, crystal, celery bowl #393......................**$28.00**
Narrow Flute, crystal, creamer, individual; #392 ....**$17.00**

New Era, crystal, plate, 9x7" $25.00
No 394, crystal, nut dish, 3½" $12.00
Octagon, crystal, ice tub, #500 ....$80.00
Octagon, crystal, platter, oval, 12⅞" $20.00
Octagon, pink, bowl, cream soup; 5¼" $17.00
Octagon, pink, cup & saucer................................$17.00
Octagon, yellow, bowl, comport; #1229, footed, 8" ...$35.00
Old Colony, crystal, sugar bowl, dolphin foot...........$17.50
Old Colony, green, bowl, flared, footed, 13" $45.00
Old Colony, marigold, stem, champagne; #380, 6-oz. $25.00
Old Colony, yellow, tumbler, soda; #3380, footed, 10" .$20.00
Old Sandwich, crystal, stem, oyster cocktail $14.00
Old Sandwich, pink, stem, sherbet; 4-oz....................$17.00

Old Williamsburg, crystal, tumbler, iced tea; $50.00.

Orchid, crystal, bowl, dressings; oval, Waverly, 6½", 2-part $47.00
Orchid, crystal, candlestick, Flame, 2-light $145.00
Orchid, crystal, plate, demi-torte; cupped, 10"...........$50.00
Orchid, crystal, stem, cocktail; #5025, 4-oz $37.00
Orchid, crystal, stem, saucer champagne....................$28.00
Orchid, crystal, stem, sherbet $22.00
Orchid, crystal, stem, water $37.00
Orchid, crystal, stem, wine; #5022 or #5025, 3-oz, each..$75.00
Plantation, crystal, bowl, salad; 9⅞"........................$80.00
Plantation, crystal, candlestick, 3-light $80.00
Plantation, crystal, champagne, 6-oz, 4⅝"..................$35.00
Plantation, crystal, goblet, 11-oz, 6½"......................$50.00
Plantation, crystal, plate, demi-torte; 10½" $50.00
Plantation, crystal, plate, luncheon; 8⅞" $30.00
Plantation, crystal, plate, salad; 7⅝" $22.50
Pleat & Panel, green, plate, luncheon; 8" $15.00
Prison Stripe, crystal, nappy, #357, 4½"...................$12.00
Provincial, crystal, cup, punch.................................$8.00
Provincial, crystal, stem, goblet; 10-oz........................$14.00
Provincial, crystal, tumbler, footed, 9-oz...................$15.00
Provincial (by Imperial), Heather, bowl, gardenia; embossed H in diamond, 12⅞".....................................$45.00
Punty & Diamond Band, crystal, custard cup, #505......$6.00
Queen Ann, crystal, candlestick, dolphin foot, 6".......$50.00
Queen Ann, crystal, tray, relish; 3-part, 10"................$18.00
Revere, yellow, plate, party; #1183, 14"....................$36.00
Ridgeleigh, crystal, ashtray, oval, 3⅞x2"....................$5.00

Ridgeleigh, crystal, ashtray, square...............................$5.00
Ridgeleigh, crystal, bowl, mayonnaise $25.00
Ridgeleigh, crystal, bowl, nut; individual.....................$8.00
Ridgeleigh, crystal, cigarette box, oval, w/lid............$65.00
Ridgeleigh, crystal, coaster, 3½".................................$5.00
Ridgeleigh, crystal, creamer, individual.......................$15.00
Ridgeleigh, crystal, cup, punch..................................$10.00
Ridgeleigh, crystal, sugar bowl, oval..........................$12.00
Saturn, crystal, bowl, shallow, 12½" $26.00
Saturn, crystal, bowl, whipped cream; footed............$15.00
Saturn, crystal, candle block, 2-light, pr $135.00
Saturn, crystal, creamer, handled...............................$15.00
Saturn, crystal, cruet, w/stopper................................$50.00
Saturn, crystal, stem, goblet; 10-oz............................$15.00
Saturn, crystal, stem, sherbet....................................$6.50
Saturn, crystal, tumbler, old fashion; 8-oz $18.00
Stanhope, crystal, stem, cordial; #4083, blown, 1-oz..$75.00

Trident, crystal, triple candle holders, from $100.00 to $125.00 for the pair.

Tudor, crystal, jelly dish, handled, #411, 5" $12.50
Twist, green, bonbon $17.00
Twist, pink, saucer...$4.00
Twist, yellow, cheese dish, 2-handled, 6"....................$35.00
Victorian, crystal, stem, wine $20.00
Waverly, crystal, bowl, divided, 3-footed, 6¼" $10.00
Waverly, crystal, bowl, 2-part, deep, oval, 8" $17.00
Waverly, crystal, cruet, w/#122 stopper, 3-oz.............$60.00
Waverly, crystal, epergne/candle holder, fits in epergnette ..$15.00
Waverly, crystal, plate, cupped, 13½" $40.00
Yeoman, amber, plate, 8" $12.00
Yeoman, crystal, stem, cocktail; 3-oz $10.00
Yeoman, marigold, bowl, baker; 9"............................$55.00
Yeoman, orchid, plate, 8"...$12.50
Yeoman, pink, saucer, demitasse...............................$2.50
Yeoman, yellow, cruet, oil; 4-oz.................................$60.00

Figurines and Novelties

Airdale, crystal $550.00
Asiatic pheasant, crystal, 7½" L $300.00
Bunny, head down, crystal, 2½" $200.00
Clydesdale, crystal, 7½x7".......................................$400.00
Colt, kicking, amber $650.00
Colt, rearing, cobalt..$1,200.00
Colt, rearing, crystal...$200.00
Colt, standing, amber $550.00

Dolphin, candlesticks, crystal, #110, pr **$250.00**
Donkey, crystal **$275.00**
Duck, ashtray, Flamingo **$160.00**
Duck, flower block, crystal................................**$140.00**
Duck, flower block, Hawthorne.........................**$295.00**
Elephant, amber, sm.......................................**$1,600.00**
Elephant, crystal, sm.......................................**$195.00**
Fish, bookend, crystal, each **$135.00**
Fish, candlestick, crystal, 5" **$175.00**
Flying mare, crystal **$3,000.00**
Frog, cheese plate, Flamingo, #1210.................**$145.00**
Gazelle, crystal, 10⅞".....................................**$1,500.00**
Giraffe, head forward, crystal **$200.00**
Goose, wings down, crystal..............................**$425.00**
Goose, wings up, crystal..................................**$100.00**
Horse head, box, crystal, 6½"............................**$85.00**
Horse head, cocktail shaker, crystal..................**$135.00**
Irish setter, ashtray, Flamingo **$45.00**
Kingfisher, flower block, Flamingo **$175.00**
Mallard, wings down, crystal............................**$325.00**
Mallard, wings up, crystal.................................**$150.00**
Piglet, standing, crystal....................................**$100.00**
Plug horse, amber **$600.00**
Pouter pigeon, crystal, 7½" L **$700.00**
Rabbit mother, crystal, 4½x5½"........................**$800.00**
Ringneck pheasant, crystal, 11⅞".....................**$140.00**
Rooster, crystal, 5½x5".....................................**$325.00**
Rooster, Fighting; crystal frost, 7½x5½"............**$200.00**
Rooster head, cocktail shaker, crystal, 1-qt.........**$75.00**

Rooster, vase, crystal, 6½", $90.00.

Scottie, crystal **$125.00**
Show horse, crystal **$1,250.00**
Sparrow, crystal **$120.00**
Swan, crystal, 7x8½".......................................**$800.00**
Swan, master nut, crystal, #1503........................**$45.00**

Hippie Collectibles

The 'Hippies' perpetuated the 'Beatnik' genre of rebellious, free-thinking Bohemian nonconformity during the decade of the 1960s. Young people created a 'counterculture' with their own style of clothing, attitudes, music, politics, and behavior. They created new forms of art, theatre, and political activism. The center of this movement was the Haight-Ashbury district of San Francisco. The youth culture culminated there in 1967 in the 'Summer of Love.' Woodstock, in August 1969, attracted at least 400,000 people. Political activism against the Viet Nam War was intense and widespread. Posters, books, records, handbills, and other items from that era are highly collectible because of their uniqueness to this time period.

Advisor: Richard Synchef (See Directory, Hippies and Beatniks)

Handbill, Human Be-In, January 14, 1967, Bindweed Press, Kelly and Mouse artists, 8½x11", classic, $500.00. (Photo courtesy Richard Synchef)

Admission ticket, Woodstock Music & Art Fair, Globe Ticket Co, August 1969, 1- or 3-day ticket, from $100 to........**$125.00**
Book, Beat the Heat: A Radial Survival Handbook, People's Law Collective, San Francisco, Ramparts Press, 1972, 1st edition..**$100.00**
Book, Do It!, Jerry Rubin, NY, Simon & Schuster, 1970, 1st edition, primary Yippie leader............................**$200.00**
Book, Psychedelic Review, #3, Cambridge MA, 1964, 1st edition, early essays by Watts, Leary, Hoffman, others.........**$250.00**
Book, Quotations From Chairman Mao Tse-Tung (Little Red Book), Peking, Foreign Language Press, 1966, 1st printing..**$200.00**
Book, Revolution for the Hell of It, by Free (Abbie Hoffman pseudonym), Dial Press, 1968, 1st edition, author's 1st book **$300.00**
Book, The Harvard Strike, Luskin, et al, Boston, Houghton-Miffland, 1970, 1st edition, prototypical student activism..**$50.00**
Book, The Politics of Ecstasy, Timothy Leary, NY, GW Putnam Sons, 1970, 1st edition............................**$150.00**
Book, Woodstock Craftsman's Manual, Jean Young, Praeger Publishers Inc, 1972, 1st edition **$75.00**
Bumper sticker, Lyndon's Bridge Is Falling Down, blue letters on orange, 3½x15", early 1968 anti-LBJ...............**$65.00**
Bumper sticker, Pat Paulsen for President, Peter Geller Distributors, We Cannot Stand Pat, red, white & blue, 1968, 1x4" **$75.00**
Bumper sticker, The People Want McCarthy, orange letters on blue, 15x4"...**$60.00**

Comic, Underground, Conspiracy Capers, The Conspiracy, Kathleen Cleaver & Susan Sontag, 1969, ...Defense of Chicago 8 ....**$200.00**

Comic, Underground, Despair, Robert Crumb artist, The Print Mint, Berkeley CA, 1st printing (no copyright info on page 2) **$100.00**

Comic, Underground, Dr Atomic #2, Last Gasp Publishing Co, Larry Todd artist, 1973......................**$45.00**

Comic, Underground, Zap Comix #5, Apex, Novelties, 1973, many famous artists......................**$120.00**

Figurine, Hippie man w/sign marked 'Fight Hate!,' Napcoware, 6"......................................**$80.00**

Handbill, March Against the War, Los Angeles, April 22, 1970, Student Mobilization Committee, San Francisco, 8½x11" **$125.00**

Handbill, Quasar's Ice Cream Parlor, Haight-Ashbury, 1966, psychedelic, 9x5" **$100.00**

Handbill, The Diggers/Communications Co, 1967, about 300 different, info re: Summer of Love in Haight, from $400 to......................................**$350.00**

Handbill, Yippie! Chicago August 25-30, Youth International Party, pre-1968 Democratic Convention, 8½x11", classic **$400.00**

Handbill, Zenefit-Zen Mountain Center Benefit, Avalon Ballroom, Nov 13, 1966, Grateful Dead, Quicksilver, etc, 8x5½"......................................**$225.00**

Jigsaw puzzle, Richard Nixon/Spiro Agnew, 2-sided, The Puzzle Factory, NY, 1970, 22x15" **$50.00**

Magazine, Avant Garde, Ralph Ginsburg editor, NY, Issue #2, March 1968, The Marilyn Monroe Issue, Bert Stern prints......................................**$200.00**

Magazine, Life, September 9, 1966, LSD Art, early mainstream......................................**$50.00**

Magazine, Look, July 15, 1969, How Hippies Raise Their Children **$30.00**

Magazine, Ramparts, March, 1967, The Social History of the Hippies, re: Haight-Ashbury scene, important......**$75.00**

Magazine, Underground Digest, Underground Communications, Inc, NY, #1, rare, important **$125.00**

Map, Haight-Ashbury: San Francisco Hippieville, Guide & Map, WT Samhill, Sausilito CA, 1967, folding style **$75.00**

Newspaper, Rat: Subterranean News, A Closed Convention in a Closed City, RAT Publication, NYC, Sept 6, 1968, 12x18" **$100.00**

Newspaper, San Francisco Oracle, Issue #5, The Human Be-In, w/same image as a poster & handbill, 16x12" **$250.00**

Newspaper, The Berkeley Barb, CIA Buys Barb, August 1, 1969, Berkeley CA **$50.00**

Newspaper, The Black Panther, March 6, 1971, Oakland CA, Free Kathleen Cleaver & All Political Prisoners, 16x12" **$80.00**

Newspaper, The East Village Other, Special Woodstock Issue, August 1, 1969, w/Woodstock map cover, 16x12".**$250.00**

Paperback, Hair, Jerome Radny & James Rado, NY, Pocket Books, 1966, play script........................**$75.00**

Paperback, LSD on Campus, Young & Hixson, NY, Dell, 1966, early study..................................**$80.00**

Paperback, Monday Night Class, Stephen Gaskin, Santa Rosa, CA, Book Farm, 1970 ....**$85.00**

Paperback, Revolutionary Nonviolence, David Dillinger, NY, Bobbs-Merrill, 1970, significant............................**$100.00**

Paperback, The Jefferson Airplane & the San Francisco Sound, Ralph J Gleason, NY, Ballantine, 1969, important....**$90.00**

Paperback, US, The Paperback Magazine, Richard Goldstein editor, NY, Bantam Books, 1969-70, many articles, 3-book set......................................**$200.00**

Pillow, inflatable plastic, Peter Max, ca 1969-70, 16x16", any of 8 different **$100.00**

Pin-back button, Be Leary of LSD, black letters on red, ca 1969 ....**$80.00**

Pin-back button, Dump Johnson in '68, blue letters on white, 1¼", rare **$80.00**

Pin-back button, Eugene McCarthy for President, various issues, from $20 to **$100.00**

Pin-back button, Free Speech, PSM, Free Speech Movement, 1964, Berkeley CA, white letters on blue, 1"......**$150.00**

Pin-back button, March on Washington-San Francisco April 24-Out Now, NAPC, National Peace Action Coalition, 1971, 1⅝"......................................**$60.00**

Pin-back button, Psychedelicize Suburbia, blue letters on white, ca 1969, 1¼"......................................**$50.00**

Poster, Better Loving Through Chemistry, Wespac Visual Communications Inc, 1969, 29x23" **$125.00**

Poster, Bobby Hutton Murdered by Oakland Pigs, Black Panther Party, Oakland CA, April 1968, 18x23", very scarce..................................**$500.00**

Poster, Can You Pass the Acid Test?, Ken Kesey & the Merry Pranksters, artist Norman Hartweg, 1965, the 1960s poster..................................**$2,500.00**

Poster, Conference on the Draft, Glide Memorial Church, May 27, 1967, Artist: Gut, important early draft poster.**$150.00**

Poster, Death Has Many Faces, We Demand Life, April 2,3,4, People's Coalition for Peace & Justice, skull & Vietnamese peasants, Washington DC, 1970, 23x17" **$150.00**

Poster, Dick Gregory for President, Mark Lane for VP, Peace & Freedom Party, w/photos, 1968, 29x22", rare.......**$450.00**

Poster, For All Time, Compass Points, silkscreen blacklight, Iwo Jima Marines raising peace flag, 1970, 22x34"........**$100.00**

Poster, Haight-Ashbury Loves You, artist Gomez, Double-H Press, San Francisco, 1967, 22x15", excellent graphics **$80.00**

Poster, Hallucination Generation, Trans-American, for theater exploitation film, 1966, 22x13" **$275.00**

Poster, High Mass, Bob Fried artist, San Francisco, The Food, 1967, 22x26", for play in San Francisco **$250.00**

Poster, Human Be-In, A Gathering of the Tribes, Jan 14, 1967, San Francisco, Bindweed Press, Mouse & Kelley art, 14x20", important..................................**$550.00**

Poster, March & Rally Against the War, National Peace Action Coalition, April 24, 1971, peace sign on yellow, 22x14"......................................**$125.00**

Poster, Monterey Pop Festival, Monterey Co Fairgrounds, June 16-18, 1967, seminal rock festival event, very important **$1,800.00**

Poster, Peace, Dean Eller artist, Kendrick Assoc, Hippies facing riot police, red, white & blue, 1970, 22x29"........**$125.00**

Poster, The Oracle, artist Rick Griffin, Berkeley Boneparte, 1967, 20x14", for premier underground newspaper, important **$300.00**

Program, Woodstock Music & Art Fair, August 1969, 52 pages, 8x11½", very rare.....................................**$500.00**

Program, Woodstock: The Movie, Warner Bros, 48 pages, 1970 ....**$125.00**

Record, Can You Pass the Acid Test?, Ken Kesey & the Merry Pranksters, A Sound City Production, 1966, very rare..**$425.00**

Record, Confrontation at Harvard 1969-Strike, Buddah, 1969, 2-record set, live recording of events **$150.00**

Record, Dick Gregory at Kent State, Poppy Records, 1970, rare...**$200.00**

Record, Is Freedom Academic?, KPFA-Pacifica Foundation, 1964, early student Free Speech Movement protest documentary **$250.00**

Record, LSD, Capitol Records, 1966, documentary report on drug controversy...**$225.00**

Record, Murder at Kent State University, Pete Hamill, narrated by Rosko, Flying Dutchman Records, 1970...**$150.00**

Record, The Wit of Senator Eugene McCarthy, McCarthy for President Committee, 1968..................................**$50.00**

Record, Wake Up America, Abbie Hoffman, Big Toe Records, 1969, from limited edition of 1,000 ....**$300.00**

Stickers, various peace signs, Atomic Energy Group, 1967, each **$10.00**

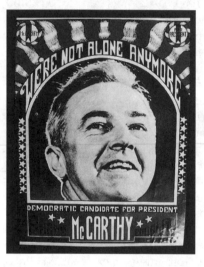

Poster, McCarthy Democratic Candidate for President, red, white, and blue, from $150.00 to $200.00. (Photo courtesy Richard Synchef)

Holt Howard

Here's one of today's newest collectibles, and dealers from all over the country tell us it's catching on fast! Now's the time to pick up the kitchenware (cruets, salt and peppers, condiments, etc.) novelty banks, ashtrays, and planters marked Holt Howard. There's a wide variety of items and decorative themes; those you're most likely to find will be from the rooster (done in golden brown, yellow, and orange), white cat (called Kozy Kitten), Santa, and pixie lines. They're not only marked but dated as well; you'll find production dates from the 1950s through the 1970s. Beware of unmarked copy-cat lines!

Advisors: Pat and Ann Duncan (See Directory, Holt Howard)

Christmas

Airwick, holly girl figural **$40.00**

Angel, cardboard cone body covered w/pink feathers, ceramic head, from $15 to....................................**$30.00**

Ashtray, Santa, med..**$25.00**

Bell, holly decoration **$20.00**

Candle holder, angel figural, pr...............................**$35.00**

Candle holder, girl w/reindeer, pr............................**$30.00**

Candle holder, Santa w/climbing mouse, pr **$35.00**

Candle holders, kneeling camels, jeweled red fabric saddle blankets & gilt harness, pr.............................**$35.00**

Candle huggers, figural snowman, pr, from $20 to **$25.00**

Candlestick, Santa handle **$25.00**

Candlestick, sleeping mouse under ruffled coverlet at side, gold trim on ring handle & rim.........................**$25.00**

Candlestick, winking Santa head as candle cup on red saucer base, white handle...**$20.00**

Candy container, w/pop-up Santa, 4¼" **$50.00**

Cookies/candy jar, roly-poly Santa figure, 3-pc **$250.00**

Demitasse pot, inverted fluting, flared cylinder, white matt w/applied holly & berries, from $50 to **$65.00**

Dish, Christmas tree form, divided, 13⅞" **$25.00**

Dish, Christmas tree form, 9⅞"...................................**$15.00**

Dish, Santa head w/scalloped beard as bowl **$25.00**

Head vase, girl w/holly headband, stylized features & heart mouth, pearl earrings, holly trim collar as base, 1949, 4"...**$140.00**

Hurricane lamp, Santa figural w/candle holder in hat inside glass chimney, red trim & ring handle, from $25 to...........**$35.00**

Hurricane lamp, standing bird w/tree cap to hold candle inside glass chimney, sponged gold trim, from $25 to **$35.00**

Mug, Christmas tree w/Santa handle...........................**$10.00**

Mug, winking Santa, mini...**$5.00**

Pitcher, juice; winking Santa, naturalistic molding, +6 sm mugs **$95.00**

Pitcher, juice; winking Santa, stylized fan-like beard, +6 sm mugs **$95.00**

Planter, candy cane..**$20.00**

Planter, reindeer, $25.00; Matching salt and pepper shakers, $30.00 for the pair. (Photo courtesy Pat and Ann Duncan)

Planter, stylized deer head w/antlers, red nose **$25.00**

Salt & pepper shakers, Christmas tree w/Santa, pr.....**$25.00**

Salt & pepper shakers, full-figured Santa, S or P on tummy, pr...**$30.00**

Salt & pepper shakers, holly girl holds lg poinsettia w/P or S at center, holly bow in hair, pr, from $15 to **$20.00**

Salt & pepper shakers, Santa's head is salt, stacks on pepper body, from $30 to $40.00

Salt & pepper shakers, 2 stacked gift boxes, 'Merry Xmas,' on top, pr..$15.00

Kozy Kitten

Ashtray, cat on square plaid base, 4 corner rests, from $60 to $75.00

Bud vase, cat in plaid cap & neckerchief, from $65 to .$75.00

Butter dish, cats peeking out on side, ¼-lb, rare $150.00

Cookie jar, head form, from $40 to $50.00

Cottage cheese keeper, cat knob on lid $100.00

Creamer & sugar bowl, stackable........................$195.00

Kozy Kitten, Powdered Cleanser, hard to find, $150.00. (Photo courtesy Pat and Ann Duncan)

Letter holder, cat w/coiled wire back $75.00

Memo minder, full-bodied cat, legs cradle note pad ..$125.00

Powdered cleanser shaker, full-bodied lady cat wearing apron, w/broom..$150.00

Salt & pepper shakers, cat's head, pr.......................$30.00

Salt & pepper shakers, tall cats, pr.........................$40.00

Salt & pepper shakers, 4 individual cat heads stacked on upright dowel, from $90 to.................................$120.00

Sewing box, figural cat w/tape-measure tongue on lid ..$100.00

Shakers, head form, 1 in plaid cap, in wireware napkin-holder frame, from $50 to.......................................$75.00

Spice set, stacking $175.00

String holder, head only...$95.00

Sugar shaker, cat in apron carries sack lettered Pour, shaker holes in hat, side pour spout formed by sack, rare $145.00

Wall pocket, cat's head....................................$95.00

Pixie Ware

Candlesticks, pr...$55.00

Cherries jar, flat head finial on lid, w/cherry pick or spoon ..$150.00

Chili sauce, rare, minimum value..............................$300.00

Cocktail olives, winking green head finial on lid $150.00

Creamer $55.00

Cruets, oil & vinegar, Sally & Sam, pr, minimum value ..$200.00

Decanter, Devil Brew, striped base, 10½", rare, minimum value $200.00

Decanter, flat-head stopper w/300 Proof & red nose, minimum value $200.00

Decanter, winking head stopper w/Whiskey, minimum value $200.00

Dish, flat-head handle w/crossed eyes & pickle nose, green stripes, minimum value $100.00

French dressing bottle, minimum value....................$200.00

Honey, very rare, minimum value $300.00

Hors d'oeuvre, head on body pierced for toothpicks, exagerated tall hairdo, saucer base, minimum value....$200.00

Instant coffee jar, brown-skinned blond head finial, hard to find, minimum value $250.00

Italian dressing bottle, minimum value....................$300.00

Jam & jelly jar, flat-head finial on lid $75.00

Ketchup jar, orange tomato-like head finial on lid $75.00

Mayonnaise jar, winking head finial on lid, minimum value $250.00

Mustard jar, yellow head finial on lid, from $45 to $75.00

Olive jar, winking green head finial on lid.................$95.00

Onion jar, flat onion-head finial on lid, 1958 ....$95.00

Pixie, Mayonnaise, hard to find, minimum value, $250.00. (Photo courtesy Pat and Ann Duncan)

Russian dressing bottle, minimum value $300.00

Salt & pepper shakers, gourd form, pointed beak & 'eye' suggests bird-like appearance, stripes, no pixie, pr ..$30.00

Salt & pepper shakers, Salty & Peppy, attached flat head w/painted wood handle, pr.................................$65.00

Salt & pepper shakers, squat w/wide angled shoulder, stripes, no pixie, pr.......................................$25.00

Stacking spice set $150.00

Sugar bowl, Lil' Sugar w/spoon & pixie lid, +cream crock, pr $150.00

Towel hook, flat head w/sm loop hanger, rare, minimum value $200.00

Ponytail Girl

Candle holder, girl shares figure-8 platform w/flower-head candle cup, from $50 to.......................................$60.00

Lipstick holder, from $60 to $75.00

Salt & pepper shakers, pr $45.00

Tray, double; 2 joined flower cups, girl between.......$65.00

Rooster

Bowl, cereal; 6"...$25.00

Butter dish, embossed rooster, ¼-lb $50.00

Chocolate pot, tall & narrow w/flaring sides, embossed rooster on front $95.00

Cigarette holder, wooden w/painted-on rooster, wall mount, holds several packs $150.00

Coffeepot, electric...$100.00

Coffeepot, embossed rooster $100.00

Cookie jar, embossed rooster $200.00

Creamer & sugar bowl, embossed rooster, pr............$75.00

Cup & saucer $25.00

Egg cup, double; figural rooster $40.00

Jam & jelly jar, embossed rooster..............................$75.00

Ketchup jar, embossed rooster $75.00

Mug, embossed rooster (3 sizes), each.....................$20.00

Napkin holder $40.00

Pitcher, embossed rooster on front, cylindrical w/indents on side for gripping, no handle, tall..........................$60.00

Pitcher, water; flaring sides, tail handle, tall...............$60.00

Plate, embossed rooster, 8½"......................................$25.00

Platter, embossed rooster, oval $35.00

Recipe box, wood w/painted-on rooster..................$100.00

Rooster, candle holder, $20.00 each; Bud vase, from $30 to $35.00; Syrup pitcher, $40.00; Mustard jar, $75.00; Dish, figural with open-body receptacle, $30.00.

Salt & pepper shakers, embossed rooster, pr.............$10.00

Salt & pepper shakers, figural rooster, tall, pr, from $25 to..$30.00

Spoon rest, figural rooster, from $30 to $35.00

Tray, facing left $25.00

Trivet, tile w/rooster in iron framework $50.00

Miscellaneous

Ash receiver, comical man in yellow shirt & blue pants, opening/cigarette rest in stomach, from $100 to $125.00

Ashtray, lady w/bottle $110.00

Ashtray/coaster, mouse...$25.00

Atomizer, kneeling nude child w/pink bow in hair in recess on side of flared white bottle $75.00

Bank, Coin Clown, bobbing head, from $150 to......$185.00

Bank, Dandy Lion, bobbing head, from $140 to $160.00

Bank, full-bodied kangaroo, lettered Kangaroo Bank .$85.00

Candle holder, baby chick, from $20 to $25.00

Candle holder, boy on shoe $22.00

Candle holder, kneeling girl, 2-light.........................$20.00

Cherry jar, Cherries If You Please lettered on sign held by butler, minimum value $200.00

Child's dish, Braille ABCs..$25.00

Cocktail shaker, bartender theme, +4 tumblers..........$75.00

Creamer & sugar bowl, fruit cold painted on heavy pottery, marked Holt Howard Italy $40.00

Desk accessory, spread-winged eagle figure on marble base, holds 1 pen $100.00

Desk set, figural chickens in white, gold & brown, sharpener, pencil holder & pen holder, 3-pc set...............$95.00

Ice cream toppings, 2 covered containers & 2 pitchers modeled like layer cakes, 4-pc set...............................$75.00

Jam 'n Jelly jar, yellow w/red lettering on white band, dome lid w/handle, wood-handle spoon......................$50.00

Mug, Nursery Rhymes, footed, verse printed in wide graphic band...$25.00

Note pad holder, 3-dimensional lady's hand...............$45.00

Olives jar, Olives If You Please lettered on sign held by butler, minimum value..$200.00

Onions jar, Onions If You Please lettered on sign held by butler, minimum value $200.00

Plant feeder, bird form $35.00

Planter, camel...$20.00

Planter, mother deer & fawn, white w/gold bow, from $22 to...$35.00

Plate, Rake 'N Spade, MIB $20.00

Playing card holder, on base w/3-dimensional bust of granny holding playing cards, from $45 to $55.00

Razor bank, barber figure $30.00

Salt & pepper shakers, bride & groom, pr $30.00

Salt & pepper shakers, bull head, white w/yellow forelock, lg side-glancing eyes, pr $30.00

Salt & pepper shakers, bunnies in wicker baskets, pr..$45.00

Salt & pepper shakers, mice in wicker baskets, pr.....$35.00

Salt & pepper shakers, Rock 'N Roll kids, heads on springs $150.00

Salt & pepper shakers, Salty & Peppy raccoons, pr ...$30.00

Salt & pepper shakers, tomatoes, pr $15.00

Snack set, tomato cup & lettuce leaf plate, 1962........$25.00

Soup tureen, fruit cold painted on heavy pottery, marked Holt Howard Italy, lg, +6 mugs.........................$150.00

Soup tureen, tomato form, lg, from $85 to $100.00

Spoon rest, apple form..$15.00

Tape dispenser, pelican...$130.00

Tape dispenser, stylized poodle w/red neck band & pencil sharpener..$50.00

Wall pocket, pheasant, marked Holt Howard 1958, rare, minimum value, $150.00. (Photo courtesy Pat and Ann Duncan)

Homer Laughlin China Co.

Since well before the turn of the century, the Homer Laughlin China Company of Newell, West Virginia, has been turning out dinnerware and kitchenware lines in hundreds of styles and patterns. Most of their pieces are marked either 'HLC' or 'Homer Laughlin.' As styles changed over the years, they designed several basic dinnerware shapes that they used as a basis for literally hundreds of different patterns simply by applying various decals and glaze treatments. A few of their most popular lines are represented below. If you find pieces stamped with a name like Virginia Rose, Rhythm, or Nautalis, don't assume it to be the pattern name; it's the shape name. Virginia Rose, for instance, was decorated with many different decals. If you have some you're trying to sell through a mail or phone contact, it would be a good idea to send the prospective buyer a zerox copy of the pattern.

For further information see *The Collector's Encyclopedia of Homer Laughlin Pottery* and *American Dinnerware, 1880s to 1920s*, both by Joanne Jasper and *Collector's Guide to Homer Laughlin's Virginia Rose* by Richard Racheter. *The Collector's Encyclopedia of Fiesta* by Sharon and Bob Huxford has photographs and prices of several of the more collectible lines we mentioned above.

Note: For Harlequin, the high range of values should be used to price maroon, dark green, gray, and spruce green; chartreuse, rose, red, light green, and mauve blue will run about 10% less. The low range is for evaluating turquoise and yellow. Prices for medium green Harlequin are soaring; we would suggest that you at least double the high side of the high range when evaluating this very rare color.

See also Fiesta.

Newsletter: *The Laughlin Eagle*
c/o Richard Racheter
1270 63rd Terrace South, St. Petersburg, FL 33705; published quarterly

Amberstone

Ashtray, rare	$30.00
Butter dish, black decoration	$45.00
Cup & saucer, black decoration	$7.00
Mustard, w/lid	$60.00
Pie plate, black decoration	$40.00
Plate, black decoration, 10"	$7.00
Sauce boat stand	$25.00
Tea server	$53.00

Americana

Bowl, coupe soup	$12.00
Bowl, vegetable; round, 8"	$22.00
Egg cup	$16.00
Plate, 7"	$7.00
Platter, 13"	$24.00
Sauce boat	$24.00
Teapot	$80.00

Blue Willow

Bowl, flat soup; 8"	$15.00
Bowl, serving; oval or round	$30.00
Bowl, 5"	$6.00
Bowl, 5⅞"	$8.00
Casserole, w/lid	$45.00
Creamer	$18.00
Egg cup	$25.00
Plate, 6¼"	$8.00
Plate, 7¼"	$10.00
Plate, 9¼"	$15.00
Plate, 9⅞"	$18.00
Platter, 11"	$20.00
Platter, 13"	$30.00
Sauce boat	$30.00
Saucer	$4.00
Sugar bowl, w/lid	$20.00
Teacup	$10.00
Teapot	$60.00

Dogwood

Bowl, cereal; gold trim, 6"	$10.00
Bowl, mixing; KK, gold trim, 8⅞"	$35.00
Creamer, gold trim	$12.00
Plate, gold trim, 7"	$10.00
Platter, gold trim, 11⅞"	$20.00
Sauce boat, gold trim	$20.00

Embossed Line

Bowl, soup; tab-handled, w/decal, 7"	$15.00
Bowl, w/decals, 4"	$8.25
Casserole, w/decals, 8½"	$45.00
Pie plate, 9"	$20.00
Pitcher, batter	$50.00
Saucer, 5⅞"	$2.00

Epicure

Bowl, nappy; 8⅞"	$35.00
Bowl, vegetable; w/lid	$75.00
Creamer	$20.00
Nut dish, 4"	$35.00
Plate, 8"	$25.00
Sugar bowl, w/lid	$30.00

Harlequin

Ashtray, basketweave, high	$58.00
Bowl, '36s; high	$40.00
Bowl, nappy; high, 9"	$40.00
Bowl, salad; individual, high	$35.00
Butter dish, low, ½-lb	$115.00
Creamer, individual; high	$35.00
Creamer, regular, low	$14.00
Cup, tea; high	$11.00
Egg cup, double, low	$20.00

Marmalade, low	**$200.00**
Nut dish, basketweave, low	**$13.00**
Pitcher, jug-style, 22-oz, high	**$68.00**
Plate, deep; high	**$30.00**
Plate, high, 6"	**$5.50**
Plate, low, 10"	**$24.00**
Plate, low, 7"	**$6.00**
Platter, high, 13"	**$32.00**
Platter, med green, 13"	**$250.00**
Saucer, high	**$4.00**
Syrup, red or yellow	**$175.00**
Tumbler, high	**$58.00**

Harlequin, relish tray, scarce, from $280.00 to $300.00.

Jubilee

Bowl, cereal/soup	**$8.00**
Bowl, mixing; KK, 8"	**$115.00**
Coffeepot	**$45.00**
Egg cup	**$9.00**
Plate, 10"	**$9.00**
Platter, 11"	**$9.00**
Salt & pepper shakers, pr	**$8.00**
Teapot	**$45.00**

Kitchen Kraft; Oven Serve

Bowl, mixing; 8"	**$25.00**
Cake server	**$45.00**
Jug, w/lid	**$95.00**
Spoon	**$40.00**
Underplate	**$25.00**

Mexican Decaled Lines

Use the values below to evaluate Hacienda, Mexicana, and Conchita on Century shapes and Max-I-Cana on Yellowstone. Kitchen Kraft items will be designated KK within the line.

Batter jug, w/lid, KK	**$170.00**
Bowl, fruit; 5"	**$14.00**
Bowl, mixing; KK, 6"	**$35.00**
Bowl, mixing; KK, 8"	**$40.00**

Bowl, vegetable; 9½"	**$32.00**
Cake plate, KK, 10½"	**$40.00**
Casserole	**$135.00**
Casserole, individual, KK	**$95.00**
Fork, KK	**$70.00**

Hacienda: Butter dish, ½-lb, from $125.00 to $140.00; Teapot, from $140.00 to $160.00; Cream soup bowl, from $60.00 to $80.00.

Jar, w/lid, KK, lg	**$160.00**
Plate, deep, 8"	**$25.00**
Plate, 6"	**$7.00**
Platter, oval well, 11½"	**$40.00**
Platter, square well, 15"	**$50.00**
Salt & pepper shakers, KK, pr	**$55.00**
Sauce boat	**$35.00**
Sugar bowl, w/lid	**$30.00**
Tumbler, fired-on design, 6-oz	**$13.00**
Tumbler, fired-on design, 10-oz	**$19.00**
Underplate, KK, 9"	**$40.00**

Priscilla

Bowl, fruit; gold trim, 5"	**$7.00**
Bowl, vegetable; gold trim, oval, 9"	**$22.00**
Coffeepot, gold trim, KK	**$80.00**
Plate, gold trim, 8"	**$10.00**
Platter, gold trim, 9"	**$20.00**
Sugar bowl, w/lid, gold trim	**$22.00**
Teapot, Republic, gold trim, rare	**$85.00**

Rhythm

Bowl, mixing; KK, 8" (except gray)	**$105.00**
Bowl, nappy	**$12.00**
Bowl, soup	**$10.00**
Cup & saucer	**$11.00**
Plate, 7"	**$8.00**
Plate, 10"	**$13.00**

Riviera

Casserole	**$110.00**
Jug, w/lid	**$130.00**
Pitcher, juice; yellow	**$120.00**
Plate, 10"	**$55.00**
Platter, closed handles, 11¼"	**$30.00**
Sauce boat	**$30.00**

Teacup	**$11.00**
Tumbler, juice	**$55.00**

Serenade

Bowl, fruit	**$11.00**
Bowl, nappy; 9"	**$25.00**
Casserole base, KK, complete w/matching lid	**$115.00**
Plate, chop	**$30.00**
Plate, 6"	**$5.00**
Plate, 7"	**$7.00**
Sauce boat	**$25.00**
Teapot	**$100.00**

Virginia Rose

Bowl, deep, 5"	**$17.00**
Bowl, oatmeal; 6"	**$12.00**
Bowl, vegetable; oval, 9"	**$22.00**
Butter dish, ½-lb	**$105.00**
Creamer	**$25.00**
Egg cup	**$85.00**
Pie plate, KK, 9½"	**$30.00**
Pitcher, milk; 5"	**$40.00**
Plate, 7"	**$11.00**
Platter, 11½"	**$22.00**
Sauce boat	**$25.00**

Virginia Rose: Salt and pepper shakers, KK, from $150.00 to $175.00 for the pair; Tray, 8", from $28.00 to $35.00; Casserole, straight sides, KK, from $150.00 to $175.00.

Wells Art Glaze

Wells Art Glaze, batter set, three-piece, from $175.00 to $200.00.

Bowl, fruit; 5"	**$13.00**

Coffeepot, individual	**$120.00**
Cup, coffee; 4⅞"	**$20.00**
Muffin, w/lid	**$70.00**
Plate, deep	**$20.00**
Plate, 7"	**$12.00**
Sauce boat, fast-stand	**$32.00**
Syrup	**$115.00**
Teapot	**$90.00**

Horton Ceramics

Following the end of World War II in 1945, many new homes were being established. With this came the need for home accessories. Since it was virtually impossible to obtain overseas imports, Horace and Geri Horton established Horton Ceramics in Eastland, Texas, to help fill this need. The company produced original designs made by Mrs. Horton until it was sold in 1961. Numbers and letters listed refer to the mold number usually found as part of the backstamp along with Horton Ceramics in small script.

Advisor: Darlene Nossaman (See Directory, Horton Ceramics)

Planter/vase, sea horse, blue, 12", $35.00. (Photo courtesy Darlene Nossaman)

Ashtray, fish decor, #BS120, blues & greens	**$9.00**
Ashtray, free-form, #1811, black w/smoky-gray swirls	**$8.00**
Ashtray, horse head, #108, brown	**$8.50**
Planter, contemporary, #AT5, pink, lime or white, 6x6"	**$14.00**
Planter, contemporary, #246, fluted, pink, 6x3"	**$8.00**
Planter, contemporary, #807, gold, pink or black, 4x7"	**$14.00**
Planter, free-form, #D12, brown wood finish, 12x5"	**$11.00**
Planter, free-form, #514, 2-tone green, 14" L	**$10.00**
Planter, free-form, Art Deco, #707, black, green & mushroom, 7x5"	**$12.00**
Planter, free-form, Mood, #912, 2-tone green & black, 11x5"	**$10.00**
Planter, free-form, Skirt, #H-3, 2-tone green & yellow, 4" L	**$12.00**
Planter, window ledge, free-form, #1418, 2-tone pink, 15x5"	**$15.00**
Planter, free-form leaf, #805, black & lime green, 7x13"	**$10.00**
Planter, jack-in-the box	**$20.00**
Planter, novelty, Dutch shoe, #WBN, 10" L	**$10.00**
Planter, novelty, football, #F10, brown, 11x10"	**$10.00**
Planter, novelty, hobby horse, #H, various colors, 6"	**$10.00**

Planter, novelty, kissing boy & girl angels, #460, 6x5" .**$10.00**
Planter, novelty, lamb, #407, pink or blue, 4x6" **$8.50**
Planter, novelty, nursery block, #B1, pink or blue, 5x5" .**$6.50**
Vase, #BV19, coral, blue, black, pink or green, 9x2"..**$25.00**
Vase, #E-6, white, pink, black or green, 6x6".............**$14.00**
Vase, #211, fan form, blue, white or ivory, 11"...........**$35.00**

Hull

Hull has a look of its own. Many lines were made in soft, pastel matt glazes and modeled with flowers and ribbons, resulting in a very feminine appeal.

The company operated in Crooksville (near Zanesville), Ohio, from just after the turn of the century until they closed in 1985. From the thirties until the plant was destroyed by fire in 1950, they preferred the soft matt glazes so popular with today's collectors, though a few high gloss lines were made as well. When the plant was rebuilt, modern equipment was installed which they soon found did not lend itself to the duplication of the matt glazes, so they began to concentrate on the production of glossy wares, novelties, and figurines.

During the forties and fifties, they produced a line of kitchenware items modeled after Little Red Riding Hood. Some of this line was sent to Regal China, who decorated Hull's whiteware. All of these pieces are very expensive today. (See also Little Red Riding Hood.)

Hull's Mirror Brown dinnerware line made from about 1960 until they closed in 1985 was very successful for them and was made in large quantities. Its glossy brown glaze was enhanced with a band of ivory foam, and today's collectors are finding that its rich colors and basic, strong shapes are just as attractive now as they were back then. In addition to table service, there are novelty trays shaped like gingerbread men and fish, canisters and cookie jars, covered casseroles with ducks and hens as lids, vases, ashtrays, and mixing bowls. It's easy to find, and though you may have to pay 'near book' prices at co-ops and antique malls, bargains are out there. It may be marked Hull, Crooksville, O; HPCo; or Crestone.

If you'd like to learn more about this subject, we recommend *The Collector's Encyclopedia of Hull Pottery* and the *Ultimate Encyclopedia of Hull Pottery*, both by Brenda Roberts; and *Collector's Guide to Hull Pottery, The Dinnerware Lines*, by Barbara Loveless Gick-Burke.

Advisor: Brenda Roberts (See Directory, Hull)

Advisor, Mirror Brown: Jo-Ann Bentz (See Directory, Hull)

Bank, Corky Pig, pastel tints, 5" **$105.00**
Bank, pig figural w/embossed cold-painted floral decor, USA, 14" **$190.00**
Basket, Mardi Gras/Granada, embossed floral decor on cream to pink, simple handle, #65, 8" **$155.00**
Basket, Wildflower, embossed & painted floral decor on pink to blue, scalloped rim, smooth pink handle, W-16, 10½" **$360.00**

Basket, Woodland, 8⅞", $260.00.

Bud vase, Camellia, embossed & painted floral decor on pink to blue, low handles, #129, 7" **$135.00**
Candle holder, Blossom Flite, embossed & painted high gloss floral decor on basketweave, ring handle, T-11, 3", pr...**$60.00**
Candle holder, Bow-Knot, embossed & painted floral decor w/bow on blue to green, B-17, 4" **$120.00**
Candle holder, Serenade, embossed & painted birds on branch on blue, yellow interior, S-16, 6½"...........**$70.00**
Cornucopia, Magnolia Matte, embossed & painted flowers on pink, #19, 8½"...**$145.00**
Cornucopia, Wildflower (# series), embossed & painted florals on 2-tone pastel, #58, 6¼" **$180.00**
Cornucopia, Woodland Matte, embossed & painted floral on Dawn Rose, W-5, 6½" **$75.00**
Creamer, Ebb Tide, shell figural in shrimp & turquoise, E-15, 4" **$85.00**
Creamer, Magnolia Gloss, embossed & painted floral decor on pink, H-21, 3⅞"...**$40.00**
Creamer, Rosella, embossed & painted (pink & green) floral decor on ivory, R-3, 5½" **$65.00**

Ewer, Bow-Knot, B-1, 5½", $215.00.

Ewer, Camellia, embossed & painted floral decor on pink, bulbous, simple handle, sm foot, #105, 7" **$270.00**
Ewer, Dogwood, embossed & painted floral decor on pink to blue, #520, 4⅞"...**$155.00**
Ewer, Magnolia Matte, embossed & painted floral decor on yellow to pink, simple handle, #5, 7" **$175.00**
Ewer, Mardi Gras/Granada, embossed floral decor on cream to pale pink, simple handle & sm foot, #31, 10"......**$160.00**

Ewer, Woodland Matte, embossed & painted floral on yellow to rose, twig handle, W-3, 5½" **$55.00**

Flowerpot, Sunglow, embossed & painted (pink) floral decor on bright yellow, flared rim, #98, 7½" **$50.00**

Flowerpot w/attached saucer, Woodland Matte, embossed & painted floral on Dawn Rose, W-11, 5⅞" **$185.00**

Instant coffee server, Parchment & Pine, embossed & painted decor on green, oval handle, S-15, 8" **$125.00**

Jardiniere, Water Lily, embossed & painted floral decor on walnut to apricot, sm handles, L-23, 5½" **$125.00**

Leaf dish, swirling leaf shape in dark green shading to maroon along rim, #85, 13" **$40.00**

Novelty, dancing girl, w/flaring skirt, matt blue, #955 ....**$60.00**

Novelty, flowerpot, yellow w/embossed horizontal ribs, flared rim, #95, 4½" **$20.00**

Novelty, kitten planter, white kitten w/pink bow beside sm round planter, #61, 7½" **$45.00**

Pitcher, Sunglow, embossed & painted floral (pink) decor on bright yellow, ice lip, tilted form, #55, 7½" **$145.00**

Planter, goose figural, pink hat, yellow daisies at neck, green body, #411, 12¼" **$40.00**

Planter, heart shape, pink w/black along scalloped edge, T-21, 11¼" **$50.00**

Planter, poodle beside leafy plant, maroon & dark green, #114, 8" **$55.00**

Planter, twin geese w/heads up, dark green & white, #95, 7¼" **$60.00**

Rose bowl, Iris, embossed & painted flowers on peach, open handle, #412, 7" **$210.00**

Sugar bowl, Bow-Knot, embossed & painted floral decor on pink to blue, pink bow finial w/lid, B-22, 4" **$175.00**

Teapot, Water Lily, embossed & painted floral decor on apricot to walnut, bulbous, L-18, 6" **$200.00**

Vase, Bow-Knot, embossed & painted floral decor w/bow on blue to pink, footed, B-2, 5" **$160.00**

Vase, Butterfly, embossed & painted floral & butterfly decor on matt ivory, 3-footed, B-10, 7" **$70.00**

Vase, Camellia, embossed & hand-painted floral decor on white swan figural, #118, 6½" **$125.00**

Vase, Iris, embossed & painted flowers on peach to rose, handles, #406, 8½" **$235.00**

Vase, Iris, embossed & painted flowers on peach to rose, handles, #404, 4⅞" **$95.00**

Vase, Magnolia Gloss, embossed & painted floral decor on pink handles, footed, H-9, 8½" **$125.00**

Vase, Magnolia Matte, embossed yellow flower on pink, sm upturned handles, flared rim & foot, #13, 4⅞" **$50.00**

Vase, Poppy, embossed & painted flowers on blue to pink, sm upturned handles, #606, 10½" **$425.00**

Vase, Rosella, embossed & painted (pink & green) floral decor on ivory, square sides, sm handles, R-14, 8½" **$135.00**

Vase, Thistle, embossed & painted decor on blue, sm handles, #53, 6½" **$125.00**

Vase, Tokay, embosed & painted grapes (pink) on pink to green, twig handles, #8, 10" **$100.00**

Vase, Tuscany, embosed & painted grapes (green) on milk white, footed urn form w/sm upturned handles, #5, 5½" **$60.00**

Vase, Water Lily, embossed & painted floral decor on pink to turquoise, trumpet neck, long handles, footed, L-10, 9½" **$195.00**

Vase, Wildflower, embossed & painted floral decor on pink to yellow, handles, footed, W-1, 5½" **$50.00**

Vase, Wildflower, embossed & painted floral decor on pink to blue, ornate handles, footed, scalloped rim, W-9, 8½" **$195.00**

Vase, Woodland Matte, embossed & painted floral on yellow to green, low handles, footed, W-16, 8½" **$195.00**

Window box, Dogwood, embossed & painted floral decor on pink to blue, scalloped rectangular form, #508, 10½" **$290.00**

Dinnerware

Avocado, bowl, soup/salad; 6½" **$7.00**

Avocado, coffee cup (mug), 9-oz **$5.00**

Avocado, creamer or jug, 8-oz.............................**$9.00**

Avocado, gravy boat, w/tray.............................**$80.00**

Avocado, plate, dinner; 10¼" **$8.00**

Avocado, plate, steak; oval, individual, 11⅞x9" **$12.00**

Centennial, casserole, 4½x11" **$110.00**

Centennial, salt & pepper shakers, unmarked, 3", pr.**$60.00**

Centennial, sugar bowl, 3⅞"..........................**$50.00**

Country Belle, baker, white w/blue flower & bell stencil, square **$18.00**

Country Belle, bowl, serving; white w/blue flower & bell stencil, oval **$22.00**

Country Belle, cookie jar, white w/blue flower & bell stencil **$48.00**

Country Belle, pitcher, white w/blue flower & bell stencil, 66-oz **$57.00**

Country Belle, plate, dinner; white w/blue flower & bell stencil **$12.00**

Country Belle, quiche dish, white w/blue flower & bell stencil **$28.00**

Country Squire, bowl, spaghetti/salad; green agate w/white trim, 10¼" **$27.00**

Country Squire, jug, water; green agate w/white trim, 5-pt, 80-oz **$32.00**

Country Squire, mug, soup; green agate w/white trim, 11-oz **$8.00**

Country Squire, plate, salad; green agate w/white trim, 6½" **$5.00**

Country Squire, salt & pepper shakers, green agate w/white trim, w/corks, 3⅞", pr **$16.00**

Crestone, bowl, onion soup; turquoise, 8-oz **$8.00**

Crestone, carafe, turquoise, 2-cup **$40.00**

Crestone, casserole, turquoise, w/lid, 32-oz.............**$25.00**

Crestone, creamer, turquoise **$18.00**

Crestone, plate, dinner; turquoise, 10¼"....................**$12.00**

Crestone, plate, luncheon; turquoise, 9⅜" **$9.00**

Gingerbread Man, child's bowl, #325, Mirror Brown, from $90 to..**$110.00**

Gingerbread Man, child's cup, #324, Mirror Brown, from $90 to..**$110.00**

Gingerbread Man, coaster, #199, gray, 5x5" **$30.00**

Gingerbread Man, coaster, #299, sand, 5x5"...............**$30.00**

Gingerbread Man, coaster, #399, Mirror Brown, 5x5", from $35 to..**$40.00**

Gingerbread Man, cookie jar, #123, gray..................**$225.00**

Gingerbread Man, cookie jar, #223, sand..................**$225.00**

Gingerbread Man, cookie jar, from $295.00 to $325.00.

Gingerbread Man, tray, Mirror Brown..........................**$75.00**

Heartland, bowl, serving; brown heart stencil on ivory w/yellow trim, oval..**$22.00**

Heartland, canister set, brown heart stencil on ivory w/yellow trim..**$170.00**

Heartland, coffeepot, brown heart stencil on ivory w/yellow trim...**$50.00**

Heartland, pitcher, brown heart stencil on ivory w/yellow trim, 36-oz..**$40.00**

Heartland, plate, dinner; brown stencil heart on ivory w/yellow trim...**$12.00**

Heartland, platter, brown heart stencil on ivory w/yellow trim, oval..**$25.00**

Heartland, souffle dish, brown heart stencil on ivory w/yellow trim...**$29.00**

Mirror Almond, baker, square, 3-pt.............................**$10.00**

Mirror Almond, bowl, divided vegetable; 10⅞x7⅞"..........**$18.00**

Mirror Almond, bowl, soup/salad; 6½"........................**$6.00**

Mirror Almond, creamer, 8-oz....................................**$14.00**

Mirror Almond, custard cup, 6-oz...............................**$8.00**

Mirror Almond, fish platter, 11".................................**$35.00**

Mirror Almond, mug, 9-oz..**$6.00**

Mirror Almond, plate, dinner; 10¼".............................**$12.00**

Mirror Almond, plate, luncheon; 9⅜"...........................**$9.00**

Mirror Almond, soup mug, 11-oz..................................**$14.00**

Mirror Almond, sugar bowl, 12-oz...............................**$14.00**

Mirror Brown, ashtray, w/deer imprint, #563, 8", from $20 to..**$22.00**

Mirror Brown, bake 'n serve, round, #589, 6½", from $8 to..**$10.00**

Mirror Brown, bake 'n serve dish, #573, 1980s, 9½-oz, from $9...**$10.00**

Mirror Brown, bake 'n serve dish, oval, #574, 16-oz, from $9 to..**$11.00**

Mirror Brown, baker, rectangular, #534, 7-pt.............**$40.00**

Mirror Brown, baker, rectangular, #567, 1980s, from $30 to..**$35.00**

Mirror Brown, baker, square, #568, 3-pt, from $10 to..**$12.00**

Mirror Brown, baker, w/chicken lid, #560, from $150 to..**$175.00**

Mirror Brown, baker, w/rooster imprint, #558, 3" deep, from $50 to...**$60.00**

Mirror Brown, bean pot, #510, 2-qt, from $30 to.......**$35.00**

Mirror Brown, bean pot, w/lid, #524, 12-oz, individual, from $5 to...**$7.00**

Mirror Brown, beer stein, #526, 16-oz, from $10 to....**$12.00**

Mirror Brown, bowl, fruit; #503, 5¼", from $4 to.........**$5.00**

Mirror Brown, bowl, fruit; #533, 6", from $6 to...........**$7.00**

Mirror Brown, bowl, mixing; #437, 7", from $9 to......**$10.00**

Mirror Brown, bowl, mixing; #536, 6", from $7 to........**$8.00**

Mirror Brown, bowl, mixing; #538, 8"........................**$12.00**

Mirror Brown, bowl, mixing; Provincial Mold, #850H, 5¼", from $8 to...**$10.00**

Mirror Brown, bowl, mixing; Provincial Mold, #852H, 6¼", from $9 to...**$12.00**

Mirror Brown, bowl, onion soup; #535, 1980s, 12-oz, w/lid, from $8 to...**$9.00**

Mirror Brown, bowl, salad; w/rooster imprint, oval, #508, from $40 to...**$45.00**

Mirror Brown, bowl, soup or salad; #569, 6½", from $6 to.**$8.00**

Mirror Brown, bowl, spaghetti or salad; #545, 10¼", from $25 to..**$27.00**

Mirror Brown, bud vase, #870H, 9", from $14 to........**$18.00**

Mirror Brown, butter dish, #561, ¼-lb, from $11 to...**$15.00**

Mirror Brown, canister set, #556/557/558/559, hard to find in mint condition, 4-pc, from $350 to.....................**$550.00**

Mirror Brown, canister set, stacking, #360, 1980s, 4-pc, from $150 to...**$175.00**

Mirror Brown, carafe, #505, 2-cup, from $50 to.........**$65.00**

Mirror Brown, casserole, open, #543, 2-pt, 7x11", from $5 to..**$8.00**

Mirror Brown, casserole, oval, w/chicken lid, #5850, 2-qt, from $55 to...**$60.00**

Mirror Brown, casserole, oval, w/lid, #544, 2-pt, from $18 to..**$20.00**

Mirror Brown, casserole, oval, w/lid, 2-qt, from $25 to..**$30.00**

Mirror Brown, casserole, Provincial Mold, w/lid, #853H, from $20 to...**$22.00**

Mirror Brown, casserole, round, w/lid, #314, 1980s, from $12 to..**$14.00**

Mirror brown, casserole, w/duck lid, #5770, 2-qt, from $65 to..**$75.00**

Mirror Brown, casserole, w/lid, #507, 32-oz, from $20 to..**$25.00**

Mirror Brown, cheese server, #582, from $30 to.........**$32.00**

Mirror Brown, chip 'n dip, #586, 2-pc, 12x11", from $110 to..**$135.00**

Mirror Brown, chip 'n dip, 3-section, from $60 to......**$70.00**

Mirror Brown, chip 'n dip leaf, #521, 15", from $20 to...**$30.00**

Mirror Brown, chip 'n dip leaf, #591, 9x12¼", from $30 to..**$35.00**

Mirror Brown, coffee cup, #597, 7-oz, from $3 to........**$4.00**

Mirror Brown, coffee cup/mug, #502, 9-oz, from $4 to..**$5.00**

Mirror Brown, coffeepot, #522, 8-cup, from $30 to....**$35.00**

Mirror Brown, condiment set, #871H, from $75 to...**$100.00**

Mirror Brown, cookie jar, #523, from $25 to...............**$30.00**

Mirror Brown, corn-serving dish, #573, 9" L, from $40 to..**$50.00**

Mirror Brown, creamer and sugar bowl, #518/519, $13.00; Teapot, #549, $20.00.

Mirror Brown, custard cup, #576, 6-oz, from $7 to.......**$9.00**

Mirror Brown, deviled-egg plate, w/rooster imprint, #591, from $45 to..**$50.00**

Mirror Brown, Dutch oven, #565, 2-pc, from $30 to ..**$35.00**

Mirror Brown, French casserole, #513, individual, from $3 to **$5.00**

Mirror Brown, French casserole, stick handle, #562, 9-oz, from $6 to...**$7.00**

Mirror Brown, French casserole, stick handle, w/lid, #579, 9-oz, from $6 to...**$7.00**

Mirror Brown, French casserole, w/lid, #527, 1980s, from $6 to **$7.00**

Mirror Brown, French casserole, w/lid & warmer, #979, 3-pc, from $75 to...**$90.00**

Mirror Brown, garlic cellar, #3505, 1980s, 13-oz, from $30 to **$35.00**

Mirror Brown, gravy boat, #511....................................**$14.00**

Mirror Brown, gravy boat & liner, #540, from $25 to.**$28.00**

Mirror Brown, gravy boat liner, #512 ....**$8.00**

Mirror Brown, hen on nest, #592, from $65 to **$70.00**

Mirror Brown, ice jug, #514, 2-qt, from $22 to **$26.00**

Mirror Brown, jam/mustard jar, w/lid, #551, 12-oz, from $8 to **$10.00**

Mirror Brown, jug, #525, 2-pt, from $15 to **$17.00**

Mirror Brown, jug, ice; #514, 2-qt, from $22 to **$26.00**

Mirror Brown, jug, water; #509, 80-oz, from $25 to ...**$30.00**

Mirror Brown, leaf dish, #590, 7¼x4¼", from $7 to **$9.00**

Mirror Brown, leaf serve-all, #540, 7½x12", from $26 to...**$28.00**

Mirror Brown, mug, #302, 1980s, 10-oz, from $3 to **$5.00**

Mirror Brown, mug, Continental; #571, 10-oz & 12-oz, each, from $18 to...**$20.00**

Mirror Brown, oil server, #584, from $30 to **$32.00**

Mirror Brown, pie plate, #566, 9½", from $20 to........**$25.00**

Mirror Brown, plate, dinner; #500, 10¼" **$8.00**

Mirror Brown, plate, luncheon; #599, 9¼", from $7 to.**$8.00**

Mirror Brown, plate, salad; #501, 6½", from $4 to........**$5.00**

Mirror Brown, plate, steak; oval, #541, 9x11⅞", from $10 to **$12.00**

Mirror Brown, plate, steak; w/well & tree, oval, #593, 14x10", from $25 to...**$28.00**

Mirror Brown, platter, fish; #596, 11", from $40 to **$50.00**

Mirror Brown, platter, w/chicken lid, #559, from $150 to **$175.00**

Mirror Brown, platter, w/rooster imprint, oval, #557, from $50 to..**$60.00**

Mirror Brown, quiche dish, 3508, 1980s **$25.00**

Mirror Brown, ramekin, #600, 1980s, 2½-oz, from $10 to..**$12.00**

Mirror Brown, roaster, rectangular, w/lid, #535, 7-pt..**$90.00**

Mirror Brown, salad server, rectangular, #583, 6½x11", from $20 to...**$22.00**

Mirror Brown, salt & pepper shakers, #596, table size, pr, from $18 to...**$20.00**

Mirror Brown, salt & pepper shakers, mushroom form, #587/588, 3¾", pr, from $15 to **$18.00**

Mirror Brown, sauce bowl for chip 'n dip, #584, from $50 to..**$60.00**

Mirror Brown, saucer, #598, 6", from #3 to **$4.00**

Mirror Brown, server, w/handle, #873H, from $70 to..**$85.00**

Mirror Brown, serving dish, double, scalloped, #577, from $50 to **$60.00**

Mirror Brown, serving set, #872H, from $75 to........**$100.00**

Mirror Brown, skillet, #595, from $15 to....................**$17.00**

Mirror Brown, snack set, tray #554 & mug #553, from $18 to..**$20.00**

Mirror Brown, souffle dish, #517, 1980s **$28.00**

Mirror Brown, spaghetti dish, oval, #581, individual, 10⅞x8¼", from $15 to **$20.00**

Mirror Brown, spoon rest, w/Spoon Rest imprint, #594, from $25 to...**$35.00**

Mirror Brown, stein, jumbo; #572, 32-oz, from $35 to..**$40.00**

Mirror Brown, tidbit tray, 2-tier, #592, from $60 to.....**$70.00**

Mirror Brown, tray for chip 'n dip set, #584, from $60 to..**$75.00**

Mirror Brown, vegetable dish, divided, #542, 7x10⅞", from $12 to...**$14.00**

Mirror Brown, vinegar server, #585, from $30 to **$32.00**

Provincial, bowl, mixing; brown w/white trim, 6⅞"..**$20.00**

Provincial, casserole, French handle, brown w/white trim, individual, 12-oz **$12.00**

Provincial, coffeepot, brown w/white trim, 8-cup **$50.00**

Provincial, creamer or jug, brown w/white trim, 8-oz..**$16.00**

Provincial, jug, brown w/white trim, 2-pt....................**$28.00**

Provincial, plate, dinner; brown w/white trim, 10¼"..**$15.00**

Ridge, mug, gray, sand or brown, 10-oz **$5.00**

Ridge, plate, dinner; gray, sand or brown **$8.00**

Ridge, plate, steak; gray, sand or brown, 12x9½" **$11.00**

Ridge, salt & pepper shakers, gray, sand or brown, 2½x3", pr..**$18.00**

Ridge, tray, gray, sand or brown, 7x9½" **$16.00**

Ring, bowl, mixing; brown, 10"....................................**$22.00**

Ring, bowl, soup/salad; brown, 12-oz **$9.00**

Ring, coffee cup, brown, stemmed **$9.00**

Ring, custard cup, brown **$8.00**

Ring, gravy boat, brown, w/tray...................................**$25.00**

Ring, plate, dinner; brown **$12.00**

Ring, salt & pepper shakers, brown, w/handles, pr ...**$28.00**

Tangerine, ashtray w/deer imprint, 8"........................**$26.00**

Tangerine, bowl, salad/spaghetti; 10¼" **$27.00**

Tangerine, bud vase (Imperial), 9" **$18.00**

Tangerine, butter dish, ¼-lb **$18.00**

Tangerine, casserole, individual, French handle, 12-oz ..**$7.00**

Tangerine, coffee cup/mug, 9-oz..................................**$6.00**

Tangerine, cookie jar, 94-oz..................................**$45.00**
Tangerine, creamer or jug, 8-oz **$12.00**
Tangerine, Dutch oven, 2-pc, 3-pt **$30.00**
Tangerine, jug, ice; 2-qt......................................**$28.00**
Tangerine, salt & pepper shakers, w/corks, 3⅞", pr ..**$16.00**
Tangerine, water jug, 5-pt, 80-oz........................**$32.00**

Imperial Glass

Organized in 1901 in Bellaire, Ohio, the Imperial Glass Company made carnival glass, stretch glass, a line called NuCut (made in imitation of cut glass), and a limited amount of art glass within the first decade of the century. In the mid-thirties, they designed one of their most famous patterns (and one of their most popular with today's collectors), Candlewick. Within a few years, milk glass had become their leading product.

During the fifties, they reintroduced their NuCut line in crystal as well as colors, marketing it as 'Collector's Crystal.' In the late fifties they bought molds from both Heisey and Cambridge. Most of the glassware they reissued from these old molds was marked 'IG,' one letter superimposed over the other. When Imperial was bought by Lenox in 1973, an 'L' was added to the mark. The ALIG logo was added in 1981 when the company was purchased by Arthur Lorch. In 1982 the factory was sold to Robert Stahl of Minneapolis. Chapter 11 bankruptcy was filled in October that year. A plant resurgence continued plant production. Many Heisey by Imperial animals done in color were made at this time. A new mark, the NI for New Imperial, was placed on a few items. In November of 1984 the plant closed forever and the assets were sold at liquidation. This was the end of the 'Big I.'

In addition to tableware, they made a line of animal figures, some of which were made from Heisey's molds. *Glass Animals of the Depression Years* by Lee Garmon and Dick Spencer is a wonderful source of information and can help you determine the value and the manufacturer of your figures.

Numbers in the listings were assigned by the company and appeared on their catalog pages. They were used to indicate differences in shapes and stems, for instance. Collectors still use them.

For more information on Imperial we recommend *Imperial Glass* by Margaret and Douglas Archer; *Elegant Glassware of the Depression Era* by Gene Florence; *Imperial Carnival Glass* by Carl O. Burns; and *Imperial Glass Encyclopedia, Vol I, A–Cane,* and *Vol II, Cane to M*, edited by James Measell. Also refer to *Imperial's Modern Carnival Glass* by Ruth Grizel, who's address is in the Directory under Westmoreland.

See also Candlewick.

Advisor: Joan Cimini (See Directory, Imperial)

Club: National Imperial Glass Collectors' Society, Inc. 67183 Stein Rd, Belmont, OH 43781. Dues: $15 per year (+$1 for each additional member of household), quarterly newsletter: *Glasszette*, convention every June

Ashtray, caramel slag, square, #1608/1, 7"..................**$25.00**
Ashtray, Hambone, red slag, satin, Cambridge mold #1956 ....**$40.00**
Ashtray, jade slag, square, #1608/1, 7".....................**$35.00**

Ashtray, pipe; jade slag, satin, #1605, 7½" dia **$50.00**
Ashtray, red slag, square, #1608/1, 7".......................**$30.00**
Basket, jade slag w/milk glass handle, satin **$50.00**
Basket, red slag w/milk glass handle.........................**$45.00**
Bell, jade slag, satin..**$70.00**
Bell, red slag, satin...**$48.00**
Bowl, baked apple; Cape Cod, crystal, #160/53X, 6" ...**$9.00**
Bowl, Grapes, amber carnival, crimped, IG mark, 9".**$45.00**
Bowl, Open Rose, amber carnival, German Cross mk, 8" ..**$75.00**
Bowl, Pillar Flutes, light blue, deep, 5½" **$25.00**
Bowl, purple slag, footed, #737A, IG mark, 8½"........**$90.00**
Bowl, Roses, Horizon Blue carnival, crimped edge, LIG mark, 9" **$60.00**
Butter dish, Cape Cod, crystal, handled, #160/44, 5" dia ..**$45.00**

Cake stand, Cape Cod, footed, #160/670, 10½", $48.00.

Candle holders, Cape Cod, #160/175, 4½" dia, pr......**$45.00**
Candle holders, caramel slag, flat paneled sides, #352, 7⅜", pr..**$90.00**
Candlesticks, Cape Cod, crystal, #160/80, 5", pr.........**$40.00**
Candy dish, Leaf, red carnival, 3-toed, round, #3800/165, 6", w/lid **$65.00**
Champagne, Cape Cod, Azalea, #1602 ....**$22.00**
Coaster/spoon rest, Cape Cod, crystal, #160/76..........**$12.00**
Compote, purple slag, octagonal foot, #5930, 6" **$35.00**
Covered dish, dog on lid, caramel slag, #822 ....**$130.00**
Covered dish, dog on lid, purple slag, #822 ....**$140.00**
Covered dish, duck, pink carnival, #146, 5"................**$30.00**
Covered dish, duck on nest, jade slag, satin, #146.....**$65.00**
Covered dish, hen on nest, milk glass, #1950/145, 4¼" ..**$25.00**
Covered dish, lion on lacy base, amber, #159 ....**$75.00**
Covered dish, lion on lacy base, caramel slag, #159 ..**$160.00**
Covered dish, lion on lacy base, purple slag, satin, #159, 7½" **$185.00**
Covered dish, rooster on lacy base, purple slag, #158.**$170.00**
Covered dish, rooster on lacy base, satin caramel slag, #158..**$160.00**
Creamer & sugar bowl, owl, caramel slag w/glass eyes, #335, pr..**$45.00**
Creamer & sugar bowl, owl, purple slag, shiny, #335, pr **$65.00**
Cruet, jade slag, satin, #505, w/stopper......................**$75.00**
Cup & saucer, coffee; Cape Cod, crystal, #160/37......**$12.00**
Figurine, Airdale, caramel slag...................................**$95.00**
Figurine, angelfish, bookend, amber or frosted........**$180.00**

Figurine, bull, amber, very rare, 4" $725.00
Figurine, Champ Terrier, caramel slag, 5¾".............$150.00
Figurine, chick, head up, milk glass $10.00
Figurine, clydesdale, Salmon $275.00
Figurine, colt, balking, amber.................$140.00
Figurine, colt, kicking, Horizon Blue, marked HCA ...$40.00
Figurine, colt, standing, Sunshine Yellow, marked HCA..$55.00
Figurine, cygnet, caramel slag, ALIG mark.................$50.00
Figurine, donkey, caramel slag....................$50.00
Figurine, donkey, Ultra Blue......................$75.00
Figurine, donkey (wild jack), Meadow Green carnival..$90.00
Figurine, duckling, standing, Ultra Blue, 2⅝"............$45.00
Figurine, elephant, Meadow Green Carnival, #674, LIG mark, med.......................$90.00
Figurine, filly, head backward, Verde Green............$155.00
Figurine, filly, head forward, satin $75.00
Figurine, fish, canape plate, cobalt $30.00
Figurine, fish, candlestick, Sunshine Yellow, HCA mark, 5" ..$45.00
Figurine, Flying Mare, amber, NI mark, rare..........$1,450.00
Figurine, giraffe, amber, ALIG mark, rare.................$400.00
Figurine, Hootless Owl, caramel slag, #18...........$40.00
Figurine, mallard, wings down, Horizon Blue satin, HCA mark..............................$35.00
Figurine, mallard, wings up, caramel slag $40.00
Figurine, piglet, standing, amber......................$70.00
Figurine, Plug Horse, rose pink, HCA mark, 1978......$65.00
Figurine, ringneck pheasant, amber, NI mark, rare ..$260.00
Figurine, rooster, fighting, pink $175.00
Figurine, Scolding Bird, Cathay Crystal, signed Virginia B Evans $220.00
Figurine, swan, purple slag, glossy, #400, IG mark..$110.00
Figurine, terrier pup, amethyst carnival, 3½" $40.00
Figurine, tiger, paperweight, jade, 8" L $130.00
Figurine, wood duck, caramel slag, IG mark $45.00
Figurine, wood duckling, floating, Sunshine Yellow, satin, HCA mark $20.00
Figurine, wood duckling, standing, Ultra Blue............$45.00
Ivy ball, Reeded (Spun), teal w/crystal foot, 4" $55.00
Jar, Cathay Crystal, Ming, #5019 ....$300.00
Jar, owl, caramel slag, tall, w/lid, #800 ....$80.00
Jar, owl, jade slag, satin, w/lid....................$50.00
Jar, owl, purple slag, tall, w/lid, #800 ....$100.00
Marmalade, Cape Cod, crystal, #160/89, 4-pc $45.00
Mint dish, Cape Cod, crystal, handled, #160/51F, 6" dia..$25.00
Mug, robin, purple slag, glossy, #210 ....$45.00
Mug, robin, ruby slag, satin, #210 ....$40.00
Mug, Storybook, red slag, satin, #1591 ....$45.00
Mug, Storybook, Ultra Blue, #1591.................$35.00
Pepper mill, Cape Cod, crystal, #160/236....................$27.50
Pitcher, Windmill, caramel slag, #240....................$55.00
Pitcher, Windmill, jade slag, satin, #240....................$95.00
Pitcher, Windmill, milk glass, #1950/240, 1-pt............$25.00
Pitcher, Windmill, purple slag, satin, #240.................$65.00
Pitcher, Windmill, red slag, satin, #240 ....$55.00
Plate, Coin, crystal satin, 1971, 9".....................$20.00
Plate, Diamond Quilted, black, 8".....................$15.00
Plate, Pillar Flutes, blue, 8".....................$18.00
Relish, Cape Cod, crystal, 5-compartment, #160/102, 11"..$65.00
Rose bowl, jade slag, satin, crimped, #62C, 9"............$85.00

Rose bowl, red slag, satin, crimped, #62C, 9" $55.00
Sherbet, Cape Cod, ruby, #160.....................$20.00
Spider, Cape Cod, crystal, handled, #160/180, 4½" $25.00
Toothpick holder, cornucopia, red slag, satin, #123, 3"..$30.00
Toothpick holder, Diamond, caramel slag, #1, 2½"....$25.00
Toothpick holder, Meadow Green carnival, #123, 3"..$30.00
Toothpick holder, red slag, glossy.....................$20.00
Toothpick holder, ruby carnival, #402 ....$25.00
Tumbler, iced tea; Reeded (Spun), teal, #711, 12-oz ..$19.50
Tumbler, Niagara, crystal, 10-oz $10.00
Vase, Bowling Pin, Peach Blow, glossy, #4037, 10½" ..$150.00

Vase, Crocheted, #780, four-toed, $12.00; matching bowl/candle holder, 6", with mini vase peg, $30.00; sugar bowl and creamer, $12.50 each.

Vase, Katy, blue opalescent, #743N, 5½".....................$45.00
Vase, Reeded (Spun), red, #711, 5" $45.00
Vase, Rose, milk glass, #1950/108, 6"............$10.00

Indiana Glass

From 1972 until 1978, the Indiana Glass Company produced a line of iridescent 'new carnival' glass, much of which was embossed with grape clusters and detailed leaves in a line they called Harvest. It was made in blue, gold, and lime, and was evidently a good seller for them, judging from the amount around today. They also produced a line of 'press cut' iridescent glass called Heritage, which they made in amethyst and Sunset (amberina). Collectors always seem to gravitate toward lustre-coated glassware, whether it's old or recently made, and there seems to be a significant amount of interest in this line.

There was also a series of four Bicentennial Commemorative plates made in blue and ruby, and amethyst and gold carnival: American Eagle, Independence Hall, Liberty Bell, and Spirit of '76. They're valued at $12.00 for the gold and $15.00 for the blue, except for the American Eagle plate, which is worth from $12.00 to $15.00 regardless of color.

This glass is a little difficult to evaluate, since you see it in malls and at flea markets with such a wide range of 'asking' prices. On one hand, you'll have sellers who themselves are not exactly sure what it is they have but since it's 'carnival' assume it should be fairly pricey. On the other hand, you have those who've just 'cleaned house' and want to get rid of it. They may have bought it new themselves and know it's not very old and wasn't expensive to start with. This is what you'll be up against if you decide you want to collect it.

In addition to the iridescent glass lines, Indiana produced colored glass baskets, vases, etc., as well as a line called Ruby Band Diamond Point, a clear diamond-faceted pattern with a wide ruby-flashed rim band. We've listed some of the latter below; our values are for examples with the ruby-flashing in excellent condition.

Over the last ten years, the collectibles market has changed. Nowadays, some shows' criteria regarding the merchandise they allow to be displayed is 'if it's no longer available on the retail market, it's OK.' I suspect that this attitude will become more and more widespread. At any rate, this is one of the newest interests at the flea market/antique mall level, and if you can buy it right (and like its looks), now is the time!

Advisor: Ruth Grizel (See Directory, Westmoreland)

Iridescent Amethyst Carnival Glass (Heritage)

Basket, footed, 9x5x7".................................**$35.00**
Butter dish, 5x7½" dia....................................**$35.00**
Candle holder, 5½", each...............................**$30.00**
Center bowl, 4¾x8½", from $35 to.................**$40.00**
Goblet, 8-oz...**$17.50**
Pitcher, 8¼"..**$55.00**
Punch set, 10" bowl & pedestal, 8 cups, & ladle, 11-pc.**$150.00**
Swung vase, slender & footed w/irregular rim, 11x3" ...**$30.00**

Iridescent Blue Carnival Glass

Basket, Canterbury, waffled pattern, flared sides drawn in at handle, 11x8x12"....................................**$45.00**
Basket, Monticello, allover faceted embossed diamonds, square, 7x6"..**$35.00**
Butter dish, Harvest, embossed grapes, ¼-lb, 8" L **$25.00**

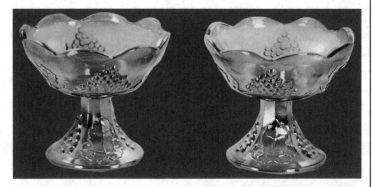

Candlesticks, Harvest, comport shape, 4x4½", $35.00 for the pair.

Candy box, Harvest, embossed grapes w/lace edge, w/lid, 6½"..**$30.00**
Candy box, Princess, diamond-point bands, pointed faceted finial, 6x6" dia, from $20 to **$25.00**
Canister/Candy jar, Harvest, embossed grapes, 7" **$30.00**
Canister/Cookie jar, Harvest, embossed grapes, 9"....**$45.00**
Canister/Snack jar, Harvest, embossed grapes, 8".......**$35.00**

Center bowl, Harvest, embossed grapes w/paneled sides, 4-footed, 4½x8½x12"......................................**$35.00**
Cooler (iced tea tumbler), Harvest, embossed grapes, 14-oz, set of 4, from $35 to.................................**$40.00**
Creamer & sugar bowl on tray, Harvest, embossed grapes, 3-pc...**$30.00**
Egg/Hors d'oeuvre tray, sectioned w/off-side holder for 8 eggs, 12¾" dia, from $30 to...................**$35.00**
Garland bowl (comport), paneled, 7½x8½" dia **$35.00**
Goblet, Harvest, embossed grapes, 9-oz, set of 4, from $25 to..**$30.00**
Hen on nest, from $10 to..................................**$15.00**
Pitcher, Harvest, embossed grapes, 10½" **$50.00**
Plate, Bicentennial; American Eagle........................**$15.00**
Plate, hostess; Canterbury, allover diamond facets, flared crimped rim, 10" **$35.00**
Punch set, Princess, 26-pc..................................**$95.00**
Tidbit, allover embossed diamond points, shallow w/flared sides, 6½" **$18.00**
Wedding bowl (sm comport), Thumbprint, footed, 5x5" ..**$25.00**

Iridescent Gold Carnival Glass

Relish tray, Vintage, six sections, 9x12¾", $20.00.

Basket, Canterbury, waffle pattern, flaring sides drawn in at handle terminals, 9½x11x8½", from $35 to..........**$40.00**
Basket, Monticello, lg faceted allover diamonds, square, 7x6"..**$25.00**
Candy box, Harvest, embossed grapes, lace edge, footed, 6½x5¾"..**$20.00**
Candy dish, Harvest, embossed grapes, lace edge, footed, 6½"...**$20.00**
Canister/Candy jar, Harvest, embossed grapes, 7" **$25.00**
Canister/Cookie jar, Harvest, embossed grapes, 9"....**$35.00**
Canister/Snack jar, Harvest, embossed grapes, 8".......**$30.00**
Center bowl, Harvest, oval w/embossed grapes & paneled sides, 4½x8½x12" **$20.00**
Console set, wide naturalistic leaves form sides, 9" bowl w/pr 4½" bowl-type candle holders, 3-pc **$30.00**
Cooler (iced tea tumbler), Harvest, 14-oz...............**$10.00**
Egg relish plate, 11"..**$25.00**
Goblet, Harvest, embossed grapes, 9-oz..................**$12.00**
Hen on nest, 5½", from $10 to............................**$15.00**
Pitcher, Harvest, embossed grapes, 10½" **$45.00**

Plate, hostess; diamond embossing, shallow w/crimped & flared sides, 10"...............................**$18.00**

Punch set, Princess, 6-qt bowl w/12 cups, 12 hooks & ladle, 26-pc.............................**$95.00**

Salad set, Vintage, embossed fruit, apple-shaped rim w/applied stem, 13", w/fork & spoon, 3-pc.........**$25.00**

Wedding bowl, Harvest, embossed grapes, pedestal foot, 8½x8", from $25 to.....................................**$35.00**

Wedding bowl (sm comport), 5x5"............................**$12.00**

Iridescent Lime Carnival Glass

Candy box, Harvest, embossed grapes w/lace edge, w/lid, 6½"...**$25.00**

Canister/Candy jar, Harvest, embossed grapes, 7"......**$25.00**

Canister/Cookie jar, Harvest, embossed grapes, 9".....**$35.00**

Canister/Snack jar, Harvest, embossed grapes, 8".......**$30.00**

Center bowl, Harvest, embossed grapes, paneled sides, 4-footed, 4½x8½x12", from $25 to.........................**$30.00**

Compote, Harvest, embossed grapes, 7x6"..................**$30.00**

Console set, Harvest, embossed grapes, 10" comport w/comport-shaped candle holders, 3-pc..........................**$45.00**

Cooler (iced tea tumbler), Harvest, embossed grapes, 14-oz..**$10.00**

Creamer & sugar bowl on tray, Harvest, embossed grapes, 3-pc..**$25.00**

Egg/Relish tray, 12¾"...**$25.00**

Goblet, Harvest, embossed grapes, 9-oz....................**$10.00**

Hen on nest, from $10 to...**$15.00**

Pitcher, Harvest, embossed grapes, 10½"...................**$35.00**

Plate, hostess; allover diamond points, flared crimped sides, 10"..**$20.00**

Punch set, Princess, 26-pc...**$95.00**

Salad set, Vintage, embossed fruit, apple-shaped rim w/applied stem, 13", w/fork & spoon, 3-pc.........**$45.00**

Snack set, Harvest, embossed grapes, 4 cups & 4 plates, 8-pc..**$35.00**

Iridescent Sunset (Amberina) Carnival Glass (Heritage)

Goblet, 8-oz., from $15.00 to $20.00.

Basket, footed, 9x5x7", from $40 to..........................**$50.00**

Basket, squared, 9½x7½", from $60 to.......................**$60.00**

Bowl, crimped, 3¾x10"..**$50.00**

Butter dish, 5x7½" dia, from $35 to..........................**$45.00**

Cake stand, 7x14" dia, from $55 to...........................**$65.00**

Center bowl, 4¾x8½", from $40 to............................**$50.00**

Creamer & sugar bowl, from $45 to...........................**$55.00**

Dessert set, 8½" bowl, 12" plate, 2-pc.......................**$75.00**

Pitcher, 7¼", from $55 to...**$65.00**

Pitcher, 8¼"..**$75.00**

Plate, rim w/4 lg & 4 sm opposing lobes, 2x14", from $50 to..**$60.00**

Punch set, 10" bowl, pedestal, 8 cups, & ladle, 11-pc, from $150 to..**$175.00**

Rose bowl, 6½x6½", from $30 to...............................**$40.00**

Sauce set, 4½" bowl, 5½" plate, w/spoon, 3-pc.........**$35.00**

Swung vase, slender, footed, w/irregular rim, 11x3", from $25 to..**$35.00**

Tumbler, 3½", from $12 to...**$15.00**

Patterns

Canterbury, basket, waffle pattern, Lime, Sunset or Horizon Blue, 5½x12", from $35 to...............................**$55.00**

Decanter, Ruby Band Diamond Point, 12", $30.00.

Monticello, basket, lg faceted diamonds overall, Lemon, Lime, Sunset or Horizon Blue, square, 7x6", from $25 to....**$35.00**

Monticello, basket, lg faceted diamonds overall, Lemon, Lime, Sunset or Horizon Blue, 8¾x10½", from $35 to.........**$45.00**

Monticello, candy box, lg faceted overall diamonds, w/lid, Lemon, Lime, Sunset or Horizon Blue, 5¼x6", from $20 to......**$25.00**

Ruby Band Diamond Point, butter dish.......................**$28.00**

Ruby Band Diamond Point, chip & dip set, 13" dia...**$25.00**

Ruby Band Diamond Point, comport, 14½" dia..........**$20.00**

Ruby Band Diamond Point, cooler (iced tea tumbler), 15-oz..**$10.00**

Ruby Band Diamond Point, creamer & sugar bowl, 4½".**$15.00**

Ruby Band Diamond Point, creamer & sugar bowl, 4¾", on 6x9" tray..**$22.00**

Ruby Band Diamond Point, goblet, 12-oz...................**$12.00**

Ruby Band Diamond Point, On-the-Rocks, 9-oz.........**$10.00**

Ruby Band Diamond Point, pitcher, 8".......................**$20.00**

Ruby Band Diamond Point, plate, hostess; 12", from $12 to..**$18.00**

Ruby Band Diamond Point, relish tray, 1-part, 12" dia.......**$20.00**

Ruby Band Diamond Point, salt & pepper shakers, 4", pr..**$20.00**

Indianapolis 500 Racing Collectibles

You don't have to be a Hoosier to know that unless the weather interfers, this famous 500-mile race is held in Indianapolis every Memorial Day and has been since 1911. Collectors of Indy memorabilia have a plethora of race-related items to draw from and can zero in on one area or many, enabling them to build extensive and interesting collections. Some of the special areas of interest they pursue are autographs, photographs, or other memorabilia related to the drivers; pit badges; race programs and yearbooks; books and magazines; decanters and souvenir tumblers; and model race cars.

Advisor: Eric Jungnickel (See Directory, Indy 500 Memorabilia)

Book, Marlboro Salute to 75th Anniversary of Indy 500, 1986, hardcover..**$25.00**
Catalog, Motor Speedway Specialties Co, wholesale to souvenir concessionaires, ca 1950s, 7 pages, EX.......**$40.00**
Coaster, silver w/filigree sides, logo in scroll on white, stamped Japan, late 1940s....................................**$25.00**
Folder, 1965 Qualifying, GC Murphy Special #67 w/ad for GC Murphy Stores, from $10 to **$12.00**
Game, Indy 500 75th Running, complete w/picture card for each winning driver since 1911, VG **$25.00**
Media guide, driver biographies, car builders' information, statistics, historical information, 1958....................**$35.00**
Media Guide, driver biographies, car builders' information, statistics, historical information, 1966....................**$20.00**
Media guide, driver biographies, stats, car builders' & historical information, 1971...**$10.00**
Media guide, driver biographies, stats, car builders' & historical information, features Jimmy Bryan, 1959.......**$35.00**
Mug, 1958 Jimmy Bryan, Belond AP Special...............**$35.00**
Mug, 1983 Indy 500 w/Shell logo, Libbey, 8" **$15.00**
Pin-back button, Detroit Diesel Quality Club, red & blue enamel on gold shield, 1944..................................**$15.00**
Postcard, color photo w/Eddie Sachs in #2 Autolite Special..**$15.00**
Postcard, Wally Dallenbach & #6 Sugaripe car, w/autograph & 1967-77 statistics, 5x7"......................................**$15.00**
Program, 1932...**$140.00**
Program, 1938...**$125.00**
Program, 1951 ....**$50.00**
Program, 1960-1970, any, EX......................................**$25.00**
Program, 1970-1980, any, EX......................................**$15.00**
Program, 1982-1990, any, EX......................................**$10.00**
Program, 1984 ....**$10.00**
Program, 1988 ....**$10.00**
Record, Great Moments From The Indy 500 (1911-1974), 33 1/3 rpm, 1974, NM..**$25.00**
Ticket, shows 1962 winner Roger Ward & car, 1963, unused **$15.00**
Toy, Indy racer #1, red w/yellow wheels & blue driver, Renwal, M..**$25.00**
Tray, logo w/1978 Ford Mustang **$25.00**
Tumbler, winners through 1950 listed, winged-wheel logo on clear glass..**$20.00**
Tumbler, 1972, short..**$10.00**

Yearbook, Indy Car World Series, 1981, 144 pages **$10.00**

Italian Glass

Throughout the century, the island of Murano has been recognized as one of the major glass-making centers of the world. Companies including Venini, Barovier, Aureliano Toso, Barvini, Vistosi, AVEM, Cenedese, Cappellin, Seguso, and Archimede Seguso have produced very fine art glass, examples of which today often bring several thousand dollars on the secondary market — superior examples much more. Such items are rarely seen at the garage sale and flea market level, but what you will be seeing are the more generic glass clowns, birds, ashtrays, and animals, generally refered to simply as Murano glass. Their values are determined by the techniques used in their making more than size alone. For instance, an item with gold inclusions, controlled bubbles, fused glass patches, or layers of colors is more desirable than one that has none of these elements, even though it may be larger. For more information concerning the specific companies mentioned above, see *Schroeder's Antiques Price Guide* (Collector Books.)

Ashtray, clown figural, Venetian, original label, from $75.00 to $90.00.

Ashtray, cranberry & clear, controlled bubbles, 3 rests, 3¼x6" dia **$25.00**
Ashtray, crimped 3-D swirls on outside, emerald green to clear w/gold, controlled bubbles, 2½x6"..............**$18.00**
Ashtray, pear shape, black w/turquoise & gold inclusions, 5¾"...**$10.00**
Basket, clear, nearly rectangular w/vertical ribs, free-form pulled strands meet at center for handle, 10x8x9"..**$65.00**
Basket, clear & pink w/gold flecks, signed Salviati....**$65.00**
Basket, deep teal w/scalloped rim, polished bottom, open handle, 14x7"..**$42.00**
Bell, Diamond Quilt w/coralene **$95.00**
Bowl, amber to green rim, pinched swirled leaves on exterior, free-forms at rim, oval, 11" L............................**$34.00**
Bowl, clear to cranberry, pinched clear points, deep ruffle at rim, controlled bubbles, 2¾x7"............................**$23.00**
Bowl, multicolor end-of-day spatters w/gold, pulled & folded looped rim, 2½x8"..**$42.00**
Bowl, orange to red at rim, spiral ribbed, deep scalloped free-form rim w/pulled points, 4½x8¾" **$45.00**
Bowl, orange w/controlled bubbles, crimped & folded rim, clear tab handles, oval, 3x6x8½"..........................**$30.00**

Bowl, red to topaz, controlled bubbles, free-form pulled points form oval, 5x5x15½" **$45.00**

Bowl, star shape, aqua to plum, raised ribbed sides, 6 points curve up, 4½x12½"..**$55.00**

Bowl, topaz to emerald, 6-pointed star shape w/6 ribs & pulled clear points, 3½x11" **$45.00**

Bowl, white & aqua w/spiraling black & metallic streaks, 2¾x9" **$32.00**

Bowl, white & pink spiral bands, 4 pulled points arch at square corners, 6x10" **$75.00**

Bowl, white to pale green w/silver & multicolor spatters, green rim, 3x8½" **$34.00**

Candy dish, clown w/black hat & collar, white pompoms, face & hands, red heart-shaped bowl body, 5"....**$50.00**

Compote, ruby w/applied leaf handles, swirled & footed, crimped & flared rim, Novecento, 4x8½" **$125.00**

Cornucopia, ruby ruffled hemmed rim, clear 5-lobed leaf foot, Novecento, 9"....................................**$115.00**

Dish, amber, controlled bubbles, crimped rim, 2x8" ..**$22.00**

Dish, amber to electric blue rim, vertical ribbed base w/horizontal crimps, scalloped 5-point rim, 2¾x8½"....**$27.00**

Dish, green, free-form rolled & pinched rim, controlled bubbles, 2¾x6" L...**$18.00**

Dish, swan form, clear body, topaz & pink wings, cobalt tail, green neck & amber beak, 8"...............................**$70.00**

Figurine, cat, clear with yellow underlayer, gold-flecked bow, Venetian, ca 1950s, 6", $75.00. (Photo courtesy Marbena Fyke)

Figurine, duck, crystal w/green & gold, 7½"...............**$65.00**

Figurine, horse, millefiori, sm.....................................**$65.00**

Figurine, pelican, red & topaz w/clear beak & feet, ground pontil, 14½"...**$68.00**

Figurine, penguin, black & white w/applied eyes, beak, flippers & feet, stands on snow base, paper label, 15" **$150.00**

Lighter & ashtray set, clear w/gold flecks & bubbles.**$75.00**

Pitcher, boot shape, end-of-day w/applied studs on sides, crimped cuff, applied handle, 7" **$32.00**

Vase, clear to cranberry, 8 vertical ribs flare to 8-scallop oval rim, 5x7x10½" **$70.00**

Vase, green, cased, 4 clear raised semicircular folds, bulbous base, controlled bubbles, narrow mouth, 6" **$58.00**

Jade-ite Glassware

Jade-ite was produced by several companies from the 1940s through 1965. Many of Anchor Hocking's Fire-King lines were available in the soft opaque green Jade-ite, and Jeannette Glass as well as McKee produced their own versions.

It was always very inexpensive glass, and it was made in abundance. Dinnerware for the home as well as restaurants and a vast array of kitchenware items literally flooded the country for many years. Though a few rare pieces have become fairly expensive, most are still reasonably priced, and there are still bargains to be had.

For more information we recommend *Fire-King Fever '97* by April and Larry Tvorak; and *Kitchen Glassware of the Depression Years*; *Collectible Glassware of the '40s, '50s, and '60s*; and *Anchor Hocking's Fire King & More,* all by Gene Florence.

Advisor: April Tvorak (See Directory, Fire-King)

Bowl, cereal; Laurel, Fire-King **$12.00**

Bowl, cereal; Swirl/Shell, Fire-King............................**$10.00**

Bowl, desert; Charm/Square, Fire-King, 4¾" **$7.50**

Bowl, flanged grapefruit/cereal; Restaurant Ware, Fire-King **$12.00**

Bowl, flanged soup; Jane-Ray, Fire-King, Anchor Hocking..**$45.00**

Bowl, flat soup; Jane-Ray, Fire-King, Anchor Hocking.**$14.00**

Bowl, horizontal ribs w/flower vines, 7½" **$25.00**

Bowl, oatmeal; Jane-Ray, Fire-King, Anchor Hocking ..**$10.00**

Bowl, Restaurant Ware, Fire-King, deep, 10-oz...........**$13.00**

Bowl, rolled lip, Restaurant Ware, Fire-King, 15-oz....**$12.00**

Bowl, sauce; Jane-Ray, Fire-King, Anchor Hocking......**$5.00**

Bowl, sauce; Restaurant Ware, Fire-King **$4.50**

Bowl, sauce; Sheaf of Wheat, Fire-King.......................**$20.00**

Bowl, serving; embossed horizontal ribs & multicolor floral decoration, Jeannette, 9¾" **$35.00**

Bowl, serving; Jane-Ray, Fire-King, Anchor Hocking .**$14.00**

Bowl, serving; Laurel, Fire-King **$22.00**

Bowl, soup; Charm/Square **$22.00**

Bowl, soup; Laurel, Fire-King......................................**$16.00**

Bowl, Tom & Jerry; McKee **$75.00**

Butter dish, Anchor Hocking, ¼-lb **$25.00**

Butter dish, dark green, Jeannette................................**$45.00**

Canister, black lettering, square w/matching square lid, Jeannette, 48-oz, 5½"...**$45.00**

Canister, coffee; from $60.00 to $70.00. (Photo courtesy Gene Florence)

Creamer & sugar bowl, Charm/Square **$22.00**

Creamer & sugar bowl, Jane-Ray, w/lid, Fire-King, Anchor Hocking **$16.00**

Cup, demitasse; Restaurant Ware................................**$20.00**

Cup & saucer, Alice, Fire-King....................................**$5.00**

Cup & saucer, Charm/Square, Fire-King **$8.00**
Cup & saucer, Jane-Ray, Fire-King, Anchor Hocking....**$3.50**
Cup & saucer, Laurel, Fire-King..................................**$8.00**
Cup & saucer, Restaurant Ware, Fire-King **$6.50**
Cup & saucer, Sheaf of Wheat, Fire-King **$25.00**
Cup & saucer, Swirl/Flat, Fire-King **$15.00**
Cup & saucer, Swirl/Shell, Fire-King **$6.00**
Cup/mug, Ransom handle, Resturant Ware, Fire-King..**$7.00**
Dessert set, Leaf & Blossom, Fire-King.......................**$15.00**
Dish, refrigerator; floral lid, Jeannette, 10x5" **$40.00**
Dish, refrigerator; Hall style, McKee, 4x6" **$16.00**
Drippings jar, McKee, 4x5"...**$85.00**
Egg cup, McKee...**$12.00**
Ice bucket, metal handle, Fenton................................**$55.00**
Jar, Epsom Salt; Jeannette..**$75.00**
Jug, batter; w/lid, Jeannette **$250.00**
Measuring pitcher, light green, sunflower in bottom, Jeannette, 2-cup **$28.00**
Mug, chocolate; slim w/flared top, Restaurant Ware, Fire-King **$15.00**
Mug, coffee; Restaurant Ware, Fire-King, lightweight, 8-oz..**$7.00**
Napkin holder, Serv-All **$175.00**
Pitcher, ball form, Restaurant Ware, Fire-King, 80-oz..**$185.00**
Plate, bread & butter; Restaurant Ware, Fire-King, 5½" ...**$4.50**
Plate, dinner; Alice, Fire-King......................................**$22.00**
Plate, dinner; Jane-Ray, Fire-King, Anchor Hocking **$5.00**
Plate, dinner; Restuarant Ware, Fire-King, 9" **$8.00**
Plate, dinner; Sheaf of Wheat, Fire-King.....................**$30.00**
Plate, dinner; Swirl/Shell, Fire-King...............................**$8.00**
Plate, grill; Laurel, Fire-King, 3-compartments.............**$12.00**
Plate, grill; Restaurant Ware, Fire-King, 3-compartment..**$14.00**
Plate, grill; Restaurant Ware, Fire-King, 5-compartment..**$18.00**
Plate, luncheon; Restaurant Ware, Fire-King, 8" **$15.00**
Plate, pie/salad; Restaurant Ware, Fire-King, 6¾" **$4.50**
Plate, salad; Charm/Square, Fire-King, 6⅝" **$7.50**
Plate, salad; Jane-Ray, Fire-King, Anchor Hocking........**$6.00**
Plate, salad; Laurel, Fire-King **$10.00**
Plate, salad; Swirl/Flat, Fire-King................................**$35.00**
Plate, salad; Swirl/Shell, Fire-King................................**$6.00**
Platter, Jane-Ray, oval, Fire-King, Anchor Hocking.....**$15.00**
Platter, Laurel, oval, Fire-King, minimum value **$25.00**
Platter, oval, partitioned, Restaurant Ware, Fire-King..**$38.00**
Platter, oval, Swirl/Shell, Fire-King **$28.00**
Platter, rectangular, Charm/Square, Fire-King..............**$20.00**
Platter, Resturant Ware, Fire-King, 9½" or 11½", each..**$20.00**
Reamer, Sunkist..**$55.00**
Refrigerator dish, floral lid, Jeannette, 5x10" **$40.00**
Salt & pepper shakers, embossed Salt (Pepper), McKee, pr **$45.00**
Salt & pepper shakers, Laurel, footed, Fire-King, scarce, pr, minimum value **$45.00**
Salt & pepper shakers, souvenir; Jeannette, pr **$125.00**
Salt box, Jeannette...**$195.00**
Sauce pan, 2-spout, Resturant Ware, Fire-King.........**$85.00**
Saucer, demitasse; Restaurant Ware............................**$20.00**
Shaker, toiletry; Jeannette, each **$150.00**
Sherbet, Laurel, Fire-King...**$6.50**
Sherbet, McKee **$9.00**
Skillet, Fire-King, miniature...**$40.00**

Sugar shaker, black lettering, silver metal lid **$35.00**
Tumbler, Jeannette, 12-oz **$15.00**
Vase, Jeannette..**$15.00**

Refrigerator dish, solid lid and design, Fire-King, 3x4½x5", $18.00.

Japan Ceramics

This category is narrowed down to the inexpensive novelty items produced in Japan from 1921 to 1941 and again from 1947 until the present. Though Japanese ceramics marked Nippon, Noritake, and Occupied Japan have long been collected, some of the newest fun-type collectibles on today's market are the figural ashtrays, pincushions, wall pockets, toothbrush holders, etc., that are marked 'Made in Japan' or simply 'Japan.' In her book called *Collector's Guide to Made in Japan Ceramics*, Carole Bess White explains the pitfalls you will encounter when you try to determine production dates. Collectors refer to anything produced before WWII as 'old,' and anything made after 1952 as 'new.' Backstamps are inconsistent as to wording and color, and styles are eclectic. Generally, items with applied devices are old, and they are heavier and thicker. Often they were more colorful than the newer items, since fewer colors mean less expense to the manufacturer. Lustre glazes are usually indicative of older pieces, especially the deep solid colors. When lustre was used after the war, it was often mottled with contrasting hues.

Imaginative styling and strong colors are what give these Japanese ceramics their charm, and they also are factors to consider when you make your purchases. You'll find all you need to know to be a wise shopper in the book we recommended above.

See also Blue Willow; Cat Collectibles; Condiment Sets; Enesco; Flower Frogs; Geisha Girl; Holt Howard; Kreiss; Lamps; Lefton; Napkin Dolls; Occupied Japan Collectibles; Toothbrush Holders; Wall Pockets.

Ashtray, calico animal between 6 snuffers, 2 rests, 3", from $15 to...**$22.00**
Ashtray, calico cat w/card suit wheelbarrow, 2¼", from $15 to...**$20.00**
Ashtray, card suit form w/calico elephant standing at side, 2¼", from $17 to...**$27.00**
Bank, dog, stylized sitting pose, multicolor glossy finish, 4¾", from $15 to..**$22.00**

Bank, friar, seated pose, coin slot in tummy, multicolor glossy finish, ca mid-1940s, 5¼", from $8 to **$18.00**

Bell, Santa, traditional suit w/black belt, hole in hat for string hanger, 2¼" **$8.00**

Bisquit jar, 6-sided w/red cherry decor, cherry finial, white & multicolor glossy finish, rattan handle, 6"..............**$55.00**

Bookends, pelican, cream & multicolor matt finish, inscribed To Angel March 17, 1941, 6", pr, from $25 to **$40.00**

Bowl, applied butterflies on outside, orange lustre interior, blue & multicolor lustre exterior, 6½", from $30 to..........**$45.00**

Cake plate, cherry blossoms on white, Moriyama Ware, late 1930s, 12¼", from $20 to **$35.00**

Candle holder, chamberstick-style w/stylized floral design, yellow & multicolor glossy finish, 4½", from $30 to....**$45.00**

Candlesticks, plain form w/circular foot, amber & cream mottled lustre, 6¼", pr..**$35.00**

Candy dish, elephant figural, w/howdah lid, white w/multicolor glossy finish, 8¾", from $50 to **$75.00**

Cigarette box, block-like stylized dog, ashtray lid w/head, Goldcastle, red glossy finish, from $35 to **$55.00**

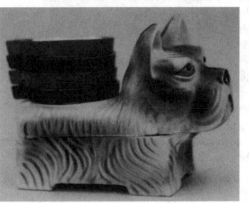

Cigarette box, Scottie dog with four stacking ashtrays, 4¼", from $45.00 to $50.00. (Photo courtesy of Carole Bess White)

Cigarette holder/humidor, elephant figural, match holder howdah lid, multicolor lustre finish, 5½", from $50 to ..**$65.00**

Creamer & sugar bowl, honey bee decor & finial, basketweave hive form, cream & multicolor glossy finish, 4¾", pr..**$28.00**

Creamer & sugar bowl, stylized hen w/blue, orange & black feathers, orange beak & gold trim, 3¼", from $45 to..........**$60.00**

Desk calendar, animal figural on tray, frame at back holds cardboard month calendar, multicolor glossy finish, 2¾".**$38.00**

Hatpin holder, elephant figural, green glossy finish, 3½", from $20 to **$30.00**

Incense burner, Egyptian girl kneeling w/burner on lap, tan lustre & multicolor glossy finish, 5½", from $50 to.......**$65.00**

Incense burner, seated gentleman in black suit & blue vest, smoking pipe, multicolor glossy finish, 4¼", from $20 to ..**$30.00**

Lemon server, checkerboard design w/gold center handle, multicolor glossy finish, 5½" dia, from $25 to......**$40.00**

Marmalade, embossed pastoral scene around sides, rattan handle, aqua & multicolor matt finish, 4", from $25 to **$35.00**

Mayonnaise set, blossom form, stork decor, multicolor enamel on white lustre, Goldcastle, 6½" wide, 3-pc, from $32 to...**$45.00**

Pincushion, calico elephant w/top hat, 3¼", from $6 to..**$10.00**

Pincushion, rhino figural, blue lustre w/brown trim, 2", from $15 to...**$25.00**

Pitcher, rooster's head, mouth as spout, multicolor glossy finish, 5", from $20 to...**$25.00**

Planter, Dutch boy w/white swan, multicolor glossy finish, 5½", from $12 to...**$22.00**

Planter, pixie sitting at tree stump, flower at side, multicolor matt finish, 3¾", from $10 to **$18.00**

Planter, swan, realistic figural, multicolor glossy finish, 7¾", from $15 to...**$25.00**

Relish dish, 3-compartment card suit form, green crackle finish w/applied floral decor at center, 8", from $15 to.....**$25.00**

Ring tray, tray lettered Just Married, couple w/dog stand at back, multicolor lustre, 3½", from $12 to **$20.00**

Tea set, child's, teapot w/creamer & sugar bowl, w/lid, blue & multicolor lustre, pot: 4½", 3-pc set, from $30 to...**$40.00**

Teapot, checkerboard design, multicolor lustre, 6", from $28 to...**$38.00**

Teapot, florals & butterfly, tan & multicolor lustre, 6¾", from $28 to...**$42.00**

Toothpick holder, stylized blue-faced dog stands to side of square holder, 3¼", from $18 to............................**$28.00**

Vase, bird at base of tall flower, domed footed base, multicolor lustre & glossy finish, 7¼", from $40 to......**$55.00**

Vase, dog on book near lg urn, multicolor semimatt finish, 3¾", from $12 to..**$18.00**

Vase, pixie on tree swing, multicolor lustre, 4¼", from $15 to...**$25.00**

Water set, stylized blue & white bamboo on white band, w/solid orange bands, Kinkozan, 4" & 6", 2-pc...**$65.00**

Flask, dog in bisque, brown-glazed bottle, All's Well That Ends Well, Black mark #1 w/Pat applied for #9634-7, 4¼", from $50.00 to $65.00. (Photo courtesy of Carole Bess White)

Jewel Tea Company

At the turn of the century, there was stiff competition among door-to-door tea-and-coffee companies, and most of them tried to snag the customer by doling out coupons that could eventually be traded in for premiums. But the thing that set the Jewel Tea people apart from the others was that their premiums were awarded to the customer first, then 'earned' through the purchases that followed. This set the tone of their business dealings which obviously contributed to their success, and very soon in addition to the basic products they started out with, the company entered the food-manufacturing field. They eventually became one of the country's largest retailers. Today their products, containers, premiums, and advertising ephemera are all very collectible.

Advisors: Bill and Judy Vroman (See Directory, Jewel Tea)

Baking powder, Jewel, script logo w/white letters, round cylindrical tin, 1950s-60s, 1-lb, from $20 to..........**$30.00**

Baking powder, logo & letters in white on red, red cylindrical tin w/red lid, from $20 to **$30.00**

Coaster set, Peasant design, nine-piece, in original box, from $25.00 to $30.00. (Photo courtesy Bill and Judy Vroman)

Coffee, Jewel Blend, white logo & letters on orange, shaded orange to brown ground, 1948, 2-lb, from $25 to...**$35.00**

Coffee, Jewel Blend, white logo & letters on orange & gold paper...**$40.00**

Coffee, Jewel Private Blend, white letters on brown, 1-lb, from $15 to...**$25.00**

Coffee, Jewel Special Blend, white & orange letters on brown circle, brown stripes on white ground, 2-lb, from $15 to **$25.00**

Coffee, Royal Jewel, brown & white on yellow, 1-lb, from $20 to...**$35.00**

Coffee, West Coast, white letters on orange & brown w/bell at top center, 1960s, 2-lb, from $25 to **$35.00**

Dishes, Melmac, 1960s, 8 place settings, from $150 to.**$170.00**

Extract, Jewel Imitation Vanilla, orange & white letters on brown rectangular box, 1960s, 4-oz, from $20 to ..**$30.00**

Extract, Jewel Lemon, orange, blue & white, 1916-19, from $40 to...**$50.00**

Flour sifter, lithographed metal, EX **$485.00**

Laundry product, Daintiflakes, marked Soft Feathery Flakes of Pure Mild Soap, blue & pink box, from $25 to..**$30.00**

Laundry product, Daybreak Laundry Set, from $15 to...**$20.00**

Laundry product, Grano Granulated Soap, marked Made For General Cleaning, blue & white box, 2-lb, from $25 to **$30.00**

Laundry product, Pure Gloss Starch, teal & white box, from $25 to **$30.00**

Malted milk mixer, Jewel-T, from $40 to **$50.00**

Mints, Jewel Mints, round green tin, 1920s, 1-lb, from $30 to **$40.00**

Mix, Jewel Sunbrite Mix, paper label on Mason jar w/metal screw-on lid, 1960s, 26-oz, from $15 to................**$25.00**

Mix, Jewel Tea Coconut Dessert, brown & white logo & letters on round tan tin, 1930s, 14-oz, from $30 to..**$40.00**

Mix, Jewel Tea Devil's Food Cake Flour, 1920s, 10-oz, from $30 to...**$40.00**

Mix, Jewel Tea Prepared Tapioca, logo & brown letters on orange w/brown stripes, tall square tin, 1930s, from $25 to...**$35.00**

Mixer, Mary Dunbar, from $40 to **$50.00**

Mixer, Mary Dunbar, white, electric, w/stand, bowl & original hang tag **$100.00**

Napkins, paper w/printed pattern, box of 200 ....**$25.00**

Pickle fork, Jewel-T, from $20 to................................**$25.00**

Prepared food, Jewel Mix Nuts, orange & brown letters on brown-striped ground, round tin, 1960s, 1-lb, from $15 to....**$20.00**

Prepared food, Jewel Quick Oats, white & orange letters on round cylindrical box, from $40 to **$50.00**

Prepared food, Jewel Tea Cocoa or Jewel Cocoa, various boxes, each, from $25 to.......................................**$40.00**

Prepared food, Jewel Tea Jellied Spiced Drops, orange & white letters on orange rectangular box, from $20 to.......**$30.00**

Prepared food, Jewel Tea Peanut Butter, multicolored paper label on glass jar w/screw-on lid, 1930s, 1-lb, from $30 to..**$40.00**

Prepared product, Jewel Tea Bags, gold & brown logo w/brown letters, green dragon to side, 1948, EX...**$65.00**

Razor blades, Jewel-T **$5.00**

Scale, Jewel-T, M, from $45 to...................................**$55.00**

Sweeper, Jewel, from $25 to **$35.00**

Sweeper, Jewel Little Bissell, from $40 to...................**$50.00**

Sweeper, Jewel Suction Sweeper, letters on lg wood case, hand-push style w/wood handle, early 1900s, lg............**$150.00**

Sweeper, Jewel Sweeper, gold letters on black, 1930s-40s, from $80 to...**$100.00**

Sweeper, Jewel Sweeper, tan letters on dark tan, 1930s-40s, from $80 to...**$100.00**

Tea bags box, 1948, EX...**$65.00**

Hot or cold tumblers in original box, from $20.00 to $30.00. (Photo courtesy Bill and Judy Vroman)

Jewelry

Today's costume jewelry collectors may range from nine to ninety and have tastes as varied as their ages, but one thing they all have in common is their love of these distinctive items of jewelry, some which were originally purchased at the corner five-&-dimes, others from department stores.

Costume jewelry became popular, simply because it was easily affordable by the average woman. Today jewelry made before 1954 is considered to be 'antique,' while the term 'collectible' jewelry generally refers to those pieces made after that time. 1954 was the year that costume jewelry was federally recognized as an American art form, and the copyright law was passed to protect the artists' designs. The copyright mark (c in a circle) found on the back of a piece identifies a post-1954 'collectible.'

Quality should always be the primary consideration when shopping for these treasures. Remember that pieces with colored rhinestones bring the higher prices. (Note: a 'rhinestone' is a clear, foil-backed, leaded glass crystal — unless it is a 'colored rhinestone' — while a 'stone' is not foiled.) A complete set (parure) increases in value by 20% over the total of its components. Check for a manufacturer's mark, since a signed piece is worth 20% more than one of comparable quality, but not signed. Some of the best designers are Miriam Haskell, Eisenberg, Trifari, Hollycraft, and Weiss.

Early plastic pieces (Lucite, Bakelite, and celluloid, for example) are very collectible. Some Lucite is used in combination with wood, and the figural designs are especially desirable.

There are several excellent reference books available if you'd like more information. Lillian Baker has written several: *Art Nouveau and Art Deco Jewelry; Twentieth Century Fashionable Plastic Jewelry; 50 Years of Collectible Fashion Jewelry;* and *100 Years of Collectible Jewelry.* Books by other authors include *Collecting Rhinestone Colored Jewelry* by Maryanne Dollan; *The Art and Mystique of Shell Cameos* by Ed Aswad and Michael Weinstein; *Christmas Pins* by Jill Gallina; *Collecting Antique Stickpins* by Jack and 'Pet' Kerins; *Collectible Costume Jewelry* by Cherri Simonds; and *Costume Jewelry, A Practical Handbook and Value Guide* by Fred Rezazadeh.

Advisor: Marcia Brown (See Directory, Jewelry)

Club/Newsletter: *Vintage Fashion and Costume Jewelry*
P.O. Box 265, Glen Oaks, NY 11004

Bar pin, Bakelite, amber w/circular carving, 3x½" **$25.00**
Bar pin, Bakelite, red diamond shape w/chrome border, 3".**$18.00**
Bracelet, Bakelite, black, linked w/metal chain & snap clasp, ca 1935, from $85 to...**$125.00**
Bracelet, Bakelite, butterscotch bangle, ribbed, 1" wide ..**$65.00**
Bracelet, Bakelite, butterscotch bangle w/carved leaf design, ½" wide **$48.00**
Bracelet, Bakelite, butterscotch w/wavy chips separated by white beads, double strung, elastic, 1½" **$38.00**
Bracelet, Bakelite, dimpled cuff style, 2-color, 1940s, from $275 to...**$325.00**
Bracelet, Bakelite, 4-color flattened bead shapes strung on stretch elastic band, 1930s, from $125 to............**$135.00**
Bracelet, Eisenberg, rhinestones set in rhodium, individually linked & flexible, wide, 1950s, from $110 to **$125.00**
Bracelet, Eisenberg, rhinestones set in rhodium, wide, 1950s, from $125 to..**$145.00**
Bracelet, Eisenberg Ice, rhinestones set in rhodium, narrow, patented safety clasp, ca 1940, from $95 to **$125.00**

Bracelet, Emmons, black plastic squares (3) set in rhodium chain, ca 1950s...**$10.00**
Bracelet, gold-tone chain w/lg jonquil square & oval rhinestones...**$18.00**
Bracelet, Nettie Rosenstein, pave-set rhinestones in 7 linked gold-tone ovals, 1950s, from $95 to....................**$125.00**
Bracelet, Renoir, copper, flowing curved design, open bangle style..**$14.00**
Bracelet, Sarah Coventry, gold-tone wheat shocks form design, ca 1950s, from $5 to **$10.00**
Bracelet, 5 rows of pink cabochons, rhinestones, white cabochons & moonstones **$18.00**
Brooch, Art, white enamel & multicolor pastel rhinestone flowers w/green, gray & white cabochons on gold-tone, 2"..**$25.00**
Brooch, Avante, textured silver-tone w/openwork, clustered ribbon shapes, 2½"...**$12.00**
Brooch, Bakelite, red tomato w/green leaves, ribbed & carved, 3x2½"..**$90.00**
Brooch, Catalin, amber pear shape w/green felt fabric stem, ca 1940 ....**$110.00**
Brooch, celluloid flower, red w/carved ivory & red center, 3"..**$12.00**
Brooch, Cini for Gumps, sterling flower form, handcrafted, 1945-50 ....**$95.00**
Brooch, Coro, gold-tone flower w/rhinestones in alternating petals, 1960-65 ....**$35.00**
Brooch, Eisenberg Ice, Christmas tree, multicolor rhinestones on brushed gold-tone, star top, 3", MOC.............**$40.00**
Brooch, Emmons, antique auto form of white rhinestones set in rhodium, ca 1970...**$35.00**
Brooch, Emmons, aurora borealis stones & cultured pearls in gold-tone star w/15 irregular points, 1950s **$30.00**
Brooch, Har, flower form w/pearl center & tiny faux seed pearls on antiqued brushed gold-tone stems, 2¾"..**$38.00**
Brooch, Hattie Carnegie, candle among holly leaves, gold-tone w/red & green enameling, ca 1960s-early 1970s, from $40 to..**$65.00**
Brooch, Hobe, 3-colored gemstones, bezel-set in gold-tone filigree, ca 1948, 2¾x1½".................................**$300.00**
Brooch, Lea Stein, Paris, thermoplastic boy on skateboard figural, 1965...**$125.00**
Brooch, olive green w/blue forget-me-not floral mosaic design in silver openwork frame, 1½" oval..........**$14.00**
Brooch, Regency Jewels, aurora borealis stones in cast mounting, 1950-60 ....**$65.00**
Brooch, Sandor, yellow enameled rose bud w/green enamel leaves, 3" **$18.50**
Brooch, Tobias Mexico, sterling bar w/lg balls & turned ends, 2" **$25.00**
Brooch, Trifari, brushed silver-tone Art Moderne spiral, 2" **$18.00**
Brooch, Trifari, feathery leaves, brushed silver-tone w/pearls & rhinestones, 2"..**$18.00**
Brooch, Trifari, gold-tone basket w/baguette & pear-shaped topaz stones & clear rhinestones, ca 1955-65.......**$45.00**
Brooch, Trifari, leafy gold-plated branch w/cultured pearls & green enamel leaves, 1960s **$65.00**
Brooch, Weisner, imitation sapphires & pave-set rhinestones form flower-like shape, 1960 ....**$65.00**

Brooch, Weiss, Christmas tree w/green, red & topaz rhinestones, crystal baguettes, & pear shape at bottom, 3" **$38.00**

Brooch, Weiss, gold-tone ribbon shape w/lg iridescent 'gold' rhinestones in oval, 2½".......................................**$28.00**

Brooch, Weiss, japanned, clear rhinestones accented by row of emerald green, $72.00. (Photo courtesy Marcia Brown)

Brooch, white baroque faux pearl w/sm faux pearls & rhinestones on silver-tone w/openwork, 2" **$30.00**

Brooch & earrings, Emmons, brushed gold-tone w/green prong-set square rhinestone, unfoiled, 1½"..........**$30.00**

Brooch & earrings, Emmons, simulated pearls & rhinestones on gold-tone, clip backs, ca 1960...........................**$45.00**

Brooch & earrings, England, porcelain horseshoe w/blue enamel forget-me-nots, 2" **$22.00**

Brooch & earrings, Lisner, butterscotch enamel leaves & smoke topaz rhinestones on brushed gold-tone, 2¾".........**$30.00**

Chain, Sarah Coventry, rhodium twist form, ca 1960 ..**$10.00**

Clip, Art Deco-style w/crystal rhinestones & emerald square rhinestone accents, 2½" L **$25.00**

Clip, Bakelite, butterscotch, amber & green berries (beads), green leaves, 4"...**$75.00**

Clip, Bakelite, deep carved, rectangular, 2x1".............**$28.00**

Critter, pin, Bakelite, black, carved, ca 1935 ....**$65.00**

Critter, pin, Boucher, angelfish, 2-tone green enamel on gold-tone, 1950s **$90.00**

Critter, pin, Brooks, gilded brass bird in flight, rhinestone accents, 1955-65 ....**$75.00**

Critter, pin, Catalin, carved navy turtle on scalloped shell, ca 1940 ....**$225.00**

Critter, pin, Coro, bird w/white enamel & amethyst rhinestones on gold-tone, 2" & 1", pr...........................**$14.00**

Critter, pin, Coro, peacock on branch, enamel on gold-plate, 1950s, from $55 to **$75.00**

Critter, pin, Doliet, France, poodle, porcelain on brass, painted details, w/chain & collar, 2½" **$32.00**

Critter, pin, Kramer, gold-tone butterfly w/multicolor blue stones overall, 1960s..**$65.00**

Critter, pin, Trifari, silver-plated elephant w/cut Bohemian crystal & rhinestone accents, 1940s.....................**$95.00**

Critter, pin, BSK, gold-tone tucan w/faux ruby eyes **$35.00**

Earrings, Alice Caviness, topaz smoke & black navette rhinestones, clip backs, 2", pr **$12.00**

Earrings, Christian Dior, gold-plated shell design, sm, 1965, pr...**$35.00**

Earrings, Coro, lime green art glass ovals w/pearls & tiny pink rhinestone on gold-tone, screw-on backs, pr.........**$10.00**

Earrings, Czechoslovakia, coral beads & drops on gold-tone, clip backs, pr...**$15.00**

Earrings, Czechoslovakia, filigree drops w/topaz rhinestones, screw-on backs, 1", pr.......................................**$15.00**

Earrings, Eisenberg Ice, blue & pink imitation zircons, clip backs, ca 1960, pr, from $55 to **$65.00**

Earrings, Eugene, white-beaded cluster w/faceted pastel crystal dangles, clip backs, pr...............................**$24.00**

Earrings, Giovanni, brushed silver-tone leaf, clip backs, pr **$6.00**

Earrings, Haskell, branch coral & white beads, clip backs, 1¼", pr...**$22.00**

Earrings, Hollycraft, pastel multicolor faceted stones in cluster set in gold-tone, clip backs, 1960s, pr.............**$30.00**

Earrings, Jomaz, carved jade-ite ovals w/tiny rhinestones, clip backs, 1", pr...**$22.50**

Earrings, KJL, thermoset plastic black & white stars, 1980, clip backs, 1980, pr...**$35.00**

Earrings, Kramer, pearl & rhinestone beads, clip backs, pr **$10.00**

Earrings, Lisner, rhinestones flank marquise stone, clip backs, 1", pr..**$10.00**

Earrings, Marvella, lg pearl domes w/crystal rhinestones, clip backs, pr...**$10.00**

Earrings, molded plastic flowers w/rhinestone centers, button style w/screw-on backs, ca 1960, pr **$20.00**

Earrings, plastic, black layered squares w/pastel multicolor rhinestones, clip backs, 2", pr..............................**$10.00**

Earrings, Trifari, apple shape w/baguette rhinestones set in rhodium, clip backs, 1950s, pr...........................**$35.00**

Earrings, Trifari, floral design w/topaz rhinestone petals, long gold rhinestone dangles, clip backs, pr **$18.00**

Earrings, Weiss, Austrian faux gemstones on japanned mounting that resembles butterfly, 1950s-60s, pr.**$85.00**

Earrings, Weiss, 3 lg clear rhinestones, sm rhinestone accents, clip backs, 1", pr..**$14.00**

Earrings, West Germany, composition banana cluster w/leaves, clip backs, pr **$18.00**

Necklace and earrings, Mexican sterling silver and amethyst, from $200.00 to $300.00 set.

Necklace, celluloid flower buds on link chain, ca 1935, from $65 to..**$85.00**

Necklace, Coro, multistrand gold-tone chains w/gold-tone spatter-look beads...**$12.00**

Necklace, Hobe, black glass beads, rhinestone spacers & pave rhinestone drop w/black oval cabochon, 24"...**$55.00**

Necklace, Kenneth Jay Lane, faux jade, coral, jet & pearls, 6-strand, ornate clasp, 1970-80, from $175 to.......**$225.00**

Necklace, unmarked, 4-strand Austrian aurora borealis beads, ca 1960...**$95.00**

Necklace, Weiss, black rhinestones & black rhinestone baguettes on 15" black rhinestone strand.............**$32.00**

Necklace & earrings, De Mario, 3 textured chains w/red faceted beads, pearls, rhinestones & filigree leaves..**$225.00**

Necklace & earrings, Hobe, mother-of-pearl cameo jacket w/rhinestones on 24" twist chain, 1½"..............**$110.00**

Necklace & earrings, W Germany, Lucite & thermoplastic beads, 3-strand, flower clasp, flower-form earrings.............**$50.00**

Parure, blue and green brilliants, deep color, 3" brooch, bracelet, and earrings, $325.00. (Photo courtesy Marcia Brown)

Parure, Hollycraft 1954, necklace, link & cuff bracelets, drop screw-back earrings & ring, shaded pink & purple stones **$350.00**

Parure, Trifari necklace, bangle bracelet, clip-back earrings, green & clear rhinestone baguettes on gold-tone...**$125.00**

Parure, unmarked, collar-style necklace, 4" bracelet, square earrings, hand-set pink rhinestones w/lavender baguettes..**$830.00**

Parure, unmarked, 4-strand necklace, 1-strand bracelet, chandelier screw-back earrings, linked red & sm pink rhinestones..**$175.00**

Ring, class; 10k gold w/black enameling, 1965, approximately 10 grams..**$65.00**

Ring, David-Anderson, gold-wash sterling w/white enameling..**$30.00**

Ring, Hattie Carnegie, adjustable, ram's head w/faux coral horns, Lucite head w/rhinestones **$175.00**

Watch pin, Waltham size D watch, 14k gold, 1¼", hangs from simple pin..**$85.00**

Johnson Bros.

There is a definite renewal of interest in dinnerware collecting right now, and a good percentage of what you find in shops and malls today was made by this Staffordshire company. They made many scenic patterns, and these are among the most popular with collectors. Though some of their lines, Friendly Village, for instance, are being produced, most are no longer as extensive as they once were, so the secondary market is being tapped to replace broken items that are not available anywhere else.

On addition to their company logo, their dinnerware is also stamped with the pattern name. Today they're a part of the Wedgwood group.

Friendly Village, platter, 13¾x11¼", from $25.00 to $30.00.

Coaching Scenes, bowl, cereal; 6", from $7 to...........**$10.00**
Coaching Scenes, bowl, fruit; 5", from $5.50 to **$7.50**
Coaching Scenes, creamer...**$18.00**
Coaching Scenes, cup & saucer, from $10 to.............**$15.00**
Coaching Scenes, plate, dinner; 10", from $12 to **$18.00**
Coaching Scenes, platter, lg, 15", from $40 to.............**$50.00**
English Chippendale, bowl, cereal; 6", from $7 to **$10.00**
English Chippendale, bowl, vegetable; round, from $20 to **$25.00**
English Chippendale, cup & saucer, from $12 to........**$15.00**
English Chippendale, plate, dinner; 10", from $10 to.**$15.00**
English Chippendale, sugar bowl, w/lid....................**$25.00**
English Chippendale, teapot, from $55 to **$60.00**
Friendly Village, bowl, cereal; 6"..................................**$6.00**
Friendly Village, bowl, fruit..**$4.00**
Friendly Village, bowl, rim soup; from $9 to **$12.00**
Friendly Village, bowl, square, 6", from $10 to..........**$12.50**
Friendly Village, bowl, vegetable; oval, from $18 to ..**$22.00**
Friendly Village, bowl, vegetable; round, from $15 to..**$20.00**
Friendly Village, bowl, vegetable; w/lid, from $40 to...**$50.00**
Friendly Village, butter dish, from $25 to **$35.00**
Friendly Village, coaster **$15.00**
Friendly Village, coffeepot, from $45 to **$55.00**
Friendly Village, creamer...**$18.00**
Friendly Village, cup & saucer, from $7 to **$9.00**
Friendly Village, gravy boat stand...............................**$12.00**
Friendly Village, gravy boat w/stand, from $30 to......**$40.00**
Friendly Village, milk pitcher, 5½", from $25 to **$30.00**
Friendly Village, mug, from $9 to.................................**$12.00**

Friendly Village, plate, bread & butter; from $4 to.......**$5.00**
Friendly Village, plate, dinner; 10", from $12 to **$18.00**
Friendly Village, plate, luncheon; 9", from $6 to **$9.00**
Friendly Village, plate, salad...**$6.00**
Friendly Village, plate, snack; w/cup well, square **$18.00**
Friendly Village, plate, square, 7", from $6 to..............**$9.00**
Friendly Village, platter, lg, 15", from $35 to...............**$45.00**
Friendly Village, platter, sm, 11½", from $18 to..........**$20.00**
Friendly Village, platter, turkey.....................................**$125.00**
Friendly Village, salt & pepper shakers, pr, from $15 to...**$20.00**
Friendly Village, soup tureen, from $125 to..............**$140.00**
Friendly Village, sugar bowl, w/lid, from $18 to........**$25.00**
Friendly Village, teapot, from $40 to.............................**$50.00**
Harvest Time, bowl, vegetable; 8", from $20 to.........**$25.00**
Harvest Time, plate, dinner; 10", from $12 to **$15.00**

Harvest Time, tidbit tray, 3-tiered, 14", $45.00.

Heritage Hall, bowl, vegetable; 8".................................**$20.00**
Historical America, cup & saucer, jumbo.....................**$25.00**
Indian Tree, bowl, soup; 7" **$13.00**
Indian Tree, bowl, vegetable; 8½" **$25.00**
Indian Tree, creamer **$17.00**
Indian Tree, platter, 12"..**$26.00**
Indian Tree, sugar bowl w/lid..**$22.00**
Merry Christmas, bowl, cereal; 6", from $7 to.............**$10.00**
Merry Christmas, bowl, vegetable; w/lid, from $55 to...**$65.00**
Merry Christmas, creamer...**$15.00**
Merry Christmas, plate, dinner; 10", from $12 to **$18.00**
Old Britain Castles, bowl, berry; 5", from $6 to...........**$7.50**
Old Britain Castles, bowl, cereal; 6", from $7 to.........**$10.00**
Old Britain Castles, bowl, soup **$9.00**
Old Britain Castles, bowl, vegetable; oval, from $20 to...**$30.00**
Old Britain Castles, bowl, vegetable; w/lid, from $55 to.**$65.00**
Old Britain Castles, coffeepot, from $55 to **$65.00**
Old Britain Castles, cup & saucer, from $10 to..........**$15.00**
Old Britain Castles, gravy boat, from $25 to **$35.00**
Old Britain Castles, plate, bread & butter; 6", from $4 to ..**$5.00**
Old Britain Castles, plate, dinner; 10", from $12 to **$18.00**
Old Britain Castles, plate, salad....................................**$6.00**
Old Britain Castles, platter, med, 13½", from $30 to ..**$35.00**
Old Britain Castles, teapot, from $45 to......................**$55.00**
Old Mill, cup & saucer, from $10 to **$12.00**

Old Mill, plate, dinner; 10", from $10 to.....................**$12.00**

Old Mill, platter, 12", from $12.00 to $15.00.

Rose Chintz, bowl, cereal; coupe, from $8 to.............**$12.00**
Rose Chintz, bowl, fruit; round or square, from $8 to..**$10.00**
Rose Chintz, bowl, vegetable; oval, from $20 to **$30.00**
Rose Chintz, bowl, vegetable; round, from $20 to **$30.00**
Rose Chintz, chop plate, 12", from $55 to...................**$65.00**
Rose Chintz, cup & saucer, demitasse; from $7 to........**$9.00**
Rose Chintz, cup & saucer, from $8 to **$12.00**
Rose Chintz, egg cup, single, from $6 to.....................**$7.00**
Rose Chintz, gravy boat, from $25 to...........................**$35.00**
Rose Chintz, gravy boat, w/underplate, from $60 to..**$75.00**
Rose Chintz, sugar bowl, w/lid, from $26 to...............**$32.00**
Rose Chintz, mug, from $15 to......................................**$17.00**
Rose Chintz, pitcher, 5½", from $35 to **$45.00**
Rose Chintz, plate, bread & butter; from $6 to **$8.00**
Rose Chintz, plate, dinner; 10", from $8 to **$12.00**
Rose Chintz, plate, salad; round or square, from $7 to ..**$10.00**
Rose Chintz, platter, lg, 15", from $35 to.....................**$45.00**
Rose Chintz, platter, med, 13½", from $30 to..............**$35.00**
Rose Chintz, platter, sm, 11½", from $20 to **$25.00**
Rose Chintz, platter, 8"...**$17.50**
Rose Chintz, soup tureen, w/lid, from $250 to.........**$300.00**
Rose Chintz, teapot, from $65 to..................................**$75.00**
Sheraton, bowl, cereal; 6" **$6.00**
Sheraton, bowl, fruit..**$4.50**
Sheraton, bowl, soup; 8" **$10.00**
Sheraton, bowl, vegetable; oval, 9" **$20.00**
Sheraton, creamer...**$10.00**
Sheraton, cup & saucer **$9.00**
Sheraton, gravy boat w/stand.......................................**$55.00**
Sheraton, plate, dinner; 10"...**$15.00**
Sheraton, plate, square, 7¾"..**$8.00**
Sheraton, plate, 6"...**$4.00**
Sheraton, platter, 11½" **$18.00**
Sheraton, platter, 14"...**$45.00**

Josef Originals

Figurines of lovely ladies, charming girls, and whimsical animals marked Josef Originals were designed by Muriel Joseph George of Arcadia, California, from 1945 to 1985. Until 1960, they were produced in California. But production costs were high, and copies of her work were being made in Japan. To remain competitive, she and her partner, George Good, found a company in Japan to build a factory and produce her designs to her satisfaction. Muriel retired in 1982; however, Mr. Good continued production of her work and made new designs of his staff's creation. The company was sold in late 1985, and the name is currently owned by Applause; a limited number of figurines bear this name. Those made during the ownership of Muriel are the most collectible. They can be recognized by these characteristics: the girls have a high-gloss finish, black eyes, and most are signed. Brown-eyed figures date from 1982 through 1985; Applause uses a red-brown eye. The animals were nearly always made with a matt finish and were marked with paper labels. Later animals have a flocked coat. Our advisors, Jim and Kaye Whitaker have two books which we recommend for further study: *Josef Originals, Charming Figurines*; and *Josef Originals, A Second Look*. Their address is in the Directory.

See also Birthday Angels.

Advisors: Jim and Kaye Whitaker (See Directory, Josef Originals)

Newsletter: *Josef Original Newsletter*
Jim and Kay Whitaker
P.O. Box 475 Dept. GS
Lynnwood, WA 98046; Subscription (4 issues): $10 per year

Birthday Girls, #1 through #16, black eyes, Japan, 2¾" to 6½", each..**$16.00**
Birthstone Dolls, colored stone in flower, 12 in series, Japan, 4", each..**$15.00**
Buggy Bugg series, various poses w/wire antenna, Japan, 3¼", each..**$10.00**
Camel, mama standing, Japan, 6¾"..............................**$55.00**

Chinese Girls, black and white kimonos, girl on right marked 'Autumn Leaf,' California, each, from $40.00 to $45.00. (Photo courtesy Jim and Kaye Whitaker)

Christmas Girl w/Cake, red & green outfit, Japan, 5"..**$25.00**
Classical Touch, Pianist, music box plays 'Fur Elise,' Japan, 5"..**$40.00**
Classical Touch series, Flutist, green w/flute, Japan, 6"..**$35.00**

Colonial Days Series, Louise, white gown, Japan, 9½"...**$95.00**
Doll of the Month series, 12 different, trimmed w/stones, California, 3½", each..**$25.00**
Doll of the Month series, 12 different poses & colors, Japan, 4", each..**$20.00**

Duck family, Japan, from 2" to 4", set of three, from $48.00 to $58.00. (Photo courtesy Jim and Kaye Whitaker)

Favorite Sayings series, Mightly Like a Rose, rose hat, Japan, 4"..**$20.00**
First Formal series, Debby, yellow gown, holding mirror, Japan, 5¼"..**$30.00**
Flower Girl series, Lilacs, pink gown, holding lilac bouquet, Japan, 5½"..**$35.00**
Holiday Girls series, Holiday in Hawaii, girl w/lei, Japan, 5½"..**$40.00**
Kandy, blue or pink, gold trim w/colored stones, California, 4½"..**$30.00**
Kangaroo mamma w/baby in pouch, Japan, 6"..........**$55.00**
Kennel Club series, Dalmatian, Japan, 3½"................**$12.00**
Kennel Club series, Poodle, Japan, 3½"....................**$12.00**
Lara's Theme music box, couple in winter attire w/yellow bird, Japan, 6¼"..**$40.00**
Lipstick holder, lavender, aqua or pink, Japan, 4"............**$22.00**
Little International series, Japan, pink w/parasol, 4"..**$20.00**
Little International series, Panama, green gown, Japan, 4"..**$20.00**

Love's Rendezvous, aqua gown and hat, Japan, 9", from $90.00 to $125.00. (Photo courtesy Jim and Kay Whitaker)

Missy, blue or pink, gold trim w/colored stones, California, 4½" **$30.00**

Morning-Noon-Night series, Yvette, aqua gown w/scissors, California, 5½" **$60.00**

Musicale series, Tammy, girl at piano, pink, Japan, 6" ...**$35.00**

Penny, little girl sitting, blue, green, pink or white, California, 4", each..**$40.00**

Pixies, various poses, green w/red & gold trim, Japan, 2" to 3¼", each..**$12.00**

Portraits-Ladies of Song series, pink w/parasol, Japan, 6" **$45.00**

Reindeer, Christmas trim, Japan, 6" **$20.00**

Sakura, Chinese lady w/fan, white, green, blue or pink, California, 10¾"...**$90.00**

Santa w/boy on lap, Japan, 6¼"...............................**$45.00**

Skunk w/perfume atomizer, Japan, 2½" **$10.00**

Special Occasions series, The New Baby, girl holding teddy bear, Japan, 4½"..**$20.00**

Strangers in the Night, music box, blue gown w/white feather fan, Japan, 5½" **$55.00**

Sweet Memories, The Love Letter, lavender gown, Japan, 6" **$75.00**

Sylvia, lime green w/rose bouquet, California, 5¾" ...**$55.00**

Taffy, pink or green, gold trim w/colored stones, California, 4½" **$30.00**

Tammy, music box, girl at piano, pink, plays 'Humoresque,' 6½" **$40.00**

Tawny, character cat, Siamese, Japan, 4"...................**$12.00**

Victoria, holding muff, green or mauve, California, 6"......**$55.00**

Wee Folk series, Elfin Children, many poses, Japan, 4½", each **$10.00**

Wee Three, 3 kittens in basket, California, 3" **$15.00**

Wu Fu & Wu Cha, Chinese couple, ecru w/gold trim, 10", pr **$85.00**

XVII Century French series, Marie, white w/veil, Japan, 7" **$75.00**

Kanawha

This company operated in Dunbar, West Virginia, until 1986. They're noted for a line of slag (End of Day) glass made during the early seventies, some crackle glass, and a line of cased glass called peachblow. The quality of the glass is good, and it's starting to show up at flea markets and malls, so if you like its looks, now is the time to start looking for it. You can easily spot their Pastel Blue and Green slag glass, since no other company's colors match Kanawha's exactly. Their 'red' is actually a reddish-orange. For more information we recommend *Crackle Glass* by Stan and Arlene Weitman (Collector Books).

Advisor: Ruth Grizel (See Directory, Westmoreland)

Crackle Glass

Candy dish, flared ruffled rim, ring foot, 3", from $40 to **$50.00**

Creamer & sugar bowl, gold, ovoid body w/ring foot, appled C-shape handle, pr, from $50 to..........................**$75.00**

Cup, amberina, ovoid body w/ring foot, applied C-shape handle, 2¼", from $25 to **$40.00**

Dish, green, flared ruffled rim, cylindrical body w/ring foot, 3x5", from $35 to **$40.00**

Miniature, hat, amberina, 2", from $35 to.................**$40.00**

Pitcher, amberina, waisted w/wide curved top & spout, pear shape body w/low foot, drop-over handle, 3¼", from $30 to **$35.00**

Pitcher, blue, cylindrical body w/low foot, rounded top, applied handle, 4", from $25 to **$30.00**

Pitcher, emerald green, bulbous center w/flared top, cylindrical base, applied handle w/curl, 3½", from $30 to........**$35.00**

Pitcher, gold, tall waist w/flared top, flat ovoid body w/ring base, applied handle w/curl, 5¼", from $40 to....**$45.00**

Pitcher, green, cylindrical body narrowing to low foot, funnel-shape top, applied C-shape handle, 5½", from $40 to **$45.00**

Pitcher, green, waisted w/funnel-shaped top, ovoid body, applied handle, 3¼", from $35 to...........................**$40.00**

Pitcher, ruby, waisted w/funnel-shape top, ovoid body, applied handle, 3¼", from $30 to...........................**$35.00**

Pitcher, topaz, waisted w/flared ruffled top, squat & low round body w/low foot, 4¼", from $25 to..........**$30.00**

Syrup, amethyst (very collectible color), 6"..............**$60.00**

Vase, amberina, cylindrical body narrows to flared 4-lobe rim, 7¾", from $60 to **$85.00**

Vase, amberina, flared 3-lobe rim, elongated ovoid body, 5½", from $50 to **$55.00**

Peachblow (cased glass with colored lining)

Basket, embossed grapes, white w/peachblow lining, bulbous w/crimped rim, 9½", from $50 to **$60.00**

Basket, Hobnail, white w/peachblow lining, wide crimped rim, 7", from $35 to **$40.00**

Basket, waffle pattern, white w/peachblow lining, wide crimped rim, 8", from $35 to **$40.00**

Bowl, Hobnail, white w/lemon lining, wide ruffled & crimped rim, 6", from $25 to **$30.00**

Pitcher, embossed grapes, white w/lemon lining, cylinder neck, bun body, footed, 9", from $45 to **$55.00**

Pitcher, embossed grapes, white w/peachblow lining, bulbous neck & body, waisted, 7"................................**$45.00**

Pitcher, embossed grapes, white w/sapphire blue lining, 3¾"..**$25.00**

Pitcher, embossed grapes, white w/sapphire blue lining, 6½" **$35.00**

Pitcher, lobed, red to yellow (peachblow) w/white lining, waisted neck, bulbous body, 4½" **$30.00**

Vase, embossed grapes, white w/sapphire blue lining, wide ruffled rim, 6½"...**$40.00**

Vase, embossed grapes, yellow interior, ruffled rim, 9", from $45 to **$55.00**

Vase, Hobnail, blue w/white lining, elongated slender neck w/angled rim, low applied blue handle, 14"......**$125.00**

Vase, waffle pattern, white w/sapphire blue lining, flaring toward base, wide ruffled & crimped rim, 5½"....**$35.00**

Slag Glass

Pastel Blue, ashtray, apple form, 5" $15.00
Pastel Blue, basket, Hobnail, shallow, scalloped rim, 7½",
from $45 to...$55.00
Pastel Blue, candle holders, Hobnail, dome base, 2-knob
stem, 5", pr..$40.00
Pastel Blue, creamer & sugar bowl w/lid, Hobnail, scalloped
lip, 6½", pr, from $45 to..$50.00
Pastel Blue, cruet, Hobnail, 6" $25.00
Pastel Blue, salt & pepper shakers, Hobnail, 5", pr....$35.00
Pastel Blue, salt dip, bird form, 3¼" $15.00
Pastel Blue, slipper, Daisy & Button, 5½".................$35.00
Pastel Green, basket, Diamond Dot, flared ruffled top,
8¼" $65.00
Pastel Green, Basket, Threaded, 6½" $45.00
Pastel Green, pitcher, Hobnail, cylindrical body w/tall stem
foot, 4", from $10 to $15.00
Pastel Green, pitcher, Thumbprint, 4½", from $25 to.$35.00
Pastel Green, pitcher, waisted w/funnel-shape top, bulbous
body w/ring foot, 5¼"...$25.00
Pastel Green, vase, Diamond Dot, waisted w/flared ruffled
top, 5¼" $45.00
Red, bonbon, Hobnail, leaf form w/C-shape handle, 6", from
$25 to..$30.00
Red, bowl, Hob Star, incurvate w/serrated 8-lobe rim, 7½",
from $40 to...$45.00
Red, compote, Hobnail, flared, crimped & ruffled rim, lg
round foot, 5½", from $30 to...................................$35.00
Red, figurine, lady w/2 dogs, from $75 to..................$95.00
Red, pitcher, Sawtooth, 3¼", from $15 to..................$20.00
Red, pitcher, Thumbprint, 3½", from $15 to..............$20.00

Red, praying hands, 5", from $65.00 to $75.00. (Photo courtesy Frank Grizel)

Red, slipper, Rose, 6", from $35 to..............................$40.00
Red, standing rooster, 9½", from $75 to $95.00
Red, vase, Moon & Star, swung style w/foot, 10" $25.00

Kentucky Derby Glasses

Since the the late 1930s, every running of the Kentucky Derby has been commemorated with a special glass tumbler. Each year at Churchill Downs on Derby day, you can buy them, filled with mint juleps. In the early days this was the only place where these glasses could be purchased. Many collections were started when folks carried the glasses home from the track and then continued to add one for each successive year they went to the Derby.

The first glass appeared in 1938, but examples from then until 1945 are extremely scarce and are worth thousands — when they can be found. Because of this, many collectors begin with the 1945 glasses. There are three to collect: the tall version, the short regular-size glass, and a jigger. Some years, for instance 1948, 1956, 1958, 1974, and 1986, have slightly different variations, so often there are more than one to collect. To date a glass, simply add one year to the last date on the winner's list found on the back.

Each year many companies put out commemorative Derby glasses. Collectors call them 'bar' glasses (as many bars sold their own versions). Because of this, collectors need to be educated as to what the official Kentucky Derby glass looks like.

Advisor: Betty L. Hornback (See Directory, Kentucky Derby and Horse Racing)

1941, aluminum $800.00
1941-1944, plastic Beetleware, each, from $2,500 to ..$4,000.00
1945, jigger...$1,000.00
1945, regular $1,200.00
1945, tall $425.00
1946 ....$100.00
1947 ....$100.00
1948 ....$180.00
1948, frosted bottom $200.00
1949 ....$180.00
1950 ....$425.00
1951 ....$550.00
1952 ....$190.00
1953 ....$135.00
1954 ....$175.00
1955 ....$135.00
1956, 4 variations, each, from $150 to $250.00
1957 ....$110.00
1958, Gold Bar..$175.00
1958, Iron Liege $185.00

1959, gold and black on frost, $80.00.

1960 ....$80.00

1961	$100.00
1962	$65.00
1963	$50.00
1964	$50.00
1965	$60.00
1966	$50.00
1967	$47.00
1968	$47.00

1969, red and green on frost, $47.00.

1970	$55.00
1971	$45.00
1972	$40.00
1973	$38.00
1974, Federal, regular or mistake, each	$150.00
1974, mistake	$18.00
1974, regular	$16.00

1975, red, yellow, and black graphics, $10.00.

1976	$14.00
1976, plastic	$12.00
1977	$10.00
1978	$12.00
1979	$12.00
1980	$18.00
1981	$12.00
1982	$12.00
1983	$9.00

1984	$7.00
1985	$9.00
1986	$10.00
1986 ('85 copy)	$18.00
1987	$9.00
1988	$9.00
1989	$9.00
1990	$7.00
1991	$7.00
1992	$7.00
1993	$5.00
1994	$5.00
1995	$5.00
1996	$3.00
1997	$3.00
1998	$3.00

Breeders' Cup Glasses

1982	$20.00
1985	$250.00
1988	$25.00
1989	$45.00
1990	$30.00
1991	$10.00

1992, yellow, green and black graphics, $20.00. (Photo courtesy Betty Hornback/photographer Dean Langdon)

1993	$12.00
1993, 10th Running, gold	$40.00
1994	$8.00
1995	$10.00
1996	$25.00

Festival Glasses

1968	$95.00
1984	$20.00
1987-88, each	$16.00
1989-90, each	$14.00
1991-92, each	$12.00
1993	$75.00
1994-95, each	$10.00
1996-97, each	$6.00

Jim Beam Stakes Glasses

1982	$300.00
1983	$65.00
1984	$55.00
1985	$55.00

1986, red and white graphics, $35.00. (Photo courtesy Betty Hornback/phototographer Dean Langdon)

1987-88, each	$27.00
1988-90, each	$22.00
1991-93, each	$18.00
1994-95, each	$12.00
1996-97, each	$8.00

Shot Glasses

1987, 1½-oz, red or black, each	$300.00
1987, 3-oz, black	$750.00
1987, 3-oz, red	$1,000.00
1988, 1½-oz	$40.00
1988, 3-oz	$60.00
1989, 1½-oz	$35.00
1989, 3-oz	$45.00
1990, 1½-oz	$35.00
1991, 1½-oz	$35.00
1991, 3-oz	$40.00
1992, 1½-oz	$20.00
1992, 3-oz	$25.00
1993, 1½-oz or 3-oz, each	$15.00
1994, 1½-oz or 3-oz, each	$12.00
1995, 1½-oz or 3-oz, each	$12.00
1996, 1½-oz or 3-oz, each	$10.00
1997, 1½-oz or 3-oz, each	$8.00

King's Crown Thumbprint Line

Back in the late 1800s, this pattern was called Thumbprint. It was first made by the U.S. Glass Company and Tiffin, one of several companies who were a part of the US conglomerate, through the 1940s. U.S. Glass closed in the late fifties, but Tiffin reopened in 1963 and reissued it. Indiana Glass bought the molds, made some minor changes, and dur-ing the 1970s, they made this line as well. Confusing, to say the least! Gene Florence's *Collectible Glassware of the 40s, 50s, and 60s,* explains that originally the thumbprints were oval, but at some point Indiana changed theirs to circles. And Tiffin's tumblers were flared at the top, while Indiana's were straight. Our values are for the later issues of both companies, with the ruby flashing in excellent condition.

Ashtray, 5¼" square	$18.00
Bowl, flared, footed, lg	$75.00
Bowl, salad; 9¼"	$85.00
Bowl, wedding or candy; footed, 6"	$30.00
Bowl, 5¾"	$20.00

Bowl, wedding; 10½", $150.00. (Photo courtesy Gene Florence)

Cake salver, footed, 12½"	$75.00
Candle holder, 2-light, 5½"	$65.00
Compote, flat, sm	$22.00
Creamer	$22.00
Cup	$8.00
Cup, punch	$15.00
Mayonnaise, 3-pc set	$65.00
Pitcher	$175.00
Plate, bread & butter; 5"	$8.00
Plate, dinner; 10"	$37.50
Plate, salad; 7¼"	$12.00
Plate, snack; w/indent, 9¾"	$15.00
Saucer	$8.00
Stem, sundae or sherbet; 5½-oz, each	$10.00
Stem, wine; 2-oz	$7.50
Sugar bowl	$25.00
Tumbler, ice tea; 11-oz	$16.00
Tumbler, juice; 4½-oz	$14.00
Vase, bud; 9"	$75.00

Kitchen Collectibles

If you've never paid much attention to old kitchen appliances, now is the time to do just that. Check in Grandma's basement — or your mother's kitchen cabinets, for that matter. As styles in home decorating changed, so did the styles of appliances. Some have wonderful Art Deco lines, while others border on the primitive. Most of those you'll find still work, and with a thorough cleaning you'll be able to restore them to their original 'like-new' appearance. Missing parts may be impossible to replace, but if it's just a cord that's gone, you can usually find what you need at any hardware store.

Even larger appliances are collectible and are often used to add the finishing touch to a period kitchen. Please note that prices listed here are for appliances that are free of rust, pitting, or dents and in excellent working condition.

During the nineteenth century, cast-iron apple peelers, cherry pitters, and food choppers were patented by the hundreds, and because they're practically indestructible, they're still around today. Unless parts are missing, they're still usable and most are very efficient at the task they were designed to perform.

Lots of good vintage kitchen glassware is still around and can generally be bought at reasonable prices. Pieces vary widely from custard cups and refrigerator dishes to canister sets and cookie jars. There are also several books available for further information and study. If this area of collecting interests you, you'll enjoy *300 Years of Kitchen Collectibles* by Linda Campbell and *Kitchen Antiques, 1790-1940*, by Kathryn McNerney. Other books include: *Kitchen Glassware of the Depression Years* by Gene Florence; *Collector's Encyclopedia of Fry Glassware* by H.C. Fry Glass Society; *The '50s and '60s Kitchen, A Collector's Handbook and Price Guide*, by Jan Lindenberger; and *Fire-King Fever* and *Pyrex History and Price Guide*, both by April Tvorak.

See also Aluminum; Clothes Sprinkler Bottles; Fire-King; Glass Knives; Griswold; Jade-ite; Kitchen Prayer Ladies; Porcelier; Reamers.

Advisor: Jim Barker, Appliances (See Directory, Appliances)

Club/Newsletter: *KOOKS (Kollectors of Old Kitchen Stuff)*
Bob Grossman, President
354 Route 206 N
Chester, NJ 07930; Send SASE for information

Appliances

Chafing dish, Simplex #1203...**$75.00**
Coffee urn set, Westinghouse PS 124............................**$65.00**
Coffee urn set, Westinghouse PS 164, ca 1930............**$75.00**
Coffeepot, Armstrong, ca 1927 ....**$65.00**
Fan, Dominion, #2017, 1950s...**$35.00**
Fan, Emerson, #94646-D, 1959, from $25 to **$30.00**
Fan, General Electric, #FM9V1, ca 1947......................**$60.00**
Fan, Westinghouse Power-Aire, #12PA2, ca 1940s **$55.00**
Hot plate, Liberty, #601, 1930s **$25.00**
Mixer, Hamilton Beach, Model B, ca 1935 ....**$65.00**
Percolator, West Bend, Color Glo Flavo-Matic **$40.00**
Popcorn popper, Dominion Electric, 1930s..................**$50.00**
Popcorn popper, Excel, ca 1927.....................................**$65.00**
Popcorn popper, K-M Tel A Matic, ca 1939 ....**$65.00**
Popcorn popper, US Manufacturing, #10, ca 1948......**$40.00**
Sandwich iron, General Electric, 1930s........................**$30.00**
Toaster, Armstrong Tablestove, ca 1927.......................**$65.00**
Toaster, Bersted #72, ca 1935 ....**$45.00**
Toaster, Bersted #80, ca 1932 ....**$65.00**
Toaster, Dominion #1000, ca 1948 ....**$65.00**
Toaster, Electra Hot #48, ca 1932 ....**$55.00**
Toaster, Empire Toaster #759, ca 1933..........................**$55.00**

Toaster, Hold Heat Toaster, ca 1927.............................**$45.00**
Toaster, Manning Bowman #83, ca 1938 ....**$55.00**
Toaster, Proctor Pop Up, ca 1941..................................**$45.00**
Toaster, Royal Rochester #13290, ca 1932 ....**$65.00**
Toaster, Samson Tri Matic, ca 1936 ....**$140.00**
Toaster, Seneca #39, ca 1938 ....**$45.00**
Toaster, Son Chief Pop Up, 1940s.................................**$45.00**
Toaster, Star Toaster by Fitzgerald, ca 1928.................**$65.00**
Toaster, Sunbeam #4 Horizontal, ca 1932....................**$55.00**

Toaster, Sunbeam T-1-C, $75.00. (Photo courtesy Jim Barker)

Toaster, Sunbeam T-9, ca 1939......................................**$75.00**
Toaster, Torrid Reversible Toaster, ca 1930..................**$75.00**
Toaster, Universal E7722, ca 1935 ....**$55.00**
Toaster, Universal E79312, 1932 ....**$65.00**
Toaster, Universal E947, ca 1926 ....**$55.00**
Toaster, Westinghouse T-D 13, ca 1930 ....**$95.00**
Toaster, Westinghouse TT-23, 1930 ....**$75.00**
Toaster, Westinghouse TTC 33, 1931.............................**$65.00**
Vaccuum cleaner, GE, ca 1939.......................................**$85.00**
Vaccuum cleaner, Torrington, ca 1925 ....**$85.00**
Vacuum cleaner, Universal Supreme, #E440, early 1940s..**$125.00**
Waffle iron, M-B Twin O Matic, ca 1939 ....**$85.00**
Waffle iron, Royal Rochester #12290 ....**$40.00**
Waffle iron, Royal Rochester #12340 ....**$45.00**
Waffle iron, Royal Rochester #12800 ....**$95.00**
Waffle iron, Royal Rochester #12900, ca 1933............**$75.00**
Waffle iron, Westinghouse CPC-15 ....**$75.00**
Waffle iron, Westinghouse WA-4....................................**$45.00**

Gadgets and Miscellaneous Items

Apple corer, Ateco Standard, dark gray tin tube type ..**$8.00**
Apple corer/peeler, Morton Salt **$12.00**
Beater, Ladd, green glass bowl, w/crank metal top, green handles **$35.00**
Biscuit cutter, Kreamer, strap handle............................**$10.00**
Biscuit cutter, Rumford, dark tin, 1⅞" dia...................**$18.00**
Biscuit/doughnut cutter, Cottolene Shortening, loop handle **$30.00**
Bowl scraper, American Beauty Cake Flour, plastic, 6x6" ..**$25.00**
Cake mold, tin, center tube, fluted & scalloped sides, 2x8" **$8.00**
Cake pan, Snow King Baking Powder, dark tinware, square **$10.00**

Cake spatula, porcelain w/floral decals & gold trim, marked Made in Germany **$10.00**

Can opener, green-painted wooden handle **$10.00**

Can opener, Pet Milk, tin, round **$15.00**

Can opener, Red Daisy Deluxe Model 80, wall mount...**$8.00**

Can opener, Tool Steel Tempered, wood handle, old ..**$2.50**

Carving fork, nickel-plated w/self stand, antler handle, marked England **$7.00**

Carving knife, Sheffield, stainless w/antler handle........**$9.00**

Cheese grater, iron & tin w/wood top, 3-footed, marked Made in Germany **$15.00**

Chopper, double blade, green-painted wood handle ...**$6.00**

Coffee grinder, PeDe, wall mount, glass & wood w/ceramic top **$50.00**

Cream whip, Horlick, black wire w/tin plate, 2" wide beaters, 9½" **$32.00**

Cutting board, Nevco, fruit decor, Copyright 1961 ....**$4.00**

Cutting board, turtle shape, pine, shows use, fairly old, 15x9" **$38.00**

Egg & cream beater, Dunlap Sanitary **$20.00**

Egg beater, Art-Beck, rachet type, 2 fine wire movable 'springs' at bottom **$38.00**

Egg beater, Baby Bingo, sm..**$15.00**

Egg beater, Cassidy-Fairbanks, dark gray tin, oval open handle, wooden wheel knob, sm bowl-shaped beater w/slits, early **$45.00**

Egg beater, Maynard, red plastic handle.....................**$3.50**

Egg beater, Turbine, ca 1930s, 9½", $25.00.

Egg scale, Acme Specialty, put egg in bowl, weight lifts to indicate correct grade, Pat June 24, 1924, 10", EX.........**$30.00**

Egg separator, Town Talk Flour Has No Equal, dark tin .**$12.00**

Flour sifter, Androck, embossed Hand-i-Sift, squeeze-handle type, ca 1940s **$15.00**

Flour sifter, Bromwell, painted tin, ca 1940s-50s, EX .**$15.00**

Flour sifter, Calumet Baking Powder, tin, 2-cup **$15.00**

Flour sifter, Duplex, dark gray tin, lids w/flat strap handle each end, red wood handle in center, 1922, 6¾x5¾" **$30.00**

Flour sifter, Hand-I-Sift, lithographed wheat & baked goods, from $12 to...**$15.00**

Flour sifter, Kno-Bugs, tin, can shape w/bottom sifter, lid & tall strap handle **$25.00**

Flour sifter, Lee's Favorite Flour, tin, crank handle, 6x5", EX **$25.00**

Flour sifter, painted tinware w/checkered band & flowers, rotary crank handle, ca 1940s, EX.....................**$20.00**

Flour sifter, Rumford Baking Powder, ca 1950s, scarce, EX **$75.00**

Food mill, Foley, red-painted wood handle & knob, 7" dia...**$15.00**

Fork, kitchen; Androck Slyfork, green-painted wood handle, Patent Applied For, 16", EX.....................................**$5.00**

French fry cutter, sled style, red-painted wood handle...**$6.00**

Fruit knife, sterling ferrule, mother-of-pearl handle, 6"...**$7.00**

Grater, All in One Patent Pending, tin, ca 1940, 10½x4¼"..**$25.00**

Grater, aluminum disc, fits over bowl, 9" **$4.00**

Grater, Regina, cast iron, clamp-on style, wood handle, 12½" **$25.00**

Grater, tin, oval w/strap handle....................................**$6.00**

Grater combination slicer/shredder, Bromco, 9x4" **$5.00**

Green bean slicer, Germany, cast iron, fancy designs, clamps to table...**$60.00**

Hamburger press, Japan, chef flipping hamburger, 6" dia ..**$3.50**

Hamburger press, wood w/Hamburger Press below roosters, 5¾"...**$3.00**

Hot pad, birds w/cherry blossoms on tin, cardboard backing, EX **$2.00**

Ice chisel, heavy iron spikes w/wooden handle.........**$12.00**

Ice cream scoop, Japan, pink plastic handle.................**$4.00**

Ice cream scoop, Scoop Master, red-painted wood handle...**$4.50**

Ice crusher, Dazey, chrome & black, standing style...**$20.00**

Ice crusher, Ice-O-Matic, Art Deco style, plastic bottom...**$8.00**

Jar/bottle opener, Schilling, red-painted handle, $20.00; Coffee scoop, Schilling, aluminum, $10.00.

Juice extractor, Handy Andy, heavy aluminum, on 3 legs, round base, crank handle.......................................**$28.00**

Knife holder, Nuway, painted tinware, red & white w/floral spray, dated 1939, MIB..**$15.00**

Knife sharpener, Eversharp, disk type w/brown-painted wood handle **$6.00**

Knife sharpener, rotating disc style w/antler handle.....**$6.00**

Ladle, aluminum, 12" **$5.00**

Ladle, green-painted wooden handle, pierced bowl **$9.00**

Measuring cup, Mirro, aluminum w/shaker top, 1-cup...**$4.00**

Measuring cup, Rumford, dark gray tin **$30.00**

Meat grinder, Favorite No 27, Pat Feb 18 1896, complete .**$12.00**

Meat grinder, Universal #305, rotary crank handle **$25.00**

Meat grinder, Universal #323, cast metal, from $12 to..**$15.00**

Mixer, Vidrio, electric, w/green base **$100.00**

Mold, fish, marked Made in Germany, 8" **$7.50**

Noodle cutter, Titantonio's, cast iron, clamps to table **$55.00**

Nut chopper, Pamco, glass base w/measure marks, push wood top to chop **$6.00**

Nutmeg grater, perforated tin half-cylinder, strap handle each end, late $8.00

Pie pan, BlueBird Pies, embossed bird in flight, gray tinware $24.00

Pie pan, Snow King Baking Powder, gray tinware $22.00

Pie pan, tin w/screen 'sifter' bottom $15.00

Pot holder, crocheted, doll-dress design, from $3 to $5.00

Pot holder, crocheted, lady's panties design, from $2 to ..$4.00

Pot holder, crocheted, w/applied flower, from $3 to $5.00

Pot-holder hangers, gentleman & lady pig, chalkware, pr ..$10.00

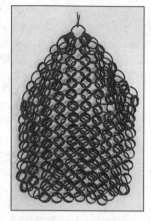

Pot scrubber, linked chain, about 6x6", $30.00.

Potato masher, cast iron, lacy round mashing end $20.00

Potato masher, old grid wire style w/wood handle $7.50

Rolling pin, turned maple, 1-pc, 16" $15.00

Rolling pin, wooden, stationary handles, late, lg $8.00

Scoop, tin, curved, 4½" $5.00

Shaker/measuring cup (for white sauce), Swirl Mixer, tin, Rochester NY $2.50

Sharpening steel, Sheffield, antler handle, England, 8" ...$8.00

Soap grater, Sunny Monday, dark tin $15.00

Spatula, Wholesome Baking Powder, open handle, 12" ..$12.00

Spoon, mixing; Rumford, slotted, 12" $18.00

Stamp saver, wood box w/S&H stamp decoration, mounts to wall, 7x4x3½" $5.00

Tea infuser, aluminum ball w/wire chain $2.50

Tea strainer, Tetley's Tea, silverplate, fancy edge & handle .$20.00

Tray, Pilgrim Art #500, tin w/multicolor florals & gold, marked Hand Decorated Tole $5.00

Tray, strutting red roosters on white tin w/red trim, 8x6" ..$2.00

Washboard, Columbus Washboard Co, glass in wood frame, Columbus Ohio, 26x13½" $30.00

Washboard, Midget Washer, all glass, original paper label ..$25.00

Whip/beater, Arthur Beck Cop, operates w/1 hand, ca 1948 ....$40.00

Wireware basket, petal-shaped sides fold in & out, reshape to make string holder, dark wire, 6¾" base $45.00

Wireware cooling tray, looped wire feet, heavy lg screen wire w/dark gray tin banding around sides, 9½x14" $55.00

Wireware tea trivet, twisted wire, 6" dia $30.00

Wireware vegetable basket, half-bushel basket shape, wire in smaller diamond design, wire bail handle, heavy $68.00

Glassware

Bowl, drippings; Dots, black on custard, McKee $33.00

Bowl, drippings; Ships, red boat fired on white, McKee, 16-oz $40.00

Bowl, mixing; Crisscross, blue transparent, Hazel Atlas, 9½" $60.00

Bowl, mixing; Green Clambroth, 8¾" $25.00

Bowl, mixing; Pyrex, Goosebery, Cinderella shape (pour handles), from $10 to $15.00

Bowl, Pyrex, Butter Print, 2½-qt $8.00

Bowl, Tulips, multicolor on white, Anchor Hocking, 9½" .$15.00

Bowl, white w/red fired-on Dutch children, deep, 7" ...$10.00

Bowl set, Jennyware, pink, vertical ribs, Jeannette, 3-pc ..$95.00

Butter box, green transparent, rectangular, w/lid, Jeannette, 2-lb $150.00

Butter box, pink transparent, embossed B, rectangular, Jeannette, 2-lb $160.00

Butter dish, Crisscross, blue transparent, Hazel Atlas, ¼-lb $95.00

Butter dish, Jennyware, ultramarine, deep bottom, Jeannette $150.00

Butter dish, Seville Yellow, rectangular, McKee, 1-lb ...$65.00

Butter dish, white w/Red Dots design, 1-lb $125.00

Cake plate & cover, clear, vertical ribs on sides, lg finial ..$55.00

Canister, clear w/decal of Dutch boy & windmill, square, Hocking $20.00

Canister, Coffee on smooth band over vertical ribbing, amber, square $90.00

Canister, Delphite Blue, Sugar in black letters, 40-oz ..$350.00

Canister, green transparent, Coffee on plain band embossed over vertical ribbing, square $275.00

Canister, green transparent, vertical ribbing, paper label, glass lid w/knob finial, 47-oz $45.00

Canisters, rooster heads, red waddle and comb, from $25.00 to $40.00. (Photo courtesy Gene Florence)

Casserole, Pyrex, Snowflake, oval w/extended handles, clear glass lid, 2½-qt, from $15 to $18.00

Dish, Pyrex, 2-part, shallow, w/handle extensions, divided clear lid w/handles doubles as serving tray, 1½-qt $15.00

Grease jar, Red Tulips, white w/fired-on red design, red lid, round w/flat front panel $25.00

Grease jar, Tulips, multicolor on white, Anchor Hocking ..$20.00

Ice bucket, clear w/fired-on pink elephants & stars ...$25.00

Ice bucket, pink transparent, vertical ribs $30.00

Measuring cup, clear, Use Silas Pierce Pure Spice, Westmoreland, 1-cup................................**$25.00**
Measuring cup, pink transparent, bowl shape w/tab handle, Jeannette, 1-cup **$50.00**
Measuring cup, Ultramarine Blue, vertical ribs, bowl shape w/tab handle, Jeannette, 1-cup................**$55.00**
Measuring pitcher, white w/Red Dots design, McKee, 2-cup................................**$28.00**
Mold, rabbit shape, in sitting position, 8" L................**$48.00**
Refrigerator dish, Chalaine Blue, w/lid, rectangular, 4x5" .**$50.00**
Refrigerator dish, cobalt blue, shallow, w/lid, 5¾" dia......**$75.00**

Refrigerator dish, Delphite, 4¼" square, from $40.00 to $45.00; Salt and pepper shakers, Delphite, 6", pr, $30.00.

Refrigerator dish, Ships, red boat fired on white, clear lid, McKee, 4x6" **$18.00**
Refrigerator jar, green transparent, Hex Optic, rectangular, w/lid, 4½x5" **$22.00**
Salt & pepper shakers, Chalaine Blue, black letters, square, pr **$150.00**
Salt & pepper shakers, clear w/blue sailboat & red lettering, red-painted lids, 12-oz, pr................**$18.00**
Salt & pepper shakers, custard w/black lettering, square, pr................................**$24.00**
Salt & pepper shakers, Tulips, multicolor on white, Anchor Hocking, pr **$15.00**
Salt & pepper shakers, yellow opaque, black lettering, square, pr **$30.00**
Tray, well-in-tree; green, Not Heat Resisting Glass, Fry, from $70 to................................**$80.00**
Water bottle, green transparent, vertical ribbing, screw-on cap to 1 side, Hocking, 32-oz................**$25.00**
Water bottle/decanter, green transparent, horizontal ribbing, Hocking, w/stopper................**$40.00**

Kitchen Prayer Ladies

The Enesco importing company of Elk Grove, Illinois, distributed a line of kitchen novelties during the 1960s that they originally called 'Mother in the Kitchen.' Today's collectors refer to them as 'Kitchen Prayer Ladies.' The line was fairly extensive — some pieces are common, others are very scarce. All are designed around the figure of 'Mother' who is wearing a long white apron inscribed with a prayer. She is more commonly found in a pink dress. Blue is harder to find and more valuable. Where we've given ranges; pink is represented by the lower end, blue by the higher. If you find her in a white dress with blue trim, add another 10% to 20%. For a complete listing and current values, you'll want to order *Prayer Lady Plus+* by April and Larry Tvorak. This line is pictured in *The Collector's Encyclopedia of Cookie Jars, Volume 1, 2, and 3* by Joyce and Fred Roerig.

Advisor: April Tvorak (See Directory, Kitchen Prayer Ladies)

Air freshener, from $125 to................................**$145.00**
Bank, from $145 to................................**$175.00**
Bell, from $75 to................................**$90.00**
Candle holders, pr, from $95 to **$110.00**
Canister, pink, each, from $200 to **$250.00**

Cookie jar, pink, $350.00; blue, $495.00. (Photo courtesy of Pat Duncan)

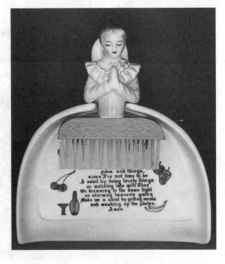

Crumb tray and brush, from $150.00 to $175.00. (Photo courtesy Pat Duncan)

Egg timer, from $135 to **$145.00**
Instant coffee jar, spoon-holder loop on side, from $85 to ..**$95.00**
Mug, from $100 to................................**$125.00**
Napkin holder, pink, from $25 to................**$30.00**

Picture frame, from $100 to $125.00
Planter, from $65 to $75.00
Plaque, full figure, from $55 to $65.00
Ring holder, from $40 to $50.00
Salt & pepper shakers, pr, from $12 to.......................$20.00
Scissors holder, wall mount, from $135 to $145.00
Soap dish, from $35 to $45.00
Spoon holder, upright, from $45 to...........................$50.00
Sprinkler bottle, blue, from $300 to $400.00
Sprinkler bottle, pink..$200.00
String holder, from $135 to $145.00
Tea set, pot, sugar & creamer, from $175 to............$275.00
Vase, bud; from $95 to $110.00

Kreiss & Co.

Collectors are hot on the trail of figural ceramics, and one of the newest areas of interest are those figurines, napkin holder dolls, salt and pepper shakers, etc., imported from Japan during the 1950s by the Kreiss company. It's so new, in fact, that we're not even sure if it's pronounced 'kriss' or 'kreese,' and dealer's asking prices also suggest an uncertainty. But there's one thing we are sure of, there's lots of activity here, and in case you haven't noticed as yet, we wanted to clue you in. There are several lines. One is a totally off-the-wall group of caricatures called Psycho-Ceramics. There's a Beatnick series, Bums, and Cave People (all of which are strange little creatures), as well as some that are very well done and tasteful. Others you find will be inset with colored 'jewels.' Many are marked either with an ink stamp or an in-mold trademark (some are dated), so you'll need to start turning likely looking items over to check for the Kreiss name just like you did last year for Holt Howard!

See also Napkin Ladies.

Advisors: Phil and Nyla Thurston (See Directory, Figural Ceramics)

Ashtray, Psycho-Ceramics, from $75.00 to 85.00. (Photo courtesy Phil and Nyla Thurston)

Ashtray, man w/tomahawk, marked Psycho-Ceramics ..$35.00

Ashtray, Wild Man head...$18.00
Bank, pink poodle..$75.00
Cookie jar, Beatnik $45.00
Egg cup, Mrs Claus...$35.00
Figurine, beatnick w/hair, NM....................................$95.00
Figurine, bum in trash can, w/rhinestones $95.00
Figurine, Christmas Party...$85.00
Figurine, Cinderella..$65.00
Figurine, devil, 5"..$32.00
Figurine, dinosaurs, set of 3...$25.00
Figurine, elephant w/drunk.......................................$125.00
Figurine, farm boy w/bee on hat $18.00
Figurine, farmer $25.00
Figurine, Happy Birthday Bum, on wood base w/plaque, M $85.00
Figurine, male, 9"..$25.00
Figurine, Merrywolf $60.00
Figurine, Santa, marked Psycho-Ceramics $50.00
Figurine, Siamese Dancer, 8" $25.00
Mug, figural bum, M...$50.00
Mug, man in garbage can $30.00
Mug, prehistoric golfer dinosaur, Oh It's That Big Snoop, EX $45.00
Mug, 3-D caveman & cavewoman, M.........................$50.00
Napkin lady...$75.00
Perfume bottle, skunk $80.00
Salt & pepper shaker, puppy, lg, pr............................$25.00
Salt & pepper shakers, bluebird, pr $35.00
Shelf sitter, Oriental figure, pr $30.00

Lamps

Aladdin Electric Lamps

Aladdin lamps have been made continually since 1908 by the Mantle Lamp Company of America, now Aladdin Industries Inc. in Nashville, Tennessee. Their famous kerosene lamps are highly collectible, and some are quite valuable. Most were relegated to the storage shelf or thrown away after electric lines came through the country. Today many people keep them on hand for emergency light.

Few know that Aladdin was one of the largest manufacturers of electric lamps from 1930 to 1956. They created new designs, colorful glass, and unique paper shades. These are not only collectible but are still used in some homes today. Many Aladdin lamps, kerosene as well as electric, can be found at garage sales, antique shops, and flea markets. You can learn more about them in the books *Aladdin Electric Lamps* and *Aladdin — The Magic Name in Lamps, Revised Edition*, written by J.W. Courter, who also periodically issues updated price guides for both kerosene and electric Aladdins.

Advisor: J.W. Courter (See Directory, Lamps)

Newsletter: *Mystic Lights of the Aladdin Knights*
J.W. Courter
3935 Kelley Rd., Kevil, KY 42053. Subscription: $25 (6 issues, postpaid 1st class) per year with current buy-sell-trade infor-

mation. Send SASE for information about other publications

Boudoir, powder dish, w/shade, G-50......................**$750.00**

Boudoir lamp, Alacite, raised floral & leaf design, fired-on color, G-48, 16"..**$70.00**

Boudoir lamp, slim cylindrical wood body w/round metal foot, W-148, 1937...**$75.00**

Bridge lamp, swing arm; Mogul socket w/8" glass reflector, #7005, 56", from $150 to **$200.00**

Bridge lamp, Whip-o-lite shade, B-135, from $100 to .**$150.00**

Floor lamp, Torchier, ornate Aladdin glass reflector, #3760, from $250 to..**$350.00**

Floor lamp, Torchier, reflector #T-172 w/embossed swirl pattern, #4598, from $200 to...................................**$250.00**

Table lamp, Alacite, electric, G-312, 1949; Base, from $40.00 to $50.00; Shade, from $50.00 to $75.00; Bride and groom finial, from $250.00 to $275.00. (Photo courtesy Bill and Treva Courter)

Table lamp, Alacite, hollow-blown pedestal design, pedestal as integral part of base, G-172, 23¼".....................**$75.00**

Table lamp, Alacite, illuminated base, metal foot, G-304..**$50.00**

Table lamp, Alacite, slim urn body, narrow neck w/double ring handles, scalloped round base, G-266 ....**$40.00**

Table lamp, all metal urn form, M-174, 21"................**$50.00**

Table lamp, clear prismic column body, metal openwork base, G-169, 23"...**$175.00**

Table lamp, Opalique, ball body w/gold-tone metal foot, G-190, 23½"...**$100.00**

TV lamp, black iron base, spun glass shade, M-367, 18" ..**$30.00**

Aladdin Kerosene Mantle Lamps

Model A, Corinthian, clear crystal, table lamp, B-100, 1935-36, from $80 to...**$125.00**

Model B, Beehive, green crystal, table lamp, B-81, 1937-38, from $125 to..**$150.00**

Model B, floor lamp, bronze & gold, B-281, 1937, from $150 to...**$200.00**

Model B, Lincoln Drape, table lamp, Alacite, scalloped design on top of foot, B-75, 1940, from $350 to.............**$400.00**

Model B, Quilt, green moonstone, table lamp, B-86, from $250 to...**$300.00**

Model B, Vertique, green moonstone, table model, B-92, 1938, from $300 to.......................................**$375.00**

Model B, Washington Drape, clear crystal, bell stem, table lamp, B-47, 1940-41, from $150 to **$200.00**

Model C-224 hanging, Brazil w/white paper shade, from $75 to..**$125.00**

Model 21C, table lamp, aluminum font, B-139, 1963-69, from $35 to...**$50.00**

Model 23, caboose lamp, aluminum, complete w/burner & white shade, B23000, from $50 to......................**$75.00**

Table lamp, Model 12, $85.00; with 601-S shade, from $300.00 to $375.00. (Photo courtesy Bill and Treva Courter)

Figural Lamps

Many of the figural lamps on the market today are from the 1930s, 1940s, and 1950s. You'll often see them modeled as matching pairs, made primarily for use in the boudoir or the nursery. They were sometimes made of glass, and *Bedroom and Bathroom Glassware of the Depression Years* by Margaret and Kenn Whitmyer (Collector Books) will prove to be an invaluable source of further information, if you're primarily interested in the glass variety. But most were ceramic, so unless another material is mentioned in our descriptions, assume that all our figural lamps are ceramic.

See also Occupied Japan.

Advisor: Dee Boston (See Directory, Lamps)

Ballerina holding flower garland, marked Germany & Schneider #17282, 6½"................................**$135.00**

Boy w/scythe & girl w/pitcher, doubled-figured base, pastel colors w/floral & heavy gold trim, 9".................**$185.00**

Clown, bashful expression, blue outfit, marked Bavaria #3614, 8"...**$150.00**

Clown, frowning child holds mandolin, marked Germany, 5½" figure on 8" base...**$135.00**

Colonial couple (double figure), bright green, pink & white, marked Germany, Schneider #15120, 6½"...............**$90.00**

Colonial couple (double figure), seated girl holds wreath, man in breeches, marked Germany #5388, 8" ...**$210.00**

Colonial couple (double figure) in green, rose & white w/gold trim, marked Germany #15120 & Schneider, 6½"......**$95.00**

Colonial couple w/decalcomania floral trim, incised #1360 Crown & Sitzendorf, w/Germany at base back, 9½", pr **$350.00**

Colonial girl in rose & yellow dress, holding blue reticule, hair piled high w/plumes, unmarked, 6"............**$110.00**

Colonial girl seated in white chair & holding Pekingese puppy, marked Germany, 5½"...........................**$145.00**

Colonial lady in yellow dress, pancake hat, holding green purse, marked Germany #3001I, 8¼" **$185.00**

Colonial lady w/fan, pink dress w/yellow trim, intaglio eyes, marked Germany #647, 8¼" figure on 9½" base ..**$165.00**

Couple (double figure) in Empire-styled dress & Napoleonic-styled blue uniform, marked #13096, 6" on 7" base.............**$175.00**

Dancing girl w/tambourine to head, marked #2923II, 7" ..**$175.00**

Dutch couple, frosted aqua glass base, frosted windmill shade depicts girl chasing geese around bottom edge, unmarked, 11½", $85.00. (Photo courtesy Dee Boston)

Flapper in blue harem outfit w/yellow trim & black hair, unmarked, 6¾" **$125.00**

Flapper in orange & white lustre evening dress w/gold star & floral trim, marked Germany #5914, 6½" **$145.00**

Flapper in orange strapless top & purple shorts holding out skirt, marked DRPa Germany #852, 7"................**$195.00**

Girl in lavender & yellow lustre short formal w/pink headband, marked Germany #15964, 6¼"..................**$135.00**

Girl seated in ornate black chair playing mandolin, yellow dress w/green trim, marked Made in Germany, 6"...........**$135.00**

Girl w/book, boy w/mandolin (double figure), lustre finish, marked Schneider & Germany #16760, 7"..........**$185.00**

Girl w/Dutch-type bonnet & lg basket bouquet, marked Germany #32438, 6" figure on 7" base **$175.00**

Girl w/lg bouquet, boy w/guitar & puppy holding basket, Cupid under floral urn at center, marked Germany #7318, 6½"...**$195.00**

Girls (3) in yellow, pink & green formals sit on base, pedestal at center w/decalcomania flowers, Bavaria, 1930s, pr.**$375.00**

Jack & Jill, Colonial-styled green & lavender outfits, holding water bucket or pitcher, marked Germany #13334 MHB, 8", pr...**$250.00**

Lady holding grape cluster & chalice, little detail, simple attire, marked Germany #6028, 6", pr................**$160.00**

Lady in blue flounced dress w/lg rose bouquet, marked Germany #23728, 6" **$135.00**

Lady in Colonial dress w/high stand-up collar, holds blue rose garland mirror, marked Germany #495, 6" **$135.00**

Lady in short dress w/orange top holding mirror, tree trunk base w/leaves, marked Germany #11636, 4¾".....**$95.00**

Pierette holding mandolin & standing in lg pink rose, marked Germany #4134, 6¾" **$135.00**

Pierette in short white dress w/black trim & top, detailed pedestal base, marked Sitzendorf & Germany #13047, 6½"...**$225.00**

Pierrot holding nosegay of roses, well-painted face, marked 1314, 6"...**$115.00**

Young girl, holding skirt out, bright multicolor w/gold trimmed base, marked Germany #89, 5½" **$145.00**

Young girl's torso atop lg pink rose skirt, marked Germany #14598, 5½", M **$175.00**

Lady in pink dress, marked Germany #15567, 5½", $175.00. (Photo courtesy Dee Boston)

Motion Lamps

Though some were made as early as 1920 and as late as the 1970s, motion lamps were most popular during the 1950s. Most are cylindrical with scenes such as waterfalls and forest fires and attain a sense of motion through the action of an inner cylinder that rotates with the heat of the bulb. Linda and Bill Montgomery have written a book called *Motion Lamps, 1920s to the Present*, containing full-page color photographs and lots of good information if you'd like to learn more about these lamps.

Advisors: Jim and Kaye Whitaker (See Directory, Lamps)

Davy Crockett, clock on top, United Clock Co, rare, 10", $650.00. (Photo courtesy Phil Helley)

Antique Autos, Econolite, 1957 ....**$110.00**

Bicycles, Econolite, 1959, 11" **$125.00**

Birches w/ducks, LA Goodman, 1956, 11" **$95.00**

Blacksmith, Gritt Co, 1920s, 11" **$75.00**

Boy & Girl Scout, Rotovue Jr, 1950, 10" **$150.00**

Butterflies, Econolite, 1954, 11" **$85.00**

Christmas Tree, Econolite, many colors, paper, 1951, various sizes, from $40 to..**$75.00**

Church in snow scene, Econolite, 1957, 11" **$110.00**
Colonial Fountain, Scene in Action Co, 1930s, 10"...**$140.00**
Forest Fire, Econolite, gold wire base, 1955, 11"........**$85.00**
Forest Fire, Ignition Co, 1940s, 8" **$35.00**
Forest Fire, LA Goodman, 1956, 11" **$65.00**

Forest Fire, Roto-Vue Jr., 1940, 10", $125.00.

Fountain of Youth, Econolite (Roto-Vue Jr), 1950, 10", from
    $75 to...**$125.00**
Hawaiian Scene, Econolite, 1959, 11" **$75.00**
Hopalong Cassidy, Econolite (Roto-Vue Jr), 1949, 10"..**$210.00**
Indian Chief, plaster, Gritt Inc, 1920s, 11", from $45 to..**$95.00**
Indian Maiden, plaster, Gritt Inc, 1920s, 11"................**$45.00**
Japanese Twilight, Scene in Action, 1931, 13" **$125.00**
Mill Stream, Econolite, 1956, 11", from $65 to **$95.00**
Miss Liberty, Econolite, 1957, 11"...............................**$135.00**
Mother Goose, Econolite, 1948, 11" **$90.00**
Mountain Waterfall (Campers), LA Goodman, 1956, 11"..**$55.00**
Niagara Falls, Econolite, 1955, 11", from $50 to..........**$85.00**
Niagara Falls, Econolite (Roto-Vue Jr), 1950, 10" **$55.00**
Niagara Falls, LA Goodman, 1957, 11"........................**$35.00**
Niagara Falls, Rainbow, Econolite, oval, 1960, 11" **$60.00**
Niagara Falls, Scene in Action, 1931, 10"....................**$95.00**
Op Art Lamp, black plastic, Visual Effects Inc, 1970s, 13"..**$25.00**
Oriental Fantasy (w/volcano), LA Goodman, 1957, 11"..**$65.00**
Seattle World's Fair, Econolite, 1962, 11"....................**$90.00**
Ships, Rev-O-Lite, 1930s, 10", from $75 to **$110.00**
Spirit of '76, Creative Light Products, 1973, 11"...........**$45.00**
Steamboats, Econolite, 1957, 11", from $95 to **$110.00**
Story Book (Hey Diddle Diddle) LA Goodman, 1956, 11"..**$80.00**
The Bar Is Open, black plastic, Visual Effects, 1970s, 13"...**$25.00**
Trains, Econolite, 1956, 11"..**$90.00**
Trains Racing, LA Goodman, 1957, 11".......................**$85.00**
Truck & Bus, Econolite, 1962, 11"..............................**$110.00**
Venice Grand Canal, Econolite, 1963, 11" **$125.00**
White Christmas, flat front, Econolite, 1953, 11", from $85
    to...**$95.00**

TV Lamps

By the 1950s, TV was commonplace in just about every
home in the country but still fresh enough to have our undi-
vided attention. Families gathered around the set together
and for the rest of the evening were entertained by Ed
Sullivan or stumped by the $64,000 Question. Pottery pro-
ducers catered to this scenario by producing TV lamps by the
score, and with the popularity of anything from the 'fifties'
being what it is today, suddenly these lamps are making an
appearance at flea markets and co-ops everywhere.

See also Maddux of California; Morton Potteries; Royal
Haeger.

Advisors: John and Peggy Scott (See Directory, Florence
Ceramics)

Bird, black & white, on brown log planter, 11x13"....**$65.00**
Conch shell, brown & lime gloss, 13" L.......................**$40.00**
Crane, white w/gold spatter, on deep planter base, 16"..**$80.00**
Deer, spike buck on rocky ledge, naturalistic colors, from $60
    to..**$65.00**
Deer pr, Deco styling, tan w/gold trim, Kron, 15x8"..**$60.00**
Dove pr, white w/gold spatter, Royal Fleet CA, 10x13½"..**$60.00**
Duck, flying, black gloss, 12½" L................................**$50.00**

Exotic bird, coral with gold spray and trim, L-710, 13x12", from $75.00 to $80.00. (Photo courtesy John and Peggy Scott)

Glass w/black silhouette riders, reverse-painted mountainous
    background, flat metal base, 8x10" **$50.00**
Horse, black w/gold trim, rearing, on reticulated base w/bulb
    inside, 18", from $85 to......................................**$100.00**
Horse standing on rock ledge, white, 12½x9½".........**$60.00**
Leda & Swan, terra cotta or turquoise high gloss, Lane, 16",
    minimum value...**$100.00**

Poodle and pug, glass eyes, Kron, 13", from $70.00 to $80.00. (Photo courtesy John and Peggy Scott)

Siamese mother w/kitten, blue marble eyes, Enchanto
    CA..**$65.00**

L.E. Smith

Originating just after the turn of the century, the L.E. Smith company continues to operate in Mt. Pleasant, Pennsylvania, at the present time. In the 1920s they introduced a line of black glass that they are famous for today. Some pieces were decorated with silver overlay or enameling. Using their own original molds, they made a line of bird and animal figures in crystal as well as in colors. The company is currently producing these figures, many in two sizes. They're one of the main producers of the popular Moon and Star pattern which has been featured in their catalogs since the 1960s in a variety of shapes and colors.

If you'd like to learn more about their bird and animal figures, *Glass Animals of the Depression Era* by Lee Garmon and Dick Spencer has a chapter devoted to those made by L.E. Smith.

See also Eye Winker; Moon and Star.

Advisor: Ruth Grizel (See Directory, Westmoreland)

Newsletter: *The Glass Post*
P.O. Box 205
Oakdale, IA 52319-0205; Subscription: $25 per year for 12 issues

Aquarium, King Fish, green, 7¼x15" $265.00
Basket, fireside; ruby, 13x12" $125.00

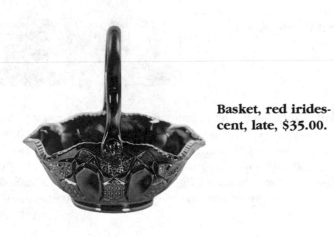

Basket, red iridescent, late, $35.00.

Bookend, horse, rearing, amber, each $38.00
Bookend, horse, rearing, crystal, each........................$25.00
Bookend, horse, rearing, ruby, each...........................$40.00
Bookend, rearing horse, slag, each, from $50 to $60.00
Bookends, horse head, milk glass, pr..........................$90.00
Bowl, berry; robin blue, footed, 4"..............................$16.00
Bowl, Doily, red carnival $38.00
Bowl, turkey, dark blue, footed, oval, 7".....................$65.00
Bowl, wedding; milk glass w/red & blue flowers, 4" square, w/lid $35.00
Bowl, Wigman, flared...$30.00
Cake plate, Veined Onyx, black, footed, 10"...............$48.00
Candle holder, kneeling angel, slag, each $25.00
Candle holders, kneeling angel, green, pr...................$26.00
Candy box, marigold iridescent, heart shape $27.00
Candy nappy, Almond Nouveau slag, heart shape, 6" .$25.00

Canoe, Daisy & Button, purple carnival $25.00
Covered dish, duck, crystal, Herter's 1893, 7" $65.00
Covered dish, hen on woven base, amberina, 7" $35.00
Covered dish, rooster, standing; white carnival $75.00
Covered dish, turkey, amethyst $65.00
Covered dish, turkey, crystal $35.00
Creamer, Homestead, pink...$8.00
Creamer & sugar bowl, Hobstar, amethyst carnival....$25.00
Figurine, bird, Almond Nouveau slag, head up or down, 5", pr...$65.00
Figurine, bird, frosted w/red & green painted flowers & buds, 8½", from $45 to....................................$50.00
Figurine, camel, amber, recumbent, 4½x6" $55.00
Figurine, camel, cobalt, recumbent, 4½x6" $65.00
Figurine, camel, crystal, recumbent, 4½x6" $45.00
Figurine, cow, crystal, miniature, 1¾"........................$10.00
Figurine, elephant, crystal, miniature, 1¾" $10.00
Figurine, Goose Girl, amber, 5½"................................$35.00
Figurine, Goose Girl, crystal frosted w/pink, yellow & green stain, 5½"..$35.00
Figurine, Goose Girl, ice green carnival, 5½" $60.00
Figurine, Goose Girl, red, 5½"......................................$50.00
Figurine, horse, amberina, recumbent, 9" L $125.00
Figurine, horse, blue, recumbent, 9" L......................$115.00
Figurine, horse, crystal satin, standing, pr $75.00
Figurine, horse, green, recumbent, 9" L....................$100.00
Figurine, praying Madonna, crystal $35.00
Figurine, rabbit, crystal, ears down, 3½", pr $40.00
Figurine, rabbit, crystal, miniature..............................$10.00
Figurine, Scottie, black w/red trim, 6" $75.00
Figurine, Scottie, crystal, 6"...$65.00
Figurine, sparrow, head up, 3½"..................................$15.00
Figurine, swan, Almond Nouveau slag, 5"...................$55.00
Figurine, swan, crystal lustre, limited edition, w/certificate, lg $55.00
Figurine, swan, ice pink carnival, 2"............................$15.00
Figurine, swan, light green carnival or light blue carnival, Levay, 2", each $20.00
Figurine, swan, milk glass w/decoration, 8½".............$45.00
Figurine, unicorn, pink, miniature...............................$20.00
Flower block, swan, Pink Mist w/gold beak & flower, 8"..$135.00
Lamp, fairy; turtle figural, green $25.00
Novelty, boot on pedestal, green or amber, each.......$12.00
Novelty, hat, amberina carnival $17.50
Novelty, shoe skate, ice blue, limited edition, 4"........$25.00
Novelty, slipper, Daisy & Button, amber $8.00
Novelty, slipper, Daisy & Button, purple carnival.......$25.00
Pitcher, water; Heritage, red carnival $40.00
Pitcher, water; Hobstar, ice green, w/6 tumblers......$125.00
Pitcher, water; Near-Cut, amber..................................$40.00
Pitcher, water; Tiara Eclipse, green.............................$70.00
Plate, Abraham Lincoln, purple carnival, #706/1195, 9" .$40.00
Plate, Do-Si-Do, black, 8" square $15.00
Plate, Herald, Christmas 1972, purple carnival, lg $40.00
Plate, Jefferson Davis, purple carnival, 1972, lg..........$40.00
Plate, John F Kennedy, purple carnival, lg..................$40.00
Plate, Robert E Lee, purple carnival, 1972, lg $40.00
Plate, Silver Dollar Eagle, purple carnival, 1972, lg $40.00
Punch bowl, Grape, amethyst, w/12 cups & ladle ...$195.00

Soap dish, swan figural, clear, 8½" $22.50
Sugar bowl, Homestead, pink...$8.00
Toothpick holder, Daisy & Button, amberina.............$12.50
Toothpick holder, Daisy & Button, light green carnival, Levay $15.00
Tumbler, Bull's Eye, red carnival................................$22.00
Urn, black, 2-handled, footed, 8" $20.00
Vase, corn, crystal lustre, very lg...............................$37.00

Butter dish, Almond Nouveau slag, 1980, $45.00.

Lefton China

China, porcelain, and ceramic items with that now familiar mark, Lefton, have been around since the early 1940s and are highly sought after by collectors in the secondary market place today. The company was founded by Mr. George Zoltan Lefton, an immigrant from Hungary. In the 1930s he was in the designing and manufacturing of sportswear, and his hobby of collecting fine china and porcelain led him to the creation of his own ceramic business.

When the bombing of Pearl Harbor occurred on December 7, 1941, Mr. Lefton came to the aid of a Japanese-American friend and helped him protect his property from anti-Japanese groups. After this event, Mr. Lefton was introduced to a Japanese factory owned by Kowa Koki KK. Up until 1980 this factory produced thousands of pieces that were marketed by the Lefton company with the initials KW preceding the item number. Figurines and animals plus many of the whimsical pieces such as Bluebirds, Dainty Miss, Miss Priss, Cabbage Cutie, Elf Head, Mr. Toodles, and Dutch Girl are eagerly collected today. As with any antique or collectible, the prices vary depending on location, condition, and availability. For the history of Lefton China, information about Lefton factories, marks, and other identification methods, we highly recommend the *Collector's Encyclopedia of Lefton China*, Volumes I and II, by our advisor, Loretta DeLozier.

See also Birthday Angels; Cookie Jars.

Advisor: Loretta DeLozier (See Directory, Lefton)

Club: National Society of Lefton Collectors

Newsletter: *The Lefton Collector*
c/o Loretta DeLozier
1101 Polk St.
Bedford, IA 50833; 712-523-2289 (Mon.-Fri. 9:00-4:00), Fax 712-523-2624, or E-mail: LeftonLady@aol.com, Dues. $25 per year (includes quarterly newsletter)

Angel, standing on flowers, #4152, 4½" $12.00
Angel, w/flowers, Happy Birthday, #5079, 6" $45.00
Angel, w/musical instrument, #1592, 3¼".....................$8.00
Ashtray, collar, #1581, 5" $25.00
Ashtray, golf tees & ball, #2139, 5¼" $18.00
Ashtray, Rose Chintz, #683, 5" dia.............................$35.00
Bank, bowling pin, #2644, 10"......................................$28.00
Bank, piggy style, boy in overalls, #2729, 5"...............$22.00
Bird, bluebird, 2 babies on base, #5157, 7"................$42.00
Bird, cockatoo, #5062, 9¾", pr $90.00
Bird, white dove, #5159, 9¼", pr.................................$80.00
Bottle, Russian Dressing, #2090, 9" $55.00
Box, candy; Paisley Fantazia, #6809, 4½" $35.00
Box, Double Bardender's, #5072, 8" $55.00
Box, Garden Bouquet, footed, w/lid, #1894, 4" dia....$40.00
Box, Green Holly, package w/red bow atop, from $30 to..$35.00
Bust, boy or girl, white w/gold trim, #3902, 5½", each..$22.00
Butter dish, Country Squire, #2393, 5¼"....................$28.00
Cake stand, Green Holly, from $65 to $70.00
Coffeepot, Blue Rose, #3037......................................$100.00
Coffeepot, Cuddles, #1448 ....$85.00
Coffeepot, Heirloom, #5381.......................................$165.00
Coffeepot, Yuletide Hollyberry, #7802......................$110.00
Cookie jar, Country Squire, #1609, 7¼" $95.00
Cookie jar, Cuddles, #3324...$75.00
Cookie jar, Scottish girl, #1173, 9¼"..........................$295.00

Creamer and sugar bowl, elf heads, #3970, $75.00 for the set. (Photo courtesy Loretta DeLozier)

Creamer & sugar bowl, Miss Priss, #1505....................$55.00
Cup & saucer, demitasse; Blue Rose............................$16.00
Cup & saucer, demitasse; Magnolia, #2524..................$30.00
Cup & saucer, Green Heritage, #512............................$30.00
Dish, Hollyberry, #10409, 7" $20.00
Dish, triple candy; Rose, gold trim, #2121, 8" $50.00
Egg cup, comical face, #220, 4"....................................$36.00
Egg cup, Country Squire, #1970, 3½" $18.00
Figurine, British Colonial couple, #856, 8", pr $150.00
Figurine, Colonial boy & girl, #5155, 10", pr.............$180.00
Figurine, Colonial lady, Elizabeth, #343, 7½" $75.00
Jam server, Strawberry, 3-compartment, #2379, 7¾"...$40.00

Figurines, poodles with applied white lilacs and stones, #157, 5", $80.00 for the pair. (Photo courtesy Loretta DeLozier)

Figurines, young children in period attire, each with a dog, #5642, from $160.00 to $210.00 for the pair. (Photo courtesy Loretta DeLozier)

Jar, Instant Coffee, coffee bag shape, #2121, 5".........$36.00
Mug, Roosevelt, #2379, 5½"...$45.00
Napkin holder, Christmas tree w/gold star, #7272......$15.00
Planter, angel on cloud w/stones, #165.....................$40.00
Planter, horse head, #1953, 6" $30.00
Planter, rainbow trout, matt finish, #1465, 10½".........$27.00
Salt & pepper shakers, Blue Paisley, #2346, pr...........$22.00
Salt & pepper shakers, Cabbage Cutie, #2126, pr.......$30.00
Salt & pepper shakers, chickens, #3024, 4", pr..........$18.00
Salt & pepper shakers, Magnolia, #2639, pr...............$22.00
Salt & pepper shakers, Mr & Mrs Humpty Dumpty, #7782, pr...$18.00
Salt & pepper shakers, speckled roosters, #3136, 3", pr.$28.00
Sleigh, Green Holly, #2637, 10½"................................$60.00
Snack set, Heirloom, #5385.......................................$22.00
Snack set, lobster design, w/cup, #2757, 8" tray........$30.00
Sugar bowl & creamer, Blue Paisley, #2374, pr $65.00
Sugar bowl & creamer, elf head figural, #3970, pr $75.00
Sugar bowl & creamer, flowers w/gold trim, #292, 4¼", pr $40.00
Sugar bowl & creamer, Magnolia, #2520, pr...............$65.00
Teapot, Hollyberry, #10419, 7" $85.00
Teapot, Miss Priss $145.00
Teapot, Modern Design, #2417...................................$85.00
Teapot, Red Cardinal, #01246 ....$110.00
Teapot, Rose Chintz, musical, #7543.........................$95.00

Toothpick holder, Christmas tree, #151, 6¼", w/Christmas tree salt & pepper shakers, 3-pc...........................$45.00
Vase, Christmas Rose, #07678 ....$22.00
Vase, Hands Floral Bisque Bouquet, #4198, 5½" $28.00
Vase, pink roses & ribbons, #70039, 6".......................$85.00
Vase, white milk china w/roses, #1189, 6¼" dia.........$50.00

Wall lantern, Green Holly, 9x6x4½", $75.00. (Photo courtesy Doug Dezso)

Wall plaque, Four Seasons, #4927, 8½" $100.00
Wall plaque, mermaid in shell, #4489, 7", pr $80.00
Wall plaque, praying child, #984, pr $40.00
Wall plaque, sunfish, #3136, 18"................................$55.00
Wall plaque, w/Colonial boy & girl, #117, 6¼"...........$90.00

Letter Openers

If you're cramped for space but a true-blue collector at heart, here's a chance to get into a hobby where there's more than enough diversification to be both interesting and challenging, yet requires very little room for display. Whether you prefer the advertising letter openers or the more imaginative models with handles sculpted as a dimensional figure or incorporating a penknife or a cigarette lighter, you should be able to locate enough for a nice assortment. Materials are varied as well, ranging from silver plate to wood. For more information, we recommend *Collector's Guide to Letter Openers,* Everett Grist (Collector Books).

Advisor: Everett Grist (See Directory, Letter Openers)

Advertising, plastic Fuller Brush Man, marked Made in USA, pink, 7¼", $12.00.

Advertising, brass, Brown & Bigelow, Remembrance advertising $30.00

Advertising, brass, Clarence A O'Brien, Registered Patent Attorney **$35.00**

Advertising, bronze, Made by Metal Arts Co, Serial Building & Loan & Savings Institution, Organized 1885 .....**$35.00**

Advertising, chrome steel, AS&W Co **$12.00**

Advertising, plastic, Fuller Brush Woman on sides **$12.00**

Advertising, plastic, RS Knapp Co Inc, figure of woman ...**$4.00**

Advertising, plastic, Yellow Pages **$3.00**

Advertising, stamped Genuine Bronze, Made by W&H Co, Newark NJ, Sealtest Ice Cream, double-sided **$40.00**

Advertising, steel, Pittsburgh Steel Co, stamped Pittsburgh Steel on nail head **$18.00**

Advertising, white metal, Mobile Asphalt Co Inc, Whistler AL **$6.00**

Antler, stag & bone, artist signed, Koras **$15.00**

Antler, stag w/sterling collar & steel, marked Pat Nov 22, 1887 ....**$25.00**

Arts & Crafts, aluminum, cut-out dogwood on handle ..**$15.00**

Arts & Crafts, aluminum, Great Smoky Mountains, w/letter opener as part of handle **$12.00**

Arts & Crafts, copper, stamped Vermont Hand Hammered Copper 705, monogrammed CVC **$12.00**

Bakelite, butterscotch w/hand-painted flowers, Ocean City MD **$25.00**

Bakelite, yellow marbelized handle w/silver, brass color, nickel blade, Chicago World's Fair, 1934 ....**$75.00**

Bone, carved & pierced handle w/painted scene, marked Souvenir of Mexico **$15.00**

Bone, cut-out totem **$20.00**

Bone w/wood handle, scrimshaw work w/dyed decoration, marked Mexico **$15.00**

Combination, bookmark/letter opener, brass, Oriental dragon inside block C, green cloth sheath, stamped FS **$12.00**

Combination, bookmark/letter opener, brass color, New Orleans French Quarter **$4.00**

Combination, bookmark/letter opener, copper, Scottie dog **$12.00**

Combination, calendar/letter opener, red plastic, Souvenir Knoxville TN, 1948-49 calender insert on handle ..**$10.00**

Combination, calendar/letter opener, steel, Gogan Machine Corp, Cleveland, 21-year perpetual calendar, 1939-1960 ....**$15.00**

Combination, desk set, brass, represents sword & stone, paperweight & letter opener **$15.00**

Combination, desk set, clear plastic & gold-tone metal, letter holder, paperweight, pen & letter opener **$15.00**

Combination, desk set, 2-tone Bakelite wax sealer, letter opener, & pen w/extra nib, Fountain Pen Co, NY, +original box **$95.00**

Combination, lighter/letter opener, plastic & steel, lighter w/fishing fly in body, ruler blade, Mardi Gras '67, Japan **$40.00**

Combination, magnifier/letter opener, clear plastic w/ruler markings **$3.00**

Combination, magnifier/letter opener, green plastic, marked SP, Made in USA **$3.00**

Combination, magnifier/letter opener, red plastic w/brass shield, Annapolis **$6.00**

Combination, magnifier/ruler/letter opener, plastic, Producers Marketing Ass'n **$3.00**

Combination, pen knife/letter opener, bronze & steel, Borman Service Co, Philadelphia, Remington UMC USA on blade **$85.00**

Combination, pen knife/letter opener, plastic & steel, Great Smoky Mountains, knife blade, Imperial USA **$10.00**

Combination, ruler/letter opener, Mobile AL, marked w/soldier holding sword & shield marked E **$4.00**

Combination, ruler/magnifier/tracing curve/letter opener, Hong Kong **$3.00**

Enamel on brass, China **$15.00**

Enamel on brass, flower motif **$30.00**

Figure, brass, derringer, Stamford CT **$10.00**

Figure, brass, gun, marked Bradley & Hubbard Mfg ..**$35.00**

Figure, brass, Pocahontas, marked Jamestown 1607 VA, Copyright 1957, Virginia Metal Workers **$25.00**

Figure, brass, 3-dimensional grasshopper, paperweight handle **$30.00**

Figure, brass, 3-dimensional nude, Great Smoky Mountains **$18.00**

Figure, cast iron, gun, sold as paperweight, Gettysburg PA, Centennial of Civil War **$18.00**

Horn, house & beach motif, florals & Philippines, EX detail **$45.00**

Horn, whale w/ivory eye, Hawaii **$25.00**

Ivory, carved burro pulling wagon **$40.00**

Ivory, carved dragon motif, double-sided **$55.00**

Ivory, scrimshawed schooner & bird **$45.00**

Ivory (French), Mille Lacs, Indian Trading Post, Onamia MN **$15.00**

Ivory & silver, Art Nouveau-styled swallow on handle, Victorian **$125.00**

Lucite, reverse-carved & filled cardinal & flowers, hand-carved handle, hand colored, Bircraft Trademark paper label **$30.00**

Lucite, stag in handle **$12.00**

Metal, white, golf clubs & bags, Metzke, 1985 ....**$15.00**

Pewter plate, sand dollar, Metzke **$6.00**

Souvenir, plastic, hollow handle w/seashells & white sand, marked Gulf Shores AL, Beach Sand **$18.00**

Souvenir, silver-painted white metal, horseshoe w/Kent & horse, KY **$8.00**

Tortoise shell, elephant head, Santo Domingo, Victorian ..**$85.00**

Tortoise shell, 3-dimensional bird's claw holding movable tortoise marble, Victorian **$125.00**

L.G. Wright

The L.G. Wright Glass Company is located in New Martinsville, West Virginia. Mr. Wright began business as a glass jobber and then began buying molds from defunct glass companies. He never made his own glass, instead many companies pressed his wares, among them the Fenton Art Glass Company, Imperial Glass Corporation, Viking Glass Company, and the Westmoreland Glass Compnay. Much of L.G. Wright's glass were reproductions of colonial and Victorian glass and lamps. Many items were made from the original molds, but the designs of some were slightly changed. His company flourished in the 1960s and 1970s; it remains open today under new ownership. For more information on many of their covered animal dishes, we recommend *Covered Animal Dishes* by Everett Grist (Collector Books).

Advisor: Ruth Grizel (See Directory, Westmoreland)

Newsletter: *The Glass Post*
P.O. Box 205
Oakdale, IA 52319-0205; Subscription: $25 per year for 12 issues; free advertising to subscribers

Ashtray, Daisy & Button, ruby, 5½" $20.00
Basket, Daisy & Button, amber, flat bottom, 4½x7½" **$35.00**
Bell, Daisy & Button, ruby, 6½" $35.00
Bowl, Daisy & Button, amber, 5" $25.00
Bowl, Daisy & Button, milk glass, w/handles, fluted rim, 9x12" $40.00
Bowl, punch; Paneled Grape, amber, footed, 9½" ...$125.00
Candy dish, Paneled Grape, amber, footed, w/lid......$25.00
Candy dish, Paneled Grape, dark green, footed, 6½"...$35.00
Candy dish, Paneled Grape, ruby, footed, 6½x4".......$35.00
Compote, Palm Beach, apple green, ca 1930, 8½".....$95.00
Covered dish, Atterbury Duck, any color, unmarked, 11"...$70.00
Covered dish, cow on basketweave base, purple or caramel slag, 5½", each...$55.00
Covered dish, duck on flange base, amethyst w/white head $65.00
Covered dish, duck on flange base, blue opaque $60.00
Covered dish, duck on flange base, milk glass or blue opaque w/milk glass head, each...........................$50.00
Covered dish, flatiron, amber, w/lid, 5x8½" $50.00
Covered dish, hen & chicks on base, custard, 5½" $75.00

Covered dish, hen on basketweave base, 7½", see listings for values. (Photography by Frank Grizel)

Covered dish, hen on basketweave base, amberina, red, or vaseline, 7½", each...$75.00
Covered dish, hen on basketweave base, amethyst w/white head or white w/amethyst head, 7½", each.........$65.00
Covered dish, hen on basketweave base, black w/white head, 7½" $75.00
Covered dish, hen on basketweave base, blue slag, 7½" $95.00
Covered dish, hen on basketweave base, chocolate, 7½" $95.00

Covered dish, hen on basketweave base, light green carnival, pink carnival, or ice blue carnival, 7½", each......$95.00
Covered dish, hen on basketweave base, purple slag or caramel slag, 5½", each....................................$55.00
Covered dish, hen on basketweave base, purple slag or caramel slag, 7½", each, from $65 to....................$75.00
Covered dish, hen on basketweave base, red slag, 7½", minimum value $125.00
Covered dish, hen on nest, red slag, 5½" $125.00
Covered dish, horse on basketweave base, purple slag or caramel slag, 5½", each....................................$55.00
Covered dish, lamb on basketweave base, amber, 5½"..$30.00
Covered dish, lamb on basketweave base, purple slag or caramel slag, 5½", each....................................$55.00
Covered dish, owl on basketweave base, amber, 5½" .$35.00
Covered dish, owl on basketweave base, Antique Blue, 5½"...$35.00
Covered dish, owl on basketweave base, blue slag, 5½" $75.00
Covered dish, owl on basketweave base, custard, caramel slag or purple slag, 5½", each $65.00
Covered dish, owl on basketweave base, custard, 5½".$50.00
Covered dish, owl on basketweave base, dark blue satin, 5½"..$50.00
Covered dish, owl on basketweave base, purple slag or caramel slag, 5½", each....................................$55.00
Covered dish, rooster on basketweave base, purple slag or caramel slag, 5½", each....................................$55.00
Covered dish, rooster on nest, red slag, 5½" $95.00
Covered dish, turkey on basketweave base, lilac mist, 5½"..$55.00
Covered dish, turkey on basketweave base, purple slag or caramel slag, 5½", each....................................$55.00
Covered dish, turtle, 'Knobby Back,' amber, lg...........$95.00
Covered dish, turtle, 'Knobby Back,' dark green, lg.$125.00
Covered dish, turtle, 'Knobby Back,' milk glass, lg..$135.00
Covered dish, turtle on basketweave base, amber, 5½" $20.00
Covered dish, turtle on basketweave base, purple slag, 5½"..$50.00
Creamer & sugar bowl, Paneled Grape, amber, 2½"..$35.00
Cruet, Thumbprint, fluted $85.00
Cup, punch; Paneled Grape, dark green, w/cup hook, set of 12 ....$120.00
Goblet, Paneled Grape, amber, 8-oz.........................$10.00
Goblet, wine; Paneled Grape, amber, 2-oz, 4"...........$10.00
Goblet, wine; Paneled Grape, ruby, 2-oz $15.00
Lamp, fairy; Thistle, crystal, 3-pc.............................$35.00
Lamp, fairy; Thousand Eye, frosted topaz $75.00
Lamp, oil; Daisy & Button, ruby, 12" $75.00
Pitcher, Cherries, green, 5"..$35.00
Pitcher, Cherries, ruby, 5"..$45.00
Plate, Log Cabin, Crystal Mist, oval, limited edition, 1971, 9"...$95.00
Plate, Paneled Grape, ruby, 7½" $25.00
Plate, Paneled Grape, ruby, 9½" $35.00
Sugar shaker, Daisy & Lattice, cobalt opalescent, pr ..$50.00
Toothpick, Cherries, red slag, 2½" $25.00
Vase, corn, yellow opalescent.....................................$75.00

Liberty Blue

'Take home a piece of American history!,' stated an ad from the 1970s for this dinnerware made in Staffordshire, England. Blue and white depictions of George Washington at Valley Forge, Paul Revere, Independence Hall — fourteen historic scenes in all — were offered on different place-setting pieces. The ad goes on to describe this 'unique...truly unusual..museum-quality...future family heirloom.'

For every five dollars spent on groceries you could purchase a basic piece (dinner plate, bread and butter plate, cup, saucer, or dessert dish) for fifty-nine cents on alternate weeks of the promotion. During the promotion, completer pieces could also be purchased. The soup tureen was the most expensive item, originally selling for $24.99. Nineteen completer pieces in all were offered along with a five-year open-stock guarantee.

For more information we recommend Jo Cunningham's book, *The Best of Collectible Dinnerware*.

Advisor: Gary Beegle (See Directory, Dinnerware)

Teapot, from $95.00 to $125.00.

Bowl, cereal; from $10 to	**$12.50**
Bowl, flat soup; 8¾", from $15 to	**$18.00**
Bowl, fruit; 5", from $4.50 to	**$5.50**
Bowl, vegetable; oval	**$40.00**
Bowl, vegetable; round	**$35.00**
Butter dish, w/lid, ¼-lb, from $20 to	**$35.00**
Casserole, w/lid, from $65 to	**$75.00**
Coaster, from $8 to	**$10.00**
Creamer	**$10.00**
Creamer & sugar bowl, w/lid, original box	**$60.00**
Cup & saucer, from $7 to	**$9.00**
Gravy boat, from $30 to	**$35.00**
Gravy boat liner	**$15.00**
Mug, from $10 to	**$12.00**
Pitcher, milk	**$95.00**
Plate, bread & butter; 6"	**$3.00**
Plate, dinner; 10", from $7 to	**$9.00**
Plate, luncheon; scarce, 8¾"	**$12.00**
Plate, scarce, 7"	**$9.50**
Platter, 12", from $35 to	**$45.00**
Platter, 14"	**$65.00**
Salt & pepper shakers, pr	**$25.00**
Soup ladle, plain white, no decal, from $30 to	**$35.00**
Soup tureen, w/lid, from $250 to	**$300.00**
Sugar bowl, no lid	**$15.00**
Sugar bowl, w/lid	**$25.00**

License Plates

Some of the early porcelain license plates are valued at more than $500.00. First-year plates (the date varies from state to state, of course) are especially desirable. Steel plates with the aluminum 'state seal' attached range in value from $150.00 (for those from 1915 to 1920) down to $20.00 (for those from the early 1940s to 1950). Even some modern plates are desirable to collectors who like those with special graphics and messages.

Our values are given for examples in good or better condition, unless noted otherwise. For further information see *License Plate Values* distributed by L-W Book Sales.

Advisor: Richard Diehl (See Directory, License Plates)

Newsletter: *Automobile License Plate Collectors*
Gary Brent Kincade
P.O. Box 712, Weston, WV 26452; 304-842-3773

Magazine: *License Plate Collectors Hobby Magazine*
Drew Steitz, Editor
P.O. Box 222
East Texas, PA 18046; Phone or FAX 610-791-7979; e-mail: PL8Seditor@aol.com or RVGZ60A@prodigy.com; Issued bimonthly; $18 per year (1st class, USA). Send $2 for sample copy

Canada, 1918, Alberta	**$50.00**
Canada, 1925, British Columbia	**$35.00**
Canada, 1925, Nova Scotia	**$40.00**
Canada, 1939, Alberta	**$16.50**
Canada, 1957, Quebec	**$5.50**
Canada, 1962, Yukon, fair	**$20.00**
Canada, 1967, Nova Scotia	**$11.50**
Canada, 1972, Ontario	**$2.00**
Canada, 1976, Saskatchewan	**$3.75**
Canada, 1979, Yukon	**$12.50**
Canada, 1983, Newfoundland	**$8.50**
Motorcycle, 1954, Nebraska	**$30.00**
Motorcycle, 1959, Arizona	**$30.00**
Motorcycle, 1959, Missouri	**$25.00**
Motorcycle, 1963, Kansas	**$6.50**
Motorcycle, 1964, Minnesota	**$10.50**
Motorcycle, 1965, Oregon	**$20.00**
Motorcycle, 1967, North Carolina	**$12.50**
Motorcycle, 1968, Montana	**$15.50**
Motorcycle, 1969, Alaska	**$15.50**
Motorcycle, 1969, Montana	**$15.50**
Motorcycle, 1970, Georgia	**$12.50**
Motorcycle, 1970, North Dakota	**$12.50**
Motorcycle, 1971, Virginia	**$6.50**
Motorcycle, 1973, Tennessee	**$10.50**
Motorcycle, 1974, Kentucky	**$15.50**

Motorcycle, 1974, Texas $8.50
Motorcycle, 1976, Mississippi $10.50
Motorcycle, 1977, Illinois $7.50
Motorcycle, 1984, Arizona $5.50
Motorcycle, 1989, Kansas $4.50
Motorcycle, 1989, South Carolina $10.50
Motorcycle, 1990, Wisconsin $4.50
Motorcycle, 1994, Nevada $10.50
Undated, Colorado, Assoc of County Clerks $10.50
Undated, Missouri, Jackson County Sheriff..............$40.00
1916, New Jersey, repainted $40.00
1917, Oklahoma...$200.00
1918, Wyoming, repainted $125.00
1920, Utah $120.00
1923, Delaware $50.00
1924, New Jersey $23.00
1925, District of Columbia, touched up $50.00
1925, Kentucky $60.00
1925, Mississippi, repainted $125.00
1925, West Virginia $30.00
1926, Connecticut $16.50
1929, Ohio, pr $35.00
1930, New York, pr $35.00
1932, Mississippi $30.00
1934, Iowa...$10.50

1934, Washington, $40.00 for the pair; 1934 Alaska, $200.00; 1934 Arizona, $80.00.

1937, Tennessee, state shape $55.00
1938, Kansas..$10.50
1939, Massachusetts...$11.50
1939, Oregon..$17.50
1942, Utah $40.00
1944, Louisiana, soybean $125.00
1948, Maryland...$20.00
1949, Minnesota, Centennial $25.00
1950, New Mexico $20.00
1953, Montana...$16.50
1957, Rhode Island $17.50
1959, Wyoming $8.50
1961, Kentucky $10.50
1962, Colorado, Ham Radio................................$10.50
1965, Indiana...$4.50
1967, South Dakota..$4.50

1969, Virginia, pr...$15.50
1971, Vermont $5.50
1973, New York, pr $15.50
1974, Ohio..$3.50
1975, Michigan $3.00
1977, Arizona, Historic Vehicle, solid copper.............$40.00
1977, Nevada $6.50
1978, Delaware..$8.50
1979, New Hampshire $4.50
1980, Maryland, Historic Vehicle $10.50
1981, North Carolina, First in Freedom....................$10.50
1983, Minnesota, Red Lake Chippewa, VG............$15.50
1984, Missouri $3.50
1986, Maryland, POW...$20.00
1987, Indiana, Disabled Veteran $5.50
1987, South Carolina, National Guard $3.50
1988, Alaska $3.50
1989, Alabama, National Guard $5.50
1990, Idaho, mountains $2.50
1991, Oregon, tree $4.00
1992, Hawaii, rainbow..$7.50
1992, Nebraska, windmill.....................................$5.50
1993, Kansas, POW...$25.00
1993, Texas, Lone Star..$3.50
1994, Florida, manatee $20.00
1994, Louisiana, pelican & USA $9.50
1994, Wyoming $3.50
1995, New Mexico, cactus.....................................$3.50
1996, Maryland, Chesapeake...............................$15.50

1948, Illinois, made from soybeans, $16.50.

Little Red Riding Hood

This line of novelty cookie jars, canisters, mugs, teapots, and other kitchenware items was made by both Regal China and Hull. Any piece today is expensive. There are several variations of the cookie jars. The Regal jar with the open basket marked 'Little Red Riding Hood Pat. Design 135889' is worth about $300.00. The same with the closed basket goes for a minimum of $50.00 more. An unmarked Regal variation with a closed basket, full skirt, and no apron books at $600.00. The Hull jars are valued at about $350.00 unless they're heavily decorated with decals and gold trim, which can add as much as $250.00 to the basic value.

The complete line is covered in *The Collector's Encyclopedia of Cookie Jars* by Joyce and Fred Roerig, and again in *Little Red Riding Hood* by Mark E. Supnick.

**Bank, standing, $600.00.
(Photo courtesy Pat and
Ann Duncan)**

Bank, wall hanging, from $1,500 to.........................**$1,700.00**

**Batter jug, $575.00. (Photo courtesy
Pat and Ann Duncan)**

Butter dish..**$425.00**
Canister, cereal..**$900.00**
Canisters, coffee, sugar, tea or flour, each..................**$800.00**
Canister, salt..**$1,200.00**
Cookie jar, closed basket, minumum value..............**$360.00**
Cookie jar, open basket, gold stars on apron, minimum
    value **$675.00**
Cookie jar, red spray w/gold bows, red shoes.........**$850.00**
Cookie jar, white..**$200.00**
Creamer, top pour, no tab handle............................**$450.00**
Creamer, top pour, tab handle **$500.00**
Grease jar, flower basket, gold trim.......................**$1,200.00**
Lamp...**$2,100.00**
Match holder, wall hanging **$800.00**
Mug, embossed figure, white (no color), minumum
    value **$450.00**
Mustard jar, w/spoon..**$400.00**
Pitcher, batter..**$575.00**
Planter, hanging **$475.00**
Shakers, Pat Design 135889, med size, pr.................**$950.00**
Shakers, 3¼", pr..**$150.00**
Spice jar, square base, from $650 to **$750.00**
String holder, from $2,800 to...................................**$3,000.00**
Sugar bowl, side pour...**$475.00**
Sugar bowl, w/lid **$675.00**
Teapot...**$365.00**

Wall pocket **$550.00**
Wolf jar, red **$1,200.00**
Wolf jar, yellow **$900.00**

Little Tikes

For more than twenty-five years, this company (a division of Rubbermaid) has produced an extensive line of toys and playtime equipment, all made of heavy-gauge plastic, sturdily built and able to stand up to the rowdiest children and the most inclement weather. As children usually outgrow these items well before they're worn out, you'll often see them at garage sales, priced at a fraction of their original cost. We've listed a few below, along with what we feel would be a high average for an example in excellent condition. Since there is no established secondary market pricing system, though, you can expect to see a wide range of asking prices.

Bench Toy Box, seats 2, pink & white w/lift-off lid, #7251,
    34x22½x27", from $10 to **$15.00**
Doll High Chair, w/baby bottle, bowl & spoon, #4429,
    24¾x16½x13½", from $5 to...................................**$7.00**
Double Easel, chalkboard or clip w/tray on side, #4428,
    28x24½x43½", from $10 to **$15.00**
Easy Hit Baseball Set, lg bat w/flat side, spring-back T-ball
    stand & 2 lg balls, stand: 24", #4140, from $4 to ...**$6.00**
Fashion Vanity, shatter-resistant mirror, 4 storage compartments & seat, #4673, 32x21¾x15½", from $8 to..**$10.00**
Junior Activity Gym, 4 interlocking walls w/climbing hand
    holds & hole for crawling, attached slide, #4498, from
    $20 to...**$25.00**
Lawn & Garden Cart, w/watering can & 2 tools, #4451,
    28x14¾x15", from $5 to **$7.00**
Lawn Mower, clear bagger to view grass clippings, engine
    sounds, #4375, 23", from $5 to **$8.00**
Log Cabin, w/fireplace, pay phone & drop-leaf table, #4814,
    57x48x59", from $45 to **$65.00**
Rocking Horse, high back & low seat, #4537, 23x12x15½",
    from $5 to..**$7.00**
Tap-a-Tune Xylophone, keyboard w/multicolor strikers,
    #0702, 19½x10", from $3 to **$5.00**
Tape Recorder, w/hand-held & built-in microphones & storage for
    3 tapes, battery-op, #1700, 13x4x8¼", from $7 to.......**$12.00**
Toddler Tractor, green w/lg black & white wheels, #4032,
    24x12x17", from $5 to...**$7.00**
Twin Slide Tunnel Climber, all-in-1 double slide, ground-level tunnel & climbing walls, #4661, 55x61x64", from $35 to..**$45.00**

Lu Ray Pastels

This was one of Taylor, Smith, and Taylor's most popular lines of dinnerware. It was made from the late 1930s until sometime in the early 1950s in five pastel colors: Windsor Blue, Persian Cream, Sharon Pink, Surf Green, and Chatham Gray.

If you'd like more information, we recommend *Collector's Guide to Lu Ray Pastels* by Kathy and Bill Meehan (Collector Books).

Bowl, fruit; 5", from $4 to **$6.00**
Bowl, lug soup; tab handles, from $15 to **$20.00**
Bowl, oatmeal; 36s, from $25 to..................................**$40.00**
Bowl, salad; lg, from $38 to..**$55.00**
Bowl, vegetable; 8½", from $10 to..............................**$15.00**
Bowl, 7", from $70 to **$90.00**
Bowl, 8¾", from $70 to..**$90.00**
Butter dish, from $35 to **$40.00**
Cake plate, from $55 to...**$75.00**
Calendar plate, 8", 9" or 10", from $35 to.................**$50.00**
Casserole, from $60 to...**$80.00**
Celery/utility tray, from $20 to....................................**$28.00**
Chop plate, 15", from $20 to **$30.00**
Coffee cup, AD; from $15 to **$22.00**
Coffeepot, AD; from $125 to **$150.00**
Creamer, AD; individual, from $35 to **$45.00**
Creamer, gray, from $20 to **$30.00**
Egg cup, double; from $12 to.......................................**$18.00**
Grill plate, from $18 to...**$25.00**
Grill plate, gray, from $60 to **$85.00**
Muffin cover, from $65 to **$80.00**
Pitcher, water; from $40 to..**$60.00**
Plate, gray, 10", from $17 to **$25.00**
Plate, gray, 7", from $12 to **$18.00**
Plate, 10", from $13 to **$18.00**
Plate, 6", from $3 to..**$5.00**
Plate, 8", from $12 to..**$18.00**
Plate, 9", from $8 to..**$12.00**
Platter, gray, 13", from $20 to **$28.00**
Platter, 11½", from $11 to **$15.00**
Salt & pepper shakers, gray, pr, from $24 to **$30.00**
Salt & pepper shakers, pr, from $10 to.......................**$16.00**
Sugar bowl, w/lid, from $10 to **$12.00**
Tea saucer, from $2 to...**$3.00**
Teacup, from $7 to **$10.00**
Teacup, gray, from $15 to...**$18.00**
Teapot, flat spout, from $60 to **$75.00**
Tumbler, from $45 to...**$65.00**

Tumbler, juice; from $30.00 to $40.00; Pitcher, juice; $115.00.

Lunch Boxes

Character lunch boxes made of metal have been very collectible for several years, but now even those made of plastic and vinyl are coming into their own.

The first lunch box of this type ever produced featured Hopalong Cassidy. Made by the Aladdin Company, it was constructed of steel and decorated with decals. But the first fully lithographed steel lunch box and matching thermos bottle was made a few years later (in 1953) by American Thermos. Roy Rogers was its featured character.

Since then hundreds have been made, and just as is true in other areas of character-related collectibles, the more desirable lunch boxes are those with easily recognizable, well-known subjects — western heroes; TV, Disney, and cartoon characters; and famous entertainers.

Values hinge on condition. Learn to grade your lunch boxes carefully. A grade of 'excellent' for metal boxes means that you will notice only very minor defects and less than normal wear. Plastic boxes may have a few scratches and some minor wear on the sides, but the graphics are completely undamaged. Vinyls must retain their original shape; brass parts may be tarnished, and the hinge may show signs of beginning splits. If the box you're trying to evaluate is in any worse condition than we've described, to be realistic, you must cut these prices drastically. Values are given for boxes without matching thermoses, unless one is mentioned in the line. If you'd like to learn more, we recommend *A Pictorial Price Guide to Metal Lunch Boxes and Thermoses* by Larry Aikins, and *Schroeder's Collectible Toys, Antique to Modern* (Collector Books).

Metal

Dick Tracy, Aladdin, 1967, EX, from $125.00 to $150.00; Thermos, metal, NM, $80.00. (Photo courtesy Larry Doucet)

Annie, w/plastic thermos, 1981, VG+ **$25.00**
Astronaut, dome top, 1960, EX..................................**$200.00**
Back in '76, 1975, VG- **$24.00**
Batman, w/thermos, 1966, EX **$168.00**
Battlestar Galactica, w/thermos, 1978, EX+ **$69.00**
Bedknobs & Broomsticks, 1972, VG **$29.00**
Berenstain Bears, 1983, EX **$52.00**
Bionic Woman, classroom & racing scenes on sides, 1978, EX+ **$85.00**
Black Hole, Walt Disney Productions, 1979, EX+ **$69.00**
Bonanza, brown rim, 1965, VG..................................**$115.00**
Bugaloos, 1971, EX+ **$100.00**
Campus Queen, w/metal thermos, 1967, EX..............**$22.00**

Care Bear Cousins, w/thermos, 1985, replaced handle, VG **$20.00**

Carnival, 1959, VG-...**$40.00**

Casey Jones, dome top, w/thermos, Universal, 1960, VG..**$455.00**

Charlie's Angels, 1978, VG.......................................**$35.00**

Corsage, 1964, VG **$23.00**

Dark Crystal, w/thermos, 1982, unused w/papers, M..**$50.00**

Denim Diner, dome top, dog w/flowers on blue denim background, Aladdin, 1975, VG **$46.00**

Disney School Bus, dome top, 1960s, EX...................**$62.00**

Dukes of Hazzard, w/thermos, 1980, EX+..................**$30.00**

ET Extra-Terrestrial, 1982, M w/original hang tag.......**$49.00**

Fall Guy, w/thermos, 1981, EX+.................................**$35.00**

Fess Parker as Daniel Boone, American Tradition Co, 1965, EX- **$110.00**

Flintstones & Dino, orange, 1962, VG+ **$139.00**

Fraggle Rock, w/thermos, 1984, EX **$26.00**

Funtastic World of Hanna-Barbera, shows Yogi Bear & Flintstones, 1977, VG..**$45.00**

Gomer Pyle USMC, 1966, VG+ **$155.00**

Gremlins, 1984, EX-..**$16.00**

Happy Days, 1976, VG..**$32.00**

He-Man & Masters of the Universe, blue, w/thermos, 1984, VG..**$15.00**

Holly Hobbie, shows Holly, cat & mouse at picnic, 1972, EX- **$25.00**

Hopalong Cassidy, full lithograph, 1954, EX............**$325.00**

How the West Was Won, 1978, VG+ **$40.00**

Incredible Hulk, 1978, EX...**$28.00**

Indiana Jones & the Temple of Doom, sword scene on front, car scene on back, 1984, EX.................................**$25.00**

Jonathan Livingston Seagull, w/thermos, 1973, VG **$35.00**

Kid Power (Wee Pals), 1974, VG+..............................**$34.00**

Kiss, NM, $100.00. (Photo courtesy June Moon)

Knight Rider, 1983, EX-..**$19.00**

Krofft Supershow, 1976, w/thermos (G), VG+............**$68.00**

Land of the Lost, w/thermos, 1975, EX......................**$88.00**

Legend of the Lone Ranger, 1980, EX-.......................**$36.00**

Looney Tunes TV Set, 1959, VG-................................**$125.00**

Mork & Mindy, w/thermos, 1979, EX **$48.00**

Muppet Babies, w/pink thermos, 1985, NM...............**$22.00**

Muppet Show, 1978, EX..**$17.00**

NFL, helmet at center w/game scenes, 1978, VG+ **$19.00**

Pebbles & Bamm-Bamm, w/plastic thermos, 1971, VG+...**$65.00**

Rambo, w/thermos, 1985, NM **$29.00**

Steve Canyon, 1959, EX **$180.00**

Walt Disney World, w/thermos (NM), 1970, EX.........**$38.00**

Monsters (Universal's), Aladdin, 1980, EX, $85.00. (Photo courtesy June Moon)

Plastic

A-Team, Thermos, 1985, EX, $22.00.

Alf, w/food around him & night sky background on red, w/thermos, 1987, EX+ **$18.00**

An American Tail, Fievel Goes West, w/purple cup, 1991, M **$3.00**

Barbie, pink, shows Barbie w/ice cream cone, Thermos, 1990, EX..**$5.00**

Barbie, purple, shows Barbie in gold bikini, 1992, VG ..**$4.00**

Barbie & the Rockers, pink, Thermos, 1987, VG **$6.00**

Batman, blue w/Joker swinging hammer at Batman, w/thermos, 1982, M...**$40.00**

Batman Returns, blue w/Batman & batrope on roof, Thermos, 1991, NM **$11.00**

Benji, blue, 1974, VG+ **$13.00**

Buck Rogers in the 25th Century, w/thermos, 1979, VG+..**$12.00**

Cabbage Patch Kids, pink, shows 3 kids in band, w/thermos, Aladdin, 1990, VG..**$12.00**

Campbell's Soup, Fuel for Fitness, Official Soup Winter Olympics Sarajevo, w/wide mouth thermos, 1984, M **$18.00**

Care Bears, lime green, no handle, 1983, NM..............**$6.00**

Care Bears, yellow, shows 5 bears painting rainbow, 1983, VG **$5.00**

Chip 'N Dale Rescue Rangers, light blue, M.................**$9.00**

Chipmunks, yellow, 1984, VG **$2.00**

Crash Dummies, Doing the Boulevard Dance on blue, w/thermos, Thermos, EX **$11.00**

Dick Tracy, red, w/thermos, 1990, EX **$4.50**

Dino-Riders, red, w/thermos, 1988, NM **$14.00**

Dinosaurs 'Kiss the Baby' (Disney TV show), plastic w/purple cup, Thermos, EX...**$3.00**

Duck Tales, red, shows pyramid & helicopter, w/thermos, 1986, EX..**$4.00**

Fisher-Price, red dome-top barn w/paper decals, w/thermos, 1962, VG..**$16.00**

Flintstones (Denny's), 1989, with thermos and Denny's Fun Book, NM, $35.00.

Flintstones (from movie), rock shaped w/decal, w/thermos, 1994?, NM **$13.00**

Furskins, purple, w/thermos, 1986, EX **$5.00**

Garfield, yellow, shows Garfield diving onto dinner table, Thermos, 1978, EX..**$8.00**

Geese, white w/pastel print, w/thermos, Peco, 1989, EX...**$4.00**

Ghostbusters, red, w/thermos, 1986, EX, from $15 to ..**$20.00**

GI Joe, Live the Adventure, blue, w/thermos, 1986, EX ...**$12.00**

GI Joe, shows General GI Joe vehicle on red, 1990, unused, M w/original hang tag...**$15.00**

Herself the Elf, Elf-Fun Is for Everyone, yellow, American Greetings, 1982, VG, from $7 to............................**$10.00**

Hugga Bunch, pink, w/thermos, Hallmark Cards Inc, 1984, EX..**$9.00**

Jetsons the Movie, red, w/thermos, 1990, unused, M w/hang tags..**$27.00**

Lisa Frank, pink w/Koala on branch, Thermos, no date, EX.**$8.00**

Lolly's New Look, pink, Merle Norman, unused old store stock, M **$20.00**

Mickey & Donald, red, Aladdin, 1986, EX....................**$9.00**

Mickey & Minnie at Mickey's Film Festival, pink, EX...**$7.00**

Micro Machines, blue, Lewis Galoob/Aladdin, VG+ **$6.00**

Mr T, orange, w/plastic thermos, 1984, EX..................**$30.00**

My Little Pony, blue w/carousel scene, Aladdin, 1989, EX ..**$11.00**

Nosy Bears, blue, Aladdin, 1988, EX+............................**$3.00**

Peanuts, yellow, shows Snoopy on skateboard w/5 birds, w/thermos (shows Snoopy as Joe Cool), EX+ **$15.00**

Pee Wee's Playhouse, red, 1987, VG+.............................**$4.00**

Pink Panther & Sons, pink, 1984, VG **$7.00**

Popples, yellow, shows Popple inside lunch box eating banana, Aladdin, 1986..**$8.00**

Rainbow Brite, yellow, shows picnic scene, 1983, EX..**$8.00**

Smurf, blue, Toughneck Thermos, Made in England, 1973, EX...**$15.00**

Superman, w/plastic thermos, 1978, VG+ **$69.00**

Treasure Trolls, purple, w/thermos, 1992, NM.............**$6.00**

Wuzzles, blue, w/thermos, 1985, EX-..............................**$9.00**

101 Dalmatians, blue, w/lithographed thermos, EX ...**$10.00**

18 Wheeler, w/thermos, 1978, G...................................**$2.00**

Vinyl

Alvin & the Chipmunks, green, EX............................**$285.00**

Animaniacs, psychedelic w/Give Us a Kiss Kid on hot pink, EX+ **$19.00**

Annie, w/plastic thermos, 1981, VG............................**$42.00**

Apple, red graphics on blue denim background, w/blue thermos, Lillian Vernon, 1985, EX **$29.00**

Betsy Clark, long strap, w/thermos, Hallmark, unused store stock w/coupons, Hallmark, M............................**$89.00**

Dawn, white, w/thermos, 1970, EX **$175.00**

Psychedelic, blue, zippered top, 1970, VG+................**$25.00**

Roy Rogers Saddlebag, brown, King Seeley, 1960, EX+ ..**$225.00**

Miscellaneous

Adopt a Norfin Troll, purple softie w/zip closure, 1992, EX **$9.00**

Always Coca-Cola Kroger, white softie w/Texas Rangers Baseball Club on diamond, red trim, EX+............**$27.00**

Avon, cologne bottle shaped, thermos cup as lid, marked Thermos Brand, M **$9.00**

Barney & Baby Bop, softie w/zipper, shoulder & hand straps, Thermos, 1992, EX+...**$7.50**

Batman Returns, odd-shaped black plastic, w/blue ice, plastic container, thermos, black lid, long strap, 1992, NM..**$17.50**

Batman the Dark Knight, softie, w/thermos, 1991, NM..**$15.00**

Beauty & the Beast, softie, pink & purple, shows them dancing w/roses in background, w/thermos, VG+ **$8.00**

Jelly Beans, softie w/zippered top flap, insulated, red top & back, NM **$10.00**

Jukebox, softie, Impact Internatio, 1991, VG................**$5.00**

Kansas City Royals, softie, white w/blue print, graphics & handle, zip top w/Missouri lottery advertisement, M...**$12.00**

Kodak Mini Cooler Bag, Know the Land & the People, softie, collapsible, w/zippered top flap, EX.................**$8.00**

Lunch Bunch, yellow softie w/blue trim, zipper & red cloth handle, insulated squeezable thermos, SGI Taiwan, VG+..**$5.00**

Mighty Morphin Power Rangers, black softie, shows Karate poses, w/thermos, 1994, EX................................**$12.00**

Mighty Morphin Power Ranges, yellow softie, shows White Ranger, w/thermos, 1995......................................**$10.00**

Minnie Mouse, figural head, w/thermos, EX..............**$17.00**

Newport Pleasure, black softie w/neon print & zippered top, NM..**$9.00**

19th Hole Golf, w/built-in straw, golf ball-shaped top, EX **$9.00**

Thermoses

Values are given for thermoses in excellent condition; all are made of metal unless noted otherwise.

Aladdin (Disney movie), EX+ **$3.50**
Alf, white plastic w/red cup, 1988, VG **$6.00**
America on Parade, blue, 1976, EX **$10.00**
Annie Oakley, w/cork stopper, missing cup, EX+ **$65.00**
Archies, plastic w/glass liner, missing cup, NM **$39.00**
Babar, plastic w/full lithograph, 1988, M **$3.00**
Baby Dinos, plastic w/paper decal, wide mouth, green cup, VG+ **$3.50**
Barbie, white, shows Barbie's name & beach umbrella, w/purple cup, Thermos, 1992, EX..........................**$2.50**
Barbie Rockers, pink w/white cup, 1987, EX+ **$4.50**
Barney (dinosaur), white plastic, Thermos, 1992, M **$2.50**
Bee Gees, yellow plastic w/white cup, 1978, VG+.....**$17.00**
Belknap, w/blue bullet-shaped cup, EX **$8.50**

Beverly Hillbillies, metal with plastic cup, EX+, $80.00.

Biker Mice From Mars, plastic w/full lithograph, 1994, EX...**$3.00**
Bionic Woman, plastic, 1977, VG **$19.00**
Boating, metal, 1959, NM...**$100.00**
Buck Rogers in the 25th Century, plastic, 1979, VG+..**$12.00**
Captain Planet, plastic w/blue base & cup, 1990, NM..**$5.00**
Captain Power, 1987, plastic, NM **$8.00**

Casper the Friendly Ghost, EX, $80.00.

Chip 'N Dale Rescue Rangers, plastic w/full lithograph, EX+..**$3.00**
Circles, red, blue & yellow on white plastic, red base & cup, Aladdin, NM **$4.00**
Colonial Bread Van Rainbo, plastic, EX **$19.00**
Cowboy in Africa, metal w/red cup, 1968, EX...........**$75.00**
Cubs Baseball, blue & white plastic w/red logo, EX....**$5.00**
Dawn, yellow & white plastic, Topper/Aladdin, 1970, EX+ ..**$29.00**
Dick Tracy, plastic, NM **$2.50**
Dino-Riders, plastic, 1988, EX **$4.00**
Disco, plastic w/orange cup, 1979, EX **$18.00**
Disney City Zoo, red, plastic, EX- **$2.50**
Disney School Bus, plastic, VG+ **$4.50**
Disneyland Castle Riverboat, metal, 1957, EX+ **$79.00**
Donny & Marie, plastic w/purple cup, long hair, 1976, NM **$15.00**
Drag Strip, plastic, 1975, EX+ **$28.00**
Empire Strikes Back, blue, 1981, NM.........................**$13.00**
Evel Knievel, plastic, 1974, EX+ **$29.00**
Fall Guy, 1981, plastic w/black cup, NM....................**$14.00**
Fess Parker As Daniel Boone, metal, 1965, EX...........**$75.00**
Firehouse, metal, 1959, EX+ **$110.00**
Floral, metal, yellow, lavender & white on peach background, American Thermos, EX **$18.00**
Game Birds & Fish, Thermos, 1973, lg, EX **$39.00**
Garfield, white plastic, Garfield pouring milk into his mouth from thermos, NM..**$3.50**
Garfield, yellow plastic w/red cup, shows Garfield at porthole, Thermos, 1978, VG+ **$3.00**
GI Joe, A Real American Hero, red cup & base, 1991, EX...**$3.00**
GI Joe, Tiger Force, plastic, 1988, EX **$3.00**
Go Bots, red w/blue cup, 1984, M...............................**$10.00**
Golf, the 19th Hole, golf-bag shaped w/ball top, EX..**$9.00**
Green Hornet, 1967, NM, from $130 to.....................**$160.00**
Gunsmoke, 1962, VG **$65.00**
Hardy Boys Mysteries, red w/white cup, 1977, EX.....**$19.00**
Heathcliff, plastic, NM **$9.00**
Holly Hobbie, plastic, shows girl pouring milk, 1979, EX+ .**$5.00**
Holly Hobbie & Robbie, plastic w/blue cup, VG..........**$3.50**
Holly Hobbie & Robby, shows Robby pulling Holly in wagon & feeding geese, 1978, EX+ **$9.00**
Hong Kong Phooey, blue plastic w/blue cup, 1975, EX+ .**$15.00**
Howdy Doody, plastic, 1977, EX................................**$25.00**
Ice Cream, pink gingham, Aladdin, 1975, EX.............**$17.00**
It's a Small World, Disneyland, metal, EX...................**$89.00**
Jetsons the Movie, plastic, 1990, NM.........................**$4.00**
Junior Nurse, metal, 1963, EX+................................**$75.00**
Kewtie Pie, metal, EX...**$60.00**
King Kong, plastic, 1977, NM **$23.00**
Kool-Aid Drink Mix, yellow plastic, Thermos, missing cup, EX+..**$9.00**
Lady Lovely Locks & the Pixietails, pink & white plastic, 1986, missing cup, EX **$3.00**
Lassie, plastic w/dark blue cup, 1978, EX **$22.00**
Life & Times of Grizzly Adams, plastic, 1977, EX.......**$40.00**
Mary Poppins, 1964, metal, EX-................................**$44.00**
Mask, plastic, 1985, VG+ **$2.50**
Masters of the Universe, plastic, 1983, EX+ **$8.00**
Mickey Mouse Club, 1977, NM **$9.00**

Mighty Morphin Power Rangers, plastic w/red base & cup, 1995, M **$3.00**

Mork & Mindy, plastic, EX....................................**$15.00**

My Little Pony, plastic w/pink base & cup, 1987, VG+ ..**$4.00**

Peanuts, metal, shows baseball scene, green cup, 1966, EX **$11.00**

Peanuts, yellow plastic, shows Charlie Brown, Snoopy & Woodstock eating cookies, EX.............................**$3.00**

Pets & Pals, metal, 1962, tall, EX................................**$25.00**

MAD Collectibles

MAD, a hotly controversial and satirical publication that was first published in 1952, spoofed everything from advertising and politics to the latest movies and TV shows. Content pivoted around a unique mix of lofty creativity, liberalism, and the ridiculous. A cult-like following has developed over the years. Eagerly sought are items relating to characters that were developed by the comic magazine such as Alfred E. Neuman or Spy Vs Spy.

Advisor: Michael Lerner (See Directory, MAD Collectibles)

Ad sheet, Spy vs Spy, full color, advertising computer game, 1989, EX, minimum value **$5.00**

Annual, Mad Follies, #7, EX....................................**$22.00**

Annual, Worst From MAD, #12, w/bonus, EX+...........**$40.00**

Bendee figure, Alfred E Neuman, Concepts Pluss, 1989, MOC (sealed), minimum value..**$15.00**

Book, Golden Trashery of MAD, 1st printing, 1960, EX.**$50.00**

Campaign kit, Alfred E Neuman for President, complete w/pin-back, cap, sign, poster & sticker, 1960, minimum value..**$1,250.00**

Comic, #11, VG...**$100.00**

Comic, #23, VG+...**$75.00**

Comic, #24, 1st magazine issue, VG-.........................**$165.00**

Doll, Alfred E. Neuman, What Me Worry tie, unlicensed issue by Baby Barry Doll Company, 1961, 20", $500.00. (Photo courtesy Michael Lerner)

Game, Spy Vs Spy, Milton Bradley, 1986, NMIB.........**$28.00**

Hair Tonic, Greasy Kid Stuff w/Alfred E Neuman portrait label on glass, 3½-oz, unused, NM+, minimum value..............**$60.00**

Lobby card, Up the Academy, 1980, 11x14", minimum value **$25.00**

Magazine, #40, VG..**$17.00**

Magazine, #88, EX **$12.00**

Magazine, MAD #102, April 1966, Branded, National Enquirer, Mad Look at Board Games, EX...............**$9.00**

Magazine, MAD #106, October 1966, Batman, 12 O'Clock High, VG+..**$6.00**

Magazine, MAD #121, 1968, Beatles on cover w/Alfred as guru, Monkees on back cover, VG+.......................**$8.00**

Magazine, MAD #232, July 1982, Greatest American Hero, NM...**$3.00**

Magazine, MAD #289, Batman the Movie, NM.............**$3.00**

Magazine, MAD #299, December 1990, Simpsons on cover, NM...**$3.00**

Magazine, MAD Follies #7, 1969, w/12 Nasty Cards (postcards), EX..**$12.00**

Magazine, More Trash From Mad #11, 1968, w/Alfred E Neuman for President bumper sticker, VG+.........**$12.00**

Magazine, More Trash From MAD #5, 1962, w/bonus stickers, EX **$12.00**

Magazine, More Trash From MAD #9, w/bonus stickers, EX...**$12.00**

Magazine, Super Special #39, Summer 1982, w/MAD Laugh Record, NM...**$5.00**

Mask, Alfred E Neuman latex head w/hair, Caesar, 1981, EX, minimum value **$50.00**

Paperback, Bedside MAD, Signet S1647 ....**$3.00**

Paperback, Dr Jekyll & Mr MAD, Warner 75-733 ....**$3.00**

Patch, Alfred E Neuman face on pink w/peel-off sticky back, unlicensed, 3", EX, minimum value......................**$10.00**

Pen, Alfred E Neuman floating in body w/toilet on top, Applause, 1988, NM, minimum value **$20.00**

Pin, Alfred E Neuman for President, 1964 & 1968, set of 2 ....**$20.00**

Pin, MAD football helmet, red & gold trim, 1", EX, minimum value **$10.00**

Pin-back button, Coos Bay MAD Art Exhibit, 2", EX..**$12.00**

Postcard, pre-MAD Alfred E Neuman, Bob Adamcik, 1950s, minimum value...**$15.00**

Poster, Alfred E Neuman for President, Bi-Rite #15-546, 1987-88, 20x28", EX **$15.00**

Poster, MAD Art Exhibit, from Raleigh NC show, 1992, EX...**$15.00**

Poster, Protect Your Wild Life, full color, Don Martin, 1970s, 21x32", EX **$10.00**

Record, Alfred E Neuman Sings What Me Worry/Potzrebie, ABC Paramount, 1959, 45-rpm, VG, minimum value **$15.00**

Record, Mad Twists Rock 'N Roll, Bigtop, 1962, 33 1/3-rpm, EX, minimum value **$40.00**

Record, Musically Mad, RCA, 1959, 33 1/3-rpm, monoral version, VG, minimum value **$10.00**

Skateboard, green w/MAD graphics, Nash, 1987, 29", edge guards missing o/w EX, minimum value **$45.00**

Slot machine, unlicensed, distributed to American military bases in Europe, Sega, 1960s **$1,200.00**

Statue, Alfred E Neuman bust, bisque w/green felt on bottom, no label, 3¾", minimum value....................**$280.00**

Statue, hand-painted full figure, Warner Bros Studio, 1994 ....**$75.00**

Statue, What Me Worry, bust portrait, 5½", minimum value **$350.00**

Stickers, complete box w/36 packs, w/advertising banner, Fleer, 1983, EX, minimum value $50.00

Slot machine, MAD Money, unlicensed issue by Sega for distribution to American military bases in Europe, 1960s, $1,200.00. (Photo courtesy Michael Lerner)

Maddux of California

Founded in Los Angeles in 1938, Maddux not only produced ceramics but imported and distributed them as well. They supplied chainstores nationwide with well-designed figural planters, TV lamps, novelty and giftware items, and during the mid-1960s their merchandise was listed in every major stamp catalog. Because of an increasing amount of foreign imports and an economic slowdown in our own country, the company was forced to sell out in 1976. Under the new management, manufacturing was abandoned, and the company was converted solely to distribution. Collectors have only recently discovered this line, and prices right now are affordable though increasing.

Planter, #510, black swan, 11", $18.00. (Photo courtesy Lee Garmon)

Ashtray, #7204, pig form, natural colors, 7" L $12.00
Bowl, seashell, #3017, white...$15.00
Candlestick, #105, double, 11"......................................$25.00
Cookie jar, Calory Hippy..$300.00
Cookie jar, Koala...$75.00
Cookie jar, Snowman...$75.00
Figurine, #914, stag, standing, natural colors, 12½"....$15.00
Figurine, #932, rooster, 10½" $30.00
Figurine, #982, horse, prancing $20.00
Figurine, cats, Deco style, black matt, facing, 12½", pr..$50.00
Figurines, ducklings, 3 on grassy base..........................$20.00
Planter, #3304, bird...$20.00

TV lamp, #839, mallard, flying, naturalistic colors, 7½x11", $35.00.

Planter, #515, flamingo, pink, 10½" $45.00
Planter, #536, bird in flight, 11½" $20.00
Planter, rearing horse, 10x7½" $22.00
Tray, #3251-L, 2-tier $20.00
TV lamp, #810, prancing stallion, 12" $20.00
TV lamp, #839, mallard, flying, natural colors, 11½"..$35.00
TV lamp, #859, Toro (bull), foot on mound, 11½".....$20.00
TV lamp, #895, swan (double), 11½" $30.00
TV lamp/planter, #3006, half-circle $25.00
TV lamp/planter, #828, swan, white, 12½"................$20.00
Vase, #2015, Antique Gold, handles, 12" $15.00
Vase, #221, swan, white, 12".......................................$20.00
Vase, #529, 2 flamingos, 5" $40.00

Magazines

There are lots of magazines around today, but unless they're in fine condition (clean, no missing or clipped pages, and very little other damage); have interesting features (cover illustrations, good advertising, or special-interest stories); or deal with sports greats, famous entertainers, or world-reknowned personalities, they're worth very little, no matter how old they are. Address labels on the front are acceptable, but if you find one with no label, it will be worth about 25% more than our listed values. For further information see *Old Magazines Price Guide* by L-W Book Sales and *Life Magazines, 1898 to 1994,* by one of our our advisors, Denis C. Jackson.

See also TV Guides.

Advisor: Denis C. Jackson (See Directory, Magazines)

Advisor: Don Smith, Rare National Geographics (See Directory, Magazines)

Newsletter: *The Illustrator Collector's News*
Denis C. Jackson, Editor
P.O. Box 1958
Sequim, WA 98382; Phone: 360-683-2559 or http://www.olypen.com/ticn; e-mail ticn@olypen.com

Action for Men, 1967, March, Vol #2, VG $3.50
Adventure for Men, 1971, April, VG..............................$4.00
Air Stories, 1928, August, G $25.00

American Detective, 1936, January, Vol 4 #2, crime cases, VG...$5.00
American Fantasy, 1982, February, Vol 1 #1, VG..........$2.00
American Legion, 1927, February, HC Christy cover, VG...$15.00
American Mercury, 1942, March, Szyk cartoons, VG....$8.00
American Review, 1900, June, VG.................................$15.00
Arizona Highways, 1980, December, VG.......................$6.00
Art Decorations, 1922, April, VG................................$10.00
Art Photography, 1956, April, Sophia Loren cover, VG ..$10.00
Auto Age, 1953, February, Vol 1 #1, VG......................$11.00
Avante Garde, 1969, #8, VG......................................$35.00
Bachelor, 1980, July, VG...$4.00
Baseball Digest, 1951, April, DiMaggio cover, VG.......$25.00
Beckett, 1989, June, Bo Jackson cover, VG..................$3.00
Behind the Scene, 1955, July, Marilyn Monroe cover, VG ..$25.00
Better Homes & Gardens, 1935, September, VG.........$22.00
Blue Book, 1965, July, VG...$6.00
Bookman, 1922, December, Arthur Rackham cover, VG ..$25.00
Boy's Life, 1937, July, HC Christy cover, VG................$10.00
Bridge Magazine, 1967, April, VG................................$2.00
Bridge Today, 1988, July-August, VG............................$3.50
Cabaret, 1956, December, Eartha Kitt, EX..................$10.00
Cabaret Quarterly, 1967, #14, VG..............................$16.00
Caper, 1961, January, VG...$7.00
Capper's Farmers, 1940, January, C Becker cover, VG .$11.00
Car Craft, 1954, April...$5.00
Car Exchange, 1979, April, Vol 1 #1, VG.....................$5.00
Chatelaine, 1957, February, Princess Margaret cover, VG ..$2.00
Classic & Custom, 1980, April, Vol 1 #1, VG...............$6.00
Classic Photography, 1956, Winter, VG......................$14.00
Click, 1938, March, Charlie Chaplin cover, VG...........$22.00
Collier's 1945, June, Truman cover, VG........................$6.00
Complete Baseball, 1953, December, Campanella cover, VG...$18.00
Confidential, 1952, December, Vol 1 #1, VG...............$18.00
Coronet, 1966, January, Marilyn Monroe cover, VG......$9.00
Cosmopolitan, 1955, October, Audrey Hepburn cover, VG...$9.00
Country Song Roundup, 1957, August, Elvis Presley cover, VG..$15.00
Cue, 1953, June 27, Marilyn Monroe cover, VG..........$30.00
Daredevil Aces, 1942, November, NM........................$35.00
Darling Detective, 1943, May, Vol 18 #104, VG...........$3.00
Debonaire, 1980, March, VG..$4.00
Delineator, 1928, May, Rose O'Neill Kewpie page, VG..$20.00
Digest, 1937, July 17, Vol 1 #1, VG............................$10.00
Dynamic Detective, 1940, September, VG.....................$4.00
Ebony, 1967, January, Star Trek cover, VG...................$5.00
Eerie Country, 1979, #2, EX...$3.00
Esquire, 1934, September, Rockwell Kent illustrations, VG..$9.00
Esquire, 1937, April, VG...$15.00
Esquire, 1978, August 15, Robert Kennedy cover, VG..$3.00
Fact, 1964, January-February, VG.................................$3.00
Family Circle, 1942, December 4, Maureen O'Hara & Tyrone Power cover, VG..$3.00
Family Circle, 1943, June 18, Barbara Stanwyck cover, VG...$7.00
Family Circle, 1944, March 24, Constance Dowling & Danny Kaye cover, VG...$3.00

Family Circle, 1945, January 19, Shirley Temple article, VG+..$16.00
Family Circle, 1946, January 25, Bob Hope cover & article, VG...$7.00
Family Circle, 1947, November, Life With Father movie ad, VG...$2.00
Family Circle, 1949, June, girl w/puppy on cover, VG .$3.00
Family Circle, 1957, April, Debbie Reynolds cover, VG...$3.00
Famous Models, 1950, April-May, VG.........................$28.00
Favorite Westerns, 1960, August, John Wayne cover, VG ..$8.00
Focus, 1953, May, Marilyn Monroe cover, VG............$35.00
Fortune, 1932, August, VG...$10.00
Future, 1978, April, #1, VG...$2.00
Galileo, 1977, July, #4, VG..$2.00
Game Players, 1990, April, VG.....................................$.50
Gentleman's Companion, 1980, May, VG....................$10.00
Glamour Photography, 1956, Summer, Jane Mansfield cover, VG...$12.00
Holiday, 1946, March, VG..$20.00
Hooker, 1981, January, VG...$5.00
Horror Show, 1985, Winter, Vol 3 #1, VG....................$1.50
Hot Rod, 1970, March...$5.00
Hound & Horn, 1927, September, Vol 1 #1, VG.........$12.00
Household, 1935, October, VG....................................$10.00
Impact, 1964, October, VG...$5.00
Inside Story, 1955, January, VG..................................$20.00
Jack & Jill, 1961, May, Roy Rogers cover, VG............$10.00
Ken, 1938, April 7, Vol 1 #1, VG................................$40.00
Ladies' Home Journal, 1939, September, VG..............$12.00
Ladies' Home Journal, 1946, October, VG+..................$3.00
Ladies' Home Journal, 1947, February, Ingrid Bergman article, EX...$5.00
Ladies' Home Journal, 1951, December, Westward the Women movie ad, VG...$3.00
Ladies' Home Journal, 1955, March, Princess Beatrix article, VG+..$2.50
Ladies' Home Journal, 1956, March, Grace Kelly article, EX...$3.50
Ladies' Home Journal, 1967, June, Twiggy cover, VG ..$2.00
Liberty, 1925, October 31, VG....................................$16.00
Liberty, 1934, October 27, John Dillinger gang article, VG..$5.00
Liberty, 1941, October 4, Dionne Quints cover, VG...$10.00
Liberty, 1946, December 21, Song of the South article, EX...$5.00
Liberty, 1947, April 5, Donna Reed cover, EX.............$4.50
Liberty, 1947, August 2, Cary Grant cover, EX $5.00
Life, 1921, July 21, FX Leyendecker cover, VG...........$50.00
Life, 1938, October 10, Carole Lombard cover, VG....$20.00
Life, 1941, March 3, VG...$7.00
Life, 1942, March 2, Ginger Rogers cover, EX............$15.00
Life, 1945, July 16, Audie Murphy cover, VG.............$10.00
Life, 1947, January 6, James Mason article, EX............$4.50
Life, 1951, July 30, Gary Crosby cover, VG.................$4.00
Life, 1951, May 7, Phyllis Kirk cover, VG....................$7.00
Life, 1953, July 20, Senator Kennedy cover, EX.........$12.00
Life, 1955, August 22, Sophia Loren cover, VG............$9.00
Life, 1959, February 2, Pat Boone cover, VG...............$5.00
Life, 1962, May 11, Bob Hope cover, VG.....................$5.00
Life, 1965, July 16, John F Kennedy cover, VG...........$10.00
Life, 1969, December 12, Apollo 12 article, VG..........$10.00

Life, 1971, July 23, Clint Eastwood cover, VG $12.00
Life, 1971, March 12, Jackie Kennedy cover, VG $5.00
Life, 1983, February, Brooke Shields cover, VG............$2.00
Lone Eagle, 1940, December, EX...$35.00

Look, 1958, June 24, Hugh O'Brien cover, EX, from $10 to $12.00.

Look, 1966, December 13, John Lennon cover, VG+ .$28.00
Look, 1971, April 6, Mickey Mouse cover, VG............$10.00
Love Magazine, 1930, July, VG $5.00
Maclean's, 1957, December 7, Queen Elizabeth article, VG..$6.00
McCall's, 1932, February, Zane Grey article, EX............$8.00
McCall's, 1944, June, Irene Dunne & Dorothy Lamour photos,
    G $4.00
McCall's, 1950, February, Esther Williams article, VG...$5.00
McCall's, 1951, August, VG $12.00
McCall's, 1951, June, Greta Garbo cover & article, VG+ ...$10.00
McCall's, 1959, March, Debbie Reynolds article, VG $8.00
McCall's, 1961, March, Jack Parr & Emily Post articles, VG..$8.00
McCall's 1956, February, Helen Hayes article, VG $8.00
Mentor, 1922, June, VG $10.00
Modern Priscilla, 1925, July, flapper cover, VG...........$15.00
Modern Romance, 1941, June, VG $11.00
Monster Fantasy, 1975, #2 ....$7.00
Monster World, 1966, #7 ....$10.00
Monsters Unleashed, 1973, #1 ....$10.00
Motor, 1929, July, VG $25.00
Motorsport, 1950, October, Vol 1 #1, VG......................$8.00
Movie Classic, 1936, October, Glenda Farrell cover, G..$22.00
Movie Story, 1948, February, Lana Turner cover, VG ...$6.00
Muscle Power, 1953, October, Mr America cover, VG ..$3.00
Musical Digest, 1928, March, Icart cover, VG..............$60.00
National Geographic Magazine, 1915-1916, each........$11.00
National Geographic Magazine, 1917-1924, each..........$9.00
National Geographic Magazine, 1925-1929, each..........$8.00
National Geographic Magazine, 1930-1945, each..........$7.00
National Geographic Magazine, 1946-1955, each..........$6.00
National Geographic Magazine, 1956-1967, each..........$5.50
National Geographic Magazine, 1968-1989, each..........$4.50
National Geographic Magazine, 1990-present, each $2.00
Needlecraft, 1924, October, Quaker ad, VG $18.00
New Movie, 1934, April, Joan Crawford cover, EX.....$30.00
New Republic, 1924, March 5, Rockwell Kent illustrations,
    VG $8.00
New Yorker, 1953, April 6, VG..$10.00
Newsweek, 1940, February 19, Walt Disney's Pinocchio arti-
    cle, VG $5.00

Nightmare, 1973, #11 ....$5.00
Now, 1953, November, VG...$12.00
Nugget, 1956, July, Vol 1 #4, Anita Ekberg, VG $8.00
Outlook & Independent, 1929, March 27, Charles Chaplin
    cover, VG...$10.00
Peek, 1940, July, Betty Grable cover, VG $10.00
Photoplay, 1966, August, Peyton Place cast cover, VG+..$5.00
Pic, 1940, April 2, Lana Turner cover, VG $10.00
Pictorial Review, 1931, April, Helen Hays & Lynn Fontaine
    photos, EX $8.00
Pictorial Review, 1935, January, Women of the Year article
    w/photos, EX...$6.00

Pictorial Review, 1938, December, Vol. 40, #3, from $5.00 to $8.00.

Picture Play, 1940, January, Bette Davis cover, VG $17.00
Picture Scope, 1955, May, Marilyn Monroe cover, VG..$25.00
Playboy, 1955, February, Jayne Mansfield, EX..........$150.00
Playboy, 1957, January, Vol 4 #1, June Blair, VG+......$18.00
Playboy, 1960, May, Ginger Young, EX.......................$18.00

Playboy, 1967, December, NM, from $25.00 to $30.00.

Playboy, 1967, March, Fran Gerard/Sharon Tate, Vargas art,
    EX..$20.00
Playboy, 1981, January, Karen Price centerfold, John Lennon
    & Yoko Ono article, VG $9.00
Playboy, 1987, January, Luann Lee centerfold, Marilyn
    Monroe article, VG...$7.00
Pleasure Magazine, 1937, Winter, Vol 1 #1, VG $12.00
Popular Photography, 1937, August, swimsuit cover, VG..$15.00
Popular Song Hits, 1947, May, Betty Grable cover, VG...$9.00
Private Affairs, 1955, August, Marilyn Monroe cover, VG...$14.00
Psycho, 1973, #12 ....$5.00
Punch, 1946, November 27, Disney spoof, VG.............$7.00

RAF Aces, 1941, Fall, NM $30.00
Rave, 1953, April, Vol 1 #1, VG $20.00
Rave, 1969, September, Paul McCartney article, VG ...$12.00
Redbook, 1932, April, VG $5.00
Redbook, 1947, May, Queen Elizabeth article, VG $4.00
Redbook, 1948, August, Gary Cooper & Lowell Thomas arti
    cles, EX $2.50
Redbook, 1949, July, Rudy Vallee article, EX $5.50
Redbook, 1955, October, Jackie Gleason cover, EX......$6.00
Redbook, 1957, January, Kim Novak cover, EX $3.50
Rod & Gun, 1957, May, Vol 1 #1, VG $15.00
Rolling Stone, 1967, #1, John Lennon cover, VG $60.00
Rolling Stone, 1986, #486, Billy Joel, VG $2.00
Romantic, 1937, November, VG $5.00
Safari, 1957, February, VG...$7.00
Saturday Evening Post, 1946, April 6, Norman Rockwell
    cover, Hawaii article, VG $10.00
Saturday Evening Post, 1948, July 12, South Pacific movie ad,
    VG $5.00
Saturday Evening Post, 1952, July 26, The Big Sky movie ad,
    VG $4.00
Saturday Evening Post, 1952, March 8, Steven Dohanos
    cover, VG...$3.00
Saturday Evening Post, 1952, November 8, Queen Elizabeth
    article, VG+ $4.00
Saturday Evening Post, 1953, March 28, Bing Crosby article,
    EX..$8.00
Saturday Evening Post, 1953, November 21, VG+ $4.00
Saturday Evening Post, 1954, December 11, Frankie Laine
    article, EX $5.00
Saturday Evening Post, 1955, July 2, Babe Didrikson article,
    VG+ $5.00
Saturday Evening Post, 1957, March 30, Victor Borge & Don
    Larson articles, VG $3.00
Saturday Evening Post, 1957, November 23, King Hussein &
    Mike Wallace articles, VG $5.00
Saturday Evening Post, 1959, January 17, Danny Thomas arti
    cle, VG $3.00
Saturday Evening Post, 1959, September 5, Dragnet article,
    VG $3.00
Saturday Evening Post, 1960, March 26, Debbie Reynolds
    article, VG..$5.00
Saturday Evening Post, 1961, June 14, Burt Lancaster article,
    VG $3.00
Saturday Evening Post, 1961, September 2, John F Kennedy
    article, VG..$4.00
Science & Invention, 1925, June, VG $20.00
Screen Guide, 1947, May, June Allyson cover, NM.....$18.00
Screen Land, 1949, February, Betty Grable & Dan Dailey
    cover, VG...$5.00
Screen Stories, 1949, May, June Allyson, Elizabeth Taylor,
    Janet Leigh & Margaret O'Brian cover, VG $6.00
Show, 1940, June, Vol 1 #1, VG $17.00
Smart Set, 1926, September, VG $15.00
Sport, 1984, July 19, Yankee's Mattingly cover, VG $5.00
Sport World, 1983, June, VG......................................$4.00
Sports Illustrated, 1979, May 28, Pete Rose cover, VG .$8.00
Sports Illustrated, 1984, April 23, Darrell Strawberry cover,
    VG $6.00

Sports Illustrated, 1988, December 12, Charles Barkley,
    VG $6.00
Sports Illustrated, 1990, August 6, Joe Montana cover,
    VG $5.00
Sports Review Wrestling, 1988, March, VG...................$6.00
Tales of the Zombie, 1973, October...........................$7.00
Teen Life, 1965, November, Beatles article, VG $12.00
The National, 1943, March, Hitler article, VG...............$7.00
Time, 1935, April 15, Dizzy Dean cover, VG $60.00
Time, 1959, June 29, Queen Elizabeth cover, VG.........$2.00
Time, 1965, December 24, Gemini 7 article, VG..........$5.00
True Confessions, 1936, May, Claudette Colbert cover,
    VG $8.00
True Confessions, 1945, September, Marie Denham cover,
    VG $5.00
True Love, 1940, May, Joan Fontaine cover, VG.........$15.00
True Love & Romance, 1941, October, Ellen Drew cover,
    VG $4.00
True Story, 1934, December, Heather Angel cover, VG...$7.00
True Story, 1938, September, Deanna Durbin cover, VG..$16.00
True Story, 1939, February, Betty Malamut cover, VG..$7.00
Tuff Stuff, 1990, July, Nolan Ryan cover, VG $5.00
Two Worlds Monthly, 1926, August, Vol 1 #1, VG......$50.00
Vogue, 1940, January, swimsuit cover, VG $8.00
Walt Disney's Magazine, 1948, February, Annette Funicello
    cover, VG...$15.00
Weird, 1966, December $7.00
Westling World, 1988, December, VG $6.00
Whisper, 1952, November, gangster article, VG $10.00
Wings, 1941, Summer $35.00
Woman's Home Companion, 1950, March, VG+...........$2.50
Woman's Home Companion, 1953, October, Jack & Mary
    Benny article, VG+...$2.50
Woman's Home Companion, 1955, November, Marlon
    Brando article, NM...$3.00
Woman's Home Companion, 1956, December, VG $2.00
World Report, 1946, May 23, Vol 1 #1, VG $6.00
Wrestling, 1985, Spring, VG $1.00
Wrestling Insider, 1986, November, VG $1.00
Wrestling Superstars, 1988, Fall, Tyson & Hogan cover,
    VG $8.00
Your Physique, 1952, April, VG $2.00

Pulp Magazines

As early as the turn of the century, pulp magazines were beginning to appear, but by the 1930s, their popularity had literally exploded. Called pulps because of the cheap wood-pulp paper they were printed on, crime and detective stories, westerns, adventure tales, and mysteries were the order of the day. Crime pulps sold for as little as 10¢; some of the westerns were 15¢. Plots were imaginative and spicy, if not downright risque. The top three publishers were Street and Smith, Popular, and the Thrilling Group. Some of the more familiar pulp-magazine authors were Agatha Christy, Clarence E. Mulford, Erle Stanley Gardner, Ellery Queen, Edgar Rice Burroughs, Louis L'Amour, and Max Brand. Until the 1950s when slick-paper magazines signed their death warrant, pulps were published by the thousands. Because of the poor quality of their paper, many have not survived. Those that have are seldom rated better than very good. A near-mint to mint example will bring a premium price, since it is almost impossible to locate one so well preserved. Except for a few very rare editions, many are in the average price range suggested below — some much lower.

Advisor: J. Grant Thiessen (Pandora's Books Ltd.). (See Directory, Magazines)

Adventure, 1935, January 1, G......................................$12.00
All Western, 1932, November, VG $15.00
Amazing Stories, 1935, April, VG $18.00
Amazing Stories, 1941, May, VG..................................$13.00
Amazing Stories, 1948, February, VG..........................$10.00
Amazing Stories Quarterly, 1949, Winter, VG.............$20.00
Argosy, 1933, September 9, VG....................................$18.00
Argosy, 1936, February 15, VG....................................$15.00
Argosy All-Story, 1928, September 29, VG..................$20.00
Astonishing, 1940, October, VG...................................$20.00
Astounding, 1937, March, VG.......................................$30.00
Astounding, 1941, May, VG $25.00
Baseball Stories, 1952, Summer, VG............................$12.00
Best Western, 1954, June, VG...$8.00
Blue Book, 1929, July, VG...$60.00
Captain Future, 1941, Fall, EX $35.00
Complete Western Book, 1939, December, G $6.00
Detective Fiction Weekly, 1938, July 16, VG $15.00
Dime Mystery, 1935, May, VG......................................$80.00
Doc Savage, 1937, June, EX..$65.00
Doc Savage, 1941, September, VG................................$55.00
Dynamic Science Fiction, 1952, December, VG $8.00
Famous Fantastic Mysteries, 1941, April, VG.............$15.00
Famous Western, 1950, February, VG..........................$25.00
Fantastic Adventures, 1941, March, VG.......................$40.00
Fantastic Novels, 1940, July, #1, VG...........................$25.00
Fantastic Story, 1951, Spring, VG..................................$8.00
Fighting Aces, 1943, July, G...$20.00
G-Men, 1939, October, VG..$25.00
International Detective Magazine, 1934, January, G ...$25.00
Mammoth Detective, 1946, October, VG $15.00
New Detective, 1947, November, VG...........................$10.00
Operator #5, 1938, September/October, VG...............$75.00
Other Worlds, 1956, February, VG...............................$10.00
Planet Stories, 1940, Winter, VG.................................$30.00
Popular Detective, 1943, June, VG..............................$18.00
Popular Magazine, 1930, March 20, G $18.00
Ranch Romances, 1935, April 1, G...............................$12.00
Range Riders, 1947, March, G..$6.00
Rio Kid Western, 1940, June, G....................................$10.00
Science Fiction Quarterly, 1940, #1, VG $30.00
Shadow, 1936, August 1, G...$60.00
Shadow, 1939, November 15, G....................................$55.00
Short Stories, 1944, August 25, VG.............................$13.00
Short Stories, 1948, March 25, VG..............................$10.00
Spider, 1936, September, G...$65.00
Startling Stories, 1941, July, EX..................................$20.00
Super Science Stories, 1940, July, EX.........................$20.00
Texas Rangers, 1947, July, VG.....................................$20.00

Thrilling Detective, 1940, August, G $15.00
Thrilling Wonder, 1938, April, EX...............................$25.00
Thrilling Wonder, 1946, Summer, VG..........................$10.00
Triple-X, 1930, October, VG...$35.00
Unknown, 1939, March, #1, VG $50.00
Weird Tales, 1934, September, VG $75.00
Weird Tales, 1943, September, VG $45.00
Western Novel & Short Stories, 1954, October, VG $12.00
Western Story, 1929, April 20, G $15.00
Wild West Weekly, 1942, July 11, VG $13.00
Wonder Stories, 1935, October, EX $23.00
10-Story Detective, 1948, December, VG....................$12.00

Marbles

There are two broad categories of collectible marbles, the antique variety and machine-made, contemporary marbles. Under those broad divisions are many classifications. Everett Grist delves into both categories in his book called *Big Book of Marbles* (Collector Books).

Sulfide marbles have figures (generally animals or birds) encased in the center. The glass is nearly always clear; a common example in excellent condition may run as low as $100.00, while those with an unusual subject or made of colored glass may go for more than $1,000.00. Many machine-made marbles are very reasonable, but if the colors are especially well placed and selected, good examples sell in excess of $50.00. Mt. Peltier comic character marbles often bring prices of $100.00 and up with Betty Boop, Moon Mullins, and Kayo being the rarest and most valuable. Watch for reproductions. New comic character marbles have the design printed on a large area of plain white glass with color swirled through the back and sides.

No matter where your interests lie, remember that condition is extremely important. From the nature of their use, mint-condition marbles are very rare and may be worth as much as three to five times more than one that is near-mint. Chipped and cracked marbles may be worth half or less, and some will be worthless. Polishing detracts considerably.

Advisor: Everett Grist (See Directory, Marbles)

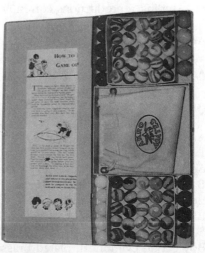

Akro Agates in metal box with bag and instructions, $1,000.00. (Photo courtesy Sally Dolly)

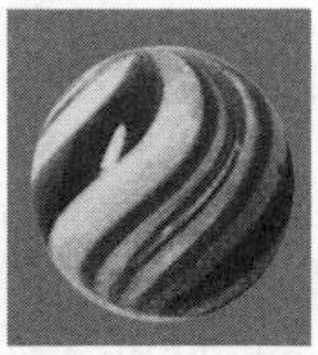

Peppermint swirl, red, white, and blue opaque, ¾", NM, $125.00. (Photo courtesy Everett Grist)

Cat's-eye, banana; Peltier, 1" **$2.00**
Comic, Annie or Sandy, Peltier, ⅝" **$100.00**
Corkscrew, clear & transparent color w/opaque ribbon, ⅝" .**$2.00**
Corkscrew, Popeye, Akro Agate, ⅝" **$25.00**
Decorated china, rose decoration in center, ¾" **$350.00**
Goldstone, glass w/copper flakes, ¾" **$35.00**
Hurricane, Christensen Agate **$10.00**
Lutz, clear swirl, ¾" **$85.00**
Lutz, Indian swirl, w/gold-colored flakes added, ¾" .. **$275.00**
Lutz, ribbon core, ¾" **$175.00**
Mica, transparent glass, clear, blue, green or amber, w/mica flakes, ¾" **$25.00**
Moonies, Akro Agate, ⅝" **$3.00**
Peppermint swirl w/mica, ¾" **$100.00**
Slag, Akro Agate, red, ⅝" **$7.00**
Slag, red, ⅝" **$5.00**
Solid core swirl, ¾" **$15.00**
Sparkler, multicolor, Akro Agate **$18.00**
Sulfide, American bison or buffalo, 2" **$250.00**
Sulfide, bear, 2" **$150.00**
Sulfide, chicken, 1¼" **$75.00**
Sulfide, pony, 2" **$150.00**
Swirl, 2-color opaque **$2.00**
Transparent swirl, solid core, ¾" **$50.00**

Match Safes

Match safes or vesta boxes, as they are known in England, evolved to keep matches dry and to protect an individual from unintentional ignition. These containers were produced in enormous quantities over a 75-year period from various materials including silver, brass, aluminum, and gold, and their shapes and designs were limitless. They can usually be recognized by the presense of a small, rough area, which is actually a striking surface. Collectors should be cautious of numerous sterling reproductions currently on the market.

Advisor: George Sparacio (See Directory, Match Safes)

Advertising furniture, black graphics, celluloid wrapped, 2¾x1½", EX **$110.00**
Agate, rectangular w/rounded end, brass trim, 2⅝x1½", EX **$125.00**
Art Nouveau, girl's face w/flowers, plated brass, 2⅞x1½", EX **$135.00**
Art Nouveau, nudes & cherubs, sterling, 2⅝x1½", EX . **$135.00**
Baby head in shirt, figural, brass, 2¾x1⅛", EX **$250.00**
Bell's #4, litho tin, 1½x3½", EX **$17.00**
Blatz Beer advertising, brass, 2⅞x1⅝", EX **$55.00**
Boot, wrinkled at ankle, figural, plated brass, 2⅝x1¾", EX .. **$225.00**
Boy Scout, cylindrical, plated brass, 3x¾", EX **$15.00**
BPOE motif, insert type, plated brass, 2¾x1½", EX ... **$65.00**
BPOE w/enameled clock, fob type, sterling, 2⅝x1½", EX **$225.00**
Cadbury, litho tin, striker on bottom, 2x3¼", EX **$30.00**
Charles Darwin portrait, plated brass, 2⅛x1⅜", EX .. **$250.00**
Cigar cutter/safe, mother-of-pearl sides, ¾x2¼", EX .. **$150.00**
Crown lid, plated brass, 2¾x1⅜", EX **$85.00**
Filigree, book shaped, silver, 2x1½", EX **$80.00**
Firemen/Home Insurance, sterling, 2½x1¾", EX **$395.00**
Gladstone bag, figural, plated brass, 1⅜x1⅞", EX **$235.00**
Gorham, engraved design, catalog #030, silverplate, 2½x1¼", EX **$55.00**
Hidden photo, sterling, 2⅞x1½", EX **$195.00**
Insert type, flag & dog motif, plated brass, 2¾x1½", EX .. **$35.00**
International Tailoring, Indians & lions, plated brass, 1⅜x2½", EX **$50.00**
King Edward VII, book shaped, vulcanite, 2x1½", EX . **$55.00**
Knights of Pythias, insert type, plated brass, 2½x1½", EX **$48.00**
Leather wrapped, burnt design, plated brass ends, 2⅝x1⅞", EX **$35.00**
Midsummer Nights Dream motif, sterling, 1⅝x1⅜", EX .. **$245.00**
Morgan & Wright Tires, slip top, gutta percha, 2¾x1⅝", EX **$40.00**
Muchline transfer, Psycho Box, wood, 3x1¼", EX **$135.00**
Owl w/glass eyes, slide profile, figural, brass, 2x1", EX **$225.00**
Pig standing on 4 feet, figural, brass, ⅞x1⅞", EX **$145.00**
Queen Victoria Jubilee/Perry & Co, plated brass, 2⅜x1⅜", EX **$110.00**
Rebecca at the Well, sterling, 2½x1¾", EX **$145.00**
Rococo motif, sterling, 2⅝x1½", EX **$65.00**
Schlitz advertising w/cigar cutter on bottom, leather wrapped, 2¾x1½", EX **$95.00**
Shoe w/cigar cutter, figural, plated brass, 2⅞x⅝", EX . **$160.00**

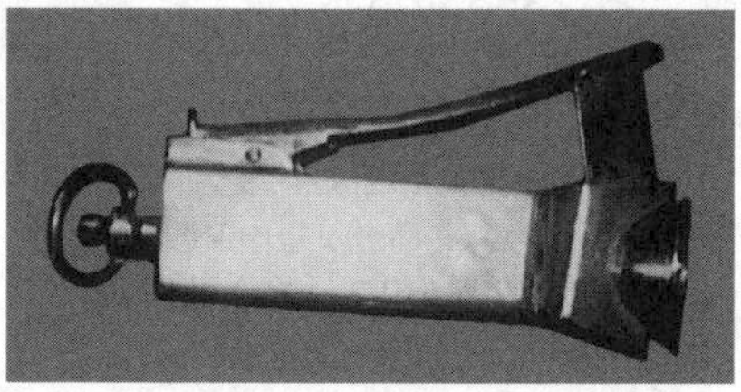

Sterling, mother-of-pearl and gold inlay, 2⅜x1⅜", EX, $325.00. (Photo courtesy George Sparacio)

Storm motif, plated brass, 2⅞x1½", EX **$55.00**
Summertime by Greenaway, copper, 3x1½", EX **$60.00**
Vacuum Oil advertising, multicolor graphics, celluloid wrapped, 2⅜x1⅜", EX **$135.00**

Matchcovers

Matchcover collecting is a relatively new hobby. Trying to get officially organized at the 1939 New York World's Fair, six lonely matchcover collectors scoured the fairground for every matchcover they could find. The fair produced quite an assortment. Over three hundred different styles are now known, including those made for this fair and others, restaurants, hotels, banks, services, and businesses in the New York area.

Matchcover clubs grew from small gatherings of the dedicated, mostly from the northeastern states — New York, New Jersey, Connecticut, and New England. At one time there were touted to be over a million matchcover collectors in this country, with many of them belonging to clubs. Those days are now gone, but many of the clubs remain. Today there are hundreds of thousands who collect matchcovers for fun and inexpensive recreation.

Note that only half the matchcovers ever produced are collectible. Of that 50%, less than 5% are worth more than a quarter. There are millions of valuable matchcovers in garages, attics, basements, and storerooms all over America.

Advisor: Bill Retskin (See Directory, Matchcovers)

Club: American Matchcover Collecting Club (AMCC)
P.O. Box 18481
Asheville, NC 28814
704-254-4487 or FAX 704-254-1066; Dues $18.00 yearly, includes *Front Striker Bulletin*. Also available: *Matchcover Collector's Price Guide* ($16.95 + $3.25 shipping and handling)

Apollo 17, Cernan, Evans, Schmitt, no photo, 30 stick **$6.50**
Apollo 7, 30 stick, front strike, 1968 ....**$40.00**
Bookbinders Sea Food House, lobster on front, fishermen on sticks, full book, front strike, Lion Match Co Giant..**$4.75**
Bundles for Britain, Coat of Arms on front, 20 stick, front strike, Universal Match Corp, 1941 ....**$6.50**
Canadian Pacific Air, Canada-Japan-Mexico-Rome/ Amsterdam, 30 stick, front strike, Eddy Match Ltd..**$3.00**
Capitol Beer, Pride of Missouri, dome in center, 20 stick, front strike, full book..**$3.00**
Christmas Giant for Luchow's Wurzburger Hofbrau & Wine Restaurant, NY, full book, front strike, Lion Match Co Giant **$2.50**
Civilian Conservation Corps Camp, Co 401, Marion NC, 1 cover, 20 stick, front strike.......................................**$6.50**
CJ Wallace photo on front, American Family Insurance ad on back, 20 stick **$2.00**
Colgate Studios, Pedigree w/Scottie dog on front & back, 20 stick, front strike, ca 1930 ....**$8.00**
Coon Chicken Dinner on front & back, Coon Chicken 50¢ on back, 20 stick, front strike....................................**$15.00**
Diamond Golf-Tee Book Matches, w/6 red golf tees, 1 full book, 20 stick, Diamond Quality.........................**$75.00**
Dixie Sandwiches, Malted Milk w/4 addresses in Denver CO on front, 20 stick, front strike, Universal Match Corp **$15.00**
Eddie Cantor in Banjo Eyes, black-faced Cantor on front, commentary on back, 20 stick, front strike **$35.00**
Enrique Freeman, New York World Checkers Champion, black & white photo on front, 20 stick, back strike..........**$2.00**
Festival of Britain, 1951, 20 stick, front strike, Bryant & May Ltd **$2.50**
Gilbert System Hotels, At Your Service in 35 Cities, Black bellhop on front, 20 stick, front strike, Lion Match Co..**$10.00**

Holiday Inns, Paris France, 30 stick, back strike...........**$2.00**
Hollywood Dog Races, opening dates on front, Hollywood FL, 20 stick **$2.00**
Hotel Jamestown in Jamestown NY, Distinctive Hotel of Chautauqua Lake Region, 1 cover, 20 stick, Diamond Quality **$4.75**
Hotel Multnomah, Portland OR, Indian on front, hotel on back, 20 stick, Diamond Quality **$6.75**
Jack Dempsey's on Broadway, 30 stick, front strike, Lion Feature **$9.50**
Margaret Peterson's Melody Lane, San Francisco, multi-color piano player on 20 sticks, photo Larry Larson inside **$6.50**
Mickey Mantle's Holiday Inn, Joplin MO, photo on front, motel map inside, 30 stick, front strike................**$27.00**
Minnesota Twins Baseball, F&M Savings Bank, William Frederick 'Billy' Gardner, 2nd Base, w/photo, 20 stick, front strike **$8.25**

Mobilgas, Merry Christmas, $5.00. (Photo courtesy Bill Retskin)

Montreal Expos, 30 stick, back strike, 1978, set of 7....**$9.50**
Nat King Cole, black & white photo, from Chez Paree series, 20 stick, front strike **$6.50**
New York World's Fair, Gas Exhibit Building, 20 stick, front strike, 1939-40 ....**$5.25**
New York World's Fair, Gimbels, 15 Minutes From...Adjoining Penn Station, 20 stick, 1939-40 ....**$6.25**
New York World's Fair, Manhattan Line, Blue Coach on back, bus on front, terminals inside, 20 stick, front strike, 1939 ....**$5.00**
Newarker Restaurant, Newark Airport, black & white, wood sticks **$30.00**
Nixon Lodge, The Matchless Ticket, Nov 8, 1960, photo on front, 20 stick **$6.75**
Ohio Federal Truck, drum majorette, 20 stick, back strike, 1941 ....**$25.00**
Pelton's Garage, Bridgeport CT on front, garage, tow truck & name on 20 sticks, full book, front striker, Lion Feature **$6.25**
Play: The Egg & I, Staring Claudette Colbert & Fred MacMurray, 20 stick, front strike...............................**$7.75**

Playboy Club, Portland OR, rabbit on front, black & white, 20 stick, front strike **$5.75**

Ponte Vedra Club, Ponte Vedra Beach Florida, sea horse logo, oversized golf ball, 20 stick, front strike, Contour **$8.00**

Re-Elect Harley Staggers Jr to Congress on saddle, ...Working for You, 30 stick, JRB Assoc, Grafton WV **$8.25**

Schodorf Truck Body & Equipment, Columbus OH, 20 stick, striker is parking lot near building on back **$8.00**

Seattle Area Boy Scout Council Jamboree, Troup 15, July 1953, 20 stick, front strike **$7.50**

Strike at the Seat of Trouble, Buy War Bonds on front, Hitler w/striker on seat of pants, full book, 20 stick, multicolor...**$65.00**

Uncle Remus Restaurant, Eatonton GA, Uncle Remus-like character on back, 20 stick, front strike **$7.50**

University of Pennsylvania Football Schedule, player on front, schedule on back, 20 stick, front strike, 1966............**$2.00**

USS Northampton, 20 stick, front strike, ca before 1944 .**$2.75**

Vote for Bob Taft for President, photo on back, Vote Republican on saddle, full book, 20 stick, front strike **$7.75**

Washington Redskins Hi Aldrich, Texas Christian, 20 stick, front strike, 1941 ....**$5.25**

Welcome Air Force Two on back, Vice Presidential seal on front, 30 stick, back strike, Universal Match Corp..**$6.25**

1939 Golden Gate Exposition, Drink Brazilian Coffee, 20 stick, front strike **$5.25**

McCoy Pottery

This is probably the best known of all American potteries, due to the wide variety of goods they produced from 1910 until the pottery finally closed only a few years ago.

They were located in Roseville, Ohio, the pottery center of the United States during the first half of the century. They're most famous for their cookie jars, of which were made several hundred styles and variations. (For a listing of these, see the section entitled Cookie Jars.) McCoy is also well known for their figural planters, novelty kitchenware, and dinnerware.

They used a variety of marks over the years, but with little consistency, since it was a common practice to discontinue an item for awhile and then bring it out again decorated in a manner that would be in sync with current tastes. All of McCoy's marks were 'in the mold.' None were ink stamped, so very often the in-mold mark remained as it was when the mold was originally created. Most marks contain the McCoy name, though some of the early pieces were simply signed 'NM' for Nelson McCoy (Sanitary and Stoneware Company, the company's original title). Early stoneware pieces were sometimes impressed with a shield containing a number. If you have a piece with the Lancaster Colony Company mark (three curved lines — the left one beginning as a vertical and terminating as a horizontal, the other two formed as 'C's contained in the curve of the first), you'll know that your piece was made after the mid-seventies when McCoy was owned by that group. Today even these later pieces are becoming collectible.

If you'd like to learn more about this company, we recommend *The Collector's Encyclopedia of McCoy Pottery* and *The Collector's Encyclopedia of Brush-McCoy Pottery*, both by Sharon and Bob Huxford, and *McCoy Pottery, Collector's Reference & Value Guide,* by Bob and Margaret Hanson and Craig Nissen. All are published by Collector Books.

A note regarding cookie jars: beware of *new* cookie jars marked McCoy. It seems that the original McCoy pottery never registered their trademark, and for several years it was legally used by a small company in Rockwood, Tennessee. Not only did they use the original mark, but they reproduced some of the original jars as well. If you're not an experienced collector, you may have trouble distinguishing the new from the old. Some (but not all) are dated #93, the '#' one last attempt to fool the novice, but there are differences to watch for. The new ones are slightly smaller in size, and the finish is often flawed. He has also used the McCoy mark on jars never produced by the original company, such as Little Red Riding Hood and the Luzianne mammy. Only lately did it become known that the last owners of the McCoy pottery actually did register the trademark; so, having to drop McCoy, he has since worked his way through two other marks: Brush-McCoy and (currently) BM Hull.

See Also Cookie Jars.

Newsletter: *The Nelson-McCoy Express*
Carol Seman, Editor
7670 Chippewa Rd., Ste. 406, Brecksville, OH 44141-2310

Jardiniere, fluting and leaves, 6x7½", $30.00.

Ashtray, 4 joined squares, dark rose w/pink seafoam, 1964, from $25 to..**$30.00**

Ashtray/novelty tray, 2 open hands form tray, tan, 1941, from $30 to..**$40.00**

Bank, Immigrant Industrial Savings, American Bald Eagle (natural colors) perched on brown box w/3 stars, from $40 to..**$50.00**

Bank, Seaman's Bank of Savings, sailor in white w/lg bag over shoulder, from $50 to **$75.00**

Basket, oval w/embossed oak leaves & acorns, cream w/rustic colors w/handle, 1952, from $40 to................**$50.00**

Bean pot, brown, embossed leaves & beans, w/handle, 1943, from $45 to..**$50.00**

Bean pot, tab handles, tan w/red apple decoration, 1960s, 2-qt, from $75 to..**$100.00**

Bookends, white swallow on green background, brown base, 1956, from $125 to.................................**$150.00**

Bowl, shoulder; nesting, tan w/colored bands (3), marked USA, 1935, from $30 to **$35.00**

Creamer, bulbous, Sunburst Gold, plain handle, 1957, from $25 to **$30.00**

Cuspidor, bulbous, flared, dark green, embossed grapes, no mark, 1926-50s, from $50 to **$60.00**

Figurine, black panther, no mark, 1950s, from $40 to ..**$50.00**

Jardiniere, light green, flying birds motif, footed, no mark, 1935, 7½", from $25 to......................................**$35.00**

Jardiniere & pedestal, light green, embossed leaves over diamonds, early 50s, from $225 to....................................**$300.00**

Lamp base, sm cowboy boots, dark brown, 1956, from $75 to **$100.00**

Lamp base, whaling man, brown, on pedestal, not many produced, from $200 to **$350.00**

Novelty, basketball, brown, no mark, 1940s, from $85 to...**$100.00**

Novelty, kitten w/basket, yellow, marked USA, 1941, from $35 to...**$45.00**

Novelty, pelican, white w/yellow feet, orange beak, black eyes, no mark, 1940s, from $100 to **$150.00**

Novelty, rabbit, yellow, marked USA, 1940s, from $75 to..**$125.00**

Novelty, rolling pin (brown) w/Boy Blue, no mark, 1952, from $75 to...**$100.00**

Novelty, standing deer, on base, white, no mark, 1940s, from $25 to..**$30.00**

Novelty, witch bust, brown, no mark, 1940s, from $100 to **$150.00**

Pitcher, chicken form, head forms spout, embossed wings on side, off-white, plain handle, footed, no mark, 1943, from $25 to...**$35.00**

Pitcher, classic shape, embossed water lilies on green, no mark, 1935, from $50 to.......................................**$75.00**

Pitcher, classic shape, green glossy glaze w/no embossing, no mark, 1926, from $50 to **$75.00**

Pitcher, cylindrical, dark rose w/sm white vertical stripes, plain handle, 1948, from $35 to **$45.00**

Pitcher, disk shape, cream w/embossed cloverleaves, 1948, from $30 to..**$45.00**

Pitcher, shape #122, classic form, embossed angelfish motif, green, 1935, from $45 to **$50.00**

Pitcher, shape #30, light brown, embossed water lilies, fish handle, no mark, 1935, from $50 to......................**$75.00**

Pitcher, tilted jug shape, ice lip, tan, no mark, 1950s, from $35 to...**$45.00**

Pitcher, waisted form, dark green, embossed buccaneer, shield mark #6, from $25 to..................................**$35.00**

Planter, bird dog w/bird, brown fence & green bushes in background, rock-like wall base, 1954, from $150 to......**$175.00**

Planter, black carriage w/white & orange wheels & separate umbrella, 1955, from $150 to.............................**$200.00**

Planter, butterfly form, green, 1940, from $50 to........**$60.00**

Planter, cradle, pink, footed, no mark, from $20 to ...**$30.00**

Planter, dog w/cart, green & brown colors, 1952, from $25 to **$35.00**

Planter, duck (yellow) w/egg (white), orange feet & beak, hard to find, from $75 to **$95.00**

Planter, duck lying down, yellow, 1951, from $25 to.**$35.00**

Planter, fawns w/forest background, brown & green colors, 1954, becoming rare, from $175 to **$200.00**

Planter, green turtle, 1950, from $35 to **$45.00**

Planter, lamb, white w/blue necktie, 1953, from $40 to ...**$50.00**

Planter, Noel, 2 angels singing w/song book, blue, scarce, 1940s, from $60 to..**$80.00**

Planter, Old Mill, brown mill w/man in white w/red cap, 1953, from $35 to..**$50.00**

Planter, pelican, pale blue, 1941, from $30 to **$40.00**

Planter, puppy, white w/black & brown markings, 1959, from $75 to...**$100.00**

Planter, pussy at the well, dark green w/white cat w/red bow, hard to find, 1956, from $85 to..................**$125.00**

Planter, quail family w/foliage behind, green & brown colors, 1955, from $40 to..**$55.00**

Planter, rodeo cowboy on horse roping calf, brown & green colors, 1950s, from $125 to.................................**$160.00**

Planter, scoop with mammy, 1953, 7½", $150.00. (Photo courtesy Hanson/Nissen)

Planter, stork and baby, marked, $45.00.

Planter, stretch horse, pale blue, head cocked to 1 side, no mark, 1941, from $45 to...**$60.00**

Planter, stretch lion, white, no mark, 1941, from $90 to **$100.00**

Planter/bookends, hunting dog w/bird in mouth, multicolored on tan base, 1955, pr, from $100 to **$130.00**

Spoon rest, butterfly motif, dark green, 1953, from $75 to **$100.00**

Spoon rest, penguin form, multicolored, 1953, from $70 to..**$100.00**

Strawberry jar, 3-D & embossed bird, light green & brown, 1950, from $30 to..**$40.00**

Sugar bowl, swirled marbleized colors, ear handles w/lid, from $40 to...**$50.00**

Tankard, banded barrel form, dark brown outside, white inside, shield mark #4, 1926, from $60 to **$70.00**

Tankard, cylindrial w/tapered bottom, dark green, Willow Ware, 1926, from $80 to...............................**$100.00**

Tankard, cylindrical, dark brown, Indian Peace Sign (swastika), no mark, 1926, from $100 to **$125.00**

Tankard, flared cylindrical shape, green, embossed grapes, no mark, 1926, from $80 to **$100.00**

Tea set, cream w/brown embossed ivy, bark-like handles, 3-pc, 1950, from $75 to......................................**$120.00**

Tea set, green & brown tones, Pine Cone pattern, 3-pc, 1946, from $75 to **$100.00**

Teapot, bulbous, Sunburst Gold, angle finial, 1957, from $60 to...**$85.00**

Teapot, cat form, black & white w/red necktie, front paw is spout, tail is handle, 1971, from $75 to **$100.00**

Urn, straight sided, dark green, Butterfly pattern, vertical bands, footed, no mark, 1940, from $45 to **$60.00**

Vase, blue hyacinth w/green leaves, brown base, 1950, from $60 to...**$75.00**

Vase, bud; white lily w/green leaves, brown base, 1947, from $60 to...**$75.00**

Vase, bulbous, blue onyx, embossed leaves & berries, footed, no mark, 1932-37, from $55 to.....................**$65.00**

Vase, bulbous, dark brown onyx, sm handles at waist, flared rim & foot, 1932-37, from $65 to............................**$85.00**

Vase, classic shape, green, embossed leaves, handled, no mark, 1926, from $85 to......................................**$110.00**

Vase, cornucopia; w/fawn, brown, 1954, from $50 to..**$65.00**

Vase, double tulip, gold trim, 6½x8", from $100.00 to $150.00. (Photo courtesy Hanson/Nissen)

Vase, pink poppies on brown log w/green leaves in background, hard to find, 1955, from $200 to..............................**$300.00**

Vase, shouldered cylindrical shape, dark brown onyx, handles at rim, 1932-37, from $50 to **$65.00**

Wall pocket, a pear w/green leaves in background, 1953, from $50 to..**$60.00**

Wall pocket, an orange w/green leaves in background, 1953, from $60 to..**$75.00**

Wall pocket, bellows, 9½x4½", from $75.00 to $90.00. (Photo courtesy Hanson/Nissen)

Wall pocket, brown bellows form w/red berries & green leaves on front, 1956, from $75 to **$90.00**

Wall pocket, clock form, pendulum style, yellow w/red cuckoo bird, 1952, from $125 to................................**$150.00**

Wall pocket, hand fan, Sunburst Gold, 1957, from $60 to...**$75.00**

Wall pocket, Mail Box, green, 'LETTERS' spelled across front, 1951, from $75 to...**$90.00**

Wall pocket, pale green birdbath w/red floral, yellow bird in bath, 1949, from $85 to....................................**$100.00**

Wall pocket, umbrella, yellow, 1955, from $60 to **$75.00**

Wall pocket, violin form, light blue w/green details, 1957, from $100 to...**$150.00**

Wall pocket, yellow iron on pale tan trivet, 1953, from $50 to **$75.00**

Wall pocket, 3 owls, red w/yellow highlights, on yellow trivet, 1953, from $50 to **$75.00**

Wall pocket, 3 yellow bananas w/green leaves in background, 1953, from $75 to **$90.00**

Window planter, Grecian, 1958, from $40 to.....................**$50.00**

Brown Drip Dinnerware

One of McCoy's dinnerware lines that was introduced in the 1960s is beginning to attract a following. It's a glossy brown stoneware-type pattern with frothy white decoration around the rims. Similar lines of brown stoneware were made by many other companies, Hull and Pfaltzgraff among them. McCoy simply called their line 'Brown Drip.'

Advisor: Jo-Ann Bentz (See Directory, Hull)

Baker, oval, 10½"...**$12.00**
Baker, oval, 12½", from $18 to...................................**$22.00**
Baker, oval, 9"...**$10.00**
Bean pot, individual, 12-oz...**$4.00**
Bean pot, 1½-qt, from $15 to.....................................**$20.00**
Bean pot, 3-qt, from $25 to..**$30.00**
Bowl, cereal; 6"..**$6.00**
Bowl, lug soup; 12-oz...**$8.00**
Bowl, lug soup; 18-oz...**$10.00**
Bowl, spaghetti or salad; 12½"...................................**$15.00**
Bowl, vegetable; 9"..**$12.00**
Bowl, vegetable; divided...**$15.00**
Butter dish, ¼-lb...**$20.00**

Candle holders, pr, from $18 to	$22.00
Canister, Coffee	$45.00
Casserole, 2-qt	$15.00
Casserole, 3½-qt	$20.00
Casserole, 3-qt, w/hen on nest lid, from $45 to	$50.00
Corn tray, individual, from $10 to	$14.00
Creamer	$4.00
Cruet, oil & vinegar, each, from $12 to	$15.00
Cup, 8-oz	$5.00
Custard cup, 6-oz	$4.00
Gravy boat, from $12 to	$15.00
Mug, pedestal base, 12-oz	$7.50
Mug, 8-oz	$5.00
Mug, 12-oz	$6.50
Pie plate, 9", from $15 to	$18.00
Pitcher, jug style, 32-oz	$20.00
Pitcher, jug style, 80-oz	$30.00
Plate, dinner; 10"	$10.00
Plate, salad; 7"	$6.50
Plate, soup & sandwich; w/lg cup ring	$10.00
Platter, fish form, 18"	$32.00
Platter, oval, 14"	$15.00

Salt and pepper shakers, $7.00 for the pair. (Photo courtesy Nissen/Hanson)

Saucer	$3.00
Souffle dish, 2-qt	$9.50
Teapot, 6-cup	$20.00

Melmac Dinnerware

The post-war era gave way to many new technologies in manufacturing. With the discovery that thermoplastics could be formed by the interaction of melamine and formaldehyde, Melmac was born. This colorful and decorative product found an eager market due to its style and affordability. Another attractive feature was its resistance to breakage. We probably all remember the sound of a Melmac plate as it bounced off the kitchen floor! It took a lot more than just being dropped to damage those dishes.

But popularity began to wane: the dinnerware was found to fade with repeated washings, the edges could chip, and the surfaces could be scratched, stained, or burned. Melmac fell from favor in the late sixties and early seventies. At that time, it was restyled to imitate china that had become popular due to increased imports.

As always, demand and availability determine price. Prices listed are for items in mint condition only; pieces with scratches, chips, or stains have no value. Lines of similar value are grouped together. As there are many more manufacturers other than those listed, for a more thorough study of the subject we recommend *Melmac Dinnerware* by Gregory R. Zimmer and Alvin Daigle Jr.

See also Russel Wright.

Advisors: Gregory R. Zimmer and Alvin Daigle Jr. (See Directory, Melmac)

Aztec, Debonaire, Flite-Lane, Mar-Crest, Restraware, Rivieraware, Stetson, Westinghouse

Aztec dinnerware, see listings for values. (Photo courtesy Zimmer/Daigle)

Bowl, cereal; from $2 to	$3.00
Bowl, fruit; from $1 to	$2.00
Bowl, serving; from $4 to	$5.00
Bowl, soup; from $3 to	$4.00
Butter dish, from $5 to	$7.00
Creamer, from $1 to	$2.00
Cup & saucer, from $2 to	$3.00
Gravy boat, from $5 to	$6.00
Plate, bread & butter; from $1 to	$2.00
Plate, dinner; from $2 to	$3.00
Plate, salad; from $2 to	$3.00
Salt & pepper shakers, pr, from $4 to	$5.00
Sugar bowl, w/lid, from $3 to	$4.00
Tumbler, 6-oz, from $6 to	$7.00
Tumbler, 10-oz, from $7 to	$8.00

Boontoon, Branchell, Brookpark, Harmony House, Prolon, Watertown Lifetime Ware

Bowl, cereal; from $4 to	$5.00
Bowl, fruit; from $3 to	$4.00
Bowl, vegetable; divided, from $8 to	$10.00
Butter dish, from $10 to	$12.00
Casserole, w/lid, from $20 to	$25.00

Creamer, from $5 to..**$6.00**
Cup & saucer, from $3 to..**$4.00**
Gravy boat, from $6 to..**$8.00**
Plate, bread & butter; from $2 to **$3.00**
Plate, compartment; from $10 to..........................**$12.00**
Plate, dinner; from $4 to..**$5.00**
Plate, salad; from $4 to..**$5.00**
Platter, from $8 to..**$10.00**
Tray, bread; from $8 to..**$10.00**
Tray, tidbit; 2-tier, from $12 to............................**$15.00**
Tumbler, 6-oz, from $10 to....................................**$12.00**
Tumbler, 10-oz, from $12 to..................................**$15.00**

Fostoria, Lucent

Bowl, cereal; from $7 to..**$9.00**
Bowl, serving; from $15 to **$18.00**
Butter dish, from $15 to..**$18.00**
Creamer, from $8 to..**$10.00**
Cup & saucer, from $8 to......................................**$12.00**
Plate, bread & butter; from $3 to **$4.00**
Plate, dinner; from $6 to..**$8.00**
Platter, from $12 to..**$15.00**
Relish tray, from $15 to..**$18.00**
Sugar bowl, w/lid, from $12 to **$15.00**

Metlox Pottery

Founded in the late 1920s in Manhattan Beach, California, this company initially produced tile and commercial advertising signs. By the early thirties, their business in these areas had dwindled, and they began to concentrate their efforts on the manufacture of dinnerware, figurines, and kitchenware. Carl Gibbs has authored *Collector's Encyclopedia of Metlox Potteries* published by Collector Books, which we recommend for more information.

Carl Romanelli was the designer responsible for modeling many of the figural pieces they made during the late thirties and early forties. These items are usually imprinted with his signature and are very collectible today. Coming on strong is their line of 'Poppets,' made from the mid-sixties through the mid-seventies. There were eighty-eight in all, whimsical, comical, sometimes grotesque. They represented characters ranging from the seven-piece Salvation Army Group to royalty, religious figures, policemen, and professionals. They came with a nametag, some had paper labels, others backstamps. If you question a piece whose label is missing, check the facial features — they're generally represented by small pierced holes.

Poppytrail was the trade name for their kitchen and dinnerware lines. Among their more popular patterns were California Ivy, Red Rooster, Homestead Provincial, and the later embossed patterns, Sculptured Grape, Sculptured Zinnia, and Sculptured Daisy.

Some of their lines can be confusing. There are two 'rooster' lines, Red Rooster (red, orange, and brown) and California Provincial (this one is in dark green and burgundy), and two 'homestead' lines, Colonial Homestead (red, orange, and brown like the Red Rooster line) and Homestead

Provincial. Just remember the Provincial patterns are done in dark green and burgundy.

See also Cookie Jars.

Bowl, lug soup, Golden Fruit, 5", $18.00; Matching plate, 10"; $12.00; Creamer, $20.00; Sugar bowl, $25.00.

Ashtray, Colonial Heritage, 1956, 12"..........................**$40.00**
Ashtray, Colonial Heritage, 1956, 4½"........................**$18.00**
Bowl, cereal; Sculptured Daisy, 1964, 7"....................**$14.00**
Bowl, cream soup; California Ivy, 1946......................**$28.00**
Bowl, fruit; Fruit Basket (Vernon), 6"..........................**$12.00**
Bowl, fruit; Patrician White (Vernon), 1959, 6"..........**$10.00**
Bowl, fruit; Red Rooster (Decorated), 1955, 6"..........**$14.00**
Bowl, salad; Sculptured Grape, 1963, 12"....................**$75.00**
Bowl, salad; Tickled Pink (Vernon), 1958, 12"............**$50.00**
Bowl, soup; Colonial Heritage, 1956..........................**$20.00**
Bowl, soup; Homestead Provincial, 1950, 8"..............**$25.00**
Bowl, vegetable; California Ivy, 1946, round, w/lid, 11"...**$75.00**
Bowl, vegetable; California Provincial, 1950, round, 10"...**$55.00**
Bowl, vegetable; Sculptured Grape, 1963, divided, round, 9½"..**$50.00**
Butter dish, Antiqua (Vernon), 1966, w/lid..................**$60.00**
Butter dish, California Contempora, 1955, w/lid.......**$100.00**
Butter dish, California Ivy, 1946, w/lid **$55.00**
Butter dish, Colonial Heritage, 1956, w/lid **$65.00**
Butter dish, Red Rooster (Decorated), 1955, w/lid **$65.00**
Canister, Homestead Provincial, 1950, Sugar, w/lid....**$75.00**
Coaster, Colonial Heritage, 1956................................**$20.00**
Coaster, Pink Lady (Vernon), 1960, 4"........................**$14.00**
Coffeepot, Antique Grape, 1964, w/lid, 8-cup **$100.00**
Coffeepot, Red Rooster (Decorated), 1955, 6-cup **$120.00**
Creamer, Sculptured Zinnia, 1964..............................**$22.00**
Cruet set, Colonial Homestead, 1956, 5-pc...............**$170.00**
Cup & saucer, California Freeform, 1954....................**$23.00**
Cup & saucer, California Ivy, 1946..............................**$14.00**
Cup & saucer, California Provincial, 1950....................**$18.00**
Cup & saucer, Colonial Heritage, 1956 ....**$15.00**
Cup & saucer, demitasse; California Ivy, 1946 ....**$28.00**
Cup & saucer, Homestead Provincial, 1950................**$18.00**
Cup & saucer, Red Rooster (Decorated), 1955............**$16.00**
Cup & saucer, Sculptured Daisy, 1964........................**$14.00**
Cup & saucer, Sculptured Zinnia, 1964......................**$14.00**
Cup & saucer, Sherwood (Vernon), 1958 ....**$12.00**

Cup & saucer, Vineyard (Vernon), 1960 ....**$14.00**
Cup & saucer, White Rose (Vernon), 1977 ....**$12.00**
Egg cup, California Ivy, 1946..................................**$25.00**
Egg cup, California Provincial, 1950 ....**$30.00**
Egg cup, Colonial Homestead, 1956 ....**$28.00**
Egg cup, Fruit Basket (Vernon), 1961 ....**$28.00**
Figurine, aardvark, Miniature Series **$85.00**
Figurine, burro, sitting, Miniature Series, 3".............**$45.00**
Figurine, Chinese Man, Miniature Series, various sizes, from
    $65 to..**$125.00**
Figurine, elephant, stylized w/upturned trunk, Miniature
    Series...**$50.00**
Gravy boat, Homestead Provincial, 1-pt **$45.00**
Gravy boat, Sculptured Daisy, 1964, attached stand, 1-pt ...**$35.00**
Mug, Autumn Leaves (Vernon), 8-oz.........................**$20.00**
Mug, Colonial Homestead, 1956, 8-oz **$22.00**
Mug, Heavenly Days (Vernon), 1958, 12-oz **$20.00**
Mug, Red Rooster (Decorated), 1955, 8-oz.................**$22.00**
Pepper mill, Homestead Provincial, 1950 ....**$50.00**
Pitcher, Antique Grape, 1964, sm, 1½-pt..................**$40.00**
Pitcher, Homestead Provincial, 1950, lg, 2¼-qt..........**$85.00**
Pitcher, water; California Contempora, 1955 ....**$230.00**
Plate, bread & butter; Homestead Provincial, 1950, 6¼" .**$10.00**
Plate, bread & butter; Meadow (Vernon), 1980, 6½" **$7.00**
Plate, bread & butter; Red Rooster (Decorated), 1955,
    6¼" **$9.00**
Plate, dinner; California Ivy, 1946, 10¼"....................**$13.00**
Plate, dinner; California Peach Blossom, 1952 ....**$15.00**
Plate, dinner; Homestead Provincial, 1950, 10"..........**$18.00**
Plate, dinner; Red Rooster (Decorated), 1955, 10" **$15.00**
Plate, dinner; Rose-A-Day (Vernon), 1958, 10"..........**$12.00**
Plate, dinner; Sculptured Daisy, 1964, 10½"................**$13.00**
Plate, luncheon; California Provincial, 1950, 9"...........**$20.00**
Plate, luncheon; Colonial Heritage, 1956, 9" **$18.00**
Plate, luncheon; San Fernando (Vernon), 1966, 9¾" .**$15.00**
Plate, salad; California Provincial, 1950, 7½"..............**$14.00**
Platter, California Ivy, 1946, oval, 11" **$40.00**
Platter, Florence (Vernon), 1969, oval, 9⅝" **$40.00**
Platter, Giftware, Chicken or Mother Hen Group, 1980s...**$70.00**
Platter, Homestead Provincial, 1950, oval, 13½" **$55.00**
Platter, Red Rooster (Decorated), 1955, oval, 11".......**$50.00**
Poppet, Bridget, maid w/tray, 8"................................**$45.00**
Poppet, Hawaiian Girl, 4¾" **$35.00**
Poppet, Huck, fishing boy, 6½" **$45.00**
Poppet, Melinda, tennis girl w/4" bowl **$55.00**
Poppet, Minnie, mermaid..**$55.00**
Poppet, Mother Goose, 8"...**$55.00**
Poppet, Nancy, girl w/dog, 6¾" **$35.00**
Salt & pepper shakers, Blue Fascination (Vernon), 1967,
    pr..**$20.00**
Salt & pepper shakers, California Provincial, 1950, pr..**$30.00**
Salt & pepper shakers, Colonial Heritage, 1956, pr **$28.00**
Salt & pepper shakers, Della Robia (Vernon), 1965, pr.....**$26.00**
Salt & pepper shakers, Giftware, Duck Group, 1980s, pr.**$70.00**
Salt & pepper shakers, Homestead Provincial, 1950, pr....**$30.00**
Salt & pepper shakers, Sculptured Zinnia, 1964, pr....**$24.00**
Salt fork & spoon set, Sculptured Grape, 1963 ....**$60.00**
Salt shaker/mill, Colonial Heritage, 1956 ....**$40.00**
Soup tureen ladle, California Provincial, 1950.............**$45.00**

Sugar bowl, Red Rooster (Decorated), 1955, w/lid, 8-oz ..**$30.00**
Sugar bowl, Sculptured Grape, 1963, w/lid, 10-oz **$28.00**
Tray, California Ivy, 2-tier **$45.00**
Tumbler, California Ivy, 1946, 13-oz **$25.00**
Vase, bud; water bearer, Carl Romanelli, 9¼" **$200.00**

Creamer, California Ivy, $22.00; Matching sugar bowl, $25.00; Plate, 9", $12.00.

Miller Studio

Imported chalkware items began appearing in local variety stores in the early fifties. Cheerfully painted hot pad holders, thermometers, wall plaques, and many other items offered a lot of decorator appeal. While not all examples will be marked Miller Studios, good indications of that manufacturer are the small holes on the back where stapled-on cardboard packaging has been torn away. There should also be a looped wire hanger on the back, although a missing hanger does not seem to affect price. Copyright dates are often found on the sides.

Advisors: Paul and Heather August (See Directory, Miller Studios)

Thermometer, fruit grouping, copyright 1966, M, from $10.00 to $14.00.

Angels, cherub's face, orange, 1954, pr, from $18 to .**$20.00**
Angels, 2 cherubs & oval mirror, gold, 1966, 3-pc set, from
    $14 to..**$16.00**
Animals, bear toothbrush holder, M17, tan & brown, 1954,
    from $16 to...**$18.00**

Animals, bunny toothbrush holder, yellow & black, from $30 to **$32.00**

Animals, cat w/pencil holder, yellow & black, 1957, from $10 to **$12.00**

Animals, elephant toothbrush holder, M16, yellow w/faded polka dots, 1954, from $16 to **$18.00**

Animals, horse head, brown, 1951, from $12 to **$14.00**

Animals, pig, blue & white, sm, from $10 to **$10.00**

Animals, poodle plaques, black & white, round, 1957, pr, from $20 to **$25.00**

Animals, poodle plaques, pink & blue, square, 1972, pr, from $8 to **$10.00**

Animals, Scottie dog head, yellow & black, pr, from $8 to..**$10.00**

Birds, bluebird, blue & yellow, 1970, sm, pr, from $5 to **$7.00**

Birds, cardinal, red, 1972, pr, from $5 to **$7.00**

Birds, crested cockatoo, M30, light blue-grey, 1957, pr, from $18 to **$20.00**

Birds, flying pheasant, M36, red, 3-pc set, from $25 to **$30.00**

Birds, owl, white, 1978, 11", pr, from $8 to **$10.00**

Birds, swan, pink, oval, 1965, pr, from $8 to.............**$10.00**

Birds, swan plaque, pink & white, round, 1958, pr, from $14 to **$16.00**

Figures, Dutch boy & girl, yellow & red, 1953, pr, from $25 to **$28.00**

Figures, Raggedy Ann & Andy, blue & orange, pr, from $28 to **$32.00**

Fish, family, blue, 9", 4-pc set, from $10 to................**$12.00**

Fish, frolicking fish pr w/starfish, yellow, 3-pc set, from $10 to **$12.00**

Fish, gaping fish pr w/bubbles, pink, 7", 4-pc set, from $8 to **$10.00**

Fish, male & female, black, 1954, pr, from $12 to......**$14.00**

Fruit, carrot bunch, orange & green, 1971, from $6 to..**$8.00**

Fruit, cherry plaque, pink, yellow & black, square, 1956, pr, from $18 to **$20.00**

Fruit, grapes on wood, gold, 1964, from $10 to **$12.00**

Fruit, lg mushrooms, yellow & brown, 1977, 2-pc set, from $10 to **$12.00**

Hot pad holder, cabbage head w/female face, green & yellow, 1959, pr, from $12 to **$14.00**

Hot pad holder, Campbell Soup Kid boy & girl, yellow, 1964, pr, from $24 to **$26.00**

Hot pad holder, peach w/funny face, yellow, 1972, pr, from $8 to **$10.00**

Hot pad holder, sunflower, Let's Be Happy, yellow & green, 1973, pr, from $12 to **$14.00**

Note pad, bird, Make a Note, yellow & red, 1954, from $16 to **$18.00**

Note pad, fruit, Don't You Forget It, blue & red, 1968, from $10 to **$12.00**

Note pad, owl w/pencil holder, red & yellow, 1970, from $10 to **$12.00**

Thermometer, fruit bunch, 1981, from $10 to...........**$12.00**

Thermometer, potbelly stove, Weather Watcher, gold, 1965, from $13 to **$15.00**

Thermometer, Sniffy Skunk, M55, black & yellow, 1954, from $28 to **$30.00**

Model Kits

By far the majority of model kits were vehicular, and though worth collecting, especially when you can find them still mint in the box, the really big news is the figure kits. Most were made by Aurora during the 1960s. Especially hot are the movie monsters, though TV and comic strip character kits are popular with collectors too. As a rule of thumb, assembled kits are priced about half as much as conservatively priced mint-in-box kits. The condition of the box is just as important as the contents, and top collectors will usually pay an additional 15% (sometimes even more) for a box that retains the factory plastic wrap still intact. For more information, we recommend *Aurora History and Price Guide* by Bill Bruegman and *Classic Plastic Model Kits* by Rick Polizzi. *Schroeder's Toys, Antique to Modern,* contains prices and descriptions of models by a variety of manufacturers.

Club: *International Figure Kit Club*
Magazine: *Kit Builders* Magazine
Gordy's
P.O. Box 201
Sharon Center, OH 44274-0201; 216-239-1657 or FAX 216-239-2991

Magazine: *Model and Toy Collector Magazine*
137 Casterton Ave., Akron, OH 44303; 216-836-0668 or Fax 216-869-8668

AMT, 1962 Corvette hard-top convertible, MIB, $25.00.

Addar, Evel Knievel, #152, 1974, 1/12, MIB (sealed)..**$120.00**

Advent, Dam Buster, VG (VG box)............................**$15.00**

AEF Designs, Aliens, Ripley #AC-1b (escape), 1980s, 1/35, MIB **$28.00**

Airfix, Bristol Bloodhound #02309, 1992, 1/76, MIB (sealed) **$11.00**

Airfix, High Chaparral #38, 1/75, MIB..........................**$8.00**

Airfix, Space Warriors #51577, 1982, MIB....................**$15.00**

Airfix, Zoo Playset #1686, 1960s, 1/75, MIB................**$30.00**

AMT, Airwolf Helicopter #6680, 1984, 1/48, MIB........**$40.00**

AMT, Flintstones Sportscar #495, 1974, MIB................**$40.00**

AMT, Interplanetary UFO #960, 1970s, 1/635, MIB...**$140.00**

AMT, Spock, 1968, complete, NM (EX+ box)............**$160.00**

AMT, Star Trek, Klingon Cruiser #971, 1979, 1/600, MIB..**$40.00**

AMT, Vegas, Thunderbird #3105, 1979, 1/25, MIB......**$24.00**
AMT/Ertl, A-Team Van #6616, 1983, 1/25, MIB..........**$26.00**
AMT/Ertl, Monkeemobile #6058, 1990, 1/24, MIB **$50.00**
AMT/Ertl, Rescue 911, Rescue Helicopter #6416, 1993, 1/25, MIB (sealed)..**$15.00**
AMT/Ertl, Star Trek, Dr McCoy #8774, 1994, 12", MIB (sealed)..**$11.00**
Aoshimo, Vostok w/Launcher #AS-4, 1/96, MIB.......**$190.00**
Arii, Barugan #26011, 1/450, MIB............................**$10.00**
Arii, Macross, Thurverl-Salan Starship #333, MIB........**$16.00**
Articles & Objects, Star Trek, Nomad #SRC-02, 9", MIB..**$30.00**
Articles & Objects, Starman Ship #SM-01, 4", MIB......**$10.00**
ATL/PAM Murray, Robocop, 1/6, MIB......................**$60.00**
Atlas, Water Tower #703, 1962, HO, MIB **$6.00**
Aurora, Batmobile #486, 1966, 1/12, assembled **$100.00**
Aurora, Black Falcon Pirate Ship #210, 1972, 1/100, MIB..**$45.00**
Aurora, Buffalo #445, 1969, 1/16, MIB......................**$40.00**
Aurora, Comic Scenes, Superman #185, 1974, 1/8, MIB (sealed) **$90.00**
Aurora, Cougar #453, 1963, 1/8, MIB..........................**$50.00**
Aurora, Cutty Sark, 1993, NM (EX box)......................**$18.00**
Aurora, Dracula #424, 1962, original issue, 1/8, MIB..**$290.00**
Aurora, Famous Fighters, US Marine #HD412, 1956, 1/8, MIB **$120.00**
Aurora, Ford T Dragster 'Spyder' #535, 1963, 1/32, MIB .**$25.00**
Aurora, Frankenstein #449, 1972, 1/8, MIB **$150.00**
Aurora, Godzilla #466, 1969, 1/600, MIB....................**$320.00**
Aurora, Green Beret #413, 1966, foreign issue, 1/18, MIB..**$135.00**
Aurora, Hunchback of Notre Dame #481, 1969, 1/6, MIB..**$190.00**
Aurora, King Kong #468, 1969, 1/25, MIB..................**$320.00**
Aurora, Land of the Giants, Spindrift #255, 1975, 1/64, MIB..**$370.00**
Aurora, Man From UNCLE, Napoleon Solo #411, 1/12, MIB..**$300.00**
Aurora, Monsters of the Movies, Mr Hyde #655, 1975, 1/12, MIB..**$110.00**
Aurora, Mummy's Chariot, 1964, assembled, complete, NM **$200.00**
Aurora, Prehistoric Scenes, Cave, EXIB **$45.00**
Aurora, Prehistoric Scenes, Neanderthal Man, EXIB ...**$40.00**
Aurora, Robin the Boy Wonder #488, 1966, 1/18, MIB..**$140.00**
Aurora, Tarzan #820, 1967, original issue, 1/11, assembled **$60.00**
Aurora, White-Tail Deer #403, 1962, 1/18, MIB **$45.00**
Aurora, Wooly Mammoth #743, 1972, 1/13, assembled ..**$35.00**
Aurora, Zorro #801, 1965, 1/12, MIB **$375.00**
Bachmann, Birds of the World, Robin #9005, 1/1, MIB **$15.00**
Bachmann, Dogs of the World, Pointer #8006, 1/5, MIB..**$16.00**
Bandai, Battleship Andromeda 4 #536044, MIB **$25.00**
Bandai, EDF Cruiser 22 #36128, MIB..........................**$20.00**
Bandai, Gamera #503543, 1984, 1/350, MIB..............**$50.00**
Bandai, Macross, VF-1J, Battroid Valkyrie #30550, 1990, 1/72, MIB **$26.00**
Bandai, Silly Samural #503565, MIB **$6.00**
Bandai, Thunderbird 2 #38602, 1971, MIB **$40.00**
Billiken, Alien Vs Predator, 1995, vinyl, MIB **$180.00**
Billiken, Frankenstein, 1988, MIB............................**$240.00**

Billiken, Kemur-Jin, 1990, vinyl, MIB.......................**$80.00**
Billiken, Mechanic Kong, 1987, vinyl, MIB...............**$180.00**
Billiken, Thing, 1984, vinyl, MIB.............................**$200.00**
Billiken, Ultra Zone, Antlar, 1987, vinyl, MIB.............**$60.00**
Billiken, Ultra Zone, Pagos, 1990, vinyl, MIB.............**$40.00**
Boyusha, Kochi Castle #JC-4, 1/5000, MIB..................**$15.00**
Dark Horse, Frankenstein #D22, 1991, 1/18, MIB **$100.00**
Entex, Space Station #8411, 1978, MIB.......................**$55.00**
Glencoe, US Paratrooper #5902, 1991, 1/10, MIB (sealed) .**$15.00**
Halcyon, Predator 2 #13, 1994, MIB............................**$20.00**

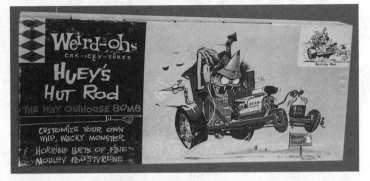

Hawk, Huey's Hut Rod #538, 1963, MIB, $40.00. (Photo courtesy June Moon)

Hawk, Indian Totem Poles, Thunderbird #555, 1966, MIB ..**$50.00**
Horizon, DC Comics, Joker #56, 1993, 1/6, MIB.........**$50.00**
Horizon, Phantom of the Opera #1, 1988, MIB **$80.00**
ITC, Neanderthal Man #3808, 1959, 1/8, MIB **$80.00**
Lifelike, Cro-Magnon Man #383, 1973, 1/8, MIB (sealed).....**$25.00**
Lifelike, Honest John w/Launcher #9656, 1974, 1/40, MIB...**$85.00**
Linberg, 13th Century Clock #339, 1969, 16", MIB......**$28.00**
Lunar Models, Batmobile #SF039, 1/25, MIB...............**$90.00**
Marusan, Ben Casey MD, Visible Man #510, 1968, 1/5, MIB **$70.00**
Monogram, A-10 Warthog Jet, MIB..............................**$15.00**
Monogram, Beer Wagon, 1995, M (NM sealed box)...**$25.00**
Monogram, Elvira Mobile, #2783, 1/24, MIB (sealed).**$30.00**
Monogram, Lion Diorama #102, 1961, MIB **$40.00**
Monogram, Mork & Mindy Jeep #2261, 1979, 1/24, MIB..**$35.00**
Monogram, Mummy #6010, 1983, 1/8, MIB (sealed) ..**$50.00**
Monogram, Space Buggy #194, 1969, 1/48, MIB **$110.00**
Monogram, Wolfman #6009, 1983 MIB (sealed)..........**$70.00**
MPC, Beatle's Yellow Submarine, MIB (sealed) **$425.00**
MPC, Good Guys Taxi #616, 1/25, MIB......................**$90.00**
MPC, Hogan's Heroes Jeep #402, 1968, 1/25, MIB **$60.00**
MPC, Ironside's Van #3012, 1970, 1/20, MIB.............**$100.00**
MPC, Six Million Dollar Man, Fight for Survival #602, 1975, 1/12, MIB (sealed) **$40.00**
MPC, Space: 1999, Hawk Spaceship #1904, 1977, 1/72, MIB **$115.00**
MPC, Star Wars, X-Wing Fighter, 1977, NM (VG box) ..**$23.00**
Nikken, Eagle Apollo Lunar Module #1, 1969, 1/80, MIB **$20.00**
Palmer, US Navy Vanguard Missile #106, 1958, 1/48, MIB.**$250.00**
Palmer Plastics, Animals of the World, Atlantic Sailfish, 1950s, NM (EX box) **$15.00**
Pyro, Indian Medicine Man #282, 1960s, 1/8, MIB ...**$100.00**
Pyro, Texas Cowboy #284, 1960s, 1/8, MIB **$65.00**
Renwal, Human Skeleton, 1950s-60s, EXIB................**$23.00**

Renwal, Reptile Science, NM (VG+ box) **$38.00**
Revell, A-7A Corsair II, MIB (sealed) **$10.00**
Revell, Apollo Spacecraft, 1969, NMIB **$65.00**
Revell, CHiPs, Helicopter #6102, 1980, 1/32, MIB **$20.00**
Revell, Discovery Shuttle #4543, 1988, 1/44, MIB
   (sealed) **$15.00**

Revell, Drag Nut, 1963, MIB, $120.00. (Photo courtesy June Moon)

Revell, GI Joe, Attack Vehicle #8901, 1982, 7½", MIB
   (sealed) **$25.00**
Revell, Jupiter C #1819, 1958, 1/96, MIB **$270.00**
Revell, Moon Ship #1825, 1957, 1/96, MIB **$200.00**
Revell, Revell, Dr Suess, Game of the Yertle #2100, 1960,
   EXIB **$125.00**
Revell, Robin Hood (Disney cartoon movie), MIB **$95.00**
Revell, Space Persuit #1850, 1969, MIB (sealed) **$310.00**
Screamin', Flash Gordon, 1993, 1/4, G (EX box) **$32.00**
Screamin', Star Wars, C-3PO #3550, 1995, 1/6, MIB **$45.00**
Screamin', Star Wars, Yoda #3300, 1992, 1/4, MIB **$40.00**
Superior Plastics, Giant American Bull Frog #4600, 1960, 1/1,
   MIB **$40.00**
Tomy, Disney, Goofy #4, 1980s, MIB **$50.00**
Tsukuda, Wolfman #40, 1985, 1/5, MIB **$40.00**
Union, Stingray (TV Show), 1983, MIB **$70.00**

Moon and Star

Moon and Star (originally called Palace) was first produced in the 1880s by John Adams & Company of Pittsburgh. But because the glassware was so heavy to transport, it was made for only a few years. In the 1960s, Joseph Weishar of Wheeling, West Virginia, owner of Island Mould & Machine Company, reproduced some of the original molds and incorporated the pattern into approximately forty new and different items. Two of the largest distributors of this line were L.E. Smith of Mt. Pleasant, Pennsylvania, who pressed their own glass, and L.G. Wright of New Martinsville, West Virginia, who had theirs pressed by Fostoria, Fenton, and Westmoreland. Both companies carried a large and varied assortment of shapes and colors. Several other companies were involved in its manufacture as well, especially of the smaller items. All in all, there may be as many as one hundred different pieces, plenty to keep you interested as you do your searching.

The glassware is already very collectible, even though it is still being made on a limited basis. Colors you'll see most often are amberina (yellow shading to orange-red), green, amber, crystal, light blue, and ruby. Pieces in ruby and light blue are most collectible and harder to find than the other colors, which seem to be abundant. Purple, pink, cobalt, amethyst, tan slag, and light green and blue opalescent were made, too, but on a lesser scale.

Current L.E. Smith catalogs contain a dozen or so pieces that are still available in crystal, pink, cobalt (lighter than the old shade), and these colors with an iridized finish. A new color, teal green, was introduced in 1992, and the water set in sapphire blue opalescent was pressed in 1993 by Weishar Enterprises. They are now producing limited editions in various colors and shapes, but they are marking their glassware 'Weishar,' to distinguish it from the old line. Cranberry Ice (light transparent pink) was introduced in 1994.

Our values are given for ruby and light blue. For amberina, green, and amber, deduct 30%. These colors are less in demand, and unless your prices are reasonable, you may find them harder to sell. Read *Mysteries of the Moon and Star* by George and Linda Breeze for more information.

Advisor: Ruth Grizel (See Directory, Westmoreland)

Newsletter: *National Moon & Star News*
George and Linda Breeze
4207 Fox Creek, Mt. Vernon, IL 62864

Ashtray, allover pattern, moons form scallops along rim, 4
   rests, 8" dia **$25.00**
Ashtray, moons at rim, star in base, 6-sided, 5½" **$18.00**
Ashtray, moons at rim, star in base, 6-sided, 8½" **$25.00**
Banana boat, allover pattern, moons form scallops along rim,
   9", from $28 to **$32.00**
Banana boat, allover pattern, moons form scallops along rim,
   12" **$45.00**
Basket, allover pattern, moons form scallops along rim, footed, incurvate upright handles, 4", from $12 to **$25.00**
Basket, allover pattern, moons form scallops along rim, solid
   handle, 9", from $50 to **$75.00**
Bell, pattern along sides, plain rim & handle, blue or pink
   opalescent, 6" **$45.00**
Bell, pattern along sides, w/plain rim & handle, 6", from $30
   to **$40.00**
Bowl, allover pattern, footed, crimped rim, 7½" **$35.00**
Butter dish, allover pattern, scalloped foot, patterned lid &
   finial, 6x5½" dia, from $45 to **$50.00**
Butter dish, allover pattern, stars form scallops along rim of
   base, star finial, oval, ¼-lb, 8½" **$45.00**
Butter/cheese dish, patterned lid, plain base, 7" dia .. **$65.00**
Cake plate, allover pattern, low collared base, 13" dia, minimum value **$65.00**
Cake salver, allover pattern w/scalloped rim, raised foot
   w/scalloped edge, 5x12" dia, minimum value **$65.00**
Cake stand, allover pattern, plate removes from standard, 2-pc, 11" dia, from $75 to **$95.00**
Candle bowl, allover pattern, footed, 8", from $28 to **$32.00**
Candle holder, allover pattern, bowl style w/ring handle,
   2x5½" **$18.00**

Candle holders, allover pattern, flared & scalloped foot, 6",
pr **$50.00**
Candle holders, allover pattern, flared base, 4½", pr .**$25.00**
Candle lamp, patterned shade, clear base, 2-pc, 7½".**$25.00**
Candy dish, allover pattern on base & lid, footed ball shape,
6" **$25.00**
Canister, allover pattern, 1-lb or 2-lb, from $12 to......**$15.00**
Canister, allover pattern, 3½-lb or 5-lb, from $18 to ..**$22.00**
Chandelier, ruffled dome shape w/allover pattern, 10"..**$100.00**
Cheese dish, patterned base, clear plain lid, 9½", from $65
to..**$70.00**
Compote, allover pattern, footed, flared crimped rim, 5"...**$22.00**
Compote, allover pattern, raised foot, patterned lid & finial,
7½x6" **$40.00**
Compote, allover pattern, raised foot on stem, patterned lid
& finial, 10x8"..**$65.00**
Compote, allover pattern, raised foot on stem, patterned lid
& finial, 12x8"..**$75.00**
Compote, allover pattern, scalloped foot on stem, patterned
lid & finial, 8x4", from $35 to **$40.00**
Compote, allover pattern, scalloped rim, footed, 5½x8"..**$35.00**
Compote, allover pattern, scalloped rim, footed, 5x6½", from
$18 to **$20.00**
Compote, allover pattern, scalloped rim, footed, 7x10"..**$45.00**

Compote with rolled edge, 12", $65.00.

Console bowl, allover pattern, scalloped rim, flared foot
w/flat edge, 8"..**$25.00**
Creamer, allover pattern, raised foot w/scalloped edge,
5¾x3" **$35.00**

Creamer and sugar bowl, LG Wright, $75.00.

Creamer & sugar bowl (open), disk foot, sm, from $25 to.**$28.00**
Cruet, vinegar; 6¾", from $65 to **$75.00**
Decanter, bulbous w/allover pattern, plain neck, foot ring, orig-
inal patterned stopper, 32-oz, 12", from $95 to......**$100.00**
Epergne, allover pattern, 1-lily, flared bowl, scalloped
foot **$95.00**
Epergne, allover pattern, 2-pc, 9"............................**$65.00**
Goblet, water; plain rim & foot, 4½" **$12.00**
Goblet, water; plain rim & foot, 5¾" **$15.00**
Jardiniere, allover pattern, patterned lid & finial, 9¾" ..**$85.00**
Jardiniere/cracker jar, allover pattern, patterned lid & finial,
7¼"...**$65.00**
Jardiniere/tobacco jar, allover pattern, patterned lid & finial,
6"...**$45.00**
Jelly dish, allover pattern, patterned lid & finial, stemmed
foot, 10½" **$65.00**
Jelly dish, patterned body w/plain flat rim & disk foot, patterned lid & finial, 6¾x3½"..................................**$35.00**

**Lamp, miniature; in amber
and green, $100.00; in red,
$175.00; in blue, $150.00;
in milk glass, $200.00.**

Lamp, oil or electric; allover pattern, all original, 24", from
$200 to..**$250.00**
Lamp, oil; allover pattern, all original, 10", from $100 to ...**$125.00**
Lighter, allover patterned body, metal fittings, from $50 to..**$60.00**
Nappy, allover pattern, crimped rim, 2¾x6" **$18.00**
Pitcher, water; patterned body, ice lip, straight sides, plain
disk foot, 1-qt, 7½" **$95.00**
Plate, patterned body & center, smooth rim, 8".........**$35.00**
Relish bowl, 6 lg scallops form allover pattern, 1½x8".**$35.00**
Relish dish, allover pattern, 1 plain handle, 2x8" dia.**$40.00**
Relish tray, patterned moons form scalloped rim, star in base,
rectangular, 8" **$35.00**
Salt & pepper shakers, allover pattern, metal tops, 4x2",
pr..**$25.00**
Salt cellar, allover pattern, scalloped rim, sm flat foot..**$8.00**
Sherbet, patterned body & foot w/plain rim & stem,
4¼x3¾"...**$25.00**
Soap dish, allover pattern, oval, 2x6" **$12.00**
Spooner, allover pattern, straight sides, scalloped rim, raised
foot, 5¼x4", from $45 to **$50.00**
Sugar bowl, allover pattern, patterned lid & finial, sm flat
foot, 5¼x4", from $35 to **$40.00**
Sugar bowl, allover pattern, straight sides, patterned lid &
finial, scalloped foot, 8x4½", from $35 to.............**$40.00**
Sugar shaker, allover pattern, metal top, 4½x3½" **$50.00**
Syrup pitcher, allover pattern, metal lid, 4½x3½".......**$75.00**

Toothpick holder, allover pattern, scalloped rim, sm flat foot **$10.00**
Tumbler, iced tea; no pattern at flat rim or on disk foot, 11-oz, 5½" **$20.00**
Tumbler, juice; no pattern at rim or on disk foot, 5-oz, 3½", from $12 to..**$14.00**
Tumbler, no pattern at rim or on disk foot, 7-oz, 4¼", from $12 to...**$15.00**

Mortens Studio

During the 1940s, a Swedish sculpturer by the name of Oscar Mortens left his native country and moved to the United States, settling in Arizona. Along with his partner, Gunnar Thelin, he founded the Mortens Studios, a firm that specialized in the manufacture of animal figurines. Though he preferred dogs of all breeds, horses, cats, and wild animals were made, too, but on a much smaller scale.

The material he used was a plaster-like composition molded over a wire framework for support and reinforcement. Crazing is common, and our values reflect pieces with a moderate amount, but be sure to check for more serious damage before you buy. Most pieces are marked with either an ink stamp or a paper label.

Beagle, recumbent..**$48.00**
Borzoi, brown or black, #749 ....**$125.00**
Chihuahua, #865 ....**$85.00**
Collie, standing, 6x7" **$90.00**
Doberman, #783 ....**$95.00**
English Setter, #848...**$65.00**
German Shepherd pup, 3½x3½".....................**$35.00**

Horse, grazing on grassy base, $90.00.

Pekingese, standing, 3½x4½" **$95.00**
Pomeranian, #739 ....**$95.00**
Poodle, gray, 4"...**$70.00**
Spaniel, black & white, #560, mini................**$65.00**
Springer Spaniel, #745 ....**$95.00**

Morton Pottery

Six different potteries operated in Morton, Illinois, during a period of ninety-nine years. The first pottery, estab-lished by six Rapp brothers who had immigrated from Germany in the mid-1870s, was named Morton Pottery Works. It was in operation from 1877 to 1915 when it was reorganized and renamed Morton Earthenware Company. Its operation, 1915 – 1917, was curtailed by World War I. Cliftwood Art Potteries, Inc. was the second pottery to be established. It operated from 1920 until 1940 when it was sold and renamed Midwest Potteries, Inc. In March 1944 the pottery burned and was never rebuilt. Morton Pottery Company was the longest running of Morton's potteries. It was in operation from 1922 until 1976. The last pottery to open was the American Art Potteries. It was in production from 1947 until 1963.

All of Morton's potteries were spin-offs from the original Rapp brothers. Second, third, and fourth generation Rapps followed the tradition of their ancestors to produce a wide variety of pottery. Rockingham and yellow ware to Art Deco, giftwares, and novelties were produced by Morton's potteries.

To learn more about these companies, we recommend *Morton's Potteries: 99 Years, Vol. II,* by Doris and Burdell Hall.

Advisors: Doris and Burdell Hall (See Directory, Morton Pottery)

Morton Pottery Works – Morton Earthenware Company, 1877 – 1917

Bank, acorn shape, advertising Acorn Stoves, Herbage Green **$50.00**
Bank, acorn shape, advertising Acorn Stoves, Rocking-ham **$40.00**
Crock, sauerkraut, 4-gal w/10" dia press, Rockingham ...**$200.00**
Jug, Dutch, cobalt, 3-pt................................**$130.00**
Jug, Dutch, Rockingham, 3-pt........................**$65.00**
Jug, yellow ware w/brown & green spatter, #245, 3-pt..**$150.00**
Marble, blue, 4½" **$18.00**
Marble, Rockingham, 4½" **$10.00**
Stein, German motto, Herbage Green, 1-pt.................**$87.50**
Stein, German motto, Rockingham, 1-pt.....................**$70.00**
Urinal, shovel shape, Rockingham **$45.00**
Urinal, shovel shape, yellow ware **$55.00**

Cliftwood Art Potteries, Inc., 1920 – 1940

Beer set, barrel pitcher+6 steins, Apple Green **$140.00**
Bowl, storage; complete nested set, drip glaze, w/lids..**$60.00**
Bowl, storage; complete nested set, Old Rose, w/lids **$50.00**
Chocolate/lemonade set, pitcher & 6 mugs, chocolate drip...**$175.00**
Clock, donut shape, Herbage Green, 8½" **$90.00**
Figurine, eagle, airbrushed natural colors..................**$95.00**
Figurine, elephant, trumpeting, Old Rose..................**$50.00**
Flower frog, lily pad, chocolate drip, 6" **$35.00**
Flower frog, lily pad, Old Rose, 4"............................**$24.00**
Flower frog, Lorelei, Herbage Green, 6½".................**$60.00**
Flower frog, turtle, blue-gray drip, 5½" **$25.00**
Flower frog, turtle, blue-pink drip, 4"........................**$20.00**
Pretzel jar, barrel shape, Apple Green, w/lid..............**$60.00**
Wine jug, w/ceramic-capped cork, chocolate drip **$50.00**

Midwest Potteries, Inc., 1940 – 1944

Bookends, leaping deer, Deco style, blue, pr **$50.00**
Bud vase, hand, right or left, matt flesh, 6½" **$20.00**
Bud vase, hand, right or left, matt white, 4½" **$15.00**
Figurine, deer, stylized, white w/gold decor, 12".......**$25.00**
Figurine, deer, stylized, 24k gold trim, 10½" **$24.00**
Figurine, deer w/antlers, white w/gold trim, 12" **$40.00**
Figurine, mountain goat, airbrushed brown, 9½" **$35.00**
Figurine, sailfish, airbrushed blue & yellow, 9" **$45.00**
Figurine, sunfish, airbrushed brown & yellow, 11".....**$50.00**

Figurine, swan, brown with gold decoration, 4½", $24.00. (Photo courtesy Doris and Burdell Hall)

Miniature, frog, green & yellow, 1"............................**$10.00**
Miniature, hen, blue & green, 1¼"............................**$10.00**
Miniature, kissing rabbits, white w/gold trim, 2½" **$25.00**
Miniature, rooster, brown & yellow, 2"......................**$10.00**
Miniature, turtle, green & yellow, 1"..........................**$10.00**
Planter, blue heron beside seashell, blue & white w/gold
    trim **$35.00**
Planter, calico cat, blue & yellow spatter....................**$20.00**
Planter, deer, reclining, brown & white **$18.00**
Planter, gingham dog, blue & yellow spatter **$18.00**
TV lamp, owl, airbrush natural colors, Kron line, 12" ..**$65.00**
TV lamp, poodle & pug, airbrushed natural colors, Kron line,
    13" **$75.00**

Morton Pottery Company, 1922 – 1976

Bookends, parrots, multicolor, pr..............................**$40.00**
Bowl, mixing; #600, blue & burgundy spatter on white, set of
    3...**$150.00**
Clock, elephant, trunk over head, brown...................**$75.00**
Figurine, Boston terrier, black & white.......................**$25.00**
Figurine, wren on tree stump, multicolor...................**$12.00**
Flowerpot soaker, hound dog **$18.00**
Humidor pipe finial on lid, brown.............................**$30.00**
Incense burner, Oriental figure, brown **$40.00**
Matchbox holder, wall-hanging style, green................**$60.00**
Milk pitcher, blue w/hand-painted Deco black cats ...**$30.00**
Pet feeding bowl, green..**$15.00**
Planter, kitten w/baby buggy.....................................**$18.00**
Planter, rocking horse...**$20.00**
Planter, rocking pig **$18.00**
Planter, rocking rooster **$22.00**
Salt box, wall-hanging style, green **$60.00**
TV lamp, black panther..**$50.00**
TV lamp, buffalo..**$100.00**

American Art Potteries, 1947 – 1963

Console set, stylized petal bowl #20+flower candle holders
    #703, airbrushed rose & gray, 3-pc **$25.00**
Creamer, bird, #67, airbrushed gray & green **$10.00**
Figurine, elephant, trumpeting, #95, gray, 7½x7½" **$35.00**
Figurine, gazelle, stylized, #503, white, 12" **$25.00**
Figurine, tiger, #506, brown & tan, 7x12" **$40.00**
Flower frog, titmouse, #98, mauve & gray, 8½"..........**$15.00**
Flower frog, turtle, #412, green, 2½" **$15.00**
Lamp, French poodle, black & pink, 15" **$45.00**
Lamp, mountain goat, airbrushed green & brown, 14"..**$54.00**
Planter, baby buggy, #452, pink & blue, 5½x7"..........**$12.00**
Planter, fish, #324, mauve & pink, 4½"......................**$14.00**
Planter, lamb, #456, white & pink, 8½" **$25.00**

Planter, rabbit by stump, multicolored, 4¾", $15.00. (Photo courtesy Doris and Burdell Hall)

TV lamp, deer w/fawn, #322, yellow & green............**$40.00**
TV lamp, horse, #327, rose & gray.............................**$38.00**
TV lamp, sunfish, #324, green & tan, pr.....................**$25.00**
TV lamp, swordfish, #307, white................................**$45.00**
Vase, double cornucopia, #208, white & gold.............**$22.00**
Vase, ruffled tulip shape, pink & mauve, 9"...............**$24.00**

Moss Rose

Though the Moss Rose pattern has been produced by Staffordshire and American pottery companies alike since the mid-1800s, the line we're dealing with here was primarily made between the late 1950s into the 1970s by Japanese manufacturers. Even today you'll occasionally see a tea set or a small candy dish for sale in some of the chain stores. (The collectors who're already picking this line up refer to it as Moss Rose, but we've seen it advertised under the name 'Victorian Rose.') The pattern consists of a briar rose with dark green mossy leaves on stark white glaze. Occasionally an item is trimmed in gold. In addition to dinnerware, many accessories and novelties were made as well.

Refer to *Schroeder's Antiques Price Guide* for information on the early Moss Rose pattern.

Advisor: April Tvorak (See Directory, Fire-King)

Bowl, sauce **$4.00**

Bowl, soup	**$6.00**
Butter dish	**$15.00**
Cottage cheese dish	**$10.00**
Cup & saucer	**$6.00**
Cup & saucer, demitasse	**$8.00**
Egg cup, sm.	**$6.00**
Incense burner, gold trim, 3-footed, w/domed lid, 3¼"	**$15.00**
Plate, dinner	**$5.00**
Plate, salad	**$4.00**
Platter	**$12.00**
Teapot	**$20.00**
Teapot, demitasse	**$25.00**

Teapot, electric; Royal Sealey label, gold trim, 7", $22.00.

Motion Clocks (Electric)

Novelty clocks with some type of motion or animation were popular in spring-powered or wind-up form for hundreds of years. Today they bring thousands of dollars when sold. Electric-powered or motor-driven clocks first appeared in the late 1930s and were produced until quartz clocks became the standard, with the 1950s being the era during which they reached the height of their production.

Four companies led their field. They were Mastercrafters, United, Haddon, and Spartus in order of productivity. Mastercrafters was the earliest and longest-lived, making clocks from the late forties until the late eighties. (They did, however, drop out of business several times during this long period.) United began making clocks in the early fifties and continued until the early sixties. Haddon followed in the same time frame, and Spartus was in production from the late fifties until the mid-sixties.

These clocks are well represented in the listings that follow; prices are for examples in excellent condition and working. With an average age of forty years, many now need repair. Dried-out grease and dirt easily cause movements and motions not to function. The other nemesis of many motion clocks is deterioration of the fiber gears. Originally intended to keep the clocks quiet, fiber gears have not held up like their metal counterparts. For fully restored clocks, add $50.00 to $75.00 to our values. (Full restoration includes complete cleaning of motor and movement, repair of same; cleaning and polishing face and bezel; cleaning and polishing case and repairing if necessary; and installing new line cord, plug,

and light bulb if needed.) Brown is the most common case color for plastic clocks. Add 10% to 20% or more for cases in onyx (mint green) or any light shade. If any parts noted below are missing, value can drop one-third to one-half. We must stress that 'as is' clocks will not bring these prices. Deteriorated, non-working clocks may be worth less that half of these values.

Note: When original names are not known, names have been assigned.

Advisors: Sam and Anna Samuelian (See Directory, Motion Clocks)

Haddon

Based in Chicago, Illinois, Haddon produced an attractive line of clocks. They used composition cases that were hand painted, and sturdy Hansen movements and motions. This is the only clock line for which new replacement motors are still available.

Granny rocking (Home Sweet Home), composition, electric, Haddon, from $100.00 to $125.00. (Photo courtesy Sam and Anna Samuelian)

Rocking Horse (Rancho), composition, electric, from $150 to	**$200.00**
Teeter Totter, children on seesaw, electric, from $125 to	**$175.00**

Mastercrafters

Based in Chicago, Illinois, this company produced many of the most appealing and popular collectible motion clocks on today's market. Cases were made of plastic, with earlier examples being a sturdy urea plastic that imparted quality, depth, and shine to their finishes. Clock movements were relatively simple and often supplied by Sessions Clock Company, who also made many of their own clocks.

Airplane, Bakelite & chrome, electric, from $175 to	**$225.00**
Blacksmith, plastic, electric, from $75 to	**$100.00**
Carousel, plastic, carousel front, from $175 to	**$225.00**
Church, w/bell ringer, plastic, electric	**$100.00**
Girl swinging, plastic, electric, from $100 to	**$125.00**
Swinging Bird, plastic, w/cage front, from $125 to	**$150.00**

Swinging Playmates, plastic, w/fence, electric, from $100 to **$125.00**
Waterfall, plastic, electric...**$100.00**

Fireplace, plastic, electric, Mastercrafters, from $60.00 to $90.00. (Photo courtesy Sam and Anna Samuelian)

Spartus

This company made clocks well into the eighties, but most later clocks were not animated. Cases were usually plastic, and most clocks featured animals.

Cat w/flirty eyes, plastic, electric, from $25 to **$40.00**
Panda bear, plastic, eyes move, electric, from $25 to........**$40.00**
Water wheel (lg style), plastic, electric, from $20 to...**$30.00**
Waterfall & wheel, plastic, electric, from $50 to **$75.00**

United

Based in Brooklyn, New York, United made mostly cast-metal cases finished in gold or bronze. Their movements were somewhat more complex than Mastercrafters'. Some of their clocks contained musical movements, which while pleasing can be annoying when continuously run.

Ballerina, wooden, electric, from $75 to....................**$125.00**
Bobbing chicks, metal case, various colors, electric, from $35 to **$50.00**
Bobbing chicks, wooden house, green & red, electric, from $40 to...**$60.00**
Cowboy w/rope, metal, wood base, electric, from $100 to...**$150.00**
Dancers, metal w/square glass dome, electric, from $100 to **$150.00**
Fireplace, metal, gold, electric, from $50 to **$75.00**
Fireplace w/man & woman, spinning wheel & moving fire, electric, from $125 to **$150.00**
Fishing boy, metal, fishing pole & fish move, electric, from $125 to...**$150.00**
Huck Finn, fishing pole & fish move, electric, from $150 to **$175.00**
Hula girl & drummer, wooden, electric, from $200 to..**$250.00**
Majorette w/rotating baton, electric, from $75 to **$100.00**
Owl, metal owl on wooden base, eyes move, electric, from $75 to...**$100.00**
Windmill, pink plastic case, electric, minor cracks in plastic, from $75 to..**$125.00**

Miscellaneous

God Bless America, flag waves, electric, from $75 to..**$100.00**
Klocker Spaniel, electric, from $50 to **$75.00**
Poodle, various colors, electric, from $75 to............**$100.00**

Motorcycle Collectibles

At some point in nearly everyone's life, they've experienced at least a brief love affair with a motorcycle. What could be more exhilarating than the open road — the wind in your hair, the sun on your back, and no thought for the cares of today or what tomorrow might bring. For some, the passion never diminished. For most of us, it's a fond memory. Regardless of which description best fits you personally, you will probably enjoy the old advertising and sales literature, books and magazines, posters, photographs, banners, etc., showing the old Harleys and Indians, and the club pins, dealership jewelry and clothing, and scores of other items of memorabilia in which collectors are now beginning to show considerable interest. For more information and lots of color photographs, we recommend *Motorcycle Collectibles With Values* by Leila Dunbar (Schiffer Publishing).

See also License Plates.

Bank, Liberty Classic, 1955 Chevy Sedan Delivery, red & gold w/Indian logo, 1/25 scale, MIB **$45.00**
Belt buckle, 1958 Motorcycle Assn of American Tour Award..**$75.00**
Book, Story of Harley-Davidson, company history, 1960s, 56 pages, 8½x11" **$35.00**
Brochure, AMF/Harley-Davidson V-Twin Motorcycles, color, 1976, 4 pages, EX **$15.00**
Brochure, Indian, America's Pioneer Motorcycle, 1942, 11x17", from $100 to **$200.00**

Brochure, Indian Motorcycles, 1940, 2-color, EX, $90.00. (Photo courtesy of Dunbar Gallery)

Brochure, Indian, the Standard Motorcycle of the World, red motorcycle w/sidecar cover, 8 pages, 4x9", w/mailer **$125.00**
Cap, Marlon Brando visor style, 1950s......................**$60.00**
Catalog, Harley-Davidson, 1975, EX...........................**$45.00**
Envelope, Indian Motorcycle logo at corner, 8x9".......**$15.00**

Folder, An Interesting Story of a Great Indian Chief & a Beautiful Indian Princess, black & white, 6½x8½", EX............**$100.00**

Folder, Indian Scout, the Universal Motorcycle, photos of Indian scaling Multnomah Falls, 6x8½" **$125.00**

Handbill, Harley-Davidson for 1940, EX......................**$65.00**

Handbill, Harley-Davidson Sportster, 1957, 12x17", M, $80.00. (Photo courtesy Dunbar Gallery)

Jacket, black leather, Harley-Davidson logo, 50th Anniversary Sturgis patch, from $100 to **$350.00**

Kidney belt, black leather, 1950s.................................**$55.00**

Letterhead, Hendee Mfg, 2-page letter from factory offering discount & 5% war tax, w/Indian logo, w/matching envelope..**$25.00**

Magazine, Big Bike, 1970, July **$5.00**

Magazine, Custom Chopper, 1971, November...............**$5.00**

Magazine, Indian News, 1928, June, from $20 to **$75.00**

Magazine, The Enthusiast, a Magazine for Motorcyclists, 1944, from $15 to..**$50.00**

Medal, AMA Third Place, 1930s, from $100 to..........**$300.00**

Money clip, AMA Award, dated 1961, MOC................**$70.00**

Patch, Harley-Davidson winged logo, 10", from $50 to...**$100.00**

Pin, AMA Gypsy Tour 1941, multicolor logo...............**$75.00**

Pin, AMA Year 1, cloisonne, clasp back **$10.00**

Pin, AMA/Gypsy Tour, motorcycle on top of AMA logo, 1941, EX...**$75.00**

Pin, Harley-Davidson Factory Visitor, silver w/motorcycle atop stylized wings **$45.00**

Pin, Outlaw Motorcycle Club..**$50.00**

Plate holder, Harley-Davidson logo on brass, marked Made in USA at bottom, EX **$20.00**

Sign, Harley-Davidson Cigarettes, tin, smiling couple on motorcycle behind product name, 1984, 17x21" ..**$55.00**

Siren cover, Harley-Davidson, stainless steel, 1958, 5½", NM..**$60.00**

Spark plugs, Harley-Davidson, gold, black & white box w/logo **$20.00**

Tie bar, AMA Gypsy Tour, 1939, gold motorcycle dangles from chain, rare **$200.00**

Tin, Harley-Davidson Leather Lacquer, orange & black paper label, pry lid, 1940s, ¼-pt.................................**$25.00**

Tin, Indian Head Hydraulic Brake Fluid, cone-top w/screw lid, 6x3½" dia..**$25.00**

Windbreaker, Harley-Davidson, 1970s **$50.00**

Movie Posters

Although many sizes of movie posters were made and all sizes are collectible, the most collected size today is still the one-sheet, 27" wide and 41" long. Movie-memorabilia collecting is as diverse as films themselves. Popular areas include specific films such as Gone With the Wind, Wizard of Oz, and others; specific stars — from the greats to character actors; directors such as Hitchcock, Ford, Speilberg, and others; specific film types such as B-Westerns, all-Black casts, sports related, Noir, fifties teen, sixties beach, musicals, crime, silent, radio characters, cartoons, and serials; specific characters such as Tarzan, Superman, Ellery Queen, Blondie, Ma and Pa Kettle, Whistler, and Nancy Drew; specific artists like Rockwell, Davis, Frazetta, Flagg, and others; specific art themes, for instance, policeman, firemen, horses, attorneys, doctors, or nurses (this list is endless). And some collectors just collect posters they like. In the past twenty years, movie memorabilia has steadily increased in value, and in the last few years the top price paid for a movie poster has reached $200,000.00. Movie memorabilia is a new field for collectors. In the past, only a few people knew where to find posters. Recently, auctions on the East and West coasts have created much publicity, attracting many new collectors. Many posters are still moderately priced, and the market is expanding, allowing even new collectors to see the value of their collections increase.

Advisors: Cleophas and Lou Ann Wooley, Movie Poster Service (See Directory, Movie Posters)

Agony & the Ecstasy, Charlton Heston & Rex Harrison, 1964, 27x41" **$45.00**

Alfred Hitchcock's Psycho, 1960, 1-sheet, NM, $695.00.

Aristocats, Disney, 1971, 27x41", NM.........................**$55.00**

Arrival, Charlie Sheen, 27x41"....................................**$10.00**

As You Like It, reissue, 1948, 14x22" **$25.00**

Beach Blanket Bingo, Annette Funicello & Frankie Avalon, 1965, 14x22" **$50.00**

Beast From the Haunted Cave, 1959, 27x41" **$185.00**

Beast Must Die, 1974, 27x41", NM..............................**$40.00**

Beast of the Yellow Night/Creature With the Blue Hand, 1971, 27x41", EX **$25.00**

Beatles' Anthology III, Their Music, Their Story, Their Video, double sided, NM..**$9.00**

Ben, 1972, 27x41", EX $40.00

Beyond the Door, 1974, 27x41", EX........................... $20.00

Boys' Town, Mickey Rooney & Spencer Tracy, reissue, 1957, 14x22" $40.00

Buddy Holly Story, 1978, 27x41", NM......................... $30.00

Butch Cassidy & the Sundance Kid, Paul Newman & Robert Redford, reissue, 1973, 27x41" $50.00

Caddy, Jerry Lewis & Dean Martin, reissue, 1964, 27x41".. $35.00

Caveman, Ringo Starr, 27x41", EX................................ $30.00

Chaplin Revue, 2-color, 1958, 27x41" $65.00

Clambake, Elvis Presley, 1967, 27x41" $65.00

Come Dance With Me, Brigitte Bardot, 1960, 27x41", NM $75.00

Countess From Hong Kong, Sophia Loren & Marlon Brando, 1967, 27x41" $40.00

Crush, Alicia Silverstone, double-sided, 27x41"........... $15.00

Dial M for Murder, Grace Kelly & Ray Milland, 1954, 27x41" $900.00

Diary of a Madman, Vincent Price, 1963, 27x41", EX. $65.00

Dirty Harry, Clint Eastwood, Belgium, 1977, 14x22"... $225.00

Dr Phibes Rises Again, 1972, 27x41", EX..................... $50.00

Eraser, Arnold Schwarzenegger & Vanessa Williams, double-sided, 27x41" $15.00

Father of the Bride, Elizabeth Taylor, Spencer Tracy & Joan Bennett, reissue, 1962, 27x41", NM $25.00

Frankenstein, the Monster From Hell, 1973, 27x41", EX+ $60.00

Frankenstein Created Woman/Curse of the Mummy's Shroud, 1967, 27x41", EX+ $45.00

Frankie & Johnny, Elvis Presley, 1966, 27x41" $75.00

Frogs, 1972, 27x41", NM... $35.00

From Beyond the Grave, 1974, 27x41", NM $45.00

From Earth to the Moon, 1958, 27x41", NM $85.00

Funny Face, Audrey Hepburn & Fred Astaire, 1957, 14x22", NM $125.00

Funny Girl, Barbara Streisand, reissue, 1972, 27x41".. $35.00

Further Perils of Laurel & Hardy, 1967, 27x41", EX+.. $45.00

Gene Krupa Story, Sal Mineo, 1960, 41x81", M.......... $75.00

Ghost & Mr Chicken, Don Knotts, 1966, 27x41"........ $40.00

Halloween II, 1981, 27x41", NM.................................. $35.00

Hawaii, Julie Andrews & Max VonSydow, 1966, 27x41".. $35.00

Horse Soldiers, John Wayne & William Holden, 1959, 27x41" $200.00

I Passed for White, 1960, 27x41", EX........................... $75.00

Island of Terror/The Projected Man, 1966, 27x41", EX. $30.00

Judge Dread, Sylvester Stallone, 1995, 27x41"............ $10.00

Kelley's Heroes, 1971, 27x41", VG............................... $65.00

Kingpin, Woody Harrelson, MGM, 27x41" $8.00

Lady & the Tramp, 1962 reissue, 27x41"....................... $95.00

Lion in Winter, Katharine Hepburn & Peter O'Toole, 1968, 14x22" $35.00

M*A*S*H, Donald Sutherland, 1970, 27x41" $85.00

Mad Love, Drew Barrymore & Chris O'Donnel, 27x41". $10.00

Magic World of Topo Gigio, Columbia, 1965, NM...... $50.00

Make Mine Mink, Terry Thomas, 1961, 27x41" $35.00

Mame, Lucille Ball, 1974, 27x41" $35.00

Man With the Golden Gun, Roger Moore, 1974, 27x41". $100.00

Merry Widow, Lana Turner & Fernando Lamas, 1952, 14x36", EX.. $50.00

Mission Impossible, Tom Cruise, 27x41"..................... $15.00

Monkey Business, Marilyn Monroe, Cary Grant & Ginger Rogers, 1952, 27x41" $225.00

My Fair Lady, Audrey Hepburn & Rex Harrison, reissue, 1971, 27x41" $100.00

Natural Born Killers, 27x41".. $25.00

One-Eyed Jacks, Marlon Brando & Karl Malden, Paramount, 1961, 14x36", EX $100.00

Painted Hills, Lassie, 1951, 27x41", EX...................... $50.00

Pat Garret & Billy the Kid, 1973, 27x41", EX+ $40.00

Patton, George C Scott, 1970, 27x41"......................... $75.00

Pinocchio in Outer Space, animation art, 1965, M...... $45.00

Please Don't Eat the Daisies, Doris Day & David Niven, 1960, 27x41" $45.00

Point of No Return, Bridget Fonda, 27x41" $10.00

Queen of Outer Space, Zsa Gabor, 1958, 24x41", EX..... $450.00

Goodbye Mr. Chips, MGM, 1939, 1-sheet, linen backed, 41x27", NM, $750.00.

Raintree County, MGM, 1957, 41x27", NM+, $125.00

Godfather, Marlon Brando, 1972, 14x22"..................... $75.00

Good Times, Sonny & Cher, 1967, 27x41".................... $45.00

Great Gatsby, Robert Redford, 1974, 27x41", NM $45.00

Guess Who's Coming to Dinner?, Kathrine Hepburn & Spencer Tracy, Academy Award style, 1967, 27x41"............... $25.00

Ride the Wild Surf, Fabian & Tab Hunter, 1964, 27x41".... $50.00

Shampoo, Warren Beatty, 1975, 14x22" $25.00

Shootist, John Wayne, 1976, 27x41"............................. $150.00

Showgirls, 1995, 27x41".. $10.00

Sons of Katie Elder, John Wayne & Dean Martin, Paramount, 1965, 27x41", NM.. $100.00

Tales From the Crypt, 1972, 27x41", EX...................... $75.00

Taxi Driver, Robert DeNiro, 1976, EX+ **$100.00**
Ten Little Indians, 1966, 27x41" **$40.00**
Terror in the Wax Museum, 1973, 27x41", EX **$50.00**
Twister, double-sided, 27x41" **$10.00**
Two on a Guillotine, 1965, 27x41", NM **$45.00**
Unfaithful, Gina Lollobrigida, 1960, 27x41" **$35.00**

Walt Disney's Beauty and the Beast, 1991, 1-sheet, M, $50.00; The Little Mermaid, 1989, 1-sheet, M, $85.00.

Wayward Bus, Joan Collins, 1957, 27x41" **$65.00**
Where the Boys Are, Connie Francis, 1961, 27x41" **$75.00**
World of Abbott & Costello, 1965, 27x41" **$65.00**
Yellow Submarine, 27x41", EX **$700.00**

Napkin Dolls

Cocktail, luncheon, or dinner..., paper, cotton, or damask..., solid, patterned, or plaid — regardless of size, color, or material, there's always been a place for napkins. In the late 1940s and early 1950s, buffet-style meals were gaining popularity. One accessory common to many of these buffets is now one of today's hot collectibles — the napkin doll. While most of the ceramic and wooden examples found today date from this period, many homemade napkin dolls were produced in ceramic classes of the 1970s and 1980s.

Advisor: Bobbie Zucker Bryson (See Directory, Napkin Dolls)

California Originals, lady holding basket for toothpicks overhead, 13¾", from $65.00 to $75.00. (Photo courtesy Bobbie Zucker Bryson)

Betson's, yellow Colonial lady, bell clapper, marked Hand
    Painted Japan, 8½" **$55.00**

California Originals, blue Spanish dancer, splits in rear only,
    foil label, 13", from $95 to **$110.00**
California Originals, toothpick holder basket over head, foil
    label, 13¾", from $65 to...**$75.00**
Enesco, Genie at Your Service, holding lantern, paper label,
    8" **$80.00**
Goebel, half doll on wire frame, marked Goebel, W
    Germany, ca 1957, 9" **$175.00**
Holland Mold, Daisy, No 514, 7¼" **$60.00**
Holland Mold, Rebecca No H-265, 10½" **$125.00**
Holland Mold, Rosie, No H-132, 10¼" **$55.00**
Holt Howard, yellow Sunbonnet Miss, marked Holt Howard
    1958, 5"..**$65.00**
Japan, lady in green w/pink umbrella, bell clapper,
    unmarked, 9" **$75.00**
Japan, lady in pink dress w/blue shawl & yellow hat, 8½",
    from $60 to..**$70.00**
Japanese angel, 5⅜" **$60.00**
Kreiss & Co, blue lady w/candle holder behind hat, from $50
    to...**$60.00**
Kreiss & Co, green doll w/poodle, jeweled eyes, necklace &
    ring, candle holder behind hat, marked Kreiss & Co,
    10¾" **$65.00**
Kreiss & Co, green doll w/yellow toothpick tray, candle
    holder in hat, marked Kreiss & Co, +pr 4¾" 'tip in' shak-
    ers **$125.00**
Kreiss & Co, green lady holding fan, candle holder behind
    fan, marked Kreiss & Co, 8¾" **$55.00**
Kreiss & Co, yellow doll w/gold trim holding muff, jeweled
    eyes, candle holder in top of hat, marked Kreiss & Co,
    10" **$75.00**
Man (bartender), holding tray w/candle holder, 8¾", from
    $95 to..**$100.00**
Metal, silhouette of Deco woman, black & gold w/wire bot-
    tom, 8⅞", from $100 to **$125.00**
Miss Versatility Cocktail Girl, 13", from $55 to **$65.00**
Rooster, white w/red & black trim, slits in tail for napkins,
    w/egg salt & pepper shakers, from $45 to...........**$55.00**
Sevy Etta, wood w/marble base, marked USD Patent No
    159,005, 11½" **$55.00**
Swedish doll, wooden, marked Patent No 113861, 12" ..**$35.00**

Swedish lady, wooden with musical base, Patent #113861, 12", MIB, $45.00. (Photo courtesy Bobbie Zucker Bryson)

Wooden Jamaican lady, movable arms, papel label: Ave 13 Nov 743, A Sinfonia, Tel 2350 Petropolis, 6".........**$85.00**

Wooden pink & blue doll w/strawberry toothpick holder on head, 8", from $50 to..**$60.00**

Yamihaya Bros, lady holding yoke w/bucket salt & pepper shakers, hat conceals candle holder **$100.00**

New Martinsville

Located in a West Virginia town by the same name, the New Martinsville Glass Company was founded in 1901, and until it was purchased by Viking in 1944, produced quality tableware in various patterns and colors that collectors admire today. They also made a line of glass animals which Viking continued to produce until they closed in 1986. In 1987 the factory was bought by Mr. Kenneth Dalzell who reopened the company under the title Dalzell-Viking. He used the old molds to reissue his own line of animals, which he marked 'Dalzell' with an acid stamp. These are usually priced in the $50.00 to $60.00 range. Examples marked 'V' were made by Viking for another company, Mirror Images. They're valued at $15.00 to $35.00, with colors sometimes higher.

Advisor: Roselle Scheifman (See Directory, Elegant Glass)

Prelude, vase, crystal, Radiance shape, 10", $75.00.

Bookends, clipper ships, crystal, pr **$85.00**
Figurine, baby bear, head straight, red, 3"...................**$70.00**
Figurine, baby seal w/ball, red, 4½" **$70.00**
Figurine, starfish, crystal, 7" **$85.00**
Figurine, wolfhound, crystal, 7".................................**$100.00**
Georgian, cup & saucer, green **$12.00**
Georgian, sugar bowl, w/lid, green, 3".........................**$40.00**
Host Master, tumbler, ruby, 4¼"..................................**$11.00**
Janice, basket, black, #4552, 11" **$200.00**
Janice, basket, crystal, 11"...**$75.00**
Janice, bowl, crystal, 10" **$37.50**
Janice, bowl, red or blue, 10"......................................**$65.00**
Janice, celery dish, light blue, 11" **$55.00**
Janice, creamer, crystal, 6-oz.......................................**$12.00**
Janice, jam jar, w/lid, red or blue, 6" **$45.00**
Janice, plate, 2-handle, crystal, 12"..............................**$25.00**
Janice, sugar bowl, red or blue, 6-oz..........................**$20.00**
Janice, tumbler, crystal **$12.00**
Janice, vase, ball shape, crystal, 9".............................**$55.00**

Oscar, tumbler, amber w/platinum trim.........................**$6.00**
Palmette Band, salt & pepper shakers, blue opaque, 2½", pr...**$60.00**
Prelude, cake stand, crystal...**$60.00**
Prelude, candlestick, single, crystal, 5" **$25.00**
Prelude, cordial, crystal **$20.00**
Radiance, bonbon, footed, amber, 6"............................**$17.50**
Radiance, bowl, flared, ice blue or red, 10" **$42.00**
Radiance, bowl, nut; 2-handled, ice blue or red, 5" ...**$20.00**
Radiance, bowl, relish; 3-part, amber, 8" **$25.00**
Radiance, bowl, relish; 2-part, ice blue or red, 7" **$30.00**
Radiance, candlesticks, ruffled, amber, 6", pr..............**$80.00**
Radiance, comport, ice blue or red, 5" **$30.00**
Radiance, creamer, amber..**$15.00**
Radiance, cup, punch; ice blue or red...........................**$15.00**
Radiance, goblet, cordial; ice blue or red, 1-oz **$42.00**
Radiance, mayonnaise set, amber, 3-pc **$40.00**
Radiance, plate, luncheon; ice blue or red, 8" **$16.00**
Radiance, plate, punch bowl liner; emerald green, 14"..**$25.00**
Radiance, plate, salad; red or blue, 8½" **$17.50**
Radiance, punch bowl, red..**$225.00**
Radiance, punch bowl liner, red **$75.00**
Radiance, saucer, amber...**$5.50**
Radiance, tray, oval ice blue or red **$30.00**
Radiance, tumbler, cobalt blue, 9-oz...........................**$28.00**
Radiance, vase, flared or crimped, amber, 10"............**$45.00**

Niloak Pottery

The Niloak Pottery company was the continuation of a quarter-century-old family business in Benton, Arkansas. Known as the Eagle Pottery in the early twentieth century, its owner was Charles Dean Hyten who continued in his father's footsteps making utilitarian wares for local and state markets. In 1909 Arthur Dovey, an experienced potter formerly from the Rookwood Pottery of Ohio and the Arkansas-Missouri based Ouachita Pottery companies, came to Benton and created America's most unusual art pottery. Introduced in 1910 as Niloak (kaolin spelled backwards), Dovey and Hyten produced art pottery pieces from swirling clays with a wide range of artifically created colors including red, blue, cream, brown, gray, and later green. Connected to the Arts & Crafts Movement by 1913, the pottery was labeled as Missionware (probably due to its seeming simplicity in the making). Missionware (or swirl) production continued alongside utilitarian ware manufacturing until the 1930s when economic factors led to the making of another type of art pottery and later to (molded) industrial castware. In 1931 Niloak Pottery introduced Hywood Art Pottery (marked as such), consisting of regular glaze techniques including overspray, mottling, and drips of two colors on vases and bowls that were primarily hand thrown. It was short-lived and soon replaced with the Hywood by Niloak (or Hywood) line to increase marketing potential through the use of the well-recognized Niloak name. Experienced potters, designers, and ceramists were involved at Niloak; among them were Frank Long, Paul Cox, Stoin M. Stoin, Howard Lewis, and Rudy Ganz. Many local families had long ties to the pottery including the

McNeills, Rowlands, and Alleys. By the mid-1930s, Niloak, experiencing tremendous financial woes, came under new management led by Hardy L. Winburn of Little Rock. To compete better, the production focused primarily on industrial castware such as vases, bowls, figurines, animals, and planters. Niloak survived into the late 1940s when it became the Winburn Tile Company of North Little Rock, which still exists today.

Virtually all of Niloak Missionware/swirl pottery is marked with die stamps. The exceptions are generally fan vases, wall pockets, lamp bases, and whiskey jugs. Be careful when you buy unmarked swirl pottery — it is usually Evans pottery (made in Missouri) which generally has either no interior glaze or is chocolate brown inside. Moreover, Evans made swirl wall pockets, lamp bases, and even hanging baskets that find their way on to today's market and are sold as Niloak. Niloak stickers are often placed on these unmarked Evans pieces — closely examine the condition of the sticker to determine if it is damaged or mutilated from the transfer process.

For more information, we recommend *The Collector's Encyclopedia of Niloak Pottery* by our advisor David Edwin Gifford, a historian of Arkansas pottery.

Advisor: David Edwin Gifford (See Directory, Niloak)

Castware

Planter, fish form, 9" long, $40.00. (Photo courtesy David Edwin Gifford)

Bowl, blue, vertical indents w/scalloped rim, Niloak block letters, 4"...**$30.00**
Bowl, Ozark Dawn II, oblong, 2-handled, Niloak incised, 3x14"..**$125.00**
Creamer, pale blue, ear-shaped handle, bulbous shape, Niloak low relief mark, 2"......................................**$15.00**
Ewer, dark blue, embossed floral, Niloak incised, 10¾" ...**$60.00**
Flower frog, turtle, yellow, Niloak block letters, 1½x4¾" .**$60.00**
Novelty, canoe, Ozark Dawn II, Niloak block letters, 3½x11"...**$75.00**
Novelty, cart, blue, Niloak low relief mark, 4¼".........**$40.00**
Novelty, wooden shoe, Ozark Dawn II, unmarked, 2½x5"..**$15.00**
Pitcher, blue, tilted, circular design on sides, Niloak low relief mark, 5½"...**$25.00**
Pitcher, green, Lewis glaze, embossed flowers, 1st art mark, 6¼"..**$80.00**

Planter, blue, footed window box, Niloak incised, 3x8½" ..**$60.00**
Planter, elephant, black, trunk curled back looking up, 2nd art mark, 3¾" **$80.00**
Planter, frog, blue, sitting w/head back & mouth open, unmarked, 3¼"...**$30.00**
Planter, Ozark Dawn II, half circle, Niloak incised, 3½x8" **$75.00**
Salt & pepper shakers, light green, ball shaped, 'S' & 'P' handles, Potteries sticker, 2¼", pr...................................**$30.00**
Strawberry jar, Ozark Dawn II, 4 tulip forms w/open top, Niloak low relief mark, 7"....................................**$35.00**
Vase, dark rose, tri-fluted, incised Niloak, 7¾" **$60.00**
Vase, fan; Ozark Dawn II, handled, pedestal foot, Niloak low relief mark, 5¼"...**$30.00**
Vase, Ozark Dawn II, embossed decor from shoulder to mid-body, sm ring handles, Niloak incised, 11½".......**$85.00**
Vase, Ozark Dawn II, embossed swan between palm trees, 2 twisted handles, Niloak incised, 7½" **$40.00**
Vase/flower frog, Ozark Dawn II, footed, round, Niloak block letters, 5"..**$40.00**
Wall pocket, yellow, Bouquet pattern, Niloak low relief mark, 5¼"...**$30.00**

Hywood Art Pottery/Hywood by Niloak

Bowl, Peacock Blue II, Lewis glaze, inverted scalloped rim, cast, Hywood by Niloak (2nd mark), 5½x2¾".....**$40.00**
Candlesticks, double, white, Lewis glaze, cast, Hywood incised, 2¾"..**$80.00**
Cookie jar, Delft Blue, Lewis glaze, w/lid, hand thrown, 1st Hywood by Niloak, 8½" **$120.00**
Pitcher, black, w/clay stopper, ball shape, hand thrown, Potteries sticker, 8¾x7", w/4 tumblers, unmarked, 3½"..........**$160.00**
Vase, blue, Lewis glaze, high shouldered, hand thrown, unmarked, 6¾"..**$60.00**
Vase, blue, Peacock Blue II, Lewis glaze, classic form, squared top, hand thrown, Hywood incised, 7½"................**$80.00**
Vase, bud; Ozark Dawn II colors, Lewis glaze, slightly waisted, flared foot, cast, Hywood by Niloak (2nd mark), 8"..**$45.00**
Vase, gray shaded to pink, Lewis glaze, waisted, flared scalloped rim, Ozark Dawn II, hand thrown, Niloak 71, 6".......**$50.00**
Vase, green shaded to dark rose, Stoin glaze, 3 appplied diagonal rim handles, hand thrown, Ozark Dawn I, 7½"..**$200.00**
Vase, green shaded to yellow, Lewis glaze, inverted scalloped top, hand thrown, unmarked, 4⅛".............**$30.00**
Vase, Ozark Dawn II, Lewis glaze, 3 applied diagonal rim handles, Hywood by Niloak (1st mark), 5½".....**$125.00**
Vase, red, Lewis glaze, high shouldered, hand thrown, 2nd art mark, 7"...**$60.00**
Vase, Sea Green, Stoin glaze, trumpet neck form, hand thrown, stamped Hywood Art Pottery, 6½".......**$150.00**

Missionware Swirl

Ashtray, 3-color swirl, Niloak sticker, ⅜x5½" dia **$100.00**
Ashtray, 3-color swirl, 2nd art mark, 5x1¼" dia........**$100.00**
Candlestick, blue & white swirl, waisted, flared base, Patent Pending, 9¾"..**$350.00**

Candlestick, 3-color swirl, flared bottom, 1st art mark, 9¾" **$225.00**

Chamber pot, 4-color swirl, 2nd art mark, 6¼x2½" .**$275.00**

Cigarette jar, 4-color swirl, flared base, 1st art mark, 4¾x3¼" **$250.00**

Fern dish, 4-color swirl, w/lid, unmarked, 6½x2" **$125.00**

Gear shift knob, 4-color swirl, round, unmarked, 2" dia .**$275.00**

Humidor, 4-color swirl, shouldered, 1st art mark, 4½".....**$300.00**

Matchstick holder, 4-color swirl, embossed band at base, 2nd art mark, 1½" **$100.00**

Pitcher, 3-color swirl, Patent Pending, 10½" **$450.00**

Plate, collection; 3-color swirl, 1st art mark, 2x9¼"..**$400.00**

Rose jar, 4-color swirl, w/lid, 1st art mark, 5¾x8"....**$500.00**

Stein/mug, 4-color swirl, cylindrical w/slightly flared base, ear handle, 1st art mark, 4½" **$250.00**

Tankard, 3-color swirl, cylindrical w/slightly flared base, ear-shaped handle, 13½" **$800.00**

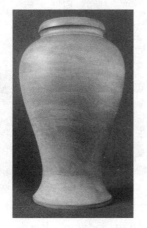

Vase, Missionware, red and brown swirl, marked with the art letter, 9½", $400.00. (Photo courtesy David Edwin Gifford)

Vase, red, gray & cream swirl, classic form, trumpet neck, 1st art mark, 9⅞" **$250.00**

Vase, 3-color swirl, cylindrical w/inverted neck, 1st art mark, 10" **$275.00**

Vase, 3-color swirl, gourd form w/trumpet neck, Patent Pending, 6½"...**$200.00**

Vase, 3-color swirl w/combed effect around gourd form, 1st art mark, 8" **$240.00**

Vase, 4-color swirl, cone shape, flared base, 1st art mark, 9½"..**$300.00**

Vase, 4-color swirl, cylindrical w/inverted neck, 1st art mark, 9⅛"..**$250.00**

Vase, 4-color swirl, gourd form, 2nd art mark, 8⅝" .**$175.00**

Vase, 4-color swirl, gourd form w/flared rim, 2nd art mark, 6¼" **$110.00**

Vase, 4-color swirl, shouldered, 2nd art mark, 3¼" **$80.00**

Vase, 4-color swirl, waisted form, 2nd art mark, 3½".**$80.00**

Vase, 4-color swirl, waisted form w/incurvate neck, 1st art mark, 10" **$300.00**

Water bottle, 4-color swirl, w/4" drinking glass lid, 2nd art mark, 7¾" **$400.00**

Noritake

Before the government restricted the use of the Nippon mark in 1921, all porcelain exported from Japan (even that made by the Noritake Company) carried the Nippon mark. The company that became Noritake had its beginning in 1904, and over the years experienced several changes in name and organization. Until 1941 (at the onset of WWII) they continued to import large amounts of their products to America. (During the occupation, when chinaware production was resumed, all imports were to have been marked 'Occupied Japan,' though because of the natural resentment on the part of the Japanese, much of it was not.)

Many variations will be found in their marks, but nearly all contain the Noritake name. Reproductions abound; be very careful. If you'd like to learn more about this subject, we recommend *The Collector's Encyclopedia of Noritake* (there are two books in the series) by Joan Van Patten; and *The Collector's Encyclopedia of Early Noritake* by Aimee Neff Alden. All are published by Collector Books.

Azalea

The Azelea pattern was produced exclusively for the Larkin Company, who offered it to their customers as premiums from 1916 until the 1930s. It met with much success, and even today locating pieces to fill in your collection is not at all difficult. The earlier pieces carry the Noritake M-in-wreath mark. Later the ware was marked Noritake, Azalea, Hand Painted, Japan.

Azalea pitcher, #100, 1-qt jug, 6", $195.00.

Bonbon, #184, 6¼" **$50.00**

Bowl, #12, 10" **$42.50**

Bowl, vegetable; oval, #172, 9¼" **$58.00**

Creamer & sugar bowl, #7 ....**$45.00**

Cup & saucer, bouillon; #124, 3½"..............................**$24.50**

Gravy boat, #40..**$48.00**

Plate, #4, 7½" **$10.00**

Plate, bread & butter; #8, 6½" **$10.00**

Plate, dinner; #13, 9¾" **$28.00**

Platter, #56, 12" **$58.00**

Relish, oval, #18, 8½" **$20.00**

Spoon holder, #399, 2-pc **$35.00**

Teapot, #15..**$110.00**

Whipped cream/mayonnaise set, #3, 3-pc...................**$38.50**

Tree in the Meadow

Made by the Noritake China Company during the 1920s and 1930s, this pattern of dinnerware is beginning to show up more and more at the larger flea markets. It's easy to spot; the pattern is hand painted, so there are variations, but the color scheme is always browns, gold-yellows, and orange-rust, and the design features a large dark tree in the foreground, growing near a lake. There is usually a cottage in the distance.

Bowl, cream soup; 2-handled	**$35.00**
Bowl, oatmeal	**$15.00**
Bowl, soup	**$15.00**
Butter pat	**$15.00**
Celery dish	**$45.00**
Condiment set, 5-pc.	**$45.00**
Creamer & sugar bowl, demitasse	**$40.00**
Cup & saucer, demitasse	**$35.00**
Egg cup	**$30.00**
Gravy boat	**$50.00**
Jam jar/dish, 4-pc.	**$70.00**
Lemon dish	**$15.00**
Mayonnaise set, 3-pc	**$50.00**

Tree in Meadow candy dish, #318, $400.00.

Various Dinnerware Patterns, ca 1930s to Present

So many lines of dinnerware have been produced by the Noritake company that to list them all would require a volume in itself. In fact, just such a book is available — *The Collector's Encyclopedia of Early Noritake* by Aimee Neff Alden (Collector Books.) And while many patterns had specific names, others did not, so you'll probably need the photographs this book contains to help you identify your pattern. Contained herein is only a general guide for the more common pieces and patterns. The low side of the range will represent more current lines, while the high side can be used to roughly evaluate lines from about 1933 until the mid-1960s.

Newsletter: *Noritake News*
David H. Spain
1237 Federal Ave. E, Seattle, WA 98102; 206-323-8102

Bowl, berry; individual, from $8 to	**$10.00**
Bowl, soup; 7½", from $10 to	**$15.00**
Bowl, vegetable; round or oval, ca 1945 to present, from $25 to	**$35.00**
Bowl, vegetable; w/lid, ca 1933-40	**$40.00**
Butter dish, 3-pc, ca 1933-64, from $35 to	**$50.00**
Creamer, from $15 to	**$25.00**

Cup, demitasse; w/saucer, from $10 to	**$17.50**
Gravy boat, from $35 to	**$45.00**
Pickle or relish dish, from $15 to	**$25.00**
Plate, bread & butter; from $8 to	**$12.00**
Plate, dinner; from $15 to	**$30.00**
Plate, luncheon; from $10 to	**$18.00**
Plate, salad; from $10 to	**$15.00**
Platter, 12" from $25 to	**$40.00**
Platter, 16" (or larger), from $40 to	**$60.00**
Salt & pepper shakers, pr, from $15 to	**$25.00**
Sugar bowl, w/lid, from $15 to	**$30.00**
Tea & toast set (sm cup & tray), from $15 to	**$25.00**
Teapot, demitasse pot, chocolate pot or coffeepot, from $45 to	**$60.00**

Miscellaneous

Ashtray, figural clown seated by bowl, 5" wide, from $275.00 to $295.00. (Photo courtesy Joan Van Patten)

Ashtray, lady in blue lustre gown, skirt forms tray, green mark, 4", from $300 to	**$325.00**
Basket vase, Deco-style florals on yellow to black, green twig handle, red mark, 10", from $200 to	**$230.00**
Bowl, exotic bird on branch painted on white lustre, blue lustre at rim and handles, green mark, 8¾", from $60 to	**$75.00**
Bowl, river & house scenic in diamond-shaped reserve on blue, pierced handles, red mark, 7¼" square, from $55 to	**$70.00**
Bowl, river scene at sunset w/bird near water, 3 pierced handles, red mark, 7¼", from $45 to	**$60.00**
Bowl, scissors-tail swallow perched along side of rim, green mark, 7½" L, from $115 to	**$135.00**
Bowl, squirrel & foliage molded in relief along side, brown & blue tones, green mark, 6½", from $125 to	**$150.00**
Butter tub, floral swag on white, tub handles, red mark, 5¼", from $20 to	**$30.00**
Cake plate, bright yellow flowers w/green foliage on white, sm gold handles, red mark, 10", from $55 to	**$65.00**
Cake plate, Deco-style flowers on red, gray rim & handles, red mark, 11", from $60 to	**$70.00**
Cake plate, parrot on branch, blue lustre rim w/sm handles, red mark, 9½", from $75 to	**$95.00**
Cake plate, river scenic w/cottage & trees, sm pierced handles, red mark, 9¾", from $55 to	**$65.00**
Candy dish, Deco-style floral design in base, sides have 8 pointed pleats, red mark, 7¼" dia, from $85 to	**$105.00**

Candy dish, Deco-style yellow tulips on white w/brown & green details, integral handles, red mark, 5½", from $75 to...**$90.00**

Candy dish, river scenic w/tree & bird, earth tones on butterfly shape w/center handle, red mark, 8½" L, from $75 to.**$95.00**

Candy dish, sampam river scene w/willows & water lilies, basket form, red mark, 7½", from $55 to.............**$60.00**

Candy jar, river scene w/swans & flowers, footed goblet form, red mark, 6", from $65 to **$75.00**

Chip 'n dip set, lovebirds on branch on white, pale yellow band along rim, green mark, 9", from $70 to.......**$80.00**

Chocolate pot, flower reserves along shoulder, white w/tan bands, black on handle & finial, 6-sided, green mark, 9¾"...**$85.00**

Cigarette holder, Deco-style lady walking dog in the wind, red mark, from $115 to **$130.00**

Compote, Deco-style flowers w/red and black on orange lustre, footed, red mark, 5¾"+handles, from $70 to.**$85.00**

Compote, multicolor butterflies on white, scalloped rim, footed, red mark, 10½", from $75 to **$85.00**

Condiment set, wide floral band on white w/gold lustre trim, 3-pc on boat-shaped tray, green mark, 7½" L, from $75 to..**$95.00**

Creamer & sugar bowl, Deco-style flowers & butterfly on black, gold lustre interior, gold angle handles, green mark...**$70.00**

Creamer & sugar bowl, Japanese lanterns on navy, white interior, rectangular shapes, red mark, 3½", from $75 to...**$90.00**

Creamer & sugar bowl, lg pink flower on white w/blue geometric design at side, w/lid, red mark, 5", from $40 to...**$60.00**

Creamer & sugar bowl, white w/blue along rim, blue lid w/red rose finial, green mark, 4", from $45 to.....**$60.00**

Dresser doll/powder shaker, yellow hat, blue dress, red mark, 6", from $275 to **$295.00**

Ferner, wide floral band on white, blue at base and flared rim, sm feet, green mark, 6½", from $85 to.......**$100.00**

Honey jar, beehive figural w/painted flowers on orange lustre, applied bees at side, bee finial, green mark, 4½"...**$75.00**

Jam jar, Deco-style florals on orange lustre, w/ladle & undertray, green mark, 5½", from $65 to.......................**$75.00**

Jar, cosmetic; blue lustre w/bird perched on lid, red mark, 4", from $100 to...**$150.00**

Lemon dish, painted floral decor on blue, applied lemon at side of rim, red mark, 5¾", from $35 to...............**$50.00**

Mayonnaise set, river scene at sunset w/blue band at rim, green mark, 3-pc, from $50 to..............................**$65.00**

Plate, Deco-style girl in striped hat, narrow blue lustre rim, red mark, 6¼", from $175 to **$195.00**

Plate, mixed flowers on creamy white to yellow, smooth rim w/narrow gold border, green mark, 7¾", from $20 to..**$30.00**

Plate, river scene w/evergreens & glimpse of building, blue lustre rim, green mark, 7¾", from $30 to **$40.00**

Plate, river scene w/swan in water, steepled building beyond, blues & pinks, smooth rim, green mark, 6¼", from $30 to...**$40.00**

Powder puff box, bird on floral branch, 8-sided, red mark, 4¾", from $175 to...**$195.00**

Powder puff box, lady checks her hair in hand mirror in reserve on lid, yellow rim & base, green mark, 3¼"............**$235.00**

Salt & pepper shakers, multicolor floral band on blue lustre, w/blue lustre figure-8 center-handled tray, green mark, pr...**$70.00**

Sandwich plate, wide floral band on blue at rim, plain white center, gold center handle, red mark, 9½", from $40 to..**$50.00**

Snack set, Deco-style landscape, black handle on cup & kidney-shaped tray w/indent for cup, green mark, 8½" L...**$115.00**

Syrup, orchids on white w/silver trim, w/lid, green mark, 4½", from $55 to..**$70.00**

Tobacco jar, lady in diamond-shaped reserve on orange lustre, pipe finial, red mark, 4½", from $200 to **$225.00**

Trivet, flower basket on white, narrow blue band along edge, green mark, 5¾" dia, from $45 to **$60.00**

Vase, jack-in-the-pulpit; butterfly on blue lustre, red mark, 6", from $140 to..**$160.00**

Vase, lg multicolor roses on black, sm gold handles, green mark, 7¼", from $95 to **$110.00**

Vase, pastoral scene on red to green, scalloped rim on slender form, red mark, 8", from $135 to..................**$150.00**

Vase, peacock figural, green mark, #27, 7", from $200 to **$225.00**

Vase, stylized tulips on blue-lustre can form w/sm handles, green mark, 7½", from $85 to **$95.00**

Vase, 3 stump forms on base, dark blue, light blue & white lustres, red mark, 6", from $175 to......................**$195.00**

Wall pocket, exotic bird painted on red, gold trim at top, red mark, 8", from $150 to **$175.00**

Candy basket, floral motif with lustre interior, 4¼", from $55.00 to $65.00. (Photo courtesy Joan Van Patten)

Novelty Radios

Novelty radios come in an unimaginable variety of shapes and sizes from advertising and product shapes, character forms, and vehicles to anything the producer might dream up. For information on this new, fun collectible read *Collector's Guide to Novelty Radios* by Marty Bunis and Robert Breed and *Schroeder's Collectible Toys, Antique to Modern* (Collector Books).

Advisor: Marty and Sue Bunis (See Directory, Novelty Radios)

Big Bird, EX **$20.00**
Blabber Mouse, EX **$35.00**
Budweiser Beer Can, NMIB **$30.00**
Camel Cigarette Pack, w/hand strap, 4" **$125.00**
Charlie Tuna, figure standing upright on base, red hat
     w/white name **$75.00**
Charlie Tuna, flat w/embossed figure, NMIB **$45.00**
Chiquita NFL 50th Anniversary, NMIB **$25.00**
Cinnamon Toast Crunch 3-Ring Binder w/built-in radio,
     cover shows 3 chefs dancing to music, Radioart/
     Taiwan **$35.00**
Coors Beer Can, EX **$26.00**
Crayola Rocks, NM **$75.00**
Del Monte Pineapple Chunks Can, replica label w/In It's
     Own Juice No Sugar Added on red dot................**$50.00**
Donald Duck, figural, transistor, 1970s, 7x4½", EX (EX
     box) **$70.00**
Double-Cola Can, EX...**$35.00**
Dutch Boy Dirt Fighter Interior Latex Flat Wall Paint Can,
     w/plastic lid & bail handle....................................**$35.00**
Flying Saucer, Pro UFO, Space Tech, 1977, 12" dia, M..**$50.00**
Fonzie (Happy Days), M..**$45.00**
Grand Old Parr Scotch Whiskey, NMIB.......................**$50.00**
Gulden's Mustard Jar Radio, MIB **$75.00**
Hair Dryer, #2401-H, marked AirWaves 2000, black w/white
     lettering & trim, J&D Brush Co/China, 9" **$25.00**
Halcite Ice Crystals, MIB **$45.00**
Hamburger Helper, MIB..**$50.00**
Heinz Catsup Bottle, EX+...**$45.00**

Superman Exiting Phone Booth, Made in Hong Kong, 7x3", from $150.00 to $175.00.

Tony Tiger, 1978, NMIB **$25.00**
Welch's Grape Juice Concentrate Can, NM.................**$35.00**
Westinghouse Cold Drinks Vending Machine, MIB...**$125.00**
1966 Lincoln Continental automobile, 1972, M **$35.00**

Novelty Telephones

Novelty telephones modeled after products or advertising items are popular with collectors. Those that are cartoon or advertising character related are highly desired by collectors. For further information we recommend *Schroeder's Collectible Toys, Antique to Modern* (Collector Books).

Alf, plush figure with phone, Hong Kong, NM, $80.00.

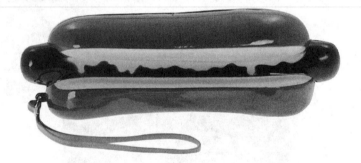

Hot Dog, plastic, Hong Kong, 8¼", $65.00.

Hubba Bubba Soda Can, reads Original Bubble Gum .**$35.00**
Kool-Aid Kool Bursts Bottle, replica w/shoulder strap, Kraft
     General Foods, 1992..**$25.00**
Kraft Macaroni & Cheese Dinomac Carton, NM..........**$35.00**
La-Co Slic-Tite Paste Compound, NM **$48.00**
Littel John, blue & white toilet, EX **$10.00**
Lunch Box, gold w/clown decals on ends, front panel
     w/dials & multicolored dots on white, Midland/Taiwan,
     5x6" **$20.00**
Olympia Beer Can, EX **$30.00**
Panasonic's Parapet 70, blue, NM **$20.00**
Planet of the Apes, pendant style w/gold chain, Introport
     Development Co/Hong Kong, 1974, 3½" dia **$35.00**
Pound Puppies, 1986, NM...**$10.00**
Sunkist Orange Fruit Drinks, NM **$35.00**

Bart Simpson, Columbia/Tel Com, 1990, MIB.............**$35.00**
Bozo, Telemania, 1988, MIB **$75.00**
Cabbage Patch Doll, EX+...**$85.00**
Ernie the Keebler Elf, 1970s NM **$50.00**
Garfield, desk-top or wall mount, EX, each................**$40.00**
Li'l Sprout, EX **$75.00**
Oscar Mayer Hot Dog, EX **$65.00**
Punchy (Hawaiian Punch), EX **$75.00**
Snoopy, as Joe Cool, 1980s, MIB **$55.00**
Spider-Man, climbing down rooftop, EX **$25.00**
Volkswagon, 8", EX...**$30.00**

Occupied Japan Collectibles

Some items produced in Japan during the period from the end of WWII until the occupation ended in 1952 were marked Occupied Japan. No doubt much of the ware from this era was marked simply Japan, since obviously the 'Occupied' term caused considerable resentment among the Japanese people, and they were understandably reluctant to use the mark. So even though you may find identical items marked simply Japan or Made in Japan, only those with the more limited Occupied Japan mark are evaluated here.

Assume that the items described below are ceramic unless another material is mentioned. For more information, we recommend *The Collector's Encyclopedia of Occupied Japan* (there are five in the series) by Gene Florence.

Newsletter: *The Upside Down World of an O.J. Collector*
The Occupied Japan Club
c/o Florence Archambault
29 Freeborn St., Newport, RI 02840-1821. Published bimonthly. Information requires SASE

Ashtray, Basilique Ste Anne de Beaupre embossed on metal, 3" **$5.00**
Ashtray, horseshoe tray w/horse standing at rim, silverplate, 4⅝" **$25.00**
Ashtray, souvenir, embossed scenes & names of location on silver-tone metal (various descriptions), each **$3.50**
Ashtray, Statue of Liberty/Crowd on Beach at Moor Hotel embossed on 2-lobed metal tray **$15.00**
Ashtray, Wedgwood type, white classical figures on blue, 2⅝" **$10.00**
Bowl, flower form w/handles, marked Pico, sm **$10.00**
Bowl, salad; wooden, 10" **$17.50**
Box, jewel; silver-tone metal w/embossed floral decor, footed, 3½x4½" **$15.00**
Bud vase, angel musician beside vase, bright colors, ceramic, red or black mark, 2¾" **$12.50**
Candle holders, Colonial figure between 2 flower holders, pastels on ceramic, 4", pr..............................**$55.00**
Cigarette box, floral on white, ceramic, 3½x4½", +2 matching 2½x3½" trays...**$20.00**
Cigarette lighter, champagne bottle form, metal **$20.00**
Cigarette lighter, telephone form, metal.....................**$20.00**
Creamer, flower decal on white **$15.00**
Creamer & sugar bowl, flower decal on white, silver trim, w/lid **$20.00**
Crumber, gold-tone metal dust-pan form, 5¼x6".......**$10.00**
Cup & saucer, floral chintz-like pattern on white, plain white cup interior, ear-shaped handle............................**$12.50**
Cup & saucer, floral on white, ornate handle, smooth rim, Saji Fancy China...**$12.50**
Cup & saucer, flower on white, hexagonal, from $12.50 to ..**$15.00**
Cup & saucer, flower on white w/yellow bands at rims and at foot of cup, sm flowers in interior of cup........**$12.50**
Cup & saucer, flower reserves on blue, white handle & interior on cup, Merit...**$12.50**
Cup & saucer, flowers on green inside cup, plain pale green exterior, matching flowers on saucer **$17.50**
Cup & saucer, gold horse w/gray knight, LaMore China ..**$20.00**
Cup & saucer, mixed roses on white, angular handle, straight-sided cup **$12.50**

Cup & saucer, wide blue band on white w/gold trim, orange mark..**$12.50**
Dinnerware, Livonia (Dogwood), service for 4 w/plates in 3 sizes, cups & saucers, cereals & soups, creamer & sugar w/lid **$200.00**
Dinnerware, marked Noritake China/OJ, complete set for 4 w/creamer & sugar bowl w/lid **$225.00**
Dinnerware, Orange Blossom, Kent China, 6-place ..**$250.00**
Dinnerware, Rochelle, Grace China, 4-place.............**$200.00**
Dinnerware, Wild Rose, Fuji China, 4-place.............**$200.00**
Doll, celluloid, nude, 4¾" **$15.00**
Doll, china, 3" **$20.00**
Doll, feather or go-go dancer, celluloid, 4¼" **$15.00**
Fan, folded paper, colorful flowers **$10.00**
Figurine, angel musician, bright colors, 2½" **$6.00**
Figurine, Black fiddler, bright colors, 5" **$42.50**
Figurine, boy seated w/duck, Hummel type, 3¾" **$30.00**
Figurine, boy w/broken sprinkler, Hummel type, 4½" ...**$35.00**
Figurine, boy w/dog, bright colors, brown mark, 4¾" ..**$12.50**
Figurine, boy w/parrot, bright colors, red mark, 5"....**$12.50**
Figurine, Colonial couple, flower gatherers, pastels on bisque, black mark, 10¼", pr............................**$140.00**
Figurine, Colonial couple, pastels on bisque, 15½", pr...**$235.00**

Figurine, Colonial couple, 7½", $40.00 for the pair.

Figurine, Colonial couple w/musical instruments, pastels, 9", pr...**$45.00**
Figurine, Colonial couple w/ornate hats, pastels, 12", pr..**$75.00**
Figurine, Colonial dancers, white clothes w/gold trim, 6¼", pr...**$35.00**
Figurine, Colonial lady w/fan, many ruffles, painted bisque, red mark, 10½" **$75.00**
Figurine, Colonial man, long coat, hands at hips, bisque, Mariyama, 7"...**$30.00**
Figurine, Colonial man reading letter, on base, pastels on bisque, 15½" **$150.00**
Figurine, Colonial man w/red hair, long green coat, yellow pants, Paulux, 9¾"...**$75.00**
Figurine, Colonial musicians on base, bright colors, 7x7⅞"...**$55.00**
Figurine, crane, realistic appearance, wings up, 3¼"....**$8.00**
Figurine, Cupid beside lg open flower, pastels on bisque, 4" **$32.00**
Figurine, Cupid w/moon, bright colors, 3½"..............**$10.00**

Figurine, Delft lady, much blue trim along dress, hat, ruffles, etc, blue mark, 6¼" **$35.00**

Figurine, frog w/mandolin, pastels on bisque, 3½"....**$18.00**

Figurine, girl w/basket, Hummel type, 4½" **$25.00**

Figurine, girl w/playful dog, Hummel type, EX painted details, 8" **$40.00**

Figurine, horse, white, simply styled, 2¼" **$5.00**

Figurine, Hummel-type girl with basket, 5½", $25.00.

Figurine, Indian chief, bright colors, red mark, 5½"...**$25.00**

Figurine, Oriental lady w/fan, marked Ardalt, Lenwile China, 3¾" **$35.00**

Figurine, Oriental male dancer, EX painted details, 10"..**$20.00**

Figurine, Oriental man w/mandolin & lady w/bowl, pastels on bisque, black mark, 6", pr **$45.00**

Figurine, rooster & hen on base, realistic browns & blacks w/red combs, rooster's head up, hen's down, 5"...**$5.00**

Figurine, Siamese dancers, bright colors, 8¾", pr.....**$100.00**

Figurine, spaniel, brown & white, 4½x5½" **$18.00**

Figurine, squirrels (2) on base, brown & white, 4½x5"..**$20.00**

Figurine, terrier, realistic appearance, Ucagco, 4" **$17.50**

Figurine, terriers (2), realistic appearance, on base, 4½x7".**$28.00**

Figurine, terriers (2), realistic appearance, 3½ " **$18.00**

Figurine, violinist boy, bright colors, turquoise mark, 3¾" **$12.50**

Incense burner, Oriental figure seated w/container, multicolor paint **$20.00**

Lamp, Colonial couple on base, pastels on bisque, 11", pr..**$115.00**

Mug, banded barrel form w/man as handle................**$20.00**

Mug, devil's face figural, tan, brown & gray, ceramic ..**$40.00**

Mug, flower embossed & painted on black, nude figural handle **$25.00**

Nativity set, 7 painted ceramic pieces, tallest figure: 2½"...**$40.00**

Novelty, boot, painted decoration, 2⅞" **$6.00**

Novelty, pitcher vase, applied rose on yellow, Mariyama, 3½"..**$10.00**

Planter, Black girl in pink dress stands beside open ear-of-corn planter..**$50.00**

Planter, Colonial couple w/rabbits, pastels on bisque, Paulux, 5¼x7¼" **$200.00**

Planter, Mexican boy in lg sombrero sits beside lg pot, bright colors **$10.00**

Planter, Oriental man pushing open wheelbarrow, bright colors **$7.00**

Planter, Sudanese lady (head & shoulders), gold earrings, opening in scarf at top of head............................**$35.00**

Plaque, musical couple in relief, pastels on white, rectangular, bisque **$40.00**

Plate, flower on white, open latticework at rim, Rosetti, Chicago, USA, 8¼"......................................**$22.50**

Plate, flower on white w/gold trim, 1 handle at side, 5¾"...**$15.00**

Powder jar, lady figural, wide skirt forms base of jar, bright colors, 5¾" **$40.00**

Purse, white beaded clutch type, EX **$40.00**

Salt & pepper shakers, Dutch boy & girl, bright colors, pr **$15.00**

Salt & pepper shakers, eggplant, purple w/green leaves, pr **$10.00**

Salt & pepper shakers, yellow apple & pear shakers, set on 2-lobed green basket, 3-pc set...................**$15.00**

Sugar bowl, gold-tone metal, w/lid, 2¼x5" **$12.50**

Tea set, Donald Duck on white, 4-place w/tureen & platter, child size..**$95.00**

Tea set, floral on white, child size, 2-place.................**$35.00**

Tea set, floral on white, child size, 6-place w/serving pcs ..**$125.00**

Teapot, black, simple style, 2-cup.............................**$12.50**

Toothbrush holder, Dutch children kissing, bright colors..**$30.00**

Toothpick holder, accordion player beside basket, multicolor paint **$4.00**

Toothpick holder, cowboy seated beside holder, multicolor paint **$18.00**

Towel, blue embroidery on ecru, 13x17" **$22.50**

Toy, duck, celluloid, 4½" **$20.00**

Wall pocket, iris figural, realistic colors **$20.00**

Wine goblet, lacquerware, exotic bird on black, gold interior, long stem **$15.00**

Old MacDonald's Farm

This is a wonderful line of novelty kitchenware items fashioned as the family and the animals that live on Old MacDonald's Farm. It's been popular with collectors for quite some time, and prices are astronomical, though they seem to have stabilized, at least for now.

These things were made by the Regal China Company, who also made some of the Little Red Riding Hood items that are so collectible, as well as figural cookie jars, 'hugger' salt and pepper shakers, and decanters. The Roerig's devote a chapter to Regal in their book *The Collector's Encyclopedia of Cookie Jars* and, in fact, show the entire Old MacDonald's Farm line.

Advisor: Rick Spencer (See Directory, Regal China)

Butter dish, cow's head................................**$220.00**

Canister, flour, cereal or coffee, med, each..............**$220.00**

Canister, pretzels, peanuts, popcorn, chips or tidbits, lg, each **$300.00**

Canister, salt, sugar or tea, med, each **$220.00**

Canister, soap or cookies, lg, each............................**$300.00**

Cookie jar, barn **$275.00**

Creamer, rooster **$110.00**

Grease jar, pig...**$175.00**

Pitcher, milk..**$400.00**

Salt & pepper shakers, boy & girl, pr **$75.00**
Salt & pepper shakers, churn, gold trim, pr **$90.00**
Salt & pepper shakers, feed sack w/sheep, pr..........**$195.00**

Spice set, $100.00 each.

Sugar bowl, hen..**$125.00**
Teapot, duck's head **$250.00**

Paden City Glassware

The Paden City Glass Company began operations in 1916 in Paden City, West Virginia. The company's early lines consisted largely of the usual pressed tablewares, but by the 1920s production had expanded to include colored wares in translucent as well as opaque glass in a variety of patterns and styles. The company maintained its high standards of handmade perfection until 1949, when under new management automation took the place of many operations formerly done by hand. The Paden City Glass Company closed in 1951; its earlier wares, the colored patterns in particular, are becoming very collectible.

Paden City Glass is not always easily recognized by collectors or dealers, as it was almost never marked. It is believed this was so the glass could be sold to decorating companies. The company assigned both line numbers and names to many of its blanks or sets of glassware. Colors were sometimes given more than one name, and etchings were named as well. All this makes identification of items offered for sale through mail order difficult, and labels prepared by dealers are often confusing.

A review of literature available on Paden City reveals the following names for the company's plate etchings: Ardith; California Poppy; Cupid; Delilah Bird (Peacock Reverse); Eden Rose; Frost; Gazebo; Gothic Garden; Lela Bird; Nora Bird; Orchid (three variations); Peacock and Rose (Peacock and Wild Rose); Samarkand; Trumpet Flower; Utopia. Names given to cuttings made on Paden City blanks are Yorktown and Lazy Daisy. It is not clear whether the names originated with Paden City or with secondary decorating companies.

See also Kitchen Collectibles.

Advisors: George and Mary Hurney (See Directory, Paden City Glassware). (Note: their interest is only in glassware, not the pottery.)

Bookends, American eagle head, frosted crystal, 7½", pr.**$300.00**
Bowl, Hotcha, amber, 3-footed, 12" **$26.00**

Candle holders, Gadroon, blue, 5½", $125.00 for the pair.

Candy dish, Crow's Foot, crystal, 3-part, w/lid **$70.00**
Cocktail, Glades, Hotcha, crystal w/platinum trim, footed cone, 3½" **$8.00**
Compote, Vale, ruby, floral etched, ball stem & finial, 9½x6¾" dia **$58.00**
Cotton-ball dispenser, bunny, ears back, frosted crystal..**$60.00**
Cotton-ball dispenser, bunny, ears up, frosted pink.**$150.00**
Creamer, Party, green **$3.00**
Cup, punch; Gazebo, crystal...**$8.00**
Cup & saucer, Mrs B, ruby...**$7.50**
Cup & saucer, Penny Line, ruby **$8.00**
Figurine, Dragon Swan, crystal....................................**$155.00**
Figurine, goose, crystal..**$50.00**
Figurine, goose, light blue, 5".....................................**$115.00**
Figurine, horse, rearing, crystal **$160.00**
Figurine, pheasant, Chinese; crystal, 6x13¾"...............**$90.00**
Figurine, pheasant, Chinese; med blue, 13¾" **$150.00**
Figurine, polar bear on ice, crystal, 4½".......................**$65.00**
Figurine, pony, crystal, 12" **$100.00**
Figurine, pouter pigeon, crystal w/Silver Mist highlights.**$125.00**
Figurine, rooster, Barnyard; crystal, 8¾"......................**$85.00**
Figurine, rooster, Elegant; light blue, 11"...................**$225.00**
Figurine, squirrel on curved log, crystal, 5½" **$65.00**
Goblet, water; Penny Line, ruby, 6" **$12.50**
Plate, Mrs B, amber, 8" **$6.00**

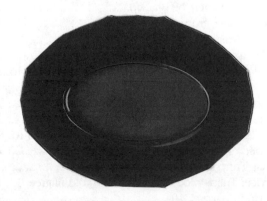

Platter, Crow's Foot, black or blue, 12", $32.50.

Powder jar, Penny Line, amber, w/lid.........................$20.00
Relish, Glade, Hotcha, crystal, 4-part, 4-lobed, handled ..$24.00
Salt & pepper shakers, Penny Line, amber, pr.............$8.00
Sandwich server, Mrs B, amber, center handle $15.00
Sandwich server, Mrs B, ruby, center handle.............$28.00
Wine, Futura, crystal, 3-oz....................................$8.50
Wine, Penny Line, ruby, 4¾"..................................$12.50

Paden City Pottery Company

Founded in 1907, this company produced many dinnerware and kitchenware lines until they closed in the 1950s. Many were decaled. In fact, this is the company credited with originating the underglaze decal process.

One of their most collectible lines is called Caliente. It was Paden City's version of the solid-color dinnerware lines that became so popular in the thirties and forties. Caliente's shapes were simple and round, but its shell-like finials, handles, and feet did little to enhance its Art Deco possibilities which the public seemed to prefer at that time. As a result, it never sold in volume comparable to Fiesta or Bauer's Ring, but with a little patience, you should eventually be able to rebuild a set. If you'd like to see photographs of this line and many others produced by Paden City, see *The Collector's Encylcopedia of American Dinnerware* by Jo Cunningham.

Bowl, cream soup; Caliente, from $12 to $15.00
Bowl, mixing; Caliente, 9".....................................$20.00
Bowl, soup; Caliente, 7"..$15.00
Bowl, soup; Elite, 7¾"..$9.00
Bowl, vegetable; Caliente, 9" $20.00
Carafe, Caliente..$45.00
Casserole, Caliente, from $30 to..............................$35.00
Casserole, Orange Blossom, in Manning Bowman chrome
    frame...$35.00
Casserole, Papoco...$22.00
Creamer & sugar bowl, Caliente, from $30 to.............$35.00
Creamer & sugar bowl, Manhattan............................$10.00
Creamer & sugar bowl, Nasturtium, Shell-Crest shape .$25.00
Creamer & sugar bowl, Papoco.................................$15.00
Cup & saucer, Cosmos, Shenandoah mark....................$7.50
Cup & saucer, Manhattan $6.00
Cup & saucer, Springblossom $7.50
Cup & saucer, Touch of Black...................................$7.50
Gravy boat, Elite, from $9 to $12.00
Gravy boat, Nasturtium, Shell-Crest shape..................$16.00
Pie plate, Bak-Serv, 10" $12.00
Plate, American Beauty, Minion shape, 10", from $10 to..$12.00
Plate, Caliente, 10"..$12.50
Plate, Corn Is Green, 10".......................................$25.00
Plate, Duchess, on Ivory Tu-Tone shoulder, 10" $6.00
Plate, novelty cartoon by Peter Arno, 6", from $6 to..$10.00
Plate, Papco, 10" $8.00
Plate, Rust Tulip, Shell-Crest shape, 9"....................$6.00
Plate, service; Tulip, wide cobalt band w/gold filigree, 12".$10.00
Plate, Springblossom, 10".......................................$10.00
Plate, Touch of Black, 10".......................................$6.00
Plate, Yellow Rose, Minion shape, 10" $7.00

Platter, Blossoms, on Shell-Crest shape, 14" $6.00
Platter, Cosmos, Shenandoah mark, 14".......................$12.00
Platter, Paden Rose, 14"..$15.00

Teapot, Caliente, $50.00.

Tray, floral-decaled insert marked Shenandoah, in Farberware frame w/handle...................................$30.00

Paper Dolls

One of the earliest producers of paper dolls was Raphael Tuck of England, who distributed many of their dolls in the United States in the late 1800s. Advertising companies used them to promote their products, and some were often included in the pages of leading ladies' magazines.

But over the years, the most common paper dolls have been those printed on the covers of a book containing their clothes on the inside pages. These were initiated during the 1920s, and because they were inexpensive, retained their popularity even during the Depression years. They peaked in the 1940s, but with the advent of television in the 1950s, children began to loose interest. Be sure to check old boxes and trunks in your attic; you just may find some!

But what's really exciting right now are those from more recent years — celebrity dolls from television shows like The Brady Bunch or The Waltons, the skinny English model Twiggy, and movie stars like Rock Hudson and Debbie Reynolds. Just remember that cut sets (even if all original components are still there) are worth only about half the price of dolls in mint, uncut, originial condition.

If you'd like to learn more about them, we recommend *Collector's Guide to Paper Dolls* (there are two in the series) and *Collector's Guide to Magazine Paper Dolls,* all by Mary Young. Other references: *Collecting Toys #6* by Richard O'Brien; *Schroeder's Collectible Toys, Antique to Modern;* and *Toys, Antique and Collectible,* by David Longest.

Advisor: Mary Young (See Directory, Paper Dolls)

Newsletter: *Paper Dolls News*
Ema Terry
P.O. Box 807
Vivian, LA 71082; Subscription: $12 per year for 6 issues; want lists, sale items and trades listed

Newsletter: *Paper Doll and Doll Diary*
Mary Longo
P.O. Box 12146
Lake Park, FL 33403; Subscription: $12 per year for 6 issues

Annette (Funicello) in Hawaii, Whitman #1969, 1961, cut, complete, VG+ **$25.00**

Archie's Girls Betty & Veronica, Samuel Lowe #2764, 1964, uncut, M, from $35 to.......................**$50.00**

Baby Tender Love, Whitman #1949, 1974, uncut, M ..**$12.00**

Beth Ann Paper Doll & Clothes, Whitman #1955, 1970, uncut, M **$35.00**

Bob Cummings Fashion Models, Samuel Lowe #2407, 1957, uncut, M, from $60 to.......................**$75.00**

Bob Hope & Dorothy Lamour Cut-Out Book, Whitman #975, 1942, uncut, M, from $175 to **$250.00**

Brenda Lee, Teen-Age Celebrity Doll Book, Samuel Lowe #2785, 1961, uncut, M, from $60 to.....................**$70.00**

Buffy, Whitman #1985, 1968, cut, complete, VG+ **$15.00**

Carol Heiss, Whitman #1964, 1961, cut, complete, EX ...**$30.00**

Charmin' Chatty, Whitman #1959, 1964, uncut, M......**$25.00**

Chitty-Chitty Bang-Bang, Whitman #1982, 1968, cut, complete, EX..**$25.00**

Crystal Barbie, Whitman #1983-46, 1984, cut, complete, NM..**$4.00**

Debbie Reynolds, Whitman #1948, 1962, uncut, M **$80.00**

Dennis the Menace Back-Yard Picnic, Whitman #1991, 1960, cut, complete, EX.......................................**$30.00**

Dorothy Provine, Whitman #1964, 1962, cut, complete, EX **$25.00**

Dr Kildare Play Book, Samuel Lowe #955, uncut, M..**$20.00**

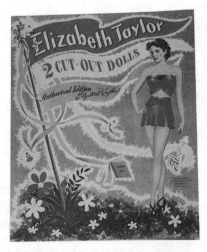

Elizabeth Taylor, Whitman #968, 1949, uncut, from $95.00 to $150.00.

Flintstones, A Great Big Punch-Out, Whitman #1982, 1961, uncut, M **$95.00**

Gene Autry's Melody Ranch Cut-Out Dolls, Whitman #990, 1950, uncut, M **$100.00**

Girls in the War, Samuel Lowe #1028, 1943, uncut, M, from $75 to...**$125.00**

Haley Mills 'That Darn Cat' Cut-Out Doll, Whitman #1955, 1965, uncut, M **$50.00**

Here Comes the Bride, Samuel Lowe #2718, 1971, uncut, M...**$10.00**

Honeymooners w/Jackie Gleason, Samuel Lowe #2560, 1956, uncut, M, from $175 to..........................**$300.00**

Jane Withers, Whitman #977, 1936, a Big-As-Life Doll, uncut, M, from $150 to **$200.00**

Jem Paper Doll, Whitman #1524, 1986, uncut, M **$6.00**

Josie & the Pussycats, Whitman #1982, 1971, cut, complete, EX..**$18.00**

June Allyson Cut-Out Dolls, Whitman #970, 1950, uncut, M...**$100.00**

King of Swing & Queen of Song, Benny Goodman & Peggy Lee, Samuel Lowe #1040, 1942, uncut, M, from $200 to **$400.00**

Lennon Sisters, Whitman #1979, 1958, cut, complete, EX..**$25.00**

Little Kiddles, Whitman #1961, 1966, cut, complete, EX+ ..**$20.00**

Lucille Ball and Desi Arnaz, Whitman #2116, 1953, uncut, from $75.00 to $100.00. (Photo courtesy Ric Wyman)

Lucy, Whitman #1963, 1964, cut, complete, NM.........**$30.00**

Malibu Francie Doll Book, Whitman #1955, 1973, uncut, M.**$20.00**

Malibu Skipper, Whitman #1952, 1972, uncut, M........**$15.00**

Margaret O'Brien, Whitman #963, 1946, uncut, M, from $75 to...**$125.00**

Marie Osmond, Saalfield #5225, 1973, uncut, from $40.00 to $50.00. (Photo courtesy Mary Young)

Maxie, Whitman #1544, 1989, uncut, M, from $3 to **$4.00**

Midge, Whitman #1962, 1963, cut, complete, EX+......**$25.00**

Moon Dreamers, Whitman #1542, 1987, uncut, M, from $3 to..**$4.00**

My Buddy, Whitman #1535, 1986, uncut, M, from $2 to...**$4.00**

Natalie Wood, Whitman #1962, 1957, cut, complete, EX.**$35.00**

New Toni Hair-Do Dress-Up Dolls, Samuel Lowe #1251, 1951, from $60 to...**$75.00**

Newborn Thumbelina, Whitman #1967, 1969, cut, complete, EX...**$8.00**

Our Gang Cut-Out Dolls, Whitman #900, 1931, uncut, M, from $175 to...**$250.00**

Pat Boone, Whitman #1968, 1959, cut, complete, EX...**$30.00**

Patti Page, Samuel Lowe #2406, 1957, uncut, M, from $60 to **$85.00**

Princess Diana, Whitman #1985-50, 1985, cut, complete, EX **$15.00**

Princess of Power, Whitman #1984-54, 1985, cut, complete, EX..**$3.00**

Punky Brewster, Whitman #1532, 1986, uncut, M, from $3 to **$5.00**

Raggedy Ann and Andy, Whitman #1988-1, 1978, uncut, from $18.00 to $25.00.

Rainbow Brite, Whitman #7407-C, 1983-84, cut, complete, EX (EX box) **$4.00**

Ricky Nelson, Whitman #2081, 1959, cut, complete, NM..**$35.00**

Rosemary Clooney, Samuel Lowe #2569, 1956, uncut, M.**$85.00**

Rub-a-Dub Dolly, Whitman #1941, 1977, uncut, M **$10.00**

Sabrina & the Archies, Whitman #1978, 1971, cut, complete, EX..**$18.00**

Shirley Temple, Whitman #1986, 1976, cut, complete, EX..**$15.00**

Star Princess & Pluta, Whitman #1839, 1979, uncut, M...**$15.00**

Super Star Barbie, Whitman #1537-2, 1989, uncut, M, from $3 to **$5.00**

Tina & Trudy, Whitman #1952, 1967, uncut, M **$35.00**

Walt Disney's Beauty & the Beast, Whitman #1675, 1991, uncut, M..**$3.00**

Walt Disney's Cinderella, Whitman #1545, 1989, uncut, M, from $3 to..**$4.00**

Walt Disney's Cinderella, Whitman #1992, 1965, cut, complete, EX+ **$35.00**

Walt Disney's Mouseketeer Linda, Whitman #1957, 1958, uncut, M **$50.00**

Pencil Sharpeners

The whittling process of sharpening pencils with pocketknives was replaced by mechanical means in the 1880s. By the turn of the century, many ingenious desk-type sharpeners had been developed. Small pencil sharpeners designed for the purse or pocket were produced in the 1890s. The typical design consisted of a small steel tube containing a cutting blade which could be adjusted by screws. Mass-produced novelty pencil sharpeners became popular in the late 1920s. The most detailed figurals were made in Germany. These German sharpeners that originally sold for less than a dollar are now considered highly collectible!

Disney and other character pencil sharpeners have been produced in Catalin, plastic, ceramic, and rubber. Novelty battery-operated pencil sharpeners can also be found. For over fifty years pencil sharpeners have been used as advertising giveaways — from Baker's Chocolates and Coca-Cola's metal figurals to the plastic 'Marshmallow Man' distributed by McDonald's. As long as we have pencils, new pencil sharpeners will be produced, much to the delight of collectors.

Advisor: Phil Helley (See Directory, Pencil Sharpeners)

Bakelite, Bambi, WDP, round, 1"................................**$50.00**

Bakelite, Br'er Fox, round & fluted, 1⅜" **$55.00**

Bakelite, Goofy, round & fluted, 1½" **$55.00**

Bakelite, Hep Cats, round & fluted, 1⅜" **$40.00**

Bakelite, Lampwick, WDP, figural, 1¾" **$65.00**

Bakelite, mantel clock, Germany, 2"..........................**$47.00**

Bakelite, Pablo, round & fluted, 1" **$45.00**

Bakelite, Panchito, WDP, round, 1"..........................**$36.00**

Bakelite, pig, 1⅜" **$70.00**

Bakelite, Snow White, WDE, figural, 1¾"..................**$75.00**

Bakelite, Thumper, WDP, round, 1" **$47.00**

Bakelite, US Army tank, 2"..**$46.00**

Bakelite, USA Army plane..**$75.00**

Bakelite, Walt Disney's train, figural, 1¾"..................**$80.00**

Bakelite, 1939 NY World's Fair **$70.00**

Celluloid, Black bride, $150.00. (Photo courtesy Phil Helley)

Celluloid, pelican, Japan, 3"......................................**$100.00**

Metal, alarm clock, Japan..**$38.00**

Metal, Charlie Chaplin, Germany, 2¼"......................**$100.00**

Metal, Coke bottle, Bavaria, 1¾" **$40.00**

Metal, cuckoo clock, Germany, 2¼" **$120.00**

Metal, Eiffel Tower, Germany, 2¼" **$85.00**

Metal, Felix the Cat, 1½"..**$165.00**

Metal, Great Dane, Germany, 2"................................**$80.00**

Metal, piano player, Germany, 2"..............................**$85.00**

Metal, soccer player, Germany, 1¾"..........................**$85.00**

Metal, stop & go light, 2¼"......................................**$70.00**

Occupied Japan, Black Uncle Sam w/bow tie **$145.00**

Occupied Japan, bulldog head, 1½" **$95.00**

Occupied Japan, clown w/bow tie **$65.00**

Occupied Japan, Indian chief head............................**$90.00**

Occupied Japan, smiling pig w/hat............................**$90.00**

Plastic, Bireley's soda bottle, 3" **$35.00**

Plastic, Ronald McDonald, 2".................................**$10.00**
Plastic, Sunbeam Bread, 1"...**$10.00**
Pot metal, pocket watch, Cracker Jack, unmarked.....**$35.00**

Pennsbury Pottery

From the 1950s throughout the 1960s, this pottery was sold in gift stores and souvenir shops along the Pennsylvania Turnpike. It was produced in Morrisville, Pennsylvania, by Henry and Lee Below. Much of the ware was hand painted in multicolor on caramel backgrounds, though some pieces were made in blue and white. Most of the time, themes centered around Amish people, barber shop singers, roosters, hex signs, and folky mottos.

Much of the ware is marked, and if you're in the Pennsylvania/New Jersey area, you'll find a lot of it. It's fairly prevalent in the Midwest as well and can still sometimes be found at bargain prices. If you'd like to learn more about this pottery, we recommend *Pennsbury Pottery Video Book* by Shirley Graff and BA Wellman.

Advisor: Shirley Graff (See Directory, Pennsbury)

Ashtray, Outen the Light...**$30.00**

Bowl, divided vegetable; Red Rooster, 9½x6¼", $50.00.

Bowl, Dutch Talk, scarce, 9"..**$70.00**
Coffee mug, eagle...**$20.00**
Coffeepot, Hex, 6-cup..**$75.00**
Creamer, Amish man, 2½"..**$30.00**
Cup, Red Rooster...**$25.00**
Figurine, chickadee, 3½"...**$150.00**
Figurine, hen, any color, 10½".....................................**$250.00**
Figurine, ring-neck pheasant, minimum value..........**$600.00**
Mug, beer; Amish...**$45.00**
Mug, beer; Gay Ninety..**$45.00**
Mug, beer; Red Barn...**$35.00**
Pie plate, Amish couple by apple tree, 9".................**$65.00**
Pitcher, Hex, 6¼"..**$55.00**
Saucer, Red Rooster...**$10.00**
Teapot, Red Rooster...**$95.00**
Wall pocket, God Bless Our Mortgaged Home..........**$90.00**

Pepsi-Cola

People have been enjoying Pepsi-Cola since before the turn of the century. Various logos have been registered over the years; the familiar oval was first used in the early 1940s. At about the same time, the two 'dots' between the words Pepsi and Cola became one, though more recent items may carry the double-dot logo as well, especially when they're designed to be reminiscent of the old ones. The bottle cap logo came along in 1943 and with variations was used through the early 1960s.

Though there are expensive rarities, most items are still reasonable, since collectors are just now beginning to discover how fascinating this line of advertising memorabilia can be. There are three books in the series called *Pepsi-Cola Collectibles* written by Bill Vehling and Michael Hunt, which we highly recommend. Another good reference is *Introduction to Pepsi Collecting* by Bob Stoddard.

Advisor: Craig and Donna Stifter (See Directory, Pepsi-Cola)

Newsletter: *Pepsi-Cola Collectors Club Express*
Bob Stoddard, Editor
P.O. Box 1275
Covina, CA 91723; Send SASE for information

Blotter, Drink...Delicious Healthful, black on brown, G..**$70.00**
Bottle carrier, tin, oval Pepsi-Cola logo, rounded handle, VG+..**$50.00**
Bottle crate, wood w/stamped Pepsi-Cola logo, EX...**$70.00**

Bottle display, foil-covered cardboard, 1930s, 18x5", EX, $385.00. (Photo courtesy Craig and Donna Stifter)

Bottle opener, wall mount, embossed Pepsi-Cola, G.**$20.00**
Calendar, 1920, cardboard w/12 months at bottom, Rolf Armstrong artwork, 5x7", EX............................**$3,800.00**
Calendar, 1941, George Petty artwork, complete, 15x23", EX...**$700.00**
Calendar, 1941, Support American Art series, complete, 15x20", EX..**$65.00**
Calendar, 1945, Support American Art series, complete, 15x20", EX..**$65.00**
Calendar, 1950, 6 pages, 13x22", EX........................**$375.00**
Calendar, 1951, shows lady walking dog, complete, 16x33", EX...**$750.00**

Can, cone-top w/cap, 1940-50s, 12-oz, EX..............$240.00

Change mat, rubber, 1960s, 8½x11", $95.00.

Clock, glass & metal, shows bottle cap on face, 1950s, 15" dia, EX...$275.00

Clock, light-up, plastic bottle cap, 1950s, 12" diameter, VG, $175.00. (Photo courtesy Gary Metz)

Game, Big League Baseball, 1950s-60s, EX.................$95.00

Paper cup, Pepsi's Best, bottle cap, red, white & blue, NM $18.00

Pocketknife, Pepsi-Cola 5¢ in blue on bone-colored handle, 3", EX...$60.00

Score sheet, Pepsi-Cola flanked by the Pepsi cops above, 8x4¼", NM...$5.00

Sign, cardboard, More Bounce to the Ounce, 1950, 11x28", EX $250.00

Sign, cardboard, Rolf Armstrong artwork, 1919, 23x28", EX...$1,800.00

Sign, cardboard cutout w/easel back, shows lady holding 6-pack, 1960, EX...$125.00

Sign, counter-top, Drink..., contour logo, lights up, 1950s, 14" dia, EX..$175.00

Sign, diecut cardboard Santa, 1951, 20", NM, from $100 to $185.00

Sign, embossed plastic Santa, cardboard back, lights up, 1956, 26", EX...$175.00

Sign, tin, Say Pepsi, Please, shows bottle, 1965, 18x48", EX...$125.00

Sign, tin, shows bottle w/5¢ on each side, 1936, 11x49", EX...$450.00

Stadium cushion, Pepsi logo on blue, M.....................$30.00

Tray, deep-dish, lg Pepsi-Cola bottle cap in center, 12" dia, EX $150.00

Perfume Bottles

Here's an area of bottle collecting that has definitely come into its own. Commercial bottles, as you can see from our listings, are very popular. Their values are based on several factors, for instance: is it sealed or full, does it have its original label, and is the original package or box present.

Figural bottles are interesting, especially the ceramic ones with tiny regal crowns as their stoppers.

Club: International Perfume and Scent Bottle Collectors Association
c/o Phyllis Dohanian
53 Marlborough St.
Boston, MA 02116-2099; 617-266-4351

Club: Perfume and Scent Bottle Collectors
Jeane Parris
2022 E Charleston Blvd.
Las Vegas, NV 89104; Membership: $15 USA or $30 foreign (includes quarterly newsletter). Information requires SASE

A'Bientot, Lucien Lelong, rectangular crystal base, flat rectangular stopper, 2½" $42.00

Apple Blossom, Lander, square base w/clock label, red scrolled base, 2½"..$32.00

Arpege, Lanvin, black ball w/gold trim, 3"..................$95.00

Asume, Coty, opaline ball base w/round foot & ball stopper, 2"..$60.00

Avon, snowman shape w/ribbon scarf, top hat cap, 2"..$8.00

Avon solid perfume, gold oval pendant/pin w/faceted jewel, 2"..$28.00

Avon solid perfume ring, cameo design, 1" $20.00

Beau Catcher, Vigny, ribbon at neck, 3¾"..................$42.00

Beverly Hills, Gale Hayman, metal leopard figural stopper, 2x1½", MIB...$65.00

Big Deal, lion figural wearing business suit, 5¾", from $35 to..$40.00

Blue Grass, Elizabeth Arden, grenade-shaped base & matching stopper, 6½"..$52.00

Blue Waltz, heart shape w/label, 4½" $5.00

Bug-sprayer perfume, metal, 2"................................$50.00

Capricci, Nina Ricci, diamond-cut bulbous base, marked Lalique, 3½" $145.00

Chanel #5, clear square base w/label, flat faceted square stopper, 2½", from $8 to $10.00

Chi Chi, crystal heart on frosted base, polished brass cap, 3½", from $70 to..$75.00

Confetti, Lentheric, bottle form w/swag ruffle, bow stopper, 7"...$48.00

Credo, Prince Obalenski, classical pillar-shaped base, crown top, 6" $32.00

Crepe de Chine, Milot, octagonal base w/flat front & back, metallic label, facted crystal stopper, 3½"............$42.00

Danger, Ciro, stepped glass base w/square foot, gold enamel labels, brass cap, 2¾" $8.00

Dubarry of London, multi-faceted base, metal cap, 2" .**$20.00**

Emeraude, Coty, foil label, green top, 4¾", drawer-type box w/tassel..**$60.00**

Evening in Paris, cobalt body w/fluted silver screw-on top, 3¾", from $7 to.....................................**$10.00**

Evening Star, Blanchard, 8-sided faceted topaz base, faceted Bakelite top, 5¾"..................................**$48.00**

Femme, Marcel Rochas, Paris, urn shape w/flat round stopper, 3", w/cylindrical box.............................**$50.00**

Flambeau, Faberge, whistle shape, 3", MIB..............**$38.00**

Forever Amber, Kathryn, stylized lady figural, 4¾" **$62.00**

Friendship Garden, Shulton, tapered cylindrical base w/florals on rounded shoulders, enameled leaves, green dome cap.......................................**$8.00**

Gay Whirl, pink Bakelite girl figural on stepped crystal base, 7¼"...**$75.00**

Ginger Blossom, Harders, glass tube bottle in faceted & stepped wooden holder, sm **$35.00**

Gipsy, George Mauret, rectangular crystal base w/embossed gold label, faceted top, 2", w/original box..........**$65.00**

Heaven, Lander, candlestick shape w/flame stopper, 5"..**$12.50**

High Lights, Stewart, table lamp shade w/3 sm bottles on metal lamp stand, 6"...............................**$55.00**

HIS, Cordovan, stylized man's torso & Bakelite head, 6¼"..**$95.00**

Honeysuckle, Houbigant, 6-sided crystal base w/domed cap, 5"...**$32.00**

Hot Date, full-length wolf figural dressed in sport suit, hat-shaped cap, 6½" **$52.00**

Imagination, Lioret, pink dress on mannequin shape, dome cap, 3¾"..**$42.00**

Joy, Jean Patou, sm square bottle w/cylindrical cap, zippered compact-shaped pouch **$20.00**

L'Heure Bleue, Guerlain, square crystal base w/scroll at shoulder, mushroom cap, 3½"............................**$45.00**

L'Heure Bleue, Guerlain, tapered cyclindrical base w/sm round indented foot, tall cylindrical cap, 3".........**$22.00**

L'Interdit, Givenchy, crystal w/square label, cylindrical top, 1", red drawer-style box......................**$22.00**

La Nuit, Worth Dans, dimpled ball base w/narrow neck, ball stopper, marked Lalique, 4" **$55.00**

Lavin set: Scandal, My Sin & Rumeur, crystal bases w/black crystal stoppers, 2", original stepped & hinged box **$85.00**

Le Dandy, D'Orsay, 6-sided bottle w/indented base & narrow neck, 6½" **$18.00**

Linetti of Italy, porcelain & glass kerosene lamp w/floral medallion, 7" **$40.00**

Lynette, bottle on red velvet ice cream chair, 3¾" **$58.00**

Meteor, Coty, tall cylindrical body w/scrollwork at base & rounded shoulder, flared cap, 3"...................**$38.00**

Meteor, Coty, tall tapered cylindrical base, w/cone-shaped stopper, gold foil label, 3"...........................**$42.00**

Mimsy, 6-sided base w/embossed florals, flat faceted stopper, 6"..**$47.50**

Mitsouko, Guerlain, tapered fluted sides, tall cylindrical cap, 3", flip-top box.......................................**$47.00**

Moment Supreme, Jean Patou, flat crescent-shaped base w/rectangular foot, fan-shaped stopper, 5½", from $30 to....**$38.00**

Moss Rose, Charles of the Ritz, waisted white bottle w/florals, teardrop stopper, 7½"...........................**$32.00**

Muse, Coty, embossed gold label, inner stopper, 4¼"..**$130.00**

My Love, Elizabeth Arden, frosted stopper, name in gold enamel, full and sealed, in original box with celluloid cover, $220.00. (Photo courtesy Monsen & Baer Auctions)

Narcisse, Caron, squatty oval base w/flat stopper, 1⅝", MIB **$42.00**

Narcisse, Jerri, triangular base w/flat button stopper, 5¾", MIB **$48.00**

Nikki, Orloff, double eagles w/outstretched wings, oval foot, metal crown top, 5".................................**$52.00**

Nina Ricci solid perfume, pocket watch shape w/stones & cameo at center, 2", from $30 to **$35.00**

Paris, Coty, flat square base w/sm label, 2¾", w/scenic flip-top box..**$38.00**

Quelques Fleurs, Houbigant, flat ovoid body, blue fluted mushroom cap, 5"......................................**$12.00**

Replique, acorn shape, marked Lalique, 2" **$150.00**

Scarlette O'Hara, Pinaud, Southern belle figural, 7"....**$60.00**

Schiaparelli, tee-shirt shape w/script letters.................**$25.00**

Sculptura, Jovan, silver torso on black base, 2¾".......**$45.00**

Seventh Heaven, Bergel, geometric Lucite base, 6"....**$68.00**

Sincerely Jenny, Gidding, 5-sided base w/applied gold foil over shoulders, round glass stopper, 6"...............**$80.00**

Stewart, tea cart w/mini bottles, w/lock & key, 3" **$70.00**

Tailspin, Lucien Lelong, metal lipstick tube shape, 3" ...**$25.00**

Ting a Ling, Lucien Lelong, urn shape w/round foot & free-hanging jingle bells, sm **$100.00**

20 Carats, Dana, gold foil inclusions in perfume, in gold and white brocade box and outer box, $80.00. (Photo courtesy Monsen & Baer Auctions)

Vantines, crystal Buddah figural w/amber glass stopper, 7"...**$70.00**

Venice, Rocher, ruby ovoid base w/gold foil label, flame stopper, 3", from $20 to **$25.00**

White Diamonds, Elizabeth Taylor, white bow-shaped stopper, 2", original pouch..............................**$20.00**

White Ginger, sm perfume tube, 2½x3¼" Hawaiian lady's bust figural holder **$42.00**

Wind Song, Prince Matchabelli, crown shape w/gold top, 2¼" **$8.00**

Yanky Clover, Richard Hudnut, flat ovoid body w/finely molded-in diagonal stripes, round label, ball stopper, 4½" **$10.00**

Zigane, Corday, crystal violin w/crystal stopper, 4½"..**$200.00**

18th Century, United Toilet Goods, red ceramic w/George Washington profile portrait in oval, coin stopper, 4¾" **$48.00**

Pez Candy Dispensers

Though Pez candy has been around since the late 1920s, the dispensers that we all remember as children weren't introduced until the 1950s. Each had the head of a certain character — a Mexican, a doctor, Santa Claus, an animal, or perhaps a comic book hero. It's hard to determine the age of some of these, but if yours have tabs or 'feet' on the bottom so they can stand up, they were made in the last ten years. Though early on, collectors focused on this feature to evaluate their finds, now it's simply the character's head that's important to them. Some have variations in color and design, both of which can greatly affect value. For instance, Batman may have a blue hood and a black mask, or both his mask and his hood may match; sometimes they're both black and sometimes they're blue. (The first one is the most valuable.)

Condition is important; watch out for broken or missing parts. If a Pez is not in mint condition, most are worthless. Original packaging can add to the value, particularly a blister card. If the card has special graphics or information, this is especially true. Early figures were sometimes sold in boxes, but these are hard to find. Nowadays you'll see them offered 'mint in package,' sometimes at premium prices. But most intense Pez collectors say that those cellophane bags add very little if any to the value.

For more information, refer to *A Pictorial Guide to Plastic Candy Dispensers Featuring Pez* by David Welch; *Schroeder's Collectible Toys, Antique to Modern;* and *Collecting Toys #6* by Richard O'Brien.

Advisor: Richard Belyski (See Directory, Pez)

Newsletter: *Pez Collector's News*
Richard and Marianne Belyski, Editors
P.O. Box 124
Sea Cliff, NY 11579; 516-676-1183; Subscription: $19 for 6 issues)

Baloo, w/feet..**$20.00**
Baseball Glove, no feet...**$150.00**
Batman, w/feet, blue or black, each, from $3 to **$5.00**
Bouncer Beagle, w/feet...**$6.00**
Bugs Bunny, no feet..**$20.00**

Captain America, no feet...**$45.00**
Captain Hook, no feet...**$35.00**
Charlie Brown, w/feet, from $1 to **$3.00**
Chick, w/feet, from $1 to..**$3.00**
Clown, w/feet, whistle head **$6.00**
Cool Cat, w/feet...**$35.00**
Daffy Duck, no feet..**$10.00**
Dino, w/feet, purple, from $1 to..................................**$3.00**

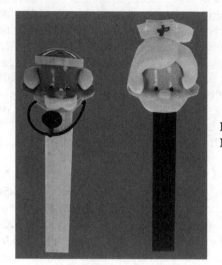

Doctor, $100.00;
Nurse, $100.00.

Donald Duck's Nephew, w/feet, green or blue hat, each.**$6.00**
Donkey, w/feet, whistle head.......................................**$6.00**
Droopy Dog (B), w/feet, painted ears..........................**$6.00**

Droopy Dog, plastic
swivel ears, $15.00.

Fat-Ears Rabbit, no feet, pink head............................**$15.00**
Fozzie Bear, w/feet, from $1 to **$3.00**
Garfield, w/feet, orange w/green hat, from $1 to.........**$3.00**
Gonzo, w/feet, from $1 to **$3.00**
Goofy, no feet, old...**$10.00**
Gyro Gearloose, w/feet..**$6.00**
Hulk, no feet, dark green...**$30.00**
Indian, w/feet, whistle head **$12.00**
Jerry Mouse, w/feet, plastic face **$15.00**
Koala, w/feet, whistle head **$25.00**
Lamb, no feet..**$10.00**
Lion w/Crown, no feet...**$55.00**
Merlin Mouse, w/feet..**$15.00**

Mickey Mouse, w/feet, from $1 to **$3.00**
Miss Piggy, w/feet, eyelashes **$10.00**
Mr Ugly, no feet..**$20.00**
Octopus, no feet, black..**$60.00**
Panda, w/feet, whistle head...**$6.00**
Parrot, w/feet, whistle head...**$6.00**
Pebbles Flintstone, w/feet, from $1 to **$3.00**
Peter Pez (B), w/feet, from $1 to **$3.00**
Pluto, no feet, red...**$10.00**
Raven, no feet, yellow beak **$30.00**
Rhino, w/feet, whistle head **$6.00**
Road Runner, w/feet..**$10.00**
Rooster, w/feet, white or yellow head, each...............**$25.00**
Santa Claus (B), no feet **$85.00**
Scrooge McDuck (B), w/feet **$6.00**
Skull (A), no feet, from $5 to **$10.00**
Snoopy, w/feet, from $1 to...**$5.00**
Spider-Man, no feet, from $10 to **$15.00**
Sylvester (A), w/feet, white whiskers..........................**$5.00**
Teenage Mutant Ninja Turtles, w/feet, 8 variations, each, from
    $1 to...**$3.00**
Tiger, w/feet, whistle head..**$6.00**
Tom (& Jerry), no feet...**$35.00**
Tom (& Jerry), w/plastic face **$15.00**
Tyke, w/feet..**$6.00**
Winnie the Pooh, w/feet..**$50.00**
Yappy Dog, no feet, orange or green, each................**$45.00**

Pfaltzgraff Pottery

Pfaltzgraff has operated in Pennsylvania since the early 1800s making redware at first, then stoneware crocks and jugs, yellow ware and spongeware in the twenties, artware and kitchenware in the thirties, and stoneware kitchen items through the hard years of the forties. In 1950 they developed their first line of dinnerware, called Gourmet Royale (known in later years as simply Gourmet). It was a high-gloss line of solid color accented at the rims with a band of frothy white, similar to lines made later by McCoy, Hull, Harker, and many other companies. Although it also came in pink, it was the dark brown that became so popular. Today these brown stoneware lines are among the newest interests of young collectors as well as those more seasoned, and they all contain more than enough unusual items to make the hunt a bit of a challenge and loads of fun.

The success of Gourmet was just the inspiration that was needed to initiate the production of the many dinnerware lines that have become the backbone of the Pfaltzgraff company.

A giftware line called Muggsy was designed in the late 1940s. It consisted of items such as comic character mugs, ashtrays, bottle stoppers, children's dishes, a pretzel jar, a cookie jar, etc. All of the characters were given names. It was very successful and continued in production until 1960. The older versions have protruding features, while the later ones were simply painted on.

Village, an almond-glazed line with a folksy, brown stenciled tulip decoration, has recently been discontinued. It's a varied line with many wonderful, useful pieces, and besides the dinnerware itself, the company catalogs carried illustrations of matching glassware, metal items, copper accessories, and hot pads. Of course, all Pfaltzgraff is of the highest quality, and all these factors add up to a new area of collecting in the making. Several dinnerware lines are features in our listings. To calculate the values of Yorktowne, Heritage, and Folk Art items not listed below, use Village prices.

For further information, we recommend *Pfaltzgraff, America's Potter,* by David A. Walsh and Polly Stetler, published in conjunction with the Historical Society of York County, York, Pennsylvania.

Advisor: Jo-Ann Bentz (See Directory, Pfaltzgraff)

Gourmet Royale, chip n' dip, in metal stand with wooden legs, #306, $30.00.

Christmas Heritage, bowl, soup/cereal; #009, 5½", from $2 to...**$3.50**
Christmas Heritage, cheese tray, #533, 10½x7½", from $5 to...**$7.00**
Christmas Heritage, pedestal mug, #290, 10-oz.............**$4.50**
Christmas Heritage, plate, dinner; #004, 10", from $4 to .**$5.50**
Gourmet Royale, ashtray, #321, 7¾", from $10 to **$12.00**
Gourmet Royale, baker, #321, oval, 7½", from $18 to..**$20.00**
Gourmet Royale, bean pot, #11-1, 1-qt, from $20 to..**$22.00**
Gourmet Royale, bean pot, #11-2, 2-qt, from $28 to..**$30.00**
Gourmet Royale, bean pot, #11-3, 3-qt.......................**$35.00**
Gourmet Royale, bean pot, #11-4, 4-qt.......................**$45.00**
Gourmet Royale, bean pot, #30, w/lip, lg, from $45 to..**$50.00**
Gourmet Royale, bowl, #241, oval, 7x10", from $15 to..**$18.00**
Gourmet Royale, bowl, cereal; #934SR, 5½", from $6 to..**$8.00**
Gourmet Royale, bowl, mixing; 6", from $8 to **$10.00**
Gourmet Royale, bowl, mixing; 8", from $12 to **$14.00**
Gourmet Royale, bowl, salad; tapered sides, 10", from $25 to...**$28.00**
Gourmet Royale, bowl, soup; 2¼x7¼", from $6 to **$8.00**
Gourmet Royale, bowl, vegetable; #341, divided, from $20 to...**$24.00**
Gourmet Royale, bowl, vegetable; 9¾" **$15.00**
Gourmet Royale, butter dish, #394, ¼-lb stick type, from $12 to...**$14.00**
Gourmet Royale, butter warmer, #301, stick handle, double spout, 9-oz, w/stand, from $18 to **$20.00**
Gourmet Royale, casserole, hen on nest, 2-qt, from $75 to...**$95.00**
Gourmet Royale, casserole, individual; #399, stick handle, 12-oz, from $10 to **$12.00**
Gourmet Royale, casserole, stick handle, 1-qt **$18.00**

Gourmet Royale, casserole, stick handle, 3-qt **$30.00**

Gourmet Royale, casserole, stick handle, 4-qt **$40.00**

Gourmet Royale, casserole, 2-qt, from $20 to............**$22.00**

Gourmet Royale, casserole-warming stand................**$10.00**

Gourmet Royale, chafing dish, w/handles, lid & stand, 8x9", from $30 to...**$35.00**

Gourmet Royale, cheese shaker, bulbous, 5¾", from $18 to..**$22.00**

Gourmet Royale, coffee server, on metal & wood stand, 10¾", from $100 to.....................................**$125.00**

Gourmet Royale, coffeepot, #303, 10-cup, from $30 to..**$35.00**

Gourmet Royale, creamer, #382, from $5 to.................**$7.00**

Gourmet Royale, cruet, coffeepot shape, fill through spout, 5", from $20 to...**$22.00**

Gourmet Royale, cup, from $2 to................................**$3.00**

Gourmet Royale, flour scoop, sm, from $12 to...........**$15.00**

Gourmet Royale, gravy boat, #426, double spout, lg, +underplate, from $14 to.....................................**$16.00**

Gourmet Royale, gravy boat, w/stick handle, 2-spout, from $15 to...**$20.00**

Gourmet Royale, jug, #384, 32-oz, from $32 to **$36.00**

Gourmet Royale, jug, #386, ice lip, from $40 to **$48.00**

Gourmet Royale, ladle, sm, from $12 to.....................**$15.00**

Gourmet Royale, ladle, 3½" dia bowl w/11" handle, from $18 to..**$20.00**

Gourmet Royale, Lazy Susan, #308, 3 sections w/center bowl, 14", from $32 to...............................**$36.00**

Gourmet Royale, mug, #391, 12-oz, from $6 to...........**$8.00**

Gourmet Royale, mug, #392, 16-oz, from $12 to........**$14.00**

Gourmet Royale, plate, egg; holds 12 halves, 7¾x12½", from $20 to...**$22.00**

Gourmet Royale, plate, grill; #87, 3-section, 11", from $18 to..**$20.00**

Gourmet Royale, plate, salad; 6¾", from $3 to.............**$4.00**

Gourmet Royale, plate, steak; 12", from $15 to..........**$20.00**

Gourmet Royale, platter, #320, 14", from $20 to........**$25.00**

Gourmet Royale, platter, #337, 16", from $25 to........**$30.00**

Gourmet Royale, rarebit, #330, w/lug handles, oval, 11", from $15 to...**$18.00**

Gourmet Royale, rarebit, w/lug handles, oval, 8½", from $10 to..**$12.00**

Gourmet Royale, relish dish, #265, 5x10", from $15 to..**$17.00**

Gourmet Royale, roaster, #325, oval, 14", from $30 to ...**$35.00**

Gourmet Royale, roaster, #326, oval, 16", from $50 to ...**$60.00**

Gourmet Royale, salt & pepper shakers, #317/318, 4½", pr, from $12 to...**$14.00**

Gourmet Royale, salt & pepper shakers, bell shape, pr, from $25 to...**$35.00**

Gourmet Royale, serving tray, round, 4-section, upright handle in center...**$20.00**

Gourmet Royale, shirred egg dish, #360, 6", from $10 to.**$12.00**

Gourmet Royale, souffle dish, #393, 5-qt +underplate, from $65 to...**$70.00**

Gourmet Royale, sugar bowl, from $5 to **$7.00**

Gourmet Royale, teapot, #381, 6-cup, from $18 to.....**$22.00**

Gourmet Royale, tray, tidbit; 2-tier, from $15 to **$18.00**

Heritage, butter dish, #002-028, from $6 to..................**$8.00**

Heritage, cake/serving plate, #002-529, 11¼" dia, from $7 to...**$10.00**

Heritage, cup & saucer, #002-002, 9-oz.......................**$3.00**

Heritage, soup tureen, #002-160, 3½-qt, from $25 to.**$35.00**

Muggsy, ashtray **$125.00**

Muggsy, bottle stopper, head, ball shape **$85.00**

Muggsy, canape holder, Carrie, lift-off hat pierced for toothpicks, from $125 to...**$150.00**

Muggsy, cigarette server...**$125.00**

Muggsy, clothes sprinkler bottle, Myrtle, Black, from $225 to...**$260.00**

Muggsy, clothes sprinkler bottle, Myrtle, white, from $195 to...**$225.00**

Muggsy, cookie jar, character face, minimum value, $250.00.

Muggsy, mug, action figure (golfer, fisherman, etc), any, from $65 to...**$85.00**

Muggsy, mug, Black action figure............................**$125.00**

Muggsy, shot mug, character face, from $45 to **$50.00**

Muggsy, tumbler **$60.00**

Muggsy, utility jar, Handy Harry, hat w/short bill as flat lid, from $175 to...**$200.00**

Planter, donkey, brown drip glaze, 10", from $15 to..**$20.00**

Planter, elephant, brown drip glaze, from $90 to **$110.00**

Village, baker, #236, rectangular, tab handles, 2-qt, from $12 to...**$15.00**

Village, baker, #237, square, tab handles, 9", from $9 to **$12.00**

Village, baker, #24, oval, 10¼", from $6 to...................**$8.00**

Village, baker, #240, oval, 7¾" **$5.50**

Village, beverage server, #490, from $20 to................**$25.00**

Village, bowl, fruit; #008, 5"...**$3.00**

Village, bowl, mixing; #453, 1-qt, 2-qt, & 3-qt, 3-pc set, from $30 to...**$35.00**

Village, bowl, rim soup; #012, 8½" **$4.50**

Village, bowl, serving; #010, 7"....................................**$6.00**

Village, bowl, soup/cereal; #009, 6" **$3.00**

Village, bowl, vegetable; #011, 8¾" **$8.50**

Village, butter dish, #028...**$8.00**

Village, canister set, #520, 4-pc, from $40 to..............**$60.00**

Village, casserole, w/lid, #315, 2-qt............................**$20.00**

Village, coffee mug, #89F, 10-oz...................................**$4.00**

Village, cookie jar, #540, 3-qt, from $15 to.................**$20.00**

Village, creamer & sugar bowl, #020, from $9 to **$12.00**

Village, cup & saucer, #001 & #002.............................**$3.50**

Village, gravy boat, #443, w/saucer, 16-oz, from $9 to..**$12.00**

Village, onion soup crock, #295, stick handle, sm........**$6.00**

Village, pedestal mug, #90F, 10-oz **$4.50**

Village, pitcher, #416, 2-qt, from $15.00 to $20.00; Bowl, from $12.00 to $15.00.

Village, plate, dinner; #004, 10¼" **$3.00**
Village, platter, #016, 14", from $12 to **$14.00**
Village, soup tureen, #160, w/lid & ladle, 3½-qt, from $25 to...**$35.00**
Village, spoon rest, #515, 9" L **$6.00**
Village, table light, #620, clear glass chimney on candle holder base, from $8 to **$12.00**

Photographica

A photograph is a moment in time caught on copper, glass, tin, or paper. Since the Parisian artist Daugerre perfected the first practical photographic process in 1839, countless images have been produced.

Paper images were first introduced by W.H. Talbot in 1841. Since then, numerous processes have been developed. By the 1860s the wet-plate albumen print process (paper coated with egg white mixture) was being widely employed by traveling photographers across our country and the world. The Civil War was our first widely photographed historical event. Civil War images are constantly increasing in value. Snapshots, however, are of little value unless they are of high quality and of an extremely rare subject. Content and condition are two vital considerations in determining the value of a photograph. Even a rare image is of little value if it is in poor condition.

Early cases are collectible in their own right; often the case is worth more than the image. Cased images are fragile and extreme caution must be used when examining them. In addition to studying the case, mat shape, and preserver style, be sure to look for hallmarks, imprints, and production information. The size of a cased image is determined according to the size plate used to produce it (there is no agreement on the exact measurements): Full plate, 1/2 plate, 1/4 plate, 1/6 plate, 1/9 plate, and 1/16 plate.

Though made well before the time frame we've established for this book, old photographs are so plentiful both at yard sales and flea markets as well (often preserved above even the family silver or jewelry!), we wanted to include some guidelines to help you evaluate them.

Advisor: Betty Davis (See Directory, Photographica)

Ambrotype: (1855 – 1865) – Black negative image on glass; its black backing produces positive view

Civil War soldier holding weapons, 1/2 plate, cased, hand-tinted scenery, coat, etc **$750.00**
Common image, 1/16 plate, common case **$35.00**
Girl & boy, 1/4 plate, ca 1860 ....**$100.00**

Daguerreotype: (1839 –1865) – Copper plate coated with silver

Civil War soldier in coffin, parents standing near, identified, w/military records & sm diary, 1/9 plate.........**$1,000.00**
Common photo, 1/16 plate..**$30.00**
Couple (young), 1/9 plate, pc of hair attached to case, early **$110.00**
Family portrait, 1/16 plate, ca 1851.............................**$85.00**

Girl in bonnet, 1/16 plate, ca 1845, thermoplastic case, $95.00. (Photo courtesy Betty Davis)

Girl in bonnet, 1/16 plate, thermoplastic case, ca 1845..**$95.00**
Postmortem, 1/16 plate, ca 1853 ....**$110.00**

Tintype: (1856 – 1867) – Image on tin, cased until ca 1860s; sold in paper mats at fairs until ca 1930

Black couple (young), very well dressed, 1/16 plate .**$35.00**
Common image, 1/16 plate, no mat or case, from $1 to .**$2.00**
Enlisted man in US Colored Regiment, 1/6 plate......**$275.00**
Occupational, blacksmith, 1/16 plate, ca 1870..........**$105.00**
Postmortem of child, 1/6 plate, full case...................**$125.00**

Wet Plate and Albumen Prints: (1860 – 1880s) – Glass plate process used to produce most paper prints

Albumen, early logging crew.......................................**$55.00**
Albumen on mat, Indian, ca 1875 ....**$120.00**
Albumen on mat, railroad depot **$45.00**
Albumen on mat, Western street scene, ca 1870.........**$65.00**
Cabinet card, common, from $1 to **$4.00**
Cabinet card, Indian w/papoose **$245.00**
Cabinet card, laundry wagons, Dayton OH.................**$65.00**
Cabinet card, postmortem of baby..............................**$40.00**
Cabinet card, President McKinley................................**$35.00**

Cartes de viste, Civil War soldier, unidentified...........**$45.00**
Cartes de viste, common, from $1 to **$2.00**
Cartes de viste, General Tom Thumb & his bride, trimmed **$22.00**
Cartes de viste, PT Barnum, autographed **$200.00**
Cartes de viste, unidentified officer, from $45 to......**$175.00**
Cartes de viste, 2 men w/violins **$35.00**

Albumen print, 'old uncle Bill,' ca 1870, of West Virginia origin, no established value. (Copyright Mike Swink 1997)

Pie Birds

Pie birds were known as pie funnels in the 1800s in England and Wales. They originated as center supports for top crusts on meat pies and were used to prevent sogginess. Meat pies did not have bottom crusts. There was also a second purpose — to vent the steam and prevent juice/gravy overflow. There are many new pie birds on the US market. Basically, the new pie birds are figural and, most importantly, they're hand painted, not airbrushed like the old ones. The older figural pie vents were the black-faced chefs with airbrushed smocks (not bright colors), an elephant with CCC embossed on the back of his drum, Benny the Baker holding a pie crimper, and a cake tester marked Pat. Pend. As we know, most of the new designs are original — just don't be fooled into buying them for old ones. There are new black birds everywhere, though. They'll have yellow beaks and no eyes. If they're on a white base and have an orange beak, they're old. There were no old holiday-related pie vents, these are all new. You'll find Santas, pilgrims, pumpkins, rabbits, holiday trees, posies, and leprechauns. New figural pie vents are sold from $6.50 to $30.00 by the original designer/potter.

Advisor: Lillian M. Cole (See Directory, Pie Birds)

Newsletter: *Pie Birds Unlimited*
Lillian M. Cole
14 Harmony School Rd., Flemington, NJ 08822

Bird, all-black or all-white, imported, 4".....................**$4.00**
Bird, black or white, wide mouth, marked England...**$35.00**
Bird, blue w/black speckles, mustard beak.................**$25.00**

Bird, multicolor, Morton Pottery................................**$18.00**

Birds on nest, USA, 1950, copyright mark, rare, 5", $85.00.

Black-faced chef & cook, red, yellow & white paint, Taiwan, pr..**$10.00**

Bluebird, speckled, black detail on head, wings and tail, USA, 1940s – 50s, 4½", $25.00. (Photo courtesy Lillian Cole)

Boy, marked Pie Boy, w/green sombrero **$85.00**
Chefs, all white, pinhole vent, 1995 reproductions, each....**$5.00**
Decaled, marked New Devon Pottery, Made in England .**$50.00**
England, white, new, 1996, embossed logo: Tala 1899.....**$10.00**
Fred Flour Grader, England, copyright (c in circle) mark on back **$50.00**
Funnel, aluminum, England..**$25.00**
Funnel, England, plain white, sizes vary, each, from $15 to...**$25.00**
Funnel, terra-cotta, marked Wales..............................**$35.00**
Funnel, TG Green motif/logo on white, 1993 to present...**$10.00**
Grimwade, funnel, England **$50.00**
Pyrex, funnel, sizes vary, each **$15.00**
Rooster, multicolor, marked Cleminson or Cb.............**$28.00**
Rowland's Hygienic Patent, England...........................**$70.00**
SB signed, England, 1980s to present.........................**$30.00**

Pierce, Howard

Of the studio potters opening businesses in California in the 1930s and 1940s, Howard Pierce probably offered more artistic choices than any other artists. William Manker, a talented California ceramist, was instrumental in Pierce's future, and his influence can be seen in the bowls and vases created by Pierce in the early 1940s. Generally those pieces had one glaze inside and a complementary glaze outside such as light and dark green or burgundy and yellow. Then Howard moved on to vases with a Wedgwood-type Jasper ware body in matt pale pink or light green. These items are not plentiful. A few years later and along the same lines, Mr. Pierce created porcelain bisque children, plants, and animals that were inserted into the center of open areas of highly glazed vases.

Mr. Pierce was fascinated with wildlife and turned his attention to creating roadrunners, panthers, raccoons, elephants, egrets, birds, and so on. In this genre, he excelled and became a well-known figure in the pottery world.

Always in tune to the world around him, Mr. Pierce used ash from Mount St. Helens when the volcano erupted. Since he had only a small amount of ash, those creations are hard to find. The ash texture should not be confused with 'lava,' which, according to Pierce, 'bubbled up from the bottom.'

Mr. Pierce also created two other treatments that cause confusion: gold leaf and what I term, 'Sears gold.' Gold leaf, most often covering the entire item, is an elegant, eye-appealing glaze. 'Sears gold' was made for Sears, Roebuck & Company in a large quantity, and even though the items are completely covered in a gold glaze, the undercoat red treatment shows through. Howard was not pleased with the 'Sears gold' glaze, and while collectors do not particularly like it either, they probably buy it as a piece of history from a talented artist and a representation of his work. Many of the overall gold pieces collectors are seeing today were made by Freeman-McFarlin and are often confused with Howard Pierce pieces.

Mr. Pierce's products were basically brown, gray, or white but in the latter part of the 1970s, he began incising numbers into the clay when he was using an experimental glaze. Each number represented a formula for the glaze so that he could duplicate it. Some of the most beautiful colors came out of this experimentation: deep purple, pale blue, cobalt, bright green tinged with yellow, pink, muted red, with some of them having an iridized finish. These experimental colors have become favorites of many collectors.

Squirrels, chipmunks, and other small wildlife would come to Howard's studio window, and he would gently feed them from his hand. These animals presented an enormous outlet for his talent, and the pieces they inspired were the mainstay of his studio for over fifty years. In 1992 Howard and his wife, Ellen, destroyed all the molds he had made. Then, in 1993, he purchased a small kiln and began making smaller versions of his larger pieces, working only one day a week. The smaller pieces were marked 'Pierce' in small letters. Very few items were made before Howard Pierce died in February 1994. For further information see *Collector's Encyclopedia of Howard Pierce Porcelain,* by Darlene Hurst Dommel (Collector Books).

Advisor: Susan Cox (See Directory, California Pottery)

Bowl, free-form, scalloped rim, #P-1, 2½" **$30.00**
Bowl, gondola style, oval, 7½x5" **$40.00**
Figurine, cat, stylized, brown & white, 8" **$50.00**
Figurine, dolphin on base, experimental green & yellow glaze **$175.00**

Figurine, dove, 6" **$60.00**
Figurine, duck, speckled brown, 1950s, 9½" **$60.00**
Figurine, Eskimo man, brown & white, #206P, 1953, 7". **$85.00**
Figurine, girl seated w/book, gray w/brown, 6½x3½" ... **$85.00**

Figurine, girl standing with basket, gray, 9½", $80.00.

Figurine, horned owl, 8" **$100.00**
Figurine, kneeling girl, 7" **$60.00**
Figurine, native couple, brown, pr **$145.00**
Figurine, owl, 5" & 3", pr **$70.00**
Figurine, raccoon, sitting, brown w/stripes, 9x3½" **$80.00**
Figurine, rooster & hen, white & brown, #215P, pr .. **$165.00**
Figurine, water bird, green & white, 5½" **$30.00**
Figurine, water bird, 14" **$75.00**
Figurines, girl feeding swan, pr **$75.00**
Figurines, quail, brown, 3-pc set **$55.00**
Magnet, turtle, experimental blue glaze, 2¼x1½" **$30.00**
Vase, brown, 5x7½" **$45.00**
Vase, green, horse w/white tree insert, #P500 .... **$85.00**

Pin-back Buttons

Literally hundreds of thousands of pin-back buttons are available; pick a category and have fun! Most fall into one of three fields — advertising, political, and personality related, but within these three broad areas are many more specialized groups. Just make sure you buy only those that are undamaged, are still bright and unfaded, and have well-centered designs and properly aligned printing. The older buttons (those from before the 1920s) may be made of celluloid and the cardboard backing printed with the name of a company or a product.

See also Political.

Newsletter: *The Button Pusher*
P.O. Box 4
Coopersburg, PA 18036. Subscriptions: 1 yr - $19.94 US.

Afghan (dog), celluloid, 1930s, ⅞" **$10.00**
America's Getting Into Training, Amtrak logo, black & gold, 2¼" **$3.00**
American Bicentennial 1776-1976, Paul Revere's Ride April 1775, multicolor, 1¾" **$2.00**

Hopalong Cassidy Savings Club, 1950, 3", EX, $45.00.

American Federation Employees, State, County, Municipal, AFL-CIO, 1962, blue & white, 1¼", EX $7.00

American Model Car Racing Congress, eagle & checkered flag logo, dark red cloisonne, late 1940s.............$35.00

American Red Star Animal Relief, red, white & blue, ¾"..$6.00

Ask Me About My Beer Belly, shows belly w/Pabst Blue Ribbon Light, multicolor, 2¼", EX $4.00

Ask Your Grocer for Ferguson's White Seal Bread, blue & white, 1¼", EX $4.50

Astronaut, Tony Tiger photo, 1960s, EX $18.00

Back Bunker at center, star border, red, white & blue, 1972, 1½" $3.50

Beverly Hills 90210, multicolor cast portrait, 4" $2.00

Bond Bread Brings You Vitamin D, yellow & green, 1¼", EX $4.50

Bring Back Volpe, blue & white, 1", EX $2.00

Bruce Lee Game of Death, 1979, M $20.00

Bruce Springsteen, red, white & blue, M.....................$2.00

Captain Cook Bicentennial, British Columbia Canada, masted ship & 1778-1978 at center, red, black & white, 2¼".$4.00

Catwoman, DC Comics, multicolor, 2" $4.00

Certified Hershey's Chocolate Lover...........................$5.00

Charter Member Batman & Robin Society, shows Batman & Robin, multicolor, Button World, 1966, 3" $12.00

Chessie, shows mascot kitten, black & white, 1½".......$2.00

Curse You, Red Baron w/Snoopy on doghouse, 1¾", EX......$8.00

Davy Crockett, Sunbeam Bread, red, yellow & black, 1¼" $15.00

Debbye Turner, Miss America 1990, blue & white, 3½".$2.00

Disneyland, 35 Years of Magic, multicolor, M $2.00

Donald Duck's 50th Birthday, multicolor, M $7.50

ET, w/portrait, multicolor, 2"..$3.00

First American in Orbit, shows John Glenn w/Well Done, Col Glenn, 1962, 1¼" $22.50

Florida State Nurses Association, Sarasota, shows skyline, 1938, 1½", EX..$8.00

Foist Family, Edith Bunker photo, 1972, EX................$18.00

Frankenstein, Universal Studios Tours, red, white & black, 2¼" $3.00

Garfield, I Was Just Another Cat Until I Went to School, multicolor, 1¾" $2.50

GE Safety Committee, red gold & green, ⅞", EX..........$8.00

Go Get 'Em Tigers, NBD (National Bank of Detroit, lithographed metal w/tab, 1940s...........................$10.00

God Bless America, shows flag, multicolor, 1¼", EX....$3.00

GOP Means Good Old Punchy (Hawaiian Punch), 1960s, 4" $18.00

Hard Rock Cafe, Save the Planet, multicolor, NM........$5.00

I Belong Peter Frampton Fan Club................................$8.00

I Gave Hope, Quake Aid 1994, shows outline of California w/quake site, multicolor, 2¼" ....$.50

I Go Pogo, 1956, ⅞", NM..$22.00

I Go to Church Sundays, aqua & orange, ⅝", EX.........$1.00

I Love Lucy 1911-1989, 1989, 3½", EX......................$12.50

I Support Nipper, 1930s, ½", EX................................$45.00

I'm a Barbara Mandrell Fan, multicolor, 3" $2.00

I'm a Batman Crimefighter, shows Batman & Robin, multicolor, 1969, 1½" $2.50

I'm an Official Monkees Fan, blue & white, bootleg, M..$4.00

I'm Bugs About the Beatles, 3½"................................$15.00

I'm Doing My Share for Air, American Lung Association, South Coast Quality Air Management, black, white & orange, 2" $3.00

I'm the Greatest, Ali, March 8, 1971, 3½" $5.00

I've Just Quit Smoking Please Bear With Me, American Cancer Society, shows bear, black & white, 2¼" ..$2.00

Jackie Gleason, The Loud-Mouth, VIP Corp, 1955, 1¾", EX $12.00

Joe Louis 1914-1981, The Brown Bomber, 1981, 3½", EX...$12.50

Join the Colonel's Great Chicken Outing, 1960s, 2", M ..$25.00

Junior Member of Grange, shows wheat sheaf, red & yellow, ⅞", EX $1.50

Jurassic Park, multicolor, 1¾" $3.00

Kentucky Free Masons, Louisville KY, 1978, gold, blue & white, 1¾" $3.50

Kiss Me I Don't Smoke, American Cancer Society, shows frog, multicolor, 2" $1.50

Lion King & Simba at center, Happy Birthday at rim, multicolor, 2" $3.50

Lionel Railroader Club, shows speeding train car, multicolor, 2½" $3.00

Los Angeles Shakespeare Festival, black & yellow, 1½"..$3.00

Lucky Strikes Again w/bull's eye, red, silver, black & white, 2½" $4.00

Massachusetts Fruit Growers' Association 1931, black, white & orange, 1¼" $4.00

Minister, 1940 Rzadu Jednosci Narodowej, w/photo, ⅞".$10.00

Morro Bay State Park Museum of Natural History, Morro Bay CA, black & orange, 2"....................................$2.00

Nixon's the One, red & white, 1⅜", EX......................$3.00

North Fort Worth Pioneer Days Celebration, red, white & blue, ca 1960s, 2¼"..$7.50

Official Member Hawkman Super Hero Club, Button World, 1966, 3", EX+..$32.00

Official Member Superman Club, Button World, 1966, 3", NM $22.00

Official Monkees Fan, Raybert, 1966, 2", EX $8.00

Orange County Florida, multicolor w/orange blossoms at top, 1" $2.50

Orel Hershiser, Los Angeles Dodgers, multicolor, 1⅛".$3.00

Pebbles Flintstone, 1972, 2", EX $15.00

Philadelphia Sesquicentennial, 1776-1926, celuloid, 1¼" ..$15.00

Pump It Up! Reebok, blue & orange, EX.....................$2.00

Reno, Biggest Little City in the World $3.50

Ron Davis, Minnesota Twins, multicolor, 1⅛", EX........**$3.00**
Sacramento Dixieland Jubilee, United Airlines logo at center, 1988, EX...**$3.00**
Sal Mineo Fan Club, multicolor, 3"................................**$5.00**
San Diego Chargers, 1960s logo, ¾" **$5.00**
School Police Parents, shows Yogi Bear wearing DARE shirt, multicolor, 2¼"...**$3.50**
Sea World, Shamu & His Crew, multicolor, 2½" **$4.00**
Six Flags Over Mid-America, Bell Blaster, multicolor w/red & white ribbon, 3" **$3.00**
Snoopy for President, black & white letters, EX **$5.00**
Spindizzy #3 (figural), late 1940s.................................**$35.00**
St Louis Zoo Friends, I Attended Zoofest '95, zebra background, 3½"...**$4.50**

Sundial Shoes Club, from $12.00 to $15.00.

Tea Keeps You Cool, blue & white, 1⅜", EX................**$3.00**
The Colonel Sanders Memorial March of Dimes Campaign, ca 1980, 3"..**$18.00**
United Electric Radio & Machine Workers, red, white & blue, 1¼"...**$6.00**
United Rubber Workers of America, CIO, 1942, tan & white, ⅞", EX...**$8.00**
US Good Roads Assn Member, Birmingham AL, green, red & white, NM **$3.50**
Widows' & Orphans' Day Sponsored by Honor Legion Police Dept City of New York, blue & white, 1¼" **$1.50**
Wild Bill Hickok & Jingles, We're Partners, early 1950s, 1½", NM **$27.50**
Wildflower Preservation Society & Bitter Root at rim, blossom at center, multicolor, NM......................................**$4.00**
Woodstock 1969, purple, red & white, M...................**$18.00**
World Famous Clydesdales, multicolor, 2¼", EX...........**$4.00**
You'll Sleep Better in a Winnebago, shows man in the moon, red & white, 2¼", EX...**$3.00**
4-H clover w/motto, green & white, 1¼" **$2.50**

Kellogg's Pep Pins

Chances are if you're over forty, you remember them, one in each box of PEP (Kellogg's wheat-flake cereal that was among the first to be vitamin fortified). There were eighty-six in all, each carrying the full-color image of a character from one of the popular cartoon strips of the day — Maggie and Jiggs, the Winkles, Dagwood and Blondie, Superman, Dick Tracy, and many others. Very few of these cartoons are still in print.

The pins were issued in five sets, the first in 1945, three in 1946, and the last in 1947. They were made in Connecticut by the Crown Bottle Cap Company, and they're marked PEP on the back. You could wear them on your cap, shirt, coat, or the official PEP pin beanie, an orange and white cloth cap made for just that purpose. The Superman pin — he was the

only D.C. Comics Inc. character in the group — was included in each set.

Not all are listed below. These are the most valuable. If you find an unlisted pin, it will be worth from $10.00 to $15.00. Values are given for pins in near mint condition.

Advisor: Doug Dezso (See Directory, Candy Containers)

Bo Plenty, NM...**$30.00**
Corky, NM **$16.00**
Dagwood, NM..**$30.00**
Dick Tracy, NM..**$30.00**
Early Bird, NM...**$6.00**
Fat Stuff, NM..**$15.00**
Felix the Cat, NM **$85.00**
Flash Gordon, NM **$30.00**
Flat Top, NM **$30.00**
Jiggs, NM..**$25.00**
Kayo, NM..**$20.00**
Maggie, NM **$25.00**
Mama De Stross, NM **$30.00**
Mama Katzenjammer **$25.00**
Navy Patrol, NM..**$6.00**
Olive Oyl, NM...**$30.00**

Orphan Annie, NM, $25.00.

Phantom, NM..**$80.00**
Popeye, NM...**$30.00**
Rip Winkle, NM...**$20.00**
Superman, NM **$42.00**

Uncle Walt, NM, $20.00.

Winkles Twins, NM **$90.00**

Pinup Art

Some of the more well-known artists in this field are Vargas, Petty, DeVorss, Elvgren, Moran, Ballantyne, Armstrong, and Phillips, and some enthusiasts pick a favorite and concentrate their collections on only his work. From the mid-thirties until well into the fifties, pinup art was extremely popular. Female movie stars from this era were ultra-glamorous, voluptuous, and very sensual creatures, and this type of media influence naturally impacted the social and esthetic attitudes of the period. As the adage goes, 'Sex sells.' And well it did. You'll find calendars, playing cards, magazines, advertising, and merchandise of all types that depict these unrealistically perfect ladies. Though not all items will be signed, most of these artists have a distinctive, easily identifiable style that you'll soon be able to recognize.

Unless noted otherwise, values listed below are for items in at least near-mint condition; blotters are unused.

Advisor: Denis Jackson (See Directory, Pinup Art)

Newsletter: *The Illustrator Collector's News*
Denis Jackson, Editor
P.O. Box 1958
Sequim, WA 98382; 206-683-2559; http://www.olypen.com/ticn; e-mail ticn@olypen.com

Ad for Glint Shampoo, Armstrong, Motion Picture magazine, June 1927...**$30.00**
Blotter, Bolles, Bedtime Stories, girl lifting top, wine & flowers, October 1933...................................**$40.00**
Blotter, Elvgren, Anchors A-Wow, 1951 ....**$11.00**
Blotter, Elvgren, Blind Date, 1951 ....**$11.00**
Blotter, Elvgren, In the Dough, brunette in apron & hose w/bread dough, 7½x9½" **$13.00**
Blotter, Elvgren, Retirement Plan, redhead in pink teddy, blue bed, 5¾x17"......................................**$24.00**
Blotter, Moran, Chief Attraction, Indian girl, 1944......**$12.00**
Blotter, Moran, Sheer Charm, blond on purple pillows, black bikini bottom & hose, 1942, 12x16".....**$55.00**
Blotter, Munson, I'm Awfully Easy on the Pupils, teacher at blackboard, 1945...............................**$12.00**
Book, Stolen Sweets, FW Smith, 1970s.....................**$42.00**
Calendar, Armstrong, 1925, Betty portrait girl, ornate silk headdress, 8x10" **$60.00**
Calendar, Armstrong, 1934, Irish Eyes Are Smiling, brunette w/roses, 12x15"...................................**$55.00**
Calendar, Armstrong, 1970s, reproduction of 1925 Betty portrait girl, ornate silk headdress, from $15 to.........**$20.00**
Calendar, desk; Playboy, 1979, EX **$12.00**
Calendar, Elliott, 1950, Delectable Dishes....................**$50.00**
Calendar, Elvgren, NAPA Auto Parts, water-skiing girl, 16x33"...**$50.00**
Calendar, Thompson, Brown & Bigelow, 12-page, 8½x13" **$35.00**
Calendar notepad, Elvgren, Always in Time **$12.00**
Date book, Randall, 1952, 12 pages, 9½x16" **$65.00**
Fan, Armstrong, brunette in red swimsuit, seated, 1930s, 8x9½"...**$75.00**
Greeting card, MacPherson, Howdy Partner, 4½x6" **$3.00**
Magazine cover, Mozert, Jean Arthur, March 1938......**$60.00**
Magazine print, Driben, brunette by fireplace, Bedtime Stories, February 1938 ....**$20.00**
Magazine print, Erbit, cover, Capper's Farmer, April 1937 ..**$15.00**
Magazine print, Varga, Rita Hayworth in red bathing suit & loosely draped red shawl, from True, 1940s **$5.00**
Matchbook cover, Petty, 1960s, unused, from $2.50 to...**$3.50**
Memo pad, Ballantyne, I Wonder if There Are Any Sharks Around, 1955, 5x6" **$10.00**

Memo pad, MacPhearson, The MacPherson Sketches of 1948, 12 pages **$90.00**
Memo pad, Thompson, In Full Bloom, 1952, 3½x6½"..**$11.00**

Mutoscope cards, 1940s – 50s, from $8.00 to $14.00 each. (Photo courtesy Denis Jackson)

Notepad, Elvgren, Hard To Suit, brunette in yellow swimwear, 3x6" **$12.00**

Notepads, from $8.00 to $12.00 each. (Photo courtesy Denis Jackson)

Playing cards, Ballantine, Quick on the Draw, double deck, 2 images, 1950s....................................**$65.00**
Playing cards, Elliott, Hit the Deck, Brown & Bigelow, 1949, NMIB..**$45.00**
Playing cards, Elvgren, American Beauties, different girl on each card, Brown & Bigelow, 1950s, NMIB **$80.00**
Playing cards, Erbit, blond in gown, double deck, 2 poses **$60.00**
Playing cards, MacPherson, Not According to Hoyle, double deck, 1946 ....**$75.00**
Playing cards, Vargas, Esquire, 1941, MIB (sealed).....**$40.00**
Postcard, Aslan, Alain; Mariane, #H280, from France, 1970s, 4x6" **$4.00**
Poster, Petty, The Petty Girl, blond in blue teddy, 14x36".**$80.00**

Poster, Ward, The Siren, brunette, 1970s, 11x14".........**$15.00**

Print, Armstrong, Hurry Back, girl in yellow sarong/swimsuit, seated, 1 leg up, 1935, 11½x13½"..........................**$50.00**

Print, Armstrong, Pick of the Crop, cowgirl feeding apples to horse, 1954, 11x12¼" **$55.00**

Print, Ballantyne, Just an Inkling, 1954, 4x6"................**$7.00**

Print, Best, Thoroughbreds, blond on rock, w/horse, 1944, 20x46" **$45.00**

Print, Buell, All American Girl, 11x13" **$18.00**

Print, calendar; Elvgren, Neat Trick, girl blowing bubble, w/dog, November 1965, 5x7" **$11.00**

Print, DeVorss, Liberty Belle, girl in patriotic attire, 16x20" **$75.00**

Print, Elvgren, Barrel of Fun, girl on barrel w/guitar, 1968, 16x20" **$40.00**

Print, Elvgren, Enchanting, nude blond on rock w/toes in water, 1955, 8x10¾"...**$75.00**

Print, Elvgren, Miss Sylvania, redhead in chair w/hand mirror, 16x20" **$140.00**

Print, Fabian, Sheer Beauty, blond in pink, on pink blanket, 1940s, 8x10"...**$18.00**

Print, Frahm, Moonlight & Roses, girl in pink gown, fountain, 6x8" **$8.00**

Print, Moran, Reflections, nude w/red hat on stool in front of mirror, 15x19"..**$90.00**

Print, Moran, Why Not?, seated blond in gold, yellow phone, 1950, 8x10" **$18.00**

Print, Mozert, Anytime, strapless white gown & flower, 1951, 11x23" **$50.00**

Print, Mozert, New Arrival, girl bottle feeding calf, 22x29" ..**$135.00**

Print, Otto, American Girl, blond in pink & white gown, 8x10"..**$10.00**

Program, Petty, Ice Capades, I'm 21, redhead against blue background, 1961 ....**$55.00**

Sheet music, Vargas, Adoring You, Ziegfield Follies, 1924...**$85.00**

Sketch pad, The Butcher Takes the Best Cuts Home, 1954, 9x14"...**$100.00**

Playing Cards

Here is another collectible that is inexpensive, easy to display (especially single cards), and very diversified. Among the endless variations are backs that are printed with reproductions of famous paintings and pinup art, carry advertising of all types, and picture tourist attractions and world's fair scenes. Early decks are scarce, but those from the forties on are usually more attractive anyway, so pick an area that interests you most and have fun! Though they're usually not dated, you may find some clues that will help you to determine an approximate date. Telephone numbers, zip codes, advertising slogans, and patriotic messages are always helpful.

Everett Grist has written an informative book, *Advertising Playing Cards*, which we highly recommend to anyone interested in playing cards with any type of advertising.

Club/Newsletter: American Antique Deck Collectors; 52 Plus Joker Club

Clear the Decks, quarterly publication
Ray Hartz, President
P.O. Box 1002
Westerville, OH 43081; 614-891-6296

Aircraft Spotters #1, 1942, USPC, 52+Joker+fact card, NMIB...**$25.00**

Amtrak, by Arrco Playing Cards, 1980s, narrow, 52+2 Jokers, M (NM box)..**$10.00**

B&O Railroad, 1953, red or blue border, MIB (sealed) .**$28.00**

Bicycle Bridge #888, 1930s, Art Deco backs, blue edges, NMIB...**$32.00**

Bodega Casino, Deadwood SD, by Gemaco, double deck, white & green backs, NMIB................................**$22.00**

Bowlers Victory Legion, Western Publishing?, WI, 1945, 52+Joker, compliments of Bowlers of America, EX (EX box) **$20.00**

Breck D Porter Co, 1920s, Young & Rudolf, Philadelphia, narrow, double deck, w/2 score cards, NMIB...........**$25.00**

Canadian Club, Hiram Walker & Sons, narrow, 1940s, 52+Joker+recipe card (cocktails), VG (VG box)...**$20.00**

Colt Firearms, Brown & Bigelow, 52+2 Jokers, M (NM box) **$50.00**

Cuba Souvenir, 1930, H-SCU3, type C photos, NMIB.**$35.00**

Death on Drugs, by Weedon Enterprises, 1985, 52 reasons not to abuse drugs, NMIB....................................**$18.00**

Delta, 1969, second series, DC-DAL 306T, NC, MIB (sealed)...**$17.00**

Eagle-Picher Lead Co, double deck, narrow, 1929, gold edges, 52+eagle Jack+scoring card, M (w/tax stamp & NM box) **$112.00**

East African Playing Cards, 1957, 52+2 Jokers, title card & fold-out color map of East Africa, M (NM box) ...**$20.00**

Eastern Steamship Lines, 1970s, USPC, narrow, color photo backs, SS Emerald Seas, 52+2 Jokers, NMIB.........**$10.00**

Fairchild Semiconductor, wide, 1968, prosaic nonstandard, electrical specifications, 52+2 Jokers+2 extra cards, NMIB...**$14.00**

Ford, 1968, info & car drawings on cards, 52 complete, EX (EX box) **$25.00**

Hawaii, double deck, 1950, VG, $15.00.

Heileman Brewing, Old Style Lager, multicolor musketeer back, 1950s, 52+2 Jokers, EX (VG+ box).............**$25.00**

Home Rubber Co, 52+special Ace of Spades & backs, VG+ (VG repaired box) **$15.00**

Hotel Del Coranado, CA, narrow, 1988, 100th Anniversary, Hoyle, 52+2 Jokers, 13 scenes, M (plastic box) ...**$12.00**

King-Size Kent Cigarettes Military Cards, 1960s, different military ranks of 4 service branchs, USPC, 52, NM (VG-box) **$28.00**

Lyon & Healy Piano Playing Cards, 1920s, 52+2 Jokers, worn gold edge, VG (EX box) **$135.00**

Masonic Zembo, Brown & Bigelow, 1930s, Shriners sphinx backs, NMIB......................................**$32.00**

Maya Good Neighbor, for American Assoc University Women, Brown & Bigelow, 1948, narrow, 52+extra card, EX+ (double box) **$42.00**

Mexicana, 50th Anniversary, Las Alas de Oro, 1971, by LaCubana, 52+Joker, MIB......................**$18.00**

Mexico Refractories, Brown & Bigelow, Mexico MO, 1930s, 52+Joker, cut corners, special Joker & Ace, NM (paper box) **$15.00**

Monumentos de Espana, 1950, scenes of Spain, Fournier, 52+2 Jokers, EX (EX box) **$10.00**

O'Callaghans Chicago Souvenir, city scenes, 1930, 52+Joker+extra card, red word borders w/gold edge, VG (VG box) **$100.00**

On the Spot, Saturday Evening Post, C. James Plumbing, double deck, EX, from $20.00 to $25.00.

Paris Souvenir, by Philibert, 1957, gold-framed scenes, red edges, 52+2 Jokers, NM (plastic box) **$45.00**

Pennsylvania Turnpike, 1940s, narrow, Howard Johnson's as Ace of Spades, 52+no Joker, NM (EX box) **$12.00**

Pep Boys, wide, special courts w/Manny, Moe & Jack, 1940, deluxe pinochle, crying towel extra card, MIB **$42.00**

Philadelpha, silver city seal backs, 1960s, gold edge, 52+2 fact cards, NM (VG box) **$40.00**

Philadelphia, wide scenic, silver city seal backs, 1960s, 52+2 fact cards, NM (VG box) **$40.00**

Roberts Express, Manchester NH, 1950s, MIB (sealed)..**$12.00**

Southern Pacific, 1935, scenes of the West, 52+2 Jokers, NMIB..**$12.00**

Spain-Political Twin Pack Playing Cards, by Ortuno, 1973, Fournier, double deck, 52+2 Jokers, & tax stamp, M (NM box) **$35.00**

Synchron Systems, wide, 1992, nonstandard, chemical items on all faces, 52+extra card, M (plastic box) **$10.00**

Time Magazine, 1962 domestic limited edition, odd size, nonstandard 1-way courts, slogans, 52+Joker+title card, NMIB..**$115.00**

United Carpenters & Joiners, wide, 1920s, 52+special Ace, G (G box) **$50.00**

Victory Playing Cards, by Arrco, Chicago, 1945, green backs w/shield, 52+2 Jokers, EX (EX box)....................**$65.00**

White Banner Malt Extract, 1950s, 52+special Joker+extra card, special Ace of Spades, M (EX box)..............**$25.00**

Winchester Playing Cards, Winchester Firearms, narrow, 52+scorecard, EX+ (EX box) **$45.00**

Political Memorabilia

Political collecting is one of today's fastest-growing hobbies. Between campaign buttons, glassware, paper, and other items, collectors are scrambling to aquire these little pieces of history. Before the turn of the century and the advent of the modern political button, candidates produced ribbons, ferrotypes, stickpins, banners, and many household items to promote their cause. In 1896 the first celluloid (or cello) buttons were used. Cello refers to a process where a paper disc carrying a design is crimped under a piece of celluloid (now acetate) and fastened to a metal button back. In the 1920s the lithographed (or litho) buttons were introduced.

Campaigns throughout the 1930s until today have used both types of buttons. In today's media-hyped world, it is amazing that in addition to TV and radio commercials, candidates still use some of their funding to produce buttons. Bumper stickers, flyers, and novelty items also still abound. Reproductions are sometimes encountered by collectors. Practice and experience are the best tools in order to be aware.

One important factor to remember when pricing buttons is that condition is everything. Buttons with any cracks, stains, or other damage will only sell for a fraction of our suggested values. Listed below are some of the items one is likely to find when scrutinizing today's sales.

For more information about this hobby, we recommend you read Michael McQuillen's monthly column, 'Political Parade,' in *Antique Week* newspaper.

Advisor: Michael McQuillen (See Directory, Political)

Club: A.P.I.C. (American Political Items Collectors) of Indiana
Michael McQuillen
P.O. Box 11141
Indianapolis, IN 46201-0141; National organization serving needs of political enthusiasts; send SASE for more information

Ballpoint pen, John F Kennedy, 1917-63, bust portrait...**$12.50**

Bank, Abraham Lincoln, bust w/A Lincoln at base, marked Banthrico Inc USA on bottom, 5½x3½x2", EX.....**$20.00**

Bank, John F Kennedy, bust w/name & dates on base, bank name & address on back, 5½x3½x2", EX............**$30.00**

Booklet, Voice in Wilderness, AB Lacy, 1928 election analysis **$10.00**

Brochure, Ronald Regan as host of GE Theatre, promotion for GE's role in US defense, 1954, 14x10½", EX..**$20.00**

Bumper sticker, Democrats for Nixon..........................**$2.00**

Bumper sticker, Jimmy Carter for President in '76, 12" L..**$2.00**

Button, Averell Harriman, 1952 Democratic Primary, blue & white **$10.00**

Button, Colonel North, American Hero.......................**$5.00**

Button, Elect Ford, Don't Settle for Peanuts, lg.............**$5.00**

Button, Go Home Peanut Farmer, the Reagans Are Coming, 1980...**$6.50**

Button, In Memory of LBJ, 1908-1973, 4" **$15.00**

Button, Jimmy Carter for President, photo, 3"...............**$6.00**

Button, John F Kennedy, celluloid, easel back, inaugural, 6" **$28.00**

Button, LBJ for the USA, flashes to photo, marked Copyright 1964 Democratic National Committee, 2½" **$15.00**

Button, Re-Elect Johnson, LBJ for President, w/photo, 1½" **$5.00**

Button, The Choice: Trust With Muskie, Nothing With Nixon, 1972...**$2.00**

Button, Vote Eisenhower-Nixon for a Better Future, litho, jugate, 1½"..**$25.00**

Button, Vote Gore, shows Senator Gore of Tennessee (father of Vice President Gore), blue & white flasher **$12.00**

Button, Vote President McCloskey, 1972......................**$5.00**

Button, Wallace for President, photo, 3".......................**$5.00**

Button, WIN (Whip Inflation Now), 1970s **$1.50**

Button, Win With Wilkie, red, white & blue, 1½" **$25.00**

Button, 1981 Inauguration Day, M **$2.50**

Calcndar, Theodore Roosevelt, 1921, 52 weeks, each w/dated quote, ribbon ties, 5x8", EX...................................**$22.50**

Cane, Gerald Ford, wood w/elephant handle.............**$30.00**

Decal, Al Smith for President, red, white & blue circle, 1928, 6", EX..**$18.00**

Decal, MacArthur for President, red, white & blue, 1951, 7x4¾"...**$22.50**

Figurine, John F Kennedy in rocker, plastic, 1962, NMOC .**$8.00**

Game, Meet the Presidents, SelRight, 1965, NMIB......**$20.00**

Game, Watergate Scandal, cards, complete, original box..**$25.00**

Half dollar, John F Kennedy, limited edition w/gold wash, MOC..**$5.00**

Handbill, Greet President Nixon, 1971..........................**$3.50**

Hankerchief, President Hoover, picture, 1932, 17x17"..**$100.00**

Invitation, inaugural; Ronald Reagan, 1981 ....**$15.00**

Lapel pin, white plastic elephant w/upraised trunk, Dewey across body, ¾", EX...**$20.00**

License plate attachment, Ike/Nixon Inaguration, 1953, NM, $150.00. (Photo courtesy Michael McQuillen)

Matchbook, Eisenhower/Nixon jugate portraits, January 1953, M **$4.00**

Money clip, John F Kennedy, 1917-1963, MIB...........**$10.00**

Mug, Jimmy Carter, 1977, EX..**$15.00**

Mug, Jimmy Carter caricature, brown ceramic **$20.00**

Needle book, Hoover President, Cooper Governor....**$15.00**

Newspaper, Dewey Defeats Truman, 1948 Chicago Tribune, complete, EX, $800.00. (Photo courtesy Michael McQuillen)

Pendant, GOP Republican National Convention, Chicago, 1952 ....**$25.00**

Poster, Carry on w/Franklin D Roosevelt, 1940s, 16x10½" .**$28.00**

Poster, Herbert Hoover, by John Doctoroff, 1928 ....**$22.50**

Poster, LBJ for the USA, 1960s, 18x26", M..................**$12.00**

Poster, Richard Nixon, Environmentalist, shows Pat & Dick walking on beach, for college students, 1972, 22x34", EX **$42.50**

Poster, This Time Vote Like Your Whole World Depended on It, color photo Richard Nixon, 21x14", NM **$18.00**

Puzzle, President Kennedy, 350-pc jigsaw portrait, Tuco, 1964, NMIB..**$10.00**

Stickpin, elephant w/GOP on side, plastic, 1" head.....**$1.00**

Tab clip, McGovern **$2.00**

Toy, The Prez or Ross the Boss, noise activated, 1996, $20.00 each. (Photo courtesy Michael McQuillen)

Wristwatch, Ross Perot, 1991, MIB **$40.00**

Wristwatch, Spiro Agnew, Dirty Time, running...........**$50.00**

Porcelier China

The Porcelier Manufacturing Company began in East Liverpool, Ohio, in 1926. It moved to Greensburg, Pennsylvania, in 1930, where it continued to operate until its closing in 1954. They are best known for their extensive line of vitrified china kitchenware, but it should also be noted that they made innumerable lighting fixtures.

They used many different methods of marking their ware, and each mark included the name Porcelier, usually written in script. With the exception of sugar bowls and creamers, most pieces are marked. The mark can be an ink stamp in black, blue, brown, or green; engraved into the metal bottom plate (as on electrical pieces); on a paper label (as found on lighting fixtures); incised block letters; or raised block letters.

The values below are suggested for pieces in excellent condition. Our advisor for this category, Susan Grindberg, has written the *Collector's Guide to Porcelier China, Identification and Values*.

Advisor: Susan Grindberg (See Directory, Porcelier)

Club/Newsletter: Porcelier Collectors Club
21 Tamarac Swamp Rd.
Wellingford, CT 06492; *Porcelier Paper* Newsletter, $2.50 for sample copy

Ashtray, 1939 New York World's Fair, from $150 to.**$175.00**
Beverage cooler, white barrel form, high or low........**$60.00**
Boiler, Rope Bow, embossed & painted rope at top, 6-cup...**$45.00**
Canister, Barock-Colonial, gold...................................**$55.00**

Canisters, Basketweave Cameo, $40.00 each. (Photo courtesy Susan Grindberg)

Casserole, Basketweave Cameo, embossed & painted floral cameo on ivory basketweave, w/lid, 8½"............**$55.00**
Ceiling fixture, floral on ivory, single socket...............**$40.00**
Ceiling fixture, ivory w/pink band, original pink shade hangs from 3 chains, single socket **$55.00**
Coffeepot, Serv-All, gold or red & black trim on ivory, #576-D **$35.00**
Cookie jar, Barock-Colonial, red or blue dots on ivory, #2015 ....**$105.00**
Creamer, Beehive Crisscross **$16.00**
Creamer, Double Floral **$12.00**
Creamer, Floral Trio, 3 embossed & painted floral sprays on ivory..**$15.00**

Creamer, Hearth...**$15.00**
Creamer, Hostess shape w/Field Flowers decal on ivory .**$12.00**
Creamer, Hostess shape w/Silhouette (Acceptance) decal on ivory..**$12.00**
Creamer, Leaf & Shadow, leafy decal on ivory, w/lid ..**$12.00**
Creamer, Nautical...**$25.00**
Creamer, Pink Flower Platinum...................................**$12.00**
Creamer, Serv-All, platinum trim on ivory, #3007 or #3009 ....**$12.00**
Decanter, Oriental Deco, black Oriental-style 'letters' running vertically on ivory..**$50.00**
Jug, Beehive Crisscross shape, embossed diamonds & flowers on ivory hive shape, ball form **$70.00**
Lamp, Dutch Boy & Girl, girl......................................**$40.00**
Mug, Ringed, solid...**$30.00**
Mug, Wildlife, w/gold trim..**$40.00**
Percolator, Field Flowers, electric, #710.....................**$75.00**
Percolator, Leaf & Shadow, leafy decal on ivory, long handle, electric, #31 ....**$75.00**
Percolator, Platinum shape w/Pink Flower decal, electric .**$60.00**
Percolator, Starflower, hand-painted flowers on creamy ivory, electric, #120, 1950s......................................**$70.00**
Percolator set, Miniature Rose, complete w/electric percolator, sugar bowl & creamer **$175.00**
Pitcher, batter; Serv-All, platinum trim on ivory, #3014 .**$35.00**
Pitcher, disc; Hearth (Fireplace), embossed & painted scene on ivory **$70.00**
Pitcher, 1939 New York World's Fair, disc form, 5", from $125 to...**$150.00**
Pot, American Beauty, rose decal w/gold on ivory, 6-cup **$35.00**
Pot, Cobblestone I or II, girl & flowers embossed & painted against embossed cobblestone body, 6-cup.........**$30.00**
Pot, Dutch Boy & Girl on ivory, gold trim, 6-cup **$40.00**
Pot, Flamingo, embossed & painted bird on ivory, 4-cup .**$40.00**
Pot, Goldfinches, 2 embossed & painted yellow birds on branch on ivory, 2-cup......................................**$30.00**
Pot, Mexican, man & burro on ivory, 4-cup...............**$40.00**
Pot, Paneled Rose, embossed & painted rose in center side panel on ivory, flower finial, 8-cup.....................**$35.00**
Pot, Pears, embossed & painted fruit on ivory, 4-cup ..**$25.00**
Pot, Periwinkle, sm blue flowers in ivory panels on green or black body, ivory spout, lid & handle, 4-cup.......**$30.00**
Pot, Rose & White, embossed & painted multicolor flowers w/wheat on ivory, 6-cup....................................**$25.00**
Pot, Southern Belle, embossed & painted couple in scene on ivory, 6-cup **$40.00**
Pot, Tomato, red tomato figural, 2-cup.......................**$35.00**
Pot, Tree Trunk, embossed & painted flowers on ivory tree-trunk shape, ivory branch handles, twig finial, 4-cup..........**$35.00**
Pretzel jar, Barock-Colonial, gold dots on ivory.........**$95.00**
Salt & pepper shakers, Oriental Deco, each................**$20.00**
Sandwich grill, Basketweave Wild Flowers, mixed flowers on creamy white, from $225 to.............................**$275.00**
Sandwich grill, Serv-All, w/platinum trim, from $200 to.**$250.00**
Sugar bowl, Beehive Crisscross **$16.00**
Sugar bowl, Double Floral **$12.00**
Sugar bowl, Hostess shape w/Black-Eyed Susan decal on ivory..**$12.00**

Sugar bowl, Hostess shape w/Field Flowers decal on ivory **$12.00**
Sugar bowl, Nautical **$25.00**
Sugar bowl, Pears, embossed & painted fruit on ivory, w/lid **$15.00**
Sugar bowl, Platinum shape w/Golden Fuchsia on aqua .**$20.00**
Sugar bowl, Platinum shape w/Reversed Field Flowers decal on ivory **$8.00**
Sugar bowl, Platinum shape w/White Flower decal, w/lid **$8.00**
Sugar bowl, Ribbed Cameo Flower Basket, flower basket cameo on ribbed ivory, w/lid **$10.00**
Sugar bowl, Scalloped Wild Flowers, mixed flowers on creamy white w/vertical ribs, w/lid **$15.00**
Sugar bowl, Tomato **$18.00**
Sugar bowl, Tulips decal on ivory w/gold trim, pink band at foot, pink & gold flower finial, from $18 to **$25.00**
Syrup jar, Barock-Colonial, red or blue dots on ivory, #2012 ....**$45.00**
Syrup jar, Serv-All, platinum trim on ivory, #3012 ......**$30.00**
Teapot, Barock-Colonial, gold **$45.00**
Teapot, Basketweave Wild Flowers, 6-cup **$50.00**
Teapot, Beehive Crisscross, 6-cup **$37.00**
Teapot, Colonial, Black-Eyed Susan decal on ivory, 6-cup **$45.00**
Teapot, Colonial, Silhouette decal, 6-cup **$95.00**
Teapot, Colonial, undecorated, 6-cup **$35.00**
Teapot, Country Life Series, 8-cup **$55.00**
Teapot, Dogwood II, black **$60.00**
Teapot, Dogwood II, yellow or green **$35.00**
Teapot, double; Basketweave Wild Flowers, 8-cup **$90.00**
Teapot, double; Colonial, Black-Eyed Susan decal, 6-cup .**$95.00**
Teapot, Dutch Boy & Girl, 4-cup **$35.00**
Teapot, Flight, 6-cup **$45.00**
Teapot, Flute & Curl **$40.00**
Teapot, Harlequin, 4-cup **$35.00**
Teapot, Harlequin, 6-cup **$42.00**
Teapot, Hearth, 6-cup **$35.00**
Teapot, Leaves, 2-cup **$37.00**
Teapot, Magnolia, 6-cup **$45.00**
Teapot, Mexican, 6-cup **$45.00**
Teapot, Nautical, 2-cup **$45.00**
Teapot, Nautical, 6-cup **$35.00**
Teapot, Oriental Deco, 6-cup **$45.00**
Teapot, Paneled Orb, 6-cup **$45.00**
Teapot, Pears, 2-cup **$30.00**
Teapot, Pears, 4-cup **$30.00**
Teapot, Ribbed Betty, 6-cup **$45.00**
Teapot, Rope Bow, 8-cup **$45.00**
Teapot, Rose & Wheat, 6-cup **$45.00**
Teapot, Scalloped Wild Flowers, 6-cup **$65.00**
Teapot, Serv-All, gold or red & black trim on ivory, #3011, from $35 to **$45.00**
Teapot, Southern Belle, 6-cup **$40.00**
Teapot, Tomato, 6-cup **$40.00**
Teapot, Tree Trunk, 4-cup **$45.00**
Teapot, Tree Trunk, 8-cup **$40.00**
Teapot, Trellis Bottom, 6-cup **$35.00**
Teapot, Trellis Top, 6-cup **$35.00**

Teapot, 1939 New York World's Fair, 4-cup, from $250 to ..**$300.00**
Teapot, 1939 New York World's Fair, 8-cup, from $225 to ..**$260.00**
Toaster, Barock-Colonial, gold, from $950 to **$1,100.00**
Urn, Hostess shape w/Pink Flower decal on ivory, electric **$95.00**
Urn, Hostess shape w/Silhouette (Acceptance) decal on ivory, electric **$95.00**
Urn, Platinum shape w/Field Flowers decal on ivory, electric **$95.00**
Waffle iron, Barock-Colonial, ivory, red or blue dots on ivory, from $175 to **$250.00**
Waffle iron, Colonial shape w/Silhouette decal on ivory, from $185 to **$225.00**
Waffle iron, Scalloped Wild Flowers, from $275 to ..**$325.00**
Waffle iron, Serv-All, w/gold trim, from $175 to **$225.00**
Wall sconce, floral in ivory w/pink trim, w/original shade ..**$48.00**

Sandwich grill, Scalloped Wild Flowers, from $350.00 to $425.00. (Photo courtesy Susan Grindberg)

Postcards

Postcard collecting has overtaken stamp collecting, and there are more collectors in the world seeking out postcards than any other single item. What kind of cards do people collect? A majority collect views of the towns they live in or where their familes came from and places they have been. The rest collect subject cards which can include Santa Claus, Art Nouveau, those signed by artists, and cards depicting animals, fire, trains, and ships — the list is inexhaustable. Whatever your interest, it will probably be found on postcards. Values can range from virtually nothing to thousands of dollars. The average, older card (modern cards not included) is valued from $2.00 to $4.00 for views, while subject cards with real photos are slightly higher. The golden age of postcards was from 1900 to 1920. Note that cards with tiny images and florals may be old but have almost no value.

Advisor: Pamela E. Apkarian-Russell (See Directory, Postcards)

Adolf Hitler in jail, Quick Get Cohen My Lawyer **$12.00**
Alabama state capital **$4.00**
Alligator border, Jacksonville scene **$25.00**
Anti-Black metamorphosis of the watermelon **$30.00**
Armenian National Anthem 1918, raised gold letters ..**$12.00**

Ballet dancer Nijinsky.................................$12.00
Bernhardt Wall (signed), witch chasing boy through jack-o'-
   lantern patch $15.00
Boardwalk, Atlantic City NJ...........................$2.00
Borzoi, dog w/beautiful woman......................$20.00
Charlie Chaplin, red letter series $12.00

Christmas, $15.00 each. (Photo courtesy Pamela Apkarian-Russell)

Chrome, robin ....$.50
Chrome, 2 white cats.....................................$1.00
Clapsaddle (signed), autumn leaves...............$1.25
Colombo (signed), beautiful woman w/horse............$20.00
Dental reminder, Peanuts & the gang............$2.00
Edward Gorey, for Gotham Book Mart..........$4.00
Father Christmas (full length), in yellow w/gold $25.00
Fernway Park, chrome $6.00
Gibson Publishing, Halloween, pumpkin man w/lg belly ..$4.00

Good Luck for Halloween, pre-1920, $12.00. (Photo courtesy Pamela Apkarian-Russell)

Hawaii, beautiful colored fish........................$8.00
Hold-to-light, Flat Iron Building in New York............$25.00
Holland America Line DD Nieuw-Amsterdam...............$9.00
Hyannis Airport, planes on field in Cape Cod MA $10.00
Japanese baseball, American team $200.00
Josephine Baker in feathery costume.........$85.00
Linen, advertising Indian motorcycles.........$35.00
Linen, Black child on toilet, comic.................$4.00
Linen, fisherman & mermaid, comic $5.00

Linen, flamingos at Hialeah race track, FL.................$3.50
Linen, 1939-40 World's Fair Card Pavilion $3.50
Litho, Italian regimental military, early......................$35.00
Mammoth Cave, KY, underground dining room $7.00
Man-O'-War & jockey $8.00
Mardi Gras procession, LA $3.50
Multiple babies on chamber pots $5.00
Native African women (2), unclothed, playing ping-
   pong $30.00
Niagara Falls, 1906 ....$.50
NYK Lines, Japanese Art card w/insert of MS Asama Maru ..$40.00
Ocean wave, anywhere in USA ....$.25
Ox team, Havana, Cuba $4.00
Park in Bardstown KY....................................$3.00
Pennsylvania mine interior.............................$4.00
PFB embossed angel $10.00
Philadelphia Centennial.................................$5.00
Pumpkin man in yamulka, Happy Chanulka................$2.00
Queen Victoria's Diamond Jubilee 1897, postmarked...$100.00
Real photo, Babe Ruth & actor Joe E Brown............$200.00
Real photo, Baden Powell & Boy Scouts...................$15.00
Real photo, ballroom aboard the Bremen $14.00
Real photo, CO mine....................................$10.00
Real Photo, covered bridge in VT $10.00
Real photo, girl on beach, waving British Flag, Welcome to
   Bermuda $20.00
Real photo, nude, French mark.........................$24.00

Real photo, Princess Grace and Prince Rainier of Monaco, 1957, $10.00.

Real photo, Shirley Temple, blue-tinted dress............$24.00
Real photo, sm girl sitting under Christmas tree holding teddy
   bear, tinted $15.00
Real photo, woman leading bull, VT $25.00
RMS Aquitania Crolean interior scene, smoking room .$12.00
Roses highly embossed on birthday card $1.00
Saint Patrick's Day, man dressed in green w/pig..........$5.00
Sand dunes on Cape Cod.................................$.25
Tsar Nicholas of Russia $20.00
Turkey, nicely embossed.................................$2.00
View, Boston MA, w/bean pot $3.00
View, Chicago IL, downtown..............................$2.00
View, Emory University, Atlanta GA $5.00
View, Lynn Beach...$2.00
Whitney Publishing, full-length Santa $10.00

Whitney Publishing, Halloween, green-haired pumpkin children flying on broomstick.......................................$15.00

Winch Schmucker, beautiful girl on sea horse..........$100.00

Worcester MA, Art Museum...$3.50

Woven in silk, Aquatania $45.00

1939 Plymouth 2-door sedan $15.00

3-dimensional, butterflies $8.00

Soviet issue, propaganda satirizing atrocities against minorities, $260.00. (Photo courtesy Postcards International)

Powder Jars

Glassware items such as powder jars, trays, lamps, vanity sets, towel bars, and soap dishes were produced in large quantities during the Depression era by many glasshouses who were simply trying to stay in business. They used many of the same colors as they had in the making of their colored Depression glass dinnerware that has been so popular with collectors for more than twenty years.

Some of their most imaginative work went into designing powder jars. Subjects ranging from birds and animals to Deco nudes and Cinderella's coach can be found today, and this diversity coupled with the fact that many were made in several colors provides collectors with more than enough variations to keep them interested and challenged.

For more information we recommend *Bedroom and Bathroom Glassware of the Depression Years* by Margaret and Kenn Whitmyer (Collector Books).

Advisor: Sharon Thoerner (See Directory, Powder Jars)

Annabella, pink transparent...$175.00

Annette w/2 dogs, crystal $85.00

Babs II, pink frost, 3-footed, sm version $155.00

Ballerina, pink frost...$255.00

Basset hound, pink frost, from $145 to $165.00

Cameo, green frost $275.00

Carrie, black, draped nude figural stem $215.00

Cinderella's Coach, pink frost w/black lid, rectangular body, sm footrest for coachman, lg $195.00

Cleopatra II, crystal, shallow base, deep lid, 4¾" $95.00

Crinoline Girl, crystal, off-the-shoulder gown, flowers in right hand, embossed bows on skirt..............................$40.00

Crinoline Girl, pink frost, off-the-shoulder gown, flowers in right hand, embossed bows on skirt...................$120.00

Dancing Girl, blue transparent, feminine features, rope trim at top of base..$480.00

Dancing Girl, green frost, feminine features, rope trim at top of base...$120.00

Delilah II, green frost $95.00

Dolly Sisters, green frost $225.00

Elephant w/carousel base, green frost.......................$255.00

Elephants battling, crystal...$45.00

Godiva, satin, nude seated on diamond-shaped base ..$185.00

Gretchen, pink transparent $195.00

Horse & coach, pink frost, round $350.00

Jackie, jade-ite...$275.00

Joker, green transparent $85.00

Lillian III, crystal, stippled lid, base w/hexagonal band....$50.00

Lillian VII, pink frost, cone-shaped base $250.00

Lovebirds, green frost...$120.00

Martha Washington, crystal, Colonial lady between boy & girl..$60.00

Martha Washington, green frost, Colonial lady between boy & girl...$150.00

Martha Washington, pink frost, Colonial Lady between boy and girl, $130.00. (Photo courtesy Margaret and Kenn Whitmyer)

Minstrel, crystal $50.00

Minstrel, crystal w/green paint $75.00

My Pet, 3 Scotties on lid, crystal..................................$75.00

My Pet, 3 Scotties on lid, pink transparent...............$185.00

Penguins, pink frost, dome top................................$300.00

Rapunzel, pink or green frost, each, $250.00. (Photo courtesy Margaret and Kenn Whitmyer)

Rin-Tin-Tin, green transparent..................................$225.00

Scottie, puff box, Akro Agate $115.00

Southern Belle, green frost $250.00
Spike Bulldog, pink frost $125.00
Terrier on lg base, pink transparent, rare.................$385.00
Twins, green frost.......................................$185.00
Vamp, pink frost, flapper's head forms finial $155.00
Victorian Lady, green frost...............................$250.00
Wendy, satin, flapper girl w/arms outstretched, beaded necklace..$65.00

Purinton Pottery

The Purinton Pottery Company moved from Ohio to Shippenville, Pennsylvania, in 1941 and began producing several lines of dinnerware and kitchen items hand painted with fruits, ivy vines, and trees in bold brush strokes of color on a background reminiscent of old yellow ware pieces. The company closed in 1959 due to economic reasons.

Purinton has a style that's popular today with collectors who like the country look. It isn't always marked, but you'll soon recognize its distinct appearance. Some of the rarer designs are Palm Tree and Pheasant Lady, and examples of these lines are considerably higher than the more common ones. You'll see more Apple and Fruit pieces than any, and in more diversified shapes.

For more information we recommend *Purinton Pottery, An Identification and Value Guide,* by Susan Morris.

Newsletter: *Purinton Pastimes*
P.O. Box 9394
Arlington, VA 22219; Subscription: $10 per year

Apple, bowl, cereal; 5¼"..................................$10.00
Apple, bowl, divided vegetable; 10½" L.....................$35.00
Apple, bowl, fruit; scalloped border, 12" $40.00
Apple, bowl, vegetable; 8½"................................$25.00
Apple, butter dish, 6½" $65.00
Apple, canister, half-oval, 5½".............................$65.00

Apple, coffee canister, 9", $60.00.

Apple, coffeepot, 8-cup, 8" $90.00
Apple, console bowl, Napco mold, 11" L....................$75.00
Apple, cup, 2½"..$10.00
Apple, Dutch jug, 2-pt, 5¾"...............................$55.00
Apple, Kent jug, 1-pt, 4½" $35.00
Apple, lap plate, indent for cup, 8½" $15.00

Apple, marmalade jar, w/lid, 4½"..........................$50.00
Apple, mug, handled, 8-oz, 4".............................$35.00
Apple, mug, juice; 6-oz, 2½"..............................$15.00
Apple, oil & vinegar bottles, 1-pt, 9½", pr $95.00
Apple, plate, dinner; 9¾"..................................$15.00
Apple, plate, grill; indentations on surface, 12" $45.00
Apple, platter, 12" dia....................................$40.00
Apple, pour 'n shake shaker, 4¼" $40.00
Apple, salt & pepper shakers, stacking, 2¼", pr.........$35.00
Cactus Flower, bowl, fruit; 12"............................$85.00
Crescent Flower, jar, 3½".................................$45.00
Crescent Flower, salt & pepper shakers, round, 2¾", pr .$65.00

Ducks, child's set: Bowl, $75.00; Plate, $100.00; Mug, $100.00. (Photo courtesy Pat Doyle)

Fruit, coffeepot, 8-cup, 8" $65.00
Fruit, cookie jar, oval, red trim, 9" $60.00
Fruit, creamer & sugar bowl, w/lid, 3", 4"..................$55.00
Fruit, Dutch jug, 2-pt, 5¾" $45.00
Fruit, jar, storage; stacking pr w/lid, 8¾"................$85.00
Fruit, Kent jug, 1-pt, 4½" $30.00
Fruit, mug, juice; 6-oz, 2½"..............................$15.00
Fruit, night bottle, 1-qt, 7½"..............................$45.00
Fruit, plate, breakfast; 8½"...............................$30.00
Fruit, plate, chop; 12"....................................$35.00
Fruit, plate, dinner; 9¾" $20.00
Fruit, teapot, individual, 2-cup, 4".......................$45.00
Fruit, teapot, w/drip filter, 6-cup, 9" $75.00
Fruit, tumbler, 12-oz, 5".................................$20.00
Grapes, bowl, 4½x5½"....................................$45.00
Heather Plaid, bowl, vegetable; 8½" $20.00
Heather Plaid, chop plate, 12"............................$25.00
Heather Plaid, cookie jar, oval, 9½".......................$60.00
Heather Plaid, cup, 2½" $20.00
Heather Plaid, lap plate, indent for cup, 8½"..............$15.00
Heather Plaid, plate, dinner; 9¾" $15.00
Heather Plaid, salt & pepper shakers, jug style, 2½", pr ...$20.00
Heather Plaid, teapot, 6-cup, 6"..........................$65.00
Intaglio, bean pot, 3¾"...................................$50.00
Intaglio, bowl, dessert; 4"...............................$8.00
Intaglio, bowl, divided vegetable; 10½" $30.00
Intaglio, bowl, open vegetable; 8½".......................$20.00

Intaglio, butter dish, 6½" L $55.00
Intaglio, chop plate, 12" $25.00
Intaglio, creamer & sugar bowl, w/lid, 3½", 5"..........$50.00
Intaglio, cup & saucer, 2½", 5½"........................$13.00

Intaglio: Plate, dinner; 10", $15.00; Mug jug, 8-oz, 4¾", $40.00.

Intaglio, plate, salad; 6¾"............................$10.00
Intaglio, platter, 12"..................................$20.00
Intaglio, teapot, 6-cup, 6½"............................$65.00
Ivy-Red Blossom, creamer & sugar bowl, miniature, 2"...$30.00
Ivy-Red Blossom, range bowl, w/lid, 5½" $45.00
Maywood, bowl, dessert; 4"..............................$6.00
Maywood, Kent jug, 1-pt, 4½".............................$25.00
Maywood, mug, juice; 6-oz, 2½" $8.00
Maywood, pillow vase, from Napco mold, 6¾".............$25.00
Maywood, plate, dinner; 9¾"............................$10.00
Maywood, platter, grill; indents along surface, 12" L..$25.00
Ming Tree, pillow vase, 4¼" $35.00
Ming Tree, planter, 5"..................................$35.00
Ming Tree, plate, dinner; 9¾"..........................$20.00
Mountain Rose, creamer & sugar bowl, 2" $50.00
Mountain Rose, Dutch jug, 2-pt, 5¾".....................$85.00
Mountain Rose, Kent jug, 1-pt, 4½"......................$45.00
Mountain Rose, marmalade jar, 4½".......................$65.00
Mountain Rose, teapot, 6-cup, 6½".......................$85.00
Normandy Plaid, bean pot, w/lid, 3¾"....................$50.00
Normandy Plaid, bowl, spaghetti; 14½" L $55.00
Normandy Plaid, cup & saucer, 2½", 5½"..................$13.00
Normandy Plaid, pitcher, beverage; 2-pt, 6¼"............$55.00
Normandy Plaid, plate, dinner; 9¾"......................$15.00
Normandy Plaid, platter, 12" $30.00
Normandy Plaid, salt & pepper shakers, stacking, 2¼", pr..$25.00
Normandy Plaid, tumbler, 12-oz, 5" $20.00
Palm Tree, plate, dinner; 9¾"..........................$125.00
Palm Tree, vase, 5".....................................$75.00
Peasant Garden, bowl, vegetable; 8½" $80.00
Peasant Garden, creamer & sugar bowl, w/lid, 3½", 5"..$125.00
Peasant Garden, cup, 2½"................................$35.00
Peasant Garden, plate, breakfast; 8½" $100.00
Pennsylvania Dutch, beer mug, 16-oz, 4¾"................$65.00
Pennsylvania Dutch, bowl, cereal; 5¼"...................$20.00
Pennsylvania Dutch, bowl, divided vegetable; 10½" L..$50.00
Pennsylvania Dutch, bowl, vegetable; 8½"................$40.00
Pennsylvania Dutch, candy dish, 6¼".....................$65.00
Pennsylvania Dutch, plate, dinner; 9¾".................$25.00
Pennsylvania Dutch, plate, salad; 6¾" $20.00

Pennsylvania Dutch, platter, meat; 12" L $50.00
Pennsylvania Dutch, salt & pepper shakers, stacking, 2¼",
    pr $50.00

Pennsylvania Dutch: Tea and Toast lap plate, 8½" diameter, $35.00; Cup, 2½", $20.00. (Photo courtesy Susan Morris)

Petals, bowl, fruit; 12" $50.00
Petals, covered dish, 9"................................$65.00
Petals, teapot, 2-cup, 4"...............................$45.00
Provincial Fruit, bowl, fruit; 12"......................$40.00
Provincial Fruit, grease jar, 5".......................$30.00
Provincial Fruit, relish, 3-section, center handle, 10"..$55.00
Provincial Fruit, salt & pepper shakers, range style, 4", pr..$45.00
Red Blossom, coffeepot, w/drip filter, 11"..............$85.00
Red Blossom, mug, juice; 6-oz, 2½"......................$15.00
Ribbon Flower, bowl, fruit; 12".........................$50.00
Saraband, bowl, cereal; 5¼"............................$4.00
Saraband, bowl, fruit; 12"..............................$15.00
Saraband, candle holder, 2x6" $20.00
Saraband, cup, 2½"......................................$5.00
Saraband, plate, dinner; 9¾"...........................$8.00
Saraband, range bowl, w/lid, 5½".......................$20.00
Saraband, roll tray, 11" L..............................$12.00
Seaform, bowl, dessert; 4"..............................$20.00
Seaform, coffee server, 9" $125.00
Seaform, creamer & sugar bowl, 5".......................$85.00
Seaform, plate, dinner; 10"............................$25.00
Sunflower, plate, breakfast; 8½".......................$45.00
Sunflower, tumbler, 12-oz, 5"...........................$30.00
Tea Rose, bowl, vegetable; 8½".........................$40.00
Tea Rose, plate, breakfast; 8½".........................$25.00
Tea Rose, plate, dinner; 9¾"...........................$25.00
Tea Rose, platter, 12"..................................$50.00
Tea Rose, roll tray, 11" $50.00
Turquoise, baker, 7" dia $30.00
Turquoise, bowl, fruit; 12".............................$40.00
Turquoise, Kent jug, 1-pt, 4½" $40.00
Turquoise, plate, salad; 6¾"...........................$10.00
Turquoise, soup & sandwich, Rubel mold $55.00

Puzzles

The first children's puzzle was actually developed as a learning aid by an English map maker, trying to encourage the study of geography. Most nineteenth-century puzzles were made of wood, rather boring, and very expensive. But by the Victorian era, nursery rhymes and other light-hearted themes became popular. The industrial revolution and the inception of color lithography combined to produce a stunning variety of themes ranging from technical advancements, historical scenarios, and fairy tales. Power saws made production more cost effective, and wood was replaced with less expensive cardboard.

As early as the twenties and thirties, American manufacturers began to favor character-related puzzles, the market already influenced by radio and the movies. Some of these were advertising premiums. Die-cutters had replaced jigsaws, cardboard became thinner, and puzzles became a commodity everyone could afford. During the Depression they were a cheap form of entertainment, and no family get-together was complete without a puzzle spread out on the card table for all to enjoy.

Television and movies caused a lull in puzzle making during the fifties, but advancements in printing and improvements in quality brought them back strongly in the sixties. Unusual shapes, the use of fine art prints, and more challenging designs caused sales to increase.

If you're going to collect puzzles, you'll need to remember that unless all the pieces are there, they're not of much value, especially those from the twentieth century. The condition of the box is important as well. Right now there's a lot of interest in puzzles from the fifties through the seventies that feature popular TV shows and characters from that era. Remember, though a frame-tray puzzle still sealed in its original wrapping may be worth $10.00 or more, depending on the subject matter and its age, a well-used example may well be worthless as a collectible.

To learn more about the subject, we recommend *Character Toys and Collectibles* and *Toys, Antique and Collectible*, both by David Longest; *Toys of the Sixties, A Pictorial Guide*, by Bill Bruegman; and *Schroeder's Toys, Antique to Modern* (Collector Books).

Newsletter: *Piece by Piece*
P.O. Box 12823
Kansas City, KS 66112-9998; Subscription: $8 per year

Alice in Wonderland, frame-tray, unmarked (not Disney), 1950s, EX **$25.00**
Andy Panda, frame-tray, Walter Lantz, 1962-63, 8½x11", EX+ **$10.00**
Annie, jigsaw, Milton Bradley #4285, 1983, MIB (sealed) ..**$5.00**
Aquaman, jigsaw, Aquaman & Mera battle a giant squid, Whitman, 1968, VG+ (VG+ box) **$30.00**
Baby Huey, Huey eating pies at fair, Built Rite, 1970s, 70 pcs, NM (EX box) **$8.00**
Back to the Future II, jigsaw, 1989, NMIB **$5.00**
Banana Splits, jigsaw, Whitman, NMIB **$55.00**
Batman, frame-tray, Watkins & Strathmore, 1966, EX+ .**$20.00**
Batman, jigsaw, Whitman, 1966, 150 pcs, MIB **$30.00**
Batman, 4-puzzle game, Milton Bradley, complete w/instructions, 1966, NM (EX box) **$36.00**
Black Hole, jigsaw, Whitman/WDP, 1979, 500 pcs, MIB (sealed) **$12.00**

Bonanza, jigsaw, #2 The Rescue, Milton Bradley, 1964, complete w/out bonus puzzle, 1964, NM+ (NM box) ..**$39.00**
Bozo, jigsaw, on high wire, 1969, NMIB **$10.00**
Broken Arrow, frame-tray, Built-Rite, M **$25.00**
Buck Rogers, jigsaw, HB, 1970s, MIB (sealed)...........**$15.00**
Buffalo Bill Junior Picture Puzzle, Built-Rite, 1956, 100 pcs, EX (EX box) **$25.00**
Bugs Bunny Looney Toons, frame-tray, Jaymar, 1940s, 11x14", EX **$30.00**
Bullwinkle & Rocky, frame-tray, Jaymar, 1960s, complete, 10x13", NM **$28.00**
Buzzy the Crow, jigsaw, Built Rite, 1961, 70 pcs, MIB ..**$26.00**
Captain America, frame-tray, scene saving congress, Whitman, 1966, 11x14", EX+ **$24.00**
Captain Kangaroo, jigsaw, Fairchild, 1971, complete, NM (NM box) **$10.00**
Charlie Brown & Peanuts Gang Decorate Christmas Tree, Hallmark/Springbok, MIP **$5.00**
Chilly Willy, frame-tray, Walter Lantz, 1962-63, 8½x11", EX..**$10.00**
Christmas Keepsake Puzzle, w/ornament, Hallmark/Springbok, 1992, MIB **$30.00**
Columbia Space Shuttle, jigsaw, photo of shuttle launching from pad, Jaymar, ca 1980, 800 pcs, NM (EX+ box) **$10.00**
Creature From the Black Lagoon, jigsaw, Golden, MIB (sealed) **$15.00**
Daktari, Whitman, 1967, 100 pcs, 14x18", EX+ **$12.00**
Dick Tracy, Jaymar, 1950s, NMIB **$40.00**
Dick Tracy, jigsaw, Bank Holdup, Jaymar, 1950s-60s, complete, NMIB **$65.00**
Disneyland, jigsaw, shows castle w/fireworks & characters, Jaymar, 1962, 100 pcs, EX **$25.00**
Disneyland Frontierland, Jaymar, 1950s, EXIB **$20.00**
Dondi, frame-tray, Camping Trip, Jaymar, 1961, complete, 11x14", NM **$15.00**
Dondi, frame-tray, Jaymar, 1961, 11x14", NM.............**$15.00**
Dr Dolittle, frame-tray, examining a horse, Whitman, 1967, complete, 11x14", NM **$15.00**
Dr Dolittle, jigsaw, shows Polynesia Parrot, Whitman, NMIB **$20.00**
Dracula, frame-tray, Dracula puts woman in casket beside Frankenstein, Jaymar, 1963, complete, 11x14", scarce, NM **$55.00**
Eddie Cantor, jigsaw, We Want Cantor, #1, Einson, 1933, 200+ pcs, complete, NM (EX+ box) **$28.00**
Eerie Magazine #4777-1, Milton Bradley, 1977, MIB...**$10.00**
Emergency, jigsaw, American Publishing, 1975, M (M sealed canister) **$45.00**
Family Affair, jigsaw, Whitman, 1970, 100 pcs, 14x18", NMIB **$12.00**
Family Affair, jigsaw (round), Jody & Buffy cover Mr French w/sand, Whitman, 1970, 125 pcs, 20" dia, EX (EX box) **$15.00**
Farrah Fawcett, jigsaw, Arts, 1977, MIB **$25.00**
Felix the Cat, frame-tray, Built-Rite, #1229-29, 1950s-60s, M **$30.00**
Felix the Cat, frame-tray, Built-Rite, 1949, complete, 9x12", EX..**$35.00**
Flash Gordon, jigsaw, #977, MIB................................**$36.00**

Flintstones, frame-tray, Man Called Flintstone, Whitman, 1966, complete, 11x14", NM **$30.00**

Flipper, Whitman, 1967, 100 pcs, 14x18", NM.............**$15.00**

Frankenstein, jigsaw, Golden, 1990, 200 pcs, MIB........**$6.00**

Funky Phantom, jigsaw, Funky & gang cruising streets, Whitman, 1974, 100 pcs, 14x18", NM (NM box) ..**$18.00**

Funny Company, frame-tray, Whitman #4428, 1963, NM...**$20.00**

Gabby Gator, frame-tray, Walter Lantz, 1962-63, 8½x11", EX...**$10.00**

Get Smart, jigsaw, Smart holds fire hydrant for his canine partner, Jaymar, 1965, complete, EX (VG box) **$40.00**

Gunsmoke, frame-tray, 1959, NM......................................**$20.00**

Gunsmoke, jigsaw, Whitman, 1969, NMIB **$25.00**

Gunsmoke, photo of James Arness/Amanda Blake, 1958, M (sealed) **$30.00**

Herman & Katnip, inlaid, EX.......................................**$15.00**

Howdy Doody, Is That You Clarabelle, frame-tray, 1952, EX..**$25.00**

Huckleberry Hound, frame-tray, 1961, EX...................**$22.50**

Impossibles, frame-tray, superheroes vs villians along beach, Whitman, 1967, complete, 11x14", NM **$28.00**

Jetsons, frame-tray, Whitman, 1962, EX.......................**$32.00**

King Leonardo, jigsaw, The King on Parade, Jaymar, 1962, 60+ pcs, complete, 10x14", NM (EX box).............**$16.00**

Krazy Ikes, frame-tray, Whitman, 1969, 11x14", NM (sealed)...**$15.00**

Lassie, frame-tray, real photo, Built-Rite, 1950s, 6x9", NM..**$25.00**

Laverne & Shirley, jigsaw, HG Toys, 1970s, complete, MIB **$20.00**

Liddle Kiddles, frame-tray, 4 Kiddles play in park, Whitman, 1968, 11x14", missing 1 pc o/w NM.......................**$14.00**

Liddle Kiddles, frame-tray, 9 Kiddles in summer outfits, Whitman, 1966, complete, 11x14", NM **$24.00**

Little Lulu, frame-tray, Whitman #4428, 1959, EX+ **$35.00**

Little People by Walt Scott, jigsaw, Jaymar, 1950s, NMIB..**$32.00**

Lone Ranger, jigsaw, Story Puzzle, Parker Bros, 1938, set of 4, 1 pc missing, EX (NM box) **$70.00**

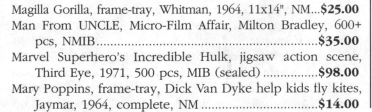

Lone Ranger and Tonto, American Publishing Corp, sealed, in original 5¾x4¼" diameter canister, $15.00.

Magilla Gorilla, frame-tray, Whitman, 1964, 11x14", NM...**$25.00**

Man From UNCLE, Micro-Film Affair, Milton Bradley, 600+ pcs, NMIB..**$35.00**

Marvel Superhero's Incredible Hulk, jigsaw action scene, Third Eye, 1971, 500 pcs, MIB (sealed) **$98.00**

Mary Poppins, frame-tray, Dick Van Dyke help kids fly kites, Jaymar, 1964, complete, NM **$14.00**

Mary Poppins, frame-tray, Dick Van Dyke on carousel horse in fox hunt, Whitman, 1966, complete, 11x14", NM **$18.00**

Mary Poppins, jigsaw, Happy Holiday, Jaymar, 1964, complete, NM (NM box, clear tape on 1 corner)........**$18.00**

Mickey Mouse Club, frame-tray, Jaymar, 1950s, M **$22.00**

Mickey Mouse Club, jigsaw, birthday party scene, Jaymar, 1950s, complete, NMIB.......................................**$12.00**

Mighty Mouse, jigsaw, Playhouse, Fairchild, 1956, complete, NMIB...**$20.00**

Mr MaGoo, frame-tray, Jaymar, 1967, complete, 10x13", EX **$18.00**

Mr Magoo, frame-tray, Magoo looking at fish in aquarium, Warren, 1978, MIP (sealed) **$27.00**

Munsters, jigsaw, Whitman, 1965, MIB **$45.00**

Oswald the Rabbit, frame-tray, Walter Lantz, 1962-63, 8½x11", EX+..**$10.00**

Pinky Lee, frame-tray, Funny Picture Puzzles, Gabriel, 1955, set of 4, 12x10", NM (EX box)...............................**$20.00**

Playland, with Popeye, Brutus, Olive Oyl, and others, Jaymar, $135.00.

Popeye, frame-tray, Jaymar, No 2764-29, 1950s, NM ..**$22.00**

Popeye, frame-tray, Jaymar, 1961, set of 4, complete, 11x14", NMIB..**$35.00**

Prince Valiant, jigsaw, Built-Rite, 1950s, 100 pcs, EX..**$25.00**

Quick Draw McGraw, frame-tray, 1963, EX **$25.00**

Quick Draw McGraw, jigsaw, Whitman, 1960, NMIB.**$35.00**

Raggedy Ann & Andy, frame-tray, Milton Bradley, 1955, EX **$15.00**

Rainbow Brite Valentine Puzzle Greeting, Hallmark/ Springbok, 1983, MIP **$5.00**

Return of the Jedi, frame-tray, shows fat green creature w/horns & tusks, 1983, EX.......................................**$8.00**

Rin-Tin-Tin, jigsaw, Whitman, No 302, 1960s, NMIB..**$30.00**

Road Runner, frame-tray, 1970s, MIB.........................**$15.00**

Roger Ramjet, frame tray, Whitman, 1966, complete, 14x11", EX...**$45.00**

Rookies, jigsaw, APC, No 1250B, 1975, NM (NM can).**$22.50**

Roy Rogers, jr jigsaw, Whitman, set of 3, 1952, EXIB...**$80.00**

Rudolph the Red-Nosed Reindeer, frame-tray, Jamar, 1950s, 11x14", NM...**$20.00**

Santa Claus, frame-tray, Lowe, 1963, 8x12", M (sealed)..**$8.00**

Santa Kermit in Christmas Box, Hallmark/Springbok, 1980, MIP **$5.00**

Shirt Tales Thanksgiving Greeting, Hallmark/Springbok, MIP **$5.00**

Shotgun Slade, jigsaw, art by Scott Brady, Milton Bradley, 1960, 100 pcs, complete, 10x18", NM (NM box)..**$24.00**

Silver Surfer (Marbel Super-Hero), jigsaw, I'm Changing, Third Eye, 1971, 500 pcs, unused, MIB (sealed)..**$18.00**

Sky Hawks, frame-tray, Whitman, 1970, EX+ **$15.00**

Smedly Ice Fishing & Catching Chilly Willy, frame-tray, Walter Lantz, 1962-63, 8½x11", EX **$10.00**

Snuffy Smith, jigsaw, The Old Gang, Jaymar, 1960s, complete, 14x10", NM (NM box).....................................**$12.00**

Space Kidettes, frame-tray, flying out of Klub House in outer space, Whitman, 1967, complete, 11x14", EX+ **$26.00**

Space Travel, frame-tray, 1959, EX+..............................**$30.00**

Space 1999, jigsaw, HG, 1970s, 150 pcs, MIB (sealed).**$15.00**

Spooky, frame-tray, Tuco, stands beside a archery target, 1960s, complete, 10x14", EX....................................**$14.00**

Star Trek, jigsaw, Battle of the Planet Klingon, HG Toys, 1974, 150 pcs, 10x14", NM (NM box) **$15.00**

Stingray, frame-tray, Whitman, 1965, complete, 11x14", NM **$26.00**

Super Six, jigsaw, 1969, EX (EX box) **$88.00**

Superman, frame-tray, Whitman, 1965, EX.................**$20.00**

Superman, jigsaw, Whitman, 1966, 150 pcs, 14x18", NMIB .**$15.00**

SWAT, jigsaw, HG No 463-03, 1975, MIB....................**$20.00**

Sword in the Stone, frame-tray, stuff flies as Merlin shows Wart his magic, Whitman, 1963, complete, 11x14", NM+ **$16.00**

Sylvester & Tweety, frame-tray, Cageman, Connor Toy, 1971, 12 pcs, EX **$15.00**

Tennessee Tuxedo, frame-tray, Whitman, 1966, complete, 11x14", EX+ **$35.00**

Tom & Jerry, frame-tray, as sultans in India, complete, 14x11", VG+ **$20.00**

Tommy Tortoise & Moe Hare, jigsaw, Built Rite, 1961, 70 pcs, MIB **$25.00**

'Twas the Night Before Christmas, frame-tray, Lowe, 1972, 8x12", M...**$6.00**

Underdog, jigsaw, Underdog & Polly fly away from bad guy, Whitman, 1975, MIB (sealed)..................................**$25.00**

Universal Monsters, frame-tray, Mummy, Jaymar, 1963, complete, NM..**$145.00**

Wagon Train, frame-tray, Whitman, EX+ **$25.00**

WC Fields, jigsaw, 1969, NMIB......................................**$25.00**

Welcome Back Kotter, frame-tray, 1977, sealed **$12.50**

Wendy the Witch, jigsaw, helping Cinderella do chores, Built Rite, 1970s, 70 pcs, complete, EX (EX+ box).......**$12.00**

Winky Dink, frame-tray, Jaymar, 1950s, complete, 10x12", VG **$30.00**

Woody Woodpecker, Splinter & Knothead, frame-tray, Walter Lantz, 1962-63, 8½x11", EX...............................**$10.00**

Woody Woodpecker Tied to Helium Balloons, frame-tray, Whitman, 1954, 11x14", EX+ **$22.00**

Wyatt Earp, frame-tray, Whitman, 1958, complete, NM..**$50.00**

Yogi Bear, frame-tray, 1960s, NM **$28.00**

Zorro, frame-tray, Jaymar #2710-29, EX......................**$22.00**

101 Dalmatians, frame-tray, Jaymar, #2720-29, M........**$40.00**

20,000 Leagues Under the Sea, frame-tray, Jaymar, 1954, NMIB..**$18.00**

Wonder Woman's Capture, frame-tray, DC Comics, 1979, 12x9½", $8.00.

Razor Blade Banks

Razor blade banks are receptacles designed to safely store used razor blades. While the double-edged disposable razor blades date back as far as 1903, ceramic and figural razor blade safes most likely only date as far back as the early 1930s. The invention of the electric razor and later disposable razors did away with the need for these items, and their production ended in the 1960s.

Shapes can include barber chairs, barbers, animals, and the more popular barber poles. Listerine produced a white donkey and elephant in 1936 with political overtones. They also made a white ceramic frog. These were used as promotional items for shaving cream. Prices are listed as a guide and reflect items in near-mint to excellent condition, based on availability. Note that regional pricing could vary.

Advisor: Debbie Gillham (See Directory, Razor Blade Banks)

Barber, wood w/Gay Blade bottom, unscrews, Woodcroft, 1950, 6", from $65 to..**$75.00**

Barber, wood w/key & metal holders for razor & brush, 9", from $85 to..**$95.00**

Barber bust w/handlebar mustache, coat & tie, from $55 to..**$65.00**

Barber chair, lg, from $100 to.....................................**$125.00**

Barber chair, sm, from $75 to.....................................**$100.00**

Barber holding pole, Occupied Japan, 4", from $50 to .**$60.00**

Barber pole, red & white, w/ or w/out attachments & various titles, from $20 to..**$25.00**

Barber pole w/barber head & derby hat, white, from $35 to..**$40.00**

Barber pole w/face, red & white, from $30 to...........**$35.00**

Barber standing in blue coat & stroking chin, from $75 to ...**$80.00**

Barber w/buggy eyes, pudgy full figure, Gleason look-alike, from $65 to..**$75.00**

Barbershop quartet, 4 singing barber heads, from $95 to ...**$125.00**

Box w/policeman holding up hand, metal, marked Used Blades, from $50 to **$65.00**

Ceramic Arts Studio, Tony the barber, from $85 to **$95.00**

Cleminson barber head, different colors on collar, from $30 to **$35.00**

Cleminson man shaving, mushroom shape, from $25 to ..**$30.00**

Dandy Dans, plastic w/brush holders, from $30 to **$40.00**

Frog, green, marked For Used Blades, from $65 to....**$75.00**

Half barber pole, hangs on wall, may be personalized w/name, from $50 to..**$60.00**

Half shaving cup, hangs on wall, marked Gay Blades w/floral design, from $65 to **$75.00**

Half shaving cup, hangs on wall, marked Gay Old Blade w/quartet, from $65 to **$75.00**

Listerine donkey, from $20 to......................................**$30.00**

Listerine elephant, from $25 to...................................**$35.00**

Listerine frog, from $15 to..**$20.00**

Looie, right- or left-hand version, from $85 to.........**$100.00**

Razor Bum, from $135 to...**$150.00**

Safe, green, marked Razor on front, from $45 to **$55.00**

Shaving brush, ceramic, wide style w/decal, from $50 to...**$60.00**

Shaving cup, hangs on wall, marked Gay Blades, floral design, from $50 to..**$65.00**

See line listings for individual values. (Photo courtesy Debbie Gillham)

Reamers

Reamers were a European invention of the late 1700s, devised as a method of extracting liquid from citrus fruits, which was used as a medicinal remedy. Eventually the concept of freshly squeezed juice worked its way across the oceans. Many early U.S. patents (mostly for wood reamers) were filed in the mid-1880s, and thanks to the 1916 Sunkist 'Drink An Orange' advertising campaign, the reamer soon became a permanent fixture in the well-equipped American kitchen. Most of the major U.S. glass companies and pottery manufacturers included juicers as part of their kitchenware lines. However, some of the most beautiful and unique reamers are ceramic figures and hand-painted, elegant china and porcelain examples. The development of frozen and bottled citrus juice relegated many a reamer to the kitchen shelf. However, the current trend for a healthier diet has garnered renewed interest for the manual juice squeezer.

Most of the German and English reamers listed here can be attributed to the 1920s and 1930s. Most of the Japanese imports are from the 1940s.

Advisor: Bobbie Zucker Bryson (See Directory, Reamers)

Club: *National Reamer Collectors Association*
Debbie Gillham
47 Midline Ct., Gaithersburg, MD 20878, 301 977 5727

Ceramic

Baby's, 2-pc, pink w/white kitten in blue pajamas, pink, blue, green & white top, Japan, 4" **$95.00**

Baby's Orange, 2-pc, red & white, Japan, 4½" **$55.00**

Camel, kneeling, 2-pc, lustre w/light green top, 4¼" ..**$225.00**

Child's, lustre w/red & yellow flowers, octagon shape, Japan, 3¼", from $95 to...**$125.00**

Child's, 2-pc, orange lustre w/red, blue & yellow flowers, 2" **$95.00**

Clown, brown body & hat, blue button & collar, 6" ..**$85.00**

Clown, saucer, orange & white, German/Goebel, 5" dia ..**$250.00**

Clown, seated, Japanese, 5½", from $65.00 to $75.00. (Photo courtesy Bobbie Zucker Bryson)

Clown, 2-pc, white, black, red & orange, Japan, 6½" ..**$95.00**

Dog, 2-pc, beige w/red & black trim, 8" **$225.00**

Elephant, 2-pc, white w/red & blue trim, 4¼", from $150 to...**$200.00**

House, 2-pc, beige w/green trees & tan branches, blue door & windmill, Japan, 4½" **$185.00**

House, 2-pc, beige w/tan & orange trim, Japan, 5½"...**$100.00**

Jiffy Juicer, maroon, US Pat 2, 130, 755, Sept 20, 1938, 5¼", $85.00. (Photo courtesy courtesy Bobbie Zucker Bryson)

Lemon, 2-pc, yellow w/green leaves, white top, Germany, 3¼", from $55 to..............................**$65.00**

Orange, 2-pc, Orange for Baby, yellow w/blue flowers, Goebel, 3½"...**$150.00**

Pear, 3-pc, yellow w/white flowers & green leaves, Japan, 4¾"...**$60.00**

Pitcher, 2-pc, beige w/multicolor flowers & black trim, Japan, 8¾"..**$50.00**

Pitcher, 2-pc, black w/gold wheat, 8"...............**$45.00**

Pitcher, 2-pc, cream w/lavender lillies & green leaves, Universal Cambridge, 9"...............................**$175.00**

Pitcher, 2-pc, rose w/yellow & lavender flowers, green leaves, Japan, 7", +6 cups.........................**$65.00**

Puddinhead, 2-pc, 6¼".....................................**$175.00**

Red Wing USA, yellow, 6¾"..............................**$125.00**

Rose, pink w/green leaves, Germany, 1¾".........**$225.00**

Saucer, cream, tan & maroon w/blue trim, England, 3¼" dia...**$90.00**

Saucer, cream w/yellow bees, Japan, 3¾" dia...........**$45.00**

Saucer, white w/pink flowers & green leaves, Germany, 4½" dia...**$75.00**

Saucer, 2-pc, France, Ivoire Corbelle, Henriot Quimper #1166, 4¼" dia...**$350.00**

Sleeping Mexican, 2-pc, green shirt, red pants, gold top, Japan, 4¾"...**$150.00**

Sourpuss, 4¾", $100.00. (Photo courtesy Bobbie Zucker Bryson)

Swan, 2-pc, cream w/rose flowers & green base, Japan, 4¼"...**$60.00**

Teapot, 2-pc, white w/blue sailboat, Germany, 3¼" ..**$65.00**

Teapot, 2-pc, white w/red flowers & trim, Prussia/ Germany/Royal Rudolstadt, 3¼".................**$150.00**

Teapot, 2-pc, white w/yellow & maroon flowers, Nippon, 3¼"...**$90.00**

Teapot, 2-pc, yellow, tan & white, England/Shelley, 3½" **$95.00**

Toby-style man, gray hair, green jacket, lavender hat, 4¾"...**$250.00**

USA, Ade-O-Matic Genuine Coorsite Porcelain, green, 9" **$150.00**

USA, Jiffy Juicer, US Pat 2,130,755, Sept 2, 1928, green, 5¼" **$85.00**

Glassware

Amber, Cambridge..**$600.00**

Amber, paneled sides, Westmoreland, lg...................**$275.00**

Amber, 2-cup measure w/reamer top, US Glass.......**$275.00**

Amber (dark), Indiana Glass, loop handle...............**$275.00**

Black opaque, Sunkist, from $650 to........................**$850.00**

Clambroth, boat shape, 5⅛" dia, from $150 to.........**$185.00**

Clear, baby's, notched top.......................................**$50.00**

Clear, embossed ASCO, Good Morning, Orange Juice......**$20.00**

Clear frosted, Baby's Orange..................................**$65.00**

Clear, loop handle, 5¼", from $10 to.......................**$15.00**

Clear, spout opposite handle, Indiana Glass.............**$12.00**

Clear w/elephant-decorated base, baby's, Fenton......**$75.00**

Clear w/flower decal, baby's, Westmoreland............**$40.00**

Custard, embossed McK, 6" dia, from $25 to............**$35.00**

Custard, Sunkist..**$30.00**

Emerald green, straight sides, Fry, 6¼" dia..............**$30.00**

Green, baby's, 2-pc, Westmoreland, 3⅜"..................**$185.00**

Green, Orange Juice Extractor................................**$50.00**

Green, paneled sides, loop handle, Federal Glass......**$25.00**

Green, Party Line, 4-cup pitcher w/reamer top, 8¾"..**$95.00**

Green, pointed cone, Federal Glass.........................**$15.00**

Green, slick handle, insert near top of cup, graduated measurements on side, US Glass.............................**$35.00**

Green, tab handle, Federal, 5¼"..............................**$12.00**

Green, 2-cup pitcher w/reamer top, Hazel Atlas........**$30.00**

Green, 4-cup pitcher marked A&J w/reamer top, Hazel Atlas...**$35.00**

Green, 4-cup pitcher w/reamer top, Hocking............**$35.00**

Green custard, embossed Sunkist............................**$85.00**

Jade-ite, McKee, 6" diameter, from $22.00 to $30.00.

Jade-ite (light), 2-cup measure w/reamer top.............**$22.50**

Milk glass, embossed Valencia, 6" dia......................**$100.00**

Milk glass, McKee, sm..**$20.00**

Mount Joy, 3-pc, green metal base w/transparent green bowl & cone, from $150 to................................**$195.00**

Pearl opalescent, straight sides, Fry.........................**$25.00**

Pink, Criss Cross, Hazel Atlas, w/tab handle, 5¼" dia..**$275.00**

Pink, Federal, sm...**$100.00**

Pink, Hex Optic, bucket container w/reamer top, Jeannette, 7¾"...**$55.00**

Pink, Jennyware..**$90.00**

Pink, Orange Juice Extractor, unembossed..............**$200.00**

Red, 2-pc, Fenton, 6⅜"...**$1,200.00**

Red & orange slag, Fleur-de-Lis, 6¼" dia, from $375 to..**$450.00**

Ultramarine, Jennyware...**$120.00**

Vitrock, orange, loop handle, Hocking.....................**$20.00**

Yellow, 2-cup measure w/reamer top, Hazel Atlas.....**$35.00**
Yellow opalescent, fluted sides, Fry, 6¼" dia............**$275.00**

Metal

Aluminum tilt-model, Seald Sweet Juice Extractor, attaches to counter, 13" **$60.00**
Green metal base, white porcelain bowl & cone, 3-pc, Presto Juice National Electric Appliance Corp, 7⅝", from $110 to **$125.00**
Metal, Quam-Nicholas Co, Chicago IL, Kwicky Juicer, 5½", from $8 to...**$10.00**
Silverplate, Meriden SP Co International, S Co, 2-pc, 4⅝" dia..**$95.00**
Silverplate, 2-pc, cocktail shaker, Germany, 7", from $85 to **$100.00**
Sterling silver, Black & Starr, 3¾" dia.......................**$300.00**

Records

Records are still plentiful at flea markets and some antique malls, but albums (rock, jazz, and country) from the fifties and sixties are getting harder to find in collectible condition (very good or better). Garage sales are sometimes a great place to buy old records, since most of what you'll find there have been stored more carefully by their original owners.

There are two schools of thought concerning what is a collectible record. While some collectors prefer the rarities — those made in limited quantities, by an unknown who later became famous, or those aimed at a specific segment of music lovers — others like the vintage Top-10 recordings. Now that they're so often being replaced with CDs, we realize that even though we take them for granted, the possibilty of their becoming a thing of the past may be reality tomorrow.

Whatever the slant your collection takes, learn to visually inspect records before you buy them. Condition is one of the most important factors to consider when assessing value. To be judged as mint, a record may have been played but must have no visual or audible deterioration — no loss of gloss to the finish, no stickers or writing on the label, no holes, no skips when it is played. If any of these are apparent, at best it is considered to be excellent and its value is at least 50% lower. Many of the records you'll find that seem to you to be in wonderful shape would be judged only very good, excellent at the most, by a knowledgeable dealer. Sleeves with no tape, stickers, tears, or obvious damage at best would be excellent; mint condition sleeves are impossible to find unless you've found old store stock.

Be on the lookout for colored vinyl or picture discs, as some of these command higher prices; in fact, older Vogue picture disks commonly sell in the $50.00 to $75.00 range, some even more. It's not too uncommon to find old radio station discards. These records will say either 'Not for Sale' or 'Audition Copy' and may be worth more than their commercial counterparts. Our values are based on original issue.

If you'd like more information, we recommend *American Premium Record Guide* by L.R. Docks.

Advisor: Dave Torzillo, 45 rpms and LPs (See Directory, Records)

45 rpm

Values for 45 rpms are 'with dust jacket'; if no jacket is present, reduce these prices by at least 50%.

Alice in Wonderland's I'm Late, Golden Records, 1951, EX...**$10.00**
Archies, Jingle Jangle, Kirshner 5002, M **$5.00**
Avalon, Frankie; Venus, Chancellor 1031, M **$10.00**

Avalon, Frankie; Where Are You/Tuxedo Junction, Chancellor C-1052, from $10.00 to $15.00.

Bambi, Walt Disney, 1966, EX **$4.00**
Batman Theme, shows Batman & Robin swinging on ropes w/harvest moon beyond on sleeve, 1966, EX......**$10.00**
Bay City Rollers, Saturday Night, Arista 0149, M...........**$1.50**
Beach Boys, Help Me Rhonda, Capitol 5372, M **$15.00**
Beatles, Free As a Bird, US issue, NM..........................**$6.00**
Beatles, I Want To Hold Your Hand, VG+....................**$45.00**
Beatles, Let It Be, VG **$15.00**
Beatles, Paperback Writer/Rain, VG+...........................**$35.00**
Big Bopper, Chantilly Lace, Mercury 71343, M, from $25 to...**$35.00**
Boone, Pat; Ain't That a Shame, Dot 15377, M...........**$15.00**
Bozo Children's Record, Little Golden, 1960, EX+......**$15.00**
Burnette, Johnny; Ballad of the One-Eyed Jacks, Liberty Records, 1963, EX+ **$10.00**
Captain & Tennille, Do That To Me One More Time, Casablanca 2215, M **$2.00**
Cher, Gypsys, Tramps & Thieves, Kapp 2146, M.........**$1.00**
Cinderella, Mickey Mouse, 1950s, NM..........................**$8.00**
Creedence Clearwater Revival, Proud Mary, Fantasy 619, M.**$5.00**
Damone, Vic; On the Street Where You Live, Columbia 40654, M **$3.00**
Dave Clark Five, Bits & Pieces, Epic 9671, M **$10.00**
Dennis the Menace, I'm Home/I Hate Spelling, Golden Records, 1960, NM..**$10.00**
Diamond, Neil; Girl, You'll Be a Woman Soon, Bang 542, M **$3.00**
Especially for Children, Impact Records, 1975, EX **$3.00**
Everly Brothers, All I Have To Do Is Dream, Cadence 1348, M **$15.00**
Francis, Connie; Who's Sorry Now, MGM 12588, M...**$10.00**
Fred Flintstone the Magician, Peter Pan, 1970s, EX......**$6.50**
Gerry & the Pacemakers, Don't Let the Sun Catch You Crying, Laurie 3251, M...**$10.00**

Gore, Lesley; It's My Party, Mercury 72119, M **$20.00**

Happy Birthday to You, Peter Pan, EX **$4.50**

Hill Street Blues, theme song, Electra, 1980, NM **$5.00**

Hunter, Tab; Young Love, Dot 15533, M **$15.00**

It's a Small World, Walt Disney, 1966, EX.................**$6.50**

Jackson, Michael; Rockin' Robin, Motown 1197, M **$5.00**

Joel, Billy; Just the Way You Are, Columbia 10646, M .**$2.50**

John, Elton; Crocodile Rock, MCA 40000, M **$5.00**

Kenny G, Songbird, Arista 9588, M **$2.00**

Lauper, Cyndi; Girls Just Want To Have Fun, Portrait 04120,
   M **$3.00**

Lee, Peggy; Fever, Capitol 3998, M **$10.00**

Loggins, Kenny; Whenever I Call You Friend, Columbia
   10794, M **$2.00**

Lovin' Spoonful, Do You Believe in Magic, Kama Sutra 201,
   M **$4.00**

Madonna, Like a Virgin, Sire 29210, M **$5.00**

Mamas & the Papas, California Dreamin', Dunhill 4020,
   M..**$6.00**

Martin, Dean; Everybody Loves Somebody, Reprise 0281,
   M **$10.00**

Mathis, Johnny; It's Not For Me To Say, Columbia 40851,
   M **$6.00**

Mel Blanc Sings Little Red Monkey & Pussycat Parade,
   Capitol, 1960s, M **$15.00**

Midler, Bette; Boogie Woogie Bugle Boy, Atlantic 2964,
   M..**$3.00**

Motley Crue, Smokin' in the Boys Room, Elektra 69625,
   M..**$2.00**

Muppets, Twiddle Bugs at Work, 1981, EX **$4.00**

My First Learning Record, ABC's 123's, 1966, EX..........**$4.00**

Nursery Songs To Read & Hear, Golden Books, 1959, EX ..**$5.00**

Ono, Yoko; My Man **$8.00**

Orbison, Roy; Only the Lonely, Monument 421, M **$20.00**

Page, Patti; Allegheny Moon, Mercury 70878, M........**$10.00**

Paper Lace, The Night Chicago Died, Mercury 73492, M ..**$4.00**

Parton, Dolly; Here You Come Again, RCA 11123, M ..**$4.00**

Perkins, Carl; Blue Suede Shoes, Sun 234, M, from $50 to ..**$75.00**

Peter Pan, A Pirate's Life, Golden Records, 1952, EX.**$10.00**

Platters, Great Pretender, Mercury 70753, M **$15.00**

Popeye the Sailor Man Children's Record, Golden Record,
   1957, EX..**$12.00**

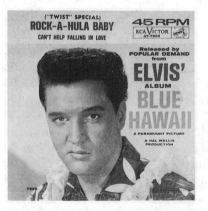

Presley, Elvis; Rock-A-Hula Baby/Can't Help Falling in Love, RCA Victor 47-7968, $35.00.

Puff the Magic Dragon, Wonderland, 1960s, EX **$4.00**

Queen, We Are the Champions/We Will Rock You, Elektra
   45441, M **$10.00**

Rascals, People Got To Be Free, Atlantic 2537, M **$5.00**

Reo Speedwagon, Keep On Loving You, Epic 50953, M.**$3.00**

Rich, Charlie; The Most Beautiful Girl, Epic 11040, M..**$3.00**

Rocky & His Friends, Golden Records, 1961, EX........**$18.00**

Rolling Stones, Time Is on My Side, London 9708, M ..**$10.00**

Romper Room Songs, Peter Pan, EX **$5.00**

Ross, Diana; Confide in Me, 1977 ....**$15.00**

Rydell, Bobby; The Door to Paradise/I Wanna Thank You, Cameo C-201, $15.00.

Rydell, Bobby; We Got Love, Cameo 169, M, from $15
   to **$20.00**

Shirelles, Mama Said, Scepter 1217, M......................**$15.00**

Simon & Garfunkel, Bridge Over Troubled Water, Columbia
   45079, M **$8.00**

Simple Simon, Little Golden, EX...............................**$3.00**

Snoopy vs the Red Baron, Peter Pan, EX **$4.50**

Snow White, Hi-Ho, Hi-Ho, Golden Records, 1949, EX .**$7.00**

Snow White, Whistle While You Work, Golden Records,
   1949, EX...**$8.00**

Spanky & Our Gang, Sunday Will Never Be the Same,
   Mercury 72679, M **$5.00**

Story of Rapunzel, Walt Disney, 1970s, EX...................**$6.00**

Turtles, Happy Together, White Whale 244, M **$6.00**

Ugly Bug Ball From Summer Magic, Disney, 1962, NM.**$6.00**

Valli, Frankie; Can't Take My Eyes Off You, Philips 40446,
   M **$4.00**

Vinton, Bobbie; Roses Are Red, Epic 9509, M..............**$8.00**

Wonder Woman Theme Song, Shadybrook, 1977, NM..**$80.00**

78 rpm

Beverly Hillbillies, Red River Valley, Brunswick 421, NM ..**$7.00**

Big Rock Candy Mountain, Golden Records, 1952, NM .**$5.00**

Carter Family, Keep on the Sunny Side, Bluebird 5006,
   NM **$10.00**

Charlie Monroe's Boys, Great Speckled Bird, Bluebird 7862,
   NM..**$7.50**

Count Basie & His Orchestra, Honeysuckle Rose, Decca
   1141, EX...**$8.00**

Crosby, Bing; Brother Can You Spare a Dime?, Brunswick
   6414, EX...**$10.00**

Deputy Dawg, Peter Pan, 1962, NM **$17.50**

Domino, Fats; Boogie Woogie Baby, Imperial 5065, EX...**$15.00**

Dorsey Brothers, Have a Little Faith in Me, Banner 0571,
   EX...**$8.00**

Durante, Jimmy; Inka Dinka Doo, Brunswick 6774, EX...**$7.50**

Ellington, Duke; Birmingham Breakdown, Brunswick 3480, EX..$12.50

Garland, Judy; Stompin' at the Savoy, Decca 848, EX..$8.00

Goodman, Benny; Japanese Sandman, Victor 25024, EX .$8.00

Hanna-Barbera 3-On-1 Children's Record, features 3 different songs, Golden Records, 1961, 6x8" stiff sleeve, VG+..$18.00

Holiday, Billie; Time on My Hands, Okeh 5991, NM .$10.00

How Much Is That Dogie in the Window, Golden Records, 1953, EX..$5.00

Imperial Dance Orchestra, Can't We Be Friends, Banner 0505, EX..$8.00

Kessinger Brothers, Arkansas Traveler, Brunswick 247, EX $8.00

Kincaid, Bradley; Old Wooden Bucket, Bluebird 5201, EX $8.00

Little Space Girl, Golden Records, 1958, NM.................$8.00

Little White Duck, Golden Records, 1954, EX..............$4.00

Magic Land of Alla-Kazam, Peter Pan, 1962, NM........$10.00

Midnight Ramblers, Kansas City Kitty, Broadway 1264, EX..$7.50

Mills Brothers, Diga Diga Doo, Brunswick 6519, EX..$12.50

Monroe Brothers, This World Is Not My Home, Bluebird 6309, EX..$10.00

Mother Goose Songs, Golden Records, 1950s, EX........$3.00

Mr Tap Toe/Glow Worm, Golden Records, 1953, EX+ .$3.00

On the Good Ship Lollipop, Golden Records, 1952, NM...$5.00

Peter Cottontail, Golden Records, 1950, NM $4.00

Red Heads, Feelin' No Pain, Melotone 12443, VG........$7.50

Ritter, Tex; Nobody's Darling but Mine, Champion 45153, NM $10.00

Scuffy the Tugboat, Golden Records, 1950, EX.............$6.00

Superman's Children's Record, Little Golden Records, ca 1950s, NM..$25.00

Ta-Ra-Ra-Boom-Der-E, Golden Records, 1954, EX.......$3.00

Tawny Scrawny Lion, Golden Records, 1950s, EX........$5.00

Taxi That Hurried, Golden Records, 1946, NM $18.00

Thumbelina, Golden Records, 1951, EX- $3.00

Williams, Hank; I Wish I Had a Nickel, MGM 12244, NM ..$12.50

LP Albums

Blues Brothers, Briefcase of Blues, Atlantic SD19217, 1978, $20.00

All in the Family, 1971, NM $12.50

Andy Griffith Show, Songs, Themes & Laughs, Capitol #T1611, NM $85.00

Annette Narrates Tubby Tuba, 1963, M $25.00

Around the World With the Chipmunks, shows Dave riding camel on sleeve, Liberty, 1961, EX.......................$15.00

Beach Boys, Best of the Beach Boys, Volume 1, Capital DT-502545, Stereo $30.00

Beach Boys, deluxe set of 3 records w/music lyrics, Capital DTCL2813, w/original box, from $100 to $150.00

Beatles, Live at Star Club, Poly Dor, Japanese import, +45-rpm record of Twist & Shout, as issued $50.00

Beatles, Rock 'N Roll Music, Capital SKBO-11537, set of 2..$35.00

Bee Gees, Spirits Having Flown, 1979, EX $4.00

Berry, Chuck; St Louis to Liverpool $50.00

Boating Songs & All That Bilge, Electra, 1960, EX......$15.00

Brigadoon, movie soundtrack, Gene Kelly photo sleeve..$6.00

Brown, James; Please, Please, Please, $45.00. (Photo courtesy Dave Torzillo)

Burnette, Johnny; Hits & Other Favorites, Liberty $25.00

Cannibal & the Head Hunters, Land of 1,000 Dances, from $30 to..$50.00

Captain Beef Heart, Trout Mask Replica.....................$40.00

Captain Kangaroo & Peter & the Wolf, Everst, 1960, EX.$10.00

Cash, Johnny; Hymns by..., Columbia 1284 ....$30.00

Cash, Johnny; Ring of Fire, Columbia, 1962, EX........$12.00

Christmas With Colonel Sanders, RCA, 1960s, NM......$25.00

Chubby Checker & Bobby Rydell Record Album, Cameo, 1960, NM $30.00

Darren, James; Love Among the Young, Colpix, 1959, EX.$25.00

Davidson, John; The Young Warm Sound of..., Colpix, 1962, EX..$10.00

Davis, Sammy; In the New Musical Golden Boy, 1964, EX..$20.00

Diamonds Are Forever, United Artists, 1971, EX+.........$8.00

Domino, Fats; Fats Domino Swings, Liberty, from $25 to..$35.00

Doors, LA Woman, Electra, die-cut cover $35.00

Douglas, Mike; The Men in My Little Girl's Life, Epic, 1965, EX..$12.00

Ed Sullivan Presents My Fair Lady, VG $5.00

Everly Brothers, Christmas With the Everly Brothers & the Boys Town Choir, Harmony HS 11350, from $10 to $15.00

Garland, Judy; Judy in Love, Capitol, 1961, M $8.00

Goldfinger, United Artist, 1963, EX+ $15.00

Good, the Bad, & the Ugly, United Artists, 1967, M...$10.00

Gore, Leslie; It's My Party, from $35 to $45.00

Grateful Dead, Blues for Allah $25.00

Grateful Dead, Live Dead, Warner Bros, 1970, set of 2, from $25 to..$40.00

Grateful Dead, Skeletons From the Closet....................$8.00

Grease, soundtrack, John Travolta & Olivia Newton John..$15.00

Greene, Lorne; Welcome to the Ponderosa, 1964, EX $12.00

Hawkins, Screamin' Jay; At Home With..., Epic 1958, from $800 to..**$1,200.00**

Heart, Dream Boat Annie/Nautilus Half-Speed Mastered, Super Disc, w/lyrics, from $25 to.........................**$45.00**

Hendrix, Jimi; Electric Ladyland, original issue (nude gatefold cover), set of 2, from $150 to......................**$300.00**

Hendrix, Jimi; Electric Ladyland, reissue, set of 2, from $30 to **$40.00**

Hendrix, Jimi; The Essential Jimi Hendrix, Vol 2, June 16, 1967...**$7.50**

Ice Station Zebra, MGM, 1968, NM **$8.00**

Ink Spots Vol 2, EX...**$6.00**

Jan & Dean, Filet of Soul, Liberty LRP-3441 ....**$25.00**

Jan & Dean, Surf City, Liberty.....................................**$30.00**

Jones, Jimmy; Good Timin', from $40 to **$50.00**

Juke Box Jive, 20 Original Hits, Original Stars, K-Tel Int'l, 1975, die-cut sleeve **$15.00**

Kaye, Danny; Mommy, Gimme a Drink of Water, Capitol, 1962, EX+ **$15.00**

Kingston Trio, Sold Out, EX..**$5.00**

KISS, Crazy Nights, M..**$10.00**

KISS, picture disc..**$30.00**

Knox, Buddy; Golden Hits, Liberty **$40.00**

Lehere, Tom; This Was the Year That Was, Reprise, 1964, NM **$12.00**

Lennon, John; Imagine, w/all inserts, from $25 to......**$40.00**

Li'l Abner, Columbia, 1959, NM **$8.00**

Limeliters, Tonight in Person **$3.00**

Linus the Lionhearted, Premier Albums, 1964, EX......**$30.00**

Little Richard, Here's Little Richard, Specialty **$100.00**

Long, Johnny; Plays for the Saturday Night Dance Date, HI-FI, VG **$4.00**

M-Squad, soundtrack, black & white cover w/Lee Marvin as Detective Frank Ballinger, RCA, 1959, NM............**$25.00**

Maharis, George; George Maharis Sings, Epic Records, 1961, EX...**$7.00**

Major Dundee, Columbia, 1964, promotional radio copy, EX...**$8.00**

Man From UNCLE & Other TV Themes, Metro, 1965, EX ..**$20.00**

Mandrake the Magician, Garabedian, 1972, NM.........**$15.00**

Marley, Bob & Wailers; Rebel Music, from $15 to **$20.00**

Mary Poppins, soundtrack, Walt Disney, EX **$7.00**

Masters of the Universe, Mattel, 1983, EX.....................**$7.50**

McDaniels, Gene; Tower of Strength, Liberty 3215.....**$40.00**

Monkees, Then & Now...The Best of the Monkees, Arista AL9-8432, 1986 reissue, set of 2, from $10 to.......**$15.00**

Moody Blues, Go Now, picture disc, AKP 5 ....**$30.00**

More Hit TV Shows, Capitol Records, 1962, NM.........**$25.00**

Newton, Wayne; Golden Archive Series, VG.................**$3.00**

Old Man & the Sea, Columbia, 1950s, EX+ **$20.00**

Orlons, Wah-Watusi, Cameo, 1960, EX+ **$20.00**

Perfect, movie soundtrack, John Travolta photo sleeve..**$8.00**

Pink Floyd, The Wall, from $15 to **$30.00**

Pink Panther Movie, RCA, 1963, NM...........................**$15.00**

Platters, Around the World, Mercury, 1950s, NM **$15.00**

Punch & Judy Record Album, Twinkle Records, 1950s, M **$5.00**

Redding, Otis; Dictionary of Soul, from $40 to **$50.00**

Redding, Otis; Dock of the Bay..................................**$20.00**

Righteous Brothers, Soul & Inspiration, Verve V6-5001, Stereo, from $25 to **$35.00**

Rolling Stones, Tattoo You, 1981, EX, from $10 to.....**$15.00**

Rydell, Bobby; We Got Love, 1960 Cameo, from $40 to ..**$50.00**

Sam & Dave, Hold On, I'm Comin', STAX 708, Monoral, from $30 to **$45.00**

Sherman, Bobby; Here Comes Bobby, Metromedia, 1970, NM **$12.00**

Shirelles, Baby It's You, Scepter **$50.00**

Sinatra, Frank; Only the Lonely, Capitol Records, 1958, EX..**$5.00**

Smothers Brothers at the Purple Onion, Mercury Records, 1959, NM **$20.00**

Snow, Hank; RCA LSP-2458, from $6.00 to $10.00.

Songs From Dr Dolittle, Disneyland Records, DQ-1325, 1967, M **$20.00**

Sonny & Cher's Greatest Hits, 1967.............................**$8.50**

Sound of Music, Julie Andrews & Christopher Plummer, 1965, NM...**$9.00**

South Pacific, RCA Victor Presents Rogers & Hammerstein's..., soundtrack, 1958, VG...**$5.00**

Spanky & Our Gang, Spanky's Greatest Hits, VG, from $10 to **$15.00**

Super Record of Superheroes Record Album, theme songs from '60s TV shows, Happy Time, 1966, EX+......**$12.00**

Three Dog Night, Joy to the World, Their Greatest Hits, 1974..**$6.00**

Uggams, Leslie; Leslie Uggams on TV Record Album, Columbia, 1961, EX **$7.00**

Van Dyke, Dick; Songs I Like, Command Records RS 860SD, M **$40.00**

Voices of the 20th Century Record Album, narrated by Henry Fonda, Coral, 1950s, EX **$8.00**

War of the Worlds Musical Record Album, CBS, 1978, set of 2 in folding sleeve, EX **$10.00**

Welk, Lawrence, TV Favorites, Coral, 1958, EX..........**$10.00**

Whistler, contains 1-hour program titled Panic, original aired April 1949, Radiola, 1974, EX+ **$15.00**

Wilson, Flip; The Devil Made Me Buy This Dress **$5.00**

Wonder, Stevie; Songs in the Key of Life, Tamla, 2-record set w/book **$15.00**

Woodstock, live soundtrack, set of 3, from $30 to **$40.00**

Zappa, Frank & Moon Unit; Valley Girl, 12" single **$20.00**

Zappa, Frank; Interviews, picture disc, from $20 to ...**$30.00**

101 Dalmatians, Disneyland Records, 1960s, EX..........**$5.00**

Red Wing

For almost a century, Red Wing, Minnesota, was the center of a great pottery industry. In the early 1900s, several local companies merged to form the Red Wing Stoneware Company. Until they introduced their dinnerware lines in 1935, most of their production centered around stoneware jugs, crocks, flowerpots, and other utilitarian items. To reflect the changes made in 1935, the name was changed to Red Wing Potteries, Inc. In addition to scores of lovely dinnerware lines, they also made vases, planters, flowerpots, etc., some with exceptional shapes and decoration.

Some of their more recognizable lines of dinnerware and those you'll most often find are Bob White (decorated in blue and brown brush strokes with quail), Tampico (featuring a collage of fruit including watermelon), Random Harvest (simple pink and brown leaves and flowers), and Village Green or Brown (solid-color pieces introduced in the fifties). Often you'll find complete or nearly complete sets, and when you do, the lot price is usually a real bargain.

If you'd like to learn more about the subject, we recommend *Red Wing Stoneware, An Identification and Value Guide,* and *Red Wing Collectibles*, both by Dan and Gail DePasquale and Larry Peterson. Also, B.L. Dollen has written a book called *Red Wing Art Pottery*. All are published by Collector Books.

Advisors: Wendy and Leo Frese, Artware (See Directory, Red Wing)

Club/Newsletter: *Red Wing Collectors Newsletter*
Red Wing Collectors Society, Inc.
Doug Podpeskar, membership information
624 Jones St., Eveleth, MN 55734-1631; 218-744-4854. Please include SASE when requesting information.

Art Ware

Ashtray, leaf shape, glossy silver green, #828, 9½", from $15 to **$20.00**
Bowl, console; ribs form scallop along edge, white semimatt, w/wing label, #1620, 10", from $36 to **$42.00**
Bowl, glossy flecked orchid, 3 sm feet, #M5010, 8", from $22 to **$28.00**
Bowl, green semimatt, rectangular, #5019, 9" L, from $24 to **$28.00**
Bowl, Tropicana Line w/embossed Desert Flower decor, glossy dark green w/lemon yellow interior, #B2102, 13", from $24 to **$30.00**
Bowl, 4-leaf clover shape, glossy burnt orange w/lime green interior, #1412, 8", from $24 to **$32.00**
Candle holders, leaf style (modern appearance), glossy flecked Zephyr Pink, #M1471, 4¾", pr, from $24 to **$30.00**
Candle holders, star shaped, white semimatt, #B1411, 4", pr, from $22 to..**$28.00**
Candle holders, white semimatt, scalloped edge, plainer style, #1619, 4½", from $18 to **$26.00**
Compote, footed cornucopia form, glossy cinnamon, #635, 7x11½", from $26 to **$32.00**

Compote, Prismatic line, octagonal, footed, Persian Blue w/white interior, #796, 8x9½", from $42 to **$58.00**
Compote, white semimatt, fluted rim, flared pedestal foot, #690, 9", from $30 to **$38.00**
Compote, white semimatt w/med pedestal, #M1597, 7", from $24 to...**$28.00**
Compote, wide oval bowl w/flared foot, glossy burnt orange, #665, 11", from $26 to **$32.00**
Figurine, bird on perch, long graceful tail up, glossy forest green, 10", from $15 to...**$22.00**

Figurine, temple lady, 10", $75.00.

Planter, embossed leaves form band, oval ribbed body, lemon yellow w/gray interior, #1402, 3½x7½", from $30 to .**$38.00**
Planter, violin form, glossy flecked Zephyr Pink, rubber band strings, #M1484, 13", from $45 to **$55.00**
Planter, yellow semimatt w/turquoise interior, tulip shape, #898, 7", from $35 to **$40.00**
Planter, 3 lg openings in teardrop shape, glossy flecked Nile Blue, hangs from chain, 10½", $28 to...................**$38.00**
Vase, blue glossy crackle w/gunmetal interior, slightly waisted form, #1301, 5", from $45 to...........................**$60.00**
Vase, bud; glossy cocoa brown w/yellow interior, square sides, #1621, 8", from $22 to...............................**$26.00**
Vase, bud; green semimatt w/silver wing label, #510, 7½", from $22 to..**$28.00**
Vase, cattails embossed on glossy lemon yellow, gray interior, #401, 7½", from $28 to **$36.00**
Vase, cornucopia form, blue glossy w/yellow interior, silver wing label, #1097, 5¾", from $26 to **$34.00**

Vase, #1162, leaves and vines, late 1930s, 9", $50.00. (Photo courtesy B.L. Dollen)

Vase, embossed magnolia blossom, ivory w/brown wiped into recesses, bulbous, flared rim, #975, 6", from $30 to ..**$42.00**

Vase, fan form, glossy cypress green w/coral interior, red wing label, #892, 7½", from $38 to **$46.00**

Vase, fan form, white semimatt w/green interior, #892, 1960s, 7½", from $32 to..**$38.00**

Vase, snail shape, pea green glossy w/brown interior, #1356, 7½", from $26 to..**$34.00**

Vase, white semimatt w/green interior, embossed spirals on cylindrical form, #1235, 9¾", from $24 to **$30.00**

Vase, white w/brass handles, footed, #M1609, 10", from $40 to...**$50.00**

Dinnerware

Anniversary, bowl, salad; pink basketweave, 10½", from $18 to..**$26.00**

Blossom Time, cup, from $4 to **$6.00**

Blossom Time, plate, dinner; 10½", from $10 to **$16.00**

Blossom Time, saucer, from $5 to.................................**$7.00**

Bob White, bowl, divided vegetable............................**$32.00**

Bob White, butter warmer, stick handle, w/lid...........**$88.00**

Bob White, creamer, from $30 to **$35.00**

Bob White, cup & saucer..**$20.00**

Bob White, hors d'oeuvre holder **$48.00**

Bob White, lazy susan w/stand, from $90 to **$100.00**

Bob White, pitcher, water; sm **$45.00**

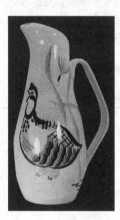

Bob White, pitcher, water; 60-oz, $50.00.

Bob White, plate, bread & butter **$6.50**

Bob White, plate, dinner; 10½" **$12.50**

Bob White, platter, 20", from $85 to **$100.00**

Bob White, relish, 2-part **$35.00**

Bob White, relish, 3-part, from $40 to **$50.00**

Bob White, salt & pepper shakers, bird form, pr **$40.00**

Bob White, salt & pepper shakers, tall, pr **$20.00**

Bob White, trivet, from $90 to...................................**$100.00**

Capistrano, bowl, lug soup; 6".....................................**$8.00**

Capistrano, bowl, lug vegetable; 8"............................**$12.00**

Capistrano, plate, dinner **$10.00**

Capistrano, platter, 13" **$35.00**

Capistrano, saucer..**$1.00**

Chevron, bowl, custard **$18.00**

Chevron, bowl, vegetable; 9".......................................**$25.00**

Chevron, drip jar...**$37.50**

Chevron, plate, bread & butter; 6" **$5.00**

Chevron, plate, salad; 8" **$7.50**

Chevron, plate, serving; 12"...**$12.00**

Chevron, platter, 12"...**$18.00**

Chevron, teapot, 6-cup...**$55.00**

Chrysanthemum, plate, dinner; 10½", from $10 to **$15.00**

Greenwichstone, bowl, sauce; from $4 to **$6.00**

Greenwichstone, plate, bread & butter; from $4 to **$6.00**

Greenwichstone, plate, dinner; 10", from $6 to **$10.00**

Hearthside, relish tray, center handle, from $15 to.....**$22.00**

Hearthstone, bowl, sauce; from $3 to **$6.00**

Hearthstone, plate, dinner; 10", from $5 to **$8.00**

Lexington Rose, bowl, berry; 5⅛" **$7.00**

Lexington Rose, cream soup...**$17.00**

Lexington Rose, plate, bread & butter **$5.50**

Lexington Rose, plate, dinner; 10¼"............................**$11.00**

Lotus, bowl, dessert; 5" **$4.00**

Lotus, bowl, vegetable; 8½"..**$8.00**

Lotus, plate, bread & butter; 6½" **$3.00**

Lotus, plate, dinnner; 10½", from $10 to **$15.00**

Lotus, plate, salad; 7", from $6 to **$8.00**

Lotus, platter, 12" **$35.00**

Magnolia, bowl, salad; lg, from $10 to **$15.00**

Magnolia, cup & saucer...**$7.00**

Magnolia, salt & papper shakers, gray, no bottom mark, pr, from $8 to...**$12.00**

Magnolia, saucer **$1.50**

Orleans, casserole, French; $45.00.

Pepe, bowl, soup; 6" **$10.00**

Pepe, coffee mug & saucer...**$12.00**

Pepe, creamer **$10.00**

Pepe, plate, dinner; 10" **$12.50**

Pepe, plate, salad; 7½" **$6.00**

Pepe, platter, 15"...**$22.00**

Pepe, sugar bowl w/lid **$12.00**

Pepe, tid-bit tray, center handle **$15.00**

Plum Blossom, bowl, sauce; from $7 to **$10.00**

Plum Blossom, cup, from $7 to...................................**$10.00**

Plum Blossom, plate, dinner; 10½", from $12 to **$16.00**

Plum Blossom, saucer..**$2.50**

Pompeii, plate, bread & butter; from $4 to **$6.00**

Pompeii, plate, salad; from $5 to..................................**$8.00**

Provincial, bean pot, tan w/red lid, 5-qt, from $16 to ..**$22.00**

Provincial Oomph, brown & aqua, w/lid, marked Red Wing USA, 60-oz, from $18 to **$24.00**

Random Harvest, coffeepot, tall **$25.00**

Random Harvest, gravy boat..**$35.00**

Random Harvest, plate, dinner; 10"............................**$12.50**

Random Harvest, relish tray, center handle, 10½", from $15 to **$22.00**
Reed, bowl, vegetable; tab handles, 9" **$22.50**
Reed, cup & saucer **$5.00**
Reed, egg cup **$16.00**
Reed, jug, ball form, 32-oz **$28.00**
Reed, mug, 10-oz **$16.00**
Reed, plate, luncheon; 9¼" **$5.00**
Reed, salt & pepper shakers, pr **$5.00**
Reed, teapot, 6-cup **$40.00**
Round-Up, bowl, cereal/salad; 6", from $32.50 to **$37.50**
Round-Up, bowl, salad; 10½", from $85 to **$95.00**
Round-Up, butter dish, ¼-lb **$200.00**
Round-Up, casserole, 2-qt, from $135 to **$165.00**
Round-Up, creamer, from $40 to **$50.00**
Round-Up, plate, bread & butter; 6½", from $10 to ...**$15.00**
Smart Set, bowl, divided vegetable; from $50 to **$60.00**
Smart Set, bowl, salad; 5½", from $12 to **$15.00**
Smart Set, bread tray, 24", from $70 to **$85.00**
Smart Set, casserole, 4-qt, from $80 to **$90.00**
Smart Set, cruets, w/stopper & stand, pr, from $165 to ..**$185.00**
Smart Set, gravy bowl, stick handle, w/lid **$80.00**
Smart Set, pepper mill, from $95 to **$115.00**
Smart Set, plate, dinner; 10½" **$35.00**
Smart Set, plate, salad; 7½", from $10 to **$14.00**

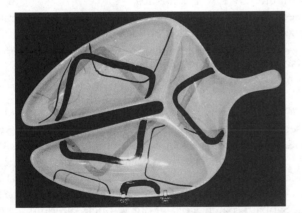

Smart Set, relish tray, 3-part, $65.00 to $75.00. (Photo courtesy Ted Haun)

Smart Set, teapot, from $185 to **$210.00**
Tampico, beverage server, w/lid **$90.00**
Tampico, bowl, cereal; from $12 to **$16.00**
Tampico, bowl, soup; from $16 to **$20.00**
Tampico, creamer, from $18 to **$22.00**
Tampico, cup & saucer **$12.50**
Tampico, mug **$45.00**
Tampico, nut bowl, 5-section **$80.00**
Tampico, plate, dinner; 10½" **$14.00**
Tampico, plate, luncheon; 8½" **$9.50**
Tampico, salt & pepper shakers, pr, from $28 to **$32.00**
Tampico, trivet, 6½", from $65 to **$75.00**
Town & Country, bowl, vegetable; sand, 8" **$35.00**
Town & Country, bowl, 5" **$15.00**
Town & Country, casserole, stick handle, w/lid, lg **$95.00**

Town & Country, creamer & sugar bowl, w/lid, minimum value **$50.00**
Town & Country, mug, coffee **$48.00**
Town & Country, mustard jar **$50.00**
Town & Country, plate, dinner; 10½" **$25.00**
Town & Country, plate, salad; 8", from $15 to **$20.00**
Town & Country, relish, 9" **$24.00**
Town & Country, salt & pepper shakers, Shmoo shape, lg, pr **$75.00**
Village Green, pitcher, brown w/aqua interior, 10-cup, from $18 to **$24.00**
Village Green, sugar bowl, brown w/aqua lid, from $6 to ..**$10.00**
Village Green, teapot, brown w/aqua lid, 5-cup, from $18 to **$26.00**

Stoneware

Bean pot, Albany slip, Boston style, NM, 1-gal **$135.00**
Bowl, Greek Key, blue & white, 12" **$225.00**
Bowl, red & blue sponging on saffron **$80.00**
Churn, red wing/#2 on white, RWUS, 2-gal **$235.00**
Cooler, Ice Water/#3/birch leaves, white, old shape ..**$800.00**
Crock, butter; Albany slip, low style, MN, 2-lb **$50.00**
Crock, butter; white low style, RW, 10-lb **$80.00**
Crock, red wing/#15, white, RWUS, 15-gal **$100.00**
Cuspidor, no seam, blue & white sponging, unmarked ..**$500.00**
Jar, wax sealer; Albany slip, MN, 1-qt **$60.00**
Jar, wax sealer; Albany slip, RW, 1-qt **$60.00**

Jug, advertising; no mark, ½-pt, $150.00. (Photo courtesy DePasquale & Peterson)

Jug, common, brown w/standard top, MN, ½-gal **$65.00**
Jug, common; white, MN, 1-gal..................................**$70.00**
Jug, fancy, white w/brown ball top, RW, 1-gal **$200.00**
Jug, fancy, white w/brown ball top, unmarked, 1-pt .**$55.00**
Jug, molded seam, brown w/bail handle, MN, ½-gal ..**$235.00**
Jug, molded seam, white, bail handle, MN, 1-gal **$100.00**
Jug, shoulder; brown & salt glaze, funnel top, MN, ½-gal **$200.00**
Jug, shoulder; brown & salt glaze, funnel top, 1-gal .**$85.00**
Jug, shoulder; white, standard top, MN, 1-qt **$90.00**
Jug, syrup; white, cone top, MN, ½-gal **$75.00**
Pan, milk; white, NM..**$100.00**
Pitcher, Albany slip, barrel form, RW **$135.00**
Pitcher, milk; Albany slip, Russian style, 1-gal **$95.00**
Spittoon, salt glaze, RW..**$800.00**
Spittoon, salt glaze, unmarked **$275.00**

Regal China

Perhaps best known for their Beam whiskey decanters, the Regal China company (of Antioch, Illinois) also produced some exceptionally well-modeled ceramic novelties, among them their 'hugger' salt and pepper shakers, designed by artist Ruth Van Telligen Bendel. Facing pairs made to 'lock' together arm-in-arm, some huggies are signed Bendel while others bear the Van Telligen mark. Another popular design is her Peek-a-Boo Bunny line, depicting the coy little bunny in the red and white 'jammies' who's just about to pop his buttons.

See also Cookie Jars; Old MacDonald's Farm.

Advisor: Rick Spencer (See Directory, Regal China)

Bendel Shakers

Bears, white w/pink & brown trim, pr	$100.00
Bunnies, white w/black & pink trim, pr	$135.00
Kissing pigs, gray w/pink trim, pr	$375.00
Love bugs, burgundy, lg, pr	$165.00
Love bugs, green, sm, pr	$65.00

Van Telligen Shakers

Sailor and mermaid, scarce, $195.00 for the pair. (Photo courtesy Pat and Ann Duncan)

Bears, brown, pr	$20.00
Boy & dog, black, pr	$120.00
Boy & dog, white, pr	$60.00
Bunnies, solid colors, pr	$22.00
Ducks, pr	$30.00
Dutch boy & girl, pr	$40.00
Mary & lamb, pr	$55.00
Peek-a-Boo, peach trim, rare, lg, pr	$575.00
Peek-a-Boo, red dots, lg, pr	$500.00
Peek-a-Boo, red dots, sm, pr	$220.00
Peek-a-Boo, solid white, lg, pr	$400.00
Peek-a-Boo, white solid, sm, pr	$200.00
Peek-a-Boo, white w/gold trim, lg, pr	$450.00

Miscellaneous

Banks, kissing pigs, Bendel, lg, pr	$425.00
Creamer, cat	$175.00
Salt & pepper shakers, A Nod to Abe, 3-pc set	$250.00
Salt & pepper shakers, clown, pr	$450.00
Salt & pepper shakers, FiFi, pr	$450.00
Salt & pepper shakers, Fish C Miller, pr	$60.00
Salt & pepper shakers, pig, pink, marked C Miller, 1-pc	$95.00
Salt & pepper shakers, tulip, pr	$50.00
Salt & pepper shakers, Vermont Leaf People, 3-pc	$150.00
Salt & peppers shakers, cat, pr	$225.00
Sugar bowl, cat	$175.00
Sugar bowl, Tulip, tall	$100.00
Teapot, Tulip, tall	$125.00

Rock 'n Roll Memorabilia

Ticket stubs and souvenirs issued at rock concerts, posters of the artists that have reached celebrity status, and merchandise such as dolls, games, clothing, etc., sold through retail stores during the heights of their careers are just the thing that interests collectors of rock 'n roll memorabilia. Some original, one-of-a-kind examples — for instance, their instruments, concert costumes, and personal items — often sell at the large auction galleries in the East where they've realized very high-dollar hammer prices. Greg Moore has written *A Price Guide to Rock and Roll Collectibles* which is distributed by L-W Book Sales.

See also Beatles Collectibles; Elvis Presley Memorabilia; Magazines; Movie Posters; Pin-Back Buttons; Records.

Advisor: Bojo/Bob Gottuso (See Directory, Character and Personality Collectibles)

AC/DC, balloon, black w/white logo, promotional, M, sealed	$6.00
AC/DC, patch, European tour, lg cut-out design, 1980-81	$7.50
Alice Cooper, concert flyer, black & white w/Alice & Monsters, 1978	$12.50
Alice Cooper, photo, on stage scene, black & white, 8x10"	$5.00
Black Sabbath, patch, gold ghoul w/brick lettering	$6.00
Black Sabbath, photo, black & white promo, Warner Bros, 1986, 8x10"	$6.50
Blondie, patch, Official Blondie Fan Club, black & yellow	$6.00
Blue Oyster Cult, poster, live shot, 1970s, 23x35", M	$15.00
Blues Brothers, shopping bag, plastic, movie promotion	$20.00
Boy George, photo, color, ca 1982, 8x10"	$18.00
Boy George, poster, color, 24x36", M	$12.00
Bruce Springsteen, backstage pass, After Show Only, 1981	$18.00
Bruce Springsteen, sticker, The River commemorative, 1980, 5x3"	$6.00
Carpenters, money cubes, Lucite cube w/shredded money, A&M Records promo, M	$28.00
David Bowie, photo, as Ziggy in gown, color, early, rare, 5x7"	$6.00
David Bowie, postcard, Tin Machine, 1989, 7x5", M	$5.00
David Bowie, shopping bag, plastic, printed both sides, 15x13", M	$10.00
David Cassidy, poster, Columbia, 1972, 1-sheet, M	$15.00

Doors, bumper sticker, radio promo, vintage................$7.00

Doors, letterhead, used by Doors Project Inc, dated March 3, 1990, w/matching envelope, M $18.00

Doors, photo, Jim Morrison head shot, black & white, 8x10"...$5.00

Duran Duran, battery pack, Toshiba Emi, w/color photo card $18.00

Duran Duran, sticker, set of 6 puffy vinyl stickers in pack..$5.00

Electric Light Orchestra, flyer, Out of the Blue, colorful, M.$7.00

Electric Light Orchestra, necklace, pewter UFO shape pendnat on chain $15.00

Elton John, card, paper photo, used for pennants, 1970s...$7.00

Elton John, pennant, Captain Fantastic, paper photo on felt, 1970s, M..$25.00

Elton John, photo, close-up portrait, black & white, 8x10"..$5.00

Elton John, poster, Elton in mink jacket, 22x32", M ...$12.50

Elvis Costello, poster, 1980, 20x28", M.........................$12.50

Fleetwood Mac, backstage pass, US tour, French Penguin on bicycle, fabric, unpeeled, 1982 ....$10.00

Fleetwood Mac, belt buckle, Penguin cutout in circle, Winterland 2st edition, 1977 ....$17.50

Fleetwood Mac, brochure, cartoon drawings, lists top albums of 1997 ....$6.00

Frank Zappa, tour program, 1980, M...........................$12.00

Genesis, postcard, drawing of man running, black & white, Duke, limited edition...$5.00

Grateful Dead, Jerry Garcia poster, Old & in the Way, 1973, 14x28", EX $22.00

Grateful Dead, postcard, Playing in the Band, St Martins' Press promo, band photo, 5x8" $4.00

Grateful Dead, postcard, Without a Net, Rick Griffin cover art, Arista, 6x4" $6.00

Grateful Dead, sticker, In the Dark promo, black, red & white, 1987, 9x4"...$6.00

Hall & Oates, belt buckle, silver & black logo on oval shape...$12.00

Hall & Oates, sticker, New Jersey concert, Canada Dry, 1983...$5.00

Hall & Oates, sticker, radio concert promo, NY, 1985..$4.00

Instant Shock, poster, American Newsprint, black & white, 1967, 26x21", M...$25.00

Jackson 5, game, Shindana, 1972, MIB (sealed) $175.00

Jackson 5, pennant, I Love the Jacksons, early 1970s, NM...$35.00

Janis Joplin, photo, hair blowing while singing into microphone, black & white, 8x10".................................$5.00

Jefferson Starship, sticker, Spitfire, girl & dragon, Winterland, 1976...$6.00

Jethro Tull, belt buckle, War Child, brass w/shield logo....$17.50

Jimi Hendrix, photo w/publicity information, Goldstein Organization Inc, 1960s, M $12.00

Jimi Hendrix, postcard, 1980s reprint of 1968 concert promo, 5x7", M..$4.00

Judas Priest, sticker, radio concert promo, NY, M.........$6.00

Kinks, booklet, TV Guise, resembles TV Guide, 1975..$10.00

Kinks, photo of Dave Davies live on stage, black & white, 8x10"..$5.00

KISS, backstage pass, Animalize World Tour, VIP, Otto, 1984-85..$15.00

KISS, backstage pass, World Tour, any area, laminated...$15.00

KISS, coin, Mardi Gras, logo & face portraits, 1979, M....$35.00

KISS, Colorforms, complete, w/instruction sheet, EX (VG+ box) $90.00

KISS, concert jacket, black paper with band and flames, M, $50.00. (Photo courtesy Bojo)

KISS, cup/megaphone, Scream Machine, Pepsi, white on blue, concert item...$90.00

KISS, cup/megaphone, Scream Machine, Pepsi, yellow, concert item..$65.00

KISS, game, On Tour, complete, VG+........................$75.00

KISS, jacket, black paper, shows band & flames, concert purchase, M...$50.00

KISS, necklace, brass cut-out logo pendant w/chain..$30.00

KISS, necklace, lightning bolt, 1¾x½" silver logo, w/chain.$25.00

KISS, pencils, set of 4, MIP (sealed)...........................$40.00

KISS, photo, group publicity shot, black & white, 8x10"..$5.00

KISS, program, 1977 World Tour, EX $40.00

KISS, ticket, 1991 convention, red & white w/glitter logo.$14.00

KISS, toy guitar, plastic w/paper photo of group & logo on front, EX $125.00

Led Zepplin, patch, Zoso original promo, 3½x1½"....$15.00

Led Zepplin, photo of Robert Plant, Esparanza Records, black & white, 8x10" $5.00

Madonna, photo, beach portrait, black & white, 8x10" ..$5.00

Marshall Tucker Band, beer mug, plastic, color logo, M ..$18.00

Meatloaf, flyer, Bat Out of Hell promo, photo, 8x10"...$5.00

Meatloaf, poster, concert promo, black & white, 1978, M...$6.00

Michael Jackson, belt, black, Triumph Merchandising, 1984, M...$10.00

Michael Jackson, figure, w/glove, microphone & stand, Thriller outfit, LJN, MIB.......................................$40.00

Michael Jackson, phonograph, Sing Along, Vanity Fair, MIB..$50.00

Michael Jackson, puppet, Moonwalker outfit, Puppet Kooler Industries, 1988, MIB...$30.00

Monkees, arcade card, biography on back, postcard size .$7.00

Monkees, ballpoint pen...$45.00

Monkees, book, Who's Got the Button?, hardcover ...$14.00

Monkees, booklet, Davy Jones Fan Club, original black & white photos, British flag cover, early.................$27.50

Monkees, bracelet, 4 color headshots in brass color disk, MOC..**$40.00**

Monkees, finger puppet, Davy, EX..........................**$28.00**

Monkees, model, Monkeemobile, reissue of original MPC model, Ertl, MIB......................................**$70.00**

Monkees, musical toy guitar, paper face, 15", EX, $110.00. (Photo courtesy Bojo)

Monkees, ring, chromed plastic w/circular photo, M.**$25.00**

Monkees, sunglasses, w/original hang tag...................**$44.00**

Monkees, tour program, for summer 1987 ....**$7.00**

Monkees, writing tablet, photo cover, 8½x11", M......**$30.00**

Motley Crue, sticker, 5 puffy vinyl stickers, MIP...........**$5.00**

Paul Revere & the Raiders, model, Raiders Coach, MPC, MIB (sealed)..**$300.00**

Pearl Jam, backstage pass, Lollapalooza, 1992.............**$28.00**

Peter, Paul & Mary, program, dated 1964, NM...........**$35.00**

Pink Floyd, ticket, CA, 1977, unused.........................**$22.00**

Pointer Sisters, sticker, color photo, 7x7"......................**$6.00**

Police, press kit, concert for Showtime Cable TV, 8x10"...**$15.00**

Red Hot Chili Peppers, photo, famous naked sock shot, black & white, 8x10"...**$4.00**

REM, photo, entire group, black & white, 8x10"...........**$5.00**

Rolling Stones, book cover set, Pepper Tree, 1969, MIP....**$25.00**

Rolling Stones, boxer shorts, stripe & patch, Steel Wheels, M...**$18.00**

Rolling Stones, greeting card, concert color design by David Byrd, 1969 tour, 1978 copyright, M.........................**$8.00**

Rolling Stones, napkins, tongue & record logo, 1983, set of 16, MIP (sealed)...**$25.00**

Rolling Stones, photo of Keith Richards, black & white, 8x10", M...**$5.00**

Rolling Stones, program, 1966, color cover w/black & white photos, VG+..**$15.00**

Rolling Stones, raincoat, plastic poncho, tongue logo, Steel wheels, MIP (sealed)...**$20.00**

Rolling Stones, transfers, rub-off type, 1983, MIP (sealed)..**$12.00**

Sex Pistols, photo, publicity shot, black & white, 8x10"..**$6.00**

Sonny & Cher, pennant, I Love Sonny & Cher, 1970s, NM...**$35.00**

Stevie Nicks, backstage pass, heart w/wings logo, 1983 tour...**$12.00**

Stray Cats, decals, set of 9 logo tattoos on sheet, M.....**$6.00**

Supremes, arm band, Gammas Invite You to Diana Ross & the Supremes, 1960s, M.......................................**$45.00**

The Who, press kit, Quadrophenia movie photo set, 8 photos, black & white, 8x10", M.................................**$18.00**

U2, ticket, Zoo TV concert, unused, 1992, 8x3".........**$18.00**

Van Halen, poster, David Lee Roth & group, 1982, 23x35", M...**$15.00**

Van Halen, stickers, puffy vinyl, set of 5, MIP.............**$4.00**

Rookwood

Although this company was established in 1879, it continued to produce commercial artware until it closed in 1967. Located in Cincinnati, Ohio, Rookwood is recognized today as the largest producer of high-quality art pottery ever to have operated in the United States.

Most of the pieces listed here are from the later years of production, but we've included some early pieces as well. With few exceptions, all early Ohio art pottery companies produced an artist-decorated brown-glaze line — Rookwood's was called Standard. Among their other early lines were Iris, Jewel Porcelain, Wax Matt, and Vellum.

Virtually all of Rookwood's pieces are marked. The most familiar mark is the 'reverse R'-P monogram. It was first used in 1886, and until 1900 a flame point was added above it to represent each passing year. After the turn of the century, a Roman numeral below the monogram indicated the current year. In addition to the dating mark, a die-stamped number was used to identify the shape.

The Cincinnati Art Galleries held two large and important cataloged auctions in 1991. The full-color catalogs contain a comprehensive history of the company, list known artists and designers with their monograms (as well as company codes and trademarks), and describe each lot thoroughly. Collectors now regard them as an excellent source for information and study. The majority of our listings are commercial artware pieces from the 1930s to the 1950s. For a more comprehensive listing, see *Schroeder's Antique Price Guide*.

Ashtray, #1139, 1947, rook figural, light brown gloss, 6½"..**$250.00**

Ashtray, #2647, 1946, fox figural, beige gloss, 6¾" dia..**$275.00**

Ashtray, no number, 1927, harp shape, light green gloss, 5½" dia...**$195.00**

Bookends, #2275, 1945, rook figural, light brown gloss, 5½", pr...**$395.00**

Bookends, #2444D, 1924, elephant, 4½", pr............**$450.00**

Bookends, #2655, 1946, owl figural, yellow-green gloss, 6", pr...**$275.00**

Bookends, #2836, 1956, cactus flower shape, brown gloss, 3½", pr..**$250.00**

Bowl, #2262C, 1921, white matt w/blue interior, 2 handles, 10½"..**$225.00**

Bowl, #2585, 1922, squaty w/banded dentil work, brown matt, 6" dia...**$175.00**

Bowl, #6038, 1928, blue gloss, w/paper label, 11½" L.**$175.00**

Compote, #6557, 1937, pelican form, wax primrose glaze, 12½" dia...**$595.00**

Cornucopia, #6983, 1948, late aventurine gloss, 5½"..**$175.00**

Face, #2457, 1949, Italian model, beige gloss, 5½" ..**$195.00**

Figurine, #2832, 1946, pheasant, lime green gloss, 13" L, from $450 to **$500.00**

Figurines: Sparrow on block, #6383, 1946, $150.00; Bird on flower branch, #6837, $175.00; Duck, #6064, $135.00.

Font, #6975, 1947, St Francis Holy Water, brown gloss, 10" **$250.00**

Humidor, #6136, 1929, green gloss, 4½" **$275.00**

Jar, peanut; no number, 1949, 6-sided, blue gloss, w/lid, 4½" **$350.00**

Lamp base, #2500C, 1946, dark green gloss, 13" **$250.00**

Loving cup, #6535, 1937, green gloss, 6½" **$250.00**

Paperweight, #6488, 1945, elephant figural, light blue matt, 3½" **$295.00**

Pin tray, #6391, 1946, pink gloss, 7" L......................**$175.00**

Platter, #6986, 1947, fish figural, yellow-green gloss, 12½" L..**$160.00**

Tankard, #587C, 1949, Advertisers Club of Cincinnati, beet red gloss, 5" **$160.00**

Tea set, #2663, 1950, gunmetal w/white drip, 3-pc set..**$575.00**

Teapot, #2800, ca 1927, blue ship on white gloss, 3½" ..**$200.00**

Tray, #6813, 1950, long leaf shape, light blue gloss, 15" L..**$135.00**

Vase, #0407, 1924, pink w/green matt, 7" **$185.00**

Vase, #2330, 1927, molded w/3 handles, light green matt, 5" **$145.00**

Vase, #2413, 1928, medium brown glaze with mistletoe embossing, 8x5", $325.00.

Vase, #2413, 1927, dark blue matt, 7¾"....................**$575.00**

Vase, #2592, 1951, embossed cattail design, light brown gloss, 5" **$155.00**

Vase, #2911, 1925, incised design, black gloss, 8¼".**$495.00**

Vase, #357F, 1923, yellow matt, 6¼" **$135.00**

Vase, #6144, 1948, magenta gloss, 2½"....................**$125.00**

Vase, #6363, 1946, floral design, brown gloss, 6" **$160.00**

Vase, #6457, 1945, butterfly form, green gloss, 4½" .**$165.00**

Vase, #6489, ca 1936, molded w/impressed rooks, matt white, 3½" dia **$425.00**

Vase, #6516, 1937, embossed storks, green matt, 11¼"...**$275.00**

Rooster and Roses

Back in the 1940s, newlyweds might conceiveably have received some of this imported Japanese-made kitchenware as a housewarming gift. They'd no doubt be stunned to see the prices it's now bringing! Rooster and Roses (Ucagco called it Early Provincial) is one of those lines of novelty ceramics from the forties and fifties that are among today's hottest collectibles. Ucagco was only one of several importers whose label you'll find on this pattern; among other are Py, ACSON, Norcrest, and Lefton. The design is easy to spot — there's the rooster, yellow breast with black crosshatching, brown head and, of course, the red crest and waddle, large full-blown roses with green leaves and vines, and a trimming of yellow borders punctuated by groups of brown lines. (You'll find another line having blue flowers among the roses; this is not considered Rooster and Roses by purist collectors.) The line is fun to collect, since shapes are so diversified. Even though there has been relatively little networking among collectors, more than seventy-five items have been reported.

Advisor: Jacki Elliott (See Directory, Rooster and Roses)

Ashtray, rectangular, 3x2"..**$9.50**

Ashtray, round or square, sm, from $15 to...............**$25.00**

Ashtray, square, lg, from $25 to **$35.00**

Basket, flared sides, 6", from $35 to **$45.00**

Bell, from $25 to..**$35.00**

Bell, rooster & chicken on opposing sides, minimum value **$35.00**

Biscuit jar, w/wicker handle, from $50 to...................**$65.00**

Bowl, cereal; from $10 to...**$14.00**

Bowl, rice; on saucer, from $25 to............................**$35.00**

Bowl, 8" **$25.00**

Box, 4½x3½", from $25 to...**$35.00**

Bread plate, minimum value.......................................**$15.00**

Butter dish, ¼-lb, from $20 to **$25.00**

Candle warmer (for tea & coffeepots), from $15 to ...**$25.00**

Candy dish, flat chicken-shaped tray w/3-dimensional chicken head, made in 3 sizes, from $30 to **$40.00**

Candy dish, w/3-dimensional leaf handle, from $17 to..**$25.00**

Canister set, round, 4-pc, from $150 to **$175.00**

Canister set, square, 4-pc, from $100 to **$150.00**

Canister set, stacking, minimum value.......................**$150.00**

Carafe, no handle, w/stopper lid, 8", from $55 to......**$65.00**

Carafe, w/handle & stopper lid, 8"..........................**$85.00**

Casserole dish, w/lid **$65.00**

Castor set in revolving wire rack, 2 cruets, mustard jar & salt & pepper shakers, from $65 to...........................**$75.00**

Chamberstick, saucer base, ring handle, from $20 to.**$25.00**

Cheese dish, slant lid, from $40 to............................**$55.00**

Cigarette box w/2 trays, from $30 to **$40.00**

Coaster, ceramic disk embedded in round wood tray, minimum value..**$35.00**

Coffee grinder, rare, from $75 to....................................**$85.00**

Condiment set, 2 cruets, salt & pepper shakers w/mustard jar on tray, miniature, from $40 to............................**$50.00**

Cookie jar, ceramic handles, from $85 to **$100.00**

Creamer & sugar bowl, w/lid, lg................................**$25.00**

Creamer & sugar bowl on rectangular tray, from $35 to ..**$40.00**

Cruets, cojoined w/twisted necks, sm.......................**$20.00**

Cruets, oil & vinegar, flared bases, pr, from $25 to **$30.00**

Cruets, oil & vinegar, square, lg, pr, from $30 to........**$35.00**

Cruets, oil & vinegar, w/salt & pepper shakers in shadow box, from $55 to **$75.00**

Cup & saucer, from $15 to...**$25.00**

Demitasse pot, w/4 cups & saucers, from $85 to **$100.00**

Demitasse pot, w/6 cups & saucers, from $100 to ...**$125.00**

Egg cup, from $20 to..**$25.00**

Egg cup on tray, from $25 to **$35.00**

Egg plate...**$28.00**

Flowerpot, buttress handles, 5", from $35 to.............**$45.00**

Hamburger press, wood w/embedded ceramic tray, round, minimum value **$24.00**

Instant coffee jar, spoon-holder tube on side, from $20 to ..**$30.00**

Jam & jelly containers, cojoined, w/lids & spoons, from $25 to **$35.00**

Jam jar, attached underplate, from $25 to....................**$35.00**

Ketchup or mustard jar, flared cylinder w/lettered label, each, from $25 to..**$30.00**

Lamp, pinup, made from either a match holder or a salt box, each **$75.00**

Lazy Susan, $150.00. (Photo courtesy Jacki Elliott)

Marmalade, round base w/tab handles, w/lid & spoon, minimum value..**$35.00**

Match holder, wall mount, from $40 to **$45.00**

Measuring cup set, 4-pc w/matching ceramic rack, from $35 to...**$45.00**

Measuring spoons on 8" ceramic spoon-shaped rack, from $35 to **$40.00**

Mug, rounded bottom, med, from $12 to....................**$15.00**

Mug, straight upright bar handle, lg, from $15 to.......**$25.00**

Napkin holder, from $30 to **$40.00**

Pipe holder/ashtray, from $30 to..................................**$40.00**

Pitcher, bulbous, 5", from $18 to..................................**$22.00**

Pitcher, lettered Milk on neck band...........................**$22.50**

Pitcher, 3½", from $12 to **$14.00**

Planter, rolling pin shape, minimum value.................**$50.00**

Plate, dinner; from $25 to...**$35.00**

Plate, luncheon; from $15 to **$25.00**

Platter, 12", from $30 to..**$35.00**

Recipe box, from $25 to..**$35.00**

Relish tray, 2 round wells w/center handle, 12", from $22 to **$28.00**

Relish tray, 3 wells w/center handle **$45.00**

Rolling pin, minimum value **$50.00**

Salad fork & spoon w/wooden handles on ceramic wall-mount rack, from $35 to...**$40.00**

Salt box, wooden lid, from $45 to **$55.00**

Toast holder, minimum value **$75.00**

Roselane Sparklers

Beginning as a husband and wife operation in the late 1930s, the Roselane Pottery Company of Pasadena, California, expanded their inventory from the figurines they originally sold to local florists to include a complete line of decorative items that eventually were shipped to Alaska, South America, and all parts of the United States.

One of their lines was the Roselane Sparklers. Popular in the fifties, these small animal and bird figures were airbrush decorated and had rhinestone eyes. They're fun to look for, and though prices are rising steadily, they're still not terribly expensive.

If you'd like to learn more, there's a chapter on Roselane in *The Collector's Encyclopedia of California Pottery* by Jack Chipman.

Elephant, jeweled headpiece, 6", $25.00. (Photo courtesy Lee Garmon)

Angelfish, 4½", from $20 to **$25.00**

Bassett hound, sitting, 4"..**$15.00**

Bassett hound pup, 2"...**$12.00**

Bulldog, fierce expression, looking right, sm.............**$12.00**

Bulldog, fierce expression, looking up & right, jeweled collar, lg...**$22.00**

Bulldog, sitting, slender body, looking right $25.00

Cat, recumbent, head turned right, tail & paws tucked under body, from $20 to...$25.00

Cat, Siamese, sitting, looking straight ahead, jeweled collar, 7" $25.00

Cat, sitting, head turned right, tail out behind, from $20 to $25.00

Cat, standing, head turned left, tail arched over back, jeweled collar, 5½", from $20 to..........................$25.00

Cat mother, looking straight ahead, 4½", w/kitten (in same pose), 2-pc set...$25.00

Chihuahua, sitting, left paw raised, looking straight ahead, 6½"...$25.00

Cocker spaniel, 4½"...$20.00

Deer, standing, head turned right, looking downward, 5½"..$25.00

Deer, upturned head, 4x3½".................................$20.00

Deer w/antlers, standing jeweled collar, 4½".............$22.00

Elephant, sitting on hind quarters, 6"....................$25.00

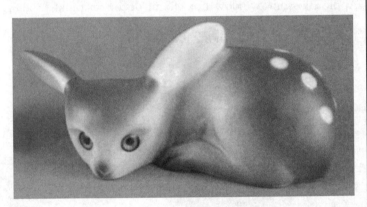

Fawn, 1½x4½", $20.00. (Photo courtesy Jack Chipman)

Kangaroo mama w/babies $35.00

Kitten, sitting, 1¾" $12.00

Owl, very stylized, lg round eyes, teardrop-shaped body, lg $25.00

Owl, 5¼" $25.00

Owl baby, 2¼"...$12.00

Pig, lg..$25.00

Pouter pigeon, 3½"...$20.00

Raccoon, 4½", $20.00. (Photo courtesy Lee Garmon)

Whippet, sitting, 7½"...$25.00

Rosemeade

The Wahpeton Pottery Company of Wahpeton, North Dakota, chose the tradename Rosemeade for a line of bird and animal figurines, novelty salt and pepper shakers, bells, and many other items which were sold from the 1940s to the 1960s through gift stores and souvenir shops in that part of the country. They were marked with either a paper label or an ink stamp; the name Prairie Rose was also used. See *Collector's Encyclopedia of the Dakota Potteries* (Collector Books) by Darlene Hurst Dommel for more information.

Advisor: Bryce Farnsworth (See Directory, Rosemeade)

Bank, bear, black w/brown details, realistic mold, 3", from $450 to...$500.00

Bell, tulip form, 3¾"...$125.00

Bookends, wolfhound, Art Deco style, metallic glaze, 6½x7½", pr, from $300 to...............................$400.00

Bowl, centerpiece; Viking ship, chartreuse, lg..........$220.00

Creamer & sugar bowl, corn pattern, 2½"................$55.00

Creamer & sugar bowl, turkey figural, 4½" & 3¾", from $150 to...$175.00

Figurine, elephant, beige w/pink details, 1¼", from $60 to..$75.00

Figurine, pony, reddish-brown & black, 4", from $200 to..$225.00

Figurine, Rocky Mountain goat on realistic rocky base, white & orange, 2¾x2¾", from $200 to.................$225.00

Figurine, skunk, black & white, 2¾x4", from $20 to..$30.00

Flower bowl, rolled-in edge $25.00

Flower frog, fish...$50.00

Jug, Minnesota Centennial 1858-1958, pink w/round foot, angled handle, 7", from $80 to...........................$100.00

Pin, prairie rose, pink w/yellow center framed by leaves, 2x2"..$500.00

Planter, dove, white w/black & pink details, open back, 4½x6", from $175 to....................................$200.00

Planter, peacock perched on stump w/tail sweeping base, multicolor, 7½", from $150 to............................$200.00

Planter, pony, blue with pink highlights, 7" long, from $50.00 to 75.00.

Planter, standing deer at tree trunk w/long grass at base, 8", from $75 to...$100.00

Plaque, mallard drake in flight, multicolor, 6½x7½", minimum value **$500.00**
Salt & pepper shakers, black bear, sitting, pr..............**$55.00**
Salt & pepper shakers, deer, recumbent, brown w/black details, 2¼", pr..**$125.00**
Salt & pepper shakers, dolphin, green, w/tail up, resting on fins, pr, from $50 to..**$65.00**
Salt & pepper shakers, duck, pink or blue, 3½", pr, from $65 to **$85.00**
Salt & pepper shakers, English toy spaniel, multicolor, 2", pr..**$50.00**
Salt & pepper shakers, greyhound dog head, 3½", pr...**$65.00**
Salt & pepper shakers, mouse, gray w/painted details, 1" & 1½", pr, from $20 to **$30.00**
Salt & pepper shakers, Paul Bunyan & Blue Ox, 2¼", pr, from $150 to..**$200.00**
Salt & pepper shakers, pink flamingo on stump base, 3¾", pr **$120.00**
Salt & pepper shakers, pink tulips, green leaves at base, 2¼", from $30 to..**$40.00**
Salt & pepper shakers, rooster & hen, multicolor, 3¼", pr..**$125.00**
Salt & pepper shakers, rooster & hen, white w/red trim, 2½", pr, from $75 to..**$100.00**
Salt & pepper shakers, swan, white w/yellow & black trim, 2½", pr, from $65 to **$85.00**
Salt & peppers shakers, cushion cactus, 1", pr............**$65.00**
Spoon rest, pansy face, 3¾" **$125.00**
Vase, lg ball shape, w/holes around edge to hold flower stems..**$35.00**

Roseville Pottery

This company took its name from the city in Ohio where they operated for a few years before moving to Zanesville in the late 1890s. They're recognized as one of the giants in the industry, having produced many lines of the finest in art pottery from the beginning to the end of their production. Even when machinery took over many of the procedures once carefully done by hand, the pottery they produced continued to reflect the artistic merit and high standards of quality the company had always insisted upon.

Several marks were used over the years as well as some paper labels. The very early art lines often carried an applied ceramic seal with the name of the line (Royal, Egypto, Mongol, Mara, or Woodland) under a circle containing the words Rozane Ware. From 1910 until 1928 an Rv mark was used, the 'v' being contained in the upper loop of the 'R.' Paper labels were common from 1914 until 1937. From 1932 until they closed in 1952, the mark was Roseville in script, or R USA. Pieces marked RRP Co Roseville, Ohio, were not made by the Roseville Pottery but by Robinson Ransbottom of Roseville, Ohio. Don't be confused. There are many jardinieres and pedestals in a brown and green blended glaze that are being sold at flea markets and antique malls as Roseville that were actually made by Robinson Ransbottom as late as the 1970s and 1980s. That isn't to say they don't have some worth of their own, but don't buy them for old Roseville.

Most of the listings here are for items produced from the 1930s on — things you'll be more likely to encounter today. If you'd like to learn more about the subject, we recommend *The Collector's Encyclopedia of Roseville Pottery, Vols 1* and *2*, and *The Catalog of Early Roseville*, all by Sharon and Bob Huxford.

Note: Watch for reproductions! They're flooding the market right now; be especially wary at flea markets and auctions. These pieces are usually marked only Roseville (no USA), though there are exceptions. These have a 'paint by number' style of decoration with little if any attempt at blending.

Newsletter: *Rosevilles of the Past*
Jack Bomm, Editor
P.O. Box 656
Clarcona, FL 32710-0656; Subscription: $19.95 per year for 6 to 12 newsletters

Apple Blossom, bowl, #326-6, 2½x6½" **$95.00**
Apple Blossom, vase, low twig handles, #388-10, 10"..**$175.00**
Apple Blossom, window box, floral decor on pink, #368-8, 2½x10"...**$95.00**
Baneda, bowl, handle, no mark, 3½x10" **$400.00**

Baneda, vase, 4", $350.00.

Baneda, vase, handles, sm silver paper label, 9" **$550.00**
Baneda, vase, low handles on footed trumpet form, paper label, 12"...**$850.00**
Baneda, vase, narrow rim w/flared body, sm handles, paper label, 4½" **$325.00**
Bittersweet, basket, twig handle, #807-8, 8½"...........**$150.00**
Bittersweet, candlestick, twig handles, #851-3, 3".......**$60.00**
Bittersweet, vase, sm twig handles at waist, #888-16, 15½", from $250 to...**$350.00**
Bittersweet, vase, twig handles, #881-6, 6".................**$85.00**
Blackberry, basket, hanging, 4½x6½".......................**$850.00**
Blackberry, jardiniere, sm handles, no mark, 7" **$375.00**
Blackberry, vase, sm brown handles, silver paper label, 6" **$350.00**
Bleeding Heart, basket, integral handle, #360-10, 9½".**$275.00**
Bleeding Heart, candlestick, silver paper label, #1139-4½...**$175.00**
Bleeding Heart, plate, 6-sided, #381-10, 10½" **$175.00**
Bushberry, console bowl, twig handles, #385-10, 13", from $125 to...**$175.00**
Bushberry, double cornucopia, #155-8, 6 " **$150.00**
Bushberry, mug, twig handle, #1-3½, 3½"...............**$125.00**
Bushberry, pitcher, twig handle, ball jug form, #1325, 8½"..**$350.00**
Bushberry, vase, integral twig handles, #39-14, 14½"..**$450.00**

Capri, leaf dish, Sandlewood Yellow, #532-16, 16", from $25 to............**$35.00**

Capri, shell, Cactus Green, #C-1120, 13½" **$60.00**

Clemana, bowl, sm handles & foot, #281-6, 4½x6½"..**$225.00**

Clemana, flower frog, #23, 4" **$175.00**

Clemana, vase, cylindrical neck, #756-9, 9½" **$350.00**

Clemana, vase, sm angle handles, #749-6, 6½".........**$225.00**

Clematis, candle holder, squatty shape w/sm angle handles, #1155-2, 2½".................................**$60.00**

Clematis, console bowl, angular handles, #458-10, 14", from $100 to..............................**$125.00**

Clematis, flower arranger, low handles, #102-5, 5½"..**$75.00**

Clematis, vase, low handles, #103-6, 6".............**$75.00**

Columbine, basket, hanging; 8½".....................**$250.00**

Columbine, candle holders, disk foot, low handles, #1146-4½, 5", pr **$150.00**

Columbine, vase, angular handles, #151-8, 8"..........**$200.00**

Cosmos, console bowl, low handles, shaped rim, #374-14, 15½" L...**$250.00**

Cosmos, vase, handles, shaped rim, #905-8, 8", from $125 to.....................................**$150.00**

Cosmos, vase, low handles, #945-5, 5" **$125.00**

Dawn, bowl, tab handles, #318-4, 16" L................**$175.00**

Dawn, ewer, slim, #834-16, 16" **$550.00**

Earlam, bowl, tan interior, handles, 3x11½"............**$160.00**

Earlam, candlestick, saucer base, black paper label, 4" ..**$275.00**

Earlam, planter, tan interior, sm angle handles, no mark, 5½x10½"......................................**$150.00**

Earlam, vase, handles, no mark, 4" **$110.00**

Falline, bowl, sm handles, no mark, 11" **$250.00**

Falline, candle holder, no mark, 4" **$200.00**

Falline, vase, ear handles, no mark, 6" **$275.00**

Falline, vase, handles, no mark, 9" **$600.00**

Ferrella, candle holder, no mark, 4½" **$250.00**

Ferrella, vase, no handles, no mark, 8" **$500.00**

Ferrella, vase, sm angle handles, footed bulb form, no mark, 6"..**$350.00**

Florane, bowl, 10", from $30 to......................**$35.00**

Florane, jar, 8", from $90 to........................**$115.00**

Florane, vase, 6", from $30 to.......................**$35.00**

Foxglove, tray, handles, 15" L **$160.00**

Foxglove, vase, footed trumpet form w/low handles, #51-10, 10", from $175 to.......................**$225.00**

Foxglove, vase, low handles, #47-8, 8½", from $125 to..**$175.00**

Freesia, basket, simple arched handle, #390-7, 7" **$150.00**

Freesia, candlestick, #1160-2, 2", pr **$110.00**

Freesia, flowerpot, w/saucer, #670-5, 5½"............**$150.00**

Freesia, vase, waisted trumpet form w/low handles, #124-9, 9"..**$150.00**

Freesia, window box, rectangular w/sm angular handles, #1392-8, 10½".....................................**$95.00**

Fuchsia, candlestick, disk foot, low handles, #1132, 2" .**$150.00**

Fuchsia, console bowl, #353-14, 4x15½", w/#37 frog....**$325.00**

Fuchsia, vase, handles, #893-6, 6", from $125 to **$150.00**

Fuchsia, vase, handles, #898-8, 8".....................**$275.00**

Gardenia, basket, integral handle, #610-12, 12" **$225.00**

Gardenia, bowl, sm handles, #641-5, 5" **$110.00**

Gardenia, tray, 4-lobed, #631-14, 15" L...............**$165.00**

Gardenia, vase, handles, disk foot, #689-14, 14½" ...**$300.00**

Iris, pillow vase, sm handles, shaped rim, #922-8, 8½" ..**$200.00**

Iris, pot, sm handles, #647-3, 3½" **$85.00**

Iris, vase, angular handles, #917-6, 6½", from $100 to .**$125.00**

Iris, vase, floral decor on turquoise to blue, handles, #924-9, 10", from $175 to................................**$250.00**

Iris, vase, handles, #923-8, 8" **$175.00**

Ivory II, basket, hanging, 3-handled, 7", from $75 to ..**$100.00**

Ivory II, candlestick, footed ball form, 2½", from $25 to ..**$30.00**

Ivory II, cornucopia, #2, 5½x12", from $45 to **$60.00**

Ivory II, ewer, embossed leafy decor on ivory, #941-10, 10½", from $50 to....................................**$75.00**

Ixia, basket, hanging, 7", from $175 to.....................**$225.00**

Ixia, candle holder, triple; #1128, 5", from $100 to...**$150.00**

Ixia, console bowl, #330-7, 3½x10½" **$125.00**

Ixia, vase, low handles, shaped rim, #858-8, silver paper label, 8½"...**$150.00**

Jonquil, bowl, low handles, no mark, 3", from $125 to..**$150.00**

Jonquil, vase, bowl form, no mark, 4", from $125 to .**$150.00**

Jonquil, vase, flared rim, sm handles, no mark, 9½", from $225 to..**$275.00**

Luffa, candlestick, sm angle handles, no mark, 5"....**$175.00**

Luffa, jardiniere, 6", 5¼" base diameter, $350.00.

Luffa, lamp base, sm angle handles, no mark, 9½"..**$600.00**

Luffa, vase, sm angle handles, no mark, 8"..............**$250.00**

Magnolia, ashtray, twig handles, #28, 7"...................**$125.00**

Magnolia, console bowl, angle handles, #5-10, 14½", from $125 to.......................................**$175.00**

Magnolia, ewer, #14-10, 10".............................**$200.00**

Magnolia, planter, twig handles, #388-6, 8½".............**$95.00**

Magnolia, vase, angle handles, #91-8, 8"..................**$150.00**

Mayfair, bowl, yellow shell form, #1119-9, 10" **$60.00**

Mayfair, candlestick, yellow shell form, #115-1, 4½", from $15 to...**$20.00**

Ming Tree, bowl, twig handles, #526-9, 4x11½".......**$110.00**

Ming Tree, vase, integral branch handles, #585-14, 14½"...**$450.00**

Mock Orange, planter, sm feet, scalloped rim, #931-8, 3½x9"..**$125.00**

Mock Orange, window box, 4 sm feet, #956-8, 4½x8½"..**$95.00**

Moderne, bowl vase, #299, 6½", from $150 to **$175.00**

Moderne, candle holder, triple; turquoise, #1112, 6" ..**$225.00**

Moderne, comport, ivory w/pedestal foot & low handles, #297-6, 6", from $100 to.......................**$150.00**

Morning Glory, basket, white, simple wishbone handle, silver paper label, 10½", from $400 to.........................**$500.00**

Morning Glory, candlestick, floral decor on green, flared foot, no mark, 5", from $150 to...........................**$200.00**

Morning Glory, console bowl, floral decor on dark green, sm angle handles, no mark, 4½x11½", from $300 to .**$350.00**

Morning Glory, pillow vase, low handles, sm silver paper label, 7", from $225 to....................................**$275.00**

Moss, bud vase, triple; #1108, 7"........................**$400.00**

Moss, vase, low handles, #290-6, 6"....................**$225.00**

Orian, candle holder, red footed form w/low handles, no mark, 4½"...**$95.00**

Orian, console bowl, green w/tan interior, sm foot & handles, no mark, 5" **$200.00**

Orian, vase, green footed acorn form w/shoulder-to-foot handles, #733-6, 6" **$125.00**

Peony, bookend, #11, 5½"...................................**$110.00**

Peony, mug, #2-3½, 3½".......................................**$125.00**

Peony, vase, handles, flared rim, #68-14, 14"...........**$300.00**

Pine Cone, basket, blue w/integral twig handle, #353-11, 11" **$425.00**

Pine Cone, planter, blue, #124, 5"......................**$225.00**

Pine Cone, vase, blue, tan interior, #747-10, 10½" ...**$400.00**

Pine Cone, vase, brown, #850-14, 14½", from $500 to.**$600.00**

Poppy, basket, tall w/simple wishbone-shaped handle, #348-12, 12½" **$400.00**

Poppy, ewer, slim form, #880-18, 18½"....................**$750.00**

Poppy, jardiniere, ring handles, #335-6, 6½", from $100 to...**$125.00**

Poppy, vase, footed U form w/low handles, #642-3, 3½"...**$85.00**

Poppy, vase, sm ring handles, #368-7, 7½"...............**$175.00**

Primrose, vase, angle handles, sm rim, #761-6, 6½".**$150.00**

Raymor, butter dish, #181, 7½", from $75 to.............**$100.00**

Raymor, casserole, #183, 11"................................**$85.00**

Raymor, casserole, #185, 13½"...............................**$95.00**

Raymor, casserole, w/lid, individual, #199, 7½", from $30 to...**$45.00**

Raymor, cruet, 5½", from $65 to **$75.00**

Raymor, gravy boat, #190, 9½", from $25 to...............**$35.00**

Raymor, pitcher, water; #189, 10", from $100 to.......**$150.00**

Raymor, ramekin, w/lid, individual, #156, 6½", from $30 to...**$40.00**

Raymor, salad bowl, #161, 11½", from $25 to............**$40.00**

Raymor, salt & pepper shakers, 3½", pr **$35.00**

Raymor, shirred egg, #200, 10", from $25 to **$45.00**

Raymor, tray, 8½", from $40 to...............................**$50.00**

Raymore, bowl, vegetable; #189, 9", from $30 to **$40.00**

Rozane, vase, trumpet form w/low handles, #10-12, 12"..**$125.00**

Silhouette, box, #740, 4½" square..............................**$125.00**

Silhouette, vase, low handles, #780-6, 6"...................**$85.00**

Snowberry, candlestick, #ICS-2, 4½".........................**$75.00**

Snowberry, console bowl, sm angle handles, #1BL-8, 11" ..**$110.00**

Snowberry, ewer, #1TK-15, 16"..............................**$400.00**

Snowberry, plate, sm handles, #IRB-6, 6"................**$125.00**

Snowberry, vase, urn form, #1UR-8, 8½" **$165.00**

Sunflower, vase, bowl form w/sm handles, no mark, 4", from $225 to...**$275.00**

Sunflower, vase, 6", $350.00.

Sunflower, window box, sm handles, no mark, 3½x11", from $350 to...**$450.00**

Teasel, vase, #888-12, 12" **$275.00**

Teasel, vase, sm handles & foot, #881-6, 6" **$110.00**

Thorn Apple, bud vase, triple; #120, 6".....................**$200.00**

Thorn Apple, vase, footed, sm handles, #820-9, 9½" ..**$225.00**

Thorn Apple, vase, stepped handles on footed globular shape, #305-6, 6½", from $125 to.......................**$175.00**

Tourmaline, vase, tan mottle, handles, silver paper label, 5½", from $100 to...**$125.00**

Tourmaline, vase, turquoise to pink mottle w/embossed rings, sm foot, no mark, 8", from $150 to..........**$175.00**

Water Lily, candlestick, handles, #1155-4½, 5"............**$85.00**

Water Lily, cookie jar, 10", $450.00.

Water Lily, flower frog, #48, 4½"...............................**$95.00**

Water Lily, vase, handles, #78-9, 9"..........................**$225.00**

White Rose, candlestick, low handles, #1143-4½, 4½" ..**$75.00**

White Rose, vase, no handles, #978-4, 4"...................**$90.00**

White Rose, vase, sm angle handles, 4-scalloped rim, #991-12, 12½" **$300.00**

Royal Capri, three-part tray, #534-16, $400.00. (Photo courtesy Pat and Ann Duncan)

White Rose, vases: #987-9, 9", $200.00; #992-15, 15½", $400.00.

Wincraft, basket, integral handle, #274-7, 7" **$175.00**
Wincraft, bowl, #227-10, 4x13½"................................**$110.00**
Wincraft, cornucopia, #221-8, 9x5"...............................**$95.00**

Wincraft, 10" vases, left to right, #284, $225.00; #290, $350.00; #285, $200.00.

Windsor, basket, mottled brown, integral handle, sm black paper label, 4½" **$350.00**
Windsor, bowl, mottled brown & green, angular handles, no mark, 3½x10½", from $150 to **$175.00**
Windsor, vase, mottled blue, rim-to-shoulder handles, no mark, 6", from $200 to **$250.00**
Zephyr Lily, bud vase, #201-7, 7½"...............................**$85.00**
Zephyr Lily, cornucopia, #204-8, 8½" **$95.00**
Zephyr Lily, urn form, #202-8, 8½"...............................**$150.00**
Zephyr Lily, vase, handles, #135-9, 9½" **$125.00**

Royal China

The dinnerware made by Royal China of Sebring, Ohio, is becoming very collectible, the lines mentioned here in particular. All are found on the same standard company shapes. The most popular are their Currier and Ives and Blue Willow patterns, both decorated with blue machine-stamped designs on white backgrounds, but interest in the other patterns is growing all the time. Memory Lane is decorated with red transfers of rural life, Colonial Homestead and Old Curiosity Shop both have green transfer prints, and Fair Oaks has brown with multicolor accents. Buck's County is decorated with gold stamping on a yellow ground. Each line has a distinctive border design that will help you identify the pattern on unmarked pieces. Of the two green lines, Old Curiosity Shop's border depicts hinges and pulls, while Colonial Homestead's represents wooden frames with nailed joints. The Willow pattern was made in both blue and pink, but pink is hard to find and not as collectible. Tradition is an allover Jacobean-type floral, and though it's often found in the pink transfer, it comes in other colors as well.

Advisor: BA Wellman (See Directory, Dinnerware)

Newsletter: *Currier and Ives China by Royal*
c/o Jack and Treva Hamlin
R.R. 4, Box 150, Kaiser St., Proctorville, OH 45669; 614-886-7644

Newsletter: *Currier and Ives Quarterly Newsletter*
c/o Patty Street
P.O. Box 504, Riverton, KS 66770; 316-848-3529

Blue Willow, ashtray, 5½"..**$12.00**
Blue Willow, bowl, cereal; 6¼" **$12.00**
Blue Willow, bowl, fruit nappy; 5½" **$4.50**
Blue Willow, bowl, soup; 8¼"..**$10.00**
Blue Willow, bowl, vegetable; 10" **$18.00**
Blue Willow, butter dish, ¼-lb.......................................**$35.00**
Blue Willow, cake plate, w/handles, 10½".................**$20.00**
Blue Willow, casserole **$65.00**
Blue Willow, creamer **$6.00**
Blue Willow, cup & saucer **$6.00**
Blue Willow, gravy boat...**$15.00**
Blue Willow, pie plate, 10", from $12 to **$15.00**
Blue Willow, plate, bread & butter; 6¼".......................**$3.00**
Blue Willow, plate, chop; 10"..**$20.00**
Blue Willow, plate, dinner; 10"......................................**$6.00**
Blue Willow, plate, salad; 7¼".......................................**$7.00**
Blue Willow, platter, 13" **$28.00**
Blue Willow, salt & pepper shakers, pr......................**$18.00**
Blue Willow, sugar bowl, w/lid....................................**$10.00**
Blue Willow, teapot..**$65.00**
Blue Willow, tray, tidbit; 2-tier **$35.00**

Blue Willow, water pitcher, $65.00.

Buck's County, ashtray, 5½" **$7.00**

Buck's County, bowl, soup; 8½" $7.00
Buck's County, bowl, vegetable; 10".................$20.00
Buck's County, cake plate, w/handles, 10½" $12.00
Buck's County, casserole, w/lid.........................$65.00
Buck's County, creamer....................................$5.00
Buck's County, cup & saucer.............................$5.00
Buck's County, gravy boat...............................$15.00
Buck's County, plate, bread & butter; 6¼" $2.00
Buck's County, plate, dinner; 10" $4.00
Buck's County, salt & pepper shakers, pr $10.00
Buck's County, sugar bowl, w/lid $7.50
Buck's County, teapot $65.00
Colonial Homestead, bowl, cereal; 6¼".................$10.00
Colonial Homestead, bowl, fruit nappy; 5½" $3.00
Colonial Homestead, bowl, soup; 8¼" $7.50
Colonial Homestead, bowl, vegetable; 10" $20.00
Colonial Homestead, cake plate, tab handles, 10½"...$12.00
Colonial Homestead, casserole, angle handles, w/lid.$50.00
Colonial Homestead, chop plate, 12"....................$18.00
Colonial Homestead, creamer.............................$5.00
Colonial Homestead, cup & saucer $5.00
Colonial Homestead, gravy boat.........................$12.00
Colonial Homestead, pie plate $15.00
Colonial Homestead, plate, bread & butter; 6"............$1.50
Colonial Homestead, plate, dinner; 10"..................$4.00
Colonial Homestead, plate, salad; rare, 7¼" $6.00
Colonial Homestead, plate, tab handles, 10½"...........$12.00
Colonial Homestead, platter, oval, 13" $18.00
Colonial Homestead, salt & pepper shakers, pr..........$12.00
Colonial Homestead, sugar bowl, w/lid...................$10.00
Currier & Ives, ashtray, 5½".............................$15.00
Currier & Ives, bowl, cereal; tab handles, 6¼"...........$30.00
Currier & Ives, bowl, cereal; 6¼" or 6⅝" $12.00
Currier & Ives, bowl, fruit nappy; 5½", from $3.50 to..$5.00
Currier & Ives, bowl, soup; 8" $12.00
Currier & Ives, bowl, vegetable; 10" $28.00
Currier & Ives, bowl, vegetable; 9" $24.00

Currier and Ives: Butter dish, ¼-lb, $35.00; Salt and pepper shakers, $25.00 for the pair.

Currier & Ives, casserole, angle handles, w/lid..........$95.00
Currier & Ives, casserole, tab handles, w/lid............$150.00
Currier & Ives, creamer & sugar bowl, w/handles......$22.00
Currier & Ives, cup & saucer $6.00
Currier & Ives, gravy boat, pour spout.................$16.00
Currier & Ives, gravy boat, tab handle, from $25 to...$30.00
Currier & Ives, lamp, candle; w/globe, from $100 to .$125.00
Currier & Ives, mug, coffee.............................$27.00

Currier & Ives, pie baker, 10" $28.00
Currier & Ives, plate, bread & butter; 6¼".....................$3.50
Currier & Ives, plate, calendar; ca 1970s-85, each, from $15 to...................................$20.00
Currier & Ives, plate, chop; marked, 11½"................$35.00
Currier & Ives, plate, chop; marked, 12¼", from $25 to..$28.00
Currier & Ives, plate, dinner; 10"........................$6.00
Currier & Ives, plate, luncheon; 9".....................$15.00
Currier & Ives, plate, salad; 7¼"........................$12.00
Currier & Ives, plate, snack; w/cup & well, 9"...........$25.00
Currier & Ives, platter, oval, 13" $30.00
Currier & Ives, platter, tab handles, 10½"...............$28.00
Currier & Ives, restyled gravy boat liner, Birthplace of Washington stamping..............................$30.00
Currier & Ives, spoon rest, wall hanging....................$30.00
Currier & Ives, sugar bowl, no handles, w/lid............$25.00
Currier & Ives, teapot....................................$125.00
Currier & Ives, tidbit tray, 3-tier.......................$75.00
Currier & Ives, tumbler, iced tea; glass, 13-oz, 5½", rare, from $12 to..$18.00
Currier & Ives, tumbler, juice; glass, 6-oz, 3½" $14.00
Currier & Ives, tumbler, old-fashioned; glass, 3¼"......$14.00
Currier & Ives, tumbler, water; glass, 4¾"...............$15.00
Fair Oaks, bowl, 9"......................................$15.00
Fair Oaks, casserole......................................$45.00
Fair Oaks, creamer..$4.50
Fair Oaks, cup & saucer..................................$5.00
Fair Oaks, plate, bread & butter.........................$2.00
Fair Oaks, plate, dinner; 10"............................$4.00
Fair Oaks, platter, 10½".................................$9.00
Fair Oaks, salt & pepper shakers, pr $12.00
Fair Oaks, sugar bowl, w/lid............................$8.00
Memory Lane, bowl, cereal; 6¼"..........................$9.00
Memory Lane, bowl, fruit nappy; 5½" $3.00
Memory Lane, bowl, soup; 8¼"............................$7.50
Memory Lane, bowl, vegetable; 10".......................$20.00
Memory Lane, butter dish, ¼-lb..........................$30.00
Memory Lane, cake plate, w/handles, 10"..................$12.00
Memory Lane, creamer.....................................$6.00
Memory Lane, gravy boat liner, from $12 to..............$15.00
Memory Lane, plate, bread & butter; 6¼"..................$2.00
Memory Lane, plate, chop; 12"...........................$20.00
Memory Lane, plate, luncheon; rare, 9¼".................$8.00
Memory Lane, plate, salad; rare, 7¼"....................$7.00
Memory Lane, platter, 13"...............................$25.00
Memory Lane, salt & pepper shakers, pr..................$12.00
Memory Lane, sugar bowl, w/lid..........................$9.00
Memory Lane, tumbler, iced tea; glass...................$12.00
Old Curiosity Shop, bowl, cereal; 6½".....................$10.00
Old Curiosity Shop, bowl, fruit nappy; 5½" $4.00
Old Curiosity Shop, bowl, vegetable; 9" $18.00
Old Curiosity Shop, cake plate, w/handles, 10"..........$15.00
Old Curiosity Shop, creamer..............................$6.00
Old Curiosity Shop, cup & saucer $5.00
Old Curiosity Shop, plate, bread & butter; 6¼" $2.50
Old Curiosity Shop, plate, dinner; 10" $4.00
Old Curiosity Shop, salt & pepper shakers, pr...........$15.00
Old Curiosity Shop, sugar bowl, w/lid....................$9.00
Tradition, bowl, fruit nappy; 5½" $3.00

Tradition, bowl, vegetable; 10".....................................$15.00
Tradition, creamer..$4.00
Tradition, cup & saucer..$4.00
Tradition, gravy boat..$15.00
Tradition, plate, dinner; 10"......................................$6.00
Tradition, platter, tab handles, 10½".............................$20.00
Tradition, sugar bowl..$8.00

Royal Copley

This is a line of planters, wall pockets, vases, and other novelty items, most of which are modeled as appealing animals, birds, or human figures. They were made by the Spaulding China Company of Sebring, Ohio, from 1942 until 1957. The decoration is underglazed and airbrushed, and some pieces are trimmed in gold (which can add 25% to 50% to their values). Not every piece is marked, but they all have a style that is distinctive. Some items are ink stamped; others have (or have had) labels.

Royal Copley is really not hard to find, and unmarked items may often be had at bargain prices. The more common pieces seem to have stabilized, but the rare and hard-to-find examples are showing a steady increase. Your collection can go in several directions; for instance, some people choose a particular animal to collect. If you're a dog or cat lover, they were made in an extensive assortment of styles and sizes. Teddy bears are also popular; you'll find them licking a lollipop, playing a mandolin, or modeled as a bank, and they come in various colors as well. Wildlife lovers can collect deer, pheasants, fish, and gazelles, and there's also a wide array of songbirds.

If you'd like more information, we recommend *Royal Copley* written by Leslie Wolfe, edited by Joe Devine.

Advisor: Joe Devine (See Directory, Royal Copley)

Ashtray, affectionate birds perched at rim of heart shape, raised letters on bottom, 5½" L $35.00
Ashtray, mallard figural, paper label only, 2".................$15.00
Bank, farmer pig, hands to front, paper label only, flat unglazed bottom, 5½"..$65.00
Bank, pig standing upright & wearing bow tie, hands visible, paper label only, 6¼"...................................$45.00
Bank, pig w/sorority emblem & Fiji Winter Formal on shirt, visible hands, 8"......................................$65.00
Figurine, cockatoo, w/paper label, 7¼"........................$35.00
Figurine, cocker spaniel, 6¼"..................................$25.00
Figurine, Oriental boy & girl, paper label only, 7½", each .$20.00
Figurine, skylark, full bodied, w/paper label, 5".............$16.00
Figurine, swallow on heavy double stump, paper label only, 7¼"..$30.00
Figurine, tanager, green stamp or raised letters on bottom, 6¼"..$20.00
Lamp, child's; white handled urn shape w/floral decals, unmarked Spaulding, 8"......................................$40.00
Lamp, dancing girl base, original shade...................$100.00
Lamp, pig, striped shirt, visible hands, unglazed bottom, 6½"..$90.00

Pitcher, Daffodil, pink, green stamp on bottom, 8" $45.00
Pitcher, Floral Beauty, 8"....................................$44.00
Planter, Bamboo, green on cream, oval, sm, 4½".......$12.00
Planter, barefooted boy & girl, paper label only, 7½", each..$35.00
Planter, bear cub clinging to stump, paper label only, 8¼"..$35.00

Planter, bear with sucker, 8", $50.00.

Planter, Blackamoor prince, raised letters on back, 8"..$40.00
Planter, cat & cello, paper label only, 7½" $80.00

Planter, cat by yellow staved bucket, $30.00.

Planter, Chinese boy w/lg hat, raised letters on back, 7½"..$26.00
Planter, coach, green stamp on bottom, 3x6".............$20.00
Planter, cocker spaniel head, raised letters on back, 5"...$25.00
Planter, cocker spaniel w/basket, paper label only, 5½".$20.00
Planter, deer & fawn, raised letters on bottom, 9"......$30.00
Planter, dog pulling wagon marked Flyer, paper label only, 5¾"..$35.00
Planter, dog w/string bass, paper label only, 7" $90.00
Planter, duck at US Mail box, paper label only, 6¾"..$50.00
Planter, Dutch boy & girl w/buckets, paper label only, 6", each $24.00
Planter, farm boy & girl, raised letters on back, 6½", each...$28.00
Planter, girl & wheelbarrow, paper label only, 7".......$26.00
Planter, Hen No 1, paper label only, 5½"....................$25.00
Planter, Hildegard, rose & ivory, raised letters on bottom, 2½x7¼"...$12.00
Planter, hummingbird on flower, paper label only, 5¼"..$45.00
Planter, Indian boy & drum, paper label only, 6½"....$24.00
Planter, kitten & book, paper label only, 6½"............$32.00

Planter, kitten & Western boot, paper label only, 7½"..**$45.00**

Planter, kitten in picnic basket, paper label only, 8" ..**$70.00**

Planter, Little Riddle, modernistic shape, paper label only, 4¾"...**$20.00**

Planter, madonna, raised letters on bottom, signed Royal Windsor, 9"..**$40.00**

Planter, mallard, paper label only, 5" **$30.00**

Planter, mallard duck on stump, paper label only, 8" ..**$35.00**

Planter, oval shape w/big blossom on side, green stamp on bottom, 3"..**$12.00**

Planter, Peter Rabbit, paper label only, 6½"...............**$50.00**

Planter, pigtail girl, raised letters on back, 7".............**$35.00**

Planter, plaque shape marked Seasons Greetings, signed Royal Windsor in gold letters on bottom, 5" **$15.00**

Planter, poodle, 6½x8", $48.00.

Planter, pup in basket, paper label only, 7"................**$35.00**

Planter, resting poodle, paper label only, 6½x8½".....**$48.00**

Planter, Siamese pr w/basketweave pot at rear, paper label only, 9"..**$95.00**

Planter, teddy bear w/concertina, paper label only, 7½" ..**$75.00**

Planter, The Mill, painting on plate shape, raised letters on back, 8"..**$50.00**

Planter, Tony, 8", $58.00.

Planter, walking rooster, raised letters on back, 5½"..**$30.00**

Planter, white poodle w/black pot, paper label only, 7" ..**$48.00**

Tray, rectangular w/tab handles, impressed fruit design at center, Spaulding, 10⅛x6¼".................................**$25.00**

Vase, Carol's Corsage, 7"...**$20.00**

Vase, cornucopia shape, white w/gold trim & rose decal, 8¼"...**$30.00**

Vase, Harmony, paper label only, 7½" **$15.00**

Vase, ivy, green on cream, tall cylinder body w/foot, 7".**$12.00**

Vase, Mary Kay, gold stamp on bottom, 6¼" **$15.00**

Vase, parrot on stump, 5"..**$18.00**

Vase, rooster, paper label only, 8"..............................**$38.00**

Vase, Trailing Leaf & Vine, paper label only, 8½" **$18.00**

Royal Haeger

Many generations of the Haeger family have been associated with the ceramic industry. Starting out as a brickyard in 1871, the Haeger Company (Dundee, Illinois) progressed to include artware in their production line as early as 1914. That was only the beginning. In the thirties they began to make a line of commercial artware so successful that as a result a plant was built in Macomb, Illinois, devoted exclusively to its production.

Royal Haeger was their premium line. Its chief designer was Royal Arden Hickman, a talented artist and sculptor who worked in mediums other than pottery. For Haeger he designed a line of wonderfully stylized animals and birds, high-style vases, and human figures and masks with extremely fine details.

Paper labels were used extensively before the mid-thirties. Royal Haeger ware has an in-mold script mark, and their Flower Ware line (1954 – 1963) is marked 'RG' (Royal Garden).

For those wanting to learn more about this pottery, we recommend *Collecting Royal Haeger* by Lee Garmon and Doris Frizzell (Collector Books), and *Haeger Potteries Through the Years* by David D. Dilley (L-W Book Sales).

Club: Haeger Pottery Collectors of America
Lanette Clarke
5021 Toyon Way
Antioch, CA 94509, 510-776-7784; Monthly newsletter available

Pitcher, Graphic Earth Wraps, 9", $50.00.

Ashtray, brown w/blue flambe, #135, triangluar, 12" L.....**$15.00**

Ashtray, Grapic Earth Wraps, #2-69, 8" dia.................**$15.00**

Bowl, 2-tone green flambe, pedestal base, 3¾x7" dia..**$25.00**

Candle holder, triple, #R-433, pink & blue mottled Mauve Agate glaze, 11" L..**$30.00**

Centerpiece, mermaid lying on stomach holding bowl, #514, gold-accented white matt, 13½" L.......................**$95.00**

Dish, Graphic Earth Wraps, #3169, swooping curved shape w/integral handles, 11" L **$25.00**

Figurine, tigress on rocky ledge, #R-314, amber & brown mottled glaze, 11x10" **$115.00**

Figurines, doves, #649 & #650, 9½", 8½", 2 pcs **$95.00**

Planter, fan-tail pouter pigeon, #R-334, blue & pink mottled glaze, 8x8" **$65.00**

Planter, florist's, square w/square pedestal, 4¾" **$8.00**

Planter, hound dog in shoe, #5080, advertising piece, Bennington Brown Foam, 7x11" **$70.00**

Planter, lion, Bennington Brown Foam, 8", $35.00.

Planter, madonna, head bowed, praying hands, #990, white matt, 13"..**$45.00**

Toe Tapper, series of 7 comical gents w/various instruments, Bennington Brown Foam, from 4¼" to 11½", each **$35.00**

TV lamp, elephant, w/planter pocket, chartreuse.......**$75.00**

TV lamp, leaping gazelle, green w/white foam, 13½" L..**$75.00**

TV lamp, sailfish **$80.00**

Vase, ballerina stands before disk, #3105, no mark, 8"..**$22.00**

Vase, double leaf, #33, blue & pink mottled, 13x17"..**$145.00**

Vase, Earth Grapic Wraps, cylindrical, 7x3½" **$25.00**

Vase, gladiola; peacock w/flared tail feathers, #R-453, pink & blue mottle, 9¾" **$45.00**

Wall pocket, birdhouse w/bird in doorway, 2nd aside, #R-287, pink & blue mottled Mauve Agate glaze, 9".**$65.00**

RumRill

RumRill-marked pottery was actually made by other companies who simply provided the merchandise that George Rumrill marketed from 1933 until his death in 1942. Rumrill designed his own lines, and the potteries who filled the orders were the Red Wing Stoneware Company, Red Wing Potteries, Shawnee (but they were involved for only a few months), Florence, and Gonder. Many of the designs were produced by more than one company. Examples may be marked RumRill or with the name of the specific pottery.

Advisors: Wendy and Leo Frese, Three Rivers Collectibles (See Directory, RumRill)

Basket, #285, white, Classic Group, 8".........................**$60.00**

Basket, #438, Pompeiian, Sylvan Group **$60.00**

Bowl, #O-40, light green, leaf design w/lily pad leaves, shallow, 14½x11", from $40 to.....................................**$50.00**

Bowl, #300, pink w/black simulated airbrushing, Fluted Group, 8½", from $75 to..**$95.00**

Bowl, #304, orange w/brown mottling, 7½" **$45.00**

Bowl, #314, Seafoam **$20.00**

Bowl, #683, white, Empire Group, 6x11" L...............**$125.00**

Bowl, melon ribbed, mottled brown & cinnamon over orange, #152, 3¼x9½".....................................**$46.00**

Candle holders, #597, yellow-gold w/brown antiquing at rims, 6½", pr...**$88.00**

Ewer, #I-26, shows bird inside circle, 10".................**$40.00**

Ewer, #1012, Pompeiian, Magnolia Line, 7", from $60 to..**$75.00**

Pitcher, #A-50, Dutch Blue................................**$45.00**

Planter, #304, Goldenrod..................................**$45.00**

Planter, #432, Shell Line, 5"..............................**$35.00**

Planter, #440, swan, Mustard Yellow w/white interior, from $60 to..**$75.00**

Planter, #537, Seafoam, Manhattan Group, 12" L........**$40.00**

Planter, double swan, pink **$75.00**

Urn, #252, Pompeiian, Continental Group, 14", from $165 to..**$225.00**

Vase, #K-6, yellow w/abstract Aztec-like bird design.**$88.00**

Vase, #279, Mustard Yellow w/white interior, Swan Group, 7½", from $40 to...**$50.00**

Vase, #290, Lilac, handled, 9½", from $35 to **$40.00**

Vase, #307, Dutch Blue, handled, 10"....................**$125.00**

Vase, #501, Riviera, white w/blue interior, Manhattan Group, from $30 to..**$45.00**

Vase, #537, fan shape, chocolate brown w/beige interior, 12" **$28.00**

Vase, #576, white, Athenia................................**$300.00**

Vase, #581, Slate Blue, 6x10" **$20.00**

Vase, cornucopia; #558, white, 3"..........................**$55.00**

Russel Wright Designs

One of the country's foremost industrial designers, Russel Wright, was also responsible for several dinnerware lines, glassware, and aluminum that have become very collectible. American Modern, produced by the Steubenville Pottery Company (1939 – 1959) is his best known dinnerware and the most popular today. It had simple, sweeping lines that appealed to tastes of that period, and it was made in a variety of solid colors. The most desirable are Canteloupe, Glacier, Bean Brown, and White. Double our values for these colors. Chartreuse is represented by the low end of our range, Cedar, Black Chutney, and Seafoam by the high end, and Coral and Gray near the middle.

Iroquois China made his Casual line, and because it was so serviceable, it's relatively easy to find today. It will be marked with both Wright's signature and 'China by Iroquois.' To price Brick Red, Aqua, and Cantaloupe Casual, double our values; for Avocado, use the low end of the range. Oyster and Charcoal are valued at 50% more than prices listed.

Wright's aluminum ware is highly valued by today's collectors, even though it wasn't so well accepted in its day, due to the fact that it was so easily damaged.

If you'd like to learn more about the subject, we recommend *The Collector's Encyclopedia of Russel Wright Designs* by Ann Kerr.

American Modern

Bowl, salad, from $75 to	**$85.00**
Bowl, vegetable, from $20 to	**$25.00**
Butter dish, w/lid, from $200 to	**$225.00**
Creamer, from $10 to	**$12.00**
Cup & saucer, from $10 to	**$15.00**

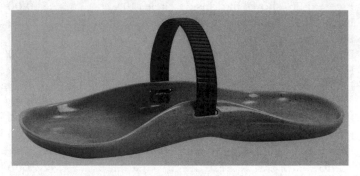

Divided relish, 10", from $150.00 to $175.00.

Hostess set, divided plate w/cup, from $75 to	**$85.00**
Ice box jar, rare, from $175 to	**$200.00**
Plate, salad; 8", from $10 to	**$12.00**
Platter, 13", from $25 to	**$30.00**
Ramekin, individual; w/lid, rare, from $150 to	**$200.00**
Salad fork & spoon set, from $80 to	**$90.00**
Salt & pepper shakers, pr, from $12 to	**$16.00**
Tumbler, rare, from $70 to	**$80.00**

Casual

Asbestos pad	**$40.00**
Bowl, soup; redesigned, 18-oz, from $15 to	**$20.00**
Cup & saucer, from $12 to	**$15.00**
Gravy boat w/attached stand, 16-oz, from $55 to	**$65.00**
Mug, restyled, 9-oz, from $65 to	**$75.00**
Mug, 13-oz, from $75 to	**$85.00**
Plate, bread & butter; 6½", from $4 to	**$5.00**
Plate, luncheon; 9½", from $6 to	**$8.00**
Platter, oval, 12¾", from $20 to	**$25.00**
Sugar bowl, redesigned, from $15 to	**$20.00**
Teapot, restyled (replaced coffeepot), from $150 to	**$175.00**

Knowles

Bowl, fruit; 5½"	**$8.00**
Centerpiece/server, 22"	**$70.00**
Cream pitcher	**$14.00**
Cup & saucer	**$14.00**
Sugar bowl, w/lid	**$20.00**

Sterling

Bouillon, 7-oz, from $12 to	**$16.00**
Bowl, fruit; 5", from $7 to	**$10.00**

Bowl, salad; 7½", from $12 to	**$15.00**
Coffee bottle, from $85 to	**$100.00**
Plate, dinner; 10¼"	**$12.00**
Platter, oval, 10½", from $17 to	**$25.00**

White Clover

Ashtray, clover decorated	**$30.00**
Bowl, cereal/soup; clover decorated	**$14.00**
Bowl, fruit; clover decorated	**$14.00**
Gravy boat, clover decorated	**$25.00**
Salt & pepper shakers, 2 sizes, per pr	**$25.00**

Aluminum

Casseroles, each	**$90.00**
Gravy boat	**$150.00**
Relish rosette, lg	**$200.00**
Sandwich humidor	**$175.00**
Smoking stand	**$450.00**

Spaghetti set, $400.00.

Wastebasket	**$125.00**

Glass

American Modern, goblet, 4", 10-oz	**$40.00**
American Modern, pilsner, 7"	**$125.00**
American Modern, tumbler, water; 4½", 11-oz	**$30.00**
Eclipse, highball, 5"	**$15.00**
Eclipse, shot glass, 2"	**$20.00**
Imperial Flair, tumbler, ice tea; 14-oz	**$65.00**
Imperial Flair, tumbler, juice; 6-oz, from $45 to	**$50.00**
Iroquois Pinch, tumbler, ice tea; 14-oz, from $30 to	**$45.00**
Iroquoise Pinch, tumbler, juice or water; 6- or 14-oz, each, from $35 to	**$40.00**
Old Morgantown, stem, cocktail; 2½", 3-oz	**$30.00**
Old Morgantown, stem, wine; 3", 4-oz	**$30.00**

Plastic

Black Velvet, cup & saucer	**$11.00**
Black Velvet, plate, dinner	**$8.00**
Copper Penny, sugar bowl, w/lid	**$16.00**
Copper Penny, tumbler	**$18.50**
Flair, lug soup	**$12.00**
Flair, platter, from $15 to	**$18.00**

Flair, sugar bowl, w/lid **$13.00**
Home Decorator, bowl, vegetable; w/lid....................**$30.00**
Home Decorator, plate, bread & butter **$3.00**
Home Decorator, tumbler **$15.00**
Ideal Adult Kitchen Ware, bowl, salad......................**$16.00**
Ideal Adult Kitchen Ware, tumbler, 2 sizes, each........**$25.00**
Meladur, bowl, cereal; 9-oz...**$9.00**
Meladur, cup & saucer **$10.00**
Meladur, plate, compartment; 9½".............................**$10.00**

Residential, Cup and saucer set, from $7.00 to $9.00; Divided vegetable bowl, from $16.00 to $18.00

Residential, onion soup, w/lid, each pc **$12.00**
Residential, plate, salad; from $4 to **$5.00**

Salt Shakers

Probably the most common type of souvenir shop merchandise from the twenties through the sixties, salt and pepper shaker sets can be spotted at any antique mall or flea market today by the dozens. Most were made in Japan and imported by various companies, though American manufacturers made their fair share as well.

'Miniature shakers' are hard to find and their prices have risen faster than any others. They were made by Arcadia Ceramics (probably an American company). They're under 1½" tall, some so small they had no space to accommodate a cork. Instead they came with instructions to 'use Scotch tape to cover the hole.'

Advertising sets and premiums are always good, since they appeal to a cross section of collectors. If you have a chance to buy them on the primary market, do so. Many of these are listed in the Advertising Character Collectibles section of this guide.

There are several good books on the market. We recommend *Salt and Pepper Shakers, Identification and Values, Vols I, II, III* and *IV*, by Helene Guarnaccia; and *The Collector's Encyclopedia of Salt and Pepper Shakers, Figural and Novelty, First* and *Second Series,* by Melva Davern.

See also Advertising Character Collectibles; Breweriana; Condiment Sets; Holt Howard; Occupied Japan; Regal China; Rosemeade; Vandor; and other specific companies.

Advisor: Judy Posner (See Directory, Salt and Pepper Shakers)

Club: Novelty Salt and Pepper Club
c/o Irene Thornburg, Membership Coordinator
581 Joy Rd.
Battle Creek, MI 49017; Publishes quarterly newsletter and annual roster. Annual dues: $20 in USA, Canada, and Mexico; $25 for all other countries

Advertising

Coppertone Suntan Lotion, from $75.00 to $100.00. (Photo courtesy Helene Guarnaccia)

Evinrude Motors, black w/silver trim, on stands, pr..**$150.00**
Firestone Tires, black at tread, green sides w/silver hub caps, 1 says Firestone, other says US Rubber, pr...........**$75.00**
French's, Seagrams 7-Crown, red 7s on white base w/red letters, pr **$25.00**
Hamm's Beer, ceramic, black & white bears w/logo on belly, 1 pours from top of head, other pours from nose, 5", pr..**$150.00**
Marathon Mile-Maker, gas pump, white w/black & red label, pr..**$40.00**
Mobilgas, ceramic, shield shaped, white w/red horse logo & blue & white lettering, 1950s, pr **$50.00**
Nabisco, Blue Bonnet Sue, white apron over blue bonnet & dress, Benjamin & Medwin, discontinued, pr.......**$30.00**
New Era, potato chip cans, yellow w/red & black letters, pr...**$10.00**
Nipper, dog & RCA phonograph, plastic, pr **$45.00**
Philgas, propane tanks, green w/black lettering, pr...**$35.00**
Sprite, soda cans, green w/white lettering, metal lids, pr..**$8.00**

Animals, Birds, and Fish

Alligators, realistic w/green & brown details, tails up, pr..**$12.00**
Alligators in hats, brown w/white chest, black bow tie, yellow hat w/black band, 1 on all 4s, 1 on hind legs, pr **$20.00**
Bark-o-lounger, dalmatian resting on chaise marked Bark-o-lounger, pr..**$18.00**
Basset hounds, natural colors, both sitting, 1 w/head back, pr...**$32.00**
Bear w/2 fish, many color variations, per set **$15.00**
Bird on stump, yellow bird w/white wings & black trim, stump is brown w/purple floral, Poinsettia Studios, pr..**$25.00**
Birds in baskets, multicolor w/yellow nest, lift top to show 2 egg shakers, set...**$15.00**

Boxer dogs w/collars, realistic paint, standing or sitting, pr **$25.00**

Buffalo, realistic paint, pr................................**$15.00**

Camel, 1 hump is salt, other is pepper, light brown w/dark brown hair, Enesco, set **$22.00**

Cat at piano, white cat w/black stripes, black piano, pr...**$18.00**

Cat in cup, fat yellow cat w/blue tie sits in white cup w/yellow band, set **$18.00**

Cats, green w/white eyes, sitting, German, pr **$22.00**

Cats, multicolor outfits, each has 1 rhinestone eye w/other eye closed, pr..**$18.00**

Cats in pajamas, standing, 1 in white w/blue vertical stripes, other in white w/red dots, pr...............................**$18.00**

Chickens, wearing black & white striped uniforms, green base, pr...**$16.00**

Chinese dragons, yellow w/green showing underneath, pr..**$24.00**

Circus elephant & tent, elephant has red hat, tent is red & cream, pr **$18.00**

Circus horse & wagon, white horse w/green hat & saddle, white wagon w/yellow roof & wheels, gold trim, pr.........**$30.00**

Collies, realistic, standing, pr **$22.00**

Cow & moon, yellow moon & sitting brown cow, pr..**$28.00**

Cow w/baby calf, mother in pink dress, baby in blue shirt, pr...**$35.00**

Cows, cartoon type, pink w/white underside, standing, pr **$10.00**

Cows, lying down, black & white w/yellow bell hanging from neck, pr **$10.00**

Crocodile in rubber raft, green w/yellow chest, wearing red sunglasses w/blue lens, orange raft w/yellow trim, set..**$18.00**

Dog in doghouse, brown dog sitting up, black & white doghouse w/brown roof, German, pr.........................**$24.00**

Dog's head in shoe, multicolored, PY Japan, pr.........**$30.00**

Donkeys, white w/black spots, tail & bridle, yellow headband, red at feet, pr.......................................**$8.00**

Dr Dog & patient, Dr w/stethoscope in white uniform, patient under white blanket in bed has yellow bow in hair, pr..**$25.00**

Dr Goat w/bag, Dr in clothes holding pipe, yellow Dr's bag, pr...**$32.00**

Ducks, painted clay pottery, Mexico, pr.....................**$10.00**

Ducks, realistic wood decoy look-alikes, pr...............**$10.00**

Elephants, realistic bone china, 1 w/upturned trunk & leg lifted, other on all 4s w/trunk down, pr....................**$26.00**

Elephants, red or green w/white tusks, sitting, German, pr...**$22.00**

Fawns, realistic paint, 1 standing, other sitting, pr **$26.00**

Fish, rainbow trout, realistic paint, swimming on blue water base, pr...**$18.00**

Fish, realistic bluegill, pr **$25.00**

Fish, yellow & white w/black vertical stripes, w/yellow tray, set...**$25.00**

Fish, yellow perch, natural colors, swimming on top of blue water base, pr...**$18.00**

Foxes, bone china, brown w/white furry tail & chest, 1 begging, 1 standing, pr..**$12.00**

Frog & mushroom, green frog & brown mushroom, pr...**$8.00**

Goats, gray w/black & rose highlights, 1 male, 1 female, both standing, pr...**$26.00**

Gorillas, orange cartoon-type boy & girl in a cage, pr..**$15.00**

Hippo on scales, gray & white w/pink trim, pr..........**$18.00**

Hippos, bone china, brown w/white underside, 1 w/mouth open, pr..**$26.00**

Hippos, light pink w/open mouths, sitting, pr...........**$12.00**

Kangaroos, mother w/baby in pouch, black over gray, pr..**$18.00**

Monkey in car, monkey w/right hand on green hat, yellow & green jacket, green car, pr **$25.00**

Monkey w/telephone, brown monkey w/receiver to ear, black phone, pr **$18.00**

Monkeys, black, in human clothes, scratching head, pr**$22.00**

Monkeys, See No Evil, Hear No Evil & Speak No Evil, set..**$28.00**

Monkeys, wearing red, white & blue-checked shirt, pr.**$22.00**

Moose, realistic bone china, male sitting, female laying down, pr...**$22.00**

Mouse on bowling ball, gray mouse w/black tail on black ball, pr **$24.00**

Mouse w/cheese wedge, gray & yellow, pr **$8.00**

Mouse w/foot through shoe, brown mouse & blue shoe, pr..**$18.00**

Native on carrot, original with color on bottom, from $50.00 to $60.00; reproduction set with white underside, $10.00. (Photo courtesy Helene Guarnaccia)

Oxen pulling wagon, brown & yellow, w/green tray, set ..**$15.00**

Pelicans, metal, white w/orange open beak on green base marked Miami, pr **$35.00**

Penguin couple in wooden boat, drink in hand, he has blue hair, she has pink bow in hair, set.......................**$22.00**

Penguins, realistic paint, 1 has umbrella, pr...............**$14.00**

Pigs, sitting, wearing green pants w/dark lines, rose-colored faces, heads cocked, pr......................................**$14.00**

Pigs, sleeping, pink, 1 cradles the other at side, pr....**$10.00**

Pigs playing bass fiddle, brown, yellow, blue & white paint, marked Otagiri, pr **$16.00**

Ponies, realistic bone china, standing, pr **$26.00**

Poodle in green bucket & cat in watering can, marked Germany, pr..**$22.00**

Poodles, white realistically painted bone china, pr **$26.00**

Rabbit playing banjo, blue & cream, German, pr.......**$35.00**

Rabbits, begging, yellow, holes in head, 1 ear up, other ear down, German, pr **$35.00**

Rabbits, white w/pink inner ears, she w/yellow hat & tie, he w/blue scarf, marked Kessler, pr......................**$12.00**

Rabbits on motorcycle, multicolored, pr...................**$25.00**

Rabbits playing musical instruments, pink, pr............**$12.00**

Seals, gray, tails tucked & heads turned, marked New England Ceramics, Torrington CT, pr....................**$12.00**

Skunk, black & white, 1-pc, elongated body.............**$10.00**

Snails, bone china, blue & white, w/blue & white floral tray, set..**$10.00**

Tiger cub w/green hat & baseball, pr.......................**$24.00**

Tigers, cartoon-like modeling, yellow w/black stripes, sitting, pr..**$12.00**

Zebras, natural black & white stripes, both standing, pr.**$12.00**

Black Americana

Babies eating watermelon, painted bisque, 1930s, 2¼", EX...**$175.00**

Bellhop in orange uniform w/2 eggs on tray, Art Deco style, set..**$110.00**

Boy on elephant, holes in eyes, marked Japan Importing Company NYC NY, pr....................................**$75.00**

Boy sitting w/green tray holding 2 red berries, set....**$95.00**

Boy sitting w/melon slice, 4", EX...............................**$95.00**

Boy w/whole watermelon & girl w/watermelon slice, pr...**$45.00**

Butler & maid, brown skin tone, 4¾", pr.................**$110.00**

Cannibal looking at man in pot, Japan, 2½", pr.........**$95.00**

Chef, lg feet, carrying 2 milk cans, 3-pc set.............**$185.00**

Chef holding pitcher attached to stand holding 3 barrels, marked Fairyland China, Japan, 5¼", set...........**$110.00**

Children in rocking chairs reading books, eyes blink as chairs rock, gold trim, holes in back of chair, pr............**$65.00**

Couple, Before & After, turnabout style, pr..............**$175.00**

Couple, chalkware busts, man w/white hat, lady w/red scarf, holes in eyes, USA ink stamp on bottom, pr.......**$75.00**

Couple, elderly man w/beard & cane, lady w/shopping basket, Japan, 3", pr...**$140.00**

Couple, huggers, lady in pink w/green hat, man w/cream pants, blue shirt & red hat, 3", pr.......................**$70.00**

Couple on green tray w/tree as handle, set.............**$115.00**

Egg couple, girl's bust & man at water's edge, marked Hand-Painted, pr...**$30.00**

Graduates, each sitting on tree stumps, he w/diploma & flower, she w/book, pr..................................**$125.00**

Luzianne Coffee Mammy, green skirt, carries teapot & cup on tray, plastic, marked F&F Die Works, 5¼", pr....**$250.00**

Luzianne Coffee Mammy, red skirt reissue, pr.........**$125.00**

Mammy, chalkware, yellow dress, red scarf, legs crossed, pr...**$35.00**

Mammy, 1 w/happy face, other w/frowning face, both w/white dress & yellow trim, 3", pr.....................**$50.00**

Mammy & butler, she w/yellow, blue & white dress, he w/black & white tuxedo, pr.................................**$175.00**

Mammy & chef heads, she w/orange scarf, he w/white chef hat, marked #7859, 3½", pr...............................**$90.00**

Man carrying yoke & 2 baskets, white hat & apron, red shirt, blue pants, brown baskets, 5", set.......................**$150.00**

Mother w/baby in lap, native style, pr.......................**$55.00**

Native in red gown & white hat w/brown & white hut, marked Japan, pr...**$45.00**

Native w/bone in hair, head 1 shaker, bone other, pr...**$95.00**

Porter w/2 barrel shakers at sides, marked Japan, 7½", 3-pc...**$35.00**

Porter w/2 suitcases, holes in suitcase, red hat & pants, blue jacket on white base, set......................................**$125.00**

Sambo on camel, bulging eyes, orange lips & green shirt, interlocking, 4½x4½" overall, EX, pr.................**$225.00**

Sea captain & ship's mate, pr.....................................**$60.00**

Shoeshine boy & shoe stand, green & brown, pr.......**$85.00**

Character

Astro Boy & sister in rocket, white rocket w/red trim, Japanese cartoon, pr, minimum value **$100.00**

Barney Google & Snuffy Smith, chalkware, Barney in blue sailor suit, Snuffy in brown army fatigues, 1940s, pr...**$40.00**

Charlie Brown & Lucy on chair, multicolor, marked Copyright Charles Schulz, set..**$60.00**

Charlie McCarthy (bust), blue jacket, white shirt, orange bow tie & base, w/monocle, pr.................................**$150.00**

Cinderella's slipper on a pillow, blue slipper w/white bow, pink pillow w/yellow trim, pr...............................**$24.00**

Daisy & bag of groceries, she sits w/hands on hips, cream bag, pr..**$30.00**

Davy Crockett-type boys in canoe, w/oars & coonskin hats, red, white & brown canoe, set...............................**$20.00**

Dish & the spoon, white w/black facial details, yellow or green base, pr...**$30.00**

Donald Duck, sitting, multicolor, Leeds, M, pr.........**$145.00**

Donald Duck (not Disney), multicolor w/black hat & pipe, pr...**$18.00**

Donald Duck & Ludwig Von Drake, 1950s, EX, pr ..**$165.00**

Felix the Cat, black w/white eyes & mouth, sm, pr.**$125.00**

Ferdinand the Bull, black & white w/florals on green base, unmarked, pr...**$75.00**

Figaro the Cat, sitting, yellow w/black markings, unmarked, pr...**$75.00**

Garfield & girlfriend, Garfield w/red shirt, blue overalls, & shovel, girlfriend w/red-dotted white apron, pr...**$50.00**

Garfield & Odie, Thanksgiving theme, pr **$50.00**

Goldilocks, green dress w/white apron, red bow in hair, holding book of The 3 Bears, pr..........................**$26.00**

Goofy & car, painted bisque, Japan, 1930s, pr **$495.00**

Goofy & Donald, Donald w/carton of milk, Goofy sits w/yellow apple, pr...**$45.00**

Humpty Dumpty, winking, sitting on blue base, yellow shirt, black jacket, brown pants, head & body as shakers, pr..**$70.00**

JFK in rocking chair, light blue shirt, dark blue pants & tie, brown hair, set...**$50.00**

Kanga & Roo, Enesco, 1964, EX, pr.........................**$235.00**

Laurel & Hardy (heads), both w/black hats & purple ties, pr...**$95.00**

Little Orphan Annie & Sandy, chalkware, Annie in yellow, brown Sandy sitting, 1940s, pr **$45.00**

Little Red Riding Hood & Big Bad Wolf, on Never Never Land bases, pr...**$75.00**

Maggie & Jiggs, she w/yellow top & red slacks, he w/black tuxedo & blue shirt, pr.....................................**$150.00**

Maggie & Jiggs outhouses, white w/blue roofs, pr.....$45.00

Martin & Lewis (heads), as though singing, w/tray, set, minimum value $300.00

Mary & lamb, she w/blond hair, blue dress & cap, white lamb w/brown collar, pr $30.00

Mickey Mouse, ceramic, marked Dan Brechner Imports, ca 1961, pr $225.00

Mickey Mouse, 1 playing bass drum, other playing guitar, multicolored, 1930s, pr..$300.00

Mickey Mouse as chef, on plain white cylinder-shaped shakers, gold trim, pr..$35.00

Mickey Mouse as Santa in sleigh, waving, w/toy bag, red, white & green..$45.00

Mickey Mouse Club hats, black w/Mickey Mouse emblem on front, 1 has red bow on top, pr $25.00

Mickey Mouse in chair & in car (both yellow), marked Walt Disney Co, by Good Co, Applause, 1989.............$20.00

Miss Piggy & Kermit, Kermit the Magician saws Miss Piggy in half, pr $75.00

Moon Mullins, black or red tie, cream pants w/checkered design, black top hat, pr......................................$35.00

Old Lady & shoe, white dress w/blue dots, brown shoe w/blue roof, gold trim, pr......................................$32.00

Paul Bunyan and Babe the Blue Ox, $30.00. (Photo courtesy Helene Guarnaccia)

Pinocchio, glazed porcelain bisque w/gold trim, 1940s, 5", pr $165.00

Pluto, ivory w/gold trim, Leeds, pr $90.00

Pluto & house, multicolor, pr $30.00

Popeye & Olive Oyl, he w/sailor uniform, she w/green skirt, white dress, hands on hips, pr............................$125.00

Shmoos, by Al Capp, white w/black details, 1 w/green scarf, other w/black tie & blue collar, pr.....................$175.00

Snow White & Dopey, Enesco, 1960s, pr..................$275.00

Stanley & Livingston, both in African fatigues in kettle over fire, pr..$45.00

Sylvester w/Tweety in nest, pr $22.00

Tasmanian Devil & wood crate marked Danger, Warner Brothers, pr $22.00

Winnie the Pooh & Rabbit, Enesco, 1950s, EX, pr ...$295.00

Woody Woodpecker & Winnie, walking w/shakers in arm, Walter Lantz Productions Inc, Napco Japan, 1958, pr..........$250.00

Ziggy & dog, w/sticker marked Universal Syndicate 1969, Japan, 2" & 2¾", pr..$45.00

Fruit, Vegetables, and Other Food

Banana & pineapple people, red or green shorts, w/boxing gloves & white shirts, pr $35.00

Banana couple, male w/sombrero plays drum, female w/Hawaiian lei dances, pr $45.00

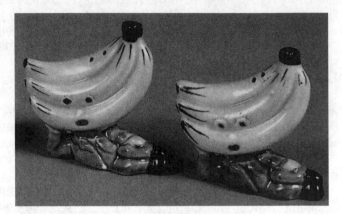

Banana People, $18.00 to $25.00. (Photo courtesy Helene Guarnaccia)

Bananas in baskets, winking, arms to face, pr............$18.00

Beer mugs, glass w/foam heads, embossed 1933 Happy Days, pr $10.00

Bunch of bananas, realistic paint, pr $12.00

Cabbage girls, blond hair w/realistic faces, pr............$10.00

Children holding tomato & garlic over heads, pr $22.00

Cookies, black w/white cream filling, pr....................$22.00

Corn on the cob, pale yellow corn wrapped in green leaves, w/green tray, set..$12.00

Corn people, brown hair, ear of corn body, arms out front, pr..$28.00

Eggplant & cabbage referees, both w/black & white-striped uniforms, whistles around necks, pr.....................$55.00

Ice cream cones, yellow cone & ice cream, holes on top, pr..$10.00

Lemon head, yellow w/green leaf hair, brown hat shaker, 1 eye closed, brown jacket w/blue bow tie, pr $12.00

Mrs Carrot Head & Mrs Peapod Head, w/broom or flower basket, pr..$45.00

Onion, pearl white bulbs, holes at top, pr..................$12.00

Onion-head people, white w/black eyes, w/green tray, set $15.00

Peanut-head people, green dress w/gold necklace, feet lifted, brown shoes, pr $35.00

Potato pancakes, fork & spoon arms raised to temples, marked Latke Salt or Latke Pepper, pr..................$22.00

Pretzels, brown w/white salt, J Rayton, California, pr ..$15.00

Squash-head people, sitting, green pants, white shirt, gold vest, feet up, pr..$20.00

Watermelon-slice-head people, white shirt w/blue pants, pr..$28.00

Watermelon slices, ceramic, pr $12.00

Holidays and Special Occasions

Bride & groom bench sitters, w/wooden park bench, set ..$18.00

Bunny & Easter egg, white w/multicolor flowers, pr.**$12.00**

Choir boys, 1 w/book, other w/accordion, white shirts, red shoes, pr...........................**$18.00**

Christmas ornaments, red or green w/silver tops, pr.**$22.00**

Father Time & clock, brown & white, pr...................**$35.00**

Halloween pumpkins, orange w/black face, Pilgrim hat w/green band & yellow buckle, 1980s, pr...........**$12.00**

Pilgrim hats, white w/black band & gold buckle, pr..**$10.00**

Santa & Mrs Claus, as cowboy or cowgirl, pr.................**$25.00**

Santa & Mrs Claus, each w/holly-decorated white rocket, pr.**$26.00**

Santa & Mrs Claus, playing tennis, pr............................**$18.00**

Santa & Mrs Claus, red, white & green w/gold trim, Poinsettia Studios, pr **$30.00**

Santa in sleigh w/reindeer, red & white sleigh, brown reindeer w/candy cane antlers & green harness, set .**$15.00**

Snowman & cane, black eyes, nose, mouth & buttons, red-tipped cane, pr...**$22.00**

Snowmen couples, many variations & colors, any, pr, from $14 to...**$18.00**

Thanksgiving Day turkeys, multicolored, pr................**$10.00**

Valentine heart, red w/golden arrow through center, 2-pc set..**$22.00**

Valentine hearts, w/embossed arrow on pedestal, pr.**$12.00**

Wedding bells, ivory w/satin bows on top, 1940s, pr.**$15.00**

Wedding ring & license, gold band w/diamond ring in black box, white license w/black lettering, pr **$28.00**

Witch & jack-o-lantern, dark orange jack-o-lantern w/big grin, witch in purple w/broom, pr........................**$15.00**

Angels, applied 'fur' trim, from $15.00 to $18.00. (Photo description Helene Guarnaccia)

Household Items

Baby shoes, bronze-look painted ceramic, pr.............**$22.00**

Binoculars & case, brown & black w/gold trim, pr....**$15.00**

Books, marked Salt or Pepper w/rooster at bottom of spine & flower at top, pr....................................**$8.00**

Chair & ottoman, brown w/white & green decoration, set..**$15.00**

Egg-in-egg-cup people, pr **$15.00**

Faucet, white china w/colored taps, old-fashion style, pr..**$15.00**

Lunch box & thermos, light green thermos w/chrome-like handle, black box w/gold handle & clasps, pr **$15.00**

Paint bucket & brush, red & yellow, pr.......................**$10.00**

Purse & pocket watch, maroon purse, clock face is white w/black numbers, both trimmed in gold..............**$22.00**

Refrigerator & stove, white w/red trim, 1940s, pr.......**$15.00**

Rolling pin & scoop, white w/floral design, pr.............**$8.00**

Telephone, dial type, red & green, receiver & base as shakers, pr...**$22.00**

Toaster, plastic, black bottom & handles, yellow top w/floral design, 1 black (pepper) & 1 white (salt) pc of toast...**$15.00**

Watering cans, white w/red, yellow & green floral design, poem in black letters on sides, pr........................**$10.00**

Miniatures

Aladdin on flying carpet & magic lamp, pr.................**$45.00**

Barbecue & picnic table, green, white, blue & gray, pr.**$28.00**

Cake on plate (minus pc) & plate w/cake slice & gold fork, pr...**$20.00**

Coffeepot w/cup & saucer set, black & white w/gold trim, pr...**$25.00**

Cowboy boots, brown w/gold spurs & buckles, pr....**$28.00**

Hurricane lamps, red globes w/clear glass, brass-like hardware, pr **$18.00**

Ice cream maker & plate of ice cream, brown, white & red w/gold trim, pr.......................................**$26.00**

Mouse & mousetrap, gray, white & yellow w/gold trim, pr...**$35.00**

Outhouses, brown w/black roof, half moon on door, antenna on 1, pr **$30.00**

Pancakes w/syrup bottle, pancakes on a plate w/knife & fork attached, bottle w/yellow lid, set **$35.00**

Pipe & slippers, black, cream & rose w/gold trim, pr..**$20.00**

Roller skates, white w/brown details & gold trim, pr.**$30.00**

Sausage & eggs on a plate, blue, brown, white & yellow, pr...**$26.00**

Shaving brush & lather mug, brown, white, cream & blue, pr...**$35.00**

Sir George & dragon, gray, maroon & red, pr, minimum value **$50.00**

Snowman & sled, red, black, white & yellow, pr.......**$40.00**

Stop sign & car, pr.......................................**$40.00**

Typewriter and telephone, from $25.00 to $30.00. (Photo courtesy Helene Guarnaccia)

Whisk broom & dustpan, green & yellow w/gold trim, pr.**$22.00**

People

Baseball players, 1 in green w/blue hat, 1 in blue w/red hat, white bases, pr.....................................**$45.00**

Bowler w/ball & 10 pins, multicolor, pr **$18.00**

Boxers squaring off, 1 in red shorts w/hands to side, other in green shorts & throwing an uppercut, white bases, pr **$18.00**

Cactus & Mexican man in red sombrero, blue shirt & black pants, sitting & sleeping, pr **$10.00**

Canadian Mounted Police, standing, yellow hat, red jacket & blue pants, marked S or P on green base, pr **$18.00**

Cartoon sports players, football, basketball or soccer, marked Napco, ca 1958, any, pr **$35.00**

Clown w/dog in lap, sitting, matching red & white outfits, pr **$20.00**

Clowns, Emmet Kelly look-alikes, white w/red-checked pants or white w/blue-checked pants, holding cane, pr..**$28.00**

Clowns, multicolored outfits, Napco, marked 1957, pr..**$24.00**

Clowns, white outfits, red nose & mouth, 'X' for eyes, 1 sitting, 1 on his head, pr.....................................**$10.00**

Deep sea diver & fish, red, blue, gray & green, pr **$28.00**

Drunk on yellow & white park bench, pr...................**$16.00**

Dutch couple in wooden shoes, dancing, blue & white, pr.**$10.00**

Eastern men, seated, 1 playing instrument, multicolor w/gold trim, marked Occupied Japan, pr **$22.00**

English bobbies, white shirt, black tie & uniform, silver shield on helmet, marked S or P, pr **$18.00**

Eskimo couple, he w/fish, she w/basket, pr...............**$15.00**

Firemen boy & girl, she w/#1 on helmet & dog, he w/#2 on helmet & axe, pr..**$15.00**

Friars, brown robes, book in left hand, unmarked, pr ..**$10.00**

Golfer, red hat, white shirt, blue pants, oversized golf ball, 4 clubs form tray, set..**$70.00**

Grandparents in rocking chairs, she knits, he smokes pipe, pr...**$15.00**

Hawaiian girls, yellow skirts, w/flower on heads & leis, dancing or playing stringed instrument, pr **$18.00**

Indian & tepee, black-haired man wrapped in red blanket, brown tepee w/gray markings, pr............................**$10.00**

Indian chief & tepee, chief in multicolor headdress & white blanket, white tepee w/brown markings, pr........**$12.00**

Indian chief boy carrying 2 drum shakers, red, white, blue & black headdress, blue pants, white & black drums, set.........**$22.00**

Indian couple (bust) in canoe, multicolor, set **$18.00**

Indian mother w/baby on backboard, multicolor, pr .**$18.00**

Indians on horseback, red headdress, yellow outfit, dark pants, carrying tomahawk & shield, gray horse, pr...............**$22.00**

Kitchen witches, yellow dresses, white aprons & yellow-dotted black scarves, yellow broom handles w/brown bristles, pr...**$10.00**

Lady on knees dressed in hearts, red or blue, pr.......**$18.00**

Lady skier, blond, red blouse & blue pants, yellow skis, white base, pr..**$24.00**

Lion tamer & lion, tamer sits w/whip in right hand, brown lion looks very meek, pr..**$15.00**

Maid & butler, black & white outfits, he w/red tie, she w/towel over arm, Kessler, pr **$12.00**

Man & woman doing pushups, she w/red pants & green shirt, he w/red shirt & black pants, pr..................**$18.00**

Man w/donkey & cart, multicolored, yellow cargo shakers, set..**$20.00**

Mexican man on burro, beige hat w/red & green trim, yellow shirt, brown pants, gray burro carrying gray sacks, set.........**$12.00**

Monks, Achoo (pepper) w/white-dotted red hankerchief, Salt of the Earth w/hands clasped at front, pr.............**$12.00**

Nuns, white hair, black robes & white dress w/blue trim, pr...**$18.00**

Oriental boy & pagoda in boat, boy in brown & yellow scratching head, white & red pagoda w/green roof, brown boat, set...**$15.00**

Oriental boy w/shakers on his back, red pants, blue shirt w/red Chinese letters gold-trimmed hat, beige backpack, pr...**$15.00**

Oriental couple, elderly man w/black robe & blue vest, lady in blue robe w/black vest, pr.................................**$18.00**

Oriental farmer carries 2 baskets w/pig head shakers, set...**$28.00**

Pilgrim couple, turquoise & white, she w/red purse, he w/black shoes, pr...**$10.00**

Pixie band leader & podium, black outfit w/wand, white podium marked The Pixy Band, pr.......................**$45.00**

Pixie band members, different colors, playing different musical instruments, any, pr...**$45.00**

Pixie chefs, white uniforms, red shoes, 1 w/fish & knife, other w/pan & yellow chicken, marked #1C2426, Napco, 1956, pr..**$14.00**

Referees, striped shirts, white pants & hat w/left hand on whistle tied around neck, ca 1940s-50s, pr **$26.00**

Sailors, comical faces, white uniforms w/blue trim & ties, binoculars around neck & flag in right hand, pr .**$10.00**

Sailors, 1 in red & white uniform, other in blue & white, both w/red oar, pr...**$22.00**

Scottish couple, 6½", $12.00. (Photo description Helene Guarnaccia)

Sea captains, both w/pipes, pr **$12.00**

Surfer on surfboard, man w/black hair & shorts, light pink board on white & blue water wave, pr **$35.00**

Souvenir

Beale Street, Memphis TN, Jazz musician playing trumpet, all black, white street sign, set.................................**$15.00**

Blinking-eye shakers, sitting on logs, arms outstretched, red bow w/white polka-dots, Souvenir of Indian Lake OH, pr .**$50.00**

Bonneville Dam OR, split scene of Dam & surroundings, pr...$22.00

Florida, green alligators in FL shirts, 1 orange w/red trim, 1 w/purple shirt w/blue trim, pr $12.00

Grand Canyon, National Park, split scene of park land, pr $20.00

Grotto of the Blessed Virgin Mary, split scene of castle-like building w/flags, pr.....................................$22.00

Hollywood, brown derby hats, marked Hollywood CA on bottom, pr..$15.00

Loretta Lynn's Dude Ranch, white cowboy hats w/black letters, pr $20.00

Mt Hood OR, split scene of calm volcano & surroundings, pr..$22.00

Mt Rainier Washington, split scene of mountain area, pr..$22.00

Old City Gateway, St Augustine FL, bisque-like ceramic, towers in gate are shakers, set.............................$30.00

Punxsutaney PA, groundhog figures, place where he sees his shadow, brown & black features, pr.....................$18.00

Salt Lake City/Mormon Temple, white oval building w/yellow window shaker, temple w/4 towers, pr $18.00

Sandia Crest NM, altitude 10,678 feet, split scene of area, pr...$22.00

Seattle World's Fair, 1962, white w/blue letters on egg shapes w/arrowheads, pr..$30.00

Springfield IL, axe & log, marked Lincoln's Tomb, pr ..$18.00

SS Lurline, George Wallace's boat, white ship w/yellow trim, smokestack shakers, set $18.00

White Sands NM, split scene of sandy desert w/blue mountains in background, pr..$22.00

Yellowstone Park/Old Faithful, split scene w/deer or bears, pr...$22.00

Miscellaneous

Ball canning jars, plastic, complete w/rubber sealing rings, metal handles, pr $7.00

Beer mugs, glass w/foam heads, embossed 1933 Happy Days, pr $10.00

Bowling-pin people, red & white w/bow tie & buttons, Made in Japan sticker, pr..$15.00

Cactus in flowerpot, 2-part, pr.......................................$18.00

Champagne bottle & ice bucket, w/original label, pr.$18.00

Cigarette pack & matchbook, marked Oldfield Cigarettes, pr $18.00

Cookies, black w/white cream filling, pr....................$22.00

Cottages, white w/blue shutters & roof, brown tree on corner, green shrubs, & white chimney, marked Kessler, pr..$12.00

Cupcakes, brown cake w/white confetti icing & cherry on top, pr $8.00

Earth & chair, blue globe-shape man w/feet sits on yellow-dotted chair, 2-part, pr.......................................$18.00

Eyeball & nose, pr...$12.00

Grater, realistic, marked S or P, pr $18.00

Gumball machine, clear globe, red bottom & lid, black mechanism, pr...$20.00

Hat rack w/2 hat shakers, multicolor plastic, set $12.00

Ice cream cones, yellow cone & ice cream, holes on top, pr...$10.00

Legs, sticking straight up or bent at knees, cream, pr..$8.00

Masks of Comedy & Tragedy, white & black, pr........$20.00

Milk shake & mixer, green, pink, white & silver, pr...$16.00

Monsters, green pumpkin-like faces, green feet & white lab coats, 1 scratching head, pr $18.00

Ocean liner, white w/blue & brown smokestack shakers, set $22.00

Playing cards, upright decks showing Ace of Diamonds & Ace of Clubs, pr...$15.00

Roll-top desk & chair, brown desk w/gold handles, white chair w/decoration, The Good Company, pr $12.00

Salty & Peppy, egg cup people (head & neck), hat (shaker) comes off for egg cup, Peppy w/blue tie, Salty w/red tie, pr..$22.00

Sea captain & whale, wood or metal, bearded captain in uniform, white whale or black whale, each pr $18.00

Sunbathing tourists, man on blue blanket w/newspaper on face, lady on orange blanket w/hat over face, pr..$35.00

Tennis balls in metal holder, recent, $10.00. (Photo courtesy Helen Guarnaccia)

Toy soldiers, 1 w/red shirt & rifle, other w/blue shirt & drum, white pants & black shoes, pr..............................$14.00

We're a Perfect Match, male & female faces fit together, male w/brown hair, female w/blond hair, pr $20.00

Windmills, white w/brown markings & blue windows, brown base & roof, Occupied Japan, pr..........................$22.00

Schoop, Hedi

One of the most successful California ceramic studios was founded in Hollywood by Hedi Schoop, who had been educated in the arts in Berlin, Germany. She had studied not only painting but sculpture, architecture, and fashion design as well. Fleeing Nazi Germany with her husband, the famous composer Frederick Holander, Hedi settled in California in 1933 and only a few years later became involved in producing novelty giftware items so popular that they were soon widely copied by other

California companies. She designed many animated human figures, some in matched pairs, some that doubled as flower containers. All were hand painted and many were decorated with applied ribbons, sgraffito work, and gold trim. To a lesser extent, she modeled animal figures as well. Until fire leveled the plant in 1958, the business was very productive. Nearly everything she made was marked.

If you'd like to learn more about her work, we recommend *The Collector's Encyclopedia of California Pottery* by Jack Chipman.

Advisors: Pat and Kris Secor (See Directory, California Pottery)

Ashtray, duck form, green & gold, 5x6½" **$30.00**
Basket, yellow w/gold trim...**$40.00**
Bowl, crimped acorn shape **$65.00**
Bowl, shell form, 7"...**$35.00**
Candle holder, 2-sided lady, 1 side w/eyes open, 1 closed, incised mark, 1962, 12½" **$375.00**
Console bowl w/2 lady figures w/umbrellas, mauve w/gold, 3-pc set, from $195 to **$225.00**
Dish, molded-in dove, w/lid..**$60.00**
Figurine, ballet dancer, ankle-length skirt, 9" **$60.00**
Figurine, ballet dancer, pink w/platinum mottling, 10", from $135 to..**$150.00**
Figurine, Dutch boy, hands on hips, vase behind, 10" **$45.00**
Figurine, French peasant couple, 13", pr....................**$195.00**
Figurine, girl, arms akimbo, tiered & ruffled skirt, heavy gold trim, 12" **$85.00**
Figurine, girl, blond hair w/bow, eyes closed, arms outstretched, full skirt, 12", pr **$150.00**

Figurine, lady in long pink and black dress with parasol, tall, $90.00.

Figurine, girl, peasant dress w/applied flowers, holds bowl above head, 13" **$65.00**
Figurine, Oriental boy musician, black & white, 10½" ..**$80.00**
Figurine, rooster, lg **$150.00**
Lamp, girl reading book..**$100.00**
Planter, horse, lg **$95.00**
Vase, fanned shell shape, gold trim, 6¾"....................**$40.00**
Vase, rooster figural, forest green, chartreuse & red, 13" **$125.00**

Scouting Collectibles

Collecting scouting memorabilia has been a popular hobby for many years. Through the years, millions of boys and girls have been a part of this worthy organization founded in England in 1907 by retired Major-General Lord Robert Baden-Powell. Scouting has served to establish goals in young people and help them develop leadership skills, physical strength, and mental alertness. Through scouting, they learn basic fundamentals of survival. The scouting movement came to the United States in 1910, and the first World Scout Jamboree was held in 1911 in England. If you would like to learn more, we recommend *A Guide to Scouting Collectibles With Values* by R.J. Sayers (ordering information is given in the Directory).

Advisor: R.J. Sayers (See Directory, Scouting Collectibles)

Knife, plastic handles, unused, ca 1940s, 3½", in original box, $100.00.

Bank, scout figural w/staff, steel, 1930s, 6" **$45.00**
Belt, First Class on buckle w/drawings, webb type....**$10.00**
Belt, Leaders, slip type, double catch, w/BSA.............**$10.00**
Binoculars, plastic, 12 power, 1950, VG **$12.00**
Blotter, various types (Coke, God & Country), 1940-50, each...**$5.00**
Book, any fiction (over 1,200 titles available), ca 1913-1940, each, from $2 to...**$5.00**
Book, Handbook for Boys, ca 1940 ....**$5.00**
Book, Handbook for Patrol Leaders, silver cover, ca 1940-60 ....**$5.00**
Book, Scoutmaster's Handbook, 1947 edition, blue cover..**$5.00**
Bookends, bronze finish, First Class, pr **$25.00**
Bookends, laminated wood pulp, pressed, 1950s, pr.**$12.00**
Booklet, Merit Badge series, white & tan cover, 1913-1938, each..**$4.00**
Booklet, Order of the Arrow, 1948 edition, rare.........**$40.00**
Booklet, Scout Service Library Edition, over 60 titles available, 1930s, each..**$4.00**
Camera, Seneca, 1940s, in litho box **$45.00**
Cameras, Kodak, green, 1930, w/case **$60.00**
Catalog, for equipment, ca 1913-40, each...................**$15.00**
Coin, Excelsior Shoe Coin, dated 1910, ca 1940s.........**$5.00**
Coin, 1964, 1969 or 1973 Jamborees, souvenir type, each..**$3.00**
Compass, Taylor type, red or black, ca 1930-50 ....**$10.00**
Diary, ca 1930-47, each **$5.00**
Equipment, backpack, Yucca, ca 1950......................**$10.00**
Equipment, canteen or eating kit, each **$10.00**
Flag, Troop, notched end, 1930-40 ....**$15.00**
Flag, 1935 or 1937 Jamboree Troop Contingent, 36x60"..**$100.00**
Hat, broad-brimmed felt, ca 1920-50..........................**$15.00**
Hat, Garrison type, ca 1940-60 ....**$15.00**
Lobby cards, movie dedicated to Scouting, set of 6 ...**$50.00**
Magazine, Boys Life, ca 1940-70, each.........................**$2.00**

Magazine, Scouting, 1930-60, each $1.50
Mug, showing various Scout events, ca 1950s to present, each...$1.00
Neckerchief, varied troop, camp, OA, Jamboree, etc, each, from $2 to.................................$10.00

Patch, Philmont Ranger, embroidery on yellow twill, blue edge, $50.00.

Patch, Scoutmasters, green, ca 1950, 3" dia $2.00
Patch, 1937 Official Jamboree, Scout, beware of reproduction...$75.00
Patch, 1950, 1953, 1957 or 1960 Jamborees, 3" dia, each ..$10.00
Record, Bugal Calls for Camp, 78-rpm, 1940 ....$10.00
Record, Dan Beard Talks With Scouts, 1940, w/book ..$30.00
Sheath knife, Remington, w/scabbard.........................$65.00
Sheath knife, Western, w/scabbard $30.00
Sheet music, BSA, over 100 various titles, 1913-40, each..$10.00
Watch, Timex, 1950s, w/original band.........................$15.00

Western Union De Luxe Radio-Telegraph Signal Set, ca 1930s, unused, EX, $25.00.

Sebastians

These tiny figures were first made in 1938 by Preston W. Baston and sold through gift stores, primarily in the New England area. In 1976 the Lance Corporation chose one hundred designs which they continued to produce under Baston's supervision. Since then, the discontinued figures have become very collectible. Baston died in 1984, but his son, P.W. Baston, Jr., continues the tradition.

The figures are marked with an imprinted signature and a paper label. Early labels (before 1977) were green and silver foil shaped like an artist's palette; these are referred to as 'Marblehead' labels (Marblehead, Massachusetts, being the location of the factory), and figures that carry one of these are becoming hard to find and are highly valued by collectors.

Advisor: Jim Waite (See Directory, Sebastians)

America Salutes Desert Storm, bronze $95.00
America's Home Town, Smith's $60.00
Aunt Polly...................................$35.00
Basketball Hall of Fame $35.00
Ben Franklin...............................$60.00
Betsy Ross $50.00
Boston Gas Tank..............................$250.00
Charles Dickens, blue label $35.00
Christmas Morning.............................$30.00
Colonial Glass Blower $25.00
Davy Crockett $200.00
Eastern Star.................................$75.00
Egg Rock Light...............................$55.00
Evangeline $50.00
First at Bat $35.00
For You....................................$40.00
Gathering Tulips $100.00
Great Stone Face..............................$700.00
Iron Master's House............................$500.00
Jack & Jill, blue label.........................$35.00
James Madison, pewter $65.00
Jamestown Ships $200.00
John Monroe $115.00
Judge Thatcher...............................$35.00
Little Sister, blue label $40.00
Lobster Man, Marblehead era $45.00
Masonic Bible................................$325.00
Mrs Obocell.................................$400.00
Old Woman in Shoe, Jell-O $375.00

Peace and Brotherhood, $45.00.

Prince Philip................................$200.00
Princess Elizabeth $200.00
Romeo $45.00
Romeo, Marblehead ear $70.00

Sampling the Stew, Marblehead era $40.00
Scottish Girl, Jell-O $375.00
Scrooge..$25.00
Scuba Diver..$375.00
Sir Frances Drake...$250.00
Swanboat, Masons $300.00
Town Crier $45.00
Uncle Mistletoe $125.00
Uncle Sam, Marblehead era $50.00
Wickford Weavers..$300.00
Williamsburg Lady $60.00

Shawnee Pottery

In 1937, a company was formed in Zanesville, Ohio, on the suspected site of a Shawnee Indian village. They took the tribe's name to represent their company, recognizing the Indians to be the first to use the rich clay from the banks of the Muskingum River to make pottery there. Their venture was very successful, and until they closed in 1961, they produced many lines of kitchenware, planters, vases, lamps, and cookie jars that are very collectible today.

They specialized in figural items. There were 'Winnie' and 'Smiley' pig cookie jars and salt and pepper shakers; 'Bo Peep,' 'Puss 'n Boots,' 'Boy Blue,' and 'Charlie Chicken' pitchers; Dutch children; lobsters; and two lines of dinnerware modeled as ears of corn.

Values sometimes hinge on the extent of an item's decoration. Most items will increase by 50% to 200% when heavily decorated and gold trimmed.

Not all of their ware was marked Shawnee; many pieces were simply marked USA with a three- or four-digit mold number. If you'd like to learn more about this subject, we recommend *Shawnee Pottery, The Full Encyclopedia,* by Pam Curran; *The Collector's Guide to Shawnee Pottery* by Duane and Janice Vanderbilt; and *Shawnee Pottery, Identification & Value Guide,* by Jim and Bev Mangus.

See also Cookie Jars.

Advisor: Rick Spencer (See Directory, Shawnee)

Club: Shawnee Pottery Collectors' Club
P.O. Box 713
New Smyrna Beach, FL 32170-0713; Monthly nationwide newsletter. SASE (c/o Pamela Curran) required when requesting information. Optional: $3 for sample of current newsletter.

Casserole, fruit lid on basketweave bottom, from $65.00 to $70.00. (Photo courtesy Duane and Janice Vanderbilt)

Ashtray, free-form, Hostess Line, pink & gold, marked Shawnee 205, from $10 to $12.00
Bank, tumbling bear, 4½", from $175 to $200.00
Bookends, Flying Geese, marked Shawnee 4000, gold trim, pr, from $50 to...$75.00
Candle holders, Crescent pattern, marked Kenwood USA 3017, pr, from $18 to $20.00
Candle holders, magnolia blossom, gold trim, 3", pr .$30.00
Canister, Dutch decal, marked USA, 2-qt....................$50.00
Cigarette box, Confetti, marked Kenwood USA 2120, 2-pc, from $35 to..$45.00
Clock, Trellis, green & white, from $85 to $100.00
Creamer, Sunflower, marked USA, embossed flower on side, from $35 to...$45.00
Figurine, pig, unmarked, miniature.............................$24.00
Figurine, rabbit, gold trim...$125.00
Figurine, raccoon, unmarked......................................$60.00
Figurine, Southern girl, marked USA, 4½"...................$20.00
Flower frog, snail, marked USA, 4x5" $35.00
Grease jar, Cottage, marked USA 8, from $250 to $275.00
Jardiniere, Petit-Point pattern, marked USA 1910, 7", from $14 to...$16.00
Jug, ball; Snowflake Kitchenware, 2-qt, from $40 to ..$50.00
Lamp, Harvest Queen, glazed inside & on base, inner strength ring, unmarked, from $50 to $55.00
Pitcher, Boy Blue, marked Shawnee 46, gold trim, 20-oz..$225.00
Pitcher, Chanticleer, marked patented Chanticleer USA, gold trim & decal, from $300 to..................................$350.00
Pitcher, Flower & Fern Kitchenware, 4-cup, from $22 to...$24.00
Pitcher, Smiley, Marked Pat Smiley USA, embossed clover bud, from $140 to..$165.00
Pitcher, Sunflower, marked USA, 48-oz, from $75 to..$80.00
Plant waterer, fish w/open mouth, marked USA, from $35 to..$40.00
Planter, bear cub w/wagon, gold trim, marked Shawnee USA 732 ....$45.00
Planter, blow fish, marked USA....................................$8.00
Planter, boy at gate, unmarked....................................$12.00
Planter, butterfly on log, gold trim, marked Shawnee USA 524 ....$22.00
Planter, Cameo pattern, bulbous body w/ring foot & ruffled top, marked Shawnee USA 2501, 5", from $8 to..$10.00
Planter, Chantilly pattern, ribbed circular gold foot, scalloped top, marked Shawnee USA 1801, 3½", from $8 to..$10.00
Planter, clown kneeling & holding pot, gold trim, marked USA 619 ....$65.00
Planter, dog in boat, marked Shawnee 736.................$22.00
Planter, Elegance pattern, urn form w/foot, marked Shawnee USA 1401, 5", from $12 to................................$14.00
Planter, Irish setter, marked USA $10.00
Planter, Medallion pattern, rooster figural, bronze glaze, marked USA 503, ca 1950s, 6", from $85 to $95.00
Planter, panda & cradle, marked Shawnee USA 2031...$30.00
Planter, Pastel Medallion pattern, leaf form, marked 1502, 5", from $20 to...$22.00
Planter, pixie & wheelbarrow w/flower wheel, unmarked ..$15.00
Planter, pony, marked Kenwood 1509.........................$65.00

Planter, poodle & carriage, marked USA 704 ....**$32.00**
Planter, rabbit & cabbage, marked USA.....................**$10.00**
Planter, Southern girl, marked USA, 8½" **$12.00**
Planter, Tony the Peddler, marked USA 621...............**$35.00**
Planter, turtle, gold trim, unmarked **$25.00**
Planter, Valencia couple, marked USA **$40.00**
Planter, 3 pigs looking through fence w/lg sunflower, marked USA **$14.00**
Salt & pepper shakers, Chanticleers, gold trim, lg, pr ..**$160.00**
Salt & pepper shakers, Fern Kitchenware, 7-oz, pr, from $30 to **$35.00**
Salt & pepper shakers, Flowerpots, gold trim, sm, pr ..**$50.00**
Salt & pepper shakers, Jumbo, sm, pr **$85.00**

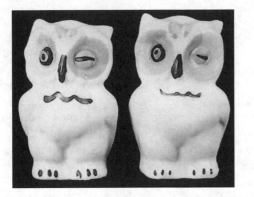

Salt and pepper shakers, owls, green eyes, sm, $30.00 for the pair. (Photo courtesy Duane and Janice Vanderbilt)

Salt & pepper shakers, Puss 'n Boots, gold trim, sm, pr..**$100.00**
Salt & pepper shakers, Smiley, gold-painted bib, sm, pr ...**$85.00**
Salt & pepper shakers, Smiley, green bib, lg, pr **$135.00**
Salt & pepper shakers, Sunflower, sm, pr....................**$35.00**
String holder, Fruit pattern, unmarked, from $100 to .**$125.00**
Sugar/utility jar, Clover Bud, marked USA...................**$60.00**
Teapot, Drape, marked USA, 4-cup, from $30 to........**$35.00**
Teapot, Elephant, marked USA, 5-cup, from $125 to .**$135.00**
Teapot, Horseshoe, marked USA, 8-cup, from $40 to ..**$45.00**
Teapot, Pennsylvania Dutch, marked USA 14, 14-oz, from $65 to...**$70.00**
Tumbler, Stars & Stripes, marked USA, 3", from $6 to..**$8.00**
Vase, bud; Tiara, marked Shawnee USA 3510, 11", from $12 to...**$14.00**
Vase, embossed philodendron, gold trim, marked Shawnee 805, 6½"...**$40.00**
Vase, Liana pattern, pillow form, lime green w/yellow interior, marked Shawnee USA 1012, 7x5", from $10 to.......**$12.00**
Wall pocket, chef w/frying pan & lg spoon, marked USA..**$35.00**
Wall pocket, cornucopia w/bird, unmarked...............**$25.00**
Window box, Fernware pattern, marked USA 1705, 11½" L, from $12 to...**$14.00**

Corn Ware

Bowl, cereal; marked #94 ....**$45.00**
Bowl, fruit; marked #92...**$40.00**
Bowl, mixing; marked #6, 6" **$30.00**
Butter dish, marked #72..**$50.00**
Casserole, individual; marked #73, from $60 to..........**$75.00**
Casserole, marked #74, lg..**$60.00**

Cookie jar, marked #66, from $200 to **$250.00**
Corn holder, marked #79 ....**$32.00**
Creamer, gold trim, marked USA, from $65 to...........**$90.00**
Creamer, marked #70..**$25.00**
Mug, marked #69..**$45.00**
Plate, marked #68, 10"..**$36.00**
Plate, marked #93, 8"...**$15.00**
Platter, marked #96, 12"..**$52.00**
Salt & pepper shakers, Indian corn, pr, from $60 to ..**$65.00**
Salt & pepper shakers, lg, pr....................................**$30.00**
Salt & pepper shakers, sm, pr **$20.00**
Snack set, 4 mugs & 4 plates, MIB **$435.00**
Sugar bowl, marked #70, gold trim...........................**$90.00**
Sugar bowl, white corn, gold trim, marked USA, from $60 to...**$75.00**
Sugar shaker, white corn w/gold, from $85 to **$100.00**
Teapot, marked #75, w/gold, 30-oz...........................**$175.00**

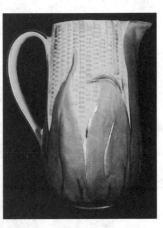

Corn, pitcher, #71, $65.00; with gold trim, $140.00. (Photo courtesy Duane and Janice Vanerbilt)

Lobster Ware

French casserole, stick handle, lobster finial, marked #900, sm **$15.00**

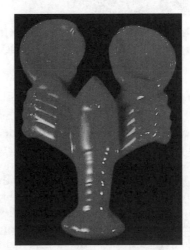

Lobsterware, spoon holder, marked USA, 7¼", $175.00.

Mustard jar, lobster finial, marked #926......................**$80.00**
Salt & pepper shakers, lobster claws, 5½", pr.............**$20.00**
Snack jar, tab handles, lobster finial, marked #925...**$250.00**
Spoon holder, lobster figural w/claw spoon rests, 8½" .**$175.00**
Sugar bowl, tab handles, lobster finial, marked #907.**$25.00**

Valencia

Ashtray..$17.00
Bud vase..$22.00
Candle holders, bulb, pr, from $26 to....................$28.00
Candle holders, tripod, pr, from $32 to $34.00
Carafe, w/lid, from $40 to $45.00
Coaster...$17.00
Coffeepot, demitasse; from $25 to.........................$30.00
Creamer & sugar bowl, w/lid $35.00
Egg cup, from $14 to..$17.00
Mustard jar, w/lid...$45.00
Nappie, 9½"...$25.00
Pie plate, 10½"..$25.00
Pitcher, ball jug, marked USA $40.00
Plate, chop; 15"...$36.00
Plate, deep, 8"...$20.00
Plate, 10"..$17.00
Plate, 7¾"...$14.00
Plate, 9¾"...$16.00
Salt & pepper shakers, pr......................................$24.00
Spoon, from $30 to...$35.00
Teacup & saucer..$25.00
Teapot, regular..$55.00
Tray, utility...$28.00

Valencia: Syrup pitcher with lid, $48.00; Water pitcher with lid, $55.00. (Photo courtesy Duane and Janice Vanderbilt)

Sheet Music

Flea markets are a good source for buying old sheet music, and prices are usually very reasonable. Most examples can be bought for less than $5.00. More often than not, it is collected for reasons other than content. Some of the cover art was done by well-known illustrators like Rockwell, Christy, Barbelle, and Starmer, and some collectors like to zero in on their particular favorite, often framing some of the more attractive examples. Black Americana collectors can find many good examples with Black entertainers featured on the covers and the music reflecting an ethnic theme.

You may want to concentrate on music by a particularly renowned composer, for instance George M. Cohan or Irving Berlin. Or you may find you enjoy covers featuring famous entertainers and movie stars from the forties through the sixties. At any rate, be critical of condition when you buy or sell sheet music. As is true with any item of paper, tears, dog ears, or soil will greatly reduce its value.

If you'd like a more thorough listing of sheet music and prices, we recommend *The Sheet Music Reference and Price Guide* by Anna Marie Guiheen and Marie-Reine A. Pafik and *The Collector's Guide to Sheet Music* by Debbie Dillon.

Afraid, Fred Rose, Rex Allen photo cover, 1949...........$5.00
Ain't It Kind of Wonderful, Wilder, Movie: The World's Greatest Lover, Gene Wilder photo cover, 1977.....$5.00
Alice in Wonderland, Irving Berlin, Movie: Puttin' on the Ritz, 1929 ....$15.00
All I've Got To Get Now Is My Man, Cole Porter, Movie: Panama Hattie, 1942 ....$8.00
Am I Blue, Grant Clarke & Harry Akst, Movie: On With the Show, 1929 ....$8.00
Amapola, Joseph M Lacalle, Jimmy Dorsey photo cover, 1924 ....$5.00
And They Say He Went to College, Seymour Furth, Eddie Foy photo cover, 1907 ....$10.00
Aren't You Glad You're You, Johnny Burke/Jimmy Van Heusen, Movie: The Bells of St Mary's, Bing Crosby photo cover, 1945...$10.00
Around the Corner, Gus Kahn & Art Kassel, Kassel photo cover, 1930 ....$5.00
At the Red Rose Cotillion, Frank Loesser, Movie: Where's Charley?, cariture of Ray Bolger, 1948.....................$5.00
Autumn Leaves, Joseph Kosma, Johnny Mercer & Jacques Prevert, Roger Williams photo cover, 1950.............$3.00
Baia, Art Barroso, Ray Gilbert, Movie: The Three Caballeros, (Disney), 1945 ....$15.00
Bananas, Marvin Hamlisch, Movie: Bananas, Woody Allen photo cover, 1971 ....$5.00
Barking Dog, Al Stillman, Crew Cuts photo cover, 1954 ..$5.00
Because of You, Hammerstein/Wilkinson, Movie: I Was American Spy, Tony Bennett photo cover, 1940 ....$3.00
Because You're Beautiful, BG DeSylva, Lew Brown & Ray Henderson, Musical: Three Cheers.........................$5.00
Beware, Mort Greene & Harry Revel, Movie: Call Out the Marines, 1942 ....$5.00
Blue Danube, Anne Caldwell & Jerome Kern, Musical: Good Morning Dearie, 1921 ....$10.00
Bluebirds in the Moonlight, Robin & Rainger, Movie: Gulliver's Travels, 1937...$10.00
Boy Named Sue, Shel Silverstein, Johnny Cash photo cover, 1969..$5.00
Brazil, Bob Russell, Movie: Amigos (Disney), 1939 ....$15.00
Bring Back the Thrill, Ruth Poll & Peter Rugolo, Eddie Fisher photo cover, 1950 ....$3.00
By Candle Light, Cole Porter, Movie: You Never Know .$5.00
By the Time I Get to Phoenix, Jim Webb, Glen Campbell photo cover, 1967 ....$3.00
Careless Rhapsody, Lorenz Hart & Richard Rodgers, Movie: All's Fair, 1942 ....$5.00
Charanga, Hal David & Marco Rizo, Merv Griffin photo cover $3.00
Chicago, Fred Fisher (signed), 1922..........................$35.00

Cocoanut Grove, Harry Owens, Movie: Cocoanut Grove, 1938......**$5.00**

Cold, Cold Heart, Hank Williams, Tony Bennett photo cover, 1951......**$3.00**

Could I Come to You?, CL Mittell, Billy Argall photo cover, 1913......**$5.00**

Crying for You, Ned Miller & Chester Cohn, Barney Rapp photo cover, 1923......**$3.00**

Cuban Pete, Jose Norman, Desi Arnaz & King Sisters photo cover, 1946......**$5.00**

Darling I, BC Hilliam, Musical: Buddies, 1919......**$10.00**

Darling Sue, Sterling, Harry Van Tilzer......**$3.00**

Darn That Dream, Eddie DeLange & Jimmy Van Heusen, Joe Venuti photo cover, 1939......**$3.00**

Dawn, Mack David & Jerry Livingston, Jaye P Morgan photo cover......**$5.00**

Destiny, Bryan & Spencer, Movie: Destiny, Dorothy Phillips photo cover, 1919......**$3.00**

Divorce Me COD, Merle Travis & Cliffe Stone, Lawrence Welk photo cover, 1946......**$3.00**

Doctor Dolittle, Bricusse, Movie: Doctor Dolittle, Rex Harrison photo cover, 1967......**$3.00**

Don Juan, Lee & Axt, Movie: Don Juan, John Barrymore & Mary Astor photo cover, 1927......**$10.00**

Down Among the Sheltering Palms, James Brockman & Abe Olman, Pied Pipers photo cover, 1915......**$5.00**

Down in Chattanooga, Irving Berlin, 1913......**$15.00**

Dreamer's Holiday, Kim Gannon & Mabel Wayne, Perry Como photo cover, 1949......**$5.00**

Dreamy Hawaiian Moon, Harry Owens, Movie: Cocoanut Grove, 1938......**$5.00**

Eileen, Ernest J Schuster, Schuster photo cover, 1912...**$10.00**

Eli, Eli, Jacob Koppel Sandler, Sandler photo cover, 1919 ..**$5.00**

Everybody's Talkin', Fred Neil, Movie: Midnight Cowboy, Harry Nilsson photo cover, 1968 ......**$2.00**

Fairy Tales, BC Hilliam, Musical: Buddies, 1919 ......**$10.00**

Fire & Rain, James Taylor, Taylor photo cover, 1969....**$5.00**

Five Minutes More, Sammy Cahn & Jule Styne, Bob Crosby photo cover, 1946 ......**$5.00**

For Once in My Life, Miller & Murden, Tony Bennett photo cover, 1967 ......**$5.00**

Forever, Buddy Kellen, Little Dippers photo cover, 1960 .**$5.00**

Furlough Waltz, Claude Marquis, Guy Lombardo photo cover, 1945......**$5.00**

Gangster's Warning, Gene Autry, Curt Poulton photo cover, 1932......**$5.00**

Ghost of the Violin, Kalmer & Snyder, Courtney Sisters photo cover, 1912 ......**$10.00**

Gigi, Alan J Lerner & Frederick Loewe, Movie: Gigi, 1958 .**$5.00**

Go Away Little Girl, Carole King, Donny Osmond photo cover, 1962 ......**$5.00**

Goddess, Murry & Richmand, Anita Stewart photo cover, 1915 ......**$10.00**

Good Man Is Hard To Find, Eddie Green, Jack Norworth photo cover, 1918 ......**$8.00**

Good Night Boat, Caldwell & Kern, Musical: The Night Boat, 1920 ......**$10.00**

Great Divide, Gimbel & Schifrin, Movie: Bullitt, Steve McQueen & Jacqueline Bisset photo cover, 1969......$5.00

Gypsy, Billy Reid, 1947, Sammy Kaye photo cover, 1947..**$5.00**

Harrigan, George M Cohan, Movie: Yankee Doodle Dandy, James Cagney & Cohan photo cover, 1933 ......**$15.00**

Haunting Waltz, MJ Gunsky & Nat Goldstein, Musical: Angel Face, 1921......**$5.00**

He's So Unusual, Sherman & Lewis & Abner Silver, Movie: Sweetie, Helen Kane photo cover, 1939 ......**$5.00**

Heart, Richard Adler & Jerry Ross, Musical: Damn Yankees, 1955......**$5.00**

Heat Wave, Irving Berlin, Musical: Easter Parade, 1933..**$10.00**

Here's a Hand, Lorenz Hart & Richard Rodgers, Movie: All's Fair, 1942......**$5.00**

Hitchy Koo, L Wolfe Gilbert & Lewis F Muir, Maude Rockwell photo cover, 1912......**$10.00**

Home on the Range, Nick Manoloff, Jackie Heller photo cover, 1935 ......**$5.00**

Honolulu Moon, Fred Lawrence, Ray West photo cover, 1926 ......**$5.00**

How About You?, Freed & Lane, Movie: Babes on Broadway, 1941......**$3.00**

I Always Knew, Cole Porter, Movie: Something To Shout About, 1943 ......**$5.00**

I Beg of You, Elvis Presley, 1957 ......**$20.00**

I Don't Want the Moon To Shine When I Make Love, Burke, Mae Burke photo cover, 1912......**$10.00**

I Double Dare You, Terry Shand & Jimmy Eaton, Rudy Vallee photo cover, 1937 ......**$5.00**

I Hate Men, Cole Porter, Musical: Kiss Me Kate, 1948..**$5.00**

I Hear a Dream, Leo Robin & Ralph Rainger, Movie: Gulliver's Travels, 1939......**$5.00**

I Love You, Cole Porter, Movie: Mexican Hayride, 1943 ..**$5.00**

I Love You Kid, Diamond & Stone, May Burke photo cover, 1912 ......**$10.00**

I Surrender Dear, Gordon Clifford & Harry Harris, Bing Crosby photo cover, 1931 ......**$5.00**

I Used To Be Color Blind, Irving Berlin, Fred Astaire & Ginger Rogers photo cover, 1938......**$15.00**

I Want To Learn Jazz Dance, Gene Buck & Dave Stamper, Musical: Ziegfeld Follies, 1918......**$15.00**

I Watch the Love Parade, Oto Harbach & Jerome Kern, Musical: The Cat & the Fiddle, 1931 ......**$10.00**

I Wrote a Song for You, Dolph Singer & Sam Morrison, Movie: Summer Wives, 1936......**$5.00**

I'd Like To Make a Million, Walt, Warner & George Weilder, Nat King Cole photo cover, 1949 ......**$5.00**

If You Are But a Dream, by Moe Jaffe, Frank Fulton, and Nat Bonx, Sinatra on cover, 1941, $3.00. (Photo courtesy Guiheen & Pafik)

I'll Follow You, Melville J Gideon, Rock & Fulton signed photo cover, 1912 ....**$10.00**

I'll Go Home With Bonnie Jean, Alan J Lerner & Fredrick Loewe, Movie: Brigadoon, 1947 ....**$5.00**

I'm an Indian Too, Irving Berlin, Movie: Annie Get Your Gun, 1946.............................**$5.00**

I'm at the Mercy of Love, Benny Davis & Fred J Coots, Musical: Cotton Club Parade, 1936.........................**$8.00**

I'm Hans Christian Anderson, Frank Loesser, Movie: Hans Christian Anderson, Danny Kaye photo cover, 1951 .**$5.00**

I'm on the Water Wagon Now, John W Bratton, Frank Daniels photo cover, 1903 ....**$5.00**

I'm Shooting High, Jimmy McHugh, Lainie Kazan photo cover, 1963 ....**$3.00**

I've Got My Washing To Do, Al Moritz, Janette Davis photo cover, ...**$5.00**

I've Gotta Be Me, Walter Marks, Musical: Golden Rainbow, Steve Lawrence & Eydie Gorme photo cover, 1967 ....**$3.00**

If I Had My Way, Lou Klein & James Kendis, Woody Herman photo cover, 1913 ....**$5.00**

If I Thought You Wouldn't Tell, Irving Berlin, 1909 ...**$10.00**

If You Knew Suzie Like I Know Suzie, BG DeSylva, Musical: Big Boy, Al Jolson photo cover, 1925 ....**$20.00**

If You Were Mine, Al Bryan & George W Meyers, Movie: Twin Beds, 1929 ....**$5.00**

In a Kingdom of My Own, George M Cohan.............**$10.00**

In a World of My Own, Bob Hilliard & Sammy Fain, Movie: Alice in Wonderland, 1951 ....**$10.00**

In the Middle of a Kiss, Sam Coslow, Movie: College Scandals, Arline Judge photo cover, 1935...............**$5.00**

In the Mood, Andy Razaf & Joe Garland, Glenn Miller photo cover, 1936 ....**$5.00**

Instant Girl, Crawford, Bobby Vee, Jackie Deshannon & Eddie Hodges, 1965 ....**$3.00**

Iron Claw, Benjamin Richmond, Pearl White photo cover, 1916 ....**$10.00**

It Might Have Been, Cole Porter, Movie: Something To Shout About, 1943 ....**$5.00**

It Was Written in the Stars, Leo Robin & Harold Arlen, Movie: Casbah, 1948 ....**$5.00**

It's Home, Jack Yellen & Jay Gorney, Movie: Home, 1942..**$5.00**

It's My Lazy Day, Burnette, Movie: Bordertown Trails, Smiley Burnette photo cover, 1946..............................**$3.00**

It's On, It's Off, Coslow & Siegel, Movie: Double or Nothing, Martha Raye photo cover, 1937 ....**$8.00**

Jealous Heart, Jenny Lou Carson, Al Morgan photo cover, 1944..............................**$3.00**

Jesse James, Jerry Livingston, Eileen Barton photo cover, 1954..............................**$5.00**

Just a Little Angel, Woolfolk & Barron, Musical: Paradise Valley, 1917 ....**$15.00**

Just a Prayer Away, Charles Tobias & David Kapp, Bing Crosby photo cover, 1944 ....**$3.00**

Just As Though You Were Here, Edgar DeLange & John Benson Brooks, Tommy Dorsey photo cover, 1942.............**$5.00**

Just the Way You Are, Billy Joel, 1977 ....**$3.00**

Keating Wheel March, Bryan, Keating Bicycle (advertisment) **$20.00**

Kokomo, Love, Melcher, Phillips & McKenzie, Movie: Cocktails, Tom Cruise photo cover, 1988...............**$3.00**

La Cucaracha, Carl Field, Don Pedro photo cover, 1935 ..**$5.00**

Laura Lee, Meredith Wilson, Vaughn Monroe photo cover, 1951 ....**$2.00**

Learn To Croon, Sam Coslow & Arthur Johnston, Movie: College Humor, Bing Crosby photo cover, 1933 ..**$10.00**

Let's Not Talk About Love, Cole Porter, Movie: Let's Face It, 1943..............................**$5.00**

Let's Take an Old Fashion Walk, Irving Berlin, Musical: Miss Liberty, 1948..............................**$10.00**

Little Angel Told Me So, Sam Coslow, Movie: One Hour Late, Joe Morrison & Helen Twelvetrees photo cover, 1934..............................**$8.00**

Little Arrows, Mike Hazelwood & Albert Hammond, Leapy Lee photo cover, 1968 ....**$2.00**

Little Mother, Erno Rapee & Lew Pollack, Musical: Four Sons, Bob Olsen photo cover, 1928..............................**$10.00**

Little Toot, Allie Wrubel, Movie: Melody Time (Disney), 1948 ....**$10.00**

Look to the Rainbow, EY Harburg & Burton Lane, Movie: Finian's Rainbow, 1946..............................**$5.00**

Lookin' Out My Backdoor, John C Fogerty, Creedence Clearwater Revival photo cover, 1970 ....**$3.00**

Love Me Tender, WW Fosdick & George R Paulton, Elvis Presley photo cover, 1956 ....**$25.00**

Love's First Kiss, Klages, Axt & Mendoza, Movie: A Woman of Affairs, Greta Garbo & John Gilbert photo cover, 1929 ....**$10.00**

Make Believe Island, Nick Kenny, Charles Kenny & Will Grosz, Glenn Miller photo cover, 1940 ....**$5.00**

Man I Love, Ira & George Gershwin, Movie: Strike Up the Band, 1945..............................**$10.00**

Many a New Day, Richard Rodgers & Oscar Hammerstein II, Musical: Oklahoma, 1943 ....**$5.00**

Mary, Mary, Quite Contrary, Frank Loesser & Burton Lane, Movie: Las Vegas Night, Frank Sinatra photo cover, 1941..............................**$5.00**

May I?, Mack Gordon & Harry Revel, Movie: We're Not Dressing, Bing Crosby & Carole Lombard photo cover, 1934..............................**$5.00**

Maybe I'll Cry Over You, Elton Britt, Britt photo cover, 1949..............................**$3.00**

Merry Widow Waltz, Carl Field & Franz Lehar, Glenn Lee photo cover, 1935 ....**$5.00**

Mexico, Charles Wolcott & Ray Gilbert, Movie: The Three Caballeros (Disney), 1945 ....**$10.00**

Mister & Mississippi, Irving Gordon, Patti Page photo cover, 1951..............................**$3.00**

Mister Pollyanna, Johnny Mercer & Hoagy Carmichael, Movie: True to Life, 1943 ....**$5.00**

Mona, Seymour Rici & E Harry Kelly, Bob Hope photo cover, 1938..............................**$5.00**

Moonlight Mood, Harold Adamson & Peter DeRose, King Sisters photo cover, 1942..............................**$4.00**

Moonshine Lullaby, Irving Berlin, Movie: Annie Get Your Gun, 1946..............................**$10.00**

My Brooklyn Love Song, Tibbles & Idress, Movie: If You Knew Suzie, Eddie Cantor photo cover, 1947 ....**$8.00**

My Caravan, Ann Caldwell & Hugo Felix, Musical: The Sweetheart Shop, 1920 ....**$5.00**

My Heart Cries for You, Carl Sigman & Percy Faith, Dinah Shore photo cover, 1950.................................**$5.00**

My Heart Is Unemployed, Harold J Rome, Musical: Sing Out the News, 1938...**$5.00**

My Mammie Rose, E Ray Goetz & Melville J Gidion, Lydia Barry photo cover, 1910 ....**$5.00**

My Meloncholy Baby, Norton, Watson & Burnett, Movie: Birth of the Blues, 1939.................................**$5.00**

My Sweetheart Went Down With the Ship, Roger Lewis & F Henri Klickman, The Sinking of the Titanic photo cover **$75.00**

My Tonia, BG DeSylva, Lew Brown & Ray Henderson, Musical: In Old Arizona, 1928.................................**$5.00**

Never Gonna Dance, Dorothy Fields & Jerome Kern, Movie: Swing Time, Fred Astaire & Ginger Rogers photo cover, 1936...**$5.00**

Night in Mahattan, Leo Robin & Ralph Rainger, Movie: The Big Broadcast of 1937, Jack Benny & many stars, 1936...**$5.00**

No Two People, Frank Loesser, Movie: Hans Christian Andersen, Danny Kaye photo cover, 1951 ....**$10.00**

Not for All the Rice in China, Irving Berlin, Musical: Easter Parade, 1933...**$10.00**

Oh Lady Be Good, Ira & George Gershwin, Movie: Lady Be Good, 1924...**$5.00**

Oh Papa, Oh Daddy, Arthur Robsham, Musical: Hoyt's Review, 1920 ....**$5.00**

Ol' Man River, Oscar Hammerstein II & Jerome Kern, Musical: Ziegfeld's Show Boat, 1927 ....**$10.00**

Old Fashion Girl, Al Jolson, 1922.................................**$10.00**

Old Home Guard, Sherman & Sherman, Movie: Bedknobs & Broomsticks, Angela Lansbury & David Tomlinson, 1971 ....**$3.00**

On the Street Where You Live, Lerner & Lowe, Movie: My Fair Lady, 1956...**$5.00**

Oop Shoop, Shirley Gunter & The Queens, The Crew Cuts photo cover, 1954 ....**$3.00**

Over the Rainbow, EY Harburg & Harold Arlen, Movie: The Wizard of Oz, Judy Garland photo cover, 1939 ...**$35.00**

Painting the Roses Red, Bob Hillard & Sammy Fain, Movie: Alice in Wonderland (Disney), 1951.....................**$10.00**

Paper Dolls, Johnny S Black, Bing Crosby photo cover, 1943 ....**$5.00**

Pecos Bill, Eliot Daniels & Johnny Lange, Movie: Melody Time (Disney), 1948 ....**$10.00**

Personality, Johnny Burke & James Van Heusen, Movie: The Road to Utopia (Disney), 1945 ....**$10.00**

Policeman's Ball, Irving Berlin, Musical: Miss Liberty, 1949 ....**$10.00**

Poor Jud, Richard Rodgers & Oscar Hammerstein II, Musical: Oklahoma, 1943...**$5.00**

Puddin' Head Jones, Alfred Bryan & Lou Handman, Ozzie Nelson photo cover, 1933 ....**$5.00**

Put Me to the Test, Ira Gershwin & Jerome Kern, Movie: Cover Girl, 1944...**$3.00**

Ramblin' Rose, Noel & Joe Sherman, Nat King Cole photo cover, 1962 ....**$3.00**

Ready To Take a Chance Again, Gimbel & Fox, Movie: Foul Play, Chevy Chase & Goldie Hawn photo cover, 1978.........**$5.00**

Ricochet, Larry Coleman, Norman Gimbel & Joe Darion, Theresa Brewer photo cover, 1953.....................**$3.00**

Rockin' Around the Christmas Tree, Johnny Marks, Brenda Lee photo cover, 1958 ....**$3.00**

Rollin' Stone, Mack Gordon, Perry Como photo cover, 1951...**$3.00**

Roses in the Rain, Al Frisch, Fred Wise & Frankie Carle, Frank Sinatra photo cover, 1947.................................**$3.00**

Ruby Tuesday, Mick Jagger & Keith Richards, Rolling Stones photo cover, 1967 ....**$5.00**

Sail Along, Sil'vry Moon, Harry Tobias & Percy Wenrich, Bing Crosby photo cover, 1937.................................**$5.00**

Say When, Jimmie Mercer, Richard Hayes photo cover, 1950...**$3.00**

Second Hand Rose, Grant Carle & James F Hanley, Barbara Streisand photo cover, 1965 ....**$3.00**

Seventy-six Trombones, Meredith Wilson, Movie: Music Man, 1957...**$3.00**

Shall We Dance, Richard Rodgers & Oscar Hammerstein II, Movie: The King & I, 1951.................................**$5.00**

Shot-Gun Boogie, Tennessee Ernie Ford, TE Ford photo cover, 1951 ....**$3.00**

Side by Side, Harry Woods, Dick Jurgens photo cover, 1927 ....**$3.00**

Sing to Me Guitar, Cole Porter, Movie: Mexican Hayride, 1943 ....**$3.00**

Singin' in the Saddle, Sherwin, Ann Sheridan photo cover, 1944...**$3.00**

Sixteen Reasons, Bill & Doree Post, Connie Stevens photo cover, 1959 ....**$3.00**

Small Talk, Richard Alder & Jerry Ross, Musical: Pajama Game, 1954...**$3.00**

Some Day, Brian Hooker & Rudolf Friml, Movie: Vagabond King, Jeannette MacDonald, 1926.....................**$5.00**

Some of These Days, Shelton Brooks, Sophie Tucker photo cover, 1937 ....**$15.00**

Someone Who Cares, Harvey, Movie: Fools, Jason Robards & Katharine Ross photo cover, 1971 ....**$3.00**

Somethin' Stupid, C Carson Parks, Frank & Nancy Sinatra photo cover, 1967 ....**$2.00**

Son of the Sheik, Rudolph Valentino photo cover, 1952 ..**$3.00**

Sooner or Later, Charles Wolcott & Ray Gilbert, Movie: Song of the South (Disney), 1946.................................**$10.00**

South of the Border, Jimmy Kennedy & Michael Carr, Bing Crosby photo cover, 1939 ....**$5.00**

Street of Dreams, Sam Lewis & Victor Young, Jane Froman photo cover, 1932 ....**$3.00**

Sugar Plum, Gus Kahn & Arthur Johnson, Movie: Thanks a Million, Dick Powell photo cover, 1935.................**$5.00**

Sunday, Richard Rodgers & Oscar Hammerstein II, Movie: Flower Drum Song, Nancy Kwan photo cover, 1961 .**$5.00**

Sweet Dreams, Don Gibson, Patsy Cline photo cover, 1955...**$2.00**

Sweet Violets, Cy Cohen & Charles Grean, Dinah Shore photo cover, 1951 ....**$5.00**

Talk to the Animals, Bricusse, Movie: Doctor Dolittle, Rex Harrison photo cover, 1967.................................**$3.00**

Tears on My Pillow, Gene Autry & Fred Rose, Dick Jergens photo cover, 1941 ....$3.00

That Silver Haired Daddy of Mine, Movie: Tumbling Tumbleweeds, 1932 ....$5.00

That's All, Alan Brandt & Bob Haymes, Nat King Cole photo cover, 1952 ....$3.00

Theme From Bullitt, Schifrin, Movie: Bullitt, Steve McQueen & Jacqueline Bisset, 1969 ....$3.00

Theme From the Monkees, Tommy Boyce & Bobby Hart, Monkees photo cover, 1966 ....$5.00

There Once Was a Man, Richard Adler & Jerry Ross, Musical: The Pajama Game, 1954......................$5.00

There She Was, Hoagy Carmichael, Movie: True to Life, 1943......................................$5.00

There's No You, Tom Adair & Hal Hopper, Frank Sinatra photo cover, 1944 ....$3.00

Thing, Charles R Green, Phil Harris photo cover, 1950 ..$5.00

This Is My Song, C Chaplin, Movie: A Countess From Hong Kong, Charlie Chaplin photo cover, 1966.............$10.00

Thumper Song, Bliss, Sour & Manners, Movie: Bambi, 1942 ....$10.00

Till There Was You, Meredith Wilson, Movie: The Music Man, 1950......................$5.00

Together, by DeSylva, Brown, and Henderson, from the movie _Since You Went Away_, 1928, $15.00. (Photo courtesy Guiheen & Pafik)

Tom, Dick or Harry, Cole Porter, Musical: Kiss Me Kate, 1948 ....$5.00

Tonight, Stephen Sondheim & Leonard Bernstein, Movie: West Side Story, 1957......................$5.00

True Confession, Sam Coslow & Fred Hollander, Movie: True Confession, Carole Lombard photo cover, 1937...$10.00

Two Lost Souls, Richard Adler & Jerry Ross, Musical: Damn Yankees, 1955......................$3.00

Ugly Duckling, Frank Loesser, Movie: Hans Christian Andersen, Danny Kaye photo cover, 1951 ....$5.00

Venus, Ed Marshall, Frankie Avalon photo cover,1959 .$3.00

Volare, Mitchell Parish & Domenico Modugno, McGuire Sisters photo cover, 1958......................$3.00

Wait & See, Harry Warren & Johnny Mercer, Movie: The Harvey Girls, Judy Garland photo cover, 1946.....$10.00

Waltz of Memory, John Burger, Movie: It Happens on Ice, 1951......................$5.00

We'll Meet Again, Ross Parker & Hughie Charles, Kate Smith photo cover, 1939 ....$10.00

We're All Together, Leo Robin & Ralph Rainger, Movie: Gulliver's Travels, 1939......................$5.00

Weddin' Day, Clancy Hayes & Carl Kalash, Jack Kilty photo cover, 1949 ....$3.00

What Is a Wife?, Gene Piller & Ruth Roberts, Steve Allen & Garry Moore photo cover, 1955......................$5.00

What More Can I Ask For?, Jack Maxus & Bernard Bierman, Guy Lombardo photo cover, 1946......................$3.00

When I Lost You, Irving Berlin, Sabelle Patricola photo cover, 1912 ....$15.00

When My Dream Boat Comes Home, Cliff Friend & Dave Franklin, Les Brown photo cover, 1936 ....$5.00

When New York Was New York, George M Cohan ...$10.00

When the Saints Go Marching In, Paul Campbell, The Weavers photo cover, 1951......................$3.00

When They Ask About You, Sam H Stept, Joan Brooks photo cover, 1943 ....$3.00

When You Were Sweet Sixteen, James Thornton, Perry Como photo cover, 1932 ....$5.00

Who Knows?, Cole Porter, Movie: Rosalie, 1937...........$5.00

Who's Got the Pain?, Richard Adler & Jerry Ross, Musical: Damn Yankee, 1955......................$5.00

Why Don't You Love Me?, Hank Williams, Williams signed photo, 1950......................$5.00

Why?, Bob Marcucci & Peter DeAngelis, Frankie Avalon signed photo cover, 1969 ....$5.00

Wilhelmina, Mack Gordon & Josef Myrow, Movie: Wabash Avenue, Betty Grable photo cover, 1950 ....$5.00

Will You?, Gene Raymond, Raymond photo cover, 1935...$3.00

Windmills of Your Mind, Michael Legrand & Alan & Marilyn Bergman, Movie: Thomas Crown Affair, 1968........$5.00

Wish You Were Here, Harold Rome, Musical: Wish You Were Here, 1952 ....$5.00

With a Little Bit of Luck, Frederich Loewe & Allan Jay Lerner, Musical: My Fair Lady, 1956......................$5.00

Without a Memory, Robinson, Judy Garland photo cover, 1953 ....$10.00

Wonderful Copenhagen, Frank Loesser, Movie: Hans Christian Andersen, 1951......................$5.00

Would You?, Arthur Freed & Nacio Herb Brown, Movie: San Francisco, 1936......................$10.00

Yes, Virginia, There is a Santa Claus, Joyce Baker, Jose Ferrer photo cover, 1960 ....$5.00

You Belong to My Heart, Augustine Lara & Ray Gilbert, Movie: The Three Caballeros (Disney), 1945 ....$10.00

You Can Do No Wrong, Cole Porter, Movie: The Pirates, 1948......................$5.00

You Can't Be True, Hal Cotton & Ken Griffin, Griffin photo cover, 1948 ....$2.00

You Know How Talk Gets Around, Fred Rose, Eddy Arnold photo cover, 1949 ....$5.00

You Light Up My Life, Joe Brooks, Movie: You Light Up My Life, Didi Conn & Joe Silver photo cover, 1977 .....$3.00

You Only Live Twice, Bricusse & Barry, Movie: You Only Live Twice, Sean Connery photo cover, 1967 ....$3.00

You Two, Sherman & Sherman, Movie: Chitty-Chitty Bang-Bang, Dick Van Dyke & Sally Ann Howes photo cover, 1968 .$3.00

You Won't Be Satisfied, Freddy James & Larry Stock, Perry Como photo cover, 1945 ....$5.00

You're in Love, Newman & Bregman, Movie: Accused of Murder, Gogi Grant photo cover, 1956 ....$3.00

You're My Girl, Sammy Cahn & Jule Styne, Musical: High Button Shoes, 1948 ....**$5.00**

Your Kiss, Auld, Auld & Cates, Movie: To Catch a Thief, Grace Kelly & Cary Grant photo cover, 1955 ....**$3.00**

Yours, Mine & Ours, Sheldon & Karlin, Movie: Yours, Mine & Ours, Henry Fonda & Lucille Ball photo cover, 1968 ..**$8.00**

You're A Grand Old Flag, by George M. Cohan, from the movie *Yankee Doodle Dandy*, Cagney and Cohan on cover, $10.00. (Photo courtesy Guiheen & Pafik)

Shell Pink Glassware

Here's something new to look for this year — lovely soft pink opaque glassware made by the Jeannette Glass Company for only a short time during the late 1950s. Prices, says expert Gene Florence, have been increasing by leaps and bounds! You'll find a wide variance in style from piece to piece, since the company chose shapes from several of their most popular lines to press in the satiny shell pink. Refer to *Collectible Glassware from the 40s, 50s, and 60s,* by Mr. Florence for photos and more information.

Advisors: April and Larry Tvorak (See Directory, Fire-King)

Ashtray, butterfly shape..**$17.50**
Bowl, Florentine, footed, 10"..**$27.50**
Bowl, fruit; Floragold, footed, 9"..................................**$25.00**
Bowl, fruit; Gondola, 17½"..**$32.00**
Bowl, Lombardi, plain center, 4-toe, 11"...................**$28.00**
Bowl, Napco #2250, footed **$15.00**
Bowl, pheasants at base, footed, 8"...........................**$45.00**
Bowl, wedding; w/lid, 6½"...**$22.50**
Bowl, wedding; w/lid, 8"..**$27.50**
Cake plate, Anniversary **$150.00**
Cake stand, Harp, 10"..**$32.00**
Candle holders, eagles as 3 feet, pr **$70.00**
Candle holders, 2-light, pr **$75.00**
Candy dish, Floragold, 4-footed, 5¼"..........................**$20.00**
Candy dish, square, w/lid, 6½" **$30.00**
Candy jar, Grapes, 4-footed, w/lid, 5½" **$20.00**
Celery tray, 3-part, Jeannette **$35.00**
Cigarette box, butterfly finial......................................**$125.00**
Cookie jar, w/lid, 6½x5¾", from $125 to **$175.00**
Creamer, Baltimore Pear..**$15.00**
Cup, punch; 5-oz **$6.00**
Honey jar, beehive shape, w/lid & clear plastic spoon, from $60 to...**$70.00**

Pitcher, Thumbprint, footed, 24-oz.............................**$30.00**
Powder jar, rose finial on lid, 4¾".................................**$45.00**
Punch bowl, w/base, 12 cups & ladle, Jeannette, 15-pc..**$185.00**
Punch ladle, pink plastic..**$20.00**
Relish, Vineyard, 4-part, octagonal, 12" **$40.00**
Stem, sherbet; Thumbprint, 5-oz **$15.00**
Stem, water goblet; Thumbprint, 8-oz.........................**$12.50**
Sugar bowl, Baltimore Pear, footed, open.................**$11.00**
Tray, Harp, 2-handled, 12½x9¾".....................................**$52.50**
Tray, snack; w/cup indent, 7¾x10"...............................**$9.00**
Tray, Venetian, 6-part, 16½"...**$45.00**
Vase, cornucopia, 5"..**$18.00**
Vase, heavy bottom, 9"...**$85.00**
Vase, 7" **$35.00**

Shirley Temple

Born April 23, 1928, Shirley Jane Temple danced and smiled her way into the hearts of America in the movie *Stand Up and Cheer*. Many, many successful roles followed and by the time Shirley was eight years old, she was #1 at the box offices around the country. Her picture appeared in publications almost daily, and any news about her was news indeed. Mothers dressed their little daughters in clothing copied after hers and coifed them with Shirley hairdos.

The extent of her success was mirrored in the unbelievable assortment of merchandise that saturated the retail market. Dolls, coloring books, children's clothing and jewelry, fountain pens, paper dolls, stationery, and playing cards are just a few examples of the hundreds of items that were available. Shirley's face was a common sight on the covers of magazines as well as in the advertisements they contained, and she was featured in hundreds of articles.

Though she had been retired from the movies for nearly a decade, she had two successful TV series in the late fifties, *The Shirley Temple Story-Book* and *The Shirley Temple Show*. Her reappearance caused new interest in some of the items that had been so popular during her childhood, and many were reissued.

Always interested in charity and community service, Shirley became actively involved in a political career in the late sixties, serving at both the state and national levels.

If you're interested in learning more about her, we recommend *Shirley Temple Dolls and Collectibles* by Patricia R. Smith; *Toys, Antique and Collectible,* by David Longest; and *Shirley in the Magazines* by Gen Jones.

Note: All of the pin-back buttons we describe below have been reproduced, so has the cobalt glassware with Shirley's likeness. Beware!

Advisor: Gen Jones (See Directory, Character and Personality Collectibles)

Newsletter: *Lollipop News*
P.O. Box 6203
Oxnard, CA 93031; Dues: $14 per year

Newsletter: *The Shirley Temple Collectors News*
8811 Colonial Rd.
Brooklyn, NY 11209; Dues: $20 per year; checks payable to
Rita Dubas

Ad sheet, from Sears catalog, 1936, NM **$10.00**
Autograph, as adult, common **$10.00**
Barrette, pink, NM **$20.00**
Bell, w/photo **$17.00**
Birthday card puzzle, Hallmark, 1986, M..................**$12.50**
Book, Breck Shampoo & NBC, storybook, M **$75.00**
Book, Heidi, by Johanna Spyri, Shirley Temple edition,
    w/dust jacket, NM..**$35.00**
Book, Shirley Temple, by Jeanine Basinger, EX..........**$20.00**
Book, Shirley Temple in the Little Colonel, Saalfield #1895,
    1935, 4½x5"..**$30.00**
Book, Shirley Temple's Favorite Tales of Long Ago, 1958,
    hardcover, 8x11", EX+ **$20.00**
Book, Shirley Temple's 21st Birthday Album, NM **$20.00**
Book, The Story of Shirley Temple, Big Little Book #1089,
    1934, M **$45.00**
Book, The Story of Shirley Temple, Saalfield #1319, 1934,
    softcover, 4½x4¾" **$30.00**
Book cover, Shirley w/dolls, 1930s, NM **$10.00**
Booklet, theater promotion item, 1935, M..................**$40.00**
Box, shows Shirley in polka-dot dress w/white collar, for sta-
    tionery, 1936, NM **$35.00**
Bracelet, w/3 charms, 1936, NM..................................**$45.00**
Bridge cards, MIB (sealed) **$100.00**
Bust, green chalkware, 12", minimum value.............**$500.00**
Calendar, 1977, Liberty, Shirley photo, M **$7.50**
Calendar, 1990, Shirley photo each month, M **$15.00**
Cereal bowl, white portrait on cobalt glass, 1930s, original
    only **$60.00**
Cereal box backs, 1930s, set of 12............................**$150.00**
Cigar bands, ca 1985, set of 10....................................**$15.00**
Clothes hanger, blue cardboard, 1934, M **$65.00**
Coloring book, Saalfield/Artcraft #4584, M................**$20.00**
Dish, figural at center, Shirley Temple Collectors'
    Convention, 1992, 6¾" **$20.00**
Doll, celluloid, all original, Japan, 5", M....................**$185.00**

Doll, Ideal, 1957, 36", EX/NM, $1,300.00 at auction. (Photo courtesy McMasters Doll Auctions)

Doll, plastic & vinyl, all original, 1982-83, 12", M.......**$40.00**

Doll, plastic & vinyl, all original, 1982-83, 8", M.........**$30.00**
Doll, vinyl, all original, 1950s, 12", M........................**$225.00**
Doll, vinyl, all original, 1950s, 15", M........................**$265.00**
Doll, vinyl, all original, 1950s, 17", M........................**$325.00**
Doll, vinyl, all original, 1950s, 19", M........................**$400.00**
Doll, vinyl, all original, 1950s, 36", M.....................**$1,600.00**
Doll, vinyl, all original, 1973, 16", M..........................**$125.00**
Doll, vinyl, Montgomery Ward, all original, 1972, 17", M..**$165.00**
Doll, vinyl, Montgomery Ward, 1972, 17", played with, EX..**$45.00**
Fan, shows Shirley as teen w/RC Cola, M **$20.00**
Figurine, porcelain, Nostalgia, 1982, M......................**$75.00**
Figurine, salt, 1930s, 4", EX..**$75.00**
Figurine, salt glaze w/red-flocked dress, marked Shirley
    Temple, 6½", very common......................................**$40.00**
Figurine, Shirley in Blue Bird, painted porcelain, Danbury
    Mint, 4½", M..**$25.00**
Hair bow card, shows Shirley on swing, 1930s, NM ..**$35.00**
Hang tag, Shirley Temple Slippers & Sandles, head portrait,
    M **$20.00**
Hankerchief, Littlest Rebel, 1936, M............................**$38.00**
Iron-on transfer, Shirley w/bear, M..............................**$6.00**
Magazine, Collier's, January 19, 1935, EX..................**$20.00**
Magazine, Doll World, 1993, Shirley on cover, w/article,
    M **$5.00**

Magazine, *Film Pictorial*, birthday issue, EX, $30.00. (Photo courtesy Pat Smith)

Magazine, Hit Parader, 1946, VG................................**$15.00**
Magazine, Movie Mirror, December 1934, Shirley at Christmas
    time, M..**$45.00**
Mug, white portrait on cobalt glass, original only **$40.00**
Paper dolls, Dell Birthday Book, 1935, uncut, EX....**$100.00**
Paper dolls, Saalfield #1715, Shirley Temple Standing Dolls,
    1935, uncut, minimum value **$150.00**
Paper dolls, Whitman #1976, 1986, uncut, M..............**$15.00**
Pen & pencil set, 1930s, minimum value....................**$75.00**
Plate, Baby Take a Bow..**$65.00**
Plate, Wee Willie Winkie, Danbury Mint, 1990, 8", MIB....**$40.00**
Pocket mirror, 1935, 1¾x2¼", EX................................**$75.00**
Program, Tournament of Roses, 1939, 38 pages, 11x8½" ..**$20.00**
Puzzle, jigsaw, Springbok, 500-pc, NMIB **$10.00**
Record, Dumbo, LP, 1960, NM......................................**$15.00**
Record, Remember Shirley, 20th Century Records, 1973, set
    of 2, M..**$25.00**
Record, Sing With Shirley Temple, LP, M, from $25 to......**$30.00**
Ring, Shirley's picture on disk w/scalloped edge, 1930s..**$50.00**
School tablet, 1935, M..**$40.00**

Sheet music, Animal Crackers in My Soup, from Curly Top, shows Shirley in Heidi dress, EX..........................**$20.00**

Sheet music, Goodnight My Love, from Stowaway, 1936, EX..**$15.00**

Sheet music, Our Little Girl, 1936, VG........................**$14.00**

Spoon, silverplate w/photo on handle......................**$12.50**

Tablet, Shirley w/kitten, 1935, unused, NM................**$35.00**

Tea set, pink plastic & metal, 1959, 9-pc..................**$150.00**

Valentine, I've Gone Overboard, 1930s, NM **$4.00**

Frosted w/gold designs, $6 to **$8.00**

General, w/enameled design, $2 to **$3.00**

General advertising, $3 to.....................................**$4.00**

General etched designs, $5 to..............................**$7.50**

General porcelain, $4 to.......................................**$6.00**

General tourist, $2 to..**$3.00**

General w/frosted designs, from $3 to **$4.00**

General w/gold designs, from $6 to **$8.00**

Inside eyes, from $5 to..**$7.50**

Pitcher, cobalt with photo in white, 4½", $40.00.

Liquor store advertising, Hi-Way Liquors, Frederick MD, in fired-on red, $4.00.

Shot Glasses

Shot glasses come in a wide variety of colors and designs. They're readily available, inexpensive, and they don't take a lot of room to display. Most sell for $5.00 and under, except cut glass, for which you would probably have to pay $100.00. Carnival glass examples go for about $50.00, pressed glass for about $75.00. Colored glass, those with etching or gold trim, or one that has an unusual shape — squared or barrel form, for instance — fall into the $3.00 to $7.00 range. Several advertising shot glasses, probably the most common type of all, are described in our listings. Soda advertising is unusual and may drive the value up to about $12.50 to $15.00.

Both new and older glasses alike sell for a little more in the Western part of the country. One-of-a-kind items or oddities are a bit harder to classify, especially sample glasses. Many depend on the elaborateness of their designs as opposed to basic lettering. These values are only estimates and should be used as a general guide. The club welcomes your suggestions and comments. For more information, we recommend *Shot Glasses: An American Tradition*, by Mark Pickvet.

Note: Values for shot glasses in good condition are represented by the low end of our ranges, while the high end reflects estimated values for examples in mint condition.

Advisor: Mark Pickvet (See Directory, Shot Glasses)

Club: The Shot Glass Club of America
Mark Pickvet, Editor
5071 Watson Dr.
Flint, MI 48506. Non-profit organization publishes 12 newsletters per year. Subscription: $6; sample: $1

Mary Gregory, from $100 to **$150.00**

Nudes, from $20 to...**$25.00**

Plain, w/or w/out flutes, from 50¢ to **$1.00**

Pop or soda advertising, from $12.50 to..................**$15.00**

Rounded European designs w/gold rims, from $4 to...**$5.00**

Ruby flashed, from $30 to....................................**$40.00**

Square, general, from $5 to..................................**$7.50**

Square w/etching, from $7.50 to **$10.00**

Square w/pewter, from $12.50 to **$15.00**

Square w/2-tone bronze & pewter, from $15 to........**$17.50**

Standard glass w/pewter, from $7.50 to..................**$10.00**

Taiwan tourist, from $1 to....................................**$2.00**

Tiffany, Galle or fancy art, from $500 to..................**$750.00**

Turquoise & gold tourist, from $5 to **$7.50**

Whiskey or beer advertising, modern, from $4 to........**$5.00**

Whiskey sample, from $25 to **$250.00**

19th-century cut patterns, from $25 to....................**$35.00**

Silhouette Pictures

These novelty pictures are familiar to everyone. Even today a good number of them are still around, and you'll often see them at flea markets and co-ops. They were very popular in their day and never expensive, and because they were made for so many years (the twenties through the fifties), many variations are available. Though the glass in some is flat, others were made with curved glass. Backgrounds may be foil, a scenic print, hand tinted, or plain. Sometimes dried flowers were added as accents. But the characteristic common to them all is that the subject matter is reverse painted on the glass. People (even complicated groups), scenes, ships, and animals were popular themes. Though quite often the silhouette was done in solid black to create a look similar to the nineteenth-century cut silhouettes, colors were sometimes used as well.

In the twenties, making tinsel art pictures became a popular pastime. Ladies would paint the outline of their subjects on the back of the glass and use crumpled tinfoil as a background. Sometimes they would tint certain areas of the glass, making the foil appear to be colored. This type is popular with with today's collectors.

If you'd like to learn more about this subject, we recommend *The Encyclopedia of Silhouette Collectibles on Glass* and *1996–97 Price Guide for Encyclopedia of Silhouette Collectibles on Glass* by Shirley Mace.

Advisor: Shirley Mace (See Directory, Silhouette Pictures)

Convex Glass

Colonial couple playing horn & viola, BG 45-170, Benton Glass Co..**$25.00**
Couple in garden archway, BG 68-139, marked Copyright Morris & Bendien, NY, Benton Glass Co..............**$20.00**
Cowboy & girl on horseback, black silhouettes on glass, multicolor print background, BG 45-208, Benton Glass Co..**$27.00**
Equestrian jumping fence, PW 5D-4, marked Hand-Painted Peter Watson's Studio **$20.00**
Fishing boy w/girl & dog on pier, BG 45-110, Benton Glass Co..**$32.00**
Lady playing piano w/girl dancing, BG 68-8B, Benton Glass Co..**$60.00**

Lady with outstretched arm looking at birdcage, Benton Glass, 6x8", $38.00. (Photo courtesy Shirley and Ray Mace)

Lady w/toes in water under willow tree, LE 6D-1, w/sticker marked Edna Lewis Studios, Pequot Lakes MN, round **$18.00**
Lady's portrait, painted white lace on glass, print portrait background, BG 45-145, Benton Glass Co **$20.00**
Sleigh ride w/tall pine tree, multicolor print background w/advertising, ER 45-3, CE Erickson Co **$30.00**
Snowland Splendor, BA 45-2, Baco Glass Plaque, copyright 1950 ....**$30.00**
This Little Piggy, BG 68-100, Benton Glass Co **$38.00**
Tropical island w/palm trees, BW 3D-1, marked Guaranteed Made From Real Butterfly Wings, round..............**$24.00**
Venetian canal scene, black painted glass w/multicolor print background, OH 45-1, marked Made in USA Ohio Art Co **$18.00**

Wonderful Mother poem, BG 68-130, marked Litho in USA, Benton Glass Co **$35.00**

Flat Glass

A Spanish Dance, BB 710-26, Buckbee-Brehm Co, 1930s.**$30.00**
Amourettes, RI 55-33, from series of 4, marked Copyright C & A Richards **$30.00**
At the Gate, DE 45-26, couple at garden gate w/cottage beyond, foil background, Deltex Co, 1930s **$22.00**
Beauty Secrets, RE 912-19, mate to Vanity Fair, Reliance ..**$40.00**

Blossom Time, Reliance, $30.00. (Photo courtesy Shirley and Ray Mace)

Boy fishing, FI44-2, dried & pressed flowers on background, Fisher **$18.00**
Colonial couple, man kissing lady's hand, FI 44-8, marked Made With California Wild Flowers, Fisher **$20.00**
Colonial lady in elaborate gown, detailed painted glass, plain background, MF 2116-17, signed Steinbrink........**$70.00**
Colors That Never Run, US flag w/advertising, marked Made in USA, Forever, plastic frame **$12.00**
Cosmos & Physalis, RE 912-50, Reliance **$25.00**
Four Seasons Spring, by Fidus, RI 35-720, marked C & A Richards, Boston MA **$30.00**
Gleam O'Gold Silhouettes Springtime of Life, GG 56-3..**$35.00**
Happiness poem by Wilbur Nesbit, VO 711-1, signed Zula Kenyon, marked copyright Emma E Koehler, PF Volland **$50.00**
Huckleberry Finn, No 6816, multicolor painted fishing boy w/geese, w/calendar dated 1939, metal frame, Newton Mfg..**$30.00**
Lady at spinning wheel, NE 68-3, Newton Mfg..........**$20.00**
Lady Faire, RE 57-126, clear wrinkled cellophane background, Reliance **$18.00**
Lady w/afghan hound standing by lake, DE 810-19, foil background, Deltex Co, 1930s....................................**$35.00**
Land of the Free, Western scout & covered wagon, w/thermometer, NE 57-14, Newton Mfg **$22.00**
Lantern Garden in Japan, RE 34-116, mate to Tea Garden in Japan, Reliance..**$12.00**
Little Red Ridng Hood, RE 810-15, Reliance..............**$35.00**
Love Letter, BB 46-3, marked Copyright Buckbee-Brehm Co, 1930 ....**$23.00**
Masted ships at sea, marked Guaranteed hand painted & real exotic butterfly wings, Made in London **$40.00**
Mother (No 53 silhouette), w/poem, marked Copyright Photoplating Co, Minneapolis, 1932....................**$20.00**

Out Where the West Begins, cowboys at campfire, mountain background, NE 810-4, metal frame, Newton Mfg..**$28.00**

Souvenir Yellowstone Park, Wyomic-Haynes Inc, cowboy & horse overlooking mountains & waterfall, NE 45-19, Newton Mfg..**$18.00**

Spring in the Park, RE 44-87, mate to Sunshine & Shower, Reliance **$18.00**

Tulip Time, RE 711-34, mate to Double Dutch, Reliance..**$30.00**

Silverplated Flatware

When buying silverplated flatware, pattern and condition are very important. Monogrammed and worn pieces are worth 30% to 50% of listed prices. Replating can be very expensive. Matching services often advertise in certain trade papers and can be very helpful in helping you locate the items you're looking for. One of the best sources we are aware of is *The Antique Trader*; they're listed with the trade papers in the back of this book.

If you'd like to learn more about the subject, we recommend *Silverplated Flatware Patterns* by Davis and Deibel.

Advisor: Rick Spencer (See Directory, Regal China)

Adam, 1917, dinner knife, Oneida Community..............**$4.00**
Adam, 1917, tablespoon, Oneida Community..............**$3.00**
Adam, 1917, teaspoon, Oneida Community..................**$2.00**
Adoration, 1930, dinner fork, International **$3.00**
Adoration, 1930, sugar spoon, International..................**$3.00**
Adoration, 1930, teaspoon, International **$2.00**
Alhambra, 1907, cold meat fork, International...........**$12.00**
Alhambra, 1907, pickle fork, long twisted handle, International **$10.00**
Ambassador, 1919, demitasse spoon, 1847 Rogers........**$7.00**
Ambassador, 1919, dinner knife, hollow handle, International **$5.00**
Ambassador, 1919, ice cream fork, 1847 Rogers........**$18.00**
Ambassador, 1919, luncheon fork, International...........**$4.00**
Ambassador, 1919, luncheon knife, solid handle, International **$2.50**
Ambassador, 1919, master butter knife, International...**$3.00**
Ambassador, 1919, round soup spoon, 1847 Rogers **$9.00**
Ambassador, 1919, sugar spoon, International..............**$4.00**
Anniversary, 1923, dinner fork, notched handle, International **$4.00**
Anniversary, 1923, round soup spoon, International....**$5.00**
Anniversary, 1923, tablespoon, International.................**$5.00**
Banbury (aka Brookwood), 1950, dinner fork, Oneida..**$4.00**
Bouquet (aka Embassy), 1939, master butter knife, International **$3.00**
Carolina, 1914, berry spoon, Holmes & Edwards **$20.00**
Carolina, 1914, cream ladle, Holmes & Edwards........**$15.00**
Carolina, 1914, dinner knife, hollow handle, Holmes & Edwards **$8.00**
Carolina, 1914, luncheon fork, Holmes & Edwards......**$5.00**
Carolina, 1914, tomato server, Holmes & Edwards.....**$20.00**
Cavalcade, 1946, individual butter knife, National Silver..**$3.00**
Cavalcade, 1946, salad fork, National Silver **$3.00**

Cavalcade, 1946, teaspoon, National Silver...................**$2.00**
Churchill, 1905, cold meat fork, Gorham **$15.00**
Churchill, 1905, dinner fork, Gorham **$8.00**
Churchill, 1905, teaspoon, Gorham.............................**$6.00**
Coronation, 1936, round soup spoon, Oneida Community **$4.00**
Coronation, 1936, salad fork, Oneida Community........**$4.00**
Coronation, 1936, teaspoon, Oneida Community **$2.00**
Danish Princess, 1938, dinner knife, hollow handle, Holmes & Edwards **$4.00**
Danish Princess, 1938, luncheon fork, Holmes & Edwards ..**$4.00**
Danish Princess, 1938, salad fork, Holmes & Edwards.**$4.00**
Danish Princess, 1938, teaspoon, Holmes & Edwards..**$2.00**
Distinction, 1951, salad fork, Oneida Prestige...............**$3.00**
Distinction, 1951, teaspoon, Oneida Prestige **$2.00**
Encore, 1934, cream ladle, Oneida..............................**$5.00**
Encore, 1934, master butter knife, Oneida **$2.00**
Engraved '05, tablespoon, Towle **$10.00**
Engraved '05, teaspoon, Towle....................................**$8.00**
Evening Star, 1950, jam spoon, Oneida **$6.00**
Fantasy, 1941, dinner knife, hollow handle, Carlton Silver Plate **$3.00**
Fantasy, 1941, salad fork, Carlton Silver Plate **$3.00**
Georgian, 1912, berry spoon, Oneida Community........**$9.00**
Georgian, 1912, teaspoon, Oneida Community.............**$3.00**
Grecian, 1915, dinner knife, solid handle, 1881 Rogers...**$5.00**
Grecian, 1915, sugar shell spoon, 1881 Rogers.............**$5.00**
Grosvenor, 1921, dinner fork, Oneida Community.......**$5.00**
Grosvenor, 1921, dinner knife, hollow handle, Oneida Community **$6.00**
Grosvenor, 1921, fruit knife, Oneida Community **$8.00**
Grosvenor, 1921, lemon fork, Oneida Community **$10.00**
Grosvenor, 1921, pickle fork, Oneida Community.......**$8.00**
Grosvenor, 1921, teaspoon, Oneida Community..........**$3.00**
Heraldic, 1916, oval soup spoon, hammered, 1847 Rogers **$4.00**
Heraldic, 1916, round soup spoon, hammered, 1847 Rogers **$5.00**
Heraldic, 1916, salad fork, hammered, 1847 Rogers.....**$4.00**
Heraldic, 1916, tablespoon, 1847 Rogers **$3.00**
Jubilee, 1953, fork, Viande..**$4.00**
Jubilee, 1953, knife, hollow handle, Viande.................**$5.00**
King Cedric, 1933, jelly slice, Community **$6.00**
Lady Fair, 1957, cucumber server, pierced...................**$6.00**
Lexington, 1934, dinner fork, Oneida **$3.00**
Lexington, 1934, dinner knife, serrated, Oneida **$3.00**
Lilyta, 1909, cold meat fork, International...................**$10.00**
Lilyta, 1909, pickle fork, International..........................**$8.00**
Lilyta, 1909, salad fork, International **$10.00**
Lovely Lady, 1937, oval soup spoon, Holmes & Edwards.**$7.00**
Lovely Lady, 1937, pastry server, Holmes & Edwards...**$20.00**
Lovely Lady, 1937, tablespoon, pierced, Holmes & Edwards **$15.00**
Marathon, 1909, coffee spoon, American......................**$6.00**
Marathon, 1909, gumbo soup spoon, American...........**$8.00**
Marathon, 1909, pastry fork, American **$8.00**
Marquise, 1933, gravy ladle, 1847 Rogers..................**$15.00**
Morning Star, 1948, dinner knife, Oneida Community .**$5.00**
Morning Star, 1948, luncheon knife, Oneida Community .**$5.00**

Morning Star, 1948, master butter knife, Oneida Community **$4.00**
Morning Star, 1948, sugar spoon, Oneida Community .**$4.00**
Oxford, 1901, tablespoon, Rogers & Bros **$4.00**
Patrician, 1914, dinner fork, Oneida Community **$4.00**
Patrician, 1914, lemon fork, Oneida Community **$8.00**
Patrician, 1914, master butter knife, Oneida Community ..**$4.00**
Remembrance, 1948, master butter knife, 1847 Rogers ..**$5.00**
Remembrance, 1948, pickle fork, 1847 Rogers **$6.00**
Rendezvous (aka Old South), 1938, sm flat pierced spoon, Wm Rogers **$8.00**
Sheraton, 1910, dinner fork, Oneida **$5.00**
Sheraton, 1910, dinner knife, solid handle, Oneida **$5.00**
Sheraton, 1910, jam spoon, Oneida..............................**$8.00**
Sheraton, 1910, teaspoon, Oneida **$3.00**
Spring Charm, 1950, cold meat fork, Wm Rogers **$8.00**
Spring Charm, 1950, tablespoon, Wm Rogers **$5.00**
Surf Club, 1938, dinner fork, 1881 Rogers **$4.00**
Surf Club, 1938, dinner knife, 1881 Rogers **$5.00**
Surf Club, 1938, gravy ladle, 1881 Rogers **$12.00**
Surf Club, 1938, oval soup spoon, 1881 Rogers............**$5.00**
Surf Club, 1938, round soup spoon, 1881 Rogers.........**$5.00**
Surf Club, 1938, salad fork, 1881 Rogers **$5.00**
Vanity Fair, 1924, dinner fork, Gorham.........................**$5.00**
Vanity Fair, 1924, tablespoon, Gorham **$5.00**
Vintage, 1904, dinner knife, hollow handle, 1847 Rogers ..**$45.00**
Vintage, 1904, gravy ladle, 1847 Rogers **$45.00**
Vintage, 1904, salad fork, 1847 Rogers **$45.00**
Vintage, 1904, teaspoon, 1847 Rogers..........................**$15.00**
White Orchid, 1953, dinner fork, Oneida Community ..**$5.00**
White Orchid, 1953, teaspoon, Oneida Community **$3.00**

Skookum Indian Dolls

Skookum Indian dolls were patented in 1914 by a Montana woman, Mary McAboy. The earliest dolls had corn-husk or dried apple heads, but the ones you're most likely to find are the later dolls with composition heads. Serious collectors avoid the plastic Skookums made in the 1940s. Skookum dolls are wrapped in Indian-style blankets, and the majority have eyes looking to their right. Those looking to their left or straight ahead are rarities.

Advisor: Jo Ann Palmieri (See Directory Skookum Dolls)

Child, wooden legs & feet, 6", from $40 to **$50.00**
Child, wooden legs & feet, 8", from $60 to **$70.00**
Female, plastic legs & feet, 4", from $20 to.................**$25.00**
Female, plastic legs & feet, 6", from $25 to.................**$35.00**
Female, plastic legs & feet, 10", from $35 to...............**$45.00**
Female, plastic legs & feet, 12", from $50 to...............**$60.00**
Female, wooden legs & feet, 10" to 12", from $125 to ..**$150.00**
Female w/baby, wooden legs & feet, 14" to 16", from $175 to...**$225.00**
Male, plastic legs & feet, 4", from $20 to.....................**$25.00**
Male, plastic legs & feet, 6", from $25 to.....................**$35.00**
Male, plastic legs & feet, 10", from $35 to...................**$45.00**
Male, plastic legs & feet, 12", from $50 to...................**$60.00**

Male, wooden legs & feet, 10" to 12", from $150 to.**$175.00**
Male, wooden legs & feet, 14" to 16", from $200 to.**$350.00**

Child, plastic feet, cloth body, 6", $45.00. (Photo courtesy Patsy Moyer)

Soda-Pop Memorabilia

A specialty area of the advertising field, soft-drink memorabilia is a favorite of many collectors. Now that vintage Coca-Cola items have become rather expensive, interest is expanding to include some of the less widely known sodas — Grapette, Hires Root Beer, and Dr. Pepper, for instance.

If you want more pricing information, we recommend *Huxford's Collectible Advertising* by Sharon and Bob Huxford. See also Coca-Cola; Pepsi-Cola.

Advisors: Craig and Donna Stifter (See Directory, Soda-Pop Memorabilia)

Newsletter: National Pop Can Collectors
P.O. Box 7862
Rockford, IL 61126; Send for free information

Bank, Vernors, metal, can shape, Original Venors, Its Different, Flavor Aged in Oak Bucket, 1960s, M......................**$15.00**
Bank, 7-Up, can shape, M..**$25.00**
Banner, Hires, canvas, for truck, 1940s, EX..............**$325.00**
Blotter, Nehi, Drink for Health & Happiness to...Nehi, 1940s **$10.00**
Blotter, Nu-Grape, 1930s, EX **$25.00**
Blotter, Royal Crown Cola (RC), 1940s, NM, from $25 to ..**$35.00**
Booklet, Nehi, lists available premiums, 1920s, EX **$5.00**
Booklet, Nehi, lists unavailable premiums, 1920s.........**$5.00**
Bottle, Orange-Crush, glass w/embossed label, 1920s, EX...**$12.00**
Bottle, Royal Crown Cola (RC), embossed glass, 1940s, EX...**$10.00**
Bottle, Royal Crown Cola (RC), glass w/applied color label, 1940s, EX..**$7.00**
Bottle cap, Cleo Cola, unused, M, from $4 to..............**$5.00**
Bottle cap, Frost King Orange Soda, M, from $1 to......**$2.00**
Bottle cap, Grape Crush, unused, M, from $2 to **$3.00**
Bottle carrier, Canada Dry, cardboard, Canada Dry Beverages With Special Sparkle Flavor, 6-pack size, M..........**$8.00**

Bottle carrier, Dad's Root Beer, cardboard, That's My Pop! That's Dad's, for 6-pack 16-oz bottles, M...............**$8.00**

Bottle carrier, Dr Pepper, cardboard, for 6-pack bottles, 1940s, EX...**$75.00**

Bottle carrier, Dr Pepper, tin, for 6-pack bottles, 1930s.**$85.00**

Bottle carrier, Hill Billy Joose, cardboard, Worth Feudin' An' Fightin' For!, for 16-oz bottles, M **$10.00**

Bottle carrier, Nehi, cardboard, family package, 1950s, 4-pack **$10.00**

Bottle carrier, Nehi, cardboard, 1940s, 6-pack.............**$15.00**

Bottle carrier, Nesbitt's, cardboard, 1940s, 6-pack.......**$25.00**

Bottle carrier, Nu-Grape, cardboard, 1940s, 6-pack **$20.00**

Bottle carrier, Royal Crown Cola (RC), cardboard, for 6-pack bottles, 1940s, EX.......................................**$25.00**

Bottle carrier, Vess Whistle Orange, cardboard, shows oranges & logo, 6-pack size.................................**$10.00**

Bottle crate, Dad's Root Beer, wood, King Size...Tastes Like Root Beer Should, VG **$15.00**

Bottle display, Orange-Crush, cardboard, baseball player boy wraps around bottle top, 1920s, EX.................**$500.00**

Bottle display, Orange-Crush, 1930s, EX, $350.00. (Photo courtesy Craig and Donna Stifter)

Bottle opener, Nehi, 1930s, EX..................................**$15.00**

Box, Cotton Club, wood, VG....................................**$15.00**

Box of straws, Royal Crown Cola (RC), RC Makes You Feel Like New!, 1940s, EX..**$200.00**

Calendar, Dr Pepper, 1944, complete **$300.00**

Calendar, Dr Pepper, 1964, complete........................**$50.00**

Calendar, Nehi, 1935, Rolf Armstrong art, girl in yellow gown w/fur cape, complete pad, from $150 to............**$275.00**

Calendar, Nehi, 1936, complete...............................**$250.00**

Calendar, Nehi, 1938, sailor girl at helm w/sailboats beyond, Rolf Armstrong artwork, complete **$250.00**

Calendar, Nesbitt's, 1953, complete...........................**$65.00**

Calendar, Nu-Grape, 1923, complete **$425.00**

Calendar, Nu-Grape, 1925, complete, from $250 to..**$400.00**

Calendar, Nu-Grape, 1930s, cardboard, girl holding up bottle, 12x36" **$250.00**

Calendar, Nu-Grape, 1939, complete.......................**$200.00**

Calendar, Nu-Grape, 1941, complete.......................**$200.00**

Calendar, Nu-Grape, 1949, complete.......................**$100.00**

Calendar, Nu-Grape, 1949, complete.......................**$100.00**

Calendar, Nu-Grape, 1949, complete.......................**$100.00**

Calendar, Nu-Grape, 1951, complete.........................**$65.00**

Calendar, Nu-Grape, 1951, complete **$65.00**

Calendar, Nu-Grape, 1956, complete **$50.00**

Calendar, Orange-Crush, 1932, complete..................**$575.00**

Calendar, Orange-Crush, 1946, complete..................**$275.00**

Calendar, Royal Crown Cola (RC), 1953, shows Arlene Dahl, complete..**$150.00**

Calendar, Royal Crown Cola (RC), 1964, complete **$65.00**

Calendar, 7-up, 1955, complete, 9½x20" **$300.00**

Calendar, 7-Up, 1960, complete, NM, from $15 to......**$25.00**

Carton display cutout, Royal Crown Cola (RC), cardboard, shows little girl, 1950s, EX.................................**$100.00**

Clock, Dr Pepper, composition frame w/glass front, 1930s, 15", EX...**$225.00**

Clock, Hires, plastic, 1960s, 15" square......................**$50.00**

Clock, Nu-Grape, light-up, face shows yellow logo over tilted bottle, 1940s, 15" dia.................................**$250.00**

Clock, Orange-Crush, glass & metal, bottle cap on face, 1950s, 15" dia, EX..**$225.00**

Clock, Royal Crown Cola (RC), glass & metal, 1950s, 16" square **$100.00**

Clock, 7-Up, glass & metal, 1950s, 14" dia, NM, from $175 to...**$275.00**

Dispenser, Nesbitt's, glass, w/original jug, 1930s......**$225.00**

Dispenser, Nesbitt's, glass, w/out jug, 1940s, from $100 to...**$175.00**

Dispenser w/pump, Ward's Orange-Crush, orange shaped, 1930s...**$1,250.00**

Display, 7-Up, plastic bottle, 1960s, 28", EX...............**$85.00**

Door push plate, Orange-Crush, tin, Come In! Drink Orange-Crush, 1930s, 3½x10", EX **$250.00**

Fan, Dr Pepper, girl holding bottle, 1937, EX...........**$275.00**

Fan, Royal Crown Cola (RC), shows all-American girl, 1950s, EX...**$30.00**

Fan pull, Orange-Crush, orange shaped, 1930s, EX ...**$50.00**

Fountain glass, Nehi, applied color label: white band w/Nehi logo, 1940...**$85.00**

Label, Dad's Root Beer, M, sm...................................**$15.00**

Label, Saegertown Ginger Ale, paper, M **$20.00**

Match holder, Dr Pepper, tin, 1930s, EX...................**$115.00**

Matchbook, Dr Pepper, 1930s-40s, each, from $10 to......**$15.00**

Matchbook, Nehi, 1940s, from $10 to **$15.00**

Matchbook, Royal Crown Cola (RC), 1940s, NM, from $5 to...**$8.00**

Menu board, Nehi, tin, Gas Today around circular chalkboard area, 1940s, 42x15".....................................**$500.00**

Menu board, Nesbitt's, tin, 1950s, 20x28", from $50 to..**$75.00**

Menu board, Orange-Crush, tin, shows Crushy figure w/bottle, 1930s, 18x24", EX.....................................**$225.00**

Miniature bottle, Nesbitt's, decal label, 1940s..............**$10.00**

Pencil, Dr Pepper, mechanical, 1940s, EX **$40.00**

Picnic cooler, Nesbitt's, 1950s....................................**$45.00**

Push bar, Nesbitt's, porcelain, 1940s, 32½" L...........**$165.00**

Push bar, Nesbitt's, tin plate on wire frame, 1950s.....**$80.00**

Salt & pepper shakers, Holly Beverages, green glass w/metal top, M, pr **$20.00**

Scoreboard, Orange-Crush, tin, chalkboard for baseball scoring, 1940s, 23x36", EX.....................................**$275.00**

Sign, Big Ben's, cardboard, Refresh! Take a Break Try...Big Ben's Lemon Bubbles, NM.................................**$15.00**

Sign, Cheer Up, cardboard, diecut bottle, 1960s, NM.**$15.00**

Sign, Cherry Smash, cardboard, shows cherries w/fountain glass, 1920s, 6x11", EX...**$150.00**

Sign, Cherry Smash, celluloid, Always Drink...Our Nation's Beverage, 1920s, 5x11", EX.................................**$275.00**

Sign, Dr. Pepper, aluminum, 1930s, 10", EX, $375.00. (Photo courtesy Craig and Donna Stifter)

Sign, Dr Pepper, cardboard, lady w/bottle leaning on railing, 1930s, 21x26", EX **$675.00**

Sign, Dr Pepper, cardboard, 1940s, 15x25", NM, each, from $225 to...**$375.00**

Sign, Dr Pepper, porcelain, Drink Dr Pepper, Good for Life, 1930s, 9x21", EX **$200.00**

Sign, Dr Pepper, tin, 10-2-4 clock above bottle & logo on yellow, 1940s, 18x54", EX...............................**$375.00**

Sign, Hazel Club Sparkling Ginger Ale, cardboard, diecut bottle, 1960s, M..**$15.00**

Sign, Hires, cardboard, shows Hires w/food specials, 1950s, 8x24", NM, from $35 to **$60.00**

Sign, Hires, celluloid, Drink Hires Root Beer, 1950s, 9", EX...**$100.00**

Sign, Hires, embossed tin, 1932, EX, 28x11", $350.00. (Photo courtesy Craig and Donna Stifter)

Sign, Hires, paper, So Good With Food, 1940s, 34x58", NM, from $250 to.......................................**$400.00**

Sign, Hires, tin, Bracing-Delicious, red, yellow & black w/embossing, 1923, 28x11", EX **$325.00**

Sign, Hires, tin, Hires to You!, shows bottle, 1940s, 13½x42", NM, from $125 to **$200.00**

Sign, Mr Newport, cardboard, diecut man in tux w/circle logo on shoulder, fits onto bottle, M **$45.00**

Sign, Nehi, cardboard, lady reading newspaper, shows bottle, 1930s, 12x18", EX.............................**$175.00**

Sign, Nehi, cardboard, diecut, hand-held bottle 20x10", NM...**$75.00**

Sign, Nehi, cardboard, ping-pong game scene, 1950s, 11x28" **$65.00**

Sign, Nehi, tin, Curb Service... Sold Here Ice Cold, 1930s, 42x15"...**$175.00**

Sign, Nehi, tin, Curb Service...Sold Here Ice Cold, 1930s, 20x28", EX...**$175.00**

Sign, Nehi, tin, Drink Nehi Beverages, slanted bottle, 1950s, 15x42"...**$125.00**

Sign, Nehi, tin, Drink Nehi Beverages left of bottle on white oval, 1940s, 17x45" **$150.00**

Sign, Nehi, tin, Drink Nehi over bottle & Ice Cold, 1940s, 42x15"...**$150.00**

Sign, Nehi, tin flange, Drink Nehi above Ice Cold, bottle on white at left, 1940s, 13x18".....................**$325.00**

Sign, Nehi, tin flange, Drink Nehi Beverages, bottle, 1940s, 13x18"...**$225.00**

Sign, Nesbitt's, cardboard, child dressed as boxer, 1950s, 22x35"...**$100.00**

Sign, Nesbitt's, cardboard, clown w/children, 1950s, 20x36"...**$325.00**

Sign, Nesbitt's, cardboard, twins sitting at table, 1950s, 20x36"...**$275.00**

Sign, Nesbitt's, cardboard diecut, lady in hat & gloves w/bottle, 1950s, 23x21"....................................**$85.00**

Sign, Nesbitt's, tin, Drink & 5¢ above image of bottle, 1940s, 49x16"...**$275.00**

Sign, Nesbitt's, tin, Drink Nesbitt's... on black, left of tilted bottle & 5¢ dot, 1940s, from $125 to **$200.00**

Sign, Nesbitt's, tin, Drink... Made From Real Oranges, tilted bottle, curved corners, 1940s, 24x24"..............**$175.00**

Sign, Nu-Grape, cardboard, It's a Thriller, 1949, 18x32".**$75.00**

Sign, Nu-Grape, cardboard, shows girl holding up bottle, 1930s, 12x36", EX **$250.00**

Sign, Nu-Grape, cardboard diecut, girl w/arm around lg bottle, 1920s, 14x24", from $200 to **$350.00**

Sign, Nu-Grape, cardboard diecut, woman w/snowman, 1940s, 14x16" **$125.00**

Sign, Nu-Grape, cardboard diecut, woman wearing beret, 1940s, 13x15" **$125.00**

Sign, Nu-Grape, tin, ...A Favorite With Millions, bottle framed at left, 1930s, 12x30"..............................**$175.00**

Sign, Nu-Grape, tin, Drink at left of colorful bottle on yellow background, 1930s, 12x4¾" **$175.00**

Sign, Nu-Grape, tin, Drink...a Flavor You Can't Forget above hand holding bottle, 1930s, 36x14"....................**$275.00**

Sign, Nu-Grape, tin, Drink...in Bottles & at Founts, bottle at left, 1920s, 10x24".....................................**$325.00**

Sign, Nu-Grape, tin, You Need a NuGrape Soda, slanted bottle at right, 1940s, 12x28", from $75 to **$125.00**

Sign, Nu-Grape, tin, You Need A on ribbon banner around neck of bottle, 1940s, 44x18".............................**$225.00**

Sign, Orange-Crush, cardboard, Have a Red Hot With Delicious Orange-Crush, diecut, hanger style, 1920s, EX.........**$200.00**

Sign, Orange-Crush, cardboard, self standing, bathing suit girl sitting on dock, 1930s, EX **$650.00**

Sign, Orange-Crush, cardboard, shows Crushy figure, 1930s, 11x17", NM, from $75 to **$125.00**

Sign, Orange-Crush, masonite, Rush-Rush for Orange-Crush, shows Crushy figure, 1940s, 18x48", EX.............**$275.00**

Sign, Orange-Crush, paper, framed, Walt Otto artwork, 1936, 31x15", EX, $425.00. (Photo courtesy Craig and Donna Stifter)

Sign, Orange-Crush, tin, amber bottle & Crushy figure on left, 1930s, 18x48", EX **$350.00**

Sign, Orange-Crush, tin, bottle at ends, 1930s, 12x32", EX .**$350.00**

Sign, Orange-Crush, tin, bottle form, 1939, 18", EX..**$300.00**

Sign, Orange-Crush, tin, flange, shows bottle in snow, 1930s, 15x22", EX **$275.00**

Sign, Royal Crown Cola (RC), cardboard, My Mom Knows Best, 1940s, 11x28", EX **$50.00**

Sign, Royal Crown Cola (RC), cardboard, shows Barbara Stanwyck, 1940s, 11x28", NM, from $50 to...........**$75.00**

Sign, Royal Crown Cola (RC), cardboard, shows Claudette Colbert, 1940s, 11x28", EX **$75.00**

Sign, Royal Crown Cola (RC), cardboard, shows Jeanette MacDonald, 1940s, 26x40", EX **$175.00**

Sign, Royal Crown Cola (RC), cardboard, shows June Haver, 1940s, 26x40", EX **$185.00**

Sign, Royal Crown Cola (RC), tin, Enjoy Royal Crown Cola, 1960s, 12x28", EX...**$75.00**

Sign, Royal Crown Cola (RC), tin, shows bottle in white oval at right, 1940s, 12x29½", EX **$175.00**

Sign, Royal Crown Cola (RC), 1940s, shows Mary Martin, 26x40", from $100 to **$150.00**

Sign, 7-Up, cardboard, Real 7-Up, Sold Here, Fresh Up, 1930s, 13x20", EX..**$40.00**

Sign, 7-Up, cardboard, So Good With..., shows bottles & popcorn, 1950s, 21x34", EX....................................**$65.00**

Sign, 7-Up, cardboard cutout, Morning Noon & Night 7-Up Likes You, 1930s, 8½x10½", EX **$50.00**

Sign, 7-Up, cardboard w/easel back, advertised w/liquor, 1930s, 4x6", EX **$35.00**

Sign, 7-Up, glass shield shape w/light, shows bottle, attached to wood base, 1930s, EX **$1,000.00**

Sign, 7-Up, tin, flange, Real 7-Up Sold Here, circular shape, 14x18", EX **$425.00**

Sign, 7-Up, tin, Fresh Up, shows bottle top, 1954, 18½x27", NM, from $75 to **$125.00**

Sign, 7-Up, tin, shows hand holding bottle, 1947, 19½x27", EX **$275.00**

Signs, 7-Up, tin, Take Some Home, for corner, 1930s, 8x10½", EX, pr..**$165.00**

Sign, 7-Up, tin, You Like It...It Likes You, 1940s, 18x27", EX **$200.00**

Straws, 7-Up, Get Real Action...7-Up Your Thirst Away!, 1960s, MIB..**$145.00**

Syrup dispenser, Cherry Smash, ceramic, potbelly shape, Always Drink above cherry branch, 1920s, 14x9", EX **$1,250.00**

Thermometer, Dr Pepper, 10-2-4 clock above bottle & logo, 1930s, EX..**$450.00**

Thermometer, Mr Cola, metal, bottle cap form w/scale at rim, Mr Cola 16-oz at center, 1960s, M.................**$125.00**

Thermometer, Nesbitt's, 1950s, 26", EX, $125.00. (Photo courtesy Craig and Donna Stifter)

Thermometer, Orange-Crush, tin, bottle shaped, 1950s, 30", EX **$125.00**

Thermometer, Royal Crown Cola (RC), tin, embossed RC logo on top & bottle on right, 1940s, EX...................**$150.00**

Thermometer, Royal Crown Cola (RC), tin, RC on top w/logo on bottom, Best By Taste-Test, 1950s, NM, from $100 to..**$150.00**

Thermometer, 7-Up, tin, The All-Family Drink, bottle at right, 1950s, NM, from $30 to **$50.00**

Tray, Dr Pepper, Drink a Bite To Eat, girl holding 2 bottles, tin, 1939, EX..**$275.00**

Tray, Evervess, tin, Evervess Sparkling Water, It's Good for You, Product of Pepsi-Cola Co, NM.....................**$65.00**

Tray, Nehi, tin, bathing beauty caught up in ocean wave, 1920s from $100 to **$200.00**

Tray, Nu-Grape, tin, hand holding bottle against bright oval background, 1920s...**$75.00**

Tray, Orange-Crush, tin, shows Crushy figure squeezing oranges, EX **$275.00**

Tumbler, Dr Pepper, Good for Life w/applied color label, glass w/tapered sides, 1940s............................**$150.00**

Soda Bottles With Painted Labels

The earliest type of soda bottles were made by soda producers and sold in the immediate vicinity of the bottling company. Many had pontil scars, left by a rod that was used to manipulate the bottle as it was blown. They had a flat bottom rather than a 'kick-up,' so for transport, they were laid on their side and arranged in layers. This served to keep the cork moist, which kept it expanded, tight, and in place. Upright the cork would dry out, shrink, and expel itself with a 'pop,' hence the name 'soda pop.'

Until the thirties, the name of the product or the bottler was embossed in the glass or printed on paper labels (sometimes pasted over reused returnable bottles). Though a few paper labels were used as late as the sixties, nearly all bottles produced from the mid-thirties on had painted-on (pyro-glazed) lettering, and logos and pictures were often added. Imaginations ran rampant. Bottlers waged a fierce competition to make their soda logos eyecatching and sales inspiring. Anything went! Girls, airplanes, patriotic designs, slogans proclaiming amazing health benefits, even cowboys and Indians became popular advertising ploys. This is the type you'll encounter most often today, and collector interest is on the increase. Look for interesting, multicolored labels, rare examples from small-town bottlers, and those made from glass other than clear or green. If you'd like to learn more about them, we recommend *The Official Guide to Collecting Applied Color Label Soda Bottles* by Thomas E. Marsh.

Advisor: Thomas E. Marsh, Painted-Label Soda Bottles (See Directory, Soda-Pop Collectibles)

A Good Beverage, clear glass, 8-oz $100.00
Anton's, clear glass, 10-oz..................................$10.00
Big Chief, clear glass, 8-oz................................$20.00
Big Ten, clear glass, 10-oz.................................$10.00
Brown Cow, clear glass, Dyersburg TN, 8-oz $15.00
Bubble Up, green glass, 10-oz..............................$10.00
California Drink-O, clear glass, 10-oz $25.00
Canada Dry Water, clear glass, 7-oz $10.00
Cardinal, clear glass, 12-oz................................$20.00
Chester Club, clear glass, 8-oz.............................$25.00
Chokola's, clear glass, 1-qt................................$15.00
Cleo Cola, aqua glass, 12-oz................................$65.00
Cleo Cola, green glass w/out belly button, 12-oz.....$150.00
Cotton Club, clear glass w/3-color label, 8-oz $25.00
Crystal, green glass, 1-qt $20.00
Delaware Punch, clear glass, 7½-oz.........................$15.00
Desert Cooler, clear glass, 10-oz..........................$20.00
Diamond Beverage, clear glass, 7-oz $10.00

Donald Duck Beverages, 6-pack with crowns, $175.00. (Photo courtesy Thomas E. Marsh)

Dybala, green glass, 1-qt...................................$15.00
Finn's, clear glass, 7-oz..................................$10.00
Five Points, green glass, 1-qt.............................$15.00
Freshy, green glass, 1-qt..................................$15.00
Frost King, clear glass, 7-oz..............................$45.00
Glengarry, clear glass, 7½-oz..............................$15.00
Good Humor, clear glass, 10-oz $20.00
Harris, green glass, 12-oz.................................$20.00
Hollywood, clear glass, 12-oz..............................$15.00
Hudson Rock, green glass, 7-oz.............................$10.00
Keck's, clear glass, 6½-oz.................................$15.00
Kik, clear glass, 12-oz....................................$25.00
Lafayette, clear glass, 7-oz...............................$20.00
Life, green glass, 10-oz...................................$10.00
Lulu, clear glass, Mexican, 7-oz...........................$65.00
Made Rite, clear glass, 10-oz..............................$10.00
Maple Spring, clear glass, 7-oz............................$15.00
Mini Pop, clear glass, 4-oz................................$10.00
Mooo Cho, clear glass, 7-oz................................$15.00
Mosso's, green glass, 1-qt.................................$15.00
Mrs Lombardi's, clear glass, 12-oz.........................$75.00
Nugget, clear glass, 12-oz $15.00
O'Joy, clear glass, 7-oz...................................$20.00

OOO Gee, Kankakee IL, clear, 12-oz, $350.00; Orange E Cola, clear, 10-oz, $15.00; Orange-Sip, Houston TX, clear, 6-oz, $45.00; Oxley's, clear, 7-oz, $20.00. (Photo courtesy Thomas E. Marsh)

Owen, clear glass, 8-oz....................................$15.00
Pep-Up, clear glass, 7-oz..................................$15.00
Plantation, green glass, 7-oz..............................$10.00
Playboy, green glass, 1-qt $25.00
Pop Stop Beverages, clear glass, 12-oz.....................$10.00
Purity, green glass, 1-qt..................................$15.00
Quench, green glass, 8-oz..................................$15.00
Richardson's, clear glass, 12-oz...........................$10.00
Royal Palm, clear glass, 6-oz..............................$15.00
Sahara Dry, green glass, 7-oz..............................$20.00
Sandy's, clear glass, 10-oz................................$10.00
Scramble, clear glass, 10-oz $10.00
Seal Rock Spring, clear glass, 7-oz $15.00
Seventy-Six, green glass, 7-oz.............................$10.00
Ski Club, clear glass, 7-oz $15.00
Smile, clear glass, 16-oz..................................$20.00
Solo, clear glass, 12-oz...................................$25.00

Split Rock, green glass, 7-oz.......................................$15.00
Sterling, clear glass, 7-oz..$10.00
Sun Crest, clear glass, 12-oz.....................................$10.00
Sun Frost, clear glass, 9-oz.......................................$15.00
Tab, clear glass, 10-oz..$10.00
Tea-Cola, clear glass, 6½-oz.....................................$15.00
Topflite, clear glass, 10-oz.......................................$15.00
Tyler's, clear glass, 10-oz...$10.00
Vincent's, green glass, 7-oz......................................$15.00
Virginia Bell, clear glass, 10-oz...............................$20.00
Walker, green glass, 7-oz..$10.00
Walker's Root Beer, amber glass, Melrose MA, 1953, 1-qt..$125.00
Waukesha, clear glass, 7-oz......................................$10.00
Wilkins, green glass, 7-oz...$10.00
Yacht Club, green glass, 7½-oz $15.00

Sporting Goods

Catalogs and other items of ephemera distributed by sporting good manufacturers, ammunition boxes, and just about any other item used for hunting and fishing purposes are collectible. In fact, there are auctions devoted entirely to collectors with these interests.

One of the most well-known companies specializing in merchandise of this kind was the gun manufacturer, The Winchester Repeating Arms Company. After 1931, the mark was changed from Winchester Trademark USA to Winchester-Western. Remington, Ithaca, Peters, and Dupont are other manufacturers whose goods are especially sought after.

Advisor: Kevin R. Bowman (See Directory, Sports Collectibles)

Ammo box, Federal Lightening 22-Long Range High Velocity No 510, NM $3.00
Ammo box, Federal Monark Skeet Shells, 12-gauge, green & black box w/red shooter, Target-8 factory seconds, empty, NM...$25.00
Ammo box, Griffin & Howe Inc 22-3000 Caliber, brown, Made by Winchester, 1938, 2-pc, +18 brass shells, EX+ ...$35.00
Ammo box, Peters Golden Bullet, 22-Long Range, red, white & blue box, M..$7.00
Ammo box, Peters High Velocity 30-30 Winchester, blue, red & white w/warning label, full, EX+ $16.00
Ammo box, Remington Kleanbore Nitro Express, 16-gauge 4C shot, full box, NM $20.00
Ammo box, Remington Kleanbore Shur Shot Shells, 20-gauge, empty, EX+ $14.00
Ammo box, Remington Kleanbore 22-Long Range Brick, No 6122, complete w/10 boxes, M...........................$45.00
Ammo box, US Cartridge Co, 32-Caliber Rifle Cartridges, red, EX..$25.00
Ammo box, Western Super-X 250 Savage, gold & blue, EX..$15.00
Ammo box, Western Xpert Super Skeet Load, 20-gauge 9-shot, blue & yellow, empty, VG+ $7.00
Ammo box, Winchester Super-Speed 22-Long Range Hollow Point, yellow & red w/warning label, M................$7.00
Belt buckle, NRA Life Member $5.00

Book, Farmers' Handbook, Du Pont Explosives, January 1917, 196 pages, 6x9", VG+ $20.00
Booklet, Hoppe's Guide to Gun Cleaning, shows products, 1950, 16 pages, 3½x6", VG $10.00
Booklet, Pennsylvania Hunting Regulations, 1947-48 ...$5.00
Brochure, US Cartridge Co, Name Your Sport Here's Your Shell, No C218 6-31, 6x6"................................$25.00
Brochure, Western, Super-X, Form No 2286, shows wolf in scope, 9x6", M..$15.00
Calendar, Remington, 1991, M $7.00
Calendar, Ruger, 1979, M (M original shipping tube) .$75.00
Call, Herter's Duck Call, NMIB $25.00
Call, Olt's Owl & Turkey Hooter No OL-40, w/papers, MIB...$20.00
Call, Thomas Game Call From Texas, Multi-Reed Duck Call, No 158-D, MIB...$15.00
Cap, baseball type w/green pinstripes & embroidered Remington, M $10.00
Catalog, Browning, 1931, shows trap shooter on cover, 32 pages, w/return envelope, NM.............................$65.00
Catalog, Herter's No 66, 1959, 218 pages, 8x11", VG .$10.00
Catalog, Ithaca Guns, 1980-81, M.............................$5.00
Catalog, Ruger, folds into poster, 1979, unopened, M (sealed)..$12.00
Comic book, Shooting Adventures of Doc Peters, Peters, 1953, M...$20.00
Counter mat, Remington 150th Anniversary, green cloth, 1966, 10x24", NM...$45.00
Counter mat, Ruger 1979, 30 years logo at center, red foam, 12x17", unused, M......................................$20.00
Decal, Thank You, Call Again! We Sell Eley Ammunition, red w/white letters, 5x6½", M................................$15.00
Fan, paper w/Winchester hardware advertisement, 9x15" w/handle, NM $35.00
Game vest, Winchester Trailblazer, sm, M..................$25.00
Gun cleaning kit, cable-style tools in round zippered canvas pouch, Ducks Unlimited, NM $15.00
Gun cleaning kit, Hooker's Flexifold Firearms Cleaner, 30-caliber, wire pull-type cleaner in tin container, EX.....$17.00
Hunting license, Illinois resident, 1929 ....$8.00
Instruction sheet, Olt's Instructions for Perfect Mallard Call, folding paper, 7x9", EX+ $3.00

Label, Pflueger Durite Dazie Nylon Limp Leader Material #7443, 1½x7½", $8.00. (Photo courtesy Kevin Bowman)

Magazine, Hunter Trader Trapper, October 1926, treed bobcat & wolf on cover, G..$20.00
Medal, July 1939 Archery Sharpshooter, metal w/pin-back clasp...$15.00
Oil bottle, Pflueger Speede No 378, reel oil, glass, EX+ ..$12.00
Oil bottle, Restorz Products, CT, gun oil, glass w/paper label, M (sealed)...$15.00
Oil can, Outer's Gun Oil, yellow & red w/lead spout, EX $15.00

Pistol, Daisy Targeteer, in original box with targets and metal spinner target, M (VG box), $175.00. (Photo courtesy Kevin Bowman)

Postcard, Fred Bear w/Kodiak bear, 1960, unused, M..**$5.00**

Postcard, Hunter Arms Co & Paper Mills, Fulton NY, LC Smith, shows factory, unused, M...........................**$25.00**

Poster, Remington Skeet Fundamentals, shows 8 stations of skeet & how to shoot them+guns, traps & ammo, 1960s, 41x31"...**$20.00**

Poster, Ruger Quality Firearms, Rifles, Pistols & Revolvers, yellow, red & black, 1978, M................................**$30.00**

Poster, Savage Stevens 22 Rifles Preferred the World Over, shows 2 hunters & squirrel, multicolor, 15x19", NM.............**$35.00**

Poster, Winchester, Model 77, 19x24", EX **$25.00**

Price list, Winchester, 1962, shows antelope on cover, 18 pages, 8x11", M...**$17.00**

Price list, Winchester Wholesale & Retail, Effective July 1, 1929, Form No 1081, 8x11", 28 pages...................**$35.00**

Printer's block, shows 2-manned canoe, Winchester No 23-2, 1½x4", NM...**$60.00**

Record, Crow Calling No WI-6, Wightman Electonics, MD, 45 rpm, M **$7.00**

Record, The Varminteer, Col Weaver Enterprises, OH, 45 rpm, M **$7.00**

Scissors, Remington D-6, 6", NM **$25.00**

Scope, Mossberg No M4D, 4-power, NM.....................**$60.00**

Scope mount, Browning, for BBR rifle, MIB **$20.00**

Shell carrier, Bob Allen, Remington, holds 4 12-gauge shell boxes, Remington green, M **$15.00**

Sign, Going Hunting? You'll Need Powerful Peters Ammunition, shows shell box, No 58-SPA-2, easel back, 10½x13½" **$30.00**

Skeet load box, Winchester Staynless, 1-pc, empty, EX, $95.00. (Photo courtesy Kevin Bowman)

Snack tray, shows mallard duck, marked Made in England, 10x12", EX **$9.00**

Tin, Du Pont Rifle Powder No 80, green, VG-............**$18.00**

Tin, Hercules 2400 Rifle Powder, paper label, circular lid unscrews to reveal lift-up pour spout, tall, VG+..**$15.00**

Talc can, Winchester After Shave, no top, VG, $120.00. (Photo courtesy Kevin Bowman)

Sports Collectibles

When the baseball card craze began sweeping the country a decade ago, memorabilia relating to many types of sports began to interest sports fans. Today ticket stubs, uniforms, autographed baseballs, sports magazines, and game-used bats are prized by baseball fans, and some items, depending on their age or the notoriety of the player or team they represent, may be very valuable. Baseball and golfing seem to be the two sports most collectors are involved with, but hockey and auto racing are gaining ground. There are several books on the market you'll want to read if you're personally interested in sports: *Value Guide to Baseball Collectibles* by M. Donald Raycraft and R. Craig Raycraft, *Collector's Guide to Baseball Memorabilia* by Don Raycraft and Stew Salowitz, and *The Encyclopedia of Golf Collectibles* by John M. Olman and Morton W. Olman.

Game-used equipment is sought out by collectors, and where once they preferred only items used by professionals, now the sports market has expanded, and collectors have taken great interest in the youth equipment endorsed by many star players now enshrined in their respective hall of fame. Some youth equipment was given as advertising premiums and bear that company's name or logo. Such items are now very desirable collectibles.

See also Autographs; Indianapolis 500 Memorabilia; Magazines; Motorcycle Memorabilia; Pin-Back Buttons; Puzzles.

Advisors: Don and Anne Kier (See Directory, Sports Collectibles)

Album, Cleveland Indians, Sohio giveaway w/tank of gas, 1956-67, 6x8", set of 18, NM................................**$100.00**

Annual, Street Smith Baseball, 1979, Ron Guidry cover, M...**$15.00**

Ashtray, Los Angeles Kings, w/logo, 1970s, M............**$20.00**

Bank, NFL football helmet, w/team stickers, Loyal Gift, 1967, MIB **$12.00**

Baseball bat, Mickey Mantle #3 K55, store model, EX .**$100.00**

Baseball glove, Gil Hodges, 1950s, store model, EX+ ...**$50.00**

Book, Golf Fore Fun, cartoons by Bill O'Malley w/forward by Bing Crosby, Prentice Hall, 1953, 100-page, hardcover, EX+ .**$8.00**

Book, Major League Baseball Facts, Figures & Official Rules, 1949, softcover, NM **$8.00**

Book, My Turn at Bat, by Ted Williams as told to John Underwood, 1969, softcover, EX **$2.00**

Book, Run to Daylight, by Vince Lombardi, 1967, VG .**$15.00**

Booklet, Harness Racing 1967, 32 pages, VG.............**$12.00**

Candy container, Jackie Robinson, gold plastic bust, EX.**$225.00**

Cap, Arizona Outlaws, USFL, 1985, unused, M...........**$25.00**

Coin, All Star Baseball w/Jim Gentile of Orioles, Salada Tea premium, 1962, VG..**$5.00**

Coloring book, All About Hank Aaron, 1974, unused, M..**$35.00**

Coloring book, Official Bruins, Watkins & Strathmore, M..**$18.00**

Decanter, Ebbet Field, Jim Bean, 1976, M **$65.00**

Figure, Harlem Globetrotter, bendable vinyl, NM.......**$30.00**

First day cover, Babe Ruth, signed by 5 former teammates, M..**$50.00**

Football, Official NFL ball, w/authentic Don Shula signature, NM **$100.00**

Football, Official NFL Pete Rozelle Comm, American Football Conference, leather, Wilson, G+ **$45.00**

Football, Official USFL ball, w/Oakland Invaders team signatures, 1984, NM...**$450.00**

Game, Championship Hockey Bagatelle, Marx, 1960s, complete, EX **$12.00**

Game, Mil Mascara's Pro Wrestling, 1983, MIB (sealed).**$20.00**

Game, Vince Lombardi's Board Game, Research Games, 1970, 15x21", NM...**$25.00**

Guide, NCAA Basketball, 1980, M...............................**$20.00**

Jersey, USFL Arizona Wranglers, worn in game........**$400.00**

Magazine, Basketball Digest, March 1980, Larry Bird cover, M..**$15.00**

Magazine, Beckett's Football Card Monthly, October 1, 1990, Jerry Rice cover, M..**$10.00**

Magazine, Sport World, Pete Rose cover, October 1978, M.**$15.00**

Magazine, Time, May 2, 1960, Arnold Palmer cover & 5-page article, VG+ **$25.00**

Media guide, Buffalo Bills, OJ Simpson cover, 1974, M...**$25.00**

Mug, Islander's Stanley Cup Champions, ceramic, 1980, M **$35.00**

Mug, Superbowl IV, Kansas City Chiefs, ceramic, 1970, M **$55.00**

Notebook binder, Baltimore Orioles, 1970s, EX.........**$20.00**

Pen and pencil set, ball bat form, Major League's Bob Faller of Cleveland Indians pen with Mel Ott of New York Giants pencil, wood and metal, $45.00.

Pen, wood bat form, w/facsimile Mickey Mantle signature, 1960s, MIP **$25.00**

Pencil clip, Detroit Tigers/Briggs Stadium, 1940s........**$10.00**

Photo card, Chicago White Sox team, black & white, American Chicle, 1936, 3¼x5½", EX.....................**$35.00**

Playset, Harlem Globetrotters Basketball, Brooklyn Products, 1971, MIP...**$22.00**

Press pin, Dodgers World Series, 1951 ....**$350.00**

Press Pin, Yankees World Series, 1978.......................**$125.00**

Program, Baltimore Orioles, 1974, M **$15.00**

Program, Cardinals World Series, 1944, M.................**$125.00**

Program, Cleveland Browns vs New York Giants, December 18, 1960, M...**$22.50**

Program, Ice Capades, 1952...**$5.00**

Program, New York Mets, 1963, EX.............................**$10.00**

Program, New York Rangers vs New York Islanders, Bryan Trottler cover, 1979-80, M **$15.00**

Program, New York Yankees, American League 50th Anniversary, 1951, EX..**$20.00**

Program, 1950 Globetrotters vs All Stars, 1950 National Tour, photographs and biographies of all players, NM, $175.00.

Program, Notre Dame Vs Purdue, Knute Rockne & The 4 Horsemen cover, September 26, 1970, EX............**$15.00**

Program, Philadelphia Phillies spring training, 1989, EX .**$15.00**

Program, Rose Bowl, Illinois vs Washington, 1964, NM ..**$65.00**

Program, Sonja Henie, ca 1939, VG **$25.00**

Program, St Louis Cardinals, 1987, NM **$10.00**

Program, Sugar Bowl, Florida State vs Florida, 1995, M.**$17.50**

Program, 1986 World's Series, EX................................**$6.00**

Puzzle, Hockey's Gary Unger, 1970s, MIB...................**$12.00**

Record, Arnold Palmer Golf Instructions, 33⅓ rpm, w/booklet, 1963, M..**$55.00**

Record, Better Golf Through Hypnosis, Keener Products/ Mirrosonic Records, 1966, 33⅓ rpm, NM................**$18.00**

Record book, NCAA Basketball, Kevin Magee & Cal Irvine cover, 1982, M...**$15.00**

Roach trap, D-Con w/Muhammad Ali photo, unused, M .**$20.00**

Roster, Boston Red Sox, 1987, Roger Clemens cover, M...**$15.00**

Roster, St Louis Cardinals, 1965, M...........................**$20.00**

Scorecard, Houston Atros, 1977, M **$15.00**

Seat cushion, Superbowl XXX, Cowboys vs Steelers, M..**$50.00**

Shoe polish, Muhammad Ali, The Champ's Greatest Shine w/photo on tin, unused, M, from $10 to **$15.00**

Snowdome, Cincinnati Reds, Fandome, EX, from $15 to .**$20.00**

Stationery, St Louis Browns, w/original logo, 1950s, 1 sheet, M..**$20.00**

Tumbler, Detroit Pistons, clear glass w/facsimile team signatures, 1969-70, M..**$45.00**

Yearbook, Boston Brave Sketch Book, 1946, NM.....**$250.00**

Yearbook, Brooklyn Dodgers, VG...............................$12.00
Yearbook, Detroit Red Wings, 1960-61, M.................$150.00
Yearbook, New York Giants, 1957, NM.....................$115.00
Yearbook, New York Mets, 1994, M..........................$15.00
Yearbook, Oakland A's, 1968, NM $65.00

St. Clair Glass

Since 1941, the St. Clair family has operated a small glasshouse in Elwood, Indiana. They're most famous for their lamps, though they've also produced many styles of toothpick holders, paperweights, and various miniatures as well. Though the paperweights are usually stamped and dated, smaller items may not be marked at all. In addition to various colors of iridescent glass, they've also made many articles in slag glass (both caramel and pink) and custard. For more information, we recommend *St. Clair Glass Collector's Book* by Bonnie Pruitt (see Directory, St. Clair).

Animal dish, dolphin, blue, Joe St Clair.....................$175.00
Ashtray, flower, sm...$70.00
Bell, ACGA 10th Annual Convention, cobalt..............$75.00
Bird, lg...$95.00
Bowl, pink slag, ruffled rim, clear pedestal foot.......$175.00
Creamer, Holly Band, aqua opal $85.00
Creamer & sugar bowl, Grape & Cable, red carnival, lg .$200.00
Fez hat, Joe St Clair...$200.00
Figurine, Scottie, black amethyst..............................$340.00
Goblet, Roses in the Snow, cobalt $30.00
Insulator, red...$200.00
Lamp, 2-ball base, signed Joe & Bob St Clair $1,250.00

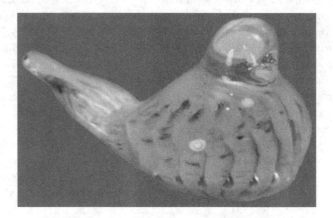

Paperweight, bird, clear with interior blue bands, 4" long, $65.00.

Paperweight, elephant, sulfide $155.00
Paperweight, owl sulfide, Joe St Clair........................$120.00
Paperweight, window flower, Paul St Clair $200.00
Paperweights, assassinated presidents, set of 4 ....$525.00
Pear, carnival glass, lg...$100.00
Plate, Lyndon Baines Johnson $25.00
Plate, Mt St Helens, May 18, 1980, chocolate.............$18.00
Ring post, floral paperweight base..............................$55.00
Statue, Scottie, any color other than dark amethyst, Bob St
   Clair $175.00

Toothpick holder, cactus form, white carnival $35.00
Toothpick holder, Daisy & Button...............................$30.00
Toothpick holder, flower paperweight base, ruffled trim..$75.00
Toothpick holder, Indian, caramel lustre, signed Joe St
   Clair...$45.00
Toothpick holder, Indian figural, yellow carnival $25.00
Toothpick holder, Nixon, cobalt carnival....................$50.00
Toothpick holder, Santa Claus, Joe St Clair $150.00
Tumbler, Cactus, cobalt carnival..................................$28.00

Tumbler, Grape and Cable, blue carnival, 4", $35.00.

Tumbler, Inverted Fan & Feather, cobalt $25.00
Vase, paperweight base...$85.00
Wine, Pinwheel...$45.00

Stanford Corn

Teapots, cookie jars, salt and pepper shakers, and other kitchen and dinnerware items modeled as ears of yellow corn with green shucks were made by the Stanford company, who marked most of their ware. The Shawnee company made two very similar corn lines; just check the marks to verify the manufacturer.

Butter dish..$45.00
Casserole, 8" L...$35.00
Creamer & sugar bowl $45.00
Pitcher, 7½" $55.00

Pitcher, 7½", $55.00.

Plate, 9" L $30.00
Relish tray...$35.00

Salt & pepper shakers, sm, pr **$25.00**
Salt & pepper shakers, 4", pr..**$25.00**
Spoon rest **$25.00**
Teapot...**$60.00**

Stangl Birds

The Stangl Pottery Company of Flemington and Trenton, New Jersey, made a line of ceramic birds which they introduced in 1940 to fulfill the needs of a market no longer able to access foreign imports due to the onset of WWII. These bird figures immediately attracted a great deal of attention. At the height of their production, sixty decorators were employed to hand paint the birds at the plant, and the overflow was contracted out and decorated in private homes. After WWII, inexpensive imported figurines once again saturated the market, and for the most part, Stangl curtailed their own production, though the birds were made on a very limited basis until as late as 1978.

Nearly all the birds were marked. A four-digit number was used to identify the species, and some pieces were signed by the decorator. An 'F' indicates a bird that was decorated at the Flemington plant.

Advisors: Popkorn Antiques (See Directory, Stangl)

Club: Stangl/Fulper Collectors Club
P.O. Box 538
Flemington, NJ 08822; Yearly membership: $25 (includes quarterly newsletter)

Allen Hummingbird, #3634, 3½" **$80.00**
Blue Jay w/leaf, #3716 ....**$650.00**
Bluebird, #3276, 5½" **$85.00**
Brewers Blackbird, #3591 ....**$130.00**

Broadbill Hummingbird, #3629, $125.00.

Broadtail Hummingbird, w/blue flower, #3626, 6" ...**$150.00**
Cardinal, pink, #3444...**$90.00**
Carolina Wren, #3590 ....**$165.00**
Cerulean Warbler, #3456, 4½"...................................**$65.00**
Chickadees, #3581 ....**$225.00**
Cliff Swallow, #3852, 3½" **$125.00**

Cock Pheasant, #3492, 6½x11"...............................**$200.00**
Cockatoo, pink, #3405...**$50.00**
Duck, flying; teal, open wings, #3443, 9½x12"........**$300.00**
Duck, grazing, #3250D...**$100.00**
Evening Grosbeak, #3813 ....**$135.00**
Feeding Duck, Antique Gold, #3250C.......................**$50.00**
Gold Finch group, #3635 ....**$200.00**
Golden Crown Kinglet, #3848 ....**$100.00**
Hen, yellow & brown, #3446, 7½".............................**$165.00**
Hummingbirds, #3599D..**$300.00**
Indigo Bunting, #3589, 3½" **$80.00**
Kentucky Warbler, #3598..**$60.00**
Kingfisher, #3406..**$75.00**
Kingfishers, teal, #3406D..**$130.00**
Lovebird, #3400, 4½" **$100.00**
Lovebirds, revised version, #3404D, 6" **$125.00**
Magpie-Jay, blue & black, #3758, 10½" **$1,000.00**
Nuthatch, #3593 ....**$55.00**
Oriole, revised version, #3402, 3½" **$60.00**
Owl, #3407...**$350.00**
Painted Bunting, #3452, 5" **$125.00**
Parakeets, green, #3582D...**$200.00**

Parrot, #3449, $150.00.

Parula Warbler, #3583...**$50.00**
Passenger Pigeon, #3450..**$1,200.00**
Penguin, #3274 ....**$500.00**
Pheasant hen, #3491...**$200.00**
Prothonatary Warbler, #3447......................................**$75.00**
Red-Faced Warbler, #3594, 3" **$85.00**
Rooster, gray, #3445 ....**$200.00**
Turkey, #3275 ....**$550.00**
White-Wing Crossbills, red matt, #3754D **$350.00**
Wren, #3401, revised **$60.00**

Stangl Dinnerware

The Stangl Company of Trenton, New Jersey, grew out of the Fulper company that had been established in Flemington early in the 1800s. Martin Stangl, president of the company, introduced a line of dinnerware in the 1920s. By 1954, 90% of their production centered around their dinnerware lines. Until 1942, the clay they used was white firing, and decoration was minimal, usually simple one-color glazes. In 1942, however, the first of the red-clay lines that have become synonomous with the Stangl name was created. Designs were hand carved into the greenware, then hand painted. More than one hundred different patterns have been cataloged. From 1974 until 1978, a few lines previously discontinued on the red clay were reintroduced with a white clay body. Soon after '78, the factory closed.

If you'd like more information on the subject, read *Stangl Pottery* by Harvey Duke.

Advisors: Popkorn Antiques (See Directory, Stangl)

Amber Glo, bowl, 8"...$20.00
Amber Glo, coffee server.....................................$75.00
Americana, tray, 7"...$8.00
Apple Delight, mug..$20.00
Apple Delight, plate, luncheon...........................$10.00
Ashtray, mallard duck, square, #3915 ....$50.00
Ashtray, pansy, pink & red, 4"............................$18.00
Ashtray, poppy, 4"...$20.00
Bachelor's Button, plate, 12"...............................$30.00
Blueberry, bowl, fruit; 5½" $15.00
Blueberry, bowl, vegetable; 10"..........................$50.00
Blueberry, butter dish..$40.00
Blueberry, gravy boat...$25.00
Blueberry, lug soup...$15.00
Blueberry, salt & pepper shakers, pr $20.00
Blueberry, sandwich tray, center handle, 10".....$10.00
Bluebird, coaster/ashtray......................................$25.00
Carnival, plate, 8"..$7.00
Carnival, salt & pepper shakers, pr $8.00
Country Garden, bowl, lug soup..........................$15.00
Country Garden, bowl, 8".....................................$30.00
Country Garden, butter dish, ¼-lb $40.00
Country Garden, cup & saucer.............................$16.00

Country Garden, flat soup bowl, $20.00.

Country Garden, jug, ½-pt $25.00
Country Garden, pitcher, 1-pt..............................$35.00
Country Life, bowl, fruit; w/pony........................$75.00
Country Life, chop plate, barn...........................$350.00
Country Life, cup & saucer $65.00
Country Life, soup, mallard, 8"..........................$150.00
Festival, bowl, cereal...$15.00
Festival, bowl, fruit $12.00

Festival, bowl, lug soup..$12.00
Festival, goblet, Terra Rose, footed, 5¾" $25.00
Festival, plate, Terra Rose, 10"............................$15.00
Flowerpot, red horizontal stripes, 3" $8.00
Fruit, bowl, fruit..$16.00
Fruit, cruet, w/stopper..$45.00
Fruit, cup & saucer..$17.00
Fruit, pitcher, ½-pt $25.00
Fruit, plate, 6"...$7.00
Fruit, relish tray..$40.00
Fruit, sugar bowl, w/lid..$18.00
Garland, plate, 8"...$12.00
Golden Blossom, cup & saucer............................$11.00
Golden Blossom, platter, 12" dia $27.50
Golden Harvest, bowl, fruit; 5½"..........................$10.00
Golden Harvest, chop plate, 12"..........................$20.00
Golden Harvest, creamer & sugar bowl, w/lid $15.00
Golden Harvest, egg cup......................................$12.00
Golden Harvest, plate, 10"....................................$12.00

Golden Harvest, relish tray, $18.00.

Golden Harvest, salt & pepper shakers, pr $15.00
Golden Harvest, teapot $50.00
Granada Gold, double pear dish, #3782.....................$18.00
Holly, creamer..$20.00
Holly, plate, dinner..$35.00
Kiddieware, cup, Indian Campfire $110.00
Kiddieware, dish, Ducky Dinner, 3-compartment, w/cup.$195.00
Magnolia, bowl, centerpiece; 12" $60.00
Magnolia, bowl, vegetable; 8"...............................$30.00
Magnolia, bowl, 5½"...$12.00
Magnolia, plate, dinner; 10"..................................$15.00
Magnolia, plate, 6" $5.00
Mediterranean, platter, Casual.............................$45.00
Orchard Song, coaster $5.00

Orchard Song, salt and pepper shakers, $16.00; gravy boat, $15.00.

Orchard Song, server, center handle, 10"......................**$6.00**
Provincial, bowl, fruit; 5½" **$9.00**
Provincial, bowl, lug soup **$12.00**
Provincial, plate, dinner **$15.00**
Sculptured Fruit, plate, 10".....................................**$14.00**
Sportsmen, plate, Canvas Back, 11" **$58.00**
Star Flower, cup & saucer **$15.00**
Thistle, bowl, casserole; knob lid, individual **$15.00**
Thistle, bowl, fruit **$12.00**
Thistle, bowl, salad; 12" **$75.00**
Thistle, bowl, vegetable; divided..............................**$40.00**
Thistle, bowl, vegetable; round, 8"...........................**$35.00**
Thistle, chop plate, 12½" **$30.00**
Thistle, coaster **$16.00**
Thistle, egg cup, double...**$15.00**
Thistle, gravy w/stand **$38.00**
Thistle, relish...**$25.00**
Thistle, salt & pepper shakers, pr **$20.00**
Thistle, teapot..**$65.00**
Town & Country, chop plate, blue **$75.00**
Town & Country, mold, blue, fluted, 6" **$50.00**
Town & Country, plate, blue, 10".............................**$45.00**
Town & Country, plate, blue, 8"...............................**$30.00**
Town & Country, teapot, blue..................................**$125.00**
Trumpet Flower, cigarette box, rectangular.................**$35.00**
Tulip, bean pot, w/lid **$55.00**

Star Trek Memorabilia

Trekkies, as fans are often referred to, number nearly 40,000 today, hold national conventions, and compete with each other for choice items of Star Trek memorabilia, some of which may go for hundreds of dollars.

The Star Trek concept was introduced to the public in the mid-1960s through a TV series which continued for many years in syndication. An animated cartoon series (1977), the release of six major motion pictures (1979 through 1989), and the success of *Star Trek, The Next Generation*, television show (Fox network, 1987) all served as a bridge to join two generations of loyal fans.

Its success has resulted in the sale of vast amounts of merchandise, both licensed and unlicensed, such as clothing, promotional items of many sorts, books and comics, toys and games, records and tapes, school supplies and party goods. Many of these are still available at flea markets around the country. An item that is 'mint in box' is worth at least twice as much as one in excellent condition but without its original packaging. For more information, refer to *Modern Toys, American Toys, 1930–1980,* by Linda Baker and *Schroeder's Collectible Toys, Antique to Modern* (Collector Books).

Bank, Applause, Klingon or Ferengi, bust image, 1992, MIB, each **$15.00**
Book, Whitman, Mission to Horatius, illustrated, hardbound, 1968, NM **$25.00**
Book & record set, Peter Pan, from 1st movie, 1979, MIB....**$10.00**
Colorforms set, 1975, MIB..**$35.00**

Coloring book, The Motion Picture, Merrigold, 1979, EX..**$12.00**
Coloring book, Whitman, Rescue at Raylo, Kirk on cover, 1978, EX+ **$10.00**
Communicators, 1974, unused...................................**$75.00**
Decanter, Mr Spock, bust image, ceramic, MIB **$60.00**
Diorama, Applause, Amok Time, 1996, M...................**$60.00**
Doll, Knickerbocker, Kirk or Spock, stuffed cloth w/vinyl head, 12", MIB, each **$50.00**
Figure, Applause, Kirk, Picard, Riker, Data, LaForge, Worf, Generations (movie), 1994, 10", MIP, each...........**$10.00**
Figure, Applause, Sisko, Odo, Quark, Kira Nerys, Deep Space 9, 1994, 10", MIP, each **$10.00**
Figure, Ertl, Kirk, Star Trek III, 3¾", MOC...............**$25.00**
Figure, Ertl, Scotty, Star Trek III, 3¾", MOC.............**$25.00**
Figure, Galoob, Data, Next Generation, 1st Series, blue face, 3¾", MOC...**$125.00**
Figure, Galoob, Data, Next Generation, 3rd Series, 3¾", MOC...**$20.00**
Figure, Galoob, LaForge, Next Generation, 3¾", MOC..**$12.00**
Figure, Mego, Decker, Motion Picture, 3¾", EX.........**$12.00**
Figure, Mego, Kirk, Motion Picture, 12", NRFB..........**$80.00**

Figure, Mego, Neptunian, 8", M, $150.00.

Figure, Mego, Scotty, Motion Picture, 3¾", EX............**$12.00**

Figure, Playmates, Lieutenant Commander Deanna Troy, 5", MOC, from $20.00 to $25.00.

Figure, Playmates, Space Talk Series, Riker, 8", MOC.**$15.00**
Figure, Presents, Classic Star Trek, set of 13 w/Enterprise, PVC, 1992, 4", M...**$50.00**
Game, Motion Picture, Milton Bradley, 1979, NMIB...**$35.00**
Game, Next Generation, for VCR, Decipher, 1993, NMIB.**$24.00**
Game, Star Trek, Ideal, 1967, complete, EX (EX box) from $50 to...**$70.00**

Game, Super Phaser II Target, battery-operated, 1976, unused, M (VG box)..$45.00

Greeting card, Kirk being attacked by alien, Beam Me Up Scotty..., California Dreamers, 1985, NM w/envelope.$5.00

Movie viewer w/filmstrips, 1960s, MOC $35.00

Ornament, Hallmark, Galileo, NRFB, from $25 to $35.00

Ornament, Hallmark, Klingon Bird of Prey, w/flickering lights, MIB $30.00

Paint-By-Numbers Set #2109, Hasbro, 1974, MIB........$60.00

Playset, Mego, Command Communication Console, 1976, MIB $80.00

Playset, Mego, Motion Picture, USS Enterprise Bridge, 1980, NRFB..$135.00

Playset, Mego, USS Enterprise Bridge, 1975, MIB.....$125.00

Puzzle, Battle on Planet Klingon, HG, 1974, 150-pc, NMIB ..$15.00

Puzzle, frame-tray; Whitman, 1978, MIP (sealed)........$12.00

Record, In Vino Veritas, 45 rpm, NM (NM sleeve)........$5.00

Silly Putty, Motion Picture, 1979, MOC.....................$20.00

Sticker book, Jeopardy at Jutterdon, Whitman, 1979, M.$17.00

Tablet, glossy photo of Kirk on cover, lined, 1960s, M ..$40.00

Vehicle, Corgi, USS Enterprise, Star Trek II, 1982, MOC, from $18 to..$25.00

Vehicle, Corgi #149, Klingon Warship, Star Trek II, MOC..$25.00

Vehicle, Dinky, Klingon Warship, MIB, from $75 to...$85.00

Vehicle, Dinky #803, USS Enterprise, Motion Picture, 1979, 4", MOC..$30.00

Vehicle, Ertl, USS Enterprise, Star Trek III, 1984, MOC, from $18 to..$25.00

Vehicle, Galoob, Ferengi Fighter, Next Generation, 1989, NRFB..$55.00

Vehicle, Galoob, Shuttlecraft Galileo, Next Generation, NRFB..$50.00

Vulcan Ears, 1976, MIP..$20.00

Water pistol, Aviva, gray phaser, 1979, 7", MOC.........$35.00

Yo-yo, Spectra Star, Data or Picard, MOC, each............$5.00

Yo-yo, Spectra Star, Star Trek Deep Space 9 graphics, 1993, MOC..$37.00

Star Wars

In the late seventies, the movie *Star Wars* became a box office hit, most notably for its fantastic special effects and its ever-popular theme of space adventure. Two more movies followed, *The Empire Strikes Back* in 1980 and *Return of the Jedi* in 1983. After the first movie, an enormous amount of related merchandise was released. A large percentage of these items was action figures, made by the Kenner company who included the logo of the 20th Century Fox studios (under whom they were licensed) on everything they made until 1980. Just before the second movie, Star Wars creator, George Lucas, regained control of the merchandise rights, and items inspired by the last two films can be identified by his own Lucasfilm logo. Since 1987, Lucasfilm, Ltd., has operated shops in conjunction with the Star Tours at Disneyland theme parks.

What to collect? First and foremost, buy what you yourself enjoy. But remember that condition is all-important. Look for items still mint in the box. Using that as a basis, if the box is missing, deduct at least half. If a major accessory or part is gone, the item is basically worthless. Learn to recognize the most desirable, most valuable items. There are lots of Star Wars bargains yet to be had!

Original packaging helps date a toy, since the package or card design was updated as each new movie was released. Naturally, items representing the older movies are more valuable than later issues. For more coverage of this subject, refer to *Schroeder's Collectible Toys, Antique to Modern* (Collector Books).

Activity set, 3-D Poster Art, poster, mask & figures to paint & assemble, 1978, MIB (sealed) $25.00

Album, Star Wars, w/insert, 1977, EX.........................$13.00

Bank, Darth Vader, ceramic, Roman Ceramic, 1977, MIB .$95.00

Bank, R2D2, ceramic, Roman Ceramics, 1977, MIB....$95.00

Bank, Yoda, ceramic, Sigma, M...................................$95.00

Book, Empire Strikes Back, pop-up, M $15.00

Book & cassette, Return of the Jedi, EX $5.00

Case, Empire Strikes Back, EX...................................$12.00

Catalog, toys, Kenner, 1980, 12 pages, 4x6", EX...........$9.00

Figure, A-Wing Pilot, Power of the Force, 3¾", MOC .$115.00

Figure, Admiral Ackbar, Return of the Jedi, w/accessories, 3¾", NM..$6.00

Figure, Anakin Skywalker, Star Wars, w/accessories, 3¾", NM..$30.00

Figure, AT-ST Driver, Return of the Jedi, 3¾", MOC ..$20.00

Figure, B-Wing Pilot, Return of the Jedi, 3¾", MOC...$15.00

Figure, Barada, Power of the Force, w/coin, complete, 3¾", NM..$40.00

Figure, Ben Obi-Wan Kenobi, 12", NM, from $100 to .$125.00

Figure, Bib Fortuna, Return of the Jedi, 3¾", EX........$10.00

Figure, Bossk, Empire Strikes Back, bounty hunter outfit, 3¾", NM..$10.00

Figure, Chewbacca, Return of the Jedi, 3¾", MOC.....$35.00

Figure, Chief Chirpa, Return of the Jedi, 3¾", MOC...$15.00

Figure, Darth Vader, Star Wars, w/accessories, 3¾", NM .$15.00

Figure, Dulok Scout, Ewoks, 3¾", MOC.....................$15.00

Figure, FX-7, Empire Strikes Back, w/accessories, 3¾", NM..$10.00

Figure, General Madine, Return of the Jedi, 3¾", MOC..$12.00

Figure, Greedo, Star Wars, w/accessories, 3¾", NM ...$10.00

Figure, Hammerhead, Star Wars, complete with accessories, from $10.00 to $12.00.

Figure, Han Solo, Empire Strikes Back, Bespin outfit, 3¾", NM $15.00

Figure, Han Solo, Return of the Jedi, trench coat, 3¾",
MOC...**$30.00**

Figure, IG-88, Empire Strikes Back, 3¾", MOC
(unpunched)...**$55.00**

Figure, Imperial Commander, Empire Strikes Back, w/acces-
sories, 3¾", NM.......................................**$8.00**

Figure, Imperial Commander, Empire Strikes Back, 3¾",
MOC, (unpunched).....................................**$35.00**

Figure, Imperial Stormtrooper, Empire Strikes Back, 3¾", M
(VG 41-back card) **$30.00**

Figure, Imperial TIE Fighter Pilot, Empire Strikes Back,
w/accessories, 3¾", NM **$12.00**

Figure, Jawa, Star Wars, w/cloth cape, 3¾", NM.........**$14.00**

Figure, Lando Calrissian, Star Wars, w/accessories, 3¾",
NM..**$12.00**

Figure, Lobot, Empire Strikes Back, w/accessories, 3¾",
NM..**$6.00**

Figure, Luke Skywalker, Empire Strikes Back, X-Wing Pilot
outfit, 3¾", M (VG card) **$65.00**

Figure, Luke Skywalker, Star Wars, w/accessories, 3¾",
NM..**$20.00**

Figure, Nikto, Return of the Jedi, 3¾", MOC..............**$15.00**

Figure, Paploo, Return of the Jedi, 3¾", MOC **$28.00**

Figure, Princess Leia Organa, Empire Strikes Back, Hoth outfit, 3¾", NM..**$15.00**

Figure, Princess Leia Organa, Return of the Jedi, combat poncho, 3¾", MOC **$40.00**

Figure, Rancor Keeper, Return of the Jedi, 3¾", MOC..**$10.00**

Figure, Rebel Commando, Return of the Jedi, 3¾", M (EX
card w/open bubble) **$12.00**

Figure, Ree-Yees, Return of the Jedi, 3¾", M (EX card w/open
bubble) **$10.00**

Figure, R2-D2, Empire Strikes Back, 3¾", MOC
(unpunched)..**$45.00**

Figure, R5-D4, Empire Strikes Back, 3¾", MOC..........**$65.00**

Figure, Security Guard, Return of the Jedi, white, 3¾",
MOC **$30.00**

Figure, Star Destroyer Commander, Star Wars, w/accessories,
3¾", NM..**$12.00**

Figure, Teebo, Tri-Logo, 3¾", MOC **$10.00**

Figure, Weequay, Return of the Jedi, w/accessories, 3¾",
NM..**$6.00**

Figure, Yoda, Empire Strikes Back, 3¾", EX **$12.00**

Figure, 2-1B, Empire Strikes Back, w/accessories, 3¾",
NM..**$10.00**

Folder, Ben Kenobi, NM...**$5.00**

Game, Destroy Death Star, G....................................**$15.00**

Game, Empire Strikes Back, Jedi Master, Kenner #41010,
1981, NMIB..**$25.00**

Magazine, People, July 1980, Empire Strikes Back cast cover,
EX..**$4.00**

Mask (Don Post), Chewbacca, hard plastic, EX **$80.00**

Mask (Don Post), Klaatu, hard plastic, EX..................**$40.00**

Movie viewer, MIB...**$45.00**

Night light, C-3PO, NM (VG card)...............................**$5.00**

Paper plate, Chewbacca, MIP (sealed)..........................**$5.00**

Pillow case, box only, Glow-in-the-Dark, 1983, EX......**$5.00**

Playset, Bespin Control Room, Micro Collection, NRFB .**$55.00**

Playset, Droid Factory, Star Wars, EXIB.....................**$100.00**

Playset, Hoth Turret Defense, Micro Collection, crack in base
otherwise EX **$25.00**

Playset, Jabba the Hutt, NRFB (Canadian/French)......**$85.00**

Playset, Sy Snootles and the Rebo Band, Return of the Jedi, 1983, MIB, $125.00. (Photo courtesy June Moon)

Playset, Tauntaun, Empire Strikes Back, EX (VG box missing
insert, proof of purchase removed)......................**$30.00**

Record, Empire Strikes Back, 45 rpm, w/booklet, M
(sealed) **$9.00**

Record, Return of the Jedi, 45 rpm, w/booklet, M
(sealed)..**$9.00**

Shoes, Clarks Jet Fighter, 1977, NM with origi-nal tags, $125.00. (Photo courtesy June Moon)

Tote bag, Return of the Jedi, blue canvas, MIP...........**$15.00**

Vehicle, B-Wing Fighter, Return of the Jedi, Kenner, 1983, MIB, $185.00. (Photo courtesy June Moon)

Vehicle, Boba Fett's Slave I, diecast, EX **$25.00**

Vehicle, Endor Forest Ranger, NRFB **$25.00**

Vehicle, Imperial TIE Fighter, Micro Collection, NM...**$30.00**

Vehicle, Interceptor (INT-4), Mini-Rigs, EX.................**$10.00**

Vehicle, Mobile Laser Cannon (MLC-3), EX...............**$10.00**

Vehicle, Side-Gunner, Droids, M (EX+ box)...............**$40.00**

Vehicle, Twin-Pod Cloud Car, diecast, EX..................**$25.00**

Vehicle, X-Wing Fighter, Micro Collection, G.............**$15.00**

Wastebasket, Return of the Jedi, litho tin, EX............**$25.00**

Steiff Animals

These stuffed animals originated in Germany around the turn of the century. They were created by Margaret Steiff, whose company continues to operate to the present day. They are identified by the button inside the ear and the identification tag (which often carries the name of the animal) on their chest. Over the years, variations in the tags and buttons help collectors determine approximate dates of manufacture.

Teddy bear collectors regard Steiff bears as some of the most valuable on the market. When assessing the worth of a bear, they use some general guidelines as a starting basis, though other features can come into play as well. For instance, bears made prior to 1912 that have long gold mohair fur start at a minimum of $75.00 per inch. If the bear has dark brown or curly white mohair fur instead, that figure may go as high as $135.00. From the 1920 to 1930 era, the price would be about $50.00 minimum per inch. A bear (or any other animal) on cast-iron or wooden wheels starts at $75.00 per inch; but if the tires are hard rubber, the value is much lower, at $27.00 per inch.

It's a fascinating study which is well covered in *Teddy Bears and Steiff Animals, First, Second, and Third Series,* by Margaret Fox Mandel. Also see Cynthia Powell's *Collector's Guide to Miniature Teddy Bears.*

Newsletter/Club: *Steiff Life*
Steiff Collectors Club
Beth Savino
c/o The Toy Store
7856 Hill Ave.
Holland, OH 43528; 419-865-3899 or 800-862-8697

Alligator, Gaty, original tag and button, 12", $95.00.

Bear, bendy type, caramel, incised button, ca 1960, 3½", NM **$35.00**

Bear, Cosy Koala, split chest tag, incised button, stock tag & hang tag, ca 1970, 5", M.....................................**$65.00**

Bear, gold mohair w/glass eyes, ca 1950, 6", EX......**$225.00**

Bear, Original Teddy, gold mohair, pet name on chest tag, 3½", M **$400.00**

Bear, Original Teddy, incised button, w/stock tag, original ribbon, ca 1960, 9", M..**$95.00**

Bear, Original Teddy, tan mohair, raised script button & original ribbon, ca 1950, 6", EX................................**$245.00**

Bear, Panda, raised script button, ca 1950, 8", EX....**$750.00**

Bear, Teddy Baby, replica of 1930s issue, brown, all identification, ca 1980s, 11½", M.....................................**$225.00**

Bear, Zotty, mohair w/plastic eyes, incised button, 11", M...**$150.00**

Bison, pet name on chest tag, raised script button & stock tag, ca 1950, 8" L, M..**$225.00**

Camel, Cosy Kamel, dralon, chest tag, raised script button & stock tag, ca 1960, 10½", M.................................**$100.00**

Camel, Original Steiff, chest tag, raised script button & stock tag, ca 1950, 11", NM.......................................**$250.00**

Camel, Original Steiff on chest tag, raised script button & stock tag, ca 1950, 5¾", NM...............................**$135.00**

Cat, Lizzy, chest tag, 2 incised buttons, stock tag & original ribbon, ca 1960, 6½", NM....................................**$135.00**

Cat, Tom cat, black velvet w/mohair tail & green glass eyes, original ribbon, no identification, NM...................**$95.00**

Cat, woolie, black & white w/jointed head, no identification, 2" L, NM...**$25.00**

Chick, felt & mohair ball-shaped body, no identification, 4½", EX..**$45.00**

Dog, Bazi, seated, chest tag, raised script button, stock tag & original collar, ca 1950, 7", NM..........................**$245.00**

Dog, Cockie, seated, black & white, original collar, 4½", EX..**$85.00**

Dog, Collie, lying down, glass eyes, no identification, ca 1950, 9" L, NM...**$95.00**

Dog, Collie, seated, no identification, 3½", NM..........**$85.00**

Dog, Dally, seated, pet name on chest tag, original red collar, 4", M..**$145.00**

Dog, Foxy, pet name on chest tag, original ribbon, ca 1950, 3¼", EX..**$85.00**

Dog, Molly, long cream mohair, FF underscored button w/full red stock tag, ca 1925, 6", NM **$395.00**

Dog, Peky, pet name on chest tag, original ribbon, ca 1950, 3", EX..**$75.00**

Dog, Snobby, gray mohair, glass eyes, pet name on chest tag, raised script button & stock tag, ca 1950, 5½", M...**$95.00**

Dog, Snobby (poodle), gray, chest tag & original collar, ca 1950, 5½", NM...**$95.00**

Dog, Waldi, pet name on chest tag, original collar, ca 1950, 10½", M...**$125.00**

Duck, Woolie, swimming position, incised button & stock tag, ca 1960, M...**$30.00**

Fox, Xorry, raised script button, ca 1950, 4", VG........**$65.00**

Frog, Froggy, velvet w/glass eyes, pet name on chest tag, raised script button & stock tag, ca 1950, 3", NM...............**$135.00**

Frog, swimming, mohair, chest tag, ca 1960, 11" L..**$125.00**

Goose, Tulla, mohair & felt w/blue glass eyes, chest tag, ca 1950, rare, EX..**$375.00**

Goose, Tulla, mohair w/blue glass eyes, no identification, ca 1950, 10", NM...**$325.00**

Hedgehog, Mucki, chest tag, incised button & stock tag, 4½", NM **$45.00**

Hen, woolie w/plastic feet, raised script button & stock tag, 2½", M..**$25.00**

Hippopotamus, mohair w/glass eyes, no teeth, ca 1950, 11", NM **$50.00**

Lady bug, woolie, no identification, NM, sm **$10.00**

Lion, Leo, pet name on chest tag, ca 1950, 4¼" L, M..**$125.00**

Lizard, Lizzy, velvet, no identification, ca 1950, 8" L, NM **$235.00**

Lobster, Crabby, pet name on chest tag, raised script button & stock tag, ca 1950, 6½" L, M..........................**$295.00**

Monkey, Jocko, bendy, incised button & stock tag, 3½", NM..**$50.00**

Monkey, Jocko type, rare striped version, ca 1926–34, 11", $850.00. (Photo courtesy Margaret Fox Mandel)

Mouse, Dormy, mohair & dralon, chest tag, raised script button & stock tag, ca 1960, 7½" across, M.............**$125.00**

Parrot, Lora, incised button & stock tag, ca 1960, 9", EX .**$135.00**

Pelican, Piccy, no identification, ca 1950, 9½", EX...**$285.00**

Penguin, Peggy, chest tag, ca 1950, 5", NM **$75.00**

Pig, Jolanthe, inised button, ca 1960, 5", NM............**$125.00**

Rabbit, woolie, black & white, raised script button & stock tag, ca 1950, 1½", M..**$40.00**

Raven, Hucky, woolie, raised script button & stock tag, 2", M...**$45.00**

Rhinoceros, Nosy, pet name on chest tag, ca 1950, 7", M...**$135.00**

Turkey, Tucky, pet name on chest tag (red print), ca 1950, 4", M...**$325.00**

Turkey, Tucky, raised script button, ca 1950, 5½", NM ..**$295.00**

Unicorn, mohair & dralon, chest tag, brass button & cloth stock tag, ca 1983, 7" L, NM **$95.00**

Walrus, Paddy, pajama bag, ca 1965, 18", $350.00. (Photo courtesy Margaret Fox Mandel)

String Holders

Today we admire string holders for their decorative nature. They are much sought after by collectors. However, in the 1800s, they were strictly utilitarian, serving as dispensers of string used to wrap food and packages. The earliest were made of cast iron. Later, advertising string holders appeared in general stores. They were made of tin or cast iron and were provided by companies pedaling such products as shoes, laundry supplies, and food. These advertising string holders command the highest prices.

These days we take cellophane tape for granted. Before it was invented, string was used to tie up packages. String holders became a staple item in the home kitchen. To add a whimsical touch, in the late 1920s and 1930s, many string holders were presented in human shapes, faces, animals, and fruits. Most of these novelty string holders were made of chalkware (plaster of Paris), ceramics, or wood fiber. If you were lucky, you might have won a plaster of Paris 'Super Hero' or comic character string holder at your local carnival. These prizes were known as 'carnival chalkware.' The Indian string holder was a popular giveaway, so was Betty Boop and Superman.

Our values reflect string holders in excellent condition.

Advisor: Ellen Bercovici (See Directory, String Holders)

Apple, many variations, chalkware, from $20 to **$35.00**

Apple w/face, ceramic, Py, from $100 to **$125.00**

Babies, 1 happy, 1 crying, ceramic, Lefton, pr, from $200 to...**$250.00**

Bananas, chalkware, from $85 to **$95.00**

Bird, 'String Nest Pull,' ceramic, from $25 to..............**$35.00**

Bird in birdcage, chalkware, from $85 to **$95.00**

Bird on branch, scissors in head, ceramic, from $75 to **$85.00**

Birdcage, red and white with green leaves and yellow bird, touches of brown, chalkware, from $85.00 to $95.00. (Photo courtesy Ellen Bercovici)

Bonzo (dog) w/bee on chest, ceramic, from $100 to **$125.00**

Boy, top hat & pipe, eyes to side, chalkware, from $50 to..**$60.00**

Bride, ceramic **$75.00**

Bride & bridesmaids, ceramic **$75.00**

Butler, Black man w/white lips & eyebrows, ceramic, minimum value **$250.00**

Chef, chalkware, from $35 to **$50.00**

Chef, Rice Crispy, chalkware, from $100 to **$125.00**

Chef w/rolling pin, full figure, chalkware, from $50 to..**$60.00**

Cherries, chalkware, from $95 to **$115.00**

Clown w/string around tooth, chalkware, from $85 to .**$95.00**
Dog, Schnauzer, ceramic, from $100 to **$125.00**
Dutch girl's head, chalkware **$50.00**
Elephant, yellow, England, ceramic, from $50 to **$60.00**
Girl in bonnet, eyes to side, chalkware, from $50 to .**$60.00**
Granny in rocking chair, Py, ceramic, from $100 to.**$125.00**
Groom & bridesmaids, ceramic **$75.00**
Heart, puffed, Cleminson, ceramic, from $40 to **$50.00**
House, Cleminson, ceramic, from $75 to....................**$85.00**
Iron w/flowers, ceramic, from $70 to **$80.00**
Jester, chalkware, from $85 to **$95.00**
Kitten w/ball of yarn, ceramic.....................................**$50.00**
Kitten w/ball of yarn, ceramic, homemade **$45.00**
Little Red Riding Hood, chalkware, minimum value ..**$200.00**
Maid, Sarsaparilla, ceramic, 1984, from $50 to............**$60.00**
Mammy, full figured, plaid & polka-dot dress, ceramic, from
    $100 to..**$125.00**
Mammy face, many variations, chalkware, from $200 to...**$250.00**
Man in top hat, head w/airbrushed accents, chalkware, 9".**$45.00**
Mouse, Josef Originals, ceramic, from $80 to.............**$90.00**
Penguin, ceramic, from $50 to......................................**$60.00**
Pig w/flowers, ceramic, from $100 to **$125.00**
Pirate & gypsy, wood fiber, pr, from $100 to............**$125.00**
Rooster, Royal Bayreuth, ceramic, from $300 to **$400.00**

Rose, red with green leaves, from $100.00 to $125.00. (Photo courtesy Ellen Bercovici)

Rosie the Riveter, chalkware, from $100 to **$125.00**
Sailor boy, chalkware, from $100 to **$125.00**
Senor, chalkware, from $40 to **$50.00**
Senora, chalkware, from $65 to **$75.00**
Soldier, head w/cap, chalkware **$50.00**
Witch in pumpkin, winking, ceramic, from $125 to .**$150.00**
Woman w/turban, chalkware, from $125 to.............**$150.00**

Swanky Swigs

These glass tumblers ranging in size from 3¼" to 4¾" were originally distributed by the Kraft company who filled them with their cheese spread. They were primarily used from the 1930s until sometime during the war, but they were brought out soon after and used to some extent until the late 1970s. Many were decorated with fired-on designs of flowers, 'Bustling Betty' scenes (assorted chores being done by a Gibson-type Betty), 'Antique' patterns (clocks, coal scuttles, lamps, kettles, coffee grinders, spinning wheels, etc.), ani-mals (in their 'Kiddie Cup' line), or solid colors of red, yellow, green, and blue (Fiestaware look alikes).

Even the lids are collectible and are valued at a minimum of $3.00, depending on condition and the advertising message they convey.

For more information we recommend *Collectible Glassware of the 40s, 50s, and 60s,* and *The Collector's Encyclopedia of Depression Glass,* both by Gene Florence; and *Collectible Drinking Glasses* by Mark Chase and Michael Kelly.

Note: All are USA issue unless noted Canadian.

Advisor: Joyce Jackson (See Directory, Swanky Swigs)

Antique #1, black, blue, brown, green, orange or red, ca
    1954, 3¾", each..**$2.50**
Antique #1, black, blue, brown, green, orange or red,
    Canadian, 3¼", each...**$10.00**
Antique #1, black, blue, brown, green, orange or red,
    Canadian, ca 1954, 4¾", each..............................**$20.00**
Antique #2, lime green, deep red, orange, blue or black,
    Canadian, ca 1974, 4⅝", each..............................**$25.00**
Bachelor Button, red, green & white, ca 1955, 3¾" **$3.00**
Bachelor Button, red, white & green, Canadian, ca 1955,
    3¼"...**$6.00**
Bachelor Button, red, white & green, Canadian, ca 1955,
    4¾"...**$15.00**
Band #1, red & black, ca 1933, 3⅜"..............................**$3.00**
Band #2, black & red, ca 1933, 3⅜"..............................**$3.00**
Band #2, black & red, Canadian, ca 1933, 4¾"...........**$20.00**
Band #3, white & blue, ca 1933, 3⅜" **$3.00**
Band #4, blue, ca 1933, 3⅜" **$3.00**
Bicentennial Tulip, green, red or yellow, ca 1975, 3¾", each..**$15.00**

Blue Tulips, ca 1937, 4¼", from $3.00 to $6.00; Bustling Betty, any color, from $2.00 to $4.00; Sailboats, #2, any color, ca 1936, from $8.00 to $10.00.

Bustlin' Betty, blue, brown, green, orange, red or yellow,
    Canadian, ca 1953, 3¼", each..............................**$10.00**
Bustlin' Betty, blue, brown, green, orange, red or yellow,
    Canadian, ca 1953, 4¾", each..............................**$20.00**
Carnival, blue, green, red or yellow, ca 1939, 3½", each .**$6.00**
Checkerboard, white w/blue, green or red, ca 1936, 3½",
    each **$20.00**
Checkerboard, white w/blue, green or red, Canadian, ca
    1936, 4¾", each..**$20.00**

Circles & Dot, any color, ca 1934, 3½", each **$4.00**

Circles & Dot, black, blue, green or red, Canadian, ca 1934, 4¾", each...**$20.00**

Coin, clear & plain w/indented coin decor around base, ca 1968, 3¾"..**$1.00**

Coin, clear & plain w/indented coin decor around base, Canadian, ca 1968, 3⅛" or 3¼", each **$2.00**

Colonial, clear w/indented waffle design around middle & base, ca 1976, 3¾", each...............................**$.50**

Colonial, clear w/indented waffle design around middle & base, ca 1976, 4⅜", each..............................**$1.00**

Cornflower #1, light blue & green, ca 1941, 3½", each ..**$3.00**

Cornflower #1, light blue & green, Canadian, ca 1941, 4⅝", each **$20.00**

Cornflower #1, light blue & green, Canadian, 3¼", each..**$10.00**

Cornflower #2, dark blue, light blue, red or yellow, ca 1947, 3½", each...**$3.00**

Cornflower #2, dark blue, light blue, red or yellow, Canadian, ca 1947, 3¼", each..............................**$10.00**

Cornflower #2, dark blue, light blue, red or yellow, Canadian, ca 1947, 4¼", each..............................**$20.00**

Crystal Petal, clear & plain w/fluted base, ca 1951, 3½", each...**$2.00**

Dots Forming Diamonds, red, ca 1935, 3½", each **$25.00**

Ethnic Series, lime green, royal blue, burgundy, poppy red or yellow, Canadian, ca 1974, 4⅝", each..................**$20.00**

Forget-Me-Not, dark blue, light blue, red or yellow, ca 1948, 3½", each...**$3.00**

Forget-Me-Not, dark blue, light blue, red or yellow, Canadian, 3¼", each...**$10.00**

Galleon, black, blue, green, red or yellow, Canadian, ca 1936, 3⅛", each..**$30.00**

Hostess, clear & plain w/indented groove base, ca 1960, 3¾", each...**$1.00**

Hostess, clear & plain w/indented groove base, Canadian, ca 1960, 3⅛" or 3¼", each **$2.00**

Hostess, clear & plain w/indented groove base, Canadian, ca 1960, 5⅝", each..**$5.00**

Jonquil (Posy Pattern), yellow & green, ca 1941, 3½", each **$3.00**

Jonquil (Posy Pattern), yellow & green, Canadian, ca 1941, 3¼"...**$10.00**

Jonquil (Posy Pattern), yellow & green, Canadian, ca 1941, 4⅝", each...**$20.00**

Kiddie Kup, black, blue, brown, green, orange or red, ca 1956, 3¾", each..**$3.00**

Kiddie Kup, black, blue, brown, green, orange or red, Canadian, ca 1956, 3¼", each.............................**$10.00**

Kiddie Kup, black, blue, brown, green, orange or red, Canadian, ca 1956, 4¾", each.............................**$20.00**

Lattice & Vine, white w/blue, green or red, ca 1936, 3½", each **$25.00**

Petal Star, clear, 50th Anniversary of Kraft Cheese Spreads, 1933-1983, ca 1983, 3¾", each.................................**$.50**

Petal Star, clear w/indented star base, ca 1978, 3¾", each...**$.25**

Petal Star, clear w/indented star base, Canadian, ca 1978, 3¼", each...**$2.00**

Plain, clear, like Tulip #1 w/out design, ca 1940, 3½", each..**$4.00**

Plain, clear, like Tulip #3 w/out design, ca 1951, 3⅞", each..**$5.00**

Provincial Crest, red & burgundy, Canadian, ca 1974, 4⅝", each **$25.00**

Sailboat #1, blue, ca 1936, 3½", each...........................**$12.00**

Special Issue, Del Monte Violet, Greetings From Kraft, ca 1942, 3½", each..**$50.00**

Special Issue, Greetings From Kraft, California Retail Grocers' Merchants' Assn, Del Monte CA 1938, red, ca 1938, 3½"..**$50.00**

Special Issue, Lewis-Pacific Dairymen's Assn, Kraft Foods Co, Sept 13, 1947, Chehalis WA, ca 1947, 3½", each..**$50.00**

Special Issue, Pasadena blue sailboat, Greetings From Kraft, blue, ca 1936, 3½"..**$50.00**

Sportsmen Series, red hockey, blue skiing, red football, red baseball, or green soccer, Canadian, ca 1976, 4⅝", each...**$25.00**

Stars #1, black, blue, green, red or yellow, Canadian, ca 1935, 4¾", each...**$20.00**

Stars #1, black, blue, green or red, ca 1935, 3½", each **$6.00**

Stars #1, yellow, ca 1935, 3½", each...........................**$25.00**

Stars #2, clear w/orange stars, Canadian, ca 1971, 4⅝", each...**$12.00**

Texas Centennial, black, blue, green or red, ca 1936, 3½", each...**$30.00**

Tulip (Posy Pattern), red & green, ca 1941, 3½", each...**$4.00**

Tulip (Posy Pattern), red & green, Canadian, ca 1941, 3¼", each **$10.00**

Tulip (Posy Pattern), red & green, Canadian, ca 1941, 4⅝", each **$20.00**

Tulip #1, black, blue, green, red or yellow, ca 1937, 3½", each...**$4.00**

Tulip #1, black, blue, green, red or yellow, Canadian, 3¼", each...**$10.00**

Tulip #1, black, blue, green or red, Canadian, ca 1937, 4⅝", each...**$20.00**

Tulip #2, black, blue, green or red, ca 1938, 3½", each ..**$20.00**

Tulip #3, dark blue, light blue, red or yellow, ca 1950, 3⅞", each...**$3.00**

Tulip #3, dark blue, light blue, red or yellow, Canadian, ca 1950, 4¾", each...**$20.00**

Tulip #3, dark blue, light blue, red or yellow, Canadian, 3¼", each...**$10.00**

Violet (Posy Pattern), blue & green, ca 1941, 3½", each ..**$4.00**

Violet (Posy Pattern), blue & green, Canadian, ca 1941, 3¼", each **$10.00**

Violet (Posy Pattern), blue & green, Canadian, ca 1941, 4⅝", each **$20.00**

Wildlife Series, black bear, Canadian goose, moose, or red fox, Canadian, ca 1975, 4⅝", each **$20.00**

Syroco

Syroco Inc. originated in New York in 1890 when a group of European woodcarvers banded together to produce original hand carvings for fashionable homes of the area. Their products were also used in public buildings throughout upstate New York, including the state capitol. Demand for those products led to the development of the original Syroco reproduction process that allowed them to copy the original carvings with no loss of detail. They later developed exclusive hand-applied color finishes to further enhance the product, which they continued to improve and refine over ninety years.

Syroco's master carvers use tools and skills handed down from father to son through many generations. Woods used, depending on the effect called for, include Swiss pear wood, oak, mahogany, and wormy chestnut. When a design is completed, it is transformed into a metal cast through their molding and tooling process. A compression mold system using wood fiber was used from the early 1940s to the 1960s. Since 1962 a process has been used where pellets of resin are injected into a press, heated to the melting point, and then injected into the mold. Because the resin is liquid, it fills every crevice, thus producing an exact copy of the carver's art. It is then cooled, cleaned, and finished.

Other companies have produced similar items, among them are Multi Products, now of Erie, Pennsylvania. It was incorporated in Chicago in 1941 but in 1976 was purchased by John Hronas. Multi Products hired a staff of artists, made some wood originals, and developed a tooling process for forms. They used a styrene-based material, heavily loaded with talc or calcium carbonate. A hydraulic press was used to get excess material out of the forms. Shapes were dried in kilns for seventy-two hours, then finished and, if the design required it, trimmed in gold. Items made included bears, memo pads, thermometers, brush holders, trays, plaques, nut bowls, napkin holders, etc., which were sold mainly as souvenirs. The large clocks and mirrors were made before the 1940s, and may sell for as much as $100.00 and more, depending on condition. Syroco used gold trim, but any other painted decoration you might encounter was very likely done by an outside firm. Some collectors prefer the painted examples and tend to pay a little more to get them. You may find similar products also stamped 'Ornawood,' 'Decor-A-Wood,' and 'Swank.'

See also Motion Clocks.

Advisor: Doris J. Gibbs (See Directory, Syroco)

Ashtray, double, glass bowls, cigarette compartment in center, from $10.00 to $20.00. (Photo courtesy Doris J. Gibbs)

Ashtray, florals at sides, rectangular receptacle, from 2 to 4 rests, Syroco, 4x6", from $6 to **$10.00**
Ashtray, florals at square sides, round receptacle, from 2 to 4 rests, Syroco, 5½x5½", from $7 to **$10.00**
Ashtray, steer and building on side, marked Alamo TX, from $3 to..**$10.00**

Barometer, ship's captain at wheel, round mechanism at wheel's center, from $10 to....................................**$15.00**
Bookends, End of the Trail, pr, from $10 to **$15.00**
Bookends, Mount Rushmore, pr, from $10 to.............**$15.00**
Box, bear, waterfall & trees on lid, marked Yellowstone Nat Park, 3½x4½", from $5 to **$7.00**
Box, cowboy boots & saddle on lid, w/paper label...**$12.50**
Box, floral design at sides & on lid, Syroco, 5½x5½", from $5 to...**$10.00**
Box, rope design on lid, velvet lining, Syroco, 6x6", from $10 to...**$15.00**
Box, standing dog on lid, 4x6", from $5 to................**$10.00**
Box, swirl design, 5½x7", from $8 to.........................**$10.00**
Brush holder, ship w/white triple mainsails, 4½", from $7 to...**$12.00**
Brush holder, 2 drunks w/keg, 5", from $5 to **$10.00**
Brush holder, 4 puppies in a basket, from $8 to........**$10.00**
Figure, Cape Cod fisherman & woman, painted, pr, from $6 to...**$15.00**
Figure, musician, painted, from $10 to **$15.00**
Figure, seated Indian, from $6 to **$10.00**
Picture frame, 3x2½"...**$6.00**
Picture frame, 8x5½", from $6 to **$12.00**
Pipe holder, 2 horses at gate, 3 rests, from $12 to **$15.00**
Plate, barn & silo pastoral scene at center, fruit & vegetables at rim, 8", from $2 to **$5.00**
Plate, pine cones & leaves, 4", from $2 to....................**$5.00**
Thermometer, captain at ship's wheel, painted, marked Copyright Thad Co, 4"..**$15.00**
Thermometer, Scottie dogs at sides, magnet at bottom, 4", from $5 to..**$10.00**
Tie rack, bartender behind bar w/bottles, painted, 6x9½", from $10 to..**$20.00**
Tie rack, pointer dog at top, metal hangers, 7x12", from $10 to...**$20.00**

Tray, embossed flowers, marked Multi Products, 11" long, from $8.00 to $14.00.

Wall plaque, crucifix, white, 8", from $5 to.................**$10.00**
Wall plaque, Our Mother of Perpetual Help, 4x5", from $5 to...**$10.00**
Wall plaque, Scottie dog, repainted, 6", from $2 to......**$8.00**
Wall shelf, floral w/acanthus leaf, bead trim at top edge, Multi Products, 9x7", pr, from $7 to.....................**$12.00**

Taylor, Smith and Taylor

Though this company is most famous for their pastel dinnerware line, Lu Ray, they made many other patterns, and some of them are very collectible. They were located in the East Liverpool area of West Virginia, the 'dinnerware capitol' of the world. Their answer to HLC's very successful Fiesta line was Vistosa. It was made in four primary colors and though quite attractive, the line was never developed to include any more than twenty items. Other lines/shapes that collectors especially look for are Taverne (also called Silhouette — similar to a line made by Hall), Conversation (a shape designed by Walter Dorwin Teague, 1950 to 1954), and Pebbleford (a textured, pastel line on the Versatile shape, 1952 to 1960).

For more information we recommend *Collector's Guide to LuRay Pastels* by Bill and Kathy Meehan (Collector Books).

Note: To evaluate King O'Dell, add 15% to the values we list for Conversation. For Boutonniere, add 15% to our Ever Yours values; and for Dwarf Pine, add the same amount to the values suggested for Versatile.

See also LuRay Pastels.

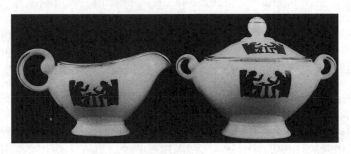

Silhouette on the Laurel shape: Creamer, $10.00; sugar bowl, $15.00. (Photo courtesy Bill and Kathy Meehan)

Conversation, bowl, vegetable; oval, sm	**$5.00**
Conversation, butter dish	**$9.00**
Conversation, cup & saucer	**$3.50**
Conversation, plate, dinner; 1950-54	**$2.50**
Conversation, salt & pepper shakers, pr	**$5.00**
Ever Yours, cake plate	**$6.00**
Ever Yours, creamer	**$2.50**
Ever Yours, plate, salad	**$1.50**
Ever Yours, platter, oval	**$3.00**
Ever Yours, tea tile	**$20.00**
Pebbleford, coupe soup	**$3.00**
Pebbleford, creamer	**$5.00**
Pebbleford, cup & saucer	**$5.00**
Pebbleford, plate, dinner	**$3.00**
Pebbleford, salt & pepper shakers, pr	**$5.00**
Petit Point Flowers, bowl, mixing; 9"	**$15.00**
Petit Point Flowers, plate, tab handles, 11"	**$10.00**
Petit Point Flowers, platter, tab handles, 12½"	**$12.00**
Revielle, bowl, 8¼"	**$22.00**
Revielle, bowl, 9"	**$24.00**
Revielle, gravy boat w/tray	**$24.00**
Revielle, plate, dinner; 10"	**$9.00**
Revielle, plate, 6½"	**$4.00**
Revielle, platter, oval, 11"	**$25.00**
Revielle, salt & pepper shakers, handles, pr	**$18.00**

Silhouette, plate, 9", Laurel shape	**$8.00**
Taverne, bowl, oval, 9¼"	**$22.00**
Taverne, bowl, soup; 7¾"	**$15.00**
Taverne, bowl, vegetable; 8¾"	**$22.00**
Taverne, creamer, footed	**$14.00**
Taverne, cup & saucer	**$15.00**
Versatile, cup & saucer	**$3.00**
Versatile, divided baker	**$15.00**
Versatile, egg cup, double	**$10.00**
Versatile, plate, chop	**$6.00**
Versatile, platter, 13"	**$4.00**
Versatile, sauce boat	**$4.00**
Vistosa, bowl, coupe soup; from $20 to	**$25.00**
Vistosa, bowl, fruit; from $10 to	**$15.00**
Vistosa, bowl, soup; lug handled, from $25 to	**$30.00**

Vistosa, chop plate, 12", from $30.00 to $40.00; Teacup and saucer, $22.00. (Photo courtesy Bill and Kathy Meehan)

Vistosa, coffee cup, AD; from $30 to	**$35.00**
Vistosa, creamer, from $15 to	**$20.00**
Vistosa, plate, 10", from $50 to	**$60.00**
Vistosa, plate, 6", from $10 to	**$15.00**
Vistosa, plate, 9", from $15 to	**$20.00**
Vistosa, salt & pepper shakers, pr, from $20 to	**$30.00**
Vistosa, sauce boat, from $100 to	**$125.00**
Vistosa, sugar bowl, w/lid, from $20 to	**$25.00**
Vistosa, teacup, from $10 to	**$15.00**
Vistosa, teapot, 6-cup, from $80 to	**$100.00**
Vistosa, water jug, 2-qt, from $75 to	**$85.00**

Vogue, covered casserole, $27.00. (Photo courtesy Bill and Kathy Meehan)

Vogue, plate, 10"	**$3.50**
Vogue, sauce boat	**$8.00**

Tiara Exclusives

Collectors are just beginning to take notice of the glassware sold through Tiara in-home parties, their Sandwich line in particular. Several companies were involved in producing the lovely colored glassware they've marketed over the years, among them Indiana Glass, Fenton, Dalzell Viking, and L.E. Smith. In the late 1960s, Tiara contracted with Indiana to produce their famous line of Sandwich dinnerware (a staple at Indiana Glass since the late 1920s). Their catalogs continue to carry this pattern, and over the years, it has been offered in many colors: ruby, teal, crystal, amber, green, pink, blue, and others in limited amounts. We've listed a few pieces of Tiara's Sandwich below, and though the market is unstable, our estimates will serve to offer an indication of current market values. Unless you're sure of what you're buying, though, don't make the mistake of paying 'old' Sandwich prices for Tiara. To learn more about the two lines, we recommend *Collectible Glassware from the 40s, 50s, and 60s* by Gene Florence (Collector Books).

Ashtray, Sandwich, 4 rests, 7⅜", from $5 to **$7.00**

**Basket, Sandwich, 10",
from $25.00 to $32.50.**

Bowl, salad; Sandwich, 5", from $2 to **$3.50**
Bowl, salad; Sandwich, 6 crimps at top edge, 10", from $14
   to **$16.00**
Bowl, vegetable; Sandwich, deep & round w/flared sides, 8"
   dia, from $10 to **$12.00**
Butter dish, Sandwich, w/high domed lid, 6", from $18
   to **$25.00**
Candle holder, Sandwich, 8½", pr, from $15 to **$18.00**
Candle lamp, Sandwich, egg-shaped top w/footed base, 5¾",
   from $8 to...**$10.00**
Canister, Sandwich, 5⅝", from $6 to **$8.00**
Canister, Sandwich, 7½", from $8 to **$10.00**
Canister, Sandwich, 8⅞", from $10 to **$12.00**
Clock, Sandwich, traditional metal face w/wide glass rim,
   battery-operated, 12", from $18 to........................**$20.00**
Creamer, Sandwich, footed, 5", from $4 to....................**$5.00**
Cruet, Sandwich, crimped top, w/stopper, 6", from $7 to .**$9.00**
Cup, Sandwich, 9-oz, from $2.50 to **$3.50**
Decanter, Sandwich, hand blown w/hand-ground stopper,
   10", from $12 to **$18.00**

Dish, relish; Sandwich, 3-compartment, 12", from $10 to ..**$12.00**
Egg tray, Sandwich, 12", from $10 to..........................**$14.00**
Goblet, wine; Sandwich, from $3 to **$6.00**
Pitcher, Sandwich, 68-oz, from $20 to **$25.00**
Plate, dinner; Sandwich, 10", from $6 to **$8.00**
Plate, salad; Sandwich, 8", from $3 to..........................**$5.00**
Platter, Sandwich, footed, from $12 to.......................**$15.00**
Platter, Sandwich, 12", from $9 to **$12.00**
Platter, Sandwich, 16" dia, from $10 to......................**$15.00**
Platter, Sandwich, 8½", from $6 to **$8.00**
Salt & pepper shakers, Sandwich, 4¾", pr, from $12 to ..**$15.00**
Saucer, Sandwich, 6", from $1 to..................................**$2.00**
Sugar bowl, Sandwich, footed, 2-handled, open, 5", from $4
   to..**$5.00**
Tray, serving; Sandwich, high rim edge, 10", from $9 to..**$12.00**
Tumbler, Sandwich, footed, 10-oz, 6½", from $4 to **$6.00**
Vase, Sandwich, footed, 3¾", from $6 to......................**$8.00**

Tire Ashtrays

Manufacturers of tires issued miniature versions that contained ashtray inserts that they usually embossed with advertising messages. Others were used as souvenirs from World's Fairs. The earlier styles were made of glass or glass and metal, but by the early 1920s, they were replaced by the more familiar rubber-tired variety. The inserts were often made of clear glass, but colors were also used, and once in awhile you'll find a tin one. The tires themselves were usually black; other colors are rarely found. Hundreds have been produced over the years; in fact, the larger tire companies still issue them occasionally, but you no longer see the details or colors that are evident in the pre-WWII tire ashtrays. Although the common ones bring modest prices, rare examples sometimes sell for up to several hundred dollars. For ladies or non-smokers, some miniature tires contained a pin tray.

For more information we recommend *Tire Ashtray Collector's Guide* by Jeff McVey.

Advisor: Jeff McVey (See Directory, Tire Ashtrays)

Atlas Bucron...**$75.00**

BF Goodrich Silvertown Lifesaver Radial HR70-15, clear insert, 100th Anniversary 1970, MIB, $50.00. (Photo courtesy Jeff McVey)

Bridgestone D-Lug 33.25.35 ....$30.00
Continental M+S $50.00
Cooper Cobra Radial GT..$25.00
Dayton Deluxe Thorobred, red glass insert $125.00
Diamond Balloon, blue glass insert $85.00
Dominion Royal Heavy Duty.......................................$90.00
Dunlop Gold Seal 78..$30.00
Firestone Deluxe Champion $35.00
Firestone Heavy Duty High Speed Balloon 6.00-18....$75.00
Firestone Super Sports Wide Oval..............................$35.00
Firestone 40 X 12..$100.00
Fisk Tuf-Lug $150.00
General Power Jet...$35.00
General XP2000H HR $25.00
Goodrich Comp T/A...$30.00
Goodrich Powersaver Radial......................................$25.00
Goodrich Silvertown 6.00-21.....................................$55.00
Goodyear Double Eagle 6.00-21...............................$125.00
Goodyear Eagle VR50..$30.00
Goodyear Nylon Hi-Miler Cross Rib...........................$40.00
Goodyear Wrangler Radial $20.00
Goodyear 6.70-15 4 Ply...$45.00
Hood Arrow $65.00
India Super Service, w/electric lighter $200.00
Jetzon..$20.00
Kelly-Springfield Tom Cat $100.00
Kelly-Springfield 9.00-20 Truck..................................$50.00
Lee of Conshohocken Truck-Bus $75.00
Miller Deluxe Long Safe Mileage Geared-To-The-Road..$80.00
Miller Farm Service Deep Cleat $40.00
Mohawk III Tissimo..$35.00
Mohawk Super Chief $40.00
Pennsylvania Low Pressure 6.50-16...........................$50.00
Pennsylvania Vacuum Cup, all glass $200.00
Phillips 66 Radial Steel Belted $25.00
Pirelli Cinturato $40.00
Republic Staghound...$125.00
Seiberling All-Tread $40.00
Seiberling Safe-Aire 7.60-15......................................$35.00
Semperit..$40.00
Toyo Radial Z-2 ....$40.00
Uniroyal Master $45.00
US Royal Heavy Duty Six...$85.00
Vogue Twin Tread Tyre $60.00
Western Auto...$30.00
Yokohama Radial 165SR14 ....$35.00
Zenith..$40.00

Tobacco Collectibles

Until lately, the tobacco industry spent staggering sums on advertising their products, and scores of retail companies turned out many types of smoking accessories such as pipes, humidors, lighters, and ashtrays. Even though the smoking habit isn't particularly popular nowadays, collecting tobacco-related memorabilia is! See *Huxford's Collectible Advertising* by Sharon and Bob Huxford for more information.

See also Cigarette Lighters.

Club: Tobacciana
Chuck Thompson and Associates
P.O. Box 11652
Houston, TX 77293; Send SASE for free list of publications

Club/Newsletter: *Tobacco Jar*
Society of Tobacco Jar Collectors
Charlotte Tarses, Treasurer
3011 Fallstaff Road #307
Baltimore, MD 21209; Dues: $30 per year ($35 outside of U.S.)

Cigar box, Counsellor, man w/long white beard holding cigar box, EX+..$45.00
Cigar box, Country Club, golfer, canoes, tennis players, rowers, EX+ $85.00
Cigar box, Red Ranger, red fox being chased by dogs, 2 for 5¢, EX $75.00
Cigar cutter, pearl handle...$95.00
Cigarette dispenser, painted wood, storage box on 1 end, bird on other, move lever forward, bird picks up cigarette....$75.00
Cigarette dispenser, plastic roll-top w/leather side inserts, Rolinx, England, ca 1950s, 2½x5¾" $30.00
Cigarette holder, brass w/leather covering, Amity, ca 1950s, 3½x2½"...$10.00
Cigarette holder, brass w/leather covering, cylindrical w/lg ring handle on lid, ca 1940s, 6x3¼"......................$20.00
Cigarette pack, Camel 75th Birthday...........................$12.00
Cigarette package holder, chromium, spring loaded, ca 1950s, 3x2¼", MIB...$60.00
Cigarette tin, Lucky Strike, 'flat fifties,' ca 1940s, 4½x5¾", EX $30.00
Clock, Kool Cigarettes, glass w/metal frame, penguins flank circle, Kools Refresh Hour After Hour, round, EX....$280.00
Dice, Marlboro, original leather pouch, MIB...............$35.00

Display box, Cremo Cigars, cardboard with dummy cigars, standard size, EX, $85.00.

Display, Kool Cigarettes, tin, Willy & open packs, Snow Fresh...., 8x7", VG+..$25.00
Door plate, Chesterfield Cigarettes, porcelain, pack of cigarettes in center, ca 1920-40s, 9x4", EX................$140.00
Door plate, L&M Cigarettes, Friendly Flavor, open pack, EX+ $40.00
Fan, Kool Cigarettes, diecut cardboard w/wooden handle, Willy w/product, 1937, 10x8", VG......................$30.00
Game, Salem Cigarettes promotional, clear plastic disk w/cigarettes & pack inside, try to get cigarettes in pack, ca '50 ....$20.00

Humidor, Prince Albert Tobacco, glass w/tin lid & paper labels, Humi-Seal, VG..............................**$20.00**

Match holder, Kool Cigarettes, tin, Willy left of Matches, 8x7", EX...**$16.00**

Matchbox, chromium, w/sliding door & bottom striker, ca 1930s, 2x1½"..**$20.00**

Nail clippers & file, Raleigh Cigarettes, chrome-plated steel, stamped w/Brown & Williamson logo, EX.............**$6.50**

Pipe, meerschaum, flowers & swirls, amber stem, 6½"..**$135.00**

Pipe, meerschaum, lady's hand as bowl, silver ferrule, 5¾"...**$110.00**

Pipe, meerschaum, turk's head, long stem, 16".......**$150.00**

Pipe & match holder, brass, figural cowboy book, Trophy Craft, ca 1940s, 4"....................................**$40.00**

Pipe rack, marquetry wood, humidor compartment centers storage space for 3 pipes each side, ca 1945, 5½x10"..**$45.00**

Sign, Bull Durham Smoking Tobacco, cardboard, Black lady w/pipe at General Store, ca 1930s, 10x25", VG.**$110.00**

Sign, Camel Cigarettes, paper, James Daly at right of Have a Real Cigarette, 11x21" EX.......................**$25.00**

Sign, Camel Cigarettes, test pilot & pack of cigarettes w/vintage warplanes beyond, ca 1942, 11x21", EX.......**$60.00**

Sign, Chesterfield Cigarettes, cardboard, actor Paul Douglas promoting product, 21x22", M..............**$65.00**

Sign, Chesterfield Cigarettes, embossed painted tin, Chesterfield above pack over tobacco leaves, 29x19", EX...**$25.00**

Sign, Kool Cigarettes, paper, Switch From Hots to..., Willy & product pack lower right, 15x10", NM...................**$10.00**

Sign, Lord Baltimore Cigars, cardboard, burning cigar, Tastes Good, ca 1930s, 7x13", EX......................**$12.00**

Sign, Lucky Strike Cigarettes, cardboard, couple floating in the air, 'flat fifties,' 50 Cigarettes 27¢, 42x26", VG **$350.00**

Sign, Lucky Strike Cigarettes, cardboard, pack of cigarettes, Have You Tried..., framed, 18x13½" **$90.00**

Sign, Lucky Strike Cigarettes, cardboard standup, Christmas scene, Give a Christmas Carton..., 30x20", M.....**$375.00**

Sign, Marlboro, embossed metal, cowboy on horse, 24x18", VG+...**$20.00**

Sign, Model Smoking Tobacco, Make a Date..., features Elyse Knox, 29½x21", EX..**$80.00**

Sign, Old Gold Cigarettes, cardboard standup, Fred Waring & His Pennsylvanians, 18x24", EX...........................**$50.00**

Sign, Philip Morris, Saftey First, heavy washable paper, 40x23", NM...**$140.00**

Sign, Philip Morris Cigarettes, cardboard, Lucy & Desi by open pack, 41x29", EX......................................**$325.00**

Sign, Philip Morris Cigarettes, tin, bellboy & 2 packs, Call for... on black background, 46x16", VG..............**$275.00**

Statuette, Raleigh Cigarettes, metal bust of Sir Walter, 5", VG+ **$3.50**

Thermometer, L&M Cigarettes, red, white & yellow, Reach for... above hand pulling cigarette from package, 13x6", G **$35.00**

Thermometer, Mail Pouch Tobacco, porcelain, Treat Yourself, 38x8", VG **$90.00**

Thermometer, Marvels Cigarettes, tin, bird & open pack, Cigarette of Quality, 12x4", EX+.........................**$125.00**

Tin, Big Ben Smoking Tobacco, horse broadside, sun in background, red w/black band at bottom, snap top, EX+...**$50.00**

Tin, Camel Cigarettes, Turkish & Domestic Blend, flat, 4½x5¾", VG..**$30.00**

Tin, Camel Cigarettes, 100's, round, EX.................**$45.00**

Tin, Dan Patch Cut Plug, black horse & writing on yellow, 4x6", VG **$25.00**

Tin, Dutch Masters, Dutchmen seated around table, slip lid, round, 5½x5", EX..**$30.00**

Tin, Dan Patch, paper label, round, EX+, $135.00.

Tin, pocket; Honeymoon, man on crescent moon, lady's head in smoke, NM..**$200.00**

Tin, pocket; Lucky Strike Roll Cut Tobacco, red bull's eye on green, VG+...**$65.00**

Tin, Red Man Chewing Tobacco, tin, 1989, 6x6", EX.**$10.00**

Toothbrush Holders

Novelty toothbrush holders have been modeled as animals of all types, in human forms, and in the likenesses of many storybook personalities. Today all are very collectible, especially those representing popular Disney characters. Some are made of bisque and are decorated over the glaze. Condition of the paint is an important consideration when trying to arrive at an evaluation.

For more information, refer to *Pictorial Guide to Toothbrush Holders* by Marilyn Cooper.

Advisor: Marilyn Cooper (See Directory, Toothbrush Holders)

Cat with Bass Fiddle, two holes, Japan, 6", $150.00. (Photo courtesy of Marilyn Cooper)

Bear w/scarf & hat, multicolored, 2 holes, Japan, 5½"..**$80.00**

Big Bird, yellow w/orange feet, 2 holes, RCC/Taiwan, 4½".**$80.00**

Bird, white w/black & brown highlights on wings, yellow beak, 1 hole, Japan, 4¾".....................................**$80.00**

Boy w/black top hat, red pants, black jacket & shoes, red & white dog at side, 2 holes, Japan, 5½" **$75.00**

Candlestick maker, blue shirt, white apron w/red vertical stripes, 1 hole, Goldcastle/Japan, 5¼" **$80.00**

Cat (Halloween), black w/yellow eyes, 1 hole, 4" ...**$140.00**

Children in auto, boy & girl, multicolored, 2 holes, Japan, 5" **$80.00**

Cowboy next to cactus, hands folded across chest, multicolored, 3 holes, Japan, 5½"..**$85.00**

Dachshund, black w/colored splotches, 2 holes, Japan, 5¼" **$80.00**

Dalmatian, natural colors, purple bow, tail is tray, 1 hole, Germany #105, 4" **$175.00**

Dog begging, brown w/black highlights, green base, 2 holes, lustre, 3¾" **$100.00**

Ducky Dandy, in black tuxedo, 2 holes, Japan, 4¼"..**$175.00**

Elephant w/tusk, white w/pink ears, 1 holes, Japan, 5½" ..**$80.00**

Genie (black), white turban, green shirt, yellow belt, red pants, 3 holes, SHOP/Japan, 5¾" **$110.00**

Humpty Dumpty, sitting on wall, green, 3 holes, Pat Pend, 5½"..**$125.00**

Indian Chief, white shirt w/red trim, beautiful headdress, 2 holes, Japan, 4½" **$250.00**

Little Red Riding Hood, standing beside green stump, 1 hole, DRGM/Germany, 5½" **$225.00**

Mexican boy, yellow sombrero, green shirt, white pants, red & yellow scarf, 2 holes, Japan, 5½" **$90.00**

Penguin, natural colors, 3 holes, Japan, 5½"...............**$95.00**

Rabbit, green w/pink ears & mouth, 1 hole, Norwood #1724/Germany, 5½"..**$90.00**

Scottie dogs, 1 red, 1 black & 1 white dog in middle, 3 holes, Goldcastle/Japan, 4⅛" **$90.00**

Three brown bears w/white bowls, 3 holes, KIM USUI/Japan, 4" **$95.00**

Three Little Pigs, two with instruments, one laying bricks, two holes, Japan, pre-war, NM, $225.00.

Toys

Toy collecting has long been an area of very strong activity, but over the past decade it has really expanded. Many of the larger auction galleries have cataloged toy auctions, and it isn't uncommon for scarce nineteenth-century toys in good condition go for $5,000.00 to $10,000.00 and up. Toy shows are popular, and there are clubs, newsletters, and magazines that cater only to the needs and wants of toy collectors. Though once buyers ignored toys less than thirty years old, in more recent years, even some toys from the eighties and nineties are sought after.

Condition has more bearing on the value of a toy than any other factor. A used toy in good condition with no major flaws will still be worth only about half (in some cases much less) as much as one in mint (like new) condition. Those mint and in their original boxes will be worth considerably more than the same toy without its box.

There are many good toy guides on the market today including *Modern Toys, American Toys, 1930 to 1980,* by Linda Baker; *Collecting Toys* and *Collecting Toy Trains* by Richard O'Brien; *Schroeder's Collectible Toys, Antique to Modern; Elmer's Price Guide to Toys* by Elmer Duellman; *Toys of the Sixties, A Pictorial Guide*, by Bill Bruegman; *Occupied Japan Toys With Prices* by David C. Gould and Donna Crevar-Donaldson; *Toys, Antique and Collectible, Antique and Collectible Toys, 1870 –1950*, and *Character Toys and Collectibles*, all by David Longest; and *Collector's Guide to Tinker Toys* by Craig Strange. More books are listed in the subcategory narratives that follow. With the exception of O'Brien's (Books Americana) and Bruegman's (Cap't Penny Productions), all are published by Collector Books.

See also Advertising Character Collectibles; Breyer Horses; Bubble Bath Containers; Character Collectibles; Disney Collectibles; Dolls; Fast-Food Collectibles; Fisher-Price; Halloween; Hartland Plastics, Inc.; Model Kits; Paper Dolls; Games; Puzzles; Star Trek; Star Wars; Steiff Animals; Trolls.

Action Figures and Accessories

Back in 1964, Barbie dolls were sweeping the feminine side of the toy market by storm. Hasbro took a risky step in an attempt to capture the interest of the male segment of the population. Their answer to the Barbie craze was GI Joe. Since no self-respecting boy would admit to playing with dolls, Hasbro called their boy dolls 'action figures,' and to the surprise of many, they were phenomenally successful. Today action figures generate just as much enthusiasm among toy collectors as they ever did among little boys.

Action figures are simply dolls with poseable bodies. The original GI Joes were 12" tall, but several other sizes were made over the years, too. Some are 8" to 9", others 6", and 3¾" figures have been favored in recent years. GI Joe was introduced in the 3¾" size in the eighties and proved to be unprecedented in action figure sales. (See also GI Joe.)

In addition to the figures themselves, each company added a full line of accessories such as clothing, vehicles, play sets, weapons, etc. — all are avidly collected. Be aware of condition! Original packaging is extremely important. In fact, when it comes to the recent issues, loose, played-with examples are seldom worth more than a few dollars.

For more information, refer to *Collectible Action Figures* by Paris and Susan Manos; *Mego Toys* by Wallace M. Chrouch; and *Collector's Guide to Dolls in Uniform* by Joseph Bourgeois.

Club: The Classic Action Figure Collector Club
Old Forest Press, Inc.
P.O. Box 2095
Halesite, NY 11743; Send SASE for information about club and official club magazine, *Collect 'Em All*

Action Jackson, outfit, Air Force Pilot, Mego, MOC....**$10.00**
Adventures of Indiana Jones, figure, Indiana Jones, Kenner, MOC..**$125.00**
Aliens, accessory, EVAC Fighter, Kenner, MIB............**$25.00**
Aliens, figure, Bishop, Gorilla, Killer Crab, Mantis or Panther, MOC, each...**$10.00**
American West, figure, Cochise, Mego, 8", M (NM box).**$55.00**
Batman, accessory, Batmobile, Toy Biz, NRFB **$50.00**
Batman, figure, Riddler or Robin, Toy Biz, MOC, each......**$15.00**
Batman Returns, figure, Catwoman or Robin, MOC, each.**$15.00**
Battlestar Galactica, figure, Daggit, Mattel, 3¾", EX ...**$15.00**
Beetlejuice, figure, Exploding Beetlejuice or Shipwreck Beetlejuice, Kenner, 2nd series, MOC, each, from $10 to **$14.00**

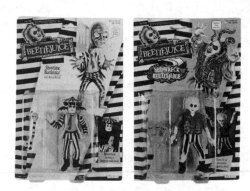

Beetlejuice Showtime figures, MOC from $10.00 to $14.00. (Photo courtesy June Moon)

Best of the West, figure, Fighting Eagle, Marx, w/accessories, EX **$160.00**
Best of the West, figure, Jaimie West, Marx, missing tether, EX **$35.00**
Best of the West, figure, Jed Gibson, Marx, M..........**$125.00**
Best of the West, figure, Johnny West, Marx, w/most accessories, EX..**$30.00**
Best of the West, figure, Sheriff Garrett, Marx, w/17 accessory pieces, NM..**$100.00**
Best of the West, figure set, Geronimo & Pinto, Marx, complete, EXIB **$135.00**
Best of the West, horse, Pancho, Marx, palomino, NM .**$20.00**
Big Jim, accessory, Kung Fu Studio, MIP...................**$50.00**
Bonanza, figure, Ben Cartwright, American Character, 8", complete w/horse & accessories, MIB................**$180.00**
Buck Rogers in the 25th Century, figure, Buck Rogers, Mego, 12", MIB..**$80.00**
Captain Action, figure, Action Boy, Ideal, complete w/space suit accessories & Panther, NM..........................**$400.00**
Captain Action, outfit, Green Hornet, complete, M (EX+ box)..**$300.00**
Clash of the Titans, figure, Charon, Mattel, NM.........**$25.00**

DC Comics Super Heroes, figure, Riddler, Toy Biz, MOC.**$15.00**
Droids, figure, any character, Kenner, 3¾", MOC, each..**$20.00**
Dukes of Hazzard, figure, Luke, Mego, 3¾", MOC.....**$20.00**
ET, figure, LJN, 3", rare, MOC..................................**$20.00**
Flash Gordon, figure set, Flash, Dr Zarkov & Thun, Mattel, 3¾", MIB..**$40.00**
Happy Days, figure, Richie, Mego, 8", NMOC (unpunched)..**$50.00**
Hook (Movie), figure, Attack Crocodile, Mattel, MOC..**$10.00**
James Bond, accessory, Oddjob karate jacket w/belt, minor stains on back, EX..**$12.00**
James Bond, figure, Goldfinger, Gilbert, 3¾", NMOC...**$15.00**
Johnny Apollo, figure, Astronaut, Marx, complete, NM (EX box) **$100.00**
Last Action Hero, accessory, Evil Eye Roadster, Mattel, MOC **$15.00**
Legends of Batman, figure, Attack Wing, Flightpak or Silver Knight, Kenner (Deluxe), MOC, each...................**$12.00**
Legends of the Lone Ranger, figure, Butch Cavendish, Gabriel, 3¾", MOC..**$20.00**
Lone Ranger Rides Again, accessory, Hidden Silver Mine, Gabriel, NRFB **$40.00**
Love Boat, figures, Mego, set of 6, MOC....................**$85.00**
Major Matt Mason, accessory, Space Crawler, Mattel, VG..**$30.00**
Man From UNCLE, figure, Illya Kuryakin, Gilbert, 12", VG (G+ box)..**$90.00**
Marvel Super Heroes, figure, Web Shooting Spider-Man, MOC..**$20.00**
Masters of the Universe, accessory, Fright Zone playset, Mattel, MIB..**$85.00**
Mike Hazard, figure, Mike Hazard Double Agent, Marx, missing several accessories, EX (VG box)................**$180.00**
Mortal Kombat, figure, any character, Hasbro, MOC, each..**$8.00**
Noble Knights, horse, Bravo the Gold-Armored Horse, Marx, complete, NM/G wheels..**$70.00**
Official Scout High Adventures, accessory, Search for the Spanish Galleon, Kenner, complete, EX...............**$20.00**
Official World's Greatest Super Heroes, accessory, Batcave, Mego, complete, NMIB **$235.00**
Official World's Greatest Super Heroes, figure, Green Arrow, 8", no accessories, otherwise G...........................**$25.00**
Official World's Greatest Super Heroes, figure, Joker, Mego, 8", complete, M..**$55.00**
Official World's Greatest Super Heroes, figure, Shazam!, Mego Bend 'n Flex, 5", MOC............................**$150.00**
Official World's Greatest Super Heroes, figure, Superman, Mego Bend 'n Flex, 5", MOC (sealed)...............**$150.00**
Planet of the Apes, accessory, Village, Mego, M (EX box).**$75.00**
Planet of the Apes, figure, Peter Burke, Mego, 8", complete, EX..**$75.00**
Power Rangers, figure, Billy (Blue Ranger), Bandai, 1st issue, MIB (triangular)..**$15.00**
Predator, figure, Cracked Tusk, Clan Leader, Scavante, Spiked Tail or Stalker, MOC, each................................**$10.00**
Real Ghostbusters, figure, Ecto-Plasm, Nasty, Terrible Teeth or Terror Tongue, Kenner, MOC, each................**$18.00**
Robin Hood Prince of Thieves, figure, Friar Tuck, Kenner, rare, MOC..**$30.00**
Robotech, figure, Roy Fokker, Matchbox, MOC..........**$15.00**

Six Million Dollar Man, figure, Fembot, Kenner, 12", NRFB **$130.00**

Spawn, figure, Badrock, Todd Toys, MOC **$12.00**

Starsky & Hutch, figure, Huggy Bear, Mego, 8", MOC .**$45.00**

Stony Smith, accessory, Stony the Sky Commando, Marx, missing few accessories, NM (NM box).............**$150.00**

Super Powers, accessory, Hall of Justice, Kenner, MIB ..**$90.00**

Super Powers, figure, Cyclotron, Kenner, M (EX card)...**$50.00**

Super Powers, figure, Hawkman, complete, NM **$40.00**

Super Powers, figure, Steppenwolf, Kenner, complete, NM **$30.00**

Swamp Thing, figure, Camouflage Swamp Thing (paint on arms & chest), Kenner, MIP **$18.00**

Teenage Mutant Ninja Turtles, figure, April O'Neil, Playmates, blue stripe, MOC...**$15.00**

Terminator 2, figure, John Conner, Kenner, MOC.......**$25.00**

Thundercats, figure, Berbil Bert or Berbil Belle, LJN, MOC, each **$45.00**

Thundercats, figure, Mumm-Ra, LJN, MOC.................**$35.00**

Waltons, figure, any character, Mego, 8", complete, EX, each...**$10.00**

Wizard of Oz, figure, Flying Monkey, Multiple Toy, 1988, MOC...**$30.00**

Wizard of Oz, figure, Scarecrow, Mego, 8", MIB **$65.00**

World of Wrestling Federation, figure, Andre the Giant, Hasbro, MOC (Spanish) **$125.00**

World Wrestling Federation, figure, Brutus Beefcake, Hasbro, MOC..**$30.00**

World Wrestling Federation, figure, Mr Perfect, Hasbro, MOC...**$30.00**

World Wrestling Federation, figure, Sgt Slaughter, Hasbro, MOC...**$30.00**

Zeroid, accessory, Action Set, Ideal, missing 2 rockets, G (VG box) **$90.00**

Raiders of the Lost Ark, Indiana Jones, Kenner, 1984, 12", MIB, minimum value, $350.00. (Photo courtesy June Moon)

Battery Operated

It is estimated that approximately 95% of the battery-operated toys that were so popular from the forties through the sixties came from Japan. The remaining 5% were made in the United States. To market these toys in America, many distributorships were organized. Some of the largest were Cragstan, Linemar, and Rosko. But even American toy mak-ers such as Marx, Ideal, Hubley, and Daisy sold them under their own names, so the trademarks you'll find on Japanese battery-operated toys are not necessarily that of the manu-facturer, and it's sometimes just about impossible to deter-mine the specific company that actually made them. After peaking in the sixties, the Japanese toy industry began a decline, bowing out to competition from the cheaper diecast and plastic toy makers.

Remember that it is rare to find one of these complex toys that have survived in good, collectible condition. Batteries caused corrosion, lubricants dried out, cycles were interrupted and mechanisms ruined, rubber hoses and bel-lows aged and cracked, so the mortality rate was extremely high. A toy rated good, that is showing signs of wear but well taken care of, is generally worth about half as much as the same toy in mint (like new) condition. Besides condition, battery-operated toys are rated on scarcity, desirability, and the number of 'actions' they perform. A 'major' toy is one that has three or more actions, while one that does only one or two is considered 'minor.' The latter, of course, are worth much less.

In addition to the books we referenced in the beginning nar-rative to the toy category, you'll find more information in *Collector's Guide to Battery Toys* by Don Hultzman (Collector Books).

Alps, Arthur-A-Go-Go Drummer, 1960s, 10", M **$475.00**

Alps, Bongo the Drumming Monkey, 3 actions, 1960s, VG+ **$65.00**

Alps, Bubble Blowing Monkey, dips wand in solution & blows bubbles, 1959, 10", NMIB **$150.00**

Alps, Happy Santa One-Man Band, 9", MIB..............**$300.00**

Alps, Jumbo the Roaring Elephant, MIB....................**$175.00**

Alps, Peter the Drumming Rabbit, 5 actions, 1950s, 13", MIB **$250.00**

Alps, Picnic Bunny, plush & tin, 1950s, 10", MIB.....**$150.00**

Alps, Reading Bear, 5 actions, 1950s, 9", M...............**$525.00**

Bandai, Musical Vegetable Truck, MIB......................**$275.00**

Bandai, Volkswagen Pickup Truck, remote control, blue w/VW hubs on black rubber tires, 8", NMIB **$300.00**

Cragstan, Bimbo the Clown, MIB..............................**$675.00**

Cragstan/Japan, Oldtimer Train Set, 1950s, MIB, $300.00. (Photo courtesy June Moon)

Cragstan, Lady Pup Tending Her Garden, 1950s, 8", NM .**$250.00**

Cragstan, Melody Band Clown, tin, EX.....................**$115.00**

Daishin, Frontline Army Jeep, MIB **$150.00**

Gakken, Musical Showboat, plays 'O Suzanna,' 13½", NMIB...**$200.00**

Hubley, Mr Magoo Car, Mr Magoo steers as car rocks & rattles, tin w/cloth top, 1961, 9", EX (VG box) **$250.00**

Ideal, Smarty Bird, 1964, EX.................................**$60.00**

Japan, Dip-ie the Whale, shoots water w/plastic spout, ears flap, tin litho w/rubber ears, 13", EX (EX box)..**$225.00**

Japan, State Trooper Motorcycle, Japan, litho tin w/rubber front tire, 10¼", EX (EX box) **$925.00**

K, Traveler Bear, 8", NM **$375.00**

KO, Airmail Helicopter, mystery action w/spinning rotors & sound, MIB...**$200.00**

Lewis Galoob, Musical Jolly Chimp, 1960s, MIB, $100.00. (Photo courtesy June Moon)

Linemar, Chevy Police Car, tin, 9", EX.....................**$110.00**

Linemar, Electro Toy Fire Engine, MIB **$175.00**

Linemar, Jalopy, 1950s style w/allover graffiti, tin w/celluloid driver, 7", driver missing arm otherwise EX (G box) **$75.00**

Linemar, Moby Dick Boat, EX **$175.00**

Linemar, Nutty Mads Car, MIB.................................**$675.00**

Linemar, Walking Elephant, 1950s, 8½", MIB............**$175.00**

Linemar, Xylophone Bear, rare, NM.........................**$275.00**

Marx, Big Parade, soldiers march together w/drum in front, 15" L, MIB...**$300.00**

Marx, Futuristic Airport, plane circles airport, remote control, 16x16" base, EX (EX box)....................................**$400.00**

Marx, Mr Mercury, advances, bends over & grasps objects, tin & plastic, remote control, 13", EX **$350.00**

Marx, Yeti the Abominable Snowman, advances w/several actions & grunts, plush, tin & vinyl, remote control, 11", NMIB...**$735.00**

Mattel, Surfing Snoopy, #3477, M.........................**$60.00**

Modern Toys, Bear the Cashier, 7½", MIB **$425.00**

MT, B-Z Porter, figure on platform truck w/3 pieces of luggage, 1950s, 7", MIB...**$375.00**

MT, Circus Fire Engine, 1960s, 10", EX....................**$225.00**

MT, Make-Up Bear, 1960s, 9", EX............................**$375.00**

MT, Mickey Mouse on Handcar, bump-&-go, litho tin w/vinyl head, 10", NM (EX box) **$365.00**

MT, Mischievous Monkey, monkey scoots up & down tree w/bone in front of doghouse, tin litho, 18", NM (EX box)......**$300.00**

MT, Tugboat Neptune, bump-&-go action w/lights & sound, tin litho, 14", NM (EX box) **$200.00**

Remco, Coney Island Penny Machine, 15", NMIB **$185.00**

Rosko, Crawling Baby (Call Me Baby), NMIB...........**$275.00**

Rosko, Dennis the Menace Playing Xylophone, 3 actions, 1950s, from $250 to...**$350.00**

Rosko, Dozo the Steaming Clown, litho tin w/cloth clothes, 1960s, 10", MIB **$575.00**

S&E, VIP Busy Boss Bear, 1950s, 8", EX....................**$275.00**

SAN, Shootin' Bear, advances w/several actions, litho tin, remote control, 11", NM **$345.00**

Santa Creations, Snowman, blows styrofoam ball on head, MIB **$275.00**

Taiwan, Batmobile, bump-&-go w/lights & sound, litho tin w/plastic figures, 10", NMIB **$275.00**

Taiyo, Volkswagen, non-fall mystery action w/flashing lights, litho tin, 9½", EX (EX box)...............................**$150.00**

TN, Ball Blowing Clown, litho tin w/cloth clothes, 1950s, 9", MIB **$350.00**

TN, Cable Express Train, locomotive & coal car travel on cable, litho tin, 8", MIB **$95.00**

TN, Cadillac Sedan, brown w/chrome detail & hood ornament, litho interior, 1940s, 8", NM.....................**$160.00**

TN, Mercedes Coupe, cream w/maroon roof, 15½", 1960s, VG+...**$175.00**

TN, Pinocchio Xylophone Player, plays 'London Bridge,' tin w/rubber band, 1962, 9", NM (EX box).............**$300.00**

TN, Santa Sled, 4 actions, 1950s, 14" L, M.................**$350.00**

TPS, Climbing Linesman, climbs up & down telephone pole, head lamp lights up, litho tin, 24", EX (EX box) .**$200.00**

TT, Porsche Sportomatic Coupe, red & blue, 11", EX (EX box)..**$185.00**

VIA, Performing Circus Lion, MIB..............................**$500.00**

Y, Acrobat, robot does acrobatics, plastic, MIB **$525.00**

Y, Blushing Cowboy, 4 actions, 1960s, NM...............**$125.00**

Y, Bubble Blowing Musician, man blows bubbles w/trumpet behind podium, 1950s, 11", NMIB **$175.00**

Y, Puffy Morris, smokes real cigarettes, 1960s, 10", EX .**$175.00**

Y, Teddy the Boxing Bear, 1950s, 9", MIB **$500.00**

Y, Waddles Family Car, EX......................................**$100.00**

Yonezawa, Ford Thunderbird Retractable Hardtop, 1962 or 1963, 11", M **$250.00**

MT/Japan, Good Time Charlie, NM (G box), $165.00. (Photo courtesy June Moon)

Guns

One of the bestselling kinds of toys ever made, toy guns were first patented in the late 1850s. Until WWII, most were made of cast iron, though other materials were used on a lesser scale. After the war, cast iron became cost prohibitive, and steel and diecast zinc were used. By 1950, most were made either of diecast material or plastic. Hundreds of names can be found embossed on these little guns, a custom which continues to the present time. Because of their tremendous popularity and durability, today's collectors can find a diversity of models and styles, and prices are still fairly affordable.

See also Western Heroes.

Newsletter: *Toy Gun Collectors of America*
Jim Buskirk, Editor and Publisher
3009 Oleander Ave., San Marcos, CA 92069; 760-559-1054; Published quarterly, covers both toy and BB guns. Dues: $15 per year

Actoy Rin-Tin-Tin Cap Pistol & Holster, 1956, diecast w/copper finish, plastic grips, black & yellow holster, 9", EX...**$250.00**

BCM Space-Outlaw Atomic Pistol, silver with red plastic windows, England, 1960s, 10", MIB, $300.00. (Photo courtesy of Plymouth Rock Toy Co.)

Carnell Dragnet 2 in 1 Combination, complete w/Hubley cap gun, M (EX box).....................................**$175.00**
Daisy Buck Rogers Atomic Pistol, 1930s, 9½", VG+.**$185.00**
Daisy Model C BB Gun, break action, wood stock, EX.**$200.00**
Daisy No 101 Model 36 BB Gun, lever action, wood stock, EX..**$35.00**
Daisy No 11 BB Gun, lever action, wood stock, EX..**$65.00**
Daisy No 50 BB Gun, copper-plated, lever action, black wood stock, EX..**$80.00**
Hubley Buck Cap Gun, cast iron w/nickel-plated finish, 3¼", VG...**$25.00**
Hubley Colt .45 Cap Pistol No 281, 1958, diecast w/nickel-plated finish, revolving gold cylinder, plastic grips, 13", VG...**$95.00**
Hubley Dagger Derringer, rotating double barrel, push button & dagger extends from middle, 7", NMOC..**$145.00**
Hubley Overland Trail Holster Set, 1960, 2 cap guns w/black simulated leather grips, double holster, MIB......**$300.00**
Hubley Texan Gold-Plated Deluxe Cap Gun, embossed longhorns on black plastic grips, 9", MIB.................**$275.00**
Ideal Clip Fire .223 Autopistol & Holster, 1966, black plastic gun w/green holster, 7", MOC.......................**$50.00**
Ives Climax Cap Gun, cast iron w/japan finish, 5", VG+.**$250.00**
Ives Liberty Cap Gun, cast iron w/japan finish, 7", G+......**$50.00**
Japan Godzilla Water Pistol, transparent blue plastic w/decals, 4x4", M....................................**$60.00**

Kenton Sheik Cap Gun, cast iron w/japan finish, 10½", VG+...**$125.00**
Kilgore Border Patrol Cap gun, cast iron w/nickel-plated finish, 4½", G+.......................................**$50.00**
Kilgore Lone Ranger Cap Gun, cast iron, sm hammer, 8½", NM...**$350.00**
Kilgore Mountie Cap Pistol, 1950 diecast w/black frame & silver highlights, lever release w/pop-up magazine, MIB...**$45.00**
Kilgore Tophand Twins, gold Mustang cap guns w/embossed horse heads on white plastic inset grips, 9", MIB..**$275.00**
King No 10 BB Gun, break action, wood stock, EX..**$30.00**
King No 22 BB Gun, lever action, wood stock, EX....**$55.00**
Leslie-Henry Matt Dillon Cap Pistol, 1950, diecast w/nickel-plated finish, embossed steer on copper grips, 10".....**$175.00**
Leslie-Henry Smoky Joe Cap Pistol & Holster, 1950s, diecast w/nickel-plated finish, plastic horse head grips, 9", EX...**$125.00**
Lone Star Lugar 9mm Cap Pistol, 1960, diecast w/black-painted finish, brown plastic grips, pop-up magazine, 8", MIB...**$65.00**
Lone Star Westerner Cap Pistol, 1960, diecast w/silver finish, reddish brown grips, 10", MIB.....................**$55.00**
Marx G-Man Automatic Gun, 1930, pressed steel w/G-Man decal, wind-up, 4", EX (EX+ box)....................**$125.00**
Marx Johnny West Ranch Rifle, 1960, built-in noisemaker & speaker, 26", EX..**$75.00**
Marx Rex Mars Planet Patrol Gun, litho tin & plastic wind-up, 21", NM (VG box)................................**$200.00**
Marx Tom Corbett Sparking Space Gun, 1950, tin & plastic wind-up, 22", NM (partial box)........................**$200.00**
Mattel Dick Tracy Power Jet Squad Gun, plastic, shoots water & caps, 31", M (EX box)...............................**$100.00**
Mattel Fanner Frontier Holster Set, 1958, complete w/smoking cap gun & leather holster, 9", MIB..............**$300.00**
Mattel Lost in Space Roto Jet Gun, 1966, changes into 4 different weapons, 15", w/10" attachment, rare, MIB (sealed)...**$350.00**
Mattel Shootin' Shell Buckle Gun, 1959, derringer pops out of belt buckle, complete, MOC.........................**$125.00**
Mattel Swivel Shot Fanner 50 Trick Holster, push down holster & gun fires, 10", EX (EX box).....................**$175.00**
Mattel-O-Matic Air Cooled Machine Gun, 1957, plastic & diecast, mounted on tripod, crank handle for action, 16", MIB.**$95.00**
Merit Dan Dare Planet Gun, 1969, plastic, MIB........**$150.00**
National Automatic Cap Gun, blue-painted cast iron, 6", EX...**$100.00**
New King BB Gun, single shot, break action, wood stock, EX...**$100.00**
Nichols Mustang 500, gold trigger & hammer w/white plastic inset grips, 12", rare, M (EX box)....................**$350.00**
Nichols Stallion .32 Six Shooter Cap Pistol, 1950s, diecast w/nickel-plated finish, black plastic grips, 8", MIB..........**$125.00**
Nichols Tophand 250 Cap Gun & Holster, 1960, diecast w/brown & white stag grips, black holster, 9½", NM...............**$125.00**
Park Plastics Squirt Ray Automatic Repeater Water Gun, 1950s-60s, black w/brass nozzle, 5½", M............**$25.00**
Randal Space Pilot Super-Sonic Gun, 1953, plastic, Interplanet Space Fleet on handle, battery-op, 9", M (EX box).**$150.00**

Remco Captain Buck Flash Buzz Ray Gun, 1965, plastic space gun w/revolving turret flashes 3 colors, 9", NM (EX box).**$125.00**

Stevens .25 Repeating Cap Pistol, nickel-plated cast iron, 4½", NM (EX box) **$50.00**

Stevens Buffalo Bill Cap Gun, cast iron w/japan finish, 11½", VG+..**$150.00**

Stevens Dead Shot Cap Gun, cast iron w/japan finish, 8¾", VG **$85.00**

Stevens Look Out Cap Gun, cast iron w/nickel-plated finish, 4½", G+ **$350.00**

Stevens Ranger Cap Gun, cast iron w/silver-painted trigger & hammer, 8", VG+ **$95.00**

Stevens 1880 Cap Gun, cast iron w/traces of original finish, 4", G+ **$150.00**

Strauss Ball Shooter, cast iron w/black finish, 8½", G ..**$110.00**

Tigrett Atom Flash Zoomeray Pistol, 1950s, fires paper roll-up into the air, 7", EX (VG box)...........................**$65.00**

Tops Dick Tracy .45 Water Pistol, 1950s, sticker on barrel shows Tracy & Sam, scarce, EX....................**$40.00**

Unknown Maker, Cat Cap Gun, cast iron w/japan finish, 4¾", EX **$850.00**

Unknown Maker, Perfect 2-Shot Monitor Pistol, cast iron w/black finish, 5¾", VG+..........................**$225.00**

Wes-Ko Thompson Automatic Sub-Machine Gun Jr, 1950s, plastic (Styron 475), fires plastic balls, 26", NMIB.............**$65.00**

Wyandotte, Hopalong Cassidy Holster Set, white plastic inset grips, black leather holster w/studs, M (EX box)..**$850.00**

Wyandotte Dart Pistol, 1950s, MIB..............................**$65.00**

Wyandotte Red Ranger Six-Shooter Repeater Pistol, pressed steel, plastic grips w/embossed bust images, 10", rare, MIB **$175.00**

Ramp Walkers

Though ramp-walking figures were made as early as the 1870s, ours date from about 1935 on. They were made in Czechoslovakia from the twenties through the forties and in this country during the fifties and sixties by Marx, who made theirs of plastic. John Wilson of Watsontown, Pennsylvania, sold his world-wide. They were known as 'Wilson Walkies' and stood about 4½" high. But the majority has been imported from Hong Kong.

Advisor: Randy Welch (See Directory, Toys)

Astro & Rosey, Hanna-Barbera, Marx...........................**$95.00**
Bear, plastic...•........**$15.00**
Big Bad Wolf & 3 Little Pigs, Marx...........................**$125.00**
Bison w/Native, Marx..**$25.00**
Bunnies Carrying Carrot, plastic **$30.00**
Camel w/2 Humps, head bobs, plastic **$20.00**
Captain Flint, Long John Silvers, 1989, w/plastic coin weight **$15.00**
Chinese Men w/Duck in Basket, plastic **$30.00**
Chipmunks Marching Band w/Drum & Horn, plastic.**$30.00**
Cow, plastic w/metal legs, sm.....................................**$15.00**
Dairy Cow, plastic **$15.00**
Donald Duck, pushing wheelbarrow, all plastic, Marx.**$25.00**
Donald Duck & Goofy, riding go-cart, Marx..............**$40.00**
Duck, plastic **$15.00**

Elephant, plastic w/metal legs, sm **$20.00**
Eskimo, Wilson **$75.00**
Farmer Pushing Wheelbarrow, plastic..........................**$20.00**
Fiddler & Fifer Pigs, Marx **$40.00**
Fred Flintstone on Dino, Hanna-Barbera, Marx **$70.00**
Goofy, riding hippo, Marx **$45.00**
Hippo w/Native **$25.00**
Horse, circus style, plastic..**$15.00**
Indian Woman Pulling Baby on Travois **$95.00**
Lion w/Clown, Marx...**$25.00**
Little King & Guards, King Features, Marx **$70.00**
Mad Hatter w/March Hare, Marx.................................**$50.00**
Man, w/carved wood hat, Czechoslovakian..................**$30.00**
Marty's Market Lady Pushing Shopping Cart, plastic ..**$45.00**
Mickey Mouse, pushing lawn roller, Marx...................**$35.00**
Mickey Mouse & Pluto, hunting, Marx........................**$50.00**
Milking Cow, plastic, lg, MIB......................................**$50.00**
Nursemaid Pushing Baby Stroller **$15.00**
Pebbles on Dino, Hanna-Barbera, Marx **$70.00**
Penguin, Wilson...**$25.00**
Pig, Czechoslovakian..**$20.00**
Pigs, 2 carrying 1 in basket...**$40.00**
Pluto, plastic w/metal legs, Marx, sm **$30.00**
Popeye, compo w/wood legs, Wilson **$175.00**

Popeye, plastic, from $40.00 to $50.00. (Photo courtesy June Moon)

Pumpkin Head Man & Woman, faces both sides........**$45.00**
Quinn Penguin, Long John Silver's, 1989, black & white, w/plastic coin weight **$15.00**
Root'n Toot'n Raspberry, Funny Face drink mix, w/plastic coin weight **$60.00**
Sailor, Wilson **$40.00**
Santa, w/gold sack, Marx...**$45.00**
Santa, w/yellow sack, Marx..**$35.00**
Santa & Snowman, faces on both sides, Marx **$40.00**
Stegosaurus w/Black Caveman, Marx **$25.00**
Sylvia Dinosaur, Long John Silver's, 1989, lavender & pink, w/plastic coin weight **$15.00**
Teeny Toddler, walking baby girls, plastic, Dolls Inc, lg...**$40.00**
Walking Baby, w/moving eyes, plastic w/cloth dress, lg..**$40.00**
Yogi Bear & Huckleberry Hound, Hanna-Barbera, Marx..**$50.00**
Zebra w/Native, Marx..**$25.00**

Rings

Toy rings are a fairly new interest in the collecting world. Earlier radio and TV mail-order premiums have been popular for some time but have increased in value considerably in the past few years. Now there is a growing interest in rings that were purchased as souvenirs from World's Fairs, gumball machines, promoting movie and TV shows, and depicting celebrities. They may be metal or plastic; most have adjustable shanks. New rings are already being sought out as future collectibles.

Note: All rings are evaluated as though in fine to very fine condition. Wear, damage and missing parts will devaluate considerably.

Advisors: Bruce and Jan Thalberg (See Directory, Toys)

Agent 007, silver-tone w/seal, 1960s, from $35 to **$50.00**

Baseball, Babe Ruth Club, baseball, glove, & bat design, gold-tone, 1934, from $150 to **$200.00**

Batman, face & clock flicker, silver-tone, 1960s, from $20 to **$30.00**

Beatles, plastic w/photo inserts, 1964, set of 4, from $50 to **$60.00**

Buster Brown Club, Buster & Tige relief, lg oval, 1940s, from $50 to **$75.00**

Capt Midnight Flight Commander, propeller wings in relief, 1941, from $350 to...**$4.50**

Capt Video Flying Saucer, 2 saucers & pull string, 1951, complete, from $1,200 to...**$1,500.00**

Cisco Kid Club, Cisco on rearing horse, gold- or silver-tone, 1950s, from $200 to..**$250.00**

Davy Crockett, profile, green or red enamel on brass, 1950s, from $75 to..**$100.00**

Dick Tracy, profile in circle, stars on sides, gold-tone, 1930s, from $200 to..**$250.00**

Donald Duck Living Toy, Donald w/magnetized Pep box, plastic, 1949, from $300 to...................................**$350.00**

Elsie Borden, assorted color shanks, plastic w/celluloid picture, 1950s, from $20 to **$30.00**

Gene Autry, Gene's face, copper or silver-tone, 1950s, from $100 to...**$150.00**

Green Hornet, flicker rings, plastic, 1960s, 12 in set, each, from $15 to...**$20.00**

Have Gun Will Travel, white or black top, 1960s, from $35 to...**$50.00**

Hopalong Cassidy Compass Hat, hat fits over compass, gold-tone, 1950s, from $150 to **$200.00**

Howdy Doody, face in relief on white or silver base, plastic, 1950s, from $100 to..**$125.00**

Jack Armstrong Siren Whistle, Egyptian design, gold-tone, 1940s, from $125 to..**$150.00**

Laugh-In Slogans, Here Come the Judge, Very Interesting, etc, 1960s, each, from $25 to **$40.00**

Lone Ranger Look Around, diagonal mirror, gold-tone, 1940s, from $125 to...**$150.00**

Man From Uncle Flicker Series, silver-tone plastic, black & white pictures, 1960s, 4 in set, each from $50 to...**$75.00**

Mickey Mouse Club, face in relief, plastic, 1960s, from $45 to **$75.00**

Movie Stars, black & white photos under glass, 1940s, from $20 to **$35.00**

Mr Softee, multicolor on cream plastic, 1950, from $25 to..**$35.00**

Orphan Annie, face, gold-tone, 1936, from $75 to...**$100.00**

Roy Rogers Saddle, silver-tone, 1950s, from $250 to ..**$400.00**

Sky King Electronic Television Picture, 4 photos, gold-tone & red plastic, 1940s, from $125 to **$200.00**

Straight Arrow, face, gold-tone, 1950s, from $35 to....**$50.00**

Super F-87 Jet Plane, Kellogg's Corn Flakes, black plastic plane on gold-tone base, 1948, from $200 to **$250.00**

Superman, from Post Toasties, 1976, EX/NM, from $25.00 to $35.00.

Tom Corbett, face, silver-tone, 1950s, from $75 to...**$100.00**

Tom Mix, lucky initial signet (various initials), gold-tone, 1930s, from $150 to...**$200.00**

World's Fair, 1933 Chicago, enameled logo on brass, from $25 to...**$40.00**

World's Fair, 1939 NY, lg oval logo in relief, gold-tone, from $35 to...**$50.00**

World's Fair, 1964 NY, Unisphere under dome, plastic, from $15 to...**$25.00**

World's Fair, 1968, San Antonio scene, metal, from $15 to ..**$25.00**

Zorro, gold on black logo, 1960, from $35 to.............**$50.00**

Robots and Space Toys

As early as 1948, Japanese toy manufactuers introduced their robots and space toys. Some of the best examples were made in the fifties, during the 'golden age' of battery-operated toys. They became more and more complex, and today some of these in excellent condition may bring well over $1,000.00. By the sixties, more and more plastic was used in their production, and the toys became inferior.

Alps, Television Spaceman, advances w/light-up space scenes in chest, litho tin, battery-op, 14", NM (EX box)..**$525.00**

Alps, Television Spaceman, advances w/revolving antenna & space scenes in chest, tin & plastic, wind-up, 7", NM (NM box) **$400.00**

Bonus Enterprises, Apollo Moon Flights Globe, 1970, litho tin globe on plastic stand, 6", NM (NM box)...........**$100.00**

Cragstan, Launching Pad w/Rocket & Satellite, battery-op, EXIB...**$375.00**

Cragstan, Moon City, 1970, battery-op, MIB..............**$250.00**

Daiya, Astro Captain, advances w/sparks & engine sound, litho tin w/plastic arms, wind-up, 6½", MIB **$325.00**

Daiya, Looping Space Tank, 1960s, battery-op, 8" L, NMIB **$500.00**

Denys-Fisher, Dr Who Giant Robot, 1976, plastic w/jointed arms, legs & torso, 10", NM (EX box)................**$245.00**

Elvin, Sparkling Space Ranger, advances w/sparks, litho tin, friction, 7", NM (EX box) **$400.00**

Gakken, Moon Explorer Vehicle, 1960s, battery-op, 11", MIB **$500.00**

German, Gama Zooming Satellite, 1958, wind-up litho tin globe on tripod joined to sm plastic satellite, 12", EXIB...**$160.00**

Gescha/Germany, Satellite-Rotaryo, 1958, wire-framed track centered on tin globe w/rotating satellite, 8", EXIB.......**$200.00**

Great Britain, Planet Special rocket, litho tin, friction, 6½", EX **$265.00**

Ideal, Mr Rembrandt, 1970, robot holds pen in base & draws on paper, complete w/6 disks, NMIB **$55.00**

Ideal, Robert the Robot, talker, gray & red plastic, remote control, 14", NM (EX box), from $400 to...........**$500.00**

Japan, Apollo Module, mystery action w/lights & sound, litho tin/plastic, battery-op, 8", scarce, MIB **$200.00**

Japan, Space Saucer, 1950s, 7½" diameter, NM, $185.00. (Photo courtesy June Moon)

Japan, V-1 Rocket, advances w/siren sound, litho tin w/rubber nose, friction, 12", NM (NM box) **$550.00**

Japan, Zoomer Robot, 1950s, black & blue, holds wrench, wind-up, EX **$200.00**

KO, Atom Robot, 1960s, bump-&-go action, battery-op, 6½", EX **$375.00**

KO, Chief Robot Man, bump-&-go w/lights & sound, litho tin, battery-op, 12", NM (EX box) **$2,100.00**

KO, Chief Robot Man, 12", EX **$850.00**

KO, Flying Saucer w/Space Pilot, litho tin & plastic, battery-op, 7½", non-working, G (G box) **$125.00**

KO, Moon Explorer, advances w/spinning antenna, red & black tin w/clear plastic helmet, lever action, 8", MIB **$900.00**

Marusan, Rocket Ranger, 2 full-figure soldiers in vehicle control gun w/attached airplane, litho tin, 5", NM (NM box).**$400.00**

Mattel, Matt Mason Space Station, 1966, plastic, battery-op, complete w/accessories, NM (EX box) **$475.00**

Modern Toys, Lavender Robot, rolls forward w/blinking eyes & mouth, battery-op, 15", VG.........................**$2,000.00**

MT, NASA Space Patrol, advances w/sound, litho tin, friction, 6", EX **$125.00**

MT, Rocket X-6, 1950s, litho tin, friction, 4", NM......**$155.00**

MT, Space Capsule w/Floating Astronaut, 1960s, battery-op, 10", MIB...**$250.00**

MT, SX-10 Space Car, advances in erratic motion, blue & red, battery-op, 9½", NM (EX+ box).........................**$200.00**

MT, X-1800 Atomic Rocket, 1950s, rare red & green version, litho tin, battery-op, 9", EXIB.............................**$450.00**

Remco, Lost in Space Robot, 1966, plastic, metallic blue w/red arms, battery-op, 12", NM (EX box)........**$850.00**

Rosko, Astronaut, blue version, advances w/lights & sound, litho tin, battery-op, 13", NM (EX box) **$1,900.00**

S&E, Spaceship SS-18, litho tin w/astronaut under clear plastic dome, friction, 9", EX (EX box).....................**$250.00**

SH, Engine Robot, advances w/swinging arms & spinning gears in chest, plastic, battery-op, 9", NMIB......**$200.00**

SH, Machine Robot, advances w/several actions & visible gears in chest, battery-op, 11½", EXIB **$250.00**

SH, Rotate-O-Matic Super Astronaut, SH, advances w/several actions, lights & sounds, litho tin, battery-op, 12", MIB **$225.00**

SH, Rotate-O-Matic Super Astronaut, 12", EX............**$100.00**

SH, Roto Robot, advances & rotates as guns fire w/lights, tin & plastic, battery-op, 9", EX (EX box) **$160.00**

SH, Space Explorer, metallic blue version, advances & chest opens, battery-op, 11½", EX................................**$100.00**

SH, Space Explorer, silver version, advances & chest opens to reveal Apollo flight, battery-op, 11½", NM (EX box).**$345.00**

SH, Star Strider Robot, 1980s, battery-op, MIB..........**$225.00**

SH, Super Space Capsule, 1960s, battery-op, 9", MIB .**$375.00**

ST, XZ-7 Space Helicopter, litho tin w/pilot in clear plastic cockpit, friction, unused, 7", MIB........................**$200.00**

Taiwan, Outer Space Spider, plastic, battery-op, 11", MIB..**$125.00**

TN, Apollo-X Moon Challenger, plastic, battery-op, 16", EX...**$185.00**

TN, Piston Action Robot, 8", EX...............................**$1,000.00**

TN, Robotank TR-2, 1960s, battery-op, 5", MIB **$325.00**

TN, Solar-X Space Rocket, rocket rises & wings extend w/lights & sound, tin & plastic, battery-op, 16", NM (EX box) **$185.00**

TN, Space Rocket Solar X, 1960s, battery-op, 16", MIB .**$200.00**

TN, Two-Stage Rocket Launching Pad, rocket propels after several actions, litho tin, battery-op, 8", MIB **$500.00**

Y, Cragstan Astronaut, 10", EX..................................**$650.00**

Y, Mighty Robot Carrying Apollo, blue & red litho tin robot w/red plastic pulling pulling blue plastic capsule, 7", EXIB...**$450.00**

Y, Mobile Satellite Tracking Station, 1950s, advances w/space scenes on screen, litho tin, battery-op, 9", MIB .**$1,200.00**

Y, Moon Rocket, 1950s, battery-op, 15", MIB...........**$325.00**

Y, Robot, easel-back robot advances w/swinging arms, litho tin, remote control, 7", scarce, NM (EX box)..**$1,200.00**

YM, Mars Patrol Spacemobile, 1950s, litho tin w/pilot under spinning dome, friction, 6", NM **$185.00**

Yonezawa, Space Saucer Mercury X-1, bump-&-go w/lights & sound, litho tin & plastic, battery-op, 8" dia, EX (G-box)...**$165.00**

Slot Car Racers

Slot cars first became popular in the early 1960s. Electric raceways set up in retail storefront windows were commonplace. Huge commercial tracks with eight and ten lanes were located in hobby stores and raceways throughout the United States. Large corporations such as Aurora, Revell, Monogram, and Cox, many of which were already manufacturing toys and hobby items, jumped on the bandwagon to produce slot cars and race sets. By the end of the early 1970s, people were losing interest in slot racing, and its popularity deminished. Today the same baby boomers that raced slot cars in earlier days are revitalizing the sport. Vintage slot cars are making a comeback as one of the hottest automobile collectibles of the 1990s. Want ads for slot cars appear more and more frequently in newspapers and publications geared toward the collector. As you would expect from their popularity, slot cars were generally well used, so finding vintage cars and race sets in like-new or mint condition is difficult. Slot cars replicating the 'muscle' cars from the sixties and seventies are extremely sought after, and clubs and organizations devoted to these collectibles are becoming more and more common-place. Large toy companies such as Tomy and Tyco still produce some slots today, but not in the quality, quantity or variety of years past.

Advisor: Gary Pollastro (See Directory, toys)

Accessory, AFX Pit Kit, black, G $15.00
Accessory, Aurora Model Motoring Auto Starter, #1507, 1960, EX (EX box) $15.00
Accessory, Aurora Model Motoring Power Pack, 18 or 20 volt, EX...........$8.00
Accessory, Aurora Model Motoring 4-Way Stop Track, EX...**$15.00**
Accessory, Strombecker Pagoda Control Tower, #9290, EX.**$20.00**
Accessory, Tyco Stick Shift 4-Speed Controller, EX **$10.00**
Aurora, AFX, Ford Escort, #1944, charcoal, blue & red, EX $14.00
Aurora AFX, Dodge Charger Daytona, #1900, orange & black, no wing, VG...........$100.00
Car, Aurora, AFX, Autoworld Beamer, #5, white w/blue stripes, EX...........$12.00
Car, Aurora, AFX, Javelin AMX, #1906, chrome & red, EX $40.00
Car, Aurora AFX, BMW MI, #1957, white w/red & blue, EX $20.00
Car, Aurora AFX, Chevelle Stock Car, #1704, yellow, red & black, EX $16.00
Car, Aurora AFX, Chevy Nomad, #1760, chrome, EX.**$25.00**
Car, Aurora AFX, Peterbilt Lighted Rig, #1156, red & yellow, EX...........$25.00
Car, Aurora AFX, Plymouth Roadrunner Stock Car, #1762, yellow & orange, EX $18.00
Car, Aurora AFX, Roarin' Rolls, white & black, EX.....**$15.00**
Car, Aurora AFX, 1929 Model A Woodie, yellow & brown, MIB $15.00
Car, Aurora G-Plus, Ferrari F1, #1734, red & white, EX..**$25.00**
Car, Aurora Screacher, Pinto Thunderbolt, white w/orange & red flames, EX...........$12.00
Car, Aurora Thunderjet, Chaparral 2F, #1410, white & blue, no wing, EX $24.00
Car, Aurora Thunderjet, Cobra GT Flamethrower, #1495, blue & white, EX $25.00

Car, Aurora Thunderjet, Dune Buggy, white w/red striped roof, EX $30.00
Car, Aurora Thunderjet, Ford GT, #1374, blue w/white stripe, G $14.00
Car, Aurora Thunderjet, Ford GT 40, #1374, red w/black stripe, EX $25.00
Car, Aurora Thunderjet, HO Dune Buggy, white w/red & white striped top, EX...........$30.00
Car, Aurora Thunderjet, Lola GT, #1378, green w/white stripe, EX...........$20.00
Car, Aurora Thunderjet, Mangusta Mongoose, #1400, green, EX...........$34.00
Car, Aurora Thunderjet, McLaren Elva, #1431, white w/red stripe, VG $22.00
Car, Aurora Thunderjet, Pontiac Firebird,#1402, white, EX...**$35.00**
Car, Aurora Thunderjet, Porsche 906GT, red w/white stripe, VG $22.00
Car, Bachman, James Bond Corvette, silver & blue striped, VG $40.00
Car, Bachman, Toyota 2000GT, white, EX...........$25.00
Car, Lionel, Corvette, blue, EX...........$28.00
Car, Strombecker, Jaguar SKE, #9620/595, red, MIB ...$50.00
Car, TCR, Mercury Stock Car, purple chrome, VG ...$14.00
Car, Tyco, Bandit Pickup, black & red, EX...........$12.00
Car, Tyco, Corvette, glow-in-the-dark, any color, EX .$10.00
Car, Tyco, Corvette Curvehanger, silver chrome w/flames, no driver, EX...........$15.00
Car, Tyco, Firebird, #6914, cream & red, VG $12.00
Car, Tyco, Firebird Turbo, red, white & black, EX $10.00
Car, Tyco, GMC Pickup Truck, cream w/flourescent pink & orange stripe, EX $15.00
Car, Tyco, Indy Lotus 440X2 #12, butterscotch, NM ...$15.00
Car, Tyco, Lighted Silverstreak Porsche 908, silver & red, EX...........$15.00
Car, Tyco, Lola 260, #8514, red, white & blue, EX.....$14.00
Car, Tyco, Porsche 908 #3, green & silver, EX...........$16.00
Car, Tyco, Silverstreak Pickup, silver w/pink & orange stripes, EX...........$15.00
Car, Tyco, Thunderbird #15, red & yellow, VG $10.00
Car, Tyco, 1940 Ford Coupe, #8534, black w/flames, EX..$20.00

Classic Industries, Manta Ray #16, orange, 1/24 scale, MIB, $125.00. (Photo courtesy Gary Pollastro)

Set, Atlas, Racing Set #1000, NMIB $185.00
Set, Aurora, Jackie Stewart Oval 9, VG (in original box) ..$85.00
Set, Cox, Ontario 8, #3070, w/Eagle & McLaren, G (in original box) $75.00
Set, Dukes of Hazzard, MIB.......................................$85.00
Set, Eldon, Sky High Triple Road Race, w/Ferrari, Lotus, Stingray & Porsche, G (in original box)................$75.00
Set, Ideal, Motorific Giant Detroit Race Track, w/Corvette, EX (EX box) $85.00
Set, Scalextric, Electric Motor Racing Set, Officially Approved by Jim Clark, made in England, NMIB...............$400.00
Set, Stirling Moss 4-Lane Racing Set, EX (EX box) ...$150.00
Set, Strombecker, Thunderbolt Monza, Montgomery Wards, 1/32 scale, VG (in original box)..........................$150.00
Set, Tyco, International Pro Racing Set #930086, EX ..$125.00

Strombecker (Canada): Ford J, #109525, yellow, MIB, $35.00; Formula One, red, MIB, $35.00; Old's Powered Special, blue, MIB, $35.00. (Photo courtesy Gary Pollastro)

Vehicles

These are the types of toys that are intensely dear to the heart of many a collector. Having a beautiful car is part of the American dream, and over the past eighty years, just about as many models, makes, and variations have been made as toys for children as the real vehicles for adults. Novices and advanced collectors alike are easily able to find something to suit their tastes as well as their budgets.

One area that is right now especially volatile covers those fifties and sixties tin scale-model autos by foreign manufacturers — Japan, U.S. Zone Germany, and English toy makers. Since these are relatively modern, you'll still be able to find some at yard sales and flea markets at reasonable prices.

There are several good references on these toys: *Collecting Toy Cars and Trucks* by Richard O'Brien; *Hot Wheels, A Collector's Guide,* by Bob Parker; *Collector's Guide to Tootsietoys* by David Richter; *Collector's Guide to Tonka Trucks, 1947 — 1963,* by Don and Barb deSalle; *Collectible Coca-Cola Toy Trucks* by Gael de Courtivron; *Matchbox Toys, 1948 to 1993,* and *Collector's Guide to Diecast Toys and Scale Models* by Dana Johnson; and *Motorcycle Toys, Antique and Contemporary,* by Sally Gibson-Downs and Christine Gentry.

Newsletter: *The Ertl Replica*
Mike Meyer, Editor
Highways 136 and 20, Dyersville, IA 52040; 319-875-2000

Newsletter: *Matchbox USA*
Charles Mack
62 Saw Mill Rd., Durham, CT 06422; 203-349-1655

AC Williams, Car Carrier, cast iron, red w/nickel-plated spoke wheels, w/bus & 2 cars, 12½", EX+....................$635.00
AC Williams, Coupe, cast iron, long blue body w/nickel-plated spoke wheels, molded rear spare, 5", EX+ ...$145.00
AC Williams, Stake Truck, cast iron, blue paint, nickel-plated tires, interchangeable tractor & trailor, 7", EX+ ..$300.00

Amaze-A-Matics, Cheverolet Astrovette car, NMIB, $45.00. (Photo courtesy June Moon)

Arcade, Coupe w/Rumble Seat, cast iron, green paint, white rubber tires, 5⅛", G.............................$150.00
Arcade, Double Decker Buse, cast iron, green w/nickel-plated grille, black rubber tires, 8", G.......................$225.00
Arcade, Ford Model T Sedan w/Center Door, cast iron, black w/gold striping, black spoke wheels, no driver, 6½", G+ $275.00
Arcade, Ford Model A Weaver Wrecker, cast iron, red w/nickel-plated spoke wheels, w/crank, no driver, 11", G $600.00
Arcade, Greyhound Lines Bus, painted cast iron, 1940, 9", MM...$650.00
Arcade, I-H Stake Truck, cast iron, green w/white rubber tires & red hubs, no driver, 1935, 12", EX.......$3,000.00
Bandai, Cadillac Sedan, light blue w/chrome trim, friction, 11", EX+ (G+ box)...............................$430.00
Bandai, Cadillac Sedan, red w/chrome detail, friction, 1963, 8", EX+...$115.00
Bandai, Chrysler Imperial Sedan, red w/black top, chrome detail, plastic taillights, friction, 1961, 8", NM (NM box)...$275.00
Bandai, Ford Falcon Sedan, red w/black top, litho interior, friction, 1960, 8", NM (EX box) $110.00
Bandai, Lincoln Mark III w/Shasta Trailer, green & white, friction, 1958, 22", M.................................$650.00
Bandai, Volkswagen Pickup Truck, blue w/VW hubs on black rubber tires, battery-op w/remote control, 8", NMIB...$300.00

Champion, Stake Truck, cast iron, red paint, C-style cab, spoke wheels, 7½", VG......$275.00
Corgi, #056, Plough, MIB......$25.00
Corgi, #102, Pony Trailer, MIB......$25.00
Corgi, #152, BRM Racer, MIB......$80.00
Corgi, #153, Bluebird Record Car, MIB......$125.00
Corgi, #159, Cooper Maserati, MIB......$50.00
Corgi, #166, Ford Mustang, MIB......$45.00
Corgi, #200, BMC Mini 1000, MIB......$50.00
Corgi, #204, Morris Mini-Minor, blue, MIB......$150.00
Corgi, #207, Standard Vanguard, MIB......$125.00
Corgi, #209, Riley Police Car, MIB......$120.00
Corgi, #210s, Citroen DS19, w/suspension, MIB......$100.00
Corgi, #217, Fiat 1800, MIB......$80.00
Corgi, #223, Chevrolet Police, MIB......$70.00
Corgi, #224, Bentley Continental, MIB......$100.00
Corgi, #240, Fiat 500 Jolly, MIB......$125.00
Corgi, #251, Hillman Imp, MIB......$100.00
Corgi, #266, Chitty-Chitty Bang-Bang, original, MIB.$350.00
Corgi, #274, Bentley Mulliner, MIB......$80.00
Corgi, #280, Rolls Royce Silver Shadow, MIB......$50.00
Corgi, #281, Metro Datapost, MIB......$20.00
Corgi, #289, VW Polo, MIB......$25.00
Corgi, #302, MGA Sports Car, MIB......$130.00
Corgi, #307, Renault, MIB......$20.00
Corgi, #310, Chevrolet Corvette, bronze, MIB......$175.00
Corgi, #315, Lotus Elite, MIB......$25.00
Corgi, #326, Chevrolet Police Car, MIB......$30.00
Corgi, #348, Pop Art Mustang Stock Car, MIB......$150.00
Corgi, #411, Mercedes 240D Taxi, cream or black, MIB.$60.00
Corgi, #454, Commer Platform Lorry, MIB......$130.00
Corgi, #470, Disneyland Bux, MIB......$40.00
Corgi, #479, Mobile Camaro Van, MIB......$150.00
Corgi, #492, VW Police Car, Polizei, MIB......$300.00
Corgi, #500, US Army Rover, MIB......$400.00
Corgi, #651, Japan Air Line Concorde, MIB......$400.00
Corgi, #801, Ford Thunderbird, MIB......$25.00
Corgi, #802, Mercedes Benz 300SL, MIB......$20.00
Corgi, #805, Mercedes Benz 300SC, MIB......$20.00
Corgi, #806, Lunar Bug, MIB......$150.00
Corgi, #931, Jet Police Helicopter, MIB......$50.00
Cragstan, Valiant Sedan, blue w/multicolor interior, white-wall tires, friction, 8", MIB......$75.00
Dinky, #100, Sunbeam Alpine, MIB......$200.00
Dinky, #102, Joe's Car, MIB......$170.00
Dinky, #106, Prisoner Mini Moke, MIB......$300.00
Dinky, #108, Sam's Car, gold, red or blue, MIB......$160.00
Dinky, #111, Cinderella's Coach, MIB......$50.00
Dinky, #114, Triumph Spitfire, purple, MIB......$170.00
Dinky, #118, Tow-Away Glider Set, MIB......$250.00
Dinky, #124, Holiday Gift Set, MIB......$1,000.00
Dinky, #129, MG Midget, MIB......$500.00
Dinky, #132, Packard Convertible, MIB......$200.00
Dinky, #140, Morris 1100, MIB......$60.00
Dinky, #147, Cadillac 62, MIB......$125.00
Dinky, #151, Triumph 1800 Saloon, MIB......$150.00
Dinky, #151b, 6-Wheeled Covered Wagon, MIB......$180.00
Dinky, #152b, Reconnaissance Car, MIB......$175.00
Dinky, #154, Ford Tanus 17m, MIB......$65.00

Dinky, #159, Morris Oxford, solid colors, MIB......$170.00
Dinky, #161, Ford Mustang, MIB......$70.00
Dinky, #162b, Trailer, MIB......$40.00
Dinky, #164, Vauxhall Cresta, MIB......$150.00
Dinky, #169, Ford Corsair, MIB......$100.00
Dinky, #171, Austin 1800, MIB......$100.00
Dinky, #173, Pontiac Parisienne, MIB......$75.00
Dinky, #175, Hillman Minx, MIB......$150.00
Dinky, #181, VW, MIB......$100.00
Dinky, #187, De Tomaso Mangusta 5000, MIB......$65.00
Dinky, #190, Caravan, MIB......$60.00
Dinky, #200, Matra 630, MIB......$50.00
Dinky, #210, Alfa Romeo 33, MIB......$50.00
Dinky, #220, Ferrari P5, MIB......$50.00
Dinky, #239, Vanwall Racer, MIB......$100.00
Dinky, #252 RCMP Car, Pontiac, MIB......$100.00
Dinky, #260, Royal Mail Van, MIB......$160.00
Dinky, #267, Paramedic Truck, MIB......$50.00
Dinky, #271, TM Motorcycle Patrol, MIB......$300.00
Dinky, #282, Land Rover Fire Appliance, MIB......$50.00

Dinky, #289, Routemaster Bus, red, Esso Safety Grip Tyres, MIB, $100.00.

Dinky, #290, Double-Decker Bus, MIB......$175.00
Dinky, #324 Hay Rake, MIB......$50.00
Dinky, #354, Pink Panther, MIB......$60.00
Dinky, #405, Universal Jeep, MIB......$50.00
Dinky, #411, Bedford Truck, MIB......$160.00
Dinky, #432, Foden Tipper, MIB......$50.00
Dinky, #449, Johnston Road Sweeper, MIB......$70.00
Dinky, #476, Morris Oxford, MIB......$100.00
Dinky, #492, Loudspeaker Van, MIB......$125.00
Dinky, #551, Trailer, MIB......$60.00
Dinky, #619, Bren Gun Carrier & Antitank Gun, MIB....$50.00
Dinky, #667, Armoured Patrol Car, MIB......$40.00
Dinky, #693, 7.2 Howitzer, MIB......$60.00
Dinky, #725, Phantom II, MIB......$135.00
Dinky, #787 Lighting Kit, MIB......$35.00
Dinky, #924, Aveling-Barford Dumper, MIB......$75.00
Dinky, #949, Wayne School Bus, MIB......$350.00
Dinky, #958, Snow Plough, MIB......$300.00
Dinky, #976, Michigan Tractor Dozer, MIB......$50.00
Ertl, #2653 Pontiac Fiero GT, maroon, MIB......$15.00
Ertl, Atlas Van Lines #1, 1926 Mack, bank, #9514......$40.00
Ertl, Campbell's Freightliner, 1/64 scale, MIB......$24.00

Ertl, Case IH Milk Truck, 1/64th scale, #648, MIB **$6.00**

Ertl, Dyversville Fire Chief, 1940 Ford, bank, #0005...**$95.00**

Ertl, FDR Associates, 1905 Ford, bank, #9378 ....**$28.00**

Ertl, Ford F-250 Pick-Up w/Livestock Trailer, 1/64th scale, #311, MIB................**$5.00**

Ertl, Great Train Store, 1950 Chevy, bank, #7536 ......**$38.00**

Ertl, Henderson Motorcycles, 1920 International, JLE, bank, #3066................**$22.00**

Ertl, Indian Motorcycle, Hubley Plane, bank, #4102...**$45.00**

Ertl, Jim Beam District 1, 1992, 1918 Ford, bank, #9332..**$24.00**

Ertl, Lakeside Speedway, 1950 Chevy, bank, #7522 ...**$25.00**

Ertl, Michelin Tires, 1931 International, JLE, bank, #5046.....**$30.00**

Ertl, NFL Super Bowl XXVIII Freightliner, 1/64 scale, MIB **$20.00**

Ertl, Oliver Tractors, Orion Plane, bank, #42501........**$32.00**

Ertl, Tobasco Sauce, 1938 Chevy, bank, #3640 ....**$28.00**

Ertl, Toy Shop, 1926 Mack, bank, #9442....................**$22.00**

Ertl, US Mail, 1938 Chevy, bank, #B447....................**$35.00**

Ertl, Winchester, Stearman Plane, bank, #37540.........**$35.00**

Ertl, 1980 Chevrolet Mountain Dew Nascar Stocker, white, black plastic tires, 1980s, M (creased card) **$64.00**

Ertl, 50th Anniversary Freightliner, 1/64 scale, MIB....**$20.00**

Gama, #9680 Mercedes Benz 350 SE, diecast, metallic gray, MIB **$25.00**

Girard, Deluxe Coupe, pressed steel, electric lights, wind-up, 1934, 14", G................**$125.00**

Haji, Ford Convertible, cream over red w/chrome detail, white walls, 11½", M................**$1,375.00**

Hot Wheels, '36 Classic Coupe, red line tires, metallic magenta, black interior, smooth black roof, 1969, M......**$30.00**

Hot Wheels, '55 Chevy, black walls, black w/white & orange '3' tampo, 1992, M (NM+ card)............................**$14.00**

Hot Wheels, '65 Mustang Convertible, white walls, white, Park 'N Plates, 1989, M (EX+ box) **$8.00**

Hot Wheels, Baja Breaker, black walls, motorcycle tampo, silver construction tires, 1989, M (NM+ Card)............**$5.00**

Hot Wheels, Bugeye, California Custom Miniatures, red, 1971 MIP................**$95.00**

Hot Wheels, Buzz Off, red line tires, flourescent lime, black interior, 1972, NM **$100.00**

Hot Wheels, Classic Cord, red line tires, ice blue, 1971, rare, EX **$300.00**

Hot Wheels, Cool One, red line tires, plum, 1976, NM ..**$34.00**

Hot Wheels, Custom Barracuda, red line tires, ice blue, 1968, NM **$100.00**

Hot Wheels, Custom Eldorado, red line tires, purple, 1968, rare, VG **$30.00**

Hot Wheels, Custom VW, red line tires, orange w/striped tampo, 1975, EX................**$125.00**

Hot Wheels, Double Vision, red line tires, red w/cream interior, 1973, NM **$90.00**

Hot Wheels, Ferrari 512S, red line tires, light green, 1972, NM................**$55.00**

Hot Wheels, Fiero 2M4, gold wheels, red w/red, white & blue stars & stripes tampo, 1987, NMOC................**$6.00**

Hot Wheels, Funny Money, red line tires, gray, complete, 1972, M................**$60.00**

Hot Wheels, Hiway Robber, red line tires, light green w/black interior, 1972, EX+................**$75.00**

Hot Wheels, Indy Eagle, Grand Prix, gold chrome, 1969, MOC................**$200.00**

Hot Wheels, Jet Threat, red line tires, light green, '15' decals, 1971, NM................**$20.00**

Hot Wheels, Land Lord, black walls, orange, 1982, M (NM card)................**$7.00**

Hot Wheels, Mustang SVO, gold wheels, black, 1985, M (NM card)................**$14.00**

Hot Wheels, Odd Rod, black walls, plum, flame tampo, rare color, 1977, M................**$300.00**

Hot Wheels, Poppa Vette, black walls, white, M (NM card) .**$34.00**

Hot Wheels, Scooper, red line tires, purple & yellow, white interior, 1971, EX................**$25.00**

Hot Wheels, Show Off, red line tires, yellow w/dark interior, 1973, EX+................**$100.00**

Hot Wheels, Street Eater, red line tires, yellow w/red & orange flame tampo, 1975, M................**$70.00**

Hot Wheels, Super Van, red line tires, plum, 1975, NM .**$75.00**

Hot Wheels, TNT Bird, red line tires, aqua w/white interior, 1970, MIP................**$65.00**

Hot Wheels, Toyota MR2 Rally, Ultra Hot Wheels, white w/red, yellow & orange tampo, 1991, NM+...........**$6.00**

Hot Wheels, VW, red line tires, orange w/black interior, bug tampo, 1974, NM................**$20.00**

Hot Wheels/Sizzler, Backfire, metallic rose, EX+ **$24.00**

Hot Wheels/Sizzler, Ferrari 512S, red, original top, German cross decal, NM................**$30.00**

Hot Wheels/Sizzler, Moon Ghost, white, scarce, EX...**$45.00**

Hot Wheels/Sizzler, Trans-Am Firebird, metallic brown, NM+................**$40.00**

Hubley, Bell Telephone Truck, cast iron, green C-style cab w/white rubber tires, no winch, 5¼", EX..........**$250.00**

Hubley, Chrysler Airflow, cast iron, beige w/nickel-plated grille & bumpers, red hubs, real spare, no driver, 4½", EX................**$200.00**

Hubley, Mack Stake Truck, cast iron, deep blue paint, white rubber tires w/red hubs, w/driver, 5½", VG **$120.00**

Hubley, Wrecker, cast iron, red & blue paint, white rubber tires, red hubs, nickel-plated hook, 5", EX........**$155.00**

Ichiko, Cadillac, friction, red w/chrome & red hubs, w/driver, 1967, 28", G+................**$500.00**

Ichiko, Mercedes 300 SE Coupe, red w/chrome detail, friction, 24", EX (G box)................**$150.00**

Ichiko, Oldsmobile 98, 2-tone blue w/chrome detail, friction, 8½", NM (EX box)................**$300.00**

Japan, Buick Sedan, friction, blue w/chrome hood ornament & detail, advances w/sound, 11", VG **$150.00**

Kelmet, Big Boy Dump Truck, pressed steel, 1920s, 25", G-................**$350.00**

Kelmet, Chemical Fire Truc, pressed steel, open cab, missing ladders & equipment, 26", restored, VG **$450.00**

Kingsbury, Ladder Truck, pressed steel, red w/wooden ladders, rubber tires, wind-up, w/driver, 10", EX ...**$385.00**

Lonestar, Chervolet Corvair, diecast, coral, M................**$45.00**

Marusan, Cadillac Sedan, friction, gray, 1950s, 12", EX..**$500.00**

Marx, Fire Hose & Ladder Truck, pressed steel, wind-up w/electric lights, open body, railed platform, 14¾", EX.....**$315.00**

Marx, First National Stores Delivery Truck, pressed steel, red & silver, 19", EX+ (EX+ box) **$550.00**

Marx, Log Trailer Truck, marked Northland Logging Co, pressed steel, complete w/chains & logs, 19", NM (EX box) $315.00

Marx, US Army Jeep w/Trailer, pressed steel, plastic driver, Radar decal on hood, 1950, 21", NM (EX box) ..$265.00

Matchbox, K-08B, Guy Warrior Car Transporter, aqua cab, orange trailer/hubs, EX+ $25.00

Matchbox, K-11C, Breakdown Truck, yellow w/black base, white booms, red hooks, AA labels, NM+ $6.50

Matchbox, K-14C, Heavy Breakdown Truck, amber windows, NM...$6.50

Matchbox, K-15A, Merryweather Fire Engine, decals, M .$38.00

Matchbox, K-21A, Mercury Cougar, red interior, NMIB....$29.00

Matchbox, K-31A, Bertone Runabout, green windows, M (NM+ window box) $9.00

Matchbox, Y-01B, 1911 Ford Model T, red, smooth black roof, brass 12-spoke wheels, NMIB......................$14.00

Matchbox, Y-03A, 1907 London E Class Tramcar, white roof, new decals, 1956, M $69.00

Matchbox, Y-04A, 1928 Sentinel Steam Wagon, blue, 1956, NM $59.00

Matchbox, Y-06B, 1926, Type 35 Bugatti, blue w/red dash & floor, #6 decal 1961, NM $26.00

Matchbox, Y-08B, 1914, Sumbeam Motrocycle & Sidecar, dark green seat, 1962, NM..................................$23.00

Matchbox, Y-12, 1899 London Horse-Drawn Bus, 1957, MIB $100.00

Matchbox, Y-12B, 1909 Thomas Flyabout, blue, smooth tan top, red seats, seat pins, B base, M......................$14.00

Matchbox, Y-21A, 1930 Model A Ford Woody Wagon, bronze hood, brown chassis, cream interior, 1981, NM+ .$12.00

Matchbox, 01-A, Diesel Road Roller, regular wheels, dark green, 1953, NM...$43.00

Matchbox, 03-B, Bedford Tipper, regular wheels (black), red dumper, 1961, M (NM+ box) $22.00

Matchbox, 03-C, Mercedes Ambulance, regular wheels (black), labels, original patient, 1968, M (EX box)................$14.00

Matchbox, 05-C, London Bus, regular wheels (black), Visco Static, 1961, EX+ $20.00

Matchbox, 08-C, Caterpillar Tractor, scarce silver plastic rollers, original treads, yellow, 1961, NM $70.00

Matchbox, 12-A, Land Rover, regular wheels (metal), no driver, 1955, EX $18.00

Matchbox, 12-D, Safari Land Rover, Superfast, gold tan luggage, 1970, NM+ $22.00

Matchbox, 14-F, Mini Ha Ha, Superfast, red, pink driver w/brown helmet, 4 labels, Maltese cross front wheels, 1975, M .$13.00

Matchbox, 16-A, Atlantic Trailer, regular wheels (metal), 1956, NM+ $34.00

Matchbox, 17-E, Horse Box, regular wheels (black), complete, 1969, M (EX box) $8.00

Matchbox, 17-F, Londoner Bus, SuperFast, silver chartreuse base, Silver Jubilee labels, 1972, MIP..................$15.00

Matchbox, 19-B, MGA Sports Car, regular wheels (metal), missing driver, 1958, NM................................$52.50

Matchbox, 23-C, Bluebird Dauphine Trailer, regular wheels (silver), tan, 1960, NM+................................$52.00

Matchbox, 25-C, BP Petrol Tanker, regular wheels (black), green, complete, 1964, M (EX box) $25.00

Matchbox, 27-D, Mercedes 230SL, regular wheels (black), 1966, M $15.00

Matchbox, 30-E, Beach Buggy, Superfast, lavender, 1970, EX+ $11.00

Matchbox, 31-D, Lincoln Continental, Superfast, green-gold, 1970, NM+ $26.00

Matchbox, 36-A, Austin A50, regular wheels (gold), 1957, M..$39.00

Matchbox, 37-E, Cattle Truck, SuperFast, orange, original cattle on tree, 1970, M $16.00

Matchbox, 37-G, Atlas Skip Truck, red & yellow, 1976, M .$12.00

Matchbox, 39-C, Ford Tractor, regular wheels (black), blue & yellow, 1967, M...$16.00

Matchbox, 42-A, Bedford Evening News, regular wheels (metal), 1957, NM+ $48.00

Matchbox, 42-C, Iron Fairy Crane, regular wheels (black), 1969, M $14.00

Matchbox, 46-C, Mercedes Benz 200 SE, regular wheels (black), metallic blue, 1968, M $15.00

Matchbox, 47-A, 1-Ton Trojan Van, regular wheels (metal), 1958, NM+ $45.00

Matchbox, 50-B, John Deere Tractor, regular wheels (black), 1964, M $25.00

Matchbox, 53-A, Aston Martin, regular wheels (metal), metallic green, 1958, NM+ $42.00

Matchbox, 54-C, Cadillac Ambulance, SuperFast, white, black base, silver grille, 1970, NM+ $22.00

Matchbox, 54-D, Ford Capri, Superfast, metallic purple, ivory interior, unpainted base, 5-spoke wheels, 1971, M.$15.00

Matchbox, 60-D, Lotus Super Seven, Superfast, orange, flame label, 1971, EX $20.00

Matchbox, 63-D, Dodge Crane Truck, SuperFast, yellow w/black axle covers, 1970, M (NM box)..............$24.00

Matchbox, 64-C, MB 1100, Superfast, rare green, 1970, NMIB $150.00

Matchbox, 71-A, Austin 200 Gallon Water Truck, regular wheels (black), 1959, NM+ $35.00

Matchbox, 73-B, Ferrari F1 Racer, regular wheels (black), gray driver, 1962, NM+ $26.00

Matchbox, 59-A, Fort Thames Singer Van, regular wheels (gray), rare Kelly green, 1958, EX+ $85.00

NASCAR Racing, Vega Plane, bank, #00312 ....$40.00

Promotional vehicle, 1960 Chevy Nova, light metallic tan, 2-door hardtop, 2 minor roof scratches, EX+........$130.00

Promotional vehicle, 1963 Ford Galaxie XL Coupe, light tan, NM $95.00

Promotional vehicle, 1964 Ford T-Bird Convertible, AMT, yellow, molded undercarriage, friction, 8½", EX $45.00

Promotional vehicle, 1966 Pontiac GTO, silver, 2-door hardtop, NM $440.00

Promotional vehicle, 1967 Chevy Firebird, red, 2-door hardtop, M $160.00

Promotional vehicle, 1976 Dodge Dart, Vintage Red, 2-door sedan, MIB $50.00

Promotional vehicle, 1984 Chevy Corvette, silver, 2-door hardtop, MIB $20.00

Promotional vehicles, 1964 Ford Falcon, white, 2-door hardtop, EX+ $115.00

Schuco, #613 BMW Turbo Coupe, diecast, orange, M..$25.00

Schuco, Mercedes 220 S, red w/white top, chrome trim, wind-up, 5", EX (VG box) **$125.00**

Solido, #107 Vanwall Racer #10, diecast, dark green, M..**$85.00**

Steelcraft, Little Jim/JC Penney Mack Dump Truck, pressed steel, red cab w/khaki bed, 1930s, 22", G-.........**$300.00**

TN, Dodge Sedan, red w/white top, chrome detail, litho interior, fancy hubs, marked D on fins, friction, 1959, 9", EX **$325.00**

TN, Mercedes Coupe, cream w/maroon roof, 1960s, 15½", VG+ **$175.00**

Tootsietoy, Chevy Cameo Pickup (1956) 1959-69, teal, plastic tires, 4", NM+ **$25.00**

Tootsietoy, Ford Texaco Oil Truck (1949), 1949-52, red, 6", NM+ **$65.00**

Tootsietoy, International K11 Standard Oil Truck, 1949-55, red, 6", NM+ **$75.00**

Tootsietoy, Mack L-Line Oil Tanker, 1954-59, red, w/ladder rear of trailer, rubber tires, 9", NM+ **$70.00**

Tootsietoy, Rambler Wagon (1960), 1961-63, dark blue, 4", NM **$30.00**

Wyandotte, Cargo Lines Moving Van, Indian logo on cab doors, 25", VG...............................**$125.00**

Wyandotte, Construction Truck w/Steam Shovel, white, blue & yellow w/black tires, 1940s, NM **$400.00**

Wyandotte, Woodie Station Wagon, maroon w/wood-look panels, lady driver lithoed in window, tin w/rubber tires, 24", EX+ **$525.00**

Y, Rambler Sedan, brown w/white top, working wipers, friction, 1950s, 8", M **$75.00**

Yonezawa, Ford Thunderbird Retractable Hardtop, battery-op, 1962 or 1963, 11", M............................**$250.00**

Matchbox, 15-K The Londoner double-decker bus, Superkings, Lesney Products, England, 1973, MIB, $45.00. (Photo courtesy June Moon)

Wind-Ups

Wind-up toys, especially comic character or personality-related, are greatly in demand by collectors today. Though most were made through the years of the thirties through the fifties, they carry their own weight against much earlier toys and are considered very worthwhile investments. Mechanisms vary, some are key wound while others depended on lever action to tighten the mainspring and release the action of the toy. Tin and celluloid were used in their manufacture, and although it is sometimes possible to repair a tin wind-up, experts advise against putting your money into a celluloid toy whose mechanism is not working, since the material may be too fragile to tolerate the repair.

Alps, Clown Drummer, multicolor clown playing snare & parade drum, litho tin, 8", EX..................**$400.00**

Arnold, Howdy Doody Acrobat, Howdy Doody performs on high bar, compo w/cloth clothes, 12", VG **$250.00**

Arnold, Monkey on Tricycle, dressed monkey steers & pedals trike, litho tin, 3½", EX..................**$300.00**

Arnold, Motorcycle Mac 700, 1950, EX, $1,000.00. (Photo courtesy Scott Smiles)

Asahitoy, Military Police Jeep, tin litho w/driver, friction, 11½", EX (VG box)............................**$100.00**

Automatic toy, Futurmatic Airport, plane circles tower & lands on base, litho tin, 15x15" base, NM (EX box)......**$225.00**

Buffalo Toys, Streak Racer, red metal w/half-figure driver, pull rod for action, 21", VG **$200.00**

Chein, Alligator w/Native Rider, 15", VG...................**$200.00**

Chein, Clown Floor Puncher, clown hits punching bag, litho tin, 8½", EX..................................**$725.00**

Chein, Disneyland Melody Player, litho tin, complete w/paper cartridge, 7x7", NM (EX box)...............**$150.00**

Chein, Drummer Boy, 1930s, 9", NM........................**$275.00**

Chein, Hand-Standing Clown, balances on hand & moves back & forth, 5", EX, from $125 to......................**$150.00**

Chein, Indian in Headdress, 1930s, EX, from $150 to .**$175.00**

Chein, Junior Truck, 220 on doors, green & red w/yellow tires, half-figure driver, 8", EX....................**$275.00**

Chein, Limousine, passengers & child w/dog in windows, litho tin, 6", EX..................................**$200.00**

Chein, Merry-Go-Round, kids spin around on horses w/bell sound, 10", NM (EX box)...................**$800.00**

Chein, Popeye Overhead Puncher, litho tin, 10", rare, EX..**$2,200.00**

Chein, Ride-a-Rocket Carousel, 18", G......................**$100.00**

Chein, Roller Coaster, w/cars & bell, 1930s, 19", NMIB, from $325 to...**$375.00**

Chein, Ski Boy, advances w/ski pole, 8", NM (G box)..**$250.00**

Creation, Chinese Man Pulling Rickshaw, painted compo & tin, 6½", NMIB **$400.00**

DRGM, Turtle Crawling, realistic movements, 7½", EX..**$275.00**

DRGM/US Zone, Punch & Judy, devil & Punch battle back & forth while Judy watches, litho tin, 9", M, from $400 to.....**$450.00**

Gama, Clown Riding Donkey Cart, w/revolving umbrella, litho tin, 8", G **$275.00**

Gibbs, See-Saw Motion Toy, 2 tin figures on rod that spins up & down pole, 14", EX **$250.00**

Girard, Blacksmith, flat-sided jointed man sharpens tool at wheel on rectangular base, litho tin, 4½", EX....**$150.00**

Irwin/WDP, Dancing Cinderella & Prince, plastic, 1950s, 5", NMIB......................**$150.00**

Japan, Bunny Cycle, white litho tin bunny w/ears back pedals litho tin tricycle as bell rings, 1950s, 5", EX+ **$250.00**

KO, Good Flavor Ice Cream Truck, mystery action, litho tin, 7", NM (NM box) **$550.00**

Lehmann, Autobus, yellow & white double-decker bus w/driver, litho tin, 7", EX......................**$1,650.00**

Lehmann, Balky Mule, clown bounces as cart advances w/crazy action, litho tin, 8", EX......................**$475.00**

Lehmann, Crocodile, advances w/jaw movement, litho tin, 9½", NM **$400.00**

Lehmann, Zebra Cart, advances as cowboy bounces up & down in seat, 7½", M (EX box)......................**$350.00**

Lindstrom, Mammy, advances & vibrates, litho tin, 8", EX..**$275.00**

Linemar, Calypso Joe the Drummer, native rocks & plays drum, litho tin, scarce, 6", MIB......................**$500.00**

Linemar, Dino (Flintstones), walks, mouth opens, purple w/pink & green litho tin, on/off switch, 1961, 7", NM **$825.00**

Linemar, Donald Duck, litho tin, friction, 3", NM **$135.00**

Linemar, Donald Duck Climbing Fireman, Donald climbs ladder on platform, litho tin,1955, 14", NM (G box)............**$725.00**

Linemar, Ferdinand the Bull, litho tin w/rubber ears & tail, 1950s, 5", NM (worn box)......................**$350.00**

Linemar, Popeye Turnover Tank, Popeye figure forces tank to turn over, litho tin, 4", EX......................**$500.00**

Linemar, Walking Pinocchio, litho tin, 6", VG **$300.00**

Linemar, Walt Disney's Television Car, litho tin, friction, 8", NMIB......................**$425.00**

Martin, Bell Ringer, jointed flat figure rings bell on post on base, rubber-band driven, painted tin/lead, 7¼", G **$325.00**

Martin, Couple Dancing, cloth-dressed couple dance & spin, painted tin, wire & lead, 7½", VG+......................**$650.00**

Marx, American Tractor, w/driver, litho tin, 8", VG ..**$200.00**

Marx, Amos 'N Andy Fresh Air Taxi, 8", G...............**$225.00**

Marx, Balky Mule, 1948, NM, $250.00; MIB, $350.00. (Photo courtesy Scott Smiles)

Marx, Boat-Tail Racer, rare purplish color w/balloon tires, litho tin, w/driver, 13½", EX......................**$300.00**

Marx, Combat Tank, advances as turret moves in & out w/firing sound, litho tin, 10", NM **$125.00**

Marx, Dagwood the Driver, Dagwood in crazy action car litho tin, 8", NMIB, $1,200 to......................**$1,300.00**

Marx, Donkey Cart, man seated on 2-wheeled cart pulled by 2 donkeys, litho tin, 9½", NMIB......................**$255.00**

Marx, Ferdinand the Bull, vibrates around w/spinning tail, tin, 6", EXIB......................**$300.00**

Marx, Goofy the Walking Gardener, Goofy pushes cart, litho tin, 9x8", EX......................**$450.00**

Marx, Magic Garage & Car, garage door flies open upon impact of car, litho tin, 10" garage, VG **$150.00**

Marx, Mickey Mouse Dipsy Car, head bobs while crazy car advances, litho tin w/plastic figure, 6", MIB, from $700 to......................**$800.00**

Marx, Pluto Twirling Tail, advances in vibrating motion w/twirling tail, plastic w/metal tail, 6x6", EX (EX box)......................**$225.00**

Marx, Popeye Express, train travels under bridges as Popeye circles in plane overhead, EX (EX box), from $1,750 to......................**$1,850.00**

Marx, Range Rider, Lone Ranger on Silver swings lasso on rocking base, litho tin, M (EX box) **$1,225.00**

Marx, Rex Mars Space Tank, marked Planet Control, w/pop-up soldier, litho tin, 10", NM **$250.00**

Marx, Rollover Plane, advances & flips over, litho tin, 6" wingspan, EX (EX box)......................**$600.00**

Marx, Scottie The Guid-A-Dog, advances w/guided leash control, 10", EX (VG box)......................**$265.00**

Marx, Tom Corbett Space Cadet Rocket Ship, advances w/sparks & sounds, litho tin, 12", EX................**$600.00**

Marx, Walking Pinocchio, moving eyes, litho tin, MIB.**$750.00**

Marx, Whirling Tail Mickey Mouse, tail spins when activated, plastic, 7", NMIB......................**$300.00**

Mattel, Dancing Dude, cowboy in cloth clothes dances atop tin stage, hand-crank, 8", NMIB......................**$150.00**

MM, See Saw Rabbit & Boy, boy & rabbit rotate around base, litho tin w/celluloid figures, 6", EX (G box) **$125.00**

MM, Teacup Merry-Go-Round, 3 bears in cups spin w/twirling umbrella above, plush, tin & plastic, 8", NM (EX box)......................**$125.00**

MT, Communication Truck, green w/equipment & lights on bed, friction w/battery-op lights, 12", NM (VG box) **$150.00**

MT, Old Smoky Joe, w/fireman driver, advances w/sparks, litho tin, friction, 8", NM (EX box)......................**$125.00**

Nifty, Donald Duck, travels in circle, mouth opens/head bobs/quacks, tin, cloth clothes, 1960s-70s, 8½", EXIB......................**$400.00**

Occupied Japan, Begging Dog, NM......................**$100.00**

Occupied Japan, Cowboy w/Trick Lasso, cowboy w/hand on hip spins lasso, celluloid, 4", NM **$175.00**

Occupied Japan, Lucky Sledge, boy rides sled as it advances & spins, celluloid & tin, 4½", MIB **$175.00**

S&E, Snapping Alligator, tin, EXIB **$200.00**

Schuco, BMW Convertible, red, #1048, 4½", NM......**$225.00**

Schuco, Coupe 3000, complete w/accessories, 4", EX+ (G box) ....:**$150.00**

Schuco, Donald Duck, moves as bill opens, tin body, plastic bill & limbs, 1960, 6", MIB......................**$400.00**

Schuco, Drinking Monk, figure raises & lowers stein, litho tin w/cloth clothes, 5", EX......................................**$250.00**

Schuco, Garage w/Auto, door opens when telephone receiver is pressed, 6x3x6", EX..............................**$150.00**

Schuco, Minnie Mouse Mascot, fabric w/plastic face & shoes, 4", NM (EX box) **$150.00**

Schuco, Solisto Clown Violinsit, tin w/cloth clothes, celluloid face, 4½", NM **$300.00**

Strauss, Air Devil, airplane w/pilot, 1926, 8½", EX, from $500 to...**$600.00**

Strauss, Chek-A-Cab, #69, yellow & black w/checked trim, 8½", VG **$650.00**

Strauss, Handcar, workmen pump yellow handcar w/2 yellow wheels, EX+ **$300.00**

Strauss, Red Flash Racer #31, red & yellow, w/driver, 9½", scarce, EX **$650.00**

Strauss, Tom Twist the Funny Clown, 8½", EX (original box), from $1,100 to **$1,200.00**

SY, Peace Corps Man, patriotic figure carries suitcase w/ringing bell in chest, litho tin, 7", VG (EX box) **$225.00**

Technofix, Loop the Loop, racer navigates track, Vacuform plastic track & litho tin racer, NM (VG box) **$250.00**

Technofix, Motorcycle w/Driver, travels in circular pattern, litho tin, 7½", EX **$250.00**

TN, Monkey the Sheriff, rocks & moves pistols, litho tin & plush, 6", EX (EX box) **$125.00**

TN, Santa Claus, Santa turns head, rings bell & waves Merry Christmas sign, litho tin, 6", EX (EX box)............**$175.00**

TN, Trumpet Player, man plays trumpet w/several other actions, tin w/cloth clothes, 10", G **$150.00**

Toyland Toys, Comical Ape, performs somersaults, celluloid w/hand-painted features, 4", NM (VG box) **$175.00**

TPS, Animal House, rabbit swing, bear & monkey see-saw, other animals in tree house, litho tin, 6", EX+ ...**$250.00**

TPS, Circus Bugler, scarce, 10", NM (G- box) **$300.00**

TPS, Lady Bug & Tortoise w/Babies, turtle flips over to reveal lady bug, litho tin, 7", NM (EX box), from $100 to..**$175.00**

TPS, Touch Down Pete, 1950s, EX, from $375.00 to $425.00. (Photo courtesy Scott Smiles)

Tri-ang Minic, Delivery Van, green tin w/black plastic wheels, 3¼", VG **$130.00**

Tri-ang Minic/L Bros Ltd, Tanker Truck, red & blue, 5¾", EX **$200.00**

Unique Art, Bambo the Monk, EXIB........................**$275.00**

Unique Art, Capital Hill Racer, 16", VG (G- box) **$225.00**

Unique Art, GI Joe & His Jouncing Jeep, forward & reverse action, litho tin, 1941, 7", G+..............................**$150.00**

Unique Art, Hee Haw, driver on 2-wheeled donkey cart, litho tin, 1930, 10¼", VG **$225.00**

Unique Art, Howdy Doody Band, Bob Smith plays piano while Howdy dances, litho tin, 8", EX............**$1,000.00**

Unique Art, Rodeo Joe, cowboy in bucking jeep, litho tin, 7", NM (EX box)..**$375.00**

US Zone, Airplanes Circle Tower, 2 litho tin planes circle silo-type tower w/lithoed airport, 4½" W, EX+ **$135.00**

US Zone, Bully Bulldog, litho tin, scarce, 8", NMIB .**$450.00**

US Zone, Motorcycle w/Driver, red & tan litho tin, #GF207, 5", VG+ **$225.00**

Wyandotte, Hoky & Poky, clowns operating hand car, litho tin, 7", NM (EX box)...**$400.00**

Y, Deluxe Open Zephyr, red & yel litho tin, friction, 1950s, 11", EX (NM box) **$275.00**

Y, Hunter Truck, truck advances as lion pushes rear door open & hunter tries to shut it, tin, friction, 9", NMIB **$250.00**

Yonezawa, Happy Chick Car, advances as rooster bounces up & down, tin, friction, 1957, 5", NM (EX box), from $300 to...**$350.00**

Transistor Radios

Introduced during the Christmas shopping season of 1954, transistor radios were at the cutting edge of futuristic design and miniaturization. Among the most desirable on today's secondary market is the 1954 four-transistor Regency TR-1 which is valued at a minimum of $750.00 in jade green. Black may go for as much as $300.00, other colors from $350.00 to $400.00. The TR-1 'Mike Todd' version in the 'Around the World in Eighty Days' leather book-look presentation case goes for $4,000.00 and up! Some of the early Toshiba models sell for $250.00 to $350.00, some of the Sonys even higher — their TR-33 books at a minimum of $1,000.00, their TR-55 at $1,500.00 and up! Certain pre-1960 models by Hoffman and Admiral represented the earliest practical use of solar technology and are also highly valued. Early collectible transistor radios all have civil defense triangle markings at 640 and 1240 on the frequency dial and nine or fewer transistors. Very few desirable sets were made after 1963.

Values in our listings are for radios in at least very good condition — not necessarily working, but complete and requiring very little effort to restore them to working order. Cases may show minor wear. All radios are battery-operated unless noted otherwise. For more information we recommend *Collector's Guide to Transistor Radios* (there are two editions), by Marty and Sue Bunis (Collector Books.)

Advisors: Marty and Sue Bunis (See Directory, Radios)

Admiral, #227, 1958, horizontal, 6-transistor, lg grill w/stylized 'A' logo, handle, AM......................................**$35.00**

Admiral, Y701R, vertical, 6-transistor, plastic; crown logo, vertical grill bars, left side strap, AM, 4x2½x1¼".**$15.00**

Advanco, #802 Super Deluxe, vertical, plastic, window dial, 8-transistor, made in Hong Kong, AM, 4¼x2½"...**$10.00**

Airline, #GEN-1249A, 1964, horizontal, 14-transistor, slide rule dial, 2 telescoping antennas, AM, FM, SW **$15.00**

Airline, GEN-1156B, vertical, plastic, 7-transistor, window dial, metal grill, AM, 4½x2½x1¼" **$20.00**

Aiwa, AR-102, horizontal, 1964, 8-transistor, slide rule dial, telescoping antenna, handle, AM/3 SWs...............**$15.00**

Allied, #24SC075, 1965, vertical, 10-transistor, window dial, lattice grill, AM **$5.00**

Americana, ST-6Z, vertical, 1962, 6-transistor, perforated grill w/logo, AM **$30.00**

Arvin, #60R58, 1960, tan cowhide, 7-transistor, round dial, checkered grill, leather handle, AM **$20.00**

Arvin, #62R65, 1962, vertical, 6-transistor, oversized round dial, textured grill w/crown logo, AM..................**$25.00**

Arvin, #68R89, 1968, horizontal, leather case, 8-transistor, slide rule dial, lg grill, crown logo, AM, AC/battery **$10.00**

Arvin, #86R29, 10-transistor, black plastic, Japan, $15.00. (Photo courtesy Marty and Sue Bunis)

Arvin, #9594, 1960, horizontal, 6-transistor, grill w/horizontal bars & starburst logo, AM **$35.00**

Bell Kamra, KTC-62, horizontal/camera radio, plastic, 6-transistor, window dial, metal grill, Made in Japan, AM ...**$100.00**

Bulova, #685, 1962, vertical, 4-transistor, round dial, grill w/oval cutouts, swing handle, AM......................**$35.00**

Channel Master, #6475, 1965, vertical, 8-transistor, round dial, telescoping antenna, AM/FM **$15.00**

Channel Master, #6509, 1960, vertical, red or black plastic, 6-transistor, metal grill w/center logo, swing handle, AM **$30.00**

Channel Master, #6522, 1963, horizontal, 10-transistor, oval dial, checkered grill, 2 telescoping antennas, feet, AM/FM **$25.00**

Columbia, #600G, 1960, vertical, green plastic, 6-transistor, circular metal grill, AM **$30.00**

Continental, TFM-1088, 1965, vertical, 9-transistor, round dial, perforated grill, telescoping antenna, AM/FM **$15.00**

Continental, TR-632, 1961, vertical, 6-transistor, window dial, perforated grill w/logo, AM **$35.00**

Coronado, RA60-9940A, 1964, horizontal, 12 transistor, round dial, crown logo, AM...**$20.00**

Crown, TR-555, 1960, vertical, 5-transistor, window dial, perforated grill, crown logo, AM...................................**$40.00**

Delmonico, #7YR707, 1965, square, 7-transistor, circular grill w/center logo, left side chain, AM **$55.00**

Elgin, R-800, 1964, vertical, 10-transistor, horizontal dial, perforated grill, AM **$15.00**

Emerson, #855, 1957, horizontal, red, blue, champagne, cinnamon or cordovan leather, 6-transistor, leather handle, AM **$40.00**

Essex, TR-6K, vertical, 6-transistor, window dial, perforated grill, Made in Taiwan, AM...............................**$15.00**

Gala, TR-824, 1965, vertical, 8-transistor, window dial, lg perforated grill, AM **$20.00**

General Electric, P-795B, 1958, horizontal, leather, plastic lattice grill, leather handle, AM.................................**$25.00**

General Electric, P740A, 1965, vertical, 8-transistor, window dial, metal perforated grill, AM....................................**$15.00**

General Electric, P791A, 1960, horizontal, plastic, 6-transistor, grill w/circular cutouts, right side curves in, AM....**$35.00**

General Electric, P840A, 1963, horizontal, leather, 7-transistor, grill w/oval cutouts, leather handle, AM...............**$25.00**

Grundig, Prima-Boy 201E, 1963, horizontal, 9-transistor, grill w/horizontal bars, telescoping antenna, handle, AM/FM/SW **$25.00**

Hi-Delity, STH-601, 1963, horizontal, 6-transistor, diagonally divided front w/right globe dial & left grill, base, AM **$25.00**

Hi-Lite, STW-6, 1964, horizontal clock/radio, 6-transistor, slide rule dial, center clock face, telescoping antenna, AM...**$15.00**

Hitachi, TH-680 Hi-Phonic, 1965, vertical, 6-transistor, round dial, lg perforated grill, AM....................................**$20.00**

Hitachi, WH-761SB, 1962, vertical, 7-transistor, 2 dials (1 SW, 1 broadcast), perforated grill, AM/SW..................**$25.00**

Hoffman, #729, 1964, 12-transistor, 2 band slide rule, lg perforated grill, 2 telescoping antennas, handle, AM/FM **$20.00**

Invicto, #8PK1, 1965, vertical, 8-transistor, window dial, perforated grill, AM..**$10.00**

ITT, #6509, 1964, vertical, 9-transistor, 2 dials, 1 AM, 1 FM, perforated grill w/logo, telescoping antenna, AM/FM **$15.00**

Jewel, #10, 1965, vertical, plastic, 9-transistor, lattice grill w/logo, swing handle, AM.....................................**$15.00**

Lafayette, #17-0102, 1965, vertical, 10-transistor, round dial, AM..**$15.00**

Lincoln, #24SC054, 1965, horizontal, 10-transistor, slide rule, grill w/horizontal bars, telescoping antenna, AM/FM.......**$20.00**

Lloyd's, TF-58, 1964, horizontal, 10-transistor, slide rule dial, lower grill, telescoping antenna, handle, AM/FM ..**$20.00**

Maco, T-16, 1960, horizontal, 6-transistor, perforated grill w/logo, AM **$40.00**

Magnavox, AM-22, 1960, horizontal, plastic, 6-transistor, window dial, metal perforated grill, AM, 2¾x4¼x1" .**$35.00**

Majestic, #6G780, vertical, plastic, 6-transistor, round dial, metal perforated grill w/bird logo, AM.................**$40.00**

Marvel, #6YR-05, 1961, vertical, 6-transistor, round dial, perforated grill, AM **$30.00**

Minute Man, #6T-170, 1960, vertical, 6-transistor, 2 perforated semi-circular wrap-around grill, AM.....................**$65.00**

Mitchell, #9X-980, 1965, horizontal, 9-transistor, round dial, perforated grill w/logo, AM **$15.00**

Motorola, #7X25P, 1959, salmon, 7-transistor, round dial over horizontal grill bars, handle, AM **$30.00**

Motorola, CX1E, 1961, horizontal/clock radio, black, fold-down front, window dial, left clock face, center grill, AM..$25.00

Motorola, X26W, 1962, vertical, white, 7-transistor, round window dial, lg checkered grill, AM......................$25.00

Motorola, X39N, 1962, horizontal, brown leather, 7-transistor, metal grill w/vertical bars & logo, leather handle, AM..$20.00

Nanola, #6TP-106, 1960, vertical, 6-transistor, round dial, perforated grill w/vertical lines & logo, AM................$30.00

Norelco, L3X09T/54, 1962, horizontal, 7-transistor, slide rule dial, top push buttons, handle, AM/2 SWs...........$25.00

Norwood, NS-901, 1964, vertical, 9-transistor, window dial, horizontal slotted grill, AM.................................$15.00

Olson, RA-315, 1960, vertical, 4-transistor, round dial, lattice grill w/logo, AM...$40.00

Olympic, #862, 1964, horizontal, 8-transistor, window dial, perforated grill, AM.......................................$20.00

Packard Bell, #6RT1, 1958, horizontal, leather, 5-transistor, round dial, checkered grill w/logo, handle, AM ..$60.00

Panasonic, RL-112, 1964, horizontal/table, 6-transistor, round dial, grill w/horizontal bars, handle, feet, AM......$10.00

Panasonic, T-81, 1964, horizontal, 9-transistor, slide rule dial, oval perforated grill, telescoping antenna, AM/FM ..$25.00

Peerless, FM-90, 1965, vertical, 9-transistor, round dial overlaps grill, telescoping antenna, AM/FM................$15.00

Petite, NTR-150, 1961, vertical, 6-transistor, window dial, perforated grill w/Oriental design, AM......................$40.00

Philco, T-50, 1959, vertical, plastic, 5-transistor, round dial, horizontal grill bars, AM....................................$30.00

Philco, T-77-124, 1962, vertical, plastic, 7-transistor, dial overlaps grill w/horizontal bars, AM $25.00

Philco, TC-47, 1960, horizontal/clock radio, 4-transistor, leather, round dial, center round grill, left clock face, AM...$30.00

Raytheon, #8TP-4, 1955, horizontal, leather, 8-transistor, company's first transistor radio, handle, AM, 7x9¼x2¾" $125.00

RCA, #1-BT-46, 1958, horizontal, 6-transistor, charcoal leather, round dial, perforated grill, leather handle, AM..$25.00

RCA, #1-T-ILE, 1960, vertical, plastic, 6-transistor, vertical grill bars w/Nipper & RCA logos, handle, AM, 7x4x2" .$25.00

RCA, #90L665, 1962, vertical, 6-transistor, window dial, perforated grill w/logo, AM.................................$30.00

Realtone, TR-1-69, 1965, 10-transistor, window dial, perforated grill, AM, 4½x3x1½".............................$10.00

Regency, TR-5, 1958, horizontal, 5-transistor, round brass dial knob, grill w/oblong cutouts & logo, leather handle, AM $45.00

Riviera, RV62, 1962, vertical, 6-transistor, window dial, perforated grill, AM......................................$25.00

Ross, RE-120, 1964, horizontal, 12-transistor, round dial over perforated grill, push buttons, telescoping antenna, AM/FM $25.00

Satelite, Boy's Radio, vertical, plastic, 2-transistor, window dial, metal perforated grill, Made in Japan, AM ...$30.00

Seminole, #1000, 1962, horizontal, 10-transistor, slide rule dial, perforated grill, telescoping antenna, AM/SW..$30.00

Sharp, BX-326, 1961, horizontal, 10-transistor, slide rule dial, band switch, perforated grill, AM/SW..................$30.00

Silvertone, #2213, '500', 1962, horizontal, 5-transistor, blue, off-centered dial overlaps horizontal grill bars, AM......$15.00

Sonic, TR-500, 1958, horizontal, leather, 4-transistor, grill w/brick-shaped cutouts, fold-down handle, AM ..$25.00

Sony, TR-609, 1962, horizontal, plastic, 6-transistor, round dial over lg lattice grill, AM...............................$60.00

Sportmaster, #47900, 1965, vertical, 6-transistor, window dial, grill w/horizontal bars, AM $15.00

Standard, SR-J716F, 1964, horizontal, 10-transistor, slide rule dial, AM/FM switch, telescoping antenna, AM/FM..$25.00

Superex, TR-66, 1960, vertical, 6-transistor, round dial knob, swing handle, AM.....................................$30.00

Tact, SF-400, 1963, horizontal, 9-transistor, 3-band dial knob over checkered grill w/logo, band switch, AM/FM/SW..$20.00

Tokai, RA-9, 1965, horizontal, 9-transistor, window dial, horizontal grill bars, AM $15.00

Toshiba, #38TP-90, 1962, vertical, 8-transistor, round window dial, round concentric circle grill, AM..................$80.00

Toshiba, #6P-10, 1963, horizontal, 6-transistor, perforated grill w/logo, AM...$25.00

Toshiba, #6TR-186, 1959, horizontal, 6-transistor, lace grill, AM $100.00

Trans-American, SR-6T60, 1962, vertical, 6-transistor, round dial, perforated grill, AM $30.00

Trav-Ler, TR-280, 1959, 6-transistor, round dial, perforated grill, swing handle, AM $45.00

Truetone, DC3459, 1963, horizontal, 10-transistor, slide rule dial, perforated grill, telescoping antenna, AM/FM $20.00

Universal, PTR-62B, 1963, vertical, plastic, 6-transistor, metal perforated grill w/logo, AM $25.00

Vesper, G-1110, 1963, horizontal, 9-transistor, slide rule dial, perforated grill, telescoping antenna, AM/FM $15.00

Vista, #10, 1965, horizontal, 10-transistor, slide rule dial, lg perforated grill, telescoping antenna, strap, AM/FM......$15.00

Vornado, V-700, 1965, vertical, 8-transistor, window dial, lg teardrop-shaped perforated grill, AM $40.00

Watterson, #601, 1958, horizontal/table, wood, 6-transistor, 3 knobs, feet, AM...$20.00

Westingham, H-697P7, 1959, vertical, charcoal gray & white plastic, round dial overlaps checkered grill, swing handle, AM $30.00

Yashica, YT-100, vertical, 6-transistor, round dial overlaps perforated grill w/vertical lines & logo, swing handle, AM...$25.00

York, TR-103, 1965, vertical, 10-transistor, round dial knob, AM...$15.00

Zenith, red plastic and chrome, AM, 2¼x2¾", $30.00. (Photo courtesy Lee Garmon)

Trolls

The legend of the Troll originated in Scandinavia. Ancient folklore has it that they were giant, supernatural beings, but in more modern times, they're portrayed as dwarfs or imps who live in underground caverns. During the seventies a TV cartoon special and movie based on J.R.R. Tolkien's books, *The Hobbit* and *The Lord of the Rings*, caused an increase in Trolls' popularity. As a result, books, puzzles, posters, and dolls of all types were available on the retail market. In the early eighties, Broom Hilda and Irwin Troll were featured in a series of books as well as Saturday morning cartoons, and today trolls are enjoying a strong comeback.

The three main manufacturers of the 'vintage' trolls are Dam Things (Royalty Des. of Florida), Uneeda (Wishniks), and A/S Nyform of Norway. Some were made in Hong Kong and Japan as well, but generally these were molded of inferior plastic.

The larger trolls (approximately 12") are rare and very desirable to collectors, and the troll animals, such as the giraffe, horse, cow, donkey, and lion made by Dam, are bringing premium prices.

For more information, refer to *Collectors Guide to Trolls* by Pat Peterson.

Advisor: Roger Inouye (See Directory, Trolls)

Ballerina, bright red mohair, green eyes, original outfit, Dam, MIP **$55.00**

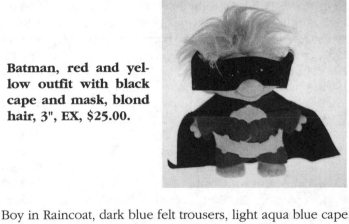

Batman, red and yellow outfit with black cape and mask, blond hair, 3", EX, $25.00.

Boy in Raincoat, dark blue felt trousers, light aqua blue cape, amber eyes, yellow hair, bank, Dam, 7½" **$50.00**

Cheerleader, hard vinyl painted body, inset plastic eyes, hair comes in many colors, Dam, 2½" **$20.00**

Cook-nik, long white apron, molded white shoes, brown eyes, black hair, bendable, Wishnik, original box, 5" **$20.00**

Cow, horns, udder, amber eyes, blond hair w/pink ribbons, tinkling cowbell, Dam, lg, 6" **$200.00**

Cow, Limited Edition, short brown hair, dark amber eyes, green felt ribbon, softer vinyl, weighs less, Dam, 1990, 7" ..**$75.00**

Double-nik Clown, 2-headed, 1 w/blue & 1 w/red hair, red & white flannel costume, red eyes, white shoes, Wishnik, 4" **$60.00**

Elephant, Blue Uglies, blue skin, red smiling mouth, gold face, poseable head, rabbit fur hair, Made in Japan, 3½" ...**$25.00**

Elephant, Limited Edition, gray body, dark amber eyes, white hair, cardboard tag, Dam, 1990, 6" **$65.00**

Elephant, poseable head, wrinkly skin texture of vinyl, amber eyes, blond mohair, Dam, 1960s, 6" **$200.00**

Giraffe, sitting on hind quarters, amber gold eyes, long blond hair, Dam, 12" **$140.00**

Guardian, molded plastic body & shield, no hair, amber eyes, Norphin Pet, Dam, 1988, 7" **$40.00**

Horse, red mane & tail, green felt saddle, Dam, 3" **$45.00**

Hula-Nik, orange hair faded to soft gold, coarse purple hula skirt, Wishnik, 5" **$30.00**

Hunt-Nik, w/rifle, red & black checkered flannel shirt, red hair & trousers, amber eyes, original Totsy box, Wishnik, 3" **$25.00**

Iggy-normous, white sailor suit w/oversized blue tie, amber eyes, blond mohair, Dam, 12" **$175.00**

Indian Girl, red headband w/yellow feather, felt costume, black hair, green eyes, Dam, 7" **$50.00**

Judge, gray hair, orange eyes, Uneeda Wishnik, 5½" .**$30.00**

Kool-Aid Troll, pink hair, 5" **$15.00**

Leprechaun, w/jacket, 1969, EX **$25.00**

Lion, Limited Edition, softer body & less hair than 1960s version, Dam, 1990, 5" **$70.00**

Lion, long blond mane & tufted tail, hard vinyl, trollish grin, Dam, 5" **$150.00**

Lucky Nik, nodder, oversized ears, long red hair, root beer brown eyes, green pedestal w/white letters, Japan, 1967, 5" **$40.00**

Luv-nik, red hair, amber eyes, red & yellow shirt w/heart & 'Luv You' decoration, blue pants, 1981 re-issue, Wishnik, 5" **$20.00**

Mama-She-Nik, yellow felt jumper w/green heart decoration, green hair ribbon, amber eyes, white mohair, Wishnik, 5" **$25.00**

Moonitik, mohair body w/rubber feet & shake eyes, rare, 18" **$100.00**

Mouse, brown molded plastic, begging, white teeth, yellow scarf w/white key, no hair, bank, Norphin Pet, Dam, 1988 ....**$50.00**

Pik-nik, red shorts, white t-shirt, red & white tennis shoes, black hair, green eyes, vinyl, bendable, Wishnik, MOC, 5" **$25.00**

Pirate (male), black felt trousers, red & white striped shirt, green belt, one earring, eyepatch, bank, Dam, 7" .**$55.00**

Poppa-He-Nik, green costume w/ felt H, faded gold hair, amber eyes, Wishnik, 5" **$23.00**

Princess, white net & felt gown w/pink rose, pearl tiara, orange hair, bank, Dam, 6" **$35.00**

Ranch-nik, long white hair, amber eyes, brown costume, black holster w/guns, neck scarf, 1980s re-issue, Wishnik, 5" **$20.00**

Seal, molded plastic, natural colors, amber eyes, 1 arm under chin, bank, no hair, Norphin Pet, Dam, 1984, 6½" .**$50.00**

Shekter, smiling monkey w/white lace diaper w/blue ribbons, white hair, amber eyes, marked USA, 3" **$40.00**

Smart-nik, black morning coat, trousers & mortarboard, pink cheeks, amber inset eyes, 1980s re-issue, Wishnik, 6" .**$20.00**

Tartan Girl, black pants, red plaid shirt w/matching ribbon in long black hair, Dam, 12" **$165.00**

Tarzan, long black hair, dark amber eyes, soft flannel leopard-skin costume, Dam, 3" **$20.00**

Turtle, molded plastic, rear feet up, chin in hands, amber eyes, no hair, green shell, bank, Norphin Pet, Dam, 4" **$50.00**

Viking, Dam, white mohair, brown eyes, blue felt robe, NM from $175.00 to $200.00. (Photo courtesy Roger Inouye)

Voodoo Doll, black plastic, cloth outfit, white fuzzy hair, red ruby eyes, 1960s **$15.00**
Weird Creature, real animal hair, 1960s, 3", MIB........**$30.00**
Werewolf Monster, 1960s, 3"...................................**$40.00**
Whale, molded plastic, blue eyes, grayish-white chest, no hair, bank, Dam, 1984, 5"......................................**$50.00**
Wiley Fox, white mohair on head & chest, blue eyes, red cape, International Passport, Leprechaun Ltd, 1970, 7"........**$65.00**
Witch Doctor, black plastic w/cloth outfit, white fuzzy hair w/simulated ruby eyes, unmarked, 1960s, M **$20.00**

TV Guides

This publication goes back to the early 1950s. And granted, those early issues are very rare, but what an interesting, very visual way to chronicle the history of TV programming!

Values in our listings are for examples in fine to mint condition. For insight into *TV Guide* collecting, we recommend *The TV Guide Catalog* by Jeff Kadet, the *TV Guide* Specialist.

Advisor: Jeff Kadet (See Directory, TV Guides)

1953, April 10, Jack Webb...**$80.00**
1953, June 19, Ed Sullivan **$42.00**
1953, November 6, Warren Hull...................................**$40.00**
1954, February 5, Jack Benny......................................**$42.00**
1954, May 14, Frank Sinatra.......................................**$54.00**
1954, September 18, Liberace **$22.00**

1955, April 30, Fess Parker as Davy Crockett, $150.00.

1955, August 20, Hal March of $64,000 Question **$30.00**
1955, February 19, Sid Caesar.....................................**$22.00**

1955, May 21, Jackie Gleason & Audrey Meadows.....**$89.00**
1955, November 26, Martha Raye...............................**$18.00**
1956, August 4, Jackie Cooper & Cleo........................**$12.00**
1956, February 11, Perry Como...................................**$12.00**
1956, May 4, George Gobel & Mitzi Gaynor **$12.00**
1956, November 10, Loretta Young.............................**$15.00**
1957, April 27, Groucho Marx **$15.00**
1957, January 19, Jerry Lewis.....................................**$20.00**
1957, July 27, Garry Moore **$8.00**
1957, November 9, James Garner of Maverick...........**$60.00**
1958, August 16, Cast of Wagon Train **$45.00**
1958, February 1, Walter Winchell..............................**$8.00**
1958, May 3, Shirley Temple.......................................**$39.00**
1958, November 1, Jack Parr **$18.00**
1959, April 25, Dick Powell **$22.00**
1959, December 12, Danny Thomas **$15.00**
1959, January 24, Red Skelton **$12.00**
1959, June 13, Pat Boone..**$12.00**
1959, October 3, June Allyson.....................................**$11.00**
1960, August 13, Nick Adams as the Rebel **$28.00**
1960, January 2, Cast of Gunsmoke **$30.00**
1960, May 7, Elvis Presley & Frank Sinatra.................**$48.00**
1960, November 12, Fred MacMurray **$10.00**
1961, August 5, Cast of My Three Sons **$15.00**
1961, December 2, Joey Bishop **$9.00**
1961, February 4, Clint Eastwood...............................**$95.00**
1961, May 6, Donna Reed..**$25.00**
1961, November 4, Dorothy Provine...........................**$18.00**
1962, April 21, Connie Stevens **$20.00**
1962, December 8, Dick Van Dyke **$35.00**
1962, January 13, Cast of Hazel.................................**$30.00**
1963, April 6, Lucille Ball **$72.00**
1963, August 31, Richard Boone..................................**$7.00**
1963, February 9, Ernest Borgnine **$15.00**
1963, June 8, Johnny Carson **$10.00**
1963, November 30, George C Scott **$13.00**
1964, December 26, Juliet Prowse...............................**$12.00**
1964, February 8, Petticoat Junction Girls.................**$36.00**
1964, May 9, Cast of Combat......................................**$40.00**
1964, September 26, Dan Blocker of Bonanza............**$26.00**
1965, April 3, Vince Edwards.......................................**$7.00**
1965, December 11, Cast of F-Troop **$27.00**
1965, January 2, Cast of The Munsters.......................**$75.00**
1965, July 3, Jimmy Dean..**$7.00**
1965, October 2, Don Adams & Barbara Feldon of Get Smart..**$35.00**
1966, December 24, Merry Christmas..........................**$11.00**
1966, January 29, Cast of Please Don't Eat the Daisies..**$10.00**
1966, July 30, Johnny Carson......................................**$7.00**
1966, May 7, Lyndon Baines Johnson **$7.00**
1966, October 8, Jim Nabors.......................................**$18.00**
1967, April 22, Cast of Family Affair **$12.00**
1967, August 12, Mike Douglas **$12.00**
1967, January 7, Ben Gazarra of Run For Your Life.......**$23.00**
1967, November 18, Shatner & Nimoy of Star Trek....**$72.00**
1968, April 27, Leslie Uggams......................................**$9.00**
1968, August 10, Cast of Gentle Ben...........................**$6.00**
1968, January 20, Cast of High Chaparral..................**$28.00**
1968, November 2, The Mod Squad.............................**$18.00**

1969, December 6, Doris Day	$18.00
1969, February 8, Cast of Mission Impossible	$15.00
1969, May 17, Marlo Thomas	$20.00
1969, October 4, Bill Cosby	$8.00
1970, January 24, Tom Jones	$18.00
1970, July 18, The Golddiggers	$12.00
1970, March 28, Rowan & Martin	$18.00
1970, May 9, David Frost	$6.00
1970, October 24, Don Knotts	$9.00
1971, April 3, Cable TV	$7.00
1971, December 11, James Garner	$8.00
1971, January 23, Flip Wilson	$13.00
1971, June 26, Cast of Adam-12	$15.00
1971, October 2, Jimmy Stewart	$6.00
1972, April 22, Don Rickles	$5.00
1972, December 9, Julie Andrews	$11.00
1972, January 29, David Janssen	$23.00
1972, July 29, Love American Style	$6.00
1972, September 23, George Peppard of Banacek	$6.00
1973, August 11, Roy Clark of Hee Haw	$6.00
1973, December 15, Katharine Hepburn	$7.00
1973, January 13, China	$10.00
1973, May 5, Peter Falk	$12.00
1974, April 13, Cast of the Waltons	$9.00
1974, August 3, Cast of Emergency	$9.00
1974, November 9, Sophia Loren	$4.00
1975, August 9, Buddy Ebsen Hits the Road	$6.00
1975, December 27, Robert Blake & Fred of Baretta	$7.00
1975, February 15, Cast of Rookies	$7.00
1976, April 24, Beatrice Arthur of Maude	$9.00
1976, August 28, The Bionic Man	$12.00
1976, February 14, Red Foxx of Sanford & Son	$9.00
1976, January 3, Telly Savalas of Kojak	$9.00
1976, July 17, The Olympics	$7.00
1976, June 5, Sonny & Cher	$8.00
1976, March 13, Cast of Chico & the Man	$9.00
1976, November 13, Dorothy Hamill	$7.00
1977, April 23, Cast of 60 Minutes	$7.00
1977, January 29, Wonder Woman	$27.00
1977, November 26, Cast of Soap	$15.00
1978, April 8, Cast of Alice	$8.00
1978, February 4, The Love Boat	$7.00
1978, November 25, Suzanne Somers	$8.00
1978, September 2, Pro Football 1978	$7.00
1979, February 10, William Shakespeare	$7.00
1979, June 9, Donna Pescow of Angie	$7.00
1980, April 12, Olivia Newton-John	$15.00
1980, August 2, Real People	$6.00
1980, December 27, Tom Selleck of Magnum PI	$15.00
1980, January 12, Estrada & Wilcox of CHiPs	$12.00
1980, October 25, Barney Miller by Hirschfield	$7.00
1981, August 1, Miss Piggy	$8.00
1981, December 26, Henry Fonda	$4.00
1981, February 14, Cast of WKRP in Cincinnati	$9.00
1981, May 23, Barbara Eden of Harper Valley PTA	$12.00
1981, October 17, World Series	$5.00
1982, January 9, Michael Landon	$15.00
1982, July 17, Rick Springfield in General Hospital	$7.00
1982, March 20, President Reagan	$5.00
1982, October 2, Genie Francis	$5.00
1983, August 13, Hall & Northrup of Days of Our Lives	$5.00
1983, December 31, Farrah Faucett	$15.00
1983, February 5, Cheryl Ladd as Grace Kelly	$8.00
1983, March 26, Chamberlain & Ward of Thorn Birds	$21.00
1984, April 14, Cast of Knight Rider	$15.00
1984, February 11, Cast of Scarecrow & Mrs King	$9.00
1984, July 7, Valerie Bertinelli	$5.00
1984, November 24, Cast of Kate & Allie	$5.00
1984, September 15, George Burns & Catherine Bach	$9.00
1985, December 21, Cast of Highway to Heaven	$8.00
1985, February 2, Cagney & Lacey by Amsel	$7.00
1985, July 6, Cast of Cheers	$9.00
1985, March 16, Lauren Tewes	$5.00
1985, September 21, Michael J Fox	$9.00
1986, January 18, Cast of Night Court	$7.00
1986, July 19, Cast of Spencer for Hire	$7.00
1986, May 17, Burt Lancaster	$7.00
1986, October 11, Cast of LA Law	$5.00
1987, April 11, Cast of Newhart	$7.00
1987, August 15, Alf	$15.00
1987, February 7, Ann-Margret	$7.00
1988, December 23, Sandy Jackson & Jason Bateman	$12.00
1988, January 9, Emma Samms	$5.00
1988, November 12, Cast of War & Remembrance	$11.00
1989, August 19, Hollywood's Drug Scene	$5.00
1989, January 28, Cast of Rosanne	$7.00
1989, May 27, Kirstie Alley of Cheers	$6.00
1989, November 25, Victoria Principal	$7.00
1990, February 24, Challenger Disaster	$5.00
1990, June 23, Arsenio Hall	$5.00
1990, May 5, Oprah Winfrey	$11.00
1990, November 17, Muppets	$7.00
1991, August 31, It's Kirk vs Picard	$9.00
1991, December 28, John Goodman	$5.00
1991, February 9, Lucy & Desi	$6.00
1992, May 23, Seinfeld	$7.00
1992, September 26, Billy Ray Cyrus & Reba McEntire	$5.00
1993, July 24, Summer Sci-Fi Issue	$9.00
1993, March 13, Mary Tyler Moore	$6.00
1993, November 27, Dolly Parton	$6.00
1994, August 27, David Letterman	$5.00
1994, January 1, Tim Allen	$8.00
1994, November 26, Ellen Degeneres	$8.00
1995, August 19, Regis	$4.00
1995, February 25, George Clooney	$8.00
1995, November 25, Jane Seymour	$6.00
1996, January 13, Morgan Fairchild	$5.00
1996, June 15, Teri Hatcher	$7.00

Twin Winton

The genius behind the designs at Twin Winton was sculptor Don Winton. He and his twin, Ross, started the company while sill in high school in the mid-1930s. In 1952 older brother Bruce Winton bought the company from his two younger brothers and directed its development nationwide. They produced animal figures, cookie jars, and matching kitchenware and household items during this time. It is important to note that Bruce was an extremely shrewd business man, and if an order came in for a nonstandard color, he would generally accomodate the buyer — for an additional charge, of course. As a result, you may find a Mopsy (Raggedy Ann) cookie jar, for instance, in a wood stain finish or some other unusual color, even though Mopsy was only offered in the Collector Series in the catalogs. This California company was active until it sold in 1976 to Roger Bowermeister, who continued to use the Twin Winton name. He experimented with different finishes. One of the most common is a light tan with a high gloss glaze. He owned the company only one year until it went bankrupt and was sold at auction. Al Levin of Treasure Craft bought the molds and used some of them in his line. Eventually, the molds were destroyed.

One of Twin Winton's most successful concepts was their Hillbilly line — mugs, pitchers, bowls, lamps, ashtrays, decanters, and novelty items molded after the mountain boys in Paul Webb's cartoon series. Don Winton was the company's only designer, though he free-lanced as well. He designed for Disney, Brush-McCoy, Revell Toys, The Grammy Award, American Country Music Award, Ronald Reagan Foundation, and numerous other companies and foundations.

Twin Winton has been revived by Don and Norma Winton (the original Don Winton and his wife). They are currently selling new designs as well as some of his original artwork through the Twin Winton Collector Club on the Internet at twinwinton.com. Some of Don's more prominent pieces of art are currently registered with the Smithsonian in Washington, D.C.

If you would like more information, read *Collector's Guide to Don Winton Designs*, written by our advisor, Mike Ellis, published by Collector Books.

Note: color codes in the listings below are as follows: A — avocado green; CS — Collectors Series, fully painted; G — gray; O — orange; P — pineapple yellow; R — red; and W — wood stain with hand-painted detail. Values are based on actual sales as well as dealer's asking prices. See also Cookie Jars.

Advisor: Mike Ellis (See Directory, Twin Winton)

Club: Twin Winton Collector Club
Also Don Winton Designs (other than Twin Winton)
266 Rose Lane
Costa Mesa, CA 92627; 714-646-7112 or Fax 7414-645-4919; internet: twinwinton.com; e-mail: ellis5@pacbell.net

Bank, Friar, wood stain with hand-painted details, $40.00. (Photo courtesy Jack Chipman)

Accent lamps, any of 11 different designs, W, each ..**$150.00**

Ashtrays, poodle, kitten, elf or Bambi, W, each........**$100.00**
Bank, cop, W, G **$50.00**
Bank, Dobbin, W, G **$50.00**
Bank, Dutch girl, W, G **$60.00**
Bank, elf on stump, W, G **$40.00**
Bank, foo dog, W, G **$50.00**
Bank, happy bull, W, G **$40.00**
Bank, Hotei, W, G **$40.00**
Bank, lamb, W, G **$50.00**
Bank, nut w/squirrel, W, G **$50.00**
Bank, owl, W, G **$50.00**
Bank, Persian cat, W, G **$50.00**
Bank, pig, W, G **$40.00**
Bank, pirate fox, W, G **$50.00**
Bank, poodle, W, G **$40.00**
Bank, rabbit, W, G **$50.00**
Bank, Ranger bear, W, G **$50.00**
Bank, sailor elephant, W, G **$40.00**
Bank, shack, W, G **$50.00**
Bank, shoe, W, G **$50.00**
Bank, squirrel, W, G **$40.00**
Bank, teddy bear, W, G **$40.00**
Bronco Group, ashtray, cowboy on saddle **$65.00**
Bronco Group, mug, cowboy handle **$25.00**
Bronco Group, pitcher, bronco on side, cowboy handle .**$150.00**
Bronco Group, pouring spouts, head & hat, each......**$40.00**
Bronco Group, stein, steer opposite cowboy handle .**$70.00**
Candy jar, bear w/lollipop on stump, W, G **$85.00**
Candy jar, Candy House, W, G **$65.00**
Candy jar, elephant w/lollipop, W, G **$65.00**
Candy jar, elf on stump, W, G **$65.00**
Candy jar, nut w/squirrel finial, W, G **$75.00**
Candy jar, old shoe, W, G **$75.00**
Candy jar, Pot O' Candy, W, G **$65.00**
Candy jar, train, W, G **$75.00**
Candy jar, turtle w/hare finial, W, G **$85.00**
Canister set, Barn, Cookies, Flour, Sugar, Coffee & Tea, W, A, P, O, R, G, 5 pcs **$275.00**
Canister set, House, Cookies, Flour, Sugar, Coffee & Tea, 5 pcs **$450.00**
Canister set, Pot O' Canister, Cookies, Flour Sugar, Coffee & Tea, W, A, P, O, G, 5 pcs **$175.00**
Canister set, Ye Old Bucket, Cookies, Flour, Sugar, Coffee, Tea & Salt, W, 6 pcs **$250.00**
Figurines, animals, green, brown or black gloss, marked Winton & # (some are unmarked), 4" to 8", each, from $15 to ..**$140.00**
Figurines, children series, marked Twinton (rarely marked Twin Winton), from 3" to 7", each, from $125 to **$175.00**
Mugs, puppy, kitten, elephant, owl, bear or lamb, W, each **$70.00**
Napkin holder, Bambi, W **$50.00**
Napkin holder, butler, W **$100.00**
Napkin holder, cocktail; elephant holding bottle, W ..**$100.00**
Napkin holder, cocktail; horse sitting down holding bottle, W **$100.00**
Napkin holder, cocktail; rabbit holding bottle, W.....**$100.00**
Napkin holder, cocktail; St Bernard head, W............**$100.00**
Napkin holder, cow, W **$85.00**
Napkin holder, Dobbin, W...**$50.00**

Napkin holder, Dutch girl, W $50.00
Napkin holder, elephant, W $50.00
Napkin holder, elf on stump, W, A, P, O, each..........$85.00
Napkin holder, goose, W $50.00
Napkin holder, Hotei, W, A, P, O, each..............$60.00
Napkin holder, kitten, W $85.00
Napkin holder, lamb, W $50.00
Napkin holder, owl, W, A, P, O, each...............$85.00
Napkin holder, pig, W $85.00
Napkin holder, poodle, W $60.00
Napkin holder, potbellied stove, W $50.00
Napkin holder, Ranger bear, W $85.00
Napkin holder, shack, W, A, P, O, R, each $85.00
Napkin holder, squirrel, W $60.00
Planter, Bambi deer, W................................$65.00
Planter, cat & boat, W $65.00
Planter, dog & drum, W................................$65.00
Planter, elephant & drum, W.........................$65.00
Planter, Ranger bear, W...............................$65.00
Planter, squirrel & stump, W.........................$65.00
Salt & pepper shakers, barrel, W, pr.................$50.00
Salt & pepper shakers, bucket, W, A, P, O, pr...........$30.00
Salt & pepper shakers, butler, W, G, pr.....................$50.00
Salt & pepper shakers, cat w/churn, W, pr $40.00
Salt & pepper shakers, cop, W, G, pr $40.00

Salt and pepper shakers, cow, wood stain with hand-painted details, $40.00 for the pair. (Photo courtesy Lee Garmon)

Salt & pepper shakers, dinosaur, W, pr $150.00
Salt & pepper shakers, Dobbin, W, G, pr....................$45.00
Salt & pepper shakers, dog, W, pr $45.00
Salt & pepper shakers, donkey, W, G, pr....................$40.00
Salt & pepper shakers, duck, W, pr $45.00
Salt & pepper shakers, Dutch girl, W, G, pr...............$35.00
Salt & pepper shakers, elephant, W, G, pr..................$30.00
Salt & pepper shakers, elf on stump, W, A, P, O, G, pr.$40.00
Salt & pepper shakers, Friar, W, G, pr.......................$35.00
Salt & pepper shakers, frog, W, pr............................$50.00
Salt & pepper shakers, goose, W, G, pr $45.00
Salt & pepper shakers, happy bull, W, G, pr $40.00
Salt & pepper shakers, hen on nest, W, pr..................$50.00
Salt & pepper shakers, Hotei, W, A, P, O, pr...............$30.00
Salt & pepper shakers, Indian, W, pr........................$60.00
Salt & pepper shakers, Jack-in-the-Box, W, pr...........$75.00
Salt & pepper shakers, kangaroo, W, pr....................$100.00
Salt & pepper shakers, kitten, W, pr.........................$40.00
Salt & pepper shakers, lamb, W, G, pr......................$30.00

Salt & pepper shakers, lion, W, A, P, O, pr...............$45.00
Salt & pepper shakers, mouse (sailor), W, A, P, O, G, pr.$30.00
Salt & pepper shakers, mouse (w/tie), W, pr.............$40.00
Salt & pepper shakers, owl, W, G, pr......................$30.00
Salt & pepper shakers, Persian cat, W, G, pr $50.00
Salt & pepper shakers, pig, W, G, pr.......................$50.00
Salt & pepper shakers, pirate fox, W, pr $45.00
Salt & pepper shakers, rabbit, W, G, pr...................$45.00
Salt & pepper shakers, raccoon, W, G, pr.................$45.00
Salt & pepper shakers, Ranger bear, W, G, pr $40.00
Salt & pepper shakers, Robin Hood & Maid Marion, hand painted, pr...................$95.00
Salt & pepper shakers, rooster, W, G, pr...................$30.00
Salt & pepper shakers, squirrel w/cookies, W, G, pr.$30.00
Salt & pepper shakers, turtle, W, G, pr...................$40.00
Spoon rests, any of 14 different designs, W, each......$35.00
Sugar bowl & creamer, cow & bull, W....................$200.00
Sugar bowl & creamer, hen & rooster, W.................$200.00
Talking picture frames, any of 10 different designs, W, each $95.00
Wall pocket/planter, bear, rabbit, elephant, lamb or puppy, W, each, from $75 to.........................$115.00

Ice buckets, bottoms up in barrel or bathing in barrel, woodstain with hand-painted details, $250.00 each. (Photo courtesy Jack Chipman)

Hillbilly Line

Ladies of the Mountains, mug w/lady handle.............$50.00
Ladies of the Mountains, pouring spouts, heads, each.$35.00
Ladies of the Mountains, salt & pepper shakers, pr ...$50.00
Ladies of the Mountains, stein w/lady handle.............$70.00
Men of the Mountains, ashtray, Clem on his back $50.00
Men of the Mountains, bowl, bathing hillbilly $70.00
Men of the Mountains, cigarette box outhouse...........$75.00
Men of the Mountains, cookie jar, outhouse, minimum value $350.00
Men of the Mountains, ice bucket, Clem w/jug sitting on barrel, W...................$200.00
Men of the Mountains, ice bucket, Clem w/suspenders holding barrel...................$200.00
Men of the Mountains, lamp, Clem w/jug on barrel ..$400.00
Men of the Mountains, mug w/hillbilly handle...........$30.00
Men of the Mountains, pitcher w/hillbilly handle.......$75.00
Men of the Mountains, pouring spout dealer plaque .$350.00
Men of the Mountains, pouring spouts, heads & hats, each...................$30.00
Men of the Mountains, pretzel bowl bathtub.............$60.00

Men of the Mountains, punch bowl, hillbilly chasing lady, minimum value **$400.00**

Men of the Mountains, punch cup w/hillbilly handle ..**$15.00**

Men of the Mountains, salt & pepper shakers, pr.......**$35.00**

Men of the Mountains, stein w/hillbilly handle **$40.00**

Universal Dinnerware

This pottery incorporated in Cambridge, Ohio, in 1934, is the outgrowth of several smaller companies in the area. They produced many lines of dinnerware and kitchenware items, most of which were marked. They're best known for their Ballerina dinnerware (simple modern shapes in a variety of solid colors) and Cat-Tail (see Cat-Tail Dinnerware). The company closed in 1960.

Ballerina, bowl, cereal...**$5.00**

Ballerina, bowl, soup..**$6.00**

Ballerina, chop plate **$15.00**

Ballerina, creamer & sugar bowl **$20.00**

Ballerina, cup & saucer, demitasse...............................**$20.00**

Ballerina, egg cup...**$12.00**

Ballerina, gravy boat...**$12.00**

Ballerina, salt & pepper shakers, pr..............................**$12.00**

Bittersweet, cup & saucer, from $12 to.........................**$14.00**

Bittersweet, platter, oval, 13½".....................................**$28.00**

Broadway Rose, plate, dinner; square, from $6 to........**$8.00**

Calico Fruit, bowl, mixing; w/lid, 8¾"..........................**$47.00**

Calico Fruit, bowl, utility; w/lid, 5" **$35.00**

Calico Fruit, creamer **$11.00**

Calico Fruit, salt & pepper shakers, pr **$20.00**

Hollyhocks, bowl, salad; from $15 to............................**$20.00**

Iris, pie plate, 10", from $18 to......................................**$20.00**

Largo, pie plate, 10", from $12 to..................................**$15.00**

Largo, salt & pepper shakers, pr, from $6 to.................**$8.00**

Largo, sugar bowl, w/lid, from $6 to **$8.00**

Poppy, cup & saucer, from $5 to **$8.00**

Poppy, plate, bread & butter; from $4 to **$6.00**

Poppy, platter, round w/tab handles, 11½", from $12 to **$18.00**

Rambler Rose, gravy boat, from $8 to **$10.00**

Rambler Rose, plate, 9", from $7 to...............................**$9.00**

Woodbine, bowl, berry; 5¼"..**$8.00**

Woodbine, bowl, soup; flat, from $4 to.........................**$6.00**

Woodbine, gravy boat liner/relish dish, from $10.00 to $12.00; Creamer and sugar bowl, from $18.00 to $22.00.

Woodbine, pitcher, milk; 6½" **$35.00**

Woodbine, utility tray, round w/tab handles, from $15 to ..**$20.00**

Zinnias, casserole..**$13.00**

Valentines

As public awareness of Valentine collecting grows, so does the demand for more categorization (ethnic, comic character, advertising, transportation, pedigree dogs and cats, artist signed, etc.). Valentine cards tend to be ephemeral in nature, but to the valentine elitest that carefully preserves each valuable example, this is not true. Collectors study their subject thoroughly, from the workings of the lithography process to the history of the manufacturing companies that made these tokens of love. Valentines are slowly making their way into more and more diversified collections as extensions of each collector's original interest. For more information we recommend *Valentines With Values* by Katherine Kreider.

Advisor: Katherine Kreider (See Directory, Valentines)

Newsletter: *National Valentine Collectors Bulletin*
Evalene Pulati
P.O. Box 1404
Santa Ana, CA 92702; 714-547-1355

Art Deco Lady w/powder puff, flat, 1920s, 4x5", NM.**$20.00**

Art Nouveau, embossed greeting card, 6½x5", EX **$35.00**

Barbie, flat, 1960s, 4½x3", EX..**$10.00**

Bear, mechanical-flat, Made in Germany, 1920s, 3½x1½", EX **$15.00**

Big-eyed children w/rabbit pull toy, 8½x6½", EX **$50.00**

Black cat, flat, 1940s, 4x1", VG.....................................**$5.00**

Black farmer boy, mechanical, 4x2½", EX...................**$15.00**

Black Uncle Tom, mechanical/flat, 4¾x4", VG **$5.00**

Cat & The Fiddle, flat, 1940s, 4½x3", VG **$10.00**

Cachet from Loveland, CO, 1940s **$10.00**

Clarabell, mechanical, 1939, EX...................................**$40.00**

Clockwork, plastic heart, 1950s, 5½x4", EX **$25.00**

Dimensional, airplane, Made in Germany, 5x4x3", EX..**$15.00**

Dimensional, car, Hallmark, 1950s, 10x6x4", EX.........**$25.00**

Dimensional, cherub w/lamp, 7½x4x3", EX...............**$45.00**

Dimensional, collie w/original chain, 7x5x3", EX.......**$40.00**

Dimensional, dove cote w/doves, 9x4x3", EX.............**$50.00**

Dimensional, Victorian house, Made in Gemany, 10x7x4", VG **$30.00**

Dimensional, windmill w/Dutch motif, 12x5x6", VG..**$50.00**

Greeting card type, Uncle Sam, 5x4", EX **$15.00**

Hansel & Gretel, mechanical/flat, 4x4", EX **$10.00**

Honeycomb paper puff, atomizer, Made in Germany, 1920s, 9½x6x4", EX...**$75.00**

Honeycomb paper puff, fan, 1920s, opens to 12", EX .**$50.00**

Honeycomb paper puff, heart, 1920s, 12x10", EX **$75.00**

Honeycomb paper puff, pedestal, w/cherubs, 1920s, 9x6", EX...**$30.00**

Honeycomb paper puff, Wheel of Love, 1920s, 9x5", EX..**$75.00**

Jack Horner, mechanical/flat, 4x4", EX **$10.00**

Kaleidoscope w/child, mechanical/flat, Made in Germany, 1940s, EX..**$10.00**

Kautz, snowman, mechanical/flat, easel back, 6½x4"...**$10.00**

Mae West, 1930s, NM, $35.00.

Paper doll, cowboy, 1940s, uncut, M...........................**$20.00**

Penny Dreadful, politician, 8½x10", EX......................**$20.00**

Pink Panther, flat, 1960s, 5x3½", EX **$5.00**

Walt Disney, Dopey, flat, 1930s, EX...........................**$25.00**

Whitney, flat, 1940s, 4x4", VG **$2.00**

Whitney, flat, 1940s, 8x6½", VG **$10.00**

Winnie the Pooh, flat, 1960s, 5x3", EX.........................**$5.00**

Vallona Starr

Triangle Studios opened in the 1930s, primarily as a ceramic gift shop that sold the work of various California potteries and artists such as Brad Keeler, Beth Barton, Cleminson, and Josef Originals. As the business grew, Leona and Valeria, talented artists in their own right, developed their own ceramic designs. In 1939 the company became known as Vallona Starr, a derivation of the three partners' names — (Val)eria Dopyera de Marsa, and Le(ona) and Everett (Starr) Frost. They made several popular ceramic lines including Winkies, Corn Design, Up Family, Flower Fairies, and the Fairy Tale Characters salt and pepper shakers. Vallona Starr made only three cookie jars: Winkie (beware of any jars made in colors other than pink or yellow); Peter, Peter, Pumpkin Eater (used as a TV prize-show giveaway); and Squirrel on Stump (from the Woodland line). For more information we recommend *Vallona Starr Ceramics* by Bernice Stamper.

See also Cookie Jars.

Advisor: Bernice Stamper (See Directory, Vallona Starr)

Bowl, Humpty Dumpty, white & pink on red brick pedestal, & cup, white, pink & green, set, minimum value.....**$125.00**

Bowl, Indian, Thunderbird design, assorted colors, lg, minimum value, each **$25.00**

Buffet dish, divided, raised design of corn on the cob divides the dish in 2, natural green & yellow, from $35 to .**$40.00**

Candy dish, cosmos design, pink, blue or white & blue, all w/gold trim, each, from $15 to.............................**$20.00**

Cigarette box, man in doghouse, multicolored, minimum value **$65.00**

Creamer & sugar bowl, snowbirds, yellow w/gold trim, from $15 to...**$20.00**

Creamer & sugar bowl, tulip form, pink w/gold trim, from $15 to...**$20.00**

Figurine, canoe & Indian boy, green & brown, minimum value **$75.00**

Honey jar, cosmos design, multicolored, bee finial, from $15 to **$20.00**

Jam jar, corn design, natural yellow & green, solid lid, from $25 to...**$30.00**

Pitcher, Bottom Up, lady pig in black dress, $60.00. (Photo courtesy Bernice Stamper)

Pitcher, corn design, natural yellow & green, 1-qt, from $50 to...**$55.00**

Plate, corn design, natural yellow & green, 10", from $25 to...**$30.00**

Platter, corn design, natural yellow & green, 14", from $35 to...**$40.00**

Relish dish, 4-leaf clover design, natural green, minimum value **$5.00**

Salt & pepper shakers, bell pepper set, natural green, 2 shapes, pr, from $20 to **$25.00**

Salt & pepper shakers, bird, yellow, on white house w/blue roof & gold trim, pr, from $30 to **$35.00**

Salt & pepper shakers, birds (2) & flower blossom, pr, from $35 to..**$40.00**

Salt & pepper shakers, brown toadstool & green frog, souvenir of Catalina Island (on sticker), pr, from $10 to **$15.00**

Salt & pepper shakers, ear of corn, natural green & yellow, 4½", pr, from $25 to **$40.00**

Salt & pepper shakers, Earth, w/yellow orb marked ?, pr.**$95.00**

Salt & pepper shakers, gold bricks, 1 says 'Gold,' 1 says 'Brick,' pr, from $20 to **$25.00**

Salt & pepper shakers, goose & golden egg, white goose w/gold trim, pr, minimum value **$55.00**

Salt & pepper shakers, In the Doghouse, man in doghouse, woman w/rolling pin, pr, minimum value **$125.00**

Salt & pepper shakers, Indian & tepee, various colors, pr, from $35 to..**$40.00**

Salt & pepper shakers, kitten, yellow w/black trim, white milk bottle, pr, from $25 to................................**$30.00**

Salt & pepper shakers, Lady Bugs, orange & black or yellow & black, each, from $25 to **$30.00**

Salt & pepper shakers, nestlings, pink & blue in brown nest, pr, from $20 to...**$25.00**

Salt & pepper shakers, Panda bears, pours through eyes, pr, from $35 to..**$40.00**

Salt & pepper shakers, peas (2) in pod, natural green, from $12 to..**$15.00**

Salt & pepper shakers, snowbirds, blue w/gold trim, pr, from $15 to..**$20.00**

Salt & pepper shakers, squirrels, brown & gray, on hind quarters, from $25 to....................................**$30.00**

Salt & pepper shakers, ten pin, ivory w/gold trim, & bowling ball, dark brown, pr, from $25 to.............**$30.00**

Salt & pepper shakers, toadstool & reclining gnome, yellow w/white beard, pr, from $40 to **$45.00**

Salt & pepper shakers, tulips, blue w/gold trim, pr, from $15 to...**$18.00**

Salt & pepper shakers, turnip & lettuce, natural colors w/gold trim, pr **$75.00**

Salt and pepper shakers, prospector & jug, colorful miner w/silver pan & gold nuggets, XXX on jug, pr, minimum value **$125.00**

Spoondrip, Honeymoon design, yellow & blue or pink & red, each, minimum value **$30.00**

Tumbler, corn design, natural yellow & green, from $15 to...**$20.00**

Vase, woodpecker on side of tree, med, from $30 to.....**$35.00**

Vandor

For more than thirty-five years, Vandor has operated out of Salt Lake City, Utah. They're not actually manufacturers, but distributors of novelty ceramic items made overseas. Some pieces will be marked 'Made in Korea,' while others are marked 'Sri Lanka,' 'Taiwan,' or 'Japan.' Many of their best things have been made in the last few years, and already collectors are finding them appealing — anyone would. They have a line of kitchenware designed around 'Cowmen Mooranda' (an obvious take off on Carmen), another called 'Crocagator' (a darling crocodile modeled as a teapot, a bank, salt and pepper shakers, etc.), character-related items (Betty Boop and Howdy Doody, among others), and some really wonderful cookie jars reminiscent of fifties radios and jukeboxes.

For more information, we recommend *The Collector's Encyclopedia of Cookie Jars, Vol II,* by Joyce and Fred Roerig.

Advisor: Lois Wildman (See Directory, Vandor)

Cowman Mooranda, spoon rest, 1989, from $18.00 to $22.00.

Betty Boop, string holder.................................**$65.00**
Cow Beach Woody, salt & pepper shakers, pr **$65.00**
Cowboy, salt & pepper shakers, 1991, pr, from $16 to .**$20.00**
Cowmen Mooranda, creamer, 1989, from $18 to........**$20.00**
Cowmen Mooranda, mug, 1989............................**$30.00**
Cowmen Mooranda, salt & pepper shakers, 1989, pr.**$40.00**
Cowmen Mooranda, teapot, 1989..........................**$65.00**
Crocagator, salt & pepper shakers, bellhop, pr...........**$20.00**
Crocagator, salt & pepper shakers, high-heeled shoes, pr.**$20.00**
Flintstones, bookends, Fred & Wilma, 1989, pr **$125.00**
Flintstones, mug, Wilma, 1990, MIB.....................**$25.00**
I Love Lucy, teapot, 1996, MIB............................**$50.00**
Miss Piggy, scissors holder.................................**$35.00**
Mona Lisa, bank, 1992.....................................**$25.00**
Popeye, bank, full figure **$160.00**
Popeye, bank, Popeye bust w/pipe, 1980...............**$125.00**

Popeye, Olive Oyl plate, $65.00. (Photo courtesy Lois Wildman)

Vernon Kilns

Founded in Vernon, California, in 1930, this company produced many lines of dinnerware, souvenir plates, decorative pottery, and figurines. They employed several well-known artists whose designs no doubt contributed substantially to their success. Among them were Rockwell Kent, Royal Hickman, and Don Blanding, all of whom were responsible for creating several of the lines most popular with collectors today.

In 1940, they signed a contract with Walt Disney to produce a line of figurines and several dinnerware patterns that were inspired by Disney's film *Fantasia.* The figurines were made for a short time only and are now expensive.

The company closed in 1958, but Metlox purchased the molds and continued to produce some of their bestselling dinnerware lines through a specially established 'Vernon Kiln' division.

Most of the ware is marked in some form or another with the company name and, in some cases, the name of the dinnerware pattern.

If you'd like to learn more, we recommend *The Collector's Encyclopedia of California Pottery* by Jack Chipman and *Collectible Vernon Kilns, An Identification and Value Guide,* by Maxine Feek Nelson.

Newsletter: *Vernon Views*
P.O. Box 945
Scottsdale, AZ 85252; Published quarterly beginning with the spring issue.

Barkwood, bowl, salad; 10½" $28.00
Barkwood, creamer, regular..................................$12.00
Barkwood, pitcher, 1-qt......................................$25.00
Barkwood, plate, dinner $15.00
Barkwood, salt & pepper shakers, pr $12.00
Barkwood, tumbler, 14-oz.....................................$14.00
Brown-Eyed Susan, bowl, soup................................$15.00
Brown-Eyed Susan, casserole, 8"............................$45.00
Brown-Eyed Susan, chop plate, 12" $22.00
Brown-Eyed Susan, egg cup $28.00
Brown-Eyed Susan, salt & pepper shakers, sm, pr.....$10.00
Brown-Eyed Susan, syrup, drip-cut top $65.00
Brown-Eyed Susan, teapot $60.00
Chintz, bowl, fruit; 5½" $8.00
Chintz, coffeepot, 8-cup $65.00
Chintz, cup & saucer $12.00
Chintz, plate, dinner; 10"..................................$13.00
Chintz, platter, 14" $35.00
Delores, bowl, serving; oval $27.00
Fantasia, bowl, goldfish, #121 ....$375.00
Fantasia, bowl, Sprite, blue, #125..........................$275.00
Fantasia, figurine, centaurette, reclining, #17 ....$635.00
Fantasia, figurine, donkey unicorn, #16.....................$475.00
Fantasia, figurine, elephant standing, Disney, from $365
   to $380.00
Fantasia, figurine, satyr, 4½", from $250 to $275.00
Fantasia, figurine, unicorn, sitting, #14 ....$365.00
Gingham, casserole..$45.00
Gingham, chicken pie, w/lid, individual $27.00
Gingham, plate, 9½"..$10.00
Gingham, salt & pepper shakers, regular, pr..............$10.00
Gingham, spoon rest $40.00
Gingham, teapot $50.00
Hawaiian Flowers, chop plate, 12 ....$95.00
Hawaiian Flowers, pickle dish, tab handles, 6"..........$30.00
Hawaiian Flowers, salt & pepper shakers, pr..............$35.00
Hawaiian Flowers, sugar bowl, w/lid, individual........$30.00
Hawaiian Flowers, tumbler, iced tea $35.00
Homespun, butter dish.......................................$25.00
Homespun, chop plate, 12" $17.50
Homespun, cup & saucer $12.00
Homespun, muffin tray, tab handles, dome lid, 9".....$75.00
Homespun, pitcher, 1-qt, 11"................................$40.00
Homespun, plate, dinner; 10½"..............................$12.00
Homespun, sugar bowl, w/lid.................................$14.00
Homespun, tumbler, lg.......................................$15.00
Lei Lani, butter tray & lid, oblong.........................$50.00
Lei Lani, chop plate, 14"...................................$145.00
Lei Lani, cup & saucer, demitasse $34.00
Lei Lani, plate, dinner; 10"................................$45.00
Lei Lani, sugar bowl, demitasse; w/lid......................$65.00
Mayflower, bowl, salad; 12" $60.00
Mayflower, butter tray & lid................................$45.00
Mayflower, cup & saucer $15.00

Mayflower, egg cup $20.00
Mayflower, plate, dinner; 10½"..............................$12.50
Mayflower, platter, 13½"....................................$20.00

Mayflower, salt and pepper shakers, 3", $15.00 for the pair.

Melinda, bowl, oval, 9¾" $37.50
Melinda, gravy boat...$25.00
Melinda, platter, 12".......................................$20.00
Melinda, salt & pepper shakers, pr $16.00
Moby Dick, bowl, fruit; 5½".................................$50.00
Moby Dick, salt & pepper shakers, pr........................$145.00
Mojave, bowl, mixing; 5" $15.00
Native California, bowl, rim soup $18.00
Native California, teapot, 6-cup $65.00
Organdie, bowl, chowder; tab hdls, 6" $10.00
Organdie, bowl, rim soup....................................$12.50
Organdie, cup & saucer $7.00
Organdie, egg cup $15.00
Organdie, pitcher, disk, w/decor, 2-qt $75.00
Organdie, pitcher, streamline, 1-pt, 6" $20.00
Organdie, sugar bowl, angular, individual...................$20.00
Organdie, teapot $45.00
Our America, cup & saucer $100.00
Our America, plate, 7".....................................$85.00
Raffia, cup & saucer..$6.00
Raffia, plate, 10" $9.00
Salamina, chop plate, 12"...................................$285.00
Salamina, cup & saucer......................................$100.00
Salamina, plate, dinner; 10.................................$175.00
Sherwood, creamer $6.00
Sherwood, relish, 3-part $16.00

Souvenir plate, Colorful San Francisco, $25.00.

Tam O'Shanter, bowl, vegetable; 8¾" $25.00
Tam O'Shanter, carafe, w/stopper $45.00

Tam O'Shanter, coffee mug...**$24.00**
Tam O'Shanter, pitcher, 2-qt **$50.00**
Tam O'Shanter, plate, luncheon; 9¾".........................**$11.00**
Tam O'Shanter, platter, oval, 12½" **$22.00**
Tickled Pink, bowl, divided, 9" **$18.00**
Tickled Pink, coffeepot..**$45.00**
Tickled Pink, cup & saucer...**$10.00**
Tickled Pink, gravy boat **$15.00**
Tickled Pink, plate, 10" **$8.50**
Tweed, chop plate, 12"...**$55.00**
Tweed, sugar bowl, w/lid..**$40.00**
Ultra California, bowl, cereal; 6"...............................**$15.00**
Ultra California, bowl, shallow, 8".............................**$18.00**
Ultra California, casserole, 8" **$55.00**
Ultra California, creamer, tall **$18.00**
Wheat, egg cup...**$18.00**
Wheat, plate, dinner **$15.00**
Wheat, salt & pepper shakers, pr..............................**$20.00**
Winchester 73, chop plate, 12"...............................**$100.00**
Winchester 73, cup & saucer **$75.00**

Winchester 73, plate, 6½", $32.00. (Photo courtesy Maxine Nelson)

Winchester 73, plate, dinner; 10".............................**$75.00**
Winchester 73, tumbler **$45.00**

View-Master Reels and Packets

View-Master, the invention of William Gruber, was introduced to the public at the 1939–1940 New York World's Fair and the Golden Gate Exposition in California. Since then, View-Master reels, packets, and viewers have been produced by five different companies — the original Sawyers Company, G.A.F. (1966), View-Master International (1981), Ideal Toys, and Tyco Toys (the present owners). Because none of the non-cartoon single reels and three-reel packets have been made since 1980, these have become collectors' items. Also highly sought after are the three-reel sets featuring popular TV and cartoon characters. The market is divided between those who simply collect View-Master as a field all its own and collectors of character-related memorabilia who will often pay much higher prices for reels about Barbie, Batman, The Addams Family, etc. Our values tend to follow the more conservative approach.

The first single reels were dark blue with a gold sticker and came in attractive gold-colored envelopes. They appeared to have handwritten letters. These were fol-lowed by tan reels with a blue circular stamp. Because these were produced for the most part after 1945 and paper supplies were short during WWII, they came in a variety of front and back color combinations: tan with blue, tan with white, and marbleized. Since print runs were low during the war, these early singles are much more desirable than the printed ones that were produced by the millions from 1946 to 1957. Three-reel packets, many containing story books, were introduced in 1955, and single reels were phased out. Nearly all viewers are very common and have little value except for the very early ones, such as the Model A and Model B. Blue and brown versions of the Model B are especially rare. Another desirable viewer, unique in that it is the only focusing model ever made, is the Model D. For more information we recommend *View-Master Single Reels, Volume I,* by Roger Nazeley.

Acapulco, B-003, NMIP....................................**$8.00**
Air Force Museum, Sawyers, A-600, MIP (sealed).......**$12.00**
Aircraft Carrier, Sawyers, #760, MIP **$35.00**
Airplanes of the World, B-773, NMIP **$18.00**
Alice in Wonderland, GAF, 1964 (1952 reissue), EX+ (EX+ envelope)...**$15.00**
Alice in Wonderland, Sawyers, 1950s, EX+ (EX+ envelope) **$18.00**
Anchorage, A-103, NMIP...................................**$10.00**
Animals of Our National Parks, H-6, 1977, MIP (sealed)..**$8.00**
Apollo Moon Landing, B-663, MIP (sealed)................**$18.00**
Australia, B-233, NMIP.....................................**$15.00**
Beverly Hillbillies, B-570, NMIP **$35.00**
Birds of the World, B-678, MIP (sealed) **$25.00**
Birth of Jesus, B-875, MIP **$12.00**
Bonanza, B-471, MIP **$35.00**
Brady Bunch, B-568, NMIP **$40.00**
Brothers Grimm, G-3, MIP (sealed).......................**$10.00**
Busch Gardens, A-988, NMIP.............................**$12.00**
Cartoon Carnival With King Leonardo, Super Car & Alvin & the Chipmunks, B-521, MIP (sealed)....................**$25.00**
Casper the Friendly Ghost, B-533, MIP (sealed) **$22.00**
Cherokee Indians, Sawyers, MIP **$10.00**
Christmas Story, B-383, MIP (sealed) **$12.00**
Cinderella, B-313, NMIP **$12.00**
Cisco Kid, #960, 1950......................................**$10.00**
Colonial Williamsburg, A-813, MIP (sealed) **$10.00**
Cowboy Stars, Sawyers, NMIP **$30.00**
Daniel Boone, B-479, MIP (sealed) **$30.00**
Dark Shadows, B-503, NMIP...............................**$85.00**
Dennis the Menace, GAF, B-539, MIP (sealed) **$28.00**
Disney World the Vacation Kingdom, GAF, MIP **$10.00**
Disneyland's Adventureland, Sawyers, 1950s, EX (EX envelope) **$18.00**
Disneyland's Frontierland, Sawyers, 1950s, EX (EX envelope)...**$18.00**
Donald Duck, Sawyers, 1957, EX (EX envelope)........**$18.00**
Egypt Land of the Pharoahs, B-140, MIP (sealed).......**$20.00**
Expo 1967, Sawyers, MIP (sealed) **$20.00**
Family Affair, B-571, MIP (sealed), from $28 to.........**$38.00**
Fiddler on the Roof by United Artists, B-390, NMIP...**$35.00**

Gene Autry and His Wonder Horse Champion, #950, 1950, MIP, from $8.00 to $10.00.

Flash Gordon, 1979, MIP (sealed) **$20.00**
Gerry Anderson's UFO, B-417, NMIP......................**$25.00**
Green Hornet, B-488, NMIP.....................................**$85.00**
Grimm's Fairy Tales, Sawyers, 1960, EX (EX envelope).**$18.00**
Gunsmoke, B-689, 1972, MIP (sealed)......................**$30.00**
Hans Christian Andersen's Fairy Tales, Sawyers, 1958, EX (EX envelope)..**$10.00**
Happy Days, the Not Making of a President, 1974, MIP (sealed) **$24.00**
Hardy Boys, 1970, MIP (sealed) **$23.00**
Hawaii Five-O, B-590, MIP (sealed) **$25.00**
Heidi, Sawyers, 1950s, EX+ (EX+ envelope) **$10.00**
Hopalong Cassidy, #955, 1950, MIP **$10.00**
Huckleberry Hound & Yogi Bear, 1960, MIP (sealed) ..**$18.00**
Iceland, Sawyers, A-085, NMIP **$20.00**
Inside Moscow, Sawyers, NMIP................................**$22.00**
Instructional Football by Don Maynard, B-951, NMIP ..**$15.00**
James Bond Live & Let Die, GAF, B-393, MIP (sealed)...**$30.00**
James Bond Moonraker, GAF, H-68, 1979, MIP (sealed)...**$25.00**
Jetsons, 1981, MIP (sealed) **$24.00**
Julia, B-572, NMIP..**$25.00**
Land of the Giants, B-494, 1968, NMIP......................**$50.00**
Lassie Look Homeward, B-480, MIP **$20.00**
Lassie Rides the Log Flume, B-489, MIP **$20.00**
Laugh-In, 1968, NMIP...**$42.00**
Los Angeles Dodgers, L-23, 1981, MIP (sealed) **$30.00**
Lost in Space, B-482, NMIP......................................**$80.00**
Love Bug, B-501, NMIP **$15.00**
Mark Twain's Huckleberry Finn, B-343, MIP (sealed) ..**$15.00**
Minnesota Twins, L-22, 1981, MIP (sealed) **$30.00**
Mister Magoo, GAF, H-56, 1977, EX (EX package) **$8.00**
Mod Squad, B-478, 1960, MIP (sealed)......................**$35.00**
Mork & Mindy, K-67, MIP (sealed) **$20.00**
Nations of the World, Five Little Countries of Europe, Sawyers, B-149, NMIP **$45.00**
New Mickey Mouse Club Mouseketeers, H-9, 1977, MIP (sealed) **$35.00**
Niagara Falls, A-655, MIP (sealed)............................**$15.00**
Night Before Christmas, B-382, MIP (sealed) **$10.00**
Our Planet Earth, World of Science: Geology, B-675, MIP (sealed) **$15.00**
Out Islands of the Bahamas, GAF, NMIP....................**$20.00**
Peter Pan, Sawyers, 1957, EX (EX envelope).............**$12.00**
Pink Panther Famous Pilot, GAF, J-12, MIP (sealed) ..**$12.00**
Planet of the Apes, B-507, NMIP...............................**$30.00**

Return From Witch Mountain, J-25, 1973, MIP............**$10.00**
Revolutionary War, America's Bicentennial Celebration, GAF, MIP (sealed) **$20.00**
Rin-Tin-Tin, Sawyers, 1955, NMIP **$22.00**
Robinson Crusoe, B-438, NMIP.................................**$18.00**
Santa's Workshop at North Pole, B-213, MIP (sealed) ..**$22.00**
Scenic USA, A-966, MIP (sealed) **$10.00**
Sleeping Beauty, Sawyers, 1959, VG (VG envelope)....**$8.00**
Snoopy & the Red Baron, B-544, NMIP......................**$10.00**
Snow White & the Seven Dwarfs, B-300, NMIP.........**$12.00**
Statue of Liberty, A-648, MIP (sealed).........................**$15.00**
Steve Canyon, 1959, EX (EX package)........................**$45.00**
Swiss Alpine Passes, Sawyers, C-127, MIP (sealed) **$28.00**
Tom Corbett Space Cadet, S-3, MIP (sealed)..............**$20.00**
US Spaceport, B-662, 1973, MIP **$10.00**
Washington DC, A-190, MIP (sealed) **$12.00**
Winnie the Pooh, GAF, 1964, EX+ (EX+ envelope)....**$15.00**
Wiz, J-14, 1978, MIP (sealed)....................................**$15.00**
Wonders of the Deep, B-612, MIP (sealed), from $10 to..**$14.00**
World of Science: Entomology, B-688, MIP (sealed) ..**$25.00**
Yellowstone National Park, GAF, 1977, MIP (sealed) .**$12.00**
Zorro, B-469, 1958, MIP **$40.00**

Viking Glass

Located in the famous glassmaking area of West Virginia, this company has been in business since the 1950s. They are best recognized for their glass animals and birds. Their Epic Line (circa 1950s and '60s) was innovative in design and vibrant in color. Rich tomato-red, amberina, brilliant blues, strong greens, black, amber, and deep amethyst were among the rainbow hues in production at that time. During the 1980s, the company's ownership changed hands, and the firm became known as Dalzell-Viking. Some of the Epic Line animals were reissued in crystal, crystal frosted, and black. If you're interested in learning more about these animals, refer to *Glass Animals of the Depression Era* by Lee Garmon and Dick Spencer (Collector Books).

Advisor: Ruth Grizel (See Directory, Westmoreland)

Bookend, elephant, amber, w/label, pr **$20.00**
Bookend, Wise Old Owl, green, pr **$30.00**
Bowl, teal, 8 deep scallops at rim, dome foot, heavy, 4½x10" **$35.00**
Bowl, teal, 9 scallops at rim, footed, 7x8"..................**$35.00**
Candle holders, dolphin, pink, hexagonal footed, 9½", pr **$150.00**
Figurine, angelfish, amber, 7x7" **$125.00**
Figurine, angelfish, milk glass...................................**$75.00**
Figurine, bird, moss green, tail up, 12".....................**$25.00**
Figurine, bird, orange, long tail, 9½" **$25.00**
Figurine, cat, green, sitting, 8" **$55.00**
Figurine, duck, dark teal, Viking's Epic Line, 9" **$35.00**
Figurine, duck, ruby, fighting, heads up & down, pr..**$100.00**
Figurine, duck, ruby, round, footed, 5" **$35.00**
Figurine, egret, orange, 12"......................................**$45.00**
Figurine, hound dog, crystal, 8" **$50.00**

Figurine, mouse, crystal mist, 4"..................................$35.00
Figurine, owl, amber, Viking's Epic..........................$45.00
Figurine, penguin, amber, w/label, 7"....................$25.00
Figurine, penguin, crystal, 7".....................................$25.00
Figurine, pony, aqua blue, tall..................................$95.00

Figurine, rooster, Viking's Epic Line, orange, 1960s, 9½", from $55.00 to $65.00.

Figurine, rabbit (Thumper), 6½"...................................$35.00
Figurine, seal, persimmon, 9¾" L...............................$15.00
Figurine, swan, bowl, amber, 6"..................................$45.00
Lamp, fairy; Fine Cut, pink satin, footed $25.00

Wade Porcelain

If you've attended many flea markets, you're already very familiar with the tiny Wade figurines, most of which are 2" and under. Wade made several lines of them, but the most common were made as premiums for the Red Rose Tea Company. Most of these sell for $3.50 to $7.00 or so. Some of the animals are much larger and may sell for more than $100.00.

The Wade company dates to 1810. The original kiln was located near Chesterton in England. The tiny pottery merged with a second about 1900 and became known as the George Wade Pottery. They continued to grow and to absorb smaller nearby companies and eventually manufactured a wide range of products from industrial ceramics to Irish porcelain giftware. In 1990 Wade changed its name to Seagoe Ceramics Limited.

If you'd like to learn more, we recommend *The World of Wade* by Ian Warner and Mike Posgay.

Advisor: Ian Warner (See Directory, Wade)

Newsletter: *The Wade Watch*
The Collector's Corner
8199 Pierson Ct.
Arvada, CO 80005; 303-421-9655 or 303-424-4401 or Fax 303-421-0317; Subscription: $8 per year (4 issues)

Bird, Barn Owl, Tom Smith, 1992-93, molded-in mark Wade England around base, 1"...$6.00
Circus Animal, Lion, Tom Smith, 1978-79, molded-in mark on drum-type base, 1½" $12.00

Circus Animal, Macaque Monkey, Tom Smith, 1978-79, molded-in mark Wade England on drum-type base, 1½" $12.00
Circus Animal, Poodle, Tom Smith, 1978-79, molded-in-mark Wade England on drum-type base, 1¾" $12.00
Farmyard, Bull, Tom Smith, 1982-83, molded-in mark Wade England around base, 1", from $12 to $14.00
Farmyard, Goose, Tom Smith, 1982-83, molded-in mark Wade England around base, 1⅜", from $8 to.......$10.00
Farmyard, Horse, Tom Smith, 1982-83, molded-in mark Wade England around base, 1½", from $12 to $14.00
Farmyard, Pig, Tom Smith, 1982-83, molded-in mark Wade England around base, 1", from $12 to $14.00
KP Friars, Father Abbot, KP Foods Limited, 1983, molded-in mark Wade on base back, 1¾"..............................$7.00
Mini-Nursery Rhyme & Fairy Tale, Baa Baa Black Sheep, Canadian Red Rose Tea, 1971-79, molded-in mark, 1" $20.00
Mini-Nursery Rhyme & Fairy Tale, Cat & the Fiddle, Canadian Red Rose Tea, 1971-79, marked England only, 1⅞x1".........$20.00
Mini-Nursery Rhyme & Fairy Tale, Hickory Dickory Dock, Canadian Red Rose Tea, 1971-79, marked Wade on base front, 1¾"..$5.00
Mini-Nursery Rhyme & Fairy Tale, Jill (Jack & Jill), Canadian Red Rose Tea, 1971-79, molded-in mark Wade England, 1¼"..$8.00
Mini-Nursery Rhyme & Fairy Tale, Little Boy Blue, Canadian Red Rose Tea, 1971-79, molded-in mark Wade England, 1⅝" $8.00
Mini-Nursery Rhyme & Fairy Tale, Little Miss Muffet, Canadian Red Rose Tea, 1971-79, molded-in mark Wade England, 1½" $8.00
Mini-Nursery Rhyme & Fairy Tale, Little Red Riding Hood, Canadian Red Rose Tea, 1971-79, molded-in mark, 1¾"..................$5.00
Mini-Nursery Rhyme & Fairy Tale, Three Bears, Canadian Red Rose Tea, 1971-79, molded-in mark Wade England, 1⅜"..$20.00
Mini-Nursery Rhyme & Fairy Tale, Tom the Piper's Son, Canadian Red Rose Tea, 1971-79, molded-in mark, 1⅝" $8.00
Mini-Nursery Rhyme & Fairy Tales, The House That Jack Built, Canadian Red Rose Tea, 1971-79, molded-in mark, 1¼"..$12.00
Painted Ladies, Pink Lady, San Francisco Mini Mansions, 1984-86, marked Wade Porcelain England SF/1, 2¼x1x1¼"..$55.00

Robin Hood and Maid Marian, 1989–1990, $30.00 each.

Safari, Musk Ox, Tom Smith, 1976-77, molded-in mark Wade England around base, 1" **$15.00**
Safari, Tiger, Tom Smith, 1976-77, molded-in mark Wade England around base, 1⅜" **$10.00**
St Bruno Pipe Tobacco, St Bernard dog, Imperial Tobacco Limited, 1986, unmarked ridged molded base, 1¼", from $8 to.**$10.00**
Survival, Armadillo, Tom Smith, 1984-85, molded-in mark Wade England around base, 1" **$12.00**
Survival, Blue Whale, Tom Smith, 1984-85, molded-in mark Wade England around base, 1" **$12.00**
Survival, Harp Seal, Tom Smith, 1984-85, molded-in mark Wade England around base, 1½" **$12.00**

Turtle mother and baby, $33.00 for the pair.

Whimsie, Angelfish, Canadian Red Rose Tea, 1967-73, molded-in mark Wade England around base, 1¼x1⅜" ..**$6.00**
Whimsie, Chimp, USA Red Rose Tea, 1983-85, single glaze, molded-in mark Wade England, 1½".......................**$6.00**
Whimsie, Hippo, USA Red Rose Tea, 1983-85, single glaze, molded-in mark Wade England, 1½" L .**$6.00**
Whimsie, Koala Bear, USA Red Rose Tea, 1985, single glaze, molded-in Wade England around base, 1⅜" **$5.00**
Whimsie, Seal, Canadian Red Rose Tea, 1967-73, tan on blue base marked Wade England, 1½x1¼" **$8.00**
Whimsie, Tiger, USA Red Rose Tea, 1985, single glaze, molded-in Wade England around base, 1⅜"...................**$5.00**
Whimsie-on-Why Village, Pump Cottage, 1980, molded-in mark Wade England on base, 1x1¼x¾" **$8.00**
Whimsie-on-Why Village, Tinker's Nook, 1982, molded-in mark Wade England on base, 1⅜x1x¾" **$12.00**
Wildlife, Badger, Tom Smith, 1980-81, molded-in mark Wade England around base, 1", from $10 to **$12.00**
Wildlife, Hare, Tom Smith, 1980-81, molded-in mark Wade England around base, 1¾", from $10 to **$12.00**
Wildlife, Mole, Tom Smith, 1980-81, molded-in mark Wade England around base, 1", from $10 to **$12.00**

Wall Pockets

A few years ago there were only a handful of really avid wall pocket collectors, but today many are finding them intriguing. They were popular well before the turn of the century. Roseville and Weller included at least one and sometimes several in many of their successful lines of art pottery, and other American potteries made them as well. Many were imported from Germany, Czechoslovakia, China, and Japan. By the 1950s, they were passé.

Some of the most popular today are the figurals. Look for the more imaginative and buy the ones you like — these are light-hearted collectibles! If you're buying to resell, look for those designed around animals, large exotic birds, children, lucious fruits, or those that are especially eyecatching. Appeal is everything. For more information, refer to *Collector's Guide to Wall Pockets, Affordable and Others,* by Marvin and Joy Gibson; *Wall Pockets of the Past* by Fredda Perkins; and *Collector's Encyclopedia of Wall Pockets* by Betty and Bill Newbound.

Bird & berry, brown & yellow tones, Czechoslovakia, 8"..**$45.00**
Cat on fishing creel, unmarked, 5½"...........................**$20.00**
Cornucopia w/applied bird, various colors, marked Patented 149244, 7" **$20.00**

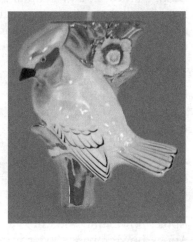

Crested bird and flowers, lustre and glossy glazes, Japan, 5", $22.00.

Dancing lady, very sm pocket in swirl of skirt, Made in Japan, 8¼"...**$55.00**
Deco flower on cone form w/lustre trim, Made in Japan, 7¼" **$35.00**
Dutch boy w/goose beside stone wall, Made in Japan, 6".**$18.00**
Fish, pink airbrushing on white w/black details, marked Pat Pend Cherm Craft, San Clemente CA, Tropic Treasures, 9½"...**$22.00**
Grape cluster on vine, bright colors, Made in Japan, 6⅝" ..**$14.00**
Little Orphan Annie & Sandy painted on cone form, lustre trim, Made in Japan, 5⅜" **$100.00**
Man's face w/mustache, bow tie, unmarked Japan, 4¼" ..**$15.00**
Oriental lady w/basket on back, bright colors, Japan, 8" .**$25.00**
Parrot perched on pocket, bright colors, Made in Japan, 9¾" **$25.00**
Rooster, white w/red & green details, Engle Studio, 12"...**$65.00**
Ruffled flower, yellow w/green leafy stem, label marked Jamy Ceramic Fashions, 6½"................................**$20.00**
Sailboat, white & gold lustre, marked Brown China Co, Sebring OH, 5¾"...**$20.00**
Shoe w/painted pine cones on toe, unmarked, 8½" ..**$14.00**
Squirrel, brown tones, eating nut, unmarked Japan, 4⅜" .**$12.00**
Straw hat, shallow crown, unmarked, 10" dia.............**$15.00**
Swallows painted on cone form, blue lustre trim, unmarked Japan, 7" **$30.00**
Swirled conical form, dark green, unmarked (European), 10" **$12.00**
Telephone, crank model, white w/multicolor floral decoration, L&F Ceramics, Hollywood, 7" **$20.00**
Umbrella, painted berries & leaves on white, sticker marked Orion, 6⅜"...**$12.00**

Watt Pottery

The Watt Pottery Company operated in Crooksville, Ohio, from 1922 until sometime in 1935. The ware they produced is easily recognized and widely available today. It appeals to collectors of country antiques, since the body is yellow ware and its decoration simple. Several pieces of Watt pottery were featured in *Country Living* magazine a few years ago, and it was this exposure that seemed to catapult it onto the collectibles market.

Several patterns were made: Apple, Autumn Foliage, Cherry, Dutch Tulip, Morning-Glory, Pansy, Rooster, Tear Drop, Starflower, and Tulip among them. All were executed in bold brush strokes of primary colors. Some items you'll find will also carry a stenciled advertising message, made for retail companies as premiums for their customers.

For further study, we recommend *Watt Pottery, An Identification and Value Guide,* by Sue and Dave Morris (see Directory, Watt Pottery).

Apple, baker, sm handle, w/lid, #96, 5¾x8½" **$125.00**
Apple, bean pot, handles, #76, 6½x7½" **$135.00**
Apple, bowl, #106, 3½x10¾" **$150.00**
Apple, bowl, #73, 4x9½" **$75.00**
Apple, bowl, cereal/salad; #52, 2¼x6½" **$35.00**
Apple, bowl, cereal/salad; #94, 1¾x6" **$35.00**
Apple, bowl, embossed ribs, w/lid, #05, 4x5" **$145.00**
Apple, bowl, mixing; #64, 5x7½" **$50.00**
Apple, bowl, mixing; #65, 5¾x8½" **$60.00**
Apple, bowl, mixing; embossed ribs, #7, 4x7" **$45.00**
Apple, bowl, mixing; embossed ribs, #9, 5x9" **$55.00**
Apple, bowl, mixing; ribbed top, #06, 3x6" **$50.00**
Apple, bowl, mixing; vertical ribs, #604, 2½x6¾" **$45.00**
Apple, bowl, spaghetti; #39, 3x13" **$150.00**
Apple, bowl, spaghetti; individual, #44, 1½x8" **$100.00**
Apple, bowl, vertical ribs, #602, 1¾x4¾" **$45.00**
Apple, canister, #72, 9½x7" **$500.00**
Apple, casserole, French handle, w/lid, #18 ....**$225.00**
Apple, cheese crock, #80, 8x8½" **$500.00**
Apple, chip 'n dip set, #120 bowl (2x5") & #110 bowl (3¾x8") w/sm metal supporting frame **$225.00**
Apple, creamer, #62, 4½x4½" **$75.00**
Apple, grease jar, #01, 5½x5¼" **$250.00**
Apple, ice bucket, w/lid, 7¼x7½" **$225.00**
Apple, mug, #121 ....**$175.00**
Apple, mug, #701 ....**$200.00**
Apple, mug, barrel shape, #501, 4½" **$225.00**
Apple, pie plate, #33, 9" **$150.00**
Apple, pitcher, no ice lip, #17, 8x8½" **$225.00**
Apple, pitcher, refrigerator; square sides, #69, 8x8½"...**$350.00**
Apple, platter, #31, 15" **$335.00**
Apple, salt & pepper shakers, barrel shaped, 4x2½", pr..**$245.00**
Apple, tumbler, #56, 4½x4" **$325.00**
Apple (Double), creamer, #62, 4¼x4½" **$125.00**
Apple (Open), bowl, mixing; #5, 2¾x5" **$85.00**
Apple (Open), bowl, mixing; #8, 4½x8" **$125.00**
Apple (Reduced Decoration), bowl, mixing; #63, 4x6½" ...**$65.00**
Autumn Foliage, bowl, #106, 3½x10¾" **$55.00**
Autumn Foliage, bowl, embossed ribs, #6, 6" **$30.00**

Autumn Foliage, ice bucket, w/lid, 7¼x7½" **$130.00**
Autumn Foliage, mug, #121, 3¾x3" **$175.00**
Autumn Foliage, platter, #31, 15" **$110.00**
Autumn Foliage, salt & pepper shakers, hourglass shape, holes depict S&P in tops, 4½", pr......................**$145.00**
Banded (Blue & White), bowl, mixing; 4x7" **$25.00**
Banded (Blue & White), casserole, w/lid, 4½x8¾" **$55.00**
Banded (Green & White), bowl, mixing; #6, 3½x6"...**$25.00**
Banded (Green & White), bowl, mixing; #9, 5x9" **$25.00**
Banded (Light Blue & White), cookie jar, 7½x7" **$65.00**
Banded (Light Blue & White), pitcher, 7x7¾" **$45.00**
Banded (White), bowl, 4½x6" **$25.00**
Banded (White), casserole, w/lid, 7x9" **$65.00**
Banded (White), pitcher, 7x7¾" **$45.00**
Cherry, bowl, berry; #4, 2x5" **$25.00**
Cherry, bowl, mixing; #6, 5" **$35.00**
Cherry, cookie jar, #21, 7½" **$160.00**
Cherry, platter, #31, 15" **$145.00**
Cut-Leaf Pansy, bowl, mixing; 7", 8" or 9", each........**$35.00**
Cut-Leaf Pansy, bowl, serving; 2x5½" **$25.00**
Cut-Leaf Pansy, bowl, serving; 3x15" **$80.00**
Cut-Leaf Pansy, casserole, stick handle, w/lid, 3¾x7½" L ..**$125.00**
Cut-Leaf Pansy, cup & saucer, 2½x4½", 6½" **$75.00**
Cut-Leaf Pansy, Dutch oven, w/lid, 7x10½" **$150.00**
Cut-Leaf Pansy, pie plate, 1½x9" **$80.00**
Cut-Leaf Pansy, platter, 15" **$100.00**
Cut-Leaf Pansy, spaghetti plate, individual, 8½" **$40.00**
Cut-Leaf Pansy (Bull's-Eye), bowl, serving; 2½x11"....**$60.00**
Cut-Leaf Pansy (Bull's-Eye), plate, 7½" **$45.00**
Cut-Leaf Pansy (Bull's-Eye), platter, 15" **$100.00**
Cut-Leaf Pansy (Bull's-Eye), saucer, w/red swirls, 6½" ..**$20.00**
Dutch Tulip, bean pot, handles, w/lid, #76, 6½x7½" ..**$225.00**
Dutch Tulip, bowl, mixing; #63, 4x6½" **$65.00**
Dutch Tulip, bowl, spaghetti; #39, 3x13" **$250.00**
Kitch-N-Queen, bowl, mixing; pink & blue stripes at rim, horizontal ribs, #9, 5x9" **$30.00**
Kitch-N-Queen, pitcher, ice lip, pink & blue bands, #17, 8x8½" **$100.00**
Morning Glory, bowl, mixing; #6, 3½x6" **$50.00**
Morning Glory, bowl, mixing; #9, 5x9" **$60.00**
Old Pansy, bowl, spaghetti; #39, 3x13" **$70.00**
Old Pansy, casserole, #3/19, w/lid, 5x9" **$65.00**
Old Pansy, casserole, w/lid, 4½x8¾" **$65.00**
Old Pansy, casserole, w/lid, 4¼x7½" **$55.00**
Old Pansy, casserole, 4 sm handles, w/lid, #8, 4¾x9½" ..**$90.00**
Old Pansy, cookie jar, 7½x7" **$140.00**
Old Pansy, pitcher, #15, 5½x5¾" **$55.00**
Old Pansy, pitcher, #17, 8x8½" **$125.00**
Old Pansy, platter, #31, 15" **$100.00**
Old Pansy, platter, #49, 12" **$100.00**
Old Pansy (Cross-Hatch), bowl, spaghetti; 3x13"....**$100.00**
Old Pansy (Cross-Hatch), pitcher, 7x7¾" **$150.00**
Old Pansy (Cross-Hatch), platter, 15" **$125.00**
Raised Pansy, casserole, French handle, individual, w/lid, 3¾x7½" L **$175.00**
Raised Pansy, creamer, 3x5½" **$85.00**
Raised Pansy, pitcher, 7x7¾" **$200.00**
Rooster, baking dish, 2¼x5¼x10" **$1,000.00**
Rooster, bean pot, handles, #76, 6½x7½" **$175.00**

Rooster, bowl, mixing; #5, 2¾x5".............................**$55.00**
Rooster, bowl, w/lid, #05, 4x5"...............................**$135.00**
Rooster, casserole, French handle, individual, w/lid, #18, 4x8" L..**$225.00**
Rooster, pitcher, #15, 5½x5¾"...............................**$75.00**
Starflower, bean pot, handles, w/lid, #76, 6½x7½" **$90.00**
Starflower, bean server, individual, #75, 2¼x3½".......**$25.00**
Starflower, bowl, #54, 3½x8½"..............................**$45.00**
Starflower, bowl, #73, 4x9½".................................**$55.00**
Starflower, bowl, cereal/salad; 352, 2½x6½"..............**$25.00**
Starflower, bowl, mixing; #04, 2x4".........................**$65.00**
Starflower, bowl, mixing; #07, 3¾x7".......................**$40.00**
Starflower, casserole, French handle, w/lid, individual, #18, 4x8" L..**$200.00**
Starflower, casserole, stick handle, w/lid, #18, 3¾x7½" L.**$150.00**
Starflower, casserole, tab handles, w/lid, #18, 4x5"..**$150.00**
Starflower, creamer, #62, 4¼x4½"...........................**$75.00**
Starflower, ice bucket, w/lid, 7¼x7½".....................**$185.00**
Starflower, mug, #121, 3¾x3"................................**$195.00**
Starflower, pitcher, #16, 6½x6¾"............................**$85.00**
Starflower, pitcher, ice lip, #17, 8x8½"...................**$165.00**
Starflower, platter, #31, 15"................................**$140.00**
Starflower, salt & pepper shakers, hourglass w/embossed letters, pr..**$175.00**
Starflower, salt & pepper shakers, red & green bands, barrel shaped, 4x2½", pr.....................................**$160.00**
Starflower, tumbler, rounded sides, #56, 4x3½"........**$275.00**
Starflower, tumbler, slant sides, #56, 4½x4"..............**$225.00**
Starflower (Green on Brown), bowl, mixing; #5, 2¾x5" .**$30.00**
Starflower (Green on Brown), casserole, tab handles, individual, #18, 4x5"..................................**$125.00**
Starflower (Green on Brown), casserole, w/lid, #54, 6x8½"...**$125.00**
Starflower (Green on Brown), cookie jar, #21, 7½" .**$125.00**
Starflower (Pink on Black), bowl, 2½x11"...............**$125.00**
Starflower (Pink on Black), casserole, w/lid, 4½x8¾"..**$125.00**
Starflower (Pink on Black), cup & saucer, 2¾x4½", 6"..**$85.00**
Starflower (Pink on Black), plate, dinner; 10"..........**$100.00**
Starflower (Pink on Green), bowl, berry; 1¾x5" **$35.00**
Starflower (Pink on Green), casserole, w/lid, 4½x8¾".**$125.00**
Starflower (Pink on Green), cup & saucer, 2¾x4½", 6"..**$65.00**
Starflower (Pink on Green), plate, bread & butter; 6½"..**$35.00**
Starflower (Pink on Green), platter, #31, 15"...........**$110.00**
Starflower (White on Blue), spaghetti bowl, #39, 3x13" .**$175.00**
Tear Drop, bean server, individual, #75, 2¼x3½".......**$25.00**
Tear Drop, bowl, #66, 3x7"...................................**$45.00**
Tear Drop, bowl, mixing; #5, 2½x5"........................**$45.00**
Tear Drop, casserole, square, w/lid, 5x8x8"............**$275.00**
Tear Drop, cheese crock, #80, 8x8¼".....................**$275.00**
Tear Drop, creamer, #62, 4½x4½".........................**$75.00**
Tear Drop, pitcher, #15, 5½x5¾"............................**$45.00**
Tear Drop, salt & pepper shakers, barrel shaped, 4x2½", pr..**$150.00**
Tulip, bowl, #73, 4x9½".......................................**$100.00**
Tulip, bowl, embossed ribs, w/lid, #600, 5½x7¾" ...**$200.00**
Tulip, bowl, from nesting set, embossed ribs, #600, 7¾"..**$85.00**
Tulip, bowl, from nesting set, embossed ribs, #604, 6¾"..**$65.00**
Tulip, bowl, mixing; #63, 4x6½"............................**$60.00**
Tulip, cookie jar, #503, 8¼x8¼".............................**$300.00**

Tulip, creamer, #62, 4¼x4½".................................**$95.00**
Tulip, pitcher, refrigerator; square sides, #69, 8x8½"..**$325.00**

Tear Drop bean pot, #76, 6½x7½", $90.00; Dutch Tulip individual French-handled casserole, #18, 8" long, $245.00; Apple, pitcher with ice lip, #17, 8", $225.00. (Photo courtesy Sue and Dave Morris)

Weeping Gold

In the mid- to late 1950s, many American pottery companies produced lines of 'Weeping Gold.' Such items have a distinctive appearance; most appear to be covered with irregular droplets of lustrous gold, sometimes heavy, sometimes fine. On others the gold is in random swirls, or there may be a definite pattern developed on the surface. In fact, real gold was used; however, there is no known successful way of separating the gold from the pottery. You'll see similar pottery covered in 'Weeping Silver.' Very often, ceramic whiskey decanters made for Beam, McCormick, etc., will be trimmed in 'Weeping Gold.' Among the marks you'll find on these wares are 'McCoy,' 'Kingwood Ceramics,' and 'USA,' but most items are simply stamped '22k (or 24k) gold.'

Basket, Dixon Art Studios, 22k gold, 8½x5"...............**$25.00**
Candy dish, flattened apple form.................................**$22.00**

Dealer sign, Kingwood Salem, 8¾", from $25.00 to $35.00. (Photo courtesy Lee Garmon)

Ewer, straight flaring sides, handle wraps from rim to base, 8"...**$16.00**
Horses, facing pr, rearing, 10".................................**$28.00**

Panther, pacing, opening in back, marked 24k gold, 14¾" L $25.00

Peafowl, 13½", from $30.00 to $40.00. (Photo courtesy Lee Garmon)

Teapot, marked McCoy, ca 1957 ....$65.00
Tidbit tray, 2-tier $20.00
Vase, dripping gold, 10-petal flower form, 5x5" dia $9.00
Vase, scalloped square, 22k gold, 3x4½" $6.00
Vase, swirls in gold, marked Swetye Salem O w/star in circle, square, 7x4¼" $12.00
Wall pocket, Apple, marked 24k gold, USA, 5" $20.00

Weil Ware

Though the Weil company made dinnerware and some kitchenware, their figural pieces are attracting the most collector interest. They were in business from the 1940s until the mid-1950s, another of the small but very successful California companies whose work has become so popular today. They dressed their 'girls' in beautiful gowns of vivid rose, light dusty pink, turquoise blue, and other lovely colors enhanced with enameled 'lacework' and flowers, sgraffito, sometimes even with tiny applied blossoms. Both paper labels and ink stamps were used to mark them, but as you study their features, you'll soon learn to recognize even those that have lost their labels over the years. Four-number codes and decorators' initials are usually written on their bases.

If you want to learn more, we recommend *The Collector's Encyclopedia of California Pottery* by Jack Chipman.

Advisors: Pat and Kris Secor (See Directory, California Pottery)

Figurine, girl stands by square vase, 10½", $35.00.

Bowl, salad; Rose, sm, from $5 to $6.00
Butter dish, Rose $15.00
Coffee server, Malay Blossom $30.00
Dish, Dogwood, divided, square, 10½" $15.00
Figurine, girl, flower vase under right arm, 2nd in skirt, 10" $40.00
Figurine, girl, hand on hip, leans to side, vase at other side, sgraffito florals, 10" $50.00
Figurine, girl holding open apron/vase, w/bonnet & open coat, 10" $35.00
Figurine, girl sits between vases, hand-painted florals, #4028, 9" $40.00
Figurine, lady w/parasol, green & lavender, #4045, 9¾" .$42.00
Figurine, Oriental girl, seated on square base, hands hold fan/vase behind head, 7" $45.00
Figurine, Southern belle, applied flowers on hat & at waist, vase each side, 10" $50.00
Figurine, young girl, short pink & blue dress, scarf on head, holds flowers, vase behind, 10" $35.00
Pitcher, Malay Blossom $30.00
Wall pocket, Oriental boy w/lg hat, #4046, 10" $40.00

Weller

Though the Weller Pottery has been closed since 1948, they were so prolific that you'll be sure to see several pieces of their ware any time you're 'antiquing.' They were one of the largest of the art pottery giants that located near Zanesville, Ohio, drawn there by rich clay deposits and natural gas the area had in abundance. In the early years, they made hand-decorated vases, jardinieres, lamps, and other decorative items for the home, many of which were signed by notable artists such as Fredrick Rhead, John Lessell, Virginia Adams, Anthony Dunlavy, Dorothy England, Albert Haubrich, Hester Pillsbury, E.L. Pickens, and Jacques Sicard, to name only a few. Some of their early lines were First and Second Dickens, Eocean, Sicardo, Etna, Louwelsa, Turada, and Aurelian. Portraits of Indians, animals of all types, lady golfers, nudes, and scenes of Dickens stories were popular themes, and some items were overlaid with silver filigree. These lines are rather hard to find at this point in time, and prices are generally high; but there's plenty of their later production still around, and most pieces are relatively inexpensive.

If you'd like to learn more, we recommend *The Collector's Encyclopedia of Weller Pottery* by Sharon and Bob Huxford.

Ardsley, fan vase, brown cattails among long green fanning leaves, flower at base, ink stamp, 8", from $125 to $175.00
Ardsley, wall pocket, double; brown cattails among long green leaves on each pocket, flower at base, ink stamp, 11½" $250.00
Ardsley, wall pocket, lg purple iris among long slim leaves, unmarked, 12", from $300 to $350.00
Balden, vase, embossed colorful apple branches on brown, sm raised rim, bulbous, unmarked, 5½", from $150 to $175.00

Baldin, vase, apples on lg branch (which also forms handles) on brown squatty form, unmarked, 9½", from $300 to..**$350.00**

Baldin, vase, embossed colorful apple branch at base of brown trumpet shape, unmarked, 7", from $65 to..............**$75.00**

Barcelona, candle holder, floral medallion on tan saucer-like base, ink stamp, 2x5", from $75 to **$100.00**

Barcelona, vase, floral medallion painted on tan, waisted form w/rim-to-hip handles, marked, 6½", from $175 to **$225.00**

Blue Drapery, planter, pink roses on shirred dark blue drapery background, impressed mark, 4", from $50 to.........**$60.00**

Blue Drapery, vase, pink roses on shirred dark blue drapery background, slim form, unmarked, 8", from $75 to.**$85.00**

Blue Ware, vase, classical woman in ivory on dark blue cylinder, impressed mark, 8½", from $200 to **$250.00**

Blue Ware, vase, 2 ivory angels amid floral swags on dark blue, footed, unmarked, 8½", from $250 to.......**$300.00**

Bonito, vase, bluebells on ivory, sm handles, marked by hand, 4", from $65 to **$95.00**

Bonito, vase, multicolor floral decor on ivory, signed NC, sm angle handles, paper label, 10", from $300 to....**$400.00**

Bouquet, bowl vase, white embossed floral decor on green, scalloped inverted rim, #B-3, script mark, 4½", from $30 to..**$35.00**

Bouquet, vase, embossed & painted flowers on blue trumpet form, #B-7, script mark, 9", from $65 to..............**$75.00**

Brighton, wall pocket, yellow bird perched on limb beside hole in stump form, impressed mark, 9½", from $350 to..**$400.00**

Burntwood, vase, 2-tone brown floral, dark brown band at rim & base, unmarked, 3½", from $90 to...........**$120.00**

Burntwood, vase, 2-tone brown floral shouldered form, brown band at rim & base, no mark, 7", from $125 to.......**$150.00**

Burntwood vases: 12", $275.00; 5½", $100.00; Jardiniere, 6½", $150.00.

Cactus, figurine, boy w/bag, brown tones, marked by hand, 5", from $85 to...**$110.00**

Cactus, figurine, frog, tan w/black eyes, marked by hand, 4", from $70 to..**$85.00**

Cameo, basket, embossed white floral decor on green, ornate handle, script mark, 7½", from $50 to **$60.00**

Cameo, vase, white floral decor on blue, waisted form w/ornate handles, unmarked, 5", from $25 to **$35.00**

Candis, ewer, embossed floral decor on ivory, shaped rim, slim form, simple handle, marked, 11", from $95 to **$110.00**

Candis, vase, embossed floral decor on ivory, handles, script mark, 9", from $55 to **$65.00**

Chase, vase, hunt scene in ivory on tan (unusual color), marked by hand, 10½", from $450 to **$500.00**

Chase, vase, hunt scene in white on blue, bulbous, marked by hand, 6½", from $250 to.............................**$350.00**

Classic, plate, cut-out scallop design along rim on white, marked, 11½", from $40 to **$45.00**

Classic, window box, cut-out scallop design along rim in light green, paper label, script mark, 4", from $60 to ..**$70.00**

Claywood, candle holder, floral in 2-tone brown w/dark brown bars, dark brown at rim & base, unmarked, 5", from $65 to..**$85.00**

Claywood, vase, floral decor on 2-tone brown w/dark brown vertical bars, unmarked, 5½", from $75 to **$85.00**

Colored Glaze, jardiniere, embossed squirrels in green & brown tones, unmarked, 8", from $225 to..........**$275.00**

Cornish, bowl, berries & leaves embossed & painted on light tan, tab handles, sm foot, script mark, 4", from $50 to..**$60.00**

Cornish, jardiniere, berries & leaves embossed & painted on brown, sm tab handles, marked, 7", from $70 to.**$80.00**

Cornish, vase, 5½", from $45.00 to $50.00.

Creamware, mug, floral decor painted on creamy white, unmarked, 5", from $100 to..................................**$125.00**

Creamware, pitcher, decalcomania on ivory, no mark, 5", from $100 to..**$150.00**

Creamware, planter, dark blue geometric decor on cream, square w/2 handles, 4 sm feet, impressed mark, 4", from $75 to..**$85.00**

Creamware, vase, dark blue cameo on cream, square sides & handles, unmarked, 7", from $50 to......................**$65.00**

Creamware, vase, lg stylized flowers painted on creamy white shouldered form, ink stamp, 11½", from $275 to **$350.00**

Darsie, vase, embossed tassels on med blue, scalloped rim, script mark, 5½", from $40 to...............................**$50.00**

Darsie, vase, embossed tassels on turquoise, flared rim, sm foot, script mark, 5½", from $40 to......................**$50.00**

Delsa, ewer, pastel flowers on green, bulbous, #10, marked, 7", from $35 to **$45.00**

Delsa, vase, pastel flowers & leaves on green, scalloped rim, script mark, 6", from $35 to **$45.00**

Dupont, jardiniere, pink potted flowers in grid-like panels on ivory, unmarked, 7½", from $100 to **$125.00**

Dupont, vase, flower basket & swag decor in grid-like reserves on ivory, cylindrical, impressed mark, 10", from $100 to................**$125.00**

Elberta, bowl, peach tones shaded to green, 3-part, marked by hand, 3½", from $65 to....................**$75.00**

Flemish, jardiniere, lg carved roses among green foliage in green panels on brown, unmarked, 7½", from $125 to.....**$150.00**

Flemish, tub, pink roses on woven brown basketweave, tub handles, impressed mark, 4½", from $100 to.....**$125.00**

Flemish, vase, embossed pastel floral decor on creamy ivory, impressed mark, 8", from $250 to......................**$350.00**

Flemish, vase, lg pastel flowers on dark blue, flared cylinder, impressed mark, 6½", from $150 to....................**$200.00**

Florenzo, planter, floral decor at base, square w/embossed ribs on ivory w/green at rim, marked, 3½", from $45 to...............................**$65.00**

Forest, basket, embossed woodland scene in earth tones, integral handle, impressed mark, 8½", from $225 to **$275.00**

Forest, pitcher, embossed woodland scene in glossy earth tones, twig handle, impressed mark, 5", from $175 to **$225.00**

Forest, vase, embossed woodland scene in earth tones, no mark, 13½", from $275 to **$375.00**

Glendale, bud vase, double; embossed bird in landscape between 2 stump-form vases on base, unmarked, 7", from $250 to.......................**$300.00**

Glendale, vase, birds on branch in landscape, shouldered form, unmarked, 8½", from $550 to...................**$650.00**

Glendale, vases: 9", $1,250.00; 13", $1,250.00.

Gloria, ewer, floral branch on brown, shape #G-12, script mark, 9", from $60 to **$70.00**

Hobart, girl w/flowers, blue, unmarked, 8½", from $250 to **$350.00**

Hudson, Blue & Decorated; vase, pink floral band on dark blue, square, impressed mark, 9½", from $150 to...........**$200.00**

Hudson, Blue & Decorated; vase, pink floral spray on dark blue, sm raised rim, impressed mark, 7½", from $175 to .**$225.00**

Hudson, vase, flower on med blue, signed Timberlake, marked by hand, 7", from $300 to **$350.00**

Hudson, vase, lg white & blue iris on black to gray, signed Axline, cylindrical, ink stamp, 8½", from $450 to .**$550.00**

Hudson, wall pocket, floral branches on white cone form, brown at rim, impressed mark, 8", from $400 to .**$500.00**

Hudson, White & Decorated; bowl, pink floral spray in ivory, unmarked, 4", from $150 to **$200.00**

Hudson, White & Decorated; vase, floral spray on white, 6-sided, impressed mark, 9½", from $200 to.........**$250.00**

Hudson-Light, vase, floral decor in creamy neutral tones, bulbous, impressed mark, 4½", from $125 to.........**$175.00**

Hudson-Light, vase, lg white flowers w/beige leaves on ivory, signed HP, shouldered form, marked, 9", from $350 to.......................................**$450.00**

Hudson-Perfecto, vase, floral decor in pink tones on pink, bulbous, sm rim, impressed mark, 5½", from $350 to **$400.00**

Ivoris, ginger jar, embossed floral decor on ivory, sm upturned handles, w/lid, marked by hand, 8½", from $100 to.......................................**$125.00**

Ivoris, vase, ivory w/ornate handles, marked by hand, 6", from $25 to.......................................**$40.00**

Ivory (Clinton Ivory), bottle vase, embossed fruit & foliage on 2-tone ivory, unmarked, 9", from $100 to.....**$125.00**

Ivory (Clinton Ivory), vase, embossed leafy panels on 2-tone ivory, cylindrical, stamped mark, 10", from $75 to .**$85.00**

Ivory (Clinton Ivory), window planter, floral relief on 2-tone ivory, stamped mark, 6x15½", from $200 to **$225.00**

Klyro, bowl, 4-footed fence-like panels w/cut-out vertical bars & embossed floral swag decor, impressed mark, 3½".....................................**$80.00**

Klyro, wall pocket, board-like trim at rim, handle & feet, floral swag on 2 sides, unmarked, 7", from $100 to......**$125.00**

Knifewood, bowl, embossed white daisies on brown, smooth rim, impressed mark, 3", from $75 to **$100.00**

Knifewood, humidor, embossed white hunting dog among foliage on brown, unmarked, 7", from $450 to..**$550.00**

Knifewood, jar, embossed bluebird & floral branches on brown, w/lid, impressed mark, 8", from $600 to .**$700.00**

Knifewood, vase, embossed white daisies w/blue butterflies on light brown, smooth rim, impressed mark, 7", from $200 to.......................................**$250.00**

Knifewood, wall pocket, embossed ivory flowers w/green leaves on light blue, impressed mark, 8", from $225 to **$275.00**

Louella, basket, floral decor on shirred ivory w/dark wash in folds, impressed mark, 6½", from $95 to............**$115.00**

Louella, hair receiver, embossed floral decor on shirred ivory w/dark wash in folds, impressed mark, 3", from $85 to.......................................**$95.00**

Louwelsa, bowl, floral on brown, half-circle seal mark, 2½", from $100 to.......................................**$125.00**

Louwelsa, pitcher vase, floral on brown, artist signed AC, marked, 3", from $125 to **$150.00**

Louwelsa, vase, floral on brown, signed V Adams, urn form, 10", from $300 to **$350.00**

Louwelsa, vase, floral on brown, shouldered form, half-circle seal, 5", from $125 to **$150.00**

Manhattan, vase, dark green leaves embossed on med green, handles, marked by hand, 8", from $60 to...........**$70.00**

Marbleized, bowl, swirling brown & ivory tones, inverted rim, impressed mark, 1½x7", from $40 to............**$50.00**

Marbleized, jardiniere, swirling blues, tans & browns, hand marked, 10", from $250 to **$350.00**

Marbleized, vase, swirled brown tones, squatty, hand marked, 4½", from $65 to **$75.00**

Marbleized, vase, swirling creamy tan & ivory tones, cylindrical, hand marked, 10½", from $125 to **$150.00**

Marvo, pitcher, embossed flowers & leaves over entire surface, brown w/green wash, ink stamp, 8", from $100 to **$125.00**

Marvo, vase, embossed leaves overall in green tones, slim cylinder, ink stamp, 9", from $60 to **$70.00**

Melrose, basket, grapes & vining decor on pale pink, twig handle, impressed mark, 10", from $175 to........**$225.00**

Melrose, vase, pink rose branch on palest pink, twig handles, scalloped rim, unmarked, 5", from $75 to **$85.00**

Mirror Black, bud base, black glossy trumpet form, unmarked, 5½", from $30 to.................................**$40.00**

Mirror Black, vase, black glossy, classic form, unmarked, 12", from $150 to...**$200.00**

Mirror Black, wall pocket, black glossy, no mark, 8", from $110 to...**$150.00**

Muskota, bowl w/goose at side of rim, ivory & brown tones, impressed mark, 4½", from $275 to....................**$375.00**

Muskota, fence, brown wood-look, 2-board style, impressed mark, 5", from $100 to **$125.00**

Noval, bowl, ivory panels w/applied colorful fruit handles, impressed mark, 3½x8", from $60 to **$70.00**

Noval, comport, ivory w/black band at rim & base, applied colorful fruit handles at rim, unmarked, 5½", from $85 to...**$95.00**

Panella, bowl, pansies on creamy beige to brown, footed, script mark, 3½", from $35 to.................................**$40.00**

Panella, vase, pansies on blue, low handles, script mark, 6½", from $40 to...**$50.00**

Paragon, vase, allover embossed blue-washed floral decor on white bulbous form, script mark, 6½", from $150 to.............**$200.00**

Paragon, vase, allover embossed floral decor on red ovoid, script mark, 7½", from $150 to...........................**$200.00**

Patra, basket, pink floral decor w/green trim on pebbly brown, marked by hand, 5½", from $150 to......**$175.00**

Patra, vase, pink & green floral decor w/green handles on pebbly brown, marked by hand, 3½", from $95 to **$110.00**

Patricia, vase, embossed foliage on streaky tan & green, swan's head & neck form handles, unmarked, 8½", from $150 to...**$175.00**

Patricia, vase, white w/duck-head handles, script mark, 4", from $65 to...**$75.00**

Pearl, basket, pink roses & pearl swags on ivory, simple style w/4 sm feet, unmarked, 6½", from $175 to **$225.00**

Pearl, bowl, pearl swags on ivory, impressed mark, 3", from $100 to...**$125.00**

Pearl, wall vase, pink roses & pearl swags on ivory, impressed mark, 8", from $175 to **$225.00**

Pumila, bowl, white water-lily form w/peach interior, ink stamp, 3½", from $30 to...**$35.00**

Pumila, candle holder, shaded green water-lily form w/peach interior, ink stamp, 3", from $75 to **$85.00**

Roba, ewer, pastel floral branch on swirling white to blue body, twig handle, script mark, 6", from $65 to ..**$75.00**

Roma, bud vase, multicolor gravevine decor on ivory, square sides w/flared base, unmarked, 6½", from $65 to...**$75.00**

Roma, bud vase, triple; multicolor floral 'horseshoe' near top of 3 tube vases on base, marked, 8", from $110 to...**$130.00**

Roma, candlestick, triple; pink flower & green leaves on ivory, unmarked, 9", from $150 to **$200.00**

Roma, comport, embossed swags on ivory, pierced decor at base, marked, 9½", from $100 to **$125.00**

Roma, console bowl, embossed pink & green floral swags on ivory, handles, oblong, sm foot, 4½x16", from $150 to...**$175.00**

Roma, vase, embossed pink & green floral swag on ivory, pierced decor, cylindrical, unmarked, 6½", from $65 to...**$75.00**

Roma, vase, pastel floral reserve on ivory, square sides, unmarked, 9", from $115 to.............................**$140.00**

Roma, wall pocket, flower basket & swag decor on ivory, unmarked, 7", from $100 to.............................**$125.00**

Rosemont, colorful fruit bowl reserves on ivory, unmarked, 8", from $175 to...**$200.00**

Softone, bud vase, double; 2 cylinders form V, curved loop joins top, all in soft pink, script mark, 9", from $22 to...**$28.00**

Softone, vase, embossed linear decor on soft blue, bulbous, script mark, 10", from $40 to.............................**$50.00**

Suevo, bowl, geometric Indian motif in brown tones, unmarked, 2½x6½", from $75 to **$100.00**

Suevo, vase, geometric American Indian motif in tan & brown, trumpet form, unmarked, 9", from $125 to............**$150.00**

Tutone, vase, embossed green floral on red, inverted rim, footed, ink mark, 4", from $30 to....................**$45.00**

Tutone, vase, floral decor on green to beige, ink mark, 11", from $150 to...**$175.00**

Velva, bowl, floral vertical panel on brown, sm upturned handles, marked by hand, 3½x12½", from $65 to **$75.00**

Velva, vase, floral decor in vertical panel on green, sm upturned handles, marked by hand, 6", from $40 to.................**$50.00**

Warwick, console bowl, buds & branches on textured brown, branches form rim & handle, marked, 10½", from $150 to...**$175.00**

Warwick, planter, bud decor on textured brown, branch handle & feet, foil label, 3½", from $60 to.................**$75.00**

Wild Rose, basket, rose embossed & painted on tan, twig handle, script mark, 5½", from $45 to **$50.00**

Wild Rose, white embossed rose on green, sm handles, script mark, 6½", from $25 to **$30.00**

Woodcraft, bowl, fruit-filled foliage on brown textured ground, unmarked, 3", from $85 to.......................**$95.00**

Woodcraft, bowl, wide band of brown twining limbs w/openwork at top, twig feet, impressed mark, 3½", from $85 to...**$95.00**

Woodcraft, bud vase, fruit & foliage on brown trunk form w/sm integral twig handles, unmarked, 6½", from $40 to...**$50.00**

Woodcraft, mug, brown trunk form w/animals peeking from knothole, twig handle, unmarked, 12½", from $225...**$275.00**

Woodcraft, vase, owls and squirrel, 18", $1,000.00; Dish, fox and cub in den, 5" high, $350.00.

Woodcraft, wall pocket, flower at base of stump form w/4 openings, impressed mark, 9", from $125 to......**$150.00**

Woodrose, vase, pink roses embossed on oaken bucket form w/tub handles, impressed mark, 4", from $40 to **$50.00**

Zona, jardiniere, multicolor floral band between black stripes at rim, black band at foot, ribbed body, unmarked, 7"..**$150.00**

Zona, pitcher, fruited multicolor branch on ivory, brown handle, smooth rim, unmarked, 6", from $75 to **$85.00**

Zona, pitcher, lg colorful flowers w/green foliage on ivory, rib decor at rim, 7", from $120 to **$140.00**

Zona, platter, fruit & berry branches along rim on ivory, slim brown twig-like trim at rim, unmarked, 12", from $50 to..**$80.00**

Zona, teapot, fruited branch on ivory w/brown bands, berry finial, 6", w/creamer & sugar bowl, marked, from $200 to...**$250.00**

Bank, tin lithograph Dude Ranch, US Metaltoys, early 1950s, EX..**$45.00**

Belt buckle, Western saddle w/brands, silver-toned metal, from Chambers, Phoenix, 2x3¾" **$10.00**

Blanket, Hudson Bay, Beaver marks, VG+.................**$75.00**

Blanket, turquoise, red & yellow geometric print, Pendleton, Beaver State, 32x46" **$75.00**

Book, The Life of a Cowboy, by George Pippen, 1st edition, 1969, w/dust jacket..**$25.00**

Book, The Settlers' West, by Martin Schmitt & Dee Brown, 1st edition, 1955, hardcover, w/dust jacket **$15.00**

Bookends, End of Trail, cast metal, 1930s, pr............**$35.00**

Game, Cowboys & Indians, cards, 1949 ....**$10.00**

Game, Roundup, cards, 1953.......................................**$10.00**

Key chain, Tony Lama Boots, 60 Yrs of Bootmaking, brass-like metal, 1½" **$5.00**

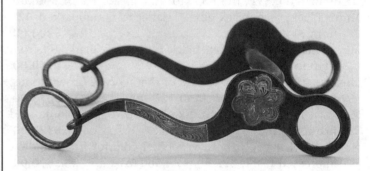

Mouth bit, Crockett & Renalde, from $85.00 to $95.00.

Purse, leather w/white inserts, Mexican, 1950s............**$45.00**

Stock certificate, Girard Gold & Silver Mining Co, Pima County AZ, June 5, 1882, VG+ **$110.00**

Vase, redware w/black & white feather design, signed D Vasquez (American Indian) **$45.00**

Western Collectibles

Although the Wild West era ended over one hundred years ago, today cowboy gear is a hot area of collecting. Prices have soared over the last five years, and the market is growing steadily stronger. Evidence of this are the seventy-five plus shows and auctions specializing in this field that are held annually across the nation.

These historic collectibles are not just found out West. Some of the most exceptional pieces have come from the East Coast states and the Midwest. But that should come as no surprise when you consider that the largest manufacturer of bits and spurs was the August Buemann Co. of Newark, New Jersey (1868–1926).

Until now, the only thing lacking in this growing market was a good reference to identify and evaluate these treasures. That gap has been filled with the publication of *Old West Cowboy Collectibles Auction Update & Price Guide*, which lists auction-realized prices of more than 650 lots, with complete descriptions and numerous photos. You can obtain a copy from our advisor, Dan Hutchins.

Advisor: Dan Hutchins (See Directory, Western Collectibles)

Westmoreland Glass

The Westmoreland Specialty Company was founded in 1889 in Grapeville, Pennsylvania. Their mainstay was a line of opalware (later called milk glass) which included such pieces as cream and sugar sets, novel tea jars (i.e., Teddy Roosevelt Bear Jar, Oriental Tea Jars, and Dutch Tea Jar), plus a number of covered animal dishes such as hens and roosters on nests. All of these pieces were made as condiment containers and originally held baking soda and Westmoreland's own mustard recipe. By 1900 they had introduced a large variety of pressed tablewares in clear glass and opal, although their condiment containers were still very popular. By 1910 they were making a large line of opal souvenir novelties with hand-painted decorations of palm trees, Dutch scenes, etc. They also made a variety of decorative vases painted in the fashion of Rookwood Pottery, plus sprayed finishes with decorations of flowers, fruits, animals, and Indians. Westmoreland gained great popularity with their line of painted, hand-decorated wares, and they also made many fancy-cut items.

These lines continued in production until 1939, when the Brainard family became full owners of the factory. The

Brainards discontinued the majority of patterns made previously under the West management and introduced dinnerware lines, primarily made of milk glass, with limited production of black glass and blue milk glass. Colored glass was not put back into full production until 1964 when Westmoreland introduced Golden Sunset, Avocado, Brandywine Blue, and ruby glass.

The company made only limited quantities of carnival glass in the early 1900s and then re-introduced it in 1972, when most of their carnival glass was made in limited editions for the Levay Distributing Company. J.H. Brainard, president of Westmoreland, sold the factory to Dave Grossman in 1981, and he, in turn, closed the factory in 1984. Westmoreland first used the stamped W over G logo in 1949 and continued using it until Dave Grossman bought the factory. Mr. Grossman changed the logo to a W with the word Westmoreland forming a circle around the W.

Milk glass was always Westmoreland's main line of production and in the 1950s, they became famous for their milk glass tableware in the #1881 'Paneled Grape' pattern. It was designed in 1950 by Jess Billups, the company's mold maker. The first piece he made was the water goblet. Items were gradually added until a complete dinner service was available. It became their most successful dinnerware, and today it is highly collectible, primarily because of the excellence of the milk glass itself. No other company has been able to match Westmoreland's milk glass in color, texture, quality, or execution of design and pattern.

For more information we recommend *Welcome Home, Westmoreland; Westmoreland Glass: Our Children's Heirlooms;* and *The Westmoreland Glass Collector's Kit*, all by our advisor Ruth Grizel.

Advisor: Ruth Grizel (See Directory, Westmoreland)

Club/Newsletter: *The Original Westmoreland Glass Collector's Newsletter*
c/o Ruth Grizel, Editor
P.O. Box 143
North Liberty, IA 52317-0143; Subscription $16 per year for 12 issues.

Covered Animal Dishes

Lion on diamond base, #1, electric blue carnival, 1/500 edition, ca 1978, $225.00. (Photo courtesy Frank Grizel)

Bulldog, Doeskin, w/WG mark, sm $30.00
Camel, blue opaque, #1 ....$125.00
Cat on nest, purple slag iridescent...........................$95.00
Cat on nest, red carnival..$85.00
Cat on rectangular lacy base, almond opaque or mint green opaque, #1, each $250.00
Cat on rectangular lacy base, milk glass, #1...............$95.00
Cat on wide-rib base, blue w/white head on blue base..$65.00
Cat on wide-rib base, Westmoreland colors, #18, 5", from $45 to..$75.00
Chick emerging from egg on lid, sitting on sm 2-handled basket, milk glass, #1...$95.00
Chicken & eggs on basket nest, milk glass, glass eyes..$95.00
Dog on wide-rib base, blue opaque or milk glass w/blue head, 5½", each...$95.00
Dove & hand on rectangular lacy base, milk glass, #1..$135.00
Duck on wavy base, almond opaque, coral opaque, mint green opaque or purple slag, #10, each.............$125.00
Fox on diamond base, blue opaque or purple (noniridized) slag,#1, each..$200.00
Hen on basketweave base, Bermuda Blue, #2, 5½"..$85.00
Hen on basketweave base, cobalt carnival, #2, Made for Levay, marked Levay, 1978, limited edition, 5½"..............$100.00
Hen on basketweave base, milk glass, #2, 5½" $30.00
Hen on basketweave base, milk glass w/red comb, #2, 5½"...$35.00
Hen on diamond base, almond opaque or coral opaque, #1, 7½", each..$150.00
Hen on diamond base, milk glass w/red comb, #1, 7½"..$40.00
Hen on lacy base, milk glass, #1, 7½" $125.00
Hen on nest, milk glass, #3, 3½".................................$20.00
Hen on nest, red carnival, 5½"....................................$85.00
Hen on nest, Westmoreland colors, #4, 3", minimum value...$35.00
Hen on 2-handled basket, milk glass w/red trim, #2 .$50.00
Hen on 2-handled basket, purple carnival or white carnival, #2, Made for Levay, limited edition, each $100.00
Lamb on picket fence base, blue opaque or purple slag iridized, 5½", each..$95.00
Lion on basketweave base, turquoise carnival, #1, 1980 .$225.00
Lion on lacy base, milk glass w/gold eyes, #1, 8"....$155.00
Lion on picket fence base, milk glass w/blue head, 5½" .$135.00
Lovebirds on nest, Golden Sunset...............................$55.00
Lovebirds on nest, milk glass or blue opaque, #20 ....$40.00
Mother eagle & babies on basketweave base, Crystal Mist on Brown Mist base $85.00
Mother eagle & babies on diamond base, chocolate or turquoise carnival, #21, Made for Levay, limited edition, each $250.00
Mule-eared rabbit on picket base, milk glass, #5 ......$50.00
Picnic basket, milk glass $35.00
Pintail duck, milk glass, 5½"..$65.00
Rabbit on diamond base, blue opaque or purple (noniridized) slag, #1, 7½", each.................................$175.00
Rabbit on diamond base, milk glass w/decorated eggs, #1, 7½"...$135.00
Rabbit on lacy base, white carnival, #1, Made for Levay, 1979, limited edition of 1,500, 7½", minimum value $200.00
Rabbit on nest, red carnival...$85.00

Rabbit on picket fence base, milk glass, decorated, #5 .**$50.00**

Rabbit on picket fence base, purple slag or blue opaque, #5, each **$95.00**

Robin on twig nest, blue opaque, #7..........................**$50.00**

Robin on twig nest, red carnival, pink carnival or turquoise carnival, Made for Levay, #7, limited edition, minimum **$125.00**

Rooster, standing; Brandywine Blue, #6, 8½" **$125.00**

Rooster, standing; Crystal Mist w/red trim, #6, 8½" **$95.00**

Rooster, standing; Golden Sunset, #6, 8½"................**$125.00**

Rooster, standing; Laurel Green, #6, 8½"..................**$125.00**

Rooster, standing; milk glass, #6, 8½"........................**$45.00**

Rooster, standing; Westmoreland colors, #6, each, from $95 to...**$125.00**

Rooster on basketweave base, blue opaque, #2, 5½" .**$65.00**

Rooster on basketweave base, Westmoreland colors, #2, 5½", each, from $85 to...**$95.00**

Rooster on diamond base, chocolate or purple slag carnival, #1, Made for Levay, 1978, limited edition, 7½", each ...**$250.00**

Rooster on diamond base, milk glass w/red comb, #1, 7½" **$60.00**

Rooster on lacy base, blue opaque, #1, 7½"............**$175.00**

Rooster on lacy base, milk glass w/red trim, #1, 8x7" ..**$75.00**

Rooster on ribbed base, milk glass, #2, 5½" **$35.00**

Santa on sleigh, milk glass, #1872............................**$75.00**

Seashell & dolphin, candy dish, blue opaque, #1048.**$50.00**

Swan (closed-neck) on basketweave base, blue opaque, 5½" **$75.00**

Swan (raised wing) on rectangular lacy base, milk glass, #1872 ....**$125.00**

Turtle, Thousand Eye, cigarette box, black, #1000 ...**$150.00**

Rabbit on diamond base, electric blue carnival, 1/500 edition, ca 1978, $250.00. (Photo courtesy Frank Grizel)

Figurines and Novelties

Butterfly, Green Mist, 2½"..**$22.00**

Cardinal, Green Mist...**$20.00**

Chick, egg cup, w/hand-painted yellow chick, handled, from $22 to...**$25.00**

Chick, salt cellar, Westmoreland colors, #3, 1", from $20 to..**$25.00**

Duck, salt cellar, clear blue..**$20.00**

Duck, salt cellar, milk glass..**$20.00**

Lovebirds on nest, Golden Sunset..............................**$55.00**

Penguin on ice floe, Brandywine Blue Mist................**$75.00**

Pouter pigeon, any color, 2½", each...........................**$35.00**

Robin, red, 5⅛"..**$35.00**

Turtle, ashtray, clear...**$15.00**

Turtle, paperweight, Green Mist, no holes, 4" L.........**$50.00**

Wren on perch, light blue on white, 2-pc....................**$40.00**

Lamps

Boudoir, English Hobnail/#555, milk glass, stick type w/flat base...**$45.00**

Candle mini, crystal w/25th anniversary decoration on shade, Crystal Mist base, #1972..**$55.00**

Candle mini, green frosted shade w/hand-painted flowers, milk glass base, 8"...**$50.00**

Electric mini, ruby w/ruby floral, #1976, 6½"..............**$95.00**

Fairy, Irish Waterford/#1932, ruby on crystal, footed .**$65.00**

Fairy, Light Blue Mist shade w/hand-painted daisies, #1972 ....**$35.00**

Mini lamp, dark blue mist with hand-painted Mary Gregory decor, #1972, ca 1970s, $35.00. (Photo courtesy Frank Grizel)

Modern Giftware

Ashtray, Beaded Grape/#1884, Brandywine Blue, 6½x6½"...**$30.00**

Ashtray, Colonial, purple slag.....................................**$30.00**

Basket, English Hobnail/#555, Light Blue Mist, 9" **$45.00**

Basket, Paneled Grape/#1881, Brandywine Blue, split handle, oval...**$45.00**

Basket, Pansy, #757, purple slag, split handle **$35.00**

Basket, Rose Trellis/#1967, milk glass w/hand-painted decor, 8½"..**$35.00**

Bell, Cameo/#754, w/Beaded Bouquet trim, Dark Blue Mist...**$35.00**

Bell, Paneled Grape/#1881, milk glass, shaped base..**$35.00**

Bonbon, Irish Waterford/#1932, ruby on crystal, handled...**$38.00**

Bonbon dish, Daisy, Brown Mist, #205.......................**$30.00**

Bowl, centerpiece; Colonial/#1776, Bermuda Blue, w/2 candle holders, 3-pc set..**$125.00**

Bowl, console; Paneled Grape/#1881, milk glass, round, 12" **$55.00**

Bowl, Lotus/#1921, black, round, lg **$50.00**

Bowl, Lotus/#1921, milk glass, oval **$30.00**

Bowl, Lotus/#1921, ruby on crystal, round, lg **$75.00**

Bowl, purple slag, leaf form, #300 ....**$45.00**

Bowl, Rose Trellis/#1967, milk glass w/hand-painted decor, 10"...**$75.00**

Bowl, Striped/#1814, Apricot Mist, round, footed, lg .**$35.00**

Bowl, wedding; ruby on crystal, #1874, 10" **$65.00**

Bowl, wedding; ruby on crystal, #1874, 8" **$50.00**

Bowl (Grandfather), Sawtooth/#556, Brandywine Blue ... **$80.00**

Box, jewel; Crystal Mist w/Blue China rose, #275, square .. **$20.00**

Box, trinket; Purple Mist, heart form, #1902 .... **$25.00**

Candle holders, ruby on crystal, #1874, matches wedding bowl, 4½", pr **$45.00**

Candy dish, Beaded Bouquet/#1700, Colonial pattern, milk glass **$35.00**

Candy dish, Beaded Grape/#1884, Bermuda Blue, 5", w/lid **$45.00**

Candy dish, Beaded Grape/#1884, Brandywine Blue, 3½", w/lid **$35.00**

Candy dish, Paneled Grape/#1881, Dark Blue Mist, crimped, 3-footed, 7½" **$35.00**

Candy dish, Paneled Grape/#1881, Dark Blue Mist, round, footed, 9" **$55.00**

Candy dish, Paneled Grape/#1881, Mist Pink, open ruffled edge, 3-toed **$35.00**

Cup plate, Stippled Hearts/#502, Brandywine Blue, 3½" .. **$15.00**

Flowerpot, purple Beaded Bouquet trim, #1707 .... **$45.00**

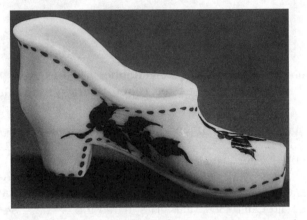

Grandma's slipper, with hand-painted Christmas decor, #1900, $40.00. (Photo courtesy Frank Grizel)

Pin tray, Heart/#1820, Blue Mist **$30.00**

Sweetmeat, ruby on crystal, 2-handled, #1700 .... **$35.00**

Urn, ruby on crystal, footed, #1943, w/lid **$95.00**

Plates

Bicentennial decoration, Paneled Grape/#1881, limited edition, 14½" **$225.00**

Blue Jay decal, Beaded Edge/#22, 7" **$18.00**

Boy fishing, Forget-Me-Not/#2 border, black **$65.00**

Fleur-de-Lis, milk glass, #4 .... **$10.00**

George Washington, purple carnival, limited edition . **$50.00**

Girl swinging, Forget-Me-Not/#2 border, black **$65.00**

Heart, Beaded Bouquet on almond opaque, #32 .... **$35.00**

Indian Head & Beaded Loop Border, purple carnival, #10, limited edition **$45.00**

Princess Feather/#201, Golden Sunset, 8" **$45.00**

Three Owls, purple carnival, 1974, limited edition **$50.00**

Wicket, Battle of Bunker Hill decoration, milk glass, #30 .... **$60.00**

Woof-Woof, milk glass, Westmoreland Specialty Co ... **$50.00**

Zodiac, crystal w/blue, ruby or yellow stain, #25, 15", each **$95.00**

Tableware

Bowl, Paneled Grape/#1881, milk glass, belled, footed, oval, 11" **$85.00**

Bowl, Paneled Grape/#1881, milk glass, belled, 9½" . **$55.00**

Bowl, Paneled Grape/#1881, milk glass, cupped, 8" .. **$45.00**

Bowl, Paneled Grape/#1881, milk glass, lipped, footed, oval, 11" **$85.00**

Bowl, Paneled Grape/#1881, milk glass, lipped, 9" **$50.00**

Bowl, Paneled Grape/#1881, milk glass, shallow, skirted foot, 6x9" **$55.00**

Bowl, Paneled Grape/#1881, milk glass w/gold trim, cupped, 8" **$50.00**

Box, chocolate; Paneled Grape/#1881, milk glass, 6½" dia, w/lid **$45.00**

Butter dish, Paneled Grape/#1881, milk glass, round, w/lid **$50.00**

Butter dish, Paneled Grape/#1881, milk glass, ¼-lb ... **$30.00**

Cake plate, Irish Waterford/#1932, ruby on crystal, low footed, 12" **$95.00**

Cake plate, Lattice, milk glass, footed **$35.00**

Cake plate, Paneled Grape/#1881, milk glass, low foot, 2x10½" dia **$75.00**

Cake salver, Beaded Grape/#1884, milk glass, footed, square **$70.00**

Candelabra, Lotus/#1921, milk glass, 3-light, pr **$68.00**

Candelabra, Lotus/#1921, Light Blue Mist, 3-light, pr . **$65.00**

Candle holders, Beaded Grape/#1884, milk glass, pr, from $25 to **$30.00**

Candle holders, Doric/#3, Bermuda Blue, pr **$35.00**

Candle holders, Doric/#3, Light Blue Mist, pr **$35.00**

Candle holders, Irish Waterford/#1932, ruby on crystal, 6", pr **$75.00**

Candle holders, Spiral/#1933, black, pr **$40.00**

Candlesticks, Paneled Grape/#1881, Bermuda Blue, 4", pr **$35.00**

Candy dish, Ball & Swirl/#1842, Dark Blue Mist, w/lid .. **$35.00**

Compote, Blue Mist, #1902, w/lid **$35.00**

Compote, Doric/#3, Brandywine Blue, 9x6" **$45.00**

Compote, Irish Waterford/#1932, ruby on crystal, crimped, low footed, 5" **$35.00**

Compote, Paneled Grape/#1881, Brandywine Blue, fluted, footed, 7½" **$50.00**

Compote, Paneled Grape/#1881, milk glass, lipped, skirted foot, 7x10" dia **$50.00**

Compote, Paneled Grape/#1881, milk glass, ruffled edge, footed, 6x8" dia **$45.00**

Creamer, Paneled Grape/#1881, milk glass, 8-oz, 5" .. **$25.00**

Cup & saucer, Paneled Grape/#1881, milk glass **$16.00**

Decanter, Paneled Grape/#1881, milk glass, +6 wine glasses **$195.00**

Egg cup, American Hobnail/#77, milk glass **$10.00**

Egg plate, Paneled Grape/#1881, milk glass, center handle, 10" **$45.00**

Fruit cocktail w/underliner, Paneled Grape/#1881, milk glass, 2-pc **$28.00**

Goblet, American Hobnail/#77, milk glass, water size....**$10.00**
Goblet, Della Robbia, milk glass, water size **$16.00**
Goblet, English Hobnail/#555, milk glass, barrel form w/ball stem, round, footed **$12.00**
Goblet, English Hobnail/#555, milk glass, water size.**$10.00**
Goblet, Paneled Grape/#1881, Brandywine Blue, round, footed, 6" **$20.00**
Goblet, Paneled Grape/#1881, milk glass, water size.**$16.00**
Gravy boat w/underplate, Paneled Grape/#1881, milk glass, from $60 to..**$65.00**
Honey dish, Old Quilt/#500, milk glass, footed, w/lid ...**$15.00**
Jam jar, Crystal Mist w/Blue China Rose......................**$25.00**
Jardiniere, Paneled Grape/#1881, milk glass, round, footed, lg **$35.00**
Mayonnaise, Lotus/#1921, black, straight up edges, footed...**$28.00**
Mayonnaise set, Paneled Grape/#1881, milk glass, 3-pc..**$40.00**
Pickle dish, Paneled Grape/#1881, milk glass, oval....**$25.00**

Place setting: Plate, American Hobnail, #77; Goblet; Cup and saucer, $35.00. (Photo courtesy Frank Grizel)

Planter, Paneled Grape/#1881, milk glass, rectangular .**$30.00**
Plate, dinner; Paneled Grape/#1881, milk glass, 10½"..**$35.00**
Plate, luncheon; Paneled Grape/#1881, milk glass, 8"..**$18.00**
Plate, salad; Della Robbia, crystal................................**$15.00**
Punch bowl, Grape, milk glass, w/12 cups & ladle, 14-pc set **$500.00**
Punch set, Fan & File, Ice Blue, miniature.................**$45.00**

Punch set, Old Quilt, #500, bowl, 12 cups, pedestal and ladle, $600.00. (Photo courtesy Frank Grizel)

Rose bowl, English Hobnail/#555, milk glass, 4½".....**$15.00**

Sherbet, American Hobnail/#77, milk glass, low foot...**$8.00**
Sherbet, Della Robbia, crystal......................................**$20.00**
Sugar bowl, Paneled Grape/#1881, Brandywine Blue, 2½x3"...**$15.00**
Sweetmeat, Colonial/#1700, ruby on crystal, 2-handled, footed...**$35.00**
Sweetmeat, Colonial/#1776, Bermuda Blue, 2-handled, hexagon foot, 7½"...**$35.00**
Tray, tidbit; Paneled Grape/#1881, Light Blue Mist, 1-tier, 8" **$35.00**
Tray, tidbit; Paneled Grape/#1881, milk glass w/hand-painted Christmas decor, 10½"...................................**$80.00**

Tumbler, footed iced tea; Della Robbia, #1058, $30.00; Water tumbler, $30.00; Juice, $35.00. (Photo courtesy Frank Grizel)

Tumbler, iced tea; American Hobnail/#77, milk glass, low foot...**$10.00**
Tumbler, water; Paneled Grape/#1881, milk glass......**$16.00**
Vase, Drape & Tassel/#1861, milk glass......................**$65.00**
Vase, Old Quilt/#500, milk glass, flared top, footed, 9"..**$65.00**
Vase, Old Quilt/#500, milk glass, flared top, 9" **$45.00**
Vase, Paneled Grape/#1881, milk glass, belled, footed, 11½"..**$65.00**
Vase, Teardrop/#231, blown milk glass **$175.00**
Water set, Old Quilt/#500, Honey Amber, 7-pc **$150.00**
Water Set, Old Quilt/#500, Ice Blue, 7-pc **$150.00**

Miscellaneous

Bank, schoolhouse, milk glass w/EX painted details..**$125.00**
Bottle, bathroom; milk glass, #1095, 7½-oz.................**$35.00**
Old Oak Bucket, milk glass, 3" **$95.00**
Ornament, Baby's First Christmas, clear, 1979, MIB ...**$45.00**

Wheaton

Though the Wheaton Company of Millville, New Jersey, made several series of bottles (examples of which are listed below), those with portraits of our country's presidents are the most collectible. Many colors have been used, including iridescents.

Bottle, Andrew Jackson, from $30 to **$35.00**
Bottle, Apollo II, 1st Man on the Moon, 4 astronauts, 1969 ..**$25.00**

Bottle, Apollo XIII, from $12.00 to $18.00.

Bottle, Benjamin Franklin, milk glass...........................$20.00
Bottle, Calvin Coolidge, from $20 to............................$25.00
Bottle, Clark Gable $12.00
Bottle, Dr Chandler Jamaica Ginger Roots Bitters.......$15.00
Bottle, elephant, Nixon/Agnew 1968, amber...............$40.00
Bottle, FDR (Franklon Delano Roosevelt), from $20 to..$25.00
Bottle, Franklin Pierce, second or corrected version, from $30
   to $35.00
Bottle, Gerald Ford, from $10 to $15.00
Bottle, Herbert Hoover, from $10 to $15.00
Bottle, Horseshoe Bitters...$40.00
Bottle, James Adams, from $20 to................................$25.00
Bottle, James K Polk, from $30 to................................$35.00
Bottle, John F Kennedy, blue carnival, lg....................$20.00
Bottle, John Tyler, from $15 to....................................$25.00
Bottle, MacArthur...$35.00

Bottle, 1968, Nixon for President, amber, 7", from $12.00 to $18.00; HH Humphrey, Democratic Campaign, 7", MIB, $22.00.

Bottle, Rutherford B Hayes, from $35 to $40.00
Bottle, Rutherford B Hayes, second or corrected version, from
   $30 to $35.00
Bottle, Ulysses S Grant, from $15 to $20.00
Bottle, William Howard Taft, from $20 to $25.00
Bottle, Zachary Taylor, second or corrected version, from $30
   to..$35.00
Doll, Colonial lady w/basket, teal blue carnival $30.00
Doll, Southern Belle, butterscotch carnival $30.00
Figurine, bull frog, emerald carnival, lg.....................$25.00
Figurine, bull frog, emerald carnival, sm....................$15.00
Paperweight, shark, teal carnival, lg $40.00
Plate, Spirit of '75, teal carnival, 1976.......................$30.00

World's Fair and Expositions

Souvenir items have been issued since the mid-1800s for every world's fair and exposition. Few fairgoers have left the grounds without purchasing at least one. Some of the older items were often manufactured right on the fairgrounds by glass or pottery companies who erected working kilns and furnaces just for the duration of the fair. Of course, the older items are usually more valuable, but even souvenirs from the past fifty years are worth hanging on to.

Newsletter: *Fair News*
World's Fair Collectors' Society, Inc.
Michael R. Pender, Editor
P.O. Box 20806
Sarasota, FL 34276; Dues: $12 (12 issues) per year in USA;
$13 in Canada; $20 for overseas members

Chicago, 1933

Ashtray, copper-tone metal w/Buckingham Fountain, 4⅝"
   dia $38.00
Book, Official World's Fair in Pictures........................$25.00
Book, World's Fair Wisecracks & Cartoons..................$12.00
Booklet, Story of the Royal Scot, Souvenir Visit of Train to
   North American Continent $10.00
Bookmark, brass w/colored background.....................$22.50
Elongated penny, Sky Ride, made from copper cent ...$7.50
Hot pad $10.00
Key, w/thermometer, Hall of Science $25.00
Needlebook, A Century of Progress, Japan $12.50
Postcard, Greeting From Chicago, A Century of Progress,
   1933 ....$10.00

Salt and pepper shakers, wooden keg design, 2⅛", MIB, $16.00 for the pair.

Spoon, EX...$10.00
Ticket $6.00

New York, 1939

Ashtray, brass w/glass insert, Trylon & Perisphere, 5x3" .$55.00
Ashtray, metal, 4½" dia $50.00
Book, Official Souvenir Book, Exposition Publications Inc .$35.00
Bookends, Trylon & Perisphere, Syroco labels, pr ...$100.00
Booklet, Visit the New York World's Fair by Rail, Penn
   Railroad...$18.00
Box, Aviation Building on lid, w/Syroco Wood paper label,
   3¾" square, M..$60.00

Cane, EX $40.00

Cigar band, set of 8 ....$2.50

Coin, commemorative, MOC.........................$35.00

Compact, enameled metal, unused, M........................$75.00

Letter opener, 25th Anniversary 1914-1939, Utica Mutual Insurance Agency..$15.00

Magazine, Life, January 31, 1938, World Tomorrow ...$30.00

Magazine, Saturday Evening Post, April 22, 1939 ....$15.00

Matchbook, Lucky Strike Building, Trylon & Perisphere, 1940 ....$12.50

Needlebook, Pilgrim Needle Co, 1938 ....$30.00

Postcard, Gimbels Round the World Flyer.................$18.00

Postcard, Italian Pavilion, real photo, 5x7" $7.00

Postcard booklet, EX $15.00

Postcard folder, World of Tomorrow, 18 cards...........$15.00

Program, Billy Rose Aquacade Revue, E Holm & Johnny Weismuller w/ads, 36 pages, 12x8½", EX.............$30.00

Spoon, Administration Building, silverplate, Wm Rogers..$8.00

Thermometer, Trylon & Perisphere, Bakelite $35.00

Ticket, dated 1940..$5.00

Tie bar, Trylon & Perisphere on chain, ½" square $30.00

Tie clip, Aviation Building on round medallion, MOC..$22.00

Tumbler, Communications Building on glass, Libbey, 6", 12-oz, from $25 to $35.00

Seattle, 1962

Book, Official Guide Book, from $15 to $18.00

First day cover, Century 21 Exposition, April 25, 1962 ..$10.00

Magazine, Life, May 4, 1962, Out of This World Fair in Seattle $12.50

Magazine, National Geographic, September 1962........$7.50

Postcard, Seattle World's Fair, Eye of the Needle..........$3.00

Program, marked Official Souvenir $12.00

Salt & pepper shakers, painted ceramic Space Needle, pr, from $25 to...$30.00

Sunday supplement, Seattle Times, April 8, 1962 ....$12.00

Tumblers, single color with black and white matt finish on frosted glass, gold trim, 16-oz, from $7.00 to $9.00 each.

New York, 1964

Ashtray, metal w/Unisphere at center, gold & black decorated rim, from $10 to $12.00

Bank, Unisphere figural, plastic, MIB.....................$45.00

Bell, ceramic w/figural handle, EX........................$30.00

Catalog, Monogram Goes to the World's Fair, 1964, M.....$20.00

Coaster, Lowenbrau, cardboard, 4" dia $3.00

Coaster, wood, M..$8.00

Comic book, The Flintstones at the New York World's Fair, EX..$12.00

Coupon booklet, Grand Union, for discount amusements $15.00

Cup & saucer set, shows Unisphere, World's Fair 1964-1965 ....$12.50

Figure, Unisphere, gold plastic on black base $18.00

Flash card, marked Official Souvenir, set of 28, MIB .$25.00

Folder, Hall of Education, vinyl, MIB.....................$10.00

Magazine, Life, May 1, 1964, World's Fair Opens $18.00

Magazine, Look, February 11, 1964.........................$15.00

Map, American Oil Co.....................................$10.00

Map, marked Official Souvenir, Time Life Publications....$12.00

Menu, Hilton Cafe International, Better Living Center $10.00

Paper dolls, Dress Up for the New York World's Fair, 1964, unused, M $20.00

Paperweight, Unisphere, US Steel, M.........................$65.00

Patch, AMF, Monorail Pioneer.................................$12.00

Postcard, Billy Graham: The Created Universe Speaks of God $3.00

Postcard, United States Pavilion, from $3 to.................$5.00

Postcard folder, 14 Official Views...........................$10.00

Rain bonnet $5.00

Record, The Triumph of Man, 33⅓ rpm, 7", folding photo sleeve, NM $5.00

Salt & pepper shakers, Unisphere, w/illustrated serving tray, 3-pc set, MIB $25.00

Salt & pepper shakers on tray, from $12 to $15.00

Souvenir book, Official Souvenir Book of New York World's Fair, color photos, 1965, M $10.00

Ticket, General Admission.................................$10.00

Tumbler, Hall of Science, blue & orange on clear frosted glass $8.00

Tumbler, Unisphere..$6.00

Yo-yo, '64-65 World on a String, MOC.....................$20.00

Montreal, Canada, 1967

Book, Official Guide, from $10 to.............................$15.00

Magazine, Life, April 28, 1967, Tomorrow Soars in at the Fair, from $10 to...$12.00

Mug, National Pavilions, glass, 5⅝", from $12 to........$15.00

Plate, shows pavilions, 6", from $10 to.......................$15.00

Knoxville, 1982

First day cover, from $15 to.................................$20.00

Knife, surgical steel, Parker Cut Co, from $18 to........$20.00

Mug, plastic thermos style, 6½"............................$15.00

Pin-back button, multicolor, M, from $3 to $5.00

Postcard, night scene......................................$2.50

Postcard, President Ronald Regan $3.00

Tray, Coca-Cola & World's Fair graphics on metal, 12" dia $25.00

Auction Houses

Many of the auction galleries we've listed here have appraisal services. Some, though not all, are free of charge. We suggest you contact them first by phone to discuss fees and requirements.

Aston Americana Auctions
2825 Country Club Rd.
Endwell, NY 13760-3349
Phone or Fax 607-785-6598
Specializing in and appraisers of Americana, folk art, other primitives, furniture, fine glassware and china

Bill Bertoia Auctions
2413 Madison Ave.
Vineland, NJ 08630
609-692-4092
Fax 609-692-8697
Specializing in antique toys and collectibles

Cincinnati Art Gallery
635 Main St.
Cincinnati, OH 45202
513-381-2128
Specializing in American art pottery, American and European fine paintings, watercolors

Collectors Auction Services
RD 2, Box 431
Oil City, PA 16301
814-677-6070
Specializing in advertising, oil and gas, toys, rare museum and investment-quality antiques

David Rago
9 S Main St.
St. Lambertville, NJ 08530
609-397-9374
Gallery: 17 S Main St.
Lambertville, NJ 08530
Specializing in American art pottery and Arts & Crafts

Don Treadway Gallery
2128 Madison Rd.
Cincinnati, OH 45208
513-321-6742
Fax 513-871-7722
Member: National Antique Dealers Association, American Art Pottery Association, International Society of Appraisers, and American Ceramic Arts Society

Dynamite Auctions
Franklin Antique Mall & Auction Gallery
1280 Franklin Ave.
Franklin, PA 16323
814-432-8577 or 814-786-9211

Early Auction Co.
123 Main St.
Milford, OH 45150

Garth's Auctions, Inc.
2690 Stratford Rd.
Box 369, Delaware, OH 43015
614-362-4771

Hake's Americana & Collectibles
P.O. Box 1444M
York, PA 17405
Specializing in character and personality collectibles along with all artifacts of popular culture for over 20 years. To receive a catalog for their next 3,000-item mail/phone bid auction, send $5.

James D. Julia
P.O. Box 210
Showhegan Rd.
Fairfield, ME 04937

Kerry and Judy's Toys
7370 Eggleston Rd.
Memphis, TN 31825-2112
901-757-1722
Specializing in 1920s through 1960s toys; consignments always welcomed

L.R. 'Les' Docks
Box 691035
San Antonio, TX 78269-1035
Providing occasional mail-order record auctions, rarely consigned (the only consignments considered are exceptionally scarce and unusual records)

Lloyd Ralston Toys
447 Stratford Rd.
Fairfield, CT 06432

Manion's International Auction House, Inc.
P.O. Box 12214
Kansas City, KS 66112
913-299-6692
Fax 913-299-6792
e-mail: manions@qni.com
URL: www.manions.com

Michael Verlangieri, California Pottery
P.O. Box 844
Cambria, CA 93428-0844
Phone or Fax 805-927-4428
e-mail: verlangieri@thegrid.net
http://www.the book.com/verlan

Noel Barrett Antiques & Auctions
P.O. Box 1001
Carversville, PA 18913
215-297-5109

Richard Opfer Auctioneering, Inc.
1919 Greenspring Dr.
Timonium, MD 21093
301-252-5035

Smith House
P.O. Box 336
Eliot, ME, 03903
207-439-4614
Fax 207-439-8554
Specializing in toys

Toy Scouts Inc.
137 Casterton Ave.
Akron, OH 44303
330-836-0668
Fax 330-869-8668;
e-mail: toyscout@newreach.net;
http:// www.scmonline.com/toyscouts/
Specializing in baby-boom era collectibles

Clubs and Newsletters

There are hundreds of clubs and newsletters mentioned throughout this book in their respective categories. There are many more available to collectors today; some are generalized and cover the entire realm of antiques and collectibles, while others are devoted to a specific interest such as toys, coin-operated machines, character collectibles, or railroadiana. We've listed several below. You can obtain a copy of most newsletters simply by requesting one. If you'd like to try placing a 'for-sale' ad or a mail bid in one of them, see the introduction for suggestions on how your ad should be composed.

AB Bookman's Weekly
P.O. Box AB
Clifton, NJ 07015
201-772-0020
Fax 201-772-9281
$80 per year bulk mail USA ($80 per year Canada or Foreign). $125 per year 1st class mail (USA, Canada, and Mexico). Foreign Air Mail: Inquire. Sample copies: $10. AB Bookman's Yearbook: $25. All advertising and subscriptions subject to acceptance.

Antique Advertising Association of America (AAAA)
P.O. Box 1121
Morton Grove, IL 60053
708-446-0904
Also *Past Times* newsletter for collectors of popular and antique advertising.
Subscription: $35 per year

Antique and Collectible News
P.O. Box 529
Anna, IL 62906
Monthly newspaper for auctions, antique shows, collectibles, and flea markets for the Midwest USA.
Subscription: $12 per year

Antique and Collectors Reproduction News
Mark Chervenka, Circulation Dept.
P.O. Box 12130
Des Moines, IA 50312-9403
800-227-5531
Monthly newsletter showing differences between old originals and new reproductions.
Subscription: $32 per year

Antique Gazette
6949 Charlotte Pky., #106
Nashville, TN 37209.
Monthly publication covering the antique and collectibles market.
Subscription: $16.95 per year

Antique Monthly magazine
Stephen C. Croft, Publisher
2100 Powers Ferry Rd.
Atlanta, GA 30339
404-955-5656
Fax 404-952-0669
Subscription: $19.95 per year (11 issues)

The Antique Trader Weekly
P.O. Box 1050 CB
Dubuque, IA 52004-1050
319-588-2073
Subscription: $35 (52 issues) per year

Antique Week
P.O. Box 90
Knightstown, IN 46148
Weekly newspaper for auctions, antique shows, antiques, collectibles, and flea markets. Write for subscription information.

Antiques and Collecting
1006 S Michigan Ave.
Chicago, IL 60605
800-221-3148
Monthly magazine with a wide variety of information and an extensive classified section.
Subscription: $28 per year; $50 for 2 years

Arts and Crafts Quarterly
P.O. Box 3592, Sta. E
Trenton, NJ 08629
800-541-5787

Ashtray Journal
Chuck Thompson, Editor Publisher
Box 11652
Houston, TX 77293
Subscription $14.95 a year (6 issues), sample $3.95

Auction Opportunities, Inc.
Doyle Auctioneers and Appraisers
109 Osborne Hill Rd.
Fishkill, NY 12524
800-551-5161
Subscription: $25 per year

Bojo
P.O. Box 1403
Cranberry Township, PA 16066-0403
724-776-0621 (9 am to 9 pm EST)
Issues fixed-price catalog containing Beatles and Rock 'n Roll memorabilia.

Bookmark Collector
Joan L. Huegel
1002 W. 25th St.
Erie, PA 16502
Quarterly newsletter: $5.50 per year ($6.50 in Canada); sample copy: $1 plus stamp or LSASE

Chicagoland Antique Advertizing
Slot Machine and Jukebox Gazette
Ken Durham, Editor
P.O. Box 2426
Rockville, MD 20852
20-page newsletter published twice a year.
Subscription: 4 issues for $10; Sample: $5

Coin-Op Newsletter
Ken Durham, Publisher
909 26th St., NW
Washington, DC 20037
Subscription (10 issues): $24; Sample: $5

The Collector
Box 158
Heyworth, IL 61745
309-473-2466
Newspaper published monthly.

Collectors' Classified
William Margolin
P.O. Box 347
Hollbrook, MA 02343-0347
617-961-1463
Covers collectibles in general; 4 issues: $1

Collector's Digest
P.O. Box 23
Banning, CA 92220
714-849-1064
Subscription: $11 (6 issues) per year

Collector's Mart magazine
P.O. Box 12830
Wichita, KS 67277
Subscription: $23.95 per year; Add $15 in Canada

Deco Echoes Publications
The Echoes Report
P.O. Box 2321
Mashpee, MA 02649
508-428-2324 or Fax 508-428-0077
Quarterly publication focusing on twentieth-century designs and styles with classified ad section.

Dorothy Kamm's Porcelain Collector's Companion
P.O. Box 7460
Port St. Lucie, FL 34985-7460
561-465-4008

Dunbar's Gallery
76 Haven St.
Milford, MA 01757
508-634-8697
Fax 508-634-8698
Specializing in quality advertising, Halloween, toys,
coin-operated machines; holding cataloged auctions
occasionally, lists available

Ephemera News
The Ephemera Society of America, Inc.
P.O. Box 37
Schoharie, NY 12157
518-295-7978

The Front Striker Bulletin
Bill Retskin
P.O. Box 18481
Asheville, NC 28814
704-254-4487
Fax 704-254-1066
Quarterly newsletter for matchcover collectors,
$17.50 per year for 1st class mailing + $2 for new
member registration

GAB! (Glass Animal Bulletin!)
P.O. Box 143
N Liberty, IA 52317
Subscription: $16 for 12 monthly issues; free ads to subscribers

Glass Collector's Digest
P.O. Box 553,
Marietta, OH 45750-0553
800-533-3433
Subscription: $22 (6 issues) per year; Add $8 for
Canada and foreign

The Glass Post
P.O. Box 205
Oakdale, IA 52319-0205
Fax 319-626-3216
Subscription: $25 per year; all ads are free to subscribers

Gonder Pottery Collectors' Newsletter
c/o John and Marilyn McCormick
P.O. Box 3174
Shawnee KS 66203

International Ivory Society
11109 Nicholas Dr.
Wheaton, MD 20902
301-649-4002
Membership: $10 per year; includes 4 newsletters
and roster

Morgantown Newscaster
Morgantown Collectors of America
Jerry Gallagher and Randy Supplee
420 1st Ave. NW
Plainview, MN 55964
Subscription: $15 per year. SASE required for
answers to queries.

Newspaper Collectors Society of America
P.O. Box 19134
Lansing, MI 48901
517-887-1255
Fax 517-887-2194; e-mail: ephemera @mail.serv.com.
Publishes booklet with current values and pertinent
information, send large SASE and $2.00.

Nutcracker Collectors' Club
Susan Otto, Editor
11204 Fox Run Dr.
Chesterland, OH 44026
216-792-2686
$10.00 annual dues, quarterly newsletters sent to mem-
bers, free classifieds

Old Stuff
Donna and Ron Miller, Publishers
336 N Davis
P.O. Box 1084
McMinnville, OR 97128
Published 6 times annually; Copies by mail: $3 each;
Annual subscription: $12 ($20 in Canada)

Paper Collectors' Marketplace
470 Main St.
P.O. Box 128
Scandinavia, WI 54977
715-467-2379 or Fax 715-467-2243
Subscription: $19.95 (12 issues) per year in USA;
Canada and Mexico add $15 per year

Paper Pile Quarterly
P.O. Box 337
San Anselmo, CA 94979-0337
415-454-5552
Fax 415-454-2947
Subscription: $20 per year in USA and Canada

Piece by Piece
P.O. Box 12823
Kansas City, KS 66112-9998
Subscription: $8 for 2 years; for Springbok puzzle collectors

The Pokey Gazette
Steve Santi
19626 Ricardo Ave.
Hayward, CA 94541
510-481-2586
A *Little Golden Book* collector newsletter

Pottery Collectors Express
Paradise Publications
P.O. Box 221
Mayview, MO 64071-0221
816-584-6309 (10 am to 10 pm CST)
Fax 816-584-6259
Subscription: $30 per year for 12 monthly issues

Salt and Pepper Illustrated Sales List
Judy Posner
May-Oct: R.D. 1, Box 273SC
Effort, PA 18330
717-629-6583 or
Nov-April: 4195 S Tamiami Trail, #183SC
Venice, FL 34293
941-497-7149
e-mail: Judyandjef@aol.com.
Send $2 and LSASE; Buy-Sell-Collect

Southern Oregon Antiques and Collectibles Club
P.O. Box 508
Talent, OR 97540
503-535-1231
Meets 1st Wednesday of the month; Promotes 2 shows a year in Medford, OR

Stanley Tool Collector News
c/o The Old Tool Shop
208 Front St.
Marietta, OH 45750
Features articles of interest, auction results, price trends, classified ads, etc.; Subscription: $20 per year; Sample: $6.95

Statue of Liberty Collectors' Club
Iris November
P.O. Box 535
Chautauqua, NY 14722
216-831-2646

Thimble Collectors International
6411 Montego Rd.
Louisville, Ky 40228

Three Rivers Depression Era Glass Society
Meetings held 1st Monday of each month at DeMartino's Restaurant, Carnegie, PA
For more information call:
Edith A. Putanko
John's Antiques & Edie's Glassware
Rte. 88 & Broughton Rd.
Bethel Park, PA 15102
412-831-2702

Tiffin Glass Collectors
P.O. Box 554
Tiffin, OH 44883
Meetings at Seneca City Museum on 2nd Tuesday of each month

Tobacciana
Chuck Thompson and Associates
P.O. Box 11652
Houston, TX 77293
Send SASE for free list of publications.

Tobacco Jar Newsletter
Society of Tobacco Jar Collectors
Charlotte Tarses, Treasurer
3011 Fallstaff Road #307
Baltimore, MD 21209
Dues: $30 per year ($35 outside of US)

Toy Gun Collectors of America Newsletter
Jim Buskirk, Editor and Publisher
175 Cornell St.
Windsor CA 95492
707-837-9949
Published quarterly, covers both toy and BB guns.
Dues: $15 per year

Toys and Prices magazine
700 E State St.
Iola, WI 54990-0001
715-445-2214
Fax 715-445-4087
Subscription: $14.95 per year

The Upside Down World of an O.J. Collector
The Occupied Japan Club
c/o Florence Archambault
29 Freeborn St.
Newport, RI 02840
Published bimonthly. Information requires SASE.

Vernon Views
P.O. Box 945
Scottsdale, AZ 85252
Published quarterly beginning with the spring issue, $6 per year

View-Master Reel Collector
Roger Nazeley
4921 Castor Ave
Philadelphia, PA 19124

Watt's News
c/o Susan Morris and Jan Seeck
P.O. Box 708
Mason City, IA 50401
Subscription: $10 per year

The Wrapper
Bubble Gum and Candy Wrapper Collectors
P.O. Box 573
St. Charles, IL 60174
708-377-7921

The '50s Flea
April and Larry Tvorak
HCR #34, Box 25B
Warren Center, PA 18851
717-395-3775 or
P.O. Box 126
Canon City, CO 81215-0126
719-269-7230
Published once a year, $4 postpaid; free classified
up to 30 words.

Special Interests

In this section of the book we have listed hundreds of dealers/collectors who specialize in many of the fields this price guide covers. Many of them have sent information, photographs, or advised us concerning current values and trends. This is a courtesy listing, and they are under no obligation to field questions from our readers, though some may be willing to do so. If you do write to any of them, don't expect a response unless you include an SASE (stamped self-addressed envelope) with your letter. If you have items to offer for sale or are seeking information, describe the piece in question thoroughly and mention any marks. You can sometimes do a pencil rubbing to duplicate the mark exactly. Photographs are still worth a 'thousand words,' and photocopies are especially good for paper goods, patterned dinnerware, or even smaller three-dimensional items.

It's a good idea to include your phone number if you write, since many people would rather respond with a call than a letter. And suggesting that they call back collect might very well be the courtesy that results in a successful transaction. If you're trying to reach someone by phone, always stop to consider the local time on the other end of your call. Even the most cordial person when dragged out of bed in the middle of the night will very likely *not* be receptive to you.

With the exception of the Advertising, Books, Bottles, Character Collectibles, and Toys sections which we've alphabetized by character or type, buyers are listed alphabetically under bold topics. A line in italics indicates only the specialized interests of the particular buyer whose name immediately follows it. Recommended reference guides not available from Collector Books may be purchased directly from the authors whose addresses are given in this section.

Abingdon
Louise Dumont
579 Old Main St.
Coventry, RI 02816
Alternative address:
319 Hawthorne Blvd.
Leesburg, FL 34749

Advertising
Aunt Jemima; fee charged for appraisal
Judy Posner
R.R. 1, Box 273
Effort, PA 18330
http://www.tias.com/stores/jpc
e-mail: judyandjef@aol.com

Big Boy
Steve Soelberg
29126 Laro Dr.
Agoura Hills, CA 91301
818-889-9909

Campbell's Soup
Dave and Micki Young
414 Country Ln. Ct.
Wauconda, IL 60084
Phone or FAX: 847-487-4917

Cereal boxes and premiums
Scott Bruce
P.O. Box 481
Cambridge, MA 02140
617-492-5004

Gasoline globes, pumps, signs, and promotional items
Author of book
Scott Benjamin
411 Forest St.
LaGrange, OH 44050
216-355-6608

Gerber Baby dolls
Author of book ($44 postpaid)
Joan S. Grubaugh
2342 Hoaglin Rd.
Van Wert, OH 45891
419-622-4411
FAX 419-622-3026

Jewel Tea products and tins
Bill and Judy Vroman
739 Eastern Ave.
Fostoria, OH 44830
419-435-5443

Mr. Peanut
Judith and Robert Walthall
P.O. Box 4465
Huntsville, AL 35815
205-881-9198

Reddy Kilowatt and Bordon's Elsie
Lee Garmon
1529 Whittier St.
Springfield, IL 62704

Smokey Bear
Glen Brady
P.O. Box 3933
Central Point, OR 97502
503-772-0350

Airline Memorabilia
Richard Wallin
P.O. Box 1784
Springfield, IL 62705
217-498-9279

Aluminum
Author of book
Dannie Woodard
P.O. Box 1346
Weatherford, TX 76086
817-594-4680

American Bisque
Author of book
Mary Jane Giacomini
P.O. Box 404
Ferndale, CA 95536-0404
707-786-9464

Angels
Specializing in birthday and Zodiac
Jim and Denise Atkinson
555 East School St.
Owatonna, MN 55060
507-455-3340

Animal Dishes
Author of book
Everett Grist
P.O. Box 91375
Chattanooga, TN 37412-3955
417-451-1910
Has authored books on aluminum, advertising playing cards, letter openers, and marbles

Appliances
Jim Barker
Toaster Master General
P.O. Box 41
Bethlehem, PA 18016

Ashtrays
Author of book
Nancy Wanvig
Nancy's Collectibles
P.O. Box 12
Thiensville, WI 53092

Autographs
Don and Anne Kier
2022 Marengo St.
Toledo, OH 43614
419-385-8211

Automobilia
Tire ashtrays
Author of book
Jeff McVey
1810 W State St., #427
Boise, ID 83702

Autumn Leaf
Gwynneth Harrison
P.O. Box 1
Mira Loma, CA 91752-0001
909-685-5434

Avon Collectibles
Author of book
Bud Hastin
P.O. Box 43690
Las Vegas, NE 89116

Tammy Rodrick
Stacey's Treasures
1509 N 300 St.
Sumner, IL 62466
Also character toys, glasses, cereal boxes and premiums; beer steins, Blue Willow, head vases, and trolls

Banks
Modern mechanical banks
Dan Iannotti
212 W Hickory Grove Rd.
Bloomfield Hills, MI 48302-1127

Barware
Especially cocktail shakers
Arlene Lederman Antiques
150 Main St.
Nyack, NY 10960

Author of book; specializing in vintage cocktail shakers
Stephen Visakay
P.O. Box 1517
W Caldwell, NJ 07707-1517

Beanie Babies
Jerry and Ellen L. Harnish
110 Main St.
Bellville, OH 44813
419-886-4782

Beatnik and Hippie Collectibles
Richard M. Synchef
22 Jefferson Ave.
San Raphael, CA 94903

Beatrix Potter
Nicki Budin
679 High St.
Worthington, OH 43085
614-885-1986
Also Royal Doulton

Beer Cans
Steve Gordon
P.O. Box 632
Olney, MD 20830-0632
301-439-4116

Bells
Unusual; no cow or school
Author of book
Dorothy Malone Anthony
802 S Eddy
Ft. Scott, KS 66701

Bicycles and Tricycles
Consultant, collector, dealer
Lorne Shields
Box 211
Chagrin Falls, OH 44022
416-744-0747 (days) or 416-733-3777 (evenings)
Fax 416-744-8042
e-mail: vintage@globalserve.net

Black Americana
Buy, sell and trade; lists available; fee charged for appraisal
Judy Posner
R.R. 1, Box 273
Effort, PA 18330
http://www.tias.com/stores/jpc
e-mail: judyandjef@aol.com

Black Glass
Author of book
Marlena Toohey
703 S Pratt Pky.
Longmont, CO 80501
303-678-9726

Blue Ridge
Author of several books; columnist for The Depression Glass Daze
Betty Newbound
2206 Nob Hill Dr.
Sanford, NC 27330
Also milk glass, wall pockets, figural planters, collectible china and glass

Blue Willow
Author of several books
Mary Frank Gaston
Box 342
Bryan, TX 77806
Also china and metals

Bobbin' Heads by Hartland
Author of guide; newsletter
Tim Hunter
1668 Golddust
Sparks, NV 89436
702-626-5029

Bookends
Author of book
Louis Kuritzky
4510 NW 17th Pl.
Gainesville, FL 32605
352-376-3884

Books
Big Little Books
Ron and Donna Donnelly
6302 Championship Dr.
Tuscaloosa, AL 35405
205-507-0789
FAX 205-507-0544

Children's
Marvelous Books
Dorothy (Dede) Kern
P.O. Box 1510
Ballwin, MO 63022
314 458-3301
Fax 314-273-5452

Children's
My Bookhouse
27 S Sandusky St.
Tiffin, OH 44883
419-447-9842

Children's illustrated, Little Golden, etc.
Ilene Kayne
1308 S Charles St.
Baltimore, MD 21230
410-685-3923
e-mail: Ilenegold@aol.com

Fine books and antique toys
Bromer Booksellers, Inc.
607 Boylston St., on Copley Sq.
Boston, MA 02116

Little Golden Books, Wonder and Elf
Author of book on Little Golden Books
Steve Santi
19626 Ricardo Ave.
Hayward, CA 94541

Paperback originals, TV and movie tie-ins, etc.
Tom Rolls
230 S Oakland Ave.
Indianapolis, IN 46201

Bottle Openers
Charlie Reynolds
2836 Monroe St.
Falls Church, VA 22042
703-533-1322

Bottles
Bitters, figurals, inks, barber, etc.
Steve Ketcham
P.O. Box 24114
Minneapolis, MN 55424
612-920-4205
Also advertising signs, trays, calendars, etc.

Dairy and milk
Author of books
John Tutton
R.R. 4, Box 929
Front Royal, VA 22630
703-635-7058

Painted-label soda
Author of books
Thomas Marsh
914 Franklin Ave.
Youngstown, OH 44502
216-743-8600
800-845-7930 (book orders)

Boyd

Joyce M. Pringle
Chip and Dale Collectibles
3708 W Pioneer Pky.
Arlington, TX 76013
Also Summit and Mosser

Boyd's Bears

Editor of secondary market price guide
Rosie Wells Enterprises, Inc.
R.R. #1
Canton, IL 61520
Also Hallmark, Precious Moments, Cherished Teddies

Breyer

Author of book
Carol Karbowiak Gilbert
2193 14 Mile Rd. 206
Sterling Hts., MI 48310

British Royal Commemoratives

Author of book
Audrey Zeder
6755 Coralite St. S
Long Beach, CA 90808

Brownies by Palmer Cox

Don and Anne Kier
2022 Marengo St.
Toledo, OH 43614
419-385-8211

Brush-McCoy Pottery

Authors of book
Steve and Martha Sanford
230 Harrison Ave.
Campbell, CA 95008
408-978-8408

Bubble Bath Containers

Matt and Lisa Adams
1234 Harbor Cove
Woodstock, GA 30189
770-516-6874

Calculators

Author of book
Guy Ball
14561 Livingston St.
Tustin, CA 92780

California Perfume Company

Not common; especially items marked Goetting Co.
Dick Pardini
3107 N El Dorado St., Dept. G
Stockton, CA 95204-3412
Also Savoi Et Cie, Hinze Ambrosia, Gertrude Recordon, Marvel Electric Silver Cleaner, and Easy Day Automatic Clothes Washer

California Pottery

Susan N. Cox
Main Street Antique Mall
237 East Main Street
El Cajon, CA 92020
619-447-0800
Want to buy: California pottery, especially Brayton, Catalina, Metlox, Kay Finch, etc.; also examples of relatively unknown companies. Must be mint. (Susan Cox has devoted much of the past 15 years to California pottery research which caught her interest when she was the editor and publisher of the *American Clay Exchange*. She would appreciate any information collectors might have about California pottery companies and artists.)

Pat and Kris Secor
P.O. Box 158
Clarksville, AR 72830
Especially Hedi Shoop, Brad Keeler, Howard Pierce, Kay Finch, Matthew Adams, Marc Bellaire, Twin Winton, Sascha Brastoff; many others

Michael John Verlangeri Gallery
P.O. Box 844
W Cambria, CA 93428-0844
Editor of *The California Pottery Trader* newsletter; holds cataloged auctions

Cleminsons
Robin Stine
P.O. Box 6202
Toledo, OH 43614
419-385-7387

Vallona Starr
Author of book
Bernice Stamper
7516 Flay Ave.
Bakersfield, CA 93308-7701
805-393-2900

Camark Pottery
Author of book, historian on Arkansas pottery
David Edwin Gifford
P.O. Box 7617
Little Rock, AR 72217

Cameras
Classic, collectible and usable
Gene's Cameras
2603 Artie St., SW Ste. 16
Huntsville, AL 35805
205-536-6893

Wooden, detective, and stereo
John A. Hess
P.O. Box 3062
Andover, MA 01810
Also old brass lenses

Candlewick
Has matching service
Joan Cimini
63680 Centerville-Warnock Rd.
Belmont, OH 43718

Candy Containers
Glass
Jeff Bradfield
90 Main St.
Dayton, VA 22821
703-879-9961
Also advertising, cast-iron and tin toys, postcards, and Coca-Cola

Glass; author of book
Doug Dezso
864 Paterson Ave.
Maywood, NJ 07607
Other interests: Tonka Toys, Shafford black cats, German bisque comic character nodders, Royal Bayreuth creamers, and Pep pins

Cape Cod, by Avon
Debbie and Randy Coe
Coes Mercantile
Lafayette School House Mall #2
748 3rd (Hwy. 99W)
Lafayette, OR 97137
Also Elegant and Depression glass, art pottery, Golden Foliage by Libbey Glass Company, and Liberty Blue dinnerware

Carnival Chalkware
Author of book
Thomas G. Morris
P.O. Box 8307
Medford, OR 97504
541-779-3164
e-mail: chalkman@cdsnet.net
Also Ginger Rogers memorabilia

Cast Iron
Door knockers, sprinklers, figural paperweights, and marked cookware
Craig Dinner
P.O. Box 4399
Sunnyside, NY 11104
718-729-3850

Cat Collectibles
Marilyn Dipboye
33161 Wendy Dr.
Sterling Hts., MI 48310
810-264-0285

Ceramic Arts Studio
BA Wellman
P.O. Box 673
Westminster, MA 01473

Cereal Boxes and Premiums
Author of book, editor of magazine Flake
Scott Bruce; Mr. Cereal Box
P.O. Box 481
Cambridge, MS 02140
617-492-5004
Buys, sells, trades, appraises

Character and Personality Collectibles

Author of books
Bill Bruegman
Toy Scouts, Inc.
137 Casterton Ave.
Akron, OH 44303
330-836-0668
Fax 330-869-8668
e-mail: toyscout@salamander.net
Dealers, publishers, and appraisers of collectible memorabilia from the '50s through today

Any and all
Terri Ivers
Terri's Toys
419 S First St.
Ponca City, OK 74601
405-762-8697 or 405-762-5174
Fax 405-765-2657
e-mail: tivers@pcok.com

Any and all
John Thurmond
Collector Holics
15006 Fuller
Grandview, MO 64030
816-322-0906

Any and all
Norm Vigue
62 Barley St.
Stoughton, MA 02072
617-344-5441

Batman, Gumby, and Marilyn Monroe
Colleen Garmon Barnes
114 E Locust
Chatham, IL 62629

Beatles
Bojo
Bob Gottuso
P.O. Box 1403
Cranberry Twp., PA 16066-0403
Phone or Fax 412-776-0621

Beatles
Rick Rann, Beatelist
P.O. Box 877
Oak Park, IL 60303
708-442-7907

Betty Boop
Leo A. Mallette
2309 Santa Anita Ave.
Arcadia, CA 91006-5154

Bubble Bath Containers
Matt and Lisa Adams
1234 Harbor Cove
Woodstock, GA 30189
770-516-6874

California Raisins
Ken Clee
Box 11412
Philadelphia, PA 19111
215-722-1979

California Raisins
Larry De Angelo
516 King Arthur Dr.
Virginia Beach, VA 23464

Children's plastic mugs
Cheryl and Lee Brown
7377 Badger Ct.
Indianapolis, IN 46260
317-253-4620

Dick Tracy
Larry Doucet
2351 Sultana Dr.
Yorktown Hts., NY 10598

Disney, Western heroes, Gone With the Wind, character watches ca 1930s to mid-1950s, premiums, and games
Ron and Donna Donnelly
Saturday Heroes
6302 Championship Dr.
Tuscaloosa, AL 35405
205-507-0789; FAX 205-507-0544

Disney, buy, sell, and trade; lists available; fee charged for appraisal
Judy Posner
R.R. 1, Box 273
Effort, PA 18330
http://www.tias.com/stores/jpc
e-mail: judyandjef@aol.com

Elvis Presley
Author of book
Rosalind Cranor
P.O. Box 859
Blacksburg, VA 24063

Elvis Presley
Lee Garmon
1529 Whittier St.
Springfield, IL 62704

Garfield
Adrienne Warren
1032 Feather Bed Ln.
Edison, NJ 08820
908-381-7083 (EST)
Also Smurfs and other characters, dolls, monsters, premiums; Lists available

I Dream of Jeannie, Barbara Eden
Richard D. Barnes
1520 W 800 N
Salt Lake City, UT 84116
801-521-4400

Lil' Abner
Kenn Norris
P.O. Box 4830
Sanderson, TX 79848-4830

The Lone Ranger
Terry and Kay Klepey
c/o The Silver Bullet Newsletter
P.O. Box 553
Forks, WA 98331

Lucille Ball
Author of book
Ric Wyman
408 S Highland Ave.
Elderon, WI 54429

Peanuts and Schulz Collectibles
Freddi Margolin
P.O. Box 5124P
Bay Shore, NY 11706
516-666-6861
Fax 516-665-7986
e-mail: snupius@li.net

Roy Rogers and Dale Evans
Author of books
Robert W. Phillips
1703 N Aster Pl.
Broken Arrow, OK 74012-1308
918-254-8205
Fax 918-252-9362
e-mail: rawhidebob@aol.com
One of the most widely-published writers in the field of cowboy memorabila and author of *Roy Rogers, Singing Cowboy Stars, Silver Screen Cowboys, Hollywood Cowboy Heroes,* and *Western Comics: A Comprehensive Reference*; research consultant for TV documentary *Roy Rogers, King of the Cowboys* (AMC-TV/Republic Pictures/Galen Films)

Shirley Temple
Gen Jones
294 Park St.
Medford, MA 02155

Smokey Bear
Glen Brady
P.O. Box 3933
Central Point, OR 97502
503-772-0350

Three Stooges
Harry S. Ross
Soitenly Stooges Inc.
P.O. Box 72
Skokie, IL 60076

Tom Mix
Author of book
Merle 'Bud' Norris
1324 N Hague Ave.
Columbus, OH 43204-2108

TV and movie collectibles
TVC Enterprises
P.O. Box 1088
Easton, MA 02334
508-238-1179

Wizard of Oz
Bill Stillman
Scarfone & Stillman Vintage Oz
P.O. Box 167
Hummelstown, PA 17036
717-566-5538

Character and Promotional Drinking Glasses
Authors of book; editors of Collector Glass News
Mark Chase and Michael Kelly
P.O. Box 308
Slippery Rock, PA 16057
412-946-2838 or 412-794-6420

Character Clocks and Watches
Author of book
Howard S. Brenner
106 Woodgate Terrace
Rochester, NY 14625

Bill Campbell
1221 Littlebrook Ln.
Birmingham, AL 35235
205-853-8227
Fax 405-658-6986
Also Character Collectibles, Advertising Premiums

Character Nodders
Matt and Lisa Adams
1234 Harbor Cove
Woodstock, GA 30189
770-516-6874

Chintz
Marge Geddes
P.O. Box 5875
Aloha, OR 97007
503-649-1041

Mary Jane Hastings
310 West 1st South
Mt. Olive, IL 62069
Phone or Fax 217-999-7519

Author of book
Joan Welsh
7015 Partridge Pl.
Hyattsville, MD 20782
301-779-6181

Christmas Collectibles
Especially from before 1920 and decorations made in Germany
J.W. 'Bill' and Treva Courter
3935 Kelley Rd.
Kevil, KY 42053
Phone or Fax 502-488-2116

Clocks
All types
Bruce A. Austin
40 Selborne Chase
Fairport, NY 14450
716-223-0711

Clothes Sprinkler Bottles
Ellen Bercovici
5118 Hampden Ln.
Bethesda, MD 20814
301-652-1140

Clothing and Accessories
Author of book
Sue Langley
101 Ramsey Ave.
Syracuse, NY 13224-1719
315-445-0133

Pat Compensa, 'The Hat Lady'
414 E Heman St.
E Syracuse, NY 13057
315-431-4441

Coca-Cola
Also Pepsi-Cola and other brands of soda
Craig and Donna Stifter
P.O. Box 6514
Naperville, IL 60540
630-789-5780

Coin-Operated Vending Machines
Ken and Jackie Durham
909 26th St., NW
Washington, D.C. 20037

Colorado Pottery (Broadmoor)
Carol and Jim Carlton
8115 S Syracuse St.
Englewood, CO 80112
303-773-8616
Also Coors, Lonhuda, and Denver White

Comic Books
Avalon Comics
Larry Curcio
P.O. Box 821
Medford, MA 02155
617-391-5614

Compacts

Unusual shapes, also vanities and accessories; Author of book
Roselyn Gerson
P.O. Box 40
Lynbrook, NY 11563

Cookbooks

Author of book; also advertising leaflets
Bob Allen
P.O. Box 56
St. James, MO 65559

Cookie Cutters

Author of book and newsletter
Rosemary Henry
9610 Greenview Ln.
Manassas, VA 22100

Cookie Jars

Joe Devine
1411 3rd St.
Council Bluffs, IA 51503
712-232-5233 or 712-328-7305
Also Russel Wright

Buy, sell, and trade; lists available; fee charged for appraisal
Judy Posner
R.R. 1, Box 273
Effort, PA 18330
http://www.tias.com/stores/jpc
e-mail: judyandjef@aol.com

Phil and Nyla Thurston
82 Hamlin St.
Cortland, NY 13045
607-753-6770
Other interests listed under Figural Ceramics

Corkscrews

Antique and unusual
Paul P. Luchsinger
1126 Wishart Pl.
Hermitage, PA 16148

Cowan

Author of book
Mark Bassett
P.O. Box 771233
Lakewood, OH 44107

Cracker Jack Items

Phil Helley
Old Kilbourn Antiques
629 Indiana Ave.
Wisconsin Dells, WI 53965
Also banks, radio premiums, and wind-up toys

Wes Johnson, Sr.
106 Bauer Ave.
Louisville, KY 40207

Author of book; has newsletter
Larry White
108 Central St.
Rowley, MA 01969

Crackle Glass

Authors of book
Stan and Arlene Weitman
101 Cypress St.
Massapequa Park, NY 11758
516-799-2619
Fax 516-797-3039

Credit Cards and Related Items

Walt Thompson
Box 2541
Yakima, WA 98907-2541

Cuff Links

National Cuff Link Society
Eugene R. Klompus
P.O. Box 346
Prospect Hts., IL 60070
Phone or Fax 847-816-0035
Also related items

Dakins

Jim Rash
135 Alder Ave.
Pleasantville, NJ 08232
609-646-4125

Decanters

Homestead Collectibles
Art and Judy Turner
R.D. 2, Rte. 150
P.O. Box 173
Mill Hall, PA 17751
717-726-3597
Fax 717-726-4488

Degenhart
Linda K. Marsh
1229 Gould Rd.
Lansing, MI 48917

deLee
Authors of book
Joanne and Ralph Schaefer
3182 Williams Rd.
Oroville, CA 95965-8300
916-893-2902 or 800-897-6263

Depression Glass
Also Elegant glassware
John and Shirley Baker
673 W Township Rd. #118
Tiffin, OH 44883
Also Tiffin glassware

Dinnerware
Cat-Tail
Ken and Barbara Brooks
4121 Gladstone Ln.
Charlotte, NC 28205

Fiesta, Franciscan, Russel Wright, Lu Ray, and Metlox
Fiesta Plus
Mick and Lorna Chase
380 Hawkins Crawford Rd.
Cookeville, TN 38501
615-372-8333
Also other Homer Laughlin patterns

Mary Frank Gaston
P.O. Box 342
Bryan, TX 77806

Homer Laughlin China, author of book
Darlene Nossaman
5419 Lake Charles
Waco, TX 76710

Liberty Blue
Gary Beegle
92 River St.
Montgomery, NY 12549
914-457-3623
Also most lines of collectible modern American dinnerware as well as character glasses

Royal China
BA Wellman
88 State Rd. W
P.O. Box 673
Homestead Farms #2
Westminster, MA 01473-1435
Also Ceramic Arts Studios

Russel Wright, Eva Zeisel, Homer Laughlin
Charles Alexander
221 E 34th St.
Indianapolis, IN 46205
317-924-9665

Dolls
Annalee Mobilitee Dolls
Jane's Collectibles
Jane Holt
P.O. Box 115
Derry, NH 03038
Extensive lists sometimes available

Boudoir dolls
Bonnie M. Groves
402 N Ave. A
Elgin, TX 78621
512-281-9551

Betsy McCall and friends
Marci Van Ausdall, Editor
P.O. Box 946
Quincy, CA 95971-0946
916-283-2770

Celebrity and character dolls
Henri Yunes
971 Main St., Apt. 2
Hackensack, NJ 07601
201-488-2236

Dolls from the 1960s–70s, including Liddle Kiddles, Dolly Darlings, Petal People, Tiny Teens, etc.; author of book on Liddle Kiddles; must send SASE for info
Paris Langford
415 Dodge Ave.
Jefferson, LA 70121
504-733-0667

Chatty Cathy; authors of book
Don and Kathy Lewis
187 N Marcello Ave.
Thousand Oaks, CA 91360
805-499-7932

Dolls from the 1960s–70s, including Liddle Kiddles, Barbie, Tammy, Tressy, etc.; co-author of book on Tammy
Cindy Sabulis
P.O. Box 642
Shelton, CT 06484
203-926-0176

Holly Hobbie
Helen McCale
1006 Ruby Ave.
Butler, MO 64730-2500

Holly Hobbie; editor of The Holly Hobbie Collectors Gazette
Donna Stultz
1455 Otterdale Mill Rd.
Taneytown, MD 21787-3032
410-775-2570

Liddle Kiddles and other small dolls from the late '60s and early '70s
Dawn Parrish
20460 Samual Drive
Saugus, CA 91530-3812
805-263-TOYS

Strawberry Shortcake
Geneva D. Addy
P.O. Box 124
Winterset, IA 50273

Vogue Dolls, Inc.
Co-author of book; available from author or Collector Books
Judith Izen
208 Follen Rd.
Lexington, MA 02173-5914

Vogue Dolls, Inc.
Co-author of book; available from author or Collector Books
Carol J. Stover
81 E Van Buren St.
Chicago, IL 60605

Dollhouse Furniture and Accessories
Renwal, Ideal, Marx, etc.
Judith A. Mosholder
R.D. #2, Box 147
Boswell, PA 15531
814-629-9277

Door Knockers
Craig Dinner
Box 4399
Sunnyside, NY 11104
718-729-3850

Egg Beaters
Author of Beat This: The Egg Beater Chronicles
Don Thornton
Off Beat Books
1345 Poplar Ave.
Sunnyvale, CA 94087

Egg Cups
Joan George, Editor
Egg Cup Collectors Corner
67 Stevens Ave.
Old Bridge, NJ 08857

Author of book
Brenda Blake
Box 555
York Harbor, ME 03911
207-363-6566

Egg Timers
Ellen Bercovici
5118 Hampden Ln.
Bethesda, MD 20814
301-652-1140

Jeannie Greenfield
310 Parker Rd.
Stoneboro, PA 16153

Elegant Glass
Cambridge, Fostoria, Heisey
Deborah Maggard Antiques
P.O. Box 211
Chagrin Falls, OH 44022
216-247-5632
Also china and Victorian art glass

Roselle Schleifman
16 Vincent Rd.
Spring Valley, NY 10977

Ertl Banks
Homestead Collectibles
P.O. Box 173
Mill Hall, PA 17751
Also decanters

Eyewinker
Sophia Talbert
921 Union St.
Covington, IN 47932
317-793-3256

Farm Collectibles
Farm Antique News
Gary Van Hoozer, Editor
812 N Third St.
Tarkio, MO 64491-0812
816-736-4528

Fast-Food Collectibles
Author of book
Ken Clee
Box 1142
Philadelphia, PA 19111
215-722-1979

Authors of several books
Joyce and Terry Losonsky
7506 Summer Leave Lane
Columbia, MD 21046-2455
Illustrated Collector's Guide to McDonald's® Happy Meal® Boxes, Premiums and Promotions ($9 plus $2 postage); McDonald's® Happy Meal® Toys in the USA and McDonald's® Happy Meal® Toys Around the World (both full color, $24.95 each plus $3 postage); and Illustrated Collector's Guide to McDonald's® McCAPS® ($4 plus $2) are available from the authors.

Bill and Pat Poe
220 Dominica Cir. E
Niceville, FL 32578-4068
850-897-4163 or Fax 850-897-2606
Also cartoon and character glasses, Pez, Smurfs, and California Raisins; Send $3 (US delivery) for 70-page catalog

Fenton Glass
Ferill J. Rice
304 Pheasant Run
Kaukauna, WI 54130

Figural Ceramics
Especially cookie jars; California pottery; Kitchen Prayer Lady, Fitz & Floyd, Head Vases, and Kreiss as well as other imports; Also American pottery
Phil and Nyla Thurston
82 Hamlin St.
Cortland, NY 13045
607-753-6770

Especially Kitchen Prayer Lady, Enesco, and Holt Howard
April and Larry Tvorak
P.O. Box 126
Canon City, CO 81215-0126
719-269-7230

Fire-King
Authors of price guide
April and Larry Tvorak
P.O. Box 126
Canon City, CO 81215-0126
719-269-7230

Fishbowl Ornaments
Sara Gifford
31 Rosemoor Dr.
Little Rock, AR 73309

Fisher-Price
Brad Cassity
1440 Texas Ave.
Grand Junction, CO 81501
970-243-7287

Fishing Collectibles
Publishes fixed-price catalog
Dave Hoover
1023 Skyview Dr.
New Albany, IN 47150
Also miniature boats and motors

Flashlights
Editor of newsletter
Bill Utley
P.O. Box 4094
Tustin, CA 92681
714-730-1252 or Fax 714-505-4067

Florence Ceramics
Author of book
Doug Foland
1811 NW Couch #303
Portland, OR 97209

John and Peggy Scott
4640 S Leroy
Springfield, MO 65810

Flower Frogs
Nada Sue Knauss
12111 Potter Rd.
Weston, OH 43569
419-669-4735

Frankoma
Authors of book
Phyllis and Tom Bess
14535 E 13th St.
Tulsa, OK 74108

Author of books
Susan N. Cox
Main Street Antique Mall
237 East Main St.
El Cajon, CA 92020
619-447-0800
Also unsharpened advertising pencils, complete matchbooks, Horlick's advertising, women's magazines from 1900 to 1950. (Susan Cox has written three books and five price guides on Frankoma pottery and is currently working on an updated price guide and a Frankoma advertising book. She has devoted much of the past 15 years to California pottery research and welcomes any information collectors might have about California companies and artists.)

Fruit Jars
Especially old, odd, or colored jars
John Hathaway
Rte. 2, Box 220
Bryant Pond, ME 04219
Also old jar lids and closures

Fulper
Douglass White
P.O. Box 5400672
Orlando, FL 32854
407-839-0004

Gambling and Related Items
Robert Eisenstadt
P.O. Box 020767
Brooklyn, NY 11202-0017

Games
Paul Fink's Fun and Games
P.O. Box 488
59 S Kent Rd.
Kent, CT 06757
203-927-4001

Paul David Morrow
1045 Rolling Point Ct.
Virginia Beach, VA 23456-6371

Gay Fad Glassware
Donna S. McGrady
154 Peters Ave.
Lancaster, OH 43130
614-653-0376

Geisha Girl Porcelain
Author of book
Elyce Litts
P.O. Box 394
Morris Plains, NJ 07950
Also ladies' compacts

Glass Animals
Author of book
Lee Garmon
1529 Whittier St.
Springfield, IL 62704

Glass Knives
Editor of newsletter
Adrienne Escoe
4448 Ironwood Ave.
Seal Beach, CA 90740-2926
562-430-6479
e-mail: escoebliss@earthlink.net

Glass Shoes
Author of book
The Shoe Lady
Libby Yalom
P.O. Box 7146
Adelphi, MD 20783

Graniteware
Author of books
Helen Greguire
716-392-2704
Also carnival glass and toasters

Griswold
Grant Windsor
P.O. Box 3613
Richmond, VA 23235-7613

Hallmark
The Baggage Car
3100 Justin Dr., Ste B
Des Moines, IA 50322
515-270-9080

Halloween
Author of books; autographed copies available from the author
Pamela Apakarian-Russell
Chris Russell & The Halloween Queen Antiques
P.O. Box 499
Winchester, NH 03470
Also other holidays, postcards, and Joe Camel

Hartland Plastics, Inc.
Author of book
Gail Fitch
1733 N Cambridge, Ave. #109
Milwaukee, WI 53202

Specializing in Western Hartlands
Kerry and Judy Irwin
Kerry and Judy's Toys
7370 Eggleston Rd.
Memphis, TN 38125-2112
901-757-1722 or Fax 901-757-0126
e-mail: kjtoys@memphisonline.com

Specializing in sports figures
James Watson
25 Gilmore St.
Whitehall, NY 12887

Holt Howard
Pat and Ann Duncan
Box 175
Cape Fair, MO 65624
417-538-2311

April and Larry Tvorak
P.O. Box 126
Canon City, CO 81215-0126
719-269-7230

Homer Laughlin
Author of book
Darlene Nossaman
5419 Lake Charles
Waco, TX 76710

Horton Ceramics
Darlene Nossaman
5419 Lake Charles
Waco, TX 76710

Hull
Mirror Brown, also Pfaltzgraff Gourmet Royal and other lines
Jo-Ann Bentz
Dealer at Shep's Grove, D15 & D16
P.O. Box 146AA
Beaver Rd., R.R. #3
Birdsboro, PA 19508-9107
610-582-0311

Author of several books on Hull
Brenda Roberts
R.R. 2
Marshall, MO 65340

Mirror Brown, also Pfaltzgraff Gourmet Royal; rare items only
Bill and Connie Sloan
4965 Valley Park Rd.
Doylestown, PA 18901

Imperial Glass
Joan Cimini
63680 Centerville-Warnock Rd.
Belmont, OH 43718
Also has Candlewick matching service

Editor of glass-oriented newsletter
Ruth Grizel
P.O. Box 143
North Liberty, IA 52317-0143

Imperial Porcelain
Geneva D. Addy
P.O. Box 124
Winterset, IA 50273

Indy 500 Memorabilia
Eric Jungnickel
P.O. Box 4674
Naperville, IL 60567-4674
630-983-8339

Insulators
Mike Bruner
6980 Walnut Lake Rd.
W Bloomfield, MI 48323
313-661-8241
Also porcelain signs, light-up advertising clocks, exit globes, lightening rod balls, and target balls

Jacqueline Linscott
3557 Nicklaus Dr.
Tutusville, FL 32780

Jewel Tea
Products or boxes only; no dishes
Bill and Judy Vroman
739 Eastern Ave.
Fostoria, OH 44830
419-435-5443

Jewelry
Marcia Brown (Sparkles)
P.O. Box 2314
White City, OR 97503
514-826-3039
Fax 541-830-5385

Men's accessories and cuff links only; edits newsletter
The National Cuff Link Society
Eugene R. Klompus
P.O. Box 346
Prospect Hts., IL 60070
Phone or Fax 847-816-0035

Josef Originals
Jim and Kaye Whitaker
Eclectic Antiques
P.O. Box 475, Dept. GS
Lynnwood, WA 98046

Kay Finch
Animals and birds, especially in pink with pastel decoration
Mike Drollinger
1202 Seventh St.
Covington, IN 47932
765-793-2392

Co-authors of book, available from authors
Mike Nickel and Cynthia Horvath
P.O. Box 456
Portland, MI, 48875
517-647-7646

Kentucky Derby and Horse Racing
B.L. Hornback
707 Sunrise Ln.
Elizabethtown, KY 42701

Kitchen Prayer Ladies; issues price guide ($6.96 plus $1 postage and handling)
April and Larry Tvorak
P.O. Box 126
Canon City, CO 81215-0126

Lamps
Aladdin; Author of books
J.W. Courter
3935 Kelley Rd.
Kevil, KY 42053
502-488-2116

Figural Lamps
Dee Boston
2299 N Pr. Rd. 475 W
Sullivan, IN 47882
Also dresser, pincushion, and half dolls

Motion lamps
Eclectic Antiques
Jim and Kaye Whitaker
P.O. Box 475, Dept. GS
Lynwood, WA 98046

Perfume Lamps
Tom and Linda Millman
231 S Main St.
Bethel, OH 45106
513-734-6884 (after 9 pm)

Law Enforcement and Crime-Related Memorabilia
Tony Perrin
1401 N Pierce #6
Little Rock, AR 72207
501-868-5005 or 501-666-6493 (after 5 pm)

Lefton

Author of books
Loretta DeLozier
1101 Polk St.
Bedford, IA 50833
712-523-2289 (M-F, 9 am to 4 pm)
Fax 712-523-2624
e-mail: LeftonLady@aol.com

Letter Openers

Author of book
Everett Grist
P.O. Box 91375
Chattanooga, TN 37412-3955
423-510-8052

License Plates

Richard Diehl
5965 W Colgate Pl.
Denver, CO 80227

Lunch Boxes

Norman's Ole and New Store
Philip Norman
126 W Main St.
Washington, NC 27889-4944
919-946-3448

Terri's Toys and Nostalgia
Terri Ivers
419 S First St.
Ponca City, OK 74601
405-762-8697 or 405-762-5174
Fax 405-765-2657
e-mail: ivers@pcok.com

MAD Collectibles

Michael Lerner
32862 Springside Ln.
Solon, OH 44139
Phone or Fax 216-349-3776

Magazines

*Issues price guide to illustrations, old magazines,
and pinups*
Denis C. Jackson
Illustrator Collector's News
P.O. Box 1958
Sequim, WA 98382
360-683-2559; http://www.olypen.com/ticn
e-mail: ticn@olypen.com

*Pre-1950 movie magazines, especially with Ginger
Rogers covers*
Tom Morris
P.O. Box 8307
Medford, OR 97504
541-779-3164
e-mail: chalkman@cdsnet.net

National Geographic; Author of guide
Don Smith's National Geographic Magazines
3930 Rankin St.
Louisville, KY 40214
502-366-7504

Pulps
J. Grant Thiessen
Pandora's Books Ltd.
Box 54
Neche, ND 58265-0054
Fax 204-324-1628 or e-mail: jgthiess@mts.net
http://www.pandora.ca/pandora
Issues catalogs on various genre of hardcover books,
paperbacks, and magazines of all types

Marbles

Author of books
Everett Grist
P.O. Box 91375
Chattanooga, TN 37412-3955
423-510-8052

Match Safes

George Sparacio
P.O. Box 791
Malaga, NJ 08328
609-694-4167

Matchcovers

Bill Retskin
P.O. Box 18481
Asheville, NC 22814

McCoy Pottery

Authors of book
Robert and Margaret Hanson, Craig Nissen
P.O. Box 70426
Bellevue, WA 98005

Melmac Dinnerware
Co-author of book
Gregg Zimmer
4017 16th Ave. S
Minneapolis, MN 55407

Co-author of book
Alvin Daigle, Jr.
Boomerang Antiques
423-915-0666

Miller Studio
Paul and Heather August
571 N 66th St.
Wauwatosa, WI 53213
414-475-0753
e-mail: packrats@execpc.com

Morton Pottery
Authors of books
Doris and Burdell Hall
B&B Antiques
210 W Sassafras Dr.
Morton, IL 61550-1245

Motion Clocks
Electric; buy, sell, trade, and restore
Sam and Anna Samuelian
P.O. Box 504
Edgmont, PA 19028-0504
610-566-7248
Also motion lamps, transistor and novelty radios

Motorcycles
Bruce Kiper
Ancient Age Motors
2205 Sunset Ln.
Lutz, FL 33549
813-949-9660
Also related items and clothing

Movie Posters
Movie Poster Service
Cleophas and Lou Ann Wooley
Box 517
Canton, OK 73724-0517
405-886-2248 or Fax 405-886-2249
e-mail: mpsposters@pldi.net
In business full time since 1972; own/operate
mail-order firm with world's largest movie poster
inventory

Napkin Dolls
Bobbie Zucker Bryson
1 St. Eleanoras Ln.
Tuckahoe, NY 10707
914-779-1405
e-mail: napkindoll@aol.com
http:/www/his.com/~judy/reamer.html

Niloak Pottery
Author of book; historian of Arkansas pottery
David Edwin Gifford
P.O. Box 7617
Little Rock, AR 72217
Autographed books available

Newspaper Collector Society
Rick Brown
P.O. Box 19134
Lansing, MI 19134

Novelty Radios
Authors of several books
Sue and Marty Bunis
R.R. 1, Box 36
Bradford, NH 03221-9102

Nutcrackers
Earl MacSorley
823 Indian Hill Rd.
Orange, CT 06477

Orientalia and Dragonware
Susie Hibbard
2570 Walnut Blvd. #20
Walnut Creek, CA 94596

Paden City Glassware
George and Mary Hurney
Glass Connection (mail-order only)
312 Babcock Dr.
Palatine, IL 50067
847-359-3839

Paper Dolls
Author of books
Mary Young
P.O. Box 9244
Wright Bros Branch
Dayton, OH 45409

Pencil Sharpeners
Phil Helley
629 Indiana Ave.
Wisconsin Dells, WI 53965
608-254-8659

Advertising and figural
Martha Hughes
4128 Ingalls St.
San Diego, CA 92103
619-296-1866

Pennsbury
Author of price guide; video book available
BA Wellman
88 State Rd. W
P.O. Box 673
Homestead Farms #2
Westminster, MA 01473-1435

Joe Devine
1411 3rd St.
Council Bluffs, IA 51503
712-232-5322 or 712-328-7305

Shirley Graff
4515 Graff Rd.
Brunswick, OH 44212

Pepsi-Cola
Craig and Donna Stifter
P.O. Box 6514
Naperville, IL 60540
630-789-5780
Other soda-pop memorablia as well

Perfume Bottles
Especially commercial, Czechoslovakian, Lalique, Baccarat, Victorian, crown top, factices, miniatures
Monsen and Baer
Box 529
Vienna, VA 22183
703-242-1357
Buy, sell, and accept consignments for auctions

Pez
Richard Belyski
P.O. Box 124
Sea Cliff, NY 11579
516-676-1183

Pfaltzgraff
Gourmet Royal as well as other dinnerware lines
Jo-Ann Bentz
Dealer Shupp's Grove, D15 & D16
Adamstown, PA or
Box 146 AA, Beaver Rd.
R.R. 3
Birdsboro, PA 19508
610-582-0311

Gourmet, Gourmet Royal
Bill and Connie Sloan
4965 Valley Park Rd.
Doylestown, PA 18901

Photographica
Antique photography and paper
Betty Davis
5291 Ravenna Rd.
Newton Falls, OH 44444
Fax 216-872-0386

Tintypes
Mike Swink
124 Town Ln.
Mt. Airy, NC 27030

Pie Birds
Also funnels
Lillian M. Cole
14 Harmony School Rd.
Flemington, NJ 08822
908-782-3198
Also old ice cream scoops

Pinup Art
Issues price guides to pinups, illustrations, and old magazines
Denis C. Jackson
Illustrator Collector's News
P.O. Box 1958
Sequim, WA 98382
360-683-2559
Fax 360-683-9708
e-mail: ticn@daka.com

Pocket Calculators
Author of book
International Assn. of Calculator Collectors
Guy D. Ball
P.O. Box 345
Tustin, CA 92781-0345
phone/fax 714-730-6140
e-mail: mrcalc@usa.net

Political
Michael and Polly McQuillen
McQuillen's Collectibles
P.O. Box 11141
Indianapolis, IN 46201-0141
317-322-8518

Before 1960
Michael Engel
29 Groveland St.
Easthampton, MA 01027

Pins, banners, ribbons, etc.
Paul Longo Americana
Box 490
Chatham Rd., South Orleans
Cape Cod, MA 02662
508-255-5482

Poodle Collectibles
Author of book
Elaine Butler
233 S Kingston Ave.
Rockwood, TN 37854

Porcelier
Jim Barker
Toaster Master General
P.O. Box 41
Bethlehem, PA 10106

Author of book
Susan Grindberg
5040 Jamaca Ave. N
Lake Elmo, MN 55042
612-779-2936
e-mail: Porcelier@visi.com
http://www.visi.com/Porcelier/
Autographed copies of *Collector's Guide to Porcelier China* available from the author for $18.95 + $2.05 postage & handling (Minnesota residents add $1.23 sales tax)

Postcards
C.J. Russell & Pamela Apakarian-Russell
Halloween Queen Antiques
P.O. Box 499
Winchester, NH 03470
Also Halloween and other holidays

Powder Jars
John and Peggy Scott
4640 S Leroy
Springfield, MO 65810

Sharon Thoerner
15549 Ryon Ave.
Bellflower, CA 90706
562-866-1555
Also slag glass

Purinton Pottery
Susan Morris
P.O. Box 656
Panora, IA 50216
515-755-3161

Purses
Veronica Trainer
P.O. Box 40443
Cleveland, OH 44140

Puzzles
Wooden jigsaw type from before 1950
Bob Armstrong
15 Monadnock Rd.
Worcester, MA 01609

Especially character related
Norm Vigue
62 Bailey St.
Stoughton, MA 02072
617-344-5441

Radio Premiums
Bill Campbell
1221 Littlebrook Ln.
Birmingham, AL 35235
205-853-8227
Fax 405-658-6986

Radios
Antique Radio Labs
James Fred
Rte. 1, Box 41
Cutler, IN 46920
Buy, sell, and trade; Repairs radio equipment using vaccuum tubes

Authors of several books on antique, novelty, and transistor radios
Sue and Marty Bunis
R.R. 1, Box 36
Bradford, NH 03221-9102

Author of book
Harry Poster
P.O. Box 1883
S Hackensack, NJ 07606
201-410-7525
Also televisions, related advertising items, old tubes, cameras, 3-D viewers and projectors, View-Master and Tru-View reels and accessories

Railroadiana
Any item; especially china and silver
John White, 'Grandpa'
Grandpa's Depot
1616 17th St., Ste. 267
Denver, CO 80202
303-628-5590
Fax 303-628-5547
Also related items; catalogs available

Also steamship and other transportation memorabilia
Fred and Lila Shrader
Shrader Antiques
2025 Hwy. 199
Crescent City, CA 95531
707-458-3525
Also Buffalo, Shelley, Niloak, and Hummels

Razor Blade Banks
David Geise
1410 Aquia Dr.
Stafford, VA 22554
703-569-5984

Debbie Gillham
47 Midline Ct.
Gaithersburg, MD 20878
301-977-5727

Reamers
Bobbie Zucker Bryson
1 St. Eleanoras Ln.
Tuckahoe, NY 10707
914-779-1405
e-mail: napkindoll@aol.com
http://www/his.com/~judy/reamer.html

Records
45 rpm and LP's
Mason's Bookstore, Rare Books, and Record Albums
Dave Torzillo
115 S Main St.
Chambersburg, PA 17201
717-261-0541

Picture and 78 rpm kiddie records
Peter Muldavin
173 W 78th St.
New York, NY 10024
212-362-9606

Especially 78 rpms
L.R. 'Les' Docks
Box 691035
San Antonio, TX 78269-1035
Write for want list

Red Wing Artware
Wendy and Leo Frese
Three Rivers Collectibles
P.O. Box 551542
Dallas, TX 75355
214-341-515
e-mail: rumrill@ix.netcom.com
Holds cataloged auctions

Regal China
Van Telligen, Bendel, Old MacDonald's Farm
Rick Spencer
Salt Lake City, UT
801-973-0805
Also Coors, Shawnee, Watt, Silverplate (especially grape patterns)

Rooster and Roses
Jacki Elliott
9790 Twin Cities Rd.
Galt, CA 95632
209-745-3860

Roselane Sparklers
Lee Garmon
1529 Whittier St.
Springfield, IL 62704

Rosemeade
NDSU research specialist
Bryce Farnsworth
1334 14½ St. S
Fargo, ND 58103
701-237-3597

Royal Bayreuth
Don and Anne Kier
2022 Marengo St.
Toledo, OH 43614
419-385-8211

Royal Copley
Author of books
Joe Devine
1411 3rd St.
Council Bluffs, IA 51503
712-323-5233 or 712-328-7305
Buy, sell, or trade; Also pie birds

Royal Haeger and Royal Hickman
Author of books
Lee Garmon
1529 Whittier St.
Springfield, IL 62704

RumRill
Wendy and Leo Frese
Three Rivers Collectibles
P.O. Box 551542
Dallas, TX 75355
214-341-5165
e-mail: rumrill@ix.netcom.com
Holds cataloged auctions

Ruby Glass
Author of book
Naomi L. Over
8909 Sharon Ln.
Arvada, CO 80002
303-424-5922

Russel Wright
Author of book
Ann Kerr
P.O. Box 437
Sidney, OH 45365

Salt and Pepper Shakers
Figural or novelty
Judy Posner
R.R. 1, Box 273
Effort, PA 18330
717-629-6583 or
http://www.tias.com/stores/jpc
e-mail: judyandjef@aol.com
Buy, sell, and trade; lists available; fee charged for appraisal

Scottie Dog Collectibles
Donna Palmer
2446 215th Ave. SE
Issaquah, WA 98027

Scouting Collectibles
Author of books
R.J. Sayers
P.O. Box 629
Brevard, NC 28712
A Guide to Scouting Collectibles With Values available by sending $30.95 (includes postage)

Sebastians
Blossom Shop Collectibles
Jim Waite
112 N Main St.
Farmer City, IL 61842
800-842-2593

Sewing Machines
Toy only; authors of book
Darryl and Roxana Matter
P.O. Box 65
Portis, KS 67474-0065

Shawnee
Rick Spencer
Salt Lake City, UT
801-973-0805

Shot Glasses
Author of book
Mark Pickvet
Shot Glass Club of America
5071 Watson Dr.
Flint, MI 48506

Silhouette Pictures (20th Century)

Author of book
Shirley Mace
Shadow Enterprises
P.O. Box 1602
Mesilla Park, NM 88047
505-524-6717
Fax 505-523-0940
e-mail: Shmace@nmsu.edu

Silverplated Flatware

Rick Spencer
Salt Lake City, UT
801-973-0805

Skookum Indian Dolls

Jo Ann Palmieri
27 Pepper Rd.
Towaco, NJ 07082-1357

Snow Domes

Author of book and newsletter
Nancy McMichael, Editor
P.O. Box 53310
Washington, DC 20009

Soda Fountain Collectibles

Harold and Joyce Screen
2804 Munster Rd.
Baltimore, MD 21234
410-661-6765

Soda-Pop Memorabilia

Craig and Donna Stifter
P.O. Box 6514
Naperville, IL 60540
630-789-5780

Painted-label soda bottles; author of books
Thomas Marsh
914 Franklin Ave.
Youngstown, OH 44502
216-743-8600
800-845-7930 (order line)

Sports Collectibles

Sporting goods
Kevin R. Bowman
P.O. Box 471
Neosho, MO 64850-0471
417-781-6418 (6pm–9pm CST)

Equipment and player-used items
Don and Anne Kier
2022 Marengo St.
Toledo, OH 43614
419-385-8211

Bobbin' head sports figures
Tim Hunter
1668 Golddust
Sparks, NV 89436
702-626-5029

Paul Longo Americana
Box 490
Chatham Rd., South Orleans
Cape Cod, MA 02662
508-255-5482
Also stocks and bonds

Golf collectibles
Pat Romano
32 Sterling Dr.
Lake Grove, NY 11202-0017

Sports Pins

Tony George
22431-B160 Antonio Pky. #252
Rancho Santa Margarita, CA 92688
714-589-6075

St. Clair Glass

Ted Pruitt
3382 W 700 N
Anderson, IN 46011
Book available ($15)

Stangl

Birds, dinnerware, artware
Popkorn Antiques
Bob and Nancy Perzel
P.O. Box 1057
4 Mine St.
Flemington, NJ 08822
908-782-9631

Statue of Liberty

Mike Brooks
7335 Skyline
Oakland, CA 94611

String Holders
Ellen Bercovici
5118 Hampden Ln.
Bethesda, MD 20814
301-652-1140

Swanky Swigs
Joyce Jackson
900 Jenkins Rd.
Aledo, TX 76008
817-441-8864

Syroco and Similar Products
Doris J. Gibbs
3837 Cuming #1
Omaha, NE 68131
402-556-4300

Teapots and Tea-Related Items
Author of book
Tina Carter
882 S Mollison
El Cajon, CA 92020

Tire Ashtrays
Author of book
Jeff McVey
1810 W State St., #427
Boise, ID 83702-3955
Book available ($12.95 postpaid)

Toothbrush Holders
Author of book
Marilyn Cooper
8408 Lofland Dr.
Houston, TX 77055
713-465-7773

Toys
Any and all
June Moon
245 N Northwest Hwy.
Park Ridge, IL 60068
847-825-1441
Fax 847-825-6090

Aurora model kits, and especially toys from 1948–1972
Author of books
Bill Bruegman
137 Casterton Dr.
Akron, OH 44303
330-836-0668
Fax 330-869-8668
e-mail: toyscout@salamander.net
Dealers, publishers, and appraisers of collectible memorabilia from the '50s through today

Building blocks and construction toys
Arlan Coffman
1223 Wilshire Blvd., Ste. 275
Santa Monica, CA 90403
310-453-2507

Die-cast vehicles
Mark Giles
P.O. Box 821
Ogallala, NE 69153-0821

Fisher-Price pull toys and playsets up to 1986
Brad Cassity
1440 Texas Ave.
Grand Junction, CO 81501
970-243-7287

Games and general line
Phil McEntee
Where the Toys Are
45 W Pike St.
Canonsburg, PA 15317

Hot Wheels
D.W. (Steve) Stephenson
11117 NE 164th Pl.
Bothell, WA 98011-4003

Model kits other than Aurora; edits publications
Gordy Dutt
Box 201
Sharon Center, OH 42274-0201

Puppets and marionettes
Steven Meltzer
670 San Juan Ave. #B
Venice, CA 90291
310-396-6007

Rings, character, celebrity, and souvenir)
Bruce and Jan Thalberg
23 Mountain View Dr.
Weston, CT 06883-1317
203-227-8175

Sand toys
Authors of book
Carole & Richard Smyth
Carole Smyth Antiques
P.O. Box 2068
Huntington, NY 11743

Slot race cars from 1960s–70s
Gary T. Pollastro
4156 Beach Dr. SW
Seattle, WA 98116
206-935-0245

Tin litho, paper on wood, comic character, penny toys, and Schoenhut
Wes Johnson, Sr.
106 Bauer Ave.
Louisville, KY 40207

Tootsietoys
Author of books
David E. Richter
6817 Sutherland
Mentor, OH 44060
216-255-6537

Tops and Spinning Toys
Bruce Middleton
5 Lloyd Rd.
Newburgh, NY 12550
914-564-2556

Toy soldiers, figures, and playsets
The Phoenix Toy Soldier Co.
Bob Wilson
P.O. Box 26365
Phoenix, AZ 85068
602-863-2891

Transformers and robots
David Kolodny-Nagy
3701 Connecticut Ave. NW #500
Washington, DC 20008
202-364-8753

Trolls
Roger Inouye
765 E Franklin Ave.
Pomona, CA 91766
909-623-1368

Walkers, ramp-walkers, and wind-ups
Randy Welch
Raven'tiques
27965 Peach Orchard Rd.
Easton, MD 21601-8203
410-822-5441

TV Guides
Price guide available
TV Guide Specialists
Jeff Kadet
P.O. Box 20
Macomb, IL 61455

Twin Winton
Author of book
Mike Ellis
266 Rose Ln.
Costa Mesa, CA 92627
714-645-4697
Fax 714-645-4697

Valentines
Author of book; fee charged for appraisal
Katherine Kreider
Kingsbury Productions
P.O. Box 7957
Lancaster, PA 17604-7957
717-892-3001

Vallona Starr
Author of book
Bernice Stamper
7516 Elay Ave.
Bakersfield, CA 93308-7701
805-393-2900

Van Briggle
Dated examples, author of book
Scott H. Nelson
Box 6081
Santa Fe, NM 87502
505-986-1176
Also UND (University of North Dakota), other American potteries

Vandor
Lois Wildman
175 Chick Rd.
Camano Island, WA 98282

Vernon Kilns
Maxine Nelson
873 Marigold Ct.
Carlsbad, CA 92009

View-Master and Tru-View
Roger Nazeley
4921 Castor Ave.
Philadelphia, PA 19124

Harry Poster
P.O. Box 1883
S Hackensack, NJ 07606
201-410-7525

Walter Sigg
3-D Entertainment
P.O Box 208
Swartswood, NJ 07877

Wade
Author of book
Ian Warner
P.O. Box 93022
Brampton, Ontario
Canada L6Y 4V8

Watt Pottery
Author of book
Susan Morris
P.O. Box 656
Panora, IA 50216
515-755-3161

Western Collectibles
Author of book
Warren R. Anderson
American West Archives
P.O. Box 100
Cedar City, UT 84720
801-586-9497
Also documents, autographs, stocks and bonds, and
other ephemera

Author of books
Dan Hutchins
Hutchins Publishing Co.
P.O. Box 529
Marion, IA 52302
505-425-3387

Western Heroes
Author of books, ardent researcher, and guest columnist
Robert W. Phillips
Phillips Archives of Western Memorabilia
1703 N Aster Pl.
Broken Arrow, OK 74012
918-254-8205 or Fax 918-252-9363

Westmoreland
Author of books; newsletter editor
Ruth Grizel
P.O. Box 143
North Liberty, IA 52317-0143

World's Fairs and Expositions
D.D. Woollard, Jr.
11614 Old St. Charles Rd.
Bridgeton, MO 63044
314-739-4662

Index

COLLECTOR BOOKS

Informing Today's Collector

For over two decades we have been keeping collectors informed on trends and values in all fields of antiques and collectibles.

DOLLS, FIGURES & TEDDY BEARS

4707	A Decade of **Barbie** Dolls & Collectibles, 1981–1991, Summers	$19.95
4631	**Barbie** Doll Boom, 1986–1995, Augustyniak	$18.95
2079	**Barbie** Doll Fashion, Volume I, Eames	$24.95
4846	**Barbie** Doll Fashion, Volume II, Eames	$24.95
3957	**Barbie** Exclusives, Rana	$18.95
4632	**Barbie** Exclusives, Book II, Rana	$18.95
4557	**Barbie**, The First 30 Years, Deutsch	$24.95
4847	**Barbie** Years, 1959–1995, 2nd Ed., Olds	$17.95
3310	**Black Dolls**, 1820–1991, Perkins	$17.95
3873	**Black Dolls**, Book II, Perkins	$17.95
3810	**Chatty Cathy Dolls**, Lewis	$15.95
1529	Collector's Encyclopedia of **Barbie** Dolls, DeWein	$19.95
4882	Collector's Encyclopedia of **Barbie** Doll Exclusives and More, Augustyniak	$19.95
2211	Collector's Encyclopedia of **Madame Alexander Dolls**, Smith	$24.95
4863	Collector's Encyclopedia of **Vogue Dolls**, Izen/Stover	$29.95
3967	Collector's Guide to **Trolls**, Peterson	$19.95
4571	**Liddle Kiddles**, Identification & Value Guide, Langford	$18.95
3826	Story of **Barbie**, Westenhouser	$19.95
1513	**Teddy Bears & Steiff** Animals, Mandel	$9.95
1817	**Teddy Bears & Steiff** Animals, 2nd Series, Mandel	$19.95
2084	**Teddy Bears, Annalee's & Steiff** Animals, 3rd Series, Mandel	$19.95
1808	Wonder of **Barbie**, Manos	$9.95
1430	World of **Barbie** Dolls, Manos	$9.95
4880	World of **Raggedy Ann** Collectibles, Avery	$24.95

TOYS, MARBLES & CHRISTMAS COLLECTIBLES

3427	**Advertising Character** Collectibles, Dotz	$17.95
2333	Antique & Collector's **Marbles**, 3rd Ed., Grist	$9.95
3827	Antique & Collector's **Toys**, 1870–1950, Longest	$24.95
3956	Baby Boomer **Games**, Identification & Value Guide, Polizzi	$24.95
4934	**Breyer Animal** Collector's Guide, Identification and Values, Browell	$19.95
3717	**Christmas** Collectibles, 2nd Edition, Whitmyer	$24.95
4976	**Christmas** Ornaments, Lights & Decorations, Johnson	$24.95
4737	**Christmas** Ornaments, Lights & Decorations, Vol. II, Johnson	$24.95
4739	**Christmas** Ornaments, Lights & Decorations, Vol. III, Johnson	$24.95
4649	Classic Plastic **Model Kits**, Polizzi	$24.95
4559	Collectible **Action Figures**, 2nd Ed., Manos	$17.95
3874	Collectible Coca-Cola Toy **Trucks**, deCourtivron	$24.95
2338	Collector's Encyclopedia of **Disneyana**, Longest, Stern	$24.95
4958	Collector's Guide to **Battery Toys**, Hultzman	$19.95
4639	Collector's Guide to **Diecast Toys & Scale Models**, Johnson	$19.95
4651	Collector's Guide to **Tinker Toys**, Strange	$18.95
4566	Collector's Guide to **Tootsietoys**, 2nd Ed., Richter	$19.95
4720	The Golden Age of **Automotive Toys**, 1925–1941, Hutchison/Johnson	$24.95
3436	Grist's Big Book of **Marbles**	$19.95
3970	Grist's Machine-Made & Contemporary **Marbles**, 2nd Ed.	$9.95
4723	**Matchbox** Toys, 1947 to 1996, 2nd Ed., Johnson	$18.95
4871	**McDonald's Collectibles**, Henriques/DuVall	$19.95
1540	**Modern Toys** 1930–1980, Baker	$19.95
3888	**Motorcycle** Toys, Antique & Contemporary, Gentry/Downs	$18.95
4953	**Schroeder's Collectible Toys**, Antique to Modern Price Guide, 4th Ed.	$17.95
1886	Stern's Guide to **Disney** Collectibles	$14.95
2139	Stern's Guide to **Disney** Collectibles, 2nd Series	$14.95
3975	Stern's Guide to **Disney** Collectibles, 3rd Series	$18.95
2028	**Toys**, Antique & Collectible, Longest	$14.95
3979	**Zany Characters** of the Ad World, Lamphier	$16.95

FURNITURE

1457	American **Oak** Furniture, McNerney	$9.95
3716	American **Oak** Furniture, Book II, McNerney	$12.95
1118	Antique **Oak** Furniture, Hill	$7.95
2271	Collector's Encyclopedia of **American** Furniture, Vol. II, Swedberg	$24.95
3720	Collector's Encyclopedia of **American** Furniture, Vol. III, Swedberg	$24.95
3878	Collector's Guide to **Oak** Furniture, George	$12.95
1755	Furniture of the **Depression Era**, Swedberg	$19.95
3906	**Heywood-Wakefield** Modern Furniture, Rouland	$18.95

1885	**Victorian** Furniture, Our American Heritage, McNerney	$9.95
3829	**Victorian** Furniture, Our American Heritage, Book II, McNerney	$9.95

JEWELRY, HATPINS, WATCHES & PURSES

1712	Antique & Collector's **Thimbles** & Accessories, Mathis	$19.95
1748	Antique **Purses**, Revised Second Ed., Holiner	$19.95
1278	Art Nouveau & Art Deco **Jewelry**, Baker	$9.95
4850	Collectible **Costume Jewelry**, Simonds	$24.95
3875	Collecting Antique **Stickpins**, Kerins	$16.95
3722	Collector's Ency. of **Compacts, Carryalls & Face Powder Boxes**, Mueller	$24.95
4854	Collector's Ency. of **Compacts, Carryalls & Face Powder Boxes**, Vol. II	$24.95
4940	**Costume Jewelry**, A Practical Handbook & Value Guide, Rezazadeh	$24.95
1716	Fifty Years of Collectible **Fashion Jewelry**, 1925–1975, Baker	$19.95
1424	**Hatpins** & Hatpin Holders, Baker	$9.95
4570	Ladies' **Compacts**, Gerson	$24.95
1181	100 Years of Collectible **Jewelry**, 1850–1950, Baker	$9.95
4729	**Sewing Tools** & Trinkets, Thompson	$24.95
2348	20th Century Fashionable Plastic **Jewelry**, Baker	$19.95
4878	Vintage & Contemporary **Purse Accessories**, Gerson	$24.95
3830	Vintage **Vanity Bags & Purses**, Gerson	$24.95

INDIANS, GUNS, KNIVES, TOOLS, PRIMITIVES

1868	Antique **Tools**, Our American Heritage, McNerney	$9.95
1426	**Arrowheads** & Projectile Points, Hothem	$7.95
4943	Field Guide to **Flint Arrowheads & Knives** of the North American Indian	$9.95
2279	**Indian Artifacts** of the Midwest, Hothem	$14.95
3885	**Indian Artifacts** of the Midwest, Book II, Hothem	$16.95
4870	**Indian Artifacts** of the Midwest, Book III, Hothem	$18.95
1964	**Indian Axes** & Related Stone Artifacts, Hothem	$14.95
2023	**Keen Kutter** Collectibles, Heuring	$14.95
4724	Modern **Guns**, Identification & Values, 11th Ed., Quertermous	$12.95
2164	**Primitives**, Our American Heritage, McNerney	$9.95
1759	**Primitives**, Our American Heritage, 2nd Series, McNerney	$14.95
4730	Standard **Knife** Collector's Guide, 3rd Ed., Ritchie & Stewart	$12.95

PAPER COLLECTIBLES & BOOKS

4633	**Big Little Books**, Jacobs	$18.95
4710	Collector's Guide to **Children's Books**, Jones	$18.95
1441	Collector's Guide to **Post Cards**, Wood	$9.95
2081	Guide to Collecting **Cookbooks**, Allen	$14.95
2080	Price Guide to **Cookbooks & Recipe Leaflets**, Dickinson	$9.95
3973	**Sheet Music** Reference & Price Guide, 2nd Ed., Pafik & Guiheen	$19.95
4654	**Victorian Trade Cards**, Historical Reference & Value Guide, Cheadle	$19.95
4733	**Whitman Juvenile Books**, Brown	$17.95

GLASSWARE

4561	Collectible **Drinking Glasses**, Chase & Kelly	$17.95
4642	Collectible **Glass Shoes**, Wheatley	$19.95
4937	Coll. **Glassware** from the 40s, 50s & 60s, 4th Ed., Florence	$19.95
1810	Collector's Encyclopedia of **American Art Glass**, Shuman	$29.95
4938	Collector's Encyclopedia of **Depression Glass**, 13th Ed., Florence	$19.95
1961	Collector's Encyclopedia of **Fry Glassware**, Fry Glass Society	$24.95
1664	Collector's Encyclopedia of **Heisey Glass**, 1925–1938, Bredehoft	$24.95
3905	Collector's Encyclopedia of **Milk Glass**, Newbound	$24.95
4936	Collector's Guide to **Candy Containers**, Dezso/Poirier	$19.95
4564	**Crackle Glass**, Weitman	$19.95
4941	**Crackle Glass**, Book II, Weitman	$19.95
2275	**Czechoslovakian Glass** and Collectibles, Barta/Rose	$16.95
4714	**Czechoslovakian Glass** and Collectibles, Book II, Barta/Rose	$16.95
4716	**Elegant Glassware** of the Depression Era, 7th Ed., Florence	$19.95
1380	Encyclopedia of **Pattern Glass**, McClain	$12.95
3981	Ever's Standard **Cut Glass** Value Guide	$12.95
4659	**Fenton** Art Glass, 1907–1939, Whitmyer	$24.95
3725	**Fostoria**, Pressed, Blown & Hand Molded Shapes, Kerr	$24.95
4719	**Fostoria**, Etched, Carved & Cut Designs, Vol. II, Kerr	$24.95
3883	**Fostoria Stemware**, The Crystal for America, Long & Seate	$24.95
4644	**Imperial Carnival Glass**, Burns	$18.95
3886	**Kitchen Glassware** of the Depression Years, 5th Ed., Florence	$19.95

4725	Pocket Guide to **Depression Glass**, 10th Ed., Florence	$9.95
5035	Standard Encyclopedia of **Carnival Glass**, 6th Ed., Edwards/Carwile	$24.95
5000	Standard **Carnival Glass** Price Guide, 11th Ed., Edwards/Carwile	$9.95
4875	Standard Encyclopedia of **Opalescent Glass**, 2nd ed., Edwards	$19.95
4731	**Stemware Identification**, Featuring Cordials with Values, Florence	$24.95
3326	**Very Rare Glassware** of the Depression Years, 3rd Series, Florence	$24.95
4732	**Very Rare Glassware** of the Depression Years, 5th Series, Florence	$24.95
4656	**Westmoreland Glass**, Wilson	$24.95

POTTERY

4927	**ABC Plates & Mugs**, Lindsay	$24.95
4929	**American Art Pottery**, Sigafoose	$24.95
4630	**American Limoges**, Limoges	$24.95
1312	**Blue & White Stoneware**, McNerney	$9.95
1958	So. Potteries **Blue Ridge Dinnerware**, 3rd Ed., Newbound	$14.95
1959	**Blue Willow**, 2nd Ed., Gaston	$14.95
4848	Ceramic **Coin Banks**, Stoddard	$19.95
4851	Collectible **Cups & Saucers**, Harran	$18.95
4709	Collectible **Kay Finch**, Biography, Identification & Values, Martinez/Frick	$18.95
1373	Collector's Encyclopedia of **American Dinnerware**, Cunningham	$24.95
4931	Collector's Encyclopedia of **Bauer Pottery**, Chipman	$24.95
3815	Collector's Encyclopedia of **Blue Ridge Dinnerware**, Newbound	$19.95
4932	Collector's Encyclopedia of **Blue Ridge Dinnerware**, Vol. II, Newbound	$24.95
4658	Collector's Encyclopedia of **Brush-McCoy Pottery**, Huxford	$24.95
2272	Collector's Encyclopedia of **California Pottery**, Chipman	$24.95
3811	Collector's Encyclopedia of **Colorado Pottery**, Carlton	$24.95
2133	Collector's Encyclopedia of **Cookie Jars**, Roerig	$24.95
3723	Collector's Encyclopedia of **Cookie Jars**, Book II, Roerig	$24.95
4939	Collector's Encyclopedia of **Cookie Jars**, Book III, Roerig	$24.95
4638	Collector's Encyclopedia of **Dakota Potteries**, Dommel	$24.95
5040	Collector's Encyclopedia of **Fiesta**, 8th Ed., Huxford	$19.95
4718	Collector's Encyclopedia of **Figural Planters & Vases**, Newbound	$19.95
3961	Collector's Encyclopedia of **Early Noritake**, Alden	$24.95
1439	Collector's Encyclopedia of **Flow Blue China**, Gaston	$19.95
3812	Collector's Encyclopedia of **Flow Blue China**, 2nd Ed., Gaston	$24.95
3813	Collector's Encyclopedia of **Hall China**, 2nd Ed., Whitmyer	$24.95
3431	Collector's Encyclopedia of **Homer Laughlin China**, Jasper	$24.95
1276	Collector's Encyclopedia of **Hull Pottery**, Roberts	$19.95
3962	Collector's Encyclopedia of **Lefton China**, DeLozier	$19.95
4855	Collector's Encyclopedia of **Lefton China**, Book II, DeLozier	$19.95
2210	Collector's Encyclopedia of **Limoges Porcelain**, 2nd Ed., Gaston	$24.95
2334	Collector's Encyclopedia of **Majolica Pottery**, Katz-Marks	$19.95
1358	Collector's Encyclopedia of **McCoy Pottery**, Huxford	$19.95
3963	Collector's Encyclopedia of **Metlox Potteries**, Gibbs Jr.	$24.95
3837	Collector's Encyclopedia of **Nippon Porcelain**, Van Patten	$24.95
2089	Collector's Ency. of **Nippon Porcelain**, 2nd Series, Van Patten	$24.95
1665	Collector's Ency. of **Nippon Porcelain**, 3rd Series, Van Patten	$24.95
4712	Collector's Ency. of **Nippon Porcelain**, 4th Series, Van Patten	$24.95
1447	Collector's Encyclopedia of **Noritake**, Van Patten	$19.95
3432	Collector's Encyclopedia of **Noritake**, 2nd Series, Van Patten	$24.95
1037	Collector's Encyclopedia of **Occupied Japan**, 1st Series, Florence	$14.95
1038	Collector's Encyclopedia of **Occupied Japan**, 2nd Series, Florence	$14.95
2088	Collector's Encyclopedia of **Occupied Japan**, 3rd Series, Florence	$14.95
2019	Collector's Encyclopedia of **Occupied Japan**, 4th Series, Florence	$14.95
2335	Collector's Encyclopedia of **Occupied Japan**, 5th Series, Florence	$14.95
4951	Collector's Encyclopedia of **Old Ivory China**, Hillman	$24.95
3964	Collector's Encyclopedia of **Pickard China**, Reed	$24.95
3877	Collector's Encyclopedia of **R.S. Prussia**, 4th Series, Gaston	$24.95
1034	Collector's Encyclopedia of **Roseville Pottery**, Huxford	$19.95
1035	Collector's Encyclopedia of **Roseville Pottery**, 2nd Ed., Huxford	$19.95
4856	Collector's Encyclopedia of **Russel Wright**, 2nd Ed., Kerr	$24.95
4713	Collector's Encyclopedia of **Salt Glaze Stoneware**, Taylor/Lowrance	$24.95
3314	Collector's Encyclopedia of **Van Briggle** Art Pottery, Sasicki	$24.95
4563	Collector's Encyclopedia of **Wall Pockets**, Newbound	$19.95
2111	Collector's Encyclopedia of **Weller Pottery**, Huxford	$29.95
3876	Collector's Guide to **Lu-Ray Pastels**, Meehan	$18.95
3814	Collector's Guide to **Made in Japan** Ceramics, White	$18.95
4646	Collector's Guide to **Made in Japan** Ceramics, Book II, White	$18.95
4565	Collector's Guide to **Rockingham**, The Enduring Ware, Brewer	$14.95
2339	Collector's Guide to **Shawnee Pottery**, Vanderbilt	$19.95
1425	**Cookie Jars**, Westfall	$9.95

3440	**Cookie Jars**, Book II, Westfall	$19.95
4924	Figural & Novelty **Salt & Pepper Shakers**, 2nd Series, Davern	$24.95
2379	Lehner's Ency. of **U.S. Marks** on Pottery, Porcelain & China	$24.95
4722	**McCoy Pottery**, Collector's Reference & Value Guide, Hanson/Nissen	$19.95
3825	**Purinton Pottery**, Morris	$24.95
4726	**Red Wing Art Pottery**, 1920s–1960s, Dollen	$19.95
1670	**Red Wing Collectibles**, DePasquale	$9.95
1440	**Red Wing Stoneware**, DePasquale	$9.95
1632	**Salt & Pepper Shakers**, Guarnaccia	$9.95
5091	**Salt & Pepper Shakers** II, Guarnaccia	$18.95
2220	**Salt & Pepper Shakers** III, Guarnaccia	$14.95
3443	**Salt & Pepper Shakers** IV, Guarnaccia	$18.95
3738	**Shawnee Pottery**, Mangus	$24.95
4629	Turn of the Century **American Dinnerware**, 1880s–1920s, Jasper	$24.95
4572	**Wall Pockets** of the Past, Perkins	$17.95
3327	**Watt Pottery** – Identification & Value Guide, Morris	$19.95

OTHER COLLECTIBLES

4704	Antique & Collectible **Buttons**, Wisniewski	$19.95
2269	Antique **Brass & Copper** Collectibles, Gaston	$16.95
1880	Antique **Iron**, McNerney	$9.95
3872	Antique **Tins**, Dodge	$24.95
4845	Antique **Typewriters & Office Collectibles**, Rehr	$19.95
1714	**Black** Collectibles, Gibbs	$19.95
1128	**Bottle** Pricing Guide, 3rd Ed., Cleveland	$7.95
4636	**Celluloid Collectibles**, Dunn	$14.95
3718	Collectible **Aluminum**, Grist	$16.95
3445	Collectible **Cats**, An Identification & Value Guide, Fyke	$18.95
4560	Collectible **Cats**, An Identification & Value Guide, Book II, Fyke	$19.95
4852	Collectible **Compact Disc** Price Guide 2, Cooper	$17.95
2018	Collector's Encyclopedia of **Granite Ware**, Greguire	$24.95
3430	Collector's Encyclopedia of **Granite Ware**, Book 2, Greguire	$24.95
4705	Collector's Guide to **Antique Radios**, 4th Ed., Bunis	$18.95
3880	Collector's Guide to **Cigarette Lighters**, Flanagan	$17.95
4637	Collector's Guide to **Cigarette Lighers**, Book II, Flanagan	$17.95
4942	Collector's Guide to **Don Winton Designs**, Ellis	$19.95
3966	Collector's Guide to **Inkwells**, Identification & Values, Badders	$18.95
4947	Collector's Guide to **Inkwells**, Book II, Badders	$19.95
4948	Collector's Guide to **Letter Openers**, Grist	$19.95
4862	Collector's Guide to **Toasters** & Accessories, Greguire	$19.95
4652	Collector's Guide to **Transistor Radios**, 2nd Ed., Bunis	$16.95
4653	Collector's Guide to **TV Memorabilia**, 1960s–1970s, Davis/Morgan	$24.95
4864	Collector's Guide to **Wallace Nutting Pictures**, Ivankovich	$18.95
1629	**Doorstops**, Identification & Values, Bertoia	$9.95
4567	Figural **Napkin Rings**, Gottschalk & Whitson	$18.95
4717	Figural **Nodders**, Includes Bobbin' Heads and Swayers, Irtz	$19.95
3968	**Fishing Lure** Collectibles, Murphy/Edmisten	$24.95
4867	**Flea Market Trader**, 11th Ed., Huxford	$9.95
4944	**Flue Covers**, Collector's Value Guide, Meckley	$12.95
4945	**G-Men and FBI Toys** and Collectibles, Whitworth	$18.95
5043	**Garage Sale & Flea Market Annual**, 6th Ed.	$19.95
3819	**General Store Collectibles**, Wilson	$24.95
4643	**Great American West** Collectibles, Wilson	$24.95
2215	Goldstein's **Coca-Cola** Collectibles	$16.95
3884	Huxford's Collectible **Advertising**, 2nd Ed.	$24.95
2216	**Kitchen Antiques**, 1790–1940, McNerney	$14.95
4950	The **Lone Ranger**, Collector's Reference & Value Guide, Felbinger	$18.95
2026	**Railroad** Collectibles, 4th Ed., Baker	$14.95
4949	**Schroeder's Antiques Price Guide**, 16th Ed., Huxford	$12.95
5007	**Silverplated Flatware**, Revised 4th Edition, Hagan	$18.95
1922	Standard **Old Bottle** Price Guide, Sellari	$14.95
4708	Summers' Guide to **Coca-Cola**	$19.95
4952	Summers' Pocket Guide to **Coca-Cola** Identifications	$9.95
3892	**Toy & Miniature Sewing Machines**, Thomas	$18.95
4876	**Toy & Miniature Sewing Machines**, Book II, Thomas	$24.95
3828	Value Guide to **Advertising Memorabilia**, Summers	$18.95
3977	Value Guide to **Gas Station** Memorabilia, Summers & Priddy	$24.95
4877	Vintage **Bar Ware**, Visakay	$24.95
4935	The W.F. Cody **Buffalo Bill** Collector's Guide with Values	$24.95
4879	**Wanted to Buy**, 6th Edition	$9.95

This is only a partial listing of the books on antiques that are available from Collector Books. All books are well illustrated and contain current values. Most of these books are available from your local bookseller, antique dealer, or public library. If you are unable to locate certain titles in your area, you may order by mail from COLLECTOR BOOKS, P.O. Box 3009, Paducah, KY 42002-3009. Customers with Visa, Discover or MasterCard may phone in orders from 7:00–5:00 CST, Monday–Friday, Toll Free 1-800-626-5420. Add $2.00 for postage for the first book ordered and $0.30 for each additional book. Include item number, title, and price when ordering. Allow 14 to 21 days for delivery.